Crossing Continents

DUNCAN CAMPBELL-SMITH

Crossing Continents

A History of Standard Chartered Bank

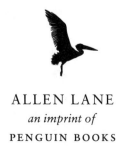

ALLEN LANE

an imprint of

PENGUIN BOOKS

ALLEN LANE

UK | USA | Canada | Ireland | Australia
India | New Zealand | South Africa

Allen Lane is part of the Penguin Random House group of companies
whose addresses can be found at global.penguinrandomhouse.com

First published 2021
001

Copyright © Standard Chartered Bank, 2021

The moral right of the author has been asserted

Set in 10.2/13.5 pt Sabon LT Std
Typeset by Jouve (UK), Milton Keynes
Printed and bound in Great Britain by Clays Ltd, Elcograf S.p.A.

The authorized representative in the EEA is Penguin Random House Ireland,
Morrison Chambers, 32 Nassau Street, Dublin D02 YH68

ISBN: 978–0–241–45873–0

Contents

List of Maps

List of Illustrations

COLOUR PLATES

1. The founders: (a) James Wilson of Chartered Bank (portrait by Sir John Watson-Gordon, 1858, reproduced courtesy of the National Portrait Gallery London); and (b) John Paterson of Standard Bank of South Africa (by permission of MetroMedia SA).
2. The real father figures: (a) Howard Gwyther of Chartered Bank (courtesy of London Metropolitan Archives CLC/B/207 (LMA), ref. CH03/01/16/002/060); and (b) Robert Stewart of Standard Bank (LMA, ref. SCB11/01/001/027/B).
3. First destinations for the Chartered Bank: (a) Calcutta in 1857 (LMA, ref. CH03/01/16/002/058); and (b) Hong Kong's Victoria waterfront in 1858 (LMA, ref. CH03/01/16/002/059).
4. Two of the earliest Chartered Bank notes: (a) a first cheque ('post bill') payable by the Singapore branch, March 1859 (LMA, ref. SCB11/06/006/74); and (b) a $10 note issued by the Chartered's branch in Hong Kong, March 1863 (photo by Stack's Bowers and Ponterio Ltd).
5. Building an imperial bank in South Africa in the 1860s: Standard Bank's branches in (a) Port Elizabeth (LMA, ref. SCB11/01/001/020/A); and (b) Cape Town (LMA, ref. SCB11/05/18/001/001).
6. The diamond rush at Kimberley: (a) the Big Hole in 1873 (LMA, ref. SCB11/01/002/004/A); and (b) Standard Bank's local branch and staff, December 1877 (LMA, ref. SCB11/01/001/017/A).
7. Standard Bank and the birth of Johannesburg: (a) Standard Bank's first branch on the Rand, opened in 1888 (LMA, ref. SCB11/05/18/005/0001); and (b) its successor on Commissioner Street in 1894 (LMA, ref. SCB11/05/18/005/004).
8. Following the Empire into Matabeleland: (a) Standard Bank's tent at Bulawayo in 1894 (LMA, ref. ST10/01/03/007/001); and (b) the Bulawayo to Gwelo stage coach, c. 1897 (LMA, ref. ST10/01/03/006/001).

TEXT ILLUSTRATIONS

The illustrations of Chartered Bank buildings on pp. 319, 335, 360 and 503 were specially commissioned by Chartered Bank in 1948 from the artist Dennis Flanders (1915–94), who worked in London and drew the overseas branches from contemporary photographs. (Drawings reproduced by courtesy of Alison and Julian Flanders.)

Acknowledgements

This book began some years ago with an invitation in May 2010 from Mike Rees, then head of Standard Chartered's Wholesale Banking division, to discuss the possibility of an authorized history of the bank. I am indebted to him for his decision to press ahead, and for his support thereafter for a project that soon outgrew the original brief. The resulting book has been a long time in the making. Most of those involved in the original commissioning of *Crossing Continents* have long since left the Group, and I must thank its current executive team under the Chairmanship of José Viñals for standing by the book in its final stages. In particular, I would like to thank Steve Atkinson, who found the book in his in-tray when he was appointed Group Head of Corporate Affairs in 2012 and never wavered in his support for what must often have looked a rather academic item compared with other, far more pressing issues on his daily agenda. His commitment to the book proved invaluable, especially after publication had to be postponed in 2016.

I am indebted to Peter Sands, who as Group Chief Executive until June 2015 set aside the time for several conversations about the period after his arrival on the Board in 2001. With his active endorsement I was able to interview a long list of executives still working in the bank, who did their best to assist my research into the most recent years of a very long history. In investigating the forty years or so before 1988, I similarly received many kindnesses from dozens of the bank's alumni who were ready to share their memories, often to a quite startling level of detail. (All former Chartered bankers, it seems, know by heart the exact date of their every reassignment, in careers typically lasting thirty years or more.) To two former Directors of Standard Chartered I owe special thanks. Michael McWilliam was Group Chief Executive from 1983 to 1988. In addition to providing innumerable insights in the course of several interviews, Michael made freely available to me the text of his personal diaries, kept daily throughout the period of his tenure, and he allowed me complete freedom to quote from them at my discretion – yielding material invaluable for an institutional history of any period, and doubly so for a modern era largely devoid of letters. The late David Millar, who joined Chartered Bank in 1947 aged eighteen and retired as Senior Executive Director in 1987, took an active interest in my research that went well beyond providing his own memories of a long career. David took pains to introduce me by email to a list of distinguished figures in Hong Kong with notable links to the bank's past there, all of whom were subsequently happy to meet me on the strength of their respect and affection for him, a legacy of his time running the business in Hong Kong in the 1970s. It is a great sadness that David did not live quite long enough to see this book in print. I also received kind introductions of a more recent vintage, and further helpful advice on how to make the most of my visits to Hong Kong, from several individuals long familiar with the city's financial past, including Mark Clifford, Leo Goodstadt, Thomas Harris, Guy de Jonquières, David Kynaston, Christopher Munn and Steve Vines. My thanks to them all.

The following individuals – third parties as well as employees, past and present – kindly agreed to be interviewed, in many cases more than once: Amit Arora, Maria Assunta, Petchsangroj Atchara, Robin Baillie, Kweku Bedu-Addo, Jaspal Bindra, Ruedi Bischof, Carol Blake, Suomen Bose, Philip Bowring, John Brinsden, Bill Brown (who kindly provided me with copies of his own personal memoirs), Lance Browne, Gareth Bullock, Peter Cameron, Ron Cannings, Dominic Casserley, Madeleine Cha, Marc Chait, Peter Chan, Y. C. Chang, Vongkusolkit Chanin, K. Kraisorn Chansiri, Andy Charlton, John Charlton, Elaine Chin, Gloria Chow, Tracy Clarke, Peter Clarke, David Cleggett, Mike Collar, George Copus, John Davidson, Mike DeNoma, Mark Devadason, Keith De Vaz, Dang Quang Do, Annemarie Durbin, Rob Edwards, Colin Endacott, Ebenezer Essoka, Richard Etemesi, David Faure, Karen Fawcett, Claire Fedder, Ray Ferguson, Theresa Foo, Alan Fung, Patty Fuster, the late Rodney Galpin, Sylvia Galpin, D. N. Ghosh, David Gibson, Rob Gilbert, Patrick Gillam, Euleen Goh, G. K. Goh, Steve Goodwin, Richard Goulding, Nick Grantham, Neville Green, Manish Gupta, Richard Hale, Philip Hampton, Derek Hewett, Peter Hibbard, Kwon Ping Ho, Peter Hodges, Judy Hsu, Aye Htun, Bill Hughes, Benjamin Hung, Andrew Hunter, Janet Hunter, John Janes, Henry Jarecki, Sarasin Kalin, Chris Keljik, Jamie Kelly, Peter Knapton, Lyn Kok (who also arranged for me the logistics of a lengthy visit to Bangkok), Ben Kruger, Ravi Kumar, William Lau, Gavin Laws (who helped to kick the whole project off in its early days), Diana Layfield, Kah Henh Lee, Richard Lee, Lawrence Leung, Sally Wong Leung, Lily Levinson, Li Ka-shing, the late Hew Liller, Jerry Liu, Norman Lyle, John Major, Anna Marrs, Bob McDonald, John McFarlane, Jeanette McKenna, P. K. Medappa, Richard Meddings (who took pains to comment very helpfully on the closing sections of the book), Tim Miller, Matthew Millett, William Mocatta, David Moir, Bill Moore, Muhammad Rawi Abdullah, Arun Murthy, Douglas Newbould, Anthony Nightingale, Barry Northrop, Helen Ocasio-Walfall, Kun Oh, Chong Hye Ong, Diane Paciello, John Peace, Simon Pilkington, Alan Plumb, Surastian Prasnee, Christopher Pratt, Agnes Pullen, Peter Rawlings, Ashia Razzaq, John Rivett, Julio Rojas, Jackie Rolf, Wangtal Salinee, V. Shankar, Christine Sheehy, R. V. Singh, Tina Singhsacha (who co-ordinated for me a memorable trip to Myanmar), Soe Win, Helmut Sohmen, Alwyn Stavert, Conrad Strauss, Bulakul Surong, Matt Sweeney, Rana Talwar, Johnny Tan, Jack Tang, S. P. Tao and his daughter Mildred Tao, Martin Taylor, Choon-Hong Tee, K. Thippathorn, Peter Thorne, Katherine Tsang, Shriti Vadera, Lalita Vadhri, Jan Verplancke, Tim Waddell, Pam Walkden, Sean Wallace, Dan Waters, Vera Waters, Simon Watson, David Weatherson, Shirley Wee, Chief Elwyn Williams, Geoff Williams, Jake Williams, Malcolm Williamson, Ian Wilson, Richard Winter, Steve Wish (who patiently explained the mechanics of trade finance on more than one occasion), Eleanor Wong, Kang Yang Wong, Alex Woo, Guy Woodford, Marjorie Yang, Kang Yao and Jerry Zhang. I am deeply indebted to all of them.

At the beginning of the project, it seemed possible that archives might be stored in various branches of the Group around the world. This turned out not to be the case, but I am grateful to the many individuals who spent time on my behalf trying in vain to track down local historical records. Fortunately, copious materials were available in three places. At the Standard Bank Heritage Centre on Simmonds Street in Johannesburg, Estranelle Lubbe and the late Letitia Mybergh provided expert guidance to the exemplary collection of archives maintained by the Standard Bank. My thanks to them, as also to my friend Richard Steyn (and his wife Elizabeth), whose work on his own history of the South African bank overlapped with my early researches. In London, the surviving pre-1969 records of Chartered Bank and many additional archives of the Standard Bank are held in the vaults of the City of London Corporation's Guildhall Library – all except for the official minute books of the two banks, which are still held by the modern Group – and they are managed by London Metropolitan Archives (LMA), a part of the City Corporation. A team of archivists at the LMA, led by Richard Wiltshire, took on the cataloguing of this material for the Group in December 2010 and their work ran alongside my own for the next three years. I am extremely grateful to Richard for his patient and diligent response to my innumerable queries over this period, as well as for his assistance in organizing the photography of archived documents, and to all those at the LMA in Islington whose professionalism helped the entire project along so smoothly, including especially Nicola Avery, Stephen Freeth, Susan Gentles, Lizzie Hunt, Melanie Kirton, David Luck, Sanita Markic, Amy Proctor, Anne-Marie Purcell, Katharine Rawson, Charlotte Scott, David Tennant and Charlie Turpie. (It seems appropriate here to acknowledge also the contribution to this book made by John Leighton-Boyce, who laboured so hard over the archives in 1950–53 and left behind a mass of notes without which much of the early history of Chartered Bank would have disappeared altogether. He died in 2007.) Once my research reached the post-1969 years, I was largely dependent on the third and last source of primary material, the boxed records still held by Standard Chartered itself. I want to thank Suzie Andrews for her unstinting help in navigating a way through the sometimes problematic indexing of the boxes, and for co-ordinating access to them.

This book involved extensive travelling and administration, which would certainly have been overwhelming but for the support provided by many members of the bank's staff. Thanks are due to Ferlis Wong in Hong Kong, Romany Parakrama in Singapore, Elaine Chin in New York and an ever-supportive team in London, including Helen Clerkin, Aimee Nicholson, Samantha Coster, Kaajal Amin Sharma and Charlotte Pierce. Simon Lau and his events-management team in Singapore always showed huge enthusiasm for the very idea of a book, which was always cheering. I am particularly indebted to Charlotte Holmes, based in London, who shepherded my dealings with the whole Group from start to finish with infinite tact and patience. In the final stages of the book's preparation, Charlotte took on the task of securing consent from all those interviewees quoted in the text, a thankless and protracted mission that she accomplished with unfailing good humour and efficiency. Shaal Karim provided some much appreciated help with appendices and charts in the closing stages.

Special thanks, as ever, are due to the many people at Penguin Allen Lane who managed to make light of all the painstaking work involved in publishing such a long book. The final stages of its preparation entailed an unusually protracted schedule, which they handled with an impressive sangfroid. I would like in particular to thank my indefatigable copy editor, Charlotte Ridings, the graphic designer Ian Moores for his work on the many charts at the back of the book, the cartographer John Gilkes for his splendid work on the maps, and the entire production team under Richard Duguid and Sandra Fuller, who both took enormous trouble over innumerable late amendments. My thanks also to two editorial assistants, Donald Futers and Ben Sinyor, both of whom were a pleasure to work with over the course of more than five years. I am particularly indebted to Penguin Press's publishing director, Stuart Proffitt, who not only edited the text but also played a crucial part in sustaining the momentum behind the book's publication, not least through the difficulties imposed on all parties by the pandemic in 2020–21.

Finally, I would like to acknowledge the huge debt I owe to many close friends, and in particular Howard Davies and Peter Stothard, who rallied with support and encouragement at several points over the course of this book's long gestation. As all of them well appreciate, there was one person without whom it would never have been possible at all. I owe its existence to my late wife, Anne-Catherine, who died suddenly in April 2014, and I dedicate *Crossing Continents* to her memory.

Author's Note

Many Asian and African place-names have changed their spelling over the course of the past 150 years. Names created by the Western colonial powers in the nineteenth century have been widely jettisoned, a process abetted in the Far East by the move away from the old Anglophone romanization of Chinese names in favour of the 'pinyin' system devised in the 1950s and more or less universally adopted in recent decades. But I would find it jarring to use today's names in the narration of past events. Contemporaries in, say, the 1890s talked of Bombay, Canton and Peking, not Mumbai, Guangzhou and Beijing. The modern names would seem just as out of place in narrating the 1890s as the old Victorian names would be misplaced in describing the recent past. As a general rule, and at the risk of straying here and there from the paths of political correctness or even strictly accurate chronology, I have therefore tried to follow common usage at the time and have noted in parenthesis, where appropriate, the switch from old to new. In just a few cases where the old has faded away sufficiently to have become unfamiliar – as in Madras, now Chennai, for example, or Hankow, now Wuhan – I have noted both at the first mention of the place in the early chapters of the book before reverting to the contemporary name.

Foreword

Over fifty years ago I joined the Standard Bank Group, some years before it merged to become Standard Chartered. After only a few months, I volunteered to work overseas in Nigeria during the Biafran War and, whilst there, learned more about life and banking than I could possibly have imagined. It was an experience that literally changed my life.

My time in Nigeria came to a premature end after a serious car accident left me badly injured. I spent some weeks in a mission hospital, staffed by non-English-speaking nurses, before I was flown home to England for further treatment. I remained in hospital for many, many months and each week, unfailingly, was visited by representatives of the Bank – even though I was one of its newest and youngest employees. I have never forgotten the care and kindness that was extended to me during that difficult and painful time.

Four years later, when I became a candidate for a Parliamentary seat that the Conservative Party had no hope of winning, the Bank were wholly supportive. They remained so beyond my second electoral defeat, and into my third election, when, at last, I entered the House of Commons as MP for Huntingdonshire.

My experience of Standard Chartered has therefore been wholly positive for over half a century and I have a lasting affection for the Bank that will never fade. This history brings together the fascinating backgrounds of Standard Bank and Chartered Bank, both of which relied for many decades on adventurous young recruits from Britain who were keen to work overseas as I was in 1966, showing how an institution built in the days of the Empire has been reshaped in more recent years to serve the needs of a very different kind of global economy.

It is an account that draws heavily on the memories of many men and women who have worked for the Bank. This helps to convey a sense of the strong corporate culture that I encountered as a young man, and which I am sure has contributed to the Bank's continuing success.

I believe this book – which is full of extraordinary stories and un-expected insights – will be seen as a valuable record of a most unusual institution.

THE RT HON SIR JOHN MAJOR KG CH

Introduction

Oh, where is the brew that is finer?
Oh, show me the drink that's diviner
Than the beer that we drank
In the old Chartered Bank
Of India, Australia and China!

For the hundreds of young Scotsmen in the Victorian era who signed up to work in the tropics for the Chartered Bank, the allure must have been self-evident. Glamorous foreign postings far from the grey drizzle of Dunbar and Dunfermline, fabulous salaries and pensions, the elevated social status due to all servants of the British Empire – as a modern City banker might exclaim, what was not to like? And for those who managed to cope with the reality – and the heavy drinking, drudgery and disease that overwhelmed too many expatriates in nineteenth-century Asia – there could be a life-long camaraderie with their peers, to be acknowledged with toasts (and perhaps even drinking songs) into a comfortable old age. Founded in 1853, the Chartered Bank of India, Australia and China deployed its starry-eyed recruits to such effect that by the end of the nineteenth century it was one of the leading 'overseas banks' in the City of London – those banks that had a City head office, but no branches in Britain. It had by that date become a bastion of the Empire's commercial life across the whole of Asia (though its triple-decker title was always a misnomer: the admission rules for banking in Australia changed just after the Chartered's launch, and it never got around to a re-christening).

Rather like the Empire itself, the bank grew to prominence across a great swathe of the globe with remarkably few home-grown managers. Its 'Foreign (that is, expatriate) Staff' – exclusively British, though not quite all of them Scottish – ran a network by the turn of the twentieth century that was largely manned by local clerks. Its activities were governed from the head office in London as strictly as pre-1914 communications would allow – which is to say, with a great deal of discretion left to those in the field from one day to the next, even as their standing instructions grew more complex and demanding with the passage of the years. Capital raised in the City was shipped out, typically as gold or silver coin in wooden crates, to fund their pursuit of 'exchange banking'. This embraced all aspects of facilitating trade, especially the currency transactions it entailed, across the main ports of the East from Bombay to Shanghai. They dealt essentially with British companies, and very largely with shipments to and from Europe – mostly London, Liverpool and Glasgow. The risks were higher than most banks in the City were ready to contemplate, but this ensured an attractive level of returns on even bread-and-butter transactions. As this book will relate, most years brought a clutch of disasters, and where they struck was something of a lottery. So the Chartered relied from its earliest days on a portfolio approach, with a spread of branches across the East (over twenty of them by the end of the 1890s) extensive enough to let shareholders sleep soundly at night. The new century brought those shareholders plenty to celebrate, albeit discreetly after 1914 to avoid attracting undue attention to the gains made in the war years. By 1928, the network had doubled in size since pre-war days, customers' deposits had soared as high as £50 million (having passed £10 million only in 1903) and the stock market's valuation of the business made it comfortably the largest of the two dozen or so overseas banks still left in the City.* It was a valuation not seen again until the end of the 1950s.

The intervening years brought no fundamental change in the purpose of Chartered's business, but a succession of calamities that might easily have swept it away. The collapse of international trade in the early 1930s was so complete as to foil the portfolio strategy for a while, and volatile commodity prices put the brakes on growth for several years thereafter. The Second World War saw two-thirds of the bank's network liquidated by the Japanese, whose conquering armies brought Tokyo accountants in their wake to wrap up the books. And the post-1945 dismantling of the European order in Asia then pulled down the shutters on some of the Chartered's core markets. Restricted to a barely token presence in Communist China and slowly strangled in India by the Licence Raj, it might easily have slipped into the past like so many famous names that had underpinned the commercial life of the Empire. (One such was Eastern Bank, an

---

* One other, based in Hong Kong, was rather larger. At around £13 million, the Chartered's market capitalization in 1928 compared with about £22 million for the Hongkong & Shanghai Banking Corporation.

erstwhile rival in India and the Middle East which only escaped a looming collapse in 1956 by becoming a Chartered subsidiary.) Against all the odds, though, Chartered Bank weathered its setbacks. Showing an astonishing resilience in the circumstances, and still managed by a tiny cadre of British expatriates, it even appeared by the end of the 1960s to have begun forging a new post-Empire role for itself – one closely aligned with the rocketing growth of Hong Kong. But in May 1969 its Directors were suddenly apprised of a different future, which they were told firmly had received the blessing of the Governor of the Bank of England. This altered the Chartered's course more decisively than any world wars or revolutions.

The Governor's involvement was precipitated by the plight of another famous overseas bank headquartered in the City. Like the Chartered, it too had grown from largely Scottish mid-Victorian roots; but it had prospered in very different ways, in a region of the Empire miraculously endowed with unparalleled mineral wealth. This was Standard Bank of (British, at first) South Africa, founded in 1862. The capital initially shipped down to the Standard Bank in the Cape had been used to buy up a string of tiny country banks, largely in anticipation of British South Africa following Australia into world markets as a leading wool exporter. By the end of the 1860s, however, the bank's London Directors were just coming to realize that they had seriously overrated the Cape economy's potential when they were rescued by the news from Kimberley of sensational diamond discoveries. By making the bank indispensable to the diamond industry from its beginning, and later by engaging actively with both the Witwatersrand gold-mining boom and the imperialist ambitions of Cecil Rhodes, the Standard's local managers assured it of a central role in the development of South Africa over the next thirty years. By the late 1890s, the bank had assumed virtually official status: its network, with almost a hundred branches, dominated the country's commercial banking sector while its close ties to government saw it serving the Province in what was effectively a central banking role. The Boer War of 1899–1902 inevitably intensified this relationship with officialdom, as the Standard – led by an expatriate British banker and a team of managers personally familiar with the workings of the London head office – provided all the essential banking services for the Empire's war effort. This proved, however, to be the high-water mark of the bank's existence as a British institution, and, in the years that followed, a subtle schism took root between London and the Cape.

In the City, Directors flush with a massive financial windfall triggered by the war against the Boers saw nothing anomalous about their long-distance control over the bank, even after the Board had lost its last members with any direct experience of South Africa. The bank was almost entirely owned by shareholders in London, who seemed happy to rely on their Directors and who saw its steady expansion as proof that their confidence was not misplaced. (The branch network doubled between 1900 and 1914. Indeed, in the years running up to the Great War the Standard's key finances bore an uncanny resemblance to those of Chartered Bank – to which at this stage it was of course completely unrelated.) Those employed by the bank at the Cape, meanwhile, were starting to see things very differently. The Standard had about 1,600 employees by 1914, and the great majority of them had been born in South Africa. The top managers were still British-born – the Standard did not have its first South African head until 1960 – but in most cases they had settled to a new life in the country: they were there as émigrés, not secondees. They already saw their bank as an essentially domestic business, albeit one with strong imperial ties. These ties were now a mixed blessing: they offered some comfort through a prolonged recession in the South African economy (there was no further growth in the balance sheet before 1914, despite the expansion of the branch network), but its imperial hue hindered the bank's attempts to navigate an often bewildering political environment. The Union of South Africa, declared in 1910, was a far cry from the British South Africa with which the Standard had become so closely identified. When the Union's leaders had to choose a bank as the official holder of the Government's account, they rejected the Standard in favour of an Afrikaner rival from the Transvaal. These were murky waters, rarely fathomed by the Board in London. The result was a growing tension between the men at the Cape and their nominal masters that seemed sure one day to see them parting ways.

The divorce took an unconscionably long time. During the interwar years, the process was robbed of any urgency by the financial collapse of the Standard's Transvaal-based competitor, the National Bank of South Africa, and the latter's absorption into the international arm of Barclays, the UK clearing bank. This left South Africa with not one 'imperial' bank but two – and together, Standard Bank and Barclays sustained a remarkable duopoly, which extended beyond the Limpopo into East and Central Africa. It buttressed the role of the Standard's London Board and discouraged any serious plans, during the Depression era, for a change to the bank's ownership. The Second World War might perhaps have heralded the end of the British connection. By 1945, the country's wartime isolation had indeed revived South African expectations – in Pretoria as well as Cape Town – that this would be a sure outcome of the war. But this view took no account of the strength of vested interests in the City of London. Its banking grandees were desperate to shore up what was left of the Empire, and they saw the Standard as a test of their resolution. This determination prolonged its imperial after-life for another decade; indeed, it might have lasted even longer had not South Africa in the 1950s become increasingly identified with the apartheid policies of its National Party regime. These badly compromised the Standard's image elsewhere in Africa, and in 1962 forced the London Board – after some undignified wrangling – to make the operations within South Africa and those outside the new-born Republic into distinct legal entities, inexorably headed for separate ownership.

The impending loss of the business in South Africa unavoidably posed a question over the future of what was left of Standard Bank. It was an issue that resonated in British banking circles in the 1960s. Many were pondering around this time how the overseas banking legacies of the disappearing Empire might be consolidated in the interests of preserving the City's influence. One of the individuals at the centre of the debate, as Executive Chairman of the Standard, was Sir Cyril Hawker, appropriately enough a former Bank of England man. For several years, starting in 1962, he plotted and cajoled in pursuit of a blueprint (he called it his 'Grand Design') that might produce a new champion of British banking across the ex-colonial world. The Standard's reach was gradually extended through East, West and Central Africa, not least via the acquisition in 1965 of the Bank of British West Africa, a long-standing stalwart of the financial sector across its region. By the late 1960s Hawker's eye was trained on the opportunities in Asia. He and his colleagues soon alighted on the notion of a merger between Standard and Chartered Bank. The idea seemed to carry less appeal for their counterparts at the Chartered, however, who wanted more time to reflect on the implications; but time, for all Britain's overseas banks, was fast running out. International banking was evolving quickly by the late 1960s, not least because the leading names in the US industry were now intent on bringing their weight to bear overseas. Hawker had not been averse to sharing his plans with one of the US behemoths, the Chase Manhattan Bank of New York. He was, however, startled in 1969 to find the Standard suddenly targeted by Chase's Chairman, David Rockefeller, for a takeover. This was decidedly not part of his Grand Design, and Hawker turned to his friends in the City for a lifeline. The Bank of England made its displeasure over the Chase's impertinence known to the market – and the merger was announced of the Standard and Chartered banks just over a week later.

Though the two proudly independent banks certainly took their time adjusting to a shared future together, the performance of Standard Chartered surpassed all expectations in its first few years. Unprecedented trading volumes in the currency and commodity markets of the world in the early 1970s helped fuel a dramatic expansion. The Group's value on the stock market doubled within three years. Nonetheless, it soon had to face an uncomfortable dilemma. In less propitious trading conditions (which arrived on the back of the oil-price shock in 1974), the Group was conspicuously short of a sound home base. Though it had built a savings-bank network in Hong Kong, none of its geographical franchises offered the remotest prospect of providing the sinews of an international bank fit to compete with Chase Manhattan, Barclays or any of the other giants of Wall Street, Tokyo and the City. The latter could rely on the deposits and retail earnings available from huge domestic markets.

Cyril Hawker retired in 1974, before this gap in his Grand Design could be properly addressed. What followed was in many ways a tragic tale. Had events been dictated by a sense of history, this product of so much nineteenth-century Scottish endeavour must surely have ended up merging with the Royal Bank of Scotland, or perhaps even its smaller Scottish rival, Clydesdale Bank (then a subsidiary of the Midland). Standard Chartered made a pitch for both, but without success. There seemed to be only two practical alternatives. One was to sell out to a bigger and better-resourced UK competitor, an option famously rejected in 1986 when the Group (with support from a trio of 'white knights' from the East) defeated a hostile bid from Lloyds Bank. The other was to try to build a Western base of its own, with extensive corporate banking operations in both Europe and the US. This goal was duly pursued, and sadly added Standard Chartered's name to a long list of British banks that rushed into the US marketplace and came to regret it. The Western strategy also exposed a harsh truth about the enduring 'overseas banking' culture of the Group. It had many virtues. Those expatriate British managers who had sustained it, in the words of a celebrated manager of one of the Chartered's overseas peers in 1950, needed to be 'men who were at the same time politicians, business-men, linguists, good mixers and accurate bank clerks' (and, as he waspishly added, 'the combination has rarely been found').[1] It was not, however, a culture at all suited to the demands of an increasingly technocratic indus-try, attracting the brightest graduates and arming them with specialist expertise. Commercial bankers by the late 1980s had to be like commer-cial pilots, adept at coping with a mass of computerized data inconceivable to their peers in earlier generations. Too many of Standard Chartered's men were still more comfortable flying romantic biplanes. The result was eventually a string of crippling losses in syndicated bank credits, sovereign loans and commercial lending. A desperate retrenchment saw the final break made with South Africa in 1987. Over the following twelve months, the Group came close to being broken up altogether.

It was saved by an influx of determined leaders, appointed externally. Standard Chartered had hitherto relied almost exclusively on a cadre of senior executives who had spent their entire careers working their way up the ladder. The 1990s saw a succession of outsiders, imposing fundamental changes of strategy and structure. They included another key arrival from the Bank of England, Rodney Galpin, and a heavyweight from the oil industry, Patrick Gillam, who was Executive Chairman for ten crucial years. Several others were senior executives from the world's largest commercial banks, most notably Barclays, Citibank and Bank of America. Their collective efforts galvanized the management ranks below them. And luckily for them, the resuscitation coincided with the timely revival of the Group's core franchises in India, Africa and China, and the growth of Asia's 'emerging markets' – most of them actually re-emerging, in the context of the Chartered's long history. This seminal change in the shape of the global economy, and in the dynamics of world trade, was just gathering momentum in the critical years between 1988 and 1992 when the Group resolved to abandon its ill-fated expansion in the West. Turning back to its roots, Standard Chartered found itself able at last to cultivate a viable home base – comprised this time of several booming markets, in both retail and corporate banking, located in the very territories from which Chartered Bank had started out under Queen Victoria.

By the turn of the millennium, the Group bundled together so unceremoniously in 1969 was coming into a possibly heady inheritance. To claim it, much still needed to be done. Indeed, a dawning appreciation of the Group's potential induced a kind of planning overload in the first years of the new century, with too many initiatives under way and too few of the required policy frameworks in place. Under a new Chief Executive and a new Finance Director, respectively Mervyn Davies and Peter Sands (later to become Chief Executive himself, with his own supportive Finance Director, Richard Meddings), a sense of order was restored and the traces were laid for Standard Chartered to pursue some carefully defined but nonetheless breathtaking goals. There followed a remarkable decade. Branch networks were acquired and expanded, giving the Group a novel presence in local retail markets across Asia and Africa. The full panoply of modern investment banking was added to the traditional skills of trade financing and foreign exchange. Huge investments were made in the technology that underpinned global customer accounts, vast trading floors and the mobile telephony of digital banking. Along with it all came an astonishing growth in the workforce – it ballooned from 30,000 in 2003 to almost 90,000 in 2012 – but an immense effort (so far, apparently, successful) went into sustaining the Group's homogeneous culture.

It was not a period entirely free of setbacks. A truly fairy-tale script might have reunited the Group with its lost franchise in South Africa, now rid of apartheid, a goal that was pursued for a while but proved elusive. It would not have included some heavy losses in one or two individual country markets – and it would certainly have had no room for a bruising and costly chastisement in New York and Washington (endured alike by several other leading international banks) for defying US sanctions on trading with Iran. The ten years nevertheless left Standard Chartered with the kind of track record very rarely achieved by any corporate body of its size, let alone one with such relatively ancient origins. The Group made light of the havoc wreaked by the global financial crisis of 2008, and emerged at the end of the period still financing around 5 per cent of the world's trade contracts (a leading position shared with HSBC, its long-standing peer and always its keenest rival). The bare numbers sported enough records to start a Wisden book of banking, with total assets up more than five-fold over the ten years, and with total revenues and pre-tax profits up more than four-fold (as recorded in an annual report that went from 120 pages in 2003 to 296 pages in 2012). It was a performance that consolidated the Group's status as one of the world's leading banks and marked a striking, not to say spectacular, vindication of the merger of 1969. It also made 2012 a natural point at which to conclude this history – though no readers with any interest in financial affairs will need reminding that the story since 2012, as a Postscript briefly notes, has seen the Group once again having to retrench and rebuild for the future.

Crossing Continents draws together into one narrative the evolution of the modern banking group and of the separate banks that preceded it – both Chartered Bank and Eastern Bank on the one hand, and Standard Bank and the Bank of British West Africa on the other. All four, even Standard in its earlier days, relied on those young men who turned their backs on careers in Britain to cross continents in search of a more adventurous life, taking with them the commercial disciplines and routines of the City. All were banks that needed managing in defiance of the huge problems posed by their cross-continental profiles. And after the four had been forged into one, it was the strategic focus of Standard Chartered itself that hopped the continents – crossing in the 1970s from Asia and Africa to Europe and the Americas and then, in the 1990s, crossing back again. The focus of the book lies mainly with the story of overseas banking and so is most closely identified with Chartered Bank – a company that broadly stuck to one business model for more than a hundred years. But the phenomenal growth of the Standard in nineteenth-century South Africa and its enduring strength thereafter is an integral part of Standard Chartered's tale. Standard's push north of the Limpopo, and later into East and West Africa, explains why Standard Chartered much later came to inherit a business scattered across sub-Saharan Africa. And it was the curious and sometimes troubled relationship between the Standard's Board of Directors in London and the senior managers in South Africa that triggered the chain of events in the 1960s that culminated, at the end of the decade, in the very creation of Standard Chartered. While the resulting enterprise is far more heavily imbued with the traditions of the Chartered than of Standard Bank, today's Group might never have existed at all without the impetus provided by Cyril Hawker and his Grand Design. While these various facets of the Standard's past all feature conspicuously in what follows, the domestic history of the South African bank since 1945 is largely ignored except insofar as it touched upon relations with the bank's own Board in London, and later with Standard Chartered.

The history of Chartered Bank up to 1969, and of Standard Chartered since then, illuminates a strand of the City's banking history that has been relatively neglected, compared with the stories of the clearing banks, the merchant banks and the many famous partnerships that for so long sustained the financial markets of the Square Mile. But the ground covered by *Crossing Continents* has not been entirely untilled. The overseas banks of the nineteenth century and their successors were the subject of two early books by A. S. J. Baster – *The Imperial Banks* (1929) and *The International Banks* (1935) – and in more recent times their collective history has been authoritatively surveyed by Professor Geoffrey Jones. Any study of an individual bank in this sector must draw heavily on his work – most notably *British Multinational Banking 1830–1990* (1993), which includes many invaluable tables of balance-sheet data – and this account of Standard Chartered's history is indebted to his research and that of his colleague, the late Frankie Bostock. The banks that eventually came together as Standard Chartered had by then already bequeathed a few dedicated histories of their own. Chartered Bank had commissioned *Realms of Silver* by Compton Mackenzie as a centenary history – though it appeared a year late, in 1954 (a curious story, recounted in Appendix A). Standard Bank had also commissioned a centenary history, J. A. Henry's *The First Hundred Years of the Standard Bank*, which was published in 1963 (and was able to draw upon a much earlier *History of the Standard Bank of South*

Africa Ltd, 1862–1913 by G. T. Amphlett, published in 1914). The story of the Bank of British West Africa then appeared in 1976 as *Bankers in West Africa*, commissioned by the Standard Chartered after its own merger and written by a former financial editor of the *Guardian* newspaper, Richard Fry. In more recent times, a third history of Standard Bank has appeared, *Hoisting the Standard: 150 Years of Standard Bank* by Richard Steyn and Francis Antonie, published by the bank itself in Johannesburg in 2012.

Compiling a modern corporate biography of Standard Chartered has entailed covering a wide canvas, and treading a careful line. Enough has to be said about the technical details of the business to convey the importance of its economic role over many decades, but not so much as to sedate the reader or smother the story of a remarkable organization, hewn from the careers and private lives of countless employees over several generations in ways not often encountered in the commercial world. At the heart of Chartered's story, in particular, lies a narrative unavoidably – and I think properly – structured around the unusual lives of just a few thousand British bankers (and, let it not be forgotten, their often long-suffering wives). More than a hundred of them were interviewed in the course of researching this book. Several joined Chartered at the start of the 1950s, just about the time that researchers for the centenary history *Realms of Silver* were chasing down the reminiscences of elderly Chartered pensioners who had themselves joined towards the end of the 1890s – and several of whom could actually remember a City head office dominated by the presence of the bank's founding father and one of his principal lieutenants, Howard Gwyther and Caleb Lewis, who were both working in Hatton Court by 1865. All these individuals in their working lives were essentially creatures of the British Empire, whether in its heyday or after it had ceased to exist in any formal sense. Indeed, the way the bank sustained the practices and traditions of the Empire until well into the last quarter of the twentieth century is one of the more striking features of its history. Its youthful expatriates flocked to the same sports clubs and drinking holes in the 1970s as in the 1920s. Its managerial hierarchies in Bombay, Singapore and Hong Kong were scarcely less sacrosanct in the early 1980s than in the 1930s. Above all, in the relations between its British and locally-recruited employees, much the same doggedly colonial mindset of the post-war years still prevailed as late as the 1990s. Chartered Bank's recruitment brochure in 1956 suggested that 'British endeavour in the East is nowhere at an end, but everywhere in progress'. In keeping with this heroic optimism, Standard Chartered clung for more than two decades to an 'Empire-staffing' model that presupposed a fundamental divide between expatriate managers (upstairs, figuratively speaking) and local hires (downstairs). Only in the 1990s was it fully replaced by a corporate culture genuinely open to all talents. This paid off, in the end, surprisingly well. The bank that had remained so steadfastly colonial in its outlook – and had thereby, in all probability, escaped the hostile takeover that had seemed for so long to be its most likely fate – very soon found itself attracting droves of ambitious and highly qualified young Asians from many different ethnic backgrounds. By the start of the twenty-first century, even the Group's Chief Executive was an Indian. The stage was set for it to become by far the most thoroughly Asian of all the Western-originated banks working in the region.*

Historians discerning broader patterns are inclined now to question the strength of the British Empire even between the two world wars, let alone after 1945. As one magisterial survey of the Great War's impact would have it, 'the British Empire came to resemble not so much a vista of power as a landscape of rebellion on which the sun never set'. The notion of the Empire 'as a self-sustaining and self-legitimating strategic unit' came to be seen in the 1920s as a 'complacent scenario [that] collapsed'.[2] But the collective view of those working at the time for Chartered Bank reminds us why even the most persuasive historical patterns need to acknowledge some deviations and counter-trends. In focusing on the biography of one institution, *Crossing Continents* affords a sideways and often revealing glimpse of many familiar historical episodes, from mining booms and market crashes to revolutions, natural disasters and the two world wars. The surviving written records can sometimes be frustratingly bare: Chartered Bank managed a comprehensive update of the Office Rules for its Vietnam branch in 1966, amended with complementary guidance in 1970 and 1973, without including a single reference anywhere to the Vietnam War raging around it.[3] But there are plenty of more rewarding instances, especially from recent decades for which oral testimonies have been at least as important as the documentary evidence – for example of the Group's experience of the 9/11 attack on the World Trade Center in New York. And, as a banking study, *Crossing Continents* offers more than just a glimpse of several seminal developments in financial history, from

---

* At the same time, the Group has shown itself capable of adapting in intriguing ways to the changing demands of its multicultural profile. The move away from Empire-staffing has been notably respectful of some old patterns. Employees from the UK and continental Europe, the US, Canada and Australia accounted in 2014 for a mere 6 per cent of the total workforce; yet they still filled 51 per cent of the top 300 jobs, according to statistics gathered by a 'Diversity and Inclusion Council'. Senior managerial practices in the Group, in fact, were not so very different from those that prevailed before the 1990s.

the emergence of the eurodollar bond market to the spread of US banking practices and the shock of the global financial crisis of 2008. In spanning so many decades, it reflects a gradual evolution in the assumptions made about the nature of banking and its role in society – an evolution underpinning, eventually, the successful transformation of Standard Chartered from a deeply conservative institution, struggling to sustain honourable but hopelessly outmoded ways of doing business, into a modern corporation with all the attributes required to compete successfully in today's international banking arena. In particular, I hope it conveys a colourful sense of how remarkably the City of London was galvanized by the Big Bang of the 1980s – an interlude of merger mania that saw almost every significant name in the City linked to a transforming deal of one kind or another. Standard Chartered passed through it with no change of ownership, though it often appeared at the time to be a bank with nine lives. This story can be narrated in detail thanks to a daily diary kept from 1983 to 1988 by its Chief Executive, Michael McWilliam, who wrote up the day's events in longhand each evening – there can surely be few, if any, comparable records left by a City banker working at this level. His regular reflections on Standard Chartered's situation portray an institution that was not so much crossing continents as being pulled apart in its attempt to straddle them.

The McWilliam diaries are the single most striking item in a voluminous archive held by London Metropolitan Archives, part of the City of London Corporation, but *Crossing Continents* has been able to draw on a wealth of primary material – not least from the Second World War – that amply reflects the archive's longevity. Much of it constitutes a written commentary in one guise or another on the social and economic context of the day, and many of the commentators brought to the task well-educated and inquiring minds. Large international banks have not generally been regarded with much sympathy or respect in the post-2008 world, to say the least. Perhaps it is salutary to be reminded, by the records left from several generations, why it is that in the past British overseas banking was usually seen – by the wider publics at home and abroad, as well as those dependent on it for a living – less as a licence for the single-minded pursuit of money for its own sake than as a hybrid of commerce and public service. As this book can attest, the perception was for the most part fully justified.

I

A Double Provenance, 1853–70

I. FREE TRADE AND A CITY BLUEPRINT

The man who began *The Economist* newspaper in 1843 led a remarkable life, cut tragically short. Born into a well-to-do Quaker family in the Scottish border country, James Wilson left for London at the age of nineteen in 1824. For the next twenty years he ran a successful hat-manufacturing business in the capital. He also read voraciously and acquired a thorough grounding in the classical economics spelled out by an earlier generation of great (and largely Scottish) Enlightenment thinkers. He started writing himself in 1839, quickly becoming one of the foremost champions of Free Trade and launching *The Economist* to advance the cause. He wrote its editorial columns almost single-handedly for several years, even after becoming an MP in 1847 and subsequently holding junior posts in government for most of the following decade. By the late 1850s, by his own admission, life had brought him everything he could have hoped for – an influential career in politics and journalism, access to the most exclusive social circles, comfortable homes in Mayfair and the country and a happy family with six daughters, one of them recently married to a brilliant young journalist, Walter Bagehot, who had bold ambitions of his own for the family's thriving periodical. Yet so compelling was the ethos of public service in Victorian Britain that, when the vagaries of political life at Westminster brought Wilson an invitation in 1859 to serve Queen and Empire in Calcutta, he saw himself as honour-bound to turn his back on England and to accept the post he had been offered.

The hazards of life in India were hardly unfamiliar. Even among the fittest young men and women of its British community, a fearsome toll was taken annually by cholera, yellow fever, malaria and a dozen other killer diseases. (Calcutta had had its own Scottish Cemetery since 1820 for some of those who never made it home: it covered six acres.) Wilson, whose own father had died of cholera in London a quarter of a century earlier, was a portly fifty-four-year-old when he set sail for the sub-continent accompanied by his wife and two of his daughters. After a six-week journey, via the Mediterranean and the usual land crossing from Alexandria to Suez, he arrived in late November 1859, just a few months after the publication of what was in effect the first travel guide to India, *Murray's Handbook*. If he ever read its many cautionary paragraphs about the grim reality of India's tropical climate, he never showed any inclination to plan for it. With characteristic vigour he worked through the pleasant Bengali winter on devising an extraordinary agenda of financial reforms for the nascent British Raj. Then, pressing on with the preparatory paperwork, he stayed in Calcutta as the temperatures soared and the city sweltered through its summer months. Having despatched his family to the safety of a hill station, Wilson remained at his desk even as the monsoon rains broke in July. He envisaged steering through a fundamental programme of what we would today call nation-building. But with a terrible suddenness, he contracted dysentery and died in the second week of August 1860. Huge crowds turned out for his funeral the next day. Subscriptions raised from local merchant firms paid for a larger-than-life marble statue – done by the Scottish sculptor Jonathan Steell, whose many other statues included that of Sir Walter Scott for Edinburgh's Scott Memorial – and it stood for decades inside one of the foremost public buildings in Calcutta, the Dalhousie Institute.

It was not just his Victorian sense of duty that had drawn Wilson to India. By 1859 he had been taking a keen interest in Anglo-Indian financial affairs for many years. And it was his firm belief in the need for more robust financial institutions in India that had led him in 1852 to join with a small group of enterprising City men in launching a new bank, to be called 'The Chartered Bank of India, Australia and China'. The true extent of his involvement is none too clear, and indeed some have questioned his role or ignored it altogether. His daughter Emilie made no reference to it in the biography she wrote of her father in 1927.[1] The bank itself, one day to become Standard Chartered, made no reference to him in any of its newspaper advertisements – presumably at his request, given his other responsibilities – though all other founding directors were carefully listed in them for years to come. Much later, it would cherish the tie enough to rescue that posthumous marble statue when the Dalhousie Institute fell into disrepair in the 1950s – it stood for years thereafter at the centre of the grandest banking hall in Calcutta – and even shipped it back to London in 1985, to add a little class to a new head office building in the City. But when office relocations in 1989 left no obvious space for it, the statue was soon deemed surplus to requirements.* Nor have recent scholars shown much interest in Wilson's link to the birth of the bank. In 1993, a history of *The Economist* suggested Wilson's status as a founder of the Chartered Bank was all a bit of a misunderstanding. The bank had made room for the statue at its City headquarters, '[p]erhaps not knowing that the relationship was more apparent than real'.[2] Many have noted Wilson's importance to Indian affairs in the 1850s and also the significance of Chartered Bank's emergence, while omitting to mention any connection between them.[3] Certainly Wilson's role lasted scarcely a year. Yet without him, the bank would almost certainly never have existed.

This is not to say he was among the initiators of the project. The men behind it at the start were all City-based London merchants – and they must have been determined characters, for the birth of the bank was to prove a long and deeply frustrating business. We know the names of the eight individuals who came together as the founding directors – John Bagshaw, Peter Bell, George Carr, William Cook, William Lindsay, Thomas Mitchell, Joseph Morrison and John Gladstone (a cousin of the future Liberal Prime Minister) – but have only the sketchiest idea of their backgrounds. (*The Directory of Directors*, a mine of information on commercial connections in the nineteenth century, was first published in abbreviated form only in 1880, and by then all but one of the founders were dead.) A diligent investigation on Chartered Bank's behalf in 1951 could do little more than establish the names and addresses of their main business interests. Most had City links and commercial interests in the East Indies – John Gladstone was one of several cousins involved in managing the extensive trading interests of the Gladstone family, with firms in Liverpool and Calcutta – though few seem actually to have worked in the East.[4] While their personal circumstances are mostly obscure, the gist of their thinking can fairly be construed from later records. They saw that the volume of trade with India was rising rapidly by the middle of the 1840s: merchant firms in Calcutta, Bombay and Madras were handling ever larger imports from Britain, especially of metal goods and manufactured textiles, while overseeing the export from India of indigo and raw cotton (both to be used in the making of those same textiles), sugar, grain and a dozen other staple commodities – including opium, which actually accounted for around 30 per

---

* Happily it was offered to the latest-in-line of Wilson's successors as editor of *The Economist*, Rupert Pennant-Rea, who was keen to have it. Cleaned and given a fresh inscription, it was moved in 1990 to the reception of the Economist Building in London's St James's. When *The Economist* relocated in 2017, the paper presented the statue as a gift to Wilson's home town of Hawick, where it stands today within sight of his birthplace.

cent of the total by value but was mostly destined for China.[5] Enticing opportunities beckoned all across Asia, and they were no longer the strict preserve of the East India Company. Its centuries-old legal monopoly on the trade routes to India and China had been repealed – in 1813 and 1833 respectively – and its influence was now (in theory, at least) restricted to political and administrative matters. Nor was it just in trade and commerce that the retreat of 'John Company' was opening the way for fresh competitors. Ambitious newcomers had made their mark, for example, in Anglo-Asian shipping – the Peninsular and Oriental Company, the P&O, had been founded in 1840 – and others were intent on laying tracks for India's first railways. No other 'collateral sphere' was of more interest to merchant firms in the City than finance and banking services. Here the sequel to John Company's monopoly had been a messy compromise for years. Much of the export/import servicing was provided by a nexus of small 'agency houses' that had long swum round the Company like shoals of pilot fish. They used cash deposits from wealthy Company employees as the basis for providing their own financial services in league with both merchant partners in India and trading firms at home, notably in Glasgow, Liverpool and Manchester as well as the City of London. But their world was in truth a very poor cousin to the City itself, as one leading economic historian of India has described:

> Fraud, disputes, cliquism and distrust were widespread because both the local and the foreign partners were driven by a mentality . . . [of] 'predatory capitalism'. The majority of the foreign partners were determined to get rich quickly and return home. In this prevailing mood, no stable rules, institutions or foundation of trust could take shape. Both the Indo-European collaborations, and the financial capacity of the ventures they floated, were thus basically unsound and fragile.[6]

By the mid-1840s, several attempts had already been made by leading figures in the City of London to improve on this state of affairs by founding a substantial bank that would be backed by City investors and establish a network of branches – a model familiar in Scotland though still alien to English banking – geared to servicing the Eastern trade routes of the Empire. They looked to the example set by other so-called 'overseas banks', anchored in the City with operations in other distant parts of the Empire, notably Canada and Australasia. They also hoped to draw lessons from the progress of several joint-stock banks in India itself, set up under British direction and providing a kind of prototype business model. With names like the Agra and United Service Bank and the North-Western Bank of India, at least a dozen of these banks had been created since

1833.* All were closely tied to the needs of Anglo-Indian trade and commerce: they had little if anything to do with indigenous banking and money-lending in the Indian interior. By 1845 the best of them, including the Agra and United, were doing rather well. But they were essentially Indian businesses, run from head offices in the sub-continent and funded, a little like the agency houses, by shareholders living in the East. Most of the City of London men, by contrast, had little direct experience of India themselves and no intention whatever of moving there. The sort of bank they had in mind would represent a more fundamental break with the past. And this explained most of the difficulties they had encountered to date. For the idea of an Eastern overseas bank was strongly resisted by the East India Company, which, according to a recent study of its decline, 'feared the arrival of large new financial institutions, the establishment of which might bring into question the rationale for its own continued existence'.[7] Such institutions would at the very least threaten the significant income that the Company still enjoyed on its own financial dealings, in flagrant denial of its revised legal status since 1833. Also actively opposed to the idea, of course, were the agency houses themselves, for whom a large City-backed rival would mean potentially disastrous competition.

In the event, many of the agency houses encountered a more immediate disaster, triggered by the worst and most far-reaching commercial crisis in living memory. The traumatic events of 1847–8 are generally most associated today with a spectacular crash in the London stock market, as the railway mania of the 1840s hit the buffers and a severe depression swept through the broader economy (not least in Ireland, where it helped precipitate the horrors of the Potato Famine). Just as conspicuous for contemporaries in the City was the ruinous impact of suddenly soaring interest rates on the complex network of relationships that tied together the financial markets of London and Calcutta, in both of which agency houses went down like nine-pins. Those few that remained cut back their services severely, leaving behind a distrust of the City of London among Bengali merchant families that would linger for a long time. Suddenly the notion of a full-blown overseas bank geared to Indian trade took on a new importance for merchants who depended on financial intermediaries. It was probably at this point that the founding Directors made common cause with the editor of *The Economist*. Just two months after the onset

---

* Two new government-controlled entities had also been established, in Bombay and Madras, to add to the official Bank of Bengal, founded in Calcutta in 1806. These three were known in India as the Presidency Banks, given their location in the three 'Presidency' territories of Bombay, Madras and Bengal into which the East India Company had long ago sub-divided its ruling presence in the sub-continent.

of the financial crisis, two of them – Thomas Mitchell and John Bagshaw – were returned to parliament in the general election of July 1847. Alongside Mitchell and Bagshaw among the newly elected Liberal MPs was James Wilson, already well-known for his journalism and keeping a close watch on the Anglo-Indian dimension of the mounting turmoil in the City.[8]

Perhaps Wilson's interest was partly attributable to the fact that he himself had once been badly burnt by the volatility of the sub-continent's roller-coaster markets. In 1837 he had speculated heavily in Bengali indigo and had lost all his money, ending up within a whisker of bankruptcy. But his fascination with India went much deeper, and was linked directly to his espousal of the Free Trade cause, as his weekly columns reflected. Top of the Free Trade school's list of grievances for years had been agricultural protectionism in England, as encapsulated in the Corn Laws that had finally been abolished in 1846 (helping, indeed, to trigger the 1847 crash). Close behind it, and still all too evident in 1847, was the state of the Indian economy – riddled with inefficiencies heaped up, as the Free Traders believed, under the aegis of the East India Company's powerful grip on British interests in Asia. True, the Company's monopolies had now been curtailed, but those who ran it from its City headquarters enjoyed a level of influence far too subtle and pervasive to have been ended at a stroke by any act of legislation. The debacle of 1847 added to the vehemence of those who criticized its lingering influence over Eastern trade. Wilson the Free Trader was determined to help make a genuine break with the past, and was soon given his chance to do so. In May 1848, he was appointed Secretary to the Indian Board of Control, the Whitehall department established in 1784 to exercise a degree of governmental supervision over the East India Company. His main brief was to find ways of encouraging British investment – a task that notably led him to instigate the creation of a railway network for the country – and it seems fair to assume he lost no time exploring ideas with the more prominent City figures interested in India, including Mitchell and Bagshaw. Certainly he appears to have been encouraged and intrigued by the readiness of Mitchell et al. to contemplate founding a new bank, not just to support their own trading activities but as a potentially attractive business in its own right.

It would be a business predicated from the start on high returns for undeniably high levels of risk, financing trade in and out of distant ports where bankers and their money could be easily separated in a thousand ways. To defray those risks as much as possible, the putative founders were keen to encompass a broad presence throughout 'the East', including Singapore and the coastal ports of China. Thomas Mitchell's family firm had long been a leading importer of flax and hemp from Russia, and he was probably searching for contacts with rival hemp producers wherever he could find them. He was soon to emerge as the leader of his small band of merchant friends. Over the next four years, little or no firm commitment was made to establishing the bank, but the scope of its prospective activities continued to grow. In the early summer of 1851, the first news arrived of gold strikes in Australia, adding hugely to the scheme's appeal. Similar reports from California in 1848 had seen hundreds of thousands of people flooding to the San Francisco region. Now a second Gold Rush phenomenon looked imminent – and the trade implications of any sizeable jump in Australia's meagre population seemed obvious. The immigrants would want tea from China, tobacco from the Philippines, sugar from Java, coffee and spices from India and Ceylon (Sri Lanka). The gold to pay for these supplies, panned in New South Wales and Victoria, would never be short of buyers in the sub-continent. Trade between Australia and the Asian markets – known as 'the country trade' and never subject to the East India Company's monopolies – was surely on the brink of explosive growth. A bank based in Australia as well as India and China might expect to flourish on the back of both trade with Britain *and* this triangular Asian trade.

However compelling the theory, though, any banking service of this kind would of course be daunting in practice – as would be the challenge of finding investors willing to risk the necessary capital. All financing activities in Asia were complicated; trying to control them from a base in the City would hugely compound the risks. Freight ships seldom made it from London via the Cape to Hong Kong – a British colony since 1841 – in less than three months, which was one measure of the geographical challenge. The ports of India and China and the harbour markets of the Eastern archipelago – including Singapore, a trading post since 1819 and part of the British 'Straits Settlements' colony since 1826 – had their own trading customs, often as impenetrable as their innumerable native languages and exotic alphabets. Sharp practice or simple misunderstandings would threaten every trade route as surely as piracy and tropical storms. And, in the event of some calamitous loss, shareholders would face the prospect of losing not just their investment in the bank but all the money they had in the world. Here was perhaps the supreme obstacle to the establishment of any joint-stock bank, whether in India or the City of London. In neither place were such banks offered the legal protection of limited liability (legislation to this effect did not arrive on the statute books until 1855). This helps explain, perhaps more than any other single factor, the merchants' reluctance to push ahead with their plan. In fact lawyers had already devised a partial solution to the liability problem and this had played an important role in spurring the formation of other 'overseas banks' since the 1830s: in exchange for complying with some basic rules laid down by the Treasury, each of them had been granted a Royal Charter. This gave them enormous kudos and the heightened credibility that came from a direct link to the Crown, but these were bits of tinsel compared with the real significance of a Charter – that it limited any shareholder's liability to a sum equivalent to twice his original outlay. With the downside risk thus limited at the stroke of a regal quill, several 'chartered' banks had had no trouble at all finding enthusiastic backers in the City. The applicability of the model to the notion of a banking network in the East must have been self-evident to Mitchell and his associates. Unfortunately, there was one huge region of the world for which Royal Charters were not available. The East India Company still enjoyed an effective right of veto over any application for a charter valid in its Asian domains – and it was a veto the Company still had no intention of surrendering.

Then, in 1852, the outlook brightened dramatically. This had nothing to do with the mounting excitement over the gold finds in Australia, though it could hardly have been better timed. One joint-stock bank in India had proved itself a cut above the rest. Founded in Bombay in 1842 as the Bank of Western India, it had grown so quickly that its directors had conceived an altogether grander future for it than originally envisaged, and in 1845 they had accordingly relocated its head office from Bombay to the City, renaming it the Oriental Bank. Four years later, they had taken over a struggling British-owned bank in Ceylon that was in possession of something almost as valuable as all the coffee on the island. (Its tea came later.) Though long occupied by British planters, Ceylon had never been a part of the East India Company's franchise. The humble Bank of Ceylon had therefore been able to distinguish itself in 1842 by acquiring a Royal Charter. In 1849 this charter had passed with all its other assets to the Oriental Bank and three years later provided the key to a scarcely suspected back door into Asian banking. Without anyone consulting the East India Company – blamed on a momentous oversight in the Treasury – the Oriental had, by early 1852, succeeded in converting the Ceylonese charter into a Royal Charter of its own, which would allow it to operate, from the City, in India and anywhere else 'east of the Cape of Good Hope'. Suddenly, albeit with some sleight of hand, the 'Chartered' formula was no longer excluded from the Asian marketplace. Within weeks, Thomas Mitchell and his friends duly hastened to take advantage of the Oriental's initiative. By now they had settled on a name for their bank: it would be called 'the Bank of British India and Australia'. They had also appointed a Company Secretary, one George Hope. Before the end of March, Hope had composed a draft prospectus to present to would-be investors.[9]

PROSPECTUS

OF THE

BANK OF BRITISH INDIA AND AUSTRALIA.

(PROVISIONALLY REGISTERED.)

TO BE INCORPORATED BY ROYAL CHARTER.

CAPITAL TWO MILLIONS, IN 100,000 SHARES OF £20 EACH.
DEPOSIT £2 10s. per Share.

(PRIVATE)

THE greatly increased and increasing intercourse with British India, and our possessions in the Southern Hemisphere, and the increasing demands which, as a natural consequence, have sprung up for further Banking Accommodation with these important divisions of the Empire,—intermediately as well as directly,—have suggested themselves to the promoters of this undertaking, as reasons sufficiently valid and substantial, to call for the establishment of such an Institution at no distant date; but when, at the same time, it is considered that the system of Agency and Banking business, hitherto conjointly carried on through the medium of the leading Commercial Houses connected with the East, has, of late years, in consequence of a continuation of periodically recurring and disastrous failures (dating from 1832 downwards) been gradually losing public confidence, until it is now well nigh exploded, it will be generally conceded that there is, at this particular moment, a wide field open for the extension of Banking enterprize, in that quarter of the World, based upon sound principles, and managed by practical and experienced men, long versed in the business of the East and of the Southern Hemisphere, in all its ramifications,—Exchange, Agency, Banking, and Commercial.

It has been said, and truly, that India is a World in itself. The population cannot be estimated at less than 150 Millions, while, from the Himalayas in the North to Cape Comorin in the South, and from Ava in the East to the Indus on the West, the extent of Territory belonging to the East India Company is estimated at about 1,700,000 square miles. This of itself is one of the noblest and most extensive fields of enterprize ever presented to any people, and when we couple this splendid territory with the surrounding islands—with China—and with our vast Empire in the Southern seas—it cannot fail to be universally admitted that, as one great whole, there never was presented to the World such a luxuriant field (comparatively unoccupied) for developement by the aid of Banking enterprize, and that too a field, to which shrewd and influential Capitalists must ever be disposed to lend their countenance and assistance.

To show clearly, and at a glance, the number and present position of the existing East India Banks, the following tabular statement is here inserted.

NAME.	When Established.	Paid up Capital.	Deposits and Circulation.	Reserve Fund.	Price of Original Shares.	Present value of Shares.	Last Dividend per Cent
METROPOLITAN.							
Bank of Bengal	1809	1,137,142	1,857,834		400	635	12
„ Madras	1809	300,000	198,049	5,316	100	120	10
„ Bombay......... ...	1840	522,500	574,699	2,158	100	115	6
Commercial Bank of Bombay	1846	362,000	86,586	7,149	100 50 paid	49	7
Oriental Bank Corporation....	1842	642,725	760,772	112,000	25	35¼	12
PROVINCIAL.							
Agra and U. S. Bank........	1833	636,450	255,906	61,031	50	56	8
North Western Bank of India	1841	238,000	107,000		50		
Simla Bank	1845	80,000	12,000		100		
Cawnpore „	1845	105,000	11,000		100		9
Delhi „	1845	160,000	42,000		50		8
Dacca ., ...	1846	50,000			50		

From which it will be observed that notwithstanding the mismanagement of several of these Institutions, (especially the Provincial or Mofussil Banks, which have been conducted more upon the principle of London Loan Societies, than that of legitimate Banking,) the majority have flourished so far, and continue to hold out encouraging prospects of success for the future, more particularly the Metropolitan ones. Nor indeed is this at all to be wondered at, for the maxim is an undisputed one that, in a Country like India, *"where the rate of Interest is high, the profits of Bankers must necessarily be high also."*

The title page of the sales prospectus drafted in March 1852 for the planned Bank of British India and Australia

Before approaching these investors, just one further ingredient was required – a prestigious chairman, preferably with excellent contacts at Westminster. There was one obvious candidate, and by a stroke of good fortune he quite unexpectedly became available. The previous month, the Whig government had fallen from power, and James Wilson was out of office. He was joined on the opposition benches by a kindred spirit in Robert Lowe, an often fiercely outspoken leader-writer for *The Times* – now at the height of its influence – who had recently returned from eight years working as a lawyer and politician in Australia. By Wilson's own account, the erstwhile Secretary of the India Board and his newly elected friend in the House were soon both approached by Mitchell and his colleagues on the newly formed Board of the bank: '[they] applied to Mr Lowe and myself to join the direction. We did so, on a belief that it was an institution in every way that [was] required for the commission of the country . . .'[10] One of the bank founders, William Lindsay, was a former merchant seaman from Ayrshire – in nine years at sea, he had risen from cabin boy to ship's captain[11] – who had joined with Mitchell in championing a reform of the Navigation Laws in 1849. (In later life he wrote a massive four-volume history of merchant shipping.) This was another cause close to Wilson's heart, and may have helped persuade the former Government minister to accept the invitation. But he evidently needed little persuading: the ambitions of the new bank were exactly in line with his Free Trade philosophy. And within weeks it was clear that he intended to be much more than a mere political figurehead.

In fact, fired by his own Free Trade goals, Wilson seems to have assumed the leadership of the project. He soon took a red pen to Hope's prospectus, for example, ditching its less-than-compelling sales pitch ('the system of Agency and Banking business [in the East] . . . has of late years . . . been gradually losing public confidence, until it is well nigh exploded') and drawing up a fresh and immeasurably more persuasive version. The new City-based bank, it proclaimed, would be

> established chiefly in order to extend the legitimate facilities of banking to the vast and rapidly expanding trade between the Australian Colonies, British India, China, and other parts of the Eastern Archipelago: – a field as yet wholly unoccupied by any similar institution. The objects of the Company will, however, also embrace in connexion therewith, an extension of Banking accommodation to the direct trade of British India, China and Australia with this country, at present so inadequately provided for.[12]

Above all, Wilson gave the bank a new name – and surely only he could have had the nerve to christen it 'The Chartered Bank of India, Australia and China' before its promoters had even formally applied for a charter.* Heedless of this little technicality, investors clamoured for stock when the prospectus was finally published in October 1852. Wilson in his own periodical described the project as 'one of the most important undertakings which has been contemplated for many years past'.[13] Initial down payments of £2 each were made on 32,200 shares (their 'fully paid-up' value to be £20, to be tapped if needed), producing immediate equity capital of £64,400. The final sum raised could be £644,000, and it was hoped this would be lifted to £1 million soon and perhaps £3 million eventually. Wilson chaired the first meeting of the Board, on 18 October 1852, and all but three of the next dozen Board meetings through the rest of the year.[14]

At some point in this process, the East India Company finally woke up to what was going on, and the Directors of its Court were not pleased. (All chartered companies had a 'Court' rather than a Board, though the difference was strictly cosmetic.) They sent for their learned friends and by the end of 1852 a counter-assault would be launched in the courts to overturn the Treasury's approval a year earlier of the Oriental's charter. In the meantime, only a few weeks after the publication of its prospectus, a letter of protest about Chartered Bank was delivered to the India Board. The Directors of the East India Company, as the India Board was indignantly informed, were

> decidedly and very strongly of [the] opinion that with due regard to the interests of the Indian community it would be highly inexpedient to confer a Charter with limited liability upon any banking company which may design to be engaged in the business of Exchange . . . It needs no argument to prove that the bank which proposes to issue notes and at the same time to engage in business of a speculative character requires every check which can be placed upon its proceedings . . . [and to grant limited liability] would in the Court's opinion be tantamount to removing the main check against improper and reckless management.[15]

Confident that the East India Company had overestimated its declining influence, the men behind the new bank pressed defiantly ahead with their plans. Certificates were posted off to the first shareholders – the register

---

* This formal name was to be retained for a hundred years, before giving way to plain The Chartered Bank as part of the centenary celebrations in 1953. In common parlance it was generally 'The Chartered'. In modern times, the bank was known to all as simply 'Chartered' (though it went on issuing banknotes as The Chartered Bank, see Plate 31). As one former executive rather indignantly explained to the author, 'well, you don't talk about The Barclays, do you?'

drawn up by
James Wilson Esq
M.P.

THE
CHARTERED BANK
OF
INDIA, AUSTRALIA,
AND
CHINA.

TO BE INCORPORATED BY ROYAL CHARTER,
BY WHICH THE LIABILITY WILL BE LIMITED.

CAPITAL £1,000,000 STERLING.

In 50,000 Shares of £20 each, with power to increase the same
to £3,000,000 Sterling.

DEPOSIT, 10 per Cent.

DIRECTORS.

T. A. MITCHELL, Esq. M.P. (firm Messrs. Sampson, Mitchell, and Co.), 9, New Broad Street.
JAMES WILSON, Esq., M.P. (late of the India Board), 15, Hertford Street, May Fair.
ROBERT LOWE, Esq., M.P. (late Member of the Legislative Assembly, Sydney), 6, Eaton Square.
PETER BELL, Esq. (firm of Messrs. Scott, Bell, and Co., London, India, and China.)
JOHN BAGSHAW, Esq. (late of Calcutta), Cliff House, Harwich.
WILLIAM COOK, Esq. (firm of Messrs. Cook, Sons, and Co., St. Paul's Churchyard.)
GEORGE BOWNES CARR, Esq., Lawrence Poultney Place.
JOHN GLADSTONE, Esq., Stockwell Lodge, Surrey.
W. S. LINDSAY, Esq. (firm of Messrs. W. S. Lindsay and Co., 8, Austin Friars.)
JOSEPH R. MORRISON, Esq. (firm of Messrs. James Morrison and Co., Australian Merchants, 2, Crown Court, Philpot Lane.)

(With power to add to their number.)

BANKERS.
Messrs. GLYN, HALLIFAX, MILLS, and CO.

AUDITORS.
GEORGE C. GLYN, Esq., Banker.

OFFICIAL AUDITORS.
Messrs. QUILTER, BALL, and CO.

SOLICITORS.
Messrs. OLIVERSON, LAVIE, AND PEACHEY.

BROKERS.
Messrs. HUTCHINSON and SON, 39, Lothbury London.
Messrs. ROSKELL and ROBERT, Liverpool.
Messrs. JOHNSTON and WALKER, Manchester.
Mr. GEORGE WISE, Leeds.
Mr. S. LEA, Birmingham.

SECRETARY PRO. TEM.
Mr. GEORGE J. HOPE.—TEMPORARY OFFICES, 21, Moorgate Street.

The Chartered Bank of India, Australia and China, is established chiefly in order to extend the
legitimate facilities of Banking to the vast and rapidly extending trade between the Australian Colonies,
British India, China, and other parts of the Eastern Archipelago:—a field as yet wholly unoccupied by
any similar institution. The objects of the Company will, however, also embrace in connexion there-
with, an extension of Banking accommodation to the direct trade of British India, China, and Australia
with this country, at present so inadequately provided for.

The title page of the finished 1852 prospectus for Chartered Bank of India,
Australia and China, 'drawn up by James Wilson Esq, M.P.'

of their names has survived, with its first line dated 5 December 1852[16] – and a first executive appointment was made in December 1852.* The Board offered 'the Bank Managership for Victoria' to one James Rae, waiting aboard a ship in the Port of London for embarkation to Melbourne – 'this of course subject to the contingency of our getting a Charter which there seems no reason to doubt', as the minutes of the next Board meeting noted.[17] It was soon apparent, however, that there were actually plenty of reasons to be doubtful. Efforts to secure the Royal Charter landed the Board in a legal quagmire, with officials at the India Board plainly disinclined to challenge the obstructive stance of the East India Company.

Moreover, at this juncture, awkwardly, the position of the parties in a highly volatile House of Commons was reversed again: a new Whig–Peelite coalition was announced just before the end of the year. Lowe and Wilson, having retained their seats in Parliament at the July 1852 general election, both accepted posts in the new Government, leaving them no choice but to leave the Board of the bank. (While Lowe joined the India Board, Wilson became Financial Secretary to the Treasury.) Their abrupt departure came close to closing Chartered Bank even before its doors had opened. For ten months, Wilson had provided much of the leadership to ensure its funding.† Even more important, he had taken the lead in the wrangling within Whitehall over the Royal Charter. The chair was now taken by the forty-year-old Thomas Mitchell. He did his best, and even continued taking discreet advice from Wilson for a while; but, since Wilson was now one of the officials at the Treasury responsible for banking matters, this unusual arrangement had its limitations and the new chairman was soon floundering. The charter negotiations grew steadily more complicated and by the spring of 1853 matters seem to have reached a complete impasse.

---

* It was not the *very* first appointment. This distinction went to a John Bullock, who had already been recruited as the bank's Head Messenger and House-Keeper. We know this only because the Court noted receipt of a medical report on him in June 1889, which was approved as the basis for his retirement after thirty-seven years' service with a pension of 20 shillings a week. (5 June 1889, JL-B notes, LMA: CH03/01/14/016.)

† Twenty years later, another of the founder members of the Board acknowledged as much. J. R. Morrison lost his place on the Board in 1872 (in slightly acrimonious circumstances) and returned as an ordinary, if distinctly quarrelsome, shareholder to make an emotional speech at the General Meeting in April 1873. Morrison told the meeting 'he still retained his interest in the bank, of which he and the late Chancellor of the Exchequer and the late President of the Board of Trade were the founders (cheers)' (*The Bankers' Magazine*, Vol. 33, 1873, pp. 463–8). Lowe had by then served as Chancellor for five years to 1873, and Wilson had served at the Board of Trade for a few months before departing for India in the autumn of 1859.

This caused Wilson serious embarrassment, not least because he had urged his fellow Directors at the start of the year to hold out for the charter as originally envisaged, when some of them had suggested scuttling their Asian challenge to the East India Company and settling instead for an exclusively Australian charter. In a further twist to the saga, the availability of an Australian charter all but disappeared early in 1853. Too many Australian banks had appeared too quickly in the course of 1852, and the Colony had taken steps to deter any further entrants for a while. By May 1853, Chartered Bank's prospects were thus looking none too hopeful. It was in danger of ending up unchartered on every front.

In some dismay, Wilson turned to his last resort – a direct appeal to the Chancellor of the Exchequer himself, William Gladstone. In a letter setting out the background at some length, he asked Gladstone to approve a petition to the Privy Council to sort out what had become 'a matter of Imperial concern as interesting to many parts of the Empire and not to any one'.[18] Though he had of course disposed of his own financial interest in the bank as propriety required, as he explained, it was plain that reputations were at stake: 'it is certain that the Treasury, and I in particular, as well as Mr Lowe are deeply committed to the granting of the charter: – and from which I do not see how we can retreat with either honour or credit'. This was a remarkably forthright stand, which would seem to have left the two men with little option but to resign, had the Chancellor ignored it. No response from the Chancellor survives; but some useful intervention might reasonably be inferred, and Gladstone must surely have known of the involvement of his cousin John.* So Wilson went on chivvying, and a few months later the India Board eventually gave way.[19] Probably not coincidentally, the Oriental Bank had in the meantime seen its right to a charter reaffirmed by the Government's Solicitor-General. The East India Company resigned itself to the idea of two 'Eastern exchange banks' flourishing under its nose, apparently preferring not to leave the Oriental with a monopoly on the new concession. Mitchell and his colleagues for their part agreed to some fine-tuning of their plans, notably giving up plans for their bank to issue its own bank-notes in India. A few months later, on 29 December 1853, Queen Victoria personally put her seal to its Royal Charter, a document running to fifteen closely written pages and setting out the parameters of the future business in considerable detail.[20]

---

* One of many enterprises linked to the Gladstones was Ogilvy, Gillanders & Co., founded in the 1820s (see Sydney Checkland, *The Gladstones: A Family Biography 1764–1851*, CUP, 1971, p. 181). John Gladstone's directorship of the Chartered bequeathed it a lasting tie with this firm.

It fell short of removing every obstacle to the Directors' plans: Australia was still out of bounds, pending further moves within the Colony itself. The Directors opted to leave that battle for another day, leaving the name of the bank unaltered in the meantime as a token of future intent.

There were other pressing battles to be fought. Securing the Royal Charter turned out to be merely the prelude to three quarrelsome years for the Directors and their investors in the City, during which time all plans for the branch network remained firmly on the drawing board. The share price had been ramped up by more than 50 per cent by the end of 1852. Falling markets in 1853, the charter difficulties and the looming prospect of a major war in the Crimea brought it back to earth with a bump. By early 1854, 'overseas banking' no longer appeared quite such an inspiring idea. Chartered Bank's Directors enjoyed belonging to a Court rather than a Board – as required by the possession of a Royal Charter, as at the East India Company, or the Bank of England itself – but the reality was less impressive. Many peeved investors had snapped up shares in the secondary market at rashly inflated prices. Shareholders accounting for no less than a third of the bank's capital now demanded their money back. At a protest meeting convened in March 1854, there was unanimous support for a motion declaring it 'highly inexpedient and hazardous to proceed with this undertaking'.[21] Soon they were pressing hard for the bank to be wound up, and court action followed. The Directors began preparing a plan that would mean abandoning their original vision in favour of tying up with an existing institution. The Company Secretary, George Hope, wrote to at least one of the Australian banks extolling the benefits of a merger with Chartered Bank.[22] A beleaguered Thomas Mitchell told shareholders at the bank's first Annual General Meeting in April 1855 that the setbacks of the past year had 'brought them to a period of pecuniary pressure . . . They had accordingly made proposals for an amalgamation with one of the banks in India . . .'[23] One way or another, the first General Meeting seemed likely to be their last. Within a few months, though, Mitchell was back reporting that the proposed merger – with the North-West Bank of India – had fallen through, 'in consequence of technical difficulties – difficulties not raised by this company, and which he did not think had any real foundation'.[24] The Directors decided to soldier on. They remained in touch with Wilson from time to time, usually via the solicitor acting for the bank, but the relationship necessarily remained delicate.[25] Wilson for his part must have watched their travails with some concern. When the time came for the bank to raise additional capital, under the terms of the charter, it seemed for a moment as though they might struggle to make any further headway at

all. An attempt to place 7,000 new shares in the City in February
1856 looked like failing ignominiously. Buyers were eventually found for
3,700 shares – but most were taken up in India, with only a few hundred
sold in the City. By the autumn of 1856, the Court was pleading with the
Treasury (in vain) to allow it to scale down its equity commitment. At
least one of the Directors was openly in favour of winding up: he told the
Court 'that in the event of the bank's going on, it was his intention to send
forward again his resignation'.[26]

But most were still determined to press ahead, if only they could circumvent the dissident shareholders. Late in 1856, Mitchell and his allies
finally found a way around them. They identified three third parties who
were keen to join the Court and ready to invest heavily in buying out the
equity held by the dissidents. It was slightly awkward, however, that these
potential white knights (to use a City idiom of a very different era) currently had insufficient cash of their own – so a scheme was devised to
provide them with the necessary funds. An obliging bank in Threadneedle
Street, City Bank, agreed to advance the money discreetly, on the back of
an indemnity from Chartered Bank itself and an undertaking that City
Bank would be Chartered's 'sole London bankers for current business and
transactions with its branches abroad'. The arrangement would probably
have looked highly improper to outsiders, if not actually illegal, but the
special committee of Chartered and City Directors that met on 23 January
1857 to seal the deal had no intention of broadcasting its details.

The solitary Minute of the meeting was scribbled on a small sheet of
notepaper, on the back of which was written: 'Certain matters connected
with the above [Minute] were afterwards the subject of private conversation by the gentlemen present and arrangements come to, a memorandum
of which was left in [the Secretary] Mr Stewart's hands for reference by
the parties and their friends interested, as they might require.' Two fair
copies have survived of that memorandum, which was simply entitled
'Outline of private Agreement January 1857'. It laid out the terms under
which City Bank would bankroll the aspiring new investors.[27] The outcome was that dissident shareholders were enabled to sell 11,000 shares,
ostensibly to William Macnaughtan, James Nelson Smith and James
Fraser – though the real buyer was City Bank and these three gentlemen
had at least two years to pay for their purchases. Meanwhile they were
qualified to join the Court 'as soon as needs be' – which hardly taxed their
patience, because two of the existing Directors quickly stepped down and
a third departed the following year. The Chartered had in the process
picked up the support of an established bank (whose own Directors had
incidentally subscribed for 6,000 shares in the bank at the outset), and

soon afterwards took up the offer of a tenancy inside City Bank, occupy-ing a two-room suite in its Threadneedle Street building. Above all, the chorus of doubters on the Share Register had at last been seen off.

By the time of the 3rd Annual General Meeting in February 1857, the Court appeared to have recovered its nerve. Mitchell as Chairman was even ready at last to voice some enthusiasm over their prospects. All plans for Australia were off, but they would have more than enough business else-where to keep them busy. He reeled off a batch of statistics, to impress upon his audience how dramatically India's overseas trade was now growing. In just three years, exports of cotton, wool, linseed, rape-seed and mustard-seed had doubled, even trebled in volume. Yet India's railways – all 300 miles of them – had hardly begun to penetrate the interior. When the line from Bombay reached the cotton districts, 'the export of cotton will take a per-fectly wonderful start'.[28] The mood of the meeting chimed with a rising confidence in the City at large: the peace treaty recently ending the Crimean War had held good, lifting the money markets. In the months that followed, the bank's shareholders – old and new alike – happily subscribed to the outstanding equity instalments on their partly-paid shares. The world seemed suddenly to be shrinking in spectacular ways. Steam-powered ves-sels were knocking as much as two months off freight voyages from London to Shanghai and Sydney via the Cape, even if finding enough room in them for both coal and passengers was still problematic. (Steamships had been leaving the Port of London for Australia on the first day of every month since 1848.) And there were surely no markets in the East that would not be embraced now within the ocean-trading routes over which the City of London's merchants presided: even the ports of Japan, effectively closed to the West for more than two hundred years, were opening up in the wake of Commodore Perry's US Navy expeditions of 1853–4.

For those focused on the sub-continent, the second half of 1857 marked a sharper and hardly less fundamental change. The Indian Mutiny – remembered in India today as the Great Rebellion – came as a terrible shock to the entire British expatriate community. It was suppressed with savage reprisals costing the lives of hundreds of thousands of Indians, but only after it had effectively demolished the old basis of British rule. One consequence of this was a curious irony. Just as the concept behind Char-tered Bank seemed ready to be tested on the ground in India, the Leviathan that had tried to block the bank's creation in London was itself swept away: in 1858 the East India Company was dismantled and replaced with the administrative machinery of the British Raj. Indeed, it was to assist with the subsequent financial reconstruction of the Indian economy that James Wilson was invited, in 1859, to take up the post of Financial Member of the new Council of India. In effect, he was to be the country's Chancellor of the Exchequer. When he turned to announcing his plans for the future in 1860, Wilson was still espousing the importance of launching a major new bank for the sub-continent. In a speech to the Legislative Council in Calcutta only eight months before his death, he spoke about

> a national banking establishment, capable of gradually embracing the great banking operations in India, and of extending its branches to the interior trading cities as opportunity might offer. That there is a growing want for such an institution and a rapidly increasing field for its operations, no-one can doubt.[29]

Plainly the bank he had helped to found seven years earlier had done nothing yet to lay claim to such a role – or, at least, nothing that had come to Wilson's attention in Calcutta. Back in London, though, its Directors were at last clawing a way forward. An editorial about India in *The Bankers' Magazine* had opined in June 1858: 'Commerce and banking in India, although their history involves a long series of calamities, must still be considered in their infancy . . . [With] India once pacified, what a field for legitimate enterprise is opened to capitalists.' Its City battles behind it, Chartered Bank had been doing its best since 1857 to vindicate this optimistic assessment.

2. TEETHING TROUBLES

Branch banking was a Scottish idea, and it was a solid, middle-aged Scotsman with experience of living in the East, George Ure Adam, who was appointed in February 1857 as Chartered Bank's first General Manager. Until this point, a handful of youthful employees in London had had little to do but pay the rent, note down the interest earned on the bank's equity capital and keep a record of the running feud between the Directors and their unruly shareholders. Now plans began to be laid for business (at last) to start in earnest. The move into 21 Threadneedle Street – the fourth change of address since 1852 – gave Adam and his team quite sufficient room for their present needs: it was not intended to keep any new home recruits long in London before despatching them to the East. Picking a first cadre of Eastern staff was the next priority.

It was intended that the 'officers' for each branch should comprise a Manager and an Accountant (a traditional post in rural Scottish banks) doubling as a 'sub-manager', with the later addition of a clerk once the workload mounted. Job applications had been trickling down from

Scotland since the earliest days of the bank's existence.* Banks with branch networks north of the border had been issuing their own bank-notes and offering customers interest on deposits for twenty years or more: they were generally far in advance of the typically small, family-run commercial banks in England. It was also a conspicuous feature of commercial life in the East, as historians have widely noted, that the British presence had long relied disproportionately on Scottish businessmen and adventurers. 'Many of the shipping lines ... relied heavily on contacts among expatriate Scots in positions of influence in the Indian and Asian ports where they provided advice, introductions and commercial intelligence.'[30] No doubt this, too, encouraged the Chartered's Directors to regard recruitment north of the border as entirely sensible. When Chartered Bank's first accountants were appointed in March 1857, both hailed from Edinburgh. Messrs Watson and Harper were promised half the cost of their passage to India, and would be on full salary from their date of embarkation. (In the event, at least one of them had to spend two months of the autumn in London on half-pay. Harper's departure was postponed at the last moment in September – a sign, perhaps, of continuing uncertainty over the aftermath of that summer's appalling events in India.)[31] While Scottish ties might prove invaluable, though, the men hired as full managers of the inaugural branches would surely also need to have had some practical experience of India. By the end of April 1857, Adam and the Directors had settled on two individuals already long resident there and enjoying good local reputations: Roger Eglinton for the Calcutta branch and Joseph Rich for Bombay. The latter had previously worked for the North-Western Bank. Another of North-Western's employees, John Mackellar, was lured away to join the putative Calcutta staff, but before the end of 1857 was invited instead to start up a branch of Chartered Bank in Shanghai (and he would be joined there early in the summer of 1858 by a sub-manager, J. W. Maclennan, from Edinburgh).[32]

It took fully twelve months to finalize these staff arrangements and to identify some appropriate premises. A first, temporary office was set up in Calcutta in April 1858, in a space made available inside the Bengal Bonded Warehouse beside the River Hooghly.[33] Two months later a proper office was opened in a suitably august building at 5 Council House Street,

---

* The first in the archive is from a forty-three-year-old accountant in Glasgow, dated 8 January 1853. His desperation to secure a post perhaps got the better of his job-seeking skills: 'I beg to apply for the situation of Accountant (Assistant) in the Head Office in London. If it should be unsuccessful, then for the situation of first cashier or clerkship; and failing those, the manager or accountantship of your Branch at Melbourne or Sydney.' (LMA: CH03/01/14/016.)

part of the central district of Calcutta already long identified with banking and commerce, where the bank would remain for the next fifty years. In Bombay, a building was rented in Rampart Row, today renamed Kaikhushru Dubash Marg, adjacent to what was then the main port area of the city. (This location served the bank well for nine years, until it moved a few streets north to Elphinstone Circle, now Horniman Circle Gardens.) Once established, these offices were to be 'agencies' in line with the terms of the 1853 Charter, which specifically precluded the bank's operations in India – along with the Head Office in London – from issuing their own banknotes. (New banks launched to operate within England had been similarly barred from note-issuance since 1844, in a move that launched the Bank of England on its way to establishing a monopoly over the issuance of notes – though existing private banks retained issuance rights for many years to come and the monopoly was finally achieved only in 1921.) But in the colonies and dominions like Australia and Hong Kong – as, indeed in any territories beyond the Empire, like Shanghai or the other new 'treaty ports' of China – additional offices of the bank would be 'branches', meaning they could issue banknotes if they chose to do so, subject only to Treasury approval.[34] Head Office would send out a letter in 1860 asking one of its top men 'to bear in mind, as there had been a good deal of misapprehension on the point, that the Court recognised no distinction whatever between branches and agencies'.[35] But the original 'banknote distinction' between them would nonetheless remain valid for many years.* For almost a century, the network would be regularly described in bank correspondence as 'all the As & Bs' – though we will stick to 'branches' for convenience.

A detailed picture of what kept the first Indian branches busy can be construed from the inaugural accounts sent home to Head Office, at the end of 1858. The bank had by then been open for business in Calcutta and Bombay for some eight months, having secured in May an inaugural line of credit for up to £50,000 from its landlord, the City Bank.† (Only

* Thus, the Singapore office started out as an agency in February 1859 but became a branch after the grant of a supplemental charter in 1861 that allowed it to join the note-issuing ranks; and the Bangkok agency picked up the same kind of promotion in 1897. The agency/branch divide would in fact survive long after its origins had been forgotten: it was only formally scrapped in 1950.

† The letter confirming its very first credit line survives in the archive. City Bank wrote to George Ure Adam on 12 May 1858 to confirm that it would extend an 'uncovered credit' on drafts worth up to £50,000 provided that no draft was outstanding for more than three months and that Chartered Bank provided full documentary evidence for the source of the cash that would eventually cover the draft plus accrued interest. The City Bank's Mr White added as a cautionary postscript for the start-up venture: 'It is of course understood . . . that

in February 1858 had the Treasury finally given it the green light, confident that the bank's shareholders would step up with all of the promised equity capital. It was fully paid by the end of 1859.) The earliest extant ledgers, in neat black copperplate handwriting across thirty-six pale blue sheets of closely lined paper, are for the Bombay branch.[36] Its year-end assets were worth just over two million rupees, roughly equivalent to £200,000 at the time or about £15 million in today's money. Assets included a sizeable quantity of silver bullion and silver Mexican dollars, shipped out from London as a basic float for all of the branch's activities. The rest consisted very largely of bills of exchange – each a written acknowledgement by the party named on the bill of a debt that would be repaid at a specified future date. Most of these 'bills receivable' had been acquired by the bank at a discount to their face value from local exporters in India who, as the original owners of the bills, were happy to take a small cut in value in order to have cash in their hands immediately. The purchase of bills by the banks was an integral part of all trade finance, in India as in England. The party ultimately responsible for honouring the bill – the 'drawee' – was typically an English importer, or an agency or bank on its behalf. After the bill was sent back to Head Office via the Royal Mail, the Chartered could await repayment by that importer, or sell the bill into the City's sophisticated secondary market: all bills were 'bearer instruments' that were actively traded, rising and falling in price in line with the level of interest rates. 'Inland bills' in India were IOUs moving in the opposite direction: the bank had paid an exporter in Britain and now held a bill to be redeemed by the importer in India. No City-style discount market existed for this paper, which was usually presented directly to the party named on the bill. All these inward and outward bills constituted the bulk of the Bombay branch's assets. Set against them were its liabilities – principally deposits received from local account-holders and 'bills payable' that it had collected in the course of buying and selling bills as a market participant in its own right. One other liability for the Bombay agency in 1858 was the debt yet to be settled for its office furniture – including two Persian carpets and (by far the most expensive single item) a fire-proof solid iron safe. In its inaugural year, Bombay scarcely managed to do better than break even in the face of its inaugural costs, but its two main sources of profit were nonetheless clear from the outset. 'Discounts on bills' represented the margin earned on bills bought and sold (or bought and held for repayment). And 'Exchange' recorded the profits earned by

on no occasion is this Bank to be placed under Cash Advance [to Chartered] in respect of this Credit.' (LMA: CH03/01/09/157.)

Bombay Agency.

Chartered Bank of India, Australia & China.

General Balance

of the Books of said Agency as at close of business on the
31 December 1858.

— Assets —

		Rs	
Cash		41164 10 11	✓
Bank of	Bombay	95323 9 5	✓
Lyall Still & Coy	Hong Kong	513314 13 2	✓
Singapore Agency	Outward Account	70000	✓
Calcutta	"	3528 2 5	✓
Local Bills	Discounted	273132 9 1	✓
Past due	Bills	22925	✓
Government Securities	5 per cent notes	387772 4 11	✓
Bills	Receivable	160068 2 4	×
Cash Credits	Accounts	92131 12 1	✓
Current deposit	"	144 15 6	✓
Office Furniture		24 2 0	
Drafts	by Head Office	224090 15 2	✓
"	" Shanghae Branch	871 732 9 1	✓
"	" Calcutta Agency	150000	✓
			2120632 8 1

Liabilities.

Agency	Capital	750000	✓
Head Office	Exchange Account	198730 5 2	✓
	General "	174327 15 6	✓
London	Exchange "	52733 6 1	✓
Shanghae Branch	General "	95158 7 7	✓
Calcutta Agency	" "	164866 14 1	✓
Agency Past	Bills	50226 5	✓
Bills	Payable	445823 8 3	✓
Deposit	Receipts	473051 2 10	✓
Current Deposit	Accounts	140369 12 6	✓
Stockholders interest	to 23 Febry 1858	2905 8	✓
			2120632 8 1

Bombay 31 December 1858

[signature] Agent

[signature] Accountant

Compared and Counterchecked

The Bombay Agency's inaugural year-end balance sheet, dated 31 December 1858

translating the sterling proceeds of 'bills on Europe' into rupees for local customers, or converting the rupee payments on 'Inland bills' into sterling for remittance to London. As indispensable to all of India's exports as the very ships that carried them away, 'exchange banking' still looked capable of becoming the formidable earner the Directors had always assumed it would be.

There was never any question, though, of trading currencies per se, independently of any underlying import or export contract. Speculative transactions for their own sake were not to be countenanced, except within narrow limits where positions could be 'overbought' or 'oversold' in direct anticipation of clients' trading requirements.* Nor was currency speculation the only activity carefully excluded by the Chartered from its model of exchange banking. A stream of official missives from London through 1858–9 constantly reminded Rich and Eglinton of all the ways they were *not* to employ the bank's funds. ('As a general rule, such advances are objected to by the Court . . .') Loans against the promise of bills to come under agreed trading contracts; loans against crops stored in any warehouses, or 'godowns' as they were everywhere known in the East, except those wholly under the branch's control; loans against the deposit of shares in local joint-stock companies – all were strictly forbidden. This was what the 1852 prospectus had meant, in asserting that the bank would refrain 'from acting in any way in a mercantile capacity'. Surplus funds were in general to be remitted 'by direct routes homewards. Any deviation from this rule, to be a rare exception and only justified by peculiarly favourable prospects.'[37]

Determined to see that their network would avoid the excesses that had brought down so many of the old agency partnerships in the past, the Directors set out to exert a degree of control that might have been ambitious between London and Birmingham, let alone London and Bombay.

---

* Indeed, the term 'foreign exchange' as used in the nineteenth century needs to be distinguished from the modern-day usage that applies almost exclusively to the buying and selling of currencies. It formerly connoted all of the clerical activities involved in the business of a commercial transaction overseas. Just as trades completed in Britain were handled by the banks as 'domestic exchange', so those completed abroad were serviced as foreign exchange – which generally entailed an exchange of currencies, but encompassed so much more. As the definitive textbook on foreign exchange would define it half a century after the Chartered's launch, the term really applied to whatever paperwork the bankers and merchants adopted by way 'of regulating their mutual indebtedness without the transfer of metallic money from one country to another'. (W. F. Spalding, *Foreign Exchange and Foreign Bills*, Pitman & Sons, 1915, p. 5. Few people can have read it for fun, but Spalding's classic tome was not the arid manual its title might suggest. As the author himself rather charmingly noted in connection with bills of exchange, 'The study of the legal side is indeed a valley of old bones, and . . . an informing spirit is needful that they may live.')

Detailed letters streamed out of Head Office at the rate of several a week. (All were numbered in sequence from the start of 1858. By the end of that year, No. 120 was being despatched to Calcutta, No. 119 to Bombay and No. 14 to Shanghai.) While lists were naturally circulated of those English firms whose bills were to be deemed a safe purchase, the Directors also seemed intent on dictating from London as much as possible the choice of local customers – in settings far removed from the clerks' rooms and gentlemen's clubs of the Victorian City. Such a stance was hopelessly optimistic once the network began to expand, as it did within a year of the first moves into India. The fundamental problem was a lack as yet of qualified young men ready to be despatched from London as managers, capable of supervising locally hired clerks and already imbued with a clear understanding of the ground rules for the bank. In their absence, the Directors had to rely heavily on British expatriates already in situ – and the results were mixed at best. The Court refused to be deterred by this from opening new branches. Instructions went off to Mackellar in Shanghai, for example, to find someone to launch an operation in Hong Kong – duly accomplished in 1859, with the opening of a branch along the Kowloon-facing edge of the island colony.*But more than 1,500 miles of open sea separated Calcutta from Singapore, and Singapore from the southern coast of China. So how were all these outposts of the bank to be, as we should say now, micro-managed from London?

Exciting reports about the potential of telegraphy via trans-oceanic submarine cables began to be received and were kept under constant review by the Court through 1859. Julius Reuter had set up his 'Submarine Telegraph' office in London all of eight years earlier, to coincide with the activation of the first such cable, between Dover and Calais. More extended routes, however, had been posing enormous difficulties, with newly laid cables invariably snagging on the seabed and fracturing. The first reference in the bank's archives to 'a telegraphic message' dates from May 1858, but it was still unclear by late 1859 how quickly this wondrous invention might conjure a transformation of the world's communications. Telegraphs were as yet traversing the globe little faster than letters, with poor forwarding

---

* Its exact location is unclear. The Chartered's centenary history placed it 'in the neighbourhood of what is now [i.e. 1953] Chinese Street, near the Central Market and abutting on Des Voeux Road. The reclamation of this area, which has completed in 1904, had the effect of moving Des Voeux Road inland, and one may presume that the bank's first office in Hong Kong was on the waterfront' (Compton Mackenzie, *Realms of Silver*, Routledge & Kegan Paul, 1954, p. 56). When the Hongkong Bank decided on its own inaugural site in 1864, this too 'backed on to a small path, later developed as Des Voeux Road, across which was the sea'. (Frank H. H. King, *History of the Hongkong Bank*, vol. 1, p. 64).

facilities in key cities and no cable connection between Bombay and Suez. This left the Directors still heavily dependent, like their predecessors in the East India Company, on ship-borne mail. A Court minute of December 1858 noted the issue of an edict 'that all operations of importance should be the subject of explanation and advice at the time, in the Official Correspondence with the Head Office . . .' But this could hardly be a substitue for local decision-making where speedy action was required. It was true the mail from London to India were now running significantly faster than in earlier generations. The old three-month voyage via the Cape – tolerated happily enough by many Company servants in the East, with little interest in shorter reins for London – had been supplanted since the 1830s (for mail and those passengers, like James Wilson, with little baggage) by the Overland Route via Egypt and the Red Sea. And this had been steadily upgraded by steamships since the 1840s, with many letters now reliably reaching London from Bombay in less than thirty days. All the same, a short month for Bombay–London mail still put London almost six weeks from Calcutta and two months from Shanghai.

Squaring this, and their reliance on locally recruited men, with their desire for close control pushed the Directors into a novel solution. They would rely on a senior colleague from London who could travel around the network – on tours of duty that might last eighteen months or more – with enough authority to hire and fire at his own discretion. The first 'Inspector of Agencies', appointed in December 1859, was Charles Iggulden. His annual salary was to be £1,300 a year, which exceeded the starting salary of £1,000 for the General Manager in London. But then, while shouldering huge responsibilities, the Inspector would also have to face the hazards of constant travelling – and these were not to be underestimated, as all were soon reminded. Iggulden set off in the New Year on one of the latest iron-built P&O steamships, the 1,080-ton SS *Malabar*. Heading for Singapore via the Cape and a stop-over in Bombay, she called at the port of Galle on the southernmost tip of Ceylon for a few days in the third week of May 1860. Just hours before its intended departure on 22 May, a violent storm broke across Galle's notoriously exposed harbour. The *Malabar* was torn from her moorings, blown across the harbour bay and dumped by the gale-force winds a mile or so along the shoreline. All aboard were saved, thanks to the captain's wise decision not to try putting out to open sea, but Iggulden lost all his papers and possessions, including a sizeable stash of Mexican silver dollars. (Other losses included 1,080 boxes of silver bullion and 725 chests of best Indian opium.) He was still in Galle three weeks later, waiting like everyone else for a fresh ship and new clothes from the local tailors.[38]

Iggulden seems to have set about his inspections (eventually) with a diligence that did nothing to abate the inevitable tension that was soon evident between London and the men on the ground in Asia. One of his first assignments was to visit Singapore in order to dismiss the local Agent, David Duff. In the course of 1859, probably at the behest of Mackellar, the bank had hired a young local expatriate in Singapore called J. Howard Gwyther as a sub-manager for Duff's office.[39] Apparently on the basis of information conscientiously despatched to London by Gwyther, the Court had come to doubt Duff's honesty. Iggulden had instructions to take charge of the Agency and then 'to form an opinion as to the fitness of the Sub-Agent [Gwyther] . . . to [assume] the office of Acting Agent'. By the time Iggulden arrived in Singapore in the middle of 1860, Duff had already left for England, having first rallied considerable support among local merchants for a fightback against the Court. Iggulden managed to defuse this situation, but soon received news from London of a change of heart over Gwyther, still only twenty-five years old: 'In view of the prejudice, however unjust, likely to lie at Singapore against Gwyther, the Court wanted him transferred to Shanghai as Sub-Manager and Accountant.'[40] A succession of similar episodes followed over the next few years, with locally popular individuals being turfed out of their jobs by a perennially suspicious Court in London. Few of the early appointees lasted long in any one place, many leaving the bank altogether. Of the first accountants hired for India, Harper had already quit late in 1858 and Watson was given six months' notice in September 1860. The manager in Calcutta, Eglinton, resigned in October 1862. The Bombay Manager, Joseph Rich, had meanwhile taken it upon himself in 1861 to lend £20,000 to a native Indian contractor ('a Mahratta Brahmin') who was providing timber sleepers for the new Great Indian Railway that was to run between Bombay and the cotton districts. This was deemed in London to be 'a gross breach of duty' and an egregious example of what could happen when the Bank employed local men with no prior exposure to the desired way of doing things. He was suspended in 1862 and even pursued in the High Court on charges of negligence 'and for sending to the company incorrect and untrue statements respecting the business transacted'.[41] (His career surprisingly survived this setback, though: Rich would retire from the bank in 1897 after forty years' service.)

Staffing proved no less problematic in China. If the Head Office's close scrutiny and the aftermath of the Mutiny put an unwelcome strain on the managers in India, those in the International Settlement adjacent to the Chinese city of Shanghai had to cope with the possibility of violence on an altogether more terrifying scale. Young Gwyther arrived there from

Singapore in the late summer of 1860, when the conflict we know as the Second Opium War was in its fourth year and serious fighting in the north of China was about to bring it to a climactic end. Of more immediate concern to Gwyther must have been the situation in and around Shanghai itself, where there seemed every prospect, that summer, of a full-scale battle between supporters of the Taiping Rebellion and the forces of the Qing imperial dynasty. The two sides were now into the tenth year of a civil war that had already left millions dead and scores of cities laid waste in central and south-western China. The Chartered's Shanghai Manager, Mackellar, had given the bank a promising start in the city: it would be known for generations to come as the Mackalee Bank, which has often been attributed to the local pronunciation of Mackellar's name.* But he was alarmed by the sight of Taiping rebels ransacking the city's outskirts – and of Chinese civilians pouring into the International Settlement as a safe refuge from the fighting – and he sent in his resignation in November 1860. Mackellar soon afterwards tried to retract it, presumably relieved to see the rebels leaving the area, but the Court had a better idea. He was reassigned to Hong Kong, and this opened up an opportunity to promote Gwyther, about whom the Court had received a string of glowing reports attesting to his good sense and natural authority. Gwyther accepted the Shanghai job and was treated with conspicuous deference by the Directors in their correspondence with him over the next twelve months. But it cannot have been an easy time to work under instructions from London, in a place swept with rumours of foreign military intervention on one day and of imminent attack by Taiping rebels on the next. In fact Gwyther resigned at the end of 1861, electing instead to go his own way as a bill-broker in the city. The bank nonetheless managed to keep its doors open in Shanghai: a fresh manager was found, and notices in the local

---

* It happens that 'Ka Li' means 'that man' in the Shanghainese dialect, so Mac-Ka-Li was a witty way of referring to a Scotsman. The nickname also had a happy ring for the bank, since the written Mandarin characters for Ma, Ka and Li represent 'wheat' (i.e. sustenance), 'plus' and 'profit'. There is another, less romantic derivation for Mackalee: it was the name of the district where the original bank was built. There is no such place-name on modern maps of Shanghai, but a note in the Chartered archive identifies 'Makalee' as 'in the area of the Cathedral and the Hovian Road' (LMA: CH03/01/14/020). Whatever the truth, the Mackalee name was adopted in other Chinese cities like Tientsin, Hankow and Peking (though Head Office never formally endorsed it) and there is no doubting its durability. Opened in 1937, the bank's Manchester branch used 'MAKALEE' as its telegraphic address. When the bank negotiated the re-opening of branches in Communist China in the 1980s, the licences granted by Beijing all referred to 'The Standard Chartered Bank (Makalee Bank)' (W. C. L. Brown, unpublished autobiography, Vol. 4, p. 29).

press went on advertising the Chartered's availability for 'all the customary business of Banking and Agency'.[42]

Mackellar fared successfully for a while in Hong Kong, then fell foul
of an embarrassing heist that illustrated another dimension of the vulnerability of overseas banking. Opium had been easily the dominant staple
of India's exports to China since the 1820s. It generated huge profits that
were critical to India's ability to fund its visible trade deficit with Britain,
once finished textiles from Lancashire began flooding into the
sub-continent. Inevitably, India's banks were integral to the export of
opium, as of all its other crops. Aside from the dubious morality of the
trade – pumping into China what the Imperial Viceroy of Canton described
in 1836 as 'the vile dirt of the foreign countries' – there was of course a
none-too-subtle difference between opium and other commodities.[43] A
boat full of tea or even indigo was hardly worth a fraction of the value of
a boat full of opium. The loss of a single cargo could be financially calamitous. Mackellar had cause to reflect on this, after advancing an astonishing
£50,000 (about £3.5 million today) in August 1862 against the security of
a shipload of opium destined for the wharfs of Hong Kong. When the time
came for it to be unloaded from its ship, the opium had disappeared and
the entire debt had eventually to be written off. The bank's chairman in
London was left to explain to the Ordinary General Meeting of April
1863 that too much reliance had been placed on it being a British ship,
with a British captain and crew – 'now expiating their crimes in penal
servitude'.[44] Angry shareholders derided the apparent naivety of the bank's
Hong Kong staff '[who] did not think it was their duty to see whether the
article [in the hold] was opium or camel's dung'. Mitchell in response could
only plead meekly that 'he believed the opium . . . was removed surreptitiously during the night'. Acknowledging that 'in these transactions great
caution was necessary on the part of the manager', he reassured the meeting that Mackellar had been dismissed. He then alluded, though, to a final
aspect of the episode that – like the local support for Duff in Singapore
three years earlier – underlined again how remote London was from the
front line of the bank's operations: 'so little did the European inhabitants
of Hong Kong share the feelings of the directors, that every one signed a
letter approving of [Mackellar's] career, and blaming the authorities of
the bank [for his dismissal]'.* Iggulden himself fell into a long-running

---

* As it happens, the earliest dated banknote of the Chartered still in existence attests to this
sad story. The Hong Kong branch began issuing its own notes in December 1862, which must
have been about the time that Mackellar and his Accountant were both dismissed. A used
HK$10 note dated 10 March 1863, and numbered only No. 5451, had to carry the signatures
of two acting officers in their place (see Plate 4). The note was auctioned in Hong Kong in

dispute with the Directors, late in 1862, and for reasons that are now obscure, left the bank in the summer of 1863.[45]

It comes as no surprise to find Mitchell admitting to the shareholders at that same 1863 General Meeting that 'the Directors had found by experience that the work of establishing a new bank in the East was not a task of ordinary difficulty'. All of their initial appointments in the field had come to grief one way or another. For the future, 'they were gradually training up gentlemen at home to be acclimatised while young in Europe'. In the meantime, the bank had no choice but to go on relying on the best local men it could find. The minutes of the Court at no point suggest any curbing of its grand ambitions. Indeed, by now it seemed determined to establish a presence in all the principal ports of the sub-continent, the East Indies and China. The network was extended before the end of 1863 to include Karachi, Hankow and Batavia (today's Jakarta) – and above all Rangoon, the main port on Burma's southern shoreline.

Eglinton of the Calcutta agency had been asked to set up a Rangoon branch in a despatch from Head Office as early as December 1861. Its principal customers would be the British companies – once again, most of them Scottish-owned – that had been establishing themselves along the banks of the Rangoon River since the Second Anglo-Burmese War of 1852. They would need help to expand their export trades, mostly of teak logs and of milled rice – the latter already thriving conspicuously on shipments to British India.[46] By one unverifiable account, an office was set up on Rangoon's Phayre Street, now Pansodan Street, in June 1862 by G. A. Whyte from the Calcutta office.[47] The timing must have seemed propitious: the British authorities were just at this point consolidating Rangoon's administration of all the coastal territories they had annexed to date in Burma, calling them 'Lower Burma'. But Whyte had to return to India to take over the Calcutta office after Eglinton himself resigned in October, and there is no record of the Phayre Street office's immediate progress. The next summer, Whyte was back. He moved the office from Phayre Street to 'a small building on the Strand near the present Port Commissioner's Office'. (The Strand ran parallel with the north bank of the river, to which Phayre Street ran down at a right angle.) He leased the new building from a local expatriate called Arthur Brooking, and their agreement took effect from the first day of September 1863. We can be sure of the date because five months later Brooking sealed a Power of Attorney for his son in London. He had agreed with Whyte that the Chartered

December 2015. (I am grateful to Nirat Lertchitvikul of auctioneers Stack's Bowers and Ponterio for drawing its sale to my attention.)

would pay its rent in sterling into his account in the City, and he wanted his son to watch over the arrangement. The document survives, and includes a reference to the 1863 lease.[48] Presumably Whyte had a junior colleague to whom he then handed over charge of the bank's Rangoon affairs, and he returned once again to Calcutta.

It was not a good time to be away for long. The leading commercial cities of Asia, and particularly Bombay and Calcutta, were in the midst of a speculative boom surpassing anything that the Chartered's young officers, or anyone else in the region, had ever seen. It had been set in motion by the American Civil War and the blockade of the Confederacy's ports that had halted the flow of raw cotton exports across the Atlantic to Liverpool after July 1861. The manufacturing of cotton textiles was Britain's biggest business and Lancashire could not go for long without alternative supplies.* Cotton prices in Liverpool had almost doubled within six months, from around 8d to 1s 3d per lb, and had gone on rising thereafter. The inflated prices prompted a dramatic surge in shipments of cotton from the rest of the world. As a contemporary wag had it,

> They sent who never sent before;
> Who sent before, now sent the more.

Despite a quintupling of the price by the end of 1864, Lancashire's consumption was by then back to fully two-thirds of its pre-war level. This remarkable rebound from the crisis of 1861 relied on first-time suppliers from China (delivering 86 million lb in 1864, nearly 10 per cent of the total imported that year) and a huge increase in imports from Bombay, which rose by almost 40 per cent in three years to reach 506 million lb in 1864.[49] The swollen volumes and inflated prices brought sterling and bullion receipts back to Bombay and the treaty ports of China in unprecedented quantities. Banking activity went wild in both regions, but the impact on Bombay was by far the greater. The export bonanza unleashed a speculative boom in every sector. As a subsequent official report of Bombay's Chamber of Commerce put it, with po-faced understatement, 'The unexpected wealth poured into the lap of Western India by the terrible incident of the American Civil War ... was not used wisely.'[50] New joint-stock companies appeared for the promotion of a colourful range of enterprises,

---

* The Union blockade coincided with a surplus of finished inventories due to recent over-production, and there were widespread reports of terrible distress in Lancashire. The merchant firms of Bombay set up a relief fund, which collected £16,000, and sent it to the Mayor of London for distribution to the needy (Raymond J. F. Sulivan, *One Hundred Years of Bombay: A History of the Bombay Chamber of Commerce 1836–1936*, Times of India Press, 1937, p. 68).

including schemes for the reclamation of land from the sea in order to join up the seven islands on which the city rested: Bombay soon had seven reclamation companies to set beside its twenty-five banks and thirty-nine finance associations. Share prices spiralled upwards through 1863–4 in a classic frenzy of speculative buying, which inevitably swept up brokers in Calcutta, too. The bust, when it came, was swift and brutal. News arrived from America in March 1865 that Richmond, the capital of the Confederacy, had fallen to Union armies. Cotton prices in Liverpool fell by 50 per cent overnight, and within weeks the largest shipping company in Bombay had declared itself bankrupt. In the ensuing panic, the Presidency Bank of Bombay suspended payment. Like the other two Presidency Banks, it had always been prohibited from any kind of exchange banking activity – but this had not prevented it from extending ill-advised advances to all and sundry within the local marketplace. Hundreds of bankruptcies followed in every corner of the Western India economy, which would take ten years to recover.

Rapidly mounting losses in all of Chartered's branches prompted consternation in London. The Directors of the bank had been struggling since 1857 with the practical limitations to their authority. Dictating instructions that would take weeks to arrive, and constantly finding their written orders hopelessly overtaken by events, they had no choice but to rely on individuals whom in many cases they had never even met. Now their frustration came to a head, and they lashed out angrily at the managers in the field, as though it had somehow been in their power to sidestep the collapse of the markets. The top men were all dismissed – *pour encourager les autres* – including Whyte in Calcutta. (The Directors later climbed down over Whyte, when admonished in a letter from Iggulden's successor, Sherwood, who 'thought it unfortunate that the Bank's name should so frequently have had to come before the public in [connection with] the dismissal of officers'.[51]) Reviewing this debacle for the shareholders' General Meeting in October 1865, chairman Thomas Mitchell was at pains to suggest the Board had a grip on the situation but had been let down by its local staff in the Eastern ports:

> Against their agents at these places he certainly made no charge of dishonesty, but he did charge them with culpable neglect, remissness and disobedience of the orders of the Directors . . . Their losses at Bombay had been unquestionably very severe . . . no such crisis had occurred in the history of the world since the famous South Sea Bubble . . . [Speculators had fuelled] all sorts of new schemes, which were driven up by stimulants to the most frantic point, and which had resulted in enormous losses . . . [In Shanghai, their agent] had allowed the bank to become the victim of a complete juggle.[52]

The bank would need in future to have officers in the field who had been recruited in Britain and given a basic training in the City. The traces had already been laid for this approach: four junior managers had been despatched from London in the spring, including a 'sub-accountant' for Calcutta called Caleb Lewis, who was to have a distinguished career with the bank.[53] But it was asking too much of these youthful pioneers to think they might reassert London's firm control overnight, and in the meantime the outlook everywhere remained deeply uncertain. Not the least worrying aspect of the situation for Mitchell and his fellow Directors was the lack of any reliable accounts to provide even a rough impression of the bank's predicament. It had notched up a respectable run of profits through the boom years since 1858. It had paid off its start-up costs of around £700,000 within its first year. Net profits since then had represented a return of 10–15 per cent on the bank's capital. This had allowed it to build up a tidy Reserve Fund of £105,000, while gradually lifting the annualized rate of dividend payments from 5 per cent up to a peak of 15 per cent in the first half of 1864. But the turmoil in Eastern markets since the spring of 1865 had thrown into question the sustainability of everything that had gone before. What proportion of the bills currently held as assets by the bank would prove to be worthless, no one knew. All would depend on the unwinding of dozens of prominent Indian family businesses and estates bankrupted by the crash. Until then, as Mitchell warned the bank's eight hundred shareholders, 'it would be absolutely impossible to furnish any statement of what had been the real losses of the bank in the East'. In the meantime, just as had happened in 1847, disasters in India were starting to bring down well-known names in the City. Two of the bank's own founding shareholders, John Gladstone and Peter Bell, had to withdraw from the Board as a result of financial misadventures elsewhere.

One consoling feature of a wretched year for the Directors was the appearance in London of one of their best former employees from the East. Still working as a bill-broker in Shanghai, Howard Gwyther came to England for a holiday in 1864.[54] Whether or not he originally intended to return to China is unclear; but he eventually decided in March 1865 to apply to his old employer's Head Office for a fresh staff position in London, and was accepted.[55] Within a month, he had been authorized to sign papers on behalf of the bank 'pro manager'. At the same time, the inaugural manager in Hong Kong, C. S. Sherwood, was hired to succeed Iggulden as the Inspector of Agencies – at a handsome salary now of £2,500 a year that marked a heightened appreciation of this post's importance. The joint counsels of Gwyther and Sherwood prompted a radical cleansing of the balance sheet after the accounts were closed for 1865. Bad and doubtful debts of £120,000 were written off, which absorbed what was left of the year's profits, after a 5 per cent dividend, and wiped out all but £20,000 of the Reserve Fund. Standing before his shareholders again in April 1866, Mitchell was proud to say they now had 'a staff such as they never had before'.* They could go forward in the confidence that their reputation in the East 'never stood better in public estimation'. Official letters out to the East, though, were sounding a different note. Head Office wrote to Sherwood, now back in the East as Inspector, that 'extraordinary vigilance and caution are needed in every quarter . . . [given] the collapse of finance and other similar companies, to say nothing of political complications'. Five days later, on Thursday 9 May, a second letter in a similar vein carried a hastily scribbled postscript that almost beggared belief. Late that afternoon, the biggest name in the City after that of the Bank of England had announced the suspension of all payments to its creditors.

The failure of Overend, Gurney & Co. in May 1866 – 'a national calamity' as *The Times* reported it next morning – stunned the City like few other events in the nineteenth century. Overends was the bankers' bank, a dominant presence in the wholesale money markets and a leading discounter of bills for every large commercial firm in Britain. Its collapse triggered a slump on the Stock Exchange (the next day's panic was the first recorded 'Black Friday') and pushed up the cost of wholesale funds to unprecedented levels for the next three months. The convulsions in the City that summer brought down thirteen of the country's joint-stock domestic banks. The impact on the overseas banking community was even more seismic. More than thirty names had been established since 1857. (*The Bankers' Magazine* had lampooned the phenomenon with a spoof prospectus for the 'North and South Poles Bank'. 'When the vast population comprised in the space between the North Pole on the one side and the South Pole on the other is considered, it is at once evident that the present banking system is totally inadequate to meet the claims made upon it.'[56]) The collapse of commodity prices in the East had already seen off several of them. The cost of money in London after Overends' failure finished off many more. Chartered and the Oriental had been joined by nine other banks in Hong Kong since the start of the decade – including,

---

* One consequence was a significantly higher outlay on salaries. One shareholder asked the Chairman why more information had not been provided on management expenses. 'The Chairman replied that he did not think it advantageous to shareholders to publish such details. The managerial expenses had been enhanced by the increased salaries which the Bank's competition in the East, and the heavy cost of living, occasioned.' (*The Bankers' Magazine*, Vol. 26, April 1866, pp. 576–80.)

as of 1865, the Hongkong (*sic*) Bank – and six of the newcomers had gone by the end of 1866. In Bombay and Calcutta, dozens of exchange banks failed. Just seven were left standing by the close of 1867.

Someone at Head Office – and we can be pretty sure it was Gwyther, though George Ure Adam as yet remained the Manager – took charge of Chartered's fortunes at this juncture decisively enough to ensure its survival. Just in the nick of time, it seems. Within weeks of the collapse of Overends, all branches were ordered to suspend their exchange operations ('very inadequate terms of remuneration . . . [being] utterly disproportionate to the risks now being run'). Across the network, loans and advances were called in wherever possible; and every branch was enjoined to remit 'without delay, all funds in their hands not necessarily required to meet their own liabilities, or to maintain the credit of the Agency'.[57] Some pruning of the network was even planned, with the Batavia branch among those scheduled for possible closure. The retrenchment did not avert a need to set aside lavish provisions against bad debts, which left little or nothing in 1866–9 to be added to the bank's Reserve Fund (a category set apart from retained earnings). But at least there was a respectable net income to report, albeit the figure was reported *before* the deduction of losses on bad debts. The Court went on paying a dividend, and signalled its confidence in the future of the bank by committing to a long-term lease for a freshly rebuilt, albeit rather anonymous-looking, four-storey brick building at 2–3 Hatton Court, a tiny paved square just off Threadneedle Street which was to remain the headquarters of the bank until 1909.[58] (Pedestrians entered the square via a narrow passage – both are now gone – that led off the street at a point directly opposite the doors of Merchant Taylors' Hall and just across the road from the City Bank, where the Chartered had previously been housed and where it still kept its main sterling account.[59]) Merely by surviving, the Chairman suggested to shareholders in 1868, Chartered would be left in command of the field – especially in India, where almost all the rest 'have lost every farthing they had'.[60]

There was cause by the start of 1869, though, to worry that (not for the first time) Mitchell might have spoken too soon. The Batavia office began disclosing sizeable loans to a local trading company, Morton Melbourne, which had suddenly failed. Gwyther found himself despatched to the Continent to represent the bank in arcane court battles with Dutch and German banks over the residual value of the Batavian company's assets. (Gwyther quickly seems to have become the Court's preferred representative for important overseas missions: he was even back in China several months later, attending to its local business there.[61]) Mitchell loftily reflected at the April 1869 General Meeting that occasional loan losses were inevitable in their line of banking, 'conducted in a peculiarly speculative part of the world'.[62] This did nothing to reassure the shareholders, who were evidently tiring of their Chairman's regular assertion at twice-yearly General Meetings that the worst of the crisis was behind them – and his dogged optimism did indeed prove to be sadly misplaced by April 1870. The Batavian losses had soared. The outbreak of the Franco-Prussian war three months later triggered another collapse in cotton prices for which the bank seemed culpably unprepared. In place of a dividend in October 1870, dismayed shareholders received a public circular, warning ominously of heavy losses in China. While the accounts for 1870 were still being drawn up, a special meeting had to be convened to invite shareholders to visit the head office in order to inspect the Bad and Doubtful Debts ledger for themselves. By April 1871 it was clear the bank was in deep trouble. A reported net profit for 1870 of almost £20,000 was eclipsed by write-offs of £127,000 on bad debts. The bank had only a vestigial Reserve Fund of £10,000 and retained earnings of £38,000 to set against them. Its shares, all originally subscribed for at £20 each a decade earlier, were down to almost half that level. (They had rarely traded as high as £20 since the Overend & Gurney crash of 1866.[63]) It was a crisis that called for drastic action by the Directors if the bank was to survive.

Chartered Bank had been founded in the 1850s by men with commercial ties to the East but scarcely any experience of living and working there. They had sometimes shown themselves more than a little naive in their expectations of those leading the bank's operations in the field; worse, on occasions they had acted behind the backs of those in the field. Alarmingly, a sizeable portion of the losses incurred in Shanghai during 1870 had arisen from a fraud linked to a huge loan made by the Directors themselves. As was admitted at the April 1871 General Meeting, they had advanced it 'without their [local] agent's knowledge . . . [It had been] perhaps an undue sum, and they blamed themselves for it now'.[64] The Court urgently needed more members whose careers had given them a personal knowledge of the East. Two such individuals, from prominent trading firms, had been attending the Court 'by invitation' since June 1870, and both were now duly elected. One was Andrew Cassels, a partner of Peel, Cassels & Co. of Bombay; the other was Ludwig Wiese of Siemssen & Co. of Shanghai. Within a year or so, they would be joined by Frederick Heilgers of Wattenbach, Heilgers of London and Calcutta, and William Paterson of Paterson, Simons of Singapore. Men from other equally illustrious Eastern firms would follow in their wake, including, before the decade was out, Directors of Jardine Matheson of Hong Kong and Jardine Skinner of Calcutta. The Chartered Bank would continue to be run from London, of course – but henceforth its affairs would be directed by men with 'extensive connections and long practical knowledge of Eastern business'.[65] It was an important change of tack, duly hailed by the City's Lord Mayor at the General Meeting on 19 April 1871: 'He could not help thinking that this was the turning point in the history of this company . . . and he thought the introduction to the Board of gentlemen connected with the various branches of Indian commerce was very essential to the prosperity of the bank.'

All this left one problem conspicuously unresolved. The bank needed fresh leadership: Mitchell's chairmanship had by now become an embarrassment to his colleagues. One prominent City shareholder had written to the Court a few days prior to the General Meeting to pass on 'the feelings of many of your constituents' that a replacement was urgently needed for the present Chairman 'who from physical or other causes evidently fails to give satisfaction or command confidence'.[66] This put the Directors in a quandary, for the man who had led them since January 1853 had himself shown no signs of wanting to go. On the contrary, at the General Meeting he told the assembled shareholders that he looked forward to their coming together a year hence in much happier times.* There followed a defenestration highly unusual in the City of any era and, by mid-Victorian standards of propriety, shockingly acrimonious. Two days after the April General Meeting, and a few hours after their weekly meeting, the Directors met secretly to plot Mitchell's removal. The impact of the new telegraphy was seized upon as a good pretext, offering him a dignified exit: any effective Chairman would now have to attend the Bank daily – which Mitchell, as a busy MP, would sadly no longer be able to do. One of the three 'white knights' of 1857, William Macnaughtan, wrote accordingly to Mitchell later that day to inform him of the Directors' 'serious conversation as to the best mode of conducting the business of the Bank in future' and to let him know that, under the circumstances, they had unanimously decided a new Chairman would be required:

> But they have so high an opinion of your ability and experience, and of the important services you have rendered the Bank since its commencement, that it is with the utmost reluctance they make this Communication to you.

---

* One shareholder asked about the remuneration of the new directors, and drew this reply from Mitchell: 'They had endeavoured to get gentlemen of eminence upon their Board – gentlemen connected with Calcutta, and they could not expect gentlemen of this stamp to join them if they offered a lower remuneration for their services than that paid by other kindred institutions in London.' (*The Bankers' Magazine*, Vol. 31, 1871, pp. 448–53.)

Their regret, however, is diminished by the recollection that you have more than once expressed a wish to be relieved from the duties and responsibilities of office.[67]

This drew a splenetic response, pointedly addressed not to Macnaughtan and the Directors but to the young Howard Gwyther.[68] Mitchell had to accept the outcome ('That letter, if, as I presume, authentic, leaves me no option as a gentleman . . .') but he was not about to quit without refuting the proffered rationale for the Directors' decision. The idea of daily attendance, he assured Gwyther, had only been mentioned for the very first time a few weeks earlier. Two of the Directors, on the day of the weekly Court meeting, 'told me that it was of no use reading the letters, as everything had been decided on the day before, thus leaving me a dummy'. As for the suggestion that he had been minded to resign anyway, Mitchell could only remember one occasion in recent years when this had been true – 'when I resisted the proposal made by you [sic] for amalgamation with the Chartered Mercantile Bank & I stated that I would not be a party to it'. Much of the letter was devoted to distancing himself from any blame for the financial calamities of 1870, but it was Mitchell's description of the Directors' initiative that caught the eye. 'As it is, I fully appreciate the underhand way in which the transaction has been carried out.' This was too much for Macnaughtan, who fired off an angry follow-up the same day:

> I cannot refrain from at once expressing in the strongest possible manner, my extreme surprise at [your letter's] contents and the tone in which it is written . . . [I must] call your attention first of all, to your want of courtesy in not replying direct to a letter addressed to you by one at the special request of my colleagues, and in the second place, to the unwarrantable liberty you have taken, in not only doubting the authenticity of the communication but in gratuitously accusing my colleagues and myself of underhand conduct.[69]

Two days later, on 26 April 1871, the Secretary officially accepted the Chairman's resignation – though not without deploring again the use of the word 'underhand', which had caused the Directors 'very great pain and surprise' – but Mitchell's letter was not, as he had requested, laid before the Court at its next meeting and minuted. After eighteen years at the helm, Mitchell simply vanished.[70] The Court elected Andrew Cassels as his successor.*

* Cassels served only two years, leaving the Court on his appointment in 1874 as a Member of the Council of the Secretary of State for India. He was succeeded as Chairman by William Paterson, whose chairmanship of the bank would leave scarcely a trace behind, though it

The press had been well aware a week earlier of the discord within the bank. Fortunately, most reports of the General Meeting chose to stress the sense of a fresh start – like this one, in a paper widely read among the expatriate trading community in China:

> At the [General] meeting . . . shareholders very wisely refrained from any hostile conduct towards the board of directors, and we attribute this entirely to the fact that the directors did not attempt to make things pleasant by disguising the serious nature of the losses. All kinds of rumour were in circulation as to the intentions of some of the shareholders to propose 'a want of confidence in the directors', while others were said to be ready to propose winding up. These gentlemen, finding they were not supported, refrained from saying anything, and this avoided a further injury to the value of the shares. Many shareholders are of opinion that with the aid of the telegraph now working to the ports in the Far East there is good reason to believe that the heavy losses which the Bank had experienced would not be repeated, and a more hopeful prospect was before them.[71]

On the potentially momentous impact of the telegraph, indeed, all could agree. Despite the wrenching upheavals in the financial sector since 1864, there had been some spectacular improvements in communications that would soon make overseas banking, at least from a technical point of view, immeasurably easier. Between 1865 and 1871, submarine cables were laid that vanquished Asia's remoteness from London for ever.[72] From Malta to Alexandria and from Suez via Aden to Bombay, gaps were plugged in the cable network that henceforth linked the City to Imperial India without a break. A line from Madras via Penang to Singapore followed by the end of the decade. For the residents of Hong Kong and Shanghai, 1871 remarkably saw the launch of not one but two cable routes to London. A Danish firm, Great Northern Telegraph Company, completed a trans-Siberian network linking the West via Vladivostock to China and Japan. And cables south from the treaty ports linked them to Singapore via Hong Kong and Saigon. The impact of all this effort and investment is etched in the pages of the Chartered Bank minutes. The telegrams read out aloud for each week's assembled Court carried news that was ever more startlingly fresh. On 26 April 1871, the Directors in London were treated to a recital of telegrams from Shanghai, Singapore

---

lasted until 1896. (He had formerly been one of Singapore's leading merchants, and would one day be commemorated by a brass plaque in the city's cathedral. It can be found today just above a stone memorial to two of his children buried in the colony, the second an infant that died in 1862 – which we can suppose may well have helped prompt Paterson and his wife to return to England the following year.)

and Bombay. All of them had been tapped out in Morse in those three distant cities that very same day. Nor was it just messages that could now traverse the globe at unprecedented speeds: in November 1869, a royal yacht bearing the French Empress Eugenie became the first vessel ever to sail from the Mediterranean into the Red Sea via the Suez crossing. A passenger ship of the P&O line followed close behind her. The opening of 'the Lesseps Canal' changed the geography of the shipping world. Select cargoes from India, the East and Australasia could now reach Europe several weeks more quickly via the Mediterranean; and even the cheapest berths would now take passengers via the Suez route that had previously been restricted to wealthier travellers who (like James Wilson in 1859) could afford the old land passage.

A welcome boost for trade in most respects, all this was of course rather less well received in the coastal ports of Britain's South African colonies – Cape Colony and Natal – where local trading firms faced losing much of their traditional business with the oceanic shipping lines. But by one of history's great coincidences, it happened that a remarkable turn of fortune for the Cape Colony would make amends within months for the prospective impact of the Canal's opening. It would also revive a badly jaded optimism over the future of the colony – and of a banking enterprise there which had brought its investors a string of disappointments since making a trumpeted debut in 1862.

3. A SCOTCH PLAN FOR SOUTH AFRICA

This was the 'Standard Bank of British South Africa'. Much like Chartered Bank, by 1869 it had only just survived a spate of early setbacks, similarly prompting some of its more impatient shareholders to ask for their money back or to press the case for merging with a rival. The Standard Bank's travails through the 1860s, however, had been in many ways the very opposite of Chartered's. The bank presided over by Mitchell and his colleagues had always been very much a City of London enterprise, and had struggled until men with more operational experience of its overseas markets had been persuaded to take charge in London. The Standard Bank, though launched in London to tap the City's capital markets, had from the outset been an essentially colonial enterprise – and had come perilously close to collapse before the City gentlemen on its Board asserted their proprietorship and despatched to the Cape a manager steeped in the ways of Scottish banking. Many versions of this story present the Standard as 'an Imperial bank', dreamt up in Lombard Street and imposing itself in the 1860s on the townships of a nascent colonial economy 6,000 miles away, where it bullied vulnerable local banks into submission.[73] What actually happened is a more curious tale – pulling those at the Cape and their backers in London together in a chequered affair that was to be entirely in keeping with the subsequent history of the bank.

At the centre of events was a Scotsman, John Paterson, who came to be the founder of the bank via an early career uncannily like James Wilson's. He was born in a village outside Aberdeen in 1822. And, like Wilson, he set off from Scotland aged nineteen to make his way in the world, though he came from a much humbler background – his father was a quarryman – and his ticket south of the border took him not to London but to South Africa, with a contract from the British government to emigrate to the Cape Colony as a schoolteacher. Assigned to a government school in Port Elizabeth – a coastal town about six days' sailing east of Cape Town, with no port as yet but plenty of Scotsmen, many of them also from Aberdeen – he four years later started a newspaper there, the *Eastern Province Herald*. (The colony was divided into a Western Province, based on Cape Town, and an Eastern Province for which Port Elizabeth was just emerging as a putative capital.) Leaving behind his days as a teacher, Paterson managed to combine editing and publishing the *Herald* from 1848 to 1857 with the pursuit of a successful business career. Driven by 'a volatile and ambitious temperament', he happily shouldered the municipal responsibilities that went with a prominent position in the commercial life of the town.[74] As Port Elizabeth's luminaries turned to establishing its first school, hospital, law court, quayside and town hall, no committee seems to have been complete without his participation – and when a Cape Parliament was set up by the British government in 1854 it was inevitable that Paterson should go to Cape Town as one of Port Elizabeth's two representatives in its new 'House of Assembly'. The energy and eloquence he brought to the House soon attracted comment, not all of it favourable. At least one waspish sketch-writer thought him too voluble by half:

> He is of Scotch extraction and his speeches [are] evidence that he has not long been 'awa' from the land o' siller birk an' gowden furse'. He is an indomitable speaker, never loses an opportunity to address the House and never sits down while his memory can supply him with a word.[75]

Paterson in Cape Town attracted criticism as an emerging leader of the regional faction (often referred to as the 'Scotch party') from the Eastern Province, at a time of lively debate over the future shape and structure of the Cape Colony. It was still a modest concern, built round a pastoral economy. It had a European population of only about 300,000, located largely around the coastal periphery, and this number included many Dutch farmers – left behind when the majority of their 'Boer' compatriots had trekked east and north in the 1830s and 1840s – as well as the mostly British settlers who had begun arriving in substantial numbers only in 1820. Though still overwhelmingly dependent on exports of wool, which accounted for around four-fifths of its total exports by value, the colony was growing remarkably quickly in the 1850s, fuelling sharp political differences over the competing merits of integration, federation and separation for the two provinces (and the younger colony of Natal beyond them). Many in Cape Town were deeply wary of politicians from the Eastern Province who seemed too overtly ambitious.

At the same time, individual townships in the Eastern Province itself were vying for a status that might at least set them notionally on a par with their more famous neighbours at the Western tip of the Cape. And as part of this rivalry most self-respecting townships of any size had their own local bank, generally owned by the leading businessmen of the community and extending credit in a none-too-rigorous fashion to the bank's own proprietors as well as local tradesmen. Indeed, some of the townships contending for regional leadership had more than bank. Port Elizabeth by 1857 had two: the Port Elizabeth Bank (founded 1846) and the Commercial Bank (founded 1853). Paterson, naturally, was a founding shareholder in both; but this did not deter him from lending his weight in 1857 to the idea of a third bank in the town. A founding committee agreed on a prospectus, but it proved an inauspicious time to launch a bank – not least because British redcoats stationed in the Cape to deal with the constant threat of 'Kaffir wars' on the eastern frontiers of the colony were departing for India, where the Empire's needs seemed greater in the wake of the Mutiny. Rising concern over the frontiers' security led this third bank to be aborted – though not before the prospectus committee had come up with a good name. It was to have been the 'Standard Bank of Port Elizabeth'.

Over the course of the next two years, the men behind it reviewed their plans and upgraded them in a remarkable fashion. The number of joint-stock banks in the Eastern Cape seemed set to go on rising in the years ahead. (Another ten would in the event be established between 1857 and 1862.[76]) All were limited to a single main office and, at best, only agency arrangements elsewhere. While yielding a healthy return for their shareholders on the back of the booming wool trade, they were strictly local affairs – in places like Cradock and Grahamstown, Graaff-Reinet and King William's Town – and they were far too small to attract the additional capital required for a more expansive strategy. Paterson and his associates – who included Alexander Croll, a leading Port Elizabeth merchant, and Alfred Jarvis, a former chairman of the Commercial Bank – now set their sights on a grander bank by far. The Commercial appears to have signalled its readiness to be acquired by a new company, which would then set out under Paterson's leadership to pursue a rapid acquisition of as many of the unitary banks as possible. They would be allowed to retain their staffs and their existing directors on local boards, but the amalgamation process would effectively convert them into a branch network on the Scottish model familiar to Paterson and many of his fellow citizens. If all went to plan, the result would eventually be tantamount to a bank covering not only the Eastern Cape but the Western as well – it would be a *national* bank for South Africa. This would be a vision ambitious enough to attract regular draughts of 'old world' capital for the colony's future growth – and would see it flowing into the country via a bank headquartered in Port Elizabeth, thus neatly promoting the latter's status as capital of the Eastern Cape.

But all would depend, of course, on the ability of Paterson and his associates to raise capital on a scale far beyond anything seen in the colony to date. The notion that they could find it was breathtakingly audacious, given the raw state of Port Elizabeth compared with the European capitals to which they would have to turn for support. One description of arriving in the town even a few years later nicely captured a sense of its remoteness:

> I can vividly remember our landing in a surf boat [in March 1864] amid what appeared appalling breakers . . . The place was singularly unattractive to a newcomer . . . [and] was in a primitive stage. The landing facilities were archaic, the streets windswept, sand storms frequent, drinking water scarce, telegraphic facilities not yet available and not a mile of railway even projected in the Eastern Province.[77]

Still, the City of London's appetite for overseas investment was widely celebrated, and had been increasingly apparent in recent years with new banks floated as joint-stock companies to operate in Egypt and Asia, as well as in the Australian colonies.[78] Why should the citizens of Port Elizabeth not use capital raised in London to pursue their vision of a bank for South Africa? In resolving to do so, the committee's immediate challenge was to find a way of gaining physical access to the City, a two-month voyage away, and of persuading its investors of the new bank's potential. It was Paterson who provided the potential solution to this dilemma early in 1859 by deciding to return to London. His wife had died in 1858, leaving him with five young children at home, so he probably had more than one motive for returning. The committee formed in 1857 met again in March 1859, putting an advert in the *Herald* to alert the public to 'a very large and profitable field . . . open to a third bank' and announcing its confidence in the support of the town's main trading families. Paterson set off four months later to find a group of willing investors in the capital of the Empire (and perhaps, with luck, a new wife as well).[79]

He proved more than equal to the task. His own career to date gave him an immediate credibility. The son of a Scottish artisan, he was returning from the Cape a wealthy man on the back of a stream of speculative land deals in the formative stages of Port Elizabeth's development: Paterson embodied the kind of success that made investment in the colonies seem enticing again after the disasters of the 1840s. He soon established himself in London as a prominent colonial figure, proposing the toast at a banquet in December in honour of the Cape Colony's distinguished Governor since 1854, Sir George Grey. His discussions in the City also moved ahead quickly – for Paterson had a compelling proposition to put before investors. Over the decade just closing, the Cape's growth had been extraordinary. (Its total exports had in fact tripled in value to just over £2 million.)[80] And while the colony's population yet remained scarcely a third of Australia's, there was another way of comparing the Cape with Australia that carried a ready appeal. Wool exports from the Cape in 1855–9 had averaged an annual volume of just over 9 million lb, which was roughly on a par with Australia's average for 1840–44.[81] By 1860, Australia's exports were running at four times that volume and were still rising sharply every year. There was every reason to suppose something similar would now happen in South Africa, where the transformational impact of telegraph and railway networks as yet lay ahead. (Bales of wool were still making their way from the interior to coastal towns like Port Elizabeth in ox-drawn wagons, often taking weeks to complete their journey.) The Australian precedent had prompted the founding of several colonial banks that were thriving. South Africa's future as a source of banking business looked similarly assured, and the profusion of Lilliputian banks already operating in the colony – with the limited capital provided by local depositors – surely attested to the promise of a well-run Cape-wide network.

Reports appeared in the Cape as early as May 1860 that a prospectus had been seen in London for the Port Elizabeth project, now shrewdly renamed by Paterson and his friends as 'The Standard Bank of British South Africa'.[82] Why exactly it should have taken two and a half years to bring the financing to fruition is not clear. A rival proposal, for a 'London and South African Bank' (L&SAB), was advertised in June 1860 and led to the opening of a head office in Cape Town just twelve months later. Possibly this bank's plans were themselves a cause of delay for the Standard Bank. Conceivably Paterson's associates in Port Elizabeth also requested more time to prepare the ground. In the meantime, anyway, he seems to have thrown himself into a career in the City, apparently abandoning his political ambitions in Cape Town. He successfully instigated at least two other significant businesses for South Africa – one for the development of irrigation schemes and another to build a railway network in the Eastern Cape – and he joined the board of an existing British bank, the Alliance Bank of London and Liverpool. Finally, in the autumn of 1862, preparations were at last in place for the launch of the Standard Bank. Its inaugural Board consisted of eight members.* Five of them – plus a solicitor from the splendidly named firm of Flux and Argles – came together for their first formal meeting at the City offices of the Alliance Bank in Lothbury on Saturday, 18 October 1862.[83]

A prospectus for the bank was published in *The Times* that morning. Rather like those published for so many start-up internet companies in the late 1990s, it put forward a good idea but could offer no track record whatever, since the bank as yet had no existing operations: it lacked even an office of its own and had no staff, other than three clerks to run the share allotment process. Instead, the prospectus reminded investors of the Cape's prodigious growth in recent years, and listed the current share prices of ten of its existing banks – all of them trading at a huge premium to their flotation prices. Readers were left to draw the obvious inference. The Directors largely confined themselves to the briefest summary of the proposed bank's ambitious agenda within the colony:

> The banking capital of the colonies has not kept pace with this increase of trade, and it has become clear that a new banking institution of considerable magnitude, and with adequate resources, is now a public necessity, and must command success.
>
> To meet this necessity, and as a profitable and safe investment of capital, the Standard Bank of British South Africa is established . . .
>
> Every description of legitimate banking business will be undertaken by the Standard Bank, and it can be stated that valuable mercantile accounts have already been promised.

---

* In addition to Paterson, they comprised a director of the Alliance Bank, John Tarrance, and another City banker, Thomas Stenhouse; two City merchants with South African connections, John Gillespie and William Duthie; and three leading members of the Port Elizabeth business community, Alfred Jarvis, James Black and Alexander Croll. Two others, Robert White and S. Bolton Edenborough, joined the Board later in the month.

> Powers are taken for the incorporation of existing banks in the colonies . . .
>
> The Head Office of the Bank will be in London.[84]

There was one other notable feature of the prospectus. As a result of the delay since 1860, whether intended or not, Paterson had been able to register the bank as one of the very first companies eligible for limited liability status under the Consolidated Limited Liability Act of 1862. (The L&SAB, by the same token, was one of the last banks to be launched on the basis of a Royal Charter.) Perhaps this helps to explain the remarkable success of the offering. Investors clamoured for the shares. Applications were received for over 15,000 shares in just the first three days, and for 43,000 by the closing date for subscriptions.[85] The prospectus offered only two tranches of 5,000 shares each in the first instance, to be followed with two more later. (The fourth and last tranche was to be issued in July 1863.) The shares would have a 'fully paid-up' value of £100, though only £25 per share would be called up, as was customary at the time, leaving the rest as a reserve to be called upon in the event of trouble. The eventual paid-up capital of £2 million would represent just over twice the aggregate paid-up capital of the other twenty-nine banks operating in the Cape Colony by 1862 (excluding the L&SAB). It was an extraordinary vindication of the founding committee's confidence that such a fund-raising might be possible, and no small tribute to Paterson's salesmanship. He and his associates in Port Elizabeth now commanded a huge treasure chest with which to pursue 'the incorporation of existing banks'.

Implementation of the plan began immediately. The Board in London agreed at the end of October 1862 that '[it] will be prepared to incorporate with itself the Commercial Bank of Port Elizabeth' and work on the merger went ahead.[86] The latter's building would in due course be the first branch of the Standard Bank, and its chief cashier, James Tudhope, its first branch manager. While Paterson's Board colleagues in the town busied themselves with the practical aspects of the merger, confirming the Commercial's directors as the Standard's first 'local board' in the colony, Paterson himself arranged in London for the initial transfer of capital to the branch via bills of exchange drawn on the City banks where the shareholders' subscription monies had been safely deposited.

Paterson was confirmed as Executive Chairman in November 1862. How he intended to divide his time between London and Port Elizabeth may not at this stage have been entirely clear, even to himself. When news arrived in December of the death of his brother-in-law, George Kemp – his partner in the firm of Paterson, Kemp & Co. – his initial reaction was to ask the Board for a leave of absence, 'to proceed to the Cape by next mail [steamer] on private business'.[87] But within a week this plan had given way to an altogether different assignment that would see the Chairman taking charge of the bank's early development on the ground. The Board to this end passed a remarkable resolution. The bank, in effect, would be based in South Africa and run from Port Elizabeth. It was resolved:

> That Mr John Paterson, the Chairman, in conjunction with Mr Alex. Croll, or Mr Robert Henry Black, or Mr Matt. C Kemp, or Mr George Impey, [all of Port Elizabeth] be authorized generally to initiate the business of the Standard Bank; and to exercise all the necessary powers of the Board, with a view to open the business of Branches at Natal, Kaffraria, or other Colonies of British South Africa; taking all necessary powers with a view thereto (including full powers for amalgamations) and without the necessity of reference to this Board for confirmation; and that a Power of Attorney for the purpose be prepared under the City Seal.[88]

A week later, with Paterson still in the chair, the Board evidently had second thoughts about this carte blanche. The notion of a Power of Attorney was set aside, and it was decided that arrangements made by these gentlemen in South Africa 'shall be conditional upon confirmation by this Board, and . . . subject to instructions from time to time conveyed from this Board by letter'.[89] How far this would be anything more than a formality, though, remained to be seen. In the meantime, a first consignment of £10,000 worth of gold coins ('specie', as distinct from gold bullion) was shipped off in boxes to Port Elizabeth. The Chairman departed for the colony – taking with him an eighteen-year-old Scottish beauty called Marizza Bowie as the new Mrs Paterson – and the Board decreed, on 20 February 1863, 'That the Bank commence business today . . .'

4. 'SEVEN CURRENT YEARS OF WANT'

For a year or so after Paterson's arrival in the Cape at the start of April, all seemed to go swimmingly. He spent four months there, leading the way. An early documentary record of the amalgamations process – actually a rather flattering description for months of plotting and scheming over share values, board positions and customer accounts – is a copy book of letters written by one James Alexander, who was sent by Paterson to Durban to negotiate directly with the directors of the local banks there. Alexander's first letter, dated 1 June 1863, is addressed to the Chairman and Directors of a bank in Durban, asking for information. 'I shall then have much pleasure in communicating the same to our chairman of the Home Board of Directors at present in Port Elizabeth.'[90] Over the winter months, initial branches were established in Durban and four other towns in addition to Port Elizabeth itself – plus Cape Town, where a branch was set up in Adderley Street, in August 1863. As envisaged from the start, many local banks – in the Western Province as well as the Eastern – were soon showing a lively interest in Paterson's plan. As his man in Durban reported to the bank's Secretary on 3 June 1863: 'The local banks are desirous of amalgamation . . .'[91] The Standard Bank was offering to buy out local shareholders with its own shares, which were trading at a healthy premium to their issue price on the London Stock Exchange, and it was evidently prepared to pay generous terms. (The Commercial Bank's shareholders had in February pocketed a 13 per cent gain on the pre-sale value of their own stock.[92]) For local proprietors who sold out, there was an additional attraction to remaining as shareholders in the Standard Bank: its limited liability status offered a degree of protection that was not available for indigenous banks in South Africa (and remained unavailable until 1879). By the time Paterson was back in London and standing in front of the Standard's shareholders at their first General Meeting, in October 1863, he was able to report on a remarkable first half-year of operations.[93] Not only had a profitable network been established in lightning time ('almost as speedily as they could have done it at home [in England]') but all had been accomplished with the tiniest possible lay-out of shareholders' capital ('very few institutions . . . could boast of having been started for the preliminary expenditure of £2,200'). Of course this owed much to the strategy of assimilating extant operations wherever possible, and even freshly established branches had been left to operate largely under the supervision of directors: 'They had local boards at all their branches, as they thought it safer to trust them than managers.' Several new branches were acquired or opened from scratch over the following six months, involving the issue to London investors of another million shares. At the second General Meeting, in April 1864, Paterson was in celebratory mood. 'It was necessary to multiply these branches, the system in South Africa being very similar to that in Scotland, where every town had its branch bank . . . His anticipations of the success of the bank had been greatly exceeded.'[94]

Over the summer of 1864, however, his fellow Directors on the Board began to have their doubts. To start with, there was a niggling concern over who was really in charge. Paterson had remained in Britain since his return the previous autumn. Alexander Croll had been Paterson's most effective lieutenant in Port Elizabeth, but in the wake of an unfortunate misunderstanding over share allotments Croll had resigned in a huff, and was even threatening to bring legal action against the Board.[95] (He later joined the Board of the Standard's rival, the L&SAB.) Early efforts to find a 'Colonial Manager' had only been pursued very half-heartedly, effectively leaving no one in the Cape senior to Tudhope as manager of the Port Elizabeth branch. But the Board's letters to Tudhope suggest that confidence in him was waning fast.[96] Even in London, staffing had proved problematic. The bank had found a solid Secretary, a former Provincial Bank of Ireland employee called Francis Searle, but the man appointed as the Chief Accountant in November 1862 had found himself totally unable to cope with the job – 'in consequence of his not having had any experience in any Bank', as the Board minutes had explained in a note that perhaps casts a revealing light on the importance originally attached to the operations at 'Head Office'.[97]

Meanwhile, and more seriously, there was mounting concern over the fundamentals of the business in South Africa. The American Civil War had closed off an important market for all wool exports. A rapid shift in European buying patterns had worked to the grave disadvantage of the Cape, by tilting demand towards 'long staple' wool and away from the 'short staple' wool produced by the colony. Above all, a severe drought since 1862 had wiped out many flocks and left thousands of farms in desperate straits. A pastoral economy that two years earlier had looked highly promising was suddenly only too dependent on a solitary export for which demand had slumped alarmingly. This harsh reality had for a while been disguised by the easy availability of credit in the colony, largely stimulated by all the capital shipped in by the Standard Bank itself. The result had disastrously aggravated the systemic weakness of a small colonial economy in which farmers lived for months off the credit extended to them by tradesmen in the towns, who were themselves dependent in tough times on ever greater quantities of discounted bills; hundreds of tradesmen were now hopelessly indebted to the banks. When interest rates jumped in September 1864, in the wake of a sharp deterioration in the City money markets, Paterson's colleagues in London called a halt to his expansionist strategy. They also decided the time had come to look more closely at what was being done with the bank's capital, still being poured into the colony in prodigious quantities.* A much more concerted attempt

---

* When a shareholder at the November 1864 General Meeting questioned the need for yet another capital subscription, Paterson responded with an explanation that would be repeated at shareholders' meetings down the generations (as at those of Chartered Bank, too, as noted already): 'The cost of living was very high there [in South Africa], and salaries were high in consequence ... and unless they paid their officers at the same rate as other similar

was now made to find a 'General Manager', someone with unimpeachable banking credentials who could be despatched to exert a firm hand in the Cape. Before the year was out – and in the wake of a collapse in wool prices in November that only made the appointment all the more urgent – the Board (still under Paterson's chairmanship) hired for the role a thirty-four-year-old Scotsman with just the right profile. He came to them recommended on the strength of a successful career to date, with first the Bank of Scotland and, more recently, as the Cardiff branch manager for the National Provincial Bank of England.[98] His name was Robert Stewart, and by February 1865 he was installed in Port Elizabeth, preparing to make his first tour of the branches.

There followed a nasty surprise. What Stewart found on his tour was a commercial sector on the edge of financial panic and a branch network in utter disarray. It seemed the Standard Bank's shareholders could hardly have chosen a worse time to invest their money in the colony. The whole of the Cape's vastly over-extended system of credits was in the process of being unwound, leaving the Standard Bank with potentially disastrous losses in many towns. This cast the willingness of so many smaller banks to contemplate amalgamation since the start of 1863 in a rather different light. It seemed to Stewart that credits had been extended with a shocking recklessness, while managers and directors had in several instances simply disguised loans going into their own accounts. It was a deeply aggrieved Scottish banker who sat down early in April 1865 to pen a detailed report for the Directors in London. By the time he despatched it, the Board was already receiving complaints from managers who had written from the Cape in January to protest at his appointment.[99] If the managers had hoped to be able to pre-empt any unfavourable comment, they were to be roundly disappointed.

While Stewart's report was crossing the oceans back to Britain, Paterson addressed another April General Meeting of shareholders. Reviewing the financial year to December 1864 that had apparently earned them a 12 per cent return on their capital and lifted the bank's 'Reserve Fund' to £56,000, he indulged himself in some exquisitely ill-timed optimism: 'He believed that banking at the Cape of Good Hope was much safer than it was in some other parts of the world.' The Standard's customers, were for the most part, only modest borrowers in small towns, and all were well known to the local managers. 'He wished them to understand distinctly that the class of business which the Standard Bank transacted was

---

institutions paid theirs, they must expect to lose them, and to be less efficiently served.' (*The Bankers' Magazine*, Vol. 24, 1864, pp. 1117–22.)

perfectly safe and sound . . . and was less speculative in its character than any banking business with which he was acquainted.'[100] Two weeks later, after an unusually swift passage from the Cape, Stewart's letter landed on the Board Secretary's desk. It was read aloud to the Directors at the Board meeting on 19 May.[101] We can suppose John Paterson was not easily embarrassed – but his presence in the chair that day must have made it an uncomfortable occasion for all, as Francis Searle regaled them with their General Manager's findings:

> The Board here [in Port Elizabeth] had practically ceased to exist, a fortu-
> nate circumstance for the bank for had it done so much longer the [local]
> Members would have absorbed all the capital of the Branch for themselves
> and their friends. I am within the truth when I state that through their
> unfaithfulness to the trust deposed in them a sum of at least £60,000 is
> now in jeopardy. The Branch has in this respect been shamefully managed.
> You have a right to know the true state of matters, and I should be failing
> in my duty were I to withhold it from you . . . I am decidedly of opinion
> that we shall manage far better without than with a [local] Board, and the
> arrangement will be attended with another advantage – we shall save £400 a
> year by it . . . I shall forward you by next mail a list of current changes
> among the Bank's officers in the Colony for the confirmation of the Court.[102]

There is no record in the minutes of any of the Directors questioning Stewart's assessment: in all probability his letter only confirmed their fears and they accepted his verdict on the state of the bank without demur. It amounted nonetheless to an instant discrediting of most of the senior personnel in South Africa and was a severe blow to Paterson's credibility. Searle's response was uncompromising on their behalf:

> . . . the Directors appreciate the valuable report sent by you on the state of
> affairs at the Cape, and they trust all [your] future statements will be
> equally candid. The mismanagement of affairs revealed in your report
> causes the Directors to withdraw all confidence from those who had been
> trusted with the Bank's business, with the honourable exception of Mr
> Campbell, and (by your representations) Mr Craik. You will be pleased to
> request Mr Kirkwood at once to withdraw from the Direction at Port
> Elizabeth, of which Board he must no longer consider himself a Member,
> and intimate to Mr Tudhope that it is the desire of the Court that he
> should at once send in his resignation as Manager. Where the duties and
> responsibilities entrusted to them as Local Directors have been so grossly
> neglected and abused, remuneration cannot be expected and must not be
> granted.[103]

Thomas Stenhouse and Alfred Jarvis seem to have emerged as the leading forces on the Board over the next few difficult months. Jarvis was a former chairman of the Commercial Bank, while Stenhouse was a professional banker who also had a seat on the Board of the Chartered Mercantile Bank of India. Jarvis was the proposer a week later of a Board motion that all executive orders in South Africa would now have to come from the London Board – which in practice would mean from Stewart in Port Elizabeth (with the assistance of an overland, albeit precarious, telegraph link between London and South Africa, inaugurated at the start of 1865).

Paterson clung to his chairmanship for several more weeks, but his position was weakened still further by news from Port Elizabeth that the rapidly worsening commercial crisis in the colony was threatening to bring down his own firm. Struggling with the impact of Paterson, Kemp's problems on his own personal finances in London, Paterson tried to push through an arrangement with the bank without the blessing of the full Board. This prompted a written complaint in the Minutes by Thomas Stenhouse, who was supported by Jarvis and other Directors.[104] Their feuding continued while rumours about Stewart's remedial treatment for the bank swirled in the City and the price of its shares slithered from well over £25 to less than £9. There was plenty of hard news to merit the sell-off: the Board in August 1865 formally took receipt of the resignations of thirty-nine local directors.[105] A circular had to be issued to shareholders later that month acknowledging 'the immense depreciation in the market value of the shares of this company', and insisting that sufficient reserves existed to protect the equity capital in the bank. By the time of the next General Meeting, in October, Paterson had finally resigned and two other founding Directors, James Black and William Duthie, had gone with him. This did little, however, to allay a series of angry exchanges at the meeting (as the deadpan pages of The Bankers' Magazine put it, 'a long and animated conversation ensued').[106] Furious shareholders were less interested in talk of a general monetary crisis in the Cape than in getting answers from the Board to their questions about losses specific to the bank. It transpired that one of Paterson's closest Port Elizabeth associates (Kirkwood) had gone bankrupt owing the bank £40,000 – substantially in excess of the entire Reserve Fund, since the latter had now been halved to take account of bad debts. By the end of the year, only £10,000 was left in the Reserve and the Board was contemplating how best to break the news to the City that no dividend would be paid for 1865.

There followed a brutal contraction of the bank's business in the Cape, under Stewart's forceful supervision. He replaced local directors with new managers and curtailed the bank's lending abruptly. He decided against any drastic reduction of the physical network – unlike the L&SAB, which chopped theirs back from eleven to just four, losing in the process most of its 'feeder' branches in the interior[107] – but he did trim it back, closing a few branches that appeared to have no real prospect of contributing to the bank's profits.* Above all, Stewart replaced the previous set-up of virtually autonomous branches with a heavily centralized reporting structure, using uniform procedures and routines that gradually imposed a quasi-Scottish stability across the network. One immediate consequence was a substantial fall in profits. For the second half of 1866, they dropped to just over £13,000, against a half-yearly average of more than £22,000 since the start of 1864. But the network survived, and when wool prices began to recover and the long drought across the interior finally broke in 1867, the scale of the bank's surviving operations – and the security offered to its customers by its deep pockets in London – allowed it to stage a slow recovery. Writing off all the book losses accruing from the earlier 'amalgamation' strategy – capitalized on the balance sheet as goodwill in modern parlance – wiped out the rest of the Reserve Fund in June 1868.

By then, at least the survival of the bank was no longer in doubt. As if to acknowledge as much, the Board in London had in April 1867 taken up a long-term lease on a new head office, at 10 Clements Lane in the heart of the City. But the Directors had had to endure an unnerving couple of years. Jarvis had confessed to shareholders at the April 1866 General Meeting: 'He could not now enter into an explanation of the circumstances which prevented this state of things being made known to the directors. He was not yet himself at the bottom of the mystery, but he thought he had a clue . . .'[108] Some in his audience that day had spoken out in

---

* One branch's closure had less to do with its banking performance than with political sensitivities over its location: the trekboers of the Orange Free State, beyond the borders of British jurisdiction, had greatly resented Standard's acquisition of the town bank in Bloemfontein. In March 1865 a vote was passed in the legislative body of the state, the Volksraad, to nullify the takeover and to bar the Standard Bank after 1865 from operating in the state at all. A spokesman for the tiny but highly profitable Bloemfontein Bank warned the Volksraad that a failure to stand up against predatory foreign banks would lead eventually to the Free State's people being forced 'to trek across the Vaal River, or be driven into the sea, leaving the dear country where the bones of their fathers and mothers had lain for ages'. There is no record of investors in London taking any heed of this episode, though it may have alerted some to the fact that political difficulties in the Cape were not entirely restricted to arguments between the Western and Eastern Provinces, or debates over how to deal with violence on the borders between the white colonies and the lands of the native peoples of Southern Africa. (See J. A. Henry, *The First Hundred Years of the Standard Bank*, OUP, 1963, pp.10–12.)

favour of a merger with the L&SAB: combining the two institutions 'would be the only way of meeting the rogues who were preying on them at the Cape'. In reply, Jarvis announced that he had in fact already led a delegation of Directors to talk to the L&SAB about a possible merger, but they had been rebuffed. It was suggested the L&SAB had objected to any association with Paterson's badly tarnished reputation. Inevitably, this disappointment – and indeed the whole sorry outcome of the bank's over-hasty expansion – was squarely blamed by several shareholders on their former chairman.

The Board, too, came to see Paterson's conduct as the principal source of their troubles. By implication, the singular structure of the bank would yet be manageable, given executive officers of greater integrity. When James Tudhope appeared in London in 1866 to give his side of the story, he produced a stream of letters that he had received from Paterson. (Tudhope had by now left the bank and found employment elsewhere, but evidently wanted the satisfaction of clearing his name.) Appalled, the Directors passed a resolution to record

> their entire disapproval of the views and instructions expressed therein: the Directors also feel it their duty to record that this is the first occasion of their having been made acquainted with these communications, which Mr Paterson, behind their backs and without their authority, most unjustifiably was in the habit of addressing to Mr Tudhope and they consider these instructions tended in great measure to that maladministration of the affairs of the Company in South Africa.[109]

For many London shareholders, Paterson had been confirmed as the villain of the piece when his own Port Elizabeth business, Paterson, Kemp, had finally collapsed early in 1866, owing the bank a substantial but unspecified sum. It was perhaps fortunate for Paterson's reputation that they were not given the full story. Prior to the failure of his business, he had spent several weeks in Port Elizabeth trying to save it. On the strength of his property holdings in the town, he had desperately sought a personal loan from the bank. Stewart's letters to the Board reported back on a series of meetings, but it is clear from his dispassionate commentary on Paterson's plight that the General Manager's one concern was to secure the money already extended to the ailing firm, and there was never the remotest possibility of his agreeing to any kind of rescue package. ('I have had several interviews with Mr Paterson in reference to Paterson Kemp & Co's liabilities, but he has not yet been able to do anything leading to a settlement.'[110]) Stewart thought the former chairman's private estate in the Cape would scarcely fetch a third of its value 'in ordinary times' and he set his face against any personal loan – a stand many times cited in later years as testimony to his strength of character and rigorous banking integrity.

The clash between Paterson and Stewart in the Cape marked the start of an increasingly vexed relationship for the bank with its founder and former chairman. Paterson was in due course declared insolvent and his private estate in South Africa was sequestered by the courts in 1867. The Directors would face questions over his debts to the bank at General Meetings for the next six years: only in 1873 was it finally asserted that they had been fully provided for, and the settlement did nothing to avert further legal quarrels. Robert Stewart, meanwhile, can fairly be said to have spent the rest of the 1860s single-handedly re-launching the Standard Bank after its brush with disaster. The good fortune of the bank's Board in selecting him for the job can hardly be overstated. It had plucked an obscure provincial bank manager from an office in Cardiff, who must have judged his career prospects in Britain to be limited indeed for him to have risked all on a job in the Cape in the mid-1860s – aptly described in one classic account as 'a number of miscellaneous territories, a ramshackle collection of polities, a congeries of peoples, united by little more than poverty . . . no one dreamed of making his future in that faraway and empty land'.[111] But Stewart did, and in pursuit of his ambition he emerged as scarcely less entitled than John Paterson to be seen as the founder of the Standard Bank.

There lingered two uncomfortable questions in the aftermath of Paterson's exit. The first concerned the nature of the ties between the Board based in London and the men on the ground in South Africa actually running the bank's operations. It was convenient to identify the lax management of the early years overwhelmingly with Paterson's shortcomings as a day-to-day manager. In reality, the whole Board had done little for two years to stop the bank perpetuating the cronyism and loose lending of the Cape banks it acquired. So what did the debacle after 1864 say about the workability of this long-distance relationship? There is no doubt that their failure to appreciate in good time what had been happening inside the bank's branches caused the Directors considerable alarm. On reflection, they decided to introduce a most unusual set of governance rules. They chose not to elect a single Chairman as Paterson's successor: instead, two Directors were asked to alternate as Chairman and Deputy Chairman. This arrangement soon gave way to an even more singular approach whereby all of the Directors on the Board took it in turns to occupy the Chair for a week at a time. The only individual with a commanding voice in the affairs of the bank would be its General Manager in the Cape. Those responsible to the shareholders in London, in setting the broad policies of the bank and watching over its finances, would work together as a collegial body.

The second question facing the bank posed a sharper dilemma. Had all of the original enthusiasm over its founding turned out, in the end, to be simply misplaced? As the end of the 1860s approached, it was becoming apparent that the City had gravely underestimated the political and geographical constraints on the future development of the Cape Colony. Stewart himself had come to broadly this conclusion after his first eighteen months, as he explained in a long letter to the Board of August 1866:

> [T]he existing Banking Capital in South Africa is far beyond the legitimate business requirements of the Country . . . To do the banking business connected with an import and export business not rising in the gross to four Millions, there is a paid up Banking Capital here of over two Millions and adding Deposits and Circulation, available Banking Capital of considerably over four Millions – an amount greatly disproportionate, as it seems to me, to the legitimate business of the colony . . . [F]rom the year 1852 to the year 1859, a period of seven years without Kaffir War or serious drought, the progress made by the Colony was great and steady . . . [B]ut not only has the former progress of South Africa not been sustained but a positive retrograde movement has set in, and . . . although I am not disposed to undervalue the probable result of a succession of seven good years of plenty after we have got through the seven current years of want, I must . . . question whether the conclusion is not forced upon us that the Colony as a merely pastoral country, has not struck something of a limit to its further progress unless some other resources are discovered.[112]

Three years on, it appears from his reports back to London that Stewart felt little cause to revise this melancholy assessment. The mid-decade crisis had passed, the price of South Africa's short staple wools had staged at least a partial recovery and the seasonal rains had come and gone with a blessed regularity. Yet the overall activity of the bank had continued to shrink, shaving net profits by 10–15 per cent with each half-year that passed, and land prices had gone on falling steadily. The substantial capital channelled into the bank since 1863 had produced a branch network capable of three times the volume of business seemingly available in the Cape. Much of Stewart's regular commentaries focused necessarily on movements in the price of wool and conditions in the farming community. But he usually laced his reports with some general remarks, and those that were included with his despatch on New Year's Day 1869 were not untypical: 'Trade all over the Colony is unprecedentedly dull and the aspect of things is altogether very gloomy . . . [W]e are drawing in our Capital.

There are loud and angry complaints at this action, but we must consult our own interests first.'[113] At the end of February 1869, he left the Cape for his first trip to Europe in four years. He was 'very cordially received' when he appeared at the shareholders' General Meeting at 10 Clements Lane in April. The meeting had to take stock of yet another set of discouraging results. Indeed, a review was presented of the bank's first six years in South Africa, disclosing that 'amalgamation expenses' and bad debts had together accounted for almost 20 per cent more than the bank had paid as dividends over the period. The General Manager nonetheless put on a brave show of optimism for the occasion. Their bank's standing in the Cape had never been higher, he told the assembled shareholders, and the balance sheet had been thoroughly cleansed with no break in dividend payments since 1865: 'to have been enabled to do this in the time we have passed through forebodes a good future, for things cannot much longer remain at the Cape in the way they have been for some time past'. After his return to Port Elizabeth late in July, though, Stewart found wool prices plummeting again, and was soon confiding in the Board as glumly as ever:

> From my remarks in recent letters I may appear to take a gloomy view of the future of this Colony, but, in the all but collapse of its staple product, and the all but entire absence of other resources to fall back immediately upon, I cannot well do otherwise. A revival in trade may be nearer at hand than I suppose, but what is to cause it, or from what quarter it is to come, it would be difficult to say.[114]

Here was a case indeed of the darkest hour coming just before the dawn. Eighteen months before his trip back to England, in August 1867, Stewart had diligently reported a story in the Cape Town newspapers about the discovery of some diamonds on the banks of the Orange River along Cape Colony's border with the Orange Free State. '[It had] not created much excitement in the Colony', he had noted, nor had a succession of smaller finds in the same area through 1868 caused much of a stir. Everyone knew diamonds only came from India (in ages past) or Brazil. A geologist sent by a London diamond merchant to the Orange River site duly confirmed the terrain was not 'diamondiferous' country; so odd gems here and there must have been deposited by ostriches which had found and swallowed them elsewhere. Then, while Stewart was still away in Europe, a monster 83.5-carat diamond turned up (one day to be known as the Star of Africa). This could only mean one thing: ostriches larger than any previously known to man. Or perhaps there was just one other possibility, the existence of a new source of diamonds, lying in wait for those enterprising enough to stake out a claim. By the time Stewart was back in Port

Elizabeth, in July 1869, thousands of 'diggers' were intent on doing so, hurrying to the Orange River and from there just a little further north to the banks of a tributary, the Vaal. By the end of the year, a canvas township had sprouted up beside the Vaal and diamonds valued at almost £25,000 had been sifted from the river banks compared with a tally of just £450 in 1868.[115] People were starting to talk of visiting 'the diamond fields'.

2

Diamonds, Silver and Gold, 1870–93

1. NO STANDING STILL AT THE CAPE

Over the course of the 1870s, the Standard Bank of British South Africa established itself not just as the leading bank of the Cape but as one of the two or three most important civic entities underpinning the emergence of the future South Africa. This was still a raw country, with few population centres of much size: even the biggest towns, like Cape Town (pop. *c*.35,000) and Port Elizabeth (pop. *c*.25,000), as yet scarcely compared with Scottish cities like Aberdeen (pop. *c*.100,000). Away from the coast, dozens of small townships across the vast interior presented a makeshift collection of iron and wooden houses, sharing dusty and cartwheel-rutted streets with just a few stone buildings, styled on Victorian lines, to announce the presence of Main Street. Early photographs of the time catch more than a hint of the American frontier territories – and the Cape had its own troubles over land ownership, too, that would soon eclipse even tales from the Wild West. (In 1879, on the borders of Natal at the north-eastern extremity of the two settled colonies, a British infantry regiment was all but wiped out by 20,000 Zulu warriors, at the Battle of Isandlwana.) But as the Cape's scattered towns evolved over the next several years and steadily acquired a greater air of permanence, there was one institution that any merchant, shopkeeper or sheep farmer could be increasingly sure of finding in an important-looking building near the centre of town. New outposts of the Standard Bank sprang up steadily over this decade: a network of fewer than twenty branches at the end of the 1860s had expanded by the end of the 1870s to embrace as many as fifty-four – though several were still prone to closing and reopening as local business ebbed and flowed – and they accounted for well over half of all the banking outlets in the Cape.[1] Half (or more) of the total was by then a fair measure of the Standard's share of banking business in the Cape by almost any measure: it held roughly half the coinage and half the deposits, half the bills under discount and half the country's paper currency.[2] As its Chairman proudly announced in London at an Annual General Meeting as early as 1872: 'Our notes are as well known in the colony as Scotch notes are in Scotland, and the majority of the people prefer a Standard bank-note to sovereigns.'[3] In a society still heavily dependent on long chains of credit stretching back from the export merchants of the coastal towns to the isolated farmsteads of the high veld, this prominence gave the 'imperial bank' a state-building role with few real parallels even among the other emerging colonial nations of the late nineteenth century.

The summer months of 1869–70 brought a buzz to Port Elizabeth, with diamond diggers on their ox-drawn wagons setting out from the town in their hundreds to begin the six-week journey north to the Vaal (see Plate 5a and Map 1 on p. 174). Amazing reports were soon being heard of men turning up precious stones in the loose earth along both banks of the river. Diamonds began to feature almost as regularly in Stewart's letters home as comments on the wool trade. In February 1870, he noted cautiously that diamonds 'still continue to be found and add a little to the wealth of the country'; in May he was bucked by 'very satisfactory intelligence . . . having reference to the finding of large numbers in a single locality'.[4] Still, more time was needed to see what new business (if any) might arise for the Standard Bank. Its nearest branch was fully four days away from the diggings, located as they were 'in as unprepossessing a spot as it is possible to imagine . . . the kind of place where one could ride for days across the gray, stony veld without seeing a soul'.[5] It was also a place beyond the effective jurisdiction either of the British colonial government or of the Dutch Boer republics to the east (the Orange Free State) and the north (the South African Republic, in the Transvaal). Technically, it was land belonging to native Africans of the Griqua nation, though no one supposed their writ would run for long if the diamond rush continued.

Leading the charge were the 'river-diggers', solitary fortune-hunters who were mostly intent on selling whatever they found to the dealers who hurried after them, adding their own tents to the local encampment. Gathering news of the camp's progress wherever he could, Stewart noted two key developments. Stocks of gold coin were fast disappearing from those branches of the bank nearest to the Vaal, since African labourers hired at the diggings would accept payment in nothing else. Much more specie would be needed soon. And second, dealers were starting to appear at those same branches, asking not just to borrow money against the security of their diamonds but also to use the bank, in effect, as a conduit to the gem markets of Europe. The diamonds needed to be insured, shipped and sold on their behalf, by a party whom they could trust to remit the sale proceeds or place them with banks in London. By September, Stewart was supervising the first such consignments out of Port Elizabeth: 'I have the pleasure to enclose herewith Bill of Lading together with Marine Policy for £205, for 8 diamonds for realization on account of Beaufort West . . .'[6] In this same letter, he made clear that he no longer had any doubt but that what was happening on the Vaal amounted to a potentially momentous development for the Cape, and therefore for the Standard Bank. It was his hope, as he explained to Francis Searle, that the shipping of diamonds back to London 'will yield handsome profits to the Bank and open up a remunerative branch [i.e. line] of business which was little contemplated when the Institution was first established'. Within weeks, he had despatched a sub-manager from Port Elizabeth to set up a branch at Klipdrift, the camp established by the diggers on the Vaal's north bank.*

The next three months, unfortunately, brought disquieting news. Vaal diamonds were soon all but impossible to find: the alluvial deposits seemed to have been picked clean. 'Boers returned to their farms, other white diggers went back to their home in the Cape and Natal. The diamond rush appeared to be at an end almost as soon as it had started.'[7] For some of the Standard Bank's competitors, this anticlimax only compounded existing anxieties about getting too involved with the diamond diggers. Bankers, after all, were not jewellers. They had no expertise in the valuation of stones presented as security for loans. Prices quoted in the Cape had turned out in many instances to be wildly in excess of those subsequently realized in London. For the Board of the Standard's old imperial rival, the London & South Africa Bank (L&SAB), rumours that the whole episode might easily prove a short-lived wonder were the last straw. Its directors issued a firm ruling at the start of 1871: the bank's four branches were ordered to make no further advances against diamonds. This seems to have crossed with letters back from senior L&SAB men in the Cape warning against such a policy, for the directors followed up with an edict shortly afterwards that 'the question be not again referred home for reconsideration'.[8]

If Stewart was ever tempted to have second thoughts on the Standard Bank's behalf, there was not a hint of it in his letters back to the Company

---

* The sub-manager did not distinguish himself in the months ahead, and almost came to grief when he reached the Vaal. A small wooden house for the branch together with its contents, including a large safe, were sent over the river by ferry. What happened next, as reported in Port Elizabeth's local newspaper, became a famous story. 'The safe weighing 1,800 lbs in crossing the Vaal slipped off the boat – or we believe two boats lashed together – into the river but, fortunately, floated like a cork, or say iron ship, never touching the ground until it reached the opposite shore.' (*Eastern Province Herald*, 23 December 1870.)

Secretary. He certainly reported to Searle that many of the 6,000 or so white diggers on the Vaal were leaving ('but it is believed, except in very few cases, only for two or three months to escape the intense summer heat there') and he had to acknowledge that digging had 'settled down to an ordinary recognised avocation' – but he never showed any sign of wavering in his belief that extraordinary events were afoot and the Standard had to be ready to respond positively to whatever might happen next.[9] Nor, far more significantly, was there any suggestion from London that the Directors wished to challenge his judgment on this. Unlike the L&SAB, the Standard Bank was an institution unmistakeably run by those in the field. Having turned to Stewart *in extremis* in 1864, its Board had come to trust him implicitly through the years of retrenchment. It was now invariably content to take his lead. Even debates in London over the balance sheet hung on Stewart's response: a proposed restructuring of the equity capital two years earlier had been ditched after he had signalled his view that it might be a damaging distraction. ('Receiving such an opinion from so high an authority', as the Chairman admitted to shareholders in October 1868, 'we have not deemed it wise to move any further in the matter.'[10]) As for operations in the Cape itself, control of these rested squarely by 1871 with the man in Port Elizabeth. So the Standard Bank stayed open for diamond business – and its stance was soon rewarded.

Increasingly desperate prospectors, hunting 20 miles or so south of the Vaal, had already come across other diamonds, scattered over some up-country farms. Turning their attention back to these as the summer heat eased in 1871, they made the astonishing discovery of not one but four new sites, even more richly endowed than the river diggings. 'The stones were so thinly covered with earth that after every heavy rain little crystals were washed free of sand and lay shining on the ground.'[11] In October, the British in effect annexed the whole territory as a Crown Colony (Griqualand), and by the end of the year a massive influx of diggers and assorted hangers-on had lifted its population to a staggering 50,000* or so – bigger by far than Cape Town's. The four main sites were turning into open-cast mines with names that would soon be known around the world: Bultfontein, Du Toits Pan, De Beers and New Rush (shortly to be renamed Kimberley). Two instant towns sprang up, New Rush/Kimberley and Beaconsfield, and Stewart by March 1872 had directed the opening of a Standard Bank branch in each of them. The reported value of the diamonds produced in 1872, at £1.6 million, was four times that of 1871. Even more astounding was the discovery, before the year was out, of what made this crop so special. The world had never encountered diamonds except as stones embedded in alluvial deposits.

Until 1872 those on the farms around Kimberley were assumed to be more of the same, and indeed they were briefly thought to be disappearing just like those on the Vaal. In fact, what had been discovered were diamond 'pipes' – formations hitherto unknown to geologists. Reaching down from the top soil into the depths of the earth, each was akin to an upside-down chimney shaft, up which liquid rocks and gases had surged millions of years ago, dragging diamonds with them towards the surface. (Alluvial diamonds resulted from rivers wearing away the surface contents of hidden pipes, carrying the stones sometimes huge distances away.) The solidified content of the pipes was not granite but eminently diggable rock, coloured a distinctive shade of blue. And when diggers hacked into it, they found something very different from alluvial deposits. The blue ground was (relatively speaking) thick with diamonds – and the deeper the diggers looked, the more diamonds they found. The economic prospects for South Africa had been dramatically transformed.

It took no time for this to be reflected in the Standard Bank's returns. Half-yearly profits had fallen well short of £10,000 from January 1868 to the end of 1870. They topped £30,000 in the half-year to June 1872 and went on rising. The diamond business made a huge and direct contribution. In addition to the agency fees charged in the Cape for making insurance, postage and sale arrangements, the branches lent against the security of the precious packages sent off to London – though they were constantly enjoined to do so with great caution, in theory lending no more than 10–15 per cent of the assessed value of the diamonds under custody. Even then, this could be highly risky business. The finances of the diamond fields, as the diggers burrowed ever deeper, could be almost as precarious as the physical conditions in Kimberley's 'Big Hole'. There, hundreds of individual diggers tried to continue excavating tiny plots directly adjacent to each other, so that dividing walls and access paths within the Hole were constantly collapsing and throwing the delineation of separate claims into chaos (see Plate 6a). The trading of diamonds was scarcely more orderly. The unprecedented volume of stones coming on to the world market led in 1873 to a disastrous collapse in prices, and many dealers were ruined before the market recovered. Shielding the bank against the wild price gyrations, and refining the complicated procedures involved in its role as an intermediary, took up huge amounts of Stewart's time – and accounted for many pages of his regular letters back to London. But, while attending to the details, he never lost sight of the wider implications of the diamond discoveries. As he wrote home in March 1871, they had 'rendered localities rich, and produced wealth in places where pastoral and agricultural pursuits previously never flourished'.[12] They had even 'wakened the lethargic

Boer to new life and fresh activities'. Successful diggers were investing their new wealth in land and stock, pushing up the values of both quite dramatically. He was reporting six months later, with no trace at all of Scottish dourness, that the bank's business had been 'completely revolutionised', which he attributed not just to the diamond finds but also to strong overseas demand for wool.[13] (By mid-1872 wool prices at the ports had doubled in three years.) The Standard Bank's response, in Stewart's view, had to go far beyond accommodating its new customers in Kimberley. Hence the energy with which he extended its network into every corner of the Cape.

The bank was soon operating on a scale that was unique in South Africa, just as its Port Elizabeth founders had envisaged in the late 1850s. There existed twenty-four other banks in the Cape as early as 1870, although all but two of them were 'unitary', that is to say restricted to a single branch. (The exceptions were the L&SAB and the largest surviving 'local' bank, the Eastern Province Bank of Grahamstown, with four branches each.) As a measure of prosperity returned to the farming community, demand rose for checking and remittance facilities across the colony, as well as for overdrafts and the discounting of trade bills. The Standard was the only bank able to offer all these services, and it made the most of it. From 1874, for example, it allowed its banknotes to be exchanged for gold at any branch, irrespective of which branch had originally issued the notes – a convenience no rival could provide. Underpinning all its operations, meanwhile, were constant (often fortnightly) injections of fresh capital borrowed in the City of London and sent by steamer from Tilbury, despatched as boxes of gold coin along with batches of crisp new £5 sterling notes. The result was a striking illustration of what competition lawyers in a different era would describe as market dominance: the Standard's size fuelled a growth rate that made the imperial bank larger still, while its competitors began to melt away. By the end of the 1870s, fewer than a dozen of the single-branch indigenous banks were left standing.

The Standard's growth did not go entirely unchallenged. Early in the decade, word of the Cape's new prosperity attracted another of the City's imperial banks into the region. This was the Oriental, whose crafty footwork in Whitehall twenty years earlier had opened up opportunities in the East for Chartered Bank. (The charter acquired by the Oriental, it might be recalled, had allowed it to operate 'east of the Cape of Good Hope', which ironically led some now to question the bank's arrival at the Cape.) Widely respected by the start of the 1870s as perhaps the leading exchange bank in the markets of Asia, the Oriental seems to have been

persuaded by none other than John Paterson that a foray into the Cape
would be worth its while. Much to the disgust of Robert Stewart, who
had had to spend countless hours since 1866 resolving arguments over the
former chairman's debts to the Standard Bank, Paterson now emerged as
an adviser to the Oriental. It has been suggested, credibly enough, that he
acted to some extent out of malice towards Stewart for denying him a
rescue loan six years earlier.[14] Having managed to win back his seat in the
Assembly at Cape Town in 1872, Paterson had regained sufficient influence
to mount a second run of banking mergers. The Oriental duly opened
in Port Elizabeth at the start of 1873, under his direction. By the end of
the year it had absorbed both the Port Elizabeth Bank and the Eastern
Province Bank of Grahamstown, and by mid-1874 had accumulated a
total of eight local branches. At this point, however, the Oriental's
growth conspicuously stalled. It added only another three branches over
the rest of the decade and never opened for business in Cape Town; nor
did it ever issue its own banknotes. (Its meagre profits in the colony were
to be overwhelmed a few years later by mounting problems in India and
Ceylon, as we shall see, and in 1878 it sold off all its Cape operations to
another City-based imperial venture, which emerged in 1879 as the Bank
of Africa.)

The Oriental's failure to emerge as a genuine competitor to the Standard
Bank must be largely attributed to its lack of an effective local leader in
the Cape. Probably Paterson's ill-defined role held it back in this respect,
for he was no day-to-day manager – as past events had amply shown – and
anyway he had far too many other calls on his time. The founder of the
Standard Bank was once again pursuing a political career in Cape Town,
even while returning periodically to Britain where his second wife insisted
on remaining to bring up their eight children. He was also embroiled in
interminable legal battles over the state of his finances, including a lawsuit
against his old bank. This was a sad turn of events, and it prompted a
string of distinctly unflattering references to the bank's first chairman in
the General Manager's letters home. In December 1874, Stewart had to
advise the Board that lawyers in Cape Town had recommended an elaborate evidence-gathering exercise in London, an expense that he accepted
was unavoidable but nonetheless found deeply galling: 'Mr Paterson is
now reaping the benefit of the [patient] policy all along pursued by the
Bank – in the consideration of his [insolvent] Estate – and the only return
he now makes for this is by putting the Bank to all the annoyance and
expense in his power.'[15] Three months later, Stewart told the Board more
about the legal preparations being made to defend the bank against Paterson's pleas in Cape Town's Supreme Court, and warned: 'This might be

an easy matter enough if he always kept to the same position, but unfortunately consistency is not a feature in Mr Paterson's character . . . [and] he has as a last resource completely turned his front, in such a way as is as novel as it is ingenious.'[16]

Paterson's shortcomings only served to underscore again the value to the Standard of being led locally by a professional banker, especially one as formidable as Stewart. It was a strength the Board fully exploited, by allowing him to act very largely at his own discretion. And Stewart's authority had been enhanced by the leap in the bank's profitability since 1870, with the Directors singing his praises at almost every General Meeting. ('His noonday thought and midnight dream is the Standard Bank', crooned Chairman David Mackenzie in 1872.[17]) He repaid them by proving himself to be that rare thing in business: an effective hatchet man, also blessed with a strong entrepreneurial drive. The bank's position in the early 1870s in no way allayed Stewart's urge to grow the business:

> There can be no standing still for a Bank in the position now occupied by us. If we cannot fairly meet the business requirements of our customers, some other bank will most assuredly push us to the rear and probably we would never thereafter be able to recover the ground we had lost.[18]

He seems to have been in no doubt by this point about his ultimate objective, which was actually little different from the vision cherished by those Port Elizabeth men who had cheered Paterson off to London as their envoy in 1859. As Stewart would put it in a letter a few years later: 'I am decidedly of opinion that we should adopt the same policy as is usually adopted in Scotland, that is to say establish a Branch in every town of any importance, not yet occupied by a Bank, even if the returns should be at first unappreciable.'[19] Once this strategy was under way, he directed every aspect of it from the head office in Port Elizabeth.

Stewart built the basis of a modern retail bank with only the barest rudiments of modern communications. The first telegraphic code for the bank was compiled in 1874, at which date just eleven of the branches could be contacted by Morse; not until 1877 was the bank's telegraphic address ('Derby') registered.[20] The first railways were not laid from Port Elizabeth until 1875 and the first under-sea telegraph cable to London until 1879 (in shocked response to that battlefield catastrophe at Isandlwana). So the General Manager had to rely on regular sea mails to London for his dealings with the Board, and on the largely horse-borne mails of the domestic Cape postal service for his supervision of the branch network. His fastidious regard for record-keeping, while a boon for later historians, must have

kept his Port Elizabeth clerks very busy indeed.* Stewart sent the Board
the most astonishingly detailed bulletins on the state of the bank, writing
at least once a week, and often more frequently, to the 'Secretary and
London Manager', Francis Searle. His letters almost always ran to ten to
fifteen pages, sometimes more, to which Searle would reply in equally
painstaking detail.[21] At the same time, a stream of correspondence between
the General Manager's Office and the branches fed a constant reappraisal
of rates and risks, customer relations and the distribution of ready assets,
as coin, bills or notes – while every prospective addition to the network
raised property and staffing questions that were seldom quickly settled.[22]
No amount of clerical work, though, could alter the fact that many
branches were awkwardly remote from Port Elizabeth: it took a few weeks
for instructions to reach some of them via the public post – or by private
courier companies, on the few routes where these existed (and they seldom
seemed to thrive for long). To cope with this challenge, Stewart had no
choice but to lean heavily – like his contemporaries at Chartered Bank – on
the work of travelling inspectors.

His inspectors toured the Cape constantly, auditing the individual
branches and submitting detailed accounts of their findings. These reports,
which eventually found their way to London, went far beyond dry assessments of bad debts and balance sheets. The Johannesburg archives of the
Standard Bank include an almost unbroken series of them from 1865 to
1900 and their contents often make for colourful reading.† The men
behind these reports had to endure lives of gruelling discomfort. The
paucity of hotels, few decent highways and, as yet, absence of trains made
life on the road a constant ordeal. Health problems of one kind or another
caught up with most of them in middle age. The very first Inspector (and
effectively Stewart's deputy) was another Scotsman, Hugh Cameron Ross,

---

* File copies of all letters were prepared using the 'copy press' technique that was the
universal procedure for duplication before the widespread introduction of typewriters and
carbon paper in the 1880s. Documents were written with a special ink containing an ingredient that stopped it running too freely when moistened. A letter could then be copied by
placing a sheet of tissue paper between it and a dampened sheet of blotting paper. When the
three of them were bundled between oil-cloth papers and then pressed hard together, the
blotting paper drew the ink up through the tissue paper and left there a clear duplicate of
the original. A 'Letter Press' in the hands of an experienced operator could turn out superb
copies; careless work could produce a barely legible brown smudge.

† One frequently quoted report was submitted in 1877 by an inspector who had arrived at
the branch in Oudtshoorn, in the Western Cape, to find the place 'in a disgusting state caused
by the housing there at night of three young ostriches belonging to the Accountant and Clerk
which had covered the floor with their filth'. (Quoted by Carolyn Terry, *A Pioneer Bank in
a Pioneer Land*, Flesch & Partners, 1979, p. 100.)

who had worked for some years in both India and the City in his youth. He had joined the bank in 1865, after working briefly in Natal as the manager of the L&SAB's Pietermaritzberg branch. By 1875 his health was ailing and he tendered his resignation. Stewart refused to accept it and instead sent him home to Britain for an extended sick leave, telling Searle in his next letter home:

> Mr Ross was at one time a strong healthy man but the hardships peculiar to his office as Inspector appear to have very seriously undermined his constitution. He has had to perform long and frequent journeys at all seasons and in all weathers, has often had to go many hours without food, and often without proper food, and proper accommodation at night. Such hardships as these Mr Ross freely encountered for several years, but though at the time he appeared to treat them lightly, and in fact never spared himself, I have no doubt that he is now paying the penalty for what he then went through, and the consequences may be serious.[23]

Living rough for so much of the time did not incline the Inspectors to be sentimental in their appraisals. Taking their cue from Stewart himself, they were notoriously forthright about any employees thought to have let the bank down.* Even branch managers with years of service behind them could come in for ferocious criticism. The first manager of the Cape Town branch, George More, had been in his post for ten years when a series of unflattering reports on his professional failings culminated in this verdict of 1874: 'His personal peculiarities have been fully reported upon at previous Inspections, and there is nothing now to say more than he is the same self-sufficient, painfully egotistical and vain man now that he was then – if anything he is worse.'[24] (Stewart was later incensed to hear that More had been relaying City of London tittle-tattle about the bank's finances, and told Searle he had to go. 'The only explanation that I can come to is that he is really mad – as many persons believe – but whether he is mad or sane, he has in my opinion proved his utter unfitness for the position of a Branch Manager.'[25])

Finding and keeping good staff to run the branches was a constant concern for the General Manager: the bank had to rely not just on sound managers but on dependable sub-managers and accountants, too. Total employee numbers climbed steadily, with about two hundred on the

---

* The reason given by Stewart to Searle for his dismissal of the first Klipdrift manager gives a flavour of his approach. 'I started him from here with a programme for his guidance which a child might follow, but no sooner does he arrive at the [diamond] fields than he would appear to have given way to other influences and followed the ideas which they suggested, instead of carrying out my views and instructions.' (Quoted in Terry, *A Pioneer Bank*, p. 50.)

payroll by 1877, and almost twice as many four years later. The ideal candidates were physically strong, self-reliant individuals, preferably fluent in Dutch – or rather its simplified Cape version, Afrikaans – as well as English. Stewart was increasingly keen on hiring men born in the Cape, who would be familiar with its very particular racial sensitivities (which to contemporaries still meant Anglo-Boer relations, since they rarely troubled to consider the non-white races at all) and he evidently had growing reservations about young hopefuls straight off the boat from England. As early as 1868, he was already suggesting to the Directors at home that

> the fact should not be overlooked that youths in such a climate as this are much more forward than those of the same age in England. A youth of 15 years here is quite as mature as one of 18 or 19 at home – some of our most valuable clerks just now are under the age of 20.[26]

This was a polite way of pointing out that, while recruits with experience of banking in Scotland might take to the life in South Africa, most young men from a genteel background in the Home Counties, sent out by parents with fond ideas about the respectability of a City banker's life, would be in for a shock. Three years later, in 1871, Stewart spelled this out with more candour:

> it would seem to be the impression of young men at home that energy is not so much a necessity in the Colony to ensure success in life as in England. Such lamentably ignorant impressions it would be an act of kindness to remove when applications of the kind come before you. The race and struggles for livelihood are perhaps greater here than in older countries; and not only energy but local knowledge is essential to success, and it does not seem to be taken into account that the best energies undergo change in this climate, especially during the summer months when the strongest constitutions are both mentally and physically very severely tested.[27]

As the bank grew larger, the proportion of local men grew with it – but its expansion rate was such that Stewart had no choice but to go on making regular requests to Head Office for new clerks from Britain, too. And whatever their origins, many of the recruits were still very young men. By the end of the 1870s, it was recorded that almost half of the bank's sixty-five managers and all but three of its accountants were under the age of thirty.[28] Profiles of the staff in individual branches were regularly supplied to Port Elizabeth by the travelling Inspectors. A report on the staffing of the branch in Kimberley, for example, was submitted early in 1878 by Rees Williams, now the most senior of the Inspectors (and another former manager, like Stewart, of the National Provincial Bank of

England). He had been sent to the diamonds town to investigate the possibility that the manager had been involved in a damaging fraud with two local dealers. Kimberley was a tough place – regarded within the bank as a hardship posting for clerks – where the Standard's employees (like everyone else) had to endure long hours working in a harsh climate with few diversions.[29] Williams nonetheless thought them not untypical of an average branch staff. They comprised eleven young bachelors (average age: twenty-three and a half) who worked – and slept – in premises built of corrugated iron, lined with brick and canvas (see Plate 6). After penning 150 pages on Kimberley's accounts and all of its current customers – including a meticulous post-mortem on the supposed fraud, clearing the manager of any wrongdoing – Williams set down a detailed, and characteristically stern, review of each of the employees, four of them born in the Cape and seven of them from Britain.[30] Most had started at Kimberley within the past year (see Appendix B).

Of course Stewart also needed more seasoned officers, and these he recruited where he could find them. Rival banks were the most obvious source of recruits with useful experience, but Stewart was always reluctant to be seen poaching their senior men. He usually waited on events, and planned accordingly. One man who greatly impressed him was the head of the L&SAB in the Cape and manager of its Port Elizabeth branch, a thirty-one-year-old from the English West Country called Lewis Michell. Known in the town for his diligence and quiet authority, Michell in 1873 brought an end to his ten years of service with the L&SAB (nine of them in the Cape) by suddenly resigning. He had no other job in prospect, but had simply lost patience with the constraints imposed on him by his directors in the City. It happened that very soon afterwards, with Stewart away on one of his rare visits to London, the manager of the Standard's Port Elizabeth branch also resigned. A day or so later Michell received an invitation to call on Hugh Cameron Ross, then deputizing in the town for Stewart. After they had spoken for some minutes, Ross offered Michell the managership of the Standard branch. Michell recorded the episode in an autobiography many years later:

> This [offer] was such an unexpected overture on his part that I asked him what Mr Stewart would say to it. Smiling broadly, he handed me the offer in Mr Stewart's own handwriting, explaining that the latter wrote it out before sailing, feeling confident that I was unlikely to stand the timid policy of my old Bank for much longer.[31]

Stewart's own career in due course took a twist that may well have surprised many of his staff in South Africa, and perhaps came as a slight shock to Stewart himself. In the middle of 1874, anxiously aware that their General Manager had already had several bouts of ill-health and was handling an ever greater workload, the Directors in London suggested to him that appointing a formal deputy in Port Elizabeth might be sensible. Stewart disagreed, reassuring them that his health was 'very greatly improved' and that he would be 'the first to request them to strengthen my hands' if ever he felt himself unequal to the running of the bank.[32] But when his health problems did indeed recur, at some point later that year or perhaps early in 1875, Stewart made no attempt to resurrect the deputy idea. Instead, and fatefully as things would turn out, he told two of the Directors privately that he would just like to keep going until Francis Searle retired – and then return to England, to take up Searle's job by way of semi-retirement from the front line. (One of the two Directors was Robert White, who spent some weeks travelling round the Cape with Stewart in October and November 1874, and visited the diamond fields with him.[33] Perhaps the two of them discussed their futures together over a camp fire on that trip.)

The progress of the business in 1875 gave no one any occasion to suspect that its General Manager might even conceive of a role for himself anywhere but in South Africa. The Standard was appointed as sole banker to the Cape Government in that year, confirming its pre-eminent status in the Colony. Even its ownership had begun to shift to the Cape, as Stewart had already noted early in 1874: 'Consulting the List of Shareholders in the Bank, I am surprised to find what a large proportion are either residents in the Colony, or have direct business relations with it. Tried by this test the Standard Bank would appear to be more purely local than any other similar Institution in South Africa.'[34] It is plain that by 1875 Stewart thought the bank had come to be seen generally as very much a South African business – with just one important qualification, as he spelled out in a remarkable conclusion to the half-yearly report dated 4 September:

> Before closing my report I may again revert for a moment to the position now occupied by the Bank – and this I do with a feeling of pardonable pride. It is no figure of speech to say that the Standard Bank is the leading institution in South Africa . . . This is now so fully recognised that it is neither necessary, nor would it be graceful towards other institutions to make further allusions to the subject . . . [The only constraint on the public's otherwise total confidence] is the idea which would seem to be abroad to some extent, that the Bank carries on banking business in the ordinary sense, in London . . . If the public could be satisfied [by a clarification from the Board] . . . that the Bank's Capital was all employed in South Africa,

that it did no discount business in London, but that its position there is *simply that of an Agency for the Branches* [author's italics], I would be able to advise without the slightest qualifications whatever, that their confidence in the Bank was quite unbounded.[35]

Alas, by the time Stewart signed off on this report, its intended recipient had been dead for three days. Searle's death was wholly unexpected, and it was not until 6 September that a letter with news of it was sent off to the Cape. It would reach Port Elizabeth on 8 October. In the meantime, the Board on 10 September noted 'with much regret' the passing of the man who had served as the bank's Secretary since its inauguration thirteen years earlier – and turned immediately to appointing a successor as 'Secretary and London Manager'. The minutes of a Board meeting just two weeks later noted:

> A vacancy having occurred in these offices through the death of Mr Searle . . . and it having also been stated by Mssrs Mackenzie and White (Directors) that the General Manager Mr Stewart had communicated to them his desire to obtain these appointments [as Secretary and London Manager] when a vacancy should occur; it was resolved that the appointments . . . be offered to Mr Stewart, at a salary of £1,500 a year . . . [At the same time] the Chairman of the week was instructed to express to him the great satisfaction of the Directors with the manner in which he had managed the affairs of the Bank during the past ten years under very difficult circumstances during its earlier stages, and their regret that the state of his health should have induced him to wish to relinquish his present high position for the less lucrative though less onerous one of London Manager.[36]

There is no record of any telegraphic communication with Stewart, and it seems he still had no idea what had happened when he wrote to the Secretary's Office on 11 October 1875 to acknowledge the news of Searle's passing. Not until 29 October did he receive a Private Official letter with news of his appointment in London, and his reply is so cryptic as to leave his feelings about the whole business rather obscure:

> I am in receipt of your Private Official letter of the 25th ulto, conveying to me certain Resolutions which have been passed by the Board of Directors, with reference to applications for the appointment of London Manager and Secretary. In reply I beg to intimate that the appointment of Mr Geo. N. Player as Assistant Secretary has been duly advised to all the Branches.[37]

He accepted the offer, but nothing was said of it officially for months. There was certainly no attempt by the Directors or Stewart himself to present his return as a promotion (though it was indeed presented in this light many years later*). Did he regret leaving his 'application' with the two Directors, or even attempt to reverse it? The documentary record gives no clue. We only know that he acceded to the Board's request that he nominate his own successor, and proceeded some months later to appoint two of his colleagues, Gilbert Farie and Hugh Cameron Ross – the latter apparently restored to health by his home leave the previous year – as Joint General Managers. Then in June 1876, a little over eleven years since his first arrival in the Cape, Stewart left to take up his new role in Clements Lane.

He was signing off letters from London as Secretary before the end of August.[38] With a small ground floor office, just two executive colleagues – an Assistant Secretary and an Accountant – and a mere handful of clerks, Stewart busied himself at first with a review of the bank's operations in the City. However disconcerted by having so few staff around him, he probably welcomed the chance to take a firmer grip on the Treasury policies of the Board. His letters in recent years had betrayed a growing exasperation with some of the wilder notions floated in London. In January 1875, for example, he had been appalled to hear of a suggestion from the Directors that the Standard might seek to build up its capital base by issuing 'mortgage debentures', a stock collateralized against physical assets that would be new to City investors. Stewart's rebuttal of the proposal (taking up no fewer than five pages of a letter to Searle) suggests that, even then, his confidence in the Board had been waning for a while:

> a moment's thought was sufficient to convince me that such a novel expedient would prove most injurious to the interests of the bank . . . [and] there appears the less reason why we should have recourse to novel and doubtful expedients from the fact that the progress of the institution has been beyond the expectations of even the most sanguine . . . [In these circumstances] it seems to me that it would be little short of madness to depart from the principles of legitimate banking to which we have hitherto adhered . . . the expedient suggested would give a serious if not fatal blow to the credit and prestige of the bank.[39]

* The first chronicler of the Standard Bank, who had himself been an employee of the bank for thirty-three years when his history was first published, put a gloss on Stewart's return to London that looked more plausible in retrospect than it would have done at the time: 'the Directors realised that the Bank's increasing responsibilities rendered it desirable that they should have at hand the best possible advice, more particularly in regard to the new business which it was entertaining, consequent upon the rapid expansion of Colonial trade, and Mr Stewart's transfer to London was thereupon arranged' (George Amphlett, *History of the Standard Bank*, Glasgow University Press, 1914, pp. 40–41).

Stewart was never offered a seat on the Board, which may seem perverse from a modern perspective but was wholly in line with contemporary City practice – and the dictates of Victorian social snobbery – which drew a clear line between being a bank director and a mere bank manager, even a highly successful one.[40] His standing with the London Directors, though, was hardly in doubt: they commissioned a portrait of him by one of the leading artists of the day.* Nor did his lowly title as Secretary and London Manager last long. It was quickly clear to all that his relocation to London had done nothing to lessen his drive, and any notion of his return amounting to semi-retirement was soon left well behind. By February 1877 Stewart had been appointed 'Chief Manager', and was bringing all his knowledge of South Africa to bear on the direction of the bank's affairs.

An early opportunity arose for him to contribute directly to the growth of operations in the Cape, when the Board was approached by the London directors of the Standard's long-standing rival, the L&SAB, proposing a set of terms on which they would be prepared to sell out. Managing the negotiations with them fell to the new Chief Manager, and by May 1877 a formal agreement looked imminent. At this point, Stewart's old bugbear showed up again. John Paterson had fired off a series of letters to the *Cape Times* earlier in the year, attacking the bank for its treatment of his affairs. Stewart had warned the General Managers: 'he is casting about for some subject of fresh quarrel with us'.[41] He soon found it. Three small banks in the Cape announced plans to merge as a 'Dominion Bank', and Paterson seized the opportunity to do some mischief, as Stewart explained in one of his regular letters. 'We understand that Mr John Paterson has written to the L&SAB in very glowing terms with reference to the prospects of the Dominion Bank, and advised them to have nothing to do with the Standard, which he represented as most unpopular in the Colony.'[42] The letter briefly derailed the merger talks, as Paterson must have intended,

---

* The portrait, by the President of the Royal Scottish Academy, Sir Daniel Macnee, was shipped out to the branch in Port Elizabeth. After Stewart's death, his widow asked for it to be returned to Scotland, a request that the Directors said had to be regretfully declined since the painting belonged to the bank in South Africa. This decision was eventually reversed more than twenty years later, largely at the behest of senior managers in the Cape who believed Stewart's family had been too little rewarded for all that he had achieved (Minutes of the Standard Bank, 23 October 1900, SCB Box 1189, Vol. 9). The family subsequently returned it to the bank in South Africa, where it hangs today in the Private Clients building of the Standard Bank in the Hyde Park suburb of Johannesburg. Unfortunately it makes Stewart look like a slightly smug family solicitor, conveying none of the strength of character to be seen in a photograph of the early 1880s (see Plate 2) – where he certainly looks much more like a man not to be crossed lightly.

and it was not until July that Stewart was finally able to bring them to a successful conclusion.

The feud with the former chairman, however, dragged on. By October 1877, Stewart had had enough and was urging his colleagues to meet the latest vexatious demand from Paterson generously enough to be shot of him: 'we think it would be well, to settle it in such a way as to give him no opportunity for further annoying us'.[43] It seems to have done the trick. By May 1878, Stewart noted 'as an item of information' in a letter to the General Managers that Paterson had just set sail for the Cape on what was apparently to be his last visit. 'He appears to have lost faith in the prosperity of South Africa and is disposed to realise his landed properties [there] . . . We may add that Mr Paterson now professes to be very friendly towards the Bank and to have no grievance whatever to complain of.'[44] It was indeed the end of a long and rather sorry sequel to Paterson's involvement with the bank, though this was not in fact to be his last trip to the Cape. Having returned to London in 1879, he set off again in April 1880 on a voyage that ended with his death in tragically bizarre circumstances. When his ship from Southampton to the Cape sank off the west coast of Africa, all aboard were rescued by a second vessel, which then itself went aground off the Canary Islands. The passengers were transferred to a lifeboat which broke up as it was being lowered. All were saved except Paterson, who fell into the sea and drowned. (It was said that he had always travelled with a good-luck charm in his baggage – a tiny box containing a piece of membrane, a 'caul', that had covered his head when he was born, and which in Scotland was thought to confer immunity from drowning. It had been lost with all Paterson's other possessions in the first wreck.)*

The acquisition of L&SAB brought two of its Directors on to the Standard's Board. (One of them was Alexander Croll, the Port Elizabeth merchant who had been one of the Standard's founding shareholders in 1862. He would remain a Director until his death in 1881.) It also gave a further boost to the growth of the bank's operations in the Cape, much

---

* Despite his troubled relationship with Stewart over many years, Paterson was to be justly commemorated as the Standard's founder. A bronze statue of him today stands beside one of James Wilson in the lift lobby of Standard Chartered's main offices in Hong Kong. His place in South African history was strongly promoted in a biography published in 1960 (Pamela Ffolliott and E. L. H. Croft, *One Titan at a Time*, Howard Timmins) which presents him in an unabashedly heroic light. He was certainly a prominent figure in South African politics through much of the 1870s, and was even apparently regarded by Lord Carnavon, the British Colonial Secretary from 1874 to 1878, 'as an ideal future premier for the Cape' (*Dictionary of South African Biography*, Vol. 1).

to Stewart's satisfaction. By 1878 he was taking a far closer interest in these than Francis Searle could ever have done – and not surprisingly had revised his earlier views on the contribution to be made by London. While of course only the men at the Cape could make detailed operational decisions, as he explained in a letter to Farie and Ross, the role played by the bank's Directors was nonetheless of great importance:

> They have still the inherent right to question, to criticise, to guide, and, if necessary, to control its operations, and to surrender this right would lay them open to the charge of neglecting their duty to the proprietors ... Though the Directors are at such a distance from the scene of operations as to preclude them from dealing immediately with passing circumstances, they have sufficient information regarding the past as to enable them to form a correct judgement with respect to the future. In fact those who are somewhat removed from the scene of events are frequently in a better position to read their character, and estimate their tendency, than others who are on the spot and immediately concerned.[45]

So much for his dismissal of Head Office three years earlier as 'an Agency for the Branches'. This letter gave Farie and Ross due notice of 'the proper spirit in which the expression of [the Directors'] views should at all times be received', and the Chief Manager thereafter passed on those views, generally indistinguishable from his own, in often quite forceful terms. Within Clements Lane, meanwhile, Stewart was presiding over a Treasury operation that was growing increasingly sophisticated to keep up with the rapid expansion of the bank. Kimberley was booming – the value of diamond shipments had risen, by one official estimate, from just over £1.6 million in 1874 (following the severe price crash of 1873) to almost £3.7 million in 1879 – and as the half-yearly report from Port Elizabeth in August 1880 happily acknowledged, 'the Bank in a large and satisfactory degree continues to participate in the general prosperity'.[46] By the end of the decade, the Standard's Reserve Fund was valued at £335,000 (up from £6,000 in 1870), its deposits stood at £5.1 million (compared with £0.5 million) and its loan book had reached £6.0 million (compared with £1.4 million).[47] These were riches indeed, especially when compared to the lean pickings of those overseas banks that had set their sights on the markets of the East.

2. 'NOT A LARGE BUT A SAFE AND SOUND BUSINESS'

The ejection of Thomas Mitchell from the chairmanship of Chartered Bank in April 1871 had signalled its Directors' determination to make a fresh start – but the outlook for the bank at that point was bleak indeed. Its finances were in an abject state: after being properly in business for thirteen years, it had a totally depleted Reserve Fund and a Retained Loss of £59,000 for the year to December 1870 that ruled out any possibility of a dividend. Nor could the Directors be sure of the outlook for the financial markets in general, given a background of tumultuous events in Europe. (Paris, besieged by German armies since September 1870 in the Franco-Prussian War, was now on the brink of starvation. Bismarck, anticipating victory, was just preparing in Versailles to proclaim the founding of a united Germany.) There was no cushion left for any further mismanagement of the bank's affairs – and it was the Court's desperate hope that the exceptional young man, effectively in charge of operations as Deputy Manager since 1869, could somehow engineer a fresh start. This was the thirty-five-year-old Howard Gwyther, now promoted to succeed George Ure Adam as General Manager (though Adam was not finally eased into retirement until the end of 1872, after almost fourteen years of service that earned him a handsome pension 'as long as he lives, and as long as the Bank has means to pay it'[48]).

Little is known of Gwyther's personal background. Born in South Wales in 1835, he was apparently educated at a private school in Kent and worked briefly for a country bank before taking up, at the age of seventeen, a City job with a small but long-established family bank, Rogers Olding & Co.[49] (Its premises, as it happened, were in Clements Lane, just yards from where the Standard Bank's head office would one day be located.) Five years later, in 1857, Gwyther moved to the City Bank in Threadneedle Street. Here he must have encountered the small staff of Chartered Bank under George Ure Adam, who had taken up a tenancy under the same roof early that year. Perhaps this had some bearing on Gwyther's decision to join Chartered Bank's Singapore agency in 1859. His subsequent career with Chartered, as we have seen, had been rather an on–off affair – he had remained less than three years on the staff before setting up as a bill-broker in Shanghai with a brother-in-law, Rowley Miller – but of the impression he had made on his peers, as a strong character and man of distinct ability, there can be no doubt.

Gwyther had only the meagrest foundations on which to rebuild the Chartered's fortunes. At his side was a relatively new Secretary, Charles Mullins, appointed after the death in 1869 of James Calder Stewart, who had held that post since succeeding George Hope in January 1854. Gwyther and Mullins together presided over a headquarters staff at Hatton Court of fewer than twenty full-time employees, with roughly the same modest number of expatriate staff, working as two- or three-man teams in seven offices across Asia, based in Rangoon and Batavia as well as Bombay and Calcutta, Singapore, Shanghai and Hong Kong. But Gwyther had other, and far more important, foundations of a different kind. He appears to have had from the outset a shrewd grasp of the extraordinary opportunities being opened up at this time by the profound changes – the Suez Canal, steampower, telegraphy, the new markets of the East and so on – that were transforming the world of international trade. And it was not just that rising volumes promised fat returns for those who could meet the service needs of the new trading routes; what Gwyther seems also to have grasped during his time in Asia was the singularly privileged position now open to British banks. For half a century, Britain had been assembling the components of what one distinguished historian of the British Empire has recently labelled a 'world-system'.[50] Its emigrants had created new settler colonies; its merchants had established new trading conduits for the output of the world's first industrialized economy; and its soldiers and sailors had consolidated their control over the great sea lanes of the globe. By the start of the 1870s, these three phenomena were starting to interact to powerful effect. While Gwyther may not have seen his world with quite such a retrospective clarity, he unquestionably shared the general conviction in the City of his day that, for as long as Britannia ruled the waves, British banks could reign over the trade that crossed them.

This gave rise to a personal (and institutional) self-confidence that, viewed from a twenty-first-century perspective, looks ever more remarkable. Leading a team comprised of just a few dozen men, Gwyther and his senior colleagues were prepared to contemplate running a complex business from their anonymous offices in Hatton Court that would straddle vast distances and countless unfamiliar cultures. Those who manned the overseas branches would have to cope with gruelling office hours and a constant stream of paperwork, as well as the physical challenge of working in the heat, dirt and humidity of the tropics – even more daunting, in many places, than the hardships of South Africa. The bank retained the services for many years of a physician, Dr James Bennett, who examined both those heading off for the first time and those temporarily back in

London on extended leave ('furlough'), before returning East.* In his letters back to the Secretary between 1872 and 1883, it is striking how often Dr Bennett could find no evidence of 'organic disease' but remarked instead on signs of stress and nervous exhaustion – sometimes in men supposedly well rested and outward bound. (Reporting back in 1872 on the condition of a Mr Dickinson, who was shortly due to return to Rangoon, the doctor took a firm line in blocking his departure: 'I do not think he has any actual disease, but his brain & nervous system are so exhausted & irritable that any thing almost is sufficient to deprive him of power for any mental duty.'[51]) And, even had it been blessed with a staff of Olympians permanently in the pink of health, the bank was still going to be heavily dependent on the readiness of hundreds of local non-European employees to work for it in subordinate positions, fulfilling essential tasks while being accorded a distinctly inferior status, socially as well as professionally. None of this seems to have daunted the men of Hatton Court for a moment, least of all the challenge of asserting their natural superiority in the workplace over the subject races of the Empire. Herein lay the incalculable value of prevailing Victorian attitudes towards the 'native peoples' of lands less superbly endowed than Britain with the glories of Christian civilization. As the same historian of the 'world-system' has put it: 'The common ingredient of most of these attitudes was a vulgar conception of "race". . . a catch-all presumption that variations in skin-shade, religion and climate were an accurate predictor of civilizational capacity. Some Victorians discovered by personal experience the limitations of this theory, but not very many.'[52]

Like all other overseas banks based in the City, the Chartered relied on having the closest possible ties with the leading British merchant houses and shipping agencies in the city ports of the East. It was unfortunate that many of the biggest names in one port, Hong Kong, had chosen to support the founding of a rival bank several years earlier, led by a Scottish shipping agent who saw the potential attraction for the local merchants of having a bank of their own that would actually be headquartered in the Colony. (As he would later recall, 'it appeared to me that, if a suitable opportunity occurred, one of the very simplest things in the world would be to start a bank in China more or less founded upon Scottish principles'.[53]) But the startling success of Thomas Sutherland's Hongkong & Shanghai Bank since 1865 had at least confirmed again the potential for well-capitalized banks that could survive the inevitable vicissitudes of trade in the

---

* The Chartered had a succession of retained physicians over the years. In the 1960s, all travelling to or from the East went via Harley Street and the surgery of a Dr Kindness.

East. Following the failure of Overend & Gurney and the banking crisis of 1866, the Hongkong Bank (as it was usually referred to) had benefited from the collapse of most of its competitors on the coast of China, just as the Chartered Bank had emerged ahead of a depleted pack in India. It would shortly complete a doubling of its initial capitalization, to bring its paid-up capital to the equivalent of just over £1.1 million – half as much again as the Chartered itself had so far raised.[54] Gwyther, with his personal experience of Shanghai, was anxious not to leave too clear a field for this upstart rival: the most senior of his managers in the field, G. A. Whyte in Calcutta (the officer defended to the Court by Sherwood in 1865), was soon being despatched as an Inspector to China, to see what more could be done to galvanize the Chartered's stuttering operations there. In the meantime, Gwyther attended to another crisis in Singapore, and set about a review of all the agency operations as a necessary precondition for any restoration of the dividend.

The communications challenge posed by this agenda far exceeded the (relatively) local difficulties encountered by Robert Stewart in the Cape. Telegrams were now being received regularly from across the whole Asian network. (Each principal outpost numbered its despatches consecutively up to No. 1,000, at which point the series was begun afresh. The five largest branches all reached 1,000 and started again in May 1871, most of them coming back to 1,000 by November 1873.) But letters continued to carry most of the information that flowed back and forth – all copy-pressed, like those of the Standard Bank – even though postage times via the Royal Mail still ranged from three to four weeks for Bombay and Calcutta to six weeks or more for Shanghai. The legacy of all this must once have been a prodigious archive, to bear comparison with the Standard's. Much of it, sadly, has been lost. But summary notes of the originals survive, compiled in 1949–52 for the writing a centenary history of the Chartered Bank.* These notes offer glimpses of the fuller story, and can be read alongside some first-hand accounts looking back as far as the 1880s:

> Each Branch and Agency [in 1883] sent periodically to Head Office [reports known as] 'States', which consisted of copies of their cash books and journals, and details of various other transactions which were copied by Head Office clerks into 'Branch Ledgers' . . . At that time, the Bank had no power to conduct a general banking business in London . . . so when cash was required for a cheque or Branch draft, the document had to be marked by

---

* See Appendix A.

the Chartered and taken across Threadneedle Street to the City Bank for payment . . . all cash and cheques received over the counter at Hatton Court were paid into the City Bank for credit of the Chartered Bank's account.[55]

From the start of his time as General Manager, Gwyther had one over-riding objective for the bank, fully endorsed by the Directors of the Court. It was alluded to regularly over the next twenty-five years or so, never more emphatically than in a Head Office despatch of 1884: 'What the Directors wished to see was not a large but a safe and sound business, and an absence of bad debts which was a sign of good management.'[56] This plain speaking was provoked by some egregiously sloppy lending in the face of a severe downturn in commodity prices in 1883–4. 'The directors had warned Agents against unsound transactions and undue risks', as the same 1884 despatch noted, 'but every mail had brought evidence of undesirable business, unsatisfactory security and large lines which it was the Bank's policy to shun at all times and under all conditions.' The consequent reprimand articulated a general approach adopted from 1871 onwards. It did not preclude opening new branches, where there appeared to be a compelling commercial case for doing so: men were sent from Hong Kong and Singapore, for example, to open new agencies in Manila in 1873 and Penang in 1875, which, it was hoped, would be able to capitalize on being the first banks ever to open there. (Manila lacked even a telegraph cable to Hong Kong until 1879.) But there was a determination not to be drawn into any premature expansion of the network. It would be far better in some instances to recruit the services of a prestigious European trading house to act as an agent with other firms on the bank's behalf: in Siam (Thailand), for example, an agency agreement was struck in the 1870s with a leading German rice exporter, A. Markwald, which remained the bank's representative in the country until a branch was finally opened in Bangkok in 1894. New branches were briefly contemplated in Java and Ceylon in 1877 and 1880 at the behest of the Inspector on his travels, but their openings were quickly postponed. (Even when the Colombo branch was eventually launched, in 1892, Head Office was less than gung-ho about the prospects in Ceylon – indeed, an over-zealous pursuit of growth by the young man appointed as its first manager, T. J. Anderson, quickly led to his recall to London and departure from the bank.*) And it was not until a full twelve years after the Meiji

---

* A former Ceylon tea planter, setting down his memories in old age, could well recall the Anderson episode and made a note of the sequel. 'T. J. Anderson returned to Ceylon a year later as a broker. He was exceptionally keen and hard-working, and did quite well in exchange and shares business for four years, 1895–9. He then sold the business and went to London,

Restoration of 1868 had opened up access to Japan that the Chartered Bank finally opened a branch there, in Yokohama. (The Hongkong Bank had set down a branch at Kobe as early as May 1870.)

What mattered far more than new branches to Gwyther and the Court was that the bank's existing operations should be infinitely better run. It would no longer be acceptable to have branches managed, as some had been in the 1860s, by men with little or no understanding of basic banking practices. (Sherwood, on one tour of inspection in 1865, had been struck at the indolence of a new agent in Karachi, whom he thought 'might with advantage have made some attempt to comprehend the meaning of, and the use for, his general ledger, the contents of which however had been as Hebrew to him'. The branch was closed down in 1868 after just five generally unprofitable years and only reopened in 1906.[57]) Inspectors from the early 1870s onwards were expected to keep the Court well informed on the performance of individual branches, while scouting all the time for ways to prod them into working more co-operatively together. The goal was a level of professionalism that would take full advantage of the wonders of telegraphy, while securing the bank against a recurrence of the crises of the 1860s that had swept away so many of their peers. G. A. Whyte, having finished his tour of inspection in China in 1872, caught the spirit of this approach exactly:

> His visit to China had confirmed the opinion which he had held all along, that . . . a most profitable business could be conducted in the way of buying and selling bills on India by the China branches. To do this, it was necessary for the Chartered Bank Managers to study their markets closely and anticipate a little more the fluctuations in the rates, which were of constant occurrence, and to be prepared to take full advantage when the rates went to extremes, from which a reaction would quickly follow . . . The telegraph wires between China and India had not been used as frequently in conveying important news as they ought to have been. Whyte had arranged for constant direct communication to be kept up between Calcutta and Hong Kong on the one hand and Bombay and Shanghai on the other . . . Hitherto many of these messages had been filtered through Singapore which Whyte thought had been a complete waste of money.[58]

Moreover, professionalism would extend, the Court decided, well beyond the intricacies of trade finance. The young Scotsmen – with a

---

where he started as a Mincing Lane share broker, doing remarkably well during the Rubber boom. He then sold the business [again] and bought a castle in Argyllshire.' Surely the definitive Happy Ending for any Chartered man. (See LMA: CH03/01/14/039.)

generous sprinkling of Sassenachs – who took up Eastern posts with the Chartered were now expected to become properly conversant with the local culture, and literally so. A Court proposal earlier in 1872 that a second branch in Malaya might be warranted, on the island of Penang, prompted the Singapore Manager to observe that 'whoever was sent ought to have some knowledge of the business of the place and also ought to be able to speak Malay'.[59] It was soon clear that the present staff contained no such person. The result was a Head Office request to Whyte, before he left for China, that

> he should urge the importance of 'cultivating an acquaintance with the vernacular or other language ordinarily used by the natives'.* To this Chinese would be an exception unless voluntarily undertaken, but where other languages were concerned, it was essential for European staff to be in a position to keep constant check on the natives, both customers and employees.[60]

It would be more than twenty years before the bank started paying gratuities to staff who could pass the Indian Government (Lower Standard) examination in Hindustani or Burmese – they were introduced in 1895, a few years after a similar arrangement had been made for those who had passed the preliminary and final exams of the Institute of Bankers – but the Court's 1872 suggestion to Whyte marked the start of a longstanding policy to encourage the learning of oriental languages. (New recruits being posted to the East were still expected to learn a local language as late as the 1950s, after which the more active promotion of local hires would finally put paid to the tradition.) How many of the bank's staff ever achieved any useful degree of fluency is hard to say – probably very few. One distinguished historian of Anglo-Indian banking has noted that the Presidency Banks made a similar effort with their British staff 'but not with outstanding success. Even when they knew the language, they were not in a position to keep in daily touch with . . . Indian traders at the

---

* This was just becoming a more practical proposition by the 1870s, thanks to the work of some pioneering philologists, most of them evangelical ministers who had lived for years in the East with Church missions, or diplomats serving as British Residents in this or that distant outpost of the Empire. A London publisher, Trubner & Co., had recently launched a ground-breaking series entitled *Collection of Simplified Grammars of the Principal Asiatic and European Languages*. A generation of Chartered bankers came to know well such august volumes as the Revd Justus Doolittle's *Vocabulary and Handbook of the Chinese Language* (2 vols., 1872) and the Revd S. H. Kellogg's *Grammar of the Hindi Language* (1876). Perhaps the best known of all such titles, appearing in Singapore in 1881, was *A Vocabulary of the English and Malay Languages* by Frank Swettenham, a brilliant young diplomat whose book went through several editions before 1914.

branches because of the social distance everybody among the official or mercantile circles considered it essential to maintain as between Europeans and Indians'.[61] Perhaps it might charitably be supposed that, in displaying at least some knowledge of the local language, many of the Chartered's expatriate staff found a little could go a long way in fostering goodwill among their non-European associates. It was anyway a common refrain, in letters back to Head Office, that genuine fluency was scarcely necessary, since anyone of any significance to the bank spoke English.[62] The truth of this reflected the whole nature of the Chartered's operations. It was providing services for the Empire, in ports like Bombay, Calcutta and Singapore that effectively constituted an overseas extension of the British economy.

All the bank's branches had nonetheless to rely, in the day-to-day running of their affairs, on locally employed clerks – men with a good command of English and unquestionable honesty. Both qualities were generally guaranteed by the policy of only employing individuals who were personally known to the bank, and preferably related to those already on the payroll. The Head Clerk in each office was also the Chief Cashier – known as the 'khazanshi' in Calcutta and the 'shroff' in Bombay – and this relatives-first staffing policy ensured the emergence over time of family dynasties whose elders succeeded each other as Chief Cashiers across the decades.* The loyalty shown by these families afforded them a degree of influence even at the Court in London by the 1890s: a campaign among them orchestrated by the Chief Cashier of Bombay, for example, led in 1895 to the inauguration of a half-pay pension for all 'native staff' who had completed thirty years of service or reached the age of fifty-five. There were always well-understood limits, of course, on the extent to which non-Europeans could hope for preferment – especially under the starchy codes of the Raj – and none could ever expect to become Managers. (An unusual proposal by British ministers in the Madras Government in 1871, that educated Indians should be recruited as managers of the Madras Presidency Bank, drew a sharp rebuttal from its Board of Directors, who pointed out '[that] such appointments would be distasteful

---

* One of the most celebrated was the Chatterjee family in Calcutta. The fourteen-year-old Baboo Okhory Coomer Chatterjee joined Eglinton's staff when he opened for business in the Bengal Bonded Warehouse in 1858. He was in his fiftieth year with the bank when he died in a railway accident in 1907. His son, Satish Chandra Chatterjee joined the bank in 1890 and died in 1925, before reaching retirement. Satish's son, Kartick Chandra Chatterjee, joined in 1917 and was still on the staff in 1951. All three rose to become the Chief Cashier in charge of the Accounts Department. (See memorandum 'The Story of the Chartered Bank in Calcutta', LMA: CH03/01/14/030.)

to a large section of shareholders, and that bank officers needed training which Indians were not in a position to secure'.[63]) The social distance between British and local staff in India would come to seem bizarre even within the lifetime of some early employees – such as Hormusji Curstaji Khan, who joined the Bombay branch in 1884 at the age of twenty. As he recalled in his eighties:

> When I first entered in the service of the Bank in 1884 there were four Officers, including the Agent, the Sub-Agent or Chief Accountant, and two other Sub-Accountants. In the beginning [of my time] the Agent used a palanquin (palkhi) supplied by the Bank to go round about. There were also four palkhi bearers . . . to guard the safe at night.[64]

Terms and conditions for the Indian staff were of course in no way comparable to the salaries of the European Officers, and any exceptional payments were closely monitored from London. When the Court decided in 1888 to award a posthumous gratuity to the family of a recently deceased Chief Cashier in Bombay, Bhasker Bapoo Josey, the branch was expressly told it was 'in consideration of his long services [sic], but this decision is in no way to be treated as a precedent'.[65] Perhaps the Court was a little wary of their Bombay manager's largesse. Four years earlier, as Hormusji Curstaji Khan also remembered, '[the manager] gave the native staff a bonus of half a month's salary, [of] which Head Office disapproved'. The occasional local initiative to pay them more money was probably not uncommon, for native staffs worked long hours. Another retired Bombay Chief Cashier left behind a good description of life in the office around 1890:

> The [European] Officers had to work in full dress at their desks during working hours. Particularly they had to put on their coats whenever called for by the Agent and the Accountant. The clerical staff also used to work in their full national dress. This discipline was very strictly observed . . . The work then was very heavy. Clerks used to attend the office at 8 o'clock in the morning and leave usually after 11 o'clock at night. At times they had to work even up to 1am. There were no typewriters and the work had to be done by hand. Of course the Office file copies were press copies . . . The Cashier used to receive cash (particularly relating to Bills) up to 8.30pm daily, according to the nature of the day's work. In this way the whole staff had to work very hard daily for more than 12 hours with comparatively small salaries.[66]

Externally, meanwhile, the prevalent use of English in the bank's dealings reflected the gulf that invariably separated its operations in this era from the domestic economies of the Asian countries in whose ports its branches were based. The British Empire was built on maritime power, and the bankers to that empire seldom strayed far from the sea. Like all the other London-based exchange banks, the Chartered was in business to facilitate maritime trade. Most of the 'external' papers over which its clerks toiled for so many hours a day – the inward and outward bills, the shipping documents and title deeds – were all about providing importers and exporters with an intermediary who could minimize the financial inconvenience of the fact that shipment and payment deadlines ran to different schedules, while also defraying much of the risk entailed at both ends of any trade for those dealing with remote third parties whose cred-itworthiness might be simply unknowable. And by making itself indispensable to this process, the Chartered automatically handled the exchanging of currencies that would accompany every transaction – swapping sterling pounds for India's silver rupees, or for the silver bullion weighed as 'taels' in China, or for the Mexican silver dollars (or their equivalent) that were used everywhere across south Asia from Singapore to Manila. The bank's counterparties for most of this business were the British trading houses of the East, with their head offices in London, Liverpool and Glasgow, whose working cultures were essentially identical to the Chartered's own. Even where the bank dealt with firms whose in-house language might be, say, Dutch as in Java or Spanish as in the Philippines, the commercial lingua franca was for all practical purposes English.

Not all its customers, though, wore stiff collars and frock coats, and some of them spoke scarcely any English at all. The European firms who comprised the bank's main clients were themselves dealing in most instances with local traders, middle-men who were typically responsible for collecting the raw crops of the host country, paying the farmers and transporting their output to the coast. As these middle-men grew in power and influence – extending their activities into milling, blending and manufacturing – the opportunities multiplied for the Chartered to deal with them directly. This did not apply in India, where doing business with native firms was still generally regarded as socially undesirable (and day-to-day dealings with the local market could be left to those fine, upstanding Chief Cashiers). But elsewhere in Asia, away from the edgy sensitivities of the Raj, the potential rewards were too obvious to be ignored. More often than not, the local entrepreneurs were Chinese – handling key markets from Malaya and Java to Siam and the Philippines, as well as in the treaty ports of China. But in reaching out to them, there was an obvious difficulty: the bank's officers could not possibly aspire to

the requisite language skills and knowledge of local commercial customs. The solution they adopted was to employ, in each key marketplace,
one of the middle-men as the bank's own agent, and to rely upon him for
the vetting of new business sourced beyond the expatriate community.

Naturally enough, the arrangement was first adopted in China itself,
where it had been refined over many decades by the now defunct East
India Company. 'Compradores' had worked for generations as the intermediaries between John Company and the Thirteen Hongs of Canton,
back in the days before the First Opium War of 1839–42 when all of
China's foreign trade had been channelled through that one port. Setting
up its own compradore was one of the Chartered's very first steps in Hong
Kong. His name was Yat Fong, plainly a well-connected local merchant,
and he was recruited in August 1859. (Taking nothing for granted, the
bank found four other compradores already working in the colony who

Extract from the bond dated 4 August 1859 securing the appointment of Yat
Fong as the first of Chartered Bank's compradores in Hong Kong

were ready to sign a bond indemnifying its manager against any future losses attributable to either Yat Fong or any of his Chinese helpers.*) Thereafter, the role of the Chartered's compradores remained essentially the same for a century, in Hong Kong and far beyond it. They earned a percentage commission on all loans advanced to customers whom they introduced to the bank; but they also stood surety for those loans, and were generally required to make good any losses. Many of them accumulated considerable wealth and a commensurate level of prestige in the local economy. This could be exploited in many different ways, as was made clear in a comprehensive overview of the compradore system published in a Hong Kong newspaper in 1871.[67] Not only were compradores in the colony typically able to trade for their own account, while overseeing their employer's business; they were also frequently invited to partner with their employers in joint ventures to their mutual benefit. Not surprisingly, many emulated the shroffs of the Chartered's Indian branches in establishing family dynasties, with rights and privileges that passed from father to son. And, like the shroffs, many took responsibility for the handling of all cash transactions within the bank – and the hiring and firing of local clerks engaged in them, no doubt to the great relief of many a young expatriate British officer.

3. MERCHANTS, MINERS AND BIMETALLISM

The Chartered's activities between 1870 and 1900 reflected the impact of Western trade all across Asia, starting with that between British India and the Empire's mother country which accounted for about 60–80 per cent of Britain's total trade with the East over the period. More than half of Britain's exports to India, as to the East in general, comprised exports of finished woollen and cotton 'piece-goods': cheap vests, socks, shirts and the like – turned out by the world-beating mills of Lancashire and Yorkshire. The bank under Gwyther's inspired guidance steadily developed simpler and cheaper ways for the mill owners to finance their shipments, culminating in a system that effectively allowed them to draw down their

---

* The four guarantors stood surety for an aggregate sum of HK$25,000 – no mean sum. Their bond indemnified C. J. Sherwood against any losses arising 'on account of any mismanagement, misusage, embezzlement, neglect, default, or procurement . . . of, in, from, or out of any money, effects or things [belonging to the bank]'. The contract survives alongside many others drawn up in the nineteenth century with compradores in Hong Kong, Kobe, Tientsin, Peking, Manila and Saigon (LMA: CH03/01/10/49).

sale proceeds (at a discount) from the bank in London even before their goods had left the country. (Title to the actual sale proceeds thereby passed to the bank, and travelled out to the East along with the shipping papers and documents of ownership, for the bank to reclaim its money from the Eastern importer. Only after the latter had handed over the money would the bank release an endorsed bill of lading, allowing the importer to extract his goods from the warehouse.) In the reverse direction, it was not just the financing procedures that evolved over time but the content of the ships' holds: the opening of the Suez Canal in 1869 meant that Indian crops could reach Britain without, as in the past, needing to cross the equator twice. The wheat trade took off as India's railways crept inland, and Chartered Bank provided shipping and foreign exchange facilities that helped to endow the main export centre, Bombay, with the largest currency-trading market in Asia. On the opposite side of the sub-continent, another crop enjoyed an even more spectacular rise. In 1870, most of the tea drunk in Britain still came from China, but new plantations thereafter began to spread quickly through the green valleys of Assam below the fringes of the eastern Himalayas. Watching the successful sale of each year's record crops, the bank's manager in Calcutta, James Simpson, made a persuasive case for making seasonal loans to the growers against the collateral of each year's output. In 1878 – a year, as it happened, after Simpson's own departure – the Court accepted the argument, and the bank became one of the leading providers of seasonal funding to India's tea industry. In the years that followed, it also lent against the security of shares in tea estates to assist with the long-term financing of packing factories, in Ceylon as well as Assam. By the 1890s, Chartered's inspectors were voicing some concern that the bank's lending to the industry might have been a little too liberal – but tea exports from India to Britain went on climbing, and by the end of the century were to be almost six times as great as China's.[68]

Several other staple Asian commodities fuelled the growth of vibrant export trades over this period. One of them was rice, cultivated in many south-east Asian lands but nowhere more intensively than in Burma. As we saw in Chapter 1, the Chartered was the first exchange bank to set up in the country's principal port, Rangoon, and soon established itself – under an agent, Alexander Watson, who remained there from 1865 until around 1890 – as a main banker to the teak yards and rice mills that lined the banks of the Rangoon River. (The latter flowed down from Rangoon to the Andaman Sea, but British engineers built a canal that joined it to the Irrawaddy in 1883, so linking the port directly to the waterways of the delta and affording access to the great Irrawaddy valley stretching far to the north. Those who ran the thriving businesses of Rangoon came to be known throughout the East as the Irrawaddy Scots.) Watson's career at the bank encompassed a tumultuous era for the region. A Third Anglo-Burmese War in 1885 extended Britain's control of 'Lower Burma' to cover the whole country, toppling the Burmese King and Queen with their royal court in Mandalay and leading directly to Burma's assimilation into the Raj as a British-ruled Indian province. Thereafter the colonial economy boomed.

The opening of the Suez Canal had an especially remarkable impact on the rice trade, opening up Europe to large steamships with capacious holds: 'In 1867 there were only two steam rice-mills in Rangoon; within a few years the number had risen to seventeen.'[69] Rice export tonnages more than trebled between 1870 and the end of the century. In addition to discounting bills for the milling companies, the bank appears also to have been quite prepared to advance working capital to money-lenders from south India to assist their funding of the paddy fields.[70] It was also providing capital for the import of machinery and equipment for City-financed businesses like the Irrawaddy Flotilla Company, the shipping line run from Glasgow with vessels shipped from the Clyde that dominated the inland waterways. These years saw Rangoon transformed into a leading capital of the Empire with a great array of imperial buildings, many of them still standing today. The main commercial thoroughfare, Phayre Street, was known to locals as 'the River' because it had banks all down both sides. Watson's Chartered Bank ought to have been one of them, but until his last day he insisted on remaining at the Strand location occupied since 1863. (By the time he retired, his office seems to have been notoriously ramshackle.[71]) After his retirement a plot of land was duly acquired in Phayre Street, on the corner of Shafraz Road. As a recent history of the city's architectural heritage has noted, though, the bank 'had to wait some ten years before constructing a new office as labour and building materials were considered too costly at the time'.[72] It was finally built in 1898-9, and would preside over a golden era for the Chartered in Burma.*

Around the same time that the British were cementing their control

---

* The destruction of the Burmese monarchy and removal of King Thibaw and his court to exile in India provide the background for an acclaimed novel, *The Glass Palace*, by Amitav Ghosh (HarperCollins, 2000). Its fictional hero, a penniless orphan from Bengal, grows up in colonial Burma and makes his fortune importing Indian labourers and establishing a teak yard in Rangoon. The yard's breakthrough contract, to provide sleepers for an Indian railway, is secured after a meeting with the contractor in the grand Phayre Street offices of Chartered Bank, where even the anteroom 'was dark and cavernous, and its deep leather chairs smelt of cigar smoke'.

over Burma, the French completed a two-stage annexation of what would
be christened 'Cochin China'. It embraced Vietnam, another country with
a flourishing export trade in rice. Unlike in Burma, the Chartered had no
physical premises in nineteenth-century Vietnam at all. It did not open a
Saigon office until 1904, but relied instead on the customers of its existing
branches elsewhere to stand surety for seasonal advances made to the
leading Vietnamese brokers:

> While these advances were outstanding, they were covered by a guarantee
> obtained in Hong Kong and by the name of the borrower. A receipt was
> obtained from the borrower. This guaranteed to hold the relative paddy
> [i.e. the defined volume of harvested rice] on the Bank's account or to repay
> the advance on demand. No further guarantee was available as the paddy
> was passed through several hands on its way to the mills [in Saigon] where
> it was converted to rice and shipped to Hong Kong. The advance was dis-
> tributed amongst many small dealers and brokers who dealt with the
> growers . . . French law recognized no lien we might take unless the rice
> was actually in our hands which was impossible to achieve. We therefore
> relied on the standing of guarantors in Hong Kong who were possessed of
> considerable means.[73]

Saigon, like Manila, was usually regarded by Head Office as belonging
within Hong Kong's sphere of influence; in a similar fashion, Bangkok
and the coastal settlements of the Malay Archipelago were seen as falling
more within Singapore's remit. (Java's main port, Batavia, was seen as a
wholly separate and independent entity.)

As these linkages would suggest, the Hong Kong and Singapore
branches were rapidly emerging in this period as impressive Asian counterweights to the bank's core activities in Calcutta and Bombay. The two
fastest growing harbour colonies of the Empire were both thriving on the
coexistence of ambitious European trading houses on the one hand and
powerful Chinese interests on the other. In both places, the discounting
of bills and of promissory notes added a valuable layer of earnings to
complement the bank's foreign exchange profits. And there was one other
activity that had proved to be surprisingly remunerative – the issuance of
banknotes. The first of the Chartered notes (aside from earlier 'post bills')
were issued in the two ports in 1862. Printed in London by Waterlow &
Sons and sent out in bound books of a hundred, each note had to be
hand-dated and signed in black ink by two local officers of the bank. The
Treasury in London stopped short of condoning them as legal tender, but
welcomed them as a boost to the liquidity and orderliness of the ports'
financial markets; and local merchants quickly adopted them as a mightily

convenient alternative to heavy bags of silver dollar coins. (A first issue in wary Shanghai was less readily accepted in 1863, and Chartered's notes in China would have a more problematic future.)

For the bank itself, as for the Hongkong Bank which soon emulated its example, private notes had several attractions. They could be issued (for a wee commission, naturally) to customers in exchange for a deposit – repayable on demand – of equal value in coins, bullion or sycee (small gold or silver ingots fashioned as Chinese currency by independent silver-smiths). Since no interest was paid on this deposit, it helped to lower the bank's average cost of funds usefully, while also alerting customers to the bank's other deposit services (always frustratingly hard to promote). And of course, private notes made cash available to the bank for its own expend-iture. This was almost but not quite a licence to print money: under rules laid down for colonial banks by the Treasury and the Board of Trade in the 1830s, the total value of any bank's private issue was strictly limited to the amount of its paid-up capital, and a third of that value had to be set aside as a cash (or equivalent) reserve. The risks inherent in any instantly convertible paper currency came to be better appreciated over time – especially after the collapse of the Oriental Bank in 1884, leaving a trail of dud notes behind it – and the Treasury steadily upped its reserve requirements. But even this process had its consolations, since a periodic correspondence on currency matters implied a quasi-official status for the bank; and a marginal shaving of the financial benefits anyway made no difference to the value of banknotes as a way of advertising the grandeur of the issuer. Eventually printed in several denominations of the Singapore/ Hong Kong silver dollar and bearing the Royal coat of arms ('Incorporated by Royal Charter') above the name of the bank, each Chartered note was a thing of beauty and as finely wrought as any government issue (see Plates 4 and 31).[74]

The Chartered's notes in circulation in Singapore rose in value from $319,000 in 1872 to $874,000 eight years later, which was equally a measure of the colony's growth and of the important role played there by the bank.[75] Founded by Sir Stamford Raffles in 1819, Singapore had acquired a population of about 100,000 by the end of the 1860s, and was then on the brink of a new era.* A young Englishman, living in a

---

* As late as 1869 one distinguished British traveller could still see it as a rather remote and untamed place: 'The island of Singapore consists of a multitude of small hills, three or four hundred feet high, the summits of many of which are still covered with virgin forest . . . There are always a few tigers roaming about Singapore and they kill, on an average, a Chinaman every day.' (Alfred Russel Wallace, *The Malay Archipelago: The Land of the Orang-Utan and the Bird of Paradise*, London 1869.)

bungalow settlement there with other European bachelor clerks – much
as the Chartered's future London General Manager must have done, several years previously – set down a sketch of their easy-going lifestyle:

> Most of the bungalows are about two miles from town; nearly all, at least,
> are within hearing range of the 68-pounder gun at Fort Canning, the dis-
> charge of which each morning at 5 o'clock ushers in the day . . . [and] six
> o'clock generally sees all dressed and out-of-doors to enjoy a couple of hours
> walk or ride through the lovely country roads, in the delicious coolness of
> morning, before the sun's rays become disagreeably powerful . . . On com-
> ing home from these morning rounds, the custom is to get into loose, free
> and easy attire, generally baju and pyjamas . . . The universal breakfast
> hour is nine o'clock . . . A little fish, some curry and rice, and perhaps a
> couple of eggs, washed down with a tumbler or so of good claret, does not
> take long to get through and yet forms a very fair foundation on which to
> begin the labours of the day.[76]

The Straits Settlements – dominated by Singapore – were reconstituted
as a Crown Colony in 1867, removing them from the governance of the
Indian Raj. The opening of the Suez Canal then ensured that most Western
trade with China passed via Singapore's deep water harbour. The Chartered's branch in the port was managed for most of the 1870s by a
long-standing resident, Thomas Neave, whose extensive contacts allowed
the bank and its four European officers a privileged position in the colony.
The Inspector T. L. Mullins – a cousin of the Company Secretary, Charles
Mullins, and not ordinarily a man given to bland praise – reported back
to Head Office in 1880: '[He] could safely declare that the Branch was the
most popular institution of its kind in Singapore and its senior officers
were looked up to and respected by the whole community.'[77] Neave and
his colleagues built strong relations both with the Chinese and with a
distinctive group of Indian banking families, the Chettiars, originally a
money-lending caste in southern India who now ran family networks
across much of southern Asia.

It was chiefly to assist the Chettiars with their dollar/rupee exchange
operations – the Chartered's own business was largely restricted to ster-
ling/dollar business – that the Court originally agreed to the opening in
1875 of the Penang branch. Within a very short time, the off-shore island
of Penang found itself at the centre of a whole new industry. It was discovered in the course of the 1870s that two of the Malay states to the east
and south of Penang – Perak and Selangor – lay astride a great swathe of
tin deposits running from Lower Burma down the Malay Archipelago to
the eastern shores of Sumatra. World demand for tin was soaring, not

least to accommodate the American food industry's passion for tinplate containers. The tin mines of Cornwall (hitherto the world's single biggest supplier) were, unluckily for them, almost exhausted. By the early 1880s, Chettiar and Chinese investors were busy establishing new mines in Malaya to take up the running, and the Chartered, through its Penang branch, became the leading banker to the industry. 'Perak and [its neighbour] Selangor all sent their tin to Penang, and were supplied in return with Coolies, Stores, Piece Goods etc . . . Many of the Chinese had become extremely wealthy.'[78] Up-country Malaya was a land of thick jungles hitherto closed to the impact of Western trade, but the boom in tin mining prompted the founding of townships far inland from the coast, at Kuala Lumpur and Taiping, and branches of the Chartered Bank were opened in both settlements in 1888. (This was a significant departure for a bank hitherto almost entirely restricted to branches in large trading ports, as the Court would observe some years later, and was 'influenced to a considerable extent . . . by the wishes of the Straits Government . . . partly for the convenience of the [Malay states'] Treasuries and partly with the idea that local trade would be greatly benefited'.[79]) Only six years after joining the bank in London, a young man called Frank Bennett arrived in Kuala Lumpur in 1889 for his second posting (after three years in Batavia):

> At that time there was only one European Officer there. The local staff consisted of Chinese Cashiers, two Eurasian Clerks and a Malay Office Boy. The Chartered was the only Bank with an office in Malaya . . . [It] occupied a two-storey Chinese house (one of a row of about six similar houses) in a small street leading from the Maidan [the town's central park] to the River. The Office was on the ground floor and the Sub-Agent's living quarters on the floor above. One or two Milner safes served instead of a strong room . . . About Chinese New Year a good deal of currency was required by Chinese clients and this was shipped up from Singapore in the form of Mexican dollars and our notes. These notes often bore only one signature so I had to sign them [as second signatory] before they were issued, a task which sometimes kept me occupied till late in the night.[80]

Over the course of the 1880s, the Chartered's operations in the Straits had to weather a period of competition from other banks that at one point seemed to threaten its recently established ascendancy in the region. (Effective competition was a challenge little encountered by the Standard Bank in the Cape at this point.) Rivals for the discount business in Singapore included two of the oldest and most powerful names in exchange banking, the Oriental and the Chartered Mercantile Bank. Both were under intense pressure in this decade to develop new business in the Straits and elsewhere after the disastrous failure of the coffee plantations in Ceylon, to which they had lent heavily for many years. (The Ceylonese plantations were overwhelmed in the years after 1878 by a fungal disease no less devastating in its way than the Phylloxera aphid that had blighted Europe's grapevines since the mid-1860s. While it killed the coffee plant, it fortunately had no taste for tea plants.) After its collapse in 1884, the Oriental Bank managed to re-launch itself as the New Oriental. Still buoyed by substantial exchange profits and a solid deposit base in India, it was ready (as was the Mercantile) to take an ever riskier line in Singapore in a bid to win fresh business.

But there was a third and far more serious rival to the Chartered whose strength derived not from exchange banking in India but from a unique domestic base further East – the Hongkong & Shanghai Bank. It had never really signed up as a fully-paid-up member of the exchange bankers' club, though in most respects it conformed to broadly the same business model. When its peers had agreed in the early 1870s to shorten the maturity of their six-month trade bills – as a response to the shorter transit times from the East to Europe, made possible by the Suez Canal – the Hongkong Bank had openly flouted the cartel, and pulled in plenty of extra business as a result. In the years that followed, there seemed to be no irritating ruse to which its managers would not happily resort in search of a commercial advantage. They would offer finer lending rates and advance cash against a higher percentage of underlying assets; they would levy finer commissions on exchange deals and blandish higher rates on deposits. It was not unknown for them to raise their flag in some newly emerging country even *after* the arrival there of Chartered Bank – and still see no harm in occupying a bigger and grander building.* (The relative size of their offices and of the residential quarters for their senior men was always a matter of huge consequence to all exchange bankers in every part of the East.) Especially galling was the readiness with which, apparently without rancour, its managers would agree to toe the line laid down for them by their Head Office in Hong Kong while paradoxically enjoying considerably more executive independence than their counterparts in the other exchange banks. This no doubt owed much, after 1876, to the personal standing of Thomas Jackson, a thirty-five-year-old Ulsterman who was appointed that

* This particular solecism incensed T. L. Mullins on his first visit to Manila. He reported back to London: 'The Hongkong Bank had an imposing building with a handsome frontage and ample accommodation inside, a fact which disposed the Spaniards and Chinese to believe that it was a more important institution than one [i.e. Chartered Bank itself] having [a local branch with] "the appearance outside of a café and inside of a small money-changing shop on the Continent".' (Mullins to Head Office, 5 June 1880, JL-B notes, LMA: CH03/01/14/064.)

year as the bank's Chief Manager. (The Hongkong Bank had only non-executive Directors and its Board, unlike the Chartered's, left executive decisions to the Chief Manager, who had formal responsibility for running the bank.)

Shrewd, charming to subordinates as well as to those above him and immensely energetic, Jackson set out to make his institution the foremost bank in the East. While Gwyther had no Board position and had to be content with exerting as firm a hand as possible from his remote office in Hatton Court, Jackson was unambiguously the man in charge and could travel regularly to most of the Hongkong Bank's branches and agencies, of which seventeen were up and running by 1883. He set great store by keeping his managers well-informed on rates in the money markets, and pressed them to help each other in the wider interests of the bank as a whole. At his personal instigation, the Hongkong Bank opened for business in Singapore in 1877, and within a few years it was posing a competitive threat that greatly concerned Gwyther and his London colleagues. The Chartered's Thomas Neave died in 1882, and he proved a hard man to replace. Jackson urged his local officers to take advantage of the Chartered's loss, and they opened a branch in Penang in 1884. Inspector Mullins was subsequently asked to investigate how the Hongkong Bank had managed to encroach so successfully upon the Chartered's business in the Straits, and in July 1885 he sent home this candid report:

> Mullins wrote that they must accept the fact that the Hongkong Bank had become 'a great power in Singapore'. It had enormous resources and overwhelming strength in China; it allowed almost unlimited freedom and independence to its Singapore manager; it ran enormous risks to secure constituents from other banks, preferably the Chartered Bank; its manager's hospitality was lavish; and there was an entire absence of those restrictions which the other banks enforced on their local managers . . . In the sale of dollar drafts, Mullins believed that both the Java and Straits branches of the Hongkong Bank worked the business on account of their Head Office at Hong Kong. In this way, no questions or arguments arose concerning the fair adjustment of rates; but in the Chartered Bank, despite Head Office intervention, this type of business continually led to ill-feeling between the branches and agencies concerned.[81]

The advantages derived by the Hongkong Bank from a greater degree of co-ordination between its different branches could hardly have been summarized more bluntly. It was perhaps the first explicit observation of a lasting difference between the two great banking rivals that would still be attracting comment a century later.

The Chartered recovered its competitive position in the region in the best possible fashion. A Scottish businessman in Singapore, James Sword, was intent on founding a joint-stock company to finance a novel method of smelting tin from the ore being mined in the archipelago. He thought he had secured the backing of the Hongkong Bank, whose local manager was a keen supporter. But the cautious directors in Hong Kong let him down – and Jackson, who would surely have backed the local man, was on leave. Sword turned instead to the Chartered, and its Singapore officers helped him raise local equity capital late in 1887. They also agreed to provide him with generous credit lines. This assured the Straits Trading Company of a successful start, and its rapid emergence as the leading smelter for the Malay tin industry opened the way for the Chartered to take on a role as the industry's principal banker.[82]

Competing against the Hongkong Bank in China itself was another matter entirely. It is said that Jackson in 1880 estimated his own bank's share of the market in Hong Kong to be about one half, with perhaps a quarter-share going to the Chartered. Perhaps he was flattering to deceive, for there were otherwise few signs of such a weighty ranking for the London bank. Constant staff changes and an overly cautious response to the new opportunities opened up by telegraphy (despite that early alert from Whyte in 1872) had held it back. The bank issued its own notes in the Colony, ran its own godowns there and advanced loans against export produce awaiting shipment with as much enterprise as Head Office would allow – but it was hard going. All the evidence supported a general belief that the Hongkong Bank had struck covert agreements with leading merchant firms like Jardine Matheson, securing it a preferred status as banker to many of the most lucrative trades with London, in both Hong Kong and Shanghai. The aggregate China market, meanwhile, had to date fallen well short of the growth that many had predicted twenty years earlier. British gunboats and diplomats in 1860 had successfully inveigled the Imperial government into allowing Western merchants to trade under their own rules within a much extended list of 'Treaty ports'. But British exports to China had still not risen to much above a quarter of the value of British exports to India. Imports of China tea into Britain had meanwhile begun to fall quite steeply, with no substitute yet in sight. The Chartered held its ground: it moved its Hong Kong branch in 1878 to a new, custom-built edifice in the Queen's Road – the colony's first street and the main thoroughfare along the northern shoreline of the island.* It also occupied an

---

* The date of this relocation from its original premises is open to some doubt. A photograph reproduced in the house magazine in 1958 purported to show the Queen's Road building

enviable position on the Bund in Shanghai, adjacent to Jardine's, which it had leased since 1873. Still, there was no disguising the slow rate of progress. Agencies set up as prospective branches on the coast in Foochow and on the Yangzi river in Hankow (a treaty port despite its inland location, given the Yangzi's size) were both closed down by the Directors on Gwyther's recommendation, in 1872 and 1875 respectively.

Some presence still needed to be retained in Hankow during the shipping season – it was a leading centre for the tea industry, in particular – and the job of representing the bank there fell in the late 1870s to a young Scotsman from Dunblane called Thomas Whitehead. Recruited in 1873 and sent out from Head Office in 1875, he had already made a strong impression on his seniors. When the Court at last decided the bank should raise a flag in Japan, in 1880, it was to the twenty-nine-year-old Whitehead that they turned as a first agent in Yokohama. He quickly proved himself a man of extraordinary drive and ability – albeit a forceful colleague whom some found insufferably overbearing – and in 1883, despite his young age, Whitehead was appointed Manager in Hong Kong.[83] His promotion might, under normal circumstances, have marked the start of a more promising period for the bank in China. In the event, the 1880s saw Jackson's Hongkong Bank buttressing its status in the Colony, expanding its business with the Chinese merchant families and consolidating its role as the de facto lead banker to the Imperial Government, for whom it organized a series of bond issues and syndicated loans. Whitehead did his best to keep his bank in contention, but had to cope with a heavy handicap. This was a result of the Hongkong Bank and Chartered Bank responding in very different ways to a mounting currency crisis in the 1880s, which posed a historic challenge for all the exchange banks of the East.

For many years prior to 1873, the world of international finance had tacitly agreed to abide by exchange values that, in effect, were pegged to the pound sterling. There were two principal media of exchange: gold, which had a fixed value in terms of sterling, and silver, which had a fixed value in terms of gold. The equally fixed standing accorded to the two

---

already occupied in 1868 (*Curry & Rice*, February 1958). But the Chartered's generally well-researched centenary history opts for 1878, describing the bank's move into 'a building that had been specially erected in what was considered a convenient and healthy site' at 4 Queen's Road (*Realms of Silver*, p. 74). The earlier date may be attributable to the fact that Queen's Road was much photographed in 1868, on the occasion of a visit to the colony by HRH Alfred, Duke of Edinburgh. The bank was to remain at 4 Queen's Road until it moved again in 1890, spending many years in 'temporary accommodation' nearby (mostly in Connaught House) until 3 Queen's Road was purchased in 1905.

metals prompted economists to refer to a 'bimetallic standard'. (Paper currencies could be used as proxies for either, so long as the issuers retained the confidence of the market in their ability to convert the paper into gold or silver at constant rates.) What happened in 1873 was unprecedented. A sudden deluge of silver into the marketplace produced a dip in its value, relative to gold. The over-supply was caused by a soaring production of silver from newly discovered mines in the United States, and from mounting sales of silver coinage by European countries (led by the newly minted Germany) whose governments had decided to store their wealth in gold alone. Neither phenomenon was temporary in nature, and nor was the fall in the price of silver. It rallied from time to time, as must all market prices, but the trend over the next twenty years was relentlessly downwards. The price of an ounce of silver, quoted at just below 60d in London in 1873, was down to almost 35d by 1893, and still falling. Silver was the prevailing store of value for almost every society in Asia at the start of the period. This protracted and bewildering devaluation posed horrendous complications for any business involved in trading with the East, while based in a Western country with a gold-based currency. Its ramifications were especially far-reaching for Britain and British rule in India. As the sterling value of the silver rupee slithered ever lower, arguments over the appropriate policy response stirred a controversy – now all but forgotten – that raged far beyond the City of London. Even before it came to a peak in the middle of the 1890s, it fuelled, by one scholarly account, 'a vast literature, with approximately one publication on the issue being produced every two days between 1881 and 1891'.[84] When Oscar Wilde's *The Importance of Being Earnest* appeared on London's West End in 1895, audiences hooted with laughter at the stern instructions given to one of the play's young ladies by her governess, Miss Prism:

> Cecily, you will read your Political Economy in my absence. The chapter on the Fall of the Rupee you may omit. It is somewhat too sensational. Even these metallic problems have their melodramatic side.

The debate pitched the 'bimetallists' against those prepared to fight to the last ditch in defence of the Gold Standard. The bimetallists blamed a doctrinaire adherence to the Gold Standard for the prevailing deflationary environment of the time; they wanted to see both gold and silver back as standard measures of value, on the basis of a comprehensive reform of existing currencies and a universal commitment to new rates for the two precious metals. Their opponents were convinced that this would in practice deal a lethal blow to the credibility of the Gold Standard, undermining the stability of the pound and with it the pre-eminent status of the City

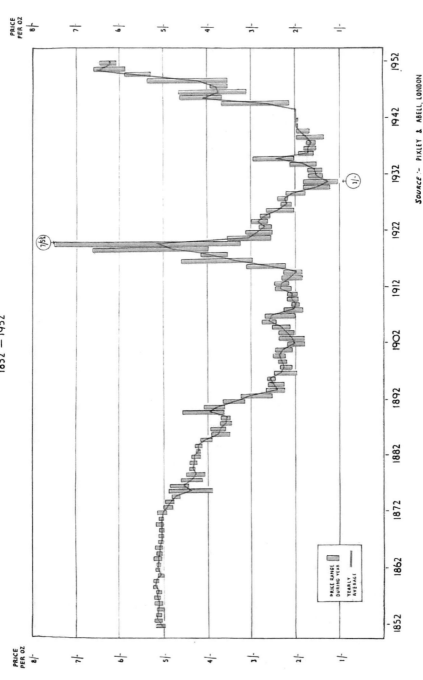

The price of silver: fluctuations in the price of bar silver in London, 1852–1952

in international monetary affairs. Bimetallism greatly appealed to Britain's manufacturers, especially those in the textile industries of the North Country who were alarmed at the prospect of their pound-valued piece-goods becoming too expensive for the Indian market, while home-spun Indian goods flooded across other Asian markets at devalued rupee prices. Most bankers and City men, meanwhile, were more than happy to go along with the benefits of a gentle deflation that lifted the real value of their loan-interest revenues and enhanced the value of the assets on their balance sheets. To these broad categories of allegiance, however, there were some notable exceptions – and a leading light of the Bimetallic League of campaigners was none other than J. Howard Gwyther, who sat on its City of London Committee. Indeed, many luminaries of the Eastern exchange banks were known to be keen bimetallists, and in Hong Kong they included both the Chartered's Thomas Whitehead and Jackson of the Hongkong Bank. The exchange banks' merchant clients were all battling every day with the volatility of the sterling/silver rate, and most of them favoured some kind of radical reform. The exchange bankers lent them their strong moral support.

Behind the closed doors of the boardroom on the third floor of Hatton Court, though, it was a different story. Gwyther and the Directors of the Court were confidently presiding over an extraordinary expansion of the bank's activities on the strength of booming exports for most of the key Asian commodities. (The range was widening, too, with the addition of newly emerging staples like smelted tin from Malaya and milled jute from Calcutta, now a significant complement to the more traditional shipments of raw jute from Bengal, much of it headed to Dundee.) But they had to contend at all times with a desperate worry that Eastern assets held in anything but sterling were exposed to the risk of a possibly quite calamitous devaluation. Gwyther appears to have taken a deeply cautious stance within three years of Germany's demonetization of its silver. At the April 1876 General Meeting, shareholders were being warned that no one could know 'whether the depreciation in silver may be permanent or not, [so] the Directors have thought it better to take the worst view, and [have] made some provision for that contingency with regard to the portion of capital which remains at the branches permanently for local employment'.[85] Three years later shareholders were told the bank had written down the sterling value of its silver assets in the East by £25,000 – equivalent to 60 per cent of the profits just reported for 1878.[86] Still the slide in silver went on, and successive shareholders' meetings could only be assured that the bank was doing what it could to limit its exposure, while sustaining the minimum levels needed for day-to-day business. But in the summer of

1885, Gwyther persuaded the Court that a truly radical step was required. All overseas activities were henceforth to be accounted in sterling, not local currencies, and all capital transferred from London was to be immediately returned. As the correspondence with the bank's Inspector recorded:

> The Directors advised [T. L.] Mullins that they had decided to bring home all the Bank's capital allotted to Branches in the East with the exception of amounts allotted to Batavia, Manila and Yokohama. Mullins considered this wise and hoped all Branches had carried out their instructions before the late important fall in silver had become an accomplished fact.[87]

Henceforth, non-sterling assets held by the overseas branches would need to be funded by locally sourced deposits, and all foreign-exchange contracts entailing an exposure to silver-based currencies would need to be strictly hedged. The bank would operate wholly on the basis of gold values.[88] There was no doubt that this would gravely disadvantage the bank in the short term while the countries of the East, including India, grappled with the implications of currency reform. (It did indeed contribute to a serious shortage of funding in Singapore and the Straits, which exacerbated the pressures on the bank in that region, already noted.) Reining back its appetite for lending in silver would also limit the Chartered's ability to challenge the dominance of its main rival in China, where there was never any question of currency reforms to introduce a Gold Standard. Hence the constraints on Whitehead's freedom to compete with Jackson's bank, which itself had little option but to align its interests, in effect, with China's Silver Standard.* (The Hongkong Bank was never slow in these years to make the most of its competitive edge in silver-based

---

* The corresponding disadvantage incurred by the Hongkong Bank, of course, was that its business, tied to the value of silver, might be looked at askance by investors in the City of London. In the event, the sheer size of the China market opening up to the bank and the latter's evident ambitions there more than countered the currency factor: the bank had no difficulty raising additional equity from City investors in 1882 and again in 1890, and the subsequent growth of its profits amply repaid their confidence. Nonetheless, silver's devaluation did inevitably cast a pall over its finances: the sterling value of the tael, Imperial China's standard weight of silver used for the denomination of transaction prices (and weighing about an ounce), dropped from 6s 8d in 1872 to 3s 2¾d in 1894. The dividend paid out by the bank in Jackson's last full year in Hong Kong, 1901, would have cost the bank 7.6 times as many local dollars as the 1877 dividend – had it not carefully accumulated sterling deposits in London to fund the pay-out – but would mark only a 75 per cent increase in the sterling value of the dividends over that period. As the bank's official historian observes in this context, 'The Bank was indeed in the land of the Red Queen.' (See Frank H. H. King, *The Hongkong Bank in Late Imperial China, 1864–1902, On an Even Keel*, Vol. 1 of the *History of the Hongkong and Shanghai Banking Corporation*, CUP, 1987, p. 263.)

Asian territories, chasing new business with an appetite that inevitably strengthened perceptions of it as the more truly local of the two institutions, and fuelled a much faster growth of its balance sheet.) Despite these grim realities, there would in Gwyther's judgment have been only one alternative course, namely to struggle on with a high-risk portfolio of Eastern assets, never trusting fully in the ability of all officers to hedge their exchange risks and desperately juggling interest revenues against capital losses with no end in sight. This course he refused to countenance.

He was proved spectacularly right in the end. Silver's decline exposed a basic lack of technical banking skills in even the largest of the other exchange banks, and led eventually to a spate of failures in the East that included the demise of both the New Oriental Bank and the Chartered Mercantile Bank in 1892 (and of the Agra Bank eight years later). Thereafter the gradual resolution of the crisis involved most of the Asian markets outside China abandoning the traditional alignment of their currencies with the value of silver. In 1893, the British government brought an end to the minting of silver coins in India, a step that led later that year to a fixed alignment of the rupee against sterling and thereafter encouraged a creeping adoption of the Gold Standard in countries all across Asia, bar China and Hong Kong: it was eventually taken up, for example, for the Japanese yen (1897), the Siamese tical (1902), the Philippine dollar (1903) and the Singapore dollar (1905).[89] By the time this process was under way, the Chartered had emerged as the pre-eminent exchange bank in Asia, second only to its Hong Kong rival. It was now significantly smaller than the Hongkong Bank by any measure – their two deposit bases in 1893 stood at £5.4 million and £10.1 million respectively (the Standard Bank's, by comparison, stood at £8.1 million and was about to jump to over £15 million)[90] – but the Chartered had more than survived, where so many of its peers had perished. While sustainable growth had proved considerably harder to achieve in the East than had been expected by the optimists of the early 1870s, Gwyther had at least sustained the shareholders' faith that exchange banking had a long-term future. His leadership of the bank was acknowledged in 1887 by his appointment, perhaps uniquely for an executive manager in the City, as a Director. In 1892 he was then made 'Managing Director', supposedly stepping aside from his daily duties as the Manager – though what exactly this would entail for the senior management cadre of the bank in Hatton Court was not immediately clear.

Meanwhile, even the theoretical arguments for bimetallism had finally had their day. Perhaps, in the end, it had come to represent an ideal that was simply unattainable in the world of practical affairs.[91] Its advocates had for many years levelled a similar accusation against devotees of the

Gold Standard – that it was ultimately impractical, insofar as a limited supply of newly mined gold would be an insufficient match for the growth of the international economy, guaranteeing chronic deflation for all. By the early 1890s, however, another momentous development in South Africa had left behind this gloomy prognosis. And, for the second time in its short history, the Standard Bank had found itself at the centre of events with a worldwide significance.

4. KRUGER AND KIMBERLEY

By far the largest and most powerful bank at the Cape by the late 1870s, the Standard had also taken on a kind of quasi-official status. The process had begun with its appointment as sole banker to the Cape Government in 1875, which was accompanied around the same time by confirmation that the Standard would be relied upon for the Imperial Government's banking needs in the Cape. This assured the bank of generous cash deposits and a close involvement in the scale and timing of official expenditure. It would also enjoy more or less total command of the exchange market. Robert Stewart himself had hailed the appointment accordingly: 'The [sole-banker] arrangement will give us the command of large sums of money and in fact the Bank will have very little difficulty in controlling the finances of the Colony.'[92] His successors in the Cape, Farie and Ross, diligently cultivated the sense on both sides that the bank was now available to facilitate government policy. As the half-yearly report early in 1877 observed: 'The Government have expressed much gratification at our having opened at places where we were before not represented, and we have been glad to consult their views . . .'[93] The bank was also glad to extend unsecured but suitably remunerative loans to the Government, and to handle the enormous flows of cash that were necessitated by the frontier wars of the next few years. (London spent about £400,000 a month in Natal alone, up to a total of about £4 million, on its 1879 war against the Zulus.[94]) Whether the bank's General Managers ever shared its half-yearly reports with officials in Cape Town is unknown, but the General Remarks in them on the state of the country's economy comprised exactly the kind of regular bulletin that might be requested of any modern central bank. The same could be said of many of the bank's inspection reports and managers' letters to Head Office, which in general were also exceptionally well-informed summaries of the economy's progress that have since proved a rich seam of data for scholars of South African history.[95]

At the same time, albeit in an accidental fashion, the Directors had installed a Chief Manager at the Head Office in London with the requisite knowledge to handle all this information flowing from the Cape. The implicit shift in the balance of power between the City and South Africa might perhaps have posed problems with the colonial staff, in other circumstances. But Stewart was so highly regarded by his peers in South Africa – and the need for a better-informed lead from London was so evident, given the remarkable expansion of the bank's operations – that his emergence as Chief Manager had for the most part been accepted without demur. It was nonetheless unclear how the Directors would react to any serious crisis in the Cape. As it happened, just such a crisis had been in the making almost since the date of Stewart's arrival in England. Exasperated by the shambolic state of governance in the Boers' South African Republic (SAR) and fearful of intrusion by other European empire-builders into the empty wilds of the Transvaal – a huge area over which a mere 8,000 Boers had boldly if rather impractically asserted their sovereignty – the British Governor of neighbouring Natal, Sir Theophilus Shepstone, had embarked in April 1877 on an outright annexation of the territory. The Boer occupants of the Transvaal were never remotely reconciled to this abrupt expansion of the Empire. They put up with it for most of the next three years, until the threat posed by the Zulus had been seen off by British troops in the aftermath to Isandlwana in 1879. Then they took up arms against the British themselves. Under the leadership of Paul Kruger, the Boers declared the Transvaal to be once again an independent state. Within weeks, a British army column marching to Pretoria was halted by a small force of Boer commandos on 20 December 1880. When the officer in command refused to turn back, the Boers opened fire, killing the officer and most of his men before they had had time to load their guns.

The very next day – though whether news of the Boer attack had yet reached them is unclear – the Standard Bank's Directors in London met to assess the situation. The prospect of serious fighting with the Boers had already generated requests for additional financial assistance from the Colonial Government in Cape Town. It was also going to pose an inevitable threat to the bank's own fledgling operations in the Transvaal. These had only been launched in 1877, because the bank's articles of association restricted it to operating within areas under British jurisdiction. Since then, the Standard had built a presence at several townships where hardened prospectors had been struggling for a few years in the hope of finding 'payable' seams of gold, which they hoped might one day launch another mining boom to set beside Kimberley's. The bank had also given assistance to the new Transvaal authorities, since the British were no more successful than the SAR had been at extracting taxes from Boer farmers: the British Governor had borrowed £150,000 from the Standard. Taking stock of all this, the Board decided to acknowledge Stewart's paramount authority and asked him to return temporarily to the Cape. As the minutes of its discussion explained,

> In view of the critical state of matters at present existing in South Africa, and the large demands that have been made, and are likely to be made on this Bank by the Cape Government in regard to the war expenditure and other matters, the Board resolved to request the Chief Manager to proceed as soon as convenient to the Cape for the purpose of assisting the Joint General Managers with his counsel and advice in the present emergency, and otherwise attending to the interests of the Bank.[96]

Farie and Ross accepted this decision as gracefully as they could, though not without complaining that news of Stewart's impending visit had reached third parties in the Cape by telegraph before they themselves knew anything about it. ('Under the circumstances, we think it would have been well had you apprized us by the same means . . .'[97]) The Chief Manager's presence in the Colony, they suggested, 'will go far towards relieving the anxiety which the Directors no doubt feel about the Bank's business at the present time'. In the event, Stewart's return to the Cape was indeed to prove extremely fortuitous – though not entirely in the way the Directors themselves had envisaged.

Within days of Stewart's arrival at Port Elizabeth in the middle of February 1881, Hugh Ross felt obliged to resign from his position on health grounds. Stewart moved quickly to replace him, appointing as 'Assistant General Manager' the very man whom he had picked out as a bright prospect eight years before – Lewis Michell. Physically small and unassuming, though with a beady eye, Michell had been the coming man for a while. A bank Inspector in 1876 had summed him up as 'remarkably cool and collected, intelligent, watchful, firm and energetic, possessing tact, judgment, promptitude and experience'.[98] There can be little doubt Stewart saw him as the man who would one day lead the bank's operations in the Cape, but he could scarcely have anticipated how immediately Michell would be required to step into this role. At the end of February, an ill-judged initiative by the British commander in the Transvaal led to a humiliating defeat at the Battle of Majuba Hill. (Their general, noted Farie in relaying the bank's shocked reactions to London, had been 'rash beyond belief'.[99]) A truce followed days later, and Stewart assigned Michell to attend the peace negotiations that soon followed in Pretoria. On his way there via Natal, Michell fell upon an unexpected opportunity to meet the three leaders of the Transvaal Boers – the so-called Triumvirate of Paul Kruger, Piet Joubert and Marthinus Pretorius – and he famously charmed them with an effusive expression of thanks for the way in which the Standard's premises and staff in the Transvaal had been kept from harm by Boer guards during the ten weeks of the hostilities. (Michell chanced to meet J. H. Brand, the President of the other Boer republic, the Orange Free State, a few nights later and charmed him too, which must have made it a memorable journey before he had even arrived in the Transvaal.)

The end of the brief 'First Boer War' led to a 'retrocession' of the 1877 annexation, and the Transvaal was soon once again a Boer republic. The Standard was faced with having to roll back its operations there in a hurry: its articles of association, already noted, left the bank with no practical alternative but to leave immediately. Even more disquieting, though, was the threat posed to its business in general by any overt clash with the restored Boer government in Pretoria. All across the Cape were branches that stood to lose ground significantly if anti-British feelings went on rising in the Dutch-speaking community and prompting hostility to the bank. How exactly the Chief Manager set about trying to defuse this threat is unclear. Farie's letters to Head Office at this time – formally addressed to the Chief Manager as though he had never left London – make surprisingly few references to Stewart at all, and it seems clear that the two men did not see eye to eye. But Stewart and Michell undoubtedly worked together effectively. They acted quickly to curtail the immediate danger to the bank's position, with the Chief Manager handling negotiations with the Colonial government while Michell navigated a delicate course for the bank in Pretoria. Over the rest of the year and into 1882, Michell would go to great lengths to rebut any notion of the Standard as an institution biased against the Dutch-speaking section of South African society.* It no doubt helped him that the defeated British authorities had the gall to try palming off their £150,000 loan from the Standard onto the books of the new Pretoria government, formed under the presidency of the fifty-five-year-old Kruger. Michell very publicly rejected this move, much to the Boer leaders' relief, and demanded repayment from Cape Town. He also moved to accommodate Kruger's ardent request that the

---

* Michell himself was anything but anti-Boer. He saw this as a matter of self-interest for the bank in more ways than one, as he noted in his autobiography. 'As a Banker, I knew by experience that, next to a canny Scot, the Boer of fair education made an excellent office man, and indeed his knowledge of both [the Dutch and English] languages gave him a position of superiority.' ('Sixty Years In and Out of South Africa', p. 54, Standard Bank Archives, Arch/2/5/Michell.)

Standard should not in fact withdraw from the Transvaal. The bank's articles were changed accordingly – a step that required an Act of Parliament in 1881, and led the Standard Bank of British South Africa to shed the 'British' from its title – and the Pretoria branch was duly kept open. Despite these measures, a lingering resentment of the bank's British ownership was still conspicuous enough across the Cape to prompt a note of concern in a half-year report in 1882: 'our operations continue to be much aggravated by the hostility of the Dutch rural population to any British Institution'.[100] This might have been a far greater problem, had it not been for Michell's sensitive approach.

Meanwhile Stewart took advantage of being in the country to assess a range of other matters, including plans to extend the size of the bank's offices in Cape Town. Above all, he took a hard look at the bank's involvement in the increasingly frenetic business centred on Kimberley. Diamonds by 1881 had come to account for at least half the value of all South Africa's exports – no one could possibly know the exact shipment figures, given the lack of any export regulations – yet the industry was still struggling to come up with a sustainable business model. The repeal in 1876 of the law limiting the size of individual territorial claims had at least helped to end the anarchic conditions of the initial rush. Market forces had then reduced the number of individual diggers significantly by 1880, but there were still hundreds of separate enterprises at work, all struggling to find and sell stones just as quickly as possible. Then, in the twelve months up to April 1881, individual proprietorship in the diamond mines had given way to an ownership structure based on joint-stock companies. About seventy companies had been formed, the largest of them – notably De Beers Mining and Kimberley Central – led by a handful of extraordinary men whose ambitions and machinations were clearly going to determine, somehow, the shape of the future industry. Initially reluctant to lend cash against any shares at all, the bank had soon been drawn into valuing company shares, like diamonds, as eligible (if risky) collateral. Loans against shares were used to fund further digging – in a manner that certainly did not meet with Stewart's approval – and when trading in company shares went from hectic to manic within months, a slew of bankruptcies among prospectors left the bank ranked among the larger proprietors in the Big Hole in its own right.

The bubble was pricked by an announcement from Standard Bank halting all lending by its branches against the security of diamond shares. There can be no question that it was Stewart who took this bold initiative, shortly before departing for London in the middle of May 1881. Farie gave an account of the episode for the Board in June which made absolutely no

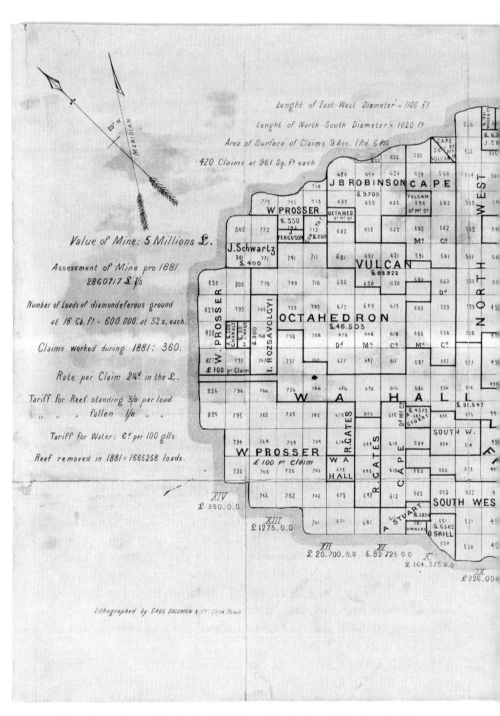

Map of proprietorships in the Big Hole at Kimberley, 1881, showing forty-two sites owned by Standard Bank

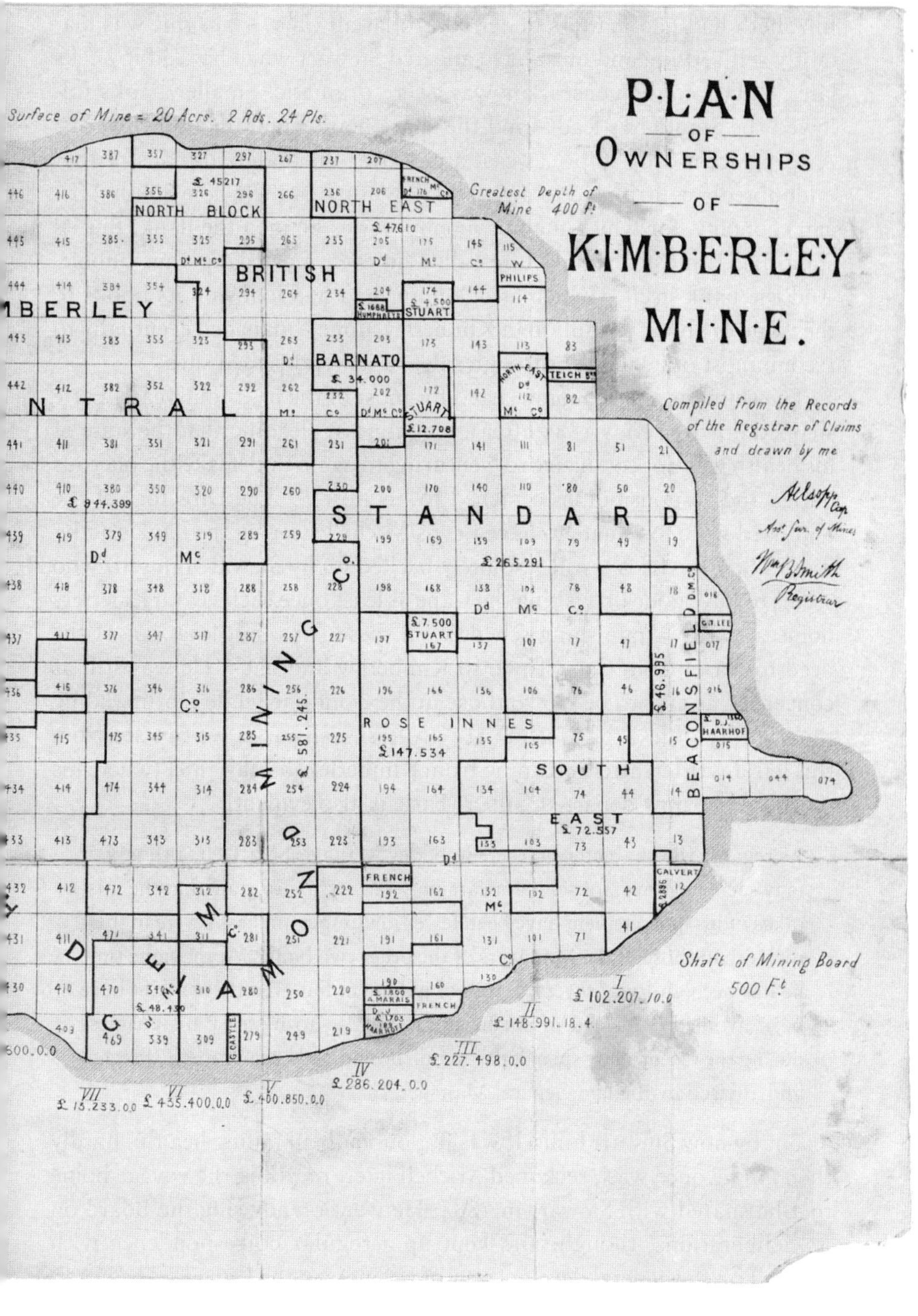

P·L·A·N
— OF —
OWNERSHIPS
— OF —
K·I·M·B·E·R·L·E·Y
M·I·N·E.

Surface of Mine = 20 Acrs. 2 Rds. 24 Pls.

Greatest Depth of Mine 400 ft

Compiled from the Records
of the Registrar of Claims
and drawn by me

Allsop
Asst. Sur. of Mines

Wal B Smith
Registrar

NORTH BLOCK

NORTH EAST

BRITISH

BARNATO
£ 34.000

STUART

ROSE INNES
£147.534

SOUTH EAST
£ 72.557

STANDARD

MINING CO.

£ 581.245.

£ 265.291

DE BEERS DIAMOND MINING CO.

BEACONSFIELD D.M.C.

Shaft of Mining Board
500 Ft

I   £ 102.207.10.0
II   £ 148.991.18.4
III £ 227.498.0.0
IV   £ 286.204.0.0
V   £ 400.850.0.0
VI   £ 455.400.0.0
VII £ 15.233.0.0

reference to the Chief Manager and insisted the management in Port Elizabeth had had matters under control at all times – but this was blatantly self-serving and must have angered Stewart when he read it weeks later.[101] The consequences, anyway, were dramatic. Smaller banks followed the Standard's lead – and the share market spiralled downwards. A 50-per-cent drop in prices cast a pall over the diamond industry that undoubtedly contributed to a general downturn in the whole South African economy, for which many contemporaries blamed the bank. But its stand had almost certainly forestalled an even more dangerous bubble. And the bank itself – which at one point had had loans on its books to the value of about £1 million in Kimberley alone – managed eventually to recoup most of its money through sales of its repossessed sites.

The slump in the economy lasted for most of the next four years. Farie stepped down in May 1883 after a long illness, pleading that the state of his health was not conducive to 'venturing to again undertake the onerous duties and responsibilities attached to his post'.[102] The Directors of the Standard were fortunate to have Lewis Michell steering the bank's activities in South Africa – still resolutely backed up by Stewart himself, who seems to have gone on visiting the Cape at least once each year. His letters home attest to a punishing schedule on these trips, not least out of the need to travel from Cape Town to Kimberley and back. He was still as concerned as ever to be fair to those in the front line while reprimanding those guilty of less than exemplary professionalism, as we can see from this letter written after returning from Kimberley in May 1884 (where his scorn for the now departed Gilbert Farie is also evident):

> As regards the character of [the Kimberley Manager] Mr Dell, although it may seem negative praise, it appears only fair to him to state that the mistakes of his management have been fewer in number and less severe in their result than those of the Managers of the other two banks. At the same time he has been guilty of several errors of judgment but even these might have been avoided if instead of encouraging him . . . to increase his business during the recent share speculative mania he had had been properly directed and advised by the late General Manager.[103]

But by now Stewart himself was undoubtedly in failing health: 'hardly the man he once was', reckoned Michell later, recalling the voyage home that he shared with Stewart in 1884. He went on advising the Board on its deliberations, though, and kept up a regular correspondence with Michell on the general development of business in the Cape.[104] The latter, for all his obvious importance to the bank, continued to share his top billing with a colleague. Farie's successor as Joint General Manager was

Edward Thomas, who stayed in Port Elizabeth and assumed responsibility for the Eastern Province and Natal. Michell, with responsibility for the rest of the country, moved to Cape Town and began weaving an impressive web of connections.* A suitably august new building, fronting on to Adderley Street in the centre of the city, was officially opened in March 1883. Two years later – and at the government's request, or so Michell would later aver – the Standard relocated its entire head office to the Adderley Street building.[105] The move coincided with news from London that on 20 March 1885 Robert Stewart had collapsed and died of a cerebral haemorrhage at the age of fifty-five.

His death came as a shock to everyone in the bank. Stewart, all were agreed, had every right to be regarded as the real architect of the institution they knew. It also prompted immediate speculation as to who would succeed him. In South Africa, no one appears to have doubted the indispensability of a Chief Manager in London, and most people assumed that the post would automatically pass to Michell – including Michell himself. By the middle of April he was writing to a colleague to reassure him that the appointment would in no way lessen his attachment to the Colony: 'were I removed to London, I could not divest myself [of] the feeling of profound interest with which S. African affairs commercial and political inspire one, after so many years residence'.[106] But he was also ready to admit around this date that he was growing tired of colonial life: it separated him from his children, whom he was determined to see educated in England, and he believed the climate was bad for his wife's health (though she had been born and raised in Port Elizabeth).[107] So London beckoned in every way. Days later, however, Michell was astounded to hear that the Directors had decided to abolish the Chief Manager's position. A London Manager would run Clements Lane, while a 'Secretary & Inspector of Colonial Returns' would handle letters to and from South Africa, rather as in Francis Searle's day. A dismayed Michell wrote to Edward Thomas in Port Elizabeth: 'A legitimate object of one's ambition is thus swept away, but putting my private feelings aside and looking at the more important

---

* By the middle of the decade, he had become a good friend of several leading government figures, including the Cape Governor, Sir Hercules Robinson. In his unpublished autobiography, Michell rather endearingly set down a list of all his appointments, some less elevated than others. He was a member of the Cape of Good Hope Board of Commissioners, a Justice of the Peace for Cape Town and vice-president of the South African Bankers' Institute. He was also a lay delegate for the Church of England Synod in the city, and a member of the Western Province's Cricket Club and Chess Club. Michell confessed he had 'entered on these and other similar affairs by way of relaxation from the rather monotonous duties at the Bank' (Arch 2/5/M, 'Sixty Years In and Out of South Africa' by Sir Lewis Michell, Kt., C.V.O. (Chapters 4–10) unpublished, p. 55).

question of its effect upon the Bank, I think you concur with me in thinking that the experiment cannot pay.'[108] The two individuals effectively
elevated in lieu of a new Chief Manager were both, in Michell's stern view,
almost laughably lightweight characters – the London Manager, John
Chumley, had never even set foot in South Africa. (News that Stewart's
widow had been offered a miserably small award for her late husband's
services added to a widespread consternation in the Cape over the actions
of the Board.) In his private correspondence – and he was a prolific letter
writer – Michell would often set out his thoughts with surprising and
sometimes brutal candour. Now he fired off a string of letters bitterly
critical of the Directors' apparent assumption that they could dictate
policy in South Africa without having any expert adviser by their side. He
wrote to a friend and client of the bank at the start of June 1885:

> I confess – as Senior Joint General Manager – I expected the appointment
> vacant by Stewart's lamented death, but the Board are endeavouring to regu-
> late affairs themselves. I am of opinion – and so is the Colonial world – that
> the decision is most disastrous, for our interests are now so large and so
> intricate that I don't see how they are [manageable without the supervi-
> sion] . . . which a Chief Manager of ample Colonial knowledge alone can
> give . . . I daresay you will agree with me that for the Standard Bank to abolish
> its chief managership in London is somewhat as if the Cape Colony were to
> abolish its Agent General [responsible for the Colony's finances] . . . [So] until
> the Board fill Stewart's place, Mr Thomas and I live in daily fear of grave
> mistakes in policy being committed through ignorance or excessive zeal.[109]

The Board's own private calculations at this time are unrecorded, but
the Directors do seem to have been aware of the problem. The only man
among them with useful personal experience of the Cape was a politician:
this was Sir Henry Barkly, a former British High Commissioner who, by
joining the Standard's Board in 1878 within months of leaving office, had
set a precedent that would be followed by a string of successors.* The
Directors saw their need for more knowledge of South African business
and brought aboard the former Joint General Manager Hugh Cameron

---

* Sir Henry Barkly (Governor and High Commissioner, 1870–77) joined the Board in
1878 and served for twenty years. Sir Hercules Robinson (Governor and High Commissioner,
1880–89) joined in 1889 but had to resign on being reappointed as High Commissioner in
1895. (His place at the Boardroom table went briefly to his younger brother, Sir William
Robinson, who knew nothing of South Africa but was a former Governor of the State of
South Australia and served for two years.) Sir Henry, later Lord, Loch (Governor, 1889–95)
served from 1895 to 1900. Sir Walter Hely-Hutchinson (Governor, 1901–10) served from
1910 to 1913.

Ross, who had retired from the bank in 1881 and settled in England. Michell wrote immediately to impress upon Ross how essential his role would be. ('I had it from Stewart's own lips that had it not been for his presence on the spot, disastrous resolutions would often have been passed.'[110]) Over the coming years, Ross would indeed prove to be a useful addition to the Board – not least as someone in whom Michell could confide, with regular and highly unofficial updates of the situation at the Cape.[111] But if the Directors were going to avoid presiding over the kind of dismal outcome to their decision that filled Michell with foreboding, there was only one truly corrective action at their disposal – which was to leave the conduct of the bank's affairs increasingly in the hands of Michell himself. This they proceeded to do, and the forty-three-year-old West Country man responded by leading the Standard Bank in some style through a momentous phase of South Africa's history.

The bank's business by 1885 had been halved in size by the impact of the depression. The slump in commodity prices that blighted most of the world's markets in 1883–4 had arrived early in South Africa, and had hit its economy with special force. The prolonged crisis had brought many small banks close to collapse, and the Standard had acknowledged its special status by stepping forward, in an ironic reversal of its stance in the 1860s, to provide emergency funding to keep these banks alive. Transcending the frailties of the banking and agricultural sectors of the economy, though, there was one fundamental problem for the country that overshadowed all else, once the worst of the depression was over: a viable model had still to be established for the running of the Kimberley diamond mines. Ways had to be found to promote essential capital investment, and to avert the over-production that remained a constant threat to prices. It had seemed evident to many observers since the 1870s – and Stewart himself had many times commented to this effect – that the problems of the industry could only be resolved in the end by a degree of common ownership for the four mines that would amount to a producers' monopoly. Inevitably, this would require a process of amalgamation that would pitch the chief protagonists against each other in a kind of no-holds-barred knock-out competition. The broad stance of the Standard Bank, spelled out in confidential papers at regular intervals, was to be supportive of this process. The managers of the bank themselves worked for an institution run on a centralized model in the Cape and fuelled with capital from the City of London. They were not slow to conclude that building deep-level mines around Kimberley would ultimately require the emergence of an analogous institution, with unitary control of the diamond industry and access to large helpings of foreign capital.[112] But of course the bank had no more idea than anyone else who would eventually emerge as the grand unifier, nor could it possibly know how long the process would take. In the meantime, it had its own shareholders' interests to promote. Customers could hardly be turned away because their activities were not thought to be conducive to the long-term evolution of the industry. So the Standard's branches in Kimberly and Beaconsfield for much of the 1880s found themselves wholly (and exhaustingly) immersed in serving the day-to-day needs of an industry in constant upheaval.

In preserving its role as an institution with a quasi-official status, the bank had perhaps three paramount concerns throughout what became an elemental battle with few parallels in the chronicles of capitalism. It needed, most obviously, to protect its own balance sheet in a febrile trading environment, while being seen to take a stand where possible against excessive mood swings in the market. In this it was broadly successful, (though its most conspicuous application of a wet flannel to the Kimberley markets, in 1881, had earned it few plaudits). The second policy imperative was that the bank should retain the Cape government's confidence and continue to be seen by officials as an institution concerned not just with its own profitability but with the broader interests of the country as a whole. Events in the diamond fields gave the Standard plenty of opportunities to demonstrate its sense of a corporate *noblesse oblige*. 'Amalgamation' was a convenient label for the way in which the number of joint-stock companies was now steadily reduced – there were four big mines and each was still being worked by a host of separate companies as of the early 1880s – but insofar as it implied a sequence of orderly and mutually agreeable takeovers, it was a misnomer for a brutal and often chaotic process. The fall in share prices, and a subsequent steep fall in carat prices for diamonds on the world market, bankrupted many companies. The Standard found itself collecting property rights within the mines in lieu of loan repayments – it owned at one point a substantial part of the Du Toits Pan mine – and thus acquired a direct interest in the work of the Mining Boards, set up at each of the four mines to try to improve the support mechanisms (roads, water-pumps and so on) shared by all. It provided the Government with regular updates on the progress of these Boards, and advised officials on what could be done to try to ensure the Boards were adequately managed and capitalized. (In 1885, for example, levies on all the extant companies in the Kimberley mine were introduced by law at the bank's suggestion, to raise funds for the mine's beleaguered Board.[113])

The third item on the Standard's scarcely concealed agenda in these years was that it should always be seen to have dealt equitably with the various parties contending for control of the diamond fields, neither pressurizing smaller companies to sell out to their larger rivals, nor favouring the schemes of any single industrialist or financier over their rivals. In this, it succeeded almost too well. For by March 1888, the struggle for control of the diamond fields finally looked like producing a clear winner in the titanic shape of Cecil John Rhodes, chairman of De Beers Mining (now to be reincorporated as De Beers Consolidated Mines) – and the record of the Standard's stance towards his long and tortuous accumulation of power over all the mines had not altogether endeared the bank to Rhodes. It had shown itself at least sympathetic in 1885 to a mooted takeover of the whole industry by a group of bankers and speculators in London and Paris. (The plan failed, but not before stoking up considerable resentment among the mining companies in the Cape.[114]) It had been opposed to the big companies' treatment of the Mining Boards and especially critical of the working conditions in the De Beers mine.[115] It had withheld its backing for Rhodes's company in the latter's long struggle to gain ascendancy over Kimberley Central, majority-owned towards the end by Barney Barnato, Rhodes's principal adversary in his climactic bid for amalgamation; and it had even toyed in the closing months of 1887 with the idea of breaking with its past neutrality to extend a huge loan to Barnato, which might have scuppered Rhodes's plans at the last moment. (This extraordinary loan proposal had Michell's personal support, but was rejected as too risky by the Directors in London.[116]) Then, within weeks of the formation of De Beers Consolidated, and while the new company was still in the throes of using its stock to complete the long-envisaged consolidation of the industry, Michell took steps to distance the Standard from yet another bout of frenzied share trading – and in the process brought the bank's stand-off with Rhodes to a head. From his office in Cape Town, Michell sent the Kimberley branch a warning that diamond shares should in general be rejected as security for any new lending – adding that shares in De Beers might just be acceptable, but only on the basis that £15 a share was their true value. Since they were currently trading at £76 each on the Kimberley exchange, the chairman of De Beers did not take well to this edict when it became general knowledge – and blamed it, rightly or wrongly, for a sharp sell-off in the market. One of Michell's friends in Kimberley wrote to him at the end of July: 'R says he intends to have it out with you, as the measure you adopted during the late crisis nearly thwarted his plans.'[117]

A meeting was arranged between the two men in August 1888. Michell's friend had offered him some thoughts in that same July letter about dealing with Rhodes: 'He is peculiar in his manners and has a rough tongue at times, but he appreciates being stood up to.' Michell took his advice.

At a meeting even more fraught with weighty implications for the Standard's future than his encounter with the Boer leaders in Natal seven years earlier, the quiet banker seems to have prevailed in his first encounter with Rhodes. As he would recall, 'I stood up to him, with excellent results'.[118] Michell set out not only the bank's commercial rationale for its recent approach, but also why that approach remained essential to the stability of the economy and the growth of the diamond industry. The man on the other side of the table could not have triumphed in the Kimberley snake pit had he not been an unusually shrewd judge of character, and he was impressed by Michell's calm analysis of the situation. At the end of their meeting, the two parted on good terms – so much so, in fact, that Michell soon found himself receiving a steady stream of requests for help with the running of Rhodes's business empire. Given the unusual ambitions of De Beers Consolidated Mines, this was a development of some consequence. The new company set up by Rhodes in 1888 was unlike any other business in the world.* Its Trust Deed authorized it 'to engage in any business enterprise, to annex land in any part of Africa, to govern foreign territories, and, if so desired, to maintain a standing army in those territories'.[119] And in addition to this rather fantastical prospectus Rhodes had other interests, too, which included equally astounding political ambitions. (He had been a Member of the Cape Legislative Assembly since 1881, representing a constituency in the diamond fields, though he had given Cape politics little attention in recent years.) Above all, like most of the other key figures at Kimberley, Rhodes was anxious to waste no time responding to the possibility – less than twenty years after the first diamond finds – of a second epoch-making discovery in the region. A potentially enormous gold reef had been discovered on an extensive ridge of land about two thirds of the way north from Kimberley towards the South African Republic's capital in Pretoria. The Transvaal government in September 1886 had declared farms along the Witwatersrand ('the Rand') to be 'public diggings', which meant they were open to licensed sales for mining purposes. By February 1887, Rhodes and his long-standing business partner, Charles Rudd, had registered a new company on the London Stock Exchange, Gold Fields of South Africa, to grab a stake in the future of the Rand. In awe of Rhodes's growing reputation at Kimberley, City investors clamoured for the stock.

---

* When die-hard opponents of his amalgamation tactics took their case to the Supreme Court in Cape Town, their legal counsel asserted – with no hyperbole intended – 'Since the time of the East India Company, no company has had such power as this' (quoted in Geoffrey Wheatcroft, *The Randlords*, Atheneum, 1986, p. 108).

The Standard Bank was even quicker off the mark: it despatched one of its managers to set up shop at the main mining site on the Rand, Ferreira's Camp, in October 1886. Plans for a town in the area had not yet got as far as confirming its name (though it was soon to be christened 'Johannesburg') and the Standard's man on the spot had to buy himself a large canvas tent from which to offer the bank's services. Today, that tent – like the manager's instant sketches of the area, portraits of the first staff on the Rand posing in front of their earliest office buildings (see Plate 7) and assorted other memorabilia – have all been transmuted into the stuff of corporate legend. In fact, the Standard's senior managers and their Board in London were initially wary of the Witwatersrand gold rush (as indeed was Rhodes, who took the capital raised by Gold Fields and promptly spent most of it in the diamond fields, which remained his real passion). Earlier discoveries of supposedly huge gold deposits, far to the east of Pretoria, had left a string of ghost towns in their wake. It was very soon clear, too, that the geology of the reef struck on the Rand was like nothing previously encountered anywhere else. Lone prospectors, sieving streams for a lucky nugget, were wasting their time: the gold was strewn in tiny fragments through a heavy conglomerate rock. Extracting it would need the rock to be smashed into rubble with huge – and very expensive – steam-driven 'stamp batteries'.

Whatever the bank's misgivings, there was no way it could stand aloof from what happened next. Mining companies sprang up by the score: 270 were registered in 1887 alone, and there were 19 Transvaal companies quoted on the London Stock Exchange by the end of 1888. The Standard began life in Johannesburg couriering modest packages of gold for sale in London – just as it had taken diamonds from Kimberley to be auctioned in Europe – and advancing money to the owners in the meantime.* Few other banks had the capacity to do this, and the Standard handled roughly half the gold leaving the Transvaal.[120] But physical mining at this stage came a poor second to financial engineering – and the proliferation of companies faced the bank with a tide of requests for long-term capital, much of it secured against little more than the owners' equity. Michell's office in Cape Town fired off a succession of telegrams urging caution on their Johannesburg colleagues. The advice was little heeded, not least

---

* The London office now had almost thirty employees. One of them, who worked for the Standard from 1889 until 1931, described in his retirement how casually the gold had been handled in the City when he first arrived at Clements Lane: 'The mail was fetched by two juniors from the Lombard Street Post Office in a large leather bag which generally included small gold bars. As these grew in size, a cab was used.' (L. Christie Smart to [?] Douglas, 2 August 1954. LMA: SBSA/0519/001.)

because the telegraph collapsed and left the boom town with no direct link to the Cape for three months. By the end of 1889, the bank's Johannesburg office had a staff of almost eighty men and a loan book valued in total at about £1 million – almost exactly as much, by chance, as Kimberley had advanced at the height of the bubble in diamond-company shares in 1881.

The sequel was much the same, too. When Barney Barnato visited the stock exchange in Johannesburg in November 1888, he found 'men taking their coats off and shrieking like maniacs – fortunes were made and lost in hours'.[121] After March 1889 they were mostly lost, as many stock prices went into free fall. The Standard's branch manager, Thomas Henderson, had assured the General Manager's Office that even a drop of 50 per cent would leave the collateral on most of his advances intact. By early 1890, the market as a whole was down by around 60 per cent from its peak, the Standard had to write off a third or so of its loan portfolio and the Johannesburg manager was out of a job. A panic over the financial viability of mining on the Witwatersrand then saw a third or so of Johannesburg's 25,000 white residents flee the town. It also prompted a run on banks across the whole of South Africa. Some failed altogether, others were lucky to attract new owners. (A new overseas bank was actually founded in London as part of this process: the African Banking Corporation was launched in 1890 and the following year acquired the bankrupt Cape of Good Hope Bank.)

The ensuing crisis of confidence in the banking sector led to a further consolidation of the Standard Bank's position in the country. This was not merely a corollary of the fact that other, smaller banks were failing. The shake-out that left Chartered Bank and the Hongkong Bank with greatly enhanced market positions in Asia early in the 1890s had no real parallel in South Africa, if only because the Standard's pre-eminence there by 1890 was already so deeply entrenched. But the banking mess coincided with a political shift in Cape Town that soon played to the Standard's advantage. The Colonial government of the 'English party' under John Gordon Sprigg fell in July 1890 – for reasons largely unconnected with events in the Transvaal – and power in the Cape Assembly passed to a coalition of his 'Afrikaner Bond' opponents. They turned for leadership to an outspoken critic of the English party who was not Dutch at all: Cecil Rhodes. And soon after the start of Rhodes's premiership, his new friend Michell found himself being asked to advise on the drafting of a new act to stabilize the banking sector. The result, the Cape Bank Act of 1891, effectively acknowledged the Standard's role as the national bank of the Colony. It made the issuance of banknotes prohibitively expensive for smaller rivals, while allowing the Standard Bank to restrict convertibility to its branch in Cape Town (thus precluding the need for large supplies of gold specie to be carted round the branch network). Unsurprisingly, Michell himself described the Act as 'that excellent measure' in his auto-biography, and noted that he had not only helped to frame it but also to persuade his Board in London 'to accept it without protest'.[122] John Gordon Sprigg wryly described it as 'an Act for the aggrandisement of the Standard Bank'.[123]

On the Rand, meanwhile, significant improvements in mining and smelting technology helped prompt a steady recovery in share prices, and gold production itself began to rise dramatically. South Africa's rail network finally reached Johannesburg in 1892. That same year, gold contributed more than diamonds to the value of the country's exports. Asian countries, as we have seen, were moving away from their dependence on a silver monetary standard. The consequent surge in demand for gold bullion assured South Africa of purchasers for whatever quantities it could ship, all at a fixed price. (Gold shares could rise and fall, but bullion, unlike diamonds, had a guaranteed value.) Under the circumstances, it struck many as anomalous that the Cape Colony itself should still be importing its gold coinage from Britain. At the instigation of the newly wealthy Boer government in the Transvaal, a conference between all the interested parties was held in Pretoria in 1893. The Cape Colony's delegate, naturally, was the Standard's General Manager. Michell strongly urged endorsement of one currency for the whole of South Africa, with all its coins to be minted in Pretoria and to carry the symbols of the country's four states as 'a very real step towards forming a nation'. Tragically, no agreement was reached. The failure of the 'Mint Conference' attested to a gulf between the British and Boer states that was wider than the optimists had been ready to acknowledge, and was about to grow wider still.

3
At the Crest of the Wave,
1893–1914

I. SHAKING THE PAGODA-TREE

> Question 4. – Which is the cheapest way of laying down Rs.100,000 in
> Calcutta –
>
> 1st By Calcutta selling T.T. on London at 1/6?
> 2nd By Calcutta selling 4 m/st on London at 1/6¼?
> 3rd By Head Office remitting Council Bills to Calcutta at 1/5¾?
>
> Reckoning interest at 3 per cent per ann. in London, and 8 per cent per ann.
> in India; Brokerage on Sales 1/8 per cent, Stamps on Drafts Rs.60 per Rs
> 100,000, and time between Calcutta and London, say 1/20th part of a year.

This and nine other equally finely calibrated brain-teasers confronted a
dozen or so young men of Chartered Bank who sat its internal exam in
September 1891, aspiring to exchange the gloomy ground floor of Hatton
Court for a glamorous posting in the East.[1] Most had by then been in
training at Head Office for two or three years, acquiring a thorough
knowledge of each department's routines. Others had arrived more
recently, having already gained at least a theoretical understanding of the
exchange markets, as attested by a certificate from the Institute of Bankers. This was a prized credential for all those intent on finding their way
into one of the City's overseas banks. Lists of those who had gained it
were published each summer, invariably followed by a surge of applicants
for advertised places with the banks. Across the 1890s and on through
the Edwardian era, the numbers attracted into working abroad went on
rising – slightly to the chagrin of some in the City, who preferred to champion the virtues of a solid career in domestic banking. As an 'educational
section' in *The Bankers' Magazine* of 1905 pointed out, life in China,
South America or the Colonies had its drawbacks, after all. 'Much has to
be given up by those who go to foreign lands . . . Most bank men never

R H-Vincent

4 — 5.45 p.m.

2nd September, 1891.

EXAMINATION PAPER.

Note.—*Each question is to be answered on separate sheet or sheets of paper, of which only one side is to be written on; each sheet must be numbered and have the name of the writer and number of the question placed at the head of it.*

When finished the sheets must be arranged in order and pinned together.

QUESTION 1.—What is the shortest method of converting—

     (a). Rupees, Dollars and Taels into Pounds sterling ?

     (b). Pounds sterling into Rupees, Dollars and Taels ?

     In both cases reckoning the Rupee at 1/8, Dollar at 3/9 and Tael at 4/6.

QUESTION 2.—What is the main factor which determines the difference between the Rates of Exchange in India for Telegraphic Transfers and Drafts at Usance on London ?

QUESTION 3.—Which is the cheaper mode of raising money in Hongkong—

     1. By Hongkong drawing T.T. on London at 3/4.

     2. By Hongkong drawing T.T. on India at 222 and India drawing T.T. on London at 1/6 ?

     In both cases disregarding Brokerage.

QUESTION 4.—Which is the cheapest way of laying down Rs.100,000 in Calcutta—

     1st. By Calcutta selling T.T. on London at 1/6 ?

     2nd. By Calcutta selling 4 m/st on London at 1/6¼ ?

     3rd. By Head Office remitting Council Bills to Calcutta at 1/5⅝ ?

     Reckoning interest at 3 per cent. per ann. in London, and 8 per cent. per ann. in India; Brokerage on Sales ⅛ per cent., Stamps on Drafts Rs.60 per Rs.100,000, and time between Calcutta and London, say 1/10th part of a year.

QUESTION 5.—What is the standard fineness of Silver in India, France and England, expressed in the usual way ?

QUESTION 6.—Compare the standard fineness of Silver in England, France and India, expressed in millièmes ?

QUESTION 7.—What is the weight of a Tola and a Canton Tael in grains, Troy ?

QUESTION 8.—What is the recognized weight of $1,000 in Hongkong, expressed in Canton Taels ?

QUESTION 9.—What is the seignorage at the Indian Mints ?

ACCOUNTS.

QUESTION 10.—Hongkong draws for Cash Tls. 100,000 d/d on Shanghai at Tls. 72·5 per $100 and pays ⅛ per cent. Brokerage. What entries have to be passed in Hongkong and Shanghai ?

The Hatton Court Examination Paper for Foreign Staff probationers, September 1891

think of India, Australia or South Africa as lands in which to make their home, but ever look forward to the time when they will be able to return to England.'[2] Intent on making its own point about career prospects at home, the magazine was guilty of glossing over a significant distinction to be made among the overseas jobs coming available. For the great majority of those lured to South Africa (as to Canada and Australasia) were in fact destined never to return. Most of the opportunities on offer for employment in the Cape were with Standard Bank, where clerical vacancies multiplied through the 1890s not least in response to the growth of Johannesburg and the repercussions of the gold boom.[3] Of those recruited at 10 Clements Lane – who were generally sent on their way within weeks of a successful interview, sailing from Southampton in one of the Castle Line cabins regularly reserved for the bank – very few ever came back. Like Lewis Michell, most would settle in the Colony as first-generation South Africans.

Being posted to the East was a different matter entirely. The same writer in *The Bankers' Magazine* thought it 'possibly' the most popular overseas destination – and 'undoubtedly' the most attractive. The proposition from the outset was that Eastern bankers would lead a peripatetic life around the trade ports of Asia, steadily expanding a precious network of colleagues and customers across the region. At the age of fifty-five, they would then either retire or ascend to the bank's top management team for a final five years in London. Whether or not all this really amounted, as the magazine seemed to be warning, to a kind of Faustian pact in reverse – instead of twenty-four years on the hog followed by eternal damnation, twenty-four years of hell would end with a blissful and well-heeled old age in the auld country, or perhaps the Home Counties – the material rewards on offer were certainly enough to turn the heads of many young men toiling at their ledgers in City counting houses, or more often in bank branches across the rain-swept Lowlands of Scotland. (Chartered men were fond of claiming their young recruits had been netted in the street, having been lured into the open by a well-placed bowl of porridge.) One City recruit was Walter Young, a clerk hired in 1878. He had actually had enough of the Far East by the start of the 1890s and was now working his way back to England having resigned from Chartered Bank; but some years later he recorded his experiences on its foreign staff in a colourful autobiography entitled *A Merry Banker in the Far East* (often less redolent of banking than of the banter in an Edwardian music hall).* Young had

---

* Young served with Chartered Bank in the Philippines for six years until 1886, and was then transferred to Hong Kong. It was not a happy move: 'my romantic life in Iloilu [*sic*], where I was feted by the sugar planters, and, when I visited their haciendas, received with

started work in the City at the age of twenty-one. After three years of monotonous routine, he took fright at the prospect ahead of him:

> When I glanced round the office and saw married men, on a salary of £140 after ten or twelve years' service, coming into the grimy old City every morning by the same old train or the same old bus, eating year after year the same old cut off the same old joint . . . I determined to try and get away from such soul-starving and abhorrent surroundings before it became too late . . . [A] married but sympathetic fellow-clerk, who worked with me on the pass-books, said: 'Why don't you try to get into an Eastern bank? Go abroad, old man, and become a rajah – shake the pagoda-tree . . .'[4]

The supposed glamour of the orient that appealed to Young in the late 1870s had become even more beguiling by the 1890s, with the British Empire in its prime and new product markets springing up as part of an even broader phenomenon, 'globalization'.

Impressive as the pace of change had been in the Chartered's world over the span of the Merry Banker's career, it was palpably quickening by the last decade of the century. The years between about 1890 and the catastrophe of 1914 have been depicted by one pioneering scholar of 'global history', the late C. J. Bayly, as The Great Acceleration: whatever their potency hitherto, several nineteenth-century trends contributing to the emergence of the modern world were now gathering a fresh intensity, not least in the context of international trade and finance. 'Many people of the time, contemplating the speed of change between 1890 and 1914, were convinced that this age was the crucible of modernity.'[5] The proliferation of cable routes across the world produced a huge jump in telegraphic traffic. Industrial production surged ahead, not just in Britain but across Western Europe and North America, generating an unprecedented flood of manufactured goods for export. Record freight levels from around the turn of the century were greatly facilitated by a boom in world shipping and advances in maritime technology that wrought a spectacular fall in transportation costs. By 1906, as another historian of the nineteenth century's impact has noted, 'it cost only twice or three times as much to ship a ton of cotton goods from Liverpool to Bombay as it did to send them 45 kilometres by train from Manchester to Liverpool'.[6] Meanwhile the

---

open arms, a brass band and a procession of virgins . . . [was swapped] for the grinding drudgery of playing second fiddle to a bald-headed Scotch taskmaster . . . It gave me a pain in my pantry' (pp. 108–9). Young quit the bank in 1889 to work briefly for a Hong Kong broking firm. After returning to Britain in 1891, he soon gave up a thoroughly unlikely position as a country banker in York and spent the rest of his career as a banker and wheeler-dealer in South America. (*A Merry Banker in the Far East*, John Lane The Bodley Head, 1916.)

capital invested since the 1870s in building railway networks, canals and modern harbours meant that the great cities and waterways of the East were open to international trade by the end of the century as never before. For the Eastern exchange banks, all this brought not just a heady expansion of business – the Chartered's balance sheet almost doubled in size between 1900 and 1913, from £14.6 million to £27.2 million – but also a qualitative improvement in their operating environment. Commodity prices started being regularly quoted and broadly aligned across the world. Cash transfers began to rely increasingly on telegraphic transfers rather than the passage of bills and related papers on fast ships. The inherent uncertainties of monetary transactions involving silver-based currencies gave way in most places (China excepted) to a simpler and safer acceptance of the Gold Standard, and of sterling as its proxy. The exchange bankers' world did also see other, less helpful developments – notably the emergence of rivals from other countries, backed by governments with a more pressing political agenda than was generally evident in Whitehall. But for the most part these decades were to be an era of unparalleled opportunity – and the young men of Chartered Bank who sallied forth to staff the Empire usually found a banker's life in the East well up to their expectations.

As a freshly posted 'covenanted officer' – legally covenanted, that is, to represent the bank on official business – any former City clerk would instantly quadruple his old salary ('to a sum', noted *The Bankers' Magazine*, 'which is higher than that which is received by most officials in the home banks at the end of their career'.) This new earning power, of course, had strings attached. It signified that he had done far more than merely swap one job for another: he had joined 'the service', becoming part of a select band of expatriate colleagues whose whole lives – far beyond the usual confines of a mere career – would be shaped by working for the bank. Though this work might at first entail a share of routine clerical chores, he would daily be reminded in Bombay, Batavia or Bangkok of his automatic elevation to a hitherto unimaginable status by the presence of the 'native' clerical staff. (That greatest of all English comic writers, P. G. Wodehouse, spent two years as a trainee exchange banker in London at the turn of the twentieth century and would later make fun of his youthful peers' expectations with a gentle lampoon of the life they looked forward to leading: 'When on an elephant's back you pass, somebody beats on a booming brass gong! The Banker of Bhong!'[7]) While directing the native employees' activities courteously but firmly, the young officer would be securely ranked in a hierarchy of men whose privileges were by the 1890s beginning to extend, for those at senior levels, to the

1. The founders. *Above:* James Wilson
MP, proprietor-editor of *The Economist*,
who wrote the City prospectus for
The Chartered Bank in 1852 before
a Royal Charter had even been applied
for. *Right:* John Paterson, another
Scotsman and journalist, whose business
and political career in the Cape Colony
made him a natural leader in 1862
for the merchants of Port Elizabeth
intent on launching a bank.

2. The real father figures.
Above: Howard Gwyther,
who took on managing the
Chartered after it had been all
but sunk by loan losses in 1870
and retired as Chairman in
1904. *Right:* Robert Stewart,
who arrived at the Cape in
1864 just in time to rescue
Standard Bank from collapse
and thereafter led its expansion
until his death in 1885.

3. Two of the Chartered's earliest destinations. *Above:* Calcutta, just before the tumultuous violence of 1857 that led to the founding of the Raj; the Chartered's first branch there was established the following year. *Below:* the waterfront of Hong Kong's Victoria harbour in 1859, when the Chartered opened up there in support of its recently established branch in Shanghai.

4. Two of the Chartered's earliest banknotes. *Above:* a first cheque ('post bill'), payable by the Singapore branch in March 1859 to Charles Sherwood, who also signed it as resident Accountant at the branch. *Below:* a $10 note issued in Hong Kong in March 1863, signed by two acting officers of the local branch after the recent dismissal by the Board of both its Manager and its Accountant.

5. Building an imperial bank in South Africa in the 1860s. *Above:* the Standard's branch in Port Elizabeth at the very end of the decade, when ox-drawn carts heading for the diamond fields to the north were a regular sight in the streets. *Below:* the Adderley Street branch in Cape Town, built within a year of the bank's inauguration as a token of the bank's ambitions.

6. The diamond rush at Kimberley. *Above:* the Big Hole in 1873, where precarious walls and access paths marked out hundreds of individual plots dug ever deeper into the earth. *Below:* the Standard's local employees outside their branch in 1877, the year a travelling inspector reviewed all their careers and deemed the staff 'upon the whole not above an average one' (see Appendix B).

7. Standard Bank and the birth of Johannesburg. *Above:* the branch on the Rand in 1888, its second full year in business, when it coordinated roughly half of the area's gold shipments. *Below:* the Standard's new branch on Commissioner Street, built just six years later in a city that had sprung from nothing since the discovery of the Rand's gold reefs in 1886.

8. Following the Empire into Matabeleland. *Above:* the Standard's tent at Bulawayo in 1894, providing clerical support for Cecil Rhodes's Chartered Company as it laid the foundations of the future Rhodesia. *Below:* the Bulawayo to Gwelo stage coach in 1897, one of the regular postal services on which the Standard's fledgling network relied, north of the Limpopo.

possession of houses more splendid and servants more numerous than were granted even to the local envoys and consuls on Her Majesty's service. Whatever his class background at home, in fact, the successful young banker would take his place in what has been nicely described, in the context of the Raj, as the 'middle-class aristocracy' of expatriate Empire society.[8] Returning to Britain for a first furlough, he would step back into Hatton Court a new man – as the Merry Banker himself described with a typically rhetorical flourish:

> [T]hose recently lassoed and unlicked Scotch cubs, who on their first arrival in London generally presented themselves at the bank with father's old topper falling over their ears and the porridge still sticking to their mugs, returned on furlough a few years later, bronzed and distinguished men of the world.[9]

In truth, many had to wait six or seven years for this first return home, sometimes even longer. (Not until 1906 was it firmly decreed that, 'subject to the exigencies of the service', all who had served six years would qualify for nine months' leave.[10]) And if on their first reappearance in London the young bucks did indeed seem to have matured out of all recognition, the greybeards of the bank knew why: most of them had by then been handed responsibilities far beyond anything entrusted to their stay-at-home peers in the grimy old City. This was of course another aspect of Eastern banking's appeal – but the reality often came as a shock. Rapid promotion was not just a function of the 'Empire-staffing' model that put chaps from home in charge of large native staffs; it was also a reflection of the physical remoteness that had often to be endured by Chartered expatriates who could find themselves despatched to some forbiddingly remote spots. In Burma, for example, during each year's rice harvest season from January to April, the Rangoon branch opened a satellite office at Akyab (now Sittwe) on Burma's Bay of Bengal coastline. It was a small port with a few mills taking paddy from the western coastal plain of Arakan. One young man, W. S. Livingstone, was assigned there in 1893 and later recalled the experience in a retirement memoir:

> On the way up to Akyab I was overcome with my own importance at taking charge, but also with an awful feeling, carefully hidden, that I might make a mess of things. Except for a small native staff, I should be alone – [with] no-one to ask 'Please, what am I to do?' It was a nice little office at Akyab, but the bungalow, where I lived, was several miles away – means of conveyance, your pony's back. The bungalow was spacious, but dilapidated, being inhabited for only three months in the year. It was looked after by a

Sikh who inhabited a small mat shed, secured by an enormously powerful padlock which seemed superfluous! Good chap, the Sikh! I found out later that he slept outside my door on the verandah 'to keep off bad men' . . .

While I was in Akyab, I received a visit from William Preston [who would rise to be the first 'Chief Manager' of the bank in 1920, but was then a mere Sub-Accountant in Calcutta] . . . Seated on the shores of the Bay of Bengal, he gave me a bit of advice that was useful to me throughout my career in the Bank. He said 'Do not be frightened of responsibility. Think your problem over at all angles and if it is within your competence and for the benefit of the Bank, ACT on your own. Report the whole matter to higher quarters and await their verdict.' As I got higher up in growing measure, I made use of this.[11]

Not everyone responded to the challenge as positively. Taking on heavy responsibilities at a relatively early age was just one aspect of a lifestyle that could be extremely testing – and pushed some beyond endurance. Young Livingstone was sent to Akyab because the Senior Sub-Accountant, who was customarily given the job, was suffering some kind of acute depression. He had been given a supposedly restorative sea voyage to Australia and back, and had apparently made a good recovery. But he was passed over for the Akyab work nonetheless, and Livingstone noted the grim sequel:

> [So] he was retained in Rangoon and I was sent there in his place. He seemed to take this quietly, but it had such an effect on him that he committed suicide a fortnight later. It was a sad business.

Another aspect of serving the bank in relatively remote corners of the East was the exposure to war and civil unrest that it sometimes involved. In 1898 – long after the Merry Banker's departure – the manager in the Philippines was caught up in the early stages of the Spanish-American War: he had to evacuate his staff to a fleet of coastal steamers organized by the local British Consul, and then opted to remain at his desk in Manila as the city braced itself for bombardment by the US Navy.[12] (He survived and no harm came to the office in the end.) The following year, and a decade after his lonely vigil in Upper Burma, W. S. Livingstone had to endure a harrowing fortnight in Hankow when the Foreign Settlement there seemed about to come under all-out attack from Imperial troops combating the Boxer Rebellion. 'When sleeping you had to have a revolver under the pillow', recalled Livingstone in his memoirs. 'I had two . . . The instructions were to fire in defence and reserve the last [bullet] for yourself as the Chinese have frightful tortures . . . Gory heads stuck on poles decorated the end of the short road where the bank was.'[13]

Even without a threat of physical violence, life in the East could be stressful enough. Everyday amenities were often far more spartan, the heat and humidity far more oppressive, than new arrivals from London had expected. Landing in Singapore as late as 1905, one made no secret of his astonishment to find 'no electric light, no fans, no tramways'.[14] Those sharing the Junior Mess in Shanghai in 1898–9 succumbed to regular illnesses, eventually attributed in an official report to some deeply suspect kitchen arrangements: 'typhoid infection if once admitted would flourish there'.[15] The rituals of departure from London included getting the all-clear from the bank's doctor in Harley Street, Dr Bennett and his successors, but did not extend to inoculations or even any proper medical advice about living in the tropics. Nor did passports, visa or health documents feature in the preparations. Few escaped health problems later, not unrelated in many cases to the less medicinal qualities of Scotch whisky. Contagious diseases then rarely seen in Europe posed a constant threat, in the absence of effective medicines. Coping with the effects of an epidemic on local staff was another challenge. Faced with a virulent outbreak of bubonic plague in Bombay in December 1896, the Agent ('without in any way wishing to pose as alarmist') had to report plans for a sharp curtailment of the bank's daily operations: 'Many of our clerks are away because their relatives are ill, the real cause being of course funk, and we have great difficulty in allaying the fears of those who have stuck to their posts. We greatly fear a general stampede if matters get much worse.'[16] His report made no mention of the fact that dead rats had been discovered under desks, which may have had some bearing on the 'funk'.[17]

Even for the physically fit, meanwhile, loneliness was always a potential problem, especially for those living in the smaller expatriate communities with little sport and limited social distractions of any kind. Marriage was strictly forbidden for all those beneath the rank of Accountant – Howard Gwyther, anxious to prevent the bank accumulating droves of dependent young widows, personally insisted on the ban – and this obliged Chartered staff to remain bachelors for the first several years of their service. Even thereafter, some delay could be entailed in finding an appropriate (i.e. white European) bride: marriage to a 'native woman', risking an involvement for the Chartered in local family disputes, was not an option for those wishing to continue their career in the bank. While single Managers and Accountants had their own residencies, other unmarried staff often lived together in a communal house – a 'mess' or, especially in the sub-continent, a 'chummery' – which was sometimes shared with bachelors working for other British companies. Most Chartered men reminiscing in old age about their days on the Foreign Staff had fond memories of the camaraderie of the mess and the relative opulence of their Asian lifestyle, at least when working at the principal branches of the network. Frank Bennett, whom we encountered signing new banknotes late into the night at Kuala Lumpur, moved on to serve briefly in Singapore in the early 1890s and found the level of accommodation there entirely satisfactory:

> The Bank was then housed in an old building in Raffles Square[;] the Manager's residence was called Cairn Hill and had a large compound with plenty of room for tennis courts . . . During the few months I was stationed here, I lived with Bruce Webster [a colleague] at a large house belonging to the Sultan of Johore called Bididari, some two or three miles out of town. There was a small Golf Course in the compound and from the back verandah of the house, which was close to thick jungle, we sometimes saw wild pig.[18]

Not all of their memories, though, were happy ones. J. A. Macgill was a clerk living in Shanghai in 1902–3 – that is to say, in the International Settlement built up by the British adjacent to the original Chinese city – who later recalled in a private memoir:

> There was one very strange broker, Roderick Campbell, who it was said got through a whole bottle of whisky per day. He did a fair amount of the Exchange broking [in Shanghai], though latterly . . . I think he had been 'plunging' in the Stock Market. It was a very old custom that Roddy came to tiffin [i.e. lunch] at our junior mess every Tuesday. On one occasion, when dear old John Alston (Accountant) was presiding over the tiffin, he and Campbell had some talk about the Highlands because Roddy was inordinately proud of his Highland ancestry; so Alston lent Campbell a copy of a Scottish magazine. Campbell went straight from that tiffin table and in his buggy he was driven to one of the Chinese back streets and there he shot himself.[19]

Crucial to the expansion of Chartered Bank was the success with which, under Gwyther's firm direction, it had already begun by the 1890s to nurture a house culture that would minimize the risk of losing its employees to the kind of personal disasters that finished off Livingstone's Rangoon colleague and poor Roddy Campbell. Senior men in the bank knew how much depended on alleviating, for young foreign staff, the pain of leaving friends and relatives behind, and on combating the (largely unacknowledged) demons of homesickness. Fundamental to this culture was the bank's insistence on hiring only school-leavers or those who had spent just a few post-school years working in a bank. Entirely shunned were university men, who would arrive with their heads full of fancy notions that might make them unpredictable colleagues and overly demanding companions in a chummery. The bank instead sought resourceful, genial and like-minded souls – a sound majority of them Scotsmen – who could spend the formative years of their young adulthood together in London, forging friendships in the Ledger Room and on the sports field that would serve them and the bank well for the rest of their working lives. A strong sense of togetherness would go along with peer pressure always to do the right thing – even in the remotest of circumstances. Or as Macgill put it in his memoir: '[once] a sense of pride in the old Bank, helped by our social and physical activities, had grown in those destined for Eastern service, there was small risk of lapses later'.[20] The old bank kept up its guard, though, just in case. Young Chartered men were never left in any doubt that they had to rank beside Caesar's wife in terms of personal propriety; nor were they short of continuing moral guidance after they had embarked on their careers. By the middle of the 1890s the Court was no longer inclined (as in the past) to spell out what was expected of staff in dour circulars that might have come from the elders of the Church of Scotland.* But it took care to see that junior employees in a mess had a senior colleague as their 'President'; and every Agent/Manager of the bank had a responsibility not only for the proficiency of his team within the office but for their well-being outside it. Howard Gwyther stressed the point in a lengthy letter of instructions that he wrote to the Inspector of the day, Thomas Forrest, before he set off on a tour in 1889:

> Whilst referring to the subject of the European Officers of each Agency, the Directors wish you to be very observant of any signs of bad habits and extravagant and speculative tendencies and exert every effort to eradicate them . . . In cases of any very grave offence, for instance intemperance, or gambling, or dishonourable conduct, it will be a question whether the offender should not be suspended awaiting the Court's decision.[21]

On a more cheery note, it was also part of the Inspector's job ('your special province, and we may add privilege') to draw the Court's attention to any juniors showing signs of outstanding ability. The business of the bank

---

* One circular had stipulated that, in addition to the total ban on marriage and on personal debt, there should be no 'falling into irregular habits of life' nor 'any impropriety of conduct, or want of courtesy and respect to seniors [which] will incur the Directors' marked displeasure'. Every sub-accountant was enjoined to seek out opportunities 'for study and improvement, whether by attending classes and lectures on subjects bearing upon the work of a Banker, or in other ways cultivating those acquirements which will be useful to one of his calling'. More than twenty serving officers in the East signed a letter to the Secretary in Hatton Court expressing their 'deep regret' over this moralizing tract. 'We venture most respectfully to add that the communication in question seems to us to touch upon points the observance of which might have been left to the self-respect and gentlemanly feeling of each member of the staff.' (David Millar, T. J. Anderson et al. to the Secretary, 31 August 1881, LMA: CH03/01/10/01/17.)

began to grow rapidly during the 1890s, and staff transfers were a constant feature of operations across the whole Eastern network. This created plenty of opportunities to promote the best men. Careful note was taken in London not only of the Inspector's recommendations but also of the regular observations made about staff by Agents and Managers in their formal letters to the Court.

Piecing together the commentaries on a single individual's career can provide a glimpse of this kaleidoscopic world, where no staffing pattern lasted long and every posting was subject to change at very short notice, as and when the Court decided. Few records of an entire career survive in much detail, but William Gibson's came to grief and so his papers were filed as evidence that he had not been treated unfairly.[22] He joined the staff in 1892, apparently in his mid-twenties and having already worked for some years in the City. As was its usual practice when taking on a qualified man for immediate despatch to the East – as opposed to a younger recruit heading for a lengthy probation at Hatton Court – the bank required a 'Fidelity Bond' worth £1,000 as a guarantee of his good behaviour. With his contract settled (and signed by three Directors), Gibson was assigned immediately as a Sub-Accountant to Singapore. He spent the next five years working up and down the Malay Archipelago, serving more than once in Penang and running the small Sub-Agencies first in Taiping and then in Kuala Lumpur. By May 1897 he was back in Singapore – by which time the accumulated verdicts on his performance were presenting a mixed picture:

> August 1892 – 'a steady gentlemanly young fellow'
> February 1893 – 'his work is always efficiently done'
> August 1893 – 'Altho appearing anxious to please, [he] is not a man after our own heart'
> March 1894 – 'the strictures I passed on him in August last may be withdrawn'
> May 1894 – 'should prove an efficient Officer'
> October 1894 – 'rather wanting in concentration of attention, and we fear inclined to be extravagant'
> May 1897 [after Gibson had returned from a sick leave] – 'seems to me to want energy, and to be without special aptitude for our business'

Whatever the occasional reservations, Gibson had done well enough by 1897 to merit a promotion and was moved to Hong Kong as head of loans and overdrafts. He thrived over the next three years and in 1901 was appointed as Sub-Accountant in Calcutta, still the most important Eastern office – but here a serious problem arose. Gibson showed a propensity for losing his temper with Indian clerks. Of all sins against the bank's code of behaviour, this had long been regarded as one of the gravest.* The head of the branch, Thomas Fraser, eventually lost patience with him and formally requested the Court to transfer Gibson to another location: 'he has not a nice way with natives and I have more than once had to task him for using harsh and abusive language to the Native Staff . . . I consider that he has lost the respect and confidence of the Native Staff in this office'.[23] When the Court demurred and suggested Gibson should be given time to settle, Fraser wrote again to provide more details. It transpired that Gibson had 'threatened before the whole office to kick our Khazanchi [i.e. the Head Cashier]'. This was doubly unfortunate, to say the least, since this Khazanchi was the young nephew of an important client, the Maharaja Doorja.[24] Gibson was transferred to Burma. Given this rather severe setback, it is striking that he remained with the bank and was able to keep his place on the ladder. He ran the Akyab office through the January–April season of 1902, after which Fraser insisted he could not return to Calcutta but was equally adamant that he should not be asked to resign. Letters were exchanged with Gwyther (by this time the Chairman of the bank) and Gibson found himself relocated to Bombay. He had been given a stiff warning, which seems to have had the desired effect, and his career resumed a more traditional trajectory. Five years later, he had served as Accountant in Batavia and Shanghai, and was back working in Hong Kong, now the most senior and experienced Accountant in the East. He was not universally popular ('He has rather an exalted opinion of his social qualifications', thought the Hong Kong Manager, 'through which he has made many enemies.'[25]) but was seen as being in line to become the Manager of a smaller branch like Penang or Colombo. Then disaster struck.

Taking up his post in Hong Kong in April 1907, Gibson inherited many customer relationships that he chose to retain in the usual way. (Newly appointed Accountants always had the option, for a brief initial period, of declining responsibility for an account handed on by their predecessor.) One of these customers was a newly established flour producer, the Hong Kong Milling Company (HKM). It had been set up in 1906 by a well-known

---

* Gwyther had emphasized as much in another Letter of Instructions for the Inspector Thomas Forrest. 'One of the points we want you to look to very particularly at each place is the bearing of the European Officers towards Natives. So much of the Bank's business now consists of direct dealing with Natives that any contemptuous or overbearing treatment of Natives on the part of the European Officers is likely to bring the Bank into serious disrepute, and must be firmly and unmistakeably put down.' (Gwyther to Forrest, 16 November 1888, LMA: CH03/01/10/26/01/A.)

Canadian entrepreneur in the Colony called Alfred Rennie, who had given all his banking business to the Chartered for over fifteen years. HKM made a sizeable profit in 1907, which perhaps encouraged Gibson to handle some trade documentation with less than meticulous timing. The details are unclear, but some irregularity appears to have exposed the bank early in 1908 to a potential loss of HK$1.3 million, well in excess of HKM's usual credit limits. As luck would have it, American competitors at this very moment began dumping cheap flour on the local market, in a transparent bid to drive HKM out of business. Flour prices dropped alarmingly, and HKM's revenues began to slide. At the same time, a 20 per cent plunge in the sterling value of the Hong Kong dollar forced Rennie to disclose that he had failed to hedge substantial forward purchases of wheat, at sterling prices that he could no longer afford. By March 1908, the Hong Kong branch needed to warn Head Office of its possible loss. The Secretary, William Hoggan, wrote immediately to Gibson: 'The position of this account . . . has caused very much surprise, and has given rise to grave misgivings in the minds of the Directors.' This, he observed darkly, was 'very disappointing', and explained why 'we have to address you personally' in requesting a full account of what had happened.[26] While Gibson was assembling his narrative in April, the wretched Rennie committed suicide, the business crashed and the bank found itself the owner of HKM's mills at Junk Bay and two godowns full of wheat, flour and bran.[27] Gibson insisted that all his dealings with the company had followed the lines laid down by his predecessors, and returned to London armed with a long list of references to earlier correspondence with Head Office. But all his pleadings were in vain, and Hoggan wrote on the Directors' behalf in late August to say that 'after consideration they think it expedient not to continue your services'.[28] Gibson was given six months' pay and a generous parting gift of £2,000 (roughly £165,000 in today's money). His career had shown how reluctant the bank could be to part with a covenanted officer, but also how ruthlessly it would drop any senior officer perceived as reckless or negligent. Especially, as in Gibson's case, where the record had suggested once too often that he was not really a pukka Chartered man.

2. GWYTHER ON GUARD

Howard Gwyther was showered with plaudits in April 1892 'on the occasion', as the inscription had it on a silver plaque presented by the home and foreign staffs, 'of his retiring from the active management of the

Chartered Bank'.[29] This turned out to be an overstatement. Some things changed in Hatton Court that year. Charles Mullins, the Secretary since 1869 and a bachelor regularly described as married to the bank, died suddenly in January – as an exceptional token of appreciation for his twenty-three years of service, the Directors granted an annual pension to his sister, with whom he had always shared his home[30] – and the Manager's desk passed to a new incumbent, the former Inspector Tom Forrest. But Gwyther's right-hand man since 1875, his fellow Welshman Caleb Lewis, remained at his post as Head Office Accountant; and it was soon apparent that Gwyther himself intended to remain a scarcely less active presence at Hatton Court than for the past twenty years, while delegating to Forrest most of the onerous paperwork that had multiplied with the growth of the bank. Gwyther had earned a fine reputation in the City.[31] No one now expected his influence to wane on the bank's Court, where the line-up in 1892 remained unchanged and where he had already been dominant for five years. Four businessmen with Eastern links and a High Court judge from Calcutta had joined it in the 1880s, but three of the City men appointed in the aftermath of Thomas Mitchell's dramatic departure in 1871 had shown a remarkable staying power: the Chairman elected in 1874, William Paterson (no relation to the Standard's John Paterson) was still in place, as were William Christian and Emile Levita.* What came as a surprise to many was the extent to which Gwyther also continued after 1892 to hold sway over the executive management of the bank – and the same deeply cautious policies he had pursued since the 1870s remained entrenched.

Few needed persuading of the need for caution in the early 1890s. While depressed trading conditions in the East and all the horrendous complications attending the decline in the value of silver were precipitating the collapse of long-established competitors like the Chartered Mercantile Bank and the New Oriental, the London money markets were going

---

* Levita (1826–1909) was a German-Jewish financier who had settled in London in the 1850s and joined the Court in 1872. He had four sons, the eldest of whom, Arthur, became a partner in the stockbroking firm of Panmure Gordon & Co., which had its head office almost adjacent to the Chartered Bank's in Hatton Court. Notwithstanding its location, Panmure Gordon had formed a close alliance by the 1890s with the Hongkong and Shanghai Bank: the senior partner in Arthur Levita's day was Ewen Allan Cameron, whose father was Sir Ewen Cameron, a close contemporary of Emile Levita's and the head of the Hongkong Bank's London office from 1890 to 1905. Perhaps it amused Emile Levita and Sir Ewen, as directors of the two great Eastern banking rivals, that their two eldest sons were partners together in the City. (In 1930 Arthur's daughter Enid married Ewen Allan Cameron's son, another Ewen, who by then had also become a partner in the broking firm. Enid and Ewen's only son, Ian, was to be not only senior partner of Panmure Gordon but the father of a Prime Minister.)

through their own banking crisis. The Chartered Bank was one of many required to earmark a sizeable figure each year as their contribution to a fund organized by the Bank of England to stave off a catastrophic collapse of Baring Brothers, one of the grandest names in the City, at the end of 1890.[32] (It remained a contingent liability until 1895. Barings had by then been restored to health – a happier sequel than would follow its second sudden collapse a century later.) The Chartered had its own troubles, too. In particular, a scandal had emerged in Calcutta, where it was discovered in April 1890 that the Indian Head Cashier – aided and abetted by his son and probably several junior clerks on his staff – had been embezzling huge sums for years to bankroll speculative trades in opium and Government securities. Confronted by the Agent with evidence of the scam, Shama Churn Sen had made a clean breast of the whole business and been indicted for criminal breach of trust. (To the dismay of every bank in India, the judge had gravely misdirected the jury at the end of a thirteen-day trial and the self-confessed embezzler had been acquitted.[33]) The episode had been a stark reminder of how much Chartered Bank necessarily relied upon the good faith of hundreds of indigenous staff in the East, whose labours were not always scrutinized daily, and it prompted a little more caution: the Head Cashier's post in each branch was no longer to be automatically awarded to the senior local employee, as hitherto. It also prompted some embarrassing write-offs. Even after £50,000 had been set aside in 1890, another £35,000 was needed the following year, which reduced 1891's net profits by almost a third and left them barely sufficient to cover the annual dividend.[34] It stayed barely covered in 1892 – and the bank's share price, which had begun to rise encouragingly in 1888–90 and had even passed the £30 mark before the Barings crisis, slipped back into the £18–£24 range recorded almost every year since the late 1870s.

Here were grounds, the Court of Directors agreed, not for questioning the bank's solidity but for clinging gratefully to the conservatism that Gwyther had always expounded and that – notwithstanding setbacks like the scam in Calcutta – had ensured its survival. Given the increased scale and complexity of the Eastern operations, it was striking how little the bank had deviated over the years from its essential principles and procedures. Managers, Accountants and Sub-Accountants were called upon to follow the elaborate guidelines laid down by Hatton Court, applying them in practice at their own discretion on the understanding that any departure from standard practice would be notified to Head Office in writing at the first opportunity. Nor, indeed, had the bank strayed far from the pay scales of an earlier era, as the four most senior department heads in

Hatton Court had recently pointed out in a carefully crafted letter to Gwyther:

> We venture to submit that at the time when the limit of salaries was fixed at £300, such an extension of the Bank's operations as has taken place was scarcely contemplated & that the altered circumstances of the work under our charge, both as to volume & variety, as well as the greater care and anxiety entailed through a vastly-increased and changing staff, have enhanced the value of our services, and justify us in asking for a substantial addition to our present emolument.[35]

This was a break with the past that Gwyther seems to have conceded readily enough, to judge by the absence of further submissions in the archive; but few details have survived of the bank's remuneration structure in these years (or indeed of Gwyther's own salary). Elsewhere, he held the line as fastidiously as ever. The Chartered Bank would aim to do as well, or slightly better, as any competitor in all its existing territories; but nowhere would the bank push for an aggressive expansion of its market position. (There would certainly be no challenging the tacit agreement with the Chartered's peers in Australasia – by now accounting for almost two-thirds of all Britain's overseas banking branches – that neither side would encroach upon the other's turf.*) The Eastern network would be kept to a practical minimum, with a dozen or so large branches closely aligned to the commerce of the main trading ports, and just a handful of smaller offices. Deposits, at present split more or less equally between the City of London and accounts held locally in the East, would not be actively chased but allowed to grow at a steady pace, as dictated by the needs of loyal customers. A heavy emphasis would be placed on the control of all branch costs, while revenues would be drawn from 'Exchange' business – that is, trade finance and related currency dealings – on the one hand (including 'Indirect Exchange' between branches, as opposed to dealing with London) and 'Local' business on the other. The latter, largely funded out of local deposits to ensure a close match between non-sterling assets and liabilities, would be subject to a super-disciplined approach to safeguarding the security of all loans and overdrafts, with regular physical inspections of all crops and godown contents accepted as collateral. The balance sheet would meanwhile be managed with a constant eye to the

---

* The most important of these were the Union Bank of Australia and the Bank of Australasia, which would eventually combine, in 1951, to form the Australia and New Zealand Bank. Other names included the English, Scottish & Australian Bank (which merged with the Australia and New Zealand Bank in 1969) and the National Bank of New Zealand. None contemplated any move into the world of the Eastern exchange banks.

changing structure of trade finance, with bills of exchange rapidly declining in importance compared to the ever growing use of telegraphic transfers
to move funds between customer accounts. As for the capitalization of
the bank, no additional funds would be sought from shareholders until a
steady accumulation of profits left it with published Reserves at least on
a par with the paid-up capital of £800,000. They stood at £250,000 in
1892 (with just £10,000 salted away in an 'Inner Reserve' that went undisclosed to the public).[36]

There was one other aspect of the bank's traditional conservatism that
Gwyther did his best to uphold, though the changing mood of the 1890s
made it harder by the year. He had always done his best to distance the
bank from any direct entanglement in politics. It was not a wholly unrealistic aspiration. The Chartered had no need to curry favour with
governments, since it had no interest in the market for sovereign lending.
Even providing capital for infrastructural projects like dams and railways
fell outside most definitions of trade finance, the bank's chosen franchise.
As the minutes of the Court put it a few years later, its business 'was commercial rather than financial'.[37] It could leave the world of high finance,
bond issues and syndicated loans to the great merchant banking houses.
Its Court Directors were hardly on a par with the grandees of banks like
Rothschilds and Barings; its typical depositors were modest merchant
firms or frugal Scottish savers, far removed from the kind of investors who
would have an appetite for newly issued international securities. That said,
the Chartered was of course an integral part of the expanding nexus of
trade, informal ties and territorial control with which the British Empire
was asserting itself across much of South and East Asia. Its branch managers invariably figured prominently on city banking associations, often
assuming the chairmanship automatically on being appointed as local
head of the Chartered (as in Calcutta). Gwyther was always careful to
ensure the bank took a seat at the table of any significant lobbying group,
such as the China Association, which was founded in London in 1889.[38]
And, as an old China hand, who had himself witnessed as a young man
the threat to Shanghai in the early 1860s – subdued in the end by General
'Chinese' Gordon and his Ever Victorious Army – Gwyther understood
well enough the reliance of all British interests in the East on their ability to fall back, ultimately, on armed intervention by the forces of the
Crown (a lesson underscored before the end of the 1890s by the course of
events in South Africa). More mundanely, he was also attentive at all
times to Hatton Court's working relationship with the Treasury, which
authorized the issuance by the bank of its own notes in the East – and,
indeed, oversaw the periodic renewal of the 1853 Charter by which the

bank was licensed to exist at all. ('Supplemental' charters had been granted in 1861, 1874 and 1884 – and others would follow in 1894 and 1897, and in the new century beyond.[39]) So no significant change of policy by the bank could ever be adopted now without at least informing the appropriate authorities, and no covert approach by Ministers or their officials for assistance could ever be simply disregarded. Nonetheless, it was always Gwyther's conviction that the bank's commercial interests should only in the rarest circumstances be compromised at the behest of any government, in London or the East, and then as little as possible.

His approach was captured perfectly by the saga of the bank's up-country sub-branches in Kuala Lumpur and Taiping. Having set them up in 1888 largely at the request of the Straits government, as part of the Empire's creeping assimilation of the Malay Archipelago, Gwyther decided in March 1895 that both should be closed. They had made no money in six years and, as he himself visited the Colonial Office to explain (according to a subsequent formal letter), 'apart from the convenience to the Government, there is no field for Banking operations'.[40] When news of the bank's intention reached the Straits government in Singapore, it was 'viewed with regret' and the decision was taken to offer a subsidy of $1,200 a year for the Taiping branch. (None was offered for the Kuala Lumpur branch, because officials were said to be 'confident that if the Chartered Bank withdraws its Agency, another financial body will be anxious to take its place'.[41]) That August, in the wake of the 1895 general election in Britain, this highly unusual subsidy was personally sanctioned for a period of six years by the newly installed Colonial Secretary, Joseph Chamberlain, who expressly conveyed to the Court his hope 'that, in consequence of this temporary assistance, the Bank will abandon its intention of retiring from the State [of Perak, where Taiping was located]'.[42] The bank took a full three months to submit its considered answer to this; and when eventually penned, it bore the clear mark of Gwyther's philosophy:

> the Directors . . . have decided to close their office at Taiping on the ground that the expenses there are more than five times as much as the proposed subsidy, having been [running] at the rate of over $6,000 a year for the last four years, while the place offers no field for profitable banking operations of any sort . . . [They] have agreed to take no action at present in the matter of the Agency at Kwala Lumpor in the Selangor state, which will be given a further trial.[43]

The record of this correspondence stops short of the story's denouement – which actually saw neither branch closed, and both complimented for their profitability in later years as the Malay economy boomed – but Gwyther had made his point.*

In reality, of course, no British overseas bank in the 1890s could truly regard itself as wholly detached from the world of politics and international affairs. The very next year, for example, Gwyther appealed directly to the Admiralty in London for the protection of a Royal Navy gunboat off the coast of the Philippines. A serious rebellion against the Spanish government in the islands had prompted rioting that was endangering the mercantile district of the capital, Manila. Gwyther requested (rather grandly) 'that instructions be given to the Admiral on the China Station to afford our Manila Branch special protection in case of need . . . In forwarding this request, I need hardly remind their Lordships that our property at Manila is very important.' He got short shrift from the Admiralty, which tartly replied that 'the Senior Naval Officer at Manila will . . . render such protection to British life and property . . . as the circumstances require and which may in his judgment be practicable'.[44]

The regions in which Chartered Bank sought to prosper were being transformed not just by steamships and telegraphy but also by the 'New Imperialism' that saw European countries engaging in an increasingly fractious competition to assert their power and influence over the undeveloped regions of Asia and Africa. Britain had led the way, with the supremely effective combination – given its overwhelming industrial might – of the Free Trade gospel, shrewd alliances with indigenous elites and a measure of (seaborne) brute force as a last resort. One inevitable consequence was that leading figures in the commercial life of the Empire were increasingly likely to be men engaged with its politics, too. Within the Chartered Bank, this trend was evident in the careers of some new arrivals to the Court. Appointed to it in 1888, Alfred Dent was the head of a great Eastern trading family ('an outstanding example of economic imperialism at work'[45]) that had once enjoyed a name as famous as any in the China trade, before collapsing in 1867. In successfully rebuilding its fortunes since the 1870s, Dent had personified the links between trade and Empire. His founding of the British North Borneo Company in 1882 had paved the way perfectly for the establishment six years later of a British protectorate in North Borneo (today the state of Sabah in East Malaysia), and one of its administrative provinces was duly christened 'Dent'. (One of Dent's closest

---

* His reluctance, on this and other occasions, to see the bank automatically align itself behind official policy surely did not go unremarked in Whitehall. It may have contributed to some notable snubs. It is perhaps relevant to note here that Gwyther never received a knighthood, unlike his counterpart at the Hongkong Bank, Thomas Jackson, or indeed the latter bank's London office manager, Sir Ewen Cameron.

associates was Sir Julian Pauncefote, the most senior official at the Foreign Office through most of the 1880s.) Knighted in 1892, Dent comfortably straddled the worlds of private enterprise and public policy, taking a seat in 1898 on one of the innumerable inquiries into the state of India's currency. Another of Gwyther's colleagues on the Court was Sir James Mackay, later to become the First Earl of Inchcape. A prominent figure in the long-running debate over the future of the silver rupee, Mackay joined the Court in 1894, a year after returning from almost two decades spent in India. He had used a brilliant career as a shipping agent to become one of the Raj's best-connected businessmen, with a leading role in half a dozen industries of the sub-continent from coal to cotton. In the process, he had struck up a firm rapport with the Viceroy from 1888, Lord Lansdowne, who subsequently served as Britain's Secretary of State for War from 1895 until 1900 and as Foreign Secretary thereafter. (Mackay was another of those archetypal Scots who had carved out illustrious careers for themselves by taking the high road out of Scotland at an early age. Addressing pupils of his old school in later life, he would urge them to follow his example: 'There is no scope in Scotland for the energy, the brains, the initiative and the ambition of all the youth in the country . . . if there is no prospect for you here, the sooner you get away the better.'[46])

Men like Dent and Mackay were in the van of a de facto alliance in the late nineteenth century between radical policy-makers and prominent City figures, exponents of what some modern historians have tagged 'gentlemanly capitalism'.[47] They were keen to expand the Empire as a means of extending the benefits of British banking and commerce to every corner of the world, preferably at the expense of empire-minded rivals in other nations. Not so Gwyther: he remained deeply mistrustful of this view of the world, all the more so as letters from the network of branches conveyed the sense of an ever more political environment for many of the bank's operations. His appointment as Chairman in 1896 (when the redoubtable William Paterson at last gave way) cemented his unassailable authority over the Court, and he appears thereafter to have run a kind of private secretariat at Head Office, monitoring all branch reports in parallel with the daily activities of the Secretary's office.[48] There is no surviving evidence of consequent tensions between him and other less cautious members of the Court (though it may be no coincidence that Mackay resigned in 1897, to become a member of the India Council that formally advised the Secretary of State for India*). Serious differences arose, though, between

---

* His place was taken by Henry Gladstone (1852–1935), the third son, and private secretary in his youth, of the great Liberal Prime Minister. Gwyther was no doubt more impressed by

Gwyther and a subordinate in the East for whom the 'gentlemanly capitalist' label might almost have been coined.

Thomas Henderson Whitehead had been appointed Manager of the Hong Kong branch in 1883 at the age of thirty-two. Since 1893, he had in addition taken on overall responsibility for the bank's branches in China, Japan, the Philippines and the Straits Settlements. Whitehead's personal ascendancy in the East was evident not just within the banking world – where he had extensive links to the Chinese business community – but in political circles, too. He took up one of the (unelected) seats on Hong Kong's Legislative Council in 1891, and established himself as one of the leading advocates of political reform in the Colony (by which was meant more self-rule for its British ratepayers). Returning to Britain on a long-postponed furlough in 1894–5, he took with him a petition to Parliament on their behalf, which successfully set in train administrative changes that eventually led to more seats at the Council for unofficial representatives. This earned him a grand formal reception on his return to Hong Kong, which can only have strengthened him in his own scarcely concealed view that politics and banking were but two sides of the same coin. With this conviction, Whitehead had constantly badgered Head Office in recent years to press the Foreign Office for a more assertive policy in China. In the early 1860s, when the treaty port world had been greatly expanded in the aftermath of the Second Opium War and the West had begun to advance its interests all across China in unprecedented ways, Britain had secured the valley of the great Yangzi river as a 'concession' where its influence would be paramount. Yet little had been done by the middle of the 1890s to consolidate the British presence there. This vexed Whitehead, who as a young man had spent the second half of the 1870s on the Yangzi at Hankow. He missed no chance to press the case for more intervention.

By the time he was back at his desk early in 1896, the world of the China treaty ports – and, indeed, of Imperial China as a whole – had been changed for ever. The devastating and wholly unexpected defeat of the Qing dynasty's forces in the Sino-Japanese war of 1894–5 had laid China wide open (or so it seemed at the time) to dismemberment by the colonial powers, among whom the Japanese now aspired to rank themselves alongside Russia, Germany and France as well as Great Britain. In the immediate wake of the war, there was a rush of new business for the bankers. The

---

the fact that for most of the twenty-five years up to 1889 Gladstone had worked in Calcutta and Rangoon as a shipping agent and successful entrepreneur. He had been a Director of the Bank of Bengal since 1886.

Qing needed huge loans to enable them to cope with extortionate reparations demanded by Japan. Unprecedentedly, one of these loans – funded
through a sale of twenty-year bonds in the City, raising the relatively
modest sum of £1 million – was formally managed by the Chartered Bank
in London, though its real instigator appears to have been a singularly
unusual City financier, Sir Ernest Cassel.[49] Whitehead had, however, been
instrumental in the completion of this loan, visiting Peking on his way
back to Hong Kong in 1895 to help finalize arrangements for future repayments into the bank's Shanghai branch.[50] No doubt this left him with a
heightened appreciation of the newly competitive nature of foreign banking in China, with state-backed institutions like the Banque de l'Indochine,
the Deutsche-Asiatische Bank and the Yokohama Specie Bank vying for
business on political as well as purely commercial grounds. This was just
one dimension of a gathering tension evident everywhere in China by early
1896, which within two years would erupt into a frenzy of violence leaving
the country '[stripped of] provinces and ports, armies and fleets, riches,
an emperor and a future'.[51] Under the circumstances, perhaps one can
sympathize with Whitehead's dismay at receiving a letter from Gwyther
in May 1896 asking him to surrender his seat on Hong Kong's Legislative
Council, in order to give the bank's affairs his 'undivided attention'. Never
a man to take criticism kindly, Whitehead wrote back a magnificently
bombastic letter, protesting at Gwyther's implication that he may have
been distracted from his duties and combining an assertion of his own
incomparable efficiency with a reminder of his critical importance to the
bank's unending struggle with its greatest rival:

> I pride myself in the Bank's progress, and in addition to possessing an
> exceptionally strong constitution, I have practically an unlimited capacity
> for work . . . [After working from 6am to 6pm every weekday] I still have
> a few spare moments in hand but I only give to the work of the Council the
> time that other men spend lounging about in the Clubs, at entertainments,
> dances, Theatres &c . . . My election to the Council was strenuously
> opposed by [Thomas] Jackson and by all the force and influence of the
> Hongkong Bank which he could bring to bear. My resigning [from the
> Council] would lessen my popularity, usefulness, and power, while it would
> gladden Jackson's heart, more than any other act . . . The only other event
> which could give him greater happiness would be your transferring me to
> some other distant field, where I could not offer them the keen competition
> they now writhe under here.[52]

Unsurprisingly, Gwyther gave way over the Council seat. But on the
far more substantive question of the British government's strategy in China

and the possibility that the bank might try to bring more influence to bear, as Whitehead argued it should, the newly appointed Chairman would have none of it. Whitehead's entreaties seem merely to have left Gwyther increasingly exasperated.* This in part reflected his less bullish view of the prospects for business in China. As he was reported telling a shareholders' meeting in October 1898, 'foreign banks [in China] found their numbers disproportionately large as regarded the requirements of external trade'.[53] Far more importantly, though, Gwyther was watching international developments in the Far East, and especially the naval posturing of the Great Powers, with mounting anxiety. Months earlier, a US fleet had made short work of a squadron of Spanish ships off Manila, in an extension of the Spanish-American War from the Caribbean to the Pacific. But the humiliation of the Spanish had been followed not by a speedy assertion of US power but by the appearance in Manila Bay of other rival fleets, and not just the Royal Navy. German warships had arrived, reminding the world that German troops had seized Tsingtao in eastern China the previous year, and were now preparing to build a new deep-water port there for the Kaiser's Far East naval squadron. Perhaps equally menacing was the novel spectacle of Japanese warships arriving uninvited and intent on signalling their government's changed view of the world since the end of the Sino-Japanese War. Gwyther at that same October 1898 meeting noted the rising assertiveness of the Japanese, which appeared not to have been curbed at all by economic problems at home ('Japan was still passing through a period of crisis induced by national extravagance and industrial over-sanguineness'). Taking stock of the prevailing climate and the potentially dangerous consequences of further empire-building in the region, he had no time at all for wild talk of deploying gunboats in furtherance of British power. Yet this was just what Whitehead seemed to have in mind.

By May 1899 Whitehead was writing from Hong Kong to explain the need to resort to full colonization of the Yangzi valley: 'While there is no

---

* He passed most of them to Tom Forrest, his successor as Head Office Manager. This can only have added to the strain on the gentle and widely liked Forrest, whose workload was already excessive and who had been diagnosed in 1896 as suffering from severe depression. He had to abandon a tour of the East in 1898, after having a nervous breakdown in Ceylon. A local doctor there, finding nothing much organically wrong with him, wrote to Gwyther that his condition 'has probably been induced amongst other causes by too constant application to work, and to want of more exercise and change. I think he should have more relaxation.' (Dr Valentine des Duke to Gwyther, 19 April 1898, LMA: CH03/01/09/181.) Alas, he never got it and died two years later, aged fifty-four. The Manager's responsibilities were then divided between two Joint Managers – initially Caleb Lewis and the Bank's Inspector, William Main – in an arrangement that worked well and was thereafter adopted as the norm.

effective occupation of the Yangtse region there can be no British sphere [of influence] . . . [and] for effective occupation a military force would be absolutely indispensable.' His Chairman responded with a public rejection of 'buccaneering projects' in China, and a measured disavowal of all those in public life who railed against any sign of other European investors stealing a march on British bankers. 'If the money can be procured from foreigners upon a second-class security and a [railway] line made for the benefit of trade, we should be the last to complain.'[54] At the Annual General Meeting of March 1900, Gwyther confessed his dismay at all the talk of constant additions to the Empire, so that trade might follow the flag. It was an impressively prescient analysis:

> If to procure trade we had to embark upon acquisitions in distant parts of the world [said the Chairman], followed by possible embroilment with some of our European rivals, then it was quite clear that we must pause, or [else] obtain a problematical benefit at the risk of weakening our centre, already severely strained by the excessive extent of our [Imperial] borders. One useful lesson taught by the present war was that even England had limitations, and could not without grave peril seek to acquire further territory from the decaying empires of Asia or in the uncivilized regions of Africa.[55]

That 'present war' was the calamitous struggle that had begun six months earlier in South Africa, pitching the British Empire into one of its gravest crises.

3. RHODES, RHODESIA AND A RIVAL

The story of the Standard Bank and the Anglo-Boer War of 1899–1902 is fraught with ironies. Lewis Michell always insisted, even more adamantly than Gwyther, that his bank and its staff had to abstain from any kind of participation in the politics of the day and sprinkled his official correspondence with references to this creed: the few who challenged it were usually dismissed. The good sense of it required little explanation, given the recent history of Anglo-Boer relations and the Standard's ubiquitous presence by the 1890s in all regions but the Orange Free State. The seven hundred or so men who ran its branches comprised 'English' and 'Dutch-speaking' employees in roughly equal measure. They served a similarly mixed customer base, which included not only 'Anglo' traders and businessmen and Afrikaner farmers but the governments of the Cape and the Transvaal, too. (Kruger and many of his closest associates, like their political counterparts in Cape Town, were in addition private clients of the bank.) So the bank had to be above the Anglo-Boer tensions of the day, ready to deal on equal terms with customers of all races – even Jews.* Yet while proclaiming the bank's neutrality, Michell in the 1890s fell utterly under the spell of Cecil Rhodes. The bond between them indirectly but inescapably linked the Standard Bank to the fortunes of the one man, above all others, whose extraordinary ambitions shaped the politics of the decade in southern Africa – and helped in no small way to precipitate the war with which it closed. Of course Michell had little option but to seek at least a cordial relationship with Rhodes: by 1890, as noted already, Rhodes had effective control of the diamond industry through De Beers Consolidated, was at the forefront of City investment in the gold mines of the Rand and was Premier of the Cape Colony. But his ties to Rhodes went far beyond the formal obligations of a bank manager, even towards such an illustrious client. Michell's key role in the drafting of the 1891 Cape Bank Act displayed a grasp of the broader issues facing the colony that greatly impressed Rhodes; his assistance with a wide range of personal matters since that first dramatic meeting in 1888 had inspired Rhodes's confidence in his grasp of detail. The outcome was a rapport between them that grew steadily closer through the first half of the 1890s. It was nowhere more vividly displayed than in the ready support that Michell offered Rhodes for his audacious campaign to extend the Empire far beyond the northern borders of South Africa.

The vehicle established by Rhodes for this extraordinary venture was the British South Africa Company, commonly referred to as the Chartered Company because it had secured in 1889 a Royal Charter from the Crown to cover its territorial ambitions. Parading its own private army like the East India Company of old, the Company in 1890 moved north of the Limpopo river and into the tribal lands of the Mashona. In June of that year it ran up the flag at a camp christened Fort Salisbury. Pioneer settlers and a telegraph line were in place within eighteen months, and Rhodes turned to the Standard Bank for help in building the new colony, soon to be known as Rhodesia. The episode has often been recounted, whereby in 1892 Michell breakfasted with him at his Groote Schuur estate, in the

---

* Michell, like so many of his contemporaries, was guilty of a casual anti-Semitism: 'Our customers are no doubt Hebraic and to that extent objectionable', he wrote to a new Sub-Manager at Kimberley in 1887, congratulating him on his appointment, 'but on the whole they are a thoroughly business-like lot and the Bank that treats them best will receive their support.' (Michell to W. Smart, 26 September 1887, ARCH 2/5/Michell.) Posterity's view of this would have amazed Michell no less than the emancipation of the black peoples of southern Africa, whose subservient status he – like almost all his contemporaries – took for granted.

hills above Cape Town, then accompanied him down to the telegraph office in the city where the line to Salisbury was cleared so that the banker could talk at length with Rhodes's right-hand man in the territory, a Dr Jameson.[56] The upshot of the discussion was Michell's decision to open a branch of the Standard in Salisbury a few months later. (The London Board had left the issue, like most other matters of any real importance, entirely to Michell's discretion.) This was the start of the Standard's expansion beyond the northern borders of present-day South Africa. Through 1893 the bank provided critical funding for the Chartered Company in a ruthless war against the tribes of the neighbouring Matabeleland, by which Rhodes greatly enlarged his new fiefdom. A second township was begun at Bulawayo – and another branch of the Standard Bank followed in short order. (Business was conducted for its first three weeks out of the bell tent depicted in Plate 8.) Pioneering settlements, railways and more armed incursions carried forward, over the years that followed, Rhodes's vision of a great British dominion across the southern continent. In close support went the Standard's men with their gold and silver specie, their code-books and ledgers, their account books and their banknotes.

Within the borders of South Africa itself, meanwhile, other momentous changes were underway, as gold production on the Witwatersrand gathered pace. The country was growing faster than ever before, and its economy was being radically reshaped. Both phenomena were reflected in the Standard's own numbers. By the middle of 1895, as compared with ten years earlier, its cash assets, loan book and deposits had all more or less doubled; annual profits were running more than twice as high, and the network comprised not sixty but almost eighty branches. Strikingly, the largest of these by far was the Johannesburg branch – and whereas the Transvaal had accounted for less than 10 per cent of its business in 1885, the Boer state now accounted for not too far short of half the bank's income. The gold boom was tilting the whole economy to the north. One result of this for the Standard was a soaring burden of paperwork. As Michell wryly noted in October 1895, fail-safe administrative routines were even more essential now that 'a great and distant mining industry [i.e. distant from Cape Town] has brought us into contact with a class of business and of persons conducting that business that may be fairly described as extra hazardous'.[57] A second consequence was a surge of competition for banking business. The few small Cape banks that remained in existence after the mergers of the past lacked the capital to exert much of a presence in Johannesburg, but there were some significant new arrivals. As noted already, City of London investors in 1890 had put up the capital for one, the African Banking Corporation, which a year later had launched itself into the country – rather as the Standard itself had done almost thirty years earlier – by scooping up a cluster of struggling local banks. Some of the Randlords themselves had decided to go into the banking business, rather than rely on third parties: Barney Barnato and J. B. Robinson had both rolled out banks of their own, withdrawing their business from the Standard in the process. One other new entrant was potentially the most significant of them all. The Boer rulers of the South African Republic, flush with a novel sense of prosperity, had created their own 'National Bank of the SAR' in 1891. They retained a 10 per cent slice of its equity for the government and devised banking rules for the Republic that would ensure the National a weighty home advantage in Johannesburg. 'We are going through the fire of <u>severe</u> competition in South Africa,' wrote Michell to Ross in August 1895, 'all the other banks are waking up and challenging our supremacy and we are in for a stiff struggle.'[58]

Here was yet another reason for the Standard to guard very carefully a relationship with Rhodes that was now crucial to the bank in several different spheres. By late 1895, Michell had already been working for him in a quasi-personal capacity for three years, having agreed in October 1892 to exercise a General Power of Attorney for him during his absences from Cape Town (and occasional bouts of illness). 'Mr Rhodes pressed the matter strongly' as Michell had explained to one of the Directors at the time, 'and I was reluctant to offend a man who . . . comes into contact with the Bank at so many points. He was at one point no friend of ours but has latterly come round and it seems good policy to stand well with him.' It seemed even better policy by the middle of the decade, with the bank under genuine pressure from competitors for the first time since the 1860s. Just how important Rhodes was to the bank, Michell had occasion to point out rather graphically in a letter to Hugh Cameron Ross towards the end of 1895. A retiring High Commissioner, ennobled as Lord Loch and duly appointed to the Standard's Board, had returned to England some months earlier leaving an extremely awkward legacy behind him:

> Certain large shareholders in the Chartered Co. and the De Beers Co . . . are at a white heat of indignation against Lord Loch who they accuse of . . . [having] worked against the interests of the Co. behind the scenes, <u>and after he became Director of the Bank</u> . . . The complainants have written out to Mr C.J. Rhodes urging him in the strongest terms to remove from the Bank the De Beers account, the Chartered Co's various accounts, the Consolidated Gold Fields a/c and those of all the mining companies it controls. If, in addition to losing the Robinson group of mines and the Barnato Group,

we are also to lose all [these] . . . and the good will of Mr Rhodes, I can
only say that our enemies may not be far out in asserting that our best days
are over.[59]

After talking to Rhodes himself – and discovering that he, too, was 'at
white heat' – Michell feared an ultimatum would soon be presented,
demanding that the Board jettison Lord Loch or face 'a rupture of all
friendly relations', as he explained in an anguished second letter to Ross
at the start of December. He urged at the very least the appointment of a
Rhodes acolyte – perhaps even Rhodes's younger brother – to the Board
as a consoling gesture. But this was dangerous territory, as Michell
obliquely acknowledged. 'The whole affair is distasteful to me and
will be so to you, and I leave it to you to move in it or not, as you may
decide.'[60]

His two outward letters crossed with one from London that landed on
his desk a few days later and confirmed his appointment as the sole General Manager of the bank, with effect from 1 January 1896. Michell
celebrated the start of his new tenure by going to watch England's cricket
XI playing South Africa on a beautiful New Year's Day at the Newlands
ground in Cape Town. How far he let his anxiety over the Loch affair
cloud his thoughts we cannot know – but he received news during the
afternoon that must instantly have consigned it to the past.[61] A telegram
arrived at the ground for him, announcing that Dr Jameson had ridden
into the Transvaal the previous day at the head of several hundred armed
men bent on inciting a general uprising against the Kruger government.
(Kruger had stubbornly resisted all calls on him to give non-Boer foreigners, the 'Uitlanders', the vote and equal status with his Boer burghers.
Jameson envisaged a flocking of the Uitlanders to his standard.) The coup
never happened – which came as no surprise to Michell, who thought the
whole scheme completely hare-brained – and the 'Jameson Raid' ended
ignominiously two days later with a handful of the raiders dead and the
rest behind prison bars in Pretoria. But there were tense days in Johannesburg before the farcical nature of the episode was entirely clear.
Through the crisis, the Standard conducted its business in the Republic
much as it had done in the weeks of the short 1880–81 War, standing back
from events in the street, while treating SAR officials and military men
with the utmost courtesy. (In the Johannesburg branch, where sandbag
barricades were hastily erected, tellers were given revolvers to protect
themselves, but Michell ruled out any distribution of rifles, which he
believed 'might justly be construed by the Government as a hostile step'.[62])
In the months that followed, it took extensive negotiations – and some

hefty payments from Rhodes, via the Standard Bank – to secure the release of Jameson and his men, along with a number of Johannesburg residents arrested on suspicion of conspiring with them.[63] But when the manager of the Johannesburg branch was asked to accompany various city worthies to Pretoria, to plead for clemency on the prisoners' behalf, he declined to do so for fear of transgressing the bank's 'no-politics' rule.[64] Michell himself, meanwhile, had had to take a hand in ensuring the release of one of the raiders – his own eldest son, Bentley, who had ridden with them as a corporal in the Mashonaland police force, and had actually been the man with the white flag who surrendered Jameson's force to a Boer commando.*

The growing dilemma posed for Michell by Anglo-Boer tensions soon threatened to cause him more than a passing family embarrassment. Rhodes lost the support of Afrikaners in the Cape with whom he had previously sustained a crucial political alliance, and with it his premiership. He seemed, briefly, to have been ruined by the Jameson fiasco. He nonetheless retained Michell's complete confidence. Indeed, Michell's personal allegiance grew steadily more intense through 1896 as he watched Rhodes gradually restoring his position – and the resources of the Standard Bank played no small part in securing the final resolution of a nasty war in Rhodesia. ('I hope you are satisfied that during the war the Bank did its best for the Company', wrote Michell to Rhodes in January 1897, 'but I can assure you it was not easy to lay down sufficient funds for charter requirements while communications were so interrupted.'[65]) One of Rhodes's motives for the founding of Rhodesia in the first place had been his desire to encircle the recalcitrant Boers of the Transvaal and so to work for the day when Kruger and all his supporters might be brushed aside in a great consolidation of the Empire in southern Africa. The arrival in Cape Town of a sympathetic new British High Commissioner, Sir Alfred Milner, helped Rhodes rebuild his political support in the Cape and added momentum to his broader campaign against Kruger. It seemed to most contemporaries increasingly likely to lead to troubles far more serious than the Jameson Raid. If this ever caused Michell any serious misgivings, they were more than outweighed by the banker's personal admiration for Rhodes, whom he regarded – idolized would hardly be too strong a word – as by far the greatest figure of his day. This led in 1897 to a decision that would be fateful for the Standard's future. The two men spent several days

---

* After his release, Bentley Michell signed up as a Trooper to fight in the Second Matabele War that saw widespread violence across much of the territories designated as Rhodesia in 1896–7. He was killed in a skirmish in Mashonaland in June 1896 at the age of twenty-four.

together, travelling in the bush country of Rhodesia and talking together over late-night camp fires. According to Michell's own account, Rhodes confided many secrets of his life that he disclosed to very few other men. Before the trip was over, Rhodes had extracted a firm promise that, in the event of his death, Michell would leave his post at the bank to act as executor of Rhodes's estate and take charge of his business empire as the head of De Beers Consolidated.[66]

For the next two years, Michell did his best to believe that Anglo-Boer difficulties in the Transvaal could be peacefully resolved, even while Rhodes furiously lobbied and connived to fuel a mounting crisis over Kruger's treatment of British interests within the SAR. Illusions were jarring with an ugly reality, and Michell's regular public protestations of neutrality for the bank, however sincerely felt, were now less than wholly consistent with his fulsome private support for Rhodes the arch-imperialist:

> I have been with the Bank for 26 years at a stretch and I can see clearly what has kept the country back [he wrote to Rhodes at the start of 1899].
> I believe you are the only man to rise – and teach others to rise – above all our little sectional jealousies and I should like to have a share, before I die, in your task of <u>lifting</u> South Africa out of its <u>littleness</u> and starting it on a great career. If the time should come when I can be useful to you, I shall not be backward.[67]

When the war finally came, in October 1899, the Standard Bank faced an acute dilemma. Not knowing how long hostilities might continue, and keen if possible to retain the confidence of both sides within the Boer republics as they had largely managed to do in 1880–81, Michell and his managers made every effort at the outset to pretend business would soon be resumed as normal. But the intensity of the fighting – and the seizure of bank assets by the Boers on a scale without precedent – soon made clear this was a forlorn hope.* The Directors in London thoughtfully sent Michell 'an extract, prepared by the Bank's Solicitors, relating to the

---

* The four British banks in Pretoria lost £265,000 in March 1900 when Kruger's government seized all the gold coins they could find, most of them (worth £150,000) from the Standard Bank. The SAR offered to deposit gold bullion of equivalent value, by way of promising repayment after the hostilities ended, but the banks were persuaded by Milner to reject this, on the grounds that it would compromise their claim for repayment by the British once the Transvaal had been re-annexed. When that day came, however, the Imperial Government turned its back on the banks, triggering a bitter correspondence that dragged on for three years. (George Amphlett felt so strongly about it that he appended the full text of the correspondence to his 1914 history, see *History of the Standard Bank*, pp. 207–51.) In support of its campaign in London, the Standard lobbied all of the overseas banks – including the Chartered Bank (see LMA: CH03/01/09/212).

English law of Treason . . . so as to avoid [the bank] rendering any aid to the Queen's enemies'; and after three months of alarming setbacks for British arms in the Cape, letters from the Home Office were being read out at the Board 'having reference to the illegality of trading with the Government of the Transvaal or the Orange Free State or with persons resident in those territories'.[68] The bank had effectively to curtail all its activities in the Transvaal, where mining on the Rand had anyway been halted. Only after British troops had overrun the two Boer republics, in the course of 1900, did the Standard return: it reopened its branches in both and seemed briefly to be prospering as never before. Certainly the chaos in the Transvaal had wiped out some profits, but this loss was more than matched by the huge sums being earned by the bank in facilitating the import of arms and supplies for the British army – along with substantial fees paid for the bank's agency services in getting cash to the troops.[69]

Having recovered from their initial alarm, the Directors in London watched their deposits and profits soaring, and seemed content to regard the war almost as an off-stage disturbance. (Remarkably, given the British public's feverish excitement over every item of news from South Africa at the time, the word 'Boer' is nowhere to be found in the Board's minutes from start to finish of the war.) But an ominous cable arrived in Clements Lane from Michell in January 1901: 'Posts much deranged and uneasy feeling owing arrival in Colony of fresh commandos. Both banks closed [in] Cradock.'[70] Here was the beginning of a third stage to the war – and Michell was right to be uneasy. In adopting the tactics of a guerrilla campaign against British troops across much of the Cape, the Boers put intense pressure on the Standard Bank as an institution that sought to serve the whole community without distinguishing one side from the other. Many branches were subjected to temporary closure; around 15 per cent of the staff were reported sick from one month to the next; and many individual employees were swept up in the fighting, some joining Boer commandos and others enlisting as British soldiers or local garrison guards.[71] Standard managers were still enjoined to think of the bank as a neutral party – but with wide areas of the country plunged into what was essentially a civil war by the middle of 1901, this stance was in many places barely tenable. In reality, the Standard was now uncompromisingly aligned behind the Imperial Government. Indeed, Michell himself was drawn into a series of important roles: these included serving on a body set up in the Cape to adjudicate on the application of martial law in civilian cases, as well as working as a financial adviser to the British authorities in the re-occupied Boer republics. (He was offered, but declined, at least one government appointment, as Agent General to South Africa.[72]) More fundamentally,

the bank took up much of the strain in providing for the financial requirements both of the British army's Paymaster General and of the Cape
Colony's government at the height of the crisis. This triggered considerable
friction between the Directors, who rather bizarrely ruled against further
advances to the Cape Colony, and Michell who saw no practical alternative but to keep lending whatever was needed. He testily explained why
in a telegram early in 1902:

> General Manager warns Board of Directors any refusal meet temporary
> requirements of Government Cape Colony means loss entire connection.
> Prime Minister Cape Colony already suggesting transfer account Cape
> Government to Bank of Africa Ltd. General Manager requests explicit
> instructions if under the circumstances he is to dishonour cheques Treasury
> Cape Colony presented over counter. Wire reply – very urgent.[73]

The hopelessly inappropriate caution of the Board – not to say its egregious naivety – was about to be tested on a more continuous basis. Cecil
Rhodes died of heart failure on 26 March. Before the end of April, true
to his promise, Michell tendered his resignation from the bank in preparation for taking up his responsibilities for Rhodes's vast estate.* Whether
he would otherwise have remained at his post is hard to say – his sixtieth
birthday was just a few months away – but given his recent rejection of a
position in government, it seems likely he would have stayed at least
through the aftermath of the war.[74] By an unhappy chance, Hugh Cameron Ross had just died, at the beginning of February. For the first time
since Robert Stewart's death in 1885, the Board in London now included
no members with any personal experience of the Cape, not even a former
High Commissioner. Its eight Directors were mostly retired Whitehall
mandarins. In their time they had run, among other stalwart institutions,
the Treasury, the Royal Mint and the Post Office – but nothing remotely
akin to the Standard Bank.† This odd state of affairs would prevail for
most of the next decade or so, with vacant seats usually going to MPs or

---

* He served as Chairman of De Beers Consolidated until 1905 and as a Director of the
Chartered Company until his death in 1928. He was also knighted and elected to the legislative assembly of Cape Colony, as the member for Cape Town, before the end of 1902. Two
years later, he was appointed a minister without portfolio in a new government – formed by
Dr Jameson. Michell's entry in the *Dictionary of South African Biography* (Vol. I) records
that 'he was never an enthusiastic politician . . . [and] kept himself and the Standard Bank
clear of controversial politics throughout a period when this was seldom easy'. In some
respects, of course, he also aligned the bank very shrewdly with the consensus politics of
his day.
† Lord Welby (appointed in 1897) had been Permanent Secretary at the Treasury 1885–94;
Sir Charles Fremantle (appointed 1898) had been head ('Deputy Master') of the Royal Mint,

ageing City gents, while much of the daily decision-making rested with a staff of more than seventy clerks in Clements Lane under a London Manager, William Smart, who had been appointed in 1900 after twenty-five years' experience in South Africa.[75] Michell's responsibilities in Cape Town were henceforth shared again between two Joint General Managers, Shelton Corbett and Hector Mackenzie – the latter would become sole General Manager in 1914 on Corbett's retirement – but none of his successors, not even Mackenzie who held sway until 1919, had the judgment or the personal authority that had made Michell such a formidable character over so many years. The result was a sudden loss of leadership for the Standard, within months of the war coming to a close at the end of May 1902. Back in 1885, immediately after the disappointment of hearing he was not needed in London, Michell had warned in a letter to Ross that, sooner or later, the Board 'will discover that slighting the General Managers by placing mere [London] clerks over them will bear bitter fruit'.[76] In the years that followed his departure, this bleak prophecy was to be fulfilled.

When the fighting was over, the Boer republics had been annexed by the Crown and no semblance of a threat remained to the strategic interests of the Empire. On the other hand, Rhodes was gone, the Boer republics had retained their self-governance, and the prospect of any renewed military action against them had vanished. Attempts by Milner as High Commissioner to forge a 'British South Africa' that would marginalize all vestiges of Afrikaner nationalism had failed by 1905. His departure (and the advent of a radical Liberal government at Westminster, inclined to let South Africa decide its own destiny) augured a new era. The country's politicians returned to the idea of a union between its four different territories – but now in a spirit far removed from the imperialist vision pushed by Rhodes and Milner. The impetus was provided not by leaders of the 'English party' but by moderate Afrikaners in the Transvaal and the Cape, led by Louis Botha and J. C. Smuts, and it was their vision of the future, not Britain's, that essentially shaped the Union of South Africa that emerged in 1910. This paradoxical political outcome of the war was mirrored in the banking world. After British forces had occupied the Transvaal and the Orange Free State in 1900, the Standard Bank had reopened its doors in both former republics while ramping up its services in aid of the Empire across the Cape Colony and Natal. At that point, the bank's position in South Africa had seemed virtually unassailable – and

---

1870–94; and Sir Spencer Walpole (appointed 1898) had been head ('Secretary') of the Post Office, 1893–9.

by the end of 1902, it could be seen that the war had brought it a massive windfall, all but doubling the size of its balance sheet from £16 million in 1898 to just over £31 million. Yet when the young Union of South Africa turned in 1912 to appointing a bank as holder of its government account, the General Manager of the Standard was only summoned to Pretoria to be told the mandate had gone elsewhere.

It went to the institution set up by Kruger's government in 1891, the National Bank of the SAR, which had engineered a dramatic restoration of its fortunes after coming close to collapse early in the war. The National Bank had flourished in the 1890s, competing against not just the Standard but two other imperial banks as well, the Bank of Africa and the African Banking Corporation. It had gained ground successfully with many of the newly arrived companies in booming Johannesburg, as the favoured local bank with an appetite for long-term loans.[77] (Cecil Rhodes had never enjoyed the dominant status in Johannesburg that he had achieved in Kimberley, and nor did the Standard Bank.) The National's links with powerful vested interests in the mining community probably saved it from disaster in 1900, when the Kruger government was toppled and the bank had to close its doors. The new British authorities treated it leniently, and it emerged from cold storage in 1902 with a new capital structure, a new name – the National Bank of South Africa – and a highly ambitious team of directors and managers. (Its general manager, Thomas Henderson, was the man who had been responsible for the Standard's Johannesburg losses in 1890, which Michell always described as the Standard's biggest ever setback.) Its new registration as a colonial bank now allowed it to expand its branch network across the whole country, but the Witwatersrand mines still provided the National's core business and by 1909 it was shipping more gold out of the Transvaal for its customers than was the Standard Bank.[78] South Africa's post-war economy was blighted by a severe recession from 1903 to 1909, but this hit the Cape-oriented Standard much harder than the National. (Net profits fell steadily at the Standard, and failed to cover the cost of its dividends in 1908.) The implications appear not to have been fully grasped by the Directors in London, whose instructions to Cape Town through these years were in general deeply cautious and often damagingly hesitant: 'in the face of the looming threat from the Transvaal bank, the Directors in London confined themselves to exhortations to local branch managers to secure more business'.[79] There was no longer a Lewis Michell in the Cape to override their innate conservatism and the Standard's profile suffered accordingly. Perhaps another factor was also at work: it must be a matter of conjecture how far residual post-war feelings of sympathy for the Boer cause might have coloured views of the imperial Standard Bank. For those who worked in the bank, its South African character was hardly in doubt.* But to some outsiders, its City provenance may still have rankled. It is evident that the idea of a locally owned national bank for the country evoked at least some measure of support among many Afrikaans-speaking South Africans. Year by year, the Standard's long-held pre-eminence in the marketplace began to fade.

The process accelerated dramatically in 1910–14. It had always been Michell's contention that the Standard would never have managed to acquire the London & South African Bank in 1879 had not Robert Stewart been in London to push through the transaction.[80] When the opportunity now arose for another round of bank mergers, the Board again dithered in its approach to negotiations, this time fatally. Early in 1910, the National Bank outbid the Standard and acquired the main local bank in the Orange Free State. Discreetly backed by government ministers in Pretoria who were keen to endorse its ambitions, the National then stepped ahead of the Standard a second time and in 1912 reversed the course of banking history in the country by taking over an imperial bank: it acquired the Bank of Africa. In fact only Board objections in London blocked the National from taking over the African Banking Corporation, too – and the latter's shaken directors were soon talking to their counterparts at the Standard, though their discussions made little immediate progress. Then, exactly two years after its move into the Free State, the National in June 1914 bought out the shareholders of the Bank of Natal, which Michell had been prevented by his Directors from buying for the Standard in 1896. In the space of four years, the National Bank had thus acquired top billing in three of the country's four provinces, had quadrupled its staff to 1,800 men (slightly more than the Standard's) and had accumulated the largest branch network in the country. By most measures it was suddenly as big an institution as its imperial rival. If the Standard still enjoyed 'the confidence of the whole country', as Stewart had once proudly proclaimed, it seemed it would now have to share that confidence with the National Bank.

---

* To illustrate this point, it is worth noting here that furlough on half-pay had long ago ceased to require that an employee return to Britain. So many of the staff were born in South Africa that the original terms of 'home leave' as laid down in the 1860s would have made no sense. The General Manager had therefore been given discretionary authority to award half-pay on furlough even though 'Colonial-born managers' would be spending their leave in South Africa. It is curious, however, to see how late in the day this approach was extended to all staff. A Board Minute noted only in 1902 that henceforth the revised furlough policy 'was extended to cover senior officers [i.e. British-born staff] as well as Colonial managers' (Minutes of the Standard Bank Board, 28 October 1902, SCB Archives, Box 1189, Vol. 10).

4. 'PIGTAIL LONDON'

By 1914, the fortunes of the Chartered had waxed as the Standard's had waned. The resilient but often beleaguered Eastern exchange bank of the Victorian era had emerged since the late 1890s as one of the City of London's foremost overseas banks (international cable address: 'Pigtail London'*). For reasons that contemporaries found a little elusive – though they noted a useful shrivelling of the bad debts provision – the year 1897 saw a sea change in the bank's profitability. At just over £89,000, net profits in 1896 were very close to the average for the previous five years. The next year, profits jumped to £160,725 and this marked a new baseline for the growth that followed (setting aside 1899, when the start of the South African war triggered heavy losses in the London money markets and was estimated to have cost the Chartered a quarter of its profits[81]). With general prices roughly stable from one year to the next, record earnings were a regular feature of the period from 1900 to 1913, which closed with £350,000 of published net profits for 1913. The profit numbers actually understated the bank's heady progress: published profits after 1896 were usually struck after 15–20 per cent (occasionally much more) had been deducted and squirrelled away to the Inner Reserves. By the end of 1913, the latter had grown to £454,000. Meanwhile the Published Reserves had accumulated at a stately pace, up to £1.8 million, and deposits held by the bank had almost doubled in value since 1900. Of the twenty or so comparable British overseas banks, only three were still larger than the Chartered in 1913 (the London & River Plate Bank, the Hongkong & Shanghai Bank and the Standard Bank).[82] Acknowledging the breakthrough, investors on the London stock market had finally put nearly forty years of scepticism behind them, driving the price of the Chartered's shares up to a new level, around £60.

The big surge started under Howard Gwyther's chairmanship (1896–1904) and unquestionably owed much to the procedures inculcated by him. It also coincided, though, with a profound evolution of the

---

* This needed changing after the Chinese Revolution. A cable was received from the Hong Kong office at the end of 1911, explaining that the entire Chinese staff had lopped off their pigtails overnight as a gesture of support for the new republic declared by Sun Yat-sen in Canton. The moment was recorded in a 1951 Memoir by A. A. Ritchie: 'The Compradore and some of the older members of the Chinese staff were still in Chinese costume but not a queue was left. Some were clad in odd lots of European dress & the Bullion Shroff had acquired an Astrakhan Coat and Bowler hat!' (LMA: CH03/01/14/019.) After a hasty assessment of the news, the bank's cable address was altered to 'Pagoda London'.

Chartered's business that gathered momentum quickly after Gwyther's final retirement. As the currencies of the East shifted one by one into line with the Gold Standard, the margins to be earned by exchanging them with the pound narrowed sharply. At the same time, clients' trade payments in the new century came to rely increasingly upon telegraphic transfers rather than bills of exchange despatched through the mail. Both trends ate into the revenues of the bank, and might once have been viewed with consternation. Not now. They were almost technicalities when set beside the sheer scale of what was happening on the trade routes serviced by the Chartered. Long familiar exports of the East were soaring. Expanding world markets for cotton, tea, jute and a score of lesser primary commodities from copra and coconuts to cinnamon and plumbago lifted the value of India's total exports from £71 million in 1893–4 to £164 million in 1912–13 (earning the surplus required to pay for all the manufactured goods it was obliged to import from Britain).[83] Government officials across the wider region all produced their own versions of much the same story, tabulating impressive export statistics boosted by the rising Western demand for south-east Asia's staple crops. And their tables now had to accommodate a few new products, too, that had not featured at all before the 1890s. Rising shipments of smelted tin from the nascent Federated Malay States were not the only item in this exciting category.

One of the foreign trading concerns established in the Japanese port of Yokohama in the 1880s was a Jewish family business run by two brothers, Sam Samuel, who spent most of his time in Japan, and his brother Marcus, who was based in London's East End. Chartered Bank, having opened up in Yokohama in 1881, helped them to ship out manufactured goods from Britain such as mechanical textile looms, vital to Meiji Japan's breakneck rate of industrialization, and to import in exchange assorted oriental goods including – as a slightly bizarre but very successful novelty line inherited from the Samuels' father, the founder of the business – knick-knack boxes covered with sea shells.[84] In 1891, Marcus Samuel seized an opportunity to launch an extraordinarily bold venture, shipping Russian kerosene from the Black Sea to Singapore and all points east. As a distillate from crude oil, kerosene ('paraffin' in Britain) was used as the fuel for lamps that burned brighter than any previous light. Its popularity had grown enormously in the US over the past twenty years, driven on by the marketing might of John D. Rockefeller's Standard Oil. Although sales in the East, and especially Japan, were potentially vast, kerosene in 1891 was still being shipped out in wooden casks and Standard Oil had as yet made no inroads into the market. Samuel conceived the idea of transporting the fuel in specially designed ships – 'tankers' – and secured permission (in the face of some initial opposition) for these slightly alarming cargoes to use the Suez Canal. He also needed agreements with wholesalers in the East who could provide him with a distribution network – and here Chartered Bank seems to have played a part. Seven of the bank's best merchant clients in Singapore set up a cartel in 1891 for the handling of all kerosene imports.[85] No records survive of their dealings with M. Samuel & Co. in 1892, when the first of its ships arrived. But they evidently found a basis on which to proceed – and sales of its kerosene soon gave the Chartered's London client a tight grip on the Asian marketplace, much to the dismay of Standard Oil. Deliveries to Japan rose especially rapidly, and saw close ties develop there between Samuel's business and the bank. (One of the principals of Samuel, Samuel & Co. of Yokohama from 1886 to 1900 was a William Foot Mitchell, who after returning to the UK would take a seat on the Chartered's Court, which he held from 1910 to 1938.[86]) Notwithstanding its general avoidance of sovereign bond business, and no doubt urged on by Whitehead from Hong Kong, the Court agreed to manage a ground-breaking bond issue for Japan in 1897, and this transaction also appears to have involved the Chartered in co-operation with Marcus Samuel.[87] That same year, Samuel overhauled the structure of his entire business, renaming it the Shell Transport and Trading Company. By the early 1900s, petroleum was overtaking kerosene as the principal derivative from crude oil, and Samuel was soon edging his company into comprehensive marketing arrangements with another company selling into the oil markets of the East, Royal Dutch, which had its own crude production from wells in the jungles of Sumatra. The expansion of these two businesses, and their merger as the Royal Dutch/Shell Group in 1907, turned petroleum into one of the region's vital exports and drew the Chartered into a hugely promising new field.*

Another new star of the Asian export sector by 1914 had also had a colourful start. Rubber trees were not indigenous to south-east Asia. They arrived there courtesy of Sir Henry Wickham, a Victorian explorer who snatched 70,000 seeds from the natural home of the 'wild' rubber tree in the Brazilian Amazon. After a brief stopover in Kew's Royal Botanical

---

* Oil production had also begun in Burma, where a syndicate of Scottish investors had founded Burmah Oil in 1886. It began to acquire its own tankers in 1899 in order to ship refined products to India, but otherwise showed no interest at this stage in exporting to world markets. Burma's crude output ran at about half the levels recorded in the Dutch East Indies for the first decade of the century, then began to close the gap. The average output in 42-gallon barrels was 7,009,000 for Burma in 1910–14, compared with 11,329,000 for the Dutch East Indies. Output in the US in these years averaged 233,400,000 (EIU Report, *Oil in South-East Asia*, 1950, LMA/CH03/01/15/024).

Gardens, some of these seeds ended up in Ceylon in the late 1870s and gave rise to the first commercial plantations. (By a curious coincidence, rubber production offered Ceylon an opportunity to fill the gap in its economy created by the collapse of its coffee plantations, which had been devastated by disease in the 1870s and were then effectively stymied in their recovery by being elbowed out of the European market by newly established coffee exporters in Brazil.) With tea prices falling sharply in the 1890s and new industrial uses in prospect for rubber – including its use in pneumatic tyres, patented in 1888 by John Boyd Dunlop (yet another Scotsman) – there were many brave individual planters ready to take a punt on rubber, in Ceylon and wider afield. After the establishment of the Federated Malay States (FMS) in 1895, plantations began spreading quickly on the Western coastal plains of the Malayan peninsula; and within a few years, the first sites were being cleared in Java and Sumatra. But the cultivation of rubber trees proved to be a more costly and time-consuming business than anyone had expected: each new plantation required intensive horticulture, road/rail links and housing for workers, and new trees took several years to begin yielding their precious latex sap. The new wonder crop had made no one's fortune by 1900, when Ceylon recorded the first ever exports of plantation rubber. The first Resident General of the FMS, Sir Frank Swettenham, observed at the time that many planters were in fact in dire straits: 'At around the year 1900, it was charity to give them a good meal.'[88]

The Chartered Bank was no charity, but undoubtedly found itself providing for many cash-starved planters around the turn of the century – and substantially more of them, we can be certain, than was deemed sensible by the Court in London. Many local managers, ready to back their own instincts, had confidence in the long-term prospects for rubber and lent accordingly. This generated a familiar stand-off between them and Head Office, whose lending guidelines tended (as ever) to be regarded by those in the field as a counsel of perfection. Then, in the early years of the new century, the industry took on a new complexion altogether. The world motor industry began to boom, triggering a suddenly insatiable demand for rubber – and for supplies of it that could match exacting technical specifications, which set wild rubber from Brazil at a serious disadvantage. British agency houses took the lead in floating joint-stock rubber companies on the London market, retaining a small slice of the equity for themselves and locking in a management contract. They were then in a position to buy up hundreds of struggling plantations, and to inject the capital that was required. Rubber emerged as one of the great new global industries – and a majority of the newly listed plantation companies had the Chartered as their registered bank. Nonetheless, and perhaps a little surprisingly, circular letters from Head Office went on warning the Branches at regular intervals against advancing loans rather than sticking to the funding of specific export (and exchange) contracts. Indeed, as demand soared and the world market for rubber showed every sign of badly overheating, Head Office's pleas for caution took on a new stridency, as here in 1911:

> The subject has been frequently dealt with, and still it is evident that the Branch Managers have not fully realised the dangers that surround commitments in Rubber . . . Application was made to us here [in London] for an advance against the title Deeds of a Rubber Company, accompanied by a statement that our Agent on the spot would favourably regard the application provided it met with our approval. We strongly disapproved, and immediately telegraphed instructions not to make any advances without our consent. This however proved too late, $17,000 having been advanced in the meantime. The Company have, we gather, expended all their funds, they find it impossible to increase their capital, the shares are at a heavy discount, and our Agent provides $17,000!! Why should he? Further troubles will no doubt arise.[89]

Ostensibly a Circular from the Secretary, the tone of this letter suggests another author, whom we find writing 'to all Rubber zone Branches' a week later. It had now emerged that the aforesaid $17,000 was intended only as the first tranche of a much bigger loan:

> The application is for $60,000 for 'clean-weeding and upkeeping 1000 acres planted' . . . Not only is this proposal advanced in all seriousness, but Head Office approval is anticipated to the extent of $17,000. It is not Banking. It is a means to obviate the necessity on the part of the Directors of the Company for confessing to the shareholders that they have no working capital left to weed the land . . . The danger to the Bank in connection with advances to develop estates, and to market the Rubber, cannot be exaggerated . . . We want to keep the resources of this Bank liquid, and largely available for Exchange business etc, our particular sphere of operation. We cannot look with approval upon any locking up of our funds in the development of Estates, even where there is some assurance of ultimate repayment.[90]

Here again was the unmistakeable voice of Thomas Whitehead – lucidly articulating the case for a strategy wedded to transactional banking rather than capital-devouring loans that would still resonate in the Standard Chartered Bank a century later.

By 1911 Whitehead had already been in London for nine years as one of the Joint Managers. He had arrived at Head Office in 1902, when William Main, like so many long-serving officers from the East, had died suddenly and prematurely.[91] Whitehead's promotion was almost certainly not to everyone's liking. His tempestuous, not to say overbearing, manner – amply reflected in all his correspondence, even including the odd postcard fired off from one capital or another in the course of his travels – irked many of his colleagues. In the autumn of 1901, the Directors had proposed to him that he should move to New York to set up a first branch in the US. This was followed by a personal communication (now lost) from Main, venturing to offer a critique of the way that the Hong Kong branch had been run in recent years. The combined effect of these missives seems to have brought Whitehead close to self-combustion. He replied to Main with another of his astonishing letters – rejecting all criticism, vilifying those whom he suspected of instigating it ('Any person who can lend himself to such a foul and infamous course of action cannot possibly be a friend of the Chartered Bank or myself') and asserting his own towering supremacy over all-comers ('No one in any employ could ever have been, or could be late and early [sic], on all occasions, more hardworking, more painstaking, more zealous, more persistent or more industrious than I have been . . .' and so on, for ten pages).[92] It was also, he pointed out, quite impossible for him to consider going to New York: he rode polo ponies every evening ('without that vigorous and health-giving exercise, I would not be so fit for work as I invariably am') and keeping polo ponies in New York would be totally unaffordable. Matters were thus awkwardly poised when Main dropped dead. Perhaps having no realistic alternative, the Directors turned back to Whitehead, inviting him to leave immediately for London. (The urgency did not preclude a send-off in Hong Kong marked by a public banquet in its City Hall and a string of handsome gifts, including a sizeable statue of Confucius in solid silver, presented by the Chinese bankers and merchants of the Colony.[93])

However intemperate his letters, Whitehead's energy and drive made him a formidable and respected leader, in London as in Hong Kong. Gwyther's chairmanship was not quite over in 1902 – he did not finally retire until 1904 – but a novel commitment to the expansion of the bank's network was evident almost from the moment of Whitehead's installation at Hatton Court. He had himself led the way in the 1890s, when he had enjoyed overall responsibility for the treaty ports of China and for the European settlements in Japan and Indo-China, where the treaty-port model was broadly replicated. He had taken the initiative in opening branches in Kobe (1895), Hankow (1895) and Tientsin (1896).[94] On his intermittent trips home to London, more than once travelling back via Moscow, he had taken every opportunity to meet foreign government ministers, impressing upon them the importance of the Chartered's expanding role in the East. (An exuberant postcard in June 1900 dashed off news for Hatton Court, in typical style, of a meeting he had had with Sergei Witte, the Tsar's Finance Minister since 1890 and the key architect by now of Russia's belated modernization – see Plate 12.) Now he urged the Court ahead with a series of bold decisions. The mooted office in New York was opened in 1902 and a similar operation was soon afterwards launched in Hamburg (1904), the two additions indicating just how quickly the list was growing of prominent American and German merchant firms in the East.* (Standard Bank also opened an agency in Hamburg in 1904, to cater for South Africa's growing trade with Germany, and followed up with a New York agency in 1905.[95]) Other new branches were established in the Philippine port of Cebu (1902), in Saigon (1904) and Karachi (1906). In all three cases, the local banking business generally adhered to the Chartered's proven model, building godowns around the port area and contacts among the shipping and export agents as diligently as ever. But the bank was also ready in some instances – mostly in south-east Asia – to develop more business 'up-country', far from the major ocean ports and a significant step beyond its traditional franchise. This was most conspicuous in the Federated Malay States, where branches were set up in the modest towns of Ipoh (1902), Klang (1909) and Seremban (1910) to service exports of smelted tin. Here again, it might be noted, the Court had to issue regular reminders that transactional banking, not term lending, was the bread and butter of its business. When the Singapore Branch advised in September 1905 that a company called Tronah Mines had sought a loan of £30,000, the Court responded that 'it is not the business of the Bank to advance against mines' – though it authorized a loan of £20,000 before the end of the month, just the same. A year later, in November 1906, Head Office was putting a limit of $200,000 on its aggregate lending to Chinese tin mines.[96]

Between 1902 and 1914 the bank opened fifteen more branches, in effect doubling the size of the network inherited from Gwyther's day. For

---

* New York and Hamburg were of course west of the Cape of Good Hope, in breach of the spirit of the bank's original 1853 Royal Charter. But the latter's wording proscribed 'branches' to the west of the Cape – and the new offices were carefully defined as 'agencies'. Such considerations had to be carefully weighed through periodic charter renewals for another half century, until a permanent 'consolidating Charter' in 1956 effectively removed all the obstacles in the small print. (India, Australia and China were to survive in the title of the bank until finally removed in that same year.)

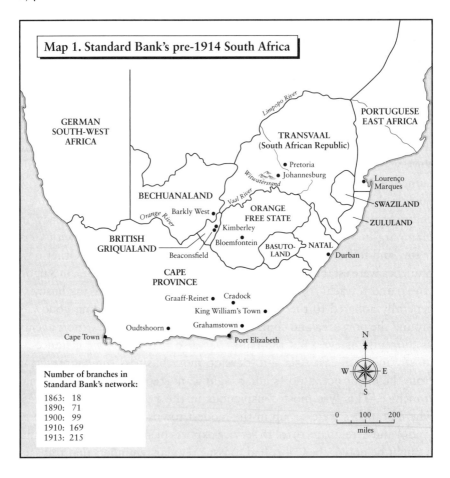

Map 1. Standard Bank's pre-1914 South Africa

GERMAN
SOUTH-WEST
AFRICA

PORTUGUESE
EAST AFRICA

Limpopo River

TRANSVAAL
(South African Republic)

● Pretoria
● Johannesburg
Witwatersrand

● Lourenço
Marques

BECHUANALAND

Vaal River

Orange River

Barkly West ●
● Kimberley

ORANGE
FREE STATE

SWAZILAND

ZULULAND

BRITISH
GRIQUALAND

● Bloemfontein
Beaconsfield

BASUTO-
LAND

NATAL

● Durban

CAPE
PROVINCE

Graaff-Reinet ● Cradock
●
King William's Town ●

Oudtshoorn ● Grahamstown ●

Cape Town   ● Port Elizabeth

N
W — E
S

Number of branches in
Standard Bank's network:
1863: 18
1890: 71
1900: 99
1910: 169
1913: 215

0   100   200
miles

the most part it responded to opportunities already apparent, on the back of what had happened to regional economies opened up by European empire-builders and an unprecedented access to capital. Agricultural output had been transformed, for example, by the re-landscaping of the delta waterways in Burma, Thailand and Vietnam of those three great rivers of south-east Asia, the Irrawaddy, the Chao Phraya and the Mekong. But the Chartered was also readier now than in the past to heed approaches from prospective clients in more remote parts of Asia, as yet scarcely touched by the modern world – none of them more remote than the peninsula of Korea. It was still often referred to by contemporaries as the 'Hermit Kingdom'. Towards the end of 1902, Gwyther heard from the head of one of the bank's largest clients, the German trading concern Mohr Bros & Co., who forwarded a letter from an overseas employee of the Hamburg-based E. Meyer & Co., Carl Wolter, requesting the bank's support. Knowing of the Mohr family's close ties with the Chartered, Wolter had sought their mediation in an enterprising effort to find additional sources of financing for a trading company he was trying to build in the tiny port of Chemulpo (modern day Inchon), on the west coast of the Korean peninsula. The Chartered had apparently been helpful to E. Meyer in Shanghai and Hong Kong in the later 1890s, after an earlier introduction from the Mohr family, and it was Wolter's hope that the bank might do the same for his nascent outpost of the Meyer business:

> Some years ago [Wolter wrote to Mohr] you were good enough to arrange with the Chartered Bank of India, Australia and China that in case of need we [i.e. E. Meyer & Co. in China] might extend our bills by three months, a facility which we have used this year for the first time. Probably I will not make use of it again for some time to come . . . but this is [*sic*] not the case if the crop in Korea is spoiled and there is absolutely no business doing. – At such times I would like to get some aid from a foreign bank and my request is therefore that you will be kind enough to put matters before Mr Gwyther. – What I would like to be able to get is a loan on the goods in our godowns, in the same way as this is done in Shanghai and Hongkong. – Perhaps an arrangement can be made, we giving Kobe a list of goods stored in our godowns with the lowest market values and Kobe allowing us a certain amount against these goods . . . Of course the Bank must trust us to some extent, as they have no representation here, but the Bank has been trusting us for some time [elsewhere] even with big amounts of money, and I believe is well satisfied with the working of the [E. Meyer] Agency at this port.[97]

Notwithstanding the eloquence of Wolter's letter, Gwyther and his colleagues were well aware that Korea in 1902 was a desperately poor country. The only surviving reference to it from earlier bank records is a decision in 1900 to steer clear of a business proposal from the government in Seoul.[98] While canals and railways were opening up other Asian economies, Korea still had scarcely any modern roads into its interior: mule paths linked the towns and villages of an overwhelmingly agrarian society. But in 1901 the Japanese, with fast-growing colonial ambitions of their own, had begun a creeping annexation. They had set up a new currency, 'reorganizing' (in the language of the official edicts) the finances of the beleaguered Korean Imperial household – through the agency of the Bank of Japan and the Dai-ichi Ginko Bank – and urging ahead a break with the past such as Japan had engineered for itself thirty years earlier following the Meiji Restoration.[99] Evidently all these signs of imminent modernization encouraged the Chartered to take a chance on Carl Wolter's Chemulpo business – and within a couple of years, the bank had gone a significant step further. By the summer of 1904, with dozens of foreign merchant firms actively exchanging commercial bills in Seoul, the Chartered was advertising its standard trade-finance and foreign-exchange services to merchants there in a newly launched English-language newspaper, the *Korean Daily News*. As its agent in the country, the bank had taken on E. Meyer in Chemulpo. The relationship deepened after 1908, when E. Meyer withdrew – one of several large German firms hit hard by a boom/bust in Hamburg's dealings with the East – and Wolter stayed to take over his former employer's stake while maintaining the Chartered Bank agency.[100] It plainly prospered, despite Japan's formal annexation of the country in 1910, for by 1912 Wolter was pressing to have its credit limit lifted to ¥400,000 (by way of comparison, Head Office was instructing Yokohama to put a limit of ¥750,000 on total lending to the entire Japanese banking sector).[101] It was growing more assertive, too – by April 1913 it was making representations to the Court in London, asking to be allowed to use simpler book-keeping procedures. The request was turned down.[102]

The Chartered's steady expansion in the East entailed discussions at the Wednesday meetings of the Court that might have amazed most contemporaries, even in the City of London. Over the course of a few hours, its Directors would each week weigh matters touching on the work of peasants and landlords, wholesalers and shippers, bankers and colonial officials in almost every part of Asia with a coastline. What survives of these meetings are Court Minutes that only occasionally go beyond a minimal description of decisions taken, and rarely stray far from the gritty practicalities of the week. No room was found to keep a record of any broad appraisals of strategy, or of individual branches' performances – and perhaps neither featured much in the Court's deliberations. Certainly the accounting practices of the day were hardly attuned to the kind of analysis found in most modern boardroom papers. Aside from debates over the allocation of profits between the bank's various hidden reserves, Directors probably engaged in little or no analysis of the bank's aggregate numbers from one year to the next. This was left to the Head Office managers, who pored over the regular returns from the branches with sharp pencils at the ready. They prepared a summary treatment of each half-year's performance to set before the Court. Begun in 1895, a small leather volume was used to keep this record of the network's figures: the Book of Profits and Losses confined each year's outcome to a single, hand-written double-page spread, assigning two lines to each of the remitting branches (see Plate

16). Remarkably, entries in this same leather volume would go on being made in precisely the same way – by just five authors in all – until 1953. (Its contents are set out in Appendix D.)

While this small book was evidently cherished for its reference value, what really engaged the attention of the Directors were the minutiae of the bank's operations – and especially any facts (or hearsay) bearing on the status of outstanding loans or the creditworthiness of actual or prospective clients. And the resulting records of their weekly trawl through the business of the network, however dry the details, have a geographical sweep about them – moving from Ceylon and Sourabaya to Singapore, Saigon and Cebu – that still conveys a sense of what made the East so alluring for the Chartered's young recruits. More prosaically, here were being taken the kind of decisions on which depended the inner workings of the truly global economy that had come to maturity over the past fifty years, linking Asia to Europe and the Americas. Nothing like it had ever existed before. It was the Chartered's great good fortune – and Howard Gwyther's signal achievement – that the bank had been able to grow organically as an integral part of the process.*

Keeping abreast of it, as the twentieth century dawned, prompted some reappraisals in London of both the physical premises of the bank and the shape of its balance sheet. A new chairman helped the process along: Gwyther's successor was Sir Montagu Cornish Turner, formerly the senior partner of one of the foremost shipping agencies in the East, Mackinnon Mackenzie. Turner (born in 1853, the same year that the Chartered was founded) had spent a quarter of a century in India – notching up a string of trophy jobs in his time, including the presidency of the Bengal Chamber of Commerce (also founded in 1853) in Calcutta – and had recently arrived home at the age of fifty, intent on becoming one of the panjandrums of the City. The headquarters building in Hatton Court was no match for his grand vision of the Chartered's future. Indeed, it didn't much impress even a new recruit to the humble clerical staff, who joined the bank around this time:

> Far from being imposing, it had a painfully dreary appearance . . . The only indication of the great Institution which the building housed was a brass plate together with a huge door-knocker which . . . were assiduously polished every morning by one of the messenger boys. Inside the door was a lift which (believe or not) sometimes worked, but during its convalescent

---

* After his departure from the bank in 1904, aged sixty-nine, Gwyther enjoyed a long and very private retirement. He died aged eighty-six at home in London, in 1921.

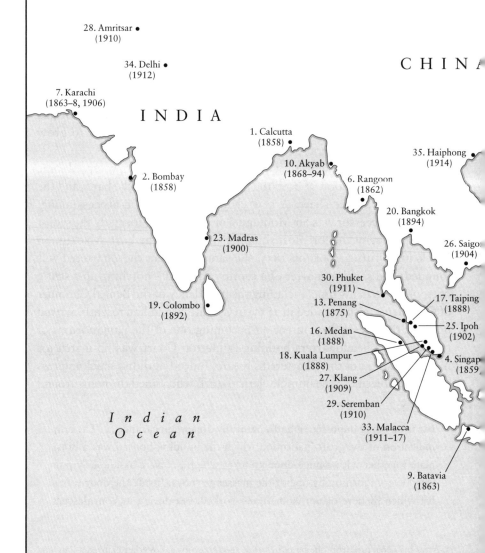

Map 2. Chartered Bank's Asian network up to 1914

Agencies and branches numbered in chronological order
(with founding dates, and closing dates where applicable)

28. Amritsar ●
(1910)

34. Delhi ●
(1912)

C H I N ⧸

7. Karachi
(1863–8, 1906)
●

I N D I A

1. Calcutta
(1858) ●

35. Haiphong ●
(1914)

10. Akyab ●
(1868–94)

6. Rangoon
(1862)
●

2. Bombay
(1858)

20. Bangkok
(1894)

23. Madras
(1900)

26. Saigo
(1904)

30. Phuket
(1911)

19. Colombo
(1892)

13. Penang
(1875)

17. Taiping
(1888)

16. Medan
(1888)

25. Ipoh
(1902)

18. Kuala Lumpur
(1888)

4. Singap
(1859

27. Klang
(1909)

29. Seremban
(1910)

I n d i a n
O c e a n

33. Malacca
(1911–17)

9. Batavia
(1863)

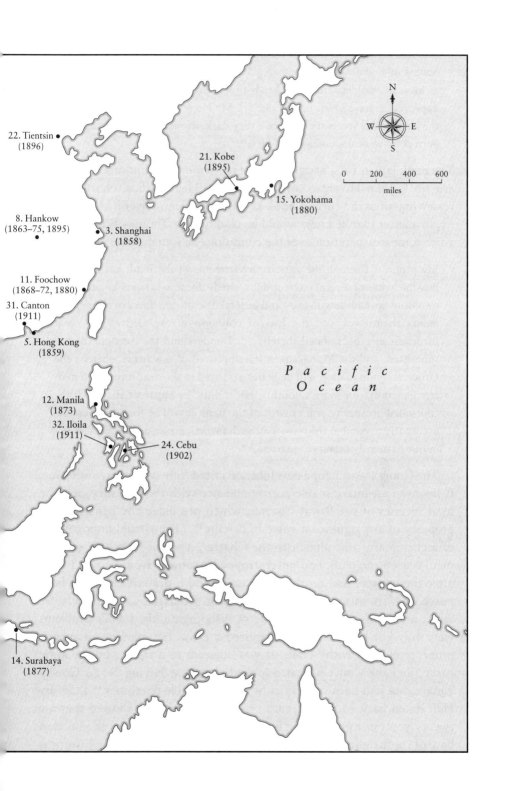

22. Tientsin ●
(1896)

21. Kobe
(1895)

15. Yokohama
(1880)

8. Hankow
(1863–75, 1895)

3. Shanghai
(1858)

11. Foochow
(1868–72, 1880) ●

31. Canton
(1911)

5. Hong Kong
(1859)

12. Manila
(1873)

32. Iloila
(1911)

24. Cebu
(1902)

14. Surabaya
(1877)

P a c i f i c
O c e a n

N
W—✦—E
S

0   200   400   600
miles

periods necessitated the climbing of seemingly hundreds of stairs . . . We also had an interior book-lift running the whole height of the building and hauled up and down by a rope . . . [The] atmosphere was very 'Dickensian' as most of the [departmental] heads functioned in long frock coats which appeared to have given life service . . . Mr Hoggan sat in a little room at the back of the Secretary's Office – very dark, dismal and surrounded by a perfect maze of documents and files.[103]

The bank late in 1904 assigned one of the senior Accountants on its Eastern staff, John Hiver, as an Inspector for Head Office, charged with reviewing all of the current book-keeping practices. Hiver had the temerity, in a letter that he knew would be read first by Thomas Whitehead, to voice some exasperation over the conditions he found there:

My progress through the various departments of the Bank has not been possible without several interruptions, partly due to what may be called the rambling up-and-down-stairs and general disconnectedness of the departments themselves and the loss of cohesion in the Office and great inconvenience occasioned thereby . . . I understand the Accountant has submitted, and the Management has approved of, a scheme whereby the Office accommodation will be better arranged in the near future and matters generally run more smoothly, but it must be apparent that with the continued prosperity and growth of the Bank it will be found impossible eventually to combat the growth of such inconvenience as is at present felt in our extremely cramped quarters.[104]

The Court's search for a new location lasted fully two years, until 1907. It involved an interminable correspondence with the Treasury over the legal niceties of the Royal Charter, which precluded the bank owning property of any significant value in Britain.[105] (The virtual impossibility of securing any amendment to the Charter, it might be noted, was the main reason the bank had never dropped Australia from its title.) Even after the lawyers had resolved this issue, and a desirable site had been purchased five minutes' walk from Hatton Court, down Threadneedle Street and across to the other side of Bishopsgate, the bank's problems were only just beginning. The acquired site was occupied by an ancient property called Crosby Hall. (It was adjacent to a square by the same name, and the Court had also looked closely at buying No. 4 Crosby Square, but had been overtaken by a more nimble purchaser.[106]) Crosby Hall dated back to the fifteenth century. City records showed that for twenty years just prior to the English Civil War, it had been the London base of the fledgling East India Company, which had a pleasing historical resonance for the Court. This did not alter the fact, unfortunately, that Crosby Hall could not possibly accommodate the 140 staff who now worked in the Chartered's Head Office. In redeveloping the site, the bank intended to demolish the existing medieval building. When this was made public, a terrible furore broke over the Directors' heads. The Hall had been a landmark for Shakespeare. It was mentioned in his plays. It had been restored early in the Victorian era on the strength of donations by the public. The Lord Mayor of London and assorted architectural, historical and antiquarian societies lined up to proclaim its magnificence. Even King Edward VII said he wanted to see it preserved. Despite all the clamour, though, no one could improve on the bank's own suggestion that Crosby Hall be dismantled and reconstructed on another site – and this, in the middle of 1908, is how the matter was finally settled.* A fresh building went up in its place, and in March 1909 the move was consummated from Hatton Court to 38 Bishopsgate, a site facing the headquarters across the road of the National Provincial Bank (which building survives to this day, as Gibson Hall).[107]

The new London Head Office was imposing (see p. 360 for a drawing done in 1948), but in truth it scarcely reflected the glamour of the buildings being commissioned in full-blown British Empire style for the bank's branches in several capitals of the East around this time. The Bangkok branch (founded 1894), for example, was relocated in May 1909 to a new building on the waterfront overlooking the Chao Phraya river.[108] (Its neighbours on the eastern bank were the Oriental Hotel and the French Consulate, both still there.) The ground floor housed the banking hall and business offices – but as with many other Chartered offices in the East, there was much more to the building than that:

> The floor above possesses a wide veranda of Italian marble extending completely round the building. On this floor are drawing, dining and billiard rooms, [and] five bedrooms each with its own bathroom, the latter being constructed on an ingenious principle whereby coolies may attend to their duties without entering any of the bedrooms.[109]

In the two principal cities of the Empire, Bombay and Calcutta, the Chartered had long been one of the most familiar institutions of the British

---

* The Court agreed to pay for the entire fabric of the Hall to be put into storage, and then donated it to London County Council. Funds were eventually raised in 1910 for the Hall's reconstruction in Cheyne Walk, Chelsea. It went up on a site that was once the garden of Sir Thomas More's Chelsea home – an appropriate outcome, since More had himself lived in the original Crosby Hall for seven years, from 1516 to 1523. The Hall can be seen from Cheyne Walk today, but is privately owned and not open to the general public.

imperial order. In recent years, it had turned accordingly to some of the best-known architects and designers charged with dreaming up buildings that could properly reflect the grandeur and permanence of the Raj. In Bombay, it had commissioned a new main office at the very centre of the city (today's 23–25 Mahatma Gandhi Road) which had taken five years to complete, from 1897 to 1902. Since the bank remains there – and the site's refurbishment in recent times was one of the earliest initiatives in the drive to preserve modern Mumbai's architectural heritage – customers and tourists alike can still see why it so impressed contemporaries when it first opened its doors. Among the carvings on its Neo-Classical façade was a sculpture above the entrance doors of the bank's heraldic arms, a shield (see facing page) bearing four images. Britannia on her rock was accompanied by an elephant for India, a junk in full sail for China – and a sheep, as if to assert that Australian ambitions had not yet been abandoned. (Motto: *Partes Per Eoas*, 'Throughout the Eastern World'.) In Calcutta, the bank left its Council House Street offices in 1908 – on the fiftieth anniversary of the bank's opening for business in the city – to take up residence in a strikingly palatial building further along the same road where it widened into Clive Street (now Netaji Subhas Road). Constructed in bands of red and white stone, 4 Clive Street had one domed turret high above its centre and four more as elaborate corner-pieces (see Plate 9). Here Chartered Bank was set magnificently at the centre of a cluster of financial institutions that included the Calcutta Stock Exchange and the Royal Exchange, home of the Bengal Chamber of Commerce (all occupying an area, as it happens, known to past generations as the Thieves' Bazaar).*

Compared with its tribulations over Crosby Hall, beefing up the balance sheet of the bank ought to have been child's play, but the Court was surprisingly slow to acknowledge the need for more capital. The Published Reserves matched the £800,000 of shareholders' equity for the first time at the end of 1903 – duly allowing Gwyther to announce this achievement with a flourish at his last General Meeting in 1904 – but three years later the equity had yet to be enlarged. Ambitious new competitors were beginning to appear in India, amid mutterings in Calcutta's English-language press about the inevitable incursion of foreign banks

---

* Even larger than its Bombay counterpart, the Calcutta building has fared less well in recent years. Originally occupied on a ninety-nine-year lease with an option to renew the tenancy for another century, it was vacated in 2005 when the Standard Chartered chose instead to develop a smaller office acquired on the other side of the street. As of 2012, the building had yet to be re-let. Modern Kolkata has none of Mumbai's resources for the conservation of its past, and the palace on Clive Street is fast becoming a sad ruin.

PARTES PER EOAS

The heraldic arms of Chartered Bank, emblazoned on a shield that hung from the wall of 38 Bishopsgate

'unless new English banks are started or those which are already here increase their capital'.[110] The Joint Managers asked their deputy, Thomas Fraser – whom we encountered in Calcutta, reminding William Gibson of his manners – to examine the bank's options. (He would succeed the long-serving Caleb Lewis as Whitehead's fellow Joint Manager in

1909.*) Fraser ruled in March 1907 against lifting deposit rates in the City, which he thought would reflect badly on the image of the bank, though he did think a lot more could be done north of the Scottish border to attract additional deposits: 'I am in favour of advertising in all the leading Scotch papers . . . Our Agents in the big Scotch towns could I think do much more in the way of obtaining money for us if they were allowed to advertise more freely.'[111] But there was no escaping the need for additional share capital. Without it, said Fraser,

> profits . . . are seriously curtailed every year and we are handicapped in competition by our inability to assist the Branches during the busy export season in India and Burma – this has been especially noticeable of late and many opportunities of making money have in consequence been lost and good business has been refused.

His recommendation was accepted, and 20,000 new shares were added to the existing 32,000. Priced at £40 each, with a par value of £20 as in 1853, they lifted the paid-up capital to £1.2 million and brought £400,000 of premiums into the Reserves (which now exceeded £1.5 million).

Part of Fraser's justification for raising the new capital in 1907 was that the Chartered had an obligation to live up to the role expected of it by the Government of India. The Directors had always to be mindful of the bank's responsibilities towards the well-being and progress of the Empire – or, at least, of how these responsibilities might be perceived by government officials on the spot and by their masters in Westminster. (All the more so, perhaps, after 1908 when a seat was taken on the Court by Lord George Hamilton, who had been Secretary of State for India from 1895 to 1903. It was probably not an appointment that Gwyther would have favoured; but Hamilton and Montagu Turner must have become well acquainted in the past, and the bank could hardly have found a better riposte to the mutterers in India.)

Around this time, the British Resident and Consul-General in Mesopotamia, Lt. Col. Ramsay, was writing to the Intelligence Department of the Board of Trade 'inviting their attention to the desirability of taking steps to induce a British Bank to open up in Baghdad'.[112] There is no record of this being discussed by the Court, but by the middle of 1908 a senior

---

* Lewis had joined Chartered Bank in 1864, and been shipped out to its six-year-old Calcutta branch early the following year. As befitted his seminal role in the bank's development, he was asked to make a world tour of the network through the first year of his retirement. At every branch he visited, a photograph was taken of the local men assembled with their august visitor – Lewis usually clutching a cigarette – and the result was a fine set of portraits of the Foreign Staff in 1910 (see Plate 13).

officer of the Chartered's Bombay branch, J. S. Bruce, had been despatched to this outpost of the increasingly rickety Ottoman Empire. His mission was to make a thorough assessment of the commercial opportunities in Baghdad and Basra, and to advise on the feasibility of opening a branch in either (or both) of these two cities at the head of the Persian Gulf. Bruce fulfilled his brief with extraordinary zeal. Arriving only in the second week of December, he cross-examined dozens of locals, from bankers and diplomats to the Arab traders of the bazaar and the numerous merchant families of Baghdad's lively Jewish quarter. By the end of January 1909, he had compiled a fifty-page report with enough statistical detail to furnish a modern Master's dissertation. It drew a fascinating picture of the economy of the region – and of the ways, too, in which the loyal servants of the Empire were hard at work as usual on contemplating its expansion. These included not just Lt. Col. Ramsay and an enthusiastic colleague from the Board of Trade (who 'had a scheme for working a wireless telegraphy between Basra & Baghdad, over the success of which he seemed very sanguine') but also Sir William Willcocks, perhaps the greatest civil engineer of his day and the foremost authority on irrigation schemes in India and Egypt. Willcocks had masterminded the building of the first dam across the Nile several years earlier. Now he had his sights fixed firmly on the waterways of Mesopotamia – with some interesting political implications, as Bruce noted in his report:

> Now Sir William told me that included in his general plans was a scheme for deepening the bar of the Shat-el-Arab which he said would not be difficult, and would remove any doubt as to Basra being the only possible terminus for the railway [currently being proposed to the Turkish government by German officials]. This being so the idea is for the British government to get a concession for a line of Railway from Basra to Baghdad . . . and thus forestall the German line, whose route as sanctioned once it gets to the south of the Euphrates traverses a lot of absolutely desert country with which nothing can be done. This would settle once and for all who was to have control of the Gulf terminus. At the present moment Sir William has a large staff of engineers out surveying on both rivers and . . . [reports so far] were more satisfactory than he had anticipated.[113]

Perhaps not surprisingly, Bruce reckoned British influence 'at present seems to be in the ascendant up the Gulf', and gave Head Office a cautious thumbs-up for the idea of two local branches: 'we should find progress slow and perhaps not very remunerative, but in view of the possible development of the country, I think the question is well worth the consideration of the Directors, if only [so] that we should be the first in the field'. Alas, the Directors were more impressed by his candid acknowledgement of the general lawlessness of the area. The Chartered could hardly expect to be given an armed guard by the military – a privilege enjoyed by the Ottoman Bank – while communications between two branches in Baghdad and Basra, as Bruce had to confess, would be stretched across 350 miles of open desert 'where Turkish authority is only in name and where the Arab does as he likes . . .' (The impudence of it!) After its review by the Court, Bruce's painstaking report was buried in the files. Pinned to it was a note from Whitehead, whose customary enthusiasm for spreading the branch network had its limits. His verdict on this occasion might just as well have been written by Gwyther:

> Politically it would no doubt be a good move for this country if a British Bank were to establish itself in Basra & Baghdad but as a business proposition the opening of agencies of this Bank in Turkish Arabia does not – at present – commend itself to me from any point of view. [PS] I know the Nat'l Bank of India was asked – I do not know by whom – some time back to open at Baghdad & Basra & declined to do so.

The intrepid William Willcocks pressed on with his surveying.* But the Manager of Bruce's office in Bombay wholly endorsed Whitehead's reservations – 'until things improve and more security exists for life and property we do not think it would be prudent to hold funds [in that part of Asia]' – and that, for the moment anyway, was the Chartered's last word.

However, Lt. Col. Ramsay and his friends did not have to wait too long before another London overseas bank opted for a bolder line. A Baghdad branch was opened in May 1912 by a name still relatively new to the City – the Eastern Bank. Launched at the end of 1909, its first objective was to capture a share of the booming exchange market in India where, as its flotation prospectus asserted (and as Thomas Fraser had warned his Chartered colleagues in 1907), 'there has been little increase in banking facilities in recent years' and the need of a new bank under European management 'is now recognized and urged by a large number of influential Natives, and is apparent to experienced observers'.[114] The Eastern had

---

* Over the course of 1908–10, Willcocks so successfully pursued the survey plans he had outlined for Bruce that the Turkish Government appointed him as head of its Irrigation Department in 1911. Work was actually begun on his brave vision for the region, which he laid out in many lectures and two acclaimed books. According to his obituary, these 'showed that his dream was nothing less than the revival by irrigation of the ancient fertility of the Chaldea; but it was soon shattered by Turkish participation in the Great War' (*The Times*, 29 July 1932).

made a respectable if unspectacular start, based on initial branches in Bombay and Calcutta. The lure of a third branch in Baghdad owed less, in 1912, to the state of trade in the Arabian Gulf than to the provenance of the mercantile dynasty behind the founding of the bank. This was the celebrated Sassoon family, Sephardic Jews who had long been based in Bombay but came originally from Baghdad: a distinguished forebear had been state treasurer to the Ottoman governor of the city for forty years, until the later 1820s when most of the family had fled to India to escape persecution. Rather like the Rothschilds – with whom they had been linked by marriage since 1887 – the Sassoons were fabled for their wealth, but had seen different branches of the family go their separate ways. The result was two very similar but rival trading firms, both with principal offices in London, Bombay and Shanghai, and both bearing the family name: David Sassoon & Co. and E. D. Sassoon & Co. The latter had been headed for three decades by Sir Jacob Sassoon, the acknowledged leader of the Jewish community in India, when he lent his weight in 1909 to a significant diversification of his firm's interests with the founding of the Eastern Bank. The shares were floated via a normal public offering, except that 40 per cent of the initial 100,000 shares were allotted to subscribers in India.[115] Sir Jacob and one of his colleagues at E. D. Sassoon, J. S. Haskell, were among the seven founding Directors – including its first chairman, a Scottish peer and former Secretary of State for Scotland, the 6th Lord Balfour of Burleigh – and the new bank actually started life in E. D. Sassoon's City offices in Fenchurch Avenue. A few months later, it established its own Head Office – at No. 4 Crosby Square, the very building that had caught the Chartered's eye three years earlier. This was the first foray into formal banking by any branch of his family, and Sir Jacob was careful from the start to impress upon his fellow Directors and the inaugural Manager, F. H. Sutton (who would stay in the job until 1938), that their neighbour in Bishopsgate – and, indeed, in both Bombay and Calcutta – was to be treated as a valued ally. The Sassoons, after all, had not built their fortunes over half a century on the trade routes between Britain, India and the treaty ports of China without occasional recourse to the services of Chartered Bank. In the event, the two banks were soon to find events forcing them into surprisingly close ties.

There was one line of Eastern trade with which the Sassoon fortunes had been especially identified since the 1840s: the export of Indian opium to China. The trade was almost as important to India itself, still accounting in the first decade of the twentieth century for a sizeable slice of India's annual exports – worth more, for example, than her exports of tea – and in the process yielding revenues that amounted to about 15 per cent of the

Indian government's annual budget. The revenues were raised partly by taxation, but also more directly by reserving cultivation of the underlying crop in Bengal to growers licensed by the Indian government itself, which had a special office of State to run the business, the Indian Opium Department. Auction sales of this 'official' Bengal opium were run by the Department in Calcutta, while unlicensed opium from the Native States of north-west India was privately cultivated and sold, under the 'Malwa' system, to traders in Bombay. The two Sassoon firms were leading buyers in both cities, transporting the nefarious drug in their own ships to coastal China where sales of standardized Indian chests of opium had of course been central to the onslaught of European commerce in the nineteenth century and to the tensions that had sparked intermittent wars between European states – especially Britain – and the Celestial Empire of the Qing. All of the Eastern exchange banks were involved in the financing of opium shipments, and the Chartered was no exception. The political and commercial pressures to back the Sassoons and other prominent shippers effectively foreclosed any real debate over this, though the British public's distaste for the trade was rising quickly by the 1890s. (The movement in Britain dedicated to banning the opium business even included among its leaders the first India Secretary in the Liberal government formed in 1905, John Morley.) As for the attitude of Chinese officialdom – as opposed to the often ambiguous stance of individual officials – its deep hostility to the importation of opium had been a source of anxiety and occasional financial embarrassment to the banks for decades.

In 1911 a long series of intermittent uprisings against the ailing empire of the Qing finally culminated in its total collapse and the declaration, on the first day of 1912, of the Chinese Republic under the presidency of Sun Yat-sen. This momentous turn of events soon prompted a crisis over the opium trade, entirely predictably given its baleful influence over China's relations with the West for so many generations past. The new Republic's leaders took even graver exception to it than the ancien regime, and their effective repudiation of an agreement with Britain – supposedly struck as a compromise in the dying days of the Empire – pitched the Indian exporters into a crisis that threatened to wipe out many firms, and to inflict grievous losses on the Sassoons.*

---

* The 'New Opium Agreement' of May 1911 was ostensibly a bargain whereby the Chinese would scale back domestic production while the British curtailed exports from India, to a seven-year timetable that would culminate in a cessation of opium sales in China altogether. In the meantime, all inland taxes and restrictions were to be lifted on the wholesale trade. Given the chaotic state of the Qing Empire by this date and the incipient violence all across China, the notion that any government in Peking could implement this kind of edict might

As coastal inventories of opium climbed steadily through 1912 and the Republican government's assault on the inland distribution of the drug showed no signs of easing, foreign merchants sought desperately to close off additional supplies which were threatening to swamp the China market. This meant persuading the Indian government to curtail its auctions in Calcutta, despite all the attendant complications for its own budget. The directors of the two Sassoon family firms led an intense lobbying effort in Shanghai, Hong Kong and London that quickly roped in the Eastern Bank and the Chartered Bank to help rally support in the banking community.[116] Whitehead and his colleagues were anxious not to be identified too publicly with the campaign, but certainly lent it effective support (endorsing, for example, an appeal to the Secretary of State for India, drawn up by E. D. Sassoon and its solicitors in London[117]). They had good reasons of their own to fear a dramatic collapse in opium prices. An urgent request to all the Chartered's branches at the start of December 1912 to remit a valuation of loans currently outstanding against stocks of the drug brought back numbers from India, Singapore and China that totalled £238,000 – roughly on a par with the Chartered's annual profits for each of the past two years.[118] It must therefore have come as a considerable relief just a few days later to hear that the Indian government had finally given way. Auction sales in Calcutta were shortly to be suspended. In the event, a permanent halt was announced in May 1913 to all government sales of opium for shipment to China. This effectively marked the end of an official trade that had lasted 150 years, as the shareholders of the Eastern Bank heard from their Chairman, Lord Balfour, at their General Meeting in March 1914: 'practically the whole of our then outstanding loans [against opium in 1913] have been repaid, and the export of the drug to China has now entirely ceased'.[119] The Chartered Bank, too, seems to have recouped its loans without serious loss.

A Manifesto issued by the Republic in the final days of 1912 had set out its objections to 'the evil effects of opium upon our nation' in terms

---

be described as wildly optimistic or supremely disingenuous, according to taste. The Agreement anyway backfired calamitously. The Indian government had to regulate its sales of opium more strictly, producing a 'certificated' category for export to China that was immediately construed as having a premium value. Demand, and auction prices, soared accordingly. When the Chinese Republic turned its back on the Agreement and outlawed the wholesale traders on whom inland distribution depended, shrill protests followed. The foreign merchants demanded protection – perhaps even military intervention – both on legal grounds (a treaty had been broken) and on 'moral' grounds (they had been lured into paying higher auction prices on false pretences). As for any outsiders' ethical objections to the sale of opium – if it was such a heinous product, why was the Government of India so dependent on it?

as plaintive as any voiced by the Qing court in the past: 'Now that we are beginning to lead a new life with our people, how could we bear to see living beings forever doomed into the deep sea?'[120] Someone at David Sassoon & Co. wrote to the Foreign Office in December 1912 offering a more cynical view. The Republic had moved against the opium trade, it was suggested, in retaliation against the British government 'for an imaginary grievance in connection with the part they took in the Loan Question, and more particularly the Crisp Loan'.[121] Here, as it happened, was another bitterly contentious episode in which the Chartered Bank and the Eastern Bank had found common cause. At the outset of the year, both banks had separately resolved to break into the market for lending to China. The Eastern Bank had actually made no secret of its intention, from the outset, to look at opportunities for sovereign lending: the Sassoons had the right kind of connections, and had given Board positions to representatives of two continental banks with extensive interests in China.[122] For the Chartered, it marked a significant change of heart since the Gwyther years and must surely have owed much to the influence of Whitehead, with his long personal experience of competing with Thomas Jackson in China. It was at least possible, as the Court argued in a letter of April 1912, that the recent Revolution might prove 'the prelude to a period of great industrial and commercial activity throughout that country'.[123] (Indeed, intense discussions were already under way in Peking, aimed at the negotiation of a 'Reorganization Loan' to help secure the post-Qing era a propitious start.) This letter from the Court was addressed to the Foreign Office, for the very good reason that all sovereign lenders in Peking had until now operated under the aegis of their home governments – and the Chartered Bank wanted official blessing for its new stance.

Unfortunately, this was not forthcoming. It suited the diplomats to have financial rivalries in China constrained by a formal agreement: loans to Peking had accordingly been handled for years by a 'Four-Power Consortium' of state-backed banks – now upgraded to a Six-Power model, with Russian and Japanese banks joining those from Britain, France, Germany and the US. The Hongkong Bank, as Britain's sole representative, was odd-man-out insofar as it had no government shareholder; but no one questioned its inclusion in the group, given its knowledge of China and long-standing readiness to lend to the Peking government. It had made a speciality of the market for China bonds in close conjunction with its friends at the stockbroking firm of Panmure Gordon. By cultivating investors in the City to whom it could sell the bonds, the bank had in effect developed a merchant banking arm in Britain to set beside its exchange and domestic banking activities in the East. The Foreign Office was not inclined to disrupt this cosy arrangement – and especially not after the irritation of seeing the Eastern Bank participate in a joint loan to China in March, co-managed with a Belgian bank. (It was conspicuously ignored by officials, thereby prompting questions in the City over the credit standing of the loan.) A token effort was made at persuading the Hongkong Bank to admit the Chartered (though not the Eastern) to a subordinate role in the Consortium, which Whitehead and the Court indignantly rejected.[124] By the early summer of 1912, an awkward impasse had been reached.

It was at this point that the Chinese themselves took a hand in proceedings. Officials in Peking had long resented the curb placed by the Consortium on their freedom to raise money at their own discretion. Now they pitched their own invitation to *non*-Consortium banks in the City to come forward with a loan of £10 million – without the backing of any Western governments at all. It was soon known as the Crisp Loan, named after the City broking firm of C. Birch Crisp & Co. which took on the management of the underwriting syndicate – and both the Chartered Bank and the Eastern Bank were among those who agreed to join it. The first half of the Loan was offered to investors with impressive speed, at the end of September, but soon came to grief.[125] Seriously under-subscribed in the City, it ran into further problems when the Chinese asked to receive their funds in silver. The task of buying the silver with the sterling proceeds of the bond sales fell mostly to the Chartered, and when it stepped into the market the Consortium banks conspired to move exchange rates heavily against it. The brunt of the work fell on the Manager of the Shanghai branch – W. S. Livingstone, who as a young man had sat on the shores of the Bay of Bengal, pondering advice about the need to act on one's own initiative – and he found it tough going, not least because of constantly changing demands from the borrower.[126] The Consortium's six governments were putting intense pressure on the Republican government in Peking to spurn the loan. As negotiations over the Reorganization Loan came to a head, City feuding over the rights and wrongs of the Birch Crisp initiative threatened to destabilize the market for all investors, and both sides welcomed a compromise under which the second half of the Crisp Loan was cancelled. The Consortium's own Reorganization Loan was signed off in March 1913 – and the Foreign Secretary, Sir Edward Grey, let it be known privately that further excursions into the sovereign bond market by the Chartered would not be appreciated.[127]

The Directors seem not to have been unduly concerned over this rebuff. It only confirmed what the Court had always known – that breaking into the world of sovereign lending in competition with the merchant bankers would not be easy. Better, surely, to stick to the traditional exchange business that was still growing so very satisfactorily. Recently opened branches included Canton (in 1911) and Delhi (1912). It might have eased Livingstone's difficulties over the Crisp Loan, as he himself had pointed out, if the bank had had a branch of its own in Peking – which it lacked until 1915. But it was striking how often local plans of this kind were now encountering competition from the 'state' banks – and from the Berlin-based Deutsche-Asiatische Bank in particular. German shippers and merchant firms had been accounting for a steadily greater share of the local market in Singapore, Bangkok and Manila for years. Their rising importance in South Asia – reflected, too, in the growth of the Chartered's operations in Hamburg – was also evident in China. The Deutsche-Asiatische had established a firm presence across the northern province of Shandong, seized by German troops in 1897–8. Its banknotes ruled there by 1913, just as most of the trade through the new port at Tsingtao was now being handled by five prominent German firms. The Chartered sent one of its officers, R. W. Robertson, to reconnoitre the Tsingtao market in September that year. The ensuing report, unlike Bruce's from Baghdad in 1909, made no mention of any wily British schemes to frustrate German expansion – it was too late for that in Shandong. Robertson simply urged that the Chartered accept an invitation to take up some space in the Tsingtao offices of a leading German broker, Arnold Karberg & Co. It should send someone, he suggested, 'as soon as possible – there is no necessity for him to talk German – he will receive any help [he needs] from Arnold Karberg and their compradore'.[128] It was an unusual proposition, of a kind that would soon be unthinkable.

4
Winners in a Shaken World, 1914–29

I. SIDEWAYS INTO A GLOBAL WAR

To many bankers in the City of London, perhaps most, the idea of a full-blown war between the Great Powers of Europe had come to seem all but unimaginable by 1914. The scale and sophistication of the global trading networks built up since the Franco-Prussian War in 1870–71 had begun to pool the commercial interests of Europe's leading powers to an extent that was binding their economies together, seemingly inextricably. Hence the notion, fondly embraced in City circles, that all statesmen were obliged now to acknowledge a blessed truth, that any thoughts of aggrandizement by force of arms amounted to nothing more than a 'great illusion' (the title of a widely quoted, if slightly misunderstood, bestseller expounding this line that had been published in 1910[1]).

There was no denying the wider public's obsession with war scares and Empire rivalries, naval statistics and military parades, nor the readiness of Europe's ruling elites to fuel it, seemingly regardless of the potential for a catastrophic outcome. A senior American diplomat, reporting to the White House on a trip made in May 1914, summed up the current mood of the continent as 'militarism run stark mad'.[2] Yet the financial world seemed strangely detached from the contagion. Market prices early that summer betrayed little hint of it, as if to confirm that those warning of war were just deluded. Even after the assassination in June in Sarajevo of Archduke Franz Ferdinand of Austria, heir to the Imperial throne, had sparked a Balkan crisis that went on mounting ominously into July, few City men saw much real cause for alarm. Only after the announcement of Austria's brutish ultimatum to Serbia on the evening of 23 July did the appalling realization dawn that serious hostilities were in the offing. Suddenly and dramatically the markets took fright, starting with an immediate sell-off in New York that night followed by a panic of historic proportions across Europe the next day. It was a change of mood that stunned the City's professionals, as a commentary in *The Bankers' Magazine* would note a few months later, and that burst upon them 'like a bombshell'.[3]

For the overseas banks, mayhem in the City soon posed a mortal threat that no one had foreseen, caused by the very complexity of the global economy that had been construed in recent years as the best reason to suppose that wars were a thing of the past. There was nothing complicated about the immediate impact of the London panic. Perhaps half of all the world's trade (and the lion's share of Britain's) was financed with sterling bills of exchange, endorsed by the accepting houses of the City and readily traded for cash in the London discount market. Within a few days of 23 July, this enormous market simply ground to a halt. Any clash of arms, however short-lived, seemed bound to preclude the automatic honouring of trade bills at maturity between parties based in countries at war with each other. This wiped out the creditworthiness of huge quantities of existing bills more or less overnight.* Secondary trading in the discount market was also impeded by a collapse in the flow of paper from overseas. Sterling bills, as a proxy for gold, were hoarded everywhere in a rush for liquidity: 'With hardly a moment's warning an incalculable stream of bills, cheques, and cable transfers came to a dead stop.'[4] By the end of the last week in July, the money markets of the City had effectively frozen over, paralysing bullion and foreign-exchange transactions as well as the provision of trade credit – and leaving London's overseas banks exposed to disaster on several counts. As *The Economist* observed on 1 August, 'the financial world has been staggering under a series of blows such as the delicate system of international credit has never before witnessed, or even imagined. Particular centres, no doubt, have had blacker experiences . . . but nothing so widespread and so world-wide has ever been known before.'[5]

How exactly the senior men at 38 Bishopsgate handled Chartered Bank's predicament is unclear: few Court records of that summer have survived. But it must have been an acutely anxious time. On a balance sheet valued at around £27 million, Chartered held trade bills and their

---

* Contemporaries valued the London discount market at around £350 million. 'It was estimated that perhaps two thirds of the overall total of bills were payable by foreigners in London, with some £70 million owed by German and Austrian clients, perhaps a further £60 million on account of Russian clients, and much of the rest by North American, Latin American and British Empire clients.' (Richard Roberts, *Saving the City, The Great Financial Crisis of 1914*, OUP, 2013, p. 31 – the most authoritative account of an episode otherwise surprisingly neglected by historians. Many chronicles of the countdown to war simply ignore the seizing up of the City's markets in the week ending 31 July 1914.)

equivalent to the value of about £18 million, compared with less than £6 million in cash and government securities.[6] Without a buyer for those bills, it had no way of paying its own creditors and was potentially insolvent – as were many of its peers. In the frenzied negotiations that ensued between the City, the Bank of England and the Treasury under the Chancellor, David Lloyd George, one of the key figures who spoke for the Eastern exchange banks was the Chartered's Thomas Fraser. On the evening of Sunday 2 August, the government responded to the banks' entreaties by proclaiming a moratorium on the repayment of all bills of exchange held in the City. It would remain in place until the middle of October, by which time Lloyd George had pushed through an electrifying initiative that authorized the Bank of England to purchase all unredeemable bills – his so-called 'cold storage scheme' which by September 1914 had seen the effective nationalization of bills worth £133 million – and a workable version had emerged of the pre-war international credit system.* This effectively marked the end of the threat posed to the Chartered's survival by the outbreak of the war, though the crisis in the markets would last a few more months: stock exchanges all over the world had closed in August and most remained shut until at least the end of the year. The London Stock Exchange reopened on 4 January 1915.

Through the last days of July, the City's overseas bankers had actually had to confront not one but two scarcely believable developments. They would soon come to be treated as a single disaster, but were not initially one and the same. First had come the shock of imminent war and paralysed markets. Only some days later, at the start of August, was it finally grasped that Britain would herself be a combatant. Hence the second shock, that the British Empire would thus be embarking on a war against her most important business partner. (Pre-war discussions in Whitehall about exactly this dilemma had prompted one senior official to table 'statistics showing that two-thirds of British exports, by value, came from selling Germany coal, fish, textiles, woollen yarns, machinery and iron and steel products'.[7]) Until the very last moment, most City bankers clung desperately to the hope that the Liberal government might keep Britain neutral. As one famous account of those terrible days notes: 'The Governor of the Bank of England called on Saturday [1 August] to inform Lloyd George that the City was "totally opposed to our intervening" in a war.'[8]

---

* An influential body in the restoration process was the Foreign Exchange Committee of the English and Foreign Banks, on which Fraser and his fellow Joint Manager Thomas Whitehead sat as Chartered Bank's representatives, alongside those of eight other banks (see Roberts, *Saving the City*, pp. 170–71).

But once the die was cast, and Britain had declared war against the Kaiser on 4 August, those banks with extensive direct links to Germany had to suspend them with immediate effect. In practice this meant putting a halt to new business while co-operating with the authorities in both London and Berlin to wind down existing commitments with the minimum of disruption. Chartered Bank's Secretary was soon circulating notices to all branches in the East accordingly. He confirmed, for example, the cancellation of credits opened with Deutsche Bank in London, 'as we are not allowed to transact any fresh business during the time the war may last'.[9] Both parties were at pains to avoid causing offence: there was no point antagonizing those with whom, it was hoped and very much expected, normal commercial dealings would soon be resumed. The same circular passed on a notice from Deutsche Bank in Berlin alerting Chartered to the withdrawal of credits arranged for two large firms in Burma and Siam, 'of which please inform your Rangoon and Bangkok friends'.

Meanwhile, arrangements were being made for the orderly contraction of Chartered's branch in Hamburg. Its annual profits were quite modest – though they had been roughly on a par in recent years with those made in Batavia – but since 1904 the branch had built up a significant network of relationships in Germany's largest port city, helping to build ties with those many German merchant houses that were expanding their activities in Asia. Like their counterparts working at German banks in the City, the British members of the Hamburg staff were quickly interned. This was especially hard on one of them, Walter Neill, who had only arrived in the city on a temporary 'holiday-cover' assignment late in July. He and a second sub-accountant were both to spend the next four years in internment, despite the bank's best efforts to negotiate their repatriation.[10] More fortunate was the forty-two-year-old Scottish manager of the branch, Murray Gibbon. As a 'colonial' (born in Ceylon) he was subject to different rules, and the individual appointed by the German government as 'Official Controller' of the branch, George Hesse, soon managed to secure his release. Perhaps Hesse was struggling to cope with his own role: just a few months later, he committed suicide. This left Gibbon to run the affairs of the bank until early 1918, when he was put under house arrest for the remainder of the war. Assisting him up to that point was the Chief Clerk, Martin Opitz, a German who had been working in the branch almost since its inception. After Gibbon's house arrest, Opitz stayed on as 'Geshäftsfuhrer' for the Chartered and at least one other bank. He was in fact the only manager of a British bank in Hamburg to remain at his desk throughout the war (and he would rise to be Joint Manager of the Hamburg branch from 1934, until his retirement five years later).[11]

Suspending direct links with Germany was one thing, but how was the bank to manage its relations with Germans and German firms in the East? In several of the more remote Asian ports, Chartered had recently been contemplating closer ties with German businesses, as with Arnold Karberg in Tsingtao. And it was generally the case across the whole of Asia that a high degree of mutual support among the European expatriates had literally entailed 'clubbing together', for business and leisure alike. Some of these close entanglements would obviously now be inappropriate. But it was occasionally awkward, not to say commercially damaging, having to sever ties with old neighbours just because they were German. Tales were told of Chartered managers helping local German merchants make a hasty exit, where local anti-German feelings ran high – in some cases even before the war had begun. In Francophile Saigon, for example, staff from one German trading house probably owed their lives to quick thinking by the bank. Speidel & Co. was a trading house that had acted as the Chartered's agent in the nineteenth century and had accommodated the Saigon branch of the bank as a tenant in its office building on Rue d'Adran since 1908. The German firm turned to the bank for help in closing down its affairs late in July 1914 – and it was said the Chartered manager had arranged to be driven in his official car to the dockside two days before the declaration of war, 'sitting at the back with a rug on his knees and the German staff of Speidel & Co underneath the rug, and that he smuggled them on to a Swedish ship while a crowd was looting the German Club'.[12] On the evening of 6 August angry crowds ransacked the premises of all the German businesses they could find in the city.*

Especially pressing for the Chartered was the need to make alternative arrangements where German businessmen had actually been taken on as agents for the bank – and this too prompted some colourful episodes. Severance instructions went off to several places, including Zanzibar and Newchwang (Yingkou today), the treaty port in north-east China. Another telegram went to the Yokohama branch where a sub-accountant, F. D. West, was instructed to leave at once for Korea. He was tasked with standing down the local agency arrangements made there with Carl Wolter a

---

* The bank later took over the whole of Speidel's premises and in due course constructed a fresh building on the same site, in what was renamed Rue Georges-Guynemer in 1920. The Saigon branch remained there until the end of 1974. A sub-accountant charged with thinning out the office's archives in the 1930s, F. A. H. Goddard, found the cash books and journals of Messrs Speidel & Co. among the bank's own records, the last entries dated 27 July 1914. Goddard was serving again in the Saigon branch in 1950, now promoted to Accountant, when he wrote to Head Office recounting his find for those researching the centenary history. (Letter to Harold Faulkner, 18 March 1950, LMA: CH03/01/14/051.)

decade earlier. He was to inaugurate instead a self-standing branch '[able] to store all goods under lien to the Bank in neutral godowns, thus relieving Messrs. Carl Wolter & Co of the control of our affairs at Chemulpo'.[13] Travelling with a Chinese servant, Sunny Jim, he made his way south on trains crammed with mobilizing Japanese troops to board a steamer from Shimonoseki and crossed the hundred miles of sea to Korea in a storm. Rail links from Fusan to Chemulpo via Seoul proved to be excellent – all built by Japan since the turn of the century – and West arrived with a couple of days to spare before the expiry of Japan's ultimatum to Germany on 23 August and the start of the war in the Far East. He was a little disarmed to receive a warm welcome from the German firm. The port had no modern hotel and so a private house had been specially found for him, complete with grand piano. His German counterpart – Carl Wolter himself seems to have departed by this point – was 'a red-whiskered individual, wearing large and powerful spectacles' called Schirbaum, who turned out to be a fine pianist. The two men struck up a warm rapport, reorganizing the bank's affairs by day and settling down to some serious Schumann and Brahms in the evenings. Alas, circulars from the British Consul in the town brought news soon enough of German atrocities in Belgium. When his new friend refused to condemn the reported behaviour of his countrymen, West announced stiffly that all future contacts between them would have to be conveyed by letter – whereupon, to his astonishment, Herr Schirbaum burst into tears. By then, fortunately, their business together had been more or less completed. The bank now had its own godown for storing imports financed on behalf of Korean customers. The British Consul helped West to find a local compradore '[who] did his work most efficiently and brought a lot of useful business to the Bank'. And the local Japanese Prefect ('a fine specimen of the old Samurai type') provided him with an armed guard to watch over the cash each night, pending the arrival of a safe which had to be ordered from Yokohama. With the transfer of all property and accounts finalized,

> [West] then proceeded to make arrangements to carry on the Bank's business. This included the sale of drafts on [the Chartered Bank branch in] Shanghai which were used in payment for imports from that place, in which there was a brisk trade . . . [Business] went on quite happily and [West], by no means overworked, was feeling perfectly pleased with the position and life in general, when one morning on opening the mail, he received advice that he had once more to be on the move. His successor arrived a week later and after handing over to him, [he] said goodbye to the quaint little backwater of Chemulpo with some regret.[14]

As already noted, Carl Wolter & Co. appears to have built up a healthy volume of business for the bank before the war – but the new set-up evidently proved a disappointment. The Chartered's Court minutes noted a decision early in November 1914 to close the new branch.[15] Days later, a better idea was submitted by West and his manager at Yokohama – and on their recommendation, the Chemulpo activities were handed back to Carl Wolter & Co. The Court minutes noted that modest credit facilities would be made available from Japan, adding cryptically: 'No fresh business however is to be entertained.'[16] How this compromise turned out, we do not know: the relevant records were almost certainly lodged at Yokohama and so were lost in the great earthquake of 1923.

The formal repudiation of new business via the German agency was probably a prudent acknowledgement of the various edicts issued in Whitehall since August against trading with the enemy. The continued provision of credit, on the other hand, was a fair reflection of the more ambivalent reality that still prevailed in many parts of Asia until well into 1915. At the outbreak of hostilities, the profound implications of a worldwide ban on trading with Germany and Austria had prompted consternation in the City, not to say widespread dismay. Unknown to the bankers, and to the public at large, an intense debate had been under way for several years in Whitehall over the extent to which Britain would be justified in seeking to throttle all international trade in the event of a war with Germany. The course of that debate and its outcome have been largely ignored in the vast historiography of the First World War until recently, but were laid out in detail in 2012 by the historian Nicholas Lambert in *Planning Armageddon, British Economic Warfare and the First World War*. Hawkish admirals had advocated a ruthless shutdown, extending far beyond a mere blockade of North Sea ports, and mobilizing the overwhelming resources of the Royal Navy (and the City) to block all shipments into Europe from Asia and the Americas. In this way, it was argued, Britain's control of the oceans could be used to cut short any serious land war on the continent. Those opposed to this strategy of 'total economic warfare', as it was called, were broadly of the view that such a massive disruption of the global trading system would effectively destroy the whole basis of Pax Britannica. It would be unacceptable to neutral countries – most especially the United States, as the Foreign Office steadfastly insisted – and would fly in the face of contemporary shipping practices that no longer allowed for a simplistic identification of individual vessels or even individual cargoes as the property of one nation or another. The warring parties in Europe, in short, would have no choice but to strike a series of compromises that would accommodate their continued trading with neutrals and even, in respect of strictly civilian cargoes, with each other. These starkly contrasting view-points implied very different prescriptions for British strategy in the event of a major war. No doubt on that account, they had elicited no consistent response from those senior politicians privy to the debate, and the government had still to choose between them when that war arrived. As a result, confusion reigned in August 1914 *inter alia* over how exactly the exchange banks were to conduct themselves in the East – and in particular over how they were to deal with German (or Austrian) customers based in neutral countries, or even in territories of the British Empire itself.

It did not take long for the overseas bankers to push back hard against the first tentative steps taken by officialdom towards total economic war-fare. Predictably, perhaps, they emphatically rejected the admirals' cure for the European war as being worse than the disease. It surely made no sense, as a response to hostilities that might well be over within a month or two, to precipitate a collapse of the international Free Trade system which was at the heart of the Empire they were fighting to defend. In the second week of the war, the Treasury put out a ruling that drew a sharp – not to say high-handed – response on 18 August from the London Manager of the Hongkong & Shanghai Bank, Sir Charles Addis:

> [The Treasury has ruled that the exchange banks should not be allowed] to negotiate bills drawn by British firms in this country upon German drawees resident in the British Colonies or in neutral countries . . . If this ruling is allowed to stand, it will, in my opinion, inflict greater injury on the trade of this country with the Orient than any damage it is likely to do to the enemy. It is desirable that an end should be put to the present dead-lock by a pronouncement on the subject by Her Majesty's Treasury. As the mail for the East closes on Thursday [20 August], it would be a favour if you could manage to let us have it by tomorrow morning.[17]

Remarkably, Addis duly received his pronouncement the next morning. The Treasury withdrew its ruling. On 20 August, Addis confirmed as much to his counterparts at Chartered Bank. By this point, it probably came as no surprise to Whitehead and Fraser. They had been conducting their own exchange of letters with the Treasury, and the drift of them was clear. The Treasury had explained, for example, that Germans and Aus-trians resident in Britain should be allowed to continue doing business with the bank. ('Indeed the probabilities are very strong that nearly all Germans and Austrians now in this country who are anxious to operate on their Banking Accounts, are people to whom the Banks ought to give as good banking facilities as they allow to their truly British customers.'[18]) Even more important, it had also provided a definition of 'enemy aliens' that left Chartered's branches extensive scope to trade with German firms in the East. As the Secretary set out in a Circular of 21 August, the Treasury had agreed that an enemy alien was 'only a person of whatever nationality resident or carrying on business in the enemy country and that consequently it is permissible to trade with a German or Austrian who is resident in British, Allied or Neutral countries'.[19] As Lambert concluded in his *Planning Armageddon*, 'aggressive implementation of economic warfare [that August] . . . had lasted for a grand total of one day at least or two weeks at most'.[20]

By October, international trade was beginning to revive and Chartered Bank set out to resume business, albeit in an often bizarre legal environment that grew more bureaucratic by the month. The surviving records are sparse but it seems clear the bank retained – for the moment, at least – its links with many German merchants in Asia, while complying with the more specific prohibition on doing business with the Central Powers directly. This involved an often delicate balancing act, a glimpse of which is provided by this Board minute of March 1915 noting a discussion about the bank's ties with Mohr Bros & Co., the powerful German firm controlling much of the Siamese rice trade:

> [Directors considered] the Bangkok Agent's advice that Mohr Bros & Co Ltd cannot work their Rice business without local advances, and approved of his action in arranging to honour their cheques . . . on condition that there is no doubt that [they] . . .are under Siamese law and not in any way subject to German jurisdiction.[21]

Without doubt, Chartered was also heavily engaged in the financing of cargoes from Asia that were being shipped into Germany via the neutral ports of Rotterdam and the Baltic. These complied with the letter of the law against trading with aliens but the bank was evidently less than confident about the Royal Navy's view of the matter, as might be inferred from a plea addressed by Whitehead to the President of the Board of Trade for a little more clarity on Government policy:

> We shall esteem it a favour if you can confirm the statement made to us that steamers of The East Asiatic Company Ltd, of Copenhagen, &c, destined for neutral ports in Denmark &c, are allowed to proceed to their destination without let or hindrance on the part of His Majesty's Government. The enquiry is made in connection with shipments of Sesame Seeds from China which we have been asked to finance.[22]

Whitehead and his colleagues were right to be concerned. The volume of trade passing through Rotterdam and the Baltic ports had, unsurprisingly, soared by the end of 1914, and Ministers in Whitehall were having serious second thoughts about their earlier, relatively relaxed views on trade links with Germany-friendly exporters in neutral countries. The Eastern exchange banks found their activities coming under ever closer scrutiny, and any mails despatched to Germany via neutral cities were plainly liable to interception by British government censors – resulting in a string of embarrassed apologies like this one from the Chartered's Secretary to the Home Office in mid-November:

> We have to acknowledge receipt of your [letter of the 9th] enclosing a letter addressed by our Hongkong Branch to Messrs. Bettmann & Kupfer, Frankfurt on Main, containing a draft for £47 – 7/-. This irregularity we can only ascribe to inadvertence and we have taken steps by which we hope to avoid any further infringement of the proclamation with regard to Trading with the Enemy. On behalf of our Hongkong Branch we tender our apologies for the mistake which has been unintentionally made.[23]

When the stalemate on the Western Front stretched into 1915, hopes of any quick end to the war had finally to be abandoned. Tougher restrictions against dealing with German firms in the East now seemed inevitable, especially after Germany's declaration in February 1915 of unrestricted submarine warfare against neutral shipping around the British Isles. As the head of the government's War Trade Department had to admit the following month, 'business as usual and crippling German trade are inconsistent'.[24] Yet commodity shipments from the East, financed by the City and often shipped in British merchant vessels, were still reaching Germany in astounding quantities. (Re-exports of cocoa from Britain to Sweden, for example, were valued at £1,150,746 in April 1915, compared with £16,500 in April 1914 – which was not down to a sudden craze for hot drinking chocolate in Stockholm.[25]) By the summer of 1915, Whitehall was ready to adopt a drastically altered approach. In June the definition of 'enemy aliens' was extended to include German and Austrian nationals in China, Siam and Persia, and the exchange banks were put under notice that any clients shipping goods to neutral Europe had to provide a written declaration of the cargoes' final destinations. By the end of the year, the government was ready to introduce sweeping constraints on most allied dealings with neutral countries. Under a fresh Proclamation of December 1915 – Trading With The Enemy (Extension of Powers) – the Royal Navy's powers were still left short of those envisaged by total economic warfare, but the gap was closing fast. The government asserted its right to blacklist any commercial operations deemed helpful to the enemy. Nor were Black Lists the last word on this score. In two of Chartered Bank's biggest markets, Siam and China, business could now only be conducted with enterprises named on so-called White Lists.[26] The die-hard defenders of unfettered international trade went on advancing their case into 1916, but theirs was a losing battle. The Foreign Office acknowledged as much, abandoning its earlier and more pragmatic stance. A naval blockade of Germany's ports had been greatly hindered since the start of the war by a lack of co-ordination between Whitehall departments. Attention now turned, with the establishment early in 1916 of a Ministry of Blockade, to a far more rigorous execution of this strategy, in effect a proxy for the abandoned option of total economic warfare. Its implementation involved gathering huge amounts of information on British trade and shipping all over the world for the rest of the war – an exercise that Chartered Bank hastened to assist, and that soon came to be incompatible with financing trade for neutral parties linked in any way to German or Austrian importers.

Whatever the costs to the Chartered of its dwindling access to this business, they were soon to be far outweighed by the positive impact of the war on the rest of the bank's activities. The Allies' demand for some of Asia's staple commodities soared from 1915 onwards and the business volumes for all the exchange banks rose accordingly – as, too, did the prices of most of those commodities and the fees payable to finance their passage from the East.* Even better, the commercial risks were increasingly defrayed by Whitehall: more and more goods were included on a Government List, which guaranteed official underpinning of any trade bills in favour of Asian exporters that were discounted by the banks. Included on the List by the end of 1916 were jute and jute bags from Calcutta (vital for the trenches), rice from Burma, hides and skins from Madras, and tea and plumbago from Ceylon (the latter much used for medicinal purposes on the Western Front), plus a variety of miscellaneous goods cited 'as articles of special National importance'.[27] Best of all, some critical foodstuffs were imported directly by the government with the financial assistance of the banks. The most extensive of these arrangements covered the shipment of wheat from India. As plans were being drawn up in 1915 for an official 'Wheat Scheme', the Eastern exchange banks took pains to remind the government of their historic role in India

---

* The fees were generally agreed in proportion to shipment values, so higher prices fed directly into increased earnings for the bank. Halfway through the war, the Chairman reviewed the percentage gains recorded for seven basic products as of March 1916 compared with March 1914. His list comprised sugar (up 50 per cent), wheat (50 per cent), jute (22 per cent), indigo (333 per cent), hemp (116 per cent), tin (47 per cent) and copper (101 per cent). (Chairman's Address to Annual General Meeting, 1 April 1916, LMA: CH01/03/05/001.)

and the disruption that would surely follow if India's Presidency banks were allowed to intrude on the workings of the sub-continent's currency-exchange market.* This pre-emptive move against fresh local competition was entirely successful – and many of the largest Indian-owned ('swadeshi') banks had anyway disappeared in the first, crisis-strewn weeks of the war. So the exchange banks retained effective control of the booming trade with India, and prospered accordingly. A telegram in April 1917 from the Foreign Office to Chartered's branch in Bombay emphasized the great importance of the 'Wheat Scheme' in particular:

> The [Exchange] Banks agree to buy sterling bills and/or TT against wheat and/or grains on Government account from Sandays Clements Robson, Strauss Co Ltd and E.D. Sassoon to the extent of £400,000 weekly or thereabouts during the next few months . . . The Banks must work in concert and loyally assist each other in every possible way to ensure the proper working of this scheme [and] there must be no hitch (full stop) This business must take precedence of [sic] all other exports.[28]

A letter a month later from Thomas Fraser as Joint Manager of the Chartered confirmed that shipments to the value of £1.64 million had been made in just three weeks.

As all this might suggest, the war transformed the finances of Chartered Bank itself. Its balance sheet roughly doubled in size, and total assets by 1919 were valued at almost £69 million – a level the bank would struggle to reach again through most of the next twenty years. Annual operating profits logged in 38 Bishopsgate – including those earned in the City by Head Office itself – more than doubled, from just under £400,000 in 1914 to just over £900,000 in 1918 (see Appendix D). True, the two years' figures were not strictly comparable, given the impact of wartime inflation (cost-of-living indices constructed retrospectively trace a rise from 100 in 1914 to 210 in 1918).[29] The bottom line was also less impressive, not least because the taxman had now to be accommodated. Inaugurated in 1911, the annual corporate tax rate rose steadily through the war. Indeed, the

---

* A Joint Letter was addressed to the India Office on 30 March 1915 by Chartered Bank, National Bank of India, Hongkong and Shanghai Bank, Mercantile Bank of India and Eastern Bank. (The sixth exchange bank was the much smaller Cox & Co., not included as a signatory on this occasion.) The merest suggestion that the government might hand some of the financing to Indian institutions would be disastrous, warned the banks. 'The uncertainty caused by doubts as to what the ultimate result of this Government action might be and the inevitable disturbance in the exchanges, must affect unfavourably the mercantile community and the masses of the population in their purchasing power, and thus affect the import of British goods into India and the revenue of the Indian Government itself.' (LMA: CH03/01/01/020.)

introduction of an Excess Profits Tax lifted the effective tax rate for the Chartered to 25 per cent for 1916, and 45 per cent for 1918. Still, the wartime finances of the bank were more than robust by any measure, and the Directors each year squirrelled away as much of the operating profits as they dared into one kind of back pocket or another: hidden reserves by the end of 1918 were just over £954,000, up from the £454,000 in 1913 that had taken decades to amass.[30] This kept published net profits within the bounds of decorum in the middle three years of the war – profits for 1916 were actually reported as slightly down on those for 1915, though in reality they had jumped by almost 30 per cent – but there was no disguising the prodigious growth of the bank from its own Directors and shareholders. They were drawn into periodic confessions of amazement at their good fortune.* As the Chairman admitted to the Annual General Meeting in April 1916, it was 'a remarkable fact that, in spite of the Empire's vast military operations . . . the trade of Great Britain, our Colonies and our dependencies has suffered comparatively so little'. An admiring shareholder was less restrained, assuring the same meeting that 'the various Indian exchange banks had had a year which, under the circumstances, could be described almost as marvellous'.[31] Other publicly quoted British banks, faced with a general contraction of their domestic retail banking operations, were slashing their dividends. The Chartered, with its trade-financing revenues rising steadily on the back of an unprecedented boom in shipments from the East, went on paying at its pre-war rate of 14 per cent – and even topping up the dividends with bonus payments that lifted shareholders' returns higher still.

The bank's employees were treated generously, too. In addition to continuing the annual staff bonuses paid regularly before the war, cost-of-living allowances were used to help defray rising inflation; and anyone

---

* From a twenty-first century perspective, the hidden reserves' role in reducing taxable profits would seem a matter of some importance. It prompted no real debate at the time, nor apparently was the taxman much exercised by the open acknowledgement of this anomaly at shareholders' meetings. It was simply accepted that banks published deeply obscure accounts, and that tax regulations were scarcely any clearer. In effect, now and for many years to come, the banks paid lower taxes – and came under less pressure to raise their dividends – as a result of running hidden reserves, in exchange for which their 'smoothing' of their profits provided the economy with a crucial (and for the most part successful) bulwark against financial instability. 'The privilege of non-disclosure was granted as part of the implicit regulatory bargain in which the banks acted as a monetary policy tool, albeit an imperfect one.' (Mark Billings and Forrest Capie, *Transparency and Financial Reporting in Mid-Twentieth Century British Banking*, Bank of England publications, 2007, p. 22.) The case for obliging the banks to abandon their hidden reserves only really gathered momentum towards the end of the 1950s, culminating in their eventual disappearance by the early 1970s. For Standard Chartered's response, see Chapter 8, p. 445 fn.

serving in the East whose home leave had to be postponed (as was invariably the case) could expect a compensatory payment equivalent to a fifth of their salary. To be sure, many of the staff more than deserved a little extra. At Head Office, in particular, Europe's sudden plunge into war kept the lights burning late into the night for seven days a week as staff struggled to keep abreast of the paperwork. Weekend duties were to remain a feature of the next four years. Normal office routines were of course heavily disrupted by the rush of men to enlist: by April 1915, all those who were eligible had already gone. Out of about 300 men employed at Head Office in 1914 – well over twice the size of Hatton Court's staff just ten years earlier – about 120 marched away, 40 per cent of the total, including virtually all the probationary Foreign Staffers. Another thirty or so followed them from London over the course of the war. The bank set a template for all of the exchange banks in keeping its enlisted married men on full pay (the bachelors got half-pay). These arrangements, though, only applied to the men from Bishopsgate. Overseas, a different story unfolded. By agreement with the British government, members of the Foreign Staff were strongly discouraged from enlisting: the Chartered's contribution to the role of the Empire as supplier of raw materials was deemed essential war work. The Chairman told shareholders at the 1915 Annual General Meeting that the enlisted men included 'at least half a dozen of the foreign staff – all that we could spare'.[32] But as the fighting wore on, and drew in vast numbers of men from across the Empire, many on the Chartered's Foreign Staff nevertheless opted to enlist, even though this meant having to resign from the bank. (Almost all of them were welcomed back after the war.) We know that over the course of the whole war, 199 Chartered men served in the armed forces.[33] This implies that as many as fifty may have signed up in the East, representing more than half of a total Foreign Staff still numbering less than a hundred men. The strain on the network must have been severe, and several of the larger overseas branches were struggling by the later stages of the war. When two men on the Foreign Staff in Hong Kong telegraphed London in April 1918 asking for permission to resign in order to enlist, the Secretary turned down their requests. Indeed, he went rather further than that, and appealed to the Colonial Office in London to instruct the government in Hong Kong to block their departures from the Colony. As he explained to the Office:

> Up to the present, the Directors of this Bank have received with all sympathy [sic] the applications of its young men abroad to place their services at the disposal of the country in an active and physical capacity, but they feel that our depleted staff in the East due to resignations for this purpose has now

reached the minimum compatible with the safe conduct of our business which has for its primary object the financing in India, Burmah, Ceylon and at most of our Branches [of] Exports of National importance and the maintenance of the country's overseas trade on which so much depends.[34]

The bank's staffing predicament across its Eastern network was more worrying than the situation in London for one very notable reason: the branches had no share in the dramatic influx of women into the workplace that transformed the City of London. Like all of its peers, the Chartered by the beginning of 1915 was starting to recruit women clerks in significant numbers to fill the gaps left by those who had gone to war. Few specifics have survived in the archives; perhaps the logistics of hiring and administering a new cohort of typists and junior clerks seemed too mundane a matter to be worth recording for posterity. But perhaps a hundred or more women must have entered the bank's service and this did not go entirely unremarked. Hitherto a strictly male preserve, Head Office had to abandon many cherished traditions – slightly to the dismay of some disgruntled old-timers, who were quick to spread word among their peers in the East that the intimate culture of Hatton Court had finally and most regrettably been left behind in the new world of 38 Bishopsgate. More generously, the Chairman assured shareholders in 1917 that 'the employment of lady clerks has been eminently satisfactory'.[35] And other oblique references survive here and there. Across the road from 38 Bishopsgate was Slaters Restaurant, where subsidized lunches were provided for the staff every day from the autumn of 1915. A meal for 1s 3d would cost the employee just 6d. Women clerks got their lunch free.[36] No doubt this was partly in recompense for the fact that they were being paid significantly less than their male counterparts.*

Those Chartered men who stuck to their civilian jobs in the East were rarely quite as insulated from the grimmer realities of the war as their peers in the City of London. In this respect, the staff's experience of the First World War had much in common with several earlier wars stretching all the way back to the young Howard Gwyther's brush with the Taiping rebels of 1860 in Shanghai. Over the course of the First World War, many members of staff found themselves unexpectedly caught up in violent episodes on the periphery of the global conflict. Not a few of them were roped into vigilante forces and guard duties, wherever expatriate

---

* Staff records for 1930 note that eighty-five female employees were being paid £90–£250 per annum, which compared with £210–£500 per annum for the most junior category of male clerks (Home Staff Salary Lists 1930–36, LMA: CH04/09/04/003). A similar differential probably applied even in 1915–18.

communities feared for their safety. Such duties were usually tedious, but could occasionally involve tasks rather different from anything ever described in a banker's manual – none more disquieting than G. A. Allen's in Singapore in February 1915. A mutiny among troops of an Indian Army regiment billeted locally led to the murder of several Europeans around the city. No Chartered families were attacked, but Allen was one of many who readily took up patrol duties in the weeks after the mutiny's suppression (and similar volunteer militias were mobilized elsewhere in the Malay Archipelago, too).[37] Allen did not hold back when volunteers were sought for a firing squad to carry out a public execution. As he recounted a few months later, it was a gruesome affair and must have seared itself into his memory for years to come:

> The Volunteers were, for some reason, given the hardest job of the lot. There were to be 5 shots at each man [of twenty-two prisoners], so we had to find a party of 110. Many men were pressed into it, but I don't mind saying I volunteered at once, thinking of the murders these chaps had committed. Imagine the long line of 110 of us, two deep, standing opposite these natives, their feet tied together and leaning against a stake. They moved about a good deal and were not blindfolded [;] some prayed, some cursed at us, some were quite quiet but watched us all the time. This went on . . . [until] our officer saw some of us getting nervy and we suddenly got the words 'Load, Aim, Fire!' very quickly. We got off quite a good volley, but didn't kill them all outright. They were finished off by some scandalously indiscriminate firing by the excited warders . . . The worst part of the whole job was standing eight paces from the row of corpses, as you couldn't help seeing the wounds . . . It was rather rotten our making such a mess of it . . . and why the deuce they gave us the most trying job of the lot, I don't know.[38]

By the end of the war, the bank's Roll of Honour listed thirty-seven Chartered men who had lost their lives in the fighting – but this took no account of those worn down at Head Office by a far greater workload. Chief among them was Thomas Fraser himself, whose ill-health had kept him from the office for long periods of 1917 – he was belatedly diagnosed as suffering from coeliac disease – and whose death in January 1918 robbed the bank of a formidable manager and a respected authority on currency matters.[39] (The news prompted all the exchange banks in Calcutta to close for a half-day as a mark of respect.) William Hoggan, Company Secretary since 1898 and now sixty-three, retired the same year. The indefatigable Thomas Whitehead was five years older, had been at the helm for sixteen years and had inevitably borne the brunt of the wartime pressures. Within months of the war's end, he too was confiding to close friends his intention to step down soon. He stayed long enough, though, to preside over a huge boost to the bank's capital – a sale of fresh equity in 1919 raised £1.6 million – and, over the course of that first year of the peace, Chartered's market capitalization jumped more than 50 per cent, to £8.1 million.[40] Whitehead presided over a continuation of the bank's wartime prosperity through 1919: published profits for the year showed another substantial rise (though they actually fell some way short of the undisclosed real profits earned in 1916 and 1917). He also saw through a key change to the executive structure. Fraser's successor, William Preston, would become the first 'Chief Manager' with the support of two colleagues in the familiar role of 'Manager'. Whitehead then announced his departure 'with immediate effect' in May 1920. True to form, he linked his statement to news that he would shortly be leaving to hunt big game in East Africa.[41]

2. EMPIRE AND EXCHANGE

Had Imperial Germany and her allies triumphed in 1918, Britain's virtually unhindered freedom to rule her own Empire far from Europe's shores would have vanished as the guns fell silent. For half a century, the Great Powers of continental Europe had effectively acquiesced in Britain's lavish application of red ink to the maps of Asia and southern Africa. Of course there had been some exceptions. The French had busied themselves carving out a mini-empire in Indo-China; the Germans had laid down markers of their future intent, not least in southern Africa and northern China. It was nonetheless broadly true that the Victorians' Pax Britannica, asserted across half the globe, had been left in peace – to the infinite benefit of, among so many others, the City of London's Eastern exchange banks. Theirs was a world in 1914 still dependent in every way on the continued ascendancy of British rules, with clubs, courts and counting houses across the great ports of the East taking their cue from London. Defeat on the Western Front, say in the wake of Tsarist Russia's implosion in October 1917, would have swept that world away. In the event, it survived. Indeed, the Empire looked better placed after 1918 than had seemed possible to many contemporaries ahead of the peace. In the words of one historian,

> It was Britain that emerged from the conflict with its political system most intact and with the majority of its strategic objectives met . . . [I]f the leaders of the British Empire emerged in a confident mood in November 1918, it was because they felt they had secured the foundations of the empire as a key pillar of the emerging, liberal world order.[42]

Over the years that followed, even while the statesmen of Europe muddled through one post-war settlement crisis after another, the primary-product economies of Asia were, accordingly, as tied as ever to the trade-financing strings pulled from the City. And London's exchange banks, exemplified by Chartered Bank, responded by re-asserting their pre-war dominance with remarkable success. It was an optimistic stance, given the breakdown of the old pre-1914 financial order and the emergence of new nationalist movements in many Asian countries. For several years, though, the optimism would be repaid. As David Lloyd George himself would observe in 1921, 'The War demonstrated – I might say revealed – to the world, including ourselves, that the British Empire was not an abstraction but a living force to be reckoned with.'[43]

The success of the Chartered's 1919 equity issue came as no surprise in the City: a year after the end of the war, almost all markets were generally still in euphoric mood. Commodity prices had soared even higher since the end of hostilities and Asian cargoes were now flooding into Europe's major ports. Investors noted that the Chartered had gone on expanding in the East even during the hostilities. A branch had been opened in Peking in 1915. The staff in Singapore had been relocated in 1916 to an august new headquarters in Raffles Place. And new premises had been acquired for sub-branches in Burma (at Tavoy) and Vietnam, in Haiphong.* Nonetheless, in snapping up Chartered's new stock, the City was making light of some signs that the bank's business environment might soon be exposed to new and potentially damaging developments. Violence and revolution had of course been more or less a permanent feature of the background to the bank's operations in China, helping to explain why the returns on business in that vast country had been a perennial source of disappointment – and why the Chartered's branches there had always been of secondary importance compared to those in Calcutta and Bombay, Rangoon and Colombo. But 1919 brought wind of a potentially far more ominous development: a concerted move by Indian nationalists to challenge the whole future of the British Raj itself. The Empire had leaned heavily on Indian resources during the war; Indian expectations of a suitable pay-back were quashed with a suddenness in 1918–19 that spawned a bitter reaction and altered the political dynamics of the Raj irreversibly. '[It] was to last no longer', in the words of one classic British account of modern India's history. 'It

---

* The lease on a much coveted address in Haiphong had eventually been approved by Head Office after the Saigon agent had cannily pointed out that a temporary arrangement in the city had left the Chartered looking 'undignified' and second-best to the Banque de l'Indo-Chine. 'What the French Bank themselves think of it we should not care to hear.' (L. R. Bremner, Saigon Agent, to Head Office, 1 February 1916, LMA: CH03/01/10/31/10.)

[would] appear to go on for another quarter-century, but it did really end in 1919 . . . Indians were no longer prepared to accept the passive role of being ruled.'[44] Gandhi launched his campaign of resistance to the British in March that year. Strikes and sporadic rioting ensued over the following weeks, involving at least one episode that must have nudged even the least attentive of the Chartered's shareholders into a sharper awareness of the changed atmosphere in the sub-continent. Mob violence swept through the Punjab, and for four days engulfed the city of Amritsar. On 13 April 1919 the rioting was brutally suppressed when orders were given to Indian Army soldiers to open fire on a crowded public square. Over three hundred died in the carnage and many more were injured.

The Amritsar Massacre would soon take on a symbolic importance that overshadowed all other aspects of the crisis in the Punjab that April – and the frightening events in the city left their mark on many Europeans caught up directly in the violence. They included the officers of three exchange banks in Amritsar, including the head of the Chartered's sub-branch in the city, J. W. Thomson. In a letter to the Karachi branch 'written [originally] on scraps of paper on the butt of a rifle' and apparently despatched on the day of the Massacre without any awareness of it, Thomson gave a graphic account of a very lucky escape. Around noon on 10 April, he spoke by telephone with the managers of the National Bank of India and the Alliance Bank, the latter confirming that 'a howling mob' had just passed his office. The three of them agreed to keep each other informed of events. Less than two hours later, Thomson and his Accountant, Alex Ross, were shaken to hear that the NBI manager and his deputy and the Alliance manager had all been seized and killed by the mob – which minutes later they saw approaching their own building at a run. With the help of their Indian Head Clerk (who afterwards wrote his own detailed and charmingly modest letter to Karachi), the two Chartered men managed just in time to conceal themselves in a cubby hole at the top of a disused stairway to the roof – having armed themselves in eccentric style:

> The only thing which I could find to make any attempt at defence with, were empty ink bottles (stone), and Mr Ross and I got one apiece . . . we could probably have knocked a few of them on the head before they got us. We both realised that it was only a question of a little time, with their numbers, before they got us, but we prepared to sell ourselves as dearly as we could . . . The mob were hammering the doors before we left the office, and soon after we got into our hole, they managed to break in. There was pandemonium . . . They were smashing tables, counters and anything they

could – windows and punkhas [fans]. The treasury was immediately below
us and we could hear them pounding at it. We also heard them now beginning in the record room with the stairway leading to our hiding place.[45]

Fortunately the Indian clerks had meanwhile retreated to the roof of the
building and had begun shouting frantically for help, which arrived just
in time to forestall the discovery of the two Englishmen. A posse of thirty
armed police drove the mob out of the building. Two hours later, and
disguised 'to make ourselves as like natives as possible', Thomson and
Ross escaped through a back door to the office garden and ran to the
safety of a nearby police station. (Some months later, the bank struck a
deal with the government, indemnifying customers against any losses at
Amritsar in exchange for the Controller of Currency agreeing to issue
duplicates of all the Government Promissory Notes that the bank reckoned
to have been destroyed in the ransacking of the branch.[46])

Civil disorder in various corners of the Empire, however shocking in
the short term, could of course be seen after four long years of war as a
regrettable part of the transition to peace. And City investors seem to have
taken the same view of another key development in 1919 – this one less
instantly troubling, but just as fundamental to the Chartered's future. The
bank's core business lay in the exchange of currencies for its customers.
Before the war, all the currencies it encountered had essentially been fixed
in value, both to each other and to their weight in gold, for many years
(albeit for rather more years in Europe than in Asia). Now this whole
edifice built around the Gold Standard had come crashing down. Governments had abandoned the Gold Standard during the war in their rush to
print more money as a complement to higher taxes. No currency except
(in theory) the US dollar was any longer convertible into gold. All others
were now floating (a term not yet in vogue) in a financial world that was
suddenly bereft of any comprehensible system at all. The consequences
were growing more bewildering by the month. Where inconvertible paper
notes had been printed ever more excessively through the war – most notably in Germany and France, but in many other countries, too – exchange
values had plummeted by the spring of 1919. They looked certain to go
on falling, since the governments behind them were plainly resigned to
accepting a steep devaluation. Their gold reserves had fallen heavily,
mostly draining away into the vaults of the US Federal Reserve Banks and
the US Treasury. Where silver coins remained the bedrock of the national
currency – as in India, with its silver rupee – the chaos was compounded
by silver's *rising* value. In contrast with the long slide in its value through
the last quarter of the nineteenth century, silver suddenly shot up in value

(see p. 111). The war had created an insatiable demand for extra silver coins in Europe to facilitate the greatly expanded trade with the East. The output of silver bullion had at the same time contracted, chiefly due to falling production in strife-torn Mexico, and the price of silver had risen accordingly. Fixed at 1s 4d against the pound since 1898, India's rupee had begun appreciating late in 1917. By late 1919 it was worth more than two shillings – a 50 per cent jump – and its value was still rising. (It would peak in 1920 at almost exactly twice its pre-war parity, at which point silver had become so valuable that it was extensively hoarded and began to disappear as a practical medium of exchange.) The gold value of the pound had, however, slumped by 40 per cent – yet the British government opted in March 1919 to part ways with its European neighbours and to seek a restoration of sterling to its pre-war value against gold and the US dollar. The markets remained deeply sceptical that this could really be achieved – not unreasonably, given the policy's severely deflationary implications – and the pound went on trading at an appreciable discount to the pre-war parity of $4.86, while still continuing to slide against the rupee.

Many supposed that more volatile exchange rates would line the bankers' pockets. Certainly opportunities opened up for some in 1919 as never before. Speculators, hitherto preoccupied with stock and bond prices, could now also make and lose fortunes by betting on currency movements. (Maynard Keynes himself made a killing in 1919 by buying – among other currencies – the Indian rupee, on which he had written a magisterial treatise just before the war, while going short on francs, Reichsmarks and lira. He lost all his gains for a while in 1920, too, when 'a spasm of optimism about Germany briefly drove the declining European currencies back up'.[47]) For Chartered Bank, though, the altered conditions were in truth a mixed blessing. As the Chairman, Sir Montagu Turner, rather charmingly put it to shareholders in 1920:

> The Hong Kong dollar, the Chinese tael and the Indian rupee have all been jumping about, so that you never know where to catch them . . . [I mention this] to show you the difficulties that exchange bankers have to contend with and the absurdity of people thinking that exchange banking means simply coining money; it is very often the reverse.[48]

It has to be assumed that shrewd positioning and superior market intelligence allowed the bank's branches, on balance, to augment their earnings marginally in the course of routine exchange dealings, though it would be difficult to prove this from their correspondence with Head Office. Meanwhile, as ever, Chartered men were strictly forbidden from 'naked' transactions, buying or selling currencies with no direct (or at least imme-diately foreseeable) linkage to customers' commercial transactions. Nor could non-sterling advances to customers be held for longer than as pre-scribed in the Head Office manual. All those years of hedging any exposure to silver, under Gwyther's stern eye, had left no room in the rules for ambiguity on that score. But while the bank's managers could not take risks in the exchange markets, their customers could – and many did, in 1919, if only by failing to hedge against strange and unprecedented cur-rency movements. Customer firms in Calcutta relying on pound sterling revenues to cope with local rupee debts fell on very hard times, and many failed – at their creditors' expense.* Here was one serious threat to the Chartered, inherent in the new order of things. And there was another: the unpegging of the world's currencies kicked off a great influx of bro-kers, intent on making a living out of this utterly transformed 'foreign exchange' market. As one authority put it a few years later, looking back on these days:

> A veritable orgy of dealing took place, and every centre seemed to be besieging London on long-distance calls. From early till late at night (6 p.m.) foreign centres called London and immense business was transacted. Brokers increased, and by 1920 there were about 40 different broking firms in the business of the banks and financial houses. There was business for all . . . The amounts turned over on the London exchange market were huge. Day after day the staffs of the brokers fed at their switchboards and went home exhausted.[49]

Close observers of this phenomenon might have questioned what would happen in future to the exchange 'spreads' that had traditionally been the core of Chartered Bank's earnings. No such concern, though, held back shareholders in 1919. Perhaps, not unreasonably, they assumed that Char-tered, with all its far-flung branches and accumulated expertise, would retain the leading position as a trader of currencies that it had enjoyed in the pre-war world.

They might have been a little less confident of this had they been able to see the entry for 1919 in the Court's Book of Profits and Losses, listing

---

* Banks failed, too. One of them, the Indian Specie Bank, collapsed early in 1919 and was unable to stand by its forward-purchase contracts in the silver market, worth about £3 mil-lion. Without a lifeboat arrangement, the silver market must have been severely disrupted. Confidence was restored by a rescue syndicate in which the Chartered took a leading role alongside the Hongkong and Shanghai Bank. The contracts were honoured, and the rising price of the metal allowed the syndicate to recoup its outlay without loss. Another member of the syndicate was the bullion broker Mocatta & Goldsmid, a firm that would feature often in the later story of Standard Chartered Bank.

the bank's results by branch. Calcutta was the network's flagship – its first branch and still its grandest, with that magnificent tailor-built temple of an office at the heart of the commercial district on Clive Street (complete with a private apartment for the Agent on the top floor). For most years since 1900 it had reported comfortably the highest annual earnings of any branch in the network, and had accounted for almost 13 per cent of the aggregate pre-tax earnings between 1895 and 1913.* In 1919, unprecedentedly and rather shockingly, Calcutta made a loss, of just over £65,000. An even bigger loss was incurred in Batavia (£95,500), though the bank was no stranger to misadventures there. Worst of all, the currency turmoil landed Shanghai with a loss of £272,455 that dwarfed any deficit reported by any branch in the history of the bank. Despite these setbacks, however, the Court was able to report a jump of almost 10 per cent in net profits for the year. In a foretaste of the pattern of profits to come, savage downturns in some branches had been offset by astonishing performances in others. Buoyed by the post-war commodities boom, Singapore, Manila and Saigon all chipped in the kinds of earnings hitherto associated only with Calcutta in its very best years; Penang and Kuala Lumpur broke all past records for the Straits Settlements; and, best of all, feverish growth in Japan's trade with the West allowed Yokohama to make a profit that came close to balancing out Shanghai's loss. Investors in the City were privy to none of this detail, but took heart from the bottom line. Even the collapse of the post-war boom in the autumn of 1920 – 'perhaps the most underrated event in the history of the twentieth century'[50] – failed to dent their faith in the Chartered's future. As the deflationary spiral of 1920–22 gathered pace (precipitating, among other price falls, a collapse in the price of silver bullion from 84d/oz to 32½d) they happily subscribed in December 1920 for another dollop of equity almost as large as the first helping in 1919. And the bank's £20 shares were split 4-for-1 – that is to say, shareholders with shares carrying a par value of £20 now received four shares in place of each one, each with a par value of £5 – to improve the marketability of the stock.

The successful issues of 1919–20 were an emphatic vote of confidence by the City in the Chartered's ability to go on prospering on the back of an Empire that might yet have its finest years ahead of it. The threat posed by Germany had been seen off, and Britain's position in India and beyond would surely now be more entrenched than ever. (The Government was not short of advice from Chambers of Commerce in the East on how to

---

* See Appendix D. Penang and Colombo were the runners-up, with about 9 per cent of the total over this period.

make sure that there would be no repetition of, for example, the pre-1914 incursions into the lands of the British Raj by German firms.*) The breadth and scale of the Chartered's network had endured, leaving it still the pre-eminent exchange bank in India and South Asia while a strong second to the Hongkong Bank in the Far East. And the performance of the bank over the next six years more than lived up to the City's expectations. Operating profits jumped astonishingly in 1920, more than doubling those of 1919 (£1,427,795 versus £700,111). That boom-year level could not be sustained, but operating profits nonetheless continued at an average annual rate of just over £1 million for each of the next six years. This was achieved despite a harsh deflationary climate, reducing the sterling value of most currencies in the East, and some shuddering falls in the price of many commodities in 1920–22. The Chartered outperformed all of its overseas banking peers in the City. It also made a substantial contribution to the Exchequer: reported net earnings fell some way short of operating profits, reflecting not just the usual discretionary transfers into 'inner reserves' but also some unprecedentedly heavy tax payments. (The Excess Profits Tax introduced in 1916 remained in place until 1922, and resulted in tax rates for 1920 and 1921 of 45 and 31 per cent respectively.[51])

Setting aside their newly elevated level, pre-tax profits in the 1920s were manifesting another significant change compared with the pre-war era. At a regional level, their geographical distribution was not so very different:

	Total pre-tax profits	
	1895–1913	1919–26
	%	%
India (including Burma)	37.1	26.5
South-east Asia	31.5	29.2
China	10.6	8.7
Other branches	5.5	9.9
Head Office	15.3	25.7
Total	100.0	100.0

* In Burma, for example, a Rangoon Chamber committee in 1917 had prepared a paper recommending that German firms be totally excluded from the country's rice trade after the war. The latter's pre-war incursions had made Germany 'the chief centre in Europe for the polishing and distribution of Burma rice'. New rules and taxes for the post-war world were proposed 'to prevent the dumping of enemy goods and the re-establishment by enemy firms of the hold in the trade in India [i.e. including Burma] which they possessed prior to the war' – though the Chartered's Rangoon manager, P. E. Beeston, persuaded the committee to drop measures aimed at dictating the exclusive use of British exchange banks for the rice trade, which he thought unlikely to be enforceable. ('Report of the Provincial Committee, appointed by the Local Government [of Burma]', 8 February 1917, LMA: CH03/01/10/50/18.)

Behind each year's aggregate numbers for all branches, though, there lurked as in 1919 a novel and disconcerting mix of winners and losers. Prior to the First World War, in a gradually expanding network – thirteen branches at the turn of the century, nineteen in 1913 – no such mix had existed. New York had had its teething troubles, in setting up accounts for US companies trading with the East, while Tientsin had several times made a loss in the face of constant political upheavals. Even so, most years saw at most just one or two loss-makers. After the war, the network almost invariably had a third or more of its twenty-two to twenty-four branches in the red every year. No consistent pattern presented itself. Only five branches (Bombay, Colombo, Kuala Lumpur, Singapore and Hong Kong) managed to avoid losses altogether; and of these only Colombo, with a usefully varied supplement of export crops in addition to its main staples of tea and rubber, achieved any real consistency. Results elsewhere rose and fell each year in quantum moves that, for the most part, must have been utterly unpredictable – not to say hugely unnerving – for the managers at Head Office. Penang earned more than mighty Bombay in 1920, then collapsed into losses two years later. Bangkok made a massive loss in 1920, and a stellar profit that outshone all other results just the following year. Singapore doubled its year-on-year earnings in 1925, as did Hong Kong in 1926. In short, the branches of the bank were adrift on a sea of volatile commodity and currency values. Most branch managers could only hope to shape each year's financial outcome to a modest extent, while those watching over them from London had even less influence on the aggregate result. It was to be some years before the Court would confront the implications of all this. In the meantime, the Directors made the most of victory in 1918 and the Empire's still sprawling geography to spread their bets, continuing to extend the network as before the war, with numerous sub-branches taking its services ever further afield.

The First World War had of course resulted in some noteworthy extensions to that Empire. To parry the wartime threat to India of a German incursion into the Middle East, Britain had built up huge military forces there by 1918. With the collapse of the Ottoman Empire, the British hastened to consolidate their presence by asserting their jurisdiction over great swathes of the region governed for centuries by the Turks. Until 1914, the task of watching over India's interests in the Gulf had been a low-key affair, left to the devices of Percy Cox, a wily Indian Army officer (famed for his command of Arabic) who held the post of 'Political Resident' and was based in the city of Bushire on the Persian side of the Gulf. (For decades the Raj had subtly exercised control within the princely states of India through Political Advisers, who comprised a kind of Foreign

Office to set beside the 'Home Office' franchise of the Indian Civil Service within British India's directly administered provinces. This system had effectively been extended to ensure British influence in the Gulf.) Following the Armistice, Cox was assigned to Tehran, and Britain set up direct military rule in Mesopotamia. As a recent history of the war's aftermath has observed, 'there was heady optimism in London that British occupation of much of the Middle East could be turned into a permanent sphere of influence'.[52] Where the Ottoman Bank had previously enjoyed a preferential status, an opportunity thus beckoned for a British bank to step up in its place. However, the Chartered held back – even though one of its top men in London was now J. S. Bruce, who as a young Accountant from Bombay had immersed himself so impressively in the bazaars of Baghdad and Basra in 1907–8 to prepare his report for the Court on the feasibility of setting up branches in the two cities. (Having seen then the potential lawlessness of the region, perhaps Bruce advised a cautious approach until the shape of the post-war settlement was clearer.) Instead, it was the Eastern Bank that grabbed its chance.

The fledgling Eastern's pre-war activities had been centred on Bombay. It had said little at its 1909 flotation about any ambitions in the Arab world, and had opened just two branches there, in Basra and Baghdad, both of which Turkish troops had closed down late in 1914.[53] Once the scale of the war had become clear, though, the bank's Directors appear to have looked more closely at the business possibilities on the Arabian side of the Gulf. The notion of carving out a commercial franchise in the territories of a defeated Ottoman empire – where it could be a pioneer, rather than a Johnny-come-lately, as it would always be in India itself – plainly had its attractions for the bank's London Board. Gaining a foothold in the tiny desert sheikhdoms of the coastal region must have looked a sensible first step: they were effectively British protectorates, where the rupee ruled in the bazaars and the dhows plied much of their trade with India, but as yet they had no modern banking facilities at all. One of the trading posts most actively linked to Bombay was the off-shore island of Bahrain, ruled for generations by the Al-Khalifa family, and the Eastern approached British officials about setting up there in 1916. Initially it encountered resistance from Bahraini merchant families who were worried about the impact on their own trading activities. ('The Bank is like a great mountain upon which anyone who fell would be broken', as the head of the leading Kanoo family darkly warned his peers.[54]) In persevering with its plans, though, the bank usefully advanced its interests in an unexpected fashion. It needed to rely heavily in Bahrain on the active support it received from Britain's Colonial Service men on the spot. This forged useful ties between them, which were strengthened when the Eastern re-opened its branches in Basra and Baghdad in 1919. Months later the military government established by the British in Mesopotamia needed to set up an official bank. The Eastern offered its services, was duly appointed and soon added more local branches in Mosul and Hillah. For its young officers posted over from India, the strategic rationale probably seemed less than compelling. In addition to the sweltering heat of the summer – which they had to endure while living in makeshift mess buildings, with no fans and few windows – they actually found themselves with very little to do aside from registering deposits and disbursing cash for the British armed forces in the region. A visiting Inspector reported back to the East-ern's Head Office in Crosby Square, early in 1920:

> It appears to me that something might be done if we could work entirely through Government, or in other words a loan would only be granted on the Political Officer's recommendation . . . I cannot say Government would be prepared to cooperate with the Bank to this extent, but it is of course impracticable [to proceed with any lending] unless they did.[55]

The bank did its best to fall in with the Government's wishes and (by now conspicuously halting) plans for the country. But after the outbreak of an Arab nationalist uprising in the Euphrates Valley in June 1920, daily life for the Eastern's half-dozen British officers must have been, in every sense, extremely uncomfortable. The level of violence in the region esca-lated rapidly, with the deployment of huge numbers of British troops – backed up by gunboats, armoured trains and several RAF squadrons – leading to heavy Arab casualties.* After the revolt was eventually suppressed, direct military rule was abandoned in favour of a far subtler approach, largely under the skilful direction once again of Percy Cox: Britain con-trived to found a new country, to be called 'Iraq' and to be ruled over from Baghdad by an Arab monarch, King Faisal, with an Indian-style British Political Adviser influencing policy behind the throne. Thereafter, stability was gradually restored. By 1923, we find the Eastern Bank adding to its Iraq staff and expanding nicely in Basra and Baghdad (after straightening

---

* The British response drew a fierce rebuke at home from the man whose name had become synonomous with the Allies' wartime support for the Arab uprising against the Turks, T. E. Lawrence. Writing in the *Sunday Times* of 22 August 1920, Lawrence despaired of the out-come: 'The people of England have been led in Mesopotamia into a trap from which it will be hard to escape with dignity and honour . . . How long will we permit millions of pounds, thousands of Imperial troops and tens of thousands of Arabs to be sacrificed on behalf of a form of colonial administration which can benefit nobody but its administrators?' (Quoted in Justin Marozzi, *Baghdad: City of Peace, City of Blood*, Allen Lane, 2014, p. 298.)

out some obscure local difficulties along the way[56]). More sub-branches in Mosul and Kirkuk would soon be added. Substantial cash deposits in the Middle East had bolstered its balance sheet rather dramatically and the bank could boast a paid-up capital a third as big as the Chartered's, though its market capitalization was scarcely a tenth as large. It had been appointed as the official banker to Faisal's new Iraqi government, which at least confirmed its status in Gulf business circles even if its subsequent support for Faisal seems not to have met with much enthusiasm in London.*

Meanwhile the Eastern's wartime initiative to set down a branch in Bahrain had finally come to fruition in July 1920, not least due to the Colonial authorities' strong encouragement. 'There was no doubt that [the] Government wished the Bank to start there immediately', an Inspector of the bank wrote home from Iraq, 'and in view of your instructions to Basra that we should open in Bahrain as soon as possible, I did not feel in a position to raise any objection.'[57] One reason for the government's enthusiasm was its desire to have a British bank on the ground that could conveniently manage the subsidies it was intent on paying to a potentially crucial figure in Arabian politics, the Emir of Najd, Abdel Aziz Ibn Saud. (The new branch handled shipments of gold specie to Ibn Saud for the next three years and held modest deposits for his agent on the island.[58]) Commercially, the local Bahraini merchants were now fully reconciled to a presence for the bank and were happy to draw on its assistance in funding the island's famous pearl fisheries: its native pearls were to remain Bahrain's principal export throughout the 1920s. The bank also picked up a few maverick European customers, like the mining engineer and former British army quartermaster Major Frank Holmes who arrived in Bahrain in 1922 with colourful ideas about a gigantic oil field that he thought might one day be discovered running down the whole eastern side of the Arabian Peninsula. The Eastern's Head Office was mildly surprised at the progress of the branch, writing to its Manager in 1923: 'We are very pleased . . . and hope that it may lead to your obtaining deposits from the

---

* When the bank organized a dinner for him at The Savoy on 18 November 1927, most of the intended guests – politicians, bankers and old soldiers including Field Marshal Allenby – found they had prior engagements. The bank sent out seventy-two invitations over the summer of 1927, but ended up with a table of just twenty-four including the hosts and Faisal's own party. The most notable guest was the man who had stepped down as High Commissioner in Iraq four years earlier, Sir Percy Cox. (Papers re Dinner for King Faisal of Iraq, 18 November 1927, LMA: MS39019.) One has to wonder whether any of those who declined the invitation later regretted it. Just over four weeks ahead of the dinner, on 14 October 1927, the first oil was struck in the former lands of the Ottoman Empire – famously exploding out of a well that had been drilled just north of Kirkuk in the new kingdom of Iraq.

minor sheikhs in your neighbourhood.'[59] And indeed, the branch took on the personal account of Bahrain's ruler, Sheikh Isa ibn Ali Al-Khalifa, the following year.

Still, as a foray into new territory opened up by the war, the Eastern's expansion into the Arab world was undeniably a cautious business, scarcely encouraged by the conspicuous lack of interest in the region among political circles in England. Meanwhile, thousands of miles to the south, defeat for German arms in southern Africa had entailed a much more forthright extension of the Empire and had posed a surprising new challenge for the Standard Bank.

3. EASING INTO AFRICA

The war had proved a boon for the Standard's South African operations in almost every respect. (As a reminder of the one obvious exception, the Cape Town branch has a fine memorial to the 812 officers of the bank who served in the war, of whom 105 were killed or died of their wounds.*) The bank had had its share of the problems that arose early in the war, when a sizeable number of Britain's old Boer foes rose up in anger against the idea of fighting a war with Germany on behalf of the King's Empire. The ensuing rebellion had forced parts of the network to close temporarily, rather as had happened in the Boer War itself though on a smaller scale; but no significant financial losses were incurred. (The depth of South Africa's problem with torn loyalties at the time is perhaps reflected in the Standard's response: having granted 300 men leave of absence for military duties in the affected areas to help suppress the troubles, the bank then made £75,000 available for emergency loans to farmers charged as rebels and hit with heavy fines by the courts.[60]) Thereafter, the country's economy had thrived in much the same way as the economies of Asia. In almost every sector, demand had risen steeply once the uncertainties of the war's first year had been survived.† Best of all, South Africa's premier export

---

* The Cape Town memorial was unveiled by J. P. Gibson on 3 February 1927 in the presence of both Lewis Michell and Hector Mackenzie. (The installation had been endlessly delayed by a lengthy refurbishment of the building.) A more elaborate memorial was unveiled a few months later in London, with a dedication by the Bishop of Pretoria. Recording only the names of those killed, the Clements Lane monument was flanked by statues of two infantrymen and straddled a staircase leading up from the Head Office's main entrance hall. Sadly, it was broken up and discarded during the modernization of the building in 1972–3.

† There was just one South African commodity market to which the war brought sudden death: European high society's long love affair with the feather boa was over, and so was the export trade in ostrich feathers.

had broken free of the constraints of a fixed price: gold had sold at steadily higher prices, just like wool, coal and diamonds. The Standard's finances had waxed on the back of all this. Deposits had soared and its balance sheet, much like the Chartered's in fact, had almost doubled in size. Every effort had been made to keep the published profits within the bounds of decency – a decline was even reported for 1915 – but a reconstruction of the real profits shows them doubling exactly, from just over £345,000 in 1914 to just over £690,000 in 1918.[61]

The war's impact on the Standard, though, involved more than a mighty boost for its finances. Just as important to the future of the bank, at least for the Directors presiding over its affairs from London, were the ramifications of the war for the Standard's future aspirations across the continent of Africa. To see how these were transformed by the middle of the 1920s, above all in the context of East Africa, we must start with a brief review of the bank's operations north of the Transvaal prior to 1914.

They had mostly been limited to a steadily growing network in Southern Rhodesia. In the two decades that followed the establishment of that first branch at Fort Salisbury in 1892, the bank had added eleven more – plus an outlying branch at Livingstone, Northern Rhodesia's designated capital on the far side of the Zambezi river, in 1907.* Elsewhere beyond the borders of the new Dominion of South Africa, exploratory moves had been distinctly half-hearted and were given scarcely any consideration by the Directors in London. To the west, neighbouring South West Africa briefly had its attractions, after the discovery of diamonds in the country in 1908. But it had been a German colony since 1884, and after Cape Town had sent one of its German-speaking managers on a reconnaissance mission, in 1909, it was decided that the Deutsche-Afrika Bank was too formidably entrenched to make any late challenge worthwhile. To the east, Portuguese East Africa had yet to develop an economy that would yield much business: branches had been set up at the two ports of Lourenço Marques and Beira and at a couple of river harbours, but these were ruggedly pioneering outposts, even by the Standard's yardstick. (One of them was actually located just to the west of the Portuguese territory, in the British Protectorate of Nyasaland. Cape Town reassigned some of its Southern Rhodesia men in 1901 to set up a branch at the tiny settlement

---

* The eleven additional Southern Rhodesian offices were at Bulawayo (founded May 1894), Umtali (July 1895), Gwelo (July 1897), Selukwe (July 1900), Hartley (July 1901), Gatooma (December 1909), Que Que (1910), Bindura (May 1911), Victoria (July 1911), Umvuma (November 1911) and Eldorado (April 1912). The branch at Livingstone was transferred there from Kalomo, the earlier capital of Northern Rhodesia, where it had existed for barely eighteen months.

of Blantyre. It is said that local tradesmen had pressed the bank to open, which might explain why it grew surprisingly quickly over the next decade.[62])

Far to the north of the Cape – in fact, roughly a third of the distance back to London from Cape Town – lay British East Africa. Here was a territory that had plenty to recommend it. One of the Standard Bank's managers went there privately to buy up farmland in 1904 and wrote back to his colleagues with a glowing account 'of grassy uplands not unlike England and of a climate in which Europeans could live normal lives and flourish'.[63] A substantial port, Mombasa, was linked by rail to a township at Nairobi that was swelling rapidly with an influx of (mostly British) settlers. There was even a scattering of Boers on the upland plains further to the west, around Eldoret. The 600-mile railway ran some way south of their farms to reach Lake Victoria, where fortnightly steamboats plied a passage across to the opposite shore and the tiny port settlements of Uganda, another British protectorate. The Standard's senior managers, however, were slow to take much interest in the region. They finally made a move only in 1910, when prodded into action by reports that a rival bank might be heading there. Over the next couple of years, men and materials were despatched to set up branches in Mombasa, Nairobi and the tiny town of Kampala, designated as the capital of Uganda. (Preparing for his journey to Kampala in 1912, its first manager, J. J. Swanson, had no luck trying to find it in the office atlas in Cape Town – and was repeatedly assured by a senior colleague 'that Uganda was in South America and he could not quite see the reason for going there'.[64] Swanson – a Scotsman who had worked at Kimberley for a few years from 1904 and had spent several months as manager of the branch at Livingstone in 1908–9 – had an aptitude for remote postings, not unconnected to his passion for hunting, and was undeterred. In retirement fifty years later, he would pen a colourful memoir of his time in East Africa.[65])

As the new branches struggled to gain momentum, the Standard's managers at the Cape found themselves encountering the kind of problems long familiar to overseas banks like the Chartered that had always run networks at a far remove from head office. Money and banking in East Africa were in effect an extension to the markets of Bombay: traders, most of them Asian, preferred silver to gold and used the Indian rupee, an unfamiliar currency to the Standard that denominated big numbers with a wayward use of the comma.* Native languages were used in preference

---

* One hundred thousand rupees (or 1 lakh) = R 1,00,000; a million rupees (10 lakhs) = R 10,00,000; and ten million rupees (100 lakhs, or 1 crore) = R 1,00,00,000.

to either English or Dutch, not just in the bazaar (Swahili) but even on the trade bills discounted by the bankers (Gujerati). Indeed, so foreign were the ways of this marketplace that the Standard's branches needed to employ intermediaries, much like Chinese compradores but known as 'brokers'. Above all, there was the simple fact that British East Africa was an unconscionably long way from the Cape. Letters took several days to reach Mombasa (and could take another three weeks to arrive in Kampala). For between the northern borders of Portuguese East Africa and British East Africa lay another giant country, stretching from the Indian Ocean in the east to Lake Tanganyika and Lake Nyasa in the west – German East Africa. This was the Kaiser's other principal colony on the continent, three times the size of Germany itself, and as of 1914 the Standard had made no headway there at all. It had briefly experimented with a branch off the coast in Zanzibar – the old centre of the Arab slave trade and another British protectorate since 1890 – but had closed it in 1913 after less than two years. No attempt had been made to open in the main port being developed by the Germans at Dar-es-Salaam, or at any of their larger settlements in the interior.

The war, however, meant a fresh start for the Standard on both sides of the continent. An invasion of South West Africa by forces under General Louis Botha, the former Boer commander and now South Africa's Premier, forced the Germans into surrendering their colony in July 1915. The Standard lost no time establishing three branches, two on the coast, at Luderitzbucht and Swakopmund, and one at the centre of the vast territory – half as big as the Union of South Africa itself – in the capital, Windhoek. Unsurprisingly, the government in Cape Town looked to the bank to help restore civil order after months of fighting. Having taken possession of the local branches of the Deutsche-Afrika Bank, with their deposits of Reichsbank notes, the Standard agreed to lend South African pounds against the security of the German currency while the latter was amassed and shipped off to New York for sale to the German banks there.* Thus commenced the Standard's operations in a land that would effectively be annexed by South Africa after the war, remaining a fifth province of the Republic in all but name until its emergence as the independent state of Namibia in

---

* The complications of the currency operation prompted a visit to South West Africa before the end of 1915 by J. P. Gibson, the bank's Deputy General Manager (and General Manager, 1919–26). The story of his visit accounts for one of the very few jokes in J. A. Henry's centenary history: Gibson's ship from the Cape to Luderitzbucht hit an off-shore reef, obliging all the passengers to take to the lifeboats and seek refuge for two days on the nearest bit of land – 'a rocky promontory, where the Standard Bank had no representative'. Doubtless, no laughing matter at the time. (*The First Hundred Years of the Standard Bank*, p. 169.)

1990. Meanwhile, the war in East Africa – one of the least familiar stories of the First World War – had become a far bloodier and more protracted affair. Several of the Standard's European staff in Mombasa and Nairobi, like many of the Chartered's in Asia, had resigned in August 1914 to enlist with the British army. After some confusion, they were offered new contracts putting them on half-pay pending their return. But they were to be gone for four years, and some never came back. The fighting, which mostly took place within German East Africa, involved hundreds of thousands of local Africans and posed huge problems of logistics for the British and allied forces. As they extended their control over the towns of the German colony, the military relied heavily on the Mombasa banks to help with cash and credit requirements. The National Bank of India was the army's official banker, while the Standard served the civil administrators who were eventually charged with absorbing the territory into the Empire. New branches followed accordingly, with the Standard opening in Tanga (in 1916), Dar-es-Salaam, Zanzibar and Tabora (1917), Mwanza (1918) and Bukoba (1919). The task of organizing the bank's operations in Dar-es-Salaam fell to the former Kampala manager, J. J. Swanson. The chaos in the town he would recall as 'almost indescribable', with 30,000 soldiers there when he arrived, but he opened over a thousand accounts in his first month.

The sheer scale of the local conflict, which came as a shock to almost all of the participants, abruptly transformed the Standard's sleepy pre-1914 approach to East Africa. Military expenditure galvanized the regional economy, even though farms and plantations in most areas were desperately neglected while hostilities lasted. In the war's aftermath, when British East Africa became Kenya and German East Africa (mostly) became the British Protectorate of Tanganyika, the Standard was faced with managing a sizeable operation across East Africa as a whole – and further additions to the East African network seemed inevitable, many at the direct behest of the Government ('[producing] a certain amount of branch extension', as Swanson put it, 'not always such as would have been merited in normal circumstances'[66]). In anticipation of all this, the London Directors had sent out their highly regarded Secretary, John Jeffrey, in 1917 to prepare a report on the region with policy recommendations for its post-war future. Noting that the General Manager in Cape Town, Hector Mackenzie, had already suggested a need for 'fresh arrangements', Jeffrey proposed that East Africa should report directly to London rather than the Cape once the war was over. This idea was not well received. '[In referring] to the necessity of making fresh arrangements,' wrote a dismayed Mackenzie, 'we did not contemplate such a radical change as the complete severance of the area from our main African system'.[67] With all of the authority he could command after sixteen years in charge at the Cape, Mackenzie insisted the requisite strengthening of the bank's control could be provided by having the East African network report to a 'District Superintendent' at Mombasa – who would report to the General Manager in Cape Town. The Directors graciously gave way, conceding that there was no need for the severance option 'at any rate in the near future'.[68]

In the same letter of June 1918, though, they also informed Mackenzie that Cape Town's broader franchise warranted an extra man at the top; and, while they were going to be losing him from Head Office 'with great regret', this man was going to be John Jeffrey, as an Assistant General Manager. Some surprisingly detailed suggestions were appended as to how Mackenzie and his immediate colleagues ought to arrange their affairs in future, with formal meetings together 'at intervals of not more than a fortnight', to ensure that London was kept fully informed on all matters of policy. This seems to have marked a significant change of outlook, even though the composition of the Board had scarcely changed since pre-war days. The Board Directors in 1918 were thus still of a kind with those whom Lewis Michell had found so frustrating during the course of the Boer War. One of the 1902 members, Sir David Barbour, was actually still there (now aged seventy-seven); and five of the six other Directors – William Arbuthnot, Robert Dickinson, Horace Peel, James Finlay and Lord Sydenham – were City figures appointed at various times between 1905 and 1913. But the sixth was William Smart, who had been London Manager since 1900. He had been given a seat on the Board during the war, and perhaps his influence lay behind a more active stance that emerged once the war was over. The minutes of the monthly Board meeting in December 1918 record his suggestion, approved by his peers, that the return of demobbed men from the forces should be taken as an opportunity to assign 'a certain number of the London Office staff' to South Africa.[69] Twelve months later, it was Smart who would travel to the Cape with another Director – 'to get into touch with local conditions' – for the first visit to South Africa by any members of the Board since 1914.[70] Whatever the explanation, anyway, the Board certainly responded to the end of the war by looking anew at the governance structure of the Standard, and seemed to be intent on some shortening of the reins.*

---

* Another idea mooted in 1919 was that an advisory board might be set up in the Cape, not as a proxy for the London Board but as a second source of intelligence from South Africa to complement the reports of the senior management. (The National Bank had established something of the kind, christened the National Bank Industrial Corporation.) The Directors envisaged appointing some of the country's business leaders to this new body, but Mackenzie

One of the reasons advanced by Mackenzie for leaving East Africa under Cape Town's control was that quite a few South African staff were now familiar with the region, having served there during the war, and also that South African farmers would be moving north to settle there. Demobbed soldiers and other adventurers were indeed soon arriving to build new lives in Kenya, but most of them turned out to be British. And when it came to finding additional managers for East Africa, events dictated that many of these were to be British, too. The need for more staff arose more quickly than expected: many of the new settlers arrived wanting to negotiate mortgage loans from the Standard to buy their land. (In the first full year of peace, the bank would record pre-tax earnings from its ten main East African branches of £78,708, compared with £22,811 from South West Africa.[71] By way of further comparison, Port Elizabeth in 1919 contributed £200,000.) Just as they were casting round for suitable candidates, the Cape Town managers heard that fifteen new clerks 'for Colonial staff' had been sent out from London, sailing by the Eastern route via the Suez Canal. A cablegram from the Secretary listed the names ('first ten chosen by J. P. Gibson, Deputy General Manager, in Scotland') and instructed Cape Town to arrange for an early disembarkation, if this would meet its needs.[72] The fifteen new recruits were duly disembarked in Mombasa on Christmas Day 1919 and added to the East African staff – whereupon, as Swanson would recall, a nicely considerate approach was taken to planning their individual assignments:

> The fifteen men were met and landed, mostly in heavy European suits, on one of the hottest days Mombasa had known. With no knowledge of their experience, an effort was made to distribute them according to their pastimes; that is to say the one who was keen on fishing went to Jinja; the keen shot to Eldoret; the low handicap golfer to Kampala . . . [73]

When Jeffrey visited East Africa again ten months later to compile a second report, his comment on the disembarkees was less cheering. 'Several of the recent arrivals who were retained en route [to Cape Town] for service in East Africa are not anxious to stay in the country.' And Jeffrey could understand why: 'Hours are long, opportunities for exercise limited, and generally speaking after a few years life is not very congenial, while

---

thought they had misjudged the likely reaction of prominent South Africans. Hearing of one proposed approach, the General Manager hastily wrote to point out that the targeted individual would not be flattered: 'he would probably regard an invitation to join the Directorate of a subsidiary concern as an effort merely to obtain the support of his name' (Mackenzie to the Secretary, 25 September 1919, LMA: ST03/01/07/061). The whole proposal was quietly ditched.

there is the ever attendant risk of fever.'[74] An acceptance of such hardships, of course, was always part of the career package for those who joined any overseas bank in London; but there was also an unspoken understanding that tougher assignments would never last too long. Swanson thought some of those diverted in 1919 later rose 'to the highest possible positions in the bank' (though he mentioned no names). Probably most were heartily relieved, anyway, when the call came to leave for Cape Town. South Africa was the real Standard territory, and Adderley Street was still at its centre – for the moment.

The evolution of the bank's stance towards West Africa owed its timing to the war, but hinged on bankers' commercial rivalries rather than the clash of armies. The outbreak of the war initially prompted all talk of further consolidation within South African banking to be set aside. But when the true extent of the country's wartime prosperity became clear, some bankers' thoughts turned again to amalgamation. There still remained one conspicuous acquisition target, even after the National Bank's flurry of initiatives in 1910–14. This was the African Banking Corporation (ABC), the London overseas bank set up in 1890. It had grown quickly in its early stages, largely through acquisition – it had a network of forty-five branches by 1913 – but it had been a lacklustre business for years. Indeed, this was the principal reason why the Standard had not picked it off in the pre-war era. In a break with their usual caution over such matters, the London Directors had actually pushed the case for a merger (in response to an initiative by the ABC's own Chairman, who in 1911 had crossed a few streets in the City to call on his counterpart for a chat).[75] But the Standard's two General Managers in Cape Town had robustly objected to the idea, fearing the ABC would be a deadweight on their shoulders and even suggesting in a long cablegram that they would prefer to see it joining forces with the National Bank '[which] would give us probably some of their best customers'.[76] Five years later, those in Cape Town took a different view. The ABC itself looked much more competitive by 1916, and the prospect of losing it to the National Bank seemed not quite such a good idea. There was also a worrying possibility that the ABC might try to reinvigorate itself by merging with yet another overseas bank, based elsewhere on the continent but rumoured to be looking for opportunities in South Africa. This was the Bank of British West Africa (BBWA).

Founded in 1894, BBWA had established a dominant position for itself in its West African home territories by 1914. (For a brief account of its early history, see Appendix C.) Seeking to expand its franchise beyond West Africa, it had opened two branches in Morocco in 1915, and an alliance of some kind with the ABC looked more than plausible, especially after January 1917 when the ABC's Chairman, the 2nd Earl of Selborne, took on the chairmanship of BBWA as well. Selborne had spent 1905–10 as High Commissioner for South Africa (and BBWA had been chaired from 1910 to the end of 1916 by the previous High Commissioner, Lord Milner). The Standard's General Managers duly pressed the case for a purchase of the ABC in 1917, to pre-empt the danger of an ABC–BBWA tie-up – only for the London Directors to announce that they too had changed their minds, and now opposed the ABC deal as a needless distraction. A stand-off ensued for more than two years, during which the ABC lost three of its most senior managers. (Its General Manager, Charles Lipp, died tragically when he was thrown from an open carriage in a street accident and struck his head on a tree.[77])

Meanwhile, the National Bank's ambition to eclipse the Standard was growing ever more blatant. The Transvaal-based bank's Directors were 'straining every nerve' to this end, reported Hector Mackenzie to the Board in October 1918. 'Their directors are active touts and J. B. Taylor, [one of the more outspoken of them] who has decided to reside in South Africa, is as active in their interests as he was in London.'[78] When the war's end spurred yet faster growth in the South African economy, the Standard's Directors dropped their objections to buying the ABC, and it seemed briefly possible in March 1920 that they might even spring a double-barrelled takeover of both the ABC *and* BBWA.[79] This idea did not appeal to J. P. Gibson, who had just taken over as General Manager on Mackenzie's retirement. Gibson flagged up several misgivings – with South West and East Africa already on his plate, he evidently had little appetite for West Africa as well – and the Directors settled for the long discussed deal with the ABC on its own.* Terms were finally ironed out

---

* Properly establishing the Standard in South West and East Africa after 1918 involved tying up a thousand and one loose ends with the German banks and colonial authorities that had run the territories before the war. Many disputes dragged on interminably, often involving tiresome paperwork for Head Office in London, and several verged on the absurd. None more so than a case known as The Stolen Gold of Bagamoyo. Three young African boys stole a bag of gold from the Standard's Mombasa office in January 1914 and fled with it into German East Africa. The German police caught up with them in the village of Bagamoyo in May and recovered what was left of the gold in their possession, valued at £127. The war broke out before it could be returned – and legal arguments over the Standard's claim to the £127 lasted from 1919 to 1925. As Claim 253 before the British Government's Clearing Office (Enemy Debts), it was vigorously contested by the German Government and a settlement worth less than £20 was indignantly rejected by the Standard in 1924. This was unfortunate, for in January 1925 the Anglo-German Mixed Arbitral Tribunal sitting in St James's ruled against the bank and awarded the German Government £3 in settlement of its costs. (Correspondence file on the Stolen Gold of Bagamoyo, LMA: SBSA 0655.)

in London, with Selborne and two colleagues joining the Board of the Standard – another bank for Selborne to chair in due course. The purchase was completed in October 1920, boosting the Standard's total assets by around 10 per cent and expanding its branch network by roughly a fifth. The Directors had not entirely abandoned their designs on BBWA, however. In fact, they had negotiated just two months earlier to acquire an 11 per cent slice of the West African bank, as one of three new investors subscribing equally to fresh shares and accounting for a third each of its expanded equity capital.[80] Thus began the Standard's association with a bank that would one day become a wholly-owned subsidiary.

By buying into BBWA in 1920, the Standard's Directors were intent on having a say in the future deliberations of a bank that looked set to make rapid progress in Africa. It had an effective City Chairman in Lord Selborne, who had briefly served in Asquith's wartime government and still retained many contacts in Africa. It enjoyed a successful relationship with the Colonial Office and with its local West African Currency Board,* and the wartime boom for commodities had transformed its finances: total assets had shot up from £3.2 million in 1914 to £16.5 million in 1919. Something less quantifiable had changed, too. The war, as Selborne told shareholders in July 1919, had created 'a new West Africa . . . and its products were now fully appreciated and sought after in both the new and old world'. BBWA still ranked among the smallest of the City's overseas banks – about the same size, as it happens, as the Eastern Bank – but with annual profits rising to just over £170,000 in the first full year of peace, it was now substantially more than just the banking arm of a successful Liverpool shipping line (which was how it had started).

The Standard also undoubtedly had an ulterior motive for investing in this West African bank, as part of a tangled web of investments that would culminate in a momentous development for banking in South Africa. It

---

* This aspect of BBWA's operations probably looked especially impressive to the Standard's Directors. An East African Currency Board (EACB) had commenced operations in December 1919 with conspicuously less success, and the resulting mess was putting a severe strain on relations between the Standard and the Colonial Office. The EACB's plans for a regional silver currency to replace the rupee in Kenya, Tanganyika and Uganda had fallen foul of the dramatic post-war fluctuations in the value of silver. The ensuing crisis over currency arrangements for East Africa was not finally surmounted until 1925, having prompted the Standard and other banks in the region to warn the Colonial Office at one point 'that unless they could rely upon some currency settlement on a permanent basis they could not carry on with any confidence' (J. A. Henry, *The First Hundred Years of the Standard Bank*, p. 202). In his fuller discussion of the crisis – 'this series of almost ridiculous calamities' – Henry claims the EACB lost over £1.5 million in the process of replacing Indian rupees and German rupees with its new currency, the East African silver shilling divisible into 100 cents.

The corporate logo of Bank of British West Africa, founded in 1894

was plain by 1920 that the City of London's 'Big Five' clearing banks –
Barclays, Lloyds, Midland, Westminster and National Provincial – having
presided over the amalgamation of well over two hundred joint-stock
banks in Britain since 1890 were now casting a covetous eye over the
prosperous markets of the overseas banks. Senior men from the English
clearers had often been a little disdainful about overseas banking in the
past, even suggesting there would be something mildly improper about
using their UK depositors' money to fund lending in distant climes.[81]
(Here was another reason, no doubt, why overseas banking had always
had a greater affinity with banking in Scotland.) Now, however, attitudes
were changing fast. A talk on current developments in the City had been
given at London's School of Oriental and African Studies by a Bank of
England official just months after the end of the war, and senior men from
several overseas banks including Standard Bank and Chartered Bank had
been in the audience to hear a lurid acknowledgement of their own mounting concerns. 'I was recently speaking to a friend of mine, an Eastern
banker and a Scotsman, who has retired from the torrid tropics to the
more bracing and congenial atmosphere of his native heather-clad hills',
warned the lecturer, C. R. Hyde, 'and he told me that his countrymen in
the north were viewing these colossal combines with growing disfavour.'[82]
Lloyds Bank was one of the more forthright of the clearers in asserting

new international ambitions, and in 1919 it had spent £255,000 on a minority stake in BBWA. Selborne went along with the idea that the resulting pact should be unveiled to the press as 'A Treaty of Alliance', but it did not stop the BBWA entering talks six months later – apparently with Lloyds Bank's blessing – with two more of the Big Five, the Westminster Bank and the National Provincial. It was these talks that the Standard's Directors took as a cue to engage with BBWA themselves. If the West African bank was going to be used by the UK clearing banks as a vehicle for investing in Africa, it would be as well for the Standard to strike a pre-emptive deal. Hence, in part, the announcement in August 1920 that the Standard had joined the three clearers: it had spent almost £210,000 on its 11 per cent stake, as part of an agreement under which the Standard and BBWA promised 'to respect each other's territory in Africa and not invade each other's sphere of influence as defined between them'.[83] The Standard's sphere, of course, included South West and East Africa.*

But the best laid schemes, as any good Burns-loving Scottish banker could always remind a customer, gang aft agley – and if the Standard's Directors thought their BBWA pact had kept the clearers out of South Africa, events were soon to dictate otherwise. Prices fell precipitously on most of the main commodity markets through the rest of 1920, triggering a severe slump in world trade. One immediate consequence was a brutal contraction of BBWA's ambitions: it was no longer in a position to contemplate expanding its activities in South Africa, or anywhere else. (It cut its dividend in half late in 1920 and retrenched impressively against the coming storm. In the event, the 1920–23 slump was weathered with no lasting harm to BBWA's finances, not least due to Selborne's impressive leadership: during the 1921–2 financial year, the sixty-two-year-old Chairman spent four months on a 4,000-mile journey round West Africa that took in visits to every branch of the bank in Nigeria and all but one of its branches in the Gold Coast.[84]) The result within South Africa itself was a period of savage deflation. This was damaging for the Standard's business, but utterly disastrous for the National Bank. The Standard's rival

---

* The distribution of its profits across the whole of this sphere was set down in its Half-Year Reports from the General Manager. The report for the six months to September 1922 – leaving behind the wilder fluctuations of the post-war boom and bust – gave a breakdown of the Net Earnings (from 322 branches) that comprised the Cape Province (with 14.5 per cent of the total), the Transvaal (37 per cent), the Orange Free State (14.5 per cent), Natal (10 per cent), Rhodesia (10 per cent), East Africa including Nyasaland (11.5 per cent) and South West Africa (2.5 per cent) (LMA: SBSA/0017). Net earnings from all these territories typically accounted for about three-quarters of the bank's income in the early 1920s, the remainder coming mostly from Head Office operations, with a small contribution from a City of London branch in London Wall and an office in New York.

had hurtled onwards with its expansion immediately after the war – a policy that Gibson described to his London Directors as 'simply rashness and aggression'[85] – lifting the number of its branches a little absurdly from 375 to 476 within eighteen months. Founded in the Transvaal as a creature of political calculation quite as much as commercial aspiration, it was still a bank with nothing like the resources to sustain this size of network through lean times. Once debtors began collapsing around it in 1921–2, the bank was soon struggling with dire liquidity problems and the prospect of its own insolvency.

Since late 1918, it had been looking intermittently at the possibility of closer ties with Barclays Bank.[86] By early 1923 a fresh top team at the National was evidently ready to contemplate a rather more binding arrangement with the UK clearer. The notion appealed to the Barclays Chairman, F. C. Goodenough, a brilliant man with his own vision of how British overseas banking might develop in the post-war world, and a protracted courtship ensued.[87] Barclays had acquired banks in Egypt and the Caribbean since the war, and in 1925 Goodenough merged them into a subsidiary, to be called Barclays (Dominion, Colonial and Overseas), invariably known as Barclays DCO. The new venture was given sufficient capital to allow it to make a full bid for ownership of the National Bank. Since Barclays would have a majority stake in the resulting combination, the outcome was in effect to be a new imperial bank for South Africa. This did not amuse those still enamoured of Kruger's original vision for the National, as a bank with its roots in Afrikanerdom; nor, apparently, did it much please the Union Government.[88] Several months of talks were needed, to reassure the politicians that the day-to-day running of the South African operations would remain under local management, supervised by a local 'National Bank Board' in Johannesburg (though the head office would of course be located in the City of London). The National's relieved shareholders, though, had no qualms, finally approving acceptance of the deal in December 1925 – and with that vote, the Standard Bank found its domestic marketplace completely transformed.

The change in the banking landscape seemed at first only to confirm how far the Standard was now removed from the dominant status it had enjoyed in South African banking twenty years earlier. Indeed, it marked the culmination in a sense of five difficult years for the bank. The long deflation in the country's economy after 1920 had led to a widespread vilification of the whole banking sector, which many blamed for fuelling the excesses of the post-war boom, and the Standard had inevitably been a prime target: it was even singled out for public criticism in September 1921 by the Prime Minister, Jan Smuts – though it was ever afterwards a matter of pride to the bank that its General Manager smartly bombarded Smuts with such a well-documented rebuttal of his attack that he retracted it in a speech the following month.* Tensions between the Standard and the country's politicians had been doubly unfortunate, insofar as they had coincided with a critical moment in the development of the country's financial system. It was a time of tortuous discussions between the bank's Cape Town managers and the Government.[89] The dilemma over how best to restore the integrity of paper money, common to so many countries after the war, was acute in South Africa: gold coins remained in common usage there, and all banknotes were still supposedly convertible into gold even while, like sterling pounds, their actual gold value had dropped sharply. (Unsurprisingly, the coins were growing rapidly scarcer, and many were being shipped abroad in defiance of an embargo on specie exports.) A series of formal conferences, inquiries and select parliamentary committees had produced legislation, in 1920, to set up a South African Reserve Bank. This was a seminal moment for overseas banking in the country, instigating a formal supervisory authority that would operate in parallel with the Bank of England. The Standard's initial reaction was relief, since its senior managers in Cape Town had feared, and strenuously opposed, the emergence of a State Bank that might have evolved into a serious commercial competitor (as had happened in the case of the Commonwealth Bank of Australia, launched in 1914). But the appointment as the first Governor of a former Chief Accountant of the Bank of England, W. H. Clegg, helped turn the new institution into a rather more robustly independent body than J. P. Gibson and his colleagues had expected. After some terse exchanges on the merits of alternative approaches to the credit and exchange markets, the Governor decided it would after all be best if the country's commercial banks did *not* have seats on the Board and select committees of the Reserve Bank, which they had been granted at the outset. This meant the Standard, much to Gibson's disgust, lost its ex officio seats in the inner circles of financial policy-making, just as it was also preparing to give up its right to issue banknotes in South Africa, henceforth to be the exclusive responsibility of the Reserve Bank (although the Standard would go on issuing its own notes in Southern

---

* Smuts had clashed with Gibson earlier in the year, too, insisting on the setting up of an arbitration tribunal that eventually obliged the bank – against its own wishes – to acknowledge a trade union launched by its employees, the South African Society of Bank Officials (SASBO). Gibson and other bankers had argued for the merits of 'internal guilds', each of which would be exclusive to their respective banks; but the outcome, in SASBO, was an industry-wide union. The basic terms and conditions of work fixed for SASBO at the tribunal would remain a point of reference for decades to come.

Rhodesia). Reasonably amicable relations were restored in due course, though, even if the Standard's General Manager remained less than complimentary in private about Clegg's abilities. ('Mr Clegg allows his pen to run away with him, and unfortunately is not too careful in what he says or the manner in which he says it.'[90]) Gibson himself retained an important role as an unofficial adviser to the Government – notably in connection with preparations for a full return to the Gold Standard in 1925.*

However, within just a year or two of the merger between National Bank and Barclays DCO, it was apparent that the emergence of a very different kind of chief rival for the Standard was going to prove surprisingly serendipitous. In fact, it signalled the start of a long and entirely satisfactory banking duopoly across the southern continent that would last many decades. As General Manager in Cape Town, Gibson managed to form a remarkably close relationship with his peers in the new entity. The resulting co-operation between the two banks would extend across the Union and beyond to both the South West African Protectorate (as it now was) and the protectorates of East Africa, where the National had established branches in virtually all the same places as the Standard. The fact that DCO had its head office in London was to prove influential in many ways over the years. At an early stage, for example, DCO opted to run its East African network from London, and this undoubtedly contributed to the decision taken by the Standard's Directors in 1926 that their own East Africa network would, after all, be better run – like the Colonial Office and the East African Currency Board – from London. Unlike in 1918, the initiative this time came from Cape Town. It was one of Gibson's last major policy recommendations, and he retired as General Manager in 1927. This, though, was not the end of his career. For the first time in the history of the Standard, the Directors offered a retiring General Manager from Cape Town a place on the Board. Gibson joined it in October 1927 (and as Chairman of the Week presided over the next General Meeting of Shareholders in June 1928).† Poor health unfortunately precipitated

---

* He was extremely lucky to be able to do so. A former clerk from one of the Johannesburg branches ('a member of a well-known old Cape family') called at his office in Cape Town one mid-morning early in 1925 to complain to the General Manager in person about his having been dismissed two years earlier. Gibson agreed to sit down with the man for a brief discussion, and soon regretted it. 'Intimating by rising that the interview was over, the General Manager said "Your case is closed, Harsant". It is alleged that Harsant then drew a revolver and fired five shots, inflicting three wounds in the neck and shoulder.' (*The Times*, 26 February 1925.) Miraculously, Gibson escaped serious injury.

† In a perhaps revealing oversight, the Standard's centenary history states that Gibson, on stepping down as General Manager, simply retired from the bank. (Henry, *The First Hundred Years*, p. 226.)

his retirement only eleven months later. But even this brief term must have allowed Gibson time to impress upon his colleagues the real nature of the Standard's relationship with Barclays DCO. The co-operation between them would extend to many aspects of their work including 'a rigid adherence to arranged rates', as a paper in 1927 made clear: 'The details of the agreement with Barclays Bank (Dominion, Colonial and Overseas) with regard to the rates for short-term deposits and for periods up to twelve months were reported to the Board.'[91] The long and often fraught history of bank amalgamations and mergers in South Africa had thus bequeathed the Standard, by the end of the 1920s, a domestic market that it could share on roughly equal terms with a competitor well attuned to what was needed for them both to enjoy a comfortable prosperity.

4. INDIA FADES, JAPAN SURGES

Across the markets of Asia, the Chartered Bank had been less fortunate. Contemporaries went on regarding the Chartered throughout the 1920s as the leader among the dozen or so exchange banks in India and South Asia. Its balance sheet, totalling close to £65 million throughout the decade, was only very slightly smaller than that of the Hongkong Bank which enjoyed an equivalent position in the Far East. (Both the Standard Bank and Barclays DCO were of a similar size, too, as was the Bank of London and South America (BOLSA) which led the market in its own region. This broad uniformity of scale is so striking as almost to suggest that bankers and City investors alike may have shared some tacit consensus about the optimal size of an overseas bank.*) But as the decade wore on, the Directors and senior managers of the Chartered nonetheless voiced a steadily mounting anxiety about the impact of new competitors. Of course most bankers invariably have a running problem with the competitiveness of their markets, as most farmers have a problem with the weather: certainly few Chartered Bank General Meetings since the 1860s had passed without a homily on the subject from someone, usually the Chairman. But the damage eventually inflicted on the Chartered by more intense competition did indeed warrant acute concern – in India, above all. For the bank as a whole, pre-tax profits dropped by a third in 1927 and struggled to revive much in 1928–9. (The published net profits hid the scale of the setback

---

* Over the four years 1926–9, their annual balance-sheet values averaged: Chartered Bank £63.3 million, Standard Bank £68.0 million, Barclays DCO £67.9 million, Hongkong and Shanghai Bank £73.0 million and BOLSA £66.9 million.

by drawing on substantial transfers from hidden reserves. As *The Bankers' Magazine* had delicately observed earlier in the 1920s: 'That the profit figures should be so good in a year of bad trade is no doubt a commentary upon the conservative disclosure of published profits in the past.'[92] So much for published profits, as any guide to a single year's performance.) Crucially, the annual contributions from Bombay, Calcutta and Rangoon – the core of the bank's prosperity since its founding days – were all but evaporating. Calcutta was everywhere still spoken of as the Chartered's flagship branch, but its image increasingly belied the financial reality. Over these three years, 1927–9, the roller-coaster unpredictability of the immediate post-war world gave way in British India to a bleakly consistent run of poor results. Calcutta itself reported losses in 1928 and 1929, reflecting the onset of a severe recession in the agrarian economy of Bengal. But the bank's difficulties were not confined to Bengal: the entire sub-continent accounted for hardly more than 6 per cent of all pre-tax profits – astonishingly, a smaller proportion than the bank derived over this same period from its Bangkok branch alone. Elsewhere in the East, a quarter of the profits were earned in the harbour cities of Singapore and Hong Kong, with the tin and rubber trades out of the Malayan Archipelago accounting for most of the rest. But the bank was left relying for half its total income on the trade-financing revenues earned in London on British exports. Largely unremarked, by outsiders at least, an era in the Chartered's history was slipping into the past.

One explanation, and the starkest, was that excessive competition had driven down margins in the foreign exchange business of the Raj to vanishing point. All those London brokers with their miraculous telephone links had accelerated a process of attrition already evident before the world war. That, however, was not the only catalyst at work through the 1920s. Attitudes to business were changing, too. The traditional exchange banks had always made the most of local 'Association Rules' under one description or another – we should call them cartel agreements today – to protect the profitability of their main activity. In economies with limited effective policing of the criminal law, never mind proper regulation of the financial markets, this was not such a surprising way of proceeding. (The largest of them, the Exchange Bankers' Association of Calcutta, had been founded in 1892 – 'to have definite and recorded agreements on certain points such as contracts, differences in rates etc' – and had been chaired almost without a break by successive heads of the Chartered's Calcutta branch.[93]) But many banks entering the marketplace for the first time in the post-war years had little or no interest in abiding by any such rules. One of the Chartered's Inspectors, a Mr Keenan, put some of the blame for this on his own colleagues, in a candid post-tour letter to the Directors of May 1922 that was subsequently distributed as a Head Office Circular to all branches:

> Conditions are now changed and the old days of agreements between Banks to maintain margins in Exchanges &c., are gone; more especially in large cities like Bombay and Calcutta where we have numerous competitors, some of them outside our [local bankers'] association.
>
> New Banks are invading what we have hitherto regarded as our preserves . . . [and have met] a generous level of support. This is not to be wondered at when we consider how these places [like Madras and Colombo] have been exploited as regards exchange by the older Banks in the last few years. I have always held that the short-sighted policy of holding out for large margins was bound in the long run to bring fresh competitors into the field to our disadvantage . . .
>
> [Now our Agencies] ought to work for each other at actual rates and . . . we must be content with one profit instead of two as formerly, in these [exchange] transactions. If we are to hold our own, Agencies must not 'stick' each other when giving transfers . . . [Above all] it should be made clear that the Chartered Bank is prepared to stand by old friends and attract new ones by quoting terms that are as satisfactory as any, if not better, than could be obtained from newly established competitors.[94]

Exhortations of this kind were to be a feature of Head Office Circulars over the next few years, as the squeeze on margins grew ever tighter. A year after the Keenan letter, one of the pushiest newcomers greatly expanded its presence in the East: all the Indian branches of Cox & Co. – private bankers to officers of the British army since the eighteenth century – were acquired by Lloyds Bank. As the Board and managers of the Standard Bank were noting by this time, all of the clearers were in fact showing a new interest in overseas markets. And other conspicuous rivals headquartered in the City of London included an institution floated quite recently on the stock market – in collaboration with Lloyds Bank, and two other clearers – and headed by a former member of the Chartered's own Court.

The P&O Banking Corporation was launched in April 1920 by James Mackay, now ennobled as Lord Inchcape (though not yet as the 1st Earl, which he would become in 1929). His shipping group, already the largest of its kind in the world, had developed a private banking business for its well-healed clients. Inchcape hived this off as a separate company which, while raising money in its own right, could aspire to an international network that would parallel the P&O shipping offices.[95] Probably Inchcape himself was none too sure at the outset how P&O Banking would evolve. It happened that early in 1920 he approached Sir Montagu Turner – one

of two Chartered Directors who had agreed to join its Board – to ask if
P&O Steam Navigation could take up a tenancy in the grand new building
that the Chartered had just commissioned for itself on the Bund in Shanghai. (See Plate 22. Begun in 1919, it would eventually be opened in 1923.
The project exactly coincided with the erection of a Bund landmark for
the Hongkong Bank two blocks away, both of them designed by the same
architect and built by the same contractor.[96]) The Chartered's standing
rules precluded any of its branches from offering a sub-lease to another
bank. Obviously this gave rise to a problem once plans for P&O Banking
became public, for in March 1920 we find a note signed by none other than
Turner, Thomas Whitehead and William Preston, being despatched from
Head Office to the Shanghai Manager: 'We are informed by the [P&O]
Chairman that, should the P & O Banking Corporation decide to establish
itself in Shanghai, it is not their intention nor aim to compete with this
Bank, and you will please therefore cancel . . . the debarring clause in the
proposed lease.'[97] It was perhaps fortunate that the sub-tenancy arrangement fell through, for P&O Banking certainly did move into competition
with the Chartered in due course, in Shanghai and several other cities.

Worse still, Inchcape's spin-off proved to be one of the most egregious
mavericks in the exchange markets of India – or so at least the members
of more than one traditional Exchange Association averred. The duplicity
of members who pretended to abide by the rules while actually flouting
them was a problem that plagued all of these Associations. Invariably,
repeat offenders had to be brought into line by the chairman. In Calcutta,
this required the occasional stiff letter to be penned by the Chartered's
Manager, R. W. Buckley, and in September 1926 he wrote an especially
terse note to P&O Banking's manager in the city. It drew a pained response,
pleading that an infringement of the rules had been an oversight, and this:
'I should like to add . . . that I consider the tone of your letter unnecessarily
aggressive; and your inference that we deliberately contravened the
rules . . . is offensive both to the writer personally and to the Bank which
he represents.'[98] Unperturbed, the tough-minded Buckley sent a copy of
this reply to London, reasserting his conviction that the P&O were guilty
as charged – 'and this is also the feeling of many of our neighbours'.[99] Sure
enough, less than a month later they transgressed again. This time the
Calcutta Association held a special meeting of all members, at which the
P&O man, Ryde, was categorically told his bank would be expelled if it
broke ranks once more. He wrote a grovelling letter of apology to Buckley,
which the latter forwarded to Head Office as 'a satisfactory surrender'.

In fact, P&O Banking was having a generally unhappy time of it by late
1926. Grabbing exchange business at knockdown margins had made it no

money. Its shipping connections had never won it much business – indeed, even its sister P&O companies had declined to drop existing bank relationships in its favour – and bad debts were piling up rapidly. Its published net profits had actually declined every year since 1921 (failing to cover its dividend for 1926). Early in 1927, probably in a conversation between Inchcape and Turner, the surprising idea was mooted that it might be merged into the Chartered. And, if there were plenty of reasons for Chartered men to be sceptical of the putative benefits, there was one aspect of acquiring the smaller bank that seems to have appealed hugely to the Court. Within months of its flotation in the City, P&O Banking had broken with all precedent in the East by taking a controlling interest in the Allahabad Bank – an Indian joint-stock company. The latter had British managers and had been founded by a group of European merchants in 1865. But it had always been proud of its pedigree as India's oldest joint-stock bank, and had evolved as an unambiguously domestic institution.* Having boldly taken a controlling stake, P&O Banking relocated the Indian bank's head office from Allahabad to Calcutta in 1923, but it still relied on a branch network linking it to native merchant firms with broad interests across the north of India.

This made P&O Banking an intriguing prospect for Turner and his colleagues in 1927. Their mounting concern over the Chartered's ailing competitiveness reflected more than just an acute awareness of the exchange market's ills. A second fundamental shift in the import/export world of the East since 1919, especially marked in India and Burma, had seen a growing share of the market slipping into the hands of locally owned businesses at the expense of the European merchant houses so dominant before 1914. As a former manager from Calcutta, J. S. Duncan, would put it in a Head Office memo a few years later: 'Whether we like it or not, Natives all over the East are now eliminating the European middleman [for import business] . . . The European firms still have the predominant share of the exports from Calcutta, but here again the Native is gradually cutting in.'[100] It was a trend that was leaving the Chartered increasingly wrong-footed, for the unavoidable truth was that the largest

---

* It had started out with nineteen European and seven Indian founding shareholders. At the first General Meeting, a resolution for the election of an Indian Director was defeated; but three years later, in 1869, one Munshi Gya Pershad was more successful: 'notice had been served . . . that the identification of Indians with what is today India's oldest joint-stock bank would brook no delay' (*The First Hundred Years, 1865–1965, The Story of the Allahabad Bank Ltd*, published by the Allahabad Bank, 1965, held in the Reserve Bank of India library). The bank was run from 1865 to 1910 by one Manager, Rutherford Deans – a worthy addition to the Founders' club made up of Robert Stewart, Howard Gwyther, George Neville and F. H. Sutton.

and oldest of the British exchange banks had never shown much interest in dealing directly with indigenous Indian firms, as Duncan's memo would concede. ('Business with Native Firms in Calcutta, if not actually frowned upon, has certainly of recent years never been encouraged . . .') The bank still stuck to the letter of its traditional documentation for trade finance, full of Victorian legalese that held few charms for a Bengali trader. Its underlying philosophy remained much as expounded by Gwyther at the turn of the century: its business lay with the European houses, leaving the locals to their own bankers:

> In the larger towns and cities [of the sub-continent] native bankers occupy a very honourable position, are highly intelligent and possess considerable means. They are also enabled by their daily contact with their own race to gauge the condition of would-be borrowers and employ their money to advantage where the white man could not venture to compete.[101]

This, however, was now a hopelessly outdated attitude. The world's leading shipping companies, which in the nineteenth century had similarly dealt almost exclusively with Europeans, were quite happy by the middle of the 1920s to deal directly with Indian firms, many of them run by former native employees ('banians') of the European houses themselves. It seemed the exchange banks might one day need to follow suit, which would mark a signal change. So when the idea of taking over control of P&O Banking surfaced, it found a ready response from the Directors. Some at 38 Bishopsgate were just beginning to wonder whether it might be possible to install local men at each of the Chartered's Indian branches in a role broadly analogous to that of the compradore in China. Linking up in some way with the branches of the Allahabad Bank might offer a useful first step in that direction. Since the deal also promised to restore a number of customer relationships which had been lost to the smaller bank since 1921, the logic seemed compelling. The Chartered launched a formal bid in October 1927 and by its closing date had acquired 75 per cent of the shares. The following January, William Preston and three more Chartered Directors joined its Board, though Inchcape remained its Chairman.[102] No real attempt was made to integrate the operations of the two banks, however. It was decided that P&O Banking should be retained in its entirety, including its branch in Calcutta's Fairlie Place, allowing full co-operation to evolve at a gentlemanly pace: 'we have a well-established business working in harmony with ourselves and ceasing to function as active opponents', as the Chairman told shareholders at the 1928 General Meeting.[103] (How this arrangement went down with Messrs Ryde and Buckley in Calcutta has sadly gone unrecorded.)

A slightly more urgent approach might have been appropriate. As Head Office Circulars from Bishopsgate had been acknowledging for some time, many cities in India and beyond had increasingly influential cliques of local merchants and bankers who had little affection for the Chartered and its peers. As one Circular noted stridently in 1925:

> There is existing in India, with their centre in Bombay, a body of Natives, Jews and Parsees, directly connected with the Cotton Mill industry, who are exceptionally clever and enterprising . . . They are aggressive and intend to press their views [on rupee exchange and lending rates] upon Government at all costs . . . They have no love whatever for the British Exchange Banks.[104]

Nor were the swelling ranks of new competitors restricted to locally owned firms. Another worry by the later 1920s was the incipient challenge being posed across Asia by international banks from other Western nations. The Deutsche-Asiatische Bank had in effect been seen off, but other rivals were emerging. In Indo-China, the principal banker to all of France's colonies in the East made no attempt to disguise its tactics, as explained to Head Office by the Chartered's Saigon Manager in 1924:

> it is quite evident that the Banque de l'Indochine is endeavouring, with the resources at its disposal, to exercise a 'freeze-out' policy towards the Foreign Banks operating here. At the moment [its allies in] the local press, in addition to conducting a campaign against the employment of foreigners in French Houses, are explaining the collapse of the Franc as being due to the machinations of Great Britain.[105]

American banks were also becoming more active. Federal regulations had long precluded US domestic banks from opening overseas branches, but the International Banking Corporation had been specially chartered for such business since the turn of the century. Starting with branches in London, Calcutta and Shanghai it had built a modest network in Asia by 1914. During the First World War, the National City Bank (NCB) of New York also began to take a serious interest in overseas markets. Already one of the largest banks in the US, it had been the first to open a Foreign Department, handling bills and letters of credit, in 1897. A change in the Fed's regulations in 1913 lifted the ban on US-owned foreign branches, and NCB in 1915 began recruiting and training university graduates for service overseas.[106] It then acquired International Banking Corporation in 1918, fully integrating the latter's Asian branches with its own US organization in 1925. American exports to Asia were rising rapidly, not least due to rising shipments of automobiles and trucks from the

Mid-West – also a lucrative source of income for the Chartered* – and NCB's Asian network by the end of the 1920s extended to more than twenty branches.

Of far greater concern to Chartered Bank than American, European or even Indian competitors, however, was a phenomenon that by the end of the 1920s was starting to look truly threatening, for the bank itself as for the broader interests of the Empire – the seemingly inexorable rise of Japanese business and finance. Prior to 1914, the speed of Imperial Japan's modernization had generally been applauded in regular reports back to Head Office from Yokohama and its sub-branch in Kobe.[107] Good profits had been made – especially in 1904–5 against the background of the Russo-Japanese war, when the Yokohama branch earned more over two years than the Calcutta branch – and the country's obvious reliance on imports for a long list of vital commodities had made it a promising market indeed. The Chartered had gladly participated, with the Hongkong Bank and the Yokohama Specie Bank – Japan's foremost overseas bank – in the management of sterling bond issues in the City for the Imperial Government. Certainly there had always been niggling concerns. The real creditworthiness of Japanese businesses could often be hard to discern; Japanese society sometimes seemed to struggle under the burdens imposed not just by a daunting pace of industrialization but a heady scale of arms procurement, too; and Japanese banks were all too obviously ambitious to stake out their own claims to a place in the markets of the East. ('We may have to face competition from Japanese banks entering into the field of exchange', the Kobe Agent had noted in 1910, 'and we should not be surprised to see the Sumitomo Bank . . . spreading itself abroad. But this will take some years.'[108] True to the usual Japanese habit of moving more quickly than expected, the Yokohama Specie Bank had opened for business in Calcutta in 1911.) But in general the Japanese had been spoken of, in bank correspondence, with respect and even a little wonderment. Their extraordinary recent achievements were so refreshingly different from the perceived corruption and ineptitude of the Chinese! And as a small off-shore

---

* Auto manufacturers in the US typically relied by the 1920s on finance companies that were given an exclusive franchise to handle the funding of their licensed wholesale dealers. But few if any of these finance companies yet had branches outside the US. They turned to banks like the Chartered to fill the gap. The Chartered's man in New York, William Baxter, agreed a first auto-financing arrangement in 1927 and several parallel schemes were established in due course for the export of American cars to Calcutta and other Asian ports including Colombo – though Chartered Managers in the field were sometimes none too impressed by the creditworthiness of the local dealers from whom they were expected to collect payments. (William Baxter to Head Office, 28 January 1927 and 9 May 1930, CH03/01/10/16/25/E.)

island putting its continental neighbours to shame, Japan had gratifying similarities with Britain and perhaps even a natural affinity – formally embodied since 1902 in a celebrated Alliance between the two nations.

The war and its aftermath had prompted second thoughts. Unable to import manufactured goods from Europe, Asian countries had turned increasingly to Japanese suppliers. One immediate result for Chartered Bank was an impressive rush of business for its Yokohama branch. It was perfectly placed to deal with Japanese companies on behalf of the Asian importers, many of them long-standing clients of the bank. Those who were privy to the bank's pre-tax returns must have been a little startled by Yokohama's consequent growth. In 1917 it reported the fourth best result; in 1918, the second best result; then for two years consecutively, it was by far the most profitable branch in the network. But the expansion of Japan's trade had a less welcome dimension, as the Yokohama branch itself noted in its half-yearly report of January 1918 (on which Thomas Whitehead scribbled 'A very sound letter'):

> To what extent the hold now obtained [by them] over old and new markets will remain after the War it is difficult to forecast, but the Japanese are very methodical and good organizers and with their Government and Foreign Consuls, who closely watch trade and commerce, assisting them, we believe they stand a good chance of holding successfully many of the markets gained during this [wartime] period.
>
> All of their first class Banks have been reaping large profits, and several of them, especially the Yokohama Specie, the Taiwan and the Sumitomo Banks are following their country's trade by opening up in most of the important ports in Asia and America, whose competition will undoubtedly be increasingly felt by our Bank wherever we have to face it.[109]

So it proved, and the Japanese banks' arrival in these ports was just one facet of a broader ambition that it was impossible to ignore: Japanese policy-makers plainly saw Asia, or more specifically East Asia, as the natural domain for an empire of their own, far grander than any built by the European powers in the East. They had taken every opportunity to further this aim during the war, seizing the German deep-water port of Tsingtao in 1914 and coercing the nascent Republic of China into a string of concessions aimed at entrenching Japan's effective control over not just Manchuria – already largely annexed, along with Korea – but much of the former German colony of Shantung as well. By 1919 the latter was well on its way to becoming virtually a Japanese colony instead.

All this provoked an intense debate among British diplomats and politicians as to the best response, and it greatly exercised the Court of the

Chartered too. Few doubted the days of slicing up China into spheres of colonial influence were over. The ultimate objective, however daunting for the moment, had to be an independent Republic committed to Open Door policies on trade. But how best to reconcile Japan to this approach: by continuing to embrace her as an ally or by adopting a fresh stance that might entail a more confrontational relationship? The Chartered's Directors assured themselves of a handy grip on events by recruiting to their number in 1920 the man widely acknowledged as Britain's greatest authority on China, who was just retiring after fourteen years as the British Minister at Peking. A forthright Ulsterman, Sir John Jordan had had a highly distinguished career in the diplomatic service – spending forty-four years in the Far East, most of them in China – and was acutely conscious of the dangers posed by, as he saw it, Japan's distinctly nineteenth-century stance. (Before leaving the Legation in Peking, he had vented his views on the continued occupation of Tsingtao, assuring his Foreign Secretary that, in all sorts of ways, 'the Japanese regime is tenfold more objectionable to foreigners and Chinese alike than the German one ever was'.[110]) The next few years saw a radical change in Anglo-Japanese relations, to which Jordan himself made a direct contribution. He attended, as an adviser to the British delegation, the international conference in Washington late in 1921 at which Britain was persuaded – principally by the US and Canada – to renounce its 1902 Alliance with Japan in favour of a vague 'Quadruple Pact' for the future security of the Pacific region. Jordan was a keen supporter of this change of tack, though it left Japanese diplomats feeling bruised and embittered.[111] How far Jordan's counsels within the Court influenced his Chartered colleagues is hard to say, but his views certainly found an echo in regular bank reports from the East about the gathering threat from Japan. This was linked by the branch managers not just to moves by Japan's government and banks to consolidate their influence in China and beyond but also to the speed with which her manufacturers were beginning to supplant Western rivals in the markets of India and South Asia.

Less than two years after the Washington Conference, albeit briefly, the growing disaffection with Japan was dramatically set aside. Just before noon on 1 September 1923, a massive earthquake hit the Yokohama–Tokyo area, followed by tsunami waves that swept across the Bay of Tokyo during the afternoon. Scarcely a single large building in Yokohama survived, and well over 100,000 people lost their lives. The Chartered bank branch was completely destroyed, and the fatalities included the branch Manager, A. H. Tait, ten local staff, and the wife and daughter of the Accountant, who were standing in the street outside the bank when the disaster struck. For some months afterwards, there was an outpouring of sympathy and admiration for the Japanese that evoked some of the old pre-war amity. The survivors' stoicism seemed remarkable; their government's success in raising international loans in London and New York to rebuild their devastated economy was, as the Chartered's Chairman declared to shareholders in April 1924, 'a testimony to the honesty and high commercial standard of Japan as one of the great powers of the world'.[112] The Chartered's was the first name on a list of corporate subscribers to a Foreign Aid Fund for reconstruction. Those who admired the efficiency of Japanese administration – contrasting it, for example, with the bandit-rule that had overwhelmed Tsingtao after its recent return to Chinese jurisdiction – felt free to voice their suspicion that a little more of it on the mainland would be no bad thing.

Within a year or two, however, the carping within the bank about Japanese competition was back in full flow. And increasingly it focused on the success of Japan's textile industry. Buying much of their raw cotton from dealers in Bombay and Amritsar, her mills were shipping back cotton piece-goods at prices that even undercut those of the Indian mills in Bombay – and left Britain's Lancashire mills trailing far behind. The impact on the Chartered from around the start of 1927 was doubly unfortunate. A precipitous decline in piece-goods shipments from Lancashire undermined a mainstay of Anglo-Indian trade. At the same time, as the bank's man in Amritsar would later lament, the export of piece-goods from Osaka brought only the briefest of bonanzas:

> As we had Agencies in Japan we were the first to finance this business [around 1924–5] and had a monopoly of it for over a year, when the National Bank of India and Lloyds [acting on behalf of the Indian importers] were able to make arrangements with Japanese banks to represent them.[113]

Addressing the shareholders in March 1928, the Chairman now had a rather different message to convey about Japan, and had to warn that textiles might be just the tip of the problem:

> In the face of such active competition from Japan, it is difficult to see how prosperity can return to the mill industry [in India] unless drastic [i.e. protectionist] remedies are adopted . . . In fact, this remark applies to nearly all Eastern markets, and it is very evident that Japan, faced with an ever-increasing population is following out the policy of pushing her exports into every possible corner of the consuming world where cheapness is the main consideration.[114]

The Directors sitting beside Sir Montagu Turner that day did not include Sir John Jordan: he had died suddenly at a council meeting of the

China Association in September 1925. In searching for a replacement, the Court displayed its penchant for making appointments with a strong element of continuity. To date, this had been a way of sustaining links with a small group of companies close to the bank, like the Eastern merchant firms of Ogilvy, Gillanders & Co. and Boustead & Co., and the Calcutta-based Bank of Bengal, each of them represented on the Court by a succession of individuals over the years. Later, in 1928, the same would apply in the case of Wallace Brothers, a long-established Eastern trading company, when one of its Directors took up a seat at the Court just as another was stepping down.[115] Following the much lamented loss of Jordan, the Court had turned in a similar fashion to another former British diplomat – and personal colleague of Jordan's – with long experience of China. Archibald Rose had served there since 1900 and had risen to become Commercial Attaché, first in Shanghai and afterwards in Peking, before retiring from the Diplomatic Service in 1921 at the early age of forty-one. He was one of no fewer than seven new Directors (on a Court of twelve) appointed between 1925 and the end of 1929. It remained to be seen how the reconstituted Court might react to any further worsening of the competitive position. And Rose for one was to prove a trenchant critic of the Chartered's performance in the field.

5
Holding Fast, 1929–41

I. FOUR BANKS AND
THE GREAT DEPRESSION

To the men presiding over the four banks that would one day come together as the Standard Chartered – as to many of their peers in the City, and beyond – the implications of the Wall Street Crash of October 1929 were not immediately apparent. It made little difference to the Standard Bank's successful co-management of a £6 million bond issue for the Union of South Africa, for which applications closed early in March 1930. Strong demand in the City seemed to bear out an ebullient optimism over South Africa's prospects, voiced at the Standard's Annual General Meeting the previous July: it was satisfactory, the Chairman of the Week had suggested then, 'to note that, whatever clouds may appear in the future, the business horizon is fairly clear at the moment'.[1] Looking back over the past twelve months at its own General Meeting in March 1930, the Chartered Bank's Chairman had to warn his shareholders that their bank was facing '[an] extraordinary decline in prices of all commodities forming the staple exports from Eastern ports'.[2] But Sir Montagu Turner was far more anxious about renewed signs of civil strife in China, and the evidence of fiendishly clever (and Lancashire-troubling) mass-production systems in Japan, than about events on the other side of the Atlantic. He made only a passing reference to New York's 'Stock Exchange boom collapse' – it explained, he said, a sharp fall in demand for Japan's silk exports – while happily acknowledging a widely held view that those Americans had let their markets run away with them (again), so that a correction was no bad thing. The Eastern Bank's Chairman, also on AGM duties that March, took a slightly less sanguine view – their problems at home, he feared, might push US companies into competing harder overseas, heightening Britain's need of protective tariffs – but he was scarcely more exercised about the debacle in New York than his counterpart at the Chartered. In the boardroom of the Bank of British West Africa (BBWA), meanwhile, the Directors were certainly concerned over sliding commodity prices, especially for cocoa and palm oil; but they were also determined in the early months of 1930 to press on with a current expansion of their West African network, planning to add eight branches to the existing fifty-one in the coming months. It seemed the best way to carry forward the legacy of the two principal figures in the forty-year history of their bank, both of whom had died in the year gone by.*

The consequences of the Crash were nonetheless to hit all the Standard Chartered's 'forerunner banks' hard over the next three years. No bank in the world could hide from the ensuing storm. Unprecedented falls in New York stock prices produced a lethal haemorrhaging of consumer confidence on Main Street, soon reflected in lower US industrial production and rising unemployment. This in turn unnerved the US commercial banks, which pulled in their lending and set in train a massive credit contraction. Flows of US capital abroad halted abruptly in the second quarter of 1930, exacerbating a growing aversion to risk among domestic lenders in London and most continental centres. With credit lines dwindling, European importers of Asian and African commodities went on reining back their orders. These had already been cut sharply in 1929 as part of what had seemed at the time a cyclical squeeze on inventories. The further reductions in 1930 broke new ground in their speed and severity, dragging world demand for many products well below levels seen in the 1920–23 recession. And the crisis took on another dimension in June 1930, when protectionist legislation in Washington – the infamous Smoot–Hawley Tariff Act – imposed effectively prohibitive tariffs on a wide range of agricultural imports into the US. By the end of 1930, the price of most internationally traded commodities had dropped by 50 per cent or more since the calamity on Wall Street fourteen months earlier – and there was worse to follow.

Assessing the damage to the world economy in two articles that December, Maynard Keynes wrote of the year's events as a 'Great Slump' and pressed the central bankers of the Western world to act decisively in agreeing on corrective action. 'We have involved ourselves in a colossal muddle', warned Keynes, 'having blundered in the control of a delicate machine, the working of which we do not understand.'[3] But the muddle was then

---

* Leslie Couper, their Manager in London since 1910, had died suddenly aged fifty-eight; George Neville, the bank's instigator in 1891 and its longest-serving Director, had died peacefully at his home in Surrey – surrounded, as one obituarist noted, by souvenirs of a punitive expedition to Benin in 1897, including two life-sized leopards cast in bronze (*The Times*, 30 November 1929).

frighteningly compounded, as central bankers and governments acquiesced in a series of ill-fated initiatives that only served further to undermine
people's confidence in their banks. A run on deposits in the US produced
a steady drain on the liquidity of its banking sector. It was in Europe,
however, that the banks succumbed first to a systemic failure. Depositors
in 1931 wanted to withdraw their funds by converting their paper money
into gold; but few countries had sufficient gold reserves to cope – a select
band that emphatically did not include either Germany or Austria, both
of them still hopelessly weighed down by the burden of war reparations
fixed (in the face of earlier dire warnings from Keynes, of course) at the
Versailles peace conference. At first it was individual banks that collapsed,
starting in May 1931 with the Credit Anstalt of Vienna, which held fully
half of Austria's bank deposits. Then withdrawals of gold threatened to
wipe out whole national reserves of the yellow metal and forced countries
into closing down *all* their banks – as Germany did, for two weeks in
July 1931 – in a last-ditch bid to defend the convertibility of their currencies. Inevitably, nothing by then could avert the need to stop defining
the value of these currencies in terms of gold. After Germany had in
effect abandoned the Gold Standard that summer, the inescapable logic
behind the Reichsbank's decision left the British Treasury and the Bank
of England faced with the same brutal outcome. The banks in Britain
were never forced into a total shutdown, but with UK gold reserves fast
disappearing, the convertibility of the pound simply could not be sustained. Sterling left the Gold Standard in September 1931, losing overnight
almost 25 per cent of its value against gold and the gold-pegged US
dollar. (The US Treasury had far greater reserves of gold, which allowed
it to preserve the dollar's convertibility – but only, eventually, at the cost
of devaluing the dollar: its worth in gold was cut by 40 per cent in
January 1934.)

By the end of the year, Keynes's colossal muddle had become the Great
Depression. International trade had been devastated and the world's
monetary system had been ruptured even more disastrously than in the
aftermath of the 1914–18 war. Shareholders' meetings in the City were
now invariably sombre occasions, only lightened by the odd shaft of
gallows humour. There had been laughter at BBWA's AGM in June 1931 –
the bank had a March year-end – when a shareholder said he had 'heard
it remarked the other day that when we were through with 1931, we
should probably be looking back on 1930 as a boom year'.[4] In fact the
well-managed BBWA retrenched itself effectively enough to avert any
worsening of its annual results after its 1930–31 year – but the quip fairly
captured the mood in many countries' export sectors, as commodity prices

hit lows in 1931 that threatened to halt shipments altogether. For the Chartered Bank's Eastern network, it proved a year like no other. Out of twenty-seven branch reports for 1931, all but a handful were awash with red ink, especially Batavia's (showing a massive loss of £394,178). Losses on the 25 per cent devaluation of sterling were partly to blame, but the curtailment of trade and a trail of bad debts to bankrupt customers had also cost the Chartered dearly in almost every Asian port: only Singapore and Colombo escaped with modest profits.[5] More typical of the times was the bank's experience in Rangoon, where a single product (rice) had dominated the local economy's exports since the turn of the century. Between 1900 and 1914, this had been enough to ensure that operating profits from the Rangoon branch accounted for 6 per cent of the Chartered network's total. (Only four other branches did better.) However, in the closing months of 1930, the price of rice dropped by more than 40 per cent – and went on falling through the next four years.[6] The Chartered's Rangoon branch lost just over £39,000 in 1931 – compared with aggregate operating profits of just over £32,000 for the whole of the 1920–30 decade – and did not report another profit until 1937.

Even more dramatic was the collapse of the bank's earnings in London. Over the three years to 1929, the Chartered's Head Office had accounted for half of total operating income. It contributed next to nothing in 1931. The aggregate pre-tax loss recorded for Head Office and all the branches in 1931 came to £963,439, roughly cancelling the profits recorded by the Chartered for the previous three years put together.[7] The scale of this reversal came as a shock, but at least the patient accumulation of Inner Reserves over so many years was vindicated. A hidden transfusion from these left the bank with a published net profit for 1931 of £381,787 – less than half the annual figure achieved through most of the 1920s, but still respectable enough to avert any serious dent in the bank's standing with depositors. A deep dip into Reserves similarly helped save Directors' blushes at the Eastern Bank, where a published profit just short of £120,000 for 1931 even appeared to mark a small gain on the previous year but actually concealed a drop in real profits to £72,444.[8] And at the Eastern, as at the Chartered and the BBWA, dividends were cut by a third.

The Standard Bank also saw a sharp fall in profits (down 30 per cent in 1931, compared with 1929) and it cut its dividend even more aggressively; but its experience of the crisis was rather different. Poor export prices (with wool down by two-thirds) badly hurt many of the bank's core customers in its rural heartlands, and a serious drought added to the South African farmer's miseries in 1932. As the bank's centenary history puts it, succinctly enough, 'Wool had the worst season in its history. The

Standard Bank did not enjoy itself.'⁹ What really caused the bank a joyless twelve months, however, had less to do with the state of the country's trade than with an awkward consequence of sterling's break with the Gold Standard. The pounds issued by the Reserve Bank of South Africa had always been effectively interchangeable with the pound sterling in London, and like sterling had been tied to the Gold Standard since 1925. After Britain had been forced into its September 1931 break with gold, the Reserve Bank rather bizarrely decreed that South Africa's pounds would retain their Gold Standard value. Given the close ties between the two countries' economies, this was a nonsense worthy of Lewis Carroll's Red Queen who could believe six impossible things before breakfast, and it caused the country's bankers no end of trouble. Within weeks of the decision, North and South Rhodesia followed in Britain's wake, and the Standard Bank had to scramble over a weekend to sign off whole crate-loads of fresh notes and fly them on a hastily hired Gypsy Moth biplane into South West Africa, hitherto dependent on Rhodesian notes which were now being shunned. Meanwhile, and much more seriously, holders of sterling were naturally rushing to exchange it for the South African currency, ostensibly valued the same but actually worth a quarter more. Capital began draining out of the country at an alarming rate, while those obliged to buy UK sterling in exchange for the Reserve Bank's pounds incurred mounting losses. Arguments in favour of retaining the South African pound's long-standing valuation drew on a proud but myopic vision of a country that could go its own way, in defiance of the rest of the world; but they had no basis in reality. (Here was a harbinger of tragedies to come.) To try to keep the markets at bay, the Reserve Bank bullied the Standard, along with Barclays DCO, into sharing the cost of a £10 million fighting fund (it was blandly christened the 'Exchange Pool') with which to stabilize the South African pound. The fund was soon under great pressure, as were relations between the Standard's managers and a newly designated Governor of the Reserve Bank, Johannes Postmus.

It might just have been possible for Pretoria to stick with the Gold Standard, had it already produced a fresh gold-linked currency of its own. Plans were in fact laid for a new currency in March 1932 – for a South African coinage based on a new gold-linked unit, to be called the Rand – but of course this came far too late to resolve the immediate problem. For several months, the country's Nationalist politicians rallied behind Postmus: a Select Committee in Pretoria backed the Reserve Bank, and government ministers tried hard to square various circles in its support. Trade partners also began adapting to the anomalies of a dual currency with two values: the Standard Bank itself made arrangements to start paying its General Managers and Inspectors directly in Cape Town rather than from London, as hitherto.[10] A sense of the Cape drifting apart was evident in other ways, too: by October, the General Managers were reporting in a cable to the Board that Postmus 'urges that interests of country demand we retain in Union of South Africa all earnings not required to meet dividends'.[11] Nothing short of an independent currency, though, could remove the underlying conundrum. As events moved to a climax, government restrictions were imposed on all exchange transactions, and steps were even taken to limit the convertibility of South African pounds into gold. By December, the mining companies of the Rand that actually sold the Pretoria government its gold were convinced that devaluation lay round the corner. Naturally, they were no longer prepared to sell gold for pounds at the old rate. The game was up for Governor Postmus, and on 29 December the Union's pound left the Gold Standard and fell into line with the value of sterling.

Just as Lewis Michell would probably have done in their position, the two Joint General Managers of the Standard in South Africa took a robust line in the following weeks over the heavy exchange losses they had incurred at the Union government's behest. They wanted some of their money back. Indeed, they contemplated submitting a formal claim for compensation, and a figure of around £750,000 was mooted – roughly equivalent to the highest annual profit ever reported by the bank.[12] This drew an indignant veto from London where the Directors thought such a combative stance most ill-advised, even though they had earlier agreed that a letter to the Finance Ministry about the losses might be a good idea. 'The Board did not intend that any claim should be made ... [and want it] placed on record that the exchange loss sustained by the Bank was the result of the support given to the Union government in their desire to maintain the Gold Standard.'[13] The notion of a formal claim was promptly dropped (and a sum of £664,000 had to be transferred from reserves to plug the gap.[14]) For the Board in London was still firmly in control – far more so, in fact, than in Michell's heyday. This did not reflect a lack of confidence in the two South African General Managers, John Schiel and F. E. King, who, on the contrary, were highly rated. It was partly a natural result of the Board's recruitment through the 1920s of several heavyweight figures with genuine banking expertise – stalwarts of the City of London establishment like Sir Roy Wilson (formerly a senior manager at the BBWA and still on the latter's Board) and R. E. Dickinson (a top man from the Westminster Bank, and also a BBWA Director), as well as City grandees like Lord Selborne and the 7th Lord Balfour of Burleigh (the son of the Eastern Bank's first Chairman). These men had never been

minded to take a back seat in the running of the Standard, and were even
less inclined to do so by 1931. Nor was their detailed scrutiny of the bank's
activities restricted to Board meetings at Clements Lane. Official letters
between London and Cape Town through the 1930s included the assembly
every six months or so of an often heroic travel itinerary for one or other
of the Directors. Most of them visited not just the Cape but the Transvaal,
the Rhodesian territories and East Africa as well, taking advantage of the
extensive rail links that had been unavailable to earlier generations, and
even taking their chances occasionally with private aeroplane
operators.[15]

A perceptible shortening of the reins between London and the Cape
can also be seen as a side-effect of the duopoly established with Barclays
DCO since 1926. The latter had proved itself a skilled exponent of decen-
tralized management and had set up a local South African board in
Pretoria, chaired by J. R. Leisk, who had been key to setting up DCO in
South Africa in the first place. Nonetheless, its General Manager, Sir John
Caulcutt, was London-based and he had around him a team that took a
daily interest in every aspect of the bank's business in South Africa.[16]
Caulcutt and his Directors engaged in a long correspondence with the
Standard's Board in the late 1920s, each letter sub-headed 'Banking Com-
petition and Arrangements: Agreement between the banks in South
Africa'. The tenor of these 'arrangements' might be inferred from a letter
that Caulcutt wrote to one of his DCO South African managers early in
1929:

> Directors here have felt that as the Standard Bank and ourselves – the two
> great banks in South Africa – have their Boards and real control [sic] in
> London, we must be particularly careful to see that we are providing in
> your territory proper banking facilities, and that such facilities are being
> offered at rates which would not permit of any serious argument against
> us . . . as you know, the Australian banks had a Cartel, which agreed that
> no accounts were to be opened for banks outside the Commonwealth . . .
> [The Government-owned State Bank] has stepped in and this arrangement
> has been altered . . . We think it quite undesirable that any discussion should
> take place about this matter as it might precipitate [in South Africa] exactly
> what we do not wish.[17]

In other words, the two banks were natural partners and would work
together – but had always to be on their guard against any overly explicit
collusion that might be countermanded by the authorities (as in Australia),
weighing in on behalf of disadvantaged customers. The best pre-emptive
defence would be a record of steady innovation, always agreed upon

between the two banks in London, that would bring South African retail banking into line with best practice in Britain. This was broadly accepted in Clements Lane, and the result for the Standard's managers in South Africa was a steady stream of comments and proposals from London about how their operations might be rendered more efficient, in ways that usually entailed a close comparison with the operations of Barclays DCO – and not infrequently seems to have irked the men in Cape Town by implying that London knew best.[18] Few aspects of banking in South Africa went untouched: the requested innovations ranged from interest-rate structures (where an early instruction decreed that deposits should in future be encouraged by varying the rates paid according to the duration of the deposit) to basic staffing issues (where, for example, employment terms for lady clerks were to be brought into line with staff rules in the City). Across a host of commercial and administrative issues, most of them thoroughly humdrum, the two banks moved as one.[19]

That South Africa's banking sector should still have been thus controlled from Britain, so many years after the ceding of political independence to the Union in 1910, was perhaps a little surprising – but the duopoly of the two 'imperial' banks was almost certainly a blessing for the country. As a leading authority on its financial history has written, the resulting stability helped shield South Africa's agricultural economy from the kind of catastrophe that overwhelmed the US farming belt. 'The "cartelised" banking structure of the inter-war years matched the needs of the South African economy well in the pre-Keynsian era of balanced budgets and [of] little support for massive state intervention in the economy.'[20] Nor did the arrangement entirely exclude meaningful competition: the two banks competed manfully over new retail customers, for instance.* And while their collusion may (*pace* Sir John Caulcutt) have deprived the country of a marginally more competitive banking sector, with some lower charges for customers, it is not easy to imagine how keener competition might have helped the South African economy to expand any faster. In the event, it enjoyed a period of steady if unexciting growth that most other nations could only envy. The Standard Bank's centenary history describes the 1930s as 'The Lean Years' – but the modern historian of British

---

* The Standard's managers in London were riled at one point to discover that former Colonial Service officers in South Africa could only draw their pensions from Barclays DCO. The Standard pressed the Crown Agents repeatedly to let it participate in the scheme. It took the top official at the Colonial Office four months, from June to November 1938, to persuade the bank to abandon its efforts to get the Barclays arrangement amended. At stake, potentially, were the current accounts of just 150 pensioners. (S. H. Wilson to Sir Cosmo Parkinson, 9 June 1938 and 18 November 1938, LMA: STo3/o3/12/oo2.)

multinational banking is surely nearer the mark in describing South Africa in this era as 'a highly desirable location for a British bank'.[21] After a relatively modest retreat in 1931–3, the Standard's balance sheet climbed steadily over the rest of the decade; and it made a respectable return on its assets, three times pushing 'real' annual profits over £1 million and accumulating inner reserves not far short of £5 million – a performance more or less paralleled, appropriately enough, by that of Barclays DCO and far in excess of anything achieved by any of Britain's other overseas banks. And behind all the figures, of course, lay one overriding feature of the domestic economy: the ever-rising output from the gold mines of the Witwatersrand. Here was the one commodity for which demand in the 1930s never sagged, and devalued currencies posed no threat at all. The sterling and dollar proceeds of its gold sales (upwardly adjusted, from 1931 and 1935 respectively) brought huge wealth to South Africa, in the process shifting the balance of the Standard Bank's deposit base from the Cape to the Transvaal – though the bank for the moment stuck stubbornly to Cape Town as its Head Office base – and leaving the whole banking sector awash with cash.[22] Much of it had to be invested in the London money markets, for there were simply too few ways to employ it domestically; but that hardly detracted from the gloss that gold bestowed.

Gold brought some relief to the economy of West Africa too, but never enough. As both Chairman of the BBWA and a regular Chairman of the Week at the Standard, Lord Selborne was especially prone to commenting on what he described in June 1935 as 'the monstrous exaltation of the value of gold', and its consequences. 'In South Africa, the passage from great depression to real prosperity has been remarkably quick . . . In West Africa, where there is considerable production of gold in the Gold Coast and a little in Nigeria, the boom in gold has not been sufficient to counterbalance the depression in agricultural produce.'[23] The frightening scale of that depression was quantified by the BBWA in its handsome annual reports, where it periodically set down the local selling prices (per ton) in Nigeria for some of its customers' most important products, as here from its 1934 Report:

	1930 £	1931 £	1932 £	1933 £	1934 £
Cocoa	29.5	16.0	19.0	15.5	12.75
Palm oil	19.0	11.5	10.5	5.25	4.25
Palm kernels	10.5	7.0	7.75	4.5	3.25
Groundnuts	7.0	6.25	9.5	3.75	2.0

Selling prices in London were meanwhile so low that – as the Chairman himself put it on one occasion towards the end of the decade – 'the [African] producer would have to give the merchant his groundnuts for nothing plus a present of £2 a ton before the latter could afford to transport them to the consuming markets'.[24] Trade shrivelled accordingly.

The BBWA's retrenchment through these years touched on every aspect of its operations – and was carried through with an impressive thoroughness under David Paterson, another founding figure, who had worked for the bank since 1894 and was its General Manager from 1929 to 1937. Its network expansion went into reverse, shrinking the number of branches from fifty-eight in 1930 to forty by 1938. Among those discontinued were the bank's two branches in the Canary Islands, imperilled by the outbreak of the Spanish Civil War. Their closure in 1937 left just a few unprofitable branches in Morocco as all that remained of the putative network beyond West Africa – and even their future now looked questionable. Closing them down would prove to be an oddly protracted business, however, not finally completed until 1945.* The Board shrank, too, from fourteen Directors to just seven by 1934. (One of the departed was Lord Kylsant, the former Sir Owen Philipps, whose shipping interests – including the Elder Dempster group and most of the other household names in Britain's shipping industry, from the Union Castle Line to the Royal Mail Steamship Company – had put him at the head of easily the biggest commercial group in the country through the 1920s.†) Bills for collection

---

* The bank's eventual plans to close the Morocco branches prompted a singular intervention in 1943 by the Governor of the Bank of England, Montagu Norman. He summoned the BBWA Chairman, Sir Frederick Eley, to express his surprise. According to a Memo written by Eley and subsequently read out to the Board: 'The Governor remarked that if the bank sustained such losses [as Eley had just set out], it should be borne by the large shareholders; this apparently was volunteered and said seriously, though the Chairman's indication [i.e. reaction?] could not have been taken as other than doubtful . . . [The Governor said] the bank could not close down Branches in foreign territory just as it wished, because British prestige had to be considered.' The closure plans were duly put in abeyance until 1945, by which time Norman had retired. A Deputy Governor, Cameron Cobbold, then proposed in a meeting with Eley that he adopt a wait-and-see approach, but this was firmly rejected. As the Minutes put it: 'Sir Frederick countered energetically . . . and introduced a note of humour when he inquired if the Bank of England would like to make us a grant . . . or even open a Branch of their own at Casablanca.' The branches were closed forthwith. (Selected Minutes of the BBWA Board, 29 September 1943 and 25 April 1945, LMA: CLC/B/207/MS28521.)

† The BBWA's Chairman told the Board on 4 November 1931 that he had only just received a letter of resignation dated 1 August 1931 – a delay perhaps attributable, though the Minutes did not say so, to the fact that Kylsant had had to write his letter from Wormwood Scrubs Prison. He had been given a twelve-month sentence at the end of July for false accounting, in the wake of a sensational collapse of his shipping empire and an emergency reconstruction

dropped by half in 1929–32 and, with ever fewer alternatives, the bank's investments in the London money markets by 1933 had more than doubled in four years. Only in 1936 did it seem that a corner might just have been turned. Prices for the staple commodities suddenly jumped almost as dramatically as they had fallen in 1931. Exports of tin ore, platinum and diamonds also began to rise encouragingly, alongside the mounting shipments of gold from the Gold Coast. Indeed, there was even talk of finding 'black gold' for which world demand was just starting to soar, as a prominent shareholder told the AGM in 1936: 'Our old friend, the late Mr George Neville, was convinced of the presence of oil in Nigeria, a country which he knew well: he had seen unmistakeable signs of it himself on the shores, so we hope that prospectors will some day be able to strike it.'[25] The upturn, though, proved short-lived – and commodity prices by late 1937 were heading rapidly back to their earlier lows.

Such a prolonged disruption of the regional economy inevitably had a lasting impact on the structure of the West African marketplace. In particular, it spawned the emergence of a uniquely powerful European firm, the United African Company (UAC). For the BBWA, this was a troubling development on at least three grounds. In the first place, the genesis of the UAC – a precursor of the giant Unilever – harked back in some ways to the old animosity shown towards the bank since the 1890s by the many local firms that resented its quasi-official status and the virtual monopoly enjoyed by the Elder Dempster shipping line. The UAC represented a consolidation of more than seventy trading companies that had been pooled together through the 1920s. Most of them, though hitherto run separately, already had the same owner: the British company built by those kings of the Victorian soap business, James and William Lever. (In every bar of Lux, Lifebuoy and Sunlight Soap, West Africa's palm oil was the essential ingredient.) To spearhead the merger initiative, Lever Brothers had employed the one firm in their portfolio, the Niger Company, that had always been at the core of the disaffection with BBWA. And not long before his death in 1925, William Lever (by then Lord Leverhulme) had put in charge of the process a former manager of one of the BBWA's rivals, Colonial Bank.[26] These were not happy antecedents, from BBWA's perspective, when in 1929 UAC was formed.

The second and rather more immediate source of misgivings over the

---

co-ordinated by the Treasury and the Bank of England. Surely a little gratuitously, the Chairman observed that Kylsant's last attendance at the Board had been on 7 May and under the Articles of Association he had therefore forfeited his Directorship on 7 August 'as he had not applied for special leave of absence'.

next couple of years was the financial position of the new group. A great many of the constituent businesses that came together as UAC had been customers of the bank for years – and not a few of them were in poor shape, even before the market turmoil of 1929–31. Indeed, it was their lingering financial frailty after the recession of the early 1920s that had motivated Lever Brothers and its various trading subsidiaries to join forces with their biggest rival, the African and Eastern Trade Corporation (AETC), as UAC. But the mere fact of the merger was not of itself enough to guarantee them a safe passage through the storms of 1929–31. Some tense negotiations ensued between the amalgamated group and its bankers, with its heavy indebtedness causing the BBWA's Directors considerable concern. This was finally allayed only in 1931 after the two parent companies behind UAC had agreed to guarantee its debts up to a value of £2½ million.[27]

The third reason for the BBWA's unease over UAC was the most vexing of all. By the middle of the 1930s, while remaining a sizeable customer of the BBWA, it had begun acting almost as a bank itself. Traditionally, the BBWA had extended credit to the region's European trading companies. They used the funds for cash loans to their own small African suppliers (in some remote places actually functioning as agents of the bank). This was perfectly agreeable to the bank, which made most of its revenues from the European companies by lending to them, handling their foreign exchange needs and financing their shipments with discounted trade bills – and it had plenty of its own African customers, too. But UAC, now reorganized as the Unilever group, had different ideas. With substantial capital resources available to it in London, it began funding ever more of its trading subsidiaries without external credit; and it went a critical step further by starting to lend to significant African customers of the BBWA. It also inaugurated a general reliance on the novel practice of cabling money transfers from London, for the financing of crop purchases in West Africa, in place of raising local funds through the discounting of trade bills drawn on the foreign customer. Here was a sea-change in trade-financing practices that was just becoming evident all over the world, but this cannot have been much of a consolation for the BBWA as it watched a valuable source of income withering away.

The bank eventually succeeded in negotiating an accord with UAC/ Unilever, which agreed to curtail its extracurricular financing initiatives in exchange for an assurance of more generous terms on its future business with the bank. Far more intriguing than the detailed terms of this agreement, though, is the way that the BBWA was able to negotiate it in cahoots with the other main bank in West Africa – Barclays DCO. According to the BBWA's own historian, no record exists of its pact with UAC.[28] But the understanding between the two banks was amply documented. Sir Roy Wilson for the BBWA met early in February 1939 with Sir John Caulcutt, who by this time had become the Chairman of his bank. They talked at some length, according to a memorandum by Wilson, about how best to respond to UAC's move 'to do without the Banks' services in West Africa, and to damage our business by offering financial facilities during the produce seasons to customers who, hitherto, had done all their business with the Banks'.[29] This close consultation was entirely in keeping with the informal co-operation struck up by Barclays DCO with the BBWA in West Africa, as indeed with the Standard Bank in South Africa. (It would give rise in 1945 to a formally codified agreement within the region, which prevailed until 1957.) But there is every indication that the BBWA would have liked to go much further. Four years earlier, in October 1935, Wilson had been entrusted by the Board to offer Barclays DCO a deal whereby the latter would have pulled out of the region altogether in exchange for a shareholding in the BBWA 'at an agreed price . . . that would give them equality with our four other shareholding Banks . . . [and] one or even two Directors [on the Board]'.[30] The proposal had in the end been rejected, but only after Barclays had mulled it over for several months. Wilson therefore pitched it to Caulcutt again at their February 1939 meeting. He got the same reply, and that was the end of it.

Within just a few weeks of this second discussion, Caulcutt's attention was drawn to another of the forerunner banks. He was offered, and accepted, a seat on the Board of the Eastern Bank. It had fallen vacant due to the death at the end of January of Jacob Haskell, one of the Eastern's seven founding Directors in 1909, and its Chairman since 1921. Caulcutt's was a logical appointment, not least because Barclays DCO had been buying shares in the Eastern Bank on the open market for several months. (Perhaps Wilson and his colleagues, noting this, had been encouraged to think quitting West Africa and taking a passive stake in their bank might appeal to Barclays DCO as part of a portfolio strategy.) It is easy to see why the Eastern's shares might have looked a good investment – far better, indeed, than any stake in the beleaguered BBWA. For the Eastern's decision to expand its network in the Arabian Gulf had paid off handsomely, albeit in ways that came as something of a surprise to the bank. It had found itself a significant, though largely unremarked, beneficiary of the emergence of the Middle East as one of the world's most promising sources of oil. First discovered in 1927, the oilfields of Iraq had been developed only very slowly in the early 1930s – lacklustre demand for oil in the worst years of the Depression had deterred the concession-owners, who had no interest in driving prices lower – but the first pipelines from the oilfields to the Mediterranean had been completed in 1934, and by 1938 the wells were in full flow. Iraq's economy was consequently expanding as never before. Meanwhile that maverick early customer of the Eastern's Bahrain branch, Major Frank Holmes, had gone one step better than Mr George Neville of the BBWA and actually found his oil – in potentially startling quantities. His first strike had been made in Bahrain in May 1932, followed by another in Kuwait in February 1938. The very next month after that, oil was discovered by other prospectors in the nascent Kingdom of Saudi Arabia, outside a village called Dammam. The Eastern Bank had had to endure its share of the Depression's miseries in India and Singapore earlier in the decade, and had seen the traditional pearl fisheries of the Gulf more or less wiped out by the impact of 'cultured' pearls from Japan. But now its prospects in the Arab world looked promising indeed.* A Trade Report on Bahrain filed by the British Political Agent in the summer of 1938 conveyed a little of what this meant for the Eastern, beyond all the bare statistics of rapidly rising crude oil shipments:

> The present prosperity which is reflected in the increased trade of Bahrain is due almost solely to the operations of the Bahrain Petroleum Company, which employs (in round numbers) 370 Europeans and Americans, 450 Asiatic foreigners and 2,360 Bahrainis. A very considerable proportion of the total wages earned is of course spent in Bahrain. There is a branch of the Eastern Bank Ltd in Bahrain which transacts all types of business.[31]

An Inspector despatched to the Gulf in December 1938 spent five weeks compiling a forty-eight-page report about the Baghdad branch and almost as long on a scarcely shorter report about the operations in tiny Bahrain.[32] The Eastern Bank had found a niche, and from now on would be steadily more identified with an expanding role in the Middle East (and a name, Sharqi Bank, to go with it – Al-Sharq being 'the East' in Arabic). Of course it would have to balance, in this niche, a heightened degree of political risk against the blessings of the oil industry, especially in Iraq. (When

---

* Barclays DCO valued its stake in Eastern not just for its inherent attractions but also as a way for it to participate indirectly in the future growth of these oil-blessed Arab countries. A more direct approach was felt to be complicated by the bank's prominent dealings with Jewish banks and customers in Palestine. One probably apocryphal story tells of the difficulties caused by this perception even in Palestine itself, where the manager, A. P. S. Clark, was on one occasion severely cross-examined by an important Arab customer. 'When Clark eventually convinced his inquisitive customer that Mr Barclay was not a Jew, he said, "But what about his partners – Dominion, Colonial and Overseas – surely are they not all Jews?"' (Julian Crossley and John Blandford, *The DCO Story, A history of banking in many countries 1925–71*, Barclays Bank International Limited 1975, p. 94.)

King Faisal's young successor, King Ghazi, died in a car crash in April 1939, he left a four-year-old son to the care of a Council of Ministers that had already shown itself ominously partial to coups, conspiracies and assassinations in Ghazi's own short reign.) But British hegemony in the region seemed assured, and the prospect of a string of oil-rich Gulf sheikh-doms loosely tied into the Empire was deeply alluring. As for political risk, by the 1930s a bank faced scarcely more of that in the Middle East than in India itself, where fundamental changes in the political environ-ment were by now adding appreciably to the economic difficulties of the Depression era – and hugely complicating life for that fourth of the fore-runners, the Chartered Bank of India, Australia and China.

2. EMPIRE-STAFFING

After being in business for seven decades, Chartered Bank was still run by an astonishingly small cadre of managers. Aggregate numbers are surprisingly elusive in the records, but about 330 officer-grade men would seem a reasonable estimate for the total in 1930.[33] This included 108 men listed on the Home Staff, and 61 young probationers on the Foreign Staff in London still eagerly awaiting their first posting. Bishopsgate's full com-plement, at about 310, including 'lady clerks and typists', was scarcely larger than in 1914. Out in the East, the Foreign Staff had grown appreci-ably larger. A top layer of a hundred or so Managers, Sub-Managers and Accountants, classified separately as 'Executives', ran the forty-seven 'Agencies and Branches' listed at the front of the Annual Report of the Directors; and below them were sixty other covenanted officers. (Career details on the latter were set down in the Eastern Staff books. Twenty-four of the sixty gave somewhere in Scotland as their home address and many more had distinctive Scottish surnames. Contemporaries still regularly alluded in passing to the comfortable majority comprised by the Scottish contingent – sometimes noting its influence in unexpected ways, as in a *Times* report of November 1929 on the annual rugby match in London against the Hongkong Bank: 'There are six Scotsmen in the Chartered Bank's pack, and this was evident from their fondness of dribbling rushes . . .'[34]) The tiny staff numbers were much in line with those of the other Eastern exchange banks – and by chance almost identical to those of the Hongkong Bank, which had an Eastern staff of 273 men in 1930 (including probationers) and probably another 60 or so in London.[35] Of course any such total represented nothing like the true scale of the workforce required by the Chartered to keep a meticulous daily record of its extensive operations. For this the bank relied on droves of other employees (even less apparent in the historical records than its lady clerks and typists, of whom there were eighty-five at Head Office in 1930). These were the 'native staff', probably numbering close to 2,000 across the network.

In all Asian countries, skilled and hard-working local clerks provided most of the basic manpower for a world of book-keeping that was now dauntingly complex, infinitely more so than the accounts department of any firm simply trading in physical goods. This staffing option was not open to the overseas banks in Africa, where few local hires were yet available with the necessary levels of education. The Standard Bank employed thousands in a management structure much like those of the British clearing banks; and the BBWA by 1930 had a network of 850 expatriates.[36] But in the largest Chartered branches of Asia, like Bombay and Calcutta, a team of a dozen or so British covenanted officers each administered well over a hundred locally hired employees (a little confusingly, the locals were the 'staff' – generally not capitalized – as opposed to the 'officers' sent from Britain, though Head Office also divided its British cohort into Home and Foreign Staffs). Senior members of the native staff, as we have already seen, could rise to trusted positions. Their skilful handling of the bank's business rendered young and inexperienced expatriates in many instances virtually surplus to requirements. 'Just sign here, sahib (or tuan)' was a familiar refrain in every Chartered counting house. No native clerk, though, was covenanted to sign on the bank's behalf, and nor – leaving aside the Chinese compradores who belonged in a special category – could they ever deal directly with a customer. They were clerks, not bankers. This was the natural order, a commercial variant on the Empire-staffing model that proverbially allowed a thousand civil servants to rule over the 250 million Indians under the Raj.

It had many laudable aspects, leaving aside its evident value to shareholders and customers of the bank. In applying it across Asia, the Chartered introduced thousands of young men to the commercial disciplines and routines of the West; many of them flourished within the bank itself, others went on to build subsequent careers very successfully outside it. They were trained by expatriates whose professionalism was everywhere acknowledged and for the most part greatly respected. Acknowledging this positive aspect of the imperial era has been unfashionable for a long time, but Empire-staffing unarguably made a contribution to the spread of Western business skills that is worth remarking.* It naturally entailed,

---

* An exception needs noting, in this context, for the work of the historian Niall Ferguson and especially his *Empire, How Britain Made The Modern World*, Allen Lane, 2003. 'The

however, an office culture inside every branch of the Chartered that was still totally imbued with the caste, class and race distinctions on which the Empire had rested for generations. Nowhere was this more evident than in India, and new arrivals from Bishopsgate could often find it all slightly overwhelming, as did a young Ulsterman, Willie MacQuitty. Having joined the bank in 1924 after a couple of years with the Belfast Bank, he landed in Bombay in January 1927 en route to a first posting in Amritsar. Before continuing his journey on the Punjab Mail, young Willie was given a tour of the city and of the Chartered's branch at its centre:

> Here I was introduced to the Burra Sahib, the 'Big Master', then to the rest of the Foreign Staff in order of rank . . . The Indian staff sat on stools at the counters, dressed in white, with long shirts hanging outside their trousers. The sahibs sat at polished desks, their *chaprassi*, or office servant, standing in readiness before them with pen, blotter, matches, a glass of water or whatever the master might need. A stream of clerks came and went, placing the folders, documents and, from time to time, telegrams on the already crowded desks . . . The scene filled me with mounting apprehension. This type of banking was more than I had bargained for.[37]

MacQuitty went on to work for the bank until March 1939, serving in Amritsar, Colombo, Bangkok, Ipoh and Shanghai. (He subsequently became a distinguished film producer – one of his best-known films being the 1958 classic *A Night to Remember*, starring Kenneth More, about the sinking of the *Titanic* – and at the age of eighty-five he turned out an engaging autobiography, *A Life to Remember*, more than half of which he devoted to a colourful narration of his years as a Chartered Sub-Accountant.*)

The fact that non-British employees were everywhere arbitrarily excluded from the officer ranks of the bank was an obvious racial snub. By the end of the 1920s this was beginning to cause serious offence wherever nationalist politicians and their supporters had set out their intentions of putting an end to the Empire itself – as in India, where civil disobedience

---

difficulty with the achievements of empire is that they are much more likely to be taken for granted than the sins of empire . . . [But] the imagination reels from the counter-factual of modern history without the British Empire' (p. xxii).

* MacQuitty did not expect his readers to have a huge interest in banking matters. He focused instead on the sports and the parties, and above all on his amorous adventures in the East (including an account of finding his predecessor's concubine in his bed on his first night as a Sub-Accountant in Bangkok). This captured an aspect of Eastern exchange banking that went unmentioned in the job adverts, but was undoubtedly treasured by many a young Chartered banker.

campaigns under Gandhi's leadership, widespread strikes and occasionally violent anti-British demonstrations were prompting many clerical workers for the first time in their lives to question the racial divide underpinning the Raj. (MacQuitty himself, proud of his Ulster roots, more than once placated an anti-British mob only by proclaiming himself an Irishman.) And growing unrest on the streets was matched by a novel assertiveness within Indian business circles, which extended to a heightened sensitivity over traditional British banking practices. Many Indian families had accumulated substantial fortunes in the Great War and through the 1920s. One result was a boom in the number of joint-stock Indian banks: their numbers had risen from sixteen in 1910 to seventy-four by 1928, bringing them rupee deposits on a par with those held by the British exchange banks.[38] Their Indian owners were now questioning the grip still exerted by Chartered Bank and its peers over the financing of the country's foreign trade. Depressed conditions in many export sectors after 1927 exacerbated this gathering resentment. The result by the end of the decade was a mounting hostility towards these British banks, which seemed to regard their powerful commercial legacy as inviolable – yet would not stoop to employing Indians as managers.

Long suppressed, this rather fundamental issue was dragged into the open by a Banking Inquiry instigated by the Indian government in May 1929. Intended as a comprehensive review of the country's banking industry – with a bevy of Provincial Committees submitting reports to a Central Committee, for expert analysis and the submission of a final report two years later – the Inquiry provided critics of the exchange banks with a perfect opportunity to try curtailing the scope of their operations. The Central Committee consisted of thirteen Indians and six Englishmen, one of whom was R. W. Buckley, the Chartered's feisty Manager in Calcutta and the chairman of the city's Exchange Banks Association. Buckley sent back periodic reports on the Committee's discussions, along with some masterly expositions of the structure of trade financing in India.[39] Some of the mooted proposals for future regulation of the exchange banks were soon causing genuine alarm in Bishopsgate. They raised the prospect of a ban on deposit-taking and term lending, a compulsory divestment of all holdings in Indian businesses (a blatant move against the Chartered's ownership of the Allahabad Bank) and even a law requiring all banks in India to register as rupee businesses, with Indians commanding a majority on the Board. Many spoke up, though, in favour of a wider franchise for the Imperial Bank, the entity created in 1921 via a merger of the three Presidency Banks and effectively the official banker to the Government. (It was still precluded from any involvement in the financing of foreign

trade, not least due to fierce lobbying by the exchange banks.) Perhaps
most disconcerting of all, insofar as they seemed much less likely to be
rejected, were measures aimed at addressing the exchange banks' failure
to promote Indians into management positions. Buckley had to report that
'Indianization' was attracting considerable support, with some even urging guidelines on the number of non-Indian managers that any bank could
retain. This was all too preposterous for the Court, which fired off a series
of letters to foreign banks in the City inquiring as to their experience of
such matters in other regions of the world – and it was made clear to
Buckley that he should have no truck with the wilder notions circulating
on the Committee:

> Obviously a section of the Central Committee have set their hearts upon
> limiting the activities of the Exchange Banks, but, fortunately, it seems to
> us that in their anxiety to stress their point they have somewhat overstepped
> themselves, in that they seem to have sunk the question of Banking
> altogether and introduced instead the entirely different question of racial
> feeling . . . and it defeats us to diagnose what is really at the back of the
> minds of our detractors if it goes beyond personal animus.[40]

Buckley and his British confrères appear to have earned their keep over
the next nine months. They had to contend with some heated opposition, as
one of the bank's Directors could confirm after visiting India for five weeks
early in 1931. 'Big changes are coming', Colin Campbell, later Lord Colgrain,
warned in a letter to Sir Montagu Turner, 'and hostility towards the Exchange
Banks, especially in Bombay, is considerable.'[41] Yet when it was published in
September that year, the Inquiry's Report delivered a broadly positive verdict
on the facilities made available by the exchange banks for the financing of
Indian trade, and it stuck mostly to technical recommendations for 'careful
consideration'. It endorsed a plan, already five years old, for a central banking
institution – to be called the Reserve Bank of India – which would one day
oversee a licensing regime for non-Indian banks. But on the critical topic of
Indianization, it trod very carefully. The exchange banks were merely urged
to contemplate the introduction of Indian 'probationary assistants', a scheme
already adopted at the Imperial Bank.

This must have come as something of a relief to the Court in London.
Campbell had led his colleagues to fear a much more drastic approach.
(Writing in April to the Chairman of the P&O Banking Corporation, M. M. Gubbay – another future Chartered Director – he had
suggested that it might be a good move to attach some young Indians
to his staff in London, thus anticipating 'a move which is bound to
develop in the future'.[42]) Press coverage of the Report in India suggested,

however, that Campbell may after all have read the runes correctly. Against the background of an increasingly acrimonious stand-off between the authorities and the Nationalists, the views of a dissenting minority on the Inquiry Committee were widely aired. Several members had been at pains to record formally the discontent of many witnesses over the anti-Indian bias, as they saw it, in the operations of the exchange banks. Two separate manifestations of this were deplored. Half a dozen of the most senior Indians on the Inquiry Committee singled out the reluctance of the banks to deal with Indian businesses. They signed a Joint Minute to the Report, stating categorically 'that every Indian commercial body that has appeared before the Committee has complained that in the matter of providing financial facilities for import and export trade the Exchange Banks have, generally speaking, been differentiating between national and non-national exporters and importers'. The second kind of bias related to the core issue of Indianization: the lack of opportunities for Indian staff. A Minority Report by Manu Subedar, a vociferous and indefatigable critic of the exchange banks, set out a list of measures that would in effect have amounted to a closure of the 'Open Door' for 'foreign' banks. Item Six stated his vision boldly enough: 'Except [for] the manager and one official in each branch under him, the whole staff shall be Indian.'[43]

The Chartered's formal response to the Report, and to these dissenting views, went off to the Indian government in Delhi in June 1932. It was written by Buckley's successor, Alex Smith. The suggestion that the bank ever took a biased view of a new business opportunity was utterly rejected – a little disingenuously, given the internal debate over recent years that had alluded frankly to the bank's conspicuous lack of engagement with the Indian business community. (One of Smith's own Sub-Accountants, Isaac Sykes, penned a private and commendably honest memorandum three months later that made the point again: 'It is a fact that the Bank has not, of recent years at any rate, attempted to foster business with Indians . . . [It is] the personal contact which is at present lacking.'[44]) As to the idea that Indian clerks might be promoted as covenanted officers, Smith simply pointed out why this was such a hopelessly Utopian notion:

As the personnel of the Covenanted Staff of the Exchange Banks is liable to be called on at a moment's notice to serve in any part of the world, this alone, we take it, presents a disability in the case of young Indians difficult to surmount. To carry this suggestion to its logical conclusion would mean that a Bank whose organisation is world wide would have for its Covenanted Staff a personnel of every race, colour and creed which is obviously impracticable.[45]

Nonetheless, the notion of at least some degree of Indianization was now unavoidably up for debate. Of course the Chartered's senior men in the early 1930s had plenty of other concerns that pressed more urgently from day to day. The devastation wrought by the Depression posed acute difficulties on an almost daily basis, chronicled in weekly letters and half-yearly reports back to London. The export of raw hides from Madras had collapsed; world demand for the output of Calcutta's jute mills was plummeting; the trade in cotton piece-goods from Lancashire had been all but demolished – this last calamity just one of the many consequences of the extraordinary rise of Japanese business on all fronts (or as the Calcutta office put it in July 1932, the rise 'of the energetic and ubiquitous Jap'.[46]) And always in the background was the nagging worry that profit margins on currency exchange had been all but eliminated by the rush of new competitors with little regard for gentlemen's rules in the marketplace ('We have seen letters from Lloyds Bank to merchants soliciting business which resemble those sent out from a third-rate grocer's shop. The same applies also to the National City Bank of New York . . .'[47]). The challenge to the Empire-staffing model, though, raised matters of an altogether more fundamental nature.

In the immediate aftermath of the Banking Inquiry, some confessed they had been scratching their heads for a while, and had now decided to bury them in the sand – as Smith explained from Calcutta:

> We often ponder what the future has in store for us as an Exchange Bank with nationalism so much in the ascendant these days . . . our thoughts are sometimes somewhat disquieting [but] we think the time is too far off for us to need to worry about it. It is, in our view, a problem which another administration of the Bank will have to tackle so we might as well carry on and ignore it entirely and formulate our Policy as if it did not exist.[48]

But by the summer of 1934, a majority of the Chartered's senior managers in India were feeling much less sanguine: that 'far-off' time seemed closer by the day. Following a managers' conference in Calcutta, the briefing for the Court included a surprising 'Item 15': 'While aware that Head Office is adverse to a change which will introduce Indianization, it is felt that the time is approaching when this question will have to be seriously considered.'[49] The next twelve months saw a dramatic change of heart in Bishopsgate. This had less to do with the entreaties of Mr Gandhi than with a sober reappraisal of the economics of banking in India. With profits looking skeletal by past standards – over the four years 1930–33, the entire sub-continent (including Rangoon and Colombo) had notched up net earnings of just £26,361 – no genuine opportunity to cut costs could be ignored. And one such opportunity was glaringly apparent – or at least, easily confirmed with a modicum of research. Both the Imperial Bank and the Chartered's own Allahabad Bank relied very heavily on Indian officers, who had proved themselves entirely interchangeable with their European colleagues while accepting salaries up to two-thirds lower. (The research established that the Imperial had 105 branches in its Bengal region, of which 63 were run by Indian managers compared with 42 under Europeans; and, of the region's 59 accountants, 46 were Indian. As for the Allahabad, it had turned over all its sub-agencies to Indian managers and given them signing powers on behalf of the bank.)

In August 1935, Head Office despatched Circular No. 394/a, alerting all offices to the fact that the Directors had decided they were 'sympathetic to the suggestion for the devolution to reliable, well-educated, members of the Local Staffs of certain executive duties, at present performed by European officers'. Henceforth, these reliable and well-educated chaps would belong to a new category of 'Assistant Officers'. It was a title exquisitely calculated to lift the holder out of mere clerical status without actually ceding a fully managerial (and covenanted) rank. Perhaps, indeed, it was overly subtle: the circular evidently failed to detonate as the Directors had expected, and was widely ignored. So two months later they put out another and very detailed Circular, headed 'Devolution of Duties to Local Staff'. Its text acknowledged much more explicitly that some traditional attitudes needed reappraising, given the increasingly evident potential of many Indians. (The Central Board of the recently established Reserve Bank of India had indeed just appointed an Indian Secretary, who was 'originally a typist in the Imperial Bank of India'!) That said, the really pressing case for change was financial. The Circular set out the seminal figures gathered from the Imperial and Allahabad Banks, 'merely as a guide ... [to] give you an idea of the extent to which the Imperial have "Indianized" – not to satisfy a political outcry, but of necessity to save overheads, as many of their up-country Branches and Pay-Offices could never, we are informed, pay their way under more expensive European management'. Here was a salutary message for the Chartered, and the Circular spelled it out:

> As we cannot help feeling that this very important question from an 'overheads' point of view is not receiving the attention we had hoped for, we must ask our individual Agents and Managers at all points to go very thoroughly into the matter ... We do not for a moment suggest that members of the Local Staff should be placed in charge of such important duties as Cash, Securities or Current Accounts, or be promoted to executive [i.e. covenanted]

rank. But, we do feel that more responsibility than hitherto could be safely given to some of the existing tried heads of certain Departments, and less routine checking by European officers . . . Under present World conditions, with margins in exchange and interest cut to ribbons, and profits in consequence so difficult to earn, we commend what we have written to your very careful consideration and attention.[50]

The prime target of the new approach was to be India, but it applied to the whole network. It seems to have been part of an initiative aimed at modernizing the bank's operations more broadly, largely orchestrated by one of the senior Inspectors, John Meldrum. In an important Memorandum of November 1935, Meldrum proposed a wider adoption of mechanized book-keeping, better monthly monitoring of credit positions, more sophisticated analysis of individual branches' true profitability, and a slew of accounting reforms to make the performance of the bank's main departments more transparent. (He proposed, for example, that interest income and exchange gains should be logged separately – an idea that seems not to have picked up much support from his peers.[51]) Meldrum had plenty of ideas to offer on staffing too. He set out a list of specific proposals aimed at dislodging some venerable practices of the bank that no longer made sense. Sub-Agencies had always been managed by experienced officers, judged to be capable of handling difficult situations without recourse to their colleagues; but a junior officer with a telephone could now do just as well. Again, Sub-Agencies had always been assigned a minimum of two officers, in case one should fall ill; but one man was surely adequate, wherever 'a relief officer can travel . . . by aeroplane to fill a gap'. Above all, he thought the notion of Assistant Officers needed to be taken a critical step further. In a section of his Memorandum euphemistically headed 'The Readjustment of Establishments', he thought newly promoted local staff – or capable new men, hired locally – could sensibly be set on a par with the young men joining from London:

> It is admitted in the [October] Circular that Asiatics have been proved capable of controlling not only Departments but BRANCHES of other Banks, and there is no reason to suppose that the benefits of economical working realised by others cannot also be acquired by us. With all due deference, I suggest that Head Office extend the scope of their reforms by authorising the appointment of Asiatics in our large Branches to the posts occupied by junior Sub-Accountants in departments carrying two or more European Officers.[52]

Meldrum stopped short of suggesting his 'Promoted Asiatics' should be appointed as covenanted officers – 'I suggest that the designation

"Departmental Supervisor" would meet the case' – and it is hard to be sure how far, if at all, his recommendation was put into effect. Conspicuously able clerks had shown up on the list of Foreign Staff Probationers in Bishopsgate from time to time in the past, and Asian names now popped up a little more regularly (S. V. Hariharan, 1936; C. A. Subramanian, 1937; Goh Poh Lim and Ching Kang in 1938). Perhaps some indeed returned home as Supervisors. What is unambiguously clear, though, is that none were admitted to the ranks of the Eastern Staff or given any kind of covenanted status. Nor, in India, was any attempt made to integrate the operations of the Allahabad Bank with the Chartered, or even to attempt a little judicious cross-fertilization. (This strictly arm's-length ownership of the Allahabad was one day to prove a costly oversight.) The essential thrust of Meldrum's 'Readjustment' was rejected. A full-blown Indianizing reorientation of the bank still remained, for most of its British officers, a thoroughly remote prospect.

Several explanations can be offered for this. The Court's appetite for a far-reaching reform was probably not enhanced in the short term by a disastrous loss in Bombay, incurred earlier in 1935: one of the city's largest grain and seed merchants, the British-owned Strauss & Co., collapsed suddenly and sensationally. Its English manager threw himself out of a fourth-floor window onto the polished central courtyard of the Taj Mahal hotel, leaving behind a suicide note to say the firm's failure 'has caused such confusion in India that I can't face this tangle'.[53] It was Chartered Bank that petitioned the High Court in London to wind up the company, and its bankruptcy left the bank's Bombay branch with a loss of £257,687 for 1935, substantially more that it had earned over the previous ten years put together. (This was by far the biggest setback of the years after 1931, and helped produce a calamitous drop in total real profits from £923,441 in 1934 to £229,910 in 1935.) But a more fundamental deterrent to reform was the resistance encountered by the Directors within Bishopsgate, especially from the young men hoping for long and remunerative careers in the East. Already worried by a fall in the number of postings, with staff numbers being whittled down everywhere in response to the wretched state of world trade, the Probationary Foreign Staffers at Head Office were quick to register their disquiet. Five members of their representative committee sent a formal letter to the Chairman and Directors of the Court in January 1936, pointing out that rumours about the idea of locally recruited officers had caused 'uneasiness'. They sought reassurance 'that [British] officers will not find themselves "dispensed with" after just three years in the East, because of Indianization'.[54] And there was resistance, too, from those in the field. Wherever isolated attempts were made to consider the possibility of promoting a local man to 'assistant officer' status, problems always seemed quick to surface. Somehow the right opportunity never jelled, for reasons that were invariably left a little vague. Here is the Manager of the branch at Ipoh in the Malay States, setting out his thoughts in July 1936 on a struggling satellite office at Sitiawan, and whether to retain it:

> Two alternatives have had our consideration, either to put an Asiatic in charge or to close down, and we regret to have to report that after much deliberation we have been unable to formulate a plan for the former which we would care to recommend to Head Office. Even if agreed in principle, a workable scheme would rob the Sub-Agency of so many of its functions that we might as well close down altogether.[55]

There was much, it seems, that 'an Asiatic' could do to fulfil the basics of managing the business, but there were also a good many additional responsibilities – attending to those undefined 'functions' – that would inevitably be beyond him. Scepticism about the wisdom of promoting local men had long been an engrained prejudice of colonial expatriates in the tropics. (Rudyard Kipling had famously noted the views of a British colliery manager in India on the subject: 'Don't you believe that the native is a fool. You can train him to everything except responsibility.'[56]) But if Chartered men were generally as inclined as their peers to cling to a sense of their own innate superiority – and it was often a case, under the Raj, of preserving class rather than racial distinctions – there were undeniably many practical obstacles to Indianization, just as Alex Smith had protested so warmly in 1932. The bank's commitment to relocating its younger British officers around the network on a regular basis was just one consideration. Another was the fact that these officers, the great majority of them unmarried, shared a lifestyle that made little distinction between office and leisure hours.* At the end of the working day, local staff went home to their families; but youthful Chartered officers gathered for supper in the chummery or the mess. Then again, there was the wider social role to which these officers were expected to aspire at each stage of their career. Diligent Chartered men were Golf Club secretaries and Yacht Club treasurers, trade-association chairmen and stalwarts of the local Church (of

---

* The traditional preponderance of bachelors was a long time passing. One retired officer, looking back in 1950, offered a rare glimpse of this feature of the bank's history. When he had gone East in 1907, it was said there were only ten married men on the whole Foreign Staff. He met two between 1907 and 1914, and none at all in Calcutta between 1914 and 1921. Of twenty-three officers who passed through Calcutta in the 1920s, he thought only two were married. (A. B. Pollock memoir, LMA: CH03/01/14/017.)

Scotland, most likely). Successful bankers sought to be fully engaged in expatriate life, and their prominence at the club stood the bank in good stead – often directly so, nurturing personal ties between the bank and its corporate clients. The day might come when being British was no longer a prerequisite for this kind of extracurricular activity, but it had not dawned yet. The 1938 edition of *Murray's Handbook for Travelling in India, Burma and Ceylon* made the point almost in passing, presumably to help readers avoid any embarrassment: the guide 'pointed out specifically that among the clubs listed (numbering 12 in Bombay, 10 in Calcutta and 9 in Madras), only the Calcutta Club was open to Indians and Europeans, though Willingdon Club in Madras was open to Indian and European ladies'.[57] An Indian man, in fact, could no more move in the social circles of the typical Chartered manager than could a European woman. The conservative governance of the bank, remarkably unchanged since Gwyther's day, provided no inducement to challenge the social norms of the day – or, indeed, to dilute the essential clubbiness of the bank itself. All officers, from the greenest Sub-Accountant to the grizzliest old Manager, came from the same cultural mould. This was seen as vital to the Foreign Staff's *esprit de corps*, truly a 'hidden reserve' worth preserving. Attitudes that we would regard today as blatantly racist were an integral part of the British management structure that was still thought necessary if the bank's overseas network was to be run from London with complete trust in the integrity of the front line. And, undeniably, that structure proved remarkably resilient through the 1930s in the face of constantly dispiriting commercial setbacks.

The half-hearted approach to Indianization had no obvious impact on profitability. There was no wholesale Indianization of India's economy, which might have set the Chartered at a penal disadvantage. Having killed off the milling of raw jute in Dundee, the jute mills of Calcutta were still run – and in many cases owned – largely by Scotsmen. (An official report on the industry twenty years later still found plenty of Mackinnons, Macneills and McLeods among its dominant personalities.[58]) British managing agencies similarly retained their substantial hold over the tea plantations of Assam, and remained almost as prominent in the Bengali coal industry. A first-time visitor to the port of Bombay in the 1930s would have had no reason to think the Empire ailing. The grandeur of the 22-acre business district adjoining the docks (the elegant Ballard Estate, completed in one giant project during the Edwardian era and entirely redolent of the smartest stone terraces of Mayfair and St James's) was still home to many of the leading shippers, insurers and managing agents, most of them British – and almost all of them clients of Chartered Bank. The Profit & Loss accounts of the Indian branches in the 1930s nonetheless tell a dispiriting story (see Appendix D). Bombay failed to break even over the four years that followed the Strauss debacle; and neither Colombo nor Rangoon were ever restored to their former profitability after 1931–2. A modest revival in Calcutta's fortunes, and a steady performance in Madras, at least ensured that the sub-continent ended with a net profit for the decade as a whole, but its contribution to the bank's aggregate earnings (3.3 per cent for 1930–39 inclusive) represented a brutal confirmation of India's greatly reduced importance, first highlighted in 1927–30. Might the business in India have flagged less conspicuously had it engaged more willingly with the sub-continent's emerging entrepreneurs and industrialists? After the Reserve Bank of India finally materialized in 1935, the Imperial Bank was given clearance to enter the foreign exchange market. Its arrival made little difference to the foreign banks as a whole – and their share of deposits held up well – but Calcutta's half-yearly report in January 1939 had to confess: 'It is probable that we have suffered more than most.'[59]

Probably nothing could have significantly allayed the decline of the Chartered's Indian business in the 1930s. In addition to the Depression's devastating impact on the export markets for agricultural commodities, there was another powerfully corrosive force undermining the bank's traditional position. The once mighty trade in cotton piece-goods from Lancashire had virtually collapsed by the beginning of the decade – and the villain of the piece-goods market (from a British perspective) had since then moved well beyond the textile sector. A prescient half-yearly report in January 1933 described a survey of the markets in Amritsar:

> Over 70 per cent of the goods displayed by the six bazaars dealing in cotton goods were of Japanese origin . . . Japan also held 90 per cent of the sundries trade. Articles imported included electric bulbs, crepe sole shoes, fountain pens, tricycles, bicycles, shell buttons, footballs, rubber toys, rubber balls etc. The Japanese also held a monopoly in the Hosiery trade, and tea from Japan was selling cheaper than that from Shanghai. German and American hardware was also losing ground to [imports from] Japan.[60]

The bank's Directors had been fretting about the impact of Japanese competition on Asian markets ever since the post-war boom that had briefly made Yokohama the busiest office in the network. But by the 1930s it seemed plain they had underestimated the threat: 'the policy of pushing her exports into every possible corner of the consuming world where cheapness is the main consideration' (as Sir Montagu Turner had put it, in that AGM speech of March 1928) had brought astounding gains for Japanese manufacturers. Nor were these restricted to the markets of India.

Indeed, Japan's expansion into China was now of rather more consequence to the Chartered and its customers – for the potential of their business in China by the 1930s transcended anything ever likely to be seen again in India.

3. A NEW ROLE FOR CHINA?

The English-language *Peking & Tientsin Times* of 24 May 1926 carried news of the official opening of a new building for the Chartered's Tientsin branch (founded in 1896) that could almost have come from the Raj.[61] His Britannic Majesty's Minister was there from Peking to open the doors with a golden key (or, at least, his wife was there to do it for him: Sir Ronald Macleay KCMG was actually in the local Victoria hospital, laid up 'by illness contracted whilst on a shooting expedition'). The British Consul General and the Chairman of the British Municipal Council for Tientsin were there to eulogize the contributions made by Chartered men to the city's growth for the past thirty years. A host of local dignitaries and diplomats – including a brace of Chinese generals and a Japanese Consul General – were on hand to hear the praises sung of a 10,000 sq ft banking hall, decked out with Italian marble columns, teak parqueted floors and 'a coffered ceiling which is lighted in the most approved modern manner'. And the newly appointed Manager of the bank, H. W. Matheson, was proud to make explicit the obvious message for the day: 'The building may be said to exemplify in Tientsin the faith of our Directors in the future of this vast and rich country.'[62] Those who read the report may also have spared a moment, though, to glance at other stories on the page, which brought news of local events to test the Directors' faith. A new currency forced on Peking by the warlord ruler of Manchuria, Zhang Zuolin, was losing its value by the day; twenty newly arrived American Church missionaries were trapped by a mob in the city of Chengchow; a militia of 100,000 men known as the Red Spear Society appeared to have captured the city of Loyang after a two-day battle with the nationalist forces of the Kuomintang; and, in Shantung, a 'Chihli Army' under warlord Wu Pei-fu was busy chasing down marauding bandits across great swathes of countryside. To scan that page today is to catch a sense of the fragility of the continued British presence on the mainland of China in the 1920s – floating above the mayhem like a bubble, bound to burst if it should touch the ground.

Through the turbulent years of the Warlord Period (1916–28) Chartered Bank clung on to hopes that the new Republic would eventually emerge

with a stable national government, capable of unleashing that long anticipated surge in the Chinese economy's growth rate. Even amid the chaos
of the 1920s, the bank had actually found it possible to thrive in the treaty
ports: Hong Kong, Tientsin and, above all, Shanghai together accounted
fairly consistently for not far short of 15 per cent of total operating profits.
Hence the Court's authorization not only of the new premises in Tientsin,
to set beside the grandeur of the 1923 building on the Shanghai Bund, but
also of new branches in the northern port of Tsingtao (in 1925) and even
Harbin (in 1928), the rapidly expanding inland capital of Manchuria. By
the end of the 1920s, the political situation appeared to have clarified –
though with an awkwardly ambiguous outcome for the Chartered. On
the one hand, real progress seemed to have been made towards a unified
government. Chiang Kai-shek's Nationalists had broken with the Communists, largely subjugated the warlords and had established an
internationally recognized government in the city of Nanking. On the
other hand, the real momentum picked up by Chinese nationalism had
effectively ended for ever the notion of Britain as an imperial power in the
country. It was true that Hong Kong remained (for the moment, at least)
a self-ruled colony, and that Shanghai's International Settlement was still
predominantly a British affair, governed by a Municipal Council with a
constitution rigged in favour of British interests and backed by a force of
expatriate British policemen. But the political climate had utterly changed.

British power had suffered another Amritsar moment back in 1925,
when police in Shanghai had opened fire on a crowded street. The casualty
figures had been slight by comparison with the massacre in the Punjab –
fewer than ten people were killed in the initial incident, though dozens
more were killed and injured in the riots that followed – but the prolonged
wave of anti-British strikes and demonstrations that had followed (the
so-called May Thirtieth Movement) had nonetheless come as a heavy blow
to the expatriate communities of Canton, Hong Kong and Shanghai.
When Chiang Kai-shek's National Revolutionary Army had then occupied
Shanghai in 1927 and turned the guns on its erstwhile Communist allies
in the city, the international community had been drawn into a de facto
alliance with the Nationalists' Generalissimo. This had sharply accelerated a dismantling of the legal and financial arrangements underpinning
Britain's imperial pretensions in the country. Shanghai's Municipal Council very soon had Chinese members; the parks of its International Settlement
could no longer be closed on racial grounds to Chinese pedestrians. Some
of the Chartered's managers could scarcely conceal their disgust at what
they saw as a humiliating retreat for Britain.[63] But a new era had undoubtedly begun in China.

This posed an obvious challenge for the Chartered. Domestic banks were growing rapidly more numerous, just as in India, and by building direct links with the foreign-owned trading companies on the coast, Chinese bankers were threatening the historic franchise of the exchange banks. Chinese currency brokers were following suit: in 1929, the foreign-exchange broking fraternity in Shanghai was restructured to admit Chinese members for the first time.[64] 'Social change followed in the wake of political compromise; Chinese and foreign elites were beginning to interact more often, and began genuinely to get along.'[65] So how was the Chartered to respond? The strong colonial flavour of the bank raised questions about its readiness to employ local managers, as in India – though few in China saw it as a pressing issue. Profits in Shanghai and Hong Kong, after all, had always drawn on taking deposits from Chinese customers, doing business with Chinese firms, and leaning heavily on the customer relationships handled by the compradores with their Chinese shroffs, clerks and coolies. But the strategic challenge appeared far broader. What mattered in China was how the bank should respond to the rise of powerful local competitors backed by a nationalist government, and how it should best position itself to participate in the awakening of China's vast economy. Given the perilous state of the international financial markets and the constant threat of renewed local wars, the risks were evident – but so too (as many thought) were the potential rewards.

The ensuing debate within the bank is of special interest because surviving papers in the archive allow a more detailed glimpse than usual of the formulation of policy at Court level. The documentary record of Court deliberations is in general quite sparse – nowhere more so than in the perfunctory Minutes of its regular meetings – and this is unfortunate since the Directors were closely involved in the running of the bank from week to week. They were not 'non-executives' expected to leave the running of the business to 'executive managers', as would come to be the norm for their successors in a later age. A huge range of executive decisions went to the Court, and its members duly took a close interest in operational matters (if not the monthly accounts of the branches – which still seem to have received scant attention from the Directors). No managers sat on the Court: Howard Gwyther's elevation had emphatically not been treated as a precedent. So the Directors relied heavily on their own collective knowledge of the bank's affairs, and lengthy tenures of service generally ensured that the Court had plenty of experience on which to draw. In this respect, though, the position in 1930 was a little atypical. The professional managers had been unchanged for ten years: William Preston had been Chief Manager since 1920, with the same two Head Office Managers (J. S. Bruce and G. Miller) below him.

But the membership of the Court, as noted already, had seen an impressive turnover since 1925. Four of the pre-1914 appointees had departed, including Sir Alfred Dent. Now seventy-six, Sir Montagu Turner remained in the Chair and still had two colleagues from pre-war days, Sir William Goschen and Sir William Mitchell. The rest of the Court were relative newcomers.[66] Perhaps this helped to promote discussion about some of the bank's more venerable traditions. One of those keenest to question them was Archie Rose, the Mandarin-speaking former diplomat and Director of British-American Tobacco who had been elected to the Chartered Court in 1925 at the age of forty-six.

Rose would occasionally profess to be a non-banker, happy to leave this or that issue of the day to his colleagues; and certainly, with a fondness for loud clothes and foreign climes, he was no typical City gent.[67] But he was one of the best-informed and most active individuals on the Court. With a private flat in Shanghai's Soochow Road, he travelled regularly in the Far East, drawing up painstaking (but often overly optimistic) appraisals of the political and commercial situation which he then set down in long, thoughtful letters to the Chairman.[68] And while affairs in China and Japan were his primary interest, he came to hold strong views on the general conduct of the bank that were to reverberate for many years. Perhaps predictably, given his own background, he pushed hard at the outset for more weight to be attached to the learning of languages by officers of the bank – 'not with any idea that they will conduct business in the vernacular', as he would later explain to a colleague, '[but as] an automatic method of bringing them in touch with the men, the ideas and the business [of the East] which are increasingly important'.[69] This was especially true, he insisted, in China: 'no business-man, banker or industrialist can pull his weight nowadays unless he can get in direct touch with the Chinese'.[70] But while his attempts to promote in-house language tuition met with plenty of support in principle, they also prompted a series of reservations from the branches – caveats, for example, about the difficulties of picking the optimal Chinese dialect, the dangers of causing a loss of face among the compradores, the costs of providing adequate study time for sub-accountants in the face of Depression-era house-keeping, and so on: a flurry of initial enthusiasm gradually petered out. (The bank paid for eighteen Foreign Staff probationers to attend the School of Oriental and African Studies in 1926–7. Largely at Rose's behest, there were forty-three at SOAS in 1928–9 – but the numbers were back to seventeen for 1931–2, and eight of these were studying Urdu.[71])

The most obvious way for the bank itself to 'get in direct touch with the Chinese' would be to put some Chinese managers on the local staff, or so it seemed to Rose. The Chartered still relied in China on the use of well-placed intermediaries; but as he wrote in a letter from Shanghai to the Chairman in February 1930 (see over page), this relic of the nineteenth century was surely fast becoming an anachronism.

> The Compradore system must remain unchanged for the present, but Mr Wong [in Shanghai] is growing old and his son has not the calibre to carry any big responsibility. If we are to hold our own against the vigorous and increasing competition of the Chinese and other Banks, we must have some real Chinese assistance in the Bank itself.

And he had found a prize candidate for the bank's first move in this direction:

> We may have an opportunity of securing the services of a young man, Mr Y. S. Liu, who belongs to a distinguished family, who is well known to and respected by the Chinese Banking community here, and who has the education and social standing to associate with them on equal terms. He has no practical knowledge of banking, but has a good theoretical knowledge of finance. He is a Ph.D. of London, and has a very good personality. I suggest that we try to secure his services experimentally, with the intention of treating him on the same basis as the Foreign Staff. He would certainly not join us on any other terms. He should be encouraged to assist and advise, with a view to a gradual increase in our Chinese interests and business.[72]

The Court turned the proposal down. (A margin note on the letter by Montagu Turner asked 'What is West's opinion?' – a reference to F. D. West, whose early career had included those happy evenings of 1914 round the piano in Korea and who was now the bank's Manager in Shanghai. Presumably he gave the idea no support.) Rose was plainly exasperated by this rebuttal, and took the opportunity fourteen months later to rub in his point. 'The man whom I had in mind last year', he wrote to Turner in April 1931, 'is now in a very responsible position in the Bank of China, and is now working, in collaboration with a delegate from the Midland Bank in London, in the reorganizing of their work . . . I trust therefore that this question [of local Chinese management] will receive urgent attention.'[73] He would go on pressing his case.

In the meantime, Rose had also been rebuffed on another, even bolder proposition that he had put to the Court in May 1930. Towards the end of a long trip in the East, he had had a series of conversations with the Chairman of one of the foremost Chinese banks, the Shanghai & Commercial Savings Bank (SCSB), a Mr K. P. Chen, and the two of them

No. ___

All Communications should be
addressed to the Bank and not
to individuals.

TELEGRAPHIC ADDRESS:
"SALAMANDER," SHANGHAI.
TELEPHONE: CENTRAL 3 (4 LINES).

S 696

Chartered Bank of India, Australia & China,
(Incorporated in England by Royal Charter 1853)
POST BOX No. 359.

SHANGHAI,

IMPORTANT
IN REPLY PLEASE QUOTE

15th February, 1930.

DEPT.

(5)

Dear Sir Montagu,

Since writing to you last I have been constantly on the move, and have been unable to concentrate on a letter which would give you a considered view of the situation.

I have seen a good deal of our men at Tientsin, Peking, Tsingtau and Hankow, and at each of these places things have been moving in a normal way and require little comment.

I can only say that I was impressed with the way in which Brearley was handling his problems and his men in Tientsin. The Peking Office will require consideration before long. There is little chance of the Capital moving back there in the near future, the place is in a state of suspended animation, and Thomas is too useful a man to be left there indefinitely without sufficient scope for his energies.

Before leaving Shanghai I must supplement my cable of February 3rd in order to make my position clear in regard to our affairs here. But first let me try to give you my general impression about conditions in China, as our business

The first and last pages of a letter to Chartered's Chairman, Sir Montagu Cornish Turner, from Archie Rose in February 1930, proposing *inter alia* the appointment of a Chinese to the executive ranks of the Shanghai branch

What is West's opinion on

advise, with a view to a gradual increase in our Chinese
interests and business. We have tried a similar man and a
similar system in the British American Tobacco Co. and the
experiment has been a marked success. I feel so strongly on
this point that I advance it as a definite recommendation,
and I hope that you will telegraph to West authorising him
to offer an appointment to Mr. Liu before he accepts some
other post. I know from experience the great difficulty of
finding men of this type and, in my opinion, this is an
opportunity which should not be missed. Mr. Liu is about 30
years old and would probably require a salary of about $700.-
per month. He has not yet been sounded so I do not know
whether he could join us, but I hope so.

I am leaving for Hongkong and Canton today and hope
to be home in the near future, but I am putting my ideas on
paper in order that you may get a clear impression of my view
of the situation as seen on the spot.

With kindest regards to all in London,

Believe me,

Yours sincerely,

Archibald Rose.

Sir Montagu C. Turner,
Chartered Bank of India, A. & C.,
London.

together produced what must have been a slightly startling proposal, that
Chartered Bank and the SCSB should establish a 'Chinese-British Bank'
as a 50/50 joint venture. From Shanghai, Rose forwarded to Montagu
Turner a letter from Chen setting out the rationale with a bracing
frankness:

> As an instance [of the JV's potential], in the case of Chinese imports the
> majority of [domestic] manufacturers or merchants place their orders
> through commission houses in view of the lack of banking facilities . . . [At
> SCSB] we have not got an organisation abroad to take such care of them
> as to enable us to perform a satisfactory service. On the other hand, due to
> its peculiar organisation [sic], the Chartered Bank is as yet unable to secure
> such desired business because of the lack of experienced and responsible
> Chinese personnel.[74]

Rose fully endorsed this analysis – and so, intriguingly, did many of
his colleagues on the Court. Not all: two Directors rejected the notion out
of hand, as incompatible with the Chartered's prestige. One anonymous
scribbler curtly pointed out in a margin-note that Chen's preliminary
figures included a Bonus to Staff in excess of the putative dividend ('Not
quite in keeping with sound European Banking, is it?'), but the Chief
Manager, William Preston, thought the branch heads in China should be
solicited for their reactions, and a meeting of the Executive Committee of
the Court at the start of June 1930 agreed with him. The subsequent replies
may have occasioned some surprise at Head Office: the men running
Shanghai and Hong Kong, as well as the tiny branches in Harbin and
Peking, all expressed strong support for the JV proposal, though views
differed on the best way to set about it.[75] They seemed agreed that proper
inland access to the domestic customer would soon be a prerequisite for
any foreign bank hoping to thrive in China: it was becoming 'more evident every day', said the Shanghai Manager, that this would mean the
demise of the old exchange banking model. (Their replies can have been
no surprise to Rose: he was encouraged by the enlightened stance of
the Chartered's men in the field. As he wrote from Shanghai on another
occasion, 'Our men in China all take a thoroughly business-like view of
the situation. The old "Tai-pan" attitude towards business is passing,
none too soon . . .'[76]) Sadly, it fell to F. D. West at the start of July
1930 to hear from Chen of the SCSB that the Depression had wrecked his
plans. Markets across China were in disarray, said Chen. The JV idea
would have to be set aside until the return of better and more stable
times.[77]

These were to be a long time coming – and not just on account of the

Depression.* The Nanking Government was once again battling with warlords by the end of 1930, while a tense stand-off prevailed between the Chinese Nationalists and the Japanese, who retained an army in their own territorial concession in (nominally Nationalist) Manchuria. Rose spent the summer of 1931 in China, and at the start of August set off on a business trip through Manchuria in the prudently balanced company of the Japanese head of Mitsui Co. (China) and the Chairman of the Bank of China. In a letter from Shanghai, posted on his departure, he was his usual optimistic self. It sometimes seemed as though China was slipping back into chaos yet again – but there were plenty of reasons to be bullish. 'It is vastly interesting here nowadays and work is most stimulating . . . China is going ahead as one of the world's economic units in spite of surface troubles.' Seven weeks later, on 18 September, his party halted for the night at Dairen (the modern Dalian) – the coastal terminus of the Japanese-built South Manchuria Railway and a day's train journey from Mukden – and Rose had occasion to see below the surface. Late that night, a bomb exploded on the railway outside Mukden. It was treated by the Japanese (who knew better) as an act of aggression by Chinese saboteurs, and their troops moved immediately to seize total control of all Manchuria. Rose had served in the Peking Legation through the terrifying Boxer Rebellion of 1900 and was unfazed by reports of local fighting and bombardments by Japanese artillery – in fact, he evidently relished finding himself at the centre of historical events, as his trip diary recorded:

Sept 19 – The Japanese boy who brought me my early tea this morning came in with a broad grin on his face and announced "Have got war". That was the end of his English. In the breakfast room the waiters were all on their toes, and an old Japanese gentleman was scanning a loose news-sheet covered with big rough characters. He could not keep his news to himself . . .

[After learning of the 'Mukden Incident', Rose and his party nonetheless took the train along the supposedly wrecked line to Mukden and travelled on from there to the city of Chang-Chun to the north.]

Sept 20 – I woke this morning with a great clattering of hoofs outside my window and found a large number of [Japanese] cavalry moving through the city, with spare horses and equipment . . . We drove down to the Chinese city to visit the merchants. The Japanese have taken over . . . Everything is perfectly quiet and the Chinese are standing about in little groups looking

---

* The inaugural branch of the first joint-venture bank between the Standard Chartered and Chinese shareholders was to be the China Bohai Bank – opened in Tianjin in February 2006.

Map 3. Full branches of Chartered Bank in pre-Communist China

N
W ⊕ E
S

0   200   400
miles

C H I N A

Standard Chartered's China network under Communism

1969–81: Shanghai alone
1982:   4 branches (including Shanghai)
1990:   10 branches
2000:   16 branches
2008:   50 branches
2013: 100 branches

Bay of Bengal

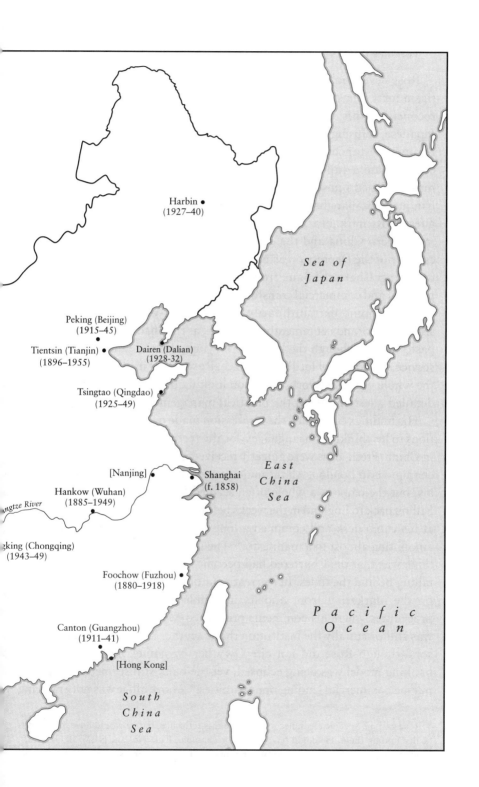

Harbin ●
(1927–40)

*Sea of
Japan*

Peking (Beijing)
(1915–45)
●
Tientsin (Tianjin) ●● Dairen (Dalian)
(1896–1955)   (1928-32)

Tsingtao (Qingdao) ●
(1925–49)

[Nanjing] ●   ● Shanghai
Hankow (Wuhan)   (f. 1858)
(1885–1949)   ●

*East
China
Sea*

ngtze River

king (Chongqing)
(1943–49)

Foochow (Fuzhou) ●
(1880–1918)

*Pacific
Ocean*

Canton (Guangzhou)
(1911–41)
●
● [Hong Kong]

*South
China
Sea*

rather puzzled and glum. One Chinese merchant with whom I had a chat asked me if this was likely to result in a world war.[78]

Rose never took this possibility very seriously, and retained his enthusiasm for a robustly expansionist strategy in China. He had no difficulty reconciling this with his own scarcely concealed admiration for the Japanese, refusing to believe – even after their establishment of a puppet regime in Manchukuo, early in 1932 – that the Japanese would ever contemplate a full-scale war against the Nanking Government.[79] (He rather fancied himself in the role of peacemaker, in fact, hosting lavish banquets in Shanghai to bring together assorted Japanese and Chinese guests.) Remarkably, he treated both the toxic political developments in northern China and the dire state of international trade in the darkest year of the Depression as passing storms that ought not to be allowed to distract Chartered Bank from planning its response to the longer-term political and commercial transformation stirring in Asia. All the branches still sent home extraordinarily detailed half-year reports and occasional memoranda commenting on these, as they had done for generations past, much as though the bank were vying with the Empire's diplomatic service as a source of local intelligence. Rose set off in 1932 to travel round the whole of the network, intent on looking beyond those reports to ask detailed questions about the practical management of the bank.

His findings confirmed the impression made on him by the earlier reactions to his thinking on languages, locally recruited staff and joint ventures in China. Fresh ideas were gingerly received and generally short of effective champions in London. All the main branches contained very able individuals, but the bank as a whole often seemed less than the sum of its parts. Sailing back to England in the weeks before Christmas 1932, Rose sat down at his cabin desk and compiled a long memorandum for the Chairman, amounting almost to a manifesto.[80] The gist of an occasionally brutal critique was that the Chartered had become hidebound in its ways and was falling behind the times. In its treatment of the Foreign Staff, its reticence on the marketing front and its inflexible accounting and inspection procedures – here his comments prefigured Meldrum's 1935 reforms – it was still essentially the institution that Gwyther had passed to his successors (though Rose did not cite Gwyther by name). The old exchange banking model was being eclipsed, yet the bank still seemed reluctant to pursue commercial lending opportunities.* Above all, it was not engaging

---

* Rose gave no specific examples to illustrate this reticence, but he would have had no difficulty finding them. He could have cited, for example, Rule No. 44, NEW BUSINESS, from the current Office Rules Book: 'When proposals for new business are received, a suitable

properly with the new nationalist mood in Asia, either in its employment practices or its approach to the marketplace. The author's remedies fell into two categories. Hard, structural changes would be needed, most notably a division of the network into three zones – based on Calcutta, Singapore and Shanghai – with their own Regional Managers. (The possibility of reviving the joint-venture idea was only referred to obliquely: a more intimate knowledge of the local banking industry might lead to 'some practical form of cooperation. The Japanese and American banks, and some of our British competitors, find it worthwhile to cultivate the Native banks and business-men in an organized way.') And soft, cultural adjustments would have to follow, changing attitudes to non-European managers and the selection criteria for Foreign Staff recruits ('[who] should include a proportion of men specially trained to meet the requirements of modern banking in an international field'). His bold letter had 'rather a dogmatic tone', Rose acknowledged in closing – but he hoped the contents would be 'more useful in their frankness and crudity than if moulded into a smoother form'.

His colleagues in Bishopsgate on the whole preferred the smoother form in such matters, and their discomfort with Rose's severe appraisal was soon apparent. Just possibly he had hoped that his report would prove timely, since the leadership of the bank was passing into new hands. Montagu Turner had stepped down earlier in 1932, after twenty-nine years as Chairman. The two Joint Managers in London since 1920, Bruce and Miller, had retired and William Preston had announced his intention to step down as Chief Manager at the end of 1933 (though he would have to wait another two years to receive his long-expected knighthood). But if Rose was looking for a Changing of the Guard, he was to be disappointed. Montagu Turner's successor in the Chair was Arthur d'Anyers Willis, a Director since 1929 and another scion of that small coterie of Eastern trading firms traditionally closely allied to the bank's Boardroom, in his case Ogilvy, Gillanders & Co. The fifty-four-year-old Willis was not inclined to see his chairmanship as a radical break with the past, and merely handed Rose's letter (and an earlier missive received by Turner in November) to the Managers' Committee. This was headed by the Chief Manager, and included Preston's two new deputies as well as Willis and Edward Mackay (one of the two Directors most vociferously opposed to the 1930 joint-venture proposal). Rose attended the meeting in January

---

reference is essential unless the applicant is personally known to the Bank. The question of references must be handled tactfully so as to avoid any possible cause of giving offence' (from Office Rules Book held in Chartered Bank, Saigon, LMA: CH03/01/06/120).

1933 at which his proposals were presented. To judge by a Memorandum of Proceedings that minuted the occasion, it must have been one of the seminal discussions in the interwar history of the bank.[81] Most of Rose's more specific recommendations were considered, weighed and carefully cut down the middle. It was then agreed the resulting half-measures would be given consideration in due course. Thus, the three regional zones were adopted – as a basis for the managers in each to meet for annual conferences, starting in 1933 – but no steps were taken to decentralize Head Office's authority to any Regional Managers. The idea of employing 'a young Native officer of good family' in each branch would be kept in mind, but nothing would be done to scale back reliance on the compradores. Attention would be given to the notion of hiring 'a few suitable recruits' from Oxbridge, but recruitment to the Foreign Staff would remain strictly a matter of personal selection by the Chairman and his Deputy – and those suitable recruits, whether from Oxbridge or any other universities, were to prove elusive for a long time yet. As for Rose's more sweeping recommendations for a 'thorough over-haul' of the whole Foreign Staff (where the bank had 'too many men of about 40 doing purely routine work'), the Memorandum recorded rather tartly 'there are no officers in the East who do purely routine work . . . and we are assured that there is no redundant staff at any point'.

Rose evidently concluded that he had little chance of remoulding the bank as a whole. No papers, at any rate, record any significant follow-up on his part in London. He turned back instead to focus on the business in China, dashing off letters to Willis and his colleagues from time to time to remind them of the potential, if only the Chartered could modernize its approach. It disappointed him in 1934 to learn from his colleagues at British-American Tobacco that they were still channelling all their Far East business to competitors. But as he wrote to the Chairman, he could hardly blame them for taking their business to those who showed the most expertise in the area – and the implication was plain. 'Banking, in China at least, is now on a highly competitive basis and banking business (as distinct from pure exchange and arbitrage) goes to those who seek business rather than to those who wait for it to come to them.'[82] And no marketing could really be effective without input from senior Chinese managers. In 1935 yet another clash of views on just this issue demolished what remaining hopes he had of setting the bank on a new course, even in China. It emerged that a Mr Percy Chu had approached the bank in Shanghai with a view to offering his services. Now thirty-seven and a postgraduate of both Columbia and New York universities, Chu had been working as a central banker in Nanking and Shanghai since 1928. His interview had been handled by the Sub-Manager, W. R. (Will) Cockburn, a popular if rather dour lowland Scot who had served in the East since 1913, and it is easy to understand why Cockburn's subsequent report to Head Office filled Rose with despair when he read it. Every sentence reeked of the Empire-staffing mindset that Rose had been struggling for ten years to dislodge:

> It would appear that [Mr Chu] had formed a rather grandiose idea of the duties he might be called upon to perform in the service of this Bank. He had apparently assumed that he would occupy the position of an adviser on Chinese affairs and business . . . [but it was] pointed out to Mr Chu that the duties which would be required of the proposed post would probably be of a more ordinary nature for some time to come . . . [We] are of opinion that, at his age of 36/37 he has already acquired set ways and we consider that he would prove difficult to guide into the desired channels. In other words we doubt whether he would be prepared to adapt himself to the multifarious duties of a less important nature which we should require of him.[83]

A draft reply to Rose from the Court towards the end of the month endorsed Cockburn's verdict, and drew a withering response from Rose two days later:

> Firstly, what are we looking for – a clerk, a broker, a political adviser? In my view we want none of these. We are seeking a man of sufficient experience and initiative to give us a lead in Chinese affairs . . . It is clear that [Mr Chu] knows the Chinese of importance in the financial-political-business world, and that he is trusted by the Chinese bankers who are very powerful. What is our problem? . . . Shanghai is growing rapidly as a commercial and industrial centre; it has a fair chance of becoming one of the busiest cities in the world in the not distant future. Its business will be Chinese with a considerable tinge of Japanese influence in all activities for some time to come . . . We do not want a clerk, but a liaison officer . . .[to be treated] as an equal – that is to say, he would require a chair which would be immediate evidence of his position, as a Sub-Manager or whatever we decide. In boom times, such a man as Mr Chu would not be available.[84]

The Court backed down, to the extent of redrafting its reply to let Cockburn know it was 'not inclined to subscribe' to his views on Mr Chu – but the real issue was ducked: 'a very great change – unfortunately for the worse – has come about in the economic conditions at Shanghai and . . . it has been decided to allow the matter to lie over in

the meantime'. There were to be no more letters to the Court from Archie
Rose.*

Certainly it was true that business had turned down sharply – and not
just in Shanghai. Results across Asia – including that calamitous failure
of Strauss & Co. in Bombay – made 1935's operating result the second
worst of the decade after 1931 (though the bank actually contrived to
publish the decade's *highest* profit in 1935, courtesy of a generous transfer
from reserves). The collapse in China, however, owed much to a critical
change in the local business environment. Over the three years since the
start of 1932, operating profits from Shanghai and Hong Kong had been
hugely boosted by manic activity in their currency markets. The collapse
of the Gold Standard in the West had been accompanied after 1931 by a
doubling in the price of silver bullion on the back of some ill-advised
policy-making in Washington. Foreign-exchange speculators had made
and lost huge fortunes. The bank, as ever, refrained from trading on its
own account; but it made enormous profits out of foreign-exchange trades
for its clients. Shanghai and Hong Kong together had accounted in 1932–
4 for an astonishing 40 per cent of the Chartered's total operating income.
(A recent study of the Chartered's operations in pre-1937 Shanghai by a
Chinese historian suggests a rapidly growing volume of business with local
Chinese customers, offering them current and deposit accounts but also
extending substantial fixed loans.[85]) All this can scarcely have helped
Archie Rose's argument that reforms were urgently required; nor did it
much enamour the Chartered to the Nationalist Government. The mayhem in the markets that so enriched the bank fatally undermined the
country's silver coinage. Greatly adding to the Nationalists' displeasure
was the fact that failing confidence in their own silver-backed currency
was confirmed by a creeping penetration of the mainland by the banknotes
issued in Hong Kong and Shanghai by Chartered Bank and the Hongkong & Shanghai Bank. A preference for the Imperialists' notes over the
Nationalists' silver coins had been a feature of the Republic for several
years.† This was much resented as an incursion on Chinese sovereignty,
and now became a serious irritant between the banks and Nanking.

---

* Or none, anyway, about strategy in China that have survived from the 1930s. But he
remained a Director into the post-war years, and his travels in the Far East were not yet done.
† After a Nationalist garrison town far inland from Shanghai had been captured by bandits
in 1928, hundreds of its residents were held for ransom – and a 'curious feature' of the episode,
as the *Times* correspondent in Shanghai reported, was that 'the bandits are everywhere
demanding Shanghai banknotes as being easier to carry, with the view, it is conjectured, of
retiring to this city when their fortunes are made' (*The Times*, 3 July 1928, quoted in Niv
Horesh, *Shanghai's Bund and Beyond – British Banks, Banknote Issuance and Monetary*

The problem had been a long time in the making. Until the middle of the 1890s, note issuance had been much more important to the Chartered in Singapore than in Hong Kong – with the annual value of issued notes in the two colonies reaching the equivalent of about £500,000 and £250,000 respectively – while Chartered notes had made no real headway in mainland China at all.[86] The British Treasury after 1892 had permitted the bank to issue well in excess of the levels ordained in the 1830s rules, not least because the plummeting value of the silver dollar meant that a fixed sterling yardstick would otherwise have meant sharply fewer notes in circulation. But as the quantity of dollar notes had risen in the Straits, the complications of a multi-layered local currency had proved too much for the colonial authorities, eventually putting paid to private notes in Singapore. Government notes had been launched in 1899. With the blessing of an official enquiry (the Barbour Commission), all other silver dollars had been demonetarized by 1904 in favour of the Government's Straits dollar, and the Chartered and Hongkong Banks had then agreed to phase out their own notes in the region.[87] As if to compensate for the benefits thus forfeited in Singapore, the Chartered had made three separate applications to the Treasury between 1905 and 1913 for scope to increase its note issue in Hong Kong – and once the wartime boom had begun in 1914, the shackles were off. The volume of new Chartered notes in the Colony soared after 1916, reaching the equivalent of £2¼ million in 1922 and settling at around £1½ million through the first half of the 1930s.[88] New issues in Shanghai trailed far behind this, but nonetheless reached the levels seen in pre-1914 Hong Kong. And just as Singapore's notes had circulated widely in the Straits, so those issued with the blessings of the British Treasury on China's doorstep found their way in ever greater numbers into the mainland economy, especially across the south to Canton and beyond.*

Policy in China 1842–1937, Yale University Press, 2009, p. 30). Literary references make the same point. In Somerset Maugham's *The Narrow Corner* published in 1932, for example, two of the novel's characters are struggling in vain to enlist the help of a doctor based in Foochow. 'Then the two brothers looked at one another and the elder took out from an inner pocket a large and shabby wallet of black leather bulging with the notes of the Chartered Bank.' That did the trick.

* The eighth and ninth characters of the Chartered's Chinese name on its notes spelled out 'Way Li' (meaning 'Handling of Remittances') whereas the Hongkong & Shanghai Bank's notes had 'Way Foong' ('Abundance of Remittances'). But one of the Chartered's first compradores had persuaded the bank to replace 'Way Li' on its street signboards with 'P'o Yuen' ('Precious Resources'). Thus, by the 1920s, the Hongkong Bank was widely known in China as Way Foong, and the Chartered as P'o Yuen. (A. J. 'Dicky' Bird to Harold Faulkner, 4 September 1951, LMA: CH03/01/14/019.)

The collapse of the Nationalists' coinage brought matters to a head. Chiang Kai-shek's government pushed through a reform of China's currency, breaking with the Silver Standard and introducing a new, Government-managed and non-convertible denomination of paper notes, usually connoted as CNC$ (Chinese National Currency dollars) and also referred to as 'Fa-pi' (the Mandarin for 'legal tender'). And the reform was backed by an assertive approach to the banking sector as a whole by officials in Nanking: the two largest domestic banks, the Bank of China and the Bank of Communications, were both nationalized. After some initial hesitation, the Chartered, along with the other British exchange banks, agreed in November 1935 to surrender their silver holdings to Nanking in exchange for the new currency. Acceptance of the CNC$ meant an end to the Chartered's note issuance in Shanghai and an abrupt end to sky-high exchange profits for the Shanghai branch. (The subsequent story of the CNC$ currency was to be horribly convoluted, with the Western powers abetted by the exchange banks doing everything possible to shore it up, while the Japanese militarists did their best to knock it down – a currency war that would last until 1944.[89]) More important to the Chartered for the longer term was the strategic implication. Denuded of their long-held dominance of the marketplace and obliged to play second fiddle to banks run by the Government, how were foreign banks to carve out a new role for themselves in China?

The answer was obvious, according to the principal architect of Nationalist policy on currency matters (and much else), T. V. Soong. Formerly Minister of Finance and now Chairman of the Bank of China – and brother to the three extraordinary Soong sisters, one now the widow of Sun Yat-sen and the other two married to Chiang Kai-shek and Dr H. H. Kung, another government finance minister – Soong was a spirited advocate for Western investment in China. He had already been pressing British bankers and diplomats for a while to seize what he presented as an historic opportunity. He thought Britain could play a vital role in the Republic's own industrial revolution, first by helping to finance vital imports of machinery and plant, then by providing long-term capital for its businesses. Quite when Soong began discussing these ideas with the Manager of the Chartered's Shanghai branch, R. D. (Robert) Murray, is unclear – but by the beginning of 1935, Murray was fully persuaded of the logic behind them. He seems also to have spent time exploring their ramifications with Archie Rose, for he was soon ready to start pushing many of the latter's recommendations on the future running of the bank. In the spring of 1935, he returned to Scotland on furlough – which explains why Cockburn, not Murray, interviewed Percy Chu – and he used his first days there to set down his thoughts for the Court. He wanted to see the bank employing Chinese bankers in senior positions, building a portfolio of term loans to Chinese borrowers and delegating significant regional autonomy to a Far East zone centred on Shanghai. Like Rose, Murray intended many of his reform proposals to apply to the network as a whole; but the main focus of his nine-page Memorandum, as its title announced, was 'the present position and future development of our business in Shanghai'.[90]

The Memorandum's arrival in Bishopsgate in May 1935 lifted the debate over the bank's policy in China to a new pitch. It acquired a special edge because the two most senior men at Head Office below the Chief Manager took up diametrically opposed positions. Broadly in sympathy with Murray was A. F. ('Fergie') Ferguson, who had served as Manager in Hong Kong for ten years before returning to London in 1932. Vehemently opposed to Murray's line was W. B. White, formerly a much acclaimed Singapore Manager and old India hand, whose instant reaction to the May missive from Scotland was a first sign of the passionate arguments to come. ('He suggests "advances of a permanent nature". Does he suggest that the Bank is to provide Capital for commercial ventures? . . . In the present chaotic state of China's Currency it would be <u>fatal</u> for us to attempt to invest our sterling funds in China.'[91]) Seemingly by chance, those inclined to side with White were much encouraged to read a remarkable briefing paper that landed at Head Office around this time. It was written by one Harold Faulkner, who had joined the bank in 1923 and had spent five of the intervening years in northern China, where he had mastered the local dialect. Faulkner's evident interest in politics had led to his appointment in Peking in 1934 as a liaison officer for the bank in its dealings with the Nationalists. He knew Murray well, but offered a very different critique of the Chinese economy: 'Many Chinese industrial undertakings are on the verge of collapse; a state of affairs that has been brought about more by corruption, nepotism, inept management and predatory profit-taking than by conditions of monetary crisis.' But it was Faulkner's devastating assessment of the political situation that must have confirmed many Directors in their aversion to any serious financial commitment in China. Nationalists in Nanking and Canton were at loggerheads, suggested Faulkner, and the north was in a state of anarchy. Chiang Kai-shek was emerging as a military dictator, yet the Communists were still far from beaten. The net result, everywhere south of the Yangzi, was a terrible uncertainty '[which is] undermining the morale of the people and causing a discernible deterioration of Chinese life. There exists an atmosphere of dismayed apprehension difficult to describe, which permeates every form of human activity.' And casting a deep shadow across the whole region, he concluded, was China's unresolved relationship with the Japanese, now the paramount power everywhere in the north of the country. The Nationalist Government was being squeezed relentlessly 'towards the most serious decision in Chinese history. They will have to choose between an exclusive entente with Japan [or] a state of hostility wherein [would lie] no hope of extraneous assistance.'[92] Neither choice, it hardly needed saying, would bring much joy for foreign bankers.

Murray initially felt crushed by the circulation of Faulkner's paper ('I wish I had his time and his facile pen . . . all I want is peace and rest'[93]); but once back in Shanghai his spirits rallied. No doubt he welcomed the appointment of Ferguson as Chief Manager in September 1935, which at least promised a chance that more encouraging views on China might get a hearing at the Court. He was also bucked to find his views shared by one of the British Treasury's foremost mandarins, Sir Frederick Leith-Ross, who arrived in China that same month on temporary secondment from London as an adviser to the Nanking Government. (Leith-Ross brought with him a close friend and assistant, Edmund Hall-Patch, who stayed on after his own departure to become Financial Counsellor to the Consulate-General in Shanghai, and was another advocate of active engagement with the Nationalists.) Murray was soon in deep discussion again with 'T. V.', who remained full of ideas for future co-operation between the Chartered and the leading Chinese banks: there were utility companies and railways, department stores and cotton mills all crying out for capital. By the summer of 1936, Soong was badgering Murray for some kind of formal agreement. The Shanghai Manager finally felt emboldened to renew his pitch to Head Office, writing in September:

> It would take a wizard to make a working profit in exchange in Shanghai today . . . [T. V. Soong] was very anxious that we should come in with the Chinese banks . . . and assist them in whatever particular finance schemes we might consider sound on a long-term basis . . . [Also] I talked the matter over with Sir Leith-Ross [sic] before he left for home and Louis Beale, H. M. Commercial Counsellor here, and they are both very anxious that we should come in if we possibly can in order to influence the Chinese Government in placing a fair proportion of their orders in Britain . . . While Mr T. V. Soong was very pleasant . . . I could not help feeling that his proposals were rather in the nature of an ultimatum, which it would be to our disadvantage to turn down . . . [I believe that we can advance] without undue risk and that in the end such procedure will give us a footing in China which will be exceedingly remunerative.[94]

The huge risks entailed in this 'procedure' are plain with hindsight. China's aspiring industrialists had to contend not just with the Japanese but with their own Nationalist politicians, too: 'the relationship between Nanking and the [Shanghai] capitalists was one of tension and hostility'.[95] Fortunately for Chartered Bank, the risks were hardly less apparent at the time, at least to W. B. White. He penned a corruscating criticism of Murray's letter that ran to twenty foolscap pages and picked apart his arguments, paragraph by paragraph.[96] A few weeks later, Ferguson hosted a lunch at the bank for Leith-Ross, and wrote privately to Murray that the Treasury man had done his best to push the case for lending to China: it was an opportunity, Leith-Ross had averred, that 'once lost, might never be regained'.[97] But he was preaching to the steadfastly unconvertible. The Directors, still mindful of Faulkner's analysis, sided firmly with White. An official letter went off to Shanghai from the Court four days later. Murray was instructed not only to avoid committing any sterling funds whatever to China, but also to prepare for the arrival in 1937 of the Cassandra from Peking. The Shanghai office, it had been decided, 'should, in the near future, prove a fruitful field for his special abilities'.[98] Sadly for Faulkner, this proved to be excessively optimistic. Shanghai turned out instead to be altogether too much for his nerves. Assigned to assist the bank in its relations with the Chinese government, he struggled with his brief, finding himself largely out of sympathy with the Chinese.[99] While Faulkner agonized over the advice he should send back to London, Murray pressed ahead with more of his enthusiastic recommendations that the bank should engage with Chinese business:

> The Japanese cotton industry is rapidly being transferred to China through large imports of Japanese machinery and . . . it is generally considered that, with the improvement in the relations between China and Japan, supplies of machinery and other equipment for industrial enterprises will tend to come more and more from Japan instead of Europe and America, and thus one more source of exchange business will pass out of our sphere . . . If therefore we are to remain a powerful institution in China, we can only do so by lending to good Chinese concerns, and with the ever growing feeling of confidence and stability, we are of opinion that we should not be running more than an average business risk.[100]

Murray thought hard over the next three months about the possibility of opening a branch in Nanking. He eventually shelved the idea, given the signs of 'a phase of extreme [Chinese] nationalism' in the city.[101] But his faith in China's potential seems to have coped with this disappointment easily enough. On 12 August 1937, he again wrote to the Directors urging them to heed the opportunities for the bank in China 'safely and profitably to develop its business in a more substantial and more constructive way than hitherto'.[102] His timing was unfortunate. The very next day, the first of what would eventually be a million Chinese and Japanese soldiers descended on Shanghai to begin a vicious and protracted battle for control of the city. The Sino-Japanese war presaged in 1931 had finally arrived. Chinese and Japanese armies were now to engage in huge set-piece battles across the country – forcing the Nationalist government to retreat deep into the interior, relocating to Chungking – and reducing the two sides to a stalemate by the end of 1939. Poor Faulkner suffered a nervous break-down and had to be invalided back to London. But the bank does appear to have acknowledged the credit that was due him for his prescient analysis of the risks in China.* The Chartered's exposure to them, which might so easily have ballooned after 1935, was still mercifully slight: its losses there in 1937 were scarcely material (even two artillery shells landing on the branch building on the Shanghai Bund in November did surprisingly little damage), and by 1938 the bank was actually reporting a modest profits revival on the back of a strong performance by that marbled and coffered branch in Tientsin. If not always for the most laudable of reasons, the Court had held fast to its most conservative traditions – and never, in more than eighty years, had these been more dramatically vindicated.

4. GLOOM AND BOOM

Looking back over a decade strewn with financial and commercial disasters, and the slow-burning crises over nationalist feelings in India and the Nationalists' struggles in China, the Directors and their Managers at Chartered Bank could have been forgiven for thinking by 1939 that mere survival had been a triumph of sorts. In fact, the singularly resilient culture of the organization, the conservatism of the Court and the sheer commitment of the bank's staff at every level had helped it do rather better than that: annual operating income for 1930–39 averaged £456,123, just about exactly half the equivalent figure for the 1920–29 period – but easily enough, with a little help from the hidden reserves, to provide a remarkably steady set of published profits. It was nonetheless true by the end of the 1930s, as

---

* His recovery took several months, but the bank looked after him well and welcomed him back to work in 1938. He was assigned to manage a new branch in Manchester, where he went on to serve with some distinction for the next twelve years, before being appointed Company Secretary.

9. Two of the Chartered's main offices in the East. *Above:* Singapore's Battery Road branch in about 1900, with the bank's heraldic shield just evident on its huge flag. *Below:* the Clive Street branch in Calcutta in about 1910, completed two years earlier and occupying pride of place in the city's financial district close by the River Hooghly.

10. Some of the Chartered's pre-1914 Chinese employees. *Left:* five clerks in the branch at Hankow (today part of Wuhan), a 'treaty port' where the bank had been helping to finance tea exports since 1863. *Below:* these clerks in the Hong Kong branch are still sporting pigtails – which they lopped off at the end of 1911 as a gesture of support for the Chinese republic newly declared by Sun Yat-sen.

11. Domestic quarters for the Chartered's foreign staff. *Above:* the interior of the Agent's bungalow in Bombay circa 1910. *Below:* the pre-1914 'chummery' in Madras (modern Chennai), shared by Sub-Accountants including J. A. Macgill (in dark blazer).

12. The postcard sent to Hatton Court from Moscow by the Chartered's Thomas Whitehead in 1900, telling of his 'long interview y'day 29.06.00 with Mr de Witte, Finance Minister'. His access to the man who had been championing Russia's industrialization efforts throughout the 1890s was a mark of Whitehead's energy and effectiveness.

13. The 1910 world tour of the Chartered's network by Caleb Lewis (who rarely posed in a group without a cigarette in his right hand). *Above:* with the branch staff in Shanghai, where the front row included F. D. West (*left*), who travelled to Korea at the outbreak of the war in 1914. *Below:* in New York, where Frank Bennett, Manager of the branch, sat next to Lewis.

14. Three of the Chartered's banknotes in the nineteenth century, shipped from contracted printers in London. *Top:* a Straits $500 note, issued in Singapore on New Year's Day 1874. *Middle:* a Straits $20 note, printed for the Penang branch but unissued. *Bottom:* a 5 Taels note, printed for the Shanghai branch but unissued.

15. Two of Chartered's pre-1914 branches in the East. *Above:* at Ipoh, in the Malay state of Perak's Kinta Valley, where credit was extended to local tin mining and smelting companies. *Below:* at Cebu in the Philippines, perhaps on St Andrew's Day, with Scottish emblems on the balcony and Scotland's Saltire flying from the flagpole.

16. Chartered's 'Book of Profits and Losses': the double page of entries for 1914, with the second half of the year recording a sizeable jump in profits for the network ('As & Bs') but a collapse into the red for the bank's beleaguered London Head Office (see Appendix D).

Archie Rose had rightly observed, that fundamental changes were needed in the Chartered's business model: the old exchange banking world was fading rapidly, and retaining the bank's franchise as a service-provider to companies engaged in seaborne trade to and from Asia was very soon going to mean finding a successful sequel to the old colonial approach. This would require a far greater commitment to doing business with indigenous companies, rather than just British agency firms and their successors. It would probably also involve a readiness to move beyond the bank's core transactional business – foreign exchange, trade financing and documentation – in order to build up more of an active loan portfolio, making term loans to local customers where regional expertise could be brought to bear. This, after all, was effectively the road taken by the other banks in the quartet of forerunners to Standard Chartered. The Standard Bank, of course, had never been limited to the exchange-banking model; but the Eastern Bank had begun building local relationships in the Gulf, especially with the nascent oil industry, which were drawing it away from its trade-financing roots; and even the BBWA, though in many ways the most comparable to the Chartered, was developing its presence in West Africa as a lender to the commodity farmers of the region as well as to the intermediary traders. As the Chartered had found in China, however, the state of the world in the late 1930s was not especially conducive to the resolution of such underlying strategic issues. And, as the possibility of war in Europe loomed menacingly, greater urgency attached to other matters.

The banks in 1938–9 had more leeway to prepare for war than had been the case in 1914, and there were lessons to be learned from 'the last time'. Thus, Standard Bank, BBWA and the Chartered all wound down their balance sheets and branch operations in Hamburg over the summer of 1939, and were quick to close their offices there when Hitler invaded Poland on 1 September. All had been trading in the German port since before the First World War. Indeed, both the Standard's office and the Chartered's in 1939 were still being run by the very same individuals who had worked for the two banks since before 1914.[103] The Chartered's men were Martin Opitz and William Haydn Evans: they had joined it as German Clerk and Chief Clerk respectively in 1905–6. The two of them, both renowned for their meticulous attention to detail and ramrod adherence to the rulebook, had combined with conspicuous success as Joint Managers since July 1934. Closure must have been all the more poignant for them, and for three clerks who had served almost as long, given the pressures under which they had worked together in the most recent years under a police state. Walter Neill, who had been interned in Germany from 1914 to 1918 and who had returned to Hamburg as a visiting Inspector in 1934, had observed even then how difficult it was to steer clear of politics during his brief visit – 'but it was hoped that the [National Socialist] Government would learn by experience that however worthy their theories might be, they were sadly lacking in practical applications'.[104] Looking back some months later, Haydn Evans was less sanguine. 'We have nowadays to cope with practically unheard of problems to maintain our business', he wrote to Neill in 1935, 'which you can well understand requires all of our energy and more of our time than can possibly be imagined by those not confronted with present day conditions ruling in Germany.'[105] Opitz took care of reports on the state of the economy – and had to be careful about withholding his signature from any reports liable to be construed as critical of the Nazi government. Few papers have survived to cast light on the events of their final days together in 1939, but it was evidently a torrid experience for Haydn Evans and his German wife. Eleven days after the outbreak of war, Head Office received a desperate telegram from him, despatched from Rotterdam: 'Wife broken down All circumstances considered hope you will not insist otherwise will endeavour cross Tuesday'. This elicited the less than wholly sympathetic reply: 'Remain Holland wait letter'. But the Directors did eventually take a compassionate view of his situation, allowing Haydn Evans to take his pension early and escape with his wife to South Africa.[106]

Another Chartered branch soon faced with closure was not in Europe but China: Canton had been overrun by Japanese forces in October 1938 and the bank now abandoned all hope of reviving its business as a neutral party in the occupied city. The Chartered Agent, A. J. ('Dicky') Bird, began laying off his Chinese clerks before the end of 1939. There ensued a three-way correspondence between Bird, the Hong Kong Manager, R. A. (Reg) Camidge, and Head Office about the treatment of the local staff: their long-standing loyalty to the bank, all were agreed, meant the bank had now to be 'fair and generous'.[107] Bird certainly lived up to this resolution. He not only urged that as many as possible be offered posts in Hong Kong, but also refunded the bank his personal motor car allowance for the past six months ('as there is little occasion to use a car under present conditions') so that it could be redistributed as redundancy payments.[108] Bird himself was due a furlough in February 1940. Some in the bank wondered if his departure might be blocked by the British government, which had put heavy constraints on the departure of men from Hong Kong so that there might be conscripts available for the local armed forces if necessary. But Camidge was reassured by Head Office that there would be no difficulty 'in view of the ruling which we received from Viscount Halifax, the Foreign Secretary . . . viz that Europeans working in

British Banks in the Far East are definitely to be regarded as "key" men'.[109] (Bird duly returned to the UK, and was fortunate still to be there at the outbreak of the Pacific War.) Another implication of the Foreign Secretary's edict was that the Foreign Staff – though not the Home Staff – would be exempted from conscription into the forces. In the event, thirty-five Foreign Staff men joined up all the same, as well as several of the new Indian Assistant Officers. At home, just short of a hundred Chartered men were eventually called up. Altogether the enrolled men represented about 40 per cent of the pre-war complement of Home and Foreign Officers. The Eastern Bank and the BBWA saw their staffs reduced by about 10 per cent each, under the same rules. At the Standard Bank, not far short of 40 per cent of those working in its branch network enlisted, along with fully half of the London staff.[110]

The early years of the war took a toll of senior managers and Directors, too. Worst hit was the Chartered. That arch-opponent of expansion into China, W. B. White, died in November 1939 and was succeeded by R. W. Buckley. Five months later, Arthur Willis took shareholders by surprise and announced at the General Meeting that poor health was forcing him to step aside as Chairman, though he was staying on the Court and he did not leave it, in the end, until 1953.* His successor was to be Vincent Alpe Grantham, another Director of one of the 'family' merchant firms – Forbes, Campbell & Co., which had now lost one of two Campbells earlier listed in its name – and a man with long experience of the East. (His family had deep roots in India, though by going into commerce he had broken with a long line of army forebears: his father had retired in 1909 as Colonel in command of the 33rd Queen Victoria's Own Light Cavalry, formerly the Bombay Light Cavalry.[111] Grantham had occupied several civic posts in Bombay including the presidency of its Chamber of Commerce, which perhaps amounted to some degree of continuity.[112]) Two days after the 1940 General Meeting, the bank's Chief Manager, 'Fergie' Ferguson, collapsed and died. Will Cockburn, who had taken such a dim view of Mr Percy Chu in 1935, took on the top job in Bishopsgate, just as the phoney war in Europe ended with the fall of France in May 1940. As Cockburn stepped up, his place as Manager alongside Buckley went to John Meldrum, but all too briefly. Meldrum's death late in 1941 was yet another reminder that long careers in the East had rarely made for old

---

* Shareholders had expected the biggest news of the day to be confirmation that the bank's amended Royal Charter had been approved. This was indeed announced, providing a new formal authorization that would run for thirty years – and which would next require their attention, as it happened, in July 1969.

bones, even without the additional weight of wartime anxieties. Cockburn himself suffered a heart attack early in 1943, though – fortunately for the Chartered, which might have struggled without him – he was able to return to the office after a three-month break. Elsewhere, deaths and resignations also weakened the Board of the BBWA, which in 1942 lost both Sir Roy Wilson and the Earl of Selborne, its Chairman since 1916. At the Eastern Bank, some of the original band of founder-directors were still hanging on – J. S. Haskell in 1939 was succeeded in the Chair by James Leigh Wood, another Board member since 1910 – but Sir John Caulcutt, the Barclays Chairman who had joined the Eastern in 1938, felt constrained by the pressure of his duties at Barclays to step down in 1941. He, too, was to die of a heart attack two years later.

In sharp contrast with the gloom and misery visited on so many private lives, a world at war appeared likely – as in 1914–18 – to mean boom times for the forerunner banks themselves, or at least for three of them. The Standard Bank, having prospered steadily through the 1930s and become essentially a domestic institution with relatively limited exposure to trade, looked like being odd man out from the start. (Its deposits rose steadily, climbing from £70 million in 1939 to almost £280 million in 1947, but the opportunities to earn more than a minimal return on them were to be limited, ensuring that profits fell back a little on their robust interwar levels.) Elsewhere, business soared in 1939–41 on the back of demand for the commodities of Asia and West Africa, and the profits earned – though emphatically *not* publicly reported – by the Chartered, the Eastern and the BBWA jumped accordingly. The Chartered's real (unpublished) profits for 1940 were three times those of 1939, and nominally the highest in its history. Earnings in India were suddenly restored almost to the golden era of the early 1920s: business in Hong Kong, Singapore and even beleaguered Shanghai steamed ahead. While some considerable discretion about the scale of this windfall was required for obvious reasons, the banks' Directors provided shareholders with fulsome operational reviews at their General Meetings – and at the Chartered, this led directly to a notable corporate innovation. In the past, it had been the standard practice for the Chairman to stand and deliver a detailed account of the prior year at the General Meeting in his Address to shareholders, a printed version of which had subsequently been posted to them. In 1941, Vincent Grantham drew up such a lengthy speech for his first AGM that he decided shareholders should be sent a copy of it ahead of the Meeting. He then announced that the Address would henceforth always be sent out in advance, as the 'Chairman's Statement', to accompany the year-end balance sheet – and though the two items went on being printed separately until 1951, the resulting package was effectively the format of the Annual Report that has survived to the present day. (Greatly reducing the importance of the General Meeting also seemed a sensible response to the difficulties of wartime travel – though nothing was done to reverse this side-effect after the war. Thus were future generations of Directors saddled with Meetings shorn of real substance, as Grantham intended, and 'confined to the necessary Resolutions'.)

When the banks were convening their General Meetings in April 1941, the London Blitz still seemed unremitting. None of their head office buildings in the City had suffered any substantial damage to date – and all were in fact to emerge from the war miraculously unscathed, amid the devastation of many surrounding streets – but all had made provisions at the outset for the aerial Armageddon that had been widely anticipated. The BBWA had moved its entire London office to the Kent countryside before the war began: one of its Directors, Lord Goschen, owned a mansion in the Weald that befitted a former Viceroy of India, and the bank had gladly accepted his offer to accommodate sixty of its clerks there for the duration (rent free).[113] The Chartered had staffed up a shadow head office at Wrexham in North Wales, and had quickly established a routine whereby records could be duplicated and stored there. 'All books, ledgers and records of importance were now photographed,' as a brief 'History of Head Office during the War' recounted later. 'By this means it was hoped that should disaster overtake the building [at 38 Bishopsgate] it would at least have been possible to build up a reasonably accurate picture of the Bank's affairs.'[114] In assessing how the Chartered dealt with the spectre of wartime disaster on this score, however, the real story has to be sought elsewhere – in the East.

6

Miracle and Mirage, 1941–53

1. WAR AND LIQUIDATION

One of the first Chartered men in the East to learn that Britain and Japan were at war was T. L. Christie, the Sub-Accountant in Haiphong, the port on the Gulf of Tonkin which was the main naval base in northern French Indo-China. Like many other Sub-Accountants, Christie lived with his family in a flat above the bank. 'At 3am on 8th December 1941 we were awakened by the noise of shutters and windows being broken in the main office and the sound of pickaxes against our building, below the bedroom windows', remembered Christie later.[1] The assailants were Japanese soldiers, slightly jumping the gun: the attack on Pearl Harbor had been launched only two hours earlier – just before 8 a.m. (Hawaii Standard Time) on 'the day of infamy', 7 December – and the Japanese Imperial Army, though roaming at will across Vietnam since the summer, had yet to seek permission from the Vichy French authorities to move against British and American nationals under their jurisdiction; it was to be granted at nine o'clock that morning.

> A few minutes later, a Japanese civilian (a client of the bank) accompanied by a Japanese officer and soldiers, fully armed and all wearing felt shoes [*sic*], broke into our apartment by way of the servants' quarters. The officer, at the point of the revolver, ordered us to dress immediately, saying no harm would come to us so long as we did what we were told.

The forty-nine-year-old Christie with his wife and young daughter – together with a junior Sub-Accountant who had just recently arrived from Singapore, A. S. M. Young – found themselves under house arrest. Christie's colleagues in Saigon were similarly taken into custody with their families before dawn broke.*

---

* While these Chartered men may have been the first to know the war had started, others had been forewarned of its imminence. In Bangkok, the entire expatriate community was at

Elsewhere, most Chartered managers across China and in Japan itself were spared such a startling experience that Monday morning and were generally able to make their way into their offices almost as though the world had not in fact changed overnight (as all must have heard that it had). The outcome was nonetheless the same. The Japanese military had been primed to strike everywhere simultaneously with the attack on the US Pacific Fleet. Soldiers arrived at the Chartered branches within an hour or so of their opening and all British staff were arrested, in Peking, Hankow and Tsingtao as in Kobe and Yokohama. Only on the Bund in Shanghai, as befitted its status, was a grander gesture made, with a contingent of the Imperial Navy Guard surrounding the Chartered Bank and its neighbours at 10 a.m., to coincide with the movement of Japanese troops into the International Settlement. Beyond the instant reach of its land forces, meanwhile, Japan's intentions were being made shockingly plain. Another of the bank's Sub-Accountants, G. A. (Gerry) Leiper in Hong Kong, having just heard the morning's momentous news on the radio, was driving down to the bank on Queen's Road from his house on the Peak when he heard the sound of distant explosions. Rounding the corner in the road at 'Magazine Gap' brought him the scarcely believable sight of a squadron of Japanese heavy aircraft dropping bombs on the Colony's Kai Tak airport. A few hours later, Leiper was snatching a quick lunchtime sandwich on the verandah of the Hong Kong Club when four planes returned to bomb the naval dockyard a quarter of a mile further along the north side of the island. 'The raid did not last long and, as . . . we emerged on to the verandah again, an elderly exchange broker, who had been sheltering under the counter with one of the bar-boys, asked him for a pink gin and kept on saying to the rest of us, "What bloody impertinence – the cheeky little bastards".'[2]

Another Scotsman notwithstanding his Dutch-sounding surname, Leiper recalled that moment in a shocking memoir of the British community's wartime sufferings in Hong Kong.* No one else on the Foreign

---

a St Andrew's Ball at the city's British Club on the night of Saturday 6 December. 'About midnight, the British Minister received a telegram which . . . told of the discovery by a Catalina Flying Boat of a Japanese convoy in the Gulf of Siam.' (P. R. Wait to Head Office, 28 September 1942, LMA: CH03/01/07/003.) It was the Malayan invasion force heading for its landing sites on the Siamese coast of the Malay Archipelago. The Minister convened a hurried meeting with the leading British men at the Ball, including the Chartered's Agent. It was agreed that no announcement needed to be made publicly. Then they all returned to the dancing.

* A Yen For My Thoughts (its flippant title redeemed by the power of the author's story) was published in 1982. It was an embellished and expanded version of six lengthy articles entitled 'Some Recollections of Duress Banking' that Leiper contributed to the staff

Staff produced anything like Leiper's elegant chronicle of his wartime experiences – but this is not to say they left no record. On the contrary, many of those located in the half-portion of the network subsequently overrun by the Japanese were eventually to set down detailed private accounts, usually in direct response to requests from Head Office that they should do so. Those few lucky enough to escape from the war-zone at the outset of hostilities generally posted back their fresh accounts from Australia or (more often) South Africa before the end of 1942. For the great majority, sadly, the same task meant recollecting years of desperate hardship and suffering in the wake of their liberation in 1945 from internment or, for those captured as members of Volunteer Defence forces, Japanese prisoner-of-war camps. Their letters, reports and private memoranda survive in the archives as four thick files of War Testimonies.[3] Together they amount to a remarkable record of the war in the Far East, as experienced by some of the many British colonials engulfed by it. And in the specific context of the Chartered's own history, the Testimonies allow a detailed reconstruction of what actually happened to the Eastern network's branches – without which, many years later, the post-war revival of the bank might have been hard to explain. Most of the narrative that follows in this section is based upon them.

Japan's astonishing conquests in 1941–2 – with all that they implied for the future of Western colonialism in the East – represented a devastating blow to the Chartered. It lost twenty-four of the forty-five branches in the pre-war network. Strikingly, it is hard to find a single wartime document or letter by an employee of the bank that questioned its long-term survival; but the brave resilience shown at the time – particularly in 1942 – denied a sombre reality. The debacle of the region's initial collapse and the trauma of the subsequent occupation must have left many wondering privately whether the Chartered would ever regain its footing in the East, even assuming, as all did, that the Japanese victories would one day be reversed. The newly appointed Sub-Manager at Head Office in 1943, H. F. Morford, perhaps came closest to acknowledging this when he wrote to one of those who had escaped internment, and was now working in India. Morford was anxious to know if his colleague could provide any details on the occupied branches: 'It is felt that even the most meagre details may be of some use ... The task of reconstruction belies

---

magazine, *Curry & Rice*, in the 1960s. He wrote them under the pseudonym 'Nijuhachi', but the 1982 book's duplication of many passages from the articles leaves no doubt about their authorship. The first appeared in November 1964 and the last in the edition of Spring 1968.

imagination, and you will appreciate our desire to file any information which may possibly be of help.'[4] Had all account balances been lost, certificates and securities been destroyed and general ledgers blown away, attempting to resume the pre-war operations in 1945 would indeed have posed all but insuperable problems. Financial insolvency for the Chartered Bank in London was probably never a threat: the bank began the war with a strong balance sheet and ended it (as we shall see) with its cash position massively bolstered. But piecing together the shattered fragments of the network east of Calcutta might have required virtually a fresh start. In the event, as the War Testimonies reveal, a different and quite unexpected story unfolded. Huge quantities of correspondence and all papers of merely historic interest were undoubtedly lost: the Japanese forces were inclined to treat filed archives as useful waste paper. To a remarkable extent, however, the operational records were saved – enabling the bank's accountants in the end to pull off their own version of a Great Escape.

This is not to suggest that comprehensive steps had been taken by December 1941 to prepare the bank against the possibility of war: they had not. Reporting lines between the branches and Head Office had been revised to allow for more local decision-making in the East, but this looked a modest step, once Chartered managers found themselves among the civilians enlisted with Volunteer Defence forces in the autumn of 1941. Senior Managers in Bishopsgate were hardly blind to the looming possibility of war with Japan. (The British, Dutch and US governments had frozen all Japanese assets within their colonial jurisdictions in July 1941, which – since it cut off her vital supplies of oil, among much else – effectively posed an ultimatum to Japan over her continuing campaign in China. With no sign from Tokyo of any readiness to capitulate, the prospect grew ever likelier that the fighting in China would turn into a wider war. By the first week of December it was widely believed to be imminent: Leiper and a friend, playing golf at one of Hong Kong's most popular clubs on 7 December, found the course eerily deserted.[5]) But, having endured the Blitz themselves, the London Managers of the bank saw little to be gained by risking any sizeable transfer of documents back to Britain. Nor were there many hatches that could sensibly be battened down without impeding the bank's services to its customers – and keeping the branches fully operational remained the clear priority. As the sense of crisis grew in the East, demand surged for letters of credit, travellers' cheques and the full gamut of remittance services. Banking halls everywhere began to fill with lines of increasingly desperate customers. Struggling to cope with unprecedented levels of business, the Chartered's managers had little time for pre-emptive measures, and just as little real inkling of what hostilities might actually entail.

As a result, the branches overrun in the first days of the war yielded a significant cash haul for the Japanese. Large quantities of CNC dollars and foreign exchange were seized in Tsingtao, as were the sterling and US dollar funds of the Stabilization Board held in the Shanghai branch. The latter's Manager, H. C. Hopkins, and his counterpart at the Hongkong Bank had laid in supplies of sulphuric acid at London's behest – a gesture that at least acknowledged the desperate times – with which to destroy their note supplies; but by the time he arrived at the office on the morning of the 8th, Hopkins felt it would be crazy to start messing about with baths of acid: 'by this time the Japanese Forces were in and about the city and, after consultation with [the Hongkong Bank's Manager], it was decided that it would be suicidal to attempt any destruction'.[6] The Chartered's deposit boxes in Shanghai proved rich pickings for the Japanese: thirty depositors a day were invited into the bank for days on end, only to be handed a receipt for their valuables and foreign bank notes, confirming their confiscation. And some assets were seized more peremptorily, as noted by Shanghai's Accountant, F. C. Lundie: 'Fourteen hundred odd boxes of silver, coin and bullion held by us in Safe Custody on behalf of the Chase Bank [of the US] were also removed.'[7]

In tackling the Chartered's China branches, however, Japanese forces were given a second objective by their commanders. While instructed to seize whatever cash and valuables they could find, they were also under orders to prevent a disorderly collapse of the banks that might bring wider disruption in its wake. To this end, front-line units had to hand over captured banks to an Army Finance Department staffed by bankers and accountants, most of them seconded from the Yokohama Specie Bank, Mitsui Bank and the Bank of Chosen. All financial institutions in newly conquered territories were to be put into liquidation in accord with recognized accounting practices. Overdrafts and loans were to be called in, accounts closed or appropriated, ledger balances struck and creditors repaid, with branches remaining open for weeks or even months to expedite the process. (It was later a matter of pride to the Chartered in Shanghai that all its creditors were repaid in full as part of the Japanese liquidation; the Hongkong Bank paid out only 85 cents to the dollar, while the Mercantile Bank of India 'paid very little'.[8]) Liquidation, in fact, seems to have been managed in China more or less in line with the closure of Japanese banks that same month by the British and American authorities in the Malayan states and the Philippines – albeit in circumstances that were generally a great deal more menacing. It could hardly have been otherwise, with officers of the much-feared Japanese military police, the Kempeitai, ever hovering in the background. But the Army Finance people assigned to working in the Chartered's branches do seem to have conformed to a Japanese stereotype that was more familiar to the bank, as they turned with meticulous courtesy to the incumbent officers and clerks for assistance. Lundie in Shanghai later noted that his counterpart from the Mitsui Bank was 'a perfect gentleman (I cannot remember his name) and, as far as regulations would allow, everything was done in my way'. Indeed, at least one Chartered man took the formality of the proceedings as a licence to behave a little haughtily. Eight days after taking over the Chartered branch in Hankow, Japanese officials appeared early in the morning with formal documents confirming that all assets were to be confiscated and all Chinese employees were to be dismissed with immediate effect. They returned again later, only to find the Manager, R. J. S. Davies, in feisty mood:

> Later that morning, we were invaded by numbers of army accountants and members of the Yokohama Specie Bank who stated that they had come to take over the cash balance and audit the books. The Gendarmerie [i.e. Kempeitai] officer in charge requested me to instruct the clerks to take out a General Ledger balance but this I refused to do, informing him that, as the staff had been dismissed as from that morning, I no longer had jurisdiction over them. He thereupon gave the orders himself.[9]

Davies was lucky to get away with this: on a different day he might easily have found himself caged in solitary confinement, like the manager of the Tsingtao branch who was so confined for five days – apparently in retribution for the branch's pre-war activities in the Chinese currency war.* (Davies stayed on as the Manager in Hankow for another seven months, assisting the manager of the Yokohama Specie Bank in his duties as the Authorized Liquidator. These included sending out letters to all of the Chartered's customers with overdrafts on their current accounts,

---

* It probably helped H. F. J. Bentinck to secure his release that he was able to show he had arrived in Tsingtao only in October 1941. Others were less fortunate, especially the British officers in Japan. Isaac Sykes, whom we encountered penning a memo about Indianization in Calcutta in 1932, was unlucky enough to find himself in Yokohama at the start of the war and was identified by the Japanese as the author of some pre-war reports on the silk industry that were construed as having been anti-Japanese. He was imprisoned days after the closure of the branch and spent several weeks in solitary confinement before suffering a nervous breakdown and being returned to house arrest. He died in April 1942, allegedly of a self-inflicted wound. His funeral was rather bizarrely attended by 'representatives of the Yokohama Specie Bank and numerous police officials'. ('Report on Yokohama', by K. W. Jones, August 1942, War Testimonies vol. 2.)

LIEBER'S STANDARD CODE,
A.B.C. CODE 4TH & 5TH EDITIONS,
BENTLEY'S COMPLETE PHRASE CODE:
PETERSON INTENATIONAL CODE 3RD EDITION.

The Yokohama Specie Bank, Limited.

TELEGRAPHIC ADDRESS:
SHOKIN

Hankow.

14th February, 1942.

Mr. R.J.S. Davies &/or Mrs. Betty,
Wah Cheong Road, S.A.D. No. 3,
Hankow.

Dear Sir, Madam,

      We beg to inform you that your currect account
with the Chartered Bank of India, Australia and China, Hankow,
shows a debit balance of $335.33 (Say local dollars Three hundred
thirty-five and 33/100.), including $16.33 for interest up to
December 16th, 1941, which please confirm and cover without
delay.

            Yours faithfully,

            The Authorized Liquidator of
            The Chartered Bank of India,
            Australia and China, Hankow.

            THE YOKOHAMA SPECIE BANK Ltd.

                      Manager

A letter from the Japanese liquidator of Chartered Bank's branch in occupied
Hankow in 1942, addressed to its Manager and demanding the repayment of an
overdraft on his personal account

requesting immediate repayment – one of the recipients, as it happened, was Davies himself.[10] The Chartered Manager and his wife secured places on a repatriation ship at the end of July 1942, and were safely evacuated via Shanghai to South Africa by September.)

In general, the Japanese in China relied more on carrots than sticks to secure the co-operation of existing bank staff – so much so, indeed, that several Chartered men were left to live in relatively tolerable conditions through this 'supervision period'. They were even paid a modest allowance, as was later noted by the managers of Peking and Hankow – and of Shanghai, too, where staff at the end of December actually received a scheduled 10 per cent bonus for the year.[11] The bankers at first debated the propriety of all this, though in reality they had little option but to comply. Comfort was drawn from the fact that other essential services, not least those providing medical care and sanitation, were similarly dependent on expatriates remaining at their posts. (In Shanghai, as five Sub-Accountants explained in a joint letter after the war, the bank 'received a recommendation from our Consul that we should continue working under the new regime as long as we were satisfied that by so doing we were serving the interests of the Allied Public'.[12] This remained the case, to their satisfaction, well into 1942.) But the lasting significance of the 'supervision arrangements', in the context of the Chartered's story, lay elsewhere: co-operation over the liquidation procedures allowed the Chartered's managers in most instances to provide for an orderly storing of the bank's closing accounts. In Peking and Tientsin, essential records were locked up in the vaults of the local Bank of Chosen (fortunately so in Peking, as the Chartered's own building there was destroyed by fire in 1944). In the critical case of Shanghai, Lundie's amicable dealings with the men from the Mitsui Bank were drawn to an especially satisfactory conclusion: 'All the Bank's records were arranged and stored personally by the Staff in the large vault at the rear of the office.' Indeed, when he came to report to Head Office in January 1946 on the wartime events on the Bund, Lundie was able to confirm that the bank had done even better than that. Its Chinese Chief Clerk had been employed by the Mitsui Bank, and so 'was able to keep a tab-on-anything that subsequently transpired'. Also hired by the Mitsui was a brave lady called Mrs Greenberger, 'a Jewish Refugee stenographer who endeavoured on several occasions, at considerable risk, to keep you advised of happenings in Shanghai'.[13]

Over the days and weeks that followed, the Chartered's branches beyond China and French Indo-China had at least a brief chance to prepare against possible occupation by the advancing Japanese (though the 'cheeky little bastards' moved at a breathtaking pace). Great importance was attached to destroying, if possible, any papers that could conceivably be of value to the enemy – meaning not just secret codebooks and confidential forms but also paper currencies, including any supplies of Chartered Bank notes as yet unsigned. The branch in Manila joined its peers in sending vanloads of paper money to the island fortress of Corregidor, where the Government took charge of burning it while US forces prepared their defences in readiness for the coming Japanese assault.[14] Sub-agencies in the Malay Archipelago trucked their notes down to Singapore, which they presumed to be a safe haven – leaving Klang, for example, soon denuded of 'all the cash except our copper supply which was too heavy and bulky to move', and Kuala Lumpur with just S$2,000 'in small coin'.[15] In many instances, last-minute opportunities were taken to pay the local staff three months' salary in advance – even while the Sub-Accountants were busy burning stockpiles of unsigned notes. And, as the enormity of Japan's strategic goals became apparent in cities all across south-east Asia, the Chartered's branches had one other principal concern. While keeping their books open to allow for business as usual until the last possible moment, they had to ensure an urgent consignment one way or another of essential copies to London, Calcutta and New York for safe keeping.

In Hong Kong, the threat of imminent attack put the local branch under intense pressure from that first day so graphically described by Gerry Leiper. The bank's main public area comprised an impressive banking hall at 4/4a Des Voeux Road.* It teemed with customers who queued through all the usual business hours (and additional hours at the weekends), most of them desperate to withdraw cash or transmit funds overseas. Of the ten British officers in Hong Kong, six joined the local Volunteer Defence Force within a day or two of Pearl Harbor – two of whom were killed in action after Japanese forces landed on the island – and a seventh joined the local Royal Navy reservists. This left only the Manager, R. A. Camidge, and the Accountant, W. A. Cruikshank, in the office, with Leiper as the senior Sub-Accountant, to prepare for the inevitable capitulation.† (In *A*

---

* The old building at 3 Queen's Road was still in use – it was not finally sold until 1951 – but most of the bank's activities had been switched to the Des Voeux Road premises, acquired from the Hongkong Bank in 1933. The two premises were connected by a stairway that led from the ground floor of Queen's Road to the first floor of Des Voeux Road.

† Camidge was very unfortunate to have returned to Hong Kong from furlough in Britain only three weeks before Pearl Harbor. By the same token, his temporary replacement, Evans Thomas, made a well-timed exit. Thomas had become something of an expert in this line over the course of a career stretching back to 1907, most of it spent in China. After four years as the Manager of the Tientsin branch, he had got away just in time in 1939 as the Japanese army launched a blockade of the foreign quarters of that city in a tense stand-off with the British authorities there. Evans had been escorted to the local port by two privates of the

Yen For My Thoughts, Leiper gave all the individuals in his narrative fictitious names. Camidge and Cruikshank were disguised as Clarkson and Walker.) They succeeded in transmitting a set of 'emergency records' just before the Colony lost its cable links to the outside world on 15 December, and over the next ten days succeeded in destroying signed notes worth about HK$5 million. (Many of them were burned in a special furnace belonging to Hongkong Bank, even though the Hongkong Bank itself decided against any large-scale destruction of notes.[16]) The banking hall remained open for business until just three hours before the formal surrender of the island on Christmas Day 1941. Thereafter, as in China, control of the Chartered (along with all of Hong Kong's other banks) was rapidly handed over by Japanese Army officers to their Army Finance Department. While most of the island's European non-combatants were herded into internment at Stanley on the south of the island – and those captured in uniform, including four of the Chartered's men, were incarcerated as prisoners of war – Leiper and his two senior colleagues found themselves in a different group. They and their families were segregated along with the other foreign banks' expatriate managers, numbering about a hundred in all, and were crammed into a former brothel (the 'Sun Wah Hotel') near the wharves in Hong Kong's Central District. They were to live there until the Japanese no longer required their assistance with the gradual liquidation of their banks, alongside a modest continuation of banking services for 'non-enemy' customers. It was not immediately apparent how long this process would last – the majority of the local Chinese and Portuguese clerks fled to Macao in the early days of the occupation – and the bankers and their new masters took some days to grasp the situation. (There was a tense moment when Japanese officials demanded to know from Leiper and his colleagues why the Chartered had only a very small reserve of unissued Hong Kong dollars. They were told that most of them had been burned during the battle to defend the island. 'How many you burn?' asked the incredulous officials. 'Almost five million dollars', came the answer – which, to the bemusement of the Chartered men, reduced the Japanese to helpless laughter.[17]) In the event, the 'supervision period' was to last until July 1943.

For eighteen months, the bankers would be marched daily along Des Voeux Road to their offices under armed guard like a white-collar chain

---

Durham Light Infantry and put safely on to a steamer for Shanghai. (His colourful career was recounted in February 1978 in *StanChart*, a staff newsletter that was briefly the successor to *Curry & Rice*. Quoted in 'Reminiscences from the East', a private memoir by Michael Brown of Standard Chartered.)

gang. Very soon, though, a not unfriendly rapport was established with the individuals of the Army Finance Department under a Mr Murata. The latter found a moment, in an early meeting with a representative committee of the bankers, to confide in his broken English 'very sorry you not in better place'.[18] And when he handed over to two liquidators from Tokyo, Mr Iishi and Mr Watanabe, the Chartered officers and their few remaining clerks continued with their work (for HK$50 a month) in a generally positive atmosphere. The Tokyo accountants were more than once at pains to caution Leiper and his colleagues against relaxing their guard ('You must understand Kempeitai very dangerous and all must be very careful') and would certainly have been aghast had they discovered that Leiper and his colleagues were secretly making duplicate records of all the banking transactions conducted since the start of the occupation. But they evidently sympathized with the desire of the Chartered bankers to safeguard the future of their accounts. The end of the supervision period did not mean the closure of the bank – its now tiny clerical staff was required to go on offering a basic service, partly in dollars and partly in military yen, the currency of the occupation forces – but it did involve Camidge, Cruikshank and Leiper leaving the Sun Wah Hotel and joining the other Europeans in internment. As they prepared to leave Des Voeux Road for the last time, the trio appealed to the liquidators for help in finding a storage space for the bank's pre-war books and records. (Two sets of the secret duplicates had been smuggled out separately, and one of them was subsequently kept up to date by the senior remaining Chinese clerk, Wan Wai In, at the risk of his life.[19]) The request appeared to have fallen on stony ground, until Camidge was suddenly summoned to the Army Finance head office for tea and biscuits – and informed that the military authorities had given Mr Iishi permission to set aside one strong room for the precious books. As Leiper later recounted:

> Our staff spent the next few days underground and took advantage of the opportunity to reorganise the storage of the entire contents of the records strong-room up to date and including the occupation period. By the time this task was completed the records were in better order than, in all probability, they had ever been in the entire history of the Branch. The liquidators took a keen interest in the work which seemed to appeal to their professional instincts. They provided brushes and disinfectants to clean down the shelves, walls and floor . . . and provided free and copious draughts of tea to wash down the dust and to relieve thirst.[20]

When the doors of the storeroom and its safes were finally locked, Iishi brandished the keys above his head and assured the Chartered men, 'I keep.'[21] Then the three British bankers were marched off, to pack their bags for Stanley. Leiper took with him a third set of secret duplicates covering the Occupation period, which he and Cruikshank later buried in a sealed bottle inside the internment camp (it was never recovered), and he even tried to continue monitoring the bank's activities by having coded messages sent to him by one of the senior Portuguese clerks. But his zeal was viewed with mixed feelings by his colleagues, who feared for the consequences. And perhaps rightly so. The Japanese discovered the messages, and the Portuguese clerk died in gaol awaiting trial. Searching his personal belongings in Kowloon, the Kempeitai came across one of the two sets of duplicate records that had been smuggled out of the bank – as a result of which in early 1944 Camidge, Cruikshank and Leiper were given heavy gaol sentences. August 1945 found them sharing a tiny prison cell in Canton, and Leiper thought all three of them would certainly have died, had the war continued much longer.*

Beyond Hong Kong at the end of 1941, other Asian branches of the Chartered had a little more time than Des Voeux Road to get their records away. Some might initially have supposed themselves beyond the reach of any likely war front, but any such illusions were very quickly dispelled. For residents of Singapore, confidence in the island as an impregnable fortress was shaken in traumatic fashion on just the fourth day of the war: having set out from the island's port to disrupt the landing of invasion forces on the eastern coast of the Malayan archipelago, the Royal Navy's two biggest ships in the Far East, HMS *Prince of Wales* and HMS *Repulse*, were both sunk by Japanese bombers with the loss of 840 men. It still seemed unthinkable that Singapore would fall to the enemy, but the possibility of fierce fighting on the island could no longer be ignored. Preparing for the worst, arrangements were made to copy the bank's most critical records and to spirit them to safety. Mechanized ledger-posting machines, only recently adopted in Singapore, failed to cope with constant breaks in the electricity supply: the office had to ship in thirty-three fresh ledgers, for all the accounts to be written up manually by twenty-five new clerks specially hired for the job.[22] Weeks were spent photographing all registered securities held by the bank, and posting off the prints. (Eastman Kodak of the US was offered the job but was too busy on Government work to spare any of its technicians. The bank had to resign itself instead

---

* Diseased and desperately thin, they were hospitalized for several weeks after the Japanese surrender, but all three did eventually recover. Of their four colleagues who were imprisoned as PoWs, three survived the war – but the fourth was less fortunate; he was included in a batch of Hong Kong prisoners despatched to Japan on a troop ship that was later sunk by an Allied submarine.

to being the first ever customer of a Chinese firm, Singapore Photo Co.[23])
Bearer bonds, freely negotiable for cash under normal circumstances, were
painstakingly converted into registered securities, details of which were
copied and posted off to Calcutta and New York.

A vivid sense of the growing panic on the island was captured in a
memorandum compiled a few months later by the Chartered's Accountant, M. E. ('Monty') Columbine. He thought it 'quite impossible, in any
written record, adequately to describe the conditions under which work
was carried on for several weeks', but he nonetheless wrote one of the best
detailed accounts that survive of the extraordinary scenes inside the
bank – and a temporary annex, Meyer Chambers, where the fugitive
up-country branches set up shop – through the terrible days of January
and early February 1942.[24] The press of customers, frantic to settle their
affairs and escape with their funds overseas, was all but overwhelming.
The Chartered felt a deep obligation towards them, which certainly precluded simply abandoning the city (as the American banks did). Hundreds
of telegraphic transfers were completed every day, the entire staff working
until well after midnight; the business of issuing travellers' cheques –
several thousand, in less than two months – continued in the basement
air-raid shelter when the bombs were falling overhead. This was in many
ways a defining hour for the bank's proud image of itself as a quasi-public
service of the Empire, as countless customers were helped to salvage a
viable future for themselves and their families.

By the first week of February 1942, with the skies full of enemy aircraft
and the island coming under intense bombardment by Japanese artillery,
the prospect of a humiliating surrender could no longer be ruled out, and
the bank's staff threw themselves into the business of actually destroying
all papers of any immediate value to the enemy that could not be despatched to safety.[25] Like the Colonial Treasury on the island, the bank
remitted huge physical shipments of cash to London and India, while
destroying most of what was left: notes worth S\$4.5 million were inciner-
ated on 11 February in front of two officials at the Treasury.[26] Wives and
lady clerks being evacuated were asked to carry with them handwritten
copies of the latest general ledgers, sometimes involving desperate
measures – as Columbine recorded of one such consignment:

> About midday [on 11 February], Mrs Williams, i/c Correspondence Depart-
> ment, informed me that she had been granted a passage and was to report
> at Clifford Pier in two hours. As the books for the 10th inst. were balanced,
> it was decided to . . . despatch them in her care if possible . . . but the typed
> copies were unfinished when Mrs Williams called to collect them; there

was no question of her being able to wait [so she departed] and as soon as
typing was completed a copy was signed without any checking, placed in
a stout cover and rushed down to Clifford Pier. The launch carrying Mrs
Williams had already cast off, but the Officer carrying the packet was able
to throw this to her on board and call out instructions to post it to the
Branch of the Chartered Bank nearest to her port of disembarkation.[27]

However, the sheer scale of the Chartered's activities meant that many
expatriates remained working in the bank as the Japanese closed in – and
this posed a delicate dilemma that had not arisen in China or Hong Kong.
Forty-three British officers of the bank were still on the island, but other
expatriates were managing to leave it – and not just women and children.
At what point would it be defensible, even advisable, to head for the
exit? Just a handful of individuals – including the most senior men at the
Chartered as at other banks and agency firms in Singapore – were offered
passes to board the last departing ships, on the afternoon of 13 February,
and they took them.[28] Among not a few of those who stayed at their desks
(or tried in vain to leave without passes), this was angrily resented and it
led to some acrimonious correspondence after the war.* One of the more
forthright accounts of the last days before the surrender on Sunday 15 February was penned by a future Chief Manager of the bank, Stafford
Northcote, who proudly asserted the contribution made by those who
remained to the bitter end:

> I feel, and so do those of my colleagues who stayed in Singapore, that it is
> only because some of us were there on the spot (in the office and actually
> at our desks) when the Japanese walked in and because we were there to

* This was perhaps less freely aired than might otherwise have been the case, once the fate
of those who made it off the island came to be known. The two last ships to leave, the SS
Kuala and the *Tien Kwong*, were both sunk by Japanese aircraft the following day. Among
the 700 survivors who made it to a tiny island called Pompong, blessed with fresh water,
were the Singapore Manager David Millar and four of his colleagues. (Four others, including
'Monty' Columbine, had left aboard different vessels.) After several terrible days all were
rescued by local boatmen, who ferried them to the mainland of Sumatra. An arduous trek
followed to the west coast port of Padang. Here the five Chartered men (and two of the other
four bank evacuees) were among hundreds rescued by the British Navy on 28 February and
taken to Colombo. Three weeks later they left by ship for South Africa – tragically without
Millar, who had contracted enteric fever in February and died while they were waiting to
sail. News of his death 'was a terrible shock to us', remembered one of those waiting with
him in Colombo, 'I had a very great admiration for him in every way' ('Singapore & Afterwards', Report by W. D. Brown to J. F. Duncan, 10 September 1942, War Testimonies vol.
2; W. M. Ritchie to J. F. Duncan, 13 August 1942, War Testimonies vol. 3; Extract from
letter by B. M. Purser to his fiancée, passed to the Chartered's Secretary, 17 May 1942, War
Testimonies vol. 3).

hand over to them, that any of our Malayan records are still in existence today ... we <u>were</u> there to hand over our records to the Japanese, thus putting ourselves at least in the position of having some justification for expecting these records to be returned to us, or otherwise made available to those interested, in good order at the end of the war.[29]

Northcote may well have been right. For within a few hours of the city's surrender, the Japanese Army Finance Department turned up at the bank in the shape of the Yokohama Specie Bank's local manager, a Mr Muto, now in uniform. It happened that one of the Chartered's staff had testified in a court case as an expert witness on Muto's behalf during 1941. This, along with the fact that the YSB's own records had been carefully preserved by the Chartered since December, left Muto well-disposed towards the bank.[30] When he and his staff began work on liquidating its affairs the next day, they treated their erstwhile peers with conspicuous politeness. The two sides worked together for the next fortnight: one of the Sub-Accountants, J. C. Kyle, wrote later that the Japanese bankers had been 'exceedingly kind and sympathetic'.[31] Another of Northcote's colleagues recalled:

They were quite obviously pleased with the Japanese Army's victory, and flattered by their consequent appointments, but nevertheless they were courteous to us and expressed their sympathy for our unfortunate predicament. I think Muto of the YSB who had been about thirty years in British Territories was genuinely sorry that the War had broken out. He promised to do the best he could to look after the Bank's books.[32]

Muto honoured his promise. The Singapore branch records were eventually transferred to a storeroom in the Hongkong Bank, whose building was appropriated by the Yokohama Specie Bank for the duration of the war, and the accounts of the up-country branches were even more carefully handled, as another Sub-Accountant remembered:

On the instructions of the Japanese we moved all the up-country books and papers ... into our own strong rooms in [the] Singapore office, which the Japanese custodian then sealed up. [Our cashier] Mr Seng Soon took away a copy of the Current Account balances which he said he would try to keep until we 'returned'.[33]

In the aftermath of Singapore's fall, attempts to keep the bank's services going in the rest of South Asia were soon abandoned. Few customers remained; the retreating British forces were pressing all civilians to evacuate; and few viable exit routes were still available. Even so, prodigious efforts were made by the Foreign Staff in the Dutch East Indies to store the Batavia branch's precious records somewhere safe from harm. They were taken by car up-country to Bandoeng, where – like the accounts left in Sourabaya at the eastern end of Java – the Japanese subsequently agreed that they could simply be locked away in safes inside branches of the Bank of Java. After the occupation of Medan, the bank's Sumatran records were illicitly copied under the very noses of the Japanese guards: 'These carbon copies were smuggled out of the Bank and thanks to the loyalty of the Local Staff were put away in safety for the duration.'[34] Several of the Batavia and Medan managers paid a high price for staying longer than was perhaps prudent and ended up, like most of their Singapore colleagues, in internment.* Other members of the Foreign Staff, including Sub-Accountants from Sourabaya in Java and Kuching in Sarawak, did manage to escape, reaching the tiny port of Tjilatjap on Java's south coast in time to board a last passage with the Royal Navy to Australia. Finding no easy way to travel east beyond Perth, six signed up as coal stokers on a merchant ship to Melbourne – where one of them wrote to the bank's Secretary in London to remind him how they had covered the last stage of their journey ' . . . and [it] being dangerous work I wired you to insure us at Lloyd's against all risks, which, if possible, no doubt had your attention'.[35]

Nowhere, though, were the bank's records more comprehensively, and dramatically, rescued than from Burma. The bank's business in pre-war Rangoon had struggled for years to cope with the impact of the Great Depression on the rice trade, but it had at least returned modest profits since 1937. Its Produce Department was once again lending heavily to millers and grain merchants in the city, to fund their seasonal purchases of the country's huge paddy crop between December and May each year

---

* Those held in Sumatra might have come across the Manager of Eastern Bank's Singapore branch, a Mr Steel, who had devised another way of safeguarding branch assets. In the days just prior to the fall of the island, he had taken all of his bank's cash and securities and had deposited them with the Singapore Government Treasury, carefully pocketing a set of receipts. On the weekend of the surrender, he and his Accountant had somehow managed to escape from the port. But they were shipwrecked on their way to Sumatra and ended up being interned there. For the next three and a half years, almost certainly at the risk of his own life, this Mr Steel served his employers in a remarkable fashion. As the first post-war Report of the Directors disclosed to the Eastern's shareholders, in a brief account of the bank's wartime misadventures: 'He took the receipts with him [to Sumatra] and in spite of many vicissitudes and risks, retained them on his person and brought them to Singapore [in August 1945] on his way to this country – a very fine and plucky performance.' Indeed so, and it apparently allowed Eastern Bank's Singapore branch to be reopened with ample funds on 1 October 1945. (Eastern Bank Report and Accounts for 1945, SCB Box 2573.)

('by far the largest business in this field compared with our competitors').[36] Showing a brave confidence in the future of the country's export trades, the Chartered had gone ahead with the building of a new branch – a splendid building, still there, erected on the site of the old 1899 branch and officially opened on Phayre Street in January 1941.[37] A new Agent, C. M. Clamp, arrived just days before Pearl Harbor to take charge of the branch and its 130 local staff. At the end of January 1942, he arranged for all of the branch's securities to be sent by steamer to Calcutta. By the time Singapore fell a fortnight later, regular air raids had left Rangoon with a severely reduced population and it was obvious it would not be able to hold off an imminent Japanese assault. Clamp judged it would be best if all the banks acted in concert together: it was he who took the initiative in organizing a 'Bankers' Train' to take the city's cash to Mandalay, and he made provision for all the banks to have carriage-space on it for their account books. (A convoy of eleven cars was also organized by the Standard Oil Company, to drive the 450 miles north to Mandalay, and some other Chartered records were sent by this route.) Clamp then led a delegation of the city's bankers, as he later described in a long letter written in 1943, to inform the authorities of the arrangements for the train and subsequent evacuation of staff:

> On arrival at his house, we found the Prime Minister at tiffin, and were shown into the dining room, where the discussion was carried on without any interruption being made in his meal. The meeting did not take up much time, and we left within a few minutes . . . to meet His Excellency [the British Governor] a few hours later. The Governor seemed very surprised that a banking crisis had arisen by exclaiming 'Struth' when the position was explained to him; he asked very few questions, and left the meeting in a very short time, after resigning himself to the decisions.[38]

After those decisions had been reported to London, however, telegrams quickly landed on the Governor's desk instructing him to block the evacuation and putting forward alternative plans. These were shown to the bankers, who 'soon unanimously agreed that the Secretary of State's proposals were completely impractical'. The loading of the train went ahead the next day, Friday 20 February, and lasted from the early hours of the morning until the middle of the afternoon (the Chartered unexpectedly found it had space for all its Safe Custody boxes as well as its account books – a weighty consignment). Shortly before the train's departure at 7 p.m., the Government relented and issued a notice proclaiming that the city would be officially evacuated on 22 February. As Clamp would later note, this happily averted possible criticism of the banks for taking

RANGOON BRANCH

Chartered Bank's new Rangoon branch, inaugurated in 1941 on Phayre (now
Pansodan) Street, and drawn in 1948

precipitate action. 'In the eyes of the public, banks are nearly always wrong, but it had to be subsequently admitted, grudgingly by some, that in this particular instance, they were right.'

The Bankers' Train pulled into Mandalay on the evening of 21 February, with two closed railway carriages containing 'over nine crores of rupees in currency notes of all denominations'. The boiler room of the Mandalay Brewery was co-opted to burn them all, which took one and a half days to complete and reportedly generated enough power for the production of 2,500 bottles of beer.[39] The Standard Oil convoy arrived three days later. Almost half the Chartered's local staff in Rangoon somehow managed to complete their own journeys north in the following days, and for the next six weeks the bank in Mandalay was one of half a dozen that ran makeshift operations in support of the British forces and civilians left in the country. As much as possible of the material so carefully transported from Rangoon was meanwhile flown to Calcutta, even including Safe Custody boxes: by early April, scarcely a dozen of these remained. By this date Japanese bombing was threatening to turn Mandalay into a ghost town, and plans were hastily made for a final exodus. Clamp and his Accountant, C. M. Jenkin, were fortunate to secure precious places on a plane to Calcutta on 15 April. They took the last of the bank's accounts with them ('The amount of baggage carried by Mr Jenkin and myself, including a suitcase of records, totalled 225 lbs . . .') and within ten days the two of them had established a 'Rangoon Evacuation Office' on the premises of the Allahabad Bank in Lahore. Here the task of reconstructing all the Rangoon customer accounts was begun more or less immediately.* Meanwhile those left behind in Burma – three Sub-Accountants and sixty employees, most of them Indians – were initially promised seats in a general airlift by the RAF to fly hundreds of civilians to safety, but it failed to materialize. All were left with little choice but to set off for the Indian border by foot. Many sought refuge along this path and died in the jungle before they reached Assam. Remarkably, the three British officers and almost forty of their staff arrived in Calcutta safely the following month.[40]

Despite all the hazards encountered on that journey, many Chartered men might gladly have tackled it rather than face internment. But

---

* One of the men who got away from Singapore, W. M. Ritchie, was already working in the Rangoon Evacuation Office by August 1942. 'I don't have time to mope, with the amount of work entailed in the reconstruction of Rangoon records which keeps us hard at it all day and every day . . . The organisation of the evacuation of their records has been practically perfect. It is the first time I have met Jenkin . . . [who] is, as you probably know, a veritable human dynamo!' (Ritchie to J. F. Duncan, 13 August 1942, War Testimonies vol. 3).

incarceration by the Japanese was the fate of most of the Foreign Staff overtaken by the course of the war. For a lucky few, the ordeal was cut short by repatriation deals struck with the Allied governments. Four of the Kobe and Yokohama officers were allowed to board a passenger ship, the *Tatuta Maru*, which left Yokohama on 30 July 1942. Other colleagues joined them when the vessel called at Shanghai, Saigon and Bangkok: altogether some sixteen of the bank's Foreign Staff – including T. L. Christie from Haiphong, with his family – managed to qualify for a berth, reaching South Africa at the end of August.[41] (The repatriation process was well described, long after the war, in a staff-magazine article written by one of the Chartered bankers' wives, who was released from Hong Kong's Stanley camp in September 1943, as part of an exchange of Canadians for Japanese citizens. Her husband had ended up in a PoW camp in Japan earlier in the war.[42]) The Chartered's Head Office had opened a line of credit with the Durban branch of the Standard Bank, to make funds available for the new arrivals from the East. Unfortunately this arrangement fell foul of stiff wartime exchange control laws, 'but the Manager and other members of the [Standard's] staff assisted us, some from their own pockets . . . and all from the Manager down could not do enough for us'.[43] Most of the evacuees were encouraged by Head Office to take their time recuperating before plotting a return passage to India, and several took the opportunity to visit tourist spots across Natal and the Cape. Everywhere they were warmly received by local managers of the Standard Bank – planting the first seeds, perhaps, of what was to be a long and fateful relationship.[44] The Chartered men were also solicitous of each other's welfare, of course. After the Peking Manager, E. W. Bilton, had had the bottom of his left leg bitten off by a shark while swimming from the beach at Durban, the intrepid R. J. S. Davies (late of Hankow) took care of him and kept Head Office posted on his recovery. 'The doctors told me that . . . it should be possible to fix an artificial foot that would cause no disability for his work and might even permit golf or dancing. I ventured to relieve Mr Bilton's mind from his anxieties which I trust was in order.'[45]

There was to be no golf or dancing for those held in Singapore's Changi Gaol, the Stanley Internment Camp on the south shore of Hong Kong, or any of half a dozen other prisons where Chartered men were held for the next three and a half years.* Ninety-nine officers of the bank remained

---

* In keeping with its reputation before the war as a city with a night life that made New York's seem tame, Shanghai saw 350 Allied internees – including seven Chartered men – put into a camp in a league of its own. A decent diet, sports facilities and a Japanese dental clinic

behind bars, some of them with wives and young children, and all were soon forced into living conditions that ranged from the severely frugal to the criminally deprived.[46] Gone were the days of settling down to a friendly accommodation with civilian aides to the Imperial Japanese Army. Living with the consequences of military defeat now turned out to be a matter in many instances of just clinging on against the odds. The Singapore office's J. C. Kyle, who had found Mr Muto and his team so kind and sympathetic, would emerge from his cell in August 1945 weighing 7st 13lbs and in urgent need, like many others, of hospitalization. Worst placed of all were those classified as Prisoners of War. They were assigned to different camps, including one in the Sarawak capital of Kuching where three out of five Chartered inmates died of disease and malnutrition.[47] Most of the PoWs were pressed into forced labour units. Ten Chartered men (and one Eastern Bank officer) were sent to work on the infamous Burma–Siam Railway. Miraculously, all but one survived that ordeal.[48] Their post-war accounts of the experience were extraordinarily brief and understated, none more so than that submitted to Head Office by D. A. Blunt in November 1945:

> On November 1st [1942] we started work on a portion of the Burma-Siam Railway and continued working on this railway up and down the river until March 16th 1944. There is no need for me to say more about the work and conditions whilst engaged on the Railway as I'm sure you must have read details in the Press and heard from reports on the wireless in this connection. All I can say is that these reports have not, in any way, been exaggerated ... During the whole time of my captivity I kept very good health, only contracting mild doses of malaria about a dozen times – I was very lucky.[49]

It would be easy to compile a book of some length from the many detailed accounts that turned up after 1945 of the wartime sufferings of the bank's Foreign Staff and their families. An envelope arrived at 38 Bishopsgate, for example, postmarked Sydney with the barely legible date '11.06.45B'. It contained three long typescript memoranda that had been written in 1944 by internees of the Fukushima camp in Japan, where nine Chartered men (three of them with families) had spent the war. Having escaped from south-east Asia to Australia, they had embarked on the long voyage to South Africa in May 1942 but their ship, the SS *Nankin*, had

---

were among its amenities. 'On one occasion, the Japanese procured professional entertainers and also provided four or five cinema shows.' (Memorandum by F. C. Lundie, January 1946, War Testimonies vol. 1.)

been captured by a German raider in the Indian Ocean and they had been handed over to the Japanese.* Evidently compiled by them in the hope of reaching out to the International Red Cross, the papers gave a harrowing account of their situation and must have been read in London with some dismay. One of the 'Fukushima Nine' (Plate 25c), who had lived in Japan for three years early in the 1930s and had come to admire its people, wrote of his 'surprise and horror at the harsh and brutal treatment . . . dangerous criminals are looked after better in our country and the dumb animals better treated than we have been'.[50] Again, one of the detainees in Singapore, G. A. P. Sutherland, emerged from internment in August 1945 clutching a school-exercise book in which he had kept a diary of the early weeks in captivity, discussed and agreed with his fellow internees as an accurate account of their experiences: it had been seized by the Kempeitai in October 1943 'but was returned to me six months later without comment'.[51] The contents of the book were promptly typed up by the bank after liberation – using scraps of Japanese accounting stationery – and copies were widely circulated.[52] After returning home to Scotland, Sutherland also compiled a forty-five-page report on the story of the Singapore camps from March 1942 to the end of the war, which he posted to the bank from his Inverness home in November 1945.[53] It tells a remarkable tale of how those who were crowded into Changi Gaol – three thousand of them, in cells designed for six hundred prisoners – built an ordered and civilized existence in the face of dire adversity.

Liberation, when it came, arrived suddenly and unexpectedly. Amid the chaos and celebrations of August–September 1945, and in many cases on the very first day of their freedom, most of the Chartered's Eastern staff made the same excursion. They went to see what had become of their bank. And as they stood and gazed at the buildings or wandered through despoiled banking halls and offices, several found familiar faces awaiting them. The loyalty shown by many of the bank's local staff in the perilous days of 1941–2 had made a strong impression on the British officers. Over the intervening years, there had also been several cases, from Shanghai and Hong Kong to Singapore and Bandoeng, of former clerks and cashiers risking their lives to smuggle food and news of the war into the camps. Now there were many affecting reunions between British managers and members of their pre-war staffs all across Asia. (Leiper recorded one such encounter in Hong Kong: 'One day in late August 1945, two of our officers entered the side door of the Chartered Bank building in Queens Road

---

* The nine men were D. Murray, J. Shewan, E. C. Phillips, H. J. M. Cook, T. E. D. Edwards, A. P. Daniels, M. R. Hannah, J. M. Jack and J. Miller.

Fukushima Internment Camp,
Japan.
13th March, 1944.

To The Representative,
The International Red Cross Committee,
J A P A N.

Sir,
We should be most grateful if something could be done to improve our conditions here as at the moment we are treated not as Civilian Internees but as Criminal Prisoners. We should like to be treated as adult human beings - to be given freedom of movement within the limits of this building and grounds, and above all to be relieved of the constant nerve strain under which we live as a result of the numerous petty regulations (numbering   a copy of which is attached) which serve no useful purpose but only make our lives unbearable.

We rise at 6.30 a.m. and go to bed at 8.40 p.m. during the winter. In the summer those hours are altered to 6 a.m. and 9 p.m. Despite the fact that we have absolutely nothing whatever to do all day since we have never been given books, writing material or games, and are not allowed to lie down and rest even on our bare tatamies without first asking permission (presumably one would have to have a headache or some minor ailment to obtain this concession), we are not allowed to cover ourselves with the blankets provided by the authorities and even our own blankets may not be wrapped around higher than the waist during the day. We would point out that the heating is only on for 2 to 2½ months during the winter.

Under the regime existing for the first year of our stay here our treatment was especially disgraceful. The guards were given the right to hit us at will, and they took full advantage of this. Constant cases of face slapping took place, and on one occasion a guard unmercifully attacked one of the women in the course of which he threw her to the ground and kicked her several times in the face: she was compelled to remain in bed for a week to recover from her physical injuries, and it was many weeks before she recovered from the nervous shock. Another woman was struck sharply on the head with a key for closing a dining room window. She immediately went to the office to lodge a complaint. The guard followed her and in front of the Commandant slapped her face. Becoming more and more enraged he followed her out of the office, grasped her by the throat and bent her back across a table preparatory to hitting her again. He was however, pulled off by the interpreter whereupon he seized a chair and went for her again.

Extract from the letter addressed by the Fukushima Nine internees in Japan to the International Red Cross Committee in March 1944

where they were greeted by a Chinese clerk who had remained with the bank during the entire occupation period.'[54]) It was obvious in many places – not least in China, but in tense city streets of former French and Dutch territories, too – that restoring even a semblance of the pre-war world was going to be difficult if not impossible. Whether the bank's erstwhile 'native staff' would be ready to resume their personal careers with the Chartered, however, was a question that scarcely needed asking. (Some actually wrote to Head Office to pre-empt any doubts: 'Regarding the Chartered Bank, Kuala Lumpur', wrote one clerk, 'the premises is intact, and the staff from cook to chief clerk available.'[55]) As for the next most pressing question, none of the newly released Foreign Staff men can have posed it without deep misgivings. What, if anything, had come of all their despairing efforts to store away those accounting records in the final days and hours of the 1941–2 collapse? The answer, on which hung at least the immediate future of the bank, could hardly have been more gratifying. On 26 October 1945, the bank's Secretary sent out a circular, 'To all liberated officers', requesting information on any happy discoveries they might have made. Back flowed a stream of replies, most of them from men still recovering in the East, and sixty-one of them remain in a numbered collection today, in the fourth file of the War Testimonies. In letter after letter, the same three magical words were to recur, or something very like them: 'everything is intact'.[56]

2. PEACE AND RECONSTRUCTION

Most of the Chartered Bank's branches in the vanquished and unlamented Co-Prosperity Sphere thus recovered enough of their pre-war ledgers, records and accounts to be able to start reassembling their affairs within weeks of the Japanese surrender. This prompted some surprise, and occasionally utter disbelief, among both the newly liberated members of its Foreign Staff and their colleagues despatched from Head Office to take forward the business of reconstruction. Week by week, the books in one city after another were returned to the shelves, though the shelves themselves in many places took a while to be reinstalled. The salvage stories were legion. British army procedures, not necessarily attuned to the accounting needs of a commercial bank, had in many instances to be adroitly side-stepped.[57] In many places mountainous piles of boxed accounts from different banks in shared vaults had to be disentangled and sorted. In Rangoon, the branch building newly completed in 1941 had somehow escaped any serious structural damage whatever – but it had 365 locks, all the keys to which had disappeared, necessitating their removal and the installation of 365 new door handles.[58] Missing records in more than one location had to be dug up with the aid of hastily drawn sketch-maps where 'X' marked the burial spot, as for the pirates in Stevenson's *Treasure Island*. In the Philippines, the pre-war Sub-Agent at Cebu had been W. G. Hollyer. On the very day of the Japanese invasion, 10 April 1942, Hollyer and a colleague, Guy Wolford, had placed a full set of the Cebu branch accounts into a tin box which they had buried in a local garden. (Hollyer must have been a remarkable banker: after being interned by the Japanese, he had also managed to recreate the bank's accounts as of 9 April 1942 in a thirty-seven-page memo – entirely from memory. The memo survived the war, and was posted to Bishopsgate as a report 'of considerable historic interest'.[59]) Much effort went into trying to locate this buried tin box after the war was over, by which time both Hollyer and Wolford had died. The bank turned for help to one of Hollyer's Sub-Accountants, R. M. McGregor, who had been interned alongside Hollyer and Wolford and had been told by them of the box's whereabouts. Young McGregor did his best, but could only offer a bare sketch that placed 'X' next to a 'clump of bamboos', perhaps a less than definitive landmark.[60] The box seems never to have been found. This fortunately proved in the end to be of little consequence. Yet another complete set of the bank's papers was somehow located by a US Army officer, A. P. Mustard, who wrote to Chartered's local staff in July confirming that he 'had located and moved the stuff to what I consider a safe place'.[61] It all made a curious sequel to the demolition of the Cebu branch by shellfire in 1942, after which Japanese officers had assured all the Chartered men in their custody that the bank's papers had been completely destroyed.

Perhaps the most complete recovery story, though, belonged to Hong Kong. It transpired after the Japanese surrender that those strongroom keys pocketed by Mr Iishi in July 1943 had not in fact been kept by him for very long, but instead had been passed through various military and civilian hands. Gerry Leiper recorded what happened next:

> The investigation into this chain of succession commenced with our liquidators who, in defeat, were dignified and most helpful. For several days various Japanese, whom the liquidators specified as having worked in our building, were taken from their internment camp for interrogation in our office . . . Eventually the keys were traced to a senior Kempeitai officer who had occupied a suite in a Chinese hotel. When the locked door of his room was forced it was found that he had committed suicide with ritual accompaniments. A large collection of keys, which included many of our more

the day of the invasion. he & her Guy Walford had prepared a tin box to contain Consular papers + our full records. This box they buried themselves in the garden of the Smith Bell House. I presume that Mr Walford, before his death, revealed the place of burial either to his wife or to a member of his staff but will try + draw a plan as it was shown to me

Smith Bell House ——— Hedge or road between S.B. House + next door

front of house x [ ] — path   🌳 🏠 clump of Bamboos   [ ] — chicken House

[ ] (S.B) House

Walking from the back of the Smith Bell House there is a pathway roughly along the dividing hedge which pathway eventually reaches the chicken house. Just before you bear to the right to go to the chicken house there is a clump of bamboos in front of which there was a dump for garbage + old cans. The tin box was buried under this garbage.

Possibly Walford gave a much better description than the above but as I don't know the garden at all my attempt at visualising the position cannot be too good.

Kindly advise me of any further particulars you may require

Yours faithfully.

m velapuran

R. M. McGregor

Page from a Sub-Accountant's post-war letter in the Philippines, sketching the supposed location of a buried box containing the Cebu branch's 1942 records

important ones, were found in a small safe in the bedroom . . . [Of] our four strong-rooms, the records room was the only one in which the contents were recovered intact after the war and in the same condition as when the door had been locked before our staff vacated the building.[62]

The recovered accounts were updated on the back of the secret duplicates kept by Wan Wai In, which comprised an invaluable record of all of the bank's local transactions since January 1942, and Hong Kong was back in business.*

Oddly, the whole story of the network's missing accounts was passed over in silence by the Directors in London, as though the bank's records had simply survived much as anyone might have expected. Confirming to the shareholders in May 1946 that most of the network had been reopened, the Chairman rejoiced that 'no major damage was done to any of our offices' and spoke at length of the war's impact on crops, currencies and staff – but said nothing at all of the accounts.[63] Presumably he thought the bank's resumption of business would speak for itself. Of the forty-one branches listed on the report sent off to shareholders in the spring of 1946, just eleven were shown as 'Not yet re-opened', and most of these were back in business within a few months.

Of course, reconstruction was not accomplished at the same brisk pace everywhere. Tientsin's surviving accounts turned out to be rather meagre, for example; and the Malayan Sub-Agency at Alor Star had lost everything by handing their books to some local Siamese officials, who were never seen again. Restoring the bank's accounts proved a challenge in both places – as indeed in Bangkok itself, where reconstruction lasted well into 1947. Probably the toughest problems were encountered in the capital of the Philippines, and the travails of the Manila branch might suggest the fate that could so easily have befallen far more of the network. The port of Manila had thrived before the war on the Philippines' rapidly expanding production of raw sugar (despite heavy tariffs on sugar imports into the US). The Chartered had prospered accordingly: in fact, its consistent profitability had made the Manila branch the second biggest earner of the entire network in the 1930s, trailing only Shanghai.[64] Head Office was

---

* Wan Wai In and three of his clerical colleagues were each given a special bonus of HK\$2,000 after the war in acknowledgement of their services during the occupation. The awards took a little while to process. In fact, Leiper had to urge the process ahead before he left the Colony on furlough at the end of 1949. A new Manager shortly afterwards confirmed they had finally been made, 'and great care has been taken to effect payment in a discreet manner'. (A. J. Bird to Head Office, 28 January 1950, SP&C Letters to Head Office, 1937–53, private papers of W. C. L. Brown.)

accordingly anxious to restore the bank's presence there as quickly as possible, and Will Cockburn despatched a new Manager within weeks of the US liberation of the islands in March 1945. As he noted in a legal affidavit for the US courts many years later:

> I gave instructions . . . that he was to reopen . . . and to re-commence active business as soon as possible, setting up the books . . . by re-establishing, inter alia, all current and deposit accounts as they stood in the books of the Branch at the date of its occupation by the Japanese.

The man selected for the job was P. R. Wait, formerly the bank's Manager in Bangkok in 1942, who had managed to get himself and his family repatriated from Siam on the strength of a pre-war position held by his wife in the local British Legation office.* Wait found his assignment heavy going. Reporting to Head Office in August 1945, he set down a long account of his work, suggesting it 'may perhaps be some guide to what is in store for us at other points' – fortunately, he was wrong there – and explaining their difficult situation. 'The position in Manila was that all principal books and files were missing, presumably destroyed . . . [and] the only records recovered after the departure of the Japanese were . . . yearly balances of the books and summaries of collections and set-offs [made by the Liquidators between 1942 and 1945].'[65] It took years to reinstate current and deposit accounts for customers; and, in fixing these at a total value of 4,665,562 pesos, the bank resigned itself to accepting a net loss of 3,179,537 pesos.

We know of both these sums precisely, because they were confirmed for the bank by its Manila auditors in 1956, as part of an interminable legal battle fought by the Chartered in pursuit of war damages.[66] The Directors clung for years to the hope that official compensation might reduce their net losses; but, here again, the war's aftermath in the Philippines proved frustrating. The bank lodged a hefty claim with the US War Damages Commission in January 1948, on the basis that its branch operations in Cebu and Iloilo had retained large cash balances (captured by the Japanese) only at the behest of the US armed forces and their quartermasters in 1941–2.[67] The claim was rejected the following year – because the bank had never been incorporated under US law – but a second, slightly

---

* During his brief internment, Wait had been delighted to receive visits at the camp from a junior official in the Ministry of Finance, Nai Chaloke, who reassured him that all the records of the British banks had been handed over to the Ministry by the Japanese. Chaloke had taken charge of keeping them safe – a happy turn of events, as Wait later reported, probably attributable to the young man's Anglophilia and the fact that he was 'one time cox of the Oxford boat'. (P. R. Wait to Head Office, 28 September 1942, War Testimonies vol. 3.)

smaller claim was filed under a Philippines property statute in 1954. This dragged on for two years alongside an unedifying, and ultimately academic, squabble between two US law firms, one in the Philippines and the other in Washington, DC, both vying for a success-based fee. Finally, the bank appealed to the US Court of Claims in 1956 for the recovery of losses at Cebu attributable to its support for the US military. This, too, was dismissed – and the US Court added to the bank's disenchantment a few weeks later by making a handsome award to the Philippines National Bank in settlement of a not dissimilar claim.[68]

Much more typical of the Chartered's reconstruction process was the success with which many branches identified overdrafts outstanding at the outbreak of hostilities – and then, remarkably, set about reclaiming the interest due on them for the intervening years. Some of the resulting debts were waived, at the discretion of the local branch, but most were not. The second post-war Manager in Hong Kong, 'Dicky' Bird, submitted a report in December 1949 with several schedules attached, showing how conscientiously his branch had set about the task: Schedule D listed thirty-four corporate accounts, and the interest paid or payable by most of them for the period since December 1941.* The Hong Kong branch had also been scrupulously attentive to payments that were owed to customers, notably on deposit accounts in credit at the close of business in 1941, and provisions were set aside where account holders had disappeared.[69] Where the resulting provisions were still untouched four years later, the branch was accounting for them at the end of 1949 as 'surpluses'. Bird's 1949 report pulled together the net balance of all his interest payments and surpluses, less his contingent liabilities and accrued fees, and he appears to have sent off a sizeable remittance to Head Office.

Across the network, other managers had been busy since the war's end on a host of similar exercises – netting a wide range of credits and (actual or potential) debits. The majority reported net losses, taking account of the damage done by the Japanese liquidators and the cost of capital and interest payments foregone for one reason or another. By the end of 1951,

---

* The notion of charging interest on loans frozen in wartime may seem ruthless, but was the only practical way to proceed, at least as a first step. Indeed, in one famous case, clients insisted on paying more than the bank had intended charging. Manchester firms had borrowed about £3,000,000 against bills outstanding in September 1939, on cargoes being shipped to the East. By re-routing the cargoes during the hostilities, the bank had managed to collect the cash due on most of these bills. After the war, it had to be agreed how much the bank should charge before netting the proceeds against the Manchester loans. 'By agreement with the Bank of England 3 per cent p.a. interest was charged, but a number of firms preferred to pay 5 per cent p.a. in gratitude for the bank's services.' (JL-B notes, LMA: CH03/01/14/072.)

Head Office was almost ready to produce a summary balance for the bank as a whole, but one further category of stock-taking still needed to be completed. All branches were asked to quantify the costs of the Japanese occupation, in terms of the damage done to their properties and possessions. This drew forth dozens of slightly surreal lists, relating to staff houses as well as bank premises, and noting the bill for lost sherry glasses and stolen whisky decanters, damaged Venetian blinds and torn mosquito nets, wrecked kitchen cabinets and broken chairs. No loss-adjusters could ever have been more thorough: scarcely a misplaced paper-clip can have gone unrecorded. The damage estimates were then added during the course of 1952 to the banking spreadsheets – and at the end of that year, Head Office delivered itself of a singularly precise audit of the war.[70] It read:

Losses Arising Out of the Japanese Occupation of the Branches of the Chartered Bank

1. Losses due to the operations of the Japanese Liquidators	£ 627,620
2. Costs of rehabilitation of premises damaged or destroyed	£ 135,577
3. Cost of renewing furniture and equipment looted or destroyed	£ 105,817
	£ 869,014
4. Loss of interest on advances occasioned by Debtor/Creditor Ordinances and other compromises	£ 758,597
	£1,627,611

Bankers and accountants prefer exact numbers, and no doubt this precise tally helped with the pursuit of insurance and war-damage claims. (The latter were received with conspicuously more sympathy by the British authorities than the American, though even the British baulked at any claims that included a kitchen sink rather too blatantly. Some overly optimistic claims appear to have been counter-productive, eliciting a less than generous response. The Chartered's Kuala Lumpur branch, for example, filed for S$5.3 million in 1954, including 'loss of rent', and saw this whittled down to a 'Final Award' of S$468,281 – of which just 70 per cent was eventually paid out by March 1955 in 'full and final settlement'.[71]) But no one could have supposed that a gross loss of £1,627,611 – plus the lives, it should not be forgotten, of thirty-two employees at the final count, fifteen from the Home Staff and seventeen from the Foreign Staff – really represented the net impact of the war. Against it had to be set a pattern of wartime earnings that had proved remarkably robust in the circumstances.

The two years prior to Pearl Harbor brought a boost to profits that far exceeded the stimulus initially provided by the First World War (see Appendix D). The Allied war effort re-booted the Indian economy, and the importance of the Chartered's operations in Calcutta in particular. Earnings on British trade with Bengal rose to levels not seen since the early 1920s. A small satellite office had been opened in 1939, in Fairlie Place across the road from the red and white towers of the main branch in Clive Street, and the timing proved fortuitous – though the burden of dealing with a huge surge of paperwork may nonetheless have taken its toll: the Calcutta Agent, D. R. Kinloch, died suddenly just before Christmas 1941. Then came Japan's entry into the war, and the liquidation of every Chartered branch east of India. With so much of the network lost, and its combined pre-war Home and Foreign Staffs reduced by enlistment and imprisonment from around 350 to not many more than 100 men, the Chartered might be supposed to have seen its profits retreating as fast as the Empire. In the event, brisk business for all the bank's main branches in the sub-continent – Bombay, Colombo and Madras as well as Calcutta – brought substantial compensation, while Head Office earnings at 38 Bishopsgate soared: as a result, over the four years of 1942–5, the Chartered's total annual operating income averaged £790,874 – a 30 per cent jump on the average achieved over the 1932–9 period. The cash position also showed a dramatic improvement.[72] Total deposits jumped to about £80 million through the war, having run along at about £45 million through the 1930s, while dividend payments halved on the back of a cut in the dividend rate at the outbreak of hostilities. The reduced pay-out cannot have enamoured the bank to its shareholders. Its market value dipped ominously in the first years of the war, closing 1942 at less than £4 million, compared with £5.6 million at the start of 1939 (and over £12 million in the late 1920s). But once the bank's survival seemed assured, the market capitalization began to recover – and had risen to almost £6.5 million even by the end of 1944, when the timing of Japan's final defeat was still far from clear.

After August 1945, the speed of the bank's return to normality was extraordinary. It was much assisted not just by the recovery of so many ledgers but also by the return to work of large numbers of the bank's pre-war employees – their loyalty no doubt greatly reinforced by the fact that the Chartered paid out in arrears all the wages it had had to suspend

across the network as part of the liquidation process. Perhaps in acknowledgement of the key role played by the more senior local clerks, many of
them appear in the post-war years to have been appointed as 'Assistant
Officers', that enigmatic ranking created in the 1930s and still just short
of covenanted status. (Many Portuguese clerks in Hong Kong, for example,
were so promoted – and were plainly the backbone of the Chartered's
workforce in the post-war Colony.) The bank's revival also owed much to
the recuperative powers – not to say, stiff upper lip – of the Foreign Staff,
most of whom could hardly wait to resume the ordered routines of their
pre-war existence.* Years of internment had done nothing to reduce their
sense of allegiance to the Chartered, as H. C. Hopkins, the Shanghai
Manager, insisted in a zealous letter home even before the end of August
1945. 'The officers here with me wish to assure you of their continued
loyalty to the Bank and of their earnest desire to place the affairs of the
Bank before their personal interests. They realize that the rehabilitation
of the Chartered Bank is of primary importance.'[73] Such sentiments were
welcome indeed at Head Office, where a shortage of eligible men for the
East was already a serious concern, as it was to remain for the next few
years. As Cockburn wrote to a colleague in New York: '[staffing] has
become so difficult as to threaten the effective working of the Bank, unless
our officers – at the risk of impairing their health – are willing to continue
to sacrifice their rights to furlough relief for some time longer'.[74] In the
event, many agreed to forego home leave; several in urgent need of a break
had to be persuaded to leave the East; and, of those who did return home,
most were back within a few months.

We can catch a flavour of what the post-war reconstruction entailed
for these impressively dedicated individuals, from a confidential report
written in 1948 by three visitors to the East from the Midland Bank's
Overseas Department in the City.[75] (The Midland had no overseas branches
of its own, and had opted instead to build a strong international presence
by spinning a web of close correspondent relationships with local banks
across the globe.) The trio spent almost four months travelling between
Karachi and Shanghai, charged with assessing the competitive position of
all the exchange banks. They not only called on every main office of the
Chartered, but also resided in many places as guests of the local Chartered

---

* Probably the same was true of the Yokohama Specie Bank men who had served with the
Imperial Japanese Army in south-east Asia. One of them, a Mr Iijima, had been classified as
a war criminal by the Occupation Forces in Tokyo and was fortunate to land a post-war job
with the Chartered Bank as its Japanese Business Adviser. Perhaps fortified by the inside
knowledge he had gained in the war, Mr Iijima proved a great success. (W. C. L. Brown,
letter to the author, 5 October 2011.)

managers, staying in their homes and enjoying some lavish hospitality. They were struck again and again by the pressure of work across the Chartered's network and the application shown by the staff. The intensity of the activity in many branches surprised them almost as much as the affluence on display in local shops – by comparison, anyway, with the straitened standards of post-war Britain (' "window-shopping" in Singapore is an unforgettable experience'). Shanghai made an especially strong impression, and they noted of the Chartered's offices on the Bund:

> Guards with fixed bayonets were at the doors and a 'White Russian' superintended the long queues of Chinese anxious to exchange their US dollars into gold yuan [just launched by the Nationalists as a new currency for the country]. The Chinese staff in the bank are most efficient and work extremely long hours, as do in fact the European staff. We were often in the office at 8.30am by which time work was in full swing, yet lights were always burning at 8pm. Life in the Chartered Bank out East is not an easy one and Shanghai Branch is no exception.

The Manager there by 1948 was the diligent G. A. P. Sutherland, who had chronicled life in Changi so carefully (and, true to character, was now busying himself with lessons in Mandarin before starting work every day). Other managers encountered on the trip included two of the three Hong Kong men incarcerated in Canton at the end of the war: Reg Camidge was now running the Colombo office and Gerry Leiper was back in Hong Kong as the Accountant (though his wife, Helen, had never properly recovered from internment, and after returning with her husband to Hong Kong had died in 1947).* Above all, there was H. C. Hopkins himself, late of Shanghai and now at the head of what had emerged since the war as easily the biggest and most glamorous of all the Chartered's branches – Singapore.

---

* Leiper's other close colleague, W. A. Cruikshank, was also back at work, having initially been flown urgently to an Allied hospital in Japan, and had accepted a fresh posting – back to Japan. This prompts one to wonder if their wartime hardships left any of the former internees disinclined to serve again in the East, let alone in Japan itself. There are almost no records of any such reaction. Indeed, few members of the Foreign Staff ever asked to be reassigned to Head Office. A rare exception was David Gibson, a Glaswegian who had been captured as an army conscript in Malaya in 1942 and had then endured almost three years labouring on the Burma–Siam Railway. Having only joined the Chartered in December 1947 aged twenty-seven, he was posted nine months later to Indonesia and found the regimented existence of a Sub-Accountant living in a bank mess in Asia altogether too reminiscent of his days as a PoW. 'Two Dutch doctors came to see me. I said, "I can't stay here, I've got to get back to England." So after a few weeks the bank got me back.' Gibson subsequently had a distinguished career at 38 Bishopsgate, becoming Head of the Foreign Exchange Department in 1967. He retired in 1982. (Interview with author, 7 June 2011.)

SINGAPORE BRANCH

Chartered Bank's Raffles Square branch in Singapore, opened in 1916 and drawn in 1948

The Midlanders stayed for eleven days with Hopkins in his magnificent bank house that had formerly been the official residence of the Sultan of Johore. They thus had plenty of time to savour the full measure of their host's lofty status in the Colony. While a Committee Member at the Singapore Club (the most prestigious watering hole of the expatriate business classes), at the Golf Club and at the Chamber of Commerce, he was also Steward of the Singapore Turf Club, President of the Tanglin Club (Singapore's version of the clubs of St James's) and Chairman of the all-important Malayan Exchange Bankers' Association. His was a personal portfolio verging perilously on that of the *Mikado*'s Grand Poobah and Lord High Everything Else, but Hopkins held down more than a string of fancy titles. As the Singapore Manager, he ran a huge operation now at the heart of the Chartered's network, employing 22 Foreign Staff and 250 Malay and Chinese employees. By way of comparison, the Midlanders noted a total complement of around ninety in Colombo, eighty in Hong Kong and thirty in Batavia.

Powering the rise of the Singapore business was the dramatic growth of tin and rubber exports from the Malay states, now the core of the Chartered's franchise. (The bank had eight branches along the archipelago, in addition to Penang, Kuala Lumpur and Singapore itself.) Monthly shipments for rubber had shot past the record levels of 1941 by the end of 1946; and tin, which as an industry had taken rather longer to rehabilitate, was well on its way to doubling the 1940 export volume for the full year of 1948. The fortunes of both figured large in all discussions in the Chartered's Court through these years. (Several members of the Court had a substantial personal stake in the Malaysian rubber and tin trades. Only tea held a comparable place in the Directors' private business affairs beyond the confines of the City. Another Director of the Eastern merchant firm Boustead & Co., Cecil Cherry, joined the Court in 1948 and declared his interests as a Director in four of the largest rubber plantation companies in Malaya. James Milne, who had been on the Court since 1942, was a member of the Council of the Rubber Growers' Association and held directorships in more than thirty Eastern businesses, the majority of them tea and rubber concerns.[76]) Most of the rubber and tin shipments were crossing the Pacific to North America. Just as the collapse of the US auto industry had dealt a shattering blow to the region in 1931, so now boom times in Detroit were fuelling an extraordinary resurgence. This gave South Asia a special significance for the City of London, given the parlous state of Britain's currency. Dollars paid by US companies to Malayan exporters had to be exchanged for sterling or Straits dollars, under the rules of the Sterling Area in place since 1939 – and this made the region a hugely important source of foreign reserves for the Treasury. As the Midlanders noted in 1948, 'Singapore and Malaya earn more hard currency than does the United Kingdom itself'. Unsurprisingly, the Malayan Communist Party's attempts to drive the British out of Malaya after the war prompted a harsh response, and by the summer of 1948 British and Commonwealth troops were fighting Communist guerrillas in the jungles of the archipelago. Tin mines and rubber plantations were a prime target for the insurgency, and were protected accordingly. This entailed not just a shrewd deployment of soldiers in the field but official backing to lock in London insurance policies, so averting any suspension of the precious exports. (Government support on the insurance front was reflected in the steadfast description of the crisis as the 'Malayan Emergency', which allowed – as the declaration of a colonial *war* would not have done – the continuation of insurance cover from a war-shy Lloyd's of London.)

Meanwhile opportunities to extend Britain's colonial (and dollar-earning) assets beyond Malaya had not been neglected. The North Borneo Chartered Company's rubber-rich territories, badly damaged by the war, had been assimilated in 1946 as the Crown Colony of North Borneo – today's Malaysian state of Sabah – as had the neighbouring territory of Sarawak, hitherto ruled by the Brooke family as a British protectorate. Export businesses prospered in both states, and the Chartered opened five new branches to help finance them.* Like the operations in the Western Malay states, all were co-ordinated and funded from Singapore. 'The customers of the Chartered include most of the rubber and tin firms', observed the Midlanders, 'with the result that there is a steady flow of bills [to the Singapore branch] which enable Mr Hopkins to have much the largest share of the "exchange business".' Hopkins reckoned that the fixed expenses of his branch were more or less covered by its domestic

---

* The only pre-war branch in the region had been established at Kuching, on the mouth of the Sarawak River in 1924. Opened in the immediate post-war years were branches at Sandakan (1946) and Kota Kinabalu (1946) in British North Borneo (now a Crown Colony), and in Sibu (1947) and Miri (1950) in Sarawak. Staffing these extensions to the network was a challenge for the Chartered. One of its young Singapore officers, Richard McGregor, was sent off in 1947 to reconnoitre the prospects on the east coast of North Borneo, where European managers of local rubber and tobacco plantations were struggling to modernize their operations. McGregor spent several days tramping the territory from tiny coastal ports and put up the case for an office at the remote settlement of Lahad Datu (Report, 28 May 1947, CH03/01/10/02/A). Within days of his report's submission, it was announced that the Hongkong Bank had opened a branch at the next town along the coast, Tawau, which must have greatly strengthened McGregor's case. But the Chartered, unlike its much bigger rival in Hong Kong, simply could not spare the men to run another remote outpost (Head Office to Singapore Manager, 9 June 1947) and Lahad Datu had to wait until 1956 for its Chartered branch. Tawau got its own three years later.

lending, leaving the exchange operations (which he ran himself, on a very short rein) to account for its profits. And very substantial they were, too. Starting in 1947, the Singapore branch was for years the highest single contributor to the operating earnings of the Chartered's overseas network by a country mile, accounting for just over 15 per cent of the aggregate earnings for the 1946–53 years. In 1953, it earned more than 38 Bishopsgate.

Most of the Chartered's other principal South Asian operations were also flourishing by the late 1940s. Rapidly improving results in Kuala Lumpur, Bangkok and Djakarta – as well as in other traditional centres like Bombay, Calcutta and Hong Kong, to which we will return – helped fuel a steep rise in the bank's 'real profits' through the post-war years: one analysis suggests that they more than doubled between 1946 and 1949.[77] The total figure then went on growing impressively – though after 1949, of course, it measured pounds worth $2.30 each instead of just over $4.00. The devaluation of sterling in September that year, unlike sterling's divorce from the Gold Standard in 1931, cost the Chartered nothing. On the contrary, reserves had been held in dollars against the possibility, and the devaluation accounted for one-third of a modest growth in the sterling-denominated balance sheet over the course of the year.[78] More importantly, subsequent income streams were boosted by the higher sterling value of commodities that were largely dollar-priced on world markets. Of all the key Asian exporting countries where the Chartered had branches, only Pakistan failed to devalue in line with sterling's fall. The others, including the rest of the sub-continent, the Malayan Federation and Hong Kong, all belonged to the bloc of countries treated as one – the 'Sterling Area' – for the purposes of foreign-exchange controls as supervised by the Bank of England and accommodated within the international arrangements agreed at Bretton Woods in 1944. The bank's operating costs thus remained largely unchanged, while the sterling value of its mostly dollar-denominated revenues jumped ahead. The result was a performance as encouraging as it was unexpected. Shy of parading its good fortune, the Court took to revealing a 'published profit' of only around 40 per cent of the 'real' profit from 1950 onwards. (The UK Companies Act of 1948 had obligingly excluded banks from the general ruling that companies needed henceforth to keep shareholders informed of their true profits.)

The combination of briskly reviving demand for commodities, supportive British government policies and a weaker pound after 1949 proved especially restorative for the Chartered – but it also served as a tonic for the other forerunner banks of Standard Chartered through the immediate post-war era. Rising demand for vegetable oils, cocoa and the many other basic commodities of West Africa soon perked up the profitability of the Bank of British West Africa, whose operations had been effectively marooned for much of the war. The new firmness in world markets was accompanied by a government-led restructuring of the domestic links between farmers, official marketing boards, merchants and shippers that had the side-effect – not unwelcome to the BBWA – of further boosting the need for local seasonal advances.[79] The resulting post-war growth itself posed some difficulties for the bank. Having relentlessly cut back on its cost base through the 1930s, it was barely able to keep up with the staffing demands made by an expanding business. A generation of British managers hired before and after the First World War was now retiring, and the bank had trouble replacing them. The physical discomforts of living in remote branches, usually bereft of running water, let alone electricity, seemed less alluring to their prospective successors. Nor did Head Office find it easy to abandon the skinflint approach to salaries that had helped it eke out a profit through the Depression.* In rebuilding its network, the bank had increasingly to turn to local African clerks: by 1953 it had more than 1,100 employees in the region, of whom only 428 were expatriates, compared with 850 in 1930.[80] The increased reliance on local recruits seems not to have impeded its growth: after an initial dip below £165,000 in 1947, real profits climbed steadily and were fast approaching the £½ million mark as the bank took on a new Chairman in 1951 and a new General Manager in 1952.

Staffing shortages were similarly a problem on the other side of the continent, for the Standard Bank in Kenya, Uganda and Tanganyika. The Nairobi branch was the Standard's largest in East Africa, and had one-third fewer British staff at the end of 1946 than in 1939.[81] The bank could hardly find enough expatriates to fill the gaps left by the war in its existing East Africa network, let alone the officers needed for six additional branches that it felt compelled to open in the face of an unprecedented growth in trade. (Mechanized ledgers were hastily adopted to make up the shortfall, with sometimes chaotic consequences.) But while its business in East

---

* This drew a singular rebuke from a British judge in Nigeria in 1950, passing sentence on an expatriate manager of the local BBWA branch convicted of defrauding the bank. 'I find it difficult, if not impossible, to understand how your late employers expect a man in your position, who has a certain standard to maintain, to keep up that standard or even do more than merely exist, on the salary which was being paid to you . . . I cannot do better than describe your salary as a niggardly, wretched salary for the manager of a branch of the importance of the one in Port Harcourt.' He sent the man down for thirteen months, all the same. (Richard Fry, *Bankers in West Africa*, pp. 175–6.)

Africa was undoubtedly showing a lot more promise, it remained small beer for the Standard by comparison with burgeoning operations in the three territories grouped together as Central Africa – Nyasaland, Northern Rhodesia and, above all, Southern Rhodesia. Staffing was no problem here: the total number of employees rose from about 360 in 1945 (roughly the same size, we might note, as the Chartered's combined Home and Foreign Staffs that year) to about 900 in 1953.[82] Recruits were drawn from a rapidly growing population of European settlers, especially in Southern Rhodesia. (The latter attracted well over 100,000 immigrants between 1945 and 1953, compared with just a few thousand a year before 1939.) Keeping its new young bankers busy was a regional economy that by the 1950s was setting new records almost every year, powered by agricultural commodities from Southern Rhodesia and Nyasaland, and a quantum jump in copper exports from Northern Rhodesia. As the Standard's Central African network grew from fifteen to twenty branches, the Directors in London decided the time had come to carve it out as a discrete entity. In 1950 it was given its own administration under a General Manager based in Salisbury – a step that shrewdly anticipated the formation of the Central African Federation less than three years later. Within South Africa itself, meanwhile, the huge domestic franchise of the Standard Bank had prospered in line with the fortunes of the whole country, amply reflected in a powerful post-war bull market on the Johannesburg Stock Exchange. The bank's network of branches grew steadily, rising by about 20 per cent between 1945 and 1953.[83] The nature of its South African operations remained, in all essentials, unchanged – though its earnings from trade finance assumed greater importance, with the export of diamonds and many other commodities reaching record levels. And, no less than the Chartered Bank in Asia, the Standard of course gained handsomely from operating within the Sterling Area. The sterling value of gold rose 44 per cent on the back of the 1949 devaluation – to which the government in Pretoria this time aligned itself with alacrity.

The fourth of the Standard Chartered's forerunners, the Eastern Bank, seemed well-positioned after the war to take advantage of a momentous development for potentially the biggest dollar-earning commodity of them all, greater even than gold. The immensity of the Arabian Peninsula's oil fields had been confirmed in 1943–4: 'In those two years the size of the potential treasure seemed to increase almost beyond imagination.'[84] The Eastern was a little slow off the mark in the first years of peace. It had already been shut out of Kuwait, much to its frustration, by an exclusive twenty-year licence awarded by the Emirate's ruling family to the Imperial Bank of Iran in 1941; and it hesitated over plans to open a branch in Saudi

Arabia, where US banks looked certain to call the tune, given the strangle-
hold over the kingdom's nascent oil industry established by 1945 for US
oil interests (meaning essentially Aramco, the jointly owned subsidiary of
Standard Oil of California and Texaco).[85] But with its strong presence in
Iraq and its own monopoly status in Bahrain, the Eastern seemed sure
eventually to enjoy a significant share of the Gulf's radically altered prospects. It opened another branch in the lower Gulf in 1949, at the port of
Doha, in the Emirate of Qatar – by which time even hardened US oil men
were expressing awe at the strikes made in the desert sands just north of
the Saudi–Qatar border. A British banker in California wrote to a colleague in New York at the start of the year, passing on a typical snippet
to illustrate the US industry's excitement: 'One of the Standard Oil officials mentioned to me a while back that some of the Arabian wells are
yielding 5,000 barrels per day; the average yield in this country is 27 barrels per day!'[86] Once oil shipments from the region began rising in earnest,
and pouring dollar royalties into the coffers of the ruling families, local
economies along the Gulf coast were plunged into a new era. Small towns
that had hitherto scarcely changed at all for generations started to acquire
a first airport, a first electricity power station, a first sea-water distillation
plant, a first modern hospital. Leading merchant families, setting up
import agencies for Western companies, were now potentially valuable
banking customers – as, of course, were the rulers themselves. When the
Emir of Bahrain, Sheikh Salman bin Hamad Al-Khalifa, visited London
for the Coronation of Queen Elizabeth in June 1953, the Directors of the
Eastern Bank threw a huge lunch in his honour at the Savoy Hotel. Unlike
those arranging the dinner for King Faisal in 1927, they do not appear to
have had a problem finding guests.

The retention of British influence in the Gulf, along with the rush of
new white settlers into Central and Eastern Africa and the resurgence of
the successful British colonies in Singapore and Hong Kong, encouraged
a widespread belief among the British ruling classes in these years that the
Empire was far from finished. It was sensible to give it a new incarnation
as the British Commonwealth, or even (after 1949) just plain 'Commonwealth', but the paramount importance of British political traditions and
institutions across the former lands of the Empire would remain, many
hoped and believed, just as vital as ever to their progress. And their grateful adherence to the same would, by the same token, continue to underpin
Britain's place in the world. In fact, given her critical need to feed her
besieged home economy and to earn US dollars with which to rebuild her
domestic industry, Britain's dependence on the Empire would be more
important than ever. 'In the new economics of siege,' as a recent study has

noted, 'the commercial value of empire rose like a rocket . . . The result by 1950 was that Britain sent a larger proportion of its exports to empire countries than at any time in its history.'[87] The overseas British banks prospered accordingly, and took some pride in their success at facilitating the much needed resuscitation of the country's colonial businesses. None more so than Chartered Bank. It was around this time that the Chartered commissioned an official history to help commemorate its centenary in 1953.* (The principal architect of the project was Harold Faulkner, the former political officer in China, who had managed the Manchester branch since 1938 and returned to Head Office as Secretary in 1949.) The history's brief summary of the years since the war, which we can assume carried the imprimatur of the Court, made a point of celebrating the revival of Britain's trade with the East and its consequences for the bank:

> When the General Management in Head Office had reviewed the immediate post-war situation in the East and the capacity of the Bank's reconstituted branch organization to resume business . . . the necessity of helping British commercial enterprises that were seeking to rehabilitate their businesses in the East became of paramount urgency. The officers of the Bank everywhere were instructed to meet the financial requirements of all who were making their way homeward [to the East]. Few of the British firms and companies which had succeeded in regaining footholds in their former spheres of activity were in a position to prove their credit-worth and to satisfy the conventional requirements of a lending banker. The Bank, trusting to its past experience of the integrity of its former customers and conscious of its duty to commerce, decided that no reasonable request for accommodation of banking services should be refused . . . It is pleasant to set on record that the Bank's policy, despite its financial hazards, led to a vast accession of business on a scale unprecedented in any previous phase of the Bank's history.

This 'vast accession of business' produced a surge in the Chartered's operating income, which jumped from £1.5 million to £2.3 million and then to £3.1 million in the two full years after the 1949 devaluation. The prospects for the Chartered struck its own staff as being in many ways brighter than at any time since the early 1920s – and the same was true for most of Britain's overseas banks, including the other forerunner banks. They shared an optimism that their longstanding franchises would survive the realignments of the post-war world. Given the virtual elimination of German and Japanese competitors – and of most French and Russian banks,

---

* This was *Realms of Silver*, eventually published in 1954 – see Appendix A.

too – those franchises might even prove a richer legacy of Empire than the City in general seemed to be expecting.

The financial markets took a more nuanced view – indeed, their general stance appeared conspicuously less bullish. City investors since the war had never rediscovered their long-lost enthusiasm for the overseas banks: share prices in the sector, as a multiple of real profits, by the early 1950s had slipped significantly lower. In 1953, real profits at the BBWA were 2.6 times higher than in 1946, yet the bank's market value was almost 20 per cent lower. The market value of the Eastern Bank had similarly fallen 20 per cent over these seven years, despite all the excitement over Middle Eastern oil (which, admittedly, had yet to make much difference to earnings at the Eastern itself). The value of the Standard Bank of South Africa in 1953 was still down almost 14 per cent, even after recovering from a collapse in 1951–2 that had at one stage seen its market capitalization fall close to half that of 1946. The numbers for the Chartered were better, but not by much: the bank in 1953 was valued 10 per cent higher than in 1946 – but its real profits over the period had almost exactly trebled (from £533,974 to £1,606,394). As ever, there were accounting quirks to be allowed for. Most obviously, real profits were undisclosed and reported profits were in all cases very substantially lower; allowances had also to be made for the distorting effect of sterling's devaluation. Nonetheless, the general message from the stock market was unmistakeable. Investors by the early 1950s had a much keener appreciation of the risks entailed in overseas banking. Politicians, diplomats and brigadiers could talk up the continued importance of Britain's imperial traditions all day long, but the City had its doubts. Might not a fresh vision for the Empire turn out in the end to be no more than a mirage?

Patterns of trade that had underpinned the Empire for a century or more were undergoing profound changes, and investors had begun adjusting to them. The proportion of Britain's exports going to the Empire may have held up surprisingly, but Britain's share of world exports was falling steadily – from 23 per cent in 1929, it was down to 16 per cent by 1953 (and would be 8 per cent by 1970).[88] Economic ties with the white settler economies of the Empire were rapidly loosening – not least in South Africa, where the election of a Nationalist government in 1948 did nothing to dampen the growth of some alarmingly strident anti-British sentiments in the business community (on which, more later). The Sterling Area survived the 1949 devaluation of the pound, but doubts inevitably lingered about the sustainability of the Bank of England's currency regime that had always been integral to the overseas banks' activities. Most obviously of all, many of the great commodity-exporting territories of the world

were now riven with hostility towards their former colonial masters, especially in Asia. By the early 1950s it was plain that the British in Malaya
and Singapore had found a more effective response to this than had the
Dutch in their East Indies or the French in Indo-China. By then, though,
investors had already had to come to terms with a new map of the overseas
banking world, abruptly redrawn by the collapse of the Raj and the culmination of the Chinese civil wars in victory for Mao Zedong's
Communists. Shareholders in the Chartered Bank of India, Australia and
China might even have been wondering to themselves whether it was
perhaps time their bank opted at last for a different name.

3. PARTING WITH THE PAST

In neither India nor China did the epochal events of 1947 and 1949,
respectively, cause the Chartered's Directors any surprise; both had been
a long time gestating. But the outcome for the bank's operations on the
ground was a different matter – which came as a cause for some satisfaction in the one case and an unpleasant shock in the other.

The days of the Raj were already numbered well before the end of the
war, and work on the transition to an independent India began shortly
afterwards. The preparations triggered a revival of Nationalist antipathy
towards the position enjoyed in the country by the British exchange banks.
They had, after all, always been an integral part of the administrative
machinery of the Raj.* The Chartered was regularly singled out for particular attention, not only as the largest of the seven banks in the group
but also as the (94 per cent) owner of the Allahabad Bank.[89] When the
country's Central Legislature in 1946 began debating a Bill for the future

---

* This was exemplified by a colourful episode in March 1946, when the governments in
London and Delhi asked the bank to handle all security arrangements for the shipment of a
spectacular collection of diamonds from London to Bombay. The gems were needed as the
centrepiece of a ceremony marking the Diamond Jubilee of the Aga Khan: he had to be
weighed in diamonds. The mandate tested the initiative of the Chartered's management,
when the precious cargo – in eighteen sealed boxes – went missing. Only by despatching a
senior man from London, G. P. Cooke, to work with the Viceroy's Private Secretary in Delhi
was it possible for the bank to establish what had happened. The diamonds had been sent
from Britain on a Royal Navy vessel as an unspecified (and uninspected) diplomatic consignment, without informing either the War Office or the captain of the ship – which, as it
happened, had been diverted on its way to Bombay and sent off to Basra. Cooke needed to
pull a lot of strings to get a BOAC flying-boat to collect the diamonds and fly them to Karachi,
whence he accompanied them, under armed guard, on their onward journey to Bombay. They
arrived safely on the eve of the ceremony – in which the Aga Khan was duly weighed and not
found wanting. (H. C. MacColl Memorandum, July 1951, pp.79–82, LMA: CB101, File 2.)

regulation of the banking sector, a Select Committee tried to add a provision that no single shareholder could own more than 10 per cent of a joint-stock bank – a blatant move to nobble the Chartered's ownership of the Allahabad. This marked the return of an old adversary, Manu Subedar, whose vitriolic observations about the Chartered and its ownership of the Allahabad had been such a feature of the 1931 Banking Inquiry. From London, a former Calcutta Agent (R. W. Buckley) wrote to warn the current Agent (C. O. Tasker) about the cut of Subedar's jib – both Chartered men were keen sailors – and he quoted from the 1931 Report some of Subedar's more outspoken views on the purchase of the P&O Bank and thereby the Allahabad (as from para. 215: 'It would be impossible to estimate, but no one can deny, that in a million little ways Indian interests must have receded and foreign interests advanced in trade through this acquisition.').[90] Tasker had already begun orchestrating a counter-offensive, drawing on his influence as a leading figure in the Bengal Chamber of Commerce, so he was probably vexed to read later in the same letter that the Court had nonetheless settled on instructions even more cautious and risk-averse than usual: ' . . . we are of the opinion that the least said about our fears the better, and that . . . no action whatever, either directly or indirectly, should be taken to plead our case. If and when it should become necessary we must just face the facts.' (In the event, the threatened amendment was dropped.)

The animosity towards the Chartered was partly driven by exasperation over its stalled progress with Indianization. The war had accelerated the delegation of responsibilities to local staff, willy nilly, and there were now many more Assistant Officers – often referred to in many countries simply as 'staff officers' or 'staff assistants' – than in pre-war days; but they received little or no formal training, and the bank's covenanted ranks were still as closed as ever to Indians. Many of the bank's critics also had scarcely concealed commercial motives for their antipathy. The number of Indian joint-stock banks had risen from 100 in 1935 to more than 250 by 1946. Yet their share in the financing of India's overseas trade, at about 15 per cent, was little higher than it had been in 1930; Indian shipping and insurance businesses had likewise made slow headway. Worse, the pressures of the wartime economy had seen the exchange banks beginning to encroach much more on the financing of shipments from the interior to the ports. The establishment of the Reserve Bank of India had so far made little difference to the status of the exchange banks – the RBI had a British Governor until 1943 – but many looked forward to the demotion of the banks as a natural sequel to the ending of the Raj.

When Independence finally arrived, the future of banking regulation was of far less immediate concern to the Chartered's managers than dealing with the momentous consequences of Partition. 'In their haste to get shot of India, [the British] left behind a chaos that almost undid two centuries of orderly government.'[91] The decision was taken by the last British Viceroy, Lord Mountbatten, to bring forward the legal date for the creation of India and Pakistan to 15 August 1947 – it had originally been envisaged that the Raj would end in the second half of 1948 – and the authorities were utterly unprepared for the atrocities that ensued. The flight of millions of dispossessed migrants across the redrawn map of the sub-continent sparked appalling violence that lasted for several months. The Chartered's eight branches seem not to have been deliberately targeted in any of the rioting – the experience of the leading Dutch banks in the mayhem that accompanied the end of the Dutch East Indies was far worse in this respect – but random violence was a constant danger: in Delhi, a young British Assistant Manager was shot dead while walking in the street. The Foreign Staff relied heavily on the advice of their most experienced senior clerks – many of whom had worked for the bank all their lives* – to provide as much protection as possible for the several hundred local men on the payroll, the majority of whom were Hindus. As it happened, this was even the case at the branch in Karachi that was now the financial centre of the new Muslim state of Pakistan. Inevitably, with millions of Hindu refugees streaming south from the old West Punjab, the situation of the Karachi staff gave rise to some concern. But Hindus actually still made up the majority of Karachi's population, and as late as the end of 1947 it was still hoped the Chartered's local staff could remain in place. Then the status quo was brutally disrupted. On 5 January 1948, the authorities in the city had to arrange an overnight stay for two hundred Sikhs who were travelling from the West Punjab to Bombay. They were asked to bed down in a Sikh temple in the middle of the city – and just before dawn all two hundred had their throats slit by a Muslim mob. Every Hindu family in Karachi now feared for their lives. The Chartered branch, faced with a twenty-four-hour curfew and martial law in the streets, needed to act quickly to safeguard its terrified Hindu employees, as someone in the branch itself recounted two years later:

> Through the good offices of our Agent, Mr D. W. Henderson, the European officers of our staff obtained passes [to travel in the city] and on arrival at the office found a large percentage of the Hindu staff inside, not daring to

---

* A list of clerks drawn up in Calcutta in 1951 included fourteen men who had worked for the bank for thirty-five years or more ('The Story of the CBIAC in Calcutta', LMA: CH03/01/14/030).

leave. They were without food and very anxious about their families. At this time about 80 per cent of the staff were Hindus, the remainder being Parsees, and it was the prime consideration of the Agent and his European Officers to care for the Hindu members of the staff who were in such a desperate plight. Food was brought in and as many families as possible were brought in to the office where they lived with their menfolk.[92]

The four Foreign Staff and the Parsee clerks barricaded the entrances to the office against unwanted visitors, and then ferried food and water into the building for the next six days, until the mobs in the city had dispersed. All the Hindus were eventually helped to travel safely to India, and the bank set about the recruitment of a new, and Muslim, staff. (It was to be trained under the watchful eye of a Parsee clerk, N. M. Dinshaw, Karachi's Chief Cashier since 1908 – and he appears to have done a good job. After a volatile few years, the Chartered thrived as never before in Karachi. It soon had ten British managers to handle the city's emergence as effectively the only port for the exports from West Punjab that had hitherto flowed through Bombay. The Karachi branch in 1950 was actually the second most profitable of the entire network.)

Other aspects of dealing with Partition were less dramatic, entailing more familiar challenges. A decision had to be made, for example, over the possible launch of an additional branch in the newly formed East Pakistan (now Bangladesh). East Bengal's jute growers had lost access to the port of Calcutta, and by late 1947 were pressing the bank to open in Chittagong, where some relatively primitive port facilities were soon the target of ambitious expansion plans to be funded by the Pakistani government. The Manager in Calcutta, A. C. Watkins, proposed sending one of his senior colleagues, James Forsyth, on a brief visit to Chittagong to scout its prospects, en route to returning to Britain on furlough. This idea drew a typically forthright response in London from Buckley, the former Calcutta Agent who was now in the final weeks of his career as Manager at Bishopsgate. As ever, Buckley had his eye on the competition, and especially the Hongkong Bank:

> I am not in favour of Forsyth inspecting the place unless we are prepared to open at once which I think we should do. For him to go there and report on his arrival home would only encourage another Bank to get in before us. I feel we should start in temporary premises . . . [93]

This view prevailed and, before the end of the year, the Chartered had committed itself to a Chittagong branch and had assigned a Sub-Accountant from Calcutta, J. F. Vicars, to take charge – though it meant his leaving his wife and new-born child behind in Calcutta, perhaps for some months.* The new branch posed plenty of logistical problems – it was to be regarded as a hardship posting for years to come – and had to be run wholly independently of Calcutta from the start. Its cash requirements were met from Karachi (in new Pakistani rupees), and within a few months it was providing much needed financing for the jute exporters of East Bengal.

Once the upheavals of 1947–8 had been survived, and the last formal vestiges of the Raj had been swept away, those in India anticipating the demise of Chartered Bank must have welcomed a flurry of regulatory proposals intended to restrict the activities of the exchange banks – one new Reserve Bank Order, for example, required them 'to maintain 75 per cent of their "assets" in India'[94] – and moves were made to inaugurate a new licensing regime. Without doubt India's legal environment became more complicated overnight, and within a few years the authorities (in the shape of the All India Industrial Tribunal on Banking Disputes of 1950) would be laying down terms and conditions of local employment. Nevertheless, one of the most striking features of the banking landscape in the immediate post-1947 years was not the demise of the Chartered Bank but its remarkable prosperity. In Bombay, profits dipped briefly then soared from early 1949. In Calcutta, the old P&O Banking branch in Fairlie Place, closed in 1944, had to be reopened for four years in 1947 to help the bank cope with the rush of business until a permanent 'annex' branch could be established (at 41 Chowringhee, and still there).

For this scarcely predicted outcome of Indian independence for the bank, there were perhaps two main explanations. In the first place, the disappearance of the Raj made surprisingly little immediate difference to British commercial activity in India. British corporate clients were the mainstay of the Chartered's business, and they went on flourishing. When the bank's Madras Agent suggested in 1950 that a Sub-Agency should be established in Cochin, he set down a profile of the customer base on which he was confident it would prosper.[95] Of twenty-five companies, twenty-one were more or less household names of British business (including tea

---

* The families of the Chartered Bank's British officers had always had to make sacrifices of this kind in the interests of the bank's advancement. In the 1920s, these passed without comment. By the 1970s, they were likely to prompt difficulties, needing to pass muster with expatriate wives. In 1947, a delicate balance prevailed. So the Calcutta Agent who recommended Vicars was not insensitive to his situation: 'before finally deciding to select him, we asked him for his reactions in the matter because it will probably be some time before his wife will be able to join him'. But the outcome was never really in much doubt. 'After due consideration, Mr Vicars has accepted the assignment.' (A. C. Watkins to Head Office, 19 December 1947, LMA: CH03/01/10/50/33.)

plantation agents like Harrison & Crosfield, textile manufacturers like J&P Coats, petroleum traders like Burmah-Shell Oil, and pharmaceutical outfits like ICI and Boots). When the Indian government set up an inquiry into the state of the country's jute-milling industry, which reported in 1954, it found 75 per cent of the mills still under the control of a dozen managing agency houses, almost all of them still British (including many names famous since the nineteenth century, like Bird/Heilgers, Thomas Duff, Jardine Henderson, McLeod's and Andrew Yule) – and most of them clients, naturally, of the Chartered.[96] A study of the British-owned plantations in Ceylon from the 1880s to the 1950s found that, while sales and closures began to thin their ranks after 1948, a majority (eighty-three tea companies and thirty-four rubber companies) were still going strong in May 1959.[97] And as if to cock a snook at those who had carped over its ownership of the Allahabad, the Chartered happily oversaw a fresh expansion of its Indian subsidiary: the Allahabad opened thirteen additional branches in 1949–51, only one fewer than it had added through the whole of the 1930s.[98]

The other key to the Chartered's post-independence record in the sub-continent lay in the strength of some formidable local managers – men like Reg Camidge, the former Manager in Hong Kong who had survived the ordeals of the war and now headed the branch in Colombo. In all the main offices of the region, the bank was fortunate to be led by individuals determined to consolidate its strengths, and confident that India would continue to need the Chartered's services, with or without the Raj. One of the more remarkable of these men was H. C. MacColl, the Agent in Bombay since 1944. A tall man with a commanding presence, he had worked for the bank in India since 1916 and had an unrivalled knowledge of its past. (When Head Office sought contributions from the field to the writing of the centenary history, he sent in by far the longest submission of all, an eighty-six-page memorandum on the story of the Bombay branch alone.[99]) Intensely proud of the achievements of the Raj, MacColl was forthright in his views of the post-Independence Government, as the three visitors from the Midland Bank recorded in the autumn of 1948: 'He deprecated in the strongest terms the efforts made by certain elements in the Government to eliminate British influence in the economic field.' Even so, he also impressed upon them that the start of a new political era in India was far from disastrous for the exchange banks – rather to the contrary, in fact.

> Mr McCall [sic] thought that their position today was far stronger than before Partition. Amenities for the Europeans were being slowly but systematically reduced (for example, two 'dry' days a week and the closing of

the old Yacht Club House in Bombay!), but Indian banks had neither the
resources nor the staff to take over the exchange banks' functions.*

Nor, he might have added, were they yet happy sharing business among
themselves, generally preferring instead to go on dealing with British
banks if this allowed them to avoid helping a domestic rival to prosper.

Another prominent Chartered manager in South Asia during the
post-war years was R. S. Wilson, who ran the Rangoon branch in Burma.
Having become a separately administered colony in 1937 (where previously it had been a province of the Raj), Burma had been devastated by
the war. One post-war assessment thought there had been 'a higher degree
of destruction [in Burma] than in any other area in the East'.[100] The country endured a stormy transition to full independence, featuring widespread
strikes in 1946, constant disruptions to foreign trade and bitter internecine
fighting among its political classes (triggering the assassination in 1947 of
Aung San, the prospective leader of post-independence Burma who had,
six months earlier, agreed the terms of Britain's withdrawal at a conference
in London). Burma escaped the kind of horrors seen in India's Partition,
but bitter ethnic rivalries helped fuel a protracted civil war after the break
from Britain in January 1948, and a recent history characterizes the
post-independence era as 'from the start an economic nightmare'.[101] It is
surprising, perhaps, that the Chartered Bank managed to revive its operations at all in these circumstances. But in Wilson it obviously had a man
on the ground with all the diplomatic talents traditionally required of
the Chartered manager in adversity. On his retirement in February 1950,
the local Burmese, Indian and Chinese Chambers of Commerce ('and the
Well-Wishers of the CBIAC') all rallied round to sign off an encomium
to his services:

> Sir, we like to emphasize here that by your untiring help to all the merchants
> in the sphere of paddy, rice, export and import enterprises [in] our new
> born Independent Union, you have indeed indirectly, if not directly,
> enhanced the greatly hampered progress of the most desirable works in
> constructing and rehabilitating our beloved war-shattered country . . . You
> have indeed done more than a thousand clever diplomats could do to bring
> about successful goodwill mission between our Union and any other foreign
> country in the wide world.[102]

---

* There is no record of the Royal Bombay Yacht Club (founded 1846) closing around this
time, and it flourishes to this day in its grand Gothic mansion around the corner from the
Taj Mahal Hotel. 'Dry days' involved a temporary ban on the sale of alcohol, though not on
its consumption.

The Chartered's profits during Wilson's time had been minimal, but its restored links with the millers on the Irrawaddy paid off over the next three years. The Korean War produced a steep rise in the price of rice, and for four years starting in 1950 the Rangoon branch outperformed many others in the Eastern network, with yearly earnings on a level not seen since the Great War.

Its success in weathering – however briefly – abrupt changes of the political climate in India and Burma attested again to the Chartered's enduring resilience, which many contemporaries supposed would continue to see it through the inevitable crises of the post-war world. Optimists, like those visitors from the Midland Bank in 1948, saw no reason to suppose otherwise:

> From our observations, the Exchange Banks as a whole are doing more business than ever before . . . [Indeed] their long standing, stability, soundness and integrity coupled with their experienced staff have made them more than ever before of great use to the Indian and Pakistani businessmen. In due course . . . the exchange banks will find their share of the business decreasing, but this cannot be envisaged for many years to come if normal factors alone are to play their part in the functioning of the banking system.

Perhaps this might have applied no less to China – but there, 'normal factors' were far from the only consideration. The end of the Second World War brought only a brief and bizarre interlude in the long war between the Nationalist and Communist forces. Coaxed into a personal meeting by the Americans, whom both sides wished to appease, Mao in September 1945 spent three weeks in talks with the Nationalist leader in Chungking. 'At a dinner and at a tea party, Mao shouted, "Long live President Chiang Kai-shek!".'[103] A pact was even announced, that hostilities were to be brought to an end. But after returning to his base in Yenan, Mao was soon ordering the Red Army back on to the offensive. By the end of the year, China was once again wracked by a civil war that had never really abated and was now fuelled by devious Soviet intervention (and abandoned Japanese weaponry). The desolation left by the long struggle against Japan was compounded in many provinces by the anarchy that now followed. In Manchuria, the looting and destruction were reckoned so catastrophic, according to a report from the Chartered's Tientsin branch, that it would take forty years just to lift economic activity back to the level left behind by the defeated Japanese army.[104] As the bank's managers set about reviving operations in Tientsin, Hankow, Tsingtao and Chungking as well as Shanghai – conditions were judged as yet too precarious to risk reopening

Dated, Rangoon, the 12th February 1950.

To,

Mr. R. S. Wilson,

The Agent,

The Chartered Bank of India, Australia & China,

Rangoon.

SIR,

WE, the well-wishers of the Chartered Bank of India, Australia & China, the Presidents and Members of The Union of Burma Chamber of Commerce & Industries, The Chinese Chamber of Commerce and The Indian Chamber of Commerce very respectfully beg to tender our humble and sincere respects in this form of address on this auspicious occasion of holding an excursion party in honour of bidding a ceremonious farewell to you.

Sir, you have indeed succeeded in leaving a well defined impression of your singular personality and virtuous morality in our memories by virtue of your foresight, sympathetic understanding and unreserved advice in all your personal contact with us in the course of our business transactions with your Bank and personal and social dealings with you.

We see in you a tremendous force of character and goodwill clothed in simplicity, constant desire to help with understanding and unbounded sympathy and unfailing advice, always wishing for the general welfare and progress of all merchants irrespective of whether big or small enterprise. Ready to help those who need help, with what is best in their interest, and with zeal, steadfastness and tremendous amount of patience, clear understanding and goodwill on your part.

Sir, we like to emphasise here that by your untiring help to all the merchants in the sphere of paddy, rice, export and import enterprises of our new born Independent Union, you have indeed indirectly, if not directly, enhanced the greatly hampered progress of the most desirable works in reconstructing and rehabilitating our beloved war shattered country, which has been in dire need of the sympathies, proper understanding, goodwill and co-operation of such persons as you have been in a position to confer.

We cannot, however, forget your kind help that you have so generously given to all of us without any reservation on your part and we are going to carry this glorious knowledge for a very long time during which time we shall pray for your long life, prosperity and happiness.

Sir, in fact, allow us to observe here before we conclude our humble address that grit of the kind displayed by you as a responsible officer of a world renowned bank is very uncommon and singularly unparallel in this country and that you have indeed done more than a thousand clever diplomats could do to bring about successful goodwill mission between our Union and any other foreign country in this wide world.

Last, but not the least, we take this opportunity of welcoming your successor, Mr. J. A. MacCullugh, and feel confident that we can always count on him for his generous help and guidance born out of ripe experience in the days to come and we, on our part, assure Mr. MacCullugh of our willing co-operation in the hard task of piloting the ship through safe channels.

Yours faithfully,

THE PRESIDENT AND THE MEMBERS OF
THE UNION OF BURMA CHAMBER OF COMMERCE & INDUSTRIES
THE CHINESE CHAMBER OF COMMERCE
THE INDIAN CHAMBER OF COMMERCE
AND
THE WELL-WISHERS OF
THE CHARTERED BANK OF INDIA, AUSTRALIA & CHINA.

The certificate presented to Chartered Bank's Rangoon Agent on his retirement in 1950

in Peking or Canton – the proximity of the front line and the scale of the fighting between Nationalists and Communists were both of acute concern. As too, on a very different level, were the interminable regulations and restrictions imposed on the banking sector by the Nationalist government, once again reinstated by early 1946 in Nanking.

But if such problems were to be seen as insuperable obstacles, the Chartered Bank would have quit China for good long ago. Pressing on in the face of such adversity was the Chartered's stock-in-trade – provided, naturally, that real demand existed for its services. Few doubted this was the case. As ever, it seemed, China remained a vast market needing a host of banks to service its foreign trade. Several American banks from New York and the West Coast were showing themselves only too keen to squeeze aside the Chartered. So the Court (once again) asserted Business as Usual: new young Foreign Staff were despatched; budgets were agreed for rebuilding work and the purchase of officers' accommodation; and British companies with pre-war links to China were politely reminded of the bank's continuing presence there. Through it all, the Directors did their best to weigh up a plethora of conflicting reports from the field. The British media were none too encouraging in their assessment of the military situation – but the Court was reassured by some of its own intelligence gathered on the spot, not least by that old champion of China's promise, Archie Rose. In his twenty-second year as a Director of the bank, the sixty-seven-year-old Rose made another Grand Tour of all the Asian offices in 1947, sending the Chairman a stream of letters and reports for the edification of colleagues just as he had done in the 1930s. He spent March and April travelling in China, and it left him 'less conscious of fundamental changes than of an upsurge of life and vitality, with reasonable prospects of recovery and prosperity'.[105] Rose thought the threat posed by Mao's Communists was being exaggerated by too many observers, and needed to be set in historical perspective:

> The persistent tendency of the Chinese to rebellion has . . . attracted undue attention both at home and abroad . . . [Mao Zedong and his men are] a party of reform, sometimes a bit violent in their methods, after the way of reformers . . . But these Communists are less drastic in their methods than were the early Communists of the 1920s . . . And the individualism of the Chinese is still his main characteristic. The best foreign military opinion assesses the two Parties [i.e. Nationalists and Communists] as about equal in effective strength – neither of them seems able to impose any real defeat on the other. The experts go so far as to suggest that the struggle is likely to be patched up before long.[106]

The Court welcomed his optimism, but it was steadily belied by events over the next eighteen months. These put huge strain on those working in the five branches still open in China. The reformed currency that was launched, as noted, just ahead of the arrival of those Midland Bank visitors in July 1948 had already slithered close to collapse by the time of their departure in October. As the Midlanders themselves reported, deposits in Shanghai were rising and falling by 40–50 per cent daily. Interest rates fluctuated violently, while foreign exchange transactions on many days were almost impossible. Both Shanghai and Tientsin actually managed to report modest profits for the year to December 1948, but elsewhere it was growing obvious that the bank had no choice but to evacuate its branches. Heavy defeats for the Nationalist forces of Chiang Kai-shek early in 1949 pointed to a Communist victory within months. The Chungking, Tsingtao and Hankow branches were all abandoned by May 1949. The best the Chartered could hope for was a clean-cut resolution of the civil war that would at least allow stability to be restored to the economy, and the Shanghai and Tientsin branches were for the moment retained. Perhaps the bank would in due course be able to adjust to the final victory of the Communists, as it had adjusted to so many regime changes in the past. Foreign trade, after all, would surely remain vital to the new government whatever its complexion.

In charge of more than a hundred local Chinese employees in the Shanghai branch were twelve British officers. One of them was a thirty-year-old Sub-Accountant, Hew Liller, who was later able to recall the events of 1949 in remarkable detail.[107] A burly Lincolnshire man with four years' pre-war service with the Midland Bank, he had been recruited to Bishopsgate in August 1946 and assigned to Shanghai a mere three months later. This rapid posting was an acknowledgement not just of his banking experience with the Midland but of an unusual talent for languages. During his wartime service in the RAF, he had learned Japanese before joining the Indian outpost of Bletchley Park at Anand Parbat outside Delhi, eavesdropping on enemy wireless traffic in Burma, and he had also mastered Hindi. (He recalled being offered a job by the Allahabad Bank before opting to be demobbed back to England.) Liller had enjoyed his time in Shanghai. He had rubbed along well with an English Manager who dubbed him 'the other Englishman' – the other ten officers being all Scots – until G. A. P. Sutherland's arrival left him in a minority of one. He shared a bachelor flat with three colleagues in the former French Concession, where a bank car collected them each morning for the short drive to Bund 18. Through the week, he worked hard as the junior in charge of the cash department; and at the weekends, he could leave the city for long expeditions shooting wildfowl in the countryside. His days, in fact, were not so very different from those of his predecessors in Shanghai over the past several decades. But Liller had an intimation of harder times to come when he was seconded for a short while to Tientsin in 1948: 'I had to fly into the city, as you couldn't go by rail any more. The Communists had surrounded it. We knew they were coming; we just didn't know what would happen when they arrived.'

Once back in Shanghai, Liller found the Foreign Staff numbers being rapidly reduced. By the early spring of 1949, he had moved into the Sub-Manager's house on his own and was working with just two other Sub-Accountants and a fresh Manager, yet another Scot. One evening, he chanced to visit the Bund and was surprised to see a string of coolies between the bank and one of the nearby wharves on the river. Silver ingots were being passed from man to man, as the Nationalists' bullion assets were decanted from the Chartered's huge vaults into a small vessel on the Whangpoo. This, as Liller shrewdly concluded, meant the fall of the city could not be far off. A few weeks later, on 27 May, he heard shooting in the night and woke to the news that the city had indeed been overrun. As he sat down to breakfast, he was surprised to find himself being called from outside:

> The Manager, 'Rusty' Forsyth was his name [previously based in Calcutta], turned up in his car and he'd got Tom Hobbs with him and Norman Saddler, and he said 'We're going to the bank.' I didn't think it was a very good idea because the streets were completely deserted apart from the odd body lying about. When we got to the bank, everything was very quiet. We went inside – there was nobody there at all. So I thought I'd go up onto the roof and have a look around, because it was a 12-storey building ... I climbed the stairs, stepped out and there was the Head Boy. His name was Beery (because he was) and he was just wandering about in his usual sodden state on the roof. I thought, Oh this is alright. I looked down, and there was nothing moving anywhere. All dead quiet. So we leaned over the parapet to look at the river and then suddenly – a couple of bangs. One bullet came whistling past me and the other hit the stone wall in front of me and ricocheted off over the river. I thought, this is getting a bit close, I think I'd better get away downstairs.[108]

They escaped home in the Manager's car, and lay low for the rest of the day. But the very next morning people returned to the streets – and the Chartered staff returned to their bank. Remarkably, the daily routine was then resumed down to the smallest detail: the Communists made no immediate attempt to disrupt the administration of the bank or its communications with London. Certainly the new regime made itself felt in savage ways. The bank's doctor, who had a room in the branch building, was interrogated so severely that he suffered a heart attack and was left in his room to die. Liller and his colleagues were also aware that many of their more well-to-do customers, and anyone suspected of having hoarded US dollars, were in great danger. ('People with money were disappearing: you didn't see them any more, they'd just gone – but they hadn't escaped. I used to go shooting with a bunch of quite wealthy Chinese and they disappeared, one after another . . . I think they were taken in and killed.') But the daily business of the bank generally went on without interruption. The (new-styled) Chief General Manager in Bishopsgate, Will Cockburn, had spent fourteen years of his career in China, from 1922 to 1936 – most of them in Shanghai – and he took an intense interest in the unfolding of events. He and his close colleagues in London were determined that the Chartered, if at all possible, should retain a presence in the country, even after the formal proclamation of the People's Republic, which followed in October 1949.[*]

But the Directors were offered scant encouragement, as the months went by. Obtaining entry and exit permits soon grew problematic. When Liller married the daughter of a local German businessman in January 1950, there was no possibility of his taking his bride on a brief honeymoon outside China. A new Accountant had been appointed to Shanghai in March 1949, John Shewan (one of the Fukushima Nine), and he had had to cool his heels in Hong Kong for over a year – now he was finally reassigned, but to Saigon. In June 1950, the Korean War broke out and the United States launched a naval blockade of all Chinese ports. The bank's Manager in Hong Kong, 'Dicky' Bird, noted drily in his half-yearly report the following month: 'Great hopes were built up in local Chinese, and certain foreign, commercial circles that Shanghai would once again be opened but the proved presence of war mines [along the coast] has dulled their optimism.'[109]

The bank's situation in China deteriorated rapidly thereafter. (The story in Hong Kong we shall return to later.) All import credits were wound down during the course of 1951. The prospect of a return to profitability looked remote by the end of that year, and the British officers felt

---

[*] There is no record of Rose's views at this time. Perhaps he clung a while longer to his earlier optimism, but he must soon have been disillusioned. He remained on the Court until 1952, retiring aged seventy-two. The Chairman replied to his resignation letter with notable grace: 'I can only be glad that I have been privileged to serve the Bank in your company for so long. We owe much to you.' (Vincent Grantham to Rose, 11 December 1952, LMA: CH03/01/10/06/07/K.) He died in 1961.

increasingly threatened by a fearful escalation of violence and intimidation that marked the next stage of Mao's revolution. Most of the remaining Foreign Staff in China (including Liller) were withdrawn, as the bank turned to extricating itself with as much dignity, and as few losses, as possible. A formal application to close both Shanghai and Tientsin completely was filed in June 1952 and all business in the country was suspended that September, when London withdrew Shanghai's telegraphic codebook. But the remaining British managers – two in Tientsin and two in Shanghai – were obliged by the Communist authorities themselves to go on attending the office, and it was soon apparent that negotiations over the bank's final withdrawal were going to be a fraught affair.[110] The Government in Peking, now 'Beijing', required the 'repayment' of all deposits held not just in the months leading up to 'Liberation', but also through the 1938–48 period *and* prior to 1937. (Any distinction between 'official' and customers' deposits seems not to have survived for long.) All were to be remitted in US dollars – badly needed in Beijing, since the Government's dollar holdings in New York had been frozen by the US authorities in 1950 – at a dollar/CNC exchange rate that prompted an expression of probably genuine disbelief from the bank in London: 'in the light of all that [has] happened, our Directors feel that this cannot represent the considered policy of the People's Government of China'.[111] But in fact it did, and the People's Government pursued it ruthlessly. The position of foreigners in China was fast reverting to their status at times of trouble in the nineteenth century, to judge from a letter sent out in 1953 by the hapless Shanghai Manager, G. K. Macfarlane (who had replaced 'Rusty' Forsyth in 1951):

> The writer was subjected to strong cross-examination by the [Government's] Inspectors ... We mention this in an endeavour to convey the unenviable position in which we are placed ... It is most difficult to apprise you of the exact atmosphere, and for humiliation we feel that in peacetime it may never have been surpassed, which is most aggravating considering the freedom enjoyed by the Bank of China overseas.[112]

Macfarlane's letter appears to have been carried to Hong Kong by his junior colleague, V. B. West, who was allowed to leave Shanghai on 12 February 1953 (being replaced by a colleague from Hong Kong, R. Stephen). West spent the next four days in the Colony writing a detailed fourteen-page report on the three years he had spent in China, and Bird forwarded it to London immediately. It gave details of the dismantling of the bank's various operations, and a glimpse of the harrowing background:

The year 1952 brought the Wu Fan (Five Anti's) movement and no one not
actually present can possibly visualize what this issue entailed. All business
ceased . . . and night and day vans removed individuals from their homes
and offices; the sirens of police vans were continuous and the later sight of
van loads of manacled prisoners being taken to execution caused an
unbelievable strain upon the whole population . . . Suicides by Chinese
persons and some foreigners were numerous and hardly a day passed without bodies falling on to the Bund. One body hit the side of the Bank, and
the roof of our chief neighbour's building was the launching ground for
many deaths.[113]

West concluded his report with a warning that it might take the bank a
long time to pull out of China ('we must expect every hindrance before
our closure') and that the three colleagues he had left behind faced 'a most
difficult period'. He was right to be pessimistic, but was wrong about the
final outcome. The talks between the bank and the Government dragged
on for more than two years, with regular telegrams to and from Macfarlane being handled by the Manager in Hong Kong on London's behalf.
The bank soon agreed in principle to settle all claims for 'pre-liberation
deposits'; but this involved trawling through several thousand accounts.
Unsurprisingly, itemizing the due amounts involved interminable negotiations and the bank was unwilling to remit any funds to Shanghai until its
British officers – Macfarlane and Stephen from Shanghai, W. Philp
and T. C. Hutchinson from Tientsin – had been released. The four men
were eventually allowed to leave at the beginning of 1955.[114] (Cockburn's
Deputy, George Pullen, had successfully led a British Trade Delegation to
Beijing in December 1954, which appears to have helped the two sides to
reach a final accommodation.[115])

Their place had to be taken by an 'Acting Manager', F. J. Hill, and he
was authorized by the bank to conclude an 'All-for-All Agreement' three
months later. Dollar 'repayments' were discreetly remitted to Shanghai –
so discreetly, in fact, that the surviving records make no mention of the
aggregate amount involved, which must have been at least a six-figure
sum – and an undertaking was given by the bank to help recover the frozen New York assets as and when US Government policy allowed (see
p. 615). Thereupon the Chinese clerks were pensioned off – but the Chartered did not close. The authorities, it seemed, had decided that a continued
presence for the bank in China might, after all, be of value to them and
Hill was invited to remain at his post. In concurring with this, the London
Directors perhaps hoped the arrangement might lead to a new era on the
Bund. If so, they were to be disappointed. After lunch on 19 April 1955,

Hill and a locally appointed assistant left Bund 18 to attend a meeting with officials for the formal signing of the All-for-All Agreement. Returning to the bank later that afternoon, they found the building had been seized by the Ta Hwa Enterprise Company, on behalf of the Government, and the two of them were escorted off to a tiny office on the city's Edinburgh Road.[116] It was a summary expulsion from the Bund and brutal confirmation, notwithstanding Hill's assignment, of a reality acknowledged by the Chartered's Chairman to the shareholders fully three years earlier: 'our usefulness in China as an Exchange Bank appears to be at an end . . . [Our record] over a period of nearly 100 years is one which we are reluctant to bring to a close, but there would appear to be no alternative.'[117]

4. A RICH CENTENNIAL

The centenary of the Chartered Bank in December 1953 fell just six months after the coronation of a new Queen for Britain and the Commonwealth. It was a bumper year for the bank's entertainment budget. Across Asia, all the branches did their best to keep up with the pace set by the likes of Calcutta, Colombo and Singapore, whose grand buildings were lit up like Christmas trees to mark the year's two auspicious occasions. There were balls and banquets, cocktail receptions and centenary parties galore. The bank's in-house magazine – *Curry & Rice*, begun in 1930, suspended for the duration of the war and relaunched in 1948 – gorged itself on snaps of beaming Managers and Accountants, entertaining Ministers, Governors and High Commissioners from Bombay to Hong Kong. In Britain, the celebrations lasted months. There were summer parties at The Wilderness, the handsome estate at East Molesey near Hampton Court to the south-west of London, acquired at the end of 1948 as home to the bank's many sporting activities.[118] In September the bank's pensioners reminisced over a special dinner at the Café Royal. In October, the Head Office danced the night away at the Empire Rooms, and the messenger staff, a fortnight later, had a knees-up at Williamson's Tavern, a celebrated pub in the City. Early in December there was a black-tie Centenary Dinner for the managers and their spouses (see Plate 26), followed three days later by a well-oiled gathering of City of London notables at the swish Palmerston Restaurant just along from the bank in Bishopsgate. (A cartoon appeared in the *Daily Mail* next day, of a perplexed customer explaining to the cashier at one of the bank's counters: 'Must have been quite a party – I've just filled my fountain-pen with gin

Head Office, London

The Chartered's Head Office at 38 Bishopsgate on the approach of its centennial celebrations, drawn in 1948

and orange.') All came to a sober end at a service of thanksgiving in Bishopsgate's parish church of St Helen's on 29 December, the day in 1853 that Queen Victoria put her signature to the bank's first charter.

Naturally the celebrations entailed endless stories from the past and fond recollections of what had been achieved by earlier generations. A sense of history came naturally to the bank, as most editions of Curry & Rice reflected: its illustrations drew on photographs of sports teams and office staffs from earlier decades almost as much as pictures of the present day. No doubt anxious to dispel any impression of being unhealthily besotted with the past, Cockburn and his Chairman, Vincent Grantham, accordingly went out of their way on many occasions to stress how successfully the bank was adjusting to the new circumstances of the post-war world. Just as the Empire had changed and adapted, so the bank had become, as Grantham put it in April 1951, a living demonstration 'that constructive British endeavour in Asia is nowhere at an end but everywhere in progress'. In his 1952 Chairman's Statement, Grantham took stock of events in India and China and the crumbling of Asia's colonial empires, and responded with some eloquence:

> A revolution on so gigantic a scale might have been expected to extinguish institutions more firmly established than the branch organisation of a commercial bank controlled and directed from Western Europe, but it is remarkable that notwithstanding the almost cataclysmic changes . . . the Chartered Bank has preserved its system of branches almost intact . . . An important factor in this signal achievement has been the readiness with which our branch managers have adapted their way of life to unfamiliar social conventions . . . and manifested an unfailing helpfulness which has won the confidence of the new generation of administrators and made possible an extensive enlargement of the Bank's clientele.

The Chief General Manager had also been peddling this same theme of flexibility for a while. As he put it in a public lecture in 1950, the Chartered and its peers (the usual code for the Hongkong & Shanghai Bank) had thus retained their essential competitiveness, which accounted for their continuing indispensability to the trade flows of the East. 'Never static, but moving with the times and adaptable to every change in the conditions ruling, they have been able to preserve their outstanding position.'[119]

Cockburn surely intended no deception, but his words here concealed a crucial half-truth. In fundamental ways, the Chartered had in fact declined to go along with more than one 'change in the conditions ruling'. Above all, it had conceded not an inch on the principle of restricting membership of the Foreign Staff to young men from Britain – despite

severe difficulties in finding the additional recruits still urgently needed
by the bank, after the ex-internees had returned to work. The loyalty and
diligence of hundreds of local clerks in 1941–2 had been deemed 'beyond
praise' by many of their British managers; in India, the bank had met the
challenges of the war successfully only because the local staff had taken
on a swathe of extra responsibilities; yet, with the return of peacetime
conditions, the bank had seen no case for abandoning the Empire-staffing
model. Indeed, quite the opposite. The Court had plainly calculated that
the more unsettled the political environment, the greater the appeal of a
British bank as firmly adherent as ever to the old verities of the Empire.
'Moving with the times, but always static' would have been a more candid
(if rather trickier) message for Cockburn to deliver – and its appeal, in
terms of enhancing the bank's competitiveness, was well understood by
his management team. When the first modern-looking annual report
appeared in 1952 – presenting the 1951 accounts and accompanying the
Chairman's Statement with tinted pen drawings of the Bombay and Singapore branches – its map of the world pointedly bore a small box with
a key to the shading: 'The Bank's Branch System under British management directed from London serves the areas shown.' In describing its
working practices and the handling of its customer relationships, the bank
seemed intent on emphasizing how little it had changed since the pre-war
era. And the same applied internally. Its recruitment practices and terms
of service, its office hierarchies and dress codes, and even its policy on
staff marriages (still subject to the bank's blessing, never granted for liai-
sons with 'native women') – all remained essentially as they had been
throughout the interwar period. It was a solid bank run by men of good
character, all well known to each other since their youth and moving
conscientiously together through lifetime careers that would end (as they
had done since 1927) at the automatic retirement age of fifty-five. Only a
few of the best would return to London as senior managers thereafter,
totally attuned to the managerial demands of an organization – 'more of
an "Institution" . . . than a mere "Corporation" ', as Cockburn nicely
expressed it in December 1953[120] – that was both a commercial enterprise
and a quasi-governmental service. The Chartered saw itself as it wanted
its customers to see it – as a rock of stability in a scarily unpredictable
world.

Whether this was fully consistent with the adaptability hailed by Cockburn and Grantham as such a key feature of the bank, some outsiders
rather doubted. Among officials at the Bank of England, in particular,
concern was mounting that the traditional overseas banking model lacked
sufficient scale and dynamism to be sustainable for much longer. 'The

Bank was particularly worried about the Eastern Exchange banks, which it believed might become a target for asset-strippers or, even worse, American banks.'[121] Any shift of strategy, though, seemed likely to be challenging: a robust and highly distinctive corporate culture brought many blessings, but had its drawbacks. Having seen the bank's earnings so dramatically eclipsed in the Far East, the Directors were quietly seeking opportunities by 1953 to expand its geographical franchise elsewhere – perhaps even by acquiring another bank. How far some justly cherished traditions might help or hinder such a move, the Chartered was about to find out.

7
Winds of Change, 1953–69

1. INCHING WESTWARDS WITH THE EASTERN

With its markets curtailed in the Far East, Chartered Bank turned for a closer look at its potential in the Near East. Its first step in this direction added a new red dot to the bank's familiar map of the world. For almost a century most of its Foreign Staff had passed between home and Asia via Aden, that tiny outpost of the Raj perched on a granite promontory on the coast of Yemen enclosing one of the world's greatest natural harbours.* Now the Staff usually travelled to and fro on BOAC aeroplanes instead, touching down at different cities nearer to routes that the proverbial crow might fly. But Aden's loss of a few of its more affluent transient ship passengers had done nothing to slow its exponential growth since 1945, and its thriving commercial port had spawned a rapidly expanding industrial zone. Hong Kong it was not; but Aden was nonetheless host to growing ranks of Western companies, law firms and accountants. The Chartered, hitherto happy to rely on a local Indian firm to represent its interests, opened the doors of a first branch in the Crater district of the city in February 1954. It added a second at Steamer Point a few months later.

Whatever the attractions of Aden, though, the southern rim of the Arabian Peninsula was hardly the focus of the financial world's interest in Arabia by 1954. When the Directors of the Chartered took stock of the bank's geography and looked for new opportunities, it was the Arabian

---

* Having been seized by the East India Company in 1839, Aden had become part of British India after the Company's demise and had remained part of the Raj until its reconstitution as a Crown Colony in 1937. In the post-war years it was still effectively the capital of a British Protectorate that extended inland and eastward along the mountainous coast to include the ancient sultanate of the Hadhramaut.

shoreline of the Persian Gulf that really drew their gaze. In Saudi Arabia and Kuwait the rulers were being deluged with oil dollars, a great torrential flood of money for which they and their peoples were utterly unprepared. King Ibn Saud, already flush with royalty payments, had turned in 1949 to the exploitation of land further north that he shared with Kuwait's Al-Sabah family (the so-called 'Neutral Zone'): he had sold his 50 per cent stake in this territory to another US oil company for $9 million plus royalties on future sales *and* a share of all the profits. The details were passed back to colleagues in London by a British overseas banker on the US West Coast, in the fervent hope that contact could somehow be made with Ibn Saud 'which would enable us to secure from the king any part of the $9,000,000'.[1] In the wake of such ground-breaking transactions, as we have noted already, there were huge dollar deposits to be garnered, exchange transactions to be made and credits to be arranged for some shopping lists of historic proportions. The surest way for Chartered Bank to land its share of this business would be to have branches on the ground that could offer services to both the ruler's immediate circle and the well-connected Arab merchant families thriving as never before. Contemplating its best approach, the Chartered enjoyed some natural advantages. Like so many of the bank's traditional bases across Asia, most of the tiny territories in the Gulf, from Kuwait and Bahrain to the Trucial States and Oman, were still actual or de facto British protectorates. Most of them used the Indian rupee as their currency and were closely tied to the money and product markets of Bombay. There was, however, one snag. Along most of the Gulf coast, a deeply personal business culture inclined the Arab rulers to favour dealing with a single Western bank on an exclusive basis. Two rivals, both British and both given critical assistance in the past by British diplomats and advisers on the ground, had already snatched up most of these singular franchises. To make a late entry into the region, the Chartered would probably have to pull off a merger with either one or the other. The choice between them would eventually be made in a dramatic and unexpected fashion.

The Eastern Bank was in some ways the more obvious partner from the start. With its Crosby Square head office directly adjacent to 38 Bishopsgate in the City, it had grown up under the Chartered's shadow before the war and had adopted broadly the same overseas banking practices across a network that now included four branches in Malaya, six in the sub-continent and five in Iraq. It was the leading bank in both Bahrain and Qatar, and even had a branch in the Hadhramaut's main port of Mukalla, surely the hardest of hardship postings.[2] It had also received permission to open a branch in Saudi Arabia's Al Khobar in 1952 (though promises in this part of the world could take time to ripen and the formal licence, two years later, had yet to arrive). Unfortunately, though, the Eastern seemed to be spoken for. Starting around the time that its Chairman, John Caulcutt, had joined the Eastern's Board in 1938 (see p. 300), Barclays DCO had been quietly accumulating shares in the bank and now held roughly 25 per cent of the total, on a par with the Sassoon family's holding. This investment provided Barclays with a stake in the Gulf's future, where a more direct involvement was thought to be precluded by its own significant business connections in the newly established state of Israel. By the same token, a full cash bid for the Eastern was unlikely.[3] But Barclays DCO was keen to pursue closer commercial ties. Its Deputy Chairman, Anthony Barnes, sat on the Board of the Eastern and regularly corresponded with managers of the two banks, sending them regular ideas for new business. There seemed no room here for the Chartered, whose Directors turned instead to the second of the two overseas banks in the Gulf – which in 1952 had modestly renamed itself the British Bank of the Middle East (BBME).

This was the old Imperial Bank of Persia, founded in London under a Royal Charter in 1889 and 'Imperial' by virtue not of the British Empire but of a concession from the Shah to run a network across his Persian Empire, with a head office in Tehran. Harried and destabilized by the forces of Iranian nationalism, by 1954 it was neither Imperial nor Persian: having stolen a march on all rivals in 1941 by capturing a fifteen-year concession as the only foreign bank in Kuwait, it had set up a string of offices in the Gulf and beyond – including an Aden branch, opened in 1952 – and had effectively pulled out of Iran (as Persia had become) altogether, in favour of the Arab world. After four years of slightly precarious manoeuvring, this bold change of horses had been accomplished with some verve. The Chairman, Lord Kennet, nonetheless remained of the view that the BBME's balance sheet was too small to sustain a successful growth strategy in a region expanding so rapidly. Probably approached by the Directors of the Chartered in the autumn of 1954 – the precise timing is unclear, as none of the relevant papers have survived – Kennet welcomed their takeover proposal. Agreement was reached on a merger that seemed to fit the bill perfectly for the Chartered: the BBME had secured exclusive concessions in Dubai and Muscat as well as Kuwait, and had muscled its way into Bahrain, as well as Al Khobar and Jeddah in Ibn Saud's kingdom. Its financial performance was considerably superior to the Eastern's, mostly on the strength of its exchange dealings for the Kuwaiti Government. Yet, having only recently shifted its head office to London, it was a relative novice in the ways of the City. The Chartered could look forward to directing its operations without hindrance from any complicated legacies of the past – and with no interference from minority shareholders, either.

By the time that Kennet came to put the merger proposition to his Board in November 1954, the Bank of England had given the deal its blessing and the Chartered's Directors might have supposed its completion almost a formality. If so, they had failed to take account of the BBME's General Manager. A crusty martinet, Howard Musker was a harsh character known as the Black Man to his office juniors on account of his less than sunny disposition. He had been with the bank almost since being demobbed after the First World War, starting off his career with three years in Bombay – where it might be surmised that he perhaps had an unfortunate brush or two with the Chartered – and thereafter rising steadily through the ranks in Persia. Returning to London in 1947, he had effectively run the BBME's operations since 1951.[4] He conformed not at all to the City's old hierarchical model, whereby its professional managers handled a bank's day-to-day business while the Directors settled all matters of policy. Musker, as autocratic as he was generally monosyllabic, took pains to ensure that few aspects of the bank's affairs ever escaped his careful direction, and served his Directors much as a good sheepdog serves its flock ('Musker used to call them bloody fools,' recalled one senior manager[5]). Kennet, now in his mid-seventies, had generally acquiesced in this, seeing the younger man as his inevitable successor. It seems, though, that for some reason the Chairman gave Musker no hint of the Chartered merger before asking him, one Friday afternoon, to make it an agenda item for the following Tuesday's Board. Probably Kennet feared a hostile reaction – which is precisely what he got, as Musker's deputy (and a future General Manager) would, years later, recall:

Musker was furious about it. I personally think [this was] chiefly because he hadn't been consulted and second because he didn't like the Chartered Bank . . . [which] seemed to be on a different wavelength to us . . . [He] spent the weekend rushing down to Sir Kenneth Cornwallis near Winchester and Hale down in Sussex and Eldrid in Devon telling [the three Directors] this dastardly plot was afoot and that he wasn't in favour of it and would like their support at the Board meeting . . . [At the meeting all three voted against it, while three Directors backed it.] And the Chairman said, 'Oh well, in that case I have the casting vote, I will vote in favour.' Pears immediately put up his hand and said, 'Mr Chairman, I'm sorry but I have a sincere and strong feeling that a matter of this importance should be unanimous, or not at all. As it isn't unanimous I wish to change my vote to a

negative.' Kennet was really very furious about it. He closed the Board
Meeting exactly, entirely and immediately. And he never spoke to Musker
again until many years later, after he'd ceased to be Chairman.[6]

The setback was a huge disappointment for Kennet and the Chartered's
Chairman, Vincent Grantham – and for the Bank of England too. After
the two chairmen had visited the Bank's Governor in December to discuss
possible ways around their problem, an Executive Director of the Bank,
Kenneth Peppiatt, noted the merger was 'such a wonderful opportunity . . .
with both Mr Grantham and Lord Kennet in favour of the scheme, it
would be absurd for it to be allowed to fail solely by reason of opposition
from one or two members of the Board of BBME'.[7] Absurd or not, this
was indeed the outcome, though talks were not finally abandoned until
April 1956. Even then, Grantham went on hoping for years that the BBME
might eventually have a change of heart.[8] But he had finally to accept
defeat in November 1959, when the BBME's Board announced that a
merger had been agreed with another party – the Hongkong & Shanghai
Bank.

Almost coinciding with the notification in 1956 that the Chartered/BBME
deal was off, the Bank of England received an anxious visitor from the
prospective partner that the Chartered had chosen not to pursue, the
Eastern Bank. Its Chairman, Sir Evan Jenkins, brought news of grim
developments in Calcutta. Huge losses were crystallizing for the Eastern
on ill-advised loans to one of post-Independence India's most colourful
businessmen, a chubby-faced bear of a man called Haridas Mundhra. And
the bank had been warned by the Reserve Bank of India that initial investigations had unearthed 'grave irregularities'.[9] As a former Civil
Commissioner of Delhi under the Raj (and the very last Governor of the
Punjab), Jenkins was not given to being alarmist – but nor could he disguise his concern. According to his own note of a conversation at the Bank
with another of its Executive Directors, Sir Cyril Hawker:

> I said . . . [that] if (a) the Central Govt or the Reserve Bank of India penal-
> ised us as a Bank, or (b) there was a big scandal in India arising, eg from
> the prosecution of our Manager, there might be a run in India followed by
> a 'chain reaction' elsewhere. This might be of considerable public import-
> ance especially if the Persian Gulf were affected . . . I also said that the affair
> had happened at an awkward time . . . We were however keeping liquid in
> London to the best of our ability.[10]

A month later, in June 1956, Jenkins was back at the Bank of England
spelling out more details.[11] Mundhra had begun his career as a successful

light-bulb salesman. The Eastern Bank had first become involved with him in 1952, when he had acquired a leading tea company on the eve of a nasty slump in tea prices. The bank's Calcutta officers had helped him survive that unfortunate bit of timing, and had been greatly impressed by his apparent resilience and energy. His methods, they had to confess, were not those of a British trading company. He was poorly educated, had a less than complete mastery of English and could barely write a simple letter.[12] Instead he ran up telephone charges of thousands of pounds a month, constantly juggling myriad business interests and dishing out verbal instructions to managers in cities across India whom he trusted to run a string of large companies on his behalf. More than one Eastern manager in Calcutta thought him the kind of brilliant entrepreneur whose vigour and intelligence might help the new India to carve out a modern industrial sector. Perhaps a little too keen to show themselves free of anti-Indian prejudice, the Eastern's local men extolled his virtues in long reports to London, each needing also to justify yet another addition to his overdraft.[13] With their assistance, Mundhra soon acquired a taste for adding to his corporate portfolio, using Eastern loans secured against stock in his target companies. Some of his acquisitions prospered, but others relied on senior European managers who were none too impressed by his style and began drifting away. And as the operating profits from his portfolio started sliding, Mundhra found stock-market transactions for their own sake ever more irresistible. By 1955, the Eastern's Head Office in London was receiving regular reassurances from its Calcutta Manager, W. A. Rushton, that all was well, or soon would be. 'He is a good deal more amenable and we think and hope his buccaneering days are over', suggested Rushton in April that year.[14] An Eastern Inspector who arrived from London the following month took a contrary, and less reassuring, view:

> Mundhra is undoubtedly very short of ready cash and is occupied for most of the day conducting what he calls his 'banking' business, which consists of highly complicated interlocking kite-flying transactions in cheques drawn on various banks and in deliveries & receipts of shares to and from Brokers . . . I am convinced that though M. is as dishonest and crooked as they make them, his object in life is to gain more and more power, and, only incidentally, more money.[15]

Hence Jenkins's conversations at the Bank. Over the next several months, Mundhra's finances duly spiralled out of control. Heavy falls on the Calcutta Stock Exchange severely depressed the value of his shares, leaving the Eastern's collateral more than a few annas short of each rupee they had lent him. Before the end of 1956, the bank had set aside a provision of R.53.3 lacs, equivalent to £400,000 and roughly equal to the bank's total operating profits for the first half of the year. The senior men in Crosby Square feared the eventual losses would be two or three times this figure. They watched in dismay as the numbers grew ever more alarming – triggering a crash, in the end, that prompted the first great political crisis of post-Independence India. Mundhra had diversified by the spring of 1957 from overt buccaneering into covert illegalities. These included foreign exchange shenanigans and the circulation of fraudulent share certificates – but also improper investments in his companies by a state-owned body, which plunged Prime Minister Nehru's ministers (and family) into a scandal over the extent of its attempts to rescue him. Meanwhile, just offstage, the Eastern Bank lost its independence.

The Chartered had its own, relatively modest, exposure to Mundhra and was involved in a joint effort by all his bank creditors to contain their losses.[16] But the Eastern's problem was on a quite different scale. Its exposure by early 1957, at around R.280 lacs, equated to more than £2 million – compared with the bank's published reserves of £1.5 million – and can only be attributed to gullibility on the part of its local managers and an egregious lack of oversight from London. Another sharp drop in the value of Mundhra's portfolio was likely to leave the bank insolvent. Its appalled minority shareholders, Barclays DCO and Victor Sassoon, now held 65 per cent of the equity between them but neither had any intention of rescuing the bank. Instead, as Vincent Grantham explained to the Bank of England in April, they were ready to sell out to the Chartered.[17] For Grantham and the Court, the chance to acquire the Eastern's network seemed too good to let slip. Despite the worrying ramifications of the previous year's Suez crisis, they remained determined to expand into the Middle East – a fresh outlook reflected in the decision, made in 1956, to drop 'India, Australia and China' from the bank's name in favour of just plain Chartered Bank. They had been frustrated over the BBME, as also over a second, much smaller merger target. (The Ionian Bank had offered a tempting spread of branches in the eastern Mediterranean. But eight of them had been nationalized in Egypt by Nasser and twenty-four had been sold off to a domestic bank in Greece – leaving the Chartered with just a pocket-sized network of six in Cyprus.) Serious talks about a purchase of the Eastern with Chartered stock began at the start of June. Sir Evan Jenkins played a poor hand as best he could, rejecting a 'final' offer '[as] whatever the real value of the Chartered's shares, [the offer] was not "obviously" attractive to the Eastern shareholder who could not be told all the facts'.[18] Indeed, as far as the real motive for the sale was concerned, the Eastern shareholder was given no facts at all: the calamitous background to the deal was kept heavily under wraps, for fear of triggering a fatal market collapse in India. In the end agreement was struck on a slightly improved (not to say generous) offer from the Chartered, which valued the Eastern at £1.62 million, a 20 per cent premium to its market capitalization on the day before the announcement and a price/earnings multiple of about 17 times the Eastern's published profits in 1956.[19] The merger was completed successfully with no last minute hiccups – doubtless to the satisfaction of Governor Cobbold at the Bank of England, who in July noted airily that 'he would shed a tear if it fell through'.[20]

The most immediate result was that the Chartered slipped into the driving seat on the Mundhra Affair. Its Accountant in Bombay, only very recently assigned there from Ceylon, found himself seconded to Calcutta at the start of 1958 to take charge of a bankers' taskforce committee. David Weatherson was also very soon appointed by the Indian High Court as Receiver to all of Mundhra's tea companies. 'But I never did get to meet the Eastern Bank's Manager – the hearsay was he'd completely disappeared.'[21] While Mundhra himself ended up in prison, measured support from the banks for the viable companies in his defunct empire reassured the Calcutta stock market and helped stabilize the value of its holdings. This in turn allowed the Chartered to pursue a gradual and surprisingly successful unwinding of the Eastern's loan portfolio. The details of the rescue certainly kept the lights on late at the Chartered's Clive Street building for several months. (Indeed, the paperwork generated by his whirlwind career went on filling bankers' files well into the 1970s.[22]) But of dents to the Chartered's balance sheet, there was to be no sign at all. The bank's hidden reserves leapt from £4.8 million in December 1957 to £8.9 million a year later, by far the biggest percentage jump ever recorded. And the Chartered's brave gamble in taking over the Eastern – and all of its sixty-eight British Foreign Staff, with the exception (presumably) of the late departed Calcutta manager – resulted in a significant expansion of its geographical coverage. Assimilating the Eastern (and the Ionian's Cyprus offices) lifted the bank's total network from fewer than seventy to almost a hundred branches. More specifically, it brought the Chartered exactly the ready-made franchise in the Middle East it had been seeking – compensating for the loss of China and persuading the *Financial Times*, at least, that it had succeeded 'in maintaining an impressive rate of progress throughout the post-war period'.[23] A Chartered Inspector tasked with writing a Post-Merger Review was not overly impressed by the standards and procedures he found inside the Eastern ('their managers do not attempt to

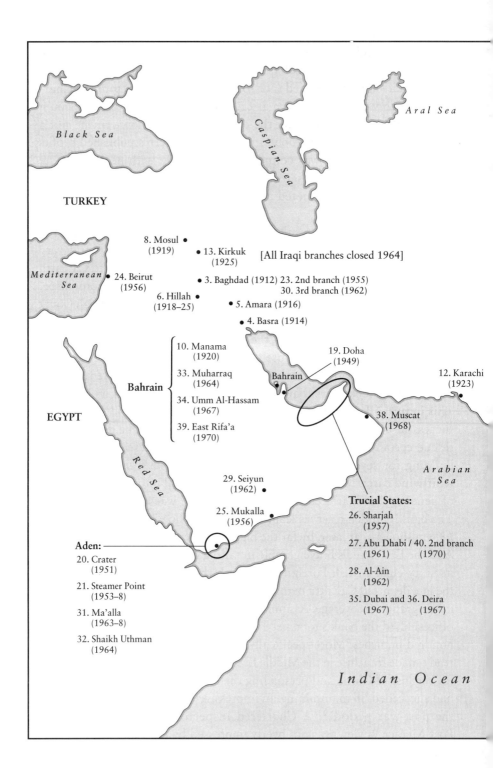

Black Sea

TURKEY

Mediterranean Sea

Caspian Sea

Aral Sea

8. Mosul ●
(1919)

● 13. Kirkuk
(1925)

[All Iraqi branches closed 1964]

● 24. Beirut
(1956)

● 3. Baghdad (1912) 23. 2nd branch (1955)
30. 3rd branch (1962)

6. Hillah ●
(1918–25)

● 5. Amara (1916)

● 4. Basra (1914)

10. Manama
(1920)

33. Muharraq
(1964)

Bahrain

34. Umm Al-Hassam
(1967)

39. East Rifa'a
(1970)

19. Doha
(1949)

Bahrain

12. Karachi
(1923)

EGYPT

38. Muscat
(1968)

Red Sea

Arabian Sea

29. Seiyun
(1962) ●

Trucial States:

25. Mukalla
(1956) ●

26. Sharjah
(1957)

Aden:

27. Abu Dhabi / 40. 2nd branch
(1961)   (1970)

20. Crater
(1951)

28. Al-Ain
(1962)

21. Steamer Point
(1953–8)

35. Dubai and 36. Deira
(1967)   (1967)

31. Ma'alla
(1963–8)

32. Shaikh Uthman
(1964)

Indian Ocean

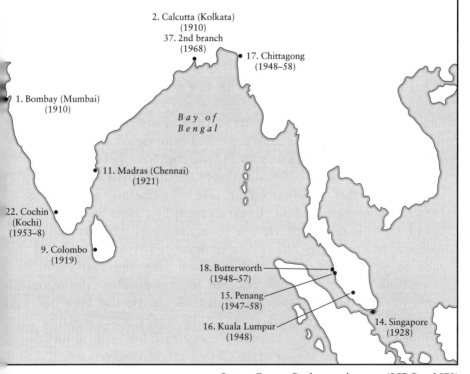

Map 4. Eastern Bank's branch network, 1910–71

Branches and sub-branches numbered in chronological order
(with founding dates, and closing dates where applicable)

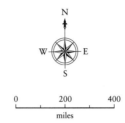

N

W — E

S

0   200   400

miles

2. Calcutta (Kolkata)
(1910)
37. 2nd branch
(1968)

17. Chittagong
(1948–58)

1. Bombay (Mumbai)
(1910)

*Bay of
Bengal*

11. Madras (Chennai)
(1921)

22. Cochin
(Kochi)
(1953–8)

9. Colombo
(1919)

18. Butterworth
(1948–57)

15. Penang
(1947–58)

16. Kuala Lumpur
(1948)

14. Singapore
(1928)

Source: Eastern Bank annual reports (SCB Box 2573)

crystallize and formulate propositions in the clear-cut way expected of Chartered Bank managers').[24] On the other hand, the mechanization of its book-keeping was well in advance of the Chartered's own progress on this score. More to the point, the standing of its twenty-two branches in the Arab world provided access to the extraordinary new markets of the Gulf.

The Eastern acquisition might also have opened up the prospect of a very different future for the Chartered. The mechanics of the takeover left Barclays Bank, as a former shareholder in the Eastern, with a 14 per cent stake in the Chartered. According to the most authoritative modern history of Britain's overseas banks, Barclays DCO's managers urged in May 1958 that its parent should add to this shareholding, presumably as a way of preparing for some kind of merger with DCO itself – 'but there were no operational consequences and DCO's proposals to increase the shareholding further were strongly opposed by Chartered'.[25] The rebuff was contained in a letter sent back within a few days to DCO's Chief Manager, Sir John Tait, by Vincent Grantham. This marked a rare intervention by the Chartered's Chairman. Now approaching the end of his second decade in office – having taken the chair in 1940, aged fifty-one – Grantham seems to have been content to play a mostly passive role in the bank's affairs since the end of the war and he cuts a shadowy figure in the records. He had played no obvious part in the production of the 1953 centenary history, for example, and even left the Preface to be written by his Chief General Manager, William Cockburn. *Realms of Silver* contains scarcely a single reference to him, beyond an airy note that, 'Mr Grantham attended the bank daily throughout the war and with Mr Cockburn, then Chief [General] Manager, concerted those measures of post-war construction which were to give the bank a new and more vigorous lease of life.' A devoted family man with six sons and two daughters, he seems to have had a modest and kindly personality that by the late 1950s was not unduly troubled by further worldly ambitions. (He was a Guernsey man, having been to school there, and an obituary written by a close friend on the island would later record: 'Despite his eminence as a banker and an authority on Far Eastern affairs, Vincent was not a "tycoon" in his attitude to people and things and remained also "un vrai homme Guernésiais".'[26]) But Grantham evidently felt strongly about the importance of retaining the Chartered's independence. He had been quite prepared to contemplate a merger with BBME in 1954, which would have left the Chartered firmly in control. He was much less ready to preside over its submergence into one of the City's giant clearing banks.

Proud of the Chartered's own pedigree, Grantham and his Court colleagues were also sensitive to the commercial case advanced by the Eastern Bank for allowing it to go forward under its old name. It was quickly agreed by both parties that opportunities in the region would in fact be exploited more effectively if the Eastern retained its identity and went on functioning, to all outward appearances, as a separate bank. A dual administration was established accordingly, and it was to last for twelve years. Senior officers were occasionally exchanged between the banks, and the Chartered's Head Office gradually took over the co-ordination of all staff movements. But the Eastern sustained its own customer relationships and business plans to a remarkable degree, even after its network had been badly shaken by the nationalization of all foreign banks in Iraq in July 1964. (The Chartered lent what assistance it could on that occasion, having had its own taste of hostile government intervention by then: it had lost all its branches to nationalization in both Burma and Indonesia in 1963. The seizure of its Rangoon branch in 1963 had been an especially wounding loss, marking the centenary of the bank's presence in Burma in a sorry fashion.*)

The correspondence between the Eastern's Crosby Square Head Office and its managers in the Gulf and Beirut would make a sizeable contribution to any comprehensive history of the Gulf's transformation through a remarkable era.[27] Banking relationships with the region's rulers and merchant families were built up by men like Neville Green (and spouses like his wife, Edna Carr Green, providing essential support). In 1957, aged

---

* None of the private banks in Rangoon, foreign or local, were given any warning of the Burmese government's intentions in 1963 – as one of the participants could later recall. About twenty-five managers from the Central Bank and the State Commercial Bank, summoned to the Government's Secretariat building on the day of the nationalization, had no idea they were about to be assigned an executive role in the process. One of the latter was a twenty-three-year-old U Soe Win, today the Managing Director of a Yangon consulting firm affiliated to Deloitte Touche Tohmatsu. 'We went into the Parliament building around 12.30 p.m. and saw all these armed guards with blank faces. We thought maybe we were going to be arrested. But our Chairman and the Chairman of the Central Bank were there and they said nothing. Then the members of the Revolutionary Council Government came in and just announced: "All the banks in this country are nationalized by the state, from this moment." They had printed the Official Ordinance, and it included all our names as the new managers of the banks.' (U Soe Win, interview with author, 17 February 2014.) He and his colleagues were then escorted to the various banks by soldiers, arriving just as they were closing their books as usual at the end of the Saturday half-day. The British officers of the Chartered stayed on for three months to advise on the handover, though the Manager's grand house was taken over immediately by the government as a state guest house. The top job at the Chartered passed in time to the General Manager of the State Commercial Bank jointly with a UK-educated Burmese manager already on the staff, U Sein Min. The Chartered's 1941 art deco building survives on the main business thoroughfare of the city, now Pansodan Street, and still houses the Myanmar Economic Bank No. 2 installed in 1963.

twenty-eight and having already served five years with the bank, Green launched the Eastern from scratch in the Trucial State of Sharjah, where 'scratch' status still attached to almost every commercial activity. For more than a year, he worked out of a tiny shop in the bazaar with no telephone, driving fifteen miles every afternoon into the adjacent sheikhdom of Dubai to open letters of credit for local firms trading with Iran, and to begin forging a link for the bank with Dubai's Sheikh Rashid, the new ruler of a territory that had formally been the preserve of the BBME since 1946. After a year's sabbatical at the British Government's celebrated Arabic language school in the Lebanon in 1960–61, he was assigned – with Edna and their three-month-old baby son – to start up a first branch in another of the Trucial States, Abu Dhabi. His wife later wrote a brief but spirited memoir of her time there – a rare record of the extraordinary pluck with which so many women, married to young Chartered bankers, served the bank royally by adapting (invariably with less help than they had expected) to living conditions of considerable hardship. Abu Dhabi in the early 1960s had none of the comforts available to expatriates in Bahrain or even Dubai: it had no doctors, no telephones and no roads. Unpleasantly hot and humid for much of the year, it had only strictly rationed supplies of drinking water, which still tasted slightly salty. The Greens had to squat at first as tenants of the local British Political Agent. Then they spent two years in a small, prefabricated house overlooking a fishermen's jetty in the centre of the town, with only the barest of amenities as Edna recorded:

> The furniture was stuff I bought in Bahrain, had loaded on to the deck of a dhow, and shipped to Abu Dhabi. Unfortunately the seas had been rough, with consequent damage, so when it arrived it was all in pieces, and a rather incompetent local carpenter had the job of sticking it all together. But at least we could sit down in a place we could call our own.[28]

Her husband's duties in the early days included handing a monthly suitcase of cash to the famously eccentric Sheikh Shakhbut, to reassure him of the Chartered's solvency. (The BBME had forfeited his confidence when the Sheikh had made an impromptu visit and been appalled to find the bank unable to produce all the cash he had on deposit with them.) After 1966, Green assisted Shakhbut's successor, Sheikh Zayed, with measures to adapt the desert kingdom to its new-found oil wealth.[29] As Gulf rulers like Sheikh Zayed grappled with the challenge of building the physical amenities of twentieth-century life, there were constant appeals to Green and the other local British officers of the Eastern Bank to provide both capital and expertise. (Many of the smaller territories had yet to strike oil, though none seemed to doubt its existence beneath the sands.)

The speed of change in the region could be bewildering, especially for officers reassigned there with no previous experience of the Arab world. One such was A. E. M. ('Tiny') Finlaison, a six-foot-five Scotsman transferred to Bahrain from Malaysia in 1966, when already in his fifties. Later to become General Manager for the Middle East (1970–75), he was forthright with his initial impressions, earning him this memorable response from Crosby Square:

> [I heard recently that] you were rather dismayed at the structure of credit in the Gulf as compared to further East and . . . I know exactly how you must feel. To be thrust into a completely new type of banking at your age with people having completely different ideas and characteristics from what you have hitherto been accustomed [to] is no joke. However, the orthodox Arab in business is generally quite an honest individual; that is, until he becomes westernised and, unfortunately, this is happening all too quickly in too many places. We fully realise that satisfactory lending in the Middle East depends to an even greater extent than further East upon the integrity and business ability of the borrowers.[30]

Like their peers in all the Western banks, the Eastern men had to deal with some wily local operators who were keenly aware of the Westerners' competitive instincts.* By leaving the long-established Eastern to go on running its own network, the Chartered could at least accommodate the inclination of Gulf rulers to deal only with those whom they had known a long time. In Dubai, despite all Green's patient efforts, it still took eight years of gentle persuasion to win Rashid's approval for a branch to be built in his territory. When he finally agreed to the new licence in 1966, it went not to the Chartered but the Eastern.[31]

Responsibility for the Middle East was not entirely delegated to the

---

* Early in 1962, for example, the Eastern had to tread carefully with Sheikh Saqr in Sharjah, who was seeking support for the construction of a first piped-water system for his main town. Frustrated by London's reluctance to back his own approach, the Eastern's Sharjah Manager wrote home to complain that the bank might be seen as lacking in public spiritedness: 'We are informed by the Ruler, with whom we have friendly relations, that a certain competitor ie The Arab Bank have expressed interest in the proposal & have tentatively agreed to underwrite it.' This brought him a stern rebuke. 'You must not be influenced by general statements concerning the alleged public spirit of the BBME or the Arab Bank, or by the belief that the Political Authorities think us inferior in this quality . . . The plain fact is that no prudent person or institution invests money without adequate information, and we must trust that the Ruler and [his adviser] do not intend to do so.' (Head Office to T. A. Barker, 3 May 1962, LMA: MS 39104.) After the Eastern's Chairman had entertained Sheikh Saqr and his Foreign Office adviser, Archie Lamb, to lunch at the Savoy, the finances appear to have become suddenly much clearer. The bank signed a funding agreement in August and the British contractors Halcrow & Partners were on site by the end of the year.

Eastern Bank: the Chartered made a few of its own forays into the region. The most important of these took it into Iran where the Eastern itself had never ventured. It set up a new business, the Irano-British Bank (IBB), to be run by a Chartered General Manager though it was only to be 49 per cent owned from London: 51 per cent of the equity was to be sold to the public and half of the fourteen seats on the Board going to Iranians, at the behest of the Tehran government.* The junior officer charged with organizing its launch was David Millar, reassigned at short notice from Calcutta in the summer of 1958. (He was the thirty-year-old son and namesake of the Singapore Manager who had died in the wake of the city's surrender to the Japanese in 1942, having seen his wife earlier evacuated to Australia.) The new venture was a coup for Chartered Bank insofar as it managed to open its doors in Tehran, in March 1959, just six weeks ahead of a return to Iran by the BBME – branded locally as Bank of Iran and the Middle East (BIME) – which had also decided the political mood there was now once again conducive to Western banking. As the first off the mark, Chartered encountered a lively reception from Iranian investors – as Millar reported back to London on the day its subscription list opened at Iran's leading commercial bank, Bank Melli: 'I went down there at 7.30am, one hour before opening time, [and] there were at least three hundred people queuing to buy shares.'[32] Notwithstanding this encouraging debut, however, Iran was to prove a disappointment. It offered none of the advantages of a colonial (or even post-colonial) setting that was the Chartered's normal habitat, and, in a host country with no British, or at least European, governing elite, the bank struggled. (It never assigned any expatriate officers with prior knowledge of the country, as managers with the rival BIME were quick to note.[33]) Though a second branch was opened at Khorramshahr only two months after IBB's launch in Tehran, progress through the 1960s was slow and Chartered's hopes for the joint venture were never to be fully realized.

Elsewhere in the region, meanwhile, British political influence in the mid-1960s still brought some undoubted benefits – most obviously, helping

---

* The minority ownership spawned a misunderstanding in later years that Chartered had bought into an Iranian bank with an existing network of branches, which was not the case. IBB did move quite quickly to open branches in Khorramshahr, Ahwaz and Abadan as well as a second branch in Tehran, but it was emphatically a Chartered initiative – and marked the first return of British bankers to Iran since the Mossadegh crisis of 1953. Initial plans envisaged the appointment of the Shah's brother, H.H. Prince Mahmood, as IBB's chairman, but this was vetoed by the Shah himself before the bank was launched. It was just one of many such complications that attended the formation of the Board – and indeed the entire history of the bank.

to provide the overseas banks with privileged access to those ruling families of the Gulf. But its blessings were now mixed. In Aden, where the Empire was clinging on, radical Arab nationalism, backed by Nasser's Egypt, had begun to make life extremely uncomfortable. Reconstituted in 1963 from a Crown Colony and Protectorate to a colonial hodge-podge entitled the 'Federation of South Arabia', Aden and its surrounding territories were torn by the middle of the decade between armed insurgents on the one hand and a large British Army presence on the other. The Chartered and Eastern Bank were still both there in 1965, facing each other from opposite sides of a major road junction at the centre of the Crater District. Plans were nonetheless pushed ahead that year for the establishment of a third operation, a local joint venture to be called the Bank of South Arabia.[34] Perhaps it was seen as a shrewd way of ensuring continuity in the future. An attempt was even made in the autumn of 1966 to float off the shares to local residents. This proved a less successful idea in Aden than it had been in Tehran seven years earlier, and the Chartered's local man on this occasion sent back a rather less encouraging note:

> The local business atmosphere is not good, due to the adverse conditions now obtaining, and there has been a regrettable lack of market interest in the subscription lists . . . The new Bank will be opening at a very difficult time and not at all with the local flourish and encouragement that one would have wished . . . I shall do all possible to keep the flag flying until Liller relieves me in November![35]

This was Hew Liller of Shanghai, whose career had taken him to India, Hong Kong and Kuala Lumpur since he had been shot at on the Bund in 1949. Now he had to spend almost a year in Aden, where badly wounded British soldiers were several times pulled from the street into the bank only to bleed to death on Liller's office floor ('on my carpet!'[36]). He himself survived a series of bomb scares, grenade attacks and random shootings before being reassigned in 1967, shortly after the end of British rule. Little or no money was being made in Aden – especially after the 1967 Middle East ('Six-Day') war, which led to a protracted closure of the Suez Canal – and the Eastern branch was closed down shortly afterwards. The Chartered, though, clung on. The bank's history had by now entrenched a deep conviction that, once added to the network, no territory should ever be voluntarily abandoned. It kept its doors open in Aden for another two years, until the People's Republic of South Yemen nationalized all foreign banks in November 1969.

2. STARTING AFRESH IN HONG KONG

Looking for opportunities in the Middle East made sense – but it was already plain by the middle of the 1950s that the Chartered would require more than just a physical expansion of its franchise if it were to prosper as an overseas bank in the post-colonial world. The social changes under way in Asia required matching adjustments to the Chartered's business culture – opening up proper management careers for local Asian employees, and strengthening the bank's ties with indigenous business groups. A big step down this path was taken in the autumn of 1952. A training college was set up outside London for Eastern probationary staff, and it was decided that its doors should also be open to Assistant Officers from around the network.* Vincent Grantham noted in his Chairman's Statement to the 1952 Annual Report that the college would 'assist in preserving and enlarging the traditions of service within the Bank, which has been the happiest feature of the cooperation between our British and Asian staffs throughout the service'. This co-operation stopped a little short of shared classrooms: the probationary expatriates lived at the college from October to May, and the Assistant Officers from across Asia took up residence through the summer months. (The first party, in the summer of 1953, comprised twenty-two 'Asian officers' from nineteen branches across nine different countries.[37]) But the latter's inclusion in the annual programme was an acknowledgement at last of the network's heavy dependence on the more senior of its local employees across Asia, who were so numerous now as to have become in effect the backbone not just of Hong Kong but of most individual branches in the network. Indeed, their strict exclusion from any prospect of promotion to covenanted-officer status, rigidly enforced since 1935, had been looking increasingly

---

* As a home for the college, the Chartered had acquired the extensive buildings and plush grounds of an erstwhile country hotel, Dormans Park, occupying four acres adjacent to the Lingfield race course in Surrey. It was rechristened Hatton Court, after the original City headquarters of the Chartered, and was put under the charge of Sir Alexander Campbell, a former Registrar of the University of Rangoon who for many years had been the Indian Civil Service's man responsible for public education in Burma. An illustrated profile of Hatton Court was included in the house magazine, Curry & Rice, in its January 1953 edition, pp. 4–5. Scores of young Chartered men began their careers there in the 1950s, but Hatton Court was not destined long to survive the decade. Too many of its British alumni appear to have cashed in the benefits of a sound training programme by resigning from the Chartered and taking a job in the City. For most of the 1960s, training of a less intensive nature was based in Bishopsgate – and, when residential courses were resumed for graduate trainees, they were to be housed at The Wilderness in East Molesey.

anomalous for years. By 1954, the refusal to open up the executive body to Asian employees was simply untenable. A formal Circular in November that year finally accepted as much. Given its significance, it was a peculiarly grudging instruction that went out to all branches, announcing that the rank of Sub-Accountant was henceforth to be considered open to Asian officers. The new men would fill the role in a 'purely local' capacity: there was no question, say, of an Indian manager being sent to work in Singapore. And Country Managers were advised that the Circular, despite its obviously far-reaching implications, had been issued 'more as a statement of principles rather than as an encouragement to precipitate action throughout the service'. Managers were sternly cautioned not to rely on mere technical qualifications as a basis for putting candidates' names forward:

> Officers selected must also be of a social standing in the community and possess a personality and bearing which will enable them to associate on an equal footing with their fellow European officers where necessary . . . It is our considered opinion that at the present time there are but few Asian officers who have all the necessary qualifications and ability to carry out with full acceptance the duties now undertaken by European sub-accountants.[38]

And indeed 'but few' made it, over the next few years (though the first Asian name appeared on the Eastern Staff list in March 1955 – K. R. Venkitaraman of Bombay.[39])

The wording of the 1954 Circular said much about the continuing reluctance in 38 Bishopsgate to tamper much either with the Empire-staffing model or the engrained preference of most branches for dealing with British customers in the marketplace. Its tone also conveyed a subtler message – that any significant shift in the culture of the bank would probably have to depend upon local initiatives from the network. But where would these initiatives surface first? Hardly in India. The social and professional etiquette of the overseas bankers' world in Calcutta and Bombay – with its dress code of black-tie for all evening occasions, and white gloves for the ladies – had long been immeasurably stuffier than anywhere else in Asia (notwithstanding Mr Venkitaraman's success). The bank was expanding at a remarkable pace in the new-styled Federation of Malaya – which still included Singapore – and in the neighbouring states to the east, Sarawak and North Borneo, where half a dozen branches had been opened since the war. But the very success of the bank in dealing with new business sectors like oil and gas production as well as the long-established rubber and tin trades suggested there was no urgent need to review its traditional approach in the region (nor did the threat posed by Communist insurgents in the early 1950s encourage much experimentation). In the event, new ways of thinking about the Chartered's role sprang from its local operations in what many feared after 1950 might become a mere backwater (at best) in the wake of China's tumultuous upheaval – the British Colony of Hong Kong.

The Chartered's managers, like many outside observers, initially feared the collapse of its trade with a Communist-run China might be a lethal blow to the Colony. Hong Kong was an entrepôt for the mainland, or it was nothing. That old China hand, Harold Faulkner, was asked by his Bishopsgate colleagues in 1951 to review the prospects of the Hong Kong branch and penned a verdict that was shrewd but deeply pessimistic: 'Political anachronisms sometimes survive for incredibly long periods and it is possible that, for reasons its founders did not foresee, the colony of Hong Kong may remain indefinitely under British jurisdiction, but . . . the peculiar conditions of trade and politics upon which its prosperity was founded have disappeared.'[40]

In fact, by 1951 the seeds of a fresh future for Hong Kong had already been sown in ways that Faulkner himself did not foresee. The growing chaos in China had begun to paralyse industrial activity in the Shanghai region two years or more before the Communist victory of October 1949. Among the most vulnerable businesses in that city were China's leading textile firms, owned by a handful of powerful families. Fearing the worst, they had begun to contemplate the possibilities of relocation overseas – to Taiwan perhaps, or even South America. One family, led by C. C. Lee, had already set up shop (as the South China Textile Company) in Hong Kong in 1946.[41] Others wanted to take more time weighing their options, but events moved quickly and many soon found themselves contemplating the same move. Another prominent Shanghai name sprang up in Hong Kong in 1947, when T. Y. Wong established Peninsula Spinners. Machine tools and other supplies en route to their plants from Europe started being unloaded in the Colony by early 1948, once a dearth of foreign exchange and a clampdown on import licences made it increasingly difficult to land them in Shanghai. But could putting them to work in Hong Kong really be a viable option? As a place to run a large spinning mill, it left much to be desired. It had no raw materials and no skilled engineers, a rotten climate for raw cotton and an incomprehensible Chinese dialect (if you came from Shanghai). Certainly there existed a lively knitting and weaving industry among the Cantonese, with roots stretching back to the 1920s, and a contemporary assessment of the first six spinning mills reckoned in 1948 that local sales of yarn would probably cover their costs quite comfortably.[42] (According to the half-yearly letters from the Chartered's branch, shirts were a staple of local production, alongside rubber shoes, enamel-ware and torches.[43]) But the Shanghainese, long accustomed to producing yarn for the whole of China, were never likely to regard local demand in Hong Kong as their target market, nor had the Cantonese ever figured much as customers for their mills in Shanghai. Exports to Indonesia before the Revolution had been of far greater importance, and exports would surely have to be the lifeblood of any industry based in Hong Kong. In this respect, it did have the priceless attraction of being an open port, free to trade with the world. True, it was perilously close to the war-torn mainland. But the British appeared to provide a (fairly) reliable haven against the Communists, and perhaps the proximity of Hong Kong might even allow one day for a return from exile. By the summer of 1948, anyway, several of the biggest textile names in Shanghai had begun establishing themselves on the western side of the New Territories, around the town of Tsuen Wan (the last stop, today, on a line of Hong Kong's MTR subway).

No doubt these families managed to spirit a fair amount of capital out of Shanghai in one way or another – it will never be known how much – but as they struggled to establish textile mills from scratch, most were soon desperately short of funds. Relief at finding some modest local demand for yarn must soon have given way to mounting anxiety over their lack of capital to support spinning operations on the large scale they had envisaged. In addition to trade financing with which to import raw cotton, mostly from the US and Pakistan, they needed the capital to invest in washing and combing machines, spindles and weaving looms. They had left behind most of their assets, which were soon to be lost for good, as the Chartered's Manager, D. J. Gilmore, noted of one of them in October 1948: 'South Sea Textiles [owned by the family of P. Y. Tang] are in rather an awkward position at the moment, owing to seizure in Shanghai by the Chinese Authorities of all their assets in that city, and the incarceration of the leading Chinese interested.'[44] The following March, Gilmore left for a long-awaited furlough, and his position was reassigned. Choosing a new Manager for Hong Kong, Head Office gave no thought to appointing one of the bank's more senior men. Instead it promoted Gilmore's deputy, A. J. ('Dicky') Bird, whose only previous experience of managing a branch had involved running down the sub-agency in Canton before the war. It might initially have seemed to him (as to Bishopsgate, perhaps) like another such unenviable role, winding down Hong Kong. But he soon began to take a lively interest in the activities of the fugitive industrialists from Shanghai.

Bird was an unusual character. Hugely overweight and at least as fond
as the next man of his evening tipple – most bankers in Hong Kong in the
1950s seem to have drunk astonishing quantities of whisky – he was a
bachelor who devoted himself entirely to the bank's business or to cultivating his social networks, which came to the same thing. (He was a prominent
figure in the freemasons, eventually becoming Grand Master of the Hong
Kong District, which effectively meant he was the most senior freemason
in the Far East.) He was far from the most meticulous manager in the
bank when it came to his accounts – he had plenty of excellent Portuguese
Assistant Officers to take good care of those – but he liked to get to know
his customers, and the Shanghainese obviously intrigued him. In years to
come, stories about a rude rebuff from the Hongkong & Shanghai Bank
for more than one of the proud fugitives would be told and retold often
enough to become part of the industry's folklore. True or not, it was certainly the case that supporting the Shanghainese appealed far more to
Bird and his colleagues, including his Accountant, Gerry Leiper, than to
their grander neighbours on Des Voeux Road. Nor were the Hong Kong
branches of the big mainland banks, or the smaller locally owned Chinese
banks, much interested in the newcomers' business.[45] The Chartered took
a different line, and soon began building a special relationship with the
nascent cotton-spinning industry.*

Within a couple of months of taking over the branch, Bird was ready
to back a facility of US$500,000 for Hong Kong Cotton Mills (General
Manager: T. Y. Wong) to cover the costs of their raw cotton supplies from
the US and of putting the final touches to their new factory at Castle Peak
Road in Kowloon. This was 'the most modern mill constructed in the Far
East', Bird reported home, and his strong support ensured completion of
the loan.[46] One of the Directors of this company (later merged with the
Wong family's Peninsula Spinners to form a third company, Hong Kong
Spinners) was an Englishman called W. C. Gomersall, who ran a large
business of his own in Hong Kong – China Engineers. The latter had long
supplied machinery from Manchester to the mills of Shanghai and had
greatly assisted some of the larger families in the immediate post-war years
by providing them with term loans. (It had also provided some of them
with a British flag to fly over the factory, which in post-war Shanghai had

---

* There was irony in this, insofar as Chartered Bank (like Hongkong Bank) had always rather
sniffily eschewed doing business with the textile industry in Singapore, which was heavily
dominated by Indian firms trading with China and the sub-continent. It happily left this sector to the Eastern Bank, whose connections with the top British names in Singapore were
so much less impressive than the Chartered's. (Neville Green, interview with the author,
19 May 2011.)

afforded some precious extra security.) In 1950, Gomersall floated the idea of a 'Cotton Pool' arrangement, under which his China Engineers would co-ordinate the funding and shipping of cotton supplies for eight of the new mills. Here again funding was sought from the banks: Gomersall wanted £750,000 from Chartered Bank – and a matching amount from the Hongkong Bank, too. 'Dicky' Bird was on furlough, but Leiper submitted the Pool proposal to London in October – and followed up two days later, for good measure, with a request to lend T. Y. Wong a further US$500,000. He explained:

> The cotton industry in Hong Kong has become one of the Colony's major enterprises, and we feel that if the Bank is to maintain its position as a leading financial institution in this port, we must be prepared to play our part in assisting the finance of such new undertakings, particularly where as in the present case no undue risks are involved and the potential profits to us appear satisfactory.[47]

Leiper's readiness to champion the cotton spinners' interests was all the more striking, given tumultuous events elsewhere in the Far East. The Korean War had broken out three months earlier, in June 1950. The Directors were still mulling over his proposals in December when the US imposed a naval embargo on all trade with the Colony using US ships or ports. Cargoes of urgently needed supplies for Hong Kong were promptly diverted elsewhere. As Leiper bitterly observed, the affected cargoes 'included such "strategic" articles as nylon stockings, lipsticks and beauty preparations, ladies' dresses and underwear '.[48] More seriously, they also included thousands of tons of raw cotton, being carried on a US merchantman from Karachi but now unceremoniously dumped in Manila. The embargo was potentially disastrous for the Shanghainese entrepreneurs, cutting off suppliers and export customers alike. However far they had succeeded in finding buyers for their yarn within the Colony, overseas markets had been essential from the start: now finished exports began piling up in their godowns at an alarming rate.[49] But Bird and Leiper stood by the struggling immigrants, and their support helped to keep the spinning mills afloat for a precious few months. Eventually, like every war, the Korean conflict sparked a boom in demand for almost all commodities – and for as much yarn and cloth as Hong Kong could produce. By importing raw cotton from Commonwealth countries and exporting their output to Britain, the new mills were able to circumvent the US embargo. For months they had struggled to avert bankruptcy, drawing on loans from the Chartered to help pay their employees' wages. Now, almost overnight, their revenues took off.

As Bird's seniors in London came to accept, his support for the embattled mills had never been quite the reckless gambit it might have appeared to the uninitiated. For their fugitive owners from Shanghai were of course no ordinary refugees. The leading names among them were businessmen whose families had been at the forefront of introducing Western technology into pre-Communist China for decades. Individuals like P. Y. Tang (b. 1898), T. Y. Wong (b. 1908) and C. C. Lee (b. 1911) – and some notable others including H. K. Liu (b. 1911) and his younger brother Jerry Liu (b. 1920), Vincent Woo (b. 1910), Cha Chi Ming (b. 1914) and H. C. Yung (b. 1923) – were in most cases the sons of highly successful entrepreneurs who had pioneered China's mass production of cotton yarn around the turn of the twentieth century.[50] Fathers and sons together had made a sizeable contribution to the emergence of Shanghai and its region by the 1930s as the industrial heartland of China, with about half of all its modern factories, half its total capital investment in manufacturing and half its skilled labour force.[51] We know from the surviving records of its pre-war branch on the Bund that the Chartered lent capital to at least one prominent name in Shanghai's textile industry in the early 1930s: a loan to the Rong family stood out in the expanding portfolio of advances to Chinese borrowers in those years.* No evidence exists of any pre-war links with any of the other families, but their names would almost certainly have been known to the Hong Kong managers. Possibly Bird himself was especially aware of their reputations, from his time in Canton. What is clear, anyway, is that the single-minded pursuit of their objectives by these families once they had arrived in Hong Kong greatly impressed him. P. Y. Tang, for example, had managed to bring a dozen or so of his most important engineers with him to the Colony. 'He bought a house which served as a dormitory for all of them to live alongside the family', recalled his son, Jack Tang, in 2012. 'So the bank thought, "it shows all

---

* An analysis of the Shanghai branch's 1934 balance sheet shows fixed loans to a dozen or so Chinese customers. The largest by far was advanced to the Mow Sing & Foh Sing Flour Mills and Sung Sing Cotton Mills, the business empire of the Rongs. (Man-han Siu, 'Foreign Banks and the Chinese Indigenous Economy: the Business of the Shanghai Branch of the Chartered Bank of India, Australia and China 1913-37', in Hubert Bonin, Nuno Valerio and Kazuhiko Yago (eds), *Asian Imperial Banking History*, Pickering & Chatto, 2014.) The head of the family, Rong Yiren, elected to stay in Shanghai in 1949, reaching an accord with the Communist authorities that allowed him to retain ownership of his companies until 1956. He became mayor of Shanghai in 1957, survived the Cultural Revolution of the 1960s and in 1979 founded the Republic's first state-owned investment company, which became the CITIC Group. He prospered under Deng Xiaoping, serving as Vice-President of the People's Republic in 1993–8, and died a rich man in 2005.

the money goes into the business, we'll bet on that" – which was a smart business judgment.'[52]

Within a few years, the output of a first thirteen mills in the New Territories had soared and their owners, already employing more than 12,000 workers, set up The Hongkong Cotton Spinners Association.[53] Some of the spinning businesses were also expanding into the weaving of basic cloth for garment manufacturing, alongside the (mostly much smaller) Cantonese weavers. The textile industry, true to its historical role in many economies as the precursor of successful industrialization, was in fact laying the foundations for large-scale manufacturing in the Colony. The Chartered's early support for it accordingly stood the bank in very good stead – and seems, too, to have prodded Head Office into an explicit acceptance of some important implications. As late as 1954, its stance on Hong Kong had been distinctly wary. 'It is perhaps difficult', observed the Chairman's Statement in the 1953 Annual Report, 'to justify the expansion of the spinning and weaving industry in the face of the lack of certain and traditional markets for its yarn and cloth . . .' But a Head Office Circular of November 1955 sounded a very different note:

> The Bank has achieved a good deal of success in adapting its operational technique to changing political and economic conditions and during the past two years an increasing proportion of our resources has been employed in the financing of infant industries and new public works. Many of the credit operations thus undertaken have necessitated the granting of loans and overdraft accommodation for periods longer than conventional bankers might regard as prudent, particularly in view of the vulnerability of our deposits. It has, however, been borne in upon us that our continuing to operate in the East can be justified only so long as we are willing to associate ourselves with the economic development of the territories we serve and with constructive measures, sponsored by governments and private enterprise.[54]

A new approach was needed, and the branch in Hong Kong was leading the way. Building on its business with the Shanghainese, the Chartered had aligned itself with the Colony's broader Chinese business community to a striking extent by the time Bird retired, in 1957. This had helped to differentiate the Chartered from the Hongkong Bank – still far more closely identified with the Colony's big trading houses – and had also done much to restore the branch's local earning power. Though not yet in the same league as those of Singapore, Kuala Lumpur and Djakarta, Hong Kong's profits by the late 1950s surpassed those earned anywhere in India.[55]

It was a performance sustained under Bird's able successor, A. O. (Alec) Small, who achieved a full mechanization of the bank's manual ledgers. (After Small took six weeks off for a holiday, the thirteen leading Shanghainese textile families marked his return with a famous dinner in his honour.[56]) Small also presided over a replacement of the existing branch office with a new one. Occupying the same site as the old nineteenth-century edifice between Des Voeux Road and Queen's Road, the new building housed a splendid banking hall and office space for more than two hundred clerical staff. It was also air-conditioned and very tall (indeed, the tallest building in the Colony at the time). Among those attending its official opening ceremony in August 1959 were the Chairman, Vincent Grantham, and a newly promoted Chief General Manager, George Pullen (known to all on the Eastern Staff, though assuredly not in his hearing, as 'Woolly Pulley').* Pullen had spent the first two decades of his career in the East – he had served in India throughout the war, rising to become Deputy Financial Adviser to the Indian Government in New Delhi – before returning to London as Secretary and working his way rapidly up the senior hierarchy in Bishopsgate.[57] Kuala Lumpur was the furthest east he had ever been posted, but since leading the 1954 UK Trade Delegation to Beijing he had followed events in China with a keen eye. It was he who insisted that the branch in Shanghai should remain open, however bleak its prospects. By 1959 he had already heard much about the Hong Kong textiles story from C. C. Lee, a frequent visitor to London whose TAL Group had emerged as one of the Colony's leading names. Pullen used his visit as head of the bank to get acquainted with some more of the industry's prominent figures. (Indeed, he had started this process before landing. On his flight from New York, Pullen found himself on the same plane as the wife and granddaughter of P. Y. Tang, who would become a close friend.[58]) As he must have heard at every turn, whether judged by the number of spindles in its mills, the size of its workforce or its output of cotton yarn, the industry was expanding at an extraordinary rate.[59] Those tiny ventures backed by Bird and his colleagues had now grown into substantial companies, and all were still banking with the Chartered. So Pullen kept a close watch on Hong Kong over the next few years, and when the time arose in 1963 for the appointment of a new

---

* William Cockburn had finally retired in January 1955 after fifteen years at the top, collecting a knighthood in the 1955 New Year's Honours List and a seat on the Chartered's Court three months later. He had been succeeded by H. F. Morford, who had been seven years ahead of Pullen in the management's pecking order throughout their careers, and who retired in December 1958. (The first professional manager to join the Court since Gwyther, Cockburn had sadly not graced it for long: he died on 1 September 1957.)

Manager – Small had been followed in 1961 by O. W. (Bill) Reynolds, but only briefly – he insisted that the post should go to one of the bank's rising men. It duly went to the person widely seen in the bank as his own eventual successor, Peter Graham.

Graham had spent several months in Hong Kong in 1947, en route to his first official posting with the Chartered after the war, during which he had served as a pilot in the Fleet Air Arm. (He bore a scar on his upper lip from a wartime crash-landing.) He now returned to the Colony with great enthusiasm, after spells in Tokyo, Amritsar and Bangkok, and he was to manage the branch through seven remarkable years. They took him into a far closer engagement with the Chinese business community than anything he had experienced in the post-war days, or than any of his predecessors might have imagined. (The zealous, polo-playing Thomas Whitehead would surely have been amazed.) Like the Chartered's earliest managers on the Island, Graham soon saw the need to have a trustworthy Chinese intermediary – or more precisely, Shanghainese intermediary – at his side. He asked a senior figure in the industry, P. Y. Tang, for help and was given an introduction to B. K. Liu, a fluent English-speaker who had trained as a Shanghainese lawyer and was currently working for Ralli Brothers, the famous Liverpool-based cotton traders.[60] Liu was extremely well connected in the global textile business. He agreed to work for the Chartered, not exactly as a compradore but in a broadly comparable role shorn of any obligations as a guarantor. His services helped consolidate the bank's position against an array of aspiring rivals, not least from the US, and emboldened it to provide what was effectively risk capital in addition to trade credits and overdrafts. The Chartered even helped to fund the expanding premises of the leading textile firms (including a new eleven-storey factory for Hong Kong Spinners, built in 1964). The bank also provided the mill owners with introductions to agents in foreign markets and logistical support for their early appearances at the biggest international textile shows. The Chartered's Hamburg office, for example, helped T. Y. Wong's son-in-law Henry Leung to set up a stand each year for his business at the Men's Fashion Week Fair in Cologne. Leung's Leighton Textiles became, as a direct result, a supplier of trousers to Ahlens AB, the biggest store group in Sweden – a relationship that was to last for thirty years.[61]

So intense were the bank's dealings with the textile sector in the 1960s that several of the leading Shanghainese industrialists came to regard the Chartered as virtually a partner in their businesses – a strong tie that would leave a lasting impression, as P. Y. Tang's son Jack could recall half a century later:

Banking was more of a profession than a business to them. The bankers were like family doctors: you could consult them and ask for their advice on family inheritance, say, or where to go for a trust . . . Peter and Lyn [Graham] were both best friends to myself and my wife – we got along famously.

Undoubtedly Graham enjoyed a remarkable personal rapport with the key families. In particular, he formed a close and lasting friendship with T. Y. Wong, whose daughter Eleanor has since recalled their relationship in a comprehensively researched family memoir:

The instant affinity between Peter Graham and my father T.Y., on both personal and business levels, meant that we could shift our banking out of the Hong Kong Bank and into the Chartered Bank, at very much more favourable rates – absolutely vital in such a capital-intensive industry as cotton-spinning, where borrowings were necessarily high and the repayments considered simply a part of the inevitable costs. Thanks in large part to my father's example, as well as that of men like C.C. Lee and P.Y. Tang, the Chartered Bank went on to finance most of the textile businesses in Hong Kong . . . [Its backing] had myriad benefits for our company. The bank certainly played a pivotal role in helping us expand through loans for new, more modern spindles and other essential equipment.[62]

Graham was regularly to be seen at public dinners happily ensconced between P. Y. Tang on the one side and T. Y. Wong on the other, and the two of them were frequent visitors to the Manager's stately residence, Abergeldie, high up on The Peak. (This was the setting for a busy social calendar: Graham and his wife entertained there on a more or less weekly basis.) The bank's standing with the Shanghainese families was further enhanced by the arrival in 1968 of David Millar as Graham's deputy. The two men had shared a mess together as young bachelors in Tokyo. Now both were married, with lively and accomplished wives whose gregariousness added another dimension to the popularity of the bank. Millar and his wife, Jackie, were soon as integral to the network of friendships as Peter and Lyn Graham (and Millar would succeed Graham as Manager in 1971). And then there were Mr and Mrs George Pullen, too. As Chief General Manager (and later as Chairman) through the 1960s Pullen retained his close interest in the Colony's development. He visited on a regular basis during his periodic 'Royal Tours' of the network – usually accompanied by his independent-minded Scottish wife, Agnes, whom the branch managers' wives all knew to be as formidable as she was famously elegant. (She had had a successful career in London's fashion world before marrying Pullen in 1960. Her Dunfermline directness provided a steady flow of useful speech material for Pullen, a Home Counties Englishman leading a largely Scottish bank, but her informality was also a good foil for his occasionally severe manner.*)

Ties with the Shanghainese were also strengthened by the assistance that was given by the bank to their younger family members (five of them pictured in Plate 29). C. C. Lee's son Richard and Vincent Woo's son Alex both spent time as students in London, staying with John Shewan who had worked in Hong Kong under Alec Small. When Richard Lee married in London, Shewan was his best man. Pullen himself acted as guardian to the two sons of T. Y. Wong during their schooldays in Britain. In time, the fathers who had fled Shanghai handed over to the next generation. Jack Tang took over South Sea Textiles from his father P. Y. Tang in 1968; Alex Woo inherited his father's Central Textiles in 1974; T. Y. Wong's daughter Eleanor and son James inherited Hong Kong Spinners, a company that later made a name for itself producing some of the finest quality yarn in the textile world (the 'Red Rose' brand); Eleanor also launched Hong Kong Knitters as a subsidiary of her father's company in 1965; that same year Richard Lee joined his father's TAL Group, which was to become the largest textile conglomerate in south-east Asia; and C. C. Lee's right-hand man at TAL, Y. L. Yang, in 1978 launched his own clothing business, Esquel, itself destined one day to be a global leader. All regarded the Chartered, as Eleanor Wong remembered in 2012, 'not just as business partners, but more like personal friends'.[63] Their warm memories of the bank, still harboured decades later, attest to the success of some good old-fashioned banking virtues – which were now serving, simultaneously, to help the Chartered adjust to a new kind of business.[64]

For its financial commitment to textiles and other light industries in Hong Kong was a fundamental departure for the Chartered, and had a lasting impact on its business model. Graham was a banker unusually ready to embrace a radical change of direction if he thought it for the best. Early on, with Pullen's support, he made a bold decision to accumulate deposits in Hong Kong with which to fund its local lending – by establishing a network of 'retail' outlets. An expansion of the bank's network in the Malaysian Archipelago in recent years had presaged this

---

* He came from modest farming stock in Surrey, and was educated at the Royal Grammar School in Guildford. Pullen had been a famous Lothario in his bachelor days and owed much to his wife's strength of character once he had landed the top job. He was fond of telling audiences in the 1960s that he had imagined it might improve his prospects if he married a Scotswoman – but he'd found himself reproved by her ever since for being a social climber. (Agnes Pullen, interview with author, 25 November 2011.)

development. The long-established branches in the Malay states were in towns like Ipoh, Alor Setar and Sitiawan, where the bank serviced local businesses that were focused respectively on the tin-mining, rice and rubber trades. Since 1955, the need to raise local capital had prompted the opening of several additional branches in and around Kuala Lumpur and in other Western Malaysian centres like Port Dickson and Port Kelang. All were essentially set up to gather deposits in support of the local loan book.[65] None of these outlets, though, approached retail banking in anything like the customer-oriented spirit now contemplated by Graham. Indeed, the retail dimension was generally of little direct concern to the bank itself. ('It was considered in the local market that if a trader or individual was considered respectable enough to be permitted to open a current account, then his cheque was good value. It was noted that many cheques circulated through the marketplace for weeks or even months, endorsed onto successive holders, before finally being presented to the bank for payment.'[66]) Graham set out to emulate the High Street branches run by the clearing banks in the UK, taking advantage of new communications technology to bind them into a coherent network.*

In 1963, the Chartered in Hong Kong had just two sub-branches, one in Tsuen Wan and a second in Kowloon. It was soon busy adding addresses at a rate of two or three a month. The new outlets were generally managed by Assistant Officers, and many were located where their savings and chequeing services could be used by employees of the bank's corporate clients. Arrangements were made for weekly wages to be paid directly via the employees' Chartered accounts. By the end of the 1960s the bank had twenty-four full branches and dozens of sub-branches, covering the Island, Kowloon and the New Territories. (Millar could later recall frequent opening ceremonies – some of them attended in person by one of Hong Kong's better-known real estate developers. Li Ka-shing, who would one day become one of the Colony's most fabled billionaires, sold the ground floor space in several of his new buildings to the Chartered: 'It was mutually beneficial. A bank is better than a shop, much nicer looking.'[67]) For a business hitherto accustomed to running each of its banks with a single, monolithic shop-front – typically with a marble-clad hall full of public counters, but only for the provision of very basic services – the management of dozens of sub-branches posed many challenges. The bank had virtually no experience of proper retail banking at all, with personal accounts merely run as a convenience here and there for a major company,

---

* The Chartered's first telex machine had gone into Singapore's Battery Road head office in 1962.

say, or the staff of a British embassy. A whole set of new banking routines had to be devised; hundreds of counter staff needed hiring and training.*

The speed of the retail network's growth ran counter to a serious loss of confidence in the local Chinese banking sector, precipitated by excessive advances against volatile property values and the disclosure of a costly fraud at one of the largest local lenders. The resulting run on deposits amounted in 1965 to a full-blown crisis and several Chinese banks failed – though both the Chartered and Hongkong Bank co-operated with the Colony's officials on efforts to stem the damage.[68] The Chartered was soon faced with a crisis of its own. Many of its new branches picked up tens of thousands of customers, all with their own savings account and passbook (not to mention a little plastic Donald Duck, to be used as a piggy bank, which became strangely popular). They were promised interest on these accounts, payable every six months. The bank was still wholly dependent, though, on the mechanical ledgers installed by NCR in the late 1950s. In charge of the retail network was W. C. L. (Bill) Brown, who had arrived in Hong Kong at about the same time as Graham, having worked under him in Bangkok. Brown pointed out to Graham late in 1965 that it was taking two to three months to calculate the interest due on all the accounts. The task was bound eventually to overwhelm them. The only solution, both men decided, would be to install a computer. No retail banking network in Britain had yet taken this step – though Hongkong Bank was known to be considering it – and the administrators in Bishopsgate did not respond too helpfully: they simply suggested that if the mechanical ledgers were struggling, the branch should buy more of them. At this point, Pullen descended on Hong Kong for a long-scheduled visit. His arrival, as Brown would later recall, proved timely:

> We had got into rather a bitter argument with London. So we had a conference and put our problem to him. Pullen hadn't heard about it from anyone in Bishopsgate. He got on the telephone immediately to the

---

* As it happened, the bank in Des Voeux Road had an ideal person to take care of the tellers. In 1965 Graham promoted a Chinese secretary to be one of the first female managers in the bank. Her name was Vera Waters, who in 1960 had married Dan Waters, a British civil servant working in the Colony. She had joined the bank aged twenty in 1956. By the time of her appointment, she had founded a charm school on the side. Graham allowed her to keep this going, though he did ask that she give up a weekly slot on one of Hong Kong's television stations offering advice on health and beauty. As Staff Relations Manager, she took charge (among other duties) of training the retail network's tellers on grooming and personal appearance. She retired, after a remarkable career, in 1988, and went on to launch a successful second career in the cosmetics business. (Vera Waters, interview with author, 20 March 2012.)

administrative people, and said he wanted everyone involved with this
argument to be in Hong Kong the next morning. Well, it took them more
than a day to get there but eventually they all arrived. They sat in a line
while we made our presentation of what we thought the problem was and
how we would solve it. Pullen ruled on the spot. He said, 'Okay, you get a
computer.' To the administration people from London he said, 'Just go
home – you're in a different world.' Which of course they were.[69]

Brown was appointed as the bank's first Computer Manager, with a
brief to build an on-line, real-time system connecting all the retail tellers
to a mainframe computer in the branch on Des Voeux Road. After a period
of leave in the UK, he spent September 1966 studying the basics of computer programming at NCR's headquarters in Dayton, Ohio, and visiting
its US banking clients to learn from their experiences. When he returned
to the Colony, he was given six months to complete the whole assignment.
The climate of Hong Kong was even less congenial to computers than to
raw cotton: the air-conditioning units necessary to protect NCR's mainframe entailed setting it inside a re-designed room the length of a
cricket-pitch, kitted out on an upper floor of the bank. Cable & Wireless
took on the work of plugging in all the retail outlets. It was often a fraught
business, which involved some long working hours – at a time when the
streets around the bank were often teeming with demonstrators, waving
their little red books in allegiance to Mao's Cultural Revolution. (Events
on the Chinese mainland reverberated in the Colony for many months,
and widespread rioting saw eight branches of the Chartered set on fire.)
But the project was successfully completed, and formally inaugurated with
250,000 savings accounts in June 1967. The Chartered had pipped its
larger Hong Kong neighbour to the post, which made it the first British
bank in the world to adopt an on-line system. For the next two years,
Brown was charged with extending computerization across the other main
administrative departments of the bank. And, by 1969, thoughts were
turning to a duplication of Hong Kong's achievement in Singapore.

The success of the Chartered's branch in Hong Kong marked out a new
future for the bank, no longer dependent on the traditional trade links of
the Empire. It had taken many years fully to acknowledge the need for a
reappraisal of its core business, perhaps too many. Adjusting its approach
across the whole of the network – as urged by Archie Rose, among others,
three decades earlier – would still take time, and there was little to spare
by the 1960s. Ironically, Hong Kong itself was the one corner of the old
colonial world least affected by the search for new constitutional structures and a post-imperial identity. At the opposite end of the spectrum

was South Africa – with consequences that had already entailed a radical upheaval for the Standard Bank.

3. STAND-OFF AT THE STANDARD

Anyone in the 1930s noting South Africa's slightly anomalous dependence on a pair of Imperial banks run from London – the Standard Bank and Barclays DCO – might well have pondered the future of this arrangement. What would become of it, were there to be a marked shift in the attitude of South Africans to the Empire (against which, of course, some of them had fought a bitter war within living memory)? It was certainly a question that the Standard's own senior men in the Cape asked themselves. One General Manager in Cape Town, F. E. King, wrote a prescient note on the subject for the London Directors as early as 1934. South Africa, he warned, had acquired a new consciousness of itself as a separate country – thanks in large part to a spread of Afrikaans and Afrikaner sentiment. 'The present and immediate future', he suggested, would be 'a period during which this Bank will undergo a gradual change in character.' The bank had to acknowledge 'the demand for a predominantly South African character in Banking policy, directed, not in London, but in South Africa, with full recognition of South African needs . . . framed in South Africa for South Africa, free of the supposedly inimical influence of the needs of London'.[70] King's views were regarded in London as alarmist, and part of a running campaign by him to have the South African Head Office moved from Cape Town to Pretoria, closer to the machinery of government and to the real centre of the country's economic growth. They preferred to stick with Cape Town, which all of them enjoyed visiting and where so many of the bank's long-standing British customers were still based. In the event, this stance probably did the bank little harm over the next several years. Though the rising wealth of the Transvaal did finally eclipse the agricultural economy of the Cape well before the 1930s were over, the Standard was not conspicuously disadvantaged by its head-office location. Nor, as it turned out, was King right to suggest the Standard would very soon be compelled to let policy be set 'in South Africa for South Africa'. Leaving aside the more strident voices of Afrikaner nationalism – as yet just a looming shadow – few people before 1939 seemed genuinely to resent the bank's policy being set in London. The Standard's ubiquitous branches had been a feature of South African towns for so long that most of its customers were probably only vaguely aware of its British connections. As we have seen already, it had made a genuine effort, in cahoots with

Barclays DCO, to deliver improved and innovatory services, if only to
avert official criticism of the powerful duopoly they enjoyed. To have
accused the two British banks of crowding out local competitors would
have been misleading, given how little demand existed for additional
banking capacity in the economy. In Johannesburg itself, the banks were
largely superfluous to the financing needs of South Africa's biggest companies: the mining groups scarcely took any heed of them at all.

However, it was King's sense of timing that let him down, not his
analysis. Once the war with Nazi Germany was under way – and the
Government in Pretoria had begun borrowing heavily from the two 'foreign banks' – their dominant role in South Africa's economy soon began
to attract more comment, much of it hostile despite South Africa's huge
commitment to the Allied cause. The altered mood was reflected in a
change of status for a co-operative savings bank, the Volkskas Beperk
('People's Bank') founded in 1934; with the active support of National
Party politicians, it became a fully fledged commercial bank in 1941.
Intent on boosting its prospects at the expense of the two British giants,
the same politicians seized on the passage of a Banking Bill through the
South African Parliament in the early months of 1942 and did their best
to ensure that it would mark the start of a new era for the country's banks,
subjecting them to close South African regulation whether their shareholders were domestic or substantially based in the City of London. This briefly
raised the prospect of a forced incorporation for the Standard in Pretoria.[71]
That danger passed, but the regulatory climate for the banks had nonetheless been transformed. By the summer of 1944, the Standard's auditors
were busy scratching their heads – in unison with those of DCO,
naturally – over the level of disclosure that would now be required in South
Africa on the transfer of profits into hidden reserves. How much of the
bank's capital would in future need to be held inside South Africa was
another of several dilemmas faced by the accountants. And Pretoria now
had a 'Registrar of Banks', to monitor the industry.*

It is not hard to imagine how all this might have prompted radical

---

* The first holder of the title was keen to impose a ceiling on any single shareholding in the
Standard, whether registered or held beneficially. The same edict posed no problem for
Barclays DCO: the Registrar was happy that all of its stock was held by Barclays, after being
assured that any sale of control by the parent was 'considered unlikely'. It was obviously a
trickier issue for the Standard. The Registrar had to be tactfully reminded that its shares
traded freely in London. All the Board could offer, by way of reassurance, was a promise
that it would refuse to register any transfer of shares to a new party who 'might not appreciate its responsibilities' (Secretary to General Manager, Cape Town, 13 April 1945, LMA:
ST03/03/12/004).

changes at the Standard in the aftermath of the war. (It went unremarked at the time, but questions over the relative responsibilities of London and Cape Town were to some extent a reprise of the uncertainties after 1918 over who would take responsibility for the expanding operations in East Africa.) Sensing a shift of mood, the Board in London might have decided the time had come to restructure the governance of the bank, ceding effective control to individuals based in South Africa, home to more than 85 per cent of its 5,570 staff.[72] Since 1936, the daily running of the bank had increasingly been left by the Directors to a successful collaboration between two accomplished General Managers, both Englishmen with many years of experience in Africa – Milton Clough in the Cape, and in London Ralph Gibson, who had risen through the ranks having begun his career as a twenty-three-year-old clerk in Durban in 1911 (not to be confused with his namesake, J. P. Gibson, whose leadership had been so vital to the bank in South Africa in the 1920s). Some outsiders, slightly puzzled that the bank still had a rota of weekly chairmen, assumed the arrangement was left in place chiefly out of respect for this Clough–Gibson partnership. By pushing this delegation one crucial stage further, in favour of the Head Office in Adderley Street, the Board could conceivably have acknowledged the spirit of the 1942 Act and resolved an ambiguity that had been a source of tension (not always of the creative variety) since the days of Robert Stewart.

It did not happen. Indeed, the Board might almost be said to have moved in the opposite direction. After the war, a clear consensus plainly still existed among powerful men in the City of London that Britain's overseas banking legacy had to be cherished and protected. Saying good-bye to the City's single most important tie with South Africa was scarcely a plausible option. Besides, almost all of Standard's shareholders were still British, or at least had their interests registered in the City. It did not require an egregious sense of *noblesse oblige* for the Square Mile's leading figures to see what was required of them on the City's behalf. Four of the Big Five clearing banks – the fifth was Barclays – had had representatives on the Standard's Board for years. Steps were taken now to ensure their influence over the bank was not lost. A soon-to-retire Director of the Standard, Stanley Christopherson, was able in 1945 to turn to a colleague on the Board of the Midland Bank who had become the latter's Deputy Chairman in 1944 – and had previously been for four years the longest-serving wartime British High Commissioner to South Africa. This was Lord (Billy) Harlech. He had not greatly enjoyed his time in South Africa.[73] But when the nudge came from Christopherson, Harlech knew his duty – as he candidly confessed to one of his new Standard colleagues: 'I may say I was not at all anxious to go on the Board of the Standard Bank and only reluctantly agreed to do so because Christopherson ... was anxious that some director of the Midland should be on the Standard Board.'[74] Those new colleagues by 1947 included the Chairman of Lloyds Bank (Lord Balfour), the Deputy Chairman of the National Provincial (Sir Jasper Ridley, also Chairman of Coutts & Co.), and two Directors of Westminster Bank (Robin Arbuthnot and Michael Berry).

All were wealthy men from families with deep roots in the City, for whom it was apparently self-evident that a bank of the Standard's importance could not possibly be handed over to its managers at the Cape. Of course the geography of the bank posed a challenge. As one Director, John Gilliat, put it in welcoming another new arrival on the Board in 1945: 'there are plenty of problems to be dealt with here, dealing with affairs so far away ... new blood [in the Boardroom] will be of vital importance in the years to come'.[75] The Cape was, however, far less remote now than it had been for their predecessors in earlier generations. Moreover, despite the war, Clements Lane had retained the two figures who had been key to its authority before 1939. Ralph Gibson was still there as one of the two General Managers. And Bertram Lowndes remained on the Board, which he had joined in 1936 having previously been London Manager for twelve years.[76] He had acquired huge influence over the bank's affairs. Indeed, Lowndes had in some ways become de facto Chairman of the Board, as Gilliat (himself a Director since the early 1930s) frankly acknowledged in a memorandum of 1947 when Lowndes was at last approaching retirement:

> When Mr Lowndes was London manager we had a succession of somewhat mediocre Cape Town Managers and it was through him, and only him, in my opinion, that the Bank got through some difficult times (eg, the Gold Affair) ... Mr Lowndes came on the Board [in 1936] and practically all matters of importance were referred to him and replies advised by him ... and to that extent he took the responsibility that a permanent Chairman would have taken in another difficult time.[77]

As for the idea of a Board in South Africa: as the London Directors perceived the world, counterparts to themselves were simply not available in South Africa – and never could be, if close links to the Colonial Office, the Bank of England and the City establishment were accepted as key credentials for any truly effective Director. After a return visit to the Cape in 1946, Harlech virtually admitted as much to the bank's Secretary:

Certainly when I was in South Africa I heard criticism that the Bank was managed too much from and by London by Directors many of whom had no knowledge or personal experience of Africa. But the more I have thought it over, the more difficult it appears to me to be able to find the personnel in South Africa for a local board or 'advisory committee'.[78]

So Harlech and his fellow Directors agreed together that the post-war Board had to take a firmer grip. One expression of this resolve would be a willingness among the Directors to make more regular trips into the field, exploiting the new convenience of air travel. Accordingly, starting in 1946, two or three of them were now to take to the road in southern Africa each year, invariably subjecting themselves to a gruelling schedule of branch visits and official receptions – not to mention nasty bouts of fever and recurring crises over stolen luggage – and returning with copious reports on how to improve the network. One of the most resilient and painstaking was John Hogg, a forceful member of the Board and a Director also of the London private bank Glyn, Mills & Co. He toured the region in 1947–8 visiting dozens of branches – including sixteen in the Johannesburg area alone – and requiring twenty-seven different hotel reservations over less than twelve weeks. He carried two black pocket-sized files, with key data for each branch of the bank and a page for his private observations about the individuals he met in them. Some were good ('Kimberley – Three damn good men at this branch. Johnston: tall, thin, outstandingly nice-looking'); some were bad ('Bulawayo Manager – Woolly headed old waffler who knows Rhodesia'); and some were ugly ('Schaafsma [on the East Rand] – An ugly little Dutchman with little hairs sticking out of his ears but brim full of personality'). But all were registered in Hogg's carefully handwritten notes for future reference, by someone plainly intent on having a hand in the detailed management of the bank.[79]

These Directors were not insensitive to the debate in South Africa over local versus external control of its banks – which, as Lord Balfour pointed out in a Board memo of 1947, 'must be regarded as more than usually delicate owing to the impending transfer of the Head Office of the Netherlands Bank to South Africa'.* But having resolved to exert more influence,

---

* Founded in 1888 with its head office in Amsterdam and a branch in Pretoria, the Netherlands Bank before the war had remained a modest trade-oriented business largely restricted to branches in Pretoria and Johannesburg. It had been rapidly expanding its network in South Africa since 1945 and by 1947 was openly planning to incorporate itself as a South African bank with its head office in Johannesburg. The changes were to be consummated in 1951, launching the 'Netherlands Bank of South Africa' (Nedbank) – though most of the shares would yet remain foreign-owned until 1962.

the Directors had by 1947 already discovered an important additional rationale for asserting the Standard's British dimension – a *raison d'être* for London's role that had been quietly gathering potency for years and was now to assume suddenly far greater significance. The bank's fortunes elsewhere in sub-Saharan Africa were booming. In the southern half of Rhodesia, rising exports of tobacco grown on new settlers' farms and the establishment of local subsidiaries by many British companies were boosting profits not just in Salisbury and Bulawayo but a dozen or so other townships with names exotic to any European ear, from Gwanda and Gatooma to Que Que, Selukwe and Umtali. The sources of growth were different in Northern Rhodesia and Nyasaland – featuring predominantly copper mining and refining in the one, cotton farming in the other – but the evidence in those territories, too, pointed to an impending transformation of the region. By 1948, the Board was approving an expansion of the bank's administrative offices in Salisbury – not least 'as an effective counter-measure to the competitive activities of the other Bank', for Barclays DCO was fast mutating from collaborator into pesky rival – and the creation there of a new post of 'Superintendent for Central Africa' along the lines adopted many years earlier for East Africa.[80] As for the progress in East Africa itself, the story here was much the same, and the growth of its economy was surpassing all forecasts. A report on the region compiled by a visiting Director in July 1948 noted that loans had doubled and profits had trebled in the year to March, versus the previous financial year, and were now scarcely comparable with anything seen in the past.[81] The Superintendent in Nairobi since 1942, Richard Gray, looked back two years later on 'a flood of new business that engulfed [East Africa] from 1946 to 1949'.[82] Office hours in Nairobi, Zanzibar, Dar-es-Salaam and a dozen smaller branches commonly began early and extended late into the night.

Whatever their prospects, though, these were scarcely yet stand-alone operations. The administration in Salisbury reported to Cape Town, and the bank's activities in both Central and East Africa were still tied closely to operations within the Union – not least in terms of staffing. Clements Lane sent out as many recruits as it could muster, and young British officers were much in demand, but most appointments were inevitably filled from South Africa. True, Gray reported directly to Home Office, via the London Manager – much to his irritation, for he thought his importance merited direct access to the Board – but even more vexing to Gray than his London reporting line was the Board's failure in 1949 to promote him to a senior post in the Union, which he reckoned his just dessert. As this suggests, East and South Africa were still viewed by most Standard men as parts of the same basic franchise, more than twenty years after the reorganization of 1926 that left the former reporting to London. So for the Directors in London to have surrendered control of the Standard to managers and local boards in South Africa would, at this juncture, undoubtedly have meant losing control over some of the most promising developments in the entire Sterling Area. This was hardly a viable option. Investors in the City by 1948 were alert to the potential of the emerging African territories, though the bank kept the full extent of their contribution under wraps (in fact, activities outside the Union were now accounting for almost 50 per cent of total trading profits[83]). British shareholders in the Standard had no interest in consigning the future direction of Central and Eastern Africa, any more than of South Africa itself, to a list of unknown names in the Cape. Better by far to stick with their existing Directors – among them Sir Dougal Malcolm, one of the most powerful figures in Northern Rhodesia's emerging copper industry, whose other positions included not only directorships of Consolidated Gold Fields and the British South Africa Company but the chairmanships also of some of the largest corporations in Southern Rhodesia and South West Africa, and seats on a string of businesses owned by South Africa's powerful Oppenheimer family.

In short, despite all the wartime developments in Pretoria, the Standard in the late 1940s remained very much under British direction – and perhaps even more so, in a host of minor ways. Clements Lane did its modest best to ease recruitment problems in South Africa by sending out men from Britain.[84] It requested that more notice be given than hitherto about managerial appointments around the South African network, and pressed suggestions for new branches on the senior team in Cape Town. Dozens of demobbed men from the South African forces had accepted invitations in 1945–6 to work in Clements Lane for a year or two before returning home, and their experience had also encouraged closer ties. Secondments to London were later reintroduced for promising young officers, under the watchful eye of a new London Manager, C. R. Hill, a former Superintendent of East Africa who in 1948 succeeded Ralph Gibson. Profit remittances from the Cape to London were put on a monthly rather than biannual basis, and a proposal to the Secretary that Cape Town's annual report to London might be truncated was summarily rejected ('It is appreciated that much labour is involved in its compilation but . . . we would not wish to see it reduced in its scope or from its present form.'[85]) Monthly cables to London on the state of the bank's finances were finally abolished in May 1949, but only because the air-mail service was now deemed reliable enough for regular letters to take their place. Meanwhile, Cape Town was left in no doubt of the Board's determination to play an assertive role in the shaping of the Central and East African businesses. As the Secretary explained in a fulsome note on future strategy in March 1948, in discussing how best to cope with the rivalry of The Other Bank in the Rhodesias and Nyasaland, 'we are inclined to the view that it would best suit us to seek close cooperation with the issuing and finance houses in London who are likely to extend their operations in Africa. This question will be explored here . . .'[86] In Nairobi, following an acrimonious exchange of letters with the Board, Richard Gray had finally agreed to remain as Superintendent for the final two years of his career but may have been regretting it, so heavy were the demands from Clements Lane: 'we have been made to feel that the order has changed . . . We appreciate that queries and explanations are necessary in connection with the control of advances, but the barrage to which we have been subjected is extraordinary.'[87]

Meanwhile, a barrage of a different and altogether more worrying kind had begun to batter the bank itself, within South Africa. In May 1948, to widespread surprise, the National Party replaced the government of Jan Smuts's United Party in a general election, heralding the start of a new era for the Union. Just as the post-war, post-Hitler world was turning its back irrevocably on any public espousal of racism, the National Party was leading South Africa uncompromisingly in the opposite direction. The immediate difficulty for the Standard was less the momentous commitment to apartheid than the National Government's undisguised ambitions for Afrikaner supremacy in the commercial life of the country at the expense of English-speaking – and especially English-owned – businesses. Local control of all the country's banks had been part of the National Party's manifesto. Within months of the election, public bodies in the Union with bank accounts at the Standard were being pressed to transfer them to the Volkskas, or 'Onse Bank' ('Our Bank') as it was increasingly referred to in Afrikaans. Managers at the Standard were privately scornful of their peers at Barclays DCO who were soon busily re-signing their branches as De Nationale Bank der Zuid-Afrikaansche Republiek Beperk – the local bank acquired by Barclays in 1925 – but there was no denying that the other bank had a useful edge here. The Standard had as yet seen no reason even to publish an Afrikaans version of its annual report: the first would not appear until 1952. A few months after he had succeeded Milton Clough as the General Manager in 1948, A. McKellar White (another Englishman) encountered the new Finance Minister, H. C. Havenga, at a dinner of the Institute of Bankers in Johannesburg. He was embarrassed when the Minister pointedly remarked to him in front of his peers that 'only Barclays had directors at the dinner'.[88] In all its dealings with the Government and the Reserve Bank, the Board had to acknowledge a greatly heightened sensitivity. The retirement of both Clough and Gibson in 1948 rekindled an overdue debate over whether or not to scrap the Weekly Chairman rota in favour of a permanent Chairman. The idea was shelved again, in case it might appear that the bank was gearing up for a fight. (At least this probably made it easier for Ralph Gibson to join the Board, which he did at the end of the year.) The Standard seemed powerless, though, to disarm a hostility in official circles that mounted steadily through 1949 and 1950. A Director who toured the Union in July and August 1950 sent the Board regular notes on the problem. He applauded the fact that two new Assistant General Managers were both bilingual South Africans. ('Mr Davies's speech in Afrikaans at the opening the other day of our new Heilbron branch was quite an historic event.') But his final conclusion was sobering: 'It seems certain that we shall eventually be forced by Union politics to adopt local direction with or without registration of a [subsidiary] company in the Union.'[89]

This, of course, ran diametrically counter to the Directors' instincts since 1945, and posed a terrible dilemma. The Board agonized for much of the next two years over how best to respond.[90] All eventually agreed in principle that rather than risk being pushed into a transfer of power to South Africa, the bank would be better to jump of its own accord. In practice, however, the debate was smothered with ambiguities. The need for some kind of local representation in South Africa evolved over 1951 into an acceptance of the case for a 'Local Board', but little was done to define the extent of its intended independence from the main Board. Early in 1952, and largely at the behest of Gibson who chaired a special committee of the Board, it was formally decided that a full-blown subsidiary had to be the bank's acknowledged destination; and the sooner it was reached the better, according to most of those senior managers in South Africa whose views were sought. But defining its nature raised some delicate questions. Would the existence of a subsidiary imply a surrender of the London Board's control? Might it even entail a dilution of existing shareholders' interests via a sale of shares in South Africa? So the Board went no further than describing the Local Board as a 'first step' towards having a full subsidiary. This rankled with some, including Sir Dougal Malcolm who shrewdly noted in May 1952:

> I am in some doubt as to whether [the Local Board] can really properly be
> so described [i.e. as a 'first step']. The formation of a subsidiary Union
> Company appears to me to be something fundamentally different from the
> establishment of a Local Board of a Company, the ultimate control and

management of which remains in London where the Board is. Between that
and the establishment of a subsidiary company, with its Board and its whole
management in the Union, there seems to me to be a great gulf fixed, and
a great gulf cannot be crossed by steps.[91]

In South Africa, meanwhile, a constitutional crisis had erupted over a
legal challenge to the Government's intended disenfranchisement of Coloured voters in the Cape. Milton Clough, who had moved into an advisory
role much as Gibson had done, was prompted by this ominous development to reverse his previous support for a subsidiary and he urged a more
cautious line. This was warmly endorsed in London by a newly appointed
Director, who within months of joining the Board in 1952 accepted its
invitation to become (with effect from January 1953) the first permanent
Chairman of the bank since 1864. This was Sir Frederick Leith-Ross, the
former Treasury mandarin who had travelled to Nanking in 1935 to advise
Chiang Kai-shek's Nationalist Government on its monetary policies.*
Leith-Ross had just returned in 1951 from five years in Cairo as Governor
of the National Bank of Egypt, but his distinguished career in international finance had not yet included any experience of South Africa. He
wanted more time to weigh the options; Clough and Gibson both
concurred.

As all these reservations surfaced, the idea of a subsidiary was tacitly
abandoned. The Board fell back on the simpler notion of a Local Board,
with no strings. In fact it settled for three Boards. A 'South Africa Board'
would meet in the bank's imposing branch on Johannesburg's Commissioner Street, while a 'Cape Board' would meet in Cape Town to watch
over the bank's affairs in the Western Cape, and Salisbury would have its
own 'Rhodesia Board'. In November 1952 Leith-Ross and Gibson set off
for South Africa with the delicate task of appointing the Board members.
There was a curious outcome. The prominent Afrikaner identified as their
first choice to chair the South African Board turned them down; and a
succession of other names were all rejected as second-raters by Gibson
(gently chided by Leith-Ross at one point as 'a hard man to please'). On
5 January 1953 the General Manager in Cape Town, McKellar White,
sent Leith-Ross a handwritten note with his own strong personal
recommendation. It turned out to be none other than Ralph Gibson. This
was awkward, because the Board had already settled on Clough as

---

* Leith-Ross was not the first man approached for the role. Both the British High Commissioner in South Africa, Evelyn Baring, and the British Government's top financial man in
Salisbury, Sir Gordon Munro, had been sounded out for it in 1950–51 as they neared the end
of their tenures – in vain.

Chairman of the Cape Board. Co-opting two former General Managers as chairmen hardly signalled much of a break with the past. After conferring with his colleagues in London, and assuring them that McKellar White had acted entirely off his own bat, Leith-Ross sat down for a chat with his travelling companion – or so he later explained in a letter to the Directors.

> I told Mr Gibson that . . . [the Directors] found it hard to understand that no suitable South African could be found for the Chairmanship and they considered that an arrangement by which the Chairmen of both the Local Boards would be Ex-General Managers of the Bank would give an entirely wrong impression.[92]

Yet, that very same day, Leith-Ross wrote a second letter home that effectively set all the Board's misgivings at naught: 'The more I think it over, the more it seems to me that it would be wisest to tide over the transition from London to South Africa by putting Gibson in the Chair at the first stage.' The Board's sharp reaction was instantly blunted, and Gibson was duly appointed. Given Leith-Ross's long experience in the devious ways of Whitehall, it is of course possible that his first letter had artfully paved the way for the second – the outcome must surely have pleased him, and seems most unlikely to have popped into his head that day. He and Gibson, anyway, resumed their task of assembling three respectable Boards. It took them another seven weeks with Gibson evidently as hard to please as ever. ('The trouble is that the Afrikaner who is available and has the qualifications for a directorship is a very rare bird.'[93])

The resulting arrangements quite unexpectedly saw out the rest of the 1950s. Real profits hovered within the same broad range each year, the network of branches and agencies across South Africa went on growing steadily, and shrewd leadership in both London and the Union sustained a pragmatic regime that, while occasionally uneasy, had almost a century's worth of momentum behind it.[94] After moving to Cape Town and becoming a South African citizen, Gibson forged a close working relationship with McKellar White and remained on the best of terms with the Secretary in London, who was a personal friend. This allowed him to preside over a gradual extension of the South African Board's de facto authority, without it being seen as a threat to the continued primacy of the Directors in London – and Milton Clough pulled off a similar feat in Cape Town. For their part, the Directors came close to behaving as though the 1952 decision in principle to have a South African subsidiary had never been taken at all. Leith-Ross, essentially a deeply cautious Treasury man, had no difficulty justifying this change of heart – as here, to Gibson in the aftermath of a second election victory for the National Party in 1954 that sealed its dominance of the country's politics:

> we contemplated the step [to a subsidiary] as likely to be welcomed as a recognition of South African 'nationhood', but we would not want it to be regarded as a sign of weakness or of surrender to the Afrikaans domination as, in present political circumstances, we gather that it would be.[95]

Gibson himself never backed away from his support for the idea of a subsidiary, which, predictably, the Local Boards' members all favoured, but he was not prepared to let the issue rupture his relations with the London Board. The stance of the authorities in Pretoria towards the bank suggested a deeply ambivalent attitude. On the one hand, Government ministers continued publicly to encourage strident expressions of Afrikaner nationalism, openly hostile to all foreign banks. They continued to press for the Standard's head office to be relocated from Cape Town to Pretoria, a move finally made in 1953. (It would have made more sense to relocate directly to Johannesburg – as happened in 1959.) On the other hand, senior officials were often far more conciliatory in private, especially after public interest in the issue appeared to fade. Intriguingly, there were those in official circles who were even starting to worry about the implications of enforcing local control. A Director of the Standard, visiting Pretoria in 1954, asked the Chairman of one of the Government's foremost investment bodies if he would applaud the foreign banks for transferring all their governance to South Africa, and was surprised by the answer: 'He felt that . . . in the long run by such action the banks would possibly be doing South Africa a disservice. The time may well come when the overseas connections provided by the banks in their present form will be invaluable to the country.'[96] A prescient response.

In April 1957, Leith-Ross stepped down as Chairman (remaining a Director) and was succeeded by his close friend, Edmund Hall-Patch. The two men had first met in 1919 – in a Paris night-club, where the twenty-four-year-old Hall-Patch was saxophonist in the band – and had worked together in China in 1935, just one of several occasions on which Leith-Ross, nine years older, had helped along the younger man's career. For all of Hall-Patch's financial expertise, though, he was a very different figure from Leith-Ross – more Foreign Office than Treasury, and cast a little in the mould of Archie Rose at Chartered Bank. 'His dress, slightly theatrical and antique, with stocks and stick-pins, an unscrutable air behind thick spectacles, and a tendency to break suddenly into French all added to the enigma.'[97] He had had a distinguished career since his time as an adviser in the Far East, representing Britain at the nascent

International Monetary Fund and accompanying the post-war Labour Government's Foreign Secretary, Ernest Bevin, on several overseas missions. His experience of international affairs had left Hall-Patch with a pessimistic view of human nature and he was sceptical of visionary schemes for the betterment of society.* But, finding himself late in life and rather unexpectedly involved with Africa's future, he came to take a lively interest in the economics of the sub-Saharan continent: the scope for labour-market reforms and the challenge of building modern townships for impoverished urban populations were topics that genuinely engaged him. When Britain's Institute of Race Relations sought his endorsement for a project in East Africa in 1959, he responded with more than token support: it was at his instigation that the bank's Superintendant for East Africa, R. G. Ridley, took on a role as local co-ordinator for the project.[98] Disdainful both of strident left-wing critics of British colonial rule in Africa and of the National Party's aspirations for Afrikanerdom, Hall-Patch tried to align the bank behind people and policies geared to sensible compromises. But time was running out for compromises in southern Africa – as he and his colleagues on the Standard Board were painfully slow to grasp, with jarring consequences.

4. SEMI-SEVERED FROM SOUTH AFRICA

At the top of Hall-Patch's in-tray on his first day at Clements Lane was a letter addressed to his predecessor from Ridley in Nairobi, reporting on complaints in the East Africa region about the name of the bank.[99] The 'wind of change' that the British Prime Minister Harold Macmillan would famously proclaim to the South African parliament in February 1960 was as yet just a stiff breeze in 1957, but the men running the Standard Bank of South Africa's branches in Kenya, Uganda and Tanganyika (and to a lesser extent Nyasaland, too) could already feel its chilling effect on their businesses. Over the next three years, the startlingly rapid rise of independence movements in these countries brought a steady intensification of the anti-apartheid movement. The Standard, nowhere perceived as a British bank, found itself classed as a legitimate target of campaigns to boycott all things South African. Nor was it just in East Africa that its name caused problems. The bank's Agency in New York handled the US

---

* His obituary in *The Times* eighteen years later would capture this side of his character with a memorable quote from his former political master. ' "Send for 'all-Patch", Ernest Bevin once said to an optimist, "'e'll make your flesh creep".' (*The Times*, 4 June 1975.)

business of the Bank of West Africa (as the old BBWA had become in 1957, the year that Ghana became an independent state), in which the Standard still held its 11 per cent stake. Bills of lading and letters of credit sent from the Agency to BWA branches in Nigeria and Ghana were increasingly rejected as unacceptable if they bore the name of the Standard Bank of South Africa. Telexes from New York had to have the bank's name carefully excised, and special stationery was adopted by the Agency for correspondence with West Africa.[100] Hall-Patch and his Board looked on in dismay as the bank's travails mounted across the continent from East to West – and knew by the middle of 1959 that the bank had no choice but to change its name if it was to survive, never mind prosper, beyond the borders of the Union. Some lively objections were anticipated from the Local Boards' members within South Africa itself, but this was not thought to be an insuperable problem. It was agreed in London by November 1959 that the words 'of South Africa' would have to be dropped everywhere.

This appraisal was at best highly optimistic in November; within a few months it had become thoroughly unrealistic. In January 1960 Prime Minister Hendrik Verwoerd announced that a referendum would be held, seeking support for the Union's conversion into a Republic; in February his hosts in Cape Town had to listen to Macmillan making his famous speech; and in March there followed the calamitous Sharpeville Massacre. Many businessmen in South Africa were appalled by the direction of events. They were also shaken by the shrillness of the international reaction. Resenting much of the overseas criticism levelled at their country, they were growing daily more sensitive to any perceived gestures of rejection. Those on the Standard's Local Boards were no different, and it posed an obvious challenge for the bank's leading figures in the Union. The most important of these was G. H. R. (Bob) Edmunds, shortly to take over the chairmanship of the South Africa Board from Ralph Gibson. A top accountant in Johannesburg and a hugely well-connected businessman – he was also Chairman of South African Associated Newspapers – the South African-born Edmunds now came to play a pivotal role in the bank's affairs.

Acutely aware of its delicate position ('we will, no doubt, find ourselves skating on an egg', as he rather curiously put it after Verwoerd's referendum speech[101]), Edmunds managed to cement the Local Boards' confidence in his leadership while at the same time shrewdly positioning himself with the London Directors as their man in South Africa. Often writing more than once a week, rather as Stewart and Michell had done in the nineteenth century, he kept up a stream of letters to Hall-Patch.[102] The correspondence evidently reassured the Directors that they were broadly in charge of the bank, even as they ceded real control to Edmunds himself. He exercised it, for the most part, with great skill – building a close rapport with the Chief General Manager who had succeeded McKellar White in 1957, Alwyn Davies, the first South African-born man in that position. But even Edmunds found it impossible to reconcile the Local Boards to the Directors' 1960 resolve to ditch 'South Africa' from the name of the bank. Polite objections were raised early in the year. Then, after a maverick shareholder backed the idea publicly at the London Annual General Meeting in June 1960, the mood among the Local Boards' members, as too among the bank's staff and a concerning number of its customers, turned darkly mutinous.* By November, Edmunds and Gibson (now Deputy Chairman) were ready to present what they saw as an inescapable conclusion – and Edmunds set it down none too gently. 'The Bank has never been thought of as anything else but a completely South African institution', he wrote in a memo to the London Board in November 1960 (the Secretary's filed copy of which has a red line under this sentence and a question mark in the margin).[103] Dropping 'South Africa' from the bank's title would have a devastating impact on its business, culling perhaps 15 per cent or more of its revenues immediately, and turning it thereafter into a 'dying bank'. Anti-English sentiment was already posing serious difficulties for the bank in the more exclusively Afrikaans-speaking areas of the country.[104] If the undeniable problems for the bank elsewhere in Africa dictated a new name there, then the bank had to go forward with two names instead of one: the 'Standard Bank of South Africa' (SBSA) would have to be retained inside the soon-to-be-created Republic, while the plain 'Standard Bank' could be adopted outside it. Implementing

---

* So prickly were the South African Directors by late 1960 that some were even affronted to hear that a planned centenary history of the bank was going to be printed outside the Union. The first draft was nearing completion of what would eventually emerge in 1963 as *The First Hundred Years of the Standard Bank*, compiled by Harry Siepmann, a former Bank of England director (1945–54), and reworked by a (slightly reluctant) Secretary to the Chief General Manager in Cape Town, J. A. Henry. Word reached South Africa in September 1960 that a contract signed with Oxford University Press involved a UK printing. One member of the Cape Town Board, Clive Corder, wrote to Edmunds that this arrangement 'on the face of it looks like a serious blunder which would affect not only the Standard Bank but give people like Volkskas valuable ammunition to fire at the Institutions which are not Afrikaner-controlled'. Edmunds replied with his customary tact, pointing out – as though it might perhaps have been overlooked – that the bank was a UK-domiciled company with its Head Office in London 'and practically all its shareholders are resident there'. So a London printing 'would not be something inconsistent with the surrounding facts'. (Corder to Edmunds and reply, 22–24 September 1960, LMA: ST03/03/01/003.)

the split would necessarily entail 'hiving off' the SBSA business into a subsidiary company.

Much might have been gained, and much ill-will avoided, had it been accepted in London at this point that the logic of the Standard Bank/SBSA split was overwhelming. Unhappily, neither Hall-Patch nor Leith-Ross had yet come to this conclusion, and they led the Board a not-so-merry dance over the next several months to try avoiding it. They dutifully set up a 'Special Working Party' to start preparing, in great secrecy, the paperwork for a South African subsidiary. Edmunds had only restated, after all, an objective already formally accepted in 1951. But the two Englishmen still hankered after a solution that might, somehow, avert the possibility of South Africa slipping from the Board's grasp. The Working Party soon confirmed this was rather more than a mere possibility, were a subsidiary to be formed. The gulf between London and Pretoria was widening by the month. (In February 1961 South Africa introduced its own currency unit, the rand, in place of pounds and shillings.) The tax and legal ramifications of setting up a subsidiary, opined the City's finest advisers, would certainly mean surrendering effective control of the South African business.[105] This so alarmed Hall-Patch and his embattled colleagues that they decided, in the first week of May 1961, that the time had come to dig in their heels. Notwithstanding the fervent objections from Johannesburg, they would insist on a clean change of name, in South Africa as everywhere else. As for the proposed subsidiary, Hall-Patch wrote to Edmunds:

> While there would be certain real advantages [to hiving-off], the Working Party have nevertheless arrived at the conclusion that it is not a practical possibility to proceed with the operation in the immediate future . . . [The Board now feels] the matter should not be pursued. If there is to be a metamorphosis, it must take some other form yet to be determined.[106]

The future shape of this mystery package, predictably, turned out to be of no interest whatever to the Local Board in Johannesburg. Convened to weigh the missive from Hall-Patch, its members reacted with a mix of outrage and dismay that Edmunds communicated straight back to London on 24 May. The Chief General Manager, Alwyn Davies, had been 'seriously concerned' about the danger of losing the loyalty of his staff, and especially of his Afrikaans-speaking managers. The bank's attorney in Johannesburg, Charles Friedman, had suggested 'that if the public turned sour in the matter, we may never regain our position in the banking world'. All were agreed the timing could hardly be more disastrous: the Verwoerd Government had just announced that the inauguration of the new Republic on 31 May 1961 would also mark the country's exit from the

Commonwealth. (Foreign-exchange controls and a ban on the sale of securities to non-residents followed soon afterwards.) As Edmunds pointed out, if news of the bank's intentions were to leak out, it would be construed as a deliberate and deeply provocative slight. The furore in the South African press would hit the Standard's credit-rating in the London markets very hard – and far harder, surely, than any foreseeable boycott of its activities elsewhere in Africa.

The day after this reply to Hall-Patch, it chanced that Davies was due at a meeting of all the commercial banks' heads at the Reserve Bank in Pretoria, followed by a group lunch with the Governor, Mike de Kock. It proved an extremely uncomfortable lunch for Davies, as he reported back to his Chairman later in the afternoon. The canny Edmunds spotted immediately how it could be turned to their advantage. He asked Davies for a detailed account of the occasion, and sent it straight to London the next day. As his covering letter explained, almost apologetically, there had been 'rather a disturbing incident during the lunch that I feel right to be reported to you'. In Davies's words:

> Speaking in Afrikaans, Dr de Kock recalled his close ties with the Standard Bank. Despite the advent of Volkskas he had stuck with them. As a young man living with his parents . . . he was anxious to pursue his studies and it was only as a result of the financial assistance the Standard Bank granted him that he was able to proceed to Harvard to complete his education. The Standard Bank sought no security but acted on their judgment of his trust-worthiness and integrity and that of his parents.
>
> Dr de Kock made the observation that he could not believe the Standard Bank would be so nonsensical as to consider seriously the suggestion which had been made to remove 'South Africa' from its title. The Standard Bank, said Dr de Kock, had operated in this country for just on 100 years and many like himself had grown up with the Bank and regarded it as belonging to South Africa.
>
> . . . [The lunch] has made it clearer than ever to me [concluded Davies] that any change in title would be a great embarrassment to those of us associated with the Bank in South Africa.[107]

As Edmunds must have anticipated, this produced consternation in London. There followed weeks of anguished debate. Hall-Patch, Leith-Ross and their fellow Directors were no keener than their predecessors on the post-war Board to be remembered as the men who scuppered the Standard's status in the City by relinquishing control of South Africa.[108] Consequently, at the start of July, the May decision to change the name was rescinded: 'we have accepted your advice', wrote Hall-Patch to Edmunds, 'we will not pursue for the present the proposal to drop the territorial designation "of South Africa" from our title. That was, I think, your main point and it has been conceded.'[109] The Board leaned heavily towards an alternative scheme, this time putting East Africa into a subsidiary with its own name. Alas, the lawyers came back later in July to say this could take years to achieve. After Edmunds had joined them in London and stopped short of utterly condemning the original plan to shorten the name everywhere, the Directors on 9 August reinstated their May decision to do just that. It was a second remarkable U-turn in six weeks. Somehow, despite the report of Dr de Kock's remarks in May, the Directors managed to persuade themselves that a firm line could be sold successfully to their colleagues in South Africa, and indeed to the Reserve Bank, if only it was presented sufficiently persuasively.

Bravely, Hall-Patch set off to make the pitch in Johannesburg with all of the considerable charm he could muster – to no avail, as he would later recount in detail.[110] Gibson was 'violently opposed to any change' in the name. The Local Boards' Directors were appalled at the prospect of defying the National Party regime 'which is becoming, in their view, quite alarmingly totalitarian'. Several senior managers, including Davies, seemed sure to resign if the plan was implemented. As for Edmunds himself, he refused at first to go with his Chairman to Pretoria, for fear of subsequent recriminations. He relented only when Hall-Patch agreed that no fait accompli would be presented there: the Reserve Bank Governor would instead be asked for his reaction to various potential schemes. And so ensued a second fateful lunch with Dr de Kock. Invited by his ever courteous guest to consider the possibility of a South Africa subsidiary as one of the options, the Governor made abruptly clear how very much Pretoria would welcome it – leaving Hall-Patch boxed into a corner from which there was no escape. The Board in London duly retreated ignominiously to the Standard Bank/SBSA split that had been proposed by Edmunds in November 1960. It was approved by the Board on 13 September 1961. 'So, for better or worse,' wrote Hall-Patch to his South Africa Chairman, 'the plunge has been taken . . .'[111] The decision, naturally, was warmly applauded by its original proposer: '[it is] a great weight off our minds here and I am certain that the Bank will benefit substantially, long term, from the wise step that you have taken'.[112]

Others took a different view. John Hogg, for many years past the most knowledgeable commercial banker on the Board and Hall-Patch's only fellow Director on the Working Party over the first half of the year, resigned in September. He was deeply upset by the way in which the Board had handled its decision-making in August, and convinced that all control over the Bank's future development would now be lost:

> As far as the Standard Bank is concerned, August 1961 has done something to me. It has burnt out something inside. I just do not feel the same about the Bank as I did, & I don't think I ever can again. The problems which used to be an interest . . . are now, I find, a weariness and a burden to the flesh . . . It would seem that you are about to enter negotiations for the formulation of a South African subsidiary because there is now no other course open to you. This South African subsidiary is a thing that should have been given willingly and accepted gratefully. It has been forced out of you. The London Board will now be under the necessity to achieve a South African subsidiary, to achieve it quickly, & to achieve it at any cost.[113]

He was right about the timetable, but a little harsh on the immediate prospects for co-operation. Plans for the hive-off were announced on 2 November, after a last-minute fiasco that seemed only too fitting.* The SBSA subsidiary would take over the bank's South African operations – comprising 700 branches out of a total African network of almost 900 – with effect from 1 March 1962, though the activities in Portuguese East Africa and the High Commission territories of Bechuanaland, Botswana and Swaziland would continue reporting directly to London. It would have a new Board, chaired by Edmunds, which would have ten South African Directors and five nominated by the Board in London. Diplomatic as ever, Bob Edmunds was careful from the outset to assert that nothing of importance was happening: 'control of the subsidiary will continue on the same lines as is now being followed'.[114] Hall-Patch and

---

* Some months earlier, the lawyers had discovered that the necessary international rights for the bank to call itself The Standard Bank were unfortunately unavailable. A Texan business-man who owned a tiny travel agency in Zurich had taken up the name in registering his firm as a bank. Frantic efforts had been made to reach a deal with him and his Swiss shareholders in time for it to be signed early on 9 October, the day scheduled for the announcement of the South African plans – but on 8 October the Texan had boarded a plane from the US to Switzerland and had died during the flight. The press conference had to be cancelled and the arrangements in Zurich were suspended pending the arrival of the Texan's widow from the US. For three weeks, the Directors lived in trepidation of their wider strategy being leaked to the media. As Hall-Patch bemoaned to the East Africa Chairman on 11 October, 'if news of our intention reached the Swiss firm they would be in a position to hold us to ransom' (LMA: SBSA/0868, File 1). Fortunately the parties in Zurich seem never to have got wind of what was afoot, and settled for the sum offered at the start – a mere SwFr 75,000, worth £6,250 then and equivalent to about £110,000 today. (Minutes of the Standard Bank Board meetings, 11 October and 1 November 1961, SCB Box 329.) Much to the Directors' disgust, *The Times* on 3 November disclosed the Zurich saga. 'The young man responsible is, apparently, a South African', wrote Hall-Patch to Edmunds the same day, 'and I hope he has his head washed.'

his fellow Directors fell in with this: Edmunds was assured in October that the Board had 'decided that we should, at the outset, go through the formal motions of transferring control to the subsidiary' – as though to imply that informal control would remain in London.[115] In reality the South African business would now be left to manage its own affairs to a far greater extent than hitherto.[116] (Hall-Patch was privately ready to acknowledge as much by March 1962, even suggesting a code for future correspondence to help avoid misunderstandings.*) That said, London would nonetheless retain a degree of oversight through the next few years that not many predicted in 1962, given the intensity of the 1960–61 crisis over the name. This was partly an acceptance of the financial reality: the Standard's shareholders had seen about £14 million of their capital tied up as liquid resources in South Africa before the hiving-off, which rose to about £25 million after it.[117] But Edmunds and Davies, as the men now charged with SBSA's success, were also conscious of an urgent need to improve its performance in the field and were open to advice from London if it was offered with tact. Edmunds set the tone from the start, reporting back on a New Year trip round the branch network and confessing that it needed 'younger and more intelligent men' in some key posts, as the Directors had been urging for a while.[118]

On these travels, Edmunds was constantly asked when it might be possible for managers to buy shares in the newly established local company. (The Netherlands Bank of South Africa had recently issued shares in its local subsidiary, for which demand had been overwhelming.[119]) This was one question left for another day, and was bound to become steadily more pressing. The same was true of another, scarcely less obvious question. If the Standard Bank in Clements Lane was no longer to be quite so readily identifiable with South Africa, what other overseas franchise might Head Office now seek to build, by way of a substitute?

5. NEW BANKS FOR OLD

The potential value to the Standard of linking up with another bank had occurred to its Chairman well before the crisis broke over its name. On a trip to California in January 1958, Hall-Patch had talked to the senior

---

* If the Directors tendered a 'suggestion', SBSA would be free to follow or disregard it. If they offered their 'advice', SBSA ought not to disregard it without at least giving London a further opportunity to assess the matter in hand. And if they made a 'recommendation', the Directors would expect it to be adopted. (Hall-Patch to Edmunds, 13 March 1962, LMA: ST03/03/01/006.)

people at the Bank of America and been intrigued by their comment that, if they ever wanted to enter the African market, they would prefer to buy their way into it rather than start from scratch – which, as he later confided to the Bank of England, he thought 'may have been a wink'. (One official at the Bank noted to another that he would have expected the Bank of America to prefer a takeover bid to any minority-stake arrangement, 'which would make what Sir Edmund took to have been a wink into rather a wolfish leer'.[120]) The Bank wasted no time making clear it would not favour the Standard ceding even a minority stake to an American bank. But banks with international ambitions were everywhere talking up the merits of basing their strategy on a well-aimed merger – or amalgamation, to use the term in vogue – and the Standard's Directors were certainly alive to the trend.

Early in July 1959, with their share price looking none too robust, they invited a partner of Lazards merchant bank to come in and talk to them about the changes afoot in the commercial banking world. With little preamble, the Lazards man reviewed the mergers currently mooted in the City and 'wondered whether this Bank might consider making some move in this direction'.[121] He noted the value to Barclays DCO of its 'big brother' – though the Board can scarcely have needed reminding of it – and suggested that '[w]ithout similar support this Bank might face a hard run in the course of time; the Chartered Bank might be looked at'. This abruptly tabled proposal was not an instant success. Some doubted there was much advantage to be had from linking with a bank saddled with such 'unsettled political conditions' in its key markets (indicating, perhaps, how little the Board was really aware, even at this late date, of the toxic nature of its own link to post-1948 South Africa). Others much preferred the idea of approaching one of the Big Five clearers: Lord Balfour confessed he had been pondering a link with the Lloyds banking group for a long time 'but had not suggested it before as he had always been very conscious of the strong independence of this Bank'.[122] Another consideration, though, strengthened the case for making an overture to the Chartered. As we have seen, Chartered's 1957 purchase of the Eastern Bank had left it with Barclays DCO as a 15 per cent shareholder. Hall-Patch warned his colleagues about a rumour that the Hongkong Bank was contemplating a merger with the Chartered's principal rival in the sub-continent, the National Bank of India – or National & Grindlays, as it had just rechristened itself (having acquired the much smaller Grindlays Bank network in India ten years earlier). Such a bold initiative by the Hongkong Bank might be enough to prod the Chartered into a counter-move, suggested Hall-Patch; in which case, its obvious partner of choice would surely be DCO. This was a sufficiently worrying possibility to warrant pre-emptive action. As another of the Directors insisted, 'a claim should be staked by approaching the Chartered Bank otherwise there was great danger of being outflanked'.[123] A 'Merger Committee' was set up 'to meet situations which might arise', and Hall-Patch – after another couple of talks with the Governor of the Bank, this time rather more encouraging – dashed off a note to Vincent Grantham at the Chartered to ask for 'half an hour of your time as soon as convenient'.[124]

The two Chairmen met for a first conversation early in September 1959. Now seventy years of age, Grantham may not have played any conspicuous role in the executive management of his bank for years, but his stance towards any putative merger affecting the Chartered's independence would still be critical. He gave the rumoured merger with National & Grindlays (N&G) little credence, but did concede that the Chartered's big rival in Asia might well be 'seeking other outlets'.* Hall-Patch, perhaps taking his cue from the Bank of England's stance, pitched the case for a merger in the context of the new threat that confronted them both: 'it was desirable that the overseas banks, in order to deal with the increasing competition in their territories of the American banks, should consolidate into larger units and so offer more effective competition with the American giants'.[125] The Standard Chairman's record of the conversation included no mention of his counterpart's response – but Grantham had never troubled in the past to conceal his scepticism about sub-Saharan Africa as a place to do business, nor his unease over the apartheid politics of South Africa. (His son remembered him as distinctly averse to any involvement with Africa on both counts: 'Temperamentally he was much more comfortable sticking to business with the sub-continent and the Middle East.'[126])

Two weeks later, Grantham paid his own visit to the Bank of England. The Governor, Lord Cobbold, was entirely sympathetic to the difficulties that Grantham laid out – including his worry that the Standard 'had all their eggs in one basket' – and certainly did not want to be seen 'trying to push the Chartered Bank into it'. But Grantham was also left in no doubt that the Bank felt some concern over the future of the British overseas banks and their vulnerability to bigger and better capitalized (i.e. American) competitors now turning to the international marketplace: it

---

* He told Hall-Patch that Hongkong Bank, while 'a very fine organisation with large reserves', had been ejected from China, squeezed out of Japan, frustrated in India and thwarted (by the Chartered) in Malaya. Given his scepticism that they would have much interest in Africa, it is not clear where Grantham thought they might turn next.

would be pleased to hear that talks about a Standard/Chartered merger were happening.[127] Grantham agreed to meet Hall-Patch again, in November 1959. This time the Standard's Chairman set aside lofty strategic overviews in favour of a more down-to-earth explanation for his wanting to explore a merger. Lacking a close tie with any of the Big Five clearers, the Standard was 'at a competitive disadvantage with Barclays (DC&O) who were extremely aggressive'.[128] Grantham reciprocated with his own candid views on the Chartered's main competitor, Hongkong Bank. He thought they would both 'have to watch the combination of the HKSB and the BBME with very keen eyes'. Even more worrying, to Grantham's mind, was the evident danger that the Hong Kong bank might exploit its low-tax status by snapping up other overseas banks, and relocating them to the Colony as subsidiaries so that they could enjoy the same manifestly unfair tax advantages. (He had complained about this on his recent visit to the Bank of England. 'To his astonishment the Governor had indicated that he was not sure he wished to intervene.') While anxious on this score, however, Grantham was not quite anxious enough to feel like pursuing a merger. He also had his own issues with the Standard. Its name was 'a great handicap . . . [which] would increase in the years ahead'. (He was of course right about that.) Its business in South Africa looked likely to absorb 'a substantial portion' of the bank's reserves if it ever split away. It was also a proudly independent bank – and in this respect, indeed, was just like the Chartered. Neither would want to submerge its identity into the other, suggested Grantham – and Hall-Patch agreed. So a gentleman's understanding was reached, that each represented the other's partner of choice and neither would enter serious discussion elsewhere without prior notice. Further than that, though, Grantham would not go.

For most of the next two years, the Standard's Directors were preoccupied with their conundrum over the bank's South African identity and its travails in East Africa. The dismantling of the British East African Federation was also a serious distraction: it posed exactly the kind of broad financial challenges that had always fascinated Hall-Patch and Leith-Ross since their days in the Far East, and their services – and those of the bank's branches on the ground – were much in demand as advisers and mediators.[129] (With the British civil servants packing their bags, white farmers were increasingly anxious over their prospects in the countries of the old East Africa: Tanganyika, Uganda and Kenya, which were to achieve independence in 1961, 1962 and 1963 respectively. The future constitutional arrangements were still fraught with uncertainty in all three, and the Federation's banking system was now under acute strain – unsurprisingly, given the impending collapse of dozens of over-extended building societies that had been funding white settlements since 1945. Relations between the colonial authorities and several departments of Whitehall were often extremely tetchy.[130]) All this left the Board little time for chasing after radical merger ideas. By late 1961, though, the pursuit was about to be resumed – partly because the Directors had finally resigned themselves to the launch of SBSA but also, and just as crucially, because of a change at the top. Hall-Patch had been increasingly dogged by ill health for some time – taking to his bed for the last two months of 1960 – and he decided before the end of 1961, at the age of sixty-five, that he would hand on the Chairmanship when a successor could be found. The search lasted but a few weeks.

One of his many close friends in the City was Sir Cyril Hawker, the Executive Director at the Bank of England whom we encountered in the context of the Eastern Bank's misadventures with Haridas Mundhra (see p. 368) – and who was due to retire in 1962. Hawker had been mostly concerned with domestic UK affairs in his forty-two years at the Bank, a career which had included being Deputy Chief Cashier and Chief Account-ant.[131] But he had latterly begun to take a special interest in the predicament of the City's overseas banks, perhaps partly as a result of the Mundhra Affair. In particular, he was intrigued by the possibility that refashioning some of the Square Mile's oldest banks as new ones might help to buttress the City's role as the pre-eminent centre for international finance. After the Suez debacle of 1956 few people had any illusions about Britain's rapidly shrinking political influence in the world. The institutions and traditions of the Empire were fading, taking with them the privileged and specialized market niches that had sustained the imperial banks. By pool-ing their inherited networks and traditions, though, it seemed to Hawker that these banks might yet produce a handful of powerful institutions, fortified by their accumulated knowledge of international trade. Sterling yet remained the trading world's dominant currency, still affording banks based in the City of London so many of their historical advantages. And other momentous opportunities were emerging in the City, too – most notably a novel availability of dollars (as 'eurodollar' deposits) that could be recycled as an alternative to sterling.* If we can assume that he and

---

* Eurodollars were simply US dollars on deposit outside the domestic US banking system – of which there were rapidly growing supplies once the US trade deficit began to widen dramati-cally in the later 1950s. A fortuitous combination of regulatory initiatives then produced one of the happier unintended consequences in the history of international finance. The US Fed-eral Reserve showed no interest in ditching a Depression-era rule ('Regulation Q') that, by keeping domestic deposit rates artificially low, added to the allure of depositing dollars outside the US; the UK Treasury in 1957 put heavier constraints on the use of sterling by

Hall-Patch mulled these developments together, Hawker's emergence in February 1962 as the next Chairman of the Standard needs little further explanation. There is no evidence that the Bank of England's new Governor, Lord Cromer, played any direct part in the appointment. On the other hand, timely moves by its former Directors into high places in the City had long been an effective tool of influence for the Bank and Hawker was treading a familiar path. One of his closest associates and a greatly respected City figure, Sir George Bolton, had left the Bank only a few years previously to become Chairman of the leading overseas bank in South America, Lloyds BOLSA. One of the Standard's newer Directors, Lance Martin, had also arrived there from the Bank of England just four years earlier. Approved in Threadneedle Street, Hawker's appointment was warmly welcomed by Hall-Patch's colleagues.

Whether the latter fully appreciated the import of his arrival might be doubted. Some, including Leith-Ross, thought a period of quiet consolidation was now needed.[132] But Hawker, while a man famous for his charm and easy-going manner, was no quiet consolidator. He set off to re-shape the bank from his first day. Even before his accession to the chairmanship in August, he had tried to bring George Bolton on to the Board beside him. This idea was frowned on by the Governor ('probably not entirely appropriate') and promptly dropped.[133] Within a year Hawker had brought on board another senior man from the Bank as his Deputy, Cyril Hamilton. Quieter and more deliberative than his new boss, Hamilton intimidated many of his colleagues and could often appear to be the *éminence grise* in the Boardroom. Justified or not, it was anyway Hawker and Hamilton together, 'the Two Cyrils', who would now shape the bank's future – though Leith-Ross remained on the Board as Vice-Chairman, a position he held until his retirement in 1966.[134] The Two Cyrils embarked from the outset on an explicit mission to regroup the City's overseas banks, for which the Standard – increasingly detached from its South African heritage after SBSA's inauguration in April 1962 – looked to them a perfect vehicle.

This is not to say that Hawker turned his back on South Africa. He had travelled there on many occasions for the Bank and knew several of the leading participants in its financial sector well. Indeed, his daughter had married the son of the Reserve Bank's Governor. He liked the country

---

countries outside the Sterling Area; and the IMF in 1958 engineered a bonfire of the post-war restrictions on the conversion of currencies by its leading member states. The result by 1962 was a vibrant market for eurodollars, to which enterprising bankers were beginning to arrange access for their customers around the world at lower rates and with infinitely less paperwork than applied to loans from the US itself.

and was a popular guest there, not least because of his interests outside banking. As the *Financial Times* noted in announcing his appointment, 'The guarded, matter-of-fact but humorous Sir Cyril has played cricket for Essex and loves all games.'[135] No one could out-talk him on sport, not even in South Africa.* He was on first-name terms with both Bob Edmunds and Alwyn Davies before he arrived in Clements Lane, and, when SBSA organized a banquet in Port Elizabeth in October 1962 to celebrate the bank's centenary, Hawker flew there and back with his wife just to be the guest of honour. But his role as the Standard's Chairman went well beyond ambassadorial visits. As he would observe at a meeting in London attended by Edmunds in July 1964, 'the Board of the parent had a responsibility to its shareholders from which it could not abdicate . . . [and had to] keep a fairly close watch on policy matters concerning the group as a whole'. (Edmunds conceded as much – 'he readily accepted what criticism there was, when justified. There were times, however, when correspondence between the managements caused a little heat – no doubt at both ends.'[136]) It was actually Hamilton, though, who was to bear the brunt of sustaining this curious and often edgy relationship, spending several weeks a year in the Republic and working with the Johannesburg Board on such testing projects as the establishment, with eight local partners, of a 'City Merchant Bank' for South Africa. Hamilton's support allowed Hawker to focus on the wider transformation of the Standard Bank, and the strategic objective that was to preoccupy him for much of the next seven years – the realization of what he fondly called his Grand Design. Any notion of a fixed and comprehensive blueprint had to be abandoned at a very early stage. The eventual outcome was nonetheless a triumph of sorts, albeit along rather different lines from those initially envisaged.

Hawker's pitch was bold and sweeping. The Standard had operations in East and Central Africa, and a stake in Bank of West Africa (BWA), as the old Bank of British West Africa had become in 1957. The winding up of Britain's colonial arrangements across all these vast regions was already well advanced. The former Gold Coast Federation had gained its independence as Ghana in 1957 and Nigeria had followed suit in 1960. The dismantling of the East African Federation was almost complete. Northern Rhodesia and Nyasaland were soon to become newly autonomous nations (as Zambia and Malawi they would achieve independence

---

* He later took up many administrative positions in UK sport, including the presidency of the MCC in 1970–71 – a case of slightly unfortunate timing, since it coincided with the cancellation of a Test tour by South Africa in 1970 and the advent of the international boycott in support of the anti-apartheid movement.

in 1964). The City's overseas bankers would have to show the ruling powers in all these fledgling countries that their activities were even more important to the continent than before – and the Standard could lead the way, provided it had the resources of a 'Big Brother' behind it. Ideally, an amalgamation with a UK clearer would also incorporate other overseas banks with links to Europe and the Far East, providing 'a network of representation and information on a worldwide scale'.[137] Directors at the Midland Bank responded with some enthusiasm at a meeting in December 1962 addressed by Hawker and Hall-Patch together. It was one of the latter's last forays – poor health forced him into final retirement six months later – and he was delighted to see the Grand Design taking forward his own efforts. His earlier notion of a link with Chartered Bank also remained embedded in Hawker's broader scheme – and it soon came to a halt, like Hall-Patch's own initiative, when confronted with Grantham's lack of interest. The Midland put the idea of a large overseas banking group to the Chartered's Chairman and his Chief General Manager, George Pullen, in March 1963. They rebuffed it, listing other unsuccessful suitors for good measure:

> Both [Grantham and Pullen] felt their bank to be firmly entrenched and to have a strong reserve position. Two years ago, a suggestion from Barclays DC&O to form an association with that bank and with the Australian and New Zealand Bank had been declined. Since that time, an American bank had approached the Chartered about a takeover. The Chartered, however, was protected, so Mr Grantham and Mr Pullen believed, because its Articles did not allow more than 20% of the equity to be in any one ownership.[138]

Hawker appealed to the Bank of England to apply some gentle pressure to the Chartered, but to no avail.[139] Appointed to his chairmanship as long ago as 1940, Grantham still appeared to be both unmoved and unmoveable. As Hawker and Hamilton put it to the Bank a year later, 'their "grand design" . . . had therefore been put on ice, at least until Mr Grantham had retired'.[140] It had in the meantime helped to generate a slightly different idea, actually examined in some depth by Hawker's own senior managers in the autumn of 1962. This was the concept of a 'consortium bank', an operation that could be set up at arm's length by a group of banks under shared ownership to explore opportunities in the euromarkets that the parent banks might find more difficult to tackle on their own.[141] The Midland Bank ran with this successfully and by the end of the year had assembled the City's very first consortium bank, Midland and International Banks, launched in March 1964. It was invariably known as

MAIBL to rhyme with table. The Standard provided one of its legs.* But Hawker never for a moment saw MAIBL as a component of his Grand Design, let alone an alternative. He was still set on building a worldwide banking group, with its partners linked via cross-holdings of equity. So the Chartered's sniffiness was not allowed to hold up talks for long. No sooner had the MAIBL contracts been signed off than Hawker was back on the trail of a slightly revised Grand Design. Leaving Grantham and his colleagues to stew for a while, he turned back to the notion of a pan-African group, with the Standard and Bank of West Africa at its heart.

We left BWA with its fortunes reviving in 1951–2 under a new Chairman, the ubiquitous Lord Harlech, and a new General Manager, John Read. Those were the years in which the bank's West African marketplace was starting to be transformed by the withdrawal of the British Empire, ebbing back there several years ahead of its retreat from East Africa. Since the old BBWA had always been so closely linked to Britain's colonial administration, not least as the agent for its management of the regional currency, the bank might easily have withered away. Most of its capital sat in London and could reasonably have been redirected into other investments, or perhaps returned to shareholders via a series of special dividends. Instead, in a process scarcely discernible even to BWA's own historian, a commitment was effectively made in the early 1950s to a broader role in the emerging post-colonial West Africa.[142] New sources of working capital were needed for the region's economy – not just to assist early pioneers of manufacturing but also, and more intriguingly, for the funding of its rural hinterlands. The moves towards independence in four new African states – Nigeria, Ghana, Sierra Leone and the Gambia – entailed a rapid eclipse of the traditional role played in the agricultural sector by the giant European trading companies like UAC, with their handling of cash and credit for small farmers. They lost their hold over the buying of crops to new state-owned Produce Marketing Boards. 'As a result, large areas of West Africa which had relied on the trading companies for banking services were going to be deprived of them.'[143] BWA stepped into the breach (alongside Barclays DCO, as usual) and so exchanged its old identity as a slightly stuffy, quasi-official bank for a new profile as a truly 'retail' bank – and a highly enterprising one, as the social setting for most of its subsequent operations demanded. It soon found itself urgently in need of retail

---

* The four shareholders were Midland Bank (45 per cent), Toronto Dominion Bank (26 per cent), Standard Bank (19 per cent) and Commercial Bank of Australia (10 per cent) – and by 1970 it was to be among the 175 largest banks in the world. (For the broader story thus initiated, see Richard Roberts, *Take Your Partners: Orion, the Consortium Banks and the Transformation of the Euromarkets*, Palgrave, 2001.)

branches to collect deposits in support of its newly energetic stance on local lending. For ten years the bank expanded its network across the region at a furious pace, following the course of new roads and railways that were gradually opening up the interior to trade that had hitherto been heavily dependent on river systems. Between 1952 and 1962 the number of the bank's branches, humbler agencies and bare tin shacks went from eighteen to fifty-five in Nigeria and fifteen to forty-four in Ghana.[144]

Dozens of young managers to run these new offices were recruited in Britain, drawn to overseas banking for all the usual reasons. Indeed, BWA was blunter than most in its advertising for new staff: 'Get out of that rut! Your place in the sun!' ran a famous BWA advertisement in *The Times* for many years.[145] (Chartered's recruitment brochure, first published in 1956, simply announced 'Opportunities in the East'.) Like those leaving London for the East or for South Africa in the nineteenth century, those headed for West Africa early in the second half of the twentieth were going to face a lifestyle that was often a touch more rugged than expected. Most found their accommodation short on frills: 'the term "furnished room" usually meant bare floors and walls with a bedstead, a small table and

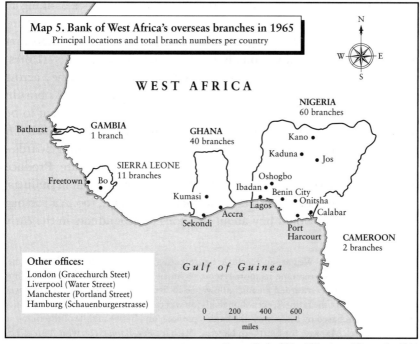

Map 5. Bank of West Africa's overseas branches in 1965
Principal locations and total branch numbers per country

WEST AFRICA

NIGERIA
60 branches

GAMBIA
1 branch

Bathurst

GHANA
40 branches

Kano

Kaduna

Jos

SIERRA LEONE
11 branches

Freetown   Bo

Oshogbo

Ibadan   Benin City

Kumasi   Onitsha

Lagos

Sekondi   Accra   Calabar

Port Harcourt

CAMEROON
2 branches

Other offices:
London (Gracechurch Steet)
Liverpool (Water Street)
Manchester (Portland Street)
Hamburg (Schauenburgerstrasse)

Gulf of Guinea

0   200   400   600

miles

Source: Bank of West Africa Annual Report for 1964

one or two chairs – and no more'.[146] Arriving in Nigeria in 1963 after joining the bank straight from university a year earlier, Bill Moore soon found himself learning how to live alone in a remote rural area:

> We had no electricity and no telephones. The mail service was erratic to say the least – though this wasn't always a bad thing. There were occasions when no news from London was very helpful. But life in general was quite difficult, with very few white people around. That was one of the reasons that I learned to speak Hausa, since without it you could be stuck. You learned to be self-sufficient because you had nobody else to rely on.[147]

The novice recruits had to fit in with local African village life if they were to have any chance of thriving as lending officers, and many pulled it off with remarkable aplomb. (Some even earned sufficient kudos to merit election as a Chief. Having originally joined the bank in Nigeria in 1957 and become a fluent speaker of Yoruba, a Welshman called Elwyn Williams later spent five years at Oshogbo, a trading centre on the main railway line from Lagos to Kano, where he acquired a considerable local celebrity. After he had acted bravely to rescue a local headman threatened by a mob, he found himself elected as Chief Elwyn Williams, Bobajiro of Oshogbo.[148] See Plate 32a.) Young BWA officers also needed plenty of initiative, to cope with business routines that often had little in common with banking in the developed world. A curious feature of banking in Nigeria, for example, was the enormous effort required each year to channel a vast flow of silver shillings into the bush. Among the most important of the crops purchased seasonally by 'Licensed Buying Agents' (LBAs) were groundnuts, cultivated in the thin sandy soils that stretched across thousands of square miles in the north of the country. The LBAs bought them directly from the farmers with cash and arranged for them to be trucked to railheads for transportation to inland mills or the ports. BWA funded the LBAs' activities under guarantees from the Marketing Boards – it was the only bank with its own dedicated expatriate Produce Inspector* – and since the farmers would only accept payment in shillings, the bank had no choice but to make its loans in shillings, too. A £100 bag of 2,000 shillings would buy about two tons of groundnuts in the early

---

* His name was J. A. Wright, an eccentric figure known throughout the bank as 'Camel Wright' for his love of roaming its more remote territories on the back of a camel. In June 1962 he was famously awarded a camel allowance in lieu of a car allowance. Wright was hugely popular with the farmers, even though his job was to check on the quality and quantity of the crops purchased by LBAs with the bank's support, and by the middle of the 1970s he was BWA's Area Manager for Northern Nigeria. (Richard Fry, *Bankers in West Africa, The Story of the Bank of British West Africa Limited*, Hutchinson Benham, 1976, pp. 204–6.)

17. The local manager of the Bank of British West Africa (BBWA), George Neville, in Lagos in 1896 with his staff, including two future luminaries of the bank, the bearded David Paterson, aged twenty-four, to his right and Roy Wilson, aged twenty, to his left.

18. BBWA as a pillar of the British presence in West Africa. *Above:* its branch at Sekondi on the Gold Coast (now part of Sekondi-Takoradi in Ghana) in 1917. *Below:* the Sekondi branch manager, Mr Grundy, and his wife setting off to town, circa 1919.

19. BBWA in the City of London. *Above:* its head office after 1922, at 37 Gracechurch Street. *Below:* a group of visiting dignitaries from West Africa in 1935, hosted by the Directors including David Paterson (*front row, left*), who had been General Manager of the bank since 1929, and Sir Roy Wilson (*front row, right*), who had quit as Assistant General Manager in 1924 to pursue a career as a Tory MP but joined the Board in 1929.

20. Eastern Bank in post-war Mesopotamia. *Above:* the branch in Mosul soon after its opening in 1919, when the Eastern was appointed as the official bank to the military government set up by Britain's occupying forces. *Right:* the long-suffering staff in Baghdad, on a balcony of their building on Christmas Day, 1920.

21. Eastern Bank in Iraq. *Above:* the interior of its Mosul branch, circa 1930. *Below:* a crowd of customers in the street waiting for the Mosul branch to open its doors for the day, circa 1932.

22. Chartered Bank in Shanghai. *Above:* its first branch on the Bund, built on land acquired in 1893, photographed circa 1900. *Below:* the new building at Bund 18, begun in 1919 and completed in 1923 by Trollope & Colls, the same contractors who in 1908–9 had built the bank's head office in London at 38 Bishopsgate.

23. Sino-Japanese hostilities reach Shanghai in 1937. *Above:* the Pudong quarter under Japanese shell-fire, photographed from the roof of Bund 18. *Below:* sandbags in the doorway of Bund 18 – but 'Business as Usual'.

24. The severe floods that hit Tientsin (today's Tianjin) in north-eastern China, in 1939. *Above:* the Chartered's local staff being ferried home from the office by punt. *Below:* dispossessed local families taking refuge on the steps of the Chartered's branch, a grand neo-classical building completed for the bank in 1926.

1960s. Given that the farmers annually supplied enough to sustain a domestic Nigerian groundnut-oil industry as well as more than a million tons for export, an awful lot of coins needed counting in and out. Bill Moore recalled:

> In one of my postings, at Nguru, specie would often come by trains that arrived in the middle of the night, to be off-loaded into trucks and driven to the bank. More often than not the volume of coins would be physically too much for the bank to hold, so I regularly kept stocks in my house and garden until it could be shipped out. The whole process would go into reverse at the end of each season, when a river of shillings would flow back in [as customer deposits]. BWA's Kano branch would pile them high in Second World War ammunition boxes in the bank's compound. They would stay there for days until the Central Bank – which had its own capacity problems – could take them as deposits. The costs of all this – with the labour, the trains, the police guards and so on – had a huge impact on the profit and loss account. Fortunately, margins were quite wide in those days![149]

Certainly the Nigerian business was making a healthy contribution to BWA's results, and these were looking promising in many parts of West Africa. The average total of its year-end advances by 1961–4 had risen to £38.4 million, up from £15.2 million for 1954–7. And what had once been known as the cocoa bank was now the largest lender to a regional economy fast developing in some surprising ways, with a flourishing diamond business in Sierra Leone and an embryonic oil industry in Nigeria. The bank's issued share capital had been almost quadrupled in the 1950s, to £4 million. Towards the end of 1963, the Directors were pondering a fresh appeal for capital when they were approached by the Standard's Chairman. Might they be prepared, asked Hawker, to consider the possibility of an altogether more radical restructuring?

The Standard still held the 11 per cent stake it had acquired in the West African bank, as part of the flurry of cross-investment in the overseas banks by the English clearers in 1920 (see p. 230). It had also, of course, greatly expanded its operations in the Central African Federation (Northern and Southern Rhodesia, and Nyasaland) and the new East Africa nations of Kenya, Uganda and Tanganyika. Hawker had just returned from the latest of his regular tours of these territories. His discussions with many of the new African leaders, including Julius Nyerere in Tanganyika and Kenneth Kaunda in Northern Rhodesia, left him in no doubt about their lack of enthusiasm for the old colonial institutions. But he sensed a readiness, at least, to acknowledge the continuing need for modern banks – even where they were run by British expatriates, as he suggested to his colleagues later:

> There is little gratitude for the efforts of the Overseas Banks, but they are being found useful. A point we repeatedly made to Ministers and their officials was the greater ability of overseas banks based in London to lend than of indigenous banks relying entirely on local resources . . . In all three countries [of East Africa] there is growing realisation that the development of their own commercial banking is a difficult and lengthy process, and that staffing is a particular problem. Consequently, the difficulties of the British banks in increasing African staff are being seen more clearly by the Africans themselves.[150]

By the start of 1964, Hawker was busy exploring how the BWA might be combined with the Standard, and perhaps National & Grindlays too. He aired several variations on this theme with BWA's Chairman, Sylvester Gates, and its other minority shareholders in the City – Lloyds, National Provincial and the Westminster – and even toyed with the idea of reviving the old African Banking Corporation name for the future bank.[151] As with the original version of the Grand Design, though, he once again ran into serious obstacles. One was the rapidly worsening relationship between the Southern Rhodesia Government, led from April 1964 by Ian Smith, and the British Government. Smith was threatening a Unilateral Declaration of Independence (UDI) if left with no other alternative but to lead the country down a path to black majority rule. The mounting crisis in Salisbury prompted Hawker to exclude Central Africa from his plans.* Another disappointment, once merger talks had begun with the BWA and its

---

* The Local Board in Salisbury was chaired by Sir Robert ('Bob') Taylor, a former Financial Secretary to the Government of Northern Rhodesia and a close friend of Hawker's. In a desperate bid to head off the UDI disaster that he could see approaching, Taylor wrote to Hawker in July 1964 urging him to co-ordinate a dramatic 12,000-mile return flight with his fellow chairmen of Barclays DCO, National & Grindlays and the Ottoman Bank: '[You should be] climbing into an aircraft and flying out here to keep an hour's appointment with the Prime Minister at which, as Chairmen of the four British banks trading in this country, you would tell him quite clearly what the financial effects were going to be . . . This is a lot to ask and I am not making the suggestion lightly. I do not think it is playing politics, and I do think that a really forceful gesture is required.' Hawker floated the idea with Sir Julian Crossley at DCO, but he was 'quite definite that he would not take part' and it was dropped. (Taylor to Hawker, 29 July 1964 and Note for the Record, 6 August 1964, LMA: ST03/03/04/003.) Hawker travelled to Salisbury alone at the start of November and cabled back to Hamilton: 'I did my best to talk sense into one or two of the leaders but HMG's harsh approach to Rhodesian question calculated to force Smith's hand. Cannot someone persuade them to hold off?' Hamilton forwarded the cable to the Commonwealth Relations Secretary, but received a predictably dusty response. (Hamilton to Arthur Bottomley,

clearing-bank shareholders, was a decision by N&G not to participate. It wanted to incorporate its Indian branches in the future bank, which Hawker would not countenance. Without N&G, the rationale for grouping the Standard's East African operations into the new business soon fell away. (The Standard's combined profits in East Africa, at around £¾ million a year, were roughly on a par with those of the BWA, and combining the two had looked a neat approach to building a balanced business across Africa but fell foul – not for the first time – of mounting legal problems.[152]) Yet one more complication was that Lloyds, with a significant minority stake in N&G, felt obliged by the latter's withdrawal to rule itself out of the discussions about a recapitalized BWA.

Here were the makings of a bewilderingly complex set of negotiations – themselves just one part of a wider series of transactions, many of them equally fraught, by which the City of London's leading bankers were coming to terms in these years with the demise of the overseas banks' old imperial franchises.[153] For months, Hawker was in and out of the Bank of England – handily, less than five minutes' walk from the Standard's own offices in Clements Lane – keeping the Governor and his staff regularly updated on the latest twists and setbacks. Gradually a pooling of several complementary businesses came to centre on Standard joining forces with BWA. The West Africa bank, proud of its long record since 1894, clung to the presentation of the deal as a match between equals though its resources were scarcely a third as big as Standard's.[154] A 'merger' was finally announced on 1 March 1965, via an offer of Standard shares worth almost £12 million. The Midland Bank took up the Lloyds holding in BWA, and the capitalization of the combined Standard/BWA bank – to be renamed Standard Bank of West Africa late in 1966, within West Africa itself though not in London – ended up with the three clearing-bank minority shareholders each retaining just about 5 per cent of the stock. Of course this implied a structure vulnerable to subsequent disputes between the shareholders, but at least a gentlemen's agreement was reached on this: none would pursue a change in their stake without prior discussion among them all. The formal terms of the transaction meanwhile left Hawker and Hamilton presiding over a reconstituted Board – pooling together most of the two banks' Directors, for the moment anyway – and a network of 1,100 branches in some twenty different territories of Africa.* They also

---

9 November 1964 (LMA: SBSA/0010). UDI was eventually announced in November 1965. On its consequences for the Standard Bank in Rhodesia, see below, pp. 449–51 and p. 513 fn.
* The spread of the new bank's territories caught the eye of a young man in the City who was keen to find a job in Africa. John Major had passed Part 1 of the Institute of Bankers exam while working in the City branch of the District Bank. He joined the staff of 10

left some unidentified gentlemen with a killing in the stock market. BWA's shares, valued by the Standard at 58 shillings each, had started the year at 28 shillings and had risen to 45 shillings on the eve of the deal's announcement. One of the City's best respected financial editors memorably deplored 'the worst leak since the Titanic'.[155]

Many at the time blamed the leak on the involvement in the transaction of so many parties in New York. For there was yet a further dimension to the BWA story. Since the summer of 1963, Hawker and Hamilton had formed a close alliance between the Standard and one of those American giants that Hall-Patch had warned Grantham about in 1959. Three had taken an active interest in Africa, and the Standard had linked up with Chase Manhattan. (The other two were Bank of America and First National City Bank.) It was ironically Hall-Patch himself who had initiated the relationship, in his last few months as a Director.[156] Hawker saw the link's potential value immediately, and was delighted when the individuals at the head of Chase responded warmly to his vision of a new banking force in Africa. Indeed, they soon decided that a 25 per cent stake in the Standard would suit their strategic needs nicely – an objective that Hawker and the Bank of England both felt a little too enthusiastic. The New York bank was tied into the restructuring that accompanied the purchase of BWA, emerging with a stake in the final outcome that was finally settled at 14.5 per cent, making it Standard's largest shareholder. In the aftermath of the deal, the two banks seemed destined for a significantly closer relationship. Chase's African operations were assimilated into Standard's network – including three branches in South Africa that were taken over by SBSA – and Chase executives, including its Chairman, George Champion, joined the Standard and SBSA Boards in London and Johannesburg. It was a slightly anomalous pairing in the field. The principal link-man delegated to the relationship by Chase was Charles (Chuck) E. Fiero, who took part in a tour of the African operations led by Hamilton late in 1965 and came away a little startled by the un-American

---

Clements Lane in September 1966 and was happy to accept a posting just three months later to a branch in the central Nigerian town of Jos – which was certainly not everyone's idea of the perfect start to a banking career. But the rigours of the 1950s had given way to a slightly more comfortable lifestyle, at least as far as Major was concerned. 'Well, compared to the living conditions I had been used to in Brixton, I didn't think it was at all bad! I shared a flat with another young Englishman, and I just absolutely loved it.' But his days as a young retail banker were cut short in May 1967 by a serious car accident that left him on his back in a London hospital for almost a year. Standard Bank kept him on as a full member of its UK staff, and colleagues paid him regular visits until he was well enough to return to Clements Lane in 1968 – for which the future Prime Minister would remain deeply grateful for the rest of his life. (Interview with Sir John Major, 9 October 2013.)

ways of British overseas banking (no university recruitment, no training programmes, no executive development courses, no structured marketing, no analysis or research about target customers). He filed a report that began with some appropriate pleasantries but soon cut to the Chase way of seeing things:

> While, in the past, competition may not have required aggressive marketing, there have been sufficient changes in the market to warrant a major re-orientation of Standard/BWA ... Now that Standard, in conjunction with the Chase, can project a new 'international' image, the tools required to do an effective job are many and much more complicated ... Is it possible to take existing [Standard] administrators, trained in traditional British banking philosophy and operating oriented, and make effective salesmen of them?[157]

Perhaps Fiero himself rather doubted it, but he was certainly game for a sustained campaign by the Chase to that end. Neither he nor any of the other Chase officers on the tour had ever been to Africa before (and there were soon to be letters back to London from Standard men about 'astonishing propositions' that had been aired by the Americans). Still, Hawker was happy to think some of Chase's professionalism might rub off on the Standard. He took on Fiero as a close confidante and the American soon became a strong, modernizing influence within the bank. This usefully complemented the meeting of minds at the top, where Hawker 'hit it off famously with George Champion', as the latter's deputy, David Rockefeller, later recorded in his memoirs.[158] Unfortunately Champion and Rockefeller often rubbed along together less easily: 'Champion remained wedded to correspondent banking and saw foreign banks as being of value chiefly to serve US customers; Rockefeller wanted a network of offices abroad to serve customers from all nations.'[159] They duly disagreed over the importance of increasing their stake in the Standard 'to ensure our real voice in their global operations and to enable us to leverage our activities in Africa', as Rockefeller remembered it. But Hawker promised Champion that he would 'bear well in mind your wish to increase your interest up to 20 per cent', and for the moment this was enough to keep the peace.[160] The growing partnership between the banks seemed, at last, to have opened up truly global horizons for Standard Bank. As Hawker announced (in English, German and Afrikaans) at a banquet in Windhoek for the Standard's first fifty years in South-West Africa: 'We are fast becoming a world bank; indeed, that is our aim.'[161]

How the Chartered Bank's Directors regarded these events cannot be traced in much detail: almost no records or correspondence files relating

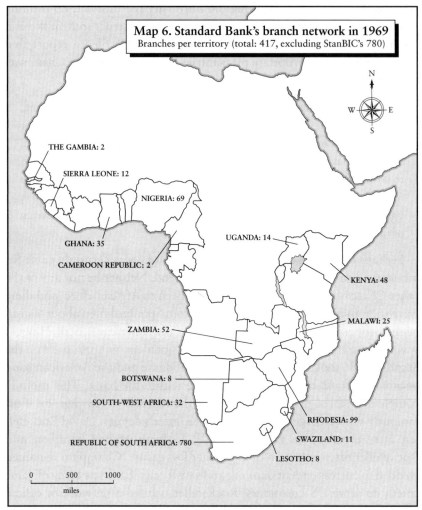

Map 6. Standard Bank's branch network in 1969
Branches per territory (total: 417, excluding StanBIC's 780)

THE GAMBIA: 2

SIERRA LEONE: 12

NIGERIA: 69

GHANA: 35

CAMEROON REPUBLIC: 2

UGANDA: 14

KENYA: 48

MALAWI: 25

ZAMBIA: 52

BOTSWANA: 8

SOUTH-WEST AFRICA: 32

RHODESIA: 99

REPUBLIC OF SOUTH AFRICA: 780

SWAZILAND: 11

LESOTHO: 8

0   500   1000
|____|____|
      miles

Source: Standard and Chartered Banking Group Annual Report, 1971

to the bank's strategy have survived from the 1960s.[162] We can infer, though, that Vincent Grantham ('le vrai homme Guernésiais') remained as uninterested as ever in global horizons: he was steadfastly opposed to any involvement in Africa and not much interested in a merger of any kind for the Chartered. But in April 1967 he did finally retire, after a remarkable twenty-seven years in the Chair (only one year less than Sir Montagu Turner's 1904–32 tenure).* George Pullen succeeded him, thus becoming

---

* His retirement was sadly a brief one: he died fifteen months later on 1 August 1968, aged seventy-nine. His obituary in *The Times* two days later noted his longevity as Chairman but

the only executive head of the bank ever to follow in the footsteps of Howard Gwyther by rising to be Chairman – and breaking, as the City editor of *The Times* noted, 'one of the most harmful taboos in the banking world'.[163] (It started a trend, with professional managers soon rising to board level elsewhere in the City.) The new man had a keener appreciation than his predecessor of the Chartered's exposed position. Recent events had cast it in a vulnerable light: the Indian Government – desperately seeking to revive an economy beset by falling industrial production, failing crops and an excessive rate of growth in the money supply – had devalued the rupee by 36.5 per cent in 1966. This had been a heavy blow to the sterling value of assets held in India and the Persian Gulf by the Chartered, Eastern and Allahabad Banks.[164] Other pressures were subtler but potentially more damaging. Pullen had watched the British clearing banks encroaching ever more worryingly on some of the Chartered's most important territories in recent years. They were marketing their deposit services in Asia, seconding British staff to indigenous banks and assisting those banks with introductions to British companies. But even the clearers' competitive threat was dwarfed by the American challenge that had surged since the early 1960s. Given the scale of their resources, the US banks (like Chase) could expand their networks in targeted markets almost regardless of the start-up costs. In this transformed environment, Pullen knew a bank as relatively small and specialized as the Chartered was perilously exposed – whatever the small print in its Articles of Association – to the designs of immeasurably bigger groups. (Even Barclays DCO was fast approaching twice its size, with total assets in 1967 of £1.48 billion compared with Chartered's £801 million.) Within months of his appointment, in September 1967, Pullen was invited to take Chartered into an amalgamation of banks on a par with the complexity of the BWA transaction. Its primary sponsor was Barclays, which with its DCO subsidiary still held almost 15 per cent of Chartered's shares. But Pullen had not yet steeled himself to a loss of his bank's independence, and he held out against any elaborate exchange of equity.[165] Perhaps fortunately so – for just a few weeks later, in November 1967, came the Wilson government's dreadfully mismanaged devaluation of sterling. A belated acknowledgement that economic policy since 1964 had failed to tackle Britain's huge current account deficit effectively, leaving the pound under constant pressure in the financial markets, the devaluation was a watershed event. It virtually

had nothing at all to say about his contribution to the bank's expansion since 1945 other than that it had involved his also being a Director of the Eastern Bank and of the Irano-British Bank. Indeed, his earlier career in India was given more space.

ended the pound's role as a reserve currency and triggered the break-up of the sterling system that had been the working milieu of the City's overseas banks for generations past.

One consequence was to be a dramatic growth in the use of eurodollars – and indeed a range of other 'eurocurrencies' deposited outside their countries of origin – as the staple denomination of international lending. It had already been clear for a few years that this was potentially another marketplace in which Britain's few surviving overseas banks could prosper. They enjoyed an advantage over the clearing banks, insofar as they had never been required to maintain liquid assets against a sizeable proportion of their deposits and so could now match eurocurrency loans and liabilities far more efficiently. And of course they had their traditional expertise at dealing with foreign exchange. On the other hand, lending in eurocurrencies required some unfamiliar book-keeping skills and a far more enterprising kind of banking in general. At the Standard, Hawker and Hamilton were well aware of the need to adopt a fundamentally new approach (and exchange banking had never really been a forte of the bank in South Africa – as Head Office was reminded when SBSA took significant exchange losses in the wake of the sterling devaluation). Hamilton began impressing upon his senior colleagues the need to think of SBSA and BWA as self-supporting subsidiaries, leaving Clements Lane to pursue opportunities in the euromarkets. As he wrote in March 1968: 'The essential point to recognise is that the London end of the Standard Bank is not an overseas bank but a London-based financial institution free to participate in the new fields which are now being developed.'[166] He seems also to have talked, in the aftermath of the devaluation, to Pullen at the Chartered. The notion that their two institutions might do well to join forces in this altered world of international banking was openly acknowledged between them, as a note from Hamilton to Hawker made clear in April 1968:

> I had a chat with George Pullen last week and went over the ground with him . . . it is obvious he still feels that we are the natural link up for his bank. He is very anxious to try and do something in London . . . I told Pullen that although we had nothing definite in mind at the moment it did not follow that we could stand still for another four months because I felt it was important to develop the London end of our business as soon as possible.[167]

Hamilton was plainly impatient to open formal discussions. Pullen, on the other hand, was scarcely a year into his chairmanship, and seems still to have been deeply ambivalent about dropping the curtain on his bank's independence. It is possible that he was also troubled by the Standard's close connections with Chase Manhattan Bank. Pullen had never given up hope of a revival in Chartered's business with the People's Republic, but he knew US sanctions against China had caused his bank difficulties in the past.[168] And in August 1968 the potential complications of a closer link with the US became suddenly much graver, when Chinese Government officials raided the one-man office that Chartered had kept going in Shanghai since the 1950s.* Nonetheless, by the end of 1968 the attractions of the Standard as a merger partner for Chartered were becoming harder to ignore. Hawker and Hamilton were gaining attention in the City with some bold initiatives. They had sought out the top official inside the Bank of England responsible for overseeing the City's eurocurrency operations – and had hired him. George Preston had moved to the Standard and begun an overhaul of its exchange operations. By December the bank had an 'International Department' that was seen by many as a benchmark for others in the Square Mile.[169] Yet still Pullen hung back.

Then, early in 1969, an unexpected turn of events drew the two banks together with a suddenness that belied all the months of hesitation. Hawker had taken care at the time of the Standard/BWA merger in 1965 to apprise Chase's leadership in New York of the gentlemen's agreement, binding on all the resulting shareholders in Standard Bank, not to change their percentage stakes without consultation.[170] It therefore came as quite a shock to him and Hamilton when a deputation of senior executives from Chase and the (soon to be merged) National Provincial and Westminster Banks turned up at Clements Lane at short notice on 24 March 1969 and declared their intention of almost doubling their combined stakes in

---

* It had briefly become a two-man office. The Chinese would only allow the British Manager to leave if he was replaced by another, and the successor had to arrive in advance. Thus, Ron Cannings landed in Shanghai in June 1968 to take over from the incumbent, David Johnston. But, during a party at Cannings' home one Saturday night, the police arrived in force and Johnston was carted off to prison. He remained incarcerated while his wife was denied an exit visa and effectively placed under house arrest, along with Hongkong Bank's man in Shanghai and his wife. The latter three were given exit visas in February 1969, but the fifty-six-year-old Johnston remained in prison for twenty-eight months, held for most of the time in solitary confinement. Pullen and his successor as Chief General Manager, Stafford Northcote, were both involved in periodic attempts by the Foreign Office and the British Ambassador in Beijing, Percy Cradock, to extricate Johnston – who was finally released on Christmas Eve 1970. He himself had no inkling of how newsworthy his plight had become when he walked across the Lowu Bridge from the Chinese mainland into Hong Kong. His wife and David Millar, now the Hong Kong Manager, were there to meet him. 'His biggest worry when he came across the bridge was that he did not have the cash for the bus fare into Hong Kong.' (Millar, letter to the author, 10 August 2011.) Johnston retired to Canada, where he died in 2001.

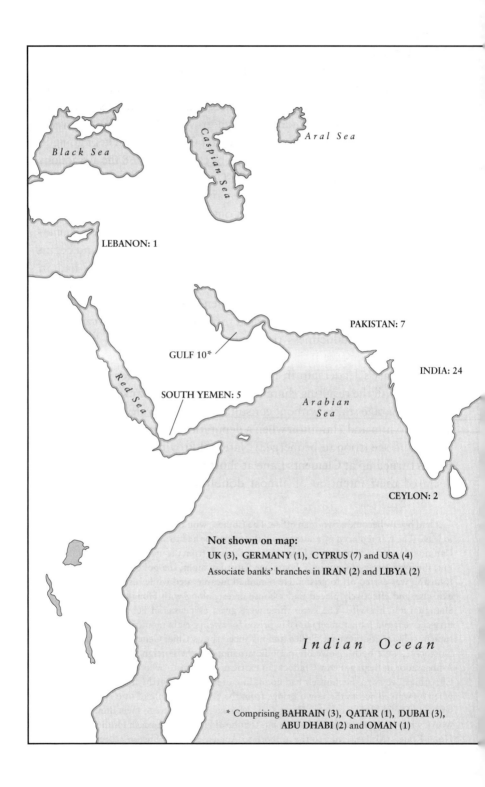

LEBANON: 1

PAKISTAN: 7

GULF 10*

INDIA: 24

SOUTH YEMEN: 5

Black Sea

Caspian Sea

Aral Sea

Red Sea

Arabian Sea

CEYLON: 2

Not shown on map:
UK (3), GERMANY (1), CYPRUS (7) and USA (4)
Associate banks' branches in IRAN (2) and LIBYA (2)

Indian Ocean

* Comprising BAHRAIN (3), QATAR (1), DUBAI (3),
ABU DHABI (2) and OMAN (1)

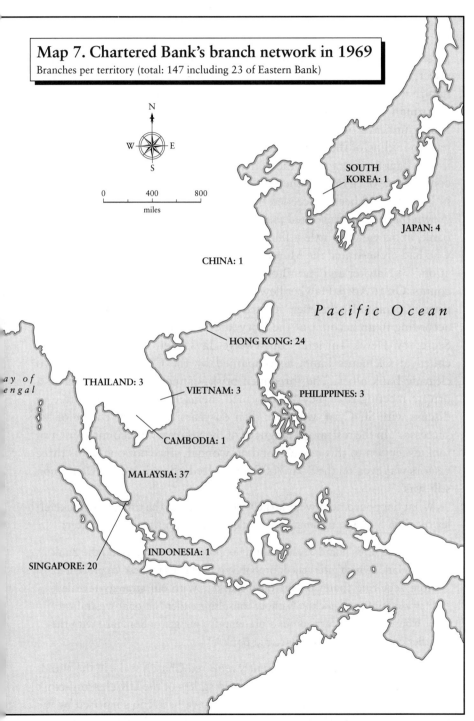

Map 7. Chartered Bank's branch network in 1969

Branches per territory (total: 147 including 23 of Eastern Bank)

N

W — E

S

0   400   800
miles

SOUTH
KOREA: 1

JAPAN: 4

CHINA: 1

Pacific Ocean

HONG KONG: 24

*ay of
engal*

THAILAND: 3

VIETNAM: 3

PHILIPPINES: 3

CAMBODIA: 1

MALAYSIA: 37

INDONESIA: 1

SINGAPORE: 20

Source: Staff magazine, *Curry & Rice*, spring 1969

Standard from their present 24.5 per cent (including Chase's 14.5 per cent) to 40 per cent. They were aware, said the visitors, of plans at Standard for an imminent sale of new shares. They wished to propose that these plans be amended to facilitate their incremental investment – which, in effect, would leave them in control of the bank. Hostile visitations of this nature would one day come to be not uncommon in the City, but for the Chairman of a prominent bank to be confronted like this in 1969 was simply unheard of. Hawker and his deputy, who until the meeting had had no inkling of the scheme, rejected it out of hand. Appalled, they saw it as a flagrant betrayal of the 1965 agreement. It was in fact the direct consequence of changes at the top of Chase. George Champion had retired in January, and been succeeded by David Rockefeller – who by now had grown thoroughly frustrated that its 1965 investment had brought the US bank, in his view, so little influence over the Standard. It was Rockefeller who had orchestrated the March initiative. ('I decided to remedy the situation.'[171]) Hawker and Hamilton strongly opposed his remedy on several counts. On 16 April, Hawker flew to New York and presented their objections in person. Rockefeller 'seemed to understand all the points made', according to an account of the story later compiled by Standard Bank's Secretary, Derek Turner.[172] But twelve days later, Rockefeller himself called at Clements Lane, accompanied by the Chairmen of his two clearing-bank allies. The three men briskly announced to Hawker in a private meeting that they 'had formed themselves into a committee to discuss with Sir Cyril, who was then 69 years of age, the choice of his successor'. In the restrained language of the Secretary's account, 'Sir Cyril took exception to this move' – and no wonder, since not one of his three visitors was even on the Board of the Standard (though, oddly, Champion still was).

What happened next went largely unrecorded at the time, but Rockefeller recalled his own understanding clearly enough thirty years later:

> Hawker and his board . . . adamantly opposed our move, as did the Bank of England, which intervened, probably at Hawker's request, to prevent us from acquiring shares on the open market. With our strategy revealed, Hawker retaliated quickly. Without consulting either National Westminster or Chase, Hawker carried out a pre-emptive merger of Standard with the other colonial giant, the Chartered Bank.[173]

The Bank of England had consistently required Chase's stake in the Standard to be kept smaller than the combined stakes of the UK clearing-bank shareholders, so Rockefeller ought not to have been too surprised by the Bank's intervention. Whether the Bank also moved to instigate the merger remedy (as many American bankers later assumed) is unclear. But there certainly followed a marriage so speedily arranged as to suggest the shadow of a shotgun somewhere in the background. No contemporary written note to this effect has survived, though many at the time must have felt badly wrong-footed. (Only in 1972 did Hawker discover that two of his colleagues on the Standard Board had been involved since the middle of 1968 in talks aimed at winning control of the bank behind his back.[174]) Most observers simply noted that Hawker appeared to have lost confidence in the future of his existing Grand Design, just at the very moment when rumours were reaching Pullen's ear that Barclays and its DCO subsidiary were planning a bid for the Chartered, perhaps in league with the National Westminster.[175] Within a week or two, anyway, Hawker and Pullen had come to an accord. On 28 May 1969, the Standard Chairman confirmed as much to his Board: his counterpart at the Chartered, as the minutes recorded, 'had proposed to him that the two Banks should commence talks with a view to merging. Both Chairmen had spoken to the Governor of the Bank of England who had given the idea his blessing.' Now they just needed to agree on terms, while keeping sweet the large shareholders they had rebuffed and selling the whole idea to their own executive managements. A triple assignment – and, it was soon clear, a tall order.

8

Trial and Error, 1969–83

I. TETHERED TOGETHER

Reaching agreement in principle to combine the Standard and Chartered banks had taken just a few weeks. Pulling them together in law would involve several months of fractious wrangling; and forging the two of them into one seamless organization would take years. The decision to begin merger talks was sprung on an unsuspecting press on 28 May 1969, hours after being formally disclosed to the two sets of Directors. The transaction was to be a 'Scheme of Arrangement', the accountants' term for an ingenious way of avoiding the appearance of a takeover by the Standard while accommodating the fact that it was of course a very much larger bank than the Chartered.* The Standard and Chartered Banking Group (S&CBG) would issue shares in exchange for those held by the two banks' shareholders, roughly in proportion to the current value of their existing shares so that all would end up where they started. The calculations to this effect produced what the stockbrokers called a '5 for 3 exchange ratio' – which in practice meant that the Chartered's shareholders would inherit 37.6 per cent of the holding company, with 62.4 per cent passing to the Standard's shareholders.[1] (The announcement made no apparent impact in the stock market: the pro forma share price of the putative Group went on trading for several days in a price range about 10 per cent below the levels of January 1969, then began drifting lower as doubts grew over the eventual outcome.) Combining two public companies with four minority shareholders – Barclays with 15 per cent of the Chartered, the

---

* After the announcement of their intention to merge, Standard Bank had a market capitalization of just under £100 million compared with Chartered's £42.5 million. Standard had total deposits of £1 billion compared with Chartered's £722 million (*The Times*, 29 May 1969). The published net profits of Standard (to March 1969) and Chartered (to December 1968) together came to £7.2 million – with Standard accounting for 66 per cent and Chartered for 34 per cent.

Midland Bank and National Westminster with 5 per cent each of the Standard, and Chase Manhattan with 14.5 per cent of the Standard – was always going to pose difficulties, with all jockeying to protect their interests. In the event, Barclays and the Midland reconciled themselves to the merger within weeks. But this left the National Westminster and Chase Manhattan (or rather the senior executives of Chase's Overseas Banking Corporation) to be squared; and here matters quickly grew more complicated. In fact, the process of completing the deal on the agreed terms soon ran foul of a whole battalion of US lawyers.

Though their own original designs on the Standard had been seen off as an unwarranted ambush, both Chase and the National Westminster were still intent in the summer of 1969 on retaining a significant stake in the enlarged future company. Indeed, Chase had not given up its hope of eventually acquiring a much bigger stake (and perhaps control, one day). But its US managers were unimpressed with several aspects of the merger, as it was initially presented to them. Over the course of four months, a series of objections were tabled by Victor Rockhill, Chase's man on the Standard Board. It emerged before the end of June, for example, that only the most careful rewiring of Standard's capital structure could prevent the New York bank getting a nasty shock from the US taxman. Again, it caused the Americans particular grief that no provision was being made for their operations in Asia to be merged with Chartered's, rather as those in Africa had been aggregated with Standard's after the BWA deal of 1965. And when the terms of the Scheme of Arrangement were disclosed, Chase executives were adamant that a 9.1 per cent stake for their bank, as dictated by the merger's arithmetic, would be unacceptably low. Above all, and remarkably late in the day, they stumbled across the fact that since 1964 Chartered had owned a small bank in San Francisco, 'Chartered Bank of London'. This was awkward. Pullen and his colleagues were proud of this US outpost and adamant that it could not be sold. But the Federal Reserve Board had a regulation that prohibited any US bank investing in an overseas bank doing domestic business inside the US.* Chase executives threatened to block the merger if, as a result of it, they were going to be forced into selling their entire stake in the future group. Negotiations over the possible solutions to this dilemma stretched into the autumn, when rumours of trouble began circulating in the City. All

---

* Readers fond of a good conspiracy theory may suspect this was an aspect of the Chartered Bank that especially recommended it to officials at the Bank of England as a merger partner for the Standard – but if this was indeed their thinking, it is most unlikely they would have said so in writing.

parties now came under intense pressure to announce agreement; but Chase refused to sign and National Westminster – for reasons none could fathom – refused to sign without them, which was enough to block the merger.

Tense meetings followed in London, New York and Washington, while the Bank of England watched from the wings. Cyril Hawker and the Chairman of Chase, David Rockefeller, went to see the Chairman of the Federal Reserve Board towards the end of September, in search of a solution to their Californian problem. They came away empty-handed. Yet for the merger to be called off at this stage was unthinkable: it would leave the two British overseas banks, as Hawker himself put it, 'in an impossible situation'.[2] Frustration over the approach taken by Chase risked an open breach between London and New York by November. In the end, the lawyers came up with the classic solution to every impossible situation: an ambiguous agreement. This one allowed the US parties, including the Washington authorities, to see the ownership of the Californian bank as temporary and thus compatible with Federal Reserve regulations, while leaving the UK parties satisfied that no binding commitment had been made to dispose of it. Some new shares were also sold to Chase to lift its equity stake to 10 per cent, easing its tax problems. Hawker privately made it clear to Rockefeller that he could no longer countenance Chase owning more than a 15 per cent stake in the new Group – and did not conceal that he felt personally betrayed by Chase's tactics over the course of 1969 – but fences were mended in public and a place was guaranteed for Rockhill on the Board (though no seat could be found for the National Westminster). Even so, a final meeting to sign off the deal kept Hawker, Pullen, Rockhill and their advisers closeted in a room at 10 Clements Lane from late afternoon on 5 December 1969 until just after midnight. According to an insider's account of the talks, they went to the brink of collapsing ('it was touch and go').[3] But agreement was reached, the formal documents were despatched and the merger was approved by the partner banks' shareholders, to take effect on 30 January 1970.

So now the quartet of forerunner banks had become one – and Hawker, in theory at least, was a giant step closer to creating that 'world bank' he had talked about for years. The headline numbers were impressive enough. The new Group, comfortably bigger than Barclays DCO, would have about 1,300 branches and almost 29,000 employees. Much play was made of the expanded geographical coverage and better spread of risks now enjoyed by each of the merged entities. Both, it seemed, were to have more eggs in more baskets – a marvellous outcome indeed. And just a glance at their Asian and African franchises was enough to see why the Standard and the Chartered appeared such ideal partners – bringing mutually exclusive geographies to bear, with a shared heritage as the two great survivors of nineteenth-century Empire banking. In reality, though, they had much less in common than met the eye, as the stock market seemed to grasp readily enough: confirmation of the merger did nothing to slow a steady decline in the share price. First quoted at 267p at the end of January 1970, it had fallen to less than £2 by April (roughly two-thirds of the pro forma quote for the two banks at the start of 1969). Waxing lyrical to his shareholders that month, Pullen spoke of the two banks as 'steeped in the same tradition, handling the same type of business' – but this was poetic licence. For the one was essentially still geared (setting aside Hong Kong) to trade financing, built on an intimate network of offices – heavily dependent on about 8,000 locally recruited clerks – that linked London on a daily basis to half a dozen of the world's great ports, with several hundred overseas British employees working under broadly uniform terms and conditions; and the other was based on four extensive and heavily decentralized branch networks, with almost 7,000 employees (not counting the 13,000 employed in South Africa) on contracts unique to their own geographical territories, handling commercial and retail banking for largely domestic customers.* Chartered's Annual Report listed 137 full branches. Standard had 45 in Kenya alone – plus 172 in Central Africa and 125 in West Africa. Its semi-detached subsidiary in the Republic of South Africa had well over 800, counting branches and agencies together. And beyond the bare numbers were two markedly different cultures (three, counting the emphatically non-British SBSA).

Both banks, of course, had once had to deal with the problems of managing remote branches in physically demanding environments. But, since the Victorian era, far more had changed for Chartered. It was polished and cosmopolitan, with an expatriate Foreign Staff that conformed to the social manners of the privately educated British middle classes (though many of its Scotsmen were in fact grammar-school boys). It remained deeply hierarchical, in ways that Howard Gwyther would certainly have recognized – though he might not have approved of the extent to which those running many of its branches were now content to leave much of the more technical aspects of the business to highly proficient

---

* The banks' UK recruitment procedures reflected these differences. Chartered generally took younger men, trained them as covenanted officers and sent them off as compulsory bachelors to one of the big Eastern offices (most commonly Bombay, Calcutta or Singapore) where their regimental loyalties could be tested and confirmed. Standard, like the old BWA, looked for men with useful experience in a clearing bank who had decided that life in East or Central Africa might be more agreeable – Bromley in the sun.

Indian and Chinese subordinates. Standard Bank north of the Limpopo, by contrast, had kept something of its nineteenth-century ruggedness. Expanding in Central and East Africa, it had retained a flavour of its pioneering days in the old Union of South Africa – a pragmatic and no-frills culture, colourfully reinforced by the recent addition of Bank of West Africa. Successful Chartered officers still had to be quasi-diplomats, always mindful (in the spirit of that 1954 Circular) of their social standing in the community, with just the right personality and bearing. But Standard men were more truly the local bankers – professional and resourceful enough to cope without the kind of clerical support available across Asia and dealing with customers from all European and African backgrounds, many of them eking out a tough living and not especially attuned to British manners and etiquette. The resulting clash of cultures was profound. Interviewed by the author, one candid former Chartered man caught more than a flavour of this in a casual dismissal of Standard men: 'they were always slightly scruffy, not particularly well-mannered or well-dressed, they were all overweight and unfit, and they all drank a lot of beer and ate the wrong food'. Chartered had always attached enormous importance to manners and etiquette: in 1975 young London recruits were still being sent to classes at a school in East London to master the finer points of dining with senior management.[4]

For Hawker and Hamilton in their private moments the palpable tension between the two merger partners must have seemed a slightly anomalous outcome to all their patient manoeuvring through the 1960s. Events had estranged them, in effect, from the industry-leading New York bank whose top men had become close allies in the struggle to modernize the Standard. In Chase's place they were now tethered to a thoroughly traditional, not to say arch-conservative, British overseas bank that seemed intent only on sustaining strong links with its past. Chartered's Court had voted for the merger, but as the share price went on wilting (down to a low of 160p early in the summer of 1970) its senior managers in London gave every impression of having been somehow coerced into an unworkable arrangement. It was common knowledge within 38 Bishopsgate that Pullen himself had deeply resented having to cede the chairmanship to Hawker, whose knowledge of commercial banking apparently did not impress him. Pullen's Chief General Manager, Stafford Northcote, openly derided the Standard Bank in front of colleagues and could scarcely bring himself to talk to its senior managers.* Both Pullen and Northcote were

---

* For the top men at Standard, it must all have been wearisomely familiar. After their acquisition of the Bank of West Africa, its General Manager, John Read, and his counterpart

quick to warn Hawker that the merger was frightfully unpopular in Chartered's ranks. Northcote himself brushed off a former Standard man, visiting him to discuss post-merger adjustments, and told him: 'You're wasting your time!'[5] Dark hints were dropped from Bishopsgate that moves towards any genuine merger might be best avoided, since Standard's links to racist South Africa would be viewed askance by customers in the East. Once Hawker had had a chance to visit the main Asian branches for himself, he gave this no credence at all. 'Indeed, Pullen and Northcote seem to have made a bogey out of nothing', he wrote home to Hamilton from Hong Kong. 'No worries in Malaya, or in Hong Kong either . . . the Chinese rather agreed with apartheid provided it was not applied to them.'[6]

Under the circumstances, it was perhaps a credit to Hawker's shrewdness and diplomatic skills that he managed to present S&CBG to the world as a half-way plausible group at all. It necessitated having to forego, at least for the foreseeable future, any meaningful convergence of the two banks: they were allowed to continue as separate entities, headquartered in their separate buildings with separate Boards. It happened by chance that the Chartered lost seven of its fifteen Directors in 1970, mostly through death and retirement, though one director, Anthony Barber, MP, resigned after a five-year stint to take up office in the newly elected Conservative government led by Edward Heath.* The bank elected six new men, all but one exclusively for its own Court just as though it was still an independent entity. (The appointments ensured that the Court retained its traditional mix of businessmen with careers honed in Asia, plus a smattering of ex-ambassadors and former colonial administrators.) The Standard meanwhile pressed on with a few changes to its own, even bigger Board. Presiding over all this was an artfully constructed Group Board for the new S&CBG. Under Hawker were Pullen and Hamilton, ranked as Deputy and Vice-Chairman. Eight other seats on the Board were shared equally, leaving one each for the Midland Bank and Chase. And like those boarding Noah's Ark, senior men were brought on to the Group's executive

---

at Standard, R. E. Williams, had occupied adjacent offices in Clements Lane for four years without speaking to each other. For lunch every day, Read would walk to the BWA's offices in nearby Gracechurch Street.

* The other six comprised Sir Charles Miles (appointed 1955), a director of the plantations company R. G. Shaw; Ian MacEwen (1957), a director of The Borneo Company; Clifford Waite (also 1957), a director of Consolidated Tin Smelters; Kenneth Campbell (1962), formerly chairman of the British India Steam Navigation Company; Donald Hawkins (1966), a director of the Dunlop Group; and Sir Arthur Atkinson Bruce (1949), a director of Wallace Brothers who had been a founder-director of the Reserve Bank of India in 1935 and had served three times as chairman of the pre-war Burma Chamber of Commerce.

team two by two – with a General Manager from each bank, a Deputy General Manager from each bank, and so on. As an operating unit, the Group remained almost entirely notional. Its accounts even had to consolidate two principal subsidiaries that retained different financial year-ends (March for Standard, December for Chartered) and both kept their different pre-merger auditors.[7] New recruits were asked on joining whether they wanted to work for Chartered or Standard, and were soon familiar with different office terminologies. (Chartered men put their "chop" on documents, Standard men made their "mark".) The two banks stuck to their own sports grounds as well as their own head offices: teams playing for S&CBG had to argue over their venue for each home match.[8] When, three years into the merger, it was eventually agreed that the top executives should at least be obliged to sit in one building, offices were duly allocated in 10 Clements Lane – but two separate dining rooms had to be maintained, and not just for entertaining guests. Chartered's men always ate in the Eastern Room, surrounded by paintings of China's treaty ports, the godowns of Bombay and other scenes of the Orient; their Standard peers ate in the Western Room, under prints of Cape Town's Adderley Street and photographs of tented branches on the Highveld. (The lunches in both were equally renowned, even by contemporary City of London standards – 'and no doubt', as one of the regular hosts would recall, 'the somewhat lavish hospitality emanated from the fact that day in, day out we entertained visitors from overseas who in all probability had no further commitments that day'.[9]) And in Hong Kong, Chartered Bank would retain its old identity for many years to come: on the HK$ banknotes issued by the Group, 'The Chartered Bank' would go on promising 'to pay the bearer on demand at its office here . . .' until the first Standard Chartered notes appeared in 1985 (see Plate 31).

Hawker and his closest colleagues, though, were never quite as reconciled as this might suggest to the idea of taking the two banks forward like a pair of Siamese twins. The City's eurocurrency markets were growing rapidly, and Cyril Hamilton was determined from the outset that the merger should be used to fuel the growth of a market-leading International Division. Standard Bank had already been competing strongly in this area since December 1968, under George Preston's leadership.[10] Chartered had set up its own, smaller version of a eurocurrency trading unit in the middle of 1969, and leaving the two to operate separately would have made a mockery of the merger. It was resolved that here an exception would be made to the general non-convergence. Even so, some initial resistance was put up by Chartered: it had hitherto used its trading unit only to cover the needs of its overseas branches, and it argued for a measure of continued independence. Preston swept this aside in a magisterial report prepared late in 1970:

> That international banking is a specialist activity, requiring an attitude and outlook divorced from that of branch oriented banking, is clearly recognised by the majority of operators ... [In the wake of our merger] amalgamation of the two International Divisions seems a natural and almost inevitable step if benefit is to be gained from the strength and resources of the combined names ... [If Chartered's wishes are met] we do not think any satisfactory plan can be made for a merged operation ... [since] all business relating to [Chartered] branches would require to be channelled through Chartered Bank's London Office, acting as little more than a postbox in passing on transactions for execution by the joint merged division. This would lead to duplication of entries and records on a vast scale, in addition to frustrating time delays.[11]

The S&CBG Board agreed, and adopted his recommendations in January 1971. A fully integrated International Division was launched ten months later. The timing could hardly have been better. The collapse of the Bretton Woods System in August 1971 ended the post-war era in which currencies had generally been fixed against the US dollar, itself fixed in value by a guaranteed convertibility into gold at a constant price. Suddenly all participants in international trade had to cope with 'floating' (and often highly volatile) currency values – and demand for the new division's currency-trading services climbed steeply from month to month. The division also had responsibility for the merged banks' lending activities in the eurocurrency markets, and here too the volume of business took off dramatically. (The Group's share price, having staged a gradual recovery after the summer of 1970, had clawed its way back by July 1971 to the levels seen at the time of the merger's first announcement; and thereafter it began to rise quite rapidly, climbing 60 per cent higher in twelve months.) It was clear by 1972 that the international financial markets were undergoing a fundamental transformation. Hawker, Hamilton and Preston were widely and justifiably applauded for their prescience in positioning the nascent Group to take advantage of this – and its second Annual Report, published in July 1972, noted that the enlarged International Division had 'contributed substantially to the Group's profits'. These appeared generally robust, adding to a gathering impression of steady growth that left the 1969 merger looking sound.*

---

* Until March 1971 the steadiness was facilitated in the traditional way by transfers in and out of hidden reserves. This accounting convention, though, had out-lived its time. The UK

As insiders were well aware, however, the International Division's contribution needed keeping in perspective. It was growing quickly and
seemed to presage much for the future, but its profits over the next financial period, ending in March 1973, were still only £4 million – less than
10 per cent of the Group's trading profits – and a continued expansion of
the business seemed likely to be problematic, given the huge capital outlay
that would be required.[12] As for the broader performance of the Group,
any bank linked to international trade could scarcely have failed to flourish in the early 1970s: most of the world's commodity markets were
roaring ahead. While gratified by the buoyant current performance, therefore, Hawker and his executives by 1972 were busy trying to size up the
competitive position of their fledgling Group – not least in relation to the
ambitions that Hawker himself had publicly promoted for so many years.
On this score, there was reason to be deeply uneasy. Standard's Africa
franchise was fast losing its sheen, while Chartered offered far fewer credible growth strategies than Standard's Directors had assumed until quite
recently.

2. SEARCHING FOR A NEW BLUEPRINT

The unfolding story in Africa had three plots, none of them especially
encouraging. Standard in the early 1970s was of course still heavily reliant
on its subsidiary in South Africa. Just short of half its total consolidated
earnings came from the Republic.[13] The underlying strength of the local
operation there was not in doubt, but how long the London parent would
be able to cling on to it was another matter. Just as Edmund Hall-Patch
and his Directors had feared in 1961, the hiving-off of the South African

---

clearing banks had abandoned it with effect from December 1969. Other overseas banks,
including Barclays DCO, had followed suit in 1970. The S&CBG's Secretary wrote a memorandum for the Board pointing out that Barclays DCO's fully disclosed net profits for the
year to September 1970 were actually substantially lower than the Group's own for the same
period, yet its shares were much more highly rated by the stock market. Taking the S&CBG's
real net profits and applying the average price/earnings ratio enjoyed by the UK clearers, said
the Secretary, would produce a pro forma 14-per-cent hike in the S&CBG share price. ('Disclosure Memorandum' by H. D. M. Turner, 22 June 1971, S&CBG Board Papers, SCB Box
363.) The Directors demurred at first, musing that 'there might be advantage in being unique',
but soon changed their minds. The results reported for the year to March 1972 were 'fully
disclosed'. The net profit for S&CBG's first fiscal period ending in March 1971, which had
been reported as £7.88 million, was retrospectively restated as £16.38 million. For the year
to March 1972, net profit was £18.05 million. The impact of the accounting change was of
course impossible to quantify, but seemed positive enough: the share price by the end of
June 1972 had risen 44 per cent since the start of the year (from 350p to 504p).

business had led inexorably to a dilution of the parental stake – though this process had been staved off by Hawker for a surprisingly long time.[14] Shares in SBSA had finally been issued to South African investors at the end of 1967. Looking back on the sale in the first ever Report & Accounts of SBSA, published in June 1968, Chairman Alwyn Davies pointedly described it as 'one of the most significant events in the history of this century-old South African banking institution'. It meant 11.1 per cent of the equity was now in local hands, and both Standard Bank and SBSA henceforth had their own separate quotations on the Johannesburg Stock Exchange.* Late in 1969, more or less to coincide with the London parent's merger with Chartered, the South African business was restructured: SBSA became a full subsidiary of the newly formed Standard Bank Investment Corporation (usually referred to as 'StanBIC') and the London parent exchanged its stake in SBSA for an equal stake in StanBIC – but it came away with its 88.9 per cent stake shaved to 85.9 per cent, after another modest issue of new shares. (News of the merger with Chartered seems to have occasioned little or no interest whatever among the South Africans. Nowhere in the records is there a flicker of interest in the possibilities opened up by a commercial link to Chartered's Asian business. But, given the two merger partners' own disavowal of any real commercial integration, this is perhaps unsurprising. And those in Johannesburg were far too preoccupied with their own restructuring to spare much thought for the parent bank's change of identity.) While a gradual diminution of London's stake in StanBIC now seemed inevitable, the prospect of a robust growth in the latter's earnings at least offered some consolation, and Hawker and Hamilton in June 1971 secured an assurance from Davies and his forceful Chief Executive, W. T. (Bill) Passmore, that around 50 per cent of earnings would go on being distributed in dividend payments. It was part of a comprehensive 'gentleman's agreement' that was struck after talks in both London and Johannesburg, governing 'the aims and intentions of the Board of [StanBIC] in relation to future dividends, reserve retentions and capital investment'.[15]

Unfortunately, these generally amenable arrangements had by this point

---

* Foreign-exchange controls prevented investors arbitraging freely between the London and Johannesburg exchanges – which soon resulted in a notable pricing anomaly. In May 1969, when the terms of Standard's merger with Chartered envisaged a £100 million capitalization for the entire Group, Standard's 88.9 per cent stake in SBSA was alone worth £147 million in Johannesburg (*The Times*, 29 May 1969). This striking disparity suggested that South African investors were confident of securing a steadily greater share of SBSA in the future – and that they saw a business based exclusively inside the Republic as worth significantly more than a Group with extensive interests elsewhere in troubled Africa and Asia.

been abruptly challenged by the Vorster government in Pretoria. It had welcomed an official report in 1970 recommending that every foreign-owned bank in the Republic would have to provide for the non-residents' ownership to be cut to less than 50 per cent of the equity within ten years.[16] The threat of legislation to this effect then hung over S&CBG's relationship with StanBIC for the next three years, much to the regret of those at the head of both organizations. As Alwyn Davies protested, in a brave valedictory statement on his retirement in 1973, South Africans with any sense of history had good reason to be grateful to Standard's City owners: 'I am at a loss to understand why our overseas shareholders, who have expressed a willingness to cooperate with the Government on any reasonable and constructive basis, should now be legislated against and left in a state of uneasiness with a cloud hanging over a large part, if not the whole, of their interests.'[17] The issue came to a head in May 1973 after the South African Government went much further with its opposition to foreign ownership and mooted a legal ceiling, eventually, of 10 per cent. Hawker arranged immediately to travel to Pretoria himself for a meeting with the Finance Minister, Dr Nicolaas Diederichs. He recorded afterwards how he had reminded the Minister of Standard Bank's 111 years of service to the country:

> We had never milked South Africa but had ploughed back substantial profits so as to be in a position to continue to finance economic development . . . At the present time South Africa badly needed friends but it seemed to me that his proposals were calculated to alienate many of them . . . For a number of years now, control had been fully in the hands of South Africans. Naturally, because of our long association with South Africa we had some influence in [StanBIC] thinking and our advice was often sought. But final decision rested entirely with that Corporation.[18]

In fact, Hawker and his colleagues had already resigned themselves to striking a compromise with the authorities. In a meeting that lasted one and a half hours, he told Diederichs it was Standard's 'firm intention' to cut its stake to 50 per cent 'as and when opportunity occurred'. Returning to Pretoria again some weeks later, this time accompanied by Davies's successor in Johannesburg, Ian Mackenzie, Hawker confirmed that this would be done voluntarily, pre-empting any need for legislation – and in November Diederichs finally rescinded on the 10 per cent target. According to Hawker's own account, he had rejected out of hand a suggestion by the Finance Minister that Standard's stake could be reduced by a series of rights issues in which the parent would not participate: 'I pointed out to him that this was not a starter.' Rather, equity would be sold off in blocks to third parties, where fair prices could be agreed. In the event, the rights-issue course was in fact to be adopted (starting with a sale in December 1973 that cut Standard's stake to 78 per cent, followed by annual reductions that lowered it to 52 per cent by 1983). Either way, though, the Pretoria meetings had ended in a curious outcome for the London parent, fraught with ambiguity. It would have the semblance of real control, remaining the majority shareholder for some years – and thereby retaining ultimate responsibility, in the Bank of England's eyes, for the balance sheet and capital needs of the South African business. In the event of any substantial disagreement with the management in Johannesburg, however, the London Board would actually have no executive power whatever over its subsidiary. As a source of profits, StanBIC would remain crucial for the foreseeable future; but, as a strategic asset, it was no longer of any value at all – and seemed only too likely, given the pariah status of South Africa's apartheid regime internationally, to become a growing liability.

The outlook in Salisbury was scarcely more heartening. As noted in the previous chapter, the tensions between Ian Smith's regime and the British Government had prompted Hawker to leave Central Africa out of his wider plans in 1964–5, despite the impressive expansion of the bank as a mainstay of the Central African Federation since its founding in 1953. If a resolution to the crisis had somehow been able to restore stability to Southern Rhodesia, aligning its growth prospects with those of Zambia and Malawi – the old Northern Rhodesia and Nyasaland, newly independent since 1964 – Standard Bank might perhaps have turned back to that vast region of the continent with genuine optimism. Instead, Smith had issued his Unilateral Declaration of Independence in November 1965, and the bank had been left to juggle with competing loyalties in Salisbury and London as best it could. Two months after UDI, Cyril Hamilton had compiled a report about his tour of Africa with the Chairman of Chase Manhattan, George Champion, and had included a candid assessment of the bank's situation in Rhodesia, based on discussions in Johannesburg with its Central African Chairman, Evan Campbell:

> There was, of course, considerable bother [after UDI] over the making of payments overseas [from Rhodesia] . . . These difficulties appear now to have been overcome and new accounts abroad have been opened. Some of these accounts have been opened by the commercial banks in Salisbury, including Standard, and it would be as well to mention the legal position. Under the emergency regulations promulgated in Salisbury, banks and companies must cooperate with the Smith regime. If they fail to do so, they can be declared 'a designated company' and under the regulations an

administrator can be appointed to run the business. This does not leave our local Board with any useful option other than to carry on the business to the best of their ability.[19]

And so they had done, ever since. Formerly the Rhodesian High Commissioner in London, Evan Campbell was a wealthy farmer with top-notch connections in all corners of the country's powerful tobacco industry, and had been appointed to head the Local Board by Hawker in July 1965. The two men wrote to each other regularly over the next several years, leaving behind a trail of often emotional letters attesting to a long series of false dawns in Rhodesia and repeatedly dashed hopes that, as Campbell put it early in their correspondence, 'sanity will prevail on both sides and that a solution [will be] found before it is too late to save this wonderful country'.[20]

After international sanctions against the Smith regime had cut Rhodesia off from Britain and most other Western countries, Campbell and his Board in Salisbury ran a more or less autonomous business, with ninety-nine branches (easily the largest of Standard's country networks anywhere in Africa beyond the Republic). As late as December 1965, Hawker was still inclined to resist a proposal from Campbell that London should sever its formal ties with the Salisbury operation. The UK Government, Hawker suggested, was not pressing for any such outcome: '[the Government has] recognized the facts of life and have not embarrassed us by expecting us to give [you] instructions which would embarrass you'.[21] But a parting of the ways nonetheless followed within a few months. Powers of Attorney were sent down to the key men in Salisbury, allowing the parent bank to pretend that it had no control over the (directly owned) Rhodesian branches. The Chairman's Statement in each year's Annual Report, while always including paragraphs on 'East and Central Africa', now made no reference at all to Rhodesia. If third parties turned up at Head Office asking for endorsement of the Rhodesian branches' creditworthiness (as occasionally they did), they were sent away with polite apologies. The great risk for Standard was that its Salisbury managers might at some point renege on a financial obligation to a third party, compromising the reputation of the bank internationally and triggering calls on the parent to drop the whole charade. So far, this risk had been averted. Despite the occasional crisis over travel restrictions and a running anxiety over their own career prospects and pensions, the local managers had adjusted remarkably well to some increasingly onerous siege conditions, and had more than repaid London's trust in their professionalism. In the process they served up earnings of about £2 million a year. This the parent included in its consolidated accounts, though of course cash could not be remitted to London and could only be added to reserves in Salisbury.* But nothing could mitigate the fact that Rhodesia's tragedy effectively made Central Africa irrelevant to the Group's post-1970 strategic planning, no less than South Africa itself. George Preston noted for colleagues early in 1971 that Rhodesia's credit in the financial world was 'thoroughly damaged'. While a political settlement there might one day revitalize local banking in the country, 'I would not react very favourably to the idea of putting fresh money of our own into Rhodesian business'.[22]

And then there was Black Africa. Standard in the 1960s had never had any illusions about the risks involved in building its business under post-colonial regimes. A broad overview written in September 1965 (almost certainly by Cyril Hamilton) had observed 'a double squeeze' on profitability. The old pre-war sources of funding – including inward investment from Europe, expatriates' current accounts and local companies' deposits – had thinned out considerably. At the same time, newly independent governments were turning to overseas banks for assistance in financing everything from agriculture to social services. The altered political climate, meanwhile, had hugely exacerbated the dangers of nationalization, devaluation, illicit support for domestic competitors and nasty regulatory surprises of every kind. Perhaps, surmised the 1965 paper, the bank should just withdraw its capital and head back to the UK? But then –

> If we believe that the risks in Black Africa are so great that this is what we must do, we should never have taken over the Bank of West Africa or joined up with Chase . . . [Contrariwise] in our favour is the knowledge on the part of Africans who matter that British banks have been prepared in the past, and are still prepared, to supply funds from London at times of strain.

---

* Standard's performance earned it no plaudits from the Smith government, of which Campbell was openly critical on several occasions. A particularly outspoken letter to the newspapers in December 1968 drew Ian Smith into a vituperative public attack on both Campbell and the bank. The two men held a private meeting together at the start of the New Year. Campbell reported back to Hawker: 'The first twenty minutes were pretty rough as I did not pull any punches at all and told him exactly what I thought of him, his Party and the way in which they were running the Country down . . . I left feeling very sorry for him and the Country, and very sad. Where we go from here I do not know.' (Campbell to Hawker, 2 January 1969, LMA: ST03/03/04/005.) For his part, Hawker was ready to make a virtue of the way in which the bank had stuck by its Rhodesian customers, when he visited Pretoria in 1973. He told the Finance Minister, Dr Diederichs, that Standard Bank 'had behaved impeccably'. ('Foreign Control of South African Banks' by Cyril Hawker, Memorandum for the S&CBG Board, 13 June 1973, SCB Box 356.)

The Standard Bank has a reputation for fair dealing and responsible management – a tremendous fund of goodwill . . . [and besides, it is] unlikely that trouble will strike in all our 17 territories at once . . .[23]

Seven years later, the bank's assessment of the position was rather different – and not just because the mooted partnership with Chase appeared to have gone so awry. Confidence had taken a severe knock in 1967 when President Julius Nyerere of the now-named Tanzania (formerly Tanganyika and Zanzibar) had nationalized all of that country's banks. This was a nation that had been independent since 1961, led by a politician well-known to the business and commercial classes of Dar-es-Salaam and Zanzibar for well over a decade. His sudden espousal of radical reforms based on 'Socialism and Self Reliance' had come as a shock, and seemed at the time to open up a Pandora's Box for the British bankers of post-colonial Africa. At the Standard a bright young merchant banker, Michael McWilliam, had recently been hired by Chuck Fiero to head a 'Market Research Department', and the newcomer was asked to write a paper on the possible consequences of Nyerere's move. McWilliam was no stranger to post-colonial adjustments: the son of a senior adviser to the Kenyan government, he had grown up in East Africa and had worked for five years as an official inside the Treasury in Nairobi, leaving shortly after independence in 1963 to pursue a career in the City. He compiled a report that warned of the likely difficulties to come. Many African countries seemed certain to demand – just as South Africa had done in 1962, in fact – that Standard's local operations should be fully capitalized within their countries as self-standing subsidiaries.[24] Sizeable shareholdings, he suggested, were then likely to be demanded by the host governments – and it would be surprising if Nyerere's Tanzania emerged as the only champion of outright nationalization.

So it proved. By the time the first Annual Report & Accounts of S&CBG appeared, in July 1971, the Standard's operations in Kenya, Uganda, Zambia and Malawi, like the erstwhile BWA networks in Nigeria, Ghana and Sierra Leone, had all been locally incorporated. Share sales in the seven new companies were in the process of reducing the parent's stake almost everywhere. Much time and effort was expended in Clements Lane puzzling how best to respond to the new political environment, while retaining effective control.* But this managerial exercise was usually out of all

---

* Some in London were inclined to suggest all kinds of shenanigans that would comply with the letter of new ownership regulations while clinging to the spirit of former colonial days. Wiser counsel was provided on the S&CBG Board by Sir Robert Taylor, a former Financial Secretary to the Government of Northern Rhodesia and Standard's Chairman in pre-UDI

proportion to the size of the newly incorporated African subsidiaries' earnings (even ignoring the added complication that their dividend payments to the UK parent were generally impeded by onerous foreign-exchange controls). In the autumn of 1971, the General Manager responsible for the Standard's business within the Group, Ray Reed, set down the revenues earned by its component parts in 1970–71 as part of his planning for the next financial year. Out of a total of £70 million, almost £20 million was sourced by the London office in Clements Lane and its direct branches (including, especially, those in Rhodesia). Of the remaining £50 million, just under £35 million represented StanBIC's revenues in South Africa. This left only £15 million for those of the six largest African subsidiaries, and almost half of that sum arose in one country – Nigeria, whose potentially huge economy was only just beginning to recover from the impact of a terrible civil war.[25] To anyone posing again that rhetorical question of 1965 ('Should the bank not just head back to the UK?'), the answer now was decidedly more nuanced. As Reed, a South African by birth, had himself written to the Board six months earlier: 'We are, as you know, concerned at the declining revenue from some of our African territories and are anxious to find ways and means of making good such losses. The answer might be found largely in the UK . . .'[26] This idea, that setting up provincial branches in the UK might be a more profitable way of exploiting the Group's trade-financing capabilities, drew no immediate response from his colleagues – but its time would come.

The local difficulties in Africa were not so great as to dent the aggregate performance of the Group too seriously – and Standard's trading profits (£21 million for 1970–71) far exceeded the £8 million earned by Chartered Bank.* But the struggles of assorted tiny African subsidiaries were hardly consistent with the brave talk of complementary franchises during the merger talks of 1969 (and did nothing to allay the resentment of grumpy Chartered critics like Stafford Northcote). Hawker and Hamilton had spent much of the 1960s pursuing a Grand Design shaped around a

---

Rhodesia for three years. He stuck to the advice he had offered from Salisbury years ago for dealing with the emerging African leaders: 'I think there is a limit to which one should go in setting up a façade to make something appear to be something which it is not. These people are not fools and are not likely to be impressed by a so-called structure of management . . . which is patently contrived to bamboozle them.' (Taylor to Hawker, 4 December 1963, LMA: ST03/03/04/003.)

* The Standard's £21 million comprised £9 million earned in South Africa, £4 million in Nigeria, £5 million at Clements Lane and the remaining £3 million from other countries in West Africa. Total trading profits for the whole Group in 1970–71 were £28.9 m (S&CBG Annual Report 1972, p. 6).

pan-African banking empire in one form or another. A cautious view of Africanization, added to the Long Goodbye in South Africa and the siege of Salisbury, only confirmed again that any Grand Design for S&CBG would need a different blueprint. If they hoped at first to find one on the drawing board at Chartered, they were quickly disillusioned. On the contrary, as Hawker reported back to Hamilton during his first tour round its branches, many of the Chartered's staff were themselves hoping desperately for a fresh start, courtesy of Standard Bank:

> The attitude in the field to the merger is a very different one from the picture painted by George Pullen and Stafford Northcote. The senior officials are in no way opposed to the merger but they have not been properly briefed ... Not unnaturally Managers are wary of crossing swords with General Management in London but I sense a feeling of frustration and doubts whether Chartered Bank are moving with the times. They are frightened of the American banks and feel that the Standard Chartered Group have the resources necessary to cope with them. The younger element in particular want to see real growth and are worried that Chartered may go to the wall if they do not adopt more progressive ideas.[27]

His trip alerted Hawker to a structural weakness at Chartered that he seems not to have anticipated: career paths in the bank still ended, as they had done since the nineteenth century, in retirement at fifty-five or a summons home to serve as one of the General Managers in Bishopsgate. Control of the bank's strategy thus rested with those in general least likely to champion troublesome reappraisals of the future. Indeed, they had shown less than a sprightly interest in even mundane administrative reforms, or running repairs that could be put off until another day. In one country after another, Hawker found physical buildings and office routines that had alike seen better days. This might perhaps have prompted him to see a latent potential to do better, but it did not. He had no problem discerning the real strength of the bank ('I have been impressed with the high standard of many of the Chartered men I have met out here') and yet he still returned in little doubt that its business across Asia was fast losing momentum – as the numbers had indeed been suggesting for a while.

For half a century after the First World War, the accountants in Bishopsgate had been accustomed each year to coping with a volatile and often highly unpredictable mix of earnings from individual branches – out of which, in a good year, would emerge one or two bumper performances to set the pace. The trading results for 1971 confirmed, like those of the two previous calendar years, that an altogether steadier profile was now evident – with some deeply unsettling features.[28] For a start, roughly half of the branches' profits were now consistently coming from just three locations – Hong Kong, Singapore and Malaysia with its greatly expanded post-war network. (Keen to build on its atypical profile as a local bank in many of Malaysia's trading towns, as noted already, Chartered had opened as many branches as possible since the mid-1950s in pursuit of customers' deposits. Its rush to expand had also been motivated by well-grounded fears that nationalist sentiment was eventually going to ban new foreign branches. By the time the boom dropped in 1965, the Chartered had opened eighteen in ten years, leaving the network with a total of thirty-seven Malaysian branches.[29]) In Hong Kong, profits for 1971 were £2.3 million, and would climb to £3.5 million in 1972 – but regulatory changes across the region were making it harder to imagine that the bank's success in the Colony might be easily replicated in south-east Asia. The unveiling of the 'New Economic Policy' in Malaysia and the establishment of the Monetary Authority in Singapore (an independent state since 1965) both presaged new rules tipping the competitive field in favour of local banks. Even by 1971, net profits after local taxation had seemingly stalled at around £1 million a year in each of these two territories (though Chartered by 1970 had succeeded in capturing 19 and 13 per cent respectively of the deposits in their two banking systems[30]).

Elsewhere, there were half a dozen or so branches – usually Bangkok, Manila and Brunei in the East; New York and Hamburg in the West – chipping in a regular £¼ million or thereabouts annually. But neither in Beirut nor in the sheikhdoms of the Gulf were the newly merged Group's operations yet consistently profitable (despite fast-rising oil revenues in the OPEC states). Above all, Chartered's glory days in India were long gone. Here the passing years had done little to repay the rescue of Eastern Bank, which had continued to haemorrhage funds in the sub-continent through most of the 1960s. When it was finally resolved in 1971 to shut down most of Eastern's twenty branches, transferring their business to the nearest Chartered branch, three perennial losers had to remain open in India as Chartered sub-branches, to placate hostile trade unionists and government ministers opposed to any closures at all.[31] This was a fair reflection of Chartered's travails in a country now gripped by the Licence Raj. Its absurdities had plagued the bank in matters great and small (few smaller than a comic refusal by the authorities in Bombay in November 1959 to grant the bank an import licence for copies of the house magazine, *Curry and Rice* – a portent of things to come[32]). Earnings had also been denuded by the loss of Allahabad Bank. The Government had nationalized fourteen major banks in 1969, and it had been a simple matter for the authorities to include the Allahabad since Chartered had never treated it as anything more than a semi-detached appendage.* The nationalization policy had also meant a de facto ban on new branches for Chartered's network in the country, further curtailing any growth plans. For 1971, Chartered reported a third successive year of substantial losses in India – and in Pakistan, too, where the Indo-Pakistani War set back any hopes of an early return to profitability. For many outside observers – including an increasingly sceptical press corps in the City – Chartered's worries in the sub-continent heavily reinforced the impression of an old-fashioned overseas bank stuck in the doldrums, and flattered in its published accounts by the rising profits earned on syndication activities in the eurocurrency markets.

What Chartered badly needed, Hawker and the S&CBG Directors agreed, were some promising new markets. But Bishopsgate's own pursuit of them in recent years had been less than a total triumph. A branch had been opened in South Korea in 1967, for example, to which Hew Liller had been transferred (much to his relief) from Aden. No one in Seoul had taken pot-shots at him, but that was about the best that could be said for his new location. Annual profits to date had been nugatory, while repeated devaluations of the Korean won had eroded the capital initially injected from London. (A demand from the Government that more capital be shipped in would shortly spark a debate on the Board over the logic of remaining in the country – at which 'it was decided that, in line with the bank's policy in accepting that its presence in any particular territory is in the long term, and [given] the effect that a precipitate withdrawal from Korea might have had on expansion elsewhere, the additional injection of capital should be made'.[33]) Hopes of a much expanded banking franchise in the Eastern Mediterranean, meanwhile, had ended in disaster. Perhaps goaded into competing with a Finance Corporation set up there by Barclays DCO in 1968, the tiny network of branches in Cyprus had built up a reckless portfolio of loans: the losses over 1971–2 reached almost £½ million.† More satisfactory, so far, had been Chartered's experience as an investor in other financial-services companies. It had acquired minority

---

* This semi-detached status may in fact have suited Chartered quite well, to judge by the shape of the Allahabad's post-nationalization balance sheet. An official from the Finance Ministry, D. N. Ghosh (subsequently Chairman and Managing Director of the State Bank of India), was appointed by the Government to investigate a suspiciously high level of dud loans. His report revealed that Chartered had been accustomed for years to handing on its more dubious loans to the Allahabad, and the latter's Chairman was soon afterwards dismissed. (D. N. Ghosh, interview with author, 9 October 2012.)

† Efforts to extricate the Group from its woes in Cyprus were not helped by the island's division into two halves after the Turkish invasion of 1974 and they lasted through the rest of the 1970s and beyond. A deal was eventually struck to sell the branch network to the Bank

stakes in dozens of small businesses, offering its shareholders a suitably guarded exposure to credit cards and ship financing, private banking and oilfield exploration. But the aggregate numbers were small. Some thirty-six trade investments by the start of 1972 were valued in the books at less than £9 million in toto. Two-thirds of these investments were in Europe, where they included a trio of tiny banks in Hamburg, Zurich and the City.[34]

To date, such business ties had scarcely been of much real significance. Both the Standard and Chartered Bank were more than a century old. Minor equity stakes in small businesses encrusted their balance sheets like barnacles on the bottom of an old boat. But when the S&CBG's Directors stepped back to contemplate their strategic options, they were soon drawn to the appeal – contrary to the historic spirit of overseas banking – of building on some of these investments that had been made nearer to home. Hamilton was asked by Hawker to explore the possibilities – and a Steering Group under Hamilton's chairmanship in due course proposed that the Group should indeed seek to grow its business not just in Africa or Asia, but in the UK and Europe too. On 1 February 1972, the Board accepted this recommendation. It was plainly a decision with weighty implications for the long-term development of the bank, but this was not immediately apparent: although a remarkable spate of initiatives followed in the next three years, most were only of incremental significance. The time and paperwork devoted to them were wholly disproportionate to their financial impact. This in itself, however, was of some consequence. The glaring managerial inefficiencies prompted a change of heart over the acquiescence in two separate banking subsidiaries, with all the duplications involved. This led directly to a consummation, at last, of the 1969 merger.

Hamilton prepared the way by setting up a shared Corporate Planning Department in February 1972. It was to be run by Michael McWilliam, rapidly emerging as a man with a future. As Hamilton pointed out, 'the expansion and evolution of the two banks outside their traditional areas in Africa and the East increasingly means that they will be confronted with common problems'. A few months later, he formally proposed the amalgamation of the two General Management structures (though not, as noted, their dining facilities) and this was finally achieved in the summer of 1973 – not by chance, a few months after the retirement of Stafford Northcote. The process was aided by a major refurbishment of Standard's

---

of Cyprus for a nominal sum in December 1982. Even then, wrangling over pensions for the staff dragged on a while longer.

premises at 10 Clements Lane, adding a much grander entrance on the corner with King William Street. The creeping convergence of the two banks thereafter gathered pace. Chartered's separate annual reports, with their elegant Baedeker-style potted essays on the national economies of the East, were discontinued; adjacent branches in Hamburg and New York were required to pool their resources; and the two executive teams in London were finally merged. After Pullen and Hamilton had both retired in March 1974, the three Boards of S&CBG, Standard and Chartered were at last aligned with identical Directors – and Sir Cyril Hawker himself stepped down as Chairman in August the same year. As the passionate cricketer himself must surely have put it in many of his innumerable farewell speeches, he had had a good innings. His deft leadership through the 1960s had probably averted the break-up of Standard Bank; and his grasp of the changing fundamentals in the international banking industry had at least ensured a chance for Standard and Chartered now to work out a sustainable future together. By the time of his departure, and whatever their deeper reservations about the growth potential of the Group he had created, most City observers saw his eventual integration of the two banks as a considerable personal achievement. (He was to enjoy a long retirement, much enriched by his enduring love of cricket, and died aged ninety in 1991.)

The limited financial impact of the 1972–4 initiatives was nonetheless troubling. Two in particular had fallen short of expectations. Hamilton and George Preston had identified European trade finance as a key market for the Group, warranting a physical presence in all the major capitals on the continent. As Hamilton explained in his Board proposal:

> This strategy accords best with the opportunities offered by the strong position of the Group in so many important markets in the developing world, to extend the trade financing role . . . so as to provide a link back into the metropolitan markets in respect of exports from European countries and imports into them. Furthermore such a role would be a natural development of the traditional policies of the Chartered Bank and Standard Bank of seeking overseas banking business from a wide circle of banking friends.[35]

By the summer of 1973, representative offices had been set up or joint-ventured with local banks in Dusseldorf and Frankfurt, Brussels and Rotterdam, Paris, Milan and Madrid. Attracting business from that 'wide circle of banking friends', however, was proving to be trickier in Europe than expected. The Joint General Managers, Ronnie Lane and Ray Reed, drew some uncomfortable conclusions. Trade patterns were changing and becoming much more competitive. The Group had a strong presence in the eurocurrency market, but not as a lender to European borrowers. (Regular monthly reports to the Board listed the Group's share of a dazzling variety of credits, but all for borrowers in the developing world. In February 1973, for example, these included multimillion advances for the Dubai Dry Dock Company, South African Railways, Mazda Motors of Zaire, Thai Containers Ltd, Hyundai Construction Company, the Central Bank of the Philippines, the Government of Iran and the Korean Exchange Bank.) The Group had no deposit base in the UK, and – more surprisingly – did not enjoy the kind of access to pools of rich investors in the East that could yet allow it to participate in the eurobond market, an increasingly active sector of European banking.* In short, expansion in Europe 'cannot be expected to yield a notable profit contribution during the next five years'. This sober appraisal triggered a call, in June 1973, for alternative action: 'the desired increase in profits cannot be achieved purely from an expansion of our existing traditional business and a major acquisition [i.e. in the UK] will be necessary to protect the future'.[36]

A major, but in many ways rather eccentric, acquisition duly followed. Chartered Bank in 1968 had acquired a 22 per cent stake in a publicly quoted but family-controlled UK consumer finance business called the Hodge Group. It earned two-thirds of its profits as a lender of secondary mortgages, but had a range of other equally unglamorous activities from insurance broking to second-hand car sales and the letting of caravans in Wales. The Welsh owner of the business, Sir Julian Hodge, was not the type of tycoon normally associated with the oriental markets of Chartered, but he prided himself on a certain fame in the Principality (where various charitable and educational institutions still bear his name to this day) and he was a personal friend of several Directors of the bank, three

---

* In the eurobond market, banks were expected to act not as principals but as agents. Where a new bond was issued by a company as the alternative to raising a loan, banks agreed to purchase a slice of the bond, not to squirrel it away in their own balance sheet but to sell it on to investors. This required either an in-house customer base of such investors or else a network of relationships with other banks and asset managers in that happy position. In 1972–3, S&CBG participated in nine eurobond issues as a way of determining how successfully Chartered Bank's branches might be able to drum up demand from investors in the Middle East and the Far East. In the event, the branches reported almost no appetite for the bonds at all, and the Group made a profit on the whole exercise of 'approximately £295'. A review for the Board concluded, though, that this dismal performance only underscored the importance of expanding the Group's presence in Europe. This 'could in time form a broader basis for a Group Eurobond capability in London than the traditional areas of our two constituent banks', allowing entry into what was seen as a vital growth market. ('The Eurobond Market' by R. F. N. Clark, undated, S&CBG Board Papers, SCB Box 363.)

of whom graced his Board. He had persuaded George Pullen to serve as Deputy Chairman – and when S&CBG began looking in earnest for a UK acquisition target, Pullen himself proposed the Hodge Group as 'the outstanding opportunity' to boost the bank's home profits.[37] Sir Julian was ready to sell his family's 59 per cent stake, and was understandably happy to have Chartered buy it. Especially so, perhaps, given an ambitious expansion of his business into car manufacturing – earlier in 1973, it had acquired a majority stake in the Reliant Motor Company, which in October was to launch upon the world its Reliant Robin, a light-weight three-wheeler that would enjoy a longer commercial life than most industry pundits predicted (and an even longer life as a cherished prop in British television comedies). The bank's purchase of the family-owned and publicly traded shares was completed early in January 1974, for stock in S&CBG worth just under £45 million. (Part of this comprised a subordinated loan stock, bearing a 13.5 per cent coupon and repayable in 1980 – which marked the first appearance on Standard Chartered's balance sheet of loan capital, as distinct from equity capital.) By this point, a two-year boom in the UK economy – the so-called Barber Boom, named after the ill-starred Tory Chancellor of the day and erstwhile director of Chartered Bank, Anthony Barber – had already come to a jarring halt, with a dramatic rise in interest rates helping to trigger a collapse in house prices and a severe squeeze on 'secondary banks' lending against property. Just eight days after the public offer for the Hodge Group had gone unconditional on the stock market, a memo to the Board noted that it had always been intended that a substantial loan facility would be made available for the new subsidiary – but had to record:

> Recent developments concerning 'secondary banks' have, however, impaired Hodge's ability to attract deposits . . . [and] some of the larger commercial lenders appear to be withdrawing from the market. As a result Hodge have requested S&CBG to make available a standby facility totalling £30 million to assist them during the current difficult period.[38]

Despite its unfortunate timing, the deal attracted less criticism in the press than might have been expected. Most components of Sir Julian's conglomerate were assimilated into various Chartered subsidiaries over time – displeasing its founder, who though he remained running it for another five years resented the re-branding of the business and departed rather earlier than planned – while the stake in Reliant was quietly ditched in 1977. But as the Secondary Banking Crisis sent dozens of small mortgage lenders into a tailspin, it was plain the transaction had done a lot more for the Hodge business than for the Chartered Bank and S&CBG.

Certainly it brought the Group nothing like the additional profit stream originally envisaged.

Only in two instances did the Group's early reorientation to Western markets lead to significant and lasting investments. Both arose, over the course of 1973, in the United States – not previously identified as much of a priority, given all the complications that had arisen over the Chartered Bank of London (CBoL) in California. Since the very first days of the International Division, George Preston had been mustard keen to add to it a gold-trading business. As he argued to colleagues, succinctly enough, 'a bank group with a major position in gold-producing countries in Africa and consuming countries in the East provides a natural base for a strong bullion business and . . . S&CBG should be a prime operator on a world-wide basis'.[39] He had spent a huge amount of time in 1970–72 cultivating a close association with Johnson Matthey Bankers, one of the five firms at the heart of the London gold market, only to see it snatched away by a rival suitor.[40] When the opportunity then arose to acquire control of Mocatta & Goldsmid (M&G), the oldest and most august of the five, Preston lost no time mobilizing what was inevitably known as Project Goldfinger. The seller was Hambro Bank, which had run up heavy losses in shipping and needed to avert any possibility of further strains on its balance sheet. In addition to M&G in London, Hambro also owned 50 per cent of Mocatta Metals Corporation (MMC) of New York, a very much larger concern and the largest silver dealer in the US. Unfortunately, in striking a deal with Preston, Hambro had overlooked the terms of its contract with the co-owner of its US business. These gave the latter the option of acquiring the whole of MMC in the event of a change of ownership for M&G. An embarrassing stand-off ensued, and some protracted talks which ended eventually with the US partner taking a 70 per cent stake in MMC and a 45 per cent stake in the London business as well (plus half of a much smaller trading firm in the UK, Commercial Metals Corp., a trader in non-ferrous metals on the London Metal Exchange). S&CBG took on the balance of the two businesses, at a total cost of about £2.5 million, while lending its new American partner a substantial sum to help him fund his share of the transaction.[41] It was not the deal that Preston had originally had in mind, but it brought the Group what was to prove a long-lasting relationship with one of the more intriguing businessmen ever to cross its path.

Dr Henry Jarecki was an American Jew whose family, once a prominent German ship-owning dynasty, had fled from the Nazis in 1939. Only in recent years had he carved out a position for himself as one of the world's leading traders in precious metals – but the skill and ingenuity he had shown in the process attested to a financial brain that any bank might think worth picking on a regular basis. A prominent academic psychiatrist with a professorial chair at Yale University and a private practice in New Haven, Connecticut, Jarecki in the 1960s had grown bored of listening to patients on his couch (and always thought pills more effective than psychotherapy).[42] Letting his mind wander over oddities in the financial markets, he had noticed one day that a quarter of the US dollar bills in circulation doubled up as 'silver certificates', theoretically entitling the holder under the Bland–Allison Act of 1878 to receive ¾ oz of physical silver. He had then discovered that, in exchange for 1,333 of these bills, the Federal Reserve would indeed hand over a 1,000 oz bar of silver. With the value of the metal climbing steadily, Jarecki did not need to be an accomplished mathematician (though he was one) to see the oddity of the fact that the price of ¾ oz of silver had shot well beyond $1. He soon began collecting dollars that carried the silver-certificate smallprint and turning them into bullion, which he sold on the US Commodity Exchange. Initial profit margins of a few per cent on his turnover soon climbed well into double figures, on an arbitrage operation that required considerable energy and organization skills – Jarecki had both in spades – but which was essentially risk-free. Always deeply averse to risk but fascinated by the mathematics of arbitrage – the buying and selling of the same asset in different markets to take advantage of anomalous price discrepancies – and the potential use of computers, he had stumbled on a modern-day version of the philosopher's stone. When the US Government in 1968 annulled the long-standing prohibition on the melting of silver coins, his arbitrage activities took on another dimension. The scale of his trades prompted him in due course to fly to London to seek assistance from the slightly disbelieving experts at Mocatta & Goldsmid. After watching their singular US client at work for some months, the UK firm's partners readily acceded to Jarecki's proposal that they go into business together in New York. Hence the founding of Mocatta Metals Corporation, in which Jarecki split the equity 50/50 with M&G – and thus eventually with Hambro Bank, majority owners of M&G from 1957 until the 1973 sale to S&CBG.

The final size of the Group's deal with Hambro and Jarecki prompted an issue of 400,000 new shares. It also, and much more importantly, attracted the attention of the US Federal Reserve. Here was cause for the authorities, once again, to ask themselves how long they were prepared to tolerate the contentious stake held in S&CBG by Chase Manhattan. Chase had actually acquired a few more shares in the Group since January 1970 and now held 11.9 per cent. Since that date, recurrent discussions with the Fed had also won more time for the New York bank to sell out. But it had no intention of doing so – its $90 million investment in S&CBG represented its largest single overseas asset – and by early 1973 the issue was again becoming critical. With a month to go until the expiry of the Fed's latest deadline, and still enjoying the support of the National Westminster Bank (which had retained its own stake in the Group since 1969), Chase executives in March sent Hawker an ultimatum. Seemingly more in sorrow than anger, they informed S&CBG that it had to promise unequivocally to dispose of its Californian subsidiary, CBoL, '[or else] we will have to consider the steps that we, upon the advice of counsel, may take'.[43] Hawker himself brushed this aside almost nonchalantly, pointing out that it was Chase's problem and nothing to do with S&CBG. Others appear to have favoured a more combative response. Pullen, never much enamoured of the Chase, thought that S&CBG should reaffirm its determination to grow in the US – and as luck would have it, a perfect opportunity now arose to do so. The Manager of CBoL, Norman Eckersley, had befriended the head of a small retail bank in California called the Liberty National Bank. It had a dozen branches usefully located in both San Francisco and Los Angeles, and looked a perfect complement to CBoL's two branches. As a report recommending the acquisition put it, in reassuringly familiar terms, Liberty National was 'a cross between Hodge Group and Coutts Bank, with an element of building-society lending thrown in'.[44] In August 1973 – just as Chase's lawyers, having placated the Fed yet again, were gathering to try to repackage the bank's stake in ways acceptable to the authorities for the long term – Pullen and Eckersley drove ahead with the purchase of the Liberty National, successfully completed for $16 million in December. This of course greatly compounded Chase's problem. Nothing could have confirmed more forcefully the rejection by Clements Lane of Chase's reading of the ambiguity contrived in 1969. Lawyers in the US huffed and puffed for a while, but in May 1975 Chase finally gave up the struggle. Its shareholding was quietly shuffled off to the Midland Bank – and six months later the National Westminster Bank sold up, disposing of its S&CBG shares in the stock market.[45] (The Midland retained its enlarged stake, almost 16 per cent, until selling out in 1979.)

Resolving the complications over Chase's stake was one of two essential precursors to any substantial expansion in the US, if this was to be added to the Group's strategic agenda. The other was the emergence of a decisive chief executive, bold enough to lead the Group in such a radical new direction. No one doubted by 1975 that the coming man was the Senior General Manager responsible for Chartered Bank's Far East region, who had done

so much in the 1960s to turn Hong Kong into Chartered's most profitable
territory. Since returning to London in 1970, Peter Graham had been
preoccupied with his role in Bishopsgate and had not played any conspicuous part in the shaping of the post-1969 Group. But in July 1975 he was
appointed Deputy Managing Director with a seat on the Board, making
him the obvious successor to the two existing Joint Managing Directors
promoted to the Board in 1974, Ronnie Lane and Ray Reed. Much was
expected of Graham. He would be the first individual to reach the top in
the wake of the merger, and was already seen as personifying the coales-
cence of the two parent banks. (It was notable that Lane, Reed and
Graham all combined executive positions with seats on the Board. This
reflected a widespread shift within the City around this time, away from
the old divide between the gentlemen lording it in the Boardroom and the
players grappling with the day-to-day tasks of management. The executive
managers of the bank were increasingly to be seen as the real drivers of
the business.)

Living up to his billing from the start, Graham wasted no time in deciding that the incremental steps taken so far to reorient the Group away
from Africa and Asia had been nothing like dynamic enough. And he was
indeed minded to add North America to the list of target markets. As he
would later recall:

> When I knew I was going to become the chief executive of the bank, I
> decided to map out a strategy which would cover my period of office which
> I anticipated would be about seven years. That took place in 1975 . . . I felt
> that it was time we diversified internationally. The focal point of that strat-
> egy was that I wanted to have roughly 25 per cent of the bank's assets in
> North America. I wanted to build a base in Europe with 25 per cent roughly
> there. To balance off, what was [sic] half roughly in Africa and half roughly
> in the East, with a very small presence in the UK.[46]

His challenging numbers were readily endorsed by Sir Cyril Hawker's
successor, Anthony (now Lord) Barber, the former Chancellor. Still only
fifty-four, Barber had abandoned politics following his unhappy career at
the Treasury and the fall of the Heath government in February 1974. His
timing suited the Group perfectly. A Director of Chartered Bank for four
years up to 1970 and a tax lawyer by profession – starting out with a
first-class law degree which he had earned while still a wartime PoW in
Germany, using the International Red Cross to correspond with London
University – Barber accepted an invitation to join the Board as its Chairman. In a privately published autobiography, Barber would later explain
that he had agreed to the role in the autumn of 1974 provided he would

be 'a full-time Chairman with executive powers'.[47] In the event, he was to be rarely less than full-time – travelling tirelessly round the world on behalf of the Group – but his knowledge of banking was modest and he would always see his role as essentially supportive of the executive, and of Graham in particular with whom he quickly formed a close bond.* He had no hesitation in backing Graham's bracing agenda, and the two of them instigated a grand conference at London's Hyde Park Hotel in October 1975 to unveil it. Well over a hundred senior managers and their wives were invited from around the world. None had ever attended anything remotely like it. Though still deputy to Managing Director Ronnie Lane, it was Graham who used the two-day event to impress upon all present that they were marking the inauguration of Standard Chartered Bank (as S&CBG was soon to be renamed) as a single, cohesive organization. That the parent banks were now history was thus one of two keynote messages. The other flagged the outcome of Graham's mapping exercise. Successful international banks could not afford to rely on wobbly Third World economies. They were simply too small. As exemplified by Barclays and the top US names, all truly international banks needed strong domestic markets to balance their activities in the East. Standard Chartered would now focus accordingly on building itself up in the West. It was instantly recognized as a seminal moment in the bank's history, and it delighted the conference participants: 'those of us serving overseas felt new vistas were unfolding', recalled David Millar, who was soon to arrive in London as a General Manager and whose own weighty contributions to the event caught the attention of his peers.[48] At the closing dinner dance, there was no mistaking a palpable sense of relief. The new bank had a new plan. And most were greatly bucked by what they had heard – speeches full of Western promise.

---

* Another member of the staff with whom Barber formed an easy rapport was John Major, recently appointed as the first manager of the bank's Public Relations Department. After recovering from his 1967 car crash in Nigeria, Major had worked in various auditing and inspection roles, travelling occasionally to the Far East. By 1974 he was intent on pursuing a political career – having served on Lambeth Borough Council as a local councillor from 1968 to 1971 – but he soon made himself indispensable to the Chairman as a sort of informal *chef de cabinet*. Barber in turn helped Major to find a less demanding role at the bank towards the end of 1976 after he had finally landed a safe constituency, Huntingdon, to fight for the Tories at the next general election. Not until 1981, when he secured his first post in Government, did Major finally leave behind his career at the bank. Six years later, Margaret Thatcher appointed him Chief Secretary to the Treasury. According to his most authoritative biographer, sourcing a 'private interview', she may have been swayed in choosing him by the assumption that he had been a senior banker in his time. ' "No-one told me he'd only been in marketing at Standard Chartered Bank", Mrs Thatcher was apt to remark later.' (Anthony Seldon, *Major, A Political Life*, Weidenfeld & Nicolson, 1997, p. 72.)

3. EMPIRE-STAFFING AT HALF-MAST

The warmth of this reception was also a measure of the vague dissatisfaction felt by many of the conference's younger participants over the state of the bank in the East. Their shared anxiety could be partly blamed on widespread gloom in the commodity markets – in the aftermath of the 1973 hike in oil prices – and the rapidly rising level of competition from local banks, which together left many wondering where to look in Asia for future growth opportunities. But the malaise went deeper. It reflected, too, a sense of frustration that the merger of 1969 had so far done surprisingly little to transform the culture of the old Chartered Bank. The management restructuring of the Group in 1973–4 had left in place the Chartered's *ancien regime* of General Managers – now featuring four doughty Scotsmen who had served the Chartered with distinction in their time, but were scarcely seen as champions of change.* Nor were the Group's longer serving Chief Managers in the field universally regarded as agents of innovation, though some enjoyed a fearsome reputation. (It was only a few years since the head of the Chartered in Singapore, a celebrated martinet, had flown up to Kuala Lumpur to confront its Manager over his submission of better trading profits than Singapore's – plainly a threat to the stability of the entire region. Some additional debt provisions were hastily extracted from the Malaysian income statement, with London's connivance, and the natural order was restored.[49]) The result undoubtedly was a deepening divide between the rising men in their thirties and early forties, who – as Hawker had discovered in 1970 – were concerned over the bank's conservative ways, and those in senior management now approaching retirement, who had joined after wartime service and were inclined to worry that any radical change might imperil the stability of the bank. The culture of the Foreign Staff placed such a premium on loyalty that dissident voices were rarely heard, even now. But with scarcely more than a few hundred covenanted officers in all – graded from the most junior Sub-Accountants to the principal Country Managers – tensions of any fundamental kind were potentially debilitating. All the more so, given that many British covenanted officers felt deeply uncertain about the future direction of an organization now employing steadily

* Their careers in the East had been synonymous with the bank's recent history in India (Jimmy Russell), Singapore (John Wilson), the Arabian Gulf (A. E. M. Finlaison) and Malaysia (Charles McCulloch). All were charged in London with responsibility for their old territories, just as Howard Gwyther had ordained a century earlier. This did nothing to encourage the adoption of a broader outlook once they were installed.

greater numbers of non-British staff. Indeed, one of the more contentious issues in many countries centred on precisely this trend, and the debate over how best to respond to what was now generally known by that unlovely description, 'indigenization'.

The first real challenge to the Chartered's Empire-staffing model had resulted, as noted in Chapter 5, in the introduction of Assistant Officers in the late 1930s – but further changes had been slow to follow. Not until 1954 had the principle of Asian covenanted officers been conceded, and Head Office had even then taken two years to relinquish control over the tiniest details of Asian officers' responsibilities and career progression.[50] The pace had begun to quicken thereafter. By the end of 1959, a total Eastern Staff complement of 268 covenanted officers had included 40 Asian names – mostly Chinese and Indians, with a sprinkling of Portuguese and one or two others.[51] Vincent Grantham, in his Chairman's Statement of March 1960, had drawn attention to this development with some pride: 'in recent years an increasing number of our Asian officers have been promoted to covenanted rank where they enjoy parity of reward and, what is equally important, parity of esteem with their British colleagues'.[52] Indigenization had then gathered momentum through the 1960s, and the number of (non-covenanted) Assistant Officers also rose rapidly. The result in not a few instances reinforced a precious continuity with the past, and some individual families had remarkable stories to tell. In Calcutta, R. V. Singh was a clerk who had worked in 4 Clive Street since 1960. He had joined at the age of eighteen as a 'zamindar', an aristocratic title cheekily adopted by the bank in the days of the Raj to dignify the role of those who supervised the messengers, known as 'peons'. Unusually, 'RV' worked for a while alongside his father, Lalta Prasad Singh, who had been a zamindar since 1943. Even more notably, the two of them were following in the footsteps of RV's grandfather (Bhagwatid Singh, 1917–31), great-grandfather (Kalisahai Singh, 1895–1917) and great-great-grandfather's brother (Dar- shan Singh, 1860–91). Within a few years of joining the bank, though, RV himself had opted to break with the family tradition by leaving the role of zamindar to become a qualified clerk – and by 1975 he would surpass all his forebears by winning promotion as an Assistant Officer, which he remained until his retirement in 1994.*

But what gave indigenization its real edge was the proliferation of

---

* In the course of his career, R. V. Singh also had no fewer than ten cousins among his contemporaries in Clive Street. As of 2012, he had two sons in the Standard Chartered: Rajesh Kumar Singh was Head of Branch Banking in Dubai and Bhupesh Singh was a Com- pliance Office in Mumbai. (R. V. Singh, interview with author, 8 October 2012.)

covenanted Asian officers. At first, in the early 1960s, the bank tended simply to select the more able Assistant Officers, bringing them to London as 'officer trainees' who then returned to the East as covenanted officers alongside newly trained British recruits. In time, it became apparent that many of the men promoted in this way, having begun their careers as clerks, found it difficult growing into managerial roles. Later in the decade, the bank began hiring young Asians externally as officer trainees. By the spring of 1969, the covenanted Eastern Staff list included 102 obviously Asian names out of a total of 294.[53] Also listed, though not covenanted, were sixty-one Asian Assistant Officers cited as 'Local Officer in Charge' and responsible for the larger retail branches, the majority of them in Hong Kong and Singapore. The next big step after the Chartered's merger with the Standard Bank was the introduction in 1970 of a graduate trainee programme in the UK, for which twenty-four places were divided equally between British and Asian recruits – all of them alike 'Trainee Officers' who would go straight into covenanted positions in the long tradition of the Chartered's Eastern Staff probationers.[54] One of those on a very early programme was Shirley Wee, a Singaporean graduate who returned home to become the first female covenanted officer in the Group. (George Pullen teased her, at a chance encounter in Bishopsgate, telling her 'you won't last six months'.[55] But she did – retiring from a successful career in 2007.) As in Hong Kong in the 1960s, the bank in Singapore turned increasingly in the 1970s to local hires for its covenanted managers. Some started as Trainee Officers like Wee. Others were former clerks who had worked their way up via the Assistant Officer rank, like Johnny Tan. A Singaporean of Chinese extraction, Tan had joined the Singapore main branch on Battery Road as a young clerk in 1967. He was appointed in 1975 as Local Officer in Charge at Changi, one of the bank's eighteen sub-branches on the island, and achieved full covenanted status three years later.[56]

The logic of indigenization for Standard Chartered was essentially threefold. First and foremost, it allowed the Group to take advantage of demographic realities. The labour markets of the sub-continent and south-east Asia could boast a growing number of fresh graduates after 1970, as the first post-war generation came of age. Many aspired to work for a foreign bank. They could bring all the skills that an employer like Standard Chartered required of its recruits, plus greater local knowledge and language skills. Second was the financial argument, which had been pertinent since pre-war days – as the advocates of the Assistant Officer class had pointed out – but which had become hugely more compelling by the 1970s. Local hires would generally accept significantly lower salaries than were needed for expatriates. The benefit to the bank of hiring locally would then rise steadily as the indigenous recruits pursued their careers. Their partners and families would expect no first-class air fares on BOAC for periodic returns to Britain; they would seek no help with school fees, so that children could be privately educated in England. And, thirdly, there was the political imperative. Nationalist politicians – especially in Malaysia and Singapore, but elsewhere too – were increasingly determined by the 1970s to see good jobs in banking offered to their own citizens. Work permits had been introduced for expatriates in many countries by the start of the decade, and they became significantly harder to secure as it wore on.

However, despite all these considerations, Empire-staffing had only been half-abandoned by the start of Anthony Barber's chairmanship. It remained unmistakeably entrenched in the values and traditions of the Group, for all the effort put into local recruitment, and there were many who still saw it as core to Standard Chartered's identity. The crude cash benefits of local recruitment had to be weighed, in their view, against the subtler cost of diluting that intense camaraderie that had been such a precious feature of the Chartered's Foreign Staff for generations past. It was obvious that air travel had ended for ever the need for Chartered men to endure lengthy immersions in remote foreign postings – and bachelors on the Foreign Staff were no longer much interested in living in a chummery with a mother-hen landlady, let alone a three-man mess in ill-lit rooms above the bank. Most now enjoyed smart individual apartments. But such background changes only reinforced, by this light, the importance of clinging on to the structure of the old Foreign Staff that yet survived, so that the British flavour of the bank might somehow be retained. No doubt the opening up of the executive ranks to local recruits was a prudent and intrinsically worthwhile step. But the traditionalists saw it as a process with natural limitations. And they could take heart from the fact that most senior figures in the East – including the Managers, Deputy Managers and Accountants of all the biggest and oldest branches – were still exclusively British, as were the heads of most of the main departments. In keeping with this reality, senior positions were conceded to non-British managers with a trepidation that could sometimes surprise recruits recently arrived from the UK – men like Geoff Williams, posted to Malaysia in 1969:

> I do have some recollection of my seniors in Kuala Lumpur asking me in 1970, as I was getting ready to leave the capital to take up a branch posting, whether I would be content to report to a Malaysian manager. They asked me if I had any objections. I thought at the time, it was such a strange thing to ask! I said, 'No, it really wouldn't bother me at all.'[57]

While it was true that the majority of the twenty-four branches and sub-branches in India (though emphatically not Calcutta, Bombay or New Delhi) were now managed by Indians, the latter were local recruits who were kept conspicuously local. Not only were they excluded from the internationally mobile cadre of the Foreign Staff, but they were kept in isolation from each other. No attempt had ever been made to convene them for any discussion of the bank's strategy in India (or, more pertinently, of its tactics for dealing with hostile trade unionists, a serious problem in many cities for years). By the same token, the bank provided no career development or training – other than an initial stint at Hatton Court if they were lucky – for those clerks whose natural ability had lifted them into the Assistant Officer ranks.

But then, of course, much the same weakness applied to the expatriates of the Foreign Staff themselves, for whom Part 1 of the Institute of Bankers' examination marked the beginning and end of their training (and only in rare cases did they sit Part 2, though this was being demanded in ever more countries as the prerequisite for a work permit). This outdated facet of the Chartered's operations had quickly attracted the attention in 1972 of the Kenyan-born Standard Bank man, Michael McWilliam, after his appointment as head of the new Corporate Planning Department. As one of the few outsiders brought into Clements Lane mid-career – or at least, one of the few without a Bank of England pedigree – he took an early opportunity to air his views on staffing more generally. He set down his prescription for a radically different approach in London as well as overseas in a 1972 paper for the Board, and it was prescient:

> Almost without exception, [the bank's] policy has been not to recruit trained staff at any level . . . [but] to rely wholly on evolving appropriate skills through operating experience in the markets concerned. While not wishing to denigrate the success thereby achieved, this policy of extreme parochialism, based mainly on cadres who joined the bank straight from secondary schools, seems incompatible with a banking group of our size and importance . . . [Ideally we need] to abandon the distinction between home and overseas staff, at least as applied to officers of real promise, and to introduce much greater mobility in appointments . . . The objective needs to be an international pool of executive talent, including South Africans, Chinese and blacks and modelled perhaps on the international oil companies.[58]

In 1974, McWilliam was appointed General Manager – though he was still only forty – in charge of West Africa. It was a striking promotion that acknowledged what had made the former merchant banker with a disarmingly boyish appearance so valuable to Hamilton and Chuck Fiero. McWilliam had briefly been an Oxford academic in his youth – authoring a study of the tea industry in East Africa[59] – and he brought an intellectual rigour to his analysis of markets and strategies that few if any of his contemporaries could match. Making tours of Standard Bank's branches in Africa as a corporate planner in the years before the 1969 merger, he had encountered several old-timers behind their castle walls who regarded his fastidious and cerebral approach as an impertinence. But by nature he was also modest and straightforward, which had won round most of his colleagues – and those tours always resulted in formal reports that were as succinct and elegant as any in the files, even in a bank graced in the past by such accomplished letter-writers as Robert Stewart and Lewis Michell.[60]

McWilliam was soon grappling with indigenization, which posed at least as stark a challenge in the countries of black Africa as anywhere in Asia. By far the most important aspect of his new job was his responsibility for Nigeria. Its government had launched a formal indigenization policy in 1969, at which point the former BWA's extensive network in the country, with its thousands of local clerks, had effectively been run by 360 British managers. By 1973, when the Group had been obliged by government legislation to reduce its ownership in Standard Bank Nigeria (SBN) to 60 per cent – with the state acquiring most of the minority stake – this expatriate cadre had shrunk to about a hundred individuals and their numbers were falling steadily.[61] In making SBN a role model for indigenization in the financial sector, it seemed likely that the Nigerian government would want to increase its stake, so Clements Lane needed to respond positively if it was to succeed in retaining at least a substantial share of the business. This was a matter of some consequence, given the remarkable changes afoot in the Nigerian economy. Devastated by the impact of the civil war from 1967 to the start of 1970, the country's oil industry had begun recovering strongly: its export revenues by 1973 had reached 1 billion Nigerian Naira (NGN), compared with just NGN 116 million in 1970, and they were heading for NGN 4 billion in 1974. (They reached NGN 5.4 billion in 1976 and NGN 10 billion in 1980.) The result was a huge surge of imports to support the rebuilding of the nation and about a quarter of them came from the UK, still Nigeria's biggest trade partner. Most of the largest UK multinationals were rushing to participate in the boom, and Standard Chartered Bank offered by far the most comprehensive trade-financing services.* Loans and advances

* In the case of Nigeria, these still revolved principally round the traditional use of bills of exchange, long since abandoned by the Group in most of its Asian operations in favour of

by SBN to Nigeria's importers were soaring, and the bank's profits were rising accordingly. By the time that McWilliam took up his brief, SBN's pre-tax profits were heading for £10 million, more than twice as much as the International Division would earn in London in 1974–5 from all of its foreign exchange and eurocurrency lending activities. Rather astonishingly, in fact, the Nigerian bank was suddenly the single biggest earner in the entire Group, only setting aside South Africa (which was forecasting £21.5 million for 1974–5). It was a performance that unsurprisingly spurred ahead the Lagos government's indigenization policy.

Travelling for several weeks in the country during the winter of 1974–5, McWilliam found there were now fewer than sixty expatriates within SBN's ranks, divided between Head Office in Lagos and the five Regional Centres across the country (Port Harcourt, Benin, Ibadan, Kaduna and Kano).[62] One immediate implication was that additional training facilities were urgently needed for newly promoted Nigerian staff at the top levels. McWilliam doubted the bank had sufficiently prepared for this: 'it is hard to resist the proposition that our senior management development programme is a bit slow motion, particularly as regards head office executives, although a good cadre has been established at branch and area manager level'.[63] Some of his colleagues in London hoped that SBN's Nigerian Directors might win the Group more time to adjust to the demise of the expatriates. Local figures held eight of the fourteen seats on the Board in Lagos alongside SBN's Ghana-born Chairman, Mallam Ahmadu Coomassie. But McWilliam soon decided any notion of slowing the process was unrealistic and he took the initiative by appointing a Nigerian as Managing Director – Chief Samuel (Sam) Asabia, recruited from the Central Bank of Nigeria where he was Deputy Governor. (This bold step did not impress the UK High Commissioner, Sir Martin Le Quesne, who summoned McWilliam and took him to task 'for letting the side down'.[64]) If he had hoped for a conciliatory approach by Asabia, though, McWilliam was to be disappointed. Returning to Nigeria in 1976, he had to report back that Asabia was forcing the pace: 'He is impatient to accelerate the appointment of Nigerians to senior positions without taking much trouble to understand the issues as we see them.'[65] Asabia was backed by the Lagos government: later that same year it pushed through a purchase of shares

---

telexed letters of credit. Physical bills were sent with invoices and shipping documents from London to SBN in Nigeria, where importers had to call at a branch of the bank to sign them and so gain access to their landed goods. The much more elaborate paperwork involved in this system better accommodated the inferior creditworthiness of many of the customers, some onerous government red tape and a desperate shortage of foreign exchange in Nigeria.

to lift its stake to 60 per cent of SBN, and a quota of thirty-six expatriates was set for the years to 1980. When the last British Managing Director, C. P. (Johnny) Johnson, took early retirement in 1977, Asabia succeeded him and was soon running SBN as a business entirely independent of the Directors in London. But this outcome had its blessings, at least in the short term: Standard Chartered was left with 40 per cent of what became Nigeria's leading bank. For the year to March 1978, the Group booked associate profits at SBN of £14.3 million – with a cash dividend to match – which topped the £14 million reported (before debts and tax) by the rest of Standard Bank's African businesses in toto, except StanBIC which made £41.7 million.[66] Coomassie and Asabia made a formidable business team. Together they galvanized SBN's standing in the country, modernizing its operations and greatly expanding its branch network across a booming economy. The name of the bank was changed in 1979 to First Bank of Nigeria (as it remains today).

McWilliam's responsibilities were extended in 1975 to include India. As the first ex-Standard man to take up responsibilities in the East, albeit from London, he was bemused by much of what he found on his first few visits. It was several years since computers had been introduced to Hong Kong, Singapore and London, so it surprised him to find hand-written ledgers still being used by the clerks in Clive Street.* Indeed, he was puzzled by the fact that Clive Street remained the bank's Indian Head Office at all, given that Bombay had long ago eclipsed Calcutta as the nation's commercial and financial centre. As for the progress of indigenization, the atomized nature of the bank's operations struck McWilliam as a bizarre constraint on the contribution made by talented local Indian managers running branches like Amritsar, Cochin and Madras. He made plans to tackle this with a first all-India management conference in 1976 – to be held at a beach resort hotel in Goa – and pushed for the appointment by then of a new Chief Manager, a veteran of the Eastern Bank. Neville Green would come to India as an 'outsider' with strong views of his own on the need to nurture local talent. But, as McWilliam soon came to appreciate, making progress here would involve more than a change in the bank's regulations. The Empire-staffing culture in India ran deep. One

---

* India's trade unions had for many years fought a rearguard action against any form of automation. 'One year into my four years in Calcutta, from 1962 to 1965, London sent us twelve NCR Class 32 accounting machines to replace the twenty-five hand-posted, 1,500-page ledgers that stretched down this lovely banking hall, with its beautiful marble floor. I left three years after the machines arrived and they were still under their dust covers. The union would not permit us to put them into operation.' (Ian Wilson, interview with author, 4 October 2012.) Wilson was one of twelve Scotsmen on the fifteen-man expatriate staff in 1962.

dimension of this was brought home to him early in 1975, when he received
a visitor in Clements Lane:

> There was a young man from one of the great British India families who
> had fallen madly in love with a girl of mixed parentage in Calcutta. She
> was Afro-Indian, and it was absolutely forbidden that they could get mar-
> ried. One day I was sitting in Head Office when I was told this chap was
> outside my door and wanted to see me, please. So in he walked with his
> fiancée! He said they were just determined to get married. I said, 'Well,
> there's no way you can go back to Calcutta under our conventions.' So I
> arranged for him to be posted to Colombo, where the two of them fitted
> into the more liberal atmosphere perfectly and were an immense success
> socially. But there was a huge bristling within the India establishment that
> one of the bank's young managers had married a mixed-race girl.[67]

Young expatriate managers were still required to ask the bank's permission to marry – and the prohibition on marrying a locally born (i.e.
non-white) woman also survived, an enduring legacy of Howard Gwyther's
firm stand on the matter (see p. 139). But the wider trend away from
expatriate employment all over Asia had seen fewer European women
arriving to work there as secretaries or nurses, teachers, airline hostesses
or department-store sales assistants. Some young Chartered bankers
thought this rendered the marriage rules more than ever a glaring
anachronism, and not just in India. A few of the General Managers in
London thought otherwise, however, which triggered more than one difficult episode before this most sensitive of issues was finally consigned to
the past. The appointment later of Bill Brown to run Hong Kong – David
Millar had returned to London late in 1975 as a General Manager –
undoubtedly helped lay it to rest, for Brown had a Japanese wife. (As a
young Japanese-speaking Sub-Accountant in Tokyo, he had famously
announced his engagement in 1959 to Nachiko Sagawa, a high-society
beauty whose family included a long line of Japan's most distinguished
physicians. She was also a minor celebrity in her own right, having been
one of the first four Japanese trained as air hostesses by BOAC after the
war. Their wedding plans had in the end been accepted by the bank, but
not without considerable misgivings in London – overruled, it was said,
on advice from the Foreign Office – and outright opposition from Brown's
own Manager in Tokyo, who had a nervous breakdown over the affair.[68])
Even in 1975, Brown's family background was seen by some as barring
his eligibility for the Hong Kong post. 'Various people got very huffy about
it,' as McWilliam recalled, 'so he wasn't appointed. But the person
appointed instead needed very soon afterwards to be replaced. Then we

did appoint Bill Brown, who was hugely successful.'[69] Brown was one day to become Deputy Chairman of the bank.

Indigenization remained a familiar item on the Board agenda over the next several years, but as other apparently more urgent aspects of modernization pressed for attention – not least the adjustment to personal computers and the rapid advances in communications technology – it undoubtedly received less attention than it warranted. Even those alert to its importance often found its implementation unexpectedly problematic, as did Neville Green in India. He was accustomed to working in compact, finely networked markets. After spending many years in the Gulf, he came to India from three years as Manager of the bank's branch in Saigon, where he had worked until three months before the city's capitulation to the Communist forces of North Vietnam.* The size and complexity of India posed a different test. When Green placed an advertisement for 12 management trainees in the *The Times of India*, he received 4,000 replies (including one from the daughter of the State Governor of West Bengal and another from the daughter of New Delhi's Chief of Police, both of whom were hired but later married and left the bank).[70] He did his best to advance the cause, but had first to oversee the development of a co-ordinated Indian network in place of the historic collection of parent branches in India – not to mention steering through the relocation of the Head Office to Bombay and coping with a vertiginous decline in India's revenues. It was slow going, as McWilliam had to admit in a typically frank assessment for the Board a few years later:

---

* Green had arrived in Saigon shortly after the final withdrawal of US ground forces from South Vietnam in 1972. In the perilous stand-off that ensued between North and South, most of the country's commercial banks put up the shutters – and Green took advantage of their timidity. 'It was wide open for me, and I did an enormous amount of business with the army of South Vietnam, and with the manufacturers of their equipment and their K rations. It was all done in Saigon or within the periphery of the city.' (Green, interviews with author, 19 May and 1 June 2011.) The bank was well served by an experienced compradore and by about fifty clerical staff, most of them the wives of full-time employees who had been called up by the army. When Saigon fell, shortly after his own departure in December 1974, Green was upset to hear that only the few remaining expatriates in the bank had been airlifted out with their wives, leaving behind all of the Vietnamese staff. It later transpired that his own driver had been a Vietcong infiltrator, so the staff – including many refugees from the North – were instantly exposed to reprisals. Among the twenty or so who managed to arrange their own escape was the most senior Vietnamese officer, Do Dang Quang, who got out with his family on a plane chartered by the US Consulate on the eve of the collapse. (Recollections sent to the author, 5 November 2011.) Green's own secretary, Miss Vi, had worked for several Managers of the bank. She spent the next three years in a re-education camp before fleeing by boat to Malaysia. There she telephoned Green to let him know she was on her way to Australia – and an introduction from Green helped her into a new life as the secretary to the Manager of Standard Chartered's office in Sydney.

To my mind we are embarrassingly out of step with the rest of the Indian banking sector (including Grindlays), not to mention industry, not only on account of top posts still being held by expatriates, but also in the absence of a planned progression to a largely Indian-run bank . . . one cannot help wondering whether we have lost our way in strategic terms here.[71]

After India, Green moved on in 1979 to become the Chief Manager in Malaysia – where there was no lack of a planned progression, but it had been planned not by the bank but by the Malaysian government. Its New Economic Policy since 1971 had been pushing a programme of positive discrimination in favour of indigenous Malays, the Bumiputra. The bank at that date employed virtually no Malays at all: about three thousand local staff, spread across its thirty-nine branches, were all either Indian or Chinese. By 1980, the bank had taken on hundreds of Malay employees and some were nominally not much junior to the forty or so expatriates. As Green quickly discovered, though, the bare numbers were misleading. The expatriates were entrenched as Managers in about twenty-five branches, with an undue influence over the network: 'my pay roll included too many expensive expatriates on the one hand, some merely cruising their way to retirement, and on the other hand a lot of young and ambitious Malaysians hungry for responsibility'.[72] In a move he co-ordinated with the Central Bank, Green introduced exam-based training and promotion rules that by 1983 left only the Head Office in Kuala Lumpur run by a British Manager – by which time he had also set in train moves to have the bank locally incorporated.

Green's approach revitalized the bank in Malaysia, and buttressed its profits (now twice the size of those earned in the whole of the sub-continent) just in time to provide some cushion against a dramatic downturn in world demand for the country's tin exports. He was fortunate to have a like-minded colleague in Peter Cameron – another former Eastern Bank man and veteran of the Gulf, among many other postings – who was effectively his deputy, overseeing the many District Managers from Penang and Perak in the West to Sabah and Sarawak in the East.* Cameron was to succeed Green in 1983 and would remain as Chief Manager until 1987. When he had first arrived there, two years ahead of Green, the condition of the extensive Chartered network across the country had come as

---

* Cameron had had more than his share of wars and revolutions since joining the bank in 1955. He had been involved in the post-nationalization closure of branches in Baghdad in 1964, in Aden in 1967 and in Libya in 1971 – followed by some dangerous weeks in Karachi during the Indo-Pakistani war of 1973. A few quiet years in Qatar had since then provided a welcome respite. (Interview with author, 5 April 2013.)

something of a shock. He recalled: 'We had not been investing for the future. There were virtually no computers in place, we had no corporate identity and some of the branches were in a parlous state ... it wasn't what I had expected.'[73] Unfortunately, as of early 1977, it was pretty much exactly what Michael McWilliam might have expected. McWilliam had travelled widely in his two years as a General Manager, far beyond West Africa and India, and had come across too many instances of dire under-investment. Nor was McWilliam much impressed by the lack of drive he observed in Clements Lane. He made a private note of his reaction in January 1977: 'as a bank, we are living on our past and making almost no serious effort to generate new business with major corporate names. Our stance is essentially passive.'[74] But this was about to change. At the end of March 1977, senior management changes at last brought to the helm the architect of the 1975 Hyde Park Hotel conference, a man of prodigious energy not best known for taking a passive stance on anything.

4. BIDS BOTCHED AND BLOCKED

Peter Graham was short and stocky, with a waistline that attested to several years of wining and dining the businessmen of Hong Kong. But his energy belied his figure, and his management approach offered the kind of hard-charging, decisive leadership that had always been greatly admired by his Chinese clients. By the time he succeeded Ronnie Lane as Managing Director, in July 1976, he had already spent months familiarizing himself with the many territories of the bank that were new to him, undertaking several trips to Africa. (This perplexed not a few of his Chinese friends in the Colony, who were deeply sceptical of the merger with the Standard Bank and frankly at a loss to understand why he wanted to devote so much time to places that, compared with Hong Kong, were surely of marginal financial significance.[75]) The African agenda did not deflect him for long, though, from his primary objective – the expansion of the bank's presence in the West. Nor was he content to rely patiently on an incremental growth of the overseas network. Graham was soon shopping for a timely purchase or two that could accelerate the shift of direction. By the end of 1976, he was ready to make a first move. It soon came to appear a slightly rash false start.

An obvious priority for any expansion strategy in the US was the establishment of a larger presence on the West Coast, to service corporate clients on both ends of the trade bridge across the Pacific. This posed a challenge for the bank, since its modest network in California had so far been very largely confined to consumer banking. In the Manager of its CBoL business, however, the bank had an unusually ambitious individual for whom the challenge was an irresistible next step. Norman Eckersley had served his time in the East – he had been the Accountant in Calcutta for some years – but had been in San Francisco since 1970, long enough to have acquired as colourful a reputation as any foreign banker in the state. As a Second World War RAF bomber pilot (he had flown Lancasters and been awarded the Distinguished Flying Cross) and a hugely extrovert Glaswegian with a fund of entertaining stories about his past in Asia, Eckersley was a bird of bright plumage in the often grey world of banking and finance. His Scottish brand of chutzpah was the stuff of endless stories. For regular trips to Los Angeles, he would invariably hire a private plane. Twice a year in the soccer season, he would leave CBoL's Head Office at 365 California Street on a Friday afternoon to attend the Old Firm game between Celtic and Rangers in Glasgow – he was a fanatical Rangers fan and a shareholder in what was then still one of Europe's leading clubs – afterwards making the twelve-hour flight home again in time to start work on the Monday morning.* And, to help along the US Bicentennial Celebrations in 1976, he pulled off a remarkable coup. By sheer force of personality – linked to his London Chairman's clout within the British establishment and a lot of patient staff work by the young John Major at Barber's side[76] – Eckersley arranged for one of the only four extant copies of the Magna Carta of 1215 to be brought from Lincoln Cathedral for exhibition at the CBoL.

> So, on 30 September, thirty seconds ahead of time, a Vulcan bomber of No.9 Squadron RAF landed at Castle Air Force Base, and Magna Carta, escorted by helicopters, spotter planes and a mass of police, duly arrived at the Chartered Bank of London in San Francisco. It evoked enormous interest throughout California.[77]

Almost certainly it was Eckersley's idea that the bank should capitalize on its new-found celebrity by making a bid for the publicly quoted Bank of California. The latter's long history (it was founded in 1864), its unusual network of eighty branches in three states, run from Los Angeles, and its bias towards retail banking at home and corporate banking overseas made

---

* Over the years to come, he was to be showered with civic honours in San Francisco and beyond, not all of them guaranteed to encourage a spirit of humility. 'October 23 1984 was proclaimed Norman C. Eckersley Day in San Francisco and the California State passed a resolution expressing their commendation of Mr Eckersley for "contributions extensively to the economic betterment of California"' (Obituary, *San Francisco Chronicle*, 27 August 2012).

it in many ways an ideal target. Graham and Barber backed him and the three of them spent many weeks preparing the ground, apparently confident that a generous price would easily carry the day. Unfortunately, when Graham arrived in Los Angeles for a first face-to-face meeting, he ran into a snag: its Chairman/Chief Executive (only recently appointed) gave the idea a brisk thumbs-down – and was supported in his rebuttal by Baron Edmond de Rothschild, whose Swiss private banking group controlled almost 40 per cent of the stock. After several fruitless attempts to win over these not unimportant parties, and despite a warning from the Federal Reserve Chairman that a contested takeover would not be regarded favourably in Washington, Graham nonetheless went ahead in February 1977 with a hostile public bid. Perhaps he hoped the Magna Carta episode would endear the British bidder to small shareholders. This odd decision was followed, after the bid had predictably been rejected by the Bank of California's Board, by the even odder decision instantly to withdraw the bid, abandoning the whole idea. It was an unedifying episode that alarmed many friends of the bank. (Its American partner in the Mocatta businesses, Henry Jarecki, told McWilliam that 'the way in which we have apparently abused the confidence of private discussions has harmed our reputation in [the] US and will make it harder for us to do another deal'.[78]) Privately, though, Graham might just conceivably have seen it as a vindication of his decision, a few months earlier, to appoint Michael McWilliam as one of his two Senior General Managers.

By promoting him well ahead of his turn (again), this effectively marked McWilliam out as a future head of the bank. It also suggests that Graham was well aware of his own need for a deputy adept at the kind of trenchant analysis that he himself was inclined to skate over. Although much readier than most of his colleagues to go for the audacious option, Graham was in other ways a typical Chartered banker: his professionalism was rooted less in analysis than in long experience, sound technical knowledge and shrewd instincts. By contrast McWilliam was positively donnish – indeed, some colleagues undoubtedly considered him too academic by half – which made him in many ways an ideal match and potentially a useful brake on the kind of impulsiveness that had ended in the Bank of California fiasco. The two of them were an effective duo, with two non-executives in especially important supporting roles: the Chairman, Anthony Barber, and Leslie Fletcher, a Director of the merchant bank Schroders, who had joined the Board in 1972 and now had his own office at Clements Lane. All that said, how far anyone in Clements Lane had effective control over the evolution of the bank in its distant territories often seemed questionable in these years. The more assertive managers in the field were inclined

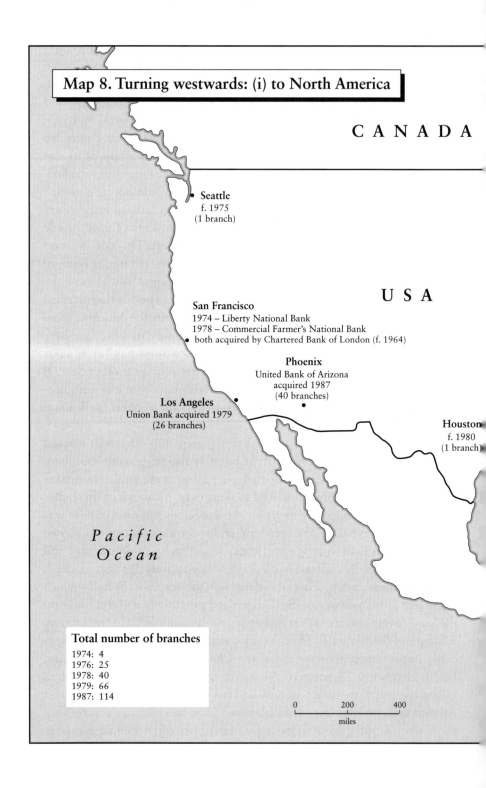

Map 8. Turning westwards: (i) to North America

CANADA

Seattle
f. 1975
(1 branch)

USA

San Francisco
1974 – Liberty National Bank
1978 – Commercial Farmer's National Bank
both acquired by Chartered Bank of London (f. 1964)

Phoenix
United Bank of Arizona
acquired 1987
(40 branches)

Los Angeles
Union Bank acquired 1979
(26 branches)

Houston
f. 1980
(1 branch)

*Pacific
Ocean*

Total number of branches
1974: 4
1976: 25
1978: 40
1979: 66
1987: 114

0   200   400
miles

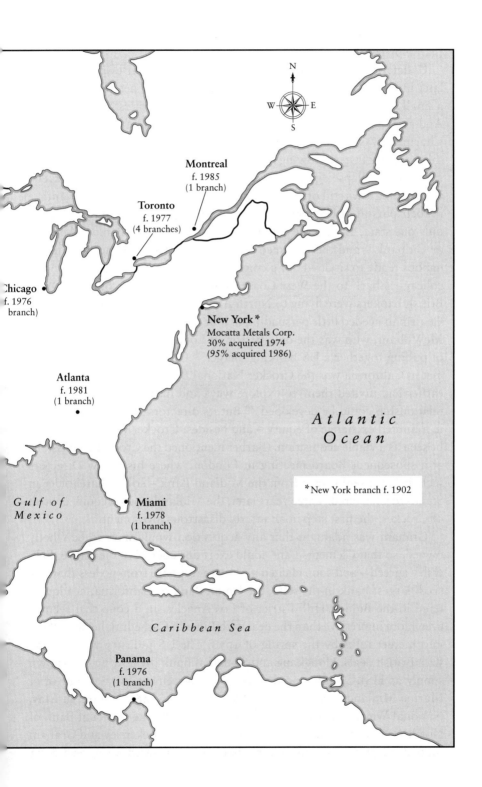

Montreal
f. 1985
(1 branch)

Toronto
f. 1977
(4 branches)

Chicago •
f. 1976
branch)

New York *
Mocatta Metals Corp.
30% acquired 1974
(95% acquired 1986)

Atlanta
f. 1981
(1 branch)
•

*Atlantic
Ocean*

*Gulf of
Mexico*

• Miami
f. 1978
(1 branch)

* New York branch f. 1902

Caribbean Sea

Panama
f. 1976
(1 branch)
•

to take the lead when it suited them, and none was bolder in this respect than Norman Eckersley.

Undeterred by the Bank of California setback, Eckersley pressed ahead later in 1977 with a modest addition to CBoL's retail network, acquiring a small agricultural lender, the Commercial and Farmers National Bank. And this, he suggested, should be seen as a mere appetizer. If Standard Chartered was to make its mark in the US, now was the time to buy into the country's fastest growing region. Sterling was recovering briskly from its 1975–6 collapse against the dollar on the foreign exchange markets. US banking laws still offered foreign banks a clear competitive advantage in their pursuit of US deposits – they were not restricted to operating in only one state, as were the big money-centre banks like Bank of America or Citibank – and there seemed to be no shortage of domestic banking nabobs ready to sit down for a conversation. Eckersley urged his London colleagues back to the West Coast to meet more of his contacts. Other British bankers were flying to North America in droves. Graham and his Chairman needed little persuading to join them – though they left behind McWilliam, who was the only person in London with direct experience of pulling together a US banking merger.[79] One of the institutions they met in California was the Crocker National Bank, which several months earlier had invited them 'to explore ways and means in which a special relationship could be developed'.[80] But its directors were only interested in a limited exchange of equity – and besides, Crocker was far too big to be seen as a viable acquisition. (Barber mentioned the Crocker discussions at a subsequent Board meeting in London, where his fellow Directors included two senior men from the Midland Bank – still a shareholder in Standard Chartered. Three years later, the Midland would acquire control of Crocker, the first step in an utterly disastrous investment.[81])

Graham was adamant that any acquisition would have to be wholly owned, so that Clements Lane could exert due control in the future. Eckersley agreed – and soon elicited a positive response from no less than the sixth largest bank in the state, the Union Bank of California, headquartered in the Bunker Hill district of Los Angeles. In a coup that seemed even more impressive than the deal with Lincoln Cathedral, he drew them into merger talks by the spring of 1978. The US industry was buzzing with British deals. Hongkong and Shanghai Bank (by now widely known simply as HSBC) announced in April an agreement to take control of Marine Midland, a leading New York bank, for $260 million; in May, National Westminster Bank unveiled plans to buy the National Bank of North America for $300 million; and, on 10 June, Eckersley and Graham topped all previous transatlantic bank mergers with an agreed $372 million bid for the Union Bank. This equated to $33 a share for a public company trading at around $14 prior to the announcement. The total outlay would equate to £204 million, not too far short of the £280 million value put on the whole of Standard Chartered by the London stock market at the time – though Union Bank's pre-tax profits were scarcely a fifth as big.[82] So it was an expensive purchase – 'received with considerable enthusiasm', as Graham would candidly recall.[83] But he had to have it. At a single stroke, the bank achieved the US presence he had envisaged for it from the outset. The Union Bank's total assets of $4.7 billion (a third as large as Crocker's) meant the future Group would have almost 25 per cent of its assets in North America. The deal, approved by the authorities in April 1979, brought it a substantial volume of dollar deposits and a highly regarded bank (founded in 1914) with strong ties to California's small and medium-sized business sector. This instantly transformed Standard Chartered's profile in the US – where the New York office was profitable but branches in Seattle, Chicago and Miami were still struggling for business – and added a new dimension to its worldwide earnings. In sterling terms, the Union Bank in 1980 and 1981 would account for 'working profits' almost exactly in line with those from Hong Kong.[84]

Within months of the deal's completion, however, a serious problem arose. The modern Union Bank was essentially the creation of Harry J. Volk, who had been its President since 1957 and was the architect of the agreement with Eckersley. But Volk's readiness to work with his counterpart from San Francisco seems to have ended there. A heavyweight luminary of California's banking and insurance industries for more than thirty years, Volk kept his own counsel once the deal was done. Both Eckersley and his young Scottish deputy, Ian Wilson, relocated to the Bunker Hill offices, taking up formal roles as Deputy Chairman and Liaison Officer, respectively. But no one in Union Bank was instructed to report to either man, nor were they given any effective authority from London. Volk remained in place, and he presented Standard Chartered to his own troops as a partner – or, indeed, as something rather less. 'We had bought them,' as Wilson would recall, 'but initially many of the Union Bank guys acted as if they had bought us.'[85] Volk had begun in recent years to build an overseas presence for Union Bank, with offices in Rio de Janeiro, Tokyo and London. Linking up with a truly international banking group, providing a handy source of extra capital without recourse to the public markets, plainly struck his senior executives as rather a masterstroke. And no serious move was made from Clements Lane to suggest otherwise. Michael McWilliam was appointed to the Union Bank's Board before the end of 1978 – it happened that he had been on a family holiday in North America that summer and had taken the opportunity to call on Volk and his colleagues, getting acquainted in timely fashion – so the London executive team was not unaware of developments in Los Angeles. No effort, though, was made to impose the Group's control. Partly to blame for this may have been a legitimate anxiety that too intrusive an approach might have prompted an exodus of senior people. California's regulators had obliged the Union Bank in 1975 to dispose of key subsidiaries that had been nurtured in insurance and mortgage banking. Decades later, one of Volk's obituaries would record: 'The bank [after 1975] never quite regained its vibrant growth. Many of its higher-level executives departed, and many of the bank's business customers followed them to their new employers.'[86] If this casts the price agreed for the 1978 bid in a less than flattering light, it also suggests why Graham was reluctant to play a forceful hand thereafter. Even with Eckersley to the fore, it would have required a small team of Standard Chartered managers to take on possibly extensive responsibilities in a deeply unfamiliar US environment. The Group had no such managers available.

So much for Graham's earlier insistence that any US subsidiary would need to be properly subject to control from London. Then, early in 1980, a tricky situation took a significant turn for the worse. The seventy-four-year-old Volk declared his intention of retiring to concentrate on his philanthropic activities, but told Clements Lane 'he was not prepared to recommend a successor from his own staff'.[87] This left Graham with little choice but to fly to California, to take charge of the situation and find someone to avert a potentially serious embarrassment for the Group. Perhaps he was given some assistance by a notable recruit to the Board: Stuart Tarrant was hired in May 1980, to become the Group's new-styled 'Chief Financial Officer'. At the time of his appointment, Tarrant was working in New York and it was agreed that he should stay on for 'a short period in the USA in the nature of a familiarisation tour to meet senior officers' – which perhaps included helping Graham to find the man they needed for Union Bank.[88] This turned out to be John F. Harrigan – another West Coast banker slightly in the Harry Volk mould. He took up his new job in July, and a flavour of what followed was nicely caught by an article in the *Los Angeles Times* a few years later:

> In January 1981, Union Bank Chief Executive John F. Harrigan summoned his top officers to a meeting at a resort in Palma Valley, north of San Diego. Harrigan, who had been brought in as Union Chairman only six months earlier ... saw a need to stem the drain of talented executives and set his own course for the bank. In his first months on the job, the new chairman

had met considerable internal resistance from managers who had grown up under former Chairman Harry J. Volk and had to move forcefully to put his stamp on the organization . . . The meeting, which Union executives describe as a watershed in the bank's history, marked the end of the 23-year-old Volk era.[89]

Harrigan moved forcefully to put his stamp on the bank's relationship with Clements Lane, too. There was to be no question of him reporting to anyone in London on the Union Bank's activities: it would be run as an autonomous unit.

After supervising the integration into the Union Bank of the CBoL's network, Eckersley departed quietly back to San Francisco. (There he soon afterwards founded a new venture, the Pacific Bank.[90] It pulled off a spectacular coup in raising deposits of $22 million from friends and business contacts before it had even opened its doors – but Eckersley would later fall foul of the state regulators and had eventually to stand down as Chairman.) Before long, a decorative building in Los Angeles was being fitted out as Standard Chartered's North American Head Office – but it was several miles away from the Union Bank, and its British occupants had no influence whatever over the Union's operations. Thrust together as unlikely colleagues, the Group's American and British bankers eyed each other's working cultures warily and with a good deal of surprise on some counts. The Americans, accustomed to just a few weeks of holiday each year, were astonished by the extended furlough arrangements still enjoyed by the former Chartered Bank expatriates in Asia. And the British for their part were no less amazed to find their West Coast counterparts being paid salaries at a multiple of their own. (For all the undoubtedly lavish housing and travel perks enjoyed by the more senior men in the East, salary levels were still distinctly modest for most expatriates in the junior and middle ranks. This was true at all of the British overseas banks – hence that admonishment of BWA by a British judge in Nigeria in 1950, noted on p. 339 – and the Chartered had traditionally rather prided itself on its parsimonious pay rates.*) Gradually, the two cultures began to converge, but this did nothing to draw the reporting lines any closer. Clements Lane was left owning a large and geographically remote

---

* In the early 1950s, a small group of Foreign Staffers had even come together, while on furlough in the UK, to form a ginger group that could lobby for less stringent pay rates. They convened at a country inn in deepest West Sussex, the Swan at Fittleworth, which subsequently became the venue for an annual lunch attended by Chartered Bank alumni. It was still going strong sixty years later – and was still known as 'The Chartered Bank Expat Lunch'.

subsidiary – with a keen appetite for capital – over which it had no day-to-day control at all. In effect, it had created a passable clone of its offspring in South Africa, with John Harrigan in much the same role as Bill Passmore. Even before this outcome of the 1978 acquisition had fully settled into place, though, Graham and his senior colleagues had become wholly preoccupied with another bid closer to home.

For half a century past, Barclays had shown how profitably a British clearer could be combined with an overseas bank within one group. The progress of Barclays DCO since the 1920s – so often entwined, in Africa, with the Standard's – had culminated in 1971 with its transmutation into Barclays Bank International, pooling the resources of the old DCO network with the foreign banking activities of the UK parent. It was a template that Graham much admired – and it carried an obvious implication. The 1975 blueprint that he later claimed to have set down for expansion in Europe and North America was oddly dismissive of the UK (only worth 'a very small presence'), but by the middle of 1976 Graham had already had second thoughts. He had come round to the idea, mooted by Ray Reed and others in 1971, of a network of UK branches that could promote the Group's trade-financing capabilities across the country. About sixty small offices run by the Hodge Group were relaunched as licensed deposit-takers, but these remained essentially geared to consumer finance. Alongside them, the Group now began opening wholly new branches, the first of them located in Sheffield, Bristol, Dundee and Leicester. Noting their appearance, the 1977 Annual Report reported a rise in the number of 'UK operations' from seventeen to eighty-four (including those newly aggrandized Hodge Group offices), and openings in other provincial UK cities extended the list steadily over the next few years. It reached 102 by the start of 1980, incorporating a string of fully-fledged provincial branches from Cardiff to Glasgow. The impact on Group profits, though, was a disappointment. The UK branches were barely profitable before 1979, and soon slipped into the red after the onset of the 1979–81 recession.

By this time, their discouraging performance had confirmed a view reached by Graham as early as 1977 – namely, that expanding in the UK market successfully would sooner or later have to entail an alliance with one of the established UK clearers. And for anyone envisaging a clearing-bank partner for Standard Chartered at this point, there could only really be one name in the frame: the Royal Bank of Scotland (RBS). For Graham in particular, the singular appeal of RBS was especially compelling. Throughout his seven years in charge of the Chartered in Hong Kong, Graham's counterpart as the Taipan of Jardine Matheson had been Michael Herries. Their tenures had coincided exactly. The two men had become good friends, both returning to Britain in 1970. Herries had joined the Board of RBS four years later – and in 1977 had become its Chairman. He had very soon received a visitor, with a suggestion to make. To Graham, the commercial logic of a merger was no less striking than the emotional resonance of bringing together Scotland's leading domestic bank (accounting for about half of Scottish bank deposits) with an overseas bank largely managed by Scotsmen across half the globe for several generations. According to an oral account taped by Graham some years later – virtually the only record of many conversations over the next few years that were kept a close secret at the time and barely noted anywhere else – Herries agreed with Graham in principle but asked for a couple of years' deferral, as 'there were things that he wanted to do first'.[91] Graham acquiesced happily enough, and turned to his US ventures. But early in 1980, rumours of another planned bid for RBS (with Lloyds Bank hotly tipped in the market) concentrated minds on both sides and serious negotiations were begun.* The potentially momentous outcome, reached surprisingly quickly, was an agreement to go forward as one Group. Overtly modelled on Barclays, it would comprise a domestic bank head-quartered in Edinburgh and an international bank running the overseas network from a head office in the City. Here, it seemed, was a Grand Design to set beside the historic merger of 1969 – with some weighty implications, also, for the UK market. Spawned in Scotland, Standard Chartered would be returning home, in a sense, and the resulting merger could look forward to having 600 branches north of the border and 320 in England (managed separately by its subsidiary, Williams and Glyn's). This prospect certainly appealed to the Bank of England, as a way of boosting competition among the clearers; it actively encouraged both parties and gave their union its blessing.[92] Herries and Graham thought it unlikely their plan would be challenged in these circumstances, even by HSBC's highly combative Michael Sandberg (its Chairman and Chief Executive since 1977 – and as it happened, also a friend of Graham's: the two men had begun their careers together in Japan in 1949). Graham felt further reassured on this score when, just a week before the announcement of the deal in March 1981, HSBC unveiled a huge rights issue in Hong Kong. A counter-bid for RBS would require it to issue yet more shares, which the

---

* It happened by chance that the Group also entered talks early in 1980 to buy the Bank of Scotland – though in this case, it was merely the headquarters building of the other Scottish bank. As part of a huge redevelopment of Chartered Bank's Head Office at 38 Bishopsgate, adjoining properties were bought from the Bank of Scotland (28–32 Bishopsgate) and smaller neighbours in Crosby Square and Great St Helens.

market would surely be reluctant to take. In effect, supposed Graham, Hongkong Bank had shot its bolt.

This, it turned out, was overly optimistic. When Sandberg read of the agreed merger in his morning paper, the price tag of £334 million amazed him. ('At first, we thought the price quoted must have been a misprint because it was so low.'[93]) He and his Board had already instigated a search for a European banking partner to balance their 1980 acquisition of a controlling stake in Marine Midland, and had been at work on a bid for the Royal Bank themselves. It took them twenty-one days to finalize their terms – and RBS's shareholders were then offered half as much again (£498 million). An incensed Gordon Richardson, Governor of the Bank of England, summoned Sandberg to his office for a dressing down: he had warned HSBC against this course, explaining why the Bank favoured the merger with Standard Chartered as a desirable evolution of the UK clearing sector, and that it was completely out of order for the Hongkong management to have pressed on regardless. Sandberg defied him, and pursued a bid that he recollected later had been taken by the Governor 'as a personal affront'.[94] On 29 April, Standard Chartered responded with a revised offer, priced a whisker ahead of HSBC's – but just days later the Bank of England stymied both bids by referring them to the Monopolies and Mergers Commission (MMC).

Thus began eight months of torrid lobbying, with all three commercial banks and their chairmen subjected to unrelenting criticism from the nationalist lobby in Scotland.[95] Only now did it really become clear that Herries and Graham had made a fatal error, worse even than the egregious under-pricing of the agreed initial bid. Given the close understanding between the two of them, it ought surely to have been possible for the merger of their banks to be presented as a takeover, led not by Standard Chartered but by RBS. Certainly this would have posed a management challenge for Graham: many of his colleagues still harboured some of that old Chartered disdain for the home clearers that had kept their bank aloof until 1969. But the envisaged structure of the future group would have needed little if any amendment and the altered finances would have posed no great obstacle. Yet the politics of the situation would have been changed utterly. The tartan army could have been enlisted as allies for a Royal Bank campaign, and its support would surely have allowed Graham to see off the Hong Kong interloper. In the event, a potential coup for Scotland was pitched as a Standard Bank campaign and so perceived as a snub for the Scots – and all was lost. Both parties to the agreed deal were equally targeted by the tartan brigade, with disastrous results. This came as a genuine surprise to Peter Graham, and was a source of bitter regret:

I felt that we had such a strong Scottish flavour in the bank that the Scottish card would be incapable of being successfully played . . . Many of them [i.e. leading figures in the Scottish business and financial establishment] were very welcoming. The only problem was that they would not say it in public . . . [And some were hostile throughout.] The Scottish Development Agency came out with a paper . . . containing a set of proposals which were completely stupid. You can't describe them as anything else . . . they were ill-informed and bordering on the ignorant! Frankly, no bank in its right mind could have gone any way towards accepting the sort of conditions they were saying should be imposed.[96]

No doubt much of the opposition had indeed taken little heed of market realities – but for the third time in four years, Graham's quest to expand Standard Chartered via a bold acquisition had landed the bank in a predicament for which it seemed less than fully prepared. In January 1982 the MMC handed over its recommendation – accepted by the Government – that both of the rival bids be blocked, despite the fact that the Bank of England in its evidence had upheld its support for Standard Chartered.[97] In Hong Kong, Sandberg had four more years in the top job and took the setback in his stride.* (Before the end of 1983, by his own account, he would be talking to Richardson's successor at the Bank of England, Robin Leigh-Pemberton, about the feasibility of a bid by HSBC for the Midland Bank.) But Graham and his colleagues were devastated. Most of the immediate press comment focused on the setback for the Edinburgh bank ('Royal Bank shanghaied') but the demolition of all the elaborate plans laid in Clements Lane was at least as damaging for its would-be partner. Giving his version of events to HSBC's official historian four years later, Graham could scarcely disguise his anguish: 'I personally feel that a great mistake was made . . . In my opinion it was a bad decision. I don't think it was substantiated by the Report . . . they were a body of men who came together to make the right decision but made the wrong one.'[98] The rebuff must have been all the more disappointing for him, insofar as the announcement of his successor was due before the end of the year: he would be retiring as Managing Director in June 1983.

---

* In a phlegmatic response to the decision, he simply acknowledged that the case for allowing either bid to proceed had 'stood and fallen on the weight of opinion as the Commission sees it in Scotland' (*Financial Times*, 16 January 1982). The sequel, as recorded in his private memoir, was not too discouraging: 'Mrs Thatcher invited me to her flat at the top of 10 Downing Street . . . She was very supportive, and without in any way apologising, she confirmed she thought the decision was wrong, and offered to help us in the future in any appropriate way. It was a kind gesture, and combined with a generous tot or two of whisky, it made for a most enjoyable evening.' (*Hurrahs and Hammerblows*, privately published 2012, p. 158.)

In the meantime, he did not allow his disappointment to deter him from pursuing other more limited transactions. One was especially notable. It involved another MMC, this time not the Monopolies and Mergers Commission but Mocatta Metals Corporation of New York, still only 30 per cent owned by the Group. Negotiations for a complete takeover of the Mocatta business in the US – along with a buy-out of Henry Jarecki's 45 per cent stake in the London business – had been mooted several times since 1974, in line with Graham's professed dislike of partnerships and his wish to see the bank always in full control. Nothing had come of the idea by 1979, but the ties between the bank and Jarecki had then grown much closer – not least as a consequence of one of the most extraordinary episodes in US financial history. This was the dramatic attempt in 1979–80 by the brothers Bunker and Herbert Hunt to corner the world's market in silver bullion. The bizarre campaign by the Texan brothers grotesquely inflated the price of silver, pushing it to a peak of around $50 an ounce compared with about $6 through the years since 1974. Half-way up this spiral, early in October 1979, the skewed market posed a problem for Jarecki. MMC made substantial forward, and fully hedged, sales of the metal in the normal course of its own business. The commodity exchanges always required percentage deposits ('margin') against these sales – so the soaring price of silver meant a stream of 'margin calls' for more cash – tens of millions of dollars. Rumours began seeping into the market about MMC's solvency. To avert a potential crisis, Standard Chartered made an extra $100 million facility available to its partner and Graham despatched Michael McWilliam to New York for a series of face-to-face meetings with the top Wall Street banks, to assure them of the Group's unwavering support. (McWilliam ended up in a meeting with the Hunt brothers themselves in Jarecki's office, 'and there were Texan boots on the table'.[99]) Together with the conspicuous support offered by MMC's major US bankers, especially Chase Manhattan, it was enough to stem the speculation.[100] Further steps were taken by Jarecki and the bank over the following days to square MMC's operations with the precarious situation on the commodity exchanges, as the Board in Clements Lane heard a week later: 'the position had been resolved as a result of an agreement entered into by MMC and the Hunt brothers, who had offset their forward purchases of silver on the Exchanges against the forward sales contracts of MMC'.[101] In the aftermath – as the Hunt brothers began disappearing under an avalanche of lawsuits that would eventually bury them in bankruptcy – it was agreed between the bank and MMC that closer reporting lines would be sensible, and the Treasury Division in London took to receiving more regular updates from New York.

This set the scene neatly for serious talks around the middle of 1980 about a takeover of MMC, reorganizing the Mocatta bullion businesses on both sides of the Atlantic into a fully owned subsidiary of Standard Chartered. What followed must have sorely tried Jarecki's patience, notwithstanding a growing friendship between him and McWilliam and the fact that a very fancy price was in the offing. First, the bid for RBS obliged Graham to suspend the whole discussion. Next, after HSBC's counter-bid and the moratorium imposed by the referral to the Monopolies Commission, Graham characteristically seized the chance to make a specific, and remarkably generous, bid proposal – only for the Board to insist that it be withdrawn, pending the authorities' decision on the Royal Bank. Then, within a few weeks of the RBS verdict in January 1982, Graham returned to Jarecki a third time with fresh terms. The subsequent negotiations lasted through the summer of 1982 but ran into some intractable difficulties, as Jarecki recounted to his Executive Directors at a private lunch in New York that October:

> The first [problem] was that [the bankers] had developed, in my view erroneously, the fear that everything in the group worked so well because I was a magician and if they didn't know how to capture me . . . then everything would fall apart . . . The second thing was that they had become increasingly concerned about how we all made so much money. They all read these books about the 1979 silver market. They thought that the companies, especially the New York company, might get sued so that all of its money would be lost. And if Standard Chartered were the majority parent, they couldn't just walk away.[102]

Underlying these concerns was the inescapable fact that almost no one in the senior echelons of the Group – with the conspicuous exception of McWilliam, who with George Preston had negotiated the bank's original investment in 1973 – grasped more than the barest bones of the bullion business, and Preston had retired from the Board in March 1979. The talks served a useful purpose in flushing this out. ('They now see that there isn't an alternative solution for them such as taking it [MMC] over by themselves', explained Jarecki at the lunch. 'They have concluded that their own managerial involvement wasn't enough to do it . . . [and] that it is best to leave the current structure as it is and to support that structure.') Jarecki called time on the whole notion, anxious to end some increasingly fraught attempts by the bank to define and contain the risks of full ownership, which were damaging what had hitherto been a generally happy relationship. As was apparent to some at the time, this outcome pointed again to an uncomfortable reality that had already been glimpsed in the aftermath of the Union Bank acquisition. For all its apparent size and worldwide reach, the Group seemed to be woefully strapped for managerial resources. Henry Jarecki had saved the day in New York, as John Harrigan had in California. It may even be that Sandberg's Hongkong Bank had saved the day in Scotland. Whatever the potential benefits of a successful acquisition of RBS – and none could doubt them – how Clements Lane might have coped with the subsequent merger was far from clear. There were grounds by 1983 for suspecting it might have been a struggle.

5. OVER-STRETCHED AND UNDER STRAIN

Legend has it that when Robert the Bruce, King of the Scots, lay dying in 1329, he was so full of remorse for never having gone on a Crusade that he bequeathed his heart to his followers, asking them to fight their way to the Holy Land with it after his death. The initial assignment was to lay the heart, carried in a casket, at the Holy Sepulchre in Jerusalem. On the way there, however, the dutiful Scottish knights with all their retainers ran into a spot of bother against the Saracens. At a critical moment in the ensuing battle, when it seemed that all might be lost, the keeper of the Bruce's Heart hurled it deep into the Saracens' ranks. It was a terrible gamble, but he reckoned the Scots would stop at nothing to retrieve it – which they duly did, winning the battle in the process. (The Heart went back to Scotland, for burial in Melrose Abbey.) Peter Graham came from Croydon, not famed for its Crusaders, and may never have heard of the expression 'throwing the Bruce's Heart' – meaning, as most of his Scottish colleagues could have told him, to risk all by setting your supporters a wildly improbable but utterly compelling objective. This was nonetheless the gist of what he had done with Standard Chartered since that 1975 conference at the Hyde Park Hotel. True, Sir Cyril Hawker and George Preston had earlier pointed the way. But it was Graham, seeing the embattled situation of the bank, who had set aside all caution in opting for a dramatic expansion in Europe and North America. He had calculated, in effect, that the bank would rally to this drastic change of direction. With the future of the Group at stake, the skills and resources would somehow be found to ensure the successful implementation of a brave if slightly reckless strategy. By 1983, when the time came for him to step aside as Managing Director, the verdict on Graham's audacity still seemed precariously balanced.

The logic behind it was as persuasive as ever – all the more so, given recent events across Asia. As a standalone bank, the Chartered's predicament by the early 1980s might have been especially sticky. Working profits in the Indian sub-continent had all but evaporated. Growth seemed to be fizzling out in Malaysia and Singapore. The Shanghai branch was a tiny apartment in a nondescript building round the corner from the Bund, with a lively telex machine but not much need of a cash register. Trade with Vietnam had been cut off by the Communists, and the markets' confidence in South Korea's future had been badly shaken by riots and insurrection. Even Hong Kong's perennial optimism was being challenged, not least by the impact on the global shipping industry of a severe trade recession that began in 1980. Of all the global fleets based in the Colony, only Y. K. Pao's World-Wide Shipping Group seemed likely to weather the storm: others looking perilously close to the rocks by 1983 included T. Y. Chao's Wah Kwong Maritime Transport – in which Standard Chartered had a small equity stake – and C. Y. Tung's OOCL. Worst of all, there was suddenly a growing disquiet in Hong Kong over the long-term future of the Colony itself: the prospect loomed of a disruptive takeover by China in 1997. The Hong Kong dollar, allowed to float freely since 1974, was plunging in value. In two days in September 1983 it fell by 13 per cent against the US dollar.* (Others forced into a reappraisal of their Eastern businesses included HSBC, which was pushing hard to expand into North America and Europe in these years, and Jardine Matheson, pillar of the Hong Kong establishment, which was to move its corporate domicile to Bermuda in 1984.) The working profits of the Chartered, publicly lost within the Group's, were falling steadily: they would amount to £91 million for the twelve months of 1983, compared with £110 million in 1980.[103]

Yet none of this caused the markets much serious concern: late in 1983, the shares of the Group, at around 425 pence, were trading at roughly the same price as in late 1981. For this, shareholders had largely to thank Graham and the ebullience with which he had pitched his Western strategy. The Group's excursion into Californian banking was now looking timely: the Union Bank in 1983 contributed £58 million to a total working profit of £405 million. (Graham would recall in 1986 that the arrangements with Harrigan had 'all slotted into place very nicely'[104]). Meanwhile South African profits were more robust than ever, at £114 million, and

---

* It reached a record low of HK$9.60, compared with HK$5.13 two years earlier and HK$4.97 when the free-float was initiated in 1974. The September crisis prompted the Colony's Government a few weeks later to abandon the free-float regime in favour of a fixed exchange rate at HK$7.80 against the US dollar – in the face of considerable scepticism voiced by both Standard Chartered and HSBC.

Atlantic Ocean

North Sea

DENMARK
f. 1975–1
1989–exit

NETHERLANDS
f. 1974–1
1975–2
1989–exit

IRELAND
f. 1977–1
1981–7
1989–exit

BELGIUM
f. 1976–1
1979–2
1980–exit

UK
1969–14
1988–137 (including 24 full branches)
2000–6

FRANCE
1969–1
1982–3
1994–exit

SWITZERLAND
f. 1976–1
1985–5
1996–exit

SPAIN
f. 1975–1
1987–exit

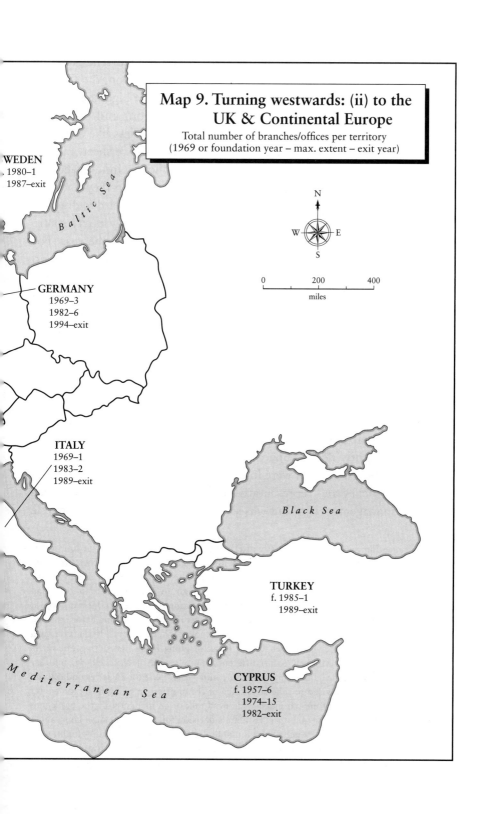

Map 9. Turning westwards: (ii) to the UK & Continental Europe

Total number of branches/offices per territory
(1969 or foundation year – max. extent – exit year)

SWEDEN
1980–1
1987–exit

Baltic Sea

N
W E
S

0   200   400
miles

GERMANY
1969–3
1982–6
1994–exit

ITALY
1969–1
1983–2
1989–exit

Black Sea

TURKEY
f. 1985–1
1989–exit

Mediterranean Sea

CYPRUS
f. 1957–6
1974–15
1982–exit

the International Division and Treasury operations remained at the forefront of the City's foreign-exchange trading and eurocurrency-lending
activities, earning £53 million for the year. By comparison, the Group's
Asian operations were now looking quite modest. The biggest contributions in 1983 came from Hong Kong (£25.9 million) and Singapore
(£24.9 million).[105] In fact, Asia was beginning to look less like a regular
earner than a source of periodic windfalls for the balance sheet. Like its
celebrated Shanghainese friends in Hong Kong – whose spinning factories
were now worth far more as property developments than they had ever
generated as textile businesses – the Group could look forward to drawing
from time to time on a new genre of 'hidden reserves', namely its city-centre
buildings across Asia that were growing more valuable by the year. For
the property market, lower returns on the banking business posed no
problem. A triennial revaluation of property values on the balance sheet
in 1981 had seen Reserves boosted 60 per cent, to £936.6 million – and
the biggest gains had been booked for Battery Road in Singapore
(£43.8 million) and various sites in Hong Kong (£29.7 million, which did
not include £16.8 million on the Des Voeux Road main office, set aside
for another day).[106]

The Group's dramatic tilt to the West was nonetheless still some way
short of fulfilment. In fact, it was disconcertingly only half implemented
in many respects. The Group's network had been expanded across the
UK, continental Europe and North America.* Now its operational performance urgently needed upgrading. Out of twenty-two full branches
across the UK, two-thirds were losing money. A steadily expanding network of branches and representative offices across Europe was a huge
drain on management time but was so far adding little to the bottom line

---

* Not to mention the Falklands. Shortly after the end of the Falklands War in June 1982,
Anthony Barber attended a meeting at 10 Downing Street where Mrs Thatcher expressed
her dismay that the islands had no commercial bank. The locals were still reliant on the
Falkland Islands Company for financial services, though an official report in 1976 had
pointed to the need for a proper bank. Barber gave an instant assurance that his bank would
remedy this oversight and hurried back to the City to set the wheels turning before the end
of that same day. (George Copus, interview with author, 24 August 2011.) In due course, a
mysterious telex was received at Des Voeux Road in Hong Kong instructing one of its
officers – known as A. J. Mitchell (61) to differentiate him from A. J. Mitchell (57), another
officer who had joined the bank four years before him – to prepare for an as yet undisclosed
reassignment. He was advised to take advantage of cheap prices in Hong Kong for winter
clothing. This naturally prompted much wide-eyed talk of an incursion by the bank into
North Korea. A press release about the Falklands decision followed some days later, and a
doubtless much relieved A. J. Mitchell (61) found himself on a non-stop military flight, with
two mid-air refuellings, to Port Stanley. ('Reminiscences from the East', private memoir by
Michael Brown, p. 28.)

(£1.9 million in 1983). It was broadly the same story in the US. Offices had been opened to handle trade-financing services in Chicago, Miami, Seattle, Houston and Atlanta. More than $2 billion was tied up in their operations. Collectively their profits were nominal, with only the New York office lending the aggregate US network's numbers a veneer of respectability. The growth of the International Division and Treasury operations in London was impressive – it accounted for almost a third of the asset growth budgeted for 1983 – but these businesses earned much lower margins than traditional commercial banking. By participating in syndicated sovereign loans managed by other banks, the International Division was also rapidly accumulating assets with none of the detailed credit checks applicable to normal corporate advances – though the implications of this were scarcely noted by anyone at the time. Another concern was the bank's mounting leverage – that is, the ratio of its total assets to shareholders' funds – which had risen from about 15:1 at the start of the 1970s to just over 20:1 by 1982. (It would top 25:1 by 1985.) Finally, adverse currency movements were fuelling concerns that the balance sheet was beginning to look over-stretched. The pound's weakness since 1979 had boosted the sterling value of overseas earnings, but less valuable sterling equity had to be supplemented with ever more debt to fund the growth of overseas assets. By 1983, cautionary papers from the Chief Financial Officer, Stuart Tarrant, were starting to sound a little exasperated at this mounting problem ('As the Board has previously been advised, SCB's capital adequacy has already fallen below acceptable levels, mainly because of the significant increase in infrastructure (premises etc) and as a result of the growth in Eurocurrency lending and interbank activity'[107]). Relations between Tarrant and some of his longer-serving colleagues, including Michael McWilliam, were becoming conspicuously scratchy.

Just as worrying as the pressure on the balance sheet was the strain on the staffing resources of the Group. In its US offices it had tried to rely heavily on British expatriates, few of whom really matched up to the job. In the UK, it had extended its franchise – and tried to offer a full range of commercial banking activities, not just a more narrowly defined set of trade services – without diluting its 'lifetime' management cadre with mid-career recruits. This had left young and inexperienced staff running newly opened branches, a problem flagged several times since the late 1970s but still not properly heeded.[108] As the newcomer on the block, the bank was struggling to compete against the clearers – and was starting to feel the effects of having taken on too much business since the mid-1970s that the clearers had turned away. For a 'Special Board Meeting and Dinner' in April 1982, several papers were presented on the problems of the new branch networks, and the staffing issue figured prominently.[109]

What emerged rather alarmingly from these stock-taking exercises was not just the fragility of the Western strategy but the extent to which the broader managerial needs of the Group were being neglected, across the board. Middle managers were receiving little or no training of any kind; senior managers were only rarely participating in the formulation of Group strategy at any level. The consequent weaknesses were exemplified by the poor response to new technology. The world's best commercial banks were being transformed by computerization, but Standard Chartered was not among them. The Group's expansion since the merger of 1969 meant that Clements Lane was now presiding over no fewer than 160 reporting units. Yet the information systems at its disposal were rudimentary at best. Consultants from Arthur Andersen were hired early in 1982 to run a forensic eye over the branches in London, New York, Hong Kong, Kuala Lumpur and Singapore. In a paper for the Board in June 1983, Michael McWilliam presented their unnerving conclusions:

(a) SCB is significantly under-invested in computers and related systems by comparison with its competitors.

(b) Management and financial control systems are underdeveloped.

(c) Technical Services Division is severely short of resources with a resultant backlog of outstanding assignments.

(d) As a result of the shortage of manpower resources, documentation of computer systems is minimal and the Group could possibly be at risk in certain circumstances.[110]

Just as important as their list of gaps that urgently needed plugging was a strong recommendation from Arthur Andersen that the Group revise its overall approach. As McWilliam pointed out to his colleagues, the report had 'strongly alerted the Bank's executive to the need to become more closely involved in the implementation process'.

Whether indigenization promised to be of help here, or hindrance, was a matter on which opinions were divided. The Board accepted the logic of indigenization, but was still inclined to regard it as a risky alternative to traditional staffing. Problems in Singapore, for example, led it to conclude that operations there were 'severely handicapped by the limited number of executives and the inadequate depth of specialisation and experience in management'. This prompted not a search for additional suitably qualified Singaporeans but a decision 'to provide further expatriate secondments of top quality staff'.[111] And it was certainly possible to argue, as did the Group's Chief Inspector in a report of 1983, that the impact of local hires remained as yet a mixed blessing. The Board's Audit Committee plainly sympathized:

> The Committee commended the new emphasis of the report on the Group's operating efficiency but was concerned that inspections carried out during the period had shown an increasing trend towards weak management control and supervision. In discussion, it was agreed that this was not a new phenomenon but had become more acute as a consequence of the Group's expansion and the dilution of expatriate management ... [The Chief Inspector] believed that a number of personnel factors were involved in the deteriorating situation reported. For instance, whereas in the past expatriate officers had received a breadth of experience from their postings to a number of territories, this could not normally be acquired by the local officers who were progressively taking their places.[112]

This reference to the limited transferability of locally recruited managers heeded a problem that had of course been flagged in some of the very first discussions of indigenization half a century earlier. If raising it again ran counter to the retreat from Empire-staffing over recent years, it was a tacit acknowledgement that the indigenization process had its complications. It had not yet been in place long enough, it seemed, to produce suitably experienced local hires at every level. Standard Chartered had lost its Empire traditions, to coin a phrase, but not yet found a post-Empire identity. Sustaining its progress in the local territories of Africa and Asia was a shrinking cohort of Foreign Staff managers, feeling increasingly remote from Head Office and irked by its dictates. Many worried that the geographical expansion in the West, though applauded in 1975, had so far done little to enhance a sense of shared purpose across the Group. Indeed, it was notably still the case at the start of the 1980s that old Africa hands and old Asia hands were very far from being interchangeable: few yet crossed successfully from the one continent to the other.[113]

It all amounted to a formidable list of challenges for whoever would succeed Peter Graham as Managing Director in 1983. The Group's extraordinary expansion since 1975 had left a slew of problems in its wake. Many were structural – inviting the kind of organizational changes that consultants were inclined to describe as fixing the plumbing. (How should the Group's regional businesses relate to the Head Office in London? How could the central functions of the bank be best adapted in London to serve the branches around the world?) But other, less structural issues would require something more akin to genetic engineering – nurturing the development of a new culture that might work as successfully for the enlarged

Standard Chartered Bank as the old expatriate culture had worked for
the Chartered. By 1983, the world of the British overseas banks had been
firmly consigned to the past. The services they had provided – trade credits
and currency exchange, seasonal loan facilities and cash remittances,
overdrafts and deposit accounts – were more in demand than ever, not
least as a result of the Bretton Woods era's passing in 1973. But they were
no longer the special preserve of a banking model invented in the nineteenth century for predominantly British customers. Now these services
were on tap from a host of banks, both local and international, working
in the context of financial markets that had scarcely existed in the 1960s.
The launch of the reconstituted Standard and Chartered Bank Group in
1970 – like the more or less simultaneous disappearance of Barclays DCO
into the reorganized Barclays Group in 1971 – could itself be seen, a decade later, as a portent of the changes to come. The merger had given the
African and Asian operations of the combined banks a vital opportunity
to spread their geographical interests. Given an extraordinarily propitious
background for many of their core activities – the soaring volume of bullion and foreign-exchange transactions, the exponential growth of the
market for syndicated loans – the merger had also opened the way for a
dramatic surge in profits (greatly accentuated in nominal terms by the
high inflation rates of the 1970s).[114] Yet as all the internal audits of the
early 1980s had made clear, the culture and workings of Standard Chartered were still in many crucial respects outdated remnants of the overseas
banking world. To survive and prosper as an independent entity it would
need to undergo many profound changes, and in short order. If it baulked
at the prospect, there was at least one other major bank already at its door
by 1983 whispering of euthanasia – or as bankers preferred to say, 'a
friendly merger'.

9

A Stymied Transition, 1983–8

I. FITNESS AND FEDERALISM

Walk along the City of London's Bishopsgate today, northwards past the junction with Threadneedle Street and across the road from Gibson Hall, and you will find no trace of a Number 38. Where the Chartered Bank built its Head Office in 1909 is once again (in 2016) a construction site, levelled in 2007–8 to make way for another towering landmark on the City skyline – this one to be simply '22' (formerly 'The Pinnacle'), rising up alongside 'The Cheese Grater' and only a few hundred yards from 'The Gherkin'. But a now-forgotten redevelopment of 38 Bishopsgate in the 1980s saw Standard Chartered itself championing post-modernist architecture, replacing the old Chartered building – relegated to more or less back-office status since 1975 – with a striking new Group headquarters. It was to provide offices for several hundred staff moving from 10 Clements Lane – which, having been continuously occupied by the Standard Bank since 1867, was to be vacated and sold. The new building in Bishopsgate, eight floors high, was all glazed windows on the outside and a passable City version of Xanadu on the inside. Mature magnolia trees filled a five-storey atrium, where streams and waterfalls ran, through channels of Brazilian granite, down to walkways adorned with a life-sized (baby) mahogany elephant and the statue of James Wilson, shipped over from Calcutta where it had stood in that branch's vast banking hall since the 1950s (see Plate 34).* Costing almost £100 million, it was a project in which Peter Graham had taken an intense personal interest from the start.[1] It offered not just a nice opportunity to upstage HSBC – their main

---

* A booklet on the bank's history, printed to accompany the opening of the new building and written by Stephen Fay, closed with a note of the Bishopsgate interior. 'It is built around an atrium full of foliage that is fertile and luxuriant; behind that façade there is a bank whose intention is to be well pruned and fruitful.'

London office was just down the street – but a way, too, of reminding the City of Standard Chartered's status.

In the past, no such reminder had been thought of much importance. This is not to say that bricks and mortar were of no consequence. On the contrary, enormous attention had always been paid to the design and location of the principal branches, not to mention the splendid houses reserved for their managers. The archives today hold hundreds of boxes labelled 'Premises', packed with architects' plans, surveyors' reports, letters to and from landlords and tenants, insurance policies, renovation proposals, inventories of fixtures and fittings. Their physical networks underpinned the success and longevity of both the Standard and the Chartered – but for the grand flagship buildings that fronted those networks, one had to look not to the City of London but to the great and exotic locations of the Empire. The white turrets of Clive Street in Calcutta and the mighty portico of Adderley Street in Cape Town, the 'French new baroque' fortress of the Standard on Johannesburg's Commissioner Street and the imposing arches of the Chartered in Colombo, its masonry adorned with elephant heads – such had been the true hallmarks of power and permanence for the two overseas banks, beside which their London offices had been mere architectural appendages. So the stately dome taking shape in Bishopsgate – eventually to be occupied in October 1985 – was a radical departure, as befitted a bank with a radical strategy. Standard Chartered was now intent on being seen not as an 'overseas bank', a lingering legacy of the old Empire, but as a top international bank with businesses on every continent and ambitious plans for all of them – 'Strength in Depth Across the World', as the Group's latest logo had it.

In truth, this transition from 'overseas' to 'international' had yet to be consummated, and still posed a challenge for its management that went far beyond the mechanics of refurbishing historic office buildings or even buying other banks. The man tasked with leading the way was Michael McWilliam. His appointment as Group Managing Director in June 1983, long expected by everyone in the bank, marked a significant break with the past. As had been evident since his recruitment in 1966, he combined a fine mind with a ferocious appetite for clear analysis and detailed planning. Christopher Fildes, the much respected financial columnist, fairly described him as 'the thinking man's banker'.[2] With his East African background, he also had a natural affinity with the bank's operations in Africa and the wider developing world, and was acutely sensitive to its role as 'a good corporate citizen', which he was determined to promote everywhere. (No doubt this was partly what Henry Jarecki of Mocatta Metals had in mind, telling his New York management team about the

COLOMBO BRANCH

Chartered Bank's branch in Colombo, Sri Lanka, drawn in 1948 – occupied by
the bank since 1892 and eventually sold by Standard Chartered in 2012

coming man after an office lunch in October 1982: 'I think we are very
fortunate in having Michael McWilliam there and I think the Bank is very
fortunate. He is a very classy, straight person and there aren't too many
of those around.'[3]) Nonetheless, his appointment put the bank into the
hands of someone out of a very different mould from his peers. Here was
an erstwhile Oxford academic economist, running a bank that had long
made a virtue of eschewing graduate recruits from any university. While
the Group's structure had in many respects been determined by the Standard since 1969 – Peter Graham, after all, had taken his cue from Hawker
and Hamilton – it had inherited most of its essential character traits from
the Chartered, and the cerebral, understated McWilliam was almost the
antithesis of a traditional Chartered man. He had never had to toil as a
young Sub-Accountant in some remote and steaming-hot branch office,
patiently awaiting his turn to move up the ladder. Grizzled Scotsmen in
Bishopsgate had won advancement for generations past by excelling at the
kind of relationship-building with traders and tycoons in Asian parlours

that made for a successful career with the Chartered. McWilliam shared none of that background. In Nairobi and the City, he had risen as (to use a latter-day label) a first-class policy wonk. He was a merchant banker, a manager and administrator, but had no experience as a day-to-day lender. His accession to the top job was in every way unprecedented.

It was plain from the start that he intended a thorough rejuvenation of the bank, and that this was all but certain to entail more friction at the top than Head Office's (mostly Eastern) senior bankers – with their lifetime careers and collegiate culture – had ever experienced in the past. Indeed, McWilliam gave notice in an address to the general management team on 2 June 1983 of the salutary approach he would be adopting:

> I think that a ruthless outside owner of this bank who was unaffected by sentimental attachment would achieve a substantial release of under-employed capital . . . It should not need a bid situation to call forth that kind of management review of our operations and . . . I therefore intend to conduct just such a wide-ranging review as if we were under the threat of outside predators.[4]

In the event, what followed his appointment was to be a marathon struggle that often saw McWilliam's intentions chafing with top colleagues and prompting dissent in the Boardroom. It was evident on many occasions that the non-Executive Directors' support for bold initiatives could not be taken for granted. Nor was Anthony Barber, for all his charm and ambassadorial skills, a Chairman much inclined to risk overt confrontation round the Board table. Meanwhile Peter Graham, who gave up the Managing Directorship only to become Deputy Chairman, remained as committed as ever to the bank's expansion and often had strong views of his own that he pushed almost as though he had never retired: as his successor noted privately, he was 'very much into every issue as of old'.[5] Perhaps inevitably, the new Managing Director's drive for modernization became an intensely politicized affair. This being so, the history of the bank over the next several years has to begin by acknowledging a highly unusual source. For Michael McWilliam kept a diary – written in long-hand almost every evening, and setting down a cool appraisal of the people and events encountered during the day – which he maintained, remarkably, throughout his tenure as Managing Director.[6] Given that few of his peers left behind much more than scraps of private correspondence, any narrative enhanced (like this one) by full access to the diary runs the risk of being unduly coloured by his view of events. But the entries invariably appear candid enough, and set on achieving as objective a record as possible – to the point of being sometimes disarmingly self-critical. They offer an illuminating supplementary guide to a fraught episode in the City of London's modern history.

As it happens, McWilliam's reference in his management address to the threat of an outside predator was not quite as hypothetical as he implied on that June day of 1983. He could hardly disclose it, but work had been under way for a year on papers designed to refute a serious bid approach. Speaking to a conference of Standard Bank executives in Johannesburg three months earlier, McWilliam had been a little more forthcoming: 'We became aware during 1980 that SCB was a potential target for a corporate predator . . .'[7] Just before his flight to Johannesburg, that predator (which he did not name) had broken cover, proposing to the Board that they begin talks about a possible friendly merger. Graham and McWilliam had declined the invitation, which came from Lloyds Bank. The giant UK clearer with the black-horse logo had been assigned the codename 'Pegasus' within Clements Lane, after the winged beast of Greek mythology. By the middle of 1983 a series of confidential Board papers had been written, arguing that the suggested merger would not fly.[8] Lloyds seemed to have dropped the idea. But its approach had made vividly clear to McWilliam from Day One that, in pursuing a fundamental reform of Standard Chartered, he would effectively be racing against the clock. Another bid, whether from Lloyds or another bank, might appear at any time. Bravely, he decided that a comprehensive modernization of the bank would be its only effective defence, if and when that day came, and he set off at a cracking pace.

The result was an avalanche of studies and analyses. Operational reports from all of the General Managers and Divisional heads led within months to sweeping reappraisals of the principal regions. 'Annual review sessions' were instigated for the country managers, involving a trip to London and levels of interrogation that came as a surprise to some of them (and drew occasional muttered references to a Star Chamber). Hard on the heels of Arthur Andersen's report into systems and technology, another external consultancy, Booz Allen Hamilton, was commissioned in July 1984 to look into the structure and processes of senior management. A cosmetic change almost coinciding with these activities concerned the formal structure of the Group: an elaborate redesignation of all its banking operations would see them integrated into one public limited company (PLC) as Standard Chartered, thus (at long last) completing the merger process launched in December 1969.[9] Above all, perhaps, McWilliam took steps to engage the Group's most senior managers from all points of the compass as a far more cohesive policy-making unit. This accorded with his conviction that Standard Chartered was not just a City of London bank with some exotic overseas operations as a heritage of its past. Rather, it was a unique kind of organization which, albeit by virtue of its history, embraced a family of local or quasi-local banking operations around the world. He duly assembled a top executive team to reflect this. It comprised not just the senior London executives and top managers from Hong Kong, Singapore and Malaysia, but also John Harrigan from California, Henry Jarecki from New York and the Managing Director of StanBIC from Johannesburg, Henri de Villiers (later to be succeeded by Conrad Strauss). They met for the first time as a unit in April 1984, at a conference centre outside London – Leeds Castle in Kent, a venerable setting with medieval foundations and a strong link with Henry VIII and the first of his six wives. Since the castle was thus a magnificent relic of the past which in recent times had been comprehensively updated to earn its keep as a modern business, it was perhaps a more appropriate venue than some of the attendees realized. Four months later, reconvening in the same place to take stock of progress, they all agreed on one overriding observation, which would set the context for much of what followed.

The Group, they concluded, was increasingly divided into two camps. On the one hand were its locally incorporated subsidiaries in California, South Africa and a handful of sub-Saharan African countries. Here operations were heavily decentralized, with local staff and agendas geared directly to the needs of local customers. Hong Kong belonged in this camp, too, by virtue of its long-standing sense of independence: its senior managers had been ignoring dictates from London for years. On the other hand were the rest of the Group's branches, across much of Asia and most notably in India and south-east Asia, where non-local senior managers were still very largely working at the behest of long-distance instructions from London. Henry Jarecki, always a compulsive note-taker and a fascinated observer of the first such meeting he had ever attended, kept a detailed record of the discussions. He summarized an unavoidable conclusion: 'Group mood: subsidiaries upbeat, branches downbeat.'[10] In general, the subsidiaries were flourishing, with good local controls and highly effective marketing teams (especially in South Africa). The branches, however, were for the most part sinking into the mire, their expatriate managers demoralized and more intent on cost-savings than business generation. As Jarecki concluded, in blunt fashion:

> Poor systems and marketing and absence of local [i.e. non-expatriate] management is, in all ex-colonial areas, seen by the local people as a racist residue of colonial mentality. Financial services' distribution systems of the future . . . not at all addressed due to the multiplicity of internal problems and the absence of a strategic planning function.

What the American perceived was a widespread failure to adjust to a rapidly changing business environment. Branch managers across all the familiar territories of the old Chartered Bank franchise were faced with a long list of local pressures. They could no longer depend on the overseas operations of UK multinational companies as their bread-and-butter customers: the commercial legacy of the Empire had been retreating rapidly since the 1960s. But, when competing for the business of Asian firms, they were up against a new generation of ambitious and rapidly expanding indigenous banks. Here was a dilemma for many of the Group's managers. If they sought to keep a distance from their new rivals, relying on the traditional aura of the Chartered, they risked appearing old-fashioned, or worse (guilty, indeed, of displaying Jarecki's 'racist residue of colonial mentality'). And if they tried approaching their customers with a new focus on marketing priorities and strict cost-containment, they were in danger of upsetting powerful families who had grown used to the old colonial ways. As one senior manager reported back to Head Office, there were certainly complaints that 'the Bank is becoming too remote and unable to provide the high quality personal service normally associated with the Chartered Bank'.[11] Meanwhile, the branches in many countries had to contend not only with much greater pressure from Head Office to improve their profitability, but also with ever closer scrutiny of their operations by the government authorities. Politicians, regulators and investors were eyeing the possibilities that might be opened up by local incorporation of the bank. (In Kuala Lumpur, the Government was still keen to acquire perhaps a quarter of the Malaysian bank.) This was a reflection of perhaps the most fundamental change of all: the old deference between expatriate manager and local clerk had gone for good, and with it the traditional business model underpinned by Empire-staffing. Yet little had been done to start forging a fresh, modern managerial culture that might properly replace it. Signs of the resulting frailty were evident across the board, from the backward state of training and computerization to the inadequacy of the accounting and management-information systems – and showed up from time to time, too, in some shocking breaches of security. In Bangkok, an office already demoralized by sagging results was badly shaken by the discovery that a local staff member had swindled the bank out of almost £3 million.[12] In Singapore, the collapse of one of the largest local companies, Pan-Electric, uncovered a scandal in the stock market that badly tarnished the reputation of the Group's local merchant-banking operation and saw one of its British officers prosecuted in the criminal courts (he just escaped receiving a prison sentence).[13]

(The demise of the Chartered's business model also spelled an end to the long tradition of employing compradores as go-betweens for British expatriates dealing with local businessmen. Sadly, it was a tradition that went out not with a wimper but a bang – a revealing episode that involved an outlandish fraud on the bank in Singapore, eventually costing the Group around £10 million and causing it considerable embarrassment. The perpetrator, Lawrence Ng, worked for the Singapore branch as a 'Deputy Business Adviser', but by 1984 had 'assumed a status equivalent to that of the Manager and his instructions carried equal weight', according to a subsequent post-mortem by the Group's Audit Committee.[14] This anomaly had much to do with the fact that Ng's father had been a celebrated compradore, Wee Mon Cheng, who had worked for the bank in the 1960s and had served as Singapore's ambassador to Japan in 1973–80. The son was a different proposition altogether. Gambling heavily on the commodity markets, he lost a fortune and concocted a series of bogus loans to prominent Singapore clients as a way of drawing emergency funds from the bank. One loan for several million dollars was purportedly made to one of his father's closest friends, who was also one of the Chartered Bank's most renowned customers, the shipping magnate Chang Yun Chung. When the branch approached him about repayment, a startled Mr Chang lost no time pointing out that his signature on the loan papers was a forgery.* The Deputy Business Adviser fled to Hong Kong shortly afterwards, and then took refuge in mainland China where he died a few years later.)

Some candid appraisals of the main south-east Asian territories by their resident managers, at Leeds Castle that summer in 1984, made a powerful impression on McWilliam and his senior colleagues. ('In both Malaysia and Singapore, one was left with a vivid impression of the failure of the bank to adapt to changing market conditions.'[15]) They prompted him to abandon the pre-arranged agenda for the last day in favour of an intense debate about the future structure of the Group – and McWilliam seized the opportunity to propose a radical decentralization. He had long held a firm belief in the principle of federalism as the key to success for many organizations. On the wall of his own office hung a framed passage from

---

* Born in 1918, Chang was by 1985 one of the great names in the shipping industry, with his own rapidly expanding fleet, Pacific International Lines (PIL), and a commanding hold over the business of providing containers for the world's maritime cargoes. But from 1949 to 1967 he had worked as the salaried General Manager of a family-owned line, Kie Hock Shipping. He had built it from scratch into a highly successful business owning more then thirty ships – with constant support from the Chartered Bank and its Singapore Managers. It proved a long and valuable relationship for the bank. Chang's advice enabled the Chartered to make substantial profits on Singapore's trade links with Indonesia. In later years, when opening up offices in new countries, PIL would always turn first to Standard Chartered for its local banking services. (Chang Yun Chung, interview with author, 30 October 2012.)

one of Alexander Hamilton's essays in *The Federalist Papers*, a seminal document of the American Revolution: 'The proposed constitution, so far from implying an abolition of State Governments, makes them constituent parts of the national sovereignty . . .' He had been talking to the Booz Allen consultants about the possible relevance of federalism to the Group's situation – as a way of re-energizing the branches and paving the way for a spate of modernization initiatives. If the Group's many branches were truly to take root now as local banks that could everywhere build for the future on a unique pedigree, their relations with London would, in his view, have to be drastically altered. To the slight dismay of the two non-Executive Directors who arrived for the final session, Peter Graham and Sir Leslie Fletcher, this bold conclusion won unanimous support at the close.* (The Deputy Chairman 'was a bit startled by the decentralisation issue, but I think got the message that it was a real issue'.[16]) Less than three months later, McWilliam won the Board's approval for a formal reorganization proposal.

There was to be 'a substantial delegation of authority to the three Far Eastern commercial banks in Hong Kong, Singapore and Malaysia', which would run three regions.[17] Hong Kong's Asia Pacific Zone would comprise South Korea, Japan, the Philippines, Taiwan and the mainland of China (where two new branches had been opened in 1982, signalling the intention to rebuild a network); Kuala Lumpur's Malaysia Area would also embrace Thailand; and a Singapore Area would include Indonesia and Brunei. The three Asian regions would be headed in future by resident Area General Managers, with their own expanded staffs to provide all the corporate muscle they would need as heads of semi-autonomous businesses. (In fact the proposal closely resembled the Three Zones scheme advocated by Archie Rose in 1932, which had envisaged Calcutta, Singapore and Shanghai as the hub branches. Strikingly, the 1984 paper made no more mention of Calcutta than of Shanghai, nor had the future of the

---

* The non-executives might have been even more dismayed had they seen a copy of Henry Jarecki's private counsel to McWilliam a few weeks later. It was uncompromising. 'Cut throats and bad businesses and reorganize now . . . Spend what it takes on systems, computerization, product development and marketing even if there is no immediate return; they are the only way to keep or expand market share . . . Warn the Board that the Bank will go through 18 months of difficulty and decreased profits while you reorganize but assure them that it will come out trim and strong at the end.' ('Leeds Weekend: Confidential Summary of Impressions' by Henry Jarecki, 18 September 1984, HJ Papers.) This of course was the advice of a brilliant maverick, who could afford to make light of delicate Boardroom dynamics and the constant pressure on management to live up to the earnings estimates put round by City analysts. Still, McWilliam had cause to regret later that he had not given more heed to Jarecki's case for a more ruthless approach.

Indian branches of the bank received more than a passing reference at Leeds Castle. Perhaps, indeed, they had no future.) As for the impact of all this on indigenization, McWilliam tacitly conceded that expatriate managers would have to remain at the helm for the moment. Replacing them all at this stage looked simply impractical – though he was privately certain the days of all-British direction for the principal branches were numbered. He looked forward to seeing the Group reshaped one day, as he had put it a couple of years earlier, round 'a truly international cadre of bankers, drawn from more than one nationality, yet still with a sense of group values and commitment'.[18]

In Hong Kong, meanwhile, there was never any doubt that a longer leash from London would be greatly welcomed. London's main concern, conversely, was that too much independence might be asserted by the men on the spot. The submission in January 1984 of a fabulously expensive proposal for the construction of a new Des Voeux Road head office had fuelled whispers about the empire-building visions of the local management. (The plans for Des Voeux Road were to be revised interminably, before agreement was finally reached to proceed with a rebuilding, at only marginally less cost, early in 1987.) But the acute political sensitivity of the bank's position in the Colony made it essential to leave as much of the decision-making as possible to Area Manager (and erstwhile computer champion) Bill Brown, and his Managing Director John Mackenzie. As a Member of the Colony's Legislative Council since 1980, Brown had been directly involved in the delicate negotiations over Hong Kong's future after the handover of its sovereignty to China in 1997. Much would depend on his ability to bring the bank's business plans into line with the Sino-British Joint Statement that was eventually issued in December 1984. At stake was not just Standard Chartered's profitability in the Colony but its repositioning over time to take advantage of the business opportunities that would surely now emerge within mainland China itself.

Empire-building was a charge also levelled from time to time at John Harrigan, boss of the Union Bank in California. It had turned out to be a bank more interested in property development than lending to companies with export business, and its deposit base was essentially inaccessible to its parent in London (nullifying much of the original acquisition rationale). But Harrigan was a forceful customer and without doubt intimidated many of his British peers. He wasted no time, after McWilliam's appointment, pitching the case for an expansion of his responsibilities to cover the Group's branch activities across the whole of the US, including (eventually) its large network-servicing centre in Manhattan. It was a logical development, sensibly implemented for the most part, but was nonetheless resented by some of the long-serving British staff in North America. Ear-lier plans to drop the Californian bank's name in favour of the Standard Chartered brand were abandoned at Harrigan's behest, as he pressed to extend the Union Bank's domain. McWilliam backed him wholeheart-edly, encouraged by Harrigan's growing readiness to engage with the Group's executive team and by the strong performance of the Union Bank itself, easily the Group's single biggest profit centre, excepting only South Africa. Hence, when an extraordinary opportunity arose in June 1984 to bid for one of the biggest banks in the US, McWilliam moved quickly to begin exploring the idea, and proposed to Harrigan that he should instal himself as Chief Executive.

The Continental Illinois Bank of Chicago had been able to boast the country's seventh largest deposit base until just a few months earlier. Dis-astrous loan losses and a run on the bank in May had brought it to the brink of insolvency. Standard Chartered was approached as part of an elaborate rescue effort orchestrated by the Federal Reserve in Washington (whose intervention prompted the first use by Wall Street reporters of the headline 'TOO BIG TO FAIL'). Stuart Tarrant, the self-styled 'CFO' in London, was despatched to Chicago to oversee preliminary talks about buying a slimmed-down version of the stricken bank and lawyers were briefed in London. In prospect was an opportunistic leap which would leave the Group with fully 50 per cent of its assets deployed in the US. When a formal negotiating mandate was sought from the Directors, how-ever, they pulled back. In a portent of what obstacles might lie ahead for any similar opportunistic bids in the future, the Board judged the difficul-ties of funding the purchase – and managing its aftermath – to be simply too daunting. After an hour's discussion, as McWilliam had to record later:

> Barber adjourned and together with [Peter Graham] and [Leslie Fletcher] we agreed we had to abort the whole project. Reconvened and decision accepted with relief. So much for the past three weeks. Moral is that our Board does not have much stomach for a big move and also does not feel that we have much management in depth.[19]

So much for 'Strength in Depth'. One surprising side-effect of the Contin-ental Illinois crisis brought a happier ending. The Chicago bank decided in December 1984 to dispose of its principal European subsidiary, based in Brussels. McWilliam again mooted the possibility of a quick purchase, and the Board again rejected it ('the correct, albeit unheroic, decision but it was a rather tense discussion'[20]). But the head of the Belgian operation, Peter McSloy, was an accomplished figure in continental European bank-ing and was keen to jump ship. Five months later he joined the Group, bringing eight of his senior colleagues with him and helping to launch a much needed revitalization of Standard Chartered's operations in Europe.

In his advocacy of federalism in August 1984, McWilliam referred to an encouraging precedent that had been set by a pilot exercise in sub-Saharan Africa. This perhaps weighed more heavily with him than with some of his fellow Directors. In the pages of his diary, business with African countries featured more regularly, from one month to the next, than Asian affairs. No doubt this in part reflected his personal background and interests. He had been a close follower of post-independence developments since the early 1970s (and was still Treasurer of the UK's Royal African Society when he succeeded Graham). He also felt a genuine optimism about banking prospects in Africa. Contrary to many people's expectations, as he reminded the Board in an overview of future strategy in May 1984, the Group's businesses had generally flourished in the post-independence period, despite all the obvious problems.[21] With only about 10 per cent of shareholders' funds committed in thirteen countries there, 'Africa' by the middle of the 1980s was generating earnings not so far short of those reported by its big neighbour to the south.[22] This Return on Equity measure, of course, would have looked less flattering had the Group not been obliged to sell 60 per cent of the business in Nigeria. In the event, it had been able to deconsolidate First Bank of Nigeria's rapidly expanding balance sheet, while continuing to book 40 per cent of its profits (and the cash dividend had gone on matching this share of the earnings). Nigeria remained by far the most powerful economy in sub-Saharan Africa and the biggest contributor to the Group's African profits. Samuel Asabia was still running First Bank, and by 1984 the bank was growing again after a difficult few years in the wake of a sharp fall in the price of oil in 1981–2 that had hurt the Nigerian economy badly. A branch of FBN had been set up in London, which had profitably pioneered a novel scheme for financing Nigerian imports from the UK, under the supervision of a seconded manager from Standard Chartered, John Rivett. By the middle of 1985, FBN was on its way to doubling the net profits earned in 1984. (This did not preclude a string of difficulties, though, in its interbank accounting with the Group: Stuart Tarrant in March 1984 expressed serious concern 'as to the accounting and administrative muddle which exists [in FBN] . . . as well as the growing level of fraud being experienced', and a provision of £4.5 million was made against the possibility of some nasty surprises.[23])

Another boost to the Group's prospects in Africa was the return to normalcy, or something close to it, of the business in Rhodesia – now Zimbabwe, since the capitulation of the Smith regime in 1979 and the subsequent transition to black-majority rule in 1980. The bank had successfully navigated its way through the political changes at the start of the decade, despite the initial delicacy of its position as a survivor from the 1970s.* (After five years in Salisbury as the General Manager, John Davidson had returned to London in 1980 as the first occupant of a new post, General Manager for Africa.) The Zimbabwean operations were incorporated locally in 1983 – and by 1984, despite signs of a worrying exodus of white farmers, the bank was accounting for well over half of the Group subsidiaries' total working profits in Africa.[24] When it was decided in London in 1985 that there should be a first Regional African Strategy Conference in July 1985, McWilliam had no hesitation assigning it to a location just outside Salisbury – or rather, now, Harare. It was attended by all thirteen of the Group's African chief executives and McWilliam himself gave the keynote address, setting the tone for three days of upbeat speeches and presentations about Africa's role in the Group, and Standard Chartered's role in Africa. The outstanding session, in McWilliam's view, was presided over by a Senior Adviser to the Group and 'our wise man of Africa', Dr Jonathan Frimpong-Ansah. A former Governor of the Bank of Ghana who had headed Standard Chartered's business in that country for five years until 1981, Frimpong-Ansah challenged the delegates to ask themselves 'whether we can make the switch from being the leading foreign bank to being the leading corporate citizen in each country as well'.[25] This appeal had its ironies, given the conference location – but the robust state of the bank that had surfaced in the new Zimbabwe of Robert Mugabe impressed all the conference delegates (as did Mugabe himself, when he made a brief appearance, welcoming them to the event).[26] Some even worried that its very success might show up a few of the Group's less flourishing subsidiaries elsewhere in Africa. McWilliam had no such reservations. The sessions in Harare, he thought, marked 'something of a watershed in our African banking, with a strong will for closer collaboration between our banks and more awareness of our communal responsibilities'. On the closing day, delegates went off with a spring in

---

* Shrewd management of the bank in Smith's Rhodesia had been crucial to the preservation of the country's access to foreign capital. This had depended through most of the 1970s on a continued link with banks in Zurich, sustained despite a complete freeze on all transactions through the City of London. When the Swiss temporarily prohibited use of their banks in 1978, it was the Standard Chartered's General Manager in the country, John Davidson, who flew immediately to Europe and succeeded in establishing alternative arrangements with a small bank in Luxembourg. (Interview with author, 13 December 2011.) Davidson's local chairman, Evan Campbell, had remained in his post to the bitter end, only retiring in 1979 after the collapse of Smith's government. Sadly, he died less than a year into his retirement.

their step – peeling off from the last session to head for the airport at intervals, as the music-loving McWilliam recorded, 'in the manner of the Farewell Symphony'.[27]

2. UNFINISHED BUSINESS

Whatever the Group's progress elsewhere in the world, though, it was now the fulfilment of the management's proclaimed objectives in the UK that was of overriding importance. It had looked obvious since the 1960s that a happy denouement for the story of Britain's overseas banks would mean some kind of alignment for each of them with a domestic clearing bank. The clearers' assorted stakes in the Standard before 1969 had at one point even seemed to prefigure a future for Sir Cyril Hawker's bank as a consortium. By contrast, the Chartered had always stood slightly sniffily aloof from the clearers – but in the wake of the bid for the Royal Bank of Scotland in 1981, Standard Chartered's destiny seemed again to lie inexorably with one of the big home banks. No developments overseas were likely to dispel the market's view of the Royal Bank episode as unfinished business. Heightening this perception significantly by the date of McWilliam's appointment in 1983 was the general air of uncertainty induced in the City of London by the Thatcher government's 'Big Bang' deregulation reforms. Though the Big Bang was not due to take effect until October 1986, preparations for it were already well under way. Those most obviously exposed to abrupt change were the tiny broking and jobbing firms of the stock market – soon to be deprived of the old demarcation lines defining and protecting their closed shops – and the British merchant banks, confronted with an influx of bigger foreign rivals offering capital as well as counselling. Big-Bang speculation effectively turned many famous City names, along with those of the world's leading banks, into a list of runners and riders. Standard Chartered was one of the more fancied, in the race to assemble new and more competitive banking/broking combinations within the UK. And this was not just a consequence of its RBS setback. It also reflected the slightly surprising fact that, as of the end of 1983, the Group owned a merchant bank that (by asset size) ranked as the sixth largest in the City.

It was almost twenty years since Hawker's Standard had taken a 19 per cent stake in the consortium bank known as MAIBL. By the end of the 1960s, it had 'so far provided a notably poor financial return'.[28] It had scarcely fared much better in the 1970s, and by the early 1980s – like other more successful consortia, such as Orion Bank – it had run out of support from its owners, all of whom had opted to grow their own rival businesses in the international capital markets. When the owners' thoughts turned to the business of finding a buyer for MAIBL, Peter Graham confessed to colleagues in November 1982 that the idea of selling to a third party had been 'a cause for hesitation and some concern'.[29] Twelve months later, Standard Chartered took over the whole of MAIBL, generously relieving the other owners of their shares at net book value. The rationale was never entirely clear. But other overseas banks had their corporate finance arms – Grindlays Bank had William Brandt's, for example, and HSBC had Wardley – and Graham essentially argued for the acquisition as a one-off opportunity to beef up the operations of the Group's own Standard Chartered Merchant Bank (SCMB).

The latter had been formed originally out of the Standard Bank's Development Corporation, largely at the behest of George Preston in the aftermath of the 1969 merger with the Chartered. It was amalgamated in 1972 with the trade-financing arm of a small City partnership called Tozer, Kemsley and Millbourn (TKM). The short-lived Tozer Standard Chartered venture was nicely known as Tosca, until TKM was bought out and the business reverted to being plain SCMB. It built up a decent business in export finance for projects backed by Whitehall's Export Credits Guarantee Department, and it developed a corporate finance arm under George Copus, a veteran of Chartered Bank who had joined Bishopsgate's payroll as a sixteen-year-old in 1941. (SCMB's most important client in these years was undoubtedly 'Tiny' Rowland's Lonrho Group, whose proprietor would occasionally sweep in and out of Bishopsgate in regal style.)

In 1977, McWilliam gave the top job at SCMB to Robin Baillie. A Glaswegian who had trained in Scotland, Baillie's banking background had included a stint as Director of the Wallace Brothers Sassoon Bank, a casualty of the secondary banking crisis of 1973-4. It was Standard Chartered's rescue of Wallace Brothers, as part of the Bank of England's lifeboat operations in 1974, that had brought Baillie into the Group. A skilled banker, he had made a considerable success of running down Wallace Brothers Sassoon, to minimize the losses to its creditors (and to the Bank of England).* Building up SCMB, inevitably, was a more difficult

---

* Founded in 1862, Wallace Brothers was for generations one of the most celebrated British trading firms in the East, and at one time enjoyed a virtual monopoly on timber exports from Burma. Several Directors of the firm had sat on Chartered Bank's Court over the years. (A private corporate history, *Wallace Brothers* by A. C. Pointon, was printed by Oxford University Press in 1974.) Its merchant banking subsidiary merged with E. D. Sassoon & Company in 1972 and operated out of 4 Crosby Square, the original home of the Eastern

assignment. Trying to break into the charmed circle of the City's leading
merchant banking names had ever been a thankless task for most who
attempted it – especially where they were answerable to commercial banking superiors – and so it proved for Baillie and his colleagues, under the
chairmanship of Sir Leslie Fletcher. George Copus ran a tidy operation,
nurturing several long-standing client relationships. Modest but worthwhile operations were managed from London in Bombay, Singapore,
Kuala Lumpur and Hong Kong, and the bank's profile was usefully
boosted by a successful leasing arm. Nonetheless, SCMB's working profits
by 1983 were still running at less than £4 million a year (well under 10 per
cent of the Group's UK-derived income). Without well-known banking
stars, it had no way of garnering lucrative corporate finance assignments
and its commercial lending and bond issuance operations were mostly
small beer. Given the geographical spread of the Group's operations, this
struck Graham among others as a wasted opportunity. He pressed for the
purchase of the rest of MAIBL as a timely boost to SCMB's performance,
and the Board backed him. Initial plans to merge the acquisition into the
main bank were set aside, and scores of MAIBL bankers were instead
found desks in SCMB's offices at 33–36 Gracechurch Street.

The combination was not a success. Less than a year after the purchase,
those running the capital-markets trading and Treasury operations of the
Group had second thoughts about leaving MAIBL's substantial
syndicated-loan portfolio and foreign exchange operations within SCMB.
All were promptly transferred to the Group International and Treasury
divisions – leaving just a skeleton crew of former MAIBL staff kicking
their heels in Gracechurch Street. (An important consequence of the move
was a further rapid expansion of the Group's activities in the marketplace
for syndicated eurocurrency loans, which attracted less attention at the
time than it should have done.) A new management team was imposed on
the merchant bank in 1984. Baillie moved upstairs to become Executive
Director responsible for Group development, to be succeeded by a

---

Bank adjacent to 38 Bishopsgate. After a collapse in its finances, it was salvaged in 1977 by
the Bank of England. The task of running it down in an orderly fashion was then passed to
Standard Chartered, which turned to Baillie as a former Director to manage the process as
part of his new role at SCMB. In a last report to Peter Graham as Managing Director, Baillie
wrote an elegant epitaph to the disappearance of an historic name: 'The shareholders of
Wallace Brothers & Co (Holdings) Ltd have lost everything, the brunt of the loss having
fallen on the Wallace family. But the other shareholders suffered greatly, many of them having lost their patrimony in the collapse. For them, and for others whose working lives had
been devoted to the group, the Wallace affair was a great personal tragedy.' (Baillie to Graham, 5 May 1983, Papers for the Board Meeting of 14 June 1983, SCB Box 1721.)

newcomer lured from Jardine Matheson in Hong Kong, Patrick Macdougall. He in turn managed to poach some blue-blooded names from Lazards but the projected take-off for SCMB never happened. (SCMB insiders would subsequently talk of the changing of the guard in 1984 as 'The Fall', still recalled with some anguish thirty years later.) Endless discussions followed over how best to allocate the origination and the funding of new business while less and less effort went into the actual graft of marketing. Former clients of MAIBL drifted away – as did most of MAIBL's more experienced executives – and the anticipated fillip to the enlarged merchant bank's corporate finance work, in the words of a 1986 post-mortem, 'did not particularly materialise although substantial project finance assets were transferred [from MAIBL] to SCMB'.[30] Annual profits fell back 40 per cent or so from the level recorded for 1984. Weighing the benefits of the MAIBL merger against its costs, the 1986 review thought 'the ultimate financial conclusion . . . had been broadly neutral', but it also noted that SCMB's growth had been severely hampered for two years. Perhaps largely as a result of this frustrating outcome to the MAIBL acquisition, McWilliam and his executive colleagues looked askance at the idea of participating in Big Bang by acquiring any of the many UK stockbroking firms up for sale at this time (though several approaches were received).

Integral to the MAIBL acquisition was a vision of the Group's merchant banking as an essentially City-driven activity, with a steady income based on a sizeable portfolio of eurocurrency assets acquired in the market for syndicated loans. This was at best a distraction from the previous merchant-banking strategy of relying on modest operations in Asia, earning their keep as fee-based corporate advisers with local expertise – ventures like Standard Chartered Merchant Bank Asia, which had been incorporated in Singapore in 1978 and had built a good local business by the early 1980s. (One of its young managers was Chris Keljik, who recalled how it ploughed its own furrow without much interaction with the staff of the bank's local branch: 'we had to go out and get our own clients, and we targeted the Chinese business population'.[31]) The income model adopted in the City was gradually imposed at the expense of these fee-earning units, and some valuable local arrangements were lost in the process, most notably in Hong Kong. Chartered Bank had formed a merchant banking venture in the Colony as long ago as 1971, sharing 80 per cent of the equity equally with the City firm of Schroders, with the remaining 20 per cent allotted to the Kadoorie family, one of Hong Kong's wealthiest and best-connected (if least publicized) business dynasties. 'Schroders and Chartered Ltd' had flourished under the leadership of a Schroders man, Win Bischoff, and had eked out an enviable reputation as

an independent corporate finance house with active support from David
Millar as head of the Hong Kong branch.[32] Clients for whom it managed
initial stock-market flotations in the 1970s included some of the Chartered's old Shanghainese friends, including Jack Tang and Jerry Liu.
Another was Li Ka-shing, whose business career since arriving in Hong
Kong from Chaozhou in Guangdong Province was already a celebrated
story and who was now one of the Colony's most successful real-estate
developers. When he decided to take his Cheung Kong property group
public in 1972 (see Plate 30), he mandated Schroders and Chartered to be
a joint manager of the issue alongside HSBC's merchant-banking arm,
Wardley. (The latter was in a better position to offer the immediate flotation date that he wanted, and could easily have handled the whole
transaction. But Li Ka-shing, who always set great store by long-established
relationships in business, opted for the joint arrangement because Bischoff's team was linked to the bank he intended should handle the cash
proceeds: 'I insisted that Chartered Bank act as the clearing bank because
they had been with me for so many years – and because Mr David Millar
was a friend worthy of my respect.'[33])

Now, in 1984, the hard-earned prestige of the Schroders and Chartered
venture was lost to the Group, when Standard Chartered withdrew from
it. (The other two shareholders took up the Group's shares in the established
business, which continued to thrive without Chartered, even though Win
Bischoff returned to Schroders' base in London – where he was appointed
as Chief Executive before the year was out.) Nor was SCMB after 1984 able
to make much of a legacy bequeathed it by the defunct Wallace Brothers.
Ever since the latter group's collapse in 1977, discussions had been continuing on what to do with a shipping, property and banking joint venture
called Ocean Leila, formed in 1976 by Wallace Brothers, Chartered Bank
and one of the Chartered's most successful customers in Asia, Shing Pee
('SP') Tao of Singapore.* The Wallace Brothers' holding had been sold

---

* Born in 1916, S. P. Tao grew up in Nanking between the wars, and was educated in
Shanghai under the Jesuits. Working for China's Nationalist Government during the Second
World War on the maintenance of its supply routes to the West, he developed a formidable
network of contacts among Burmese merchants, government officials and politicians. In the
1950s he used these to build an extensive export business in defiance of an economy always
teetering on the brink of chaos – by the early 1960s, the ubiquitous 'SP' was said to be handling about 40 per cent of Burma's rice exports, as barter trades between Eastern bloc Socialist
countries and Socialist Burma via Singapore. Tao relied on Chartered Bank to provide letters
of credit for him outside Rangoon, and in 1957 formed a lasting friendship with its Singapore
manager, John Wilson. On one occasion in the early 1970s, while on holiday in Monaco,
Tao telephoned the bank with a request that it make available in Hong Kong the next

in 1977 to a prominent Hong Kong family headed by S. S. Wong, which owned the Dah Sing Bank. It still seemed possible in the early 1980s that SCMB might make something of the Ocean Leila business, with one or both of the other shareholders. But nothing came of it. Tao felt close to Peter Graham, but sensed a change in the bank's approach after Graham's retirement in 1983. Huge amounts of time were spent dismantling Ocean Leila and agreeing on the apportionment of its assets, which included a half-share in the glamorous new headquarters building under construction for the bank on Singapore's Battery Road.

But merchant banking, whether in the City or overseas, was a mere side-show for Standard Chartered compared with the main attraction – the expansion of High Street and corporate banking activities within the UK. Application was made in 1984 to join the clearing bankers' club, about to be reorganized with the instigation in 1985 of the Clearing Houses Automated Payments System (CHAPS). Standard Chartered was granted clearing-bank status by the end of the year and membership of the company running CHAPS. Working profits in the UK were now up to more than 40 per cent of the Group total. This took account of the profits of the International Banking, Treasury and Mocatta & Goldsmid operations; it included SCMB with its 'SC Leasing' arm and the consumer-finance income of the old Hodge Group business (now 'Chartered Trust' but still based in Cardiff); and it drew above all on the UK banking network, reliably profitable at last. But another push was thought highly desirable, fully to confirm the Group's geographical reorientation. (It was also needed to satisfy the tax accountants, constantly warning of the fiscal penalties likely to be incurred soon unless more UK income could be found.[34]) McWilliam told the Board – and the Bank of England, too – that the objective was to have UK profits up to 50 per cent by 1990. Several small-scale initiatives were discussed and even piloted, as ways of raising the British public's awareness of the Standard Chartered name. The possibilities, all stymied in one way or another, included a pooling of banking services with a building society (Bristol & West), a large retail chain (British Home Stores) and even the British Post Office (via a joint venture with its wholly-owned Girobank). As McWilliam was well aware,

---

morning a HK$30 million loan to Ocean Leila and a HK$30 million deposit for the Dah Sing Bank, as part of a manoeuvre to help the latter avert an unwelcome takeover. His request was granted, and put through by David Millar in the Colony. As Tao was happy to recall forty years later, 'I had more friends in the Chartered Bank than in all the rest of the business community in Singapore put together.' (S. P. Tao, interview with author, 2 July 2013.)

though, most City observers were in little doubt that Standard Chartered's best move would still be a transformative deal with one of the clearers.

He was of much the same view himself – but with one critical caveat, which had ruled out Lloyds in 1983. No deal could be contemplated that would risk the break-up of the bank, or the subjugation of its overseas operations to an essentially UK-centric culture. This went back to his perception of Standard Chartered as a unique institution in the financial world. 'Independence' was shorthand for a commitment to sustaining that overseas status. Enormous effort was going into the work of refining the Group's strategy. (This would eventually culminate in a weighty eighty-page Corporate Plan, largely authored by the Managing Director himself at the start of 1985 and endlessly refined in Board discussions that lasted for almost another twelve months.*) The whole exercise was often expressly linked by McWilliam to ensuring the bank's continued independence. This was a strategic goal generally deprecated by the business-school professors of the day, as a matter of principle. 'Maximizing shareholder value' in the 1980s was in theory supposed to leave the ownership of a business to the dictates of the marketplace, making no allowance for sentimental notions about 'corporate loyalty'. Few companies with any pride in a long history can ever have heeded such advice in practice, and it certainly had no appeal for the lifetime-career men of Standard Chartered – as typified, say, by David Millar, appointed to the Board in 1983 and now, as Senior Executive Director, effectively McWilliam's deputy. They set great store by their allegiance to the bank, as an entity defined by more than just its market capitalization. For well over a century, the share price of the Chartered had been of little or no consequence whatever to those who served in it. McWilliam sided with them passionately, and regularly reviewed the state of the bank's defences against any unwanted suitors. (To some extent, he suggested, the Group's very complexity would offer it protection against any outright predator: it was, after all, 'a more than usually strange curate's egg'.[35]) Nonetheless, he was ready to face the paradox that, given the demands of the post-1975 reorientation, safeguarding the essence of the bank would almost certainly require a merger of some kind. 'Independence' in practice would probably (ideally, even) entail combining the bank with a front-rank

---

* McWilliam took the opportunity also to make a notable change to the Annual Report. Until now, it had continued to include a thoroughly anachronistic 'Regional Survey', airily reviewing the broad economic trends in its markets, rather than a Chief Executive's Review of Operations such as most banks now offered their shareholders. The 1984 Annual Report made the switch.

name in the UK industry – provided always that the deal could be driven by Standard Chartered itself, preserving the relevance of its past.

By the same token, its overseas franchise would yield a UK partner instant access to a unique spread of businesses, so there was never much doubt (at this stage, anyway) about Standard Chartered's potential appeal for others. The turmoil in the banking industry by the middle of the 1980s only enhanced its attractions. Every large commercial bank was under pressure to show how well it had adapted to a changing environment that sported the 'global' tag at every turn. Even the behemoths of the British High Street were facing sceptical investors, keen to hear of novel thinking about their place in the international markets. Analysts were questioning the value of the clearing bankers' retail networks in a world of automatic telling machines, while data telephony and computer systems were transforming their daily routines. Boring stay-at-home strategies were being set aside to make way for expansive corporate missions that would challenge the onward march of the Americans and Japanese, and keep abreast of the booming market in syndicated international loans. Most of the West's big banks seemed to be thinking about ideal merger opportunities – or in some cases, already rueing their choice of less than ideal ones. (Midland Bank had acquired a majority stake in California's Crocker National in 1981, and by 1983 was fast sinking under the weight of Crocker's bad debts.) During McWilliam's first six months in office, any number of permutations for Standard Chartered were being discretely aired around the Square Mile. He sounded a note of caution in his diary just before Christmas 1983, after taking stock of all the rumours with advisers at Schroders: 'I feel we should not go with the offensive and that the real danger is a move against us, when we may well prefer to turn to Lloyds or Midland.'[36] So Pegasus was not to be ruled out, after all. These two clearers' names, anyway, now began popping up quite regularly. When Barber and McWilliam called at the Bank of England for a private chat at the start of 1984, the Governor observed that a merger with Lloyds might be 'a good fit'.[37] Also that January, the Midland Bank's Finance Director, Michael Julian, telephoned Stuart Tarrant to propose a possible sale of branches and perhaps something more: 'nothing is taboo', McWilliam was told.[38] The Midland's executives were apparently 'taking very seriously the danger of a bid from Citibank'. Combining instead with Standard Chartered seemed to them a much more congenial prospect. Midland's Chief Executive, Geoffrey Taylor, candidly confessed to McWilliam at a private lunch together in May 1984 'that he would like to see a full merger'; but they both had to acknowledge little could be done 'while the Crocker situation is so bad'.[39]

The hottest prospect still seemed to be a revival of the plan for a full-blown merger with the Royal Bank of Scotland. In truth, egged on by a few senior journalists from time to time, Peter Graham had never really abandoned the idea.[40] Thoughts of a renewed campaign in Edinburgh were abruptly brought to a head in April 1984, when the London management of Citibank, out of the blue, proposed a joint bid for the Scottish clearer. Like Standard Chartered, the giant New York bank was eager to find a quick way of expanding in the UK High Street. Sharing out RBS's businesses between them, it was suggested, might suit both banks very well. McWilliam needed little persuading. ('It is really just what the doctor ordered!'[41]) Three weeks of hectic preparations followed. But when Standard Chartered's Board assembled late one afternoon in May to debate the next step, the non-Executive Directors yet again drew back:

> By 8 pm a clear consensus had emerged that directors did not like the notion of an aggressive carve-up; [they] thought there would be much political uproar and did not believe it would succeed. Final conclusion was not even to test the matter with B of E. What was even more depressing was the readiness with which several directors appeared to contemplate the desirability of a merger with one of the clearers and hence to abandon the standard of independence.[42]

Surprisingly, this rejection by the Board was not quite the end of the RBS story. At the Leeds Castle strategy conference a few months later, it was still being considered a live option – though some thought it merely a welcome distraction from deeper problems. Jarecki the psychotherapist noted wryly: 'in my former life I often saw couples with marital problems who had, or adopted, a baby as a "solution": it almost never worked'.[43] Graham was to go on yearning for a tie-up with the Scots for the next four years.* As for McWilliam, meanwhile, what really troubled him about the Board discussion of 2 May 1984 was less the timidity over the RBS plan than the readiness of some of the Directors, made explicit at that meeting, to prefer a merger with one of the clearers, whatever the

---

* Thus in March 1986, albeit in rather altered circumstances, McWilliam found himself pressed by Graham into meeting the RBS Chief Executive at a hotel bar in Venice. The two of them were taking an Easter break in the city. Graham 'was most anxious that I made contact with Sir Michael Herries. This I did and arranged to meet him for a Campari.' Herries responded sufficiently warmly to the idea of a joint venture for the two banks in the US for a further meeting to be arranged at his London flat a few days later, with Graham and Lord Barber joining them. But nothing came of it: 'Clear that H and co still like the notion of a merger but feel that the time is not right for perhaps two years.' (McWilliam Diary, 29 March and 3 April 1986, MMcW Papers.)

cost to Standard Chartered's independence. McWilliam was drawing a fine line here between what he considered the acceptable and unacceptable categories of merger partner, and perhaps – as later events would suggest – the distinction was overly subtle for some of his Boardroom colleagues. He drew some comfort immediately afterwards, anyway, from conversations with colleagues who were as opposed as himself to any talk of selling the bank ('Later talked to [David Millar] where we regretted the absence of corporate patriotism . . .'[44]). But the shift of mood at the top was unmistakeable.

A notably forthright advocate of the case for merging with one of the clearers was the Chief Financial Officer, Stuart Tarrant. He supported the idea for the same reason that he had opposed the proposed bids for both Continental Illinois and RBS: he saw the Group's balance sheet as weak, likely to be weakened much further by any outright acquisition, and in the last resort too weak to sustain the Group's ambitions to expand in the UK and Europe as a rival to the Big Four. The problem, in his view, was 'capital adequacy', or rather inadequacy – that is, a shortage of enough freely available equity capital in proportion to total assets to ensure that the ratio between them fully complied with market expectations in general and the requirements of the Bank of England in particular. As already noted, Tarrant had penned several anxious papers on this by early 1983. Talk of strategic acquisitions merely exacerbated his understandable concerns, and these grew steadily through 1984. Very much his own man, Tarrant was never slow to disparage the performance of any colleague he regarded as essentially second-rate – a bracket that sometimes seemed to include most of his peers in Clements Lane – and his relations with McWilliam were often brittle, at best. They were not improved in February 1985 when Tarrant slipped into the Bank of England, without telling his Managing Director first, to complain about the latest acquisition plans under consideration by the Board.[45] A few days later McWilliam 'tackled SST on his recent conduct in fairly blunt terms', but made no move to replace him. 'Interestingly he did not seek confrontation, managed to apologise and we eventually agreed a line for the Board.'[46] It was a bizarre episode, and perhaps an ominous portent. When the Directors later went ahead and discussed these same plans, anyway, Tarrant fired off an angry missive at McWilliam, copied to all their senior colleagues:

> [I warned in January that the Group] cannot sustain any further increase in business levels generated either internally or by acquisition unless financed by compensating disposals/contractions . . . I would have thought that any Board in these circumstances would expect a full discussion on

financial strategy . . . I am very unhappy at the way the Group's capital adequacy position had been presented . . . I am extremely concerned at the prospect of two acquisitions which will further aggravate the Group capital adequacy situation.[47]

The very next month, however, Tarrant agreed to set aside his protests when McWilliam tabled yet another merger idea – this one much more in keeping with Tarrant's own thinking.

At the end of January 1985, Midland Bank had disclosed losses at its Crocker National subsidiary that were shocking enough, ironically, to have dispelled much of the uncertainty hanging over the clearer. The markets were now more than half-convinced that the Midland was destined to be on the receiving end of a takeover. With active support from Sir Leslie Fletcher – who as Deputy Chairman of the Group, as well as Chairman of SCMB, was the most senior non-executive behind Peter Graham (who was *Senior* Deputy Chairman) – McWilliam began mulling over those 1984 discussions with the Midland's Geoffrey Taylor. Perhaps there was now a rare opportunity to engineer the acquisition of one of the clearers, on Standard Chartered's own terms. The logic of such a move, potentially resolving the Group's strategic dilemma in the UK in some style, was evident enough to win the support in March of the Leeds Castle brigade. Over a weekend session at a different Kent castle – Hever, childhood home of the ill-fated Anne Boleyn – StanBIC's Managing Director Conrad Strauss pushed ahead the resulting discussion:

> Following a strong lead from Strauss, there was a consensus for the notion that we need to make a major move in the UK by acquiring Midland Bank, if we intend to have credibility as a major international bank. The idea is that it should be opportunistic in the sense of there being a major sell-off of non-essential assets.[48]

McWilliam seems to have hesitated, not doubting the prize but unsure whether it was really attainable. ('It would be a wonder if we can pull it off.'[49]) Then, early in June 1985, he was approached for a second time by the UK boss of Citibank, Kent Price. It was a year since their plan to bid jointly for RBS had been aborted. Now Price suggested they join forces again, to plot a shared bid for the Midland. By the end of the month, enough homework had been completed for Barber and Graham to give a green light for detailed talks. McWilliam met Geoffrey Taylor for a discussion on 26 June: 'This was almost an anti-climax in the sense that [Taylor] not only welcomed the approach but seemed to agree with the federal concept, to sale of Crocker and not to take umbrage at the Citibank aspect. Almost too good to be true.'[50] Alas, it was indeed too good: after twelve more days, during which McWilliam spent many hours with Barber and Graham debating the optimal line-up for the post-acquisition board-room, name by name, Taylor called in person at McWilliam's office on 9 July with glum news. He had to report that, unfortunately, his Board had vetoed the deal until after the Crocker imbroglio was finally resolved. The resulting delay was expected to last at least several months.*

McWilliam was philosophical about this latest setback ('After all the hammering Midland has received, it is hard to blame them for playing safe'[51]). Perhaps he was also feeling more sanguine, by July 1985, about the Group's general prospects. The UK banking businesses were looking more robust. To judge by some cheering brokers' reports, the Group's strategic aims were at last gaining some credibility with the analysts. And since the spring, a vital breakthrough had been made on capital adequacy. The City's corporate bankers had invented a bond that carried no fixed maturity. Because this 'Primary Capital Floating Rate Note' never needed repaying, it was classified by the regulators as equity rather than debt. The Group had put out two of them in May – the first was the largest euro-sterling bond yet floated – and the proceeds had hugely improved its key ratios. Two more bonds were to follow in the coming months, transform-ing the balance sheet: 'free capital' was to end the year equivalent to 8.4 per cent of deposits, up from 5.5 per cent a year earlier and well beyond the Bank of England's recommended 6 per cent. Nor was this the only way in which Standard Chartered's financial profile had changed dramati-cally in recent months. It had already been a watershed year, too, for the Group's relationship with its subsidiary in South Africa.

3. 'CAUGHT IN THE LAAGER'

As of McWilliam's appointment in 1983, the Group still held a 58 per cent stake in StanBIC. The South African business that year accounted for more than a third of the Group's post-tax profits – even after deducting the portion due to minority shareholders[52] – but it had become the source of some intractable complications. Notwithstanding an occasionally frac-tious relationship in the 1970s, the Group continued to fund the Standard

---

* Less than three months later, the Midland announced that the Deputy Governor of the Bank of England since 1980, Sir Kit McMahon, would be leaving the Bank to become their Chairman and Chief Executive in 1986. McWilliam noted that it was 'perhaps the explanation for the inability to progress talks in the summer. The issue is presumably now a dead duck.' (Diary for 26 September 1985, MMcW Papers.)

Bank of South Africa on a prodigious scale. Loans to SBSA and other subsidiaries of StanBIC easily topped the table of lending to other banks by Standard Chartered. Since London in its own right also carried a substantial portfolio of loans to South African industrial companies, there was never any doubt that South Africa would head the list of country risks whenever this was reviewed. Handsome support from its parent company had become increasingly important to StanBIC as its access to other international lenders, including the major New York banks, had shrivelled in the face of anti-apartheid campaigns – though whether Standard Chartered could really afford to provide it was becoming a moot point.[53] Another snag concerned the balance sheet of StanBIC's subsidiary, the Standard Bank of South Africa itself. The capital ratios demanded by the Reserve Bank of South Africa were far less onerous than those required by the Bank of England. Naturally, SBSA managed its balance sheet to comply with the regulators' wishes in Pretoria, not London. However, the consolidation of StanBIC's generously leveraged finances with its own duly produced a significant weakening of Standard Chartered's ratios.* And of course the burden on the Group's balance sheet in London could only grow heavier if the Board in Johannesburg elected to try expanding StanBIC's business, incurring yet more debt in the process (and external borrowings by SBSA were always guaranteed, in the last resort, from the UK). Expansion was certainly in prospect: South Africa's economy was expanding at a remarkable rate in 1983–4, and StanBIC's Directors were also keen to expand its presence in South Africa's insurance industry.

Here was a Gordian knot indeed. To slice through it, and re-shape the Group balance sheet overnight, the Board in London needed only to reduce its stake in StanBIC to less than 50 per cent and so avert the consolidation of the South African finances. If it chose to disinvest altogether, the Group could even shed any moral obligation to provide capital support. Yet contemplating this radical set of options continued, as for so many decades past, to prompt deep misgivings. The view taken in Clements Lane under Peter Graham had been best articulated by a succinct paper that Graham himself wrote for the Board in October 1980.[54] The Group had already given the South African authorities a commitment, four years earlier, that Standard Chartered would reduce its stake 'to a

---

* Of the Standard Chartered Group's global top twenty corporate borrowers in March 1983, no fewer than eight were South African – and virtually all of the money advanced to them had been made as loans by SBSA. They included the Barlow Group, South African Breweries, Iscor Group and – as Standard Chartered's single largest borrower of all – the Anglo-American Corporation. ('Major Group Corporate Limits' by Peter Graham, Memorandum for the Board Meeting of 12 April 1983, SCB Box 1721.)

level no greater than 50 per cent by the year 1986 at the latest'.[55] But in the summer of 1980 a suggestion had 'emanated' from South Africa (his paper gave no names) that an accelerated disinvestment would be welcome. Graham strongly advised against it. For StanBIC, he saw no governance benefits at all, since in practice it already enjoyed complete autonomy; but it could curtail the South African bank's future access to capital, and might well encourage the anti-apartheid lobby by demonstrating how easily foreign investors in the country could be scared off. For Standard Chartered, meanwhile, turning the wholly-consolidated StanBIC into a mere associate company would knock about 20 per cent off total assets ('clearly our ranking in terms of world size and standing would drop appreciably') while reducing net income by about £2 million a year and leaving the Group with a sizeable tax bill. Graham assured his colleagues that they were under no pressure whatever from Pretoria ('if 1986 was looked upon as being inconvenient, then the South African authorities would see no difficulty in granting an extension') and urged them to set their faces against any dilution.

This remained the position in 1983, and it undoubtedly chafed with StanBIC's top men. When the Chairman, Ian Mackenzie, visited London with his colleagues for the Group's annual South African Committee Review in May 1983, it seemed briefly as though a reappraisal might be due. The South Africans stressed the reality of their Government's long-standing 1986 deadline. It was part of an argument they pushed hard, for SBSA to have its own branch in the City (a proposal resisted by the Bank of England). But three weeks later, another delegation to London sang a different tune, as McWilliam reported in his diary:

> An important meeting with Governor and Deputy Governor of South Africa Reserve Bank, with Lord Barber. We asked about the 1986 'deadline' for reducing our South African stake to 50 per cent and to our astonishment were told there was no such thing and we could make up our own minds whether we did anything at all! This is directly contrary to the advice of our own people ... When Lord Barber phoned Mackenzie, there was audible back-tracking and one must conclude that it suits StanBIC to get us down.[56]

Attempts to clarify Pretoria's position over the following weeks were a source of some embarrassment for StanBIC's executives. They suggested the Reserve Bank had simply misunderstood the official policy. Mackenzie said he would talk to Ministers about the deadline, an offer that was not well received by Barber.[57] Matters were only finally settled when the Minister of Finance, Frank Horwood, himself wrote to Barber in August 1983 to agree that the Group could retain its 58 per cent stake and would

have until 1991 to comply with the dilution request ('Red faces in Stan-
BIC!' recorded McWilliam).[58]

McWilliam's own arrival at the helm seemed at first to presage a significant strengthening of ties. An East African by birth who felt a
considerable affinity with South Africans, he had no illusions that London
could begin again to delve into the domestic management of SBSA. The
days when Cyril Hamilton had spent weeks at a time in Johannesburg
advising on personnel issues were long gone. But McWilliam admired what
had been achieved in South Africa under the executive leadership since
1974 of Henri de Villiers, an unassuming former merchant banker with
whom he had much in common, personally and professionally. De Villiers
was a corporate strategist of rare acumen – but had also made SBSA a
model of innovative consumer banking, far ahead of most other large
commercial banks in the application of computerized systems.* The figures for StanBIC's 1980–83 performance outshone those for the rest of
the Group by almost every yardstick.[59] It struck McWilliam as odd to see
Standard Chartered deriving so little benefit from this. Visiting Johannesburg in August 1983 to attend a StanBIC strategic conference – and
to make a presentation on his own priorities – he made a private note:
'One thing to emerge rather clearly . . . is the absence of any SCB Group
dimension to their thinking, yet there are so many points of interaction –
on marketing, funding, systems, people, etc.'[60] He began at once to work
for closer ties, a shift of approach to which de Villiers responded in kind.
He and McWilliam exchanged regular visits, collaborated on Group strategy sessions and encouraged renewed links on the staffing front where
training secondments had been allowed to lapse some years earlier. Indeed,
at de Villiers' request, McWilliam facilitated the secondment of John
Davidson, the Group's General Manager for Africa since leaving Harare,
to move to Johannesburg as a senior executive of SBSA. (Davidson became
its Managing Director in 1985, the same year that Ian Mackenzie retired,
de Villiers took the StanBIC chair and Conrad Strauss stepped up as
StanBIC's Managing Director.) Another, less elevated move saw the General Manager of Personnel at SBSA, Henry Fabian, visit London in
1984 and 1985 in an advisory capacity. (He would later join the Group as
a full-time executive.) These were hardly seismic developments – but they
did reflect a palpable warming of relations. And at a time when the rest

---

* The Standard's first computer, an IBM 360, had been installed in Johannesburg's Harrison
Street South branch in 1968. But South Africa is a vast country: not until 1985 was the entire
branch network put on-line, with the hooking up of the branch at Hoedspruit in the Lowveld
on the edge of the Kruger Park. (See Richard Steyn and Francis Antonie, *Hoisting the Standard*, pp. 96–9.)

of the world seemed intent on freezing South Africa out, this was welcome indeed in Johannesburg. No one there was calling now for the old 50 per cent deadline to be heeded.

None of this alleviated the capital adequacy conundrum; in fact, quite the opposite. Through the course of 1984, SBSA went on expanding its loan book – building positions in the foreign exchange market, too, that occasionally moved the head of the Group's Treasury operations, Alan Orsich, to express some concern – and McWilliam had to endure a succession of meetings with the Bank of England to talk about the implications.[61] With each conversation, the pressure on the Group to curtail its South African exposure grew a little less gentle. By October 1984, Bank of England officials were reportedly in touch with their counterparts in Pretoria to confer about the prospective implications of a sell-down decision.[62] Inside Clements Lane – now nearing the end of its days as the Group's Head Office – the Directors agonized for months. None wanted their tenure on the Board to coincide with the rupture of such a long-defended relationship. Conspicuously absent from the records of the time is any indication that political objections to its involvement with South Africa had any bearing at all on the debate in London (though it was by now ensuring an uncomfortable hour or so of hostile questions for Anthony Barber at every AGM). The financial squeeze, however, was becoming intolerable. As Tarrant put it in a typically forthright paper for the Board towards the end of 1984, the Group had a very large subsidiary that was 'under-capitalised by normal prudential criteria and is therefore perceived to be "over-trading" '.[63] It was a contentious way of summing up the situation, but there was no denying that the South African business was growing at a pace the Group balance sheet could not sustain.

By the start of 1985, tentative discussions had accordingly begun with a prospective buyer of the Group's shares in StanBIC. This was Donald Gordon, a towering figure in South African financial circles and the chairman of the country's largest life assurance business, Liberty Life, which he himself had founded in 1957. A clear exposition of all the corporate cross-holdings in Gordon's financial empire by the end of 1978 would require a short chapter of its own. Suffice to say, at his invitation StanBIC had that year taken a 25 per cent stake in 'LibLife'. Since then, Gordon, Ian Mackenzie and Henri de Villiers had emerged as a kind of de facto triumvirate, effectively controlling the fortunes of LibLife and StanBIC, and entering into a rapport that was leading, step by step, to a formal alliance between their two institutions. This had not evolved to date without some friction between Johannesburg and London. Step Two had involved a complex transaction in 1983, by which StanBIC's holding in

LibLife was raised from 25 to 50 per cent. Standard Chartered's Board had made clear its opposition to the deal ('too expensive, poor timing and nothing in it for SCB'[64]), and only relented after McWilliam had attended a Board discussion in Johannesburg, in a dissenting minority of one, and been persuaded to back the deal.[65] One of its many ramifications was a reshuffling of StanBIC's equity. The parental stake slipped again, from 58 to 52 per cent, while Gordon emerged with a 10 per cent stake. More than that, it became evident that Gordon saw himself – and was surely seen by Mackenzie and de Villiers, too – as a future controlling shareholder in place of StanBIC's erstwhile imperial parent.[66]

The South African story reached another critical point in the early months of 1985. StanBIC's lending in 1984 had grown by more than 50 per cent: its total assets had shot up to R15.7 billion against R10.8 billion a year earlier.[67] The resulting strain on the South African subsidiary's finances more than accounted for a substantial capital deficit on Standard Chartered's consolidated balance sheet, which left the Group about £137 million short of the equity needed to satisfy the Bank of England's principal ratio.[68] In February McWilliam flew down to Johannesburg again, this time to present a full analysis of the key ratios to Mackenzie, de Villiers and Strauss, and to urge remedial action. The South Africans were by now reluctant to see a fall in Standard Chartered's stake, at least for the time being. South Africa's growing political isolation was certainly weighing on their minds, after a sensational tour of the country by Senator Edward Kennedy in January, meeting Black activist leaders. But the logic of the situation was inescapable. 'Whereas their own preference would have been to adapt more gradually,' in the words of McWilliam's subsequent paper for the Board, 'it was entirely accepted that they had an obligation to take action now in order to ease the Group position.'[69] Proposals were drawn up accordingly, for StanBIC to press ahead with the largest rights issue ever made by a South African bank – and for Standard Chartered to forego its entitlement to invest in the new shares. Its stake in StanBIC would thereupon drop to 42.06 per cent. On his return to London, McWilliam pushed ahead quickly and squared these plans with his colleagues within days, for final Board approval on 19 February 1985. 'Then phoned Johannesburg and spoke to Strauss and Mackenzie', as McWilliam confided to his diary; 'they were a bit taken aback . . .'[70]

Several more weeks of tense negotiation were still required. Donald Gordon made repeated visits to London, full of ingenious schemes whereby the Group might join him in extending his financial empire outside South Africa. (None were taken up.) Arrangements for a transfer of the Group's forfeited shares to LibLife, which was to share them with the huge mining conglomerate founded by Cecil Rhodes, Consolidated Gold Fields of South Africa, were fraught with technical difficulties. Resolving these was made no easier by several attempts to extract some cash from Gordon in exchange for the Group's loss of control. (None was forthcoming.) And throughout the process, StanBIC's senior men were anxious above all to secure a guarantee that no third party would suddenly be sprung on them as a new controlling shareholder. Not for the first time, McWilliam had some difficulty persuading all of his Boardroom colleagues to adhere to the agreed line but he himself felt clear about what was at stake: 'the key point is that StanBIC regard Liberty as their means of controlling their destiny as we float down and that we must not mess up this relationship [with Gordon] – or ours with StanBIC'.[71] Assurances were given privately that Standard Chartered would not cut its stake below 35 per cent, although both sides conspicuously drew back from making any public announcement to this effect. Then Barber and McWilliam returned to Johannesburg for news of the Group's reduced shareholding to be unveiled there on 2 April. At a meeting of the StanBIC Board, one Director thought it 'a sad day for South Africa'.[72] But the local media coverage was upbeat; and in the City of London the Group's shares jumped 5 per cent.

There followed a brief few months during which Standard Chartered's exposure to South Africa faded briefly from the news. The respite ended in explosive fashion in July. Violent demonstrations plunged the country into its most severe political crisis since 1960. A breakdown of civic order in many of the Republic's black townships provoked local declarations by the Government of a State of Emergency, and marked a significant escalation of the internecine conflict over apartheid. When the President, P. W. Botha, failed to signal any fundamental change of direction in a policy address that was notoriously labelled his Rubicon Speech – he was expected to cross the proverbial river in the right direction, but spoke instead of no way back for apartheid – overseas perceptions of South Africa took a disastrous turn. Its plight made the front cover of *Time* magazine at the beginning of August, and began genuinely to alarm foreign investors. At Chase Manhattan, David Rockefeller had long since abandoned his optimistic stance of the 1960s. It was Rockefeller who now announced that Chase would not be rolling over its short-term loans to the Republic or making new corporate advances there. The news hit South Africa's finances hard. All the US banks drew back, and the rand fell heavily. About 60 per cent of South Africa's foreign debt comprised short-term borrowings, and economists began to contemplate the unprecedented phenomenon of a country combining a strong balance of payments with national insolvency. Reviewing the half-year results of Standard

Chartered, the Lex Column of the *Financial Times* in August carried a waspish suggestion that, in the shadow of events in South Africa, the Group's shares 'now show every sign of being a special situation' (the standard City euphemism for investment opportunities offering high rewards for off-the-scale risks).[73] The dividend yield on them, at 9.5 per cent, actually exceeded the yield on the Midland Bank's Crocker-crocked stock. The Lex headline was 'STANDARD CAUGHT IN THE LAAGER'. A week later, on 28 August, Pretoria announced a three-day halt to all domestic stock market and foreign-exchange trading, the introduction of exchange controls on the rand and a four-month moratorium on the repayment of foreign debts. Inevitably, the instant impact of these drastic measures caused StanBIC itself considerable difficulties in overseas markets, and especially in New York where it was suddenly short of funds it needed to fulfil immediate cash settlements. Standard Chartered stepped in to rescue the situation, providing overnight liquidity just as it might have done when still StanBIC's parent. This, noted McWilliam, 'earned us enormous gratitude in Johannesburg: Davidson said it was a pleasure being an SCB officer there today and Strauss phoned to express his appreciation'.[74] But its support for StanBIC was a growing worry for the Group's investors. They were apprehensive that, notwithstanding the dilution of its stake, Standard Chartered might find itself increasingly drawn into breaching the gaps in StanBIC's finances left by the withdrawal of other banks.[75]

Over the next several months, the Group's strong identification with South Africa proved deeply damaging. Investors took fright at the speed of the rand's depreciation: from R2.30 to the pound, it was soon plunging towards R3.80. Whatever the short-term gains in the rand/sterling exchange market – and some huge foreign-exchange profits were certainly booked, both in London and in Johannesburg – Group earnings for the full year seemed certain to be badly dented. Intense speculation in the City about Standard Chartered's true exposure to the political crisis of the apartheid regime forced the Board, in September, to make a clean breast of the numbers. A total loan book was disclosed of approximately $1.4 billion, of which $600 million was on loan to StanBIC with the rest comprising loans to South African third parties.[76] This stemmed the speculation, at the cost of confirming some of the gloomier analysts' assessments. Nor, of course, did full disclosure of the South African dimension do anything to relieve political pressure from the anti-apartheid lobbies. Here, too, attitudes to the Group were growing steadily more hostile. Most of its critics saw it simply as supportive of repressive Government policies in the Republic. It would surely have caused the anti-apartheid campaigners some surprise, to say the least, had publicity been given to the identity of the very first guests entertained in the Board dining room of the new Group Head Office just opened at 38 Bishopsgate, in October 1985. They were Oliver Tambo and Thabo Mbeki, both leading figures of the African National Congress, outlawed in South Africa. They were there as guests of APEG, a private dining group made up of executives from the leading UK companies with interests in Africa, with which McWilliam had been involved for many years and which held events at the bank occasionally under his auspices.[77] 'It was a remarkable occasion' noted McWilliam afterwards, 'in that while sticking to hard sanctions and the need for violent opposition, Tambo largely disarmed us by his manner, historical grasp and reasoning approach. I'm sure we all had a different view of [the] ANC by the end of the evening. His colleague, Mbeki, was also impressive.'[78] Perhaps, after all, a post-apartheid regime might yet emerge that would one day vindicate the Group's long-standing reluctance to let political considerations dictate a withdrawal from South Africa.

If this brought him any consolation, it can hardly have allayed for long McWilliam's concern over the more immediate financial impact of the South African crisis. A reappraisal of the Group's exposure seemed to be underpinning a broader change of attitude in the City towards its prospects. With gathering conviction, journalists and market analysts alike began referring to Standard Chartered's participation in Big Bang in disparaging terms. With each passing month, in fact, it was deemed less likely to be the architect of some bold new combination of its own than a key component of someone else's plans, with or without the bank's connivance. In Bishopsgate, there was a palpable unease over this unmistakeable shift in the wind. On 27 November, the Board dining room received another notable visitor, a Malaysian businessman who had risen from a humble background to acquire enormous wealth, courtesy of booming property values in Kuala Lumpur and Singapore:

> An intriguing lunch when we entertained Khoo Teck Puat, the great lone financier from Singapore, who has just bought a key stake in Exco [one of the City's leading money-brokers] and might well mount a full bid. He is very interested in the UK financial sector and talked of buying into Midland and into Royal Bank. We were all wondering about his intentions regarding SCB.[79]

In the weeks that followed the visit by Khoo Teck Puat, this unease turned to acute anxiety. It was becoming plain to everyone in Bishopsgate that Standard Chartered might any day be the target of a hostile bid.

4. ON RED ALERT

By the end of January 1986, Lord Barber had appointed McWilliam and Tarrant to a 'Defence Committee' of the Board alongside Peter Graham and four other non-Executive Directors. It was a dramatic acknowledgement that, after years of contemplating possible bids of their own devising, the tables had been turned with a shocking suddenness. Their slightly desperate sense of vulnerability stemmed first and foremost from the abysmal political situation in South Africa, and its financial ramifications. But the Group now seemed dogged by ill fortune. Alongside the rand's decline, the US dollar had also fallen sharply (closing 1985 at $1.45 to the pound, down from $1.16 twelve months earlier), and the two depreciations together had effectively wiped out a more than respectable year's growth in rand/dollar terms, and left 1985's sterling profits devoid of any growth at all. This in turn had ensured a dismal year for the bank's shares, which by the end of 1985 were trading at a 50-per-cent discount to their asset value. (Barclays' shares, by contrast, were not far short of matching their asset value.) The 1985 results had been especially depressing, not to say alarming, given all the endless strategic appraisals of 1983–4. And here, perhaps, was the real clue to the Boardroom atmosphere in the New Year. Many of the Directors, including the Chairman, seemed to be tiring of their Managing Director's penchant for analysis and long-term planning. It was far from evident to them, for example, that McWilliam's 'federalist' initiative had yet done much to improve results in the field, where the calibre of the bank's management was causing growing disquiet. In south-east Asia, in particular, operations seemed to have been plagued for months by a stream of discouraging stories and a trail of corporate failures that had prompted a worrying rise in the bank's exposure to bad debts.*

---

* Fears of a deep recession in Malaysia and Singapore had been aggravated by the effective bankruptcy of the International Tin Council (ITC), which since the 1950s had been 'stabilizing' prices on the tin market by soaking up surplus stocks from time to time. The ITC in October 1985 had run out of funds, and was short of £550 million to pay for purchases of tin to which it was legally committed. As one of its principal creditors, owed about £10 million, Standard Chartered agreed to lead a rescue. It was Peter Graham who co-ordinated much of the work behind a plan that was presented to the Council, and the twenty-two member states behind it, in mid-November. Over the next four months, and despite all of Graham's prodigious efforts (for which he was widely praised), disagreements between the main parties proved to be insurmountable. The ITC's affairs had eventually to be dismantled in the courts – where the Standard Chartered again led the way, with a UK High Court action in April 1986 that secured the repayment of its entire loan thanks to a watertight contract. It was the only creditor to escape unscathed. (This episode was the first occasion on which the Group

(Eventually forced into liquidation, Pan-Electric's collapse left the Singapore branch with a loss of around £30 million.[80]) Shortly before Christmas 1985, McWilliam had circulated the final version of his Corporate Plan. By comparison with any paper put to the Directors in the past, it was a Wagnerian effort on which McWilliam himself had spent huge amounts of time over the past eighteen months. Days later it was tabled formally for the Directors. Their reaction was less than acclamatory:

> The big day of presenting the Corporate Plan to the Board was a rather dispiriting flop. Pennock and Loudon did not come and the discussion was niggling in the main. Also we did not get through the document and Barber was unprepared to press on, so the whole thing is held over till 7th January . . . All rather depressing.[81]

After the follow-up meeting on the 7th, McWilliam recorded that there had been a 'much better discussion than last time and a broad endorsement of what we are up to'. But the following week the Chief Financial Officer put a memorandum to the Board reviewing the latest estimate of 1985's profits and setting out the budget for the coming twelve months, which of course took account of the Plan. 'Earnings per share budgeted for 1986 . . . reflect a trend of nil growth and inevitably this will not be acceptable in the market.'[82] As a comment on the Corporate Plan's usefulness as a cure for the City's shrinking confidence in the Group, Stuart Tarrant's verdict could hardly have been terser. The task facing the Defence Committee, set up by Barber at the end of the month, was to find an alternative and faster-acting remedy.

One slightly startling proposal was that the Directors should buy the Group themselves, taking it into private ownership with heroic levels of debt on the balance sheet. In the City, as on Wall Street, the concept of the 'management buy-out' (MBO) was much in vogue, and McWilliam had already received several discreet notes on the topic in recent months from one of Wall Street's leading investment banks, Goldman Sachs. This firm was just finding its way into the City's Mergers & Acquisitions (M&A) sector and was intent on winning mandates to help defend company boards in fear of predators. It brought a bold and imaginative approach to the work that transcended anything generally offered by the traditional British merchant banks. The latter were generally content to produce a revised profits forecast for the defending company, then leave

---

was advised by Nigel Boardman of solicitors Slaughter and May, who in time would come to be regarded by most of his contemporaries as the leading City lawyer of his generation. He would remain the Group's principal legal adviser through the next three decades.)

the market to dictate the outcome. Goldman was ready to adopt any tactic it thought might prevail – typically starting with a forensic evaluation of its client's balance sheet and an assessment of how the calculated value could best be realized for shareholders. Their 'no-holds barred' audacity delighted McWilliam – and the MBO idea drew an enthusiastic response from Graham, too.[83] It went down much less well with Barber and the rest of the Defence Committee. Two of its members, Sir Leslie Fletcher and Philip Robinson, were directors of Schroders, the blue-blooded merchant bank that was still the formal adviser to the Group, and they welcomed the notion of a role for Goldman as warmly as might have been expected. The other two members of the Committee – Sir Idwal Pugh, a retired Whitehall Permanent Secretary who had been Parliamentary Ombudsman in the 1970s and had come on to the Board via the acquisition of the Hodge Group; and John Page, a former Chief Cashier at the Bank of England – were both Directors of traditional building societies (the Halifax and the Nationwide respectively) and seemed deeply suspicious of any advice from Wall Street bankers as a matter of principle. By the middle of February it was clear that a majority of the Committee's members, notably including Tarrant, saw no practical alternative but to seek out a merger with one of the clearers. Only with some reluctance did the Committee agree to sit through a presentation by Goldman's American team leader, Bob Hamburger. The response filled McWilliam with gloom:

> Everyone agreed it was very ably done; but over a sandwich lunch the atmosphere soured: anti-Americanism surfaced; [Barber] was openly hostile to the buy-out defence; I clashed with [Barber] and with [Tarrant] on the commitment to remain independent . . . What now? The only action agreed is that Stuart and Robinson will seek to assemble a dossier of defence data. I suppose the probability is that Schroders will be called in, without Goldmans, and that soundings will be made for a white knight. The combination of [Tarrant] positively wanting to see us merged into a clearer, plus an elderly Board with no spunk for a fight, is daunting and it is hard not to feel that our days of independence are numbered.[84]

Late that same February afternoon, news broke that Lloyds Bank had contracted to sell its only US business, a subsidiary in California. The implication, that Lloyds would soon be free to bid for another bank with US operations of its own without snaring itself in a US regulatory net, was lost on no one. Pegasus was back. Next day, McWilliam cancelled plans for a skiing holiday and warned Peter Graham that they were all 'on Red Alert'.[85]

The situation had its ironies, for the Group's progress since the turn of

1986 had seen several executive initiatives that smacked of anything but a lack of self-confidence. In Europe, Peter McSloy was busy recruiting trading teams from other (mostly American) banks that had grown disillusioned with their own forays into the European marketplace. In the Far East, project managers had been appointed to proceed at last with that comprehensive redevelopment of the bank's site at 4/4a Des Voeux Road in Hong Kong – erecting a forty-five-storey new building with a striking modern design – after almost two years of deliberation over the alternative merits of a cut-price refurbishment.[86] In London and New York, the restructuring of the Mocatta Group, aborted in 1982, had since January been resuscitated with Jarecki's blessing: plans were underway to lift Standard Chartered's stake in the combined UK/US bullion-dealing business up to 80 per cent, at a net cost of £121 million based on a valuation representing roughly a 50 per cent premium to the business's net worth.[87] Even more strikingly assertive, McWilliam had won the Board's approval for a most unusual piece of new business, likely to attract extraordinary levels of publicity. Among the Group's more colourful clients was the Australian financier Robert Holmes à Court, one of the most active (and vilified) of the 'corporate raiders' turning over apple carts in the equity markets of the 1980s. He had devised a scheme whereby his privately owned Bell Group might capture control of BHP, the mining-to-steel-manufacturing giant that was the largest company in Australia. The market arithmetic left him needing £1 billion in cash, to be secured against BHP shares, which McWilliam had agreed by the end of January could be provided as a stand-by facility. It was intended that £750 million would be raised from a syndicate of other banks, but that still left Standard Chartered with an eye-watering commitment – and 'an obvious risk of black-listing by BHP' in the event of a defeat for Holmes à Court.[88] If he prevailed, on the other hand, there was the prospect of a restructuring of BHP's banking relationships and a much expanded role for Standard Chartered, which would be a timely boost for its profile in Australia.*

---

* The Group had had a small merchant bank and a money-market trading business in Australia for some years, with offices in all the state capitals, but had been trying since 1983 to persuade the authorities to grant it a full banking licence – an objective actively promoted by the merchant bank's forceful Chairman, Terry Attwood, in the face of occasional wavering in London and regulatory delays in Australia. Strong support from the Premier of South Australia stiffened London's resolve, and plans were in place by the end of 1984 for a full bank with a Head Office in Adelaide, subject to licensing. The Federal Government – making much the same mistake as the colonial authorities in the 1850s – then opened up the sector rather too enthusiastically: it invited no fewer than sixteen foreign banks to apply for licences, which significantly detracted from their appeal. By early 1986, though, Standard Chartered's Australian activities had been in the throes of preparatory restructuring for almost a year

And March brought the opportunity for a little glamour and some useful bits of theatre on the home front. Senior managers from all over the world were invited to the new Head Office at 38 Bishopsgate for another Annual Strategy Conference. (The printed List of Delegates included ninety-five smiling faces – just fourteen of them evidencing progress with indigenization.) Nine days later, the Queen descended on 38 Bishopsgate for a hugely successful opening ceremony and was treated to her very own series of five royal presentations on the bank's activities.

By March 1986, however, the schism within the Defence Committee over the best way forward had reached unsustainable levels of tension. Rumours of an imminent bid were wafting through the markets, from Hong Kong to Wall Street. Some spoke of a move by the Australia and New Zealand Banking Group (ANZ), others of a consortium led from New York by American Express. The previous November's visitor from Singapore, Khoo Teck Puat, called on Goldman Sachs in the Far East and openly declared his intention of accumulating over time a 30 per cent stake in the bank. None of this was remotely in line with an outcome acceptable to the Defence Committee. The one point on which all had agreed early in January was 'the overriding strategic need for a larger UK sterling business base . . . with a target of 50 per cent profits by 1990 [which] could not be achieved through organic growth alone'.[89] While the Managing Director turned his mind to a list of some eleven possible steps towards that target – none of them entailing a full-scale merger with anyone – others on the Committee resolved, as McWilliam had feared they might, to find a 'white knight' who could vanquish the foreigners and bring Standard Chartered home to the City of London. There were really only two viable candidates for the role. At a special session of the Defence Committee late in March, Peter Graham as ever pressed the case for renewed talks with the Royal Bank of Scotland – hence that chat over a campari between McWilliam and Herries in Venice – but 'the other lobby went for Lloyds'.[90]

Anthony Barber now decided the time had come for him to nudge things along. Colleagues were bemoaning what McWilliam described privately as their Chairman's 'lack of bias for action'. For many weeks, Barber had been understandably distracted by his involvement in a seven-man 'Eminent Persons Group', tasked by the Commonwealth with visiting

---

and there was no turning back. The duly licensed new commercial bank was finally launched in April 1986, with a 30-per-cent shareholding for the South Australia government and just under 20 per cent traded on the public market. What followed was not a happy story, as the Adelaide business raced to build up a loan portfolio among customers largely shunned by the domestic banking sector – with predictably disastrous consequences.

South Africa to find a basis for political negotiation in place of heavier Western economic sanctions.* After returning to London in mid-March, he appears to have made up his mind that a merger with Lloyds needed to happen, and the sooner the better. As he would explain in his memoirs:

> They were a very efficient domestic bank in the United Kingdom where Standard Chartered had little presence and their overseas presence complemented our own. I had known Sir Jeremy Morse, their Chairman, from way back when he was in the Bank of England and I was a Treasury Minister. I would have been quite content, in the general interest, to serve as his deputy.[91]

At some point – and exactly when can only be a matter of conjecture – Barber won confirmation from the Lloyds Board that it was intending to make a bid. (One of their non-executives was Lord Hanson, the doyen of the M&A market in the mid-1980s, who was well-known for asserting that any company with a fountain in its reception area was ripe for a takeover. The grand atrium at 38 Bishopsgate had been noted – and perhaps also the fact that the top floor of the building had been officially designated the *piano nobile*, apparently at Barber's own behest.) It would seem that Standard Chartered's Chairman then led his counterpart at Lloyds to believe a visit in person would be the most sensible way to launch talks on an amicable basis. Early on the morning of Friday 4 April, Sir Jeremy Morse duly telephoned Barber's office to ask for a short meeting. He arrived within the hour. Graham and McWilliam had meanwhile been summoned by Barber to join the discussion. The two men were appalled to realize, as soon as Jeremy Morse came into the room, that the visit was not exactly a bolt from the blue. 'We were gobsmacked', recalled McWilliam. 'Barber clearly was expecting the visit, and it was fairly clear to us that Morse and Barber had talked.'[92] But if they were taken aback, Barber himself was mortified by what happened next.

Graham and McWilliam both rejected the idea of a merger out of hand.

---

* When Barber agreed in November 1985 to serve on this body at Margaret Thatcher's request, it was misconstrued by some as a crass attempt by the Standard Chartered to hijack the initiative for its own commercial ends. In the event, though no immediate breakthrough was made with the Botha government in Pretoria, the Eminent Persons Group filed a report that would later be seen to have played its part in convincing moderate white opinion in South Africa that a basis might one day exist for political dialogue with the ANC. Barber played a prominent part in it, and his threat to resort to a Minority Report was largely responsible for persuading the EPG to drop a call for additional economic sanctions from its final text. (Anthony Barber, *Taking the Tide, A Memoir*, privately published, 1996, pp. 164–73.)

Morse beat a brisk retreat, leaving the hapless Barber to face his two perplexed colleagues. Had Graham only sided with his Chairman at this point, Standard Chartered's name must sooner or later have disappeared from the map. Instead, Graham joined McWilliam in insisting that the Board should state a bid would be unwelcome. Barber, never one to assert an executive decision, capitulated immediately. He and Graham then went round to the Bank of England to explain to the Governor what had happened. (Lloyds had given the Bank no notice of Morse's visit, fondly supposing a private chat would leave ample time later for the formalities of a bid.) According to McWilliam's diary account that evening, Barber and Graham 'were told that a merger might be "no bad thing" with Lloyds'. But Graham stood his ground. By the time the two of them returned to Bishopsgate, word of the visit had reached the market and Standard Chartered's shares had raced up to 830p (they had ended 1985 at 423p). Lloyds had no choice but to put out a press statement. Graham demanded that it make clear the initiative was entirely theirs. Standard Chartered then issued a press release, rejecting the approach unambiguously. This was publicly endorsed by the full Board on 8 April – though not until 15 April were the formal terms of the bid announced. They valued the offer at 785p, give or take a few pence, valuing the Group at just under £1.2 billion. Having set out as a putative saviour to whisk Standard Chartered from the grasp of assorted foreign predators, Lloyds had thus stumbled into launching the first ever hostile takeover bid in Britain's banking sector.

Few in the City doubted it would triumph in the end. Its earnings record and the recent market performance of its shares were both far superior to Standard Chartered's. The bid nonetheless got off to a wobbly start. It was too little, too late in several respects. The price looked mean, especially once the City had had a chance to tot up how much the Group's component parts might reasonably fetch if broken apart and sold independently. The essence of the business case for a merger – that Standard Chartered had fallen off the pace of international banking, and was wasting away a precious Asian franchise – would have been far more persuasive three years earlier. The modernization programme since 1983 was still in its early stages, and had been obscured by the South African crisis; but sufficient progress had been made for the City to be offered at least a plausible defence of the Group's current management and its strategic goals. McWilliam set about the task with extraordinary energy. He was in his element – collating presentations, refining arguments, co-ordinating the work of colleagues and of outside parties – and by late April had mobilized a campaign that surprised many press commentators and even impressed his investment banking advisers. The latter were all the more admiring of his efforts because they were privy to a delicate problem behind the scenes, which had to be concealed from the City at all costs. McWilliam was saddled on the one hand with a Chairman who hankered constantly after a rapprochement with Lloyds, and on the other with a Chief Financial Officer who was only too obviously unpersuaded that a genuine battle with Lloyds was really worth the powder. This lack of accord in the home camp added hugely to the pressures inherent in mounting the defence – which were formidable enough in themselves.

Once the bidder's formal terms were on the table, under the City's rules on such matters, the targeted management had just sixty days to persuade shareholders that rejecting the bid would not amount to forfeiting a sizeable cash windfall. So Standard Chartered had until Saturday 12 July to make its case. And McWilliam would have to make light not just of the intellectual merits (such as they were) of the bid, but also of a truth well appreciated in the City by 1986 – namely, that the great majority of hostile bids were now winning the day (as Goldman Sachs pointed out to McWilliam at the outset). There would be the usual despatch of chest-beating letters to the targeted company's shareholders from one side then the other, full of clever charts and confident predictions. The relative claims of the warring parties would be endlessly dissected in stockbrokers' reports and the financial media. Then, with just a couple of weeks to go and assuming no utterly unforeseen upset, the bidder would present shareholders with an all but irresistible embellishment of the terms initially on offer. The fact that 80 per cent of Standard Chartered's shares were held by institutional investors in the City hung like the Sword of Damocles over McWilliam's head from the start. Most of the fund managers – if true to form – would listen politely to the debate, then opt to take the money. Every ounce of effort by the defence had to be expended in the certain knowledge that most ostensible supporters in the City would prove cruelly fickle at the close.

As a former merchant banker himself, McWilliam needed no reminding of the long odds against survival – and of the futility of winning a theological disputation in the City over which bank could best manage this or that combination of overseas businesses. There was no ducking the frantic round of meetings and interviews through May that were an essential part of any defence. But McWilliam knew these would turn out to have been a sideshow if enough new, third-party investors could somehow be persuaded to acquire stakes in Standard Chartered that, in toto, would put a 50-per-cent bag beyond Lloyds' reach. He sat down with Schroders in the middle of May to talk about this tactic – or as he put it later, 'about white squires as our real back stop against the institutions'.[93] It was not a tactic to be adopted lightly, given the legal and procedural difficulties: the City's rules outlawed 'concert parties', for example, so there could be no collusion between different knights. Other problems were more mundane. Even assuming that the defence could present a compelling case for a long-term investment in the Group, any new investors at the bid-inflated share price would almost certainly have to face being heavily out of pocket for possibly a very long time, if their purchases helped to vanquish the bid. As a mere gesture of support for the bank, it might be ruinously expensive in the short term. Under the circumstances, there were really only two categories of prospective white squire – or 'white knight' in the more usual jargon – likely to be interested. Some banks or other large corporations might see investing now as a timely way of instigating a commercial alliance. (In a rather special sub-category here, perhaps, was StanBIC in South Africa – no longer owned by the Group, and legally in a position to offer vital support, as McWilliam repeatedly urged them to do.) Alternatively, some seriously wealthy individuals, with a few hundred million pounds to spare, might have a taste for the risk and potential reward while relishing the chance to influence the affairs of a big and famous bank. The general flux in the banking sector ensured a lively interest from the corporate sector; Standard Chartered's prominence in south-east Asia guaranteed a flurry of exchanges with the tycoon sector. A series of tentative proposals began to trickle in accordingly, even before the end of April. A sale of 10 per cent of the Group to Donald Gordon's Liberty Life in South Africa was agreed in principle, then abandoned a few days later.[94] Over the weeks that followed, McWilliam's diary began sporting a remarkable parade of names. The investment bankers were handling talks with several banks and conglomerates with financial divisions that had expressed a serious interest. They included Credit Suisse in Switzerland, WestPac in Australia, the British & Commonwealth Group and the tobacco giant BAT. Intermittent conversations were at the same time under way with some of the bank's more colourful individual customers, including Lonrho's Tiny Rowland as well as Singapore's Khoo Teck Puat and the Australian, Holmes à Court.* And in every corner of the

---

* Holmes à Court's plans to capture control of BHP had by this time grown more complicated. Elders IXL, run from Adelaide by his Australian rival John Elliott, had acquired 18.5 per cent of BHP on the open market. Now the Bell Group would need to capture 45 per cent of the shares in order to gain control, requiring Standard Chartered to guarantee cash resources of not A$2 million but A$2.625 million (£1.47 million). The facility was increased accordingly. (Minutes of Executive Committee, 18 April 1986.) Four days earlier, as it happens, McWilliam had been visited by another of the maverick Australians currently making

bank's network, but especially in Hong Kong and Singapore, senior managers were diligently courting less prominent but still conspicuously well-heeled customers who might each be persuaded to lock away a few hundred thousand shares.

The sheer intensity of the hunt for friendly new investors must have been deeply galling for the Chairman. Lloyds Bank was still pressing for talks on a recommended bid, and seemed to be almost the only party to whom McWilliam's door was firmly closed. A clash was inevitable, and it came in the middle of June. Morale was starting to sag in the defence camp. At a Sunday retreat on the 8th, discouraging reports about sentiment in the City, and a frustrating lack of firm commitments from prospective white knights, were glumly assessed by McWilliam and the other Directors most involved in the defence – Peter Graham, Leslie Fletcher, Philip Robinson and Robin Baillie. McWilliam noted later: 'The ghosts at the party were, of course, Lord B and SST.'[95] In fact, Barber and Tarrant were busy with their own separate plans. Barber was intent on persuading the non-Executive Directors to back his proposal for another meeting with Jeremy Morse, this time for a rather longer discussion. He sprang the idea at a Board meeting on the 13th, with open support from two of the Directors, but was eventually talked out of it by a thoroughly exasperated McWilliam.[96] Worse was to follow. Late in the afternoon on 16 June, Tarrant handed a memo to Barber setting out his views on the bid and explaining that he would himself be voting in favour of a takeover by Lloyds. Even more incendiary was a passage of the memo alleging that the Group had been offering financial support to putative white knights to help fund their share purchases – an egregious breach of company law. Next day, the Board assembled for a meeting that might have ended the battle with Lloyds – and McWilliam's career as well. Noting as much in his diary, McWilliam summarized the events of a dramatic afternoon:

> At the lunch break, Barber had the outside members to himself again and lobbied hard for support for going into immediate negotiations with [Lloyds

---

waves in the international business world, Alan Bond. He had pitched up in London 'offering to mobilise significant support through his private family corporation' (MMcW Diary, 14 April 1986). The bank's backing for Holmes à Court in the BHP battle apparently made no difference to Bond's interest in finding a role for himself in the bid defence. Within weeks, he had begun talking to the Chicago-based Pritzker family, owners of the Hyatt hotels chain, about an investment in Standard Chartered. Hence arose yet another possible lead for the bank's defence team, leaving even McWilliam occasionally bemused. ('Call from Alan Bond who has been talking to Pritzker, who has been talking to Jarecki. What a combination!' MMcW Diary 12 May 1986). The Bell Group's pursuit of BHP eventually ran foul of common sense and was quietly abandoned.

Bank]. When [Tarrant] returned from lunch, the rest of the pm was spent in trying to get him on board in various discussions. I was eventually summoned at 5 to be told by Barber in front of [Graham] and [Robinson], that they were being pressured by ST, under threat of revelations about impropriety, to abandon the defence and to start immediate talks with LB and had so agreed. No plausible evidence was produced and I said I would not accept and would make a public statement. Barber then called the Board, made his case and called on me. A vote was taken and I won 7–5, or 7–6 if ST had been there. Morse was told immediately and so was Tarrant.[97]

The vote scotched at last the notion of a meeting with Lloyds, which would inevitably have led to the Group's capitulation. As for the allegations of dodgy dealing with white knights, Tarrant told Barber two days later that he had decided not to pursue them – 'Very decent!' noted a mightily disgusted McWilliam to himself – though the details Tarrant had provided to the Board were made available by someone to the City's Takeover Panel. The Panel duly sought clarification from the bank's advisers, and they responded with a full analysis of recent business activity that might in all fairness have been misconstrued. (Most prospective white knights, almost by definition, were current customers – and no one expected the bank to freeze their accounts for the duration of the bid.) The Panel ruled that there was no case for an official inquiry, and a press release was issued by the Group to make unambiguously clear that any white knights would have nothing grey about them. Within Bishopsgate, McWilliam briefed the General Managers on the whole affair – they were 'all very loyal and indignant' – and won renewed support on the Board. Peter Graham, who had actually voted with Barber for talks, apologized in effect for doing so ('now rather shamefaced and admits to having been panicked'). McWilliam accepted this with good grace, though not without complaining to Graham 'that I thought it very poor that B had not either apologised or expressed regrets about the week'.[98]

Lloyds, meanwhile, had been preparing its final offensive. Its campaign had been maladroit in several respects, notably in its handling of the US authorities. That contract to sell its Californian subsidiary, for instance, had not been sufficient to avoid endless complications. But all obstacles now seemed to have been surmounted. On 27 June, it lifted its offer price to 822p and published a forecast of excellent results for its first half-year (which boosted the value of the revised offer again, to 840p by the end of the day). This adhered to the familiar bid-battle script, and the financial press responded with comment columns tantamount to the last rites for Standard Chartered. Since Lloyds had shrewdly indicated that a friendly response from the Group, even at this late stage, might elicit a higher price, Barber and most of the Directors were reduced to anguished hand-wringing over their fiduciary responsibilities. And in capital cities across Asia, some wry exchanges began passing between expatriate managers of the two banks – as the Manager of the branch in Korea could later recall:

> We were perfectly friendly with the manager of Lloyds Bank in Seoul, but he came to me about two weeks before it was all over and said: 'just to let you know, we will be moving into your premises because you have a lovely new office, and ours is getting a bit tired. Do you mind if I come round and have a look at your personal office because that's going to be mine?'[99]

It was the darkest hour. The City's verdict seemed clear; friendly investors had picked up as much as 15 per cent of the shares, but nowhere near enough to tip the balance; StanBIC had in the end offered no help at all, despite plenty of entreaties; and Stuart Tarrant was making no attempt to conceal from colleagues his satisfaction at the prospect of victory for Lloyds.[100] But now Bill Brown, still resident in Hong Kong and a widely respected figure in the Colony for all he had done on behalf of the Group over the past several years, popped up as a harbinger of the dawn. He telephoned McWilliam to say that, in the latest of a series of late-night discussions he had had with the ship-owning magnate Y. K. Pao, the latter had talked in earnest of investing in the Group, and even of launching a full-scale counter-bid. Apparently it bothered him not a jot that he had been a Director of HSBC until 1984 and still remained both a close adviser to the Hong Kong bank and one of its prime customers.* McWilliam had heard enough tokens of intent to respond with some reserve ('I counselled a more cautious white squire approach, to avoid dividing the board or giving the BofE palpitations') but by 4 July it was evident that Y. K. Pao had indeed begun to pick up shares in the market.[101] The same day, McWilliam learned that Holmes à Court would be arriving in London from

---

* His readiness to invest in Standard Chartered may have been related to the fact that his age was obliging him to stand down (very reluctantly) as an adviser to HSBC. It was not a universally popular move with his former colleagues at that bank, which had stood behind him almost since the start of his career. Helmut Sohmen, one of his sons-in-law who succeeded him on the HSBC Board and was soon to take over running his shipping interests, saw it as an essentially business-driven decision. Pao had done something very similar in 1985, agreeing to back the nascent Dragon Air even though he was at the time a Board Director of the Colony's flag carrier, Cathay Pacific. (Helmut Sohmen, interview with author, 24 April 2013.)

Australia over the weekend of 5–6 July with every intention of taking a significant stake in the Group.

Thus began the final week of the bid timetable.[102] Events thereafter unfolded at a breathless pace. McWilliam met privately with both Holmes à Court and Khoo Teck Puat to convince them of the Group's emerging potential. Khoo disclosed early on Wednesday 9 July that he was a holder of 5 per cent of the bank's shares. Later that morning, McWilliam called Y. K. Pao to ask for a clarification of his position. When asked outright by Pao what level of investment he wanted, McWilliam said '10 per cent by the weekend'. In that case, said Pao, he would take the evening plane to London and see McWilliam at Gatwick airport early the next morning. They duly met there, and Pao was as good as his word. Stockbrokers Cazenove had a firm order to buy 10 per cent before 9 a.m. on the Thursday. The City was stunned. Returning to Bishopsgate by midday, McWilliam was none too surprised to find himself summoned urgently to the Bank of England to see its Director of Banking Supervision, Rodney Galpin. He was prepared for a grilling – but the agenda for their meeting was not what he expected:

> [Galpin] had seen Tarrant that morning to ask what was going on and he [Tarrant] opened up with his full expose about the bid, his 'concerns' and saying he would resign if LB lose. Having explained what was happening in the market, I then went over ST's performance in some detail. Back at the office I told PAG [Peter Graham] and Lord B what had happened.[103]

But internal disagreements were now a side-show. Everything hung on the market's verdict. Cazenove had built up a comprehensive register of all the shareholdings in the City, and knew exactly which institutions (and which arbitrageurs) to pursue on behalf of the white knights. Private shareholders for the most part remained loyal holders, but the fund managers were now ready to sell. By the close of trading that Thursday afternoon, Holmes à Court's Bell Group had declared a 6 per cent stake and an interest in buying up to 10 per cent. Next day, Pao bought another 5 per cent. By the Friday evening, McWilliam could add the week's block purchases to his scorecard of smaller holdings accumulated by other friendly investors – and knew the outcome. Despite all the odds, the bid had been beaten. Lloyds confirmed as much on the Saturday morning: the bid had been accepted in the end by shareholders with only 34 per cent of the total vote. The UK press was astonished, as were most professional observers in the City. Congratulations poured in for the next few days – including a call from Conrad Strauss at StanBIC, to convey his best wishes 'despite South Africa being in disgrace' for offering no support[104] – and the champagne flowed in

Bishopsgate. Tarrant emptied his office by lunchtime on the Monday, for a quick exit that was handled as honourably and amicably as all could manage under the circumstances. Barber put on a brave face, though none doubted his retirement could not be long delayed. (He confided in Graham and McWilliam on 28 July that he would announce as much in September.[105]) For McWilliam himself, it was plainly a personal triumph. Now he had to take stock of the future he had wished for. Bob Hamburger rang him from Goldman Sachs, 'to say that the market will now expect dramatic action . . . and that I have the power base to do things!'

Financial Times Monday July 14 1986

STANDARD CHARTERED FIGHTS OFF LLOYDS

Rescued but at a price

By David Lascelles, Banking Correspondent

STANDARD CHARTERED'S last-minute escape from Lloyds Bank's £1.3bn takeover bid on Saturday has just about everything the financial thriller writer could want. The world's biggest attempted bank takeover, fabulously wealthy oriental investors riding to the rescue, hurried meetings at airports, and a nail-biting climax in the City of London.

But dramatic and unexpected as the outcome of the three-month battle was, the real themes of the Standard story may well turn out to be rather more sobering ones: the ease with which a tiny group of well-heeled, determined investors can pick up a controlling stake in a major international bank, and the highly uncertain future which that creates of Standard.

In the UK this could well influence the shape of the new Banking Act which is currently under consideration and will contain a section defining controlling interests in banks. Abroad, particularly in the Far East where Standard is one of the biggest banks in many regional markets, the bank's federal character is bound to be loosened possibly to the point

As he celebrated his victory on Saturday afternoon, with Schroders, his merchant banking advisers, Mr Michael McWilliam, the group chief executive, said: "Standard Chartered will never be the same again."

The tide in Standard's fight for survival began to turn exactly a week ago when Mr McWilliam received a telephone call from Sir Yue-Kong Pao, the Hong Kong shipping magnate, asking what he could do to help. Mr McWillian told him: "I'd like you to be a big shareholder by the end of the week." The same night, Sir Y. K. who is 68 years old, was on the Cathay Pacific flight to London. At 6 the next morning he met Mr McWilliam at Gatwick Airport, and they swung into action.

By Friday, Sir Y.K. had spent over £180m buying up 15 per cent of Standard's shares. He wiled away Saturday morning playing golf and flew home that night after what must rank as one of history's biggest shopping sprees.

Standard's ability to summon its Far Eastern friends has turned out to be crucial. Tan Sri Khoo Tack Puat, the Malaysian businesman, bought 5 per cent, Mr Robert Holmes à Court of Australia's Bell Group had 7.4 per cent, 40 smaller Hong Kong customers had up to 10 per cent. Even Mr "Tiny" Rowland of Lonrho got 2 per cent. All told, Standard could count on about 40 per cent of the vote by Friday night, and none of its friends yielded to Lloyd's last-minute efforts to turn them round.

But grateful though Standard must be for their aid, their motives and intentions are far from clear, particularly since they will all be sitting on large paper losses the moment the London stock market opens this morning if—as is widely expected — Standard's share price falls.

In the minds of the Chinese investors, at least, there appears to have been genuine concern about Standard—which they have known and dealt with for generations—passing into the hands of Lloyds which has a mixed reputation in the Far East. The Chinese Government is even believed to have asked the UK Government why it was allowing the bid to go ahead.

But while some motives may be less easy to discern in the West, the investors' support could also owe something to the give-and-take that exists in all bank-customer relations. Mr McWilliam denies that Hong Kong businessmen have been offered "funny facilities" in return for their votes. Some of the new shareholders are certainly long-time customers of the bank. Tan Sri Khoo, for instance, has known Standard for more than two decades. Standard Chartered also put up a A$2bn facility—its largest ever according to Mr McWilliam —to help Mr Holmes à Court finance his bid in May for Broken Hill Proprietary. That bid is still in the air. Mr Rowland was virtually set up in business by Standard Chartered in Africa.

Only Sir Y. K. is not a Standard customer, though as a former deputy chairman of, and now consultant to, the Hongkong and Shanghai Bank, he has a strong interest in the shape of the colony's banking community where Standard ranks No. 2. Although suggestions that he wanted to save Lloyds for a later bid by the Hongkong Bank seem a little far-fetched, he could now end up as the colony's biggest bank owner.

He will be offered a place on Standard's board. Whether the invitation will be extended to any of the other supporters remains to be seen. But Standard today is an institution with a dramatically different set of shareholders, some of whose motives and loyalty will be doubted by the market, but whose taste for good returns on their investments is not.

The most plausible explanation for this sudden show of friendship is that the investors have calculated the value of the many parts that make up Standard's far-flung global empire, and aim to realise them through some form of individual flotation. This may not amount to anything as dramatic as a break-up of Standard Chartered. But over the course of the next year or so, there are bound to be major developments.

Mr McWilliam has for some time favoured the idea of boosting value for his shareholders by realising some of the group's assets which he believes are not reflected in the share price. So he would support, and possibly even lead, efforts to sell off parts of what he calls "the federation." "We have to make values work," he said, adding that Standard now wants to get its after-tax return on capital up to 15 per cent from 10.5 per cent last year (Lloyds is expetcing 17.7 per cent in the first half of this year).

To start with, Standard could sell and lease back its new City headquarters in Bishopsgate. The Hong Kong business, which at the moment consists of 116 branches and £3.7bn in assets serving over 1m customers, could be locally incorporated and partially floated on the Hong Kong Stock Exchange. Sir Y.K. would then have the option of swapping his interest in the group for a major stake in Standard Chartered (Hong Kong).

In the US, Unon Bank, the California subsidiary now valued at close on $1bn, might issue its own shares to finance its next acquisition rather than draw on the group's cash resources. In Singapore, Malaysia and Australia (where Standard has just been admitted as one of the first batch of 16 foreign banks), similar local incorporations would be possible.

However the drawback to any scheme in which the best parts of Standard were partially sold off is that it would leave the core of the group with the worst of the business. The bank would also be left holding all of Standard's cross-border lending, which could be risky, and virtually no direct source of retail deposits. Standard would still have to pay its dividends in pounds even though most of its earnings would be overseas. Whether such a scheme would get past Standard's board, many of whose members are still "old empire" as one observer put it, remains to be seen.

A close, though silent observer of last week's events was the Bank of England. Although the Bank opened the way to the battle over Standard by raising no objection to Lloyds' bid in the first place, the outcome cannot be wholly satisfactory to Theardneedle Street.

Under the present UK Banking Act, an investor is deemed to have a "controlling interest" with 15 per cent or more. This is why Sir Y K stopped at 14.9 per cent (though he was in close touch with the Bank all week, and would be required by the Takeover Code to wait a week before buying more).

However bank takeovers are particularly sensitive matters because of the danger of a loss of confidence by depositors. Although confidence in Standard has not been damaged, it must be a matter of public concern in Britain that effective control of a large bank can pass so quickly to investors on the far side of the world, some of whom may not be accustomed to investing in delicately tuned banks.

The White Paper on Banking Supervision published last December proposed that any investor seeking to buy 15 per cent or more of a bank must seek the prior permission of the Bank of England. In the subsequent debate about the White Paper—which will be transformed into a Bill later this year—it has also been suggested that the 15 per cent ceiling be lowered. The Standard episode could reinforce that view, particularly in cases where customers end up owning large stakes in their banks and exposing themselves to possible conflicts of interest.

As Birtain's first major hostile takeover bid, the Lloyds-Standard tussle has broken new ground by showing that market forces rather than the will of the Bank of England now previal. Because of that, tougher rules may be necessary.

The final chapter in Standard's story has still to be written, and it may contain some dramatic twists for a unique institution which straddles Britain's colonial past and some of the world's most exciting and modern markets. The outcome will depend on whether the friends Standard called in at 24 hours' notice will turn out to be the catalysts who change a business that has been built up over nearly one and a half centuries.

THE THREE businessmen from Hong Kong and Australia who came to Standard Chartered's aid last week showed that the bank can count on powerful friends. But their motives are far from clear.

Sir Yue-Kong Pao, who bought 14.9 per cent, is Hong Kong's best known business magnate and one of the world's biggest shipowners. He is also a banker by training. At 68 he travels the world with a set of skipping ropes to keep fit and has amassed a personal fortune of over HK$3bn.

He would not have invested a fair portion of that in Standard without good reason since he does not have a reputation as a philanthropist.

Some observers in Hong Kong believe he may have been acting with the interests of the Hongkong and Shanghaai Bank in mind, with which he has been associated for many years. By frustrating the takeover, he could have made Lloyds Bank a ripe target for the Hongkong Bank which is looking for a European acquisition.

The alternative view—that he expects parts of Standard to be floated off—is also echoed in the colony.

Tan Sri Khoo Teck Puat, the Malaysian businessman with interests in property, hotels and banking, is a long-time customer of the Standard bank, and since last week a 5 per cent shareholder. He resides in Australia but is believed to want to shift more of his wealth to the UK, where he recently bought a 28 per cent stake in Exco, the financial services company.

Although Khoo and Pao bought their stakes in Standard separately, the extent to which they might now co-operate as shareholders could affect the bank's future. They have been depicted as bitter rivals after their takeover clash last year over Wheelock Marden, the Hong Kong shipping and trading group, but are probably less hostile than thought. Neither sold his Standard shares on learning on the other's interest.

Mr Robert Holmes à Court, the Australian who has 7.4 per cent, is one of Standard Chartered's largest customers —the bank is financing its attempted takeover of Broken Hill Proprietary with a A$2bn credit facility. In Sydney, the view is that he decided to respond to Standard's call for help in order to protect a relationship that could have been jeopardised by a Lloyds victory.

Known as both an opportunist and a masterly financial tactician, Mr Holmes à Court took over Lord Grade's Associated Communications Corp, in 1982 after a protracted struggle and now runs a worldwide business from his Perth base.

He has also amassed large profits by dealing in substantial stakes in companies such as Ansett Airlines, Elders IXL and Asarco.

All three men were in London last week and personally directed the acquisition af shares in Standard Chartered.

Sir Yue-Kong Pao: a seat on Standard's board

Mr Robert Holmes à Court

COMPONENTS OF THE BANK

	Net assets (£m)	Net assets per share (p)	Pre-tax profit £m
North America	467.9	300.8	54 (Union Bank 48.9)
Asia Pacific	352	226.3	48.7 (Hong Kong 27.6, Singapore 15 (loss), Malaysia 25.2, Australia 6.6)
Mid East and S. Asia	56.5	36.3	4.4
Tropical Africa	107.1	68.8	48.2
South Africa	136.5	87.7	35.6
Europe	92.8	59.6	4.7
UK	443.2	284.9	106.3

Source: Bid defence document

The feature article on the editorial page of the *Financial Times* on Monday, 14 July 1986, following confirmation two days earlier of the defeat of the bid for Standard Chartered by Lloyds Bank

5. ENDINGS AND EXITS

This was a happy notion – and McWilliam himself had of course alluded to the useful side-effects of a takeover scare in launching his transition project in 1983. Inevitably the battle with Lloyds had been massively distracting; but surely now, as the Executive Directors spelled out in countless speeches across the Group, the pre-bid momentum of its modernization efforts could be swiftly recaptured. And for the best part of five months, it did indeed look as though that momentum was returning. A new retail banking strategy recently launched in Hong Kong was reporting dramatic progress. Under the charismatic leadership of a former Californian banker, Fred Enlow, the Colony's 111 branches had stopped handing over all their deposits as cheap funding for the corporate bank and begun instead to recycle them as personal loans and mortgages. The market's response was so encouraging that, by October, plans were afoot to buy out two local Chinese banks in which the Group had long been a minority investor, adding perhaps another thirty or so branches to the Hong Kong network.[106] The Group was meanwhile making headway in Africa under another able senior manager, Alan Wren, and with a vision of Standard Chartered as a network of truly local operations. A struggling business in Kenya had been revived and plans were going ahead to incorporate it as a subsidiary that could be floated on the market in Nairobi; and an agricultural advisory service that had been popular in East Africa was now being extended into Zambia, Zimbabwe and Malawi. In Europe, McSloy resumed his busy expansion of the continental network by hiring new talent for the branches in Italy and Austria, and securing a rare investment banking licence in France where a Paris corporate finance operation was preparing for a launch early in 1987. And, in New York, the Group at long last completed its acquisition of the Mocatta bullion business. Having painlessly lifted its stake to 80 per cent as projected back in the spring, it seized the chance offered by Henry Jarecki in September 1986 to complete the purchase (though Jarecki retained a personal holding of 5 per cent).

Meanwhile, the more fundamental work of upgrading the Group's systems and general management culture was once again inching forward. Plans were approved to replace the current hodgepodge of different computer systems across the world with standard Group-wide systems – a topic probably deeply impenetrable for several of the Directors, but of huge consequence to all since the percentage of non-interest expenses linked to technology was growing fast (it was now over 10 per cent, twice the level of the early 1970s, and was projected to double again within ten years).[107] On the softer side of corporate rejuvenation, a new directorate for Management Development and Training was agreed. The job went to StanBIC's Dr Henri Fabian – not without some harrumphing from one or two of the old guard – and he was soon setting about a follow-up to external appraisals done by Manchester Business School in 1985. Among the senior executives more generally, it could fairly be said that confidence was reviving. By November, fresh acquisitions in the City were even being mooted.*

Then everything began to go spectacularly wrong. On 20 November, news broke of an unlikely banking scandal in one of the world's richest (albeit smallest) countries. The National Bank of Brunei had been suspended by the state authorities, pending the recall of some huge advances without which it was faced with insolvency. The 70 per cent owner of the bank – who also happened to control the companies accounting for almost all of the bank's loan portfolio – was Khoo Teck Puat, and it was chaired by his son, who was carted off to gaol along with four of his senior officers.[108] 'This could be quite damaging to us' noted McWilliam.[109] It was some understatement, even by his standards. While Khoo scrambled to raise large amounts of cash – not least to pay a de facto ransom for his son – there was a run on one of Standard Chartered's branches in Brunei. Rumours were soon abroad of fraud in high places. The Brunei bank had run up debts of more than £130 million to dozens of local and Singaporean lenders, and Standard Chartered was foremost among them. In the City, brokers speculated on the possible destination of Khoo's stake in the Group, just recently augmented from 5 to 6 per cent. In the end he clung on to his shares – for which he had paid around £200 million – and the episode made no lasting impact either on the market or on Standard Chartered's branches in Brunei. The embarrassment it caused the Group, though, was another matter. Khoo, like Y. K. Pao and Holmes à Court, had been invited on to the Board in the summer, in acknowledgement of his large shareholding. (Pao had actually picked up two seats, and had given the other to a son-in-law, Peter Woo, a former Chase Manhattan banker.) Khoo honourably resigned within days of the Brunei debacle, but this could not prevent a muffled tut-tutting round the City. For had these oriental shenanigans not shown up what desperate tactics had lain behind

---

* Among several others mentioned in McWilliam's diary, one proposal stands out. On 12 November, he had a meeting with Hamburger and his colleagues from Goldman Sachs. They aired various thoughts on the Group's future in the US, and 'also tried to provoke me into thinking about a bid for Lloyds Bank. I said we did not have strong enough management.' No one ever accused Goldman Sachs of lacking chutzpah.

the summer's triumph? Brunei seemed an almost risibly exotic place for a major bank to have put its reputation on the line. (In fact the Chartered had had a presence in Brunei since 1958, not least to provide local services for the oil industry. Its Manager early in the 1970s had also endeared the bank to the Sultan's family by introducing his country to the joys of polo.[110]) There can be little doubt that McWilliam's personal standing with his peers, especially Barber and Graham, also took a sharp knock. This was doubly harsh, in a sense. For not only had the Managing Director adopted the only effective defence ploy available – but it was plain by November 1986 that the stressful consequences of the great escape in the summer were weighing more heavily on him than anyone else.

It was a burden not much evident to the outside world, but was horribly apparent within the Boardroom. The white knights were immensely powerful personalities, and arrived on the Board in slightly truculent mood from the start. Not until after the end of the bid battle had each become aware of the others. Thereafter, they eyed each other's decisions on even the most trivial Board matters with intense suspicion, for they had disparate agendas. Pao, who had just retired from his executive position as head of World-Wide Shipping, the world's largest privately owned shipping empire, was primarily interested in the influence that he could exert through the bank, particularly vis-à-vis Hong Kong's relations with China. Peter Woo was more preoccupied with technical and procedural matters. Khoo Teck Puat, for the short while he was on the Board, seemed intent on building a banking empire. Holmes à Court had no grand blueprints but kept a beady eye on the bottom line, urging a disposal here or a big investment there. (He was especially adamant that the Union Bank in the US should be sold, for example, and that the Group's investment in South Africa should be retained.) The one thing they all had in common was a perception of Standard Chartered as a bank with huge but untapped potential.* That was why McWilliam had been able to persuade them into buying the shares in the first place. But the result was a constant badgering of the other Directors, largely in pursuit of their own designs. This regularly gummed up the deliberations of the Board, while fatally weakening its bond with the executive. Financial columnists, bemused by the signs

---

* Huge and untapped reserves seem also to have figured in Y. K. Pao's perception of the Group, until his first attendance at a meeting of the Board. As a former Director of HSBC, Pao knew of the latter's very substantial hidden reserves and had assumed that Standard Chartered was equally well endowed. 'One of the first questions he asked at the Board was "How much are your hidden reserves" and he was absolutely dumbfounded to hear that we didn't have any. He was very upset.' (David Millar, interview with author, 5 December 2011.)

of discord, began suggesting a Lloyds merger might after all have been the better option. Some within the bank probably thought so, too.

The situation demanded a strong and resourceful Chairman. Barber's accommodating style instead left the Board wide open to the white knights' machinations – especially after he had signalled his intention to step down at the next AGM. Barber also took an extraordinarily casual approach to finding a successor. After settling eventually on the choice of Peter Graham over the autumn of 1986, he made no move whatever to prepare for the handover. Opportunities tactfully to ease out some of the Board's less dynamic greybeards, for example, were simply ignored. As for Graham's emergence as the next Chairman, few turns in the history of the bank are more richly ironic. Barber was heavily swayed by his Managing Director's private counselling that Graham would be the only logical appointment – but this was advice that McWilliam came bitterly to regret. Relations between the two men, long nurtured by a mutual acknowledgement of their complementary talents, deteriorated rapidly after the Khoo episode. And once the older man was in the Chair, their working partnership was seriously compromised by an awkward truth: for Graham, rather surprisingly, turned out to have no real aptitude for the job. No longer the ebullient, decisive figure of earlier years, Graham struggled terribly. McWilliam actually provided coaching papers to help him define his role, but in a private end-of-year review for 1987 McWilliam the diarist was scathing in his assessment:

> PAG on his part made no preparations at all and assumed the Chair with no evidence of having given the role a moment's thought. It quickly became apparent that he lacks the ability to lead the Board, or to think on his feet at meetings and he was unable to handle the bullying that developed from Pao and Holmes à Court. When a meeting of non-executive directors took place in June [1987], PAG went to it in effect asking them what his role should be.[111]

The tensions at the top were an impediment to the executive management of the Group in a host of minor ways. McWilliam ran into endless difficulties, for example, in trying to make fresh appointments to the senior ranks that the Chairman thought disobliging to some of his older Chartered Bank colleagues. And the growing rift in the Boardroom began to threaten much more serious consequences, as it became ever clearer through 1987 that the Group was struggling to make headway with its 'post-war' plans. Much of the year was instead spent trying to escape the aftermath of the recent past. Two aspects of this proved especially damaging.

The first was a toxic sequel to the bid battle, which hit the bank in

February. It raised yet again the possibility that there had been something fishy about the vanquishing of the Lloyds bid. The City of London had been riveted for months by the unravelling of the Guinness/Distillers scandal. Guinness, brewers of the famous stout, had illegally funded the acquisition of its shares by friendly investors, so boosting its share price in the course of 1986 and helping it to win a contested takeover battle for Distillers Company, a Scottish drinks company. Over the first weeks of 1987, several illustrious City heads had toppled on that account, and a cloud hung over the broking firm that had acted throughout for Guinness – Cazenove, no less. At the start of February, an article in the *Financial Times* essentially charged Standard Chartered with adopting the same tactics as Guinness, lending money to the white knights to help fund their share-shopping trips the previous summer.[112] McWilliam was appalled and rushed back to London from a skiing holiday in Austria, but not in time to accompany Barber and Graham to the Bank of England for a tense meeting with Rodney Galpin. The outcome was an investigation under the Companies Act, ostensibly at the Group's own request and apparently on the initial understanding that the whole affair would last just a few weeks.[113] Given the Guinness saga, there was never the remotest chance of a speedy all-clear. In fact, independent inspectors were given the widest possible brief by the Bank of England – which only subsequently agreed to foot the bill – and they set off on a dauntingly thorough autopsy of the bid battle that lasted, in the end, three times as long as the battle itself. Several hundred questionnaires went off to branches of the bank; scores of executives were interrogated at great length, as were the knights themselves; long office tables heaved under the weight of papers deemed germane to the inquiry.[114]

The bank's own Directors were quick to satisfy themselves that the allegations were baseless – which was just as well, since a writ had been issued against the *Financial Times* on the day of the original news story's publication. But the acrimony between Stuart Tarrant and his colleagues prior to his departure had been well-aired in the financial press, as had been the sorry saga of the National Bank of Brunei and the misadventures of Khoo Teck Puat and his son. (A large loan to the National Bank just days after confirmation of Khoo's purchase of his 5 per cent stake attracted particular criticism.) With so much smoke in the air, even the most charitable outside observers had to suspect a fire or two somewhere. In the event, none was ever found.* The resulting report of the inspectors

---

* The gist of the matter was that loans, inducements or share-price guarantees given expressly to help expedite share purchases were illegal, while loans made in the ordinary

was locked away in the Bank of England – where it remains to this day, still unavailable even to Standard Chartered ('a bit of a nonsense' thought McWilliam[115]) – but its unequivocal findings, announced in January 1988, cleared the Group of any impropriety whatever.[116] By that date, though, its Directors and senior executives had had to endure an eleven-month ordeal that had done nothing for McWilliam's stature with his Board colleagues or for Peter Graham's credibility as their leader.

The other legacy of the recent past was even more fundamental. It marked, in effect, a sad denouement to three or four years during which the Group had been straining to assert itself as an international bank of the first rank – while lacking sufficient systems, credit-risk procedures or general management resources to live up to that billing. A rush for growth had stretched too many poorly trained managers to the limit of their abilities, and sometimes beyond. Now the consequences were starting to surface. First came a nasty hit in the Capital Markets Division of the merchant bank. The market for Floating Rate Notes, launched with such enthusiasm in 1985, had collapsed in December 1986. The merchant bank was embarrassed to be caught holding notes with a nominal value of $224 million, including a sizeable tranche of the Group's own issues.[117] Losses on these and other non-FRN holdings since September 1986 amounted to more than £27 million. The Audit Committee in April 1987 bemoaned 'management and operational failures', concluding ominously that 'the present situation of SCMB warranted a review of its structure and activities'.[118] In the months that followed, with the global economy slowing appreciably, a stream of bad debts began surfacing – shipping loans in Hong Kong (for which substantial provisions had been made in 1986), property deals in Singapore, corporate advances by UK branches that had been urged to make their mark against the clearers and had inevitably ended up lending to a rum assortment of companies spurned

---

course of business (or even as part of a reciprocal investment arrangement) were not. This plainly allowed some pieces of business to be construed in different ways – and exposed the bank to hostile press coverage that, perhaps understandably, skipped over some of the finer subtleties of the law. It seems more than likely that some in the bank itself were not always wholly alert to these either, and may well have needed reining back. Hence, perhaps, Stuart Tarrant's deep unhappiness. But what the inspectors established to their satisfaction (and the Bank of England's) was that no transactions had in the end fallen within the illegal category. This had nonetheless left scope for some arrangements that came as a surprise when they were uncovered in 1987, not least to Michael McWilliam. It turned out, for example, that both Holmes à Court's Bell Group and Tiny Rowland's Lonrho had paid for shares in the bank by drawing on their Standard Chartered overdraft facilities 'without thought for the implications' (McWilliam Diary: Review of 1987, MMcW Papers). Of the Managing Director's own personal dismay at the allegations of impropriety, there can be no doubt.

by the clearers themselves – all of which began to generate sizeable losses
that often spoke of poor basic lending skills. Nowhere more so than in
Canada, where the office in Toronto (founded in 1977) had set up a trio
of sub-branches since 1983 and trebled the size of its loan book. By the
spring of 1987, a new boss, posted to Canada six months earlier, was
flagging a total breakdown of lending controls that had hitherto been
concealed from Bishopsgate. Losses mounted through the summer – 'a
real horror story', noted McWilliam[119] – wiping out the Group's equity in
Canada and obliging it to inject almost £50 million extra capital in the
end. It was scant consolation that a review of the debacle by Bill Brown
could later rule out fraud, judging the staff to have been 'grossly incom-
petent but not dishonest'.[120]

Above all, and towering over the misdemeanours of mere lending officers, was the cost to the Group of its untrumpeted activities in the market
for syndicated eurocurrency loans. In May 1987, Citibank shook the
international banking fraternity by announcing that its loans to sovereign
borrowers in the Third World were sitting in its balance sheet at values
hopelessly out of line with any repayments it could realistically hope to
collect. It was therefore going to set aside 'cross-border provisions' against
the loans, equating to more than 30 per cent of their face value. This would
re-align their net book value with the discounted prices currently being
quoted for equivalent loans in the secondary trading market, but would
also involve an accounting loss of roughly $3 billion. Where the largest
bank in the US had led, it was soon apparent – albeit after several interventions by the Bank of England – that the UK's biggest banks would have
to follow.[121] One side-effect of this was that a renewed bid for the Group
by Lloyds in the summer, expected by some in the City, could now be
discounted. (It retained a sizeable shareholding, though, and would only
dispose of its last shares in April 1995 – at an average price of 292p.[122])
But the more direct impact on Standard Chartered came as a shock to
everyone in the Group. Many banks were embarrassed by the sovereign-
debt crisis; but few were as poorly placed as Standard Chartered to cope
with the consequences. Its cross-border loans – even without including
those to South Africa – amounted to $2.8 billion. The existing provisions
stood at 10 per cent of this total. Making an adjustment comparable to
Citibank's, as City analysts were quick to calculate, would involve a loss
in 1987 of about £600 million, equivalent to more than half of shareholders' equity.[123] The impact on shareholders' confidence seemed likely to be
graver still. The sheer scale of the bank's operations in the syndicated loan
market had never been very apparent to outsiders, nor indeed to many
inside the bank either. The profitability of the International Banking

Division had been evident for years, but was generally identified more with its Treasury and foreign-exchange activities. In fact a steady accumulation of assets, acquired as slices of its own or other banks' syndicated deals, had been a potent but little-remarked ingredient in its growth since the swallowing of MAIBL's books in 1983. And it was not just the volume of this business that was set to alarm shareholders. The geographical spread of the resulting portfolio was even more surprising, not to say bewildering. It was heavily skewed towards Latin America – the one area that had scarcely merited a reference in any of the bank's strategy deliberations since 1969 (or, indeed, in the pages of any of its Annual Reports).

The genesis of this exposure had been a curious business. It was initiated in the late 1970s by a newcomer to the Group called Charles Crickmore, a former Bank of America man who brought with him a genuine knowledge of Latin America and extensive contacts in Brazil. Appointed to the board of SCMB, he pressed Robin Baillie, as its Chief Executive, to let him expand the merchant bank's Latin American book – and Baillie refused. 'The merchant bank wasn't big enough to take on the scale of lending that Charles believed was good for the Group,' recalled Baillie. 'He was transferred across to the main bank because, though we were good friends, we couldn't work together. Then, when he got into Standard Chartered, he was given free rein and he built up a very large portfolio of Latin American debt.'[124] Two other developments added fuel to the fire. One was the purchase of Union Bank in 1979.* The other was the acquisition of MAIBL in 1983, which effectively put Crickmore at the head of a syndicated-loans department with ambitions to be seen as a leader in the marketplace. It duly launched into an aggressive pursuit of Latin American loan mandates, and went on chasing them even after Crickmore's untimely death in a car crash in 1985. No one else in the department had any real expertise on the region. Standard Chartered was

---

* Union Bank had tiny representative offices in Mexico and Colombia, Venezuela, Brazil and Argentina. When international lending to Latin America suddenly soared in 1979, the Union Bank took advantage of its new City parentage to participate in the boom. By June 1982, the league table of the Group's medium-term loans ranked by country was topped by Mexico ($396 million), with Brazil in fourth place ($217 million). ('Country Risk Review', Memorandum for the Board Meeting of 14 December 1982, SCB Box 1721.) Mexico's declaration of insolvency in August 1982 was a chastening experience for the Union Bank, however, and it went back to concentrating on its core business, which was lending to small and medium-sized US companies. To encourage this focus on its domestic markets and to improve its access to local funding, McWilliam decided in 1984 to move all of the Union Bank's foreign loans to the parent's balance sheet in London. The transferred book was valued at $462 million, of which Latin American credits accounted for 70 per cent. (Diary for 11 January 1985, MMcW Papers.)

thereafter as guilty as any major bank in the City of pandering to fashionable trends in global lending. Latin American sovereign credits were the hottest sector of the market. Bishopsgate filled its coffers. When Citibank's initiative brought down the shutters, the Group's stock-take came as a shock to the Board. McWilliam in July 1987 had to recommend that the Group's cross-border provisions should be lifted to 22 per cent of their nominal value. This meant a charge of $646 million (£400 million), producing a pre-tax loss at the half-year of £224 million.[125] Of the newly enlarged provisions ($832 million), almost exactly half related to Latin American loans, representing 27 per cent of the latter's $1.52 billion book value.[126]

The gathering avalanche of losses had by this point thoroughly unnerved the Board and left the Group's balance sheet in urgent need of redress. As McWilliam was himself the first to appreciate, it had probably also wrecked any chance of restoring the Corporate Plan launched early in 1986 – or indeed of sustaining the whole post-1975 vision of a Group as well grounded in the West as in Asia. Indeed, support for the vision was wearing very thin. McWilliam had been desperately disappointed in June to see yet another prospective UK merger swept aside. Under severe capital pressures of its own, the Midland Bank had offered to sell the Group its Scottish subsidiary, the Clydesdale Bank, along with two smaller regional UK banks. This had dangled the prospect of improving on the Royal Bank of Scotland bid of 1981. McWilliam had been strongly in favour of a deal ('It looks like the answer to a maiden's prayer'[127]), scenting at last a fulfilment of his long-nurtured hopes of a major UK expansion – always assuming that any counter-bid by HSBC could be kept at bay. Graham and most of the other non-executives had remained skittish through four weeks of tense negotiation, but an all-but-final agreement had nonetheless been struck with the Midland.[128] Then firm opposition to the deal had been voiced by Y. K. Pao and Holmes à Court – an increasingly dominant double-act in the Boardroom – and this had resulted in an abrupt Board decision that left McWilliam to reflect sadly on the implications:

> [Graham] invited me to speak [at the Board meeting] and a discussion of sorts ensued. No very clear explanation was given other than a rather general 'too rushed, too expensive, too complicated' theme and [there was] no suggestion that there were matters for general debate and judgement. Even more depressing, no-one was prepared to stand up to the [Y. K. Pao/Holmes à Court] juggernaut, with the result that the cornerstone of our corporate strategy for the past 10 years was torpedoed without a whimper or protest from the non executives.[129]

Managing a Clydesdale acquisition might have been problematic.* Financing it would certainly have posed an even bigger challenge. Reviewing the Group's capital adequacy back in February, the Managing Director had himself pointed out that the assets of the bank – measured in relation to its equity – were already then at the very upper limit of the range acceptable to the Bank of England.[130] Four months later, the year's mounting losses and the new cross-border provisions meant the ratio of the Group's assets to its equity had deteriorated so sharply that additional capital was required, even with no acquisition in prospect. There appeared to be little immediate possibility of raising fresh capital from shareholders.[131] And the chances of lifting the Group's profitability were also looking increasingly forlorn: commodity prices had been tumbling since late 1986 and trade volumes were now stagnating in most of its principal markets. Far from expanding the Group, there seemed no alternative but to resort to 'rationalization', the dispiriting business of cashing in 'disposable assets' – hitherto worth having, but now to be reckoned unaffordable.

Top of the list, despite all the warm words exchanged in 1985, was the Group's minority stake in StanBIC. The last stage of the divorce from the South African business is in some ways a puzzling story. The London Directors had faced down years of anti-apartheid campaigning to retain their historic link with the Standard Bank. On a visit to Johannesburg in October 1986 McWilliam had assured the Standard's senior managers that London's intention was to let its stake fall to 25 per cent but no further. At the 1987 AGM in May, Anthony Barber stuck one last time to his perennial script: the Group's outlook was immune to political lobbying. Meanwhile many ties remained in place, almost as though the 1985 dilution had never happened. Bishopsgate was still sending young managers on secondment to Johannesburg, and still taking on twenty or so young South Africans every year to give them a taste of banking in the City (and pride of place on the bank's sporting teams). Indeed, McWilliam had been ready to push the staffing exchange much further in 1986: weeks after the defeat of the Lloyds bid he had tried in vain to lure the Standard's Managing Director, Conrad Strauss, to London as a 'chief operating officer' and his designated successor.[132] For their part, the South Africans had come to appreciate the value of their ties with London ever more keenly. If Standard Chartered had had its troubles since 1985, so too of course

---

* It may be a clue to McWilliam's preparations, though, that he was able in August 1987 to lure over to the Group the ex-head of the Midland's UK banking operations, Ian Patterson. He was given a broadly similar role at Standard Chartered, as a Senior General Manager. Patterson's arrival coincided with the retirement of David Millar as Senior Executive Director, after a career that had spanned forty-one years.

had StanBIC. South Africa's economy was increasingly under siege –
Barclays had severed its links in November 1986, to the consternation of
the country's entire business community – and the Standard's senior men
were finding themselves virtually ostracized in international banking circles. The minutes of its Board meetings through 1986 made a dry note of
their discomfort on several occasions, but the gathering alarm over their
isolation could not be disguised.[133] The possibility that Standard Chartered's stake might fall to Lloyds, which made no pretence of seeing a
future for itself in South Africa, triggered much discussion in Johannesburg about conceivable endgames for the British connection; but there was
no desire to force this issue to a head. Plans were aired in the last months
of 1986 for a management buy-out of half the Standard Chartered holding,
but they came to nothing. Through the early months of 1987, Strauss and
his colleagues were more preoccupied with efforts to forge new ties with
Europe, preferably via the purchase of a bank in the UK, Germany or
Switzerland. McWilliam and his colleagues gave help and advice on several
occasions. Relations between the two banks appeared, on the surface at
least, to have weathered the storms of 1985–6 surprisingly well.

   Yet within just ten weeks or so of the crisis breaking over cross-border
provisions late in May 1987, the rupture was complete. It would often be
said later – and was vaguely asserted in press coverage at the time – that
the Group had been obliged to sell out by the tightening squeeze on its
balance sheet. Certainly the rush to sell off assets must have been a con-
tributory factor – but there is no record of any pressure in 1987 from the
Bank of England to this effect, unlike in 1985, nor was there a technical
case for the divestment at this point.[134] The substantial benefits of distancing the Group from StanBIC had already been secured by cutting its equity
stake below 50 per cent and so ending the need to consolidate StanBIC's
balance sheet. A sale of the minority stake – marginally diluted from 42
to 39 per cent since 1985 – would raise some welcome cash for the Group;
but it would actually be detrimental to the Group's capital adequacy since
the proceeds were never going to match the value of the StanBIC shares
in London's balance sheet, and the shortfall would represent yet another
sizeable loss to the income statement for 1987.[135] It would also deprive the
Group of one of its best assets. The rand's depreciation was undoubtedly
a concern, but the Standard remained a fine bank and (as more than one
shrewd City analyst pointed out, when news of the proposed sale was
leaked to the press) it made a more consistently robust contribution to
earnings than most other operations in the Group. Such considerations,
though, made little difference to the real impetus behind the split, which
was the inclination among Standard Chartered's non-Executive

Directors – and especially its white knights from Hong Kong – to see 'rationalization' as code for a stiff retrenchment in the West.

For months there had been no mistaking a sense in the Boardroom, exemplified by the forceful stance of Y. K Pao and his son-in-law Peter Woo, that the Group's Asian interests had now to be given renewed emphasis. It was, in a way, the revenge of the old Chartered Bank. Its friends in the East had made all the difference in the bid battle; now it was time to acknowledge their primacy. The crisis over cross-border provisions simply crystallized this resolve to turn away from all the troubled Western sovereign credit borrowers – and this inevitably posed a question mark over the link with South Africa, where Standard Chartered's total portfolio, bolstered by huge lines of credit for the Standard Bank, still stood at $1.1 billion, far in excess of any other single country exposure for the Group (and, as of March 1987, unaccompanied by any loss provision whatever).[136] Letting go of the StanBIC stake would open the way to curbing this anomaly. It would also shake off a wearying political liability that several of the non-executives on the Board, perhaps noting StanBIC's search for other banking connections, had undoubtedly begun to resent. All that said, however, losing South Africa as part of turning away from the misadventures in Europe and the US might be deemed in retrospect a case of letting the baby slip out with the bathwater – and there were some who argued as much at the time. The final decision to sell out was opposed on the Board by two Directors, Robert Holmes à Court and Robin Baillie. (The latter had retired from the executive team on health grounds early in 1987, but had been invited to rejoin the Board as a non-executive.) Perhaps McWilliam might also have been expected to vote against it, but it clearly emerged as part of the Clydesdale proposal which he was backing as a potentially transforming move for the Group. The seductive formula, as he jotted down early in June, seemed to be 'Out of South Africa and into Scotland'.[137] Then his Clydesdale proposal was blocked – another triumph for the retrenchers – but the momentum behind the StanBIC sale was by that point unstoppable.

Or, at least, the Board considered it unstoppable. In the event, it was almost snared by the technical difficulties of achieving the sale on terms acceptable to all. It was a thorny transaction, perhaps inevitably so, given the issues at stake for StanBIC itself. Conrad Strauss responded almost casually to news of the sale decision, at the start of June.[138] By July he was much less relaxed, telling McWilliam of his serious concern that the Group was about to sell its shares with precipitate haste – or, as he put it, 'just going to do a Barclays'.[139] Alongside a deep ambivalence about losing its London shareholder, there was also real concern over who might replace it. The StanBIC Board was desperate to ensure that, if the 39 per cent stake were to be sold, it would at least end up in friendly hands. This in practice meant Donald Gordon's Liberty Life or one of the other large South African groups allied to his cause. Liberty Life already owned almost 24 per cent, but as an insurance business it was precluded under South African rules from owning more than 30 per cent of a bank. This guaranteed a rich mix of counter-parties for London's negotiating team, in addition to which a way had to be found of squaring any agreed deal with the Reserve Bank in Pretoria. Tight rules over share sales and foreign exchange needed to be carefully finessed. It was not clear by the start of July that the Group's advisers in Johannesburg, Hill Samuel, were making much progress. McWilliam asked Robin Baillie to fly down and take charge. The erstwhile merchant banker who had begun his Standard Chartered career burying the Wallace Brothers business in as orderly a fashion as possible thus ended it by interring the London Board's historical engagement with South Africa. A sale price of R19 per share was the Group's firm demand, to produce a cash remittance of just over £146 million. StanBIC's Board thought London should accept a much steeper discount to the current share price of about R21. Baillie's negotiations with his counterpart at the Standard, Eddie Theron, involved an unexpected degree of brinkmanship ('it looks as if the whole deal is going to fall apart', noted McWilliam early in August[140]) and Donald Gordon's mediation proved crucial. The final agreement was an unsentimental affair, but London got its R19 target price.* The Standard Merchant Bank designed some ingenious dividend arrangements that enabled the payment to pass muster with the Reserve Bank, while the Standard's shareholding was comprehensively rejigged.[141] Baillie later recalled an odd ending:

> I was invited the following day [8 August] to lunch with StanBIC and was seated on De Villiers' right. Much to my surprise, neither De Villiers nor Strauss, nor any other director, made any mention of the deal. Neither, obviously, did I. Sic transit gloria mundi![142]

The Standard's share price soon bounced back to R21 in the market, and its Directors were assured by Graham and McWilliam that relations between the two banks would remain close.[143] Bishopsgate made several gestures in this direction: it obtained a UK work permit for Eddie Theron,

---

* Actually it received R18.75 and a formal R18.99 per share when the complex remittance package was unwrapped. Some weeks after the transaction, in line with City of London custom, the bankers at Hill Samuel produced a limited run of perspex 'tombstone' paperweights. Embedded in the back of each one was a new South African one cent piece.

for instance, allowing him to move to London as part of discreet prepara-
tions by the Standard to build its own presence in the City. And some in
South Africa voiced a genuine ambivalence over the final demise of the
North–South connection founded so long ago by John Paterson and his
Port Elizabeth cronies. Donald Gordon himself told the press 'it was the
severance of an old and very important business link'.[144] Given the size of
London's loan portfolio in the Republic, though, it was not long before
the two banks were eyeing each other as direct competitors – and most of
the Standard's staff seemed delighted to be free at last of the old Empire
legacy.

At Standard Chartered, meanwhile, other items on the retrenchers' hit
list included minority stakes in several smaller banks and financial-services
concerns – but by far the most important target after StanBIC was that
other Western bastion of McWilliam's federalist structure, the Union
Bank. By the middle of 1987, the Californian business had unhappily
exposed the fatal weakness of the federalist philosophy: it required that
far-flung senior executives should seek always to act in the best interests
of the Group as a whole. The management team in Los Angeles had never
exactly prided itself on being part of Standard Chartered, but John Harrigan had at least engaged regularly with his London colleagues so long
as the Group's other North American interests offered scope for the Union
Bank's expansion. Since around the start of 1985, more parochial ambitions in the US had begun to drive the Union's agenda and too little had
been done to restrain them. In September 1985 Harrigan had rushed the
London Board into approving an expensive purchase of the fourth largest
bank in Arizona.* Much weight was attached at the time to his personal
rapport with the United Bank's sixty-year-old Chairman and President,
James P. Simmons, and a close affinity between their two banks.[145] A
Board paper on the proposal was dated 3 September 1985 and a press
release went out just three days later. ('The match couldn't be better',
enthused Mr Simmons, who would be staying at the helm and joining
Union's Board.)

---

* It valued the publicly traded United Bank at $333 million – a price/earnings ratio of 18x,
based on the latter's forecast of profits for 1985, and a 2.7 multiple of net asset value. (The
equivalent numbers for the Standard Chartered on the London market were less than 5x and
about 0.5 respectively.) Admittedly, the United Bank's performance in recent years had been
impressive. Headquartered in Phoenix, its net profits had grown from $8.0 million to
$22.4 million in five years, representing a return on equity in 1984 of almost 20 per cent.
This had been achieved with forty-one branches and a thousand staff. But the principal
motive for the deal surely lay elsewhere. Once the 25th biggest bank in the country, Union
Bank was now ranked 50th in the US banks' league table – and the acquisition of United,
made possible by a creeping deregulation of the US industry, would lift it back up to 37th.

Due diligence measures supposedly followed, before the acquisition was formally completed in January 1987. But the Group accountants in Bishopsgate had scarcely had time to write off more than $110 million of goodwill before a huge bad debt was disclosed in Phoenix. It transpired that the Arizona bank had grossly misrepresented its credit controls, and had arrived inside the Group with hopelessly inadequate debt provisions. (Mr Simmons was soon to notify the Board of his decision to retire.) Running in parallel with this bleak saga over the first half of 1987 was a problematic negotiation, again led by Harrigan, to buy a second bank in Arizona – the Valley National Bank – and so to achieve a kind of 'super-regional' status for Union Bank in the Western US. The Valley National's Board dithered over its intentions, and their putative merger with Union was chopped down in June with the same axe that felled the Clydesdale project. At this point, Y. K. Pao and Peter Woo took a harder look at the Union Bank itself, and decided it, too, was now surplus to the Group's core needs. Unlike StanBIC, Union Bank sat in the Group's balance sheet at a modest valuation that implied a chance of making a useful profit from any sale. When analysts at Salomon Brothers published a paper valuing it at as much as $2.2 billion – which compared with a book value of $880 million – the Board needed no further persuading.* Both Union Bank and United went on the block (as separate lots) in September. Harrigan was given 'indefinite leave of absence' in November.[146]

By this stage, though, it was not Harrigan's departure that was really exercising minds on the Board but the possibility that McWilliam himself might soon be obliged to step down. With his broad vision of the Group's future fatally undermined and his personal relations with many Board colleagues (especially Pao and Woo) regularly stretched to the limit, his position was growing more tenuous with each passing month. The Directors had by now lost count of the number of challenging merger propositions that had been aired in vain over the past four years. None had been more frustrated over this than McWilliam himself, who had begun privately to despair of the Board's handling of most key issues under Graham's chairmanship. But his credibility as Managing Director had inevitably been diminished with each setback. Poor half-year results for 1987 and the dispiriting escalation of bad debts and write-offs heightened a mounting sense of crisis. The Wall Street crash of October 1987 added to the Group's woes in several respects. It weakened many of its corporate customers; it depressed the likely value of assets-for-sale such as the Union

---

* It was later confirmed that Salomon Brothers had got its sums wrong, and the correct valuation was nearer $1.2 billion – but by then the decision to sell was all but irreversible.

Bank; it attracted yet more criticism of the defence tactics of 1986 in some quarters, by exposing Robert Holmes à Court to possible ruin and casting doubt on his future role on the Board; and it led the Bank of England to stiffen its ratio requirements, raising again serious concern over the Group's capital position. It also brought the Group's shares crashing back to earth: having generally traded at more than £8 each since the Lloyds bid, they plunged back to £4 and levels not seen since 1985. Plainly disconcerted by the direction of events, Peter Graham had in the summer asked an outside consultant to talk privately to all the Directors and 'to advise on the strengthening, in all senses, of the Board'.[147] On 17 November, the consultant was invited to address a meeting of the Board on his findings – and, with all Directors present, he proceeded to list ten highly critical views of the Group which he presented as a shared consensus. Item six on his list was that the Managing Director had lost the confidence of the Board. Only under cross-examination did it emerge that several Directors had in fact expressly distanced themselves from this opinion. The Chairman remained conspicuously silent. McWilliam afterwards made an angry note of the affair: 'It was altogether a disgraceful episode and it will be hard to extract value from it, let alone help [sic] my endeavours.'[148] This was surely putting a brave face on matters. It is hard not to conclude that his departure was from this point just a matter of time.

The next three and a half months were to play out almost as a parody of the past three and a half years. McWilliam had a penchant for musical metaphors. His diary entries for this period track a crescendo of rising tensions that ought to have prompted a reference to Ravel's *Bolero*. Negotiations for the sale of United Bank and of Union Bank provided a steadily more desperate search for agreement with their prospective US purchasers. Debates over capital adequacy grew ever more heated, as the Board came to terms with the need to appeal to shareholders for a substantial injection of additional capital. Fresh merger possibilities began to come and go again in ever more bewildering fashion (the other parties included Barclays, Ford Motor Company – and even Lloyds Bank[149]). And, at ever shorter intervals, there were Boardroom clashes that gave warning of the approaching climax – none more extraordinary than a row on 25 January 1988, when it emerged that three of the Directors had held a secret meeting with the Bank of England's Rodney Galpin a few days earlier, apparently to discuss their concerns over the Group's capital position. McWilliam was shocked and angry to learn of this: 'It can only have been disloyal and damaging in intent and will unsettle the Bank of England.'[150] But it gave due warning that the Bank was about to call the tune. What this would mean for him had actually started to become clear some weeks earlier. In the last week of November, the American Express Group had proposed a merger. Not only had the initiative been withheld from McWilliam for several days, but it had been helped along by Galpin at the Bank, who had offered to chair a meeting between the two sides on 23 December to expedite a formal agreement as quickly as possible. The Bank had apparently known of American Express's plan since June: the American executives told Graham and McWilliam they had been 'encouraged' by the Bank.[151] Having originally favoured seeing one of the UK clearers do the job, the Bank was evidently now ready to welcome a rescue for Standard Chartered even if it was led by a bank based in New York. Here, it seemed, was vivid confirmation that all confidence had been lost in the Group's ability to resolve its own problems. Graham and McWilliam sat down with Galpin and his colleagues at the Bank on the afternoon of 1 December 'to probe their view of us':

> The result was thoroughly depressing in that they have completely bought the argument (from HàC & Pao) that we have lost our way and are in process of losing the confidence of the market. [Brian] Quinn went so far as to say that he felt something serious could happen in the next few months. They did not believe that the sale of Union [Bank] would help sentiment. In short, we have run out of time and they want a quick fix.[152]

Graham was offered the chairmanship of the putative Anglo-American combination, and he gave it his full support. After reviewing the implications of the American Express deal with the Group Executive Committee, however, McWilliam rejected it as a deeply flawed concept. He then fought tenaciously through January to avert it – thus rescuing Standard Chartered's future for the second time in the space of eight months. This finally wrecked his relationship with Graham, and can fairly be assumed not to have much endeared him to the Bank of England, either.

On 3 February, the Bank resorted to a more direct approach. The Governor, Robin Leigh-Pemberton, wrote formally to the Chairman and Directors setting out a series of acute concerns over the Group and alluding to 'growing unease in financial markets about Standard Chartered's current situation and future prospects'. The conclusion was brutal. 'The Bank now requires the Board . . . to consider, as a matter of urgency, remedial measures to secure the interests of depositors.' These included 'the strengthening of management'.[153] McWilliam orchestrated a painstaking reply on 29 February, acknowledging the gravity of the Bank's criticisms while pointing out how and where the Bank might have underestimated the Group's current remedies.[154] But by now the die was cast. In handing over his letter of 3 February, the Governor had privately confided to Graham that McWilliam's resignation was required.[155] The timing was awkward: the bank was just preparing to throw a huge party at the British Museum on 2 March to celebrate the start of an exhibition it was sponsoring, on the Ottoman Empire under Suleiman the Magnificent, to be co-hosted by Graham and McWilliam together. So the Chairman stayed his hand. The party went ahead, and was handled by Graham with all his customary bonhomie. Then, early the next morning, McWilliam was summoned to his office and asked by him and Leslie Fletcher to resign. Just two hours later, it seems quite by chance, the libel action against the *Financial Times* over its original white knights story was settled on the steps of the court. An article in the *FT* the next day, Friday 4 March, stated that the paper accepted the findings of the Bank's inquiry without reservation and would be making a contribution to Standard Chartered's legal costs.[156] It was an ironic start to a day that saw McWilliam's departure announced before the end of the afternoon.

Rodney Galpin rarely spoke of his work once he had returned home to Berkshire in the evening – he almost never stayed in town overnight – and many years later his widow had a clear memory of one of the few occasions when he did so. It was early in 1988, and Sylvia Galpin recalled: 'He just came in and said "They want me to go into Standard Chartered".'[157] And so they did. At some point, and surely prior to the Governor's aside to Graham on 3 February, Leigh-Pemberton and his deputy, George Blunden, agreed with Galpin that it would be a good idea for him to move into Standard Chartered, just as Kit McMahon had gone from the Bank into the Midland a couple of years earlier. McMahon had taken the role of 'Chairman and Chief Executive', and there can never have been much doubt that Galpin would do the same, though one of Graham's Board colleagues, Sir Derek Mitchell, did later confide to McWilliam 'the Governor insisted that Galpin become Chairman' – which perhaps suggests that someone on the Board might initially have suggested a slighter less exalted role.[158] Graham and Leslie Fletcher evidently reached an accord with the Bank, anyway, even while McWilliam was labouring over the official reply to the Governor's letter. Galpin would take up his new post later in the year, at a date yet to be decided, and Graham would in the meantime act as Chairman and Chief Executive himself. This was presented to McWilliam on 3 March as a fait accompli. Naturally all parties were then keen to play down any sense of a crisis by pitching the new appointment in public as a straightforward commercial hiring. 'I've been looking for some months with the help of headhunters for a new Chairman,' Graham blithely told the press. 'I talked to Rodney and he sounded very enthusiastic.'[159] It was true, too, that Galpin's four-year tenure as a

Director of the Bank was shortly due to expire, though at the age of fifty-six he could confidently have expected a fresh contract. Graham's blandishments were indulged by the press next day, as though he had genuinely lured Galpin across to Standard Chartered rather as Edmund Hall-Patch had enticed Cyril Hawker to accept the chairmanship of the Standard bank in 1962 (not a parallel anyone remarked upon at the time). This version of events would hardly have passed muster, had the press been aware of Galpin's critical role in the Bank's confidential dealings with Standard Chartered's Directors right up to the end of February. He could hardly have gone through the past few months wearing his Bank of England hat, after all, with a privately arranged job offer from Graham in his back pocket. But the delicate background was not apparent to out-siders in any detail. So Graham had a face-saving narrative – and Galpin himself was careful to avoid confirming any impression that he had been installed as a fireman at the Bank's behest.[160]

This was broadly how the City construed the news, just the same, since there had plainly been a Boardroom coup. The share price dipped 8 per cent lower, which the press generally attributed to market uncertainties over the Group's immediate future rather than any sense of regret at McWilliam's passing. Investors, after all, were still heavily out of pocket compared with where they might have been, had the bid from Lloyds suc-ceeded. In broad terms, the stock went on trading on either side of £5 a share for the rest of 1988 – just as it had done through the years between McWilliam's appointment and the early months of 1986 when the market had begun to scent a bid. Lloyds had offered 840p a share. Inevitably, and whatever the longer-term considerations, the opportunity cost to date of McWilliam's victory largely dictated the market's verdict on his tenure. The abruptness of his dismissal nonetheless came as a shock to many of his colleagues, not least because his difficulties had been so evident for months past that they thought a gentler and more elegant exit could have been contrived with very little effort. Among the eighty or so consoling letters that he received were several expressing dismay at the final outcome ('They've shot the wrong man', wrote Stephen Fay, author of that brief 1986 history of the Group) and an especially touching note arrived from South Africa, from StanBIC's Chairman, Henri de Villiers:

> for some time now I have had a very strong feeling that you personally were under siege and that life must have been very difficult for you. I have always regarded you as a friend of this strange country and [appreciated] that you were sympathetic to our, that is StanBIC's, endeavours to muddle our way through a rather sick society.[161]

McWilliam himself managed a remarkably dispassionate view of events, beginning with a cool appraisal on the very evening of his dismissal ('There is of course nothing that can be done to reverse events, but it is a mad, not to say embittering situation').[162] His thoughts turned within days to the start of a fresh career.* In the circumstances, there was little he could say to colleagues by way of a valedictory – though in fact, in typical fashion, he had set down some lengthy reflections on his tenure for the benefit of the Board the previous October, when storm clouds had first begun to gather. He had concluded that retrospective with his usual insight and candour:

> Looking back over four years of organisational reform and attempts to change the culture of a large and tradition-conscious company, perhaps the most powerful recollection is of the difficulty of striking the right balance between what needed to be done in objective terms, with what could be done with the executives available and without challenging too radically the accepted mores of the Board and of the institution. It is impossible to resist the conclusion that more ruthless and more radical action would have served shareholders' interests better; yet one seemed to be straining the bounds of the possible at the time and the record shows an unprecedented period of activity.[163]

As the Bank of England's choice and a man with a strong commercial streak, Rodney Galpin looked unlikely to be much daunted by those 'accepted mores'. More ruthless and more radical action beckoned.

---

* Before the end of 1988, he had been appointed Director of London University's School of Oriental and African Studies, an institution transformed under his leadership over the following seven years. He was made a KCMG in 1996, and went on to chair a variety of public and academic bodies including the Royal Commonwealth Society (1996–2002), the Royal African Society (1996–2004) and the Centre for Study of African Economies in Oxford (1997–2012). He authored *The Development Business: A History of the Commonwealth Development Corporation* (Palgrave, 2001), where he was a Board member from 1990 to 1997.

10

Re-emerging Markets, 1988–98

1. CORES, PRUNES AND BANANA SKINS

Break up or break out? That was the question for the man from the Bank of England. The business knocked together less than twenty years earlier – with more than a helping hand, in all probability, from the Bank itself – was trapped by the spring of 1988 in a terrible spiral of decline. Five years of corporate plans and merger plots had only served in the end to expose just how far the skills and systems of Standard Chartered had fallen behind the pace of modern international banking. The accounts told a bleak story: total shareholders' funds at the end of 1987 had fallen to £717 million, down from £1.29 billion a year earlier. The Group's earnings were now struggling to keep pace with shocking loan losses to which there seemed no end. To break out of the spiral would require changes altogether more drastic than anything Michael McWilliam had ever felt able to propose. Perhaps, then, a dismantling of the Group might, after all, be the more practical option – a sad but logical acceptance of the truth about old dogs and new tricks.

The post-1975 vision, of a Group looking at least as much to the West as the East, had been tried and effectively abandoned (though the disposal of the Union and United banks had yet to be finally settled, and branches were still in place, albeit rarely in profit, all across Britain and continental Europe). What lingered on was a Group *sans* its historic link with the Standard Bank of South Africa and *sans*, too, much of the pride and self-confidence it had so long enjoyed as a flagship of the Empire's exchange-banking days. No one supposed there was really much of a future for the old Chartered Bank's culture, which for generations had seen the top jobs in London taken by men who had come up through the ranks – veterans seasoned in the East, whose steadfast careers since their youth could be traced in all those photographs of sports teams and office parties, wedding days and customer receptions to be found in surviving copies of *Curry & Rice*.[1] (A successor magazine, *StanChart*, had been launched in 1976 with a similar format – which now looked sadly outdated.*) True, the Bishopsgate executive still included a few who had risen up the traditional ladder, not least Sir Peter Graham. Knighted the previous year, the sixty-six-year-old Graham had retired as Managing Director in 1983 and now found himself – in a move that encapsulated the limbo status of the Group by early 1988 – back as both Group Chairman and Chief Executive. But those around him had a wide mix of backgrounds. The old guard included wily Alan Orsich (joined 1950), still head of the bank's trading and treasury operations, and Bill Brown (joined 1953), newly returned from Hong Kong to become Managing Director of the bank. Others, like the Finance Director Richard Stein and two of the three Senior General Managers, were relative newcomers. And all were soon hanging on decisions that would have to be taken by a complete outsider – and above all on his answer to that first and fundamental question.

Rodney Galpin appears initially to have supposed that a break-up of some kind was inevitable. Several weeks after McWilliam's departure, he invited Henry Jarecki to lunch and spoke of the challenge he faced. Two days later Jarecki lunched with McWilliam and they mused together over the future Chairman's intentions. 'It appears that Galpin sees his mission as to dispose of SC as a whole or in pieces,' noted McWilliam afterwards, 'but [he] has a morale problem of [*sic*] being reluctant to discuss the matter internally.'[2] Assigned to 'gardening leave', Galpin was sitting in a temporary office at the Bank of England, contemplating the possibilities that he understandably feared might spread alarm within Bishopsgate. If he was indeed minded to dismantle the Group, this would not have come as a surprise to many people. He had been seen for years as a troubleshooter for the Bank. It had to be likely that he would deal with Standard Chartered much as he had dealt in the past with insolvent secondary banks and embattled bullion dealers, with deft use of a cleaver and no time for sentimentality.

With just a few months to go before his planned arrival at the bank, however, Galpin began taking steps that were definitely at odds with this approach. Above all, he began scouting for non-Executive Directors who would bring real authority to the Boardroom. He was well-placed to find them. Galpin had been an influential figure at the Bank since the 1950s,

---

* *Curry & Rice* had helped nurture the Chartered staff's sense of togetherness for almost half a century with a stream of gossipy articles from around the network (most of them given an alliterative headline, as in 'Penang Patter', 'Madras Musings', 'Sandakan Snippets' – even, more artfully, 'Djakarta Djottings'). It had been discontinued in 1974. *StanChart* reached its fortieth edition in 1988.

and was well-known far beyond the confines of the City. ('I was lucky enough to get some quite good jobs'[3] – including Private Secretary to Lord Cromer, Governor of the Bank for five years in the early 1960s.) Famously handsome in his younger days – secretaries, it was said, had swooned at his passing – he also had an amply deserved reputation as an unfailingly courteous and supremely urbane central banker: a mix of Clark Gable and Sir Humphrey Appleby, he had all the characteristic skills of the pro- verbial mandarin. Colleagues had fallen into line over the years, not infrequently foxed by his Delphic approach. 'Until you knew him well', in the words of one admiring Bank official, 'you could never tell when he disagreed with you.'[4] His personal charm could be irresistible, and he deployed it to great effect over the summer of 1988. By the time he took up the reins at Standard Chartered in October, Galpin had roped into the Boardroom some of the most illustrious names in British business. The best-known of them were Sir Ralph Robins, Managing Director of aero-engine manufacturer Rolls-Royce; Patrick Gillam of BP, whose exec- utive brief as one of its Managing Directors included the whole of the oil giant's operations in Asia, Africa and Australasia; and Rudolph Agnew, Chairman and Chief Executive of Consolidated Gold Fields. These were not individuals who would have been drawn to the idea of helping Galpin ride into the sunset. They joined him to help rescue the bank.

Perhaps, once he had landed his new role, Galpin had found himself not entirely immune after all to the romance of Standard Chartered's long history.* More likely, his grasp of shifting fashions in the international banking arena had prompted second thoughts about any break-up strat- egy. Selling off the Group's Asian businesses would not be the straightforward assignment that it might have been at the start of the decade. Much had changed in the intervening years. The post-1974 re- cycling of petrodollars had drawn the big banks into international lending on an unprecedented scale by the early 1980s, and this in turn had led to a general fixation with the merits of a global asset-book – full of loans to sovereign credits that could hardly go wrong (since, as Citibank's Walter Wriston had memorably observed, 'countries don't go bust'). Now bankers knew better, courtesy of endless crises over the forced 'rescheduling' of

---

* He was certainly well aware of it. Generations of boys destined for careers in the East over the first half of the nineteenth century attended the East India College in Hertfordshire. Closed after the East India Company's demise, it was reopened in 1862 as the Haileybury and Imperial Service College – and went on to become, in modern times, one of Britain's more exclusive private schools. Galpin was one of its proudest old boys – and in 1987–8 hap- pened to be serving for a year as President of its alumni association, the Haileybury Society.

loans to Mexico, Brazil and a dozen other sovereign borrowers. The long-running Third World debt crisis of the 1980s had left shareholders generally disenchanted with talk of geographical diversification. Higher marks were being awarded in London and New York by 1988 for strategies that focused again on domestic markets. This could perhaps play to Standard Chartered's advantage in two ways. As several of the leading brokers' analysts pointed out – with a dampening effect on the share price – there was unlikely to be a queue of potential suitors. The Group might be blessedly free for a while from constant takeover speculation.[5] And, second, it suggested the Group might well have more scope to prove its mettle in the East. Local banks would continue to pose ever stiffer competition, but with most of the larger international banks stepping back (Citibank was a notable exception), Standard Chartered could take fuller advantage of the unique spread of its network which so differentiated it from the pack. Or so Galpin, anyway, now felt ready to propose. To confirm and map out this potential, he turned before the end of the summer to a management consultant called Leslie Dighton.[6] The latter ran a small private consultancy, Corporate Renewal Associates (CRA), which specialized in helping large organizations to redefine themselves in the face of a rapidly changing external environment.* And in commissioning CRA, Galpin handed Dighton a wide brief. He was to conduct an audit of the Group's culture and organizational effectiveness – for the disenchantment over business with the sovereign borrowers of the Third World was not the only critical mutation in the banking world of the late 1980s.

Others needed noting, too, along with their implications for Standard Chartered. They included, for example, a sobering reappraisal of the value of 'one-stop shopping' in the financial sphere. Where many had earlier hastened to capitalize on deregulation by assembling the components of a putative universal bank, few had much interest by the end of the decade in merging with businesses only loosely aligned with their own. (Another reason to hope for a period of calm for Standard Chartered – which after all the anguished Board discussions of the 1980s had emerged from the Big Bang frenzy as one of the more conspicuous City names still intact.)

---

* Dighton came strongly recommended by the Chairman of the British Post Office, Ron Dearing, with whom he had worked closely on a remarkable revival of the UK's postal monopoly since 1983. Dearing had been intrigued by the challenges facing Standard Chartered when he heard about them from Michael McWilliam in 1985 at a Ditchley Park conference drawing together UK business leaders and senior civil servants from Whitehall. Perhaps this had sown the seed of an approach to Galpin by Dighton in the summer of 1988. Other links with the Post Office over the next year or so were to include the recruitment of its personnel guru, Martin Fish, and of its Girobank boss, Malcolm Williamson.

The corollary was a renewed determination to stick to areas of known expertise, and to offer deeper services within more narrowly defined sectors. Closely related to this was another significant trend. Commercial banks in the early 1980s had still been concerned mostly with traditional customer relationships, extending loans and living largely off net interest income. Now their ambitions stretched far beyond humdrum lending. Fierce competition had cut margins to the bone; tougher supervision was adding constantly to costs. Hugely more sophisticated capital markets were meanwhile prompting the best corporate borrowers to tap investors directly for the funds they needed. This 'disintermediation' was hardly a blessing for the banks, but it did offer them an alternative livelihood. Fees could be earned on the packaging and sale of loans refashioned as securities, and this 'securitization' business – involving the emergence of whole new secondary markets and increasingly complex 'derivative' products – was reshaping the financial landscape quite drastically. (The switch of emphasis from lending to trading was encapsulated in the success of the 'Brady Bonds', introduced by the US Treasury in March 1989 as a solution to the Third World debt crisis: they turned lead into quasi-gold by effectively replacing dud sovereign loans with US-backed securities, to be traded by banks and investors at negotiable market prices.)

Above all, and permeating every other aspect of banking's evolution through the Big Bang in the City and the 'Greed is Good' era on Wall Street, the industry had adjusted everywhere to a level of professionalism that in the 1960s had been seen almost as the preserve of the leading US banks. For the new breed of bankers, to adopt only a slight caricature, one refrain sufficed: we are all Americans now. Well educated, highly trained, relatively specialized in their duties from one year to the next, they worked hard – even after lunch – and expected to be handsomely rewarded. Collegial networks were nice to have, but it was transactional expertise that really counted, and merit-based promotion took little heed of corporate (or, indeed, customer) loyalties. Most assumed, anyway, that advancing their careers would probably involve moving periodically from one employer to another. Where all this left the typical middle-aged Standard Chartered man, towards the end of a traditional career path, was a worrying question.* Galpin handed it to Dighton for a properly documented answer.

---

* Of course not all senior managers of Standard Chartered were men. But of the 293 individuals filling the top four bands of management at the start of 1990, just 20 were women – a gender ratio starkly out of line with trends elsewhere in the City by this date. ('Management Succession' by Geoff Armstrong and Martin Fish, Memorandum for the Board, 26 February 1991, SCB Box 2390.)

In the meantime, Galpin set about making room on the Board for its newly recruited members (and others to come shortly). Three of the longest-serving Directors had already retired at the AGM in May 1988.[7] Galpin moved quickly to agree terms for several other departures. As a Bank official, he had never concealed his unease at the influence exerted over the Board from Hong Kong. Sir Y. K. Pao acknowledged this – and his seventieth birthday on 10 November – by stepping down immediately, and taking steps to dispose in the market of his 14.9 per cent shareholding. (The timing of its sale is unclear, but it appears to have been completed well before his death in 1991, and reportedly incurred a net loss of around $100 million for Pao and his family.) His son-in-law Peter Woo agreed to resign after the AGM in 1989. Robert Holmes à Court retained his seat on the Board, but his financial affairs had been in such disarray since the Wall Street crash of October 1987 – indeed, he had lost control of his heavily indebted Bell Group to his fellow Australian, Alan Bond – that it was questionable how much longer he could retain his own 14.9 per cent interest in the Group; and his associate Alan Newman stepped down in December.[8] (In the event, Holmes à Court kept hold of his shares – but they were to be sold by his family after his sudden death, aged just fifty-three, in September 1990.) Four other Directors, including Deputy Chairman Leslie Fletcher, indicated that they would be retiring at the 1989 AGM.[9] Peter Graham himself bowed out as agreed in October, handing over a balance sheet usefully strengthened by a gratifyingly well-received rights issue for £304 million in his last month in office. It also happened that completion of the two bank sales in the US fell into Graham's final days – though, in both cases, contracts had been negotiated and exchanged at McWilliam's behest eight months previously. United Bank of Arizona was sold to Citibank in June 1988. The Group was obliged to hang on to a portfolio of bad debts nominally valued at $145 million, and nonetheless incurred a book loss of $81 million. (A civil suit was filed against the United Bank's auditors, Price Waterhouse, blaming them for a fraudulent window display in 1985 and seeking compensatory damages. It would lead in 1992 to the largest damages yet awarded against an accounting firm; but the ruling was overturned in an interminable US appeals process and nothing ultimately came of it.[10]) The disposal of Union Bank to a Californian subsidiary of the Bank of Tokyo had a slightly happier outcome, insofar as a $754 million price left the Group with a capital gain of about £90 million.* But it was scarcely the outcome that Graham

---

* Majority owned by its Japanese parent, California First Bank adopted Union Bank's name after acquiring it in 1988. Eight years later, the Bank of Tokyo, familiar to generations of

had envisaged in 1978, splashing out on his Los Angeles acquisition as a first step towards establishing a significant presence for Standard Chartered in the Western hemisphere. That strategy, while in many ways entirely rational at the time, now looked ill-judged in light of its troubled implementation. Once such a popular and formidable figure in Hong Kong, Peter Graham retired to his Sussex farm with a less glowing reputation than might once have seemed his due. It was not enhanced by his decision in 1989 to take up the non-executive chairmanship of Equatorial Bank, a tiny commercial bank catering mostly for Indian and East African Asian depositors in Britain, which collapsed in 1993. It was a sad note on which to have ended a banking career that stretched back to his Chartered days in Tokyo after the Second World War.

The challenge for the man replacing him in Bishopsgate was to come up with an alternative strategy that might prove more enduring. Within his first few months, Galpin restructured the governance of the Group – separating the PLC's Board from an executives-only board of the bank itself (still referred to as 'the Court'), divorcing the non-Executive Directors from the day-to-day running of operations – and made several critical changes to the senior management.* He ordered the sale of the Bishopsgate head office, opened with such panache only three years earlier, in favour of a smaller and far less glitzy headquarters in the City's Aldermanbury Square.[11] And he tore up a first draft of the 1989 budget that had hopelessly underestimated his determination to make a break with the past. As he explained to the Board, the executive had to accept 'a greater need for a responsible re-examination of goals'.[12] Critical re-examinations soon began piling up by the dozen. (It is perhaps a measure of the disarray at the top of the Group in these early stages of Galpin's regime that the Annual Report for 1988 emerged, in March 1989, full of glaring spaces. Its Review of Operations comprised eight mostly empty pages, and the 1988 Consolidated Balance Sheet appeared with nine of its twelve figures simply missing.[13]) Insiders and outsiders alike tore into Standard Chartered's traditional ways with a ferocity that left McWilliam's patient

---

Chartered Bank men as the Yokohama Specie Bank, merged with one of its biggest domestic competitors, Mitsubishi Bank. The latter had also acquired a West Coast subsidiary in the 1980s – none other than Bank of California, the original target of Graham's foray into the US banking sector in 1977. So Union Bank and Bank of California were brought together in the end, and as one merged entity (UnionBanCal) comprise today one of the principal businesses that make up the huge Mitsubishi UFJ Financial Group.

* The non-Executive Directors at the end of 1989, in addition to Sir Ralph Robins, Patrick Gillam, Rudolph Agnew and Robert Holmes à Court, comprised The Lord Pennock, Robin Baillie, John Craig, Philip Robinson, Paul Rudder and The Rt Hon. Ian Stewart MP.

analyses looking like the merest gentle carping. Suddenly the shortcomings of the bank were seen to be legion – inadequately trained staff, hopelessly bureaucratic procedures, risibly porous credit controls, discredited personnel functions, skimpy or non-existent management-information systems, creaking IT resources, a senior management culture which had created barons in their castles with oceans in place of moats. On and on went the list.

Some of the most devastating observations, backed up with copious research findings from across the network, came from Dighton's team. The CRA consultants reported back to Galpin in March 1989.[14] They charted the Group's organizational effectiveness against a matrix of attributes. An exemplary client with a top billing on all fronts would show up as a diamond on their grid. Alas, poor Standard Chartered sparkled less radiantly. Indeed, searching for the *mot juste* with which to describe their graphic representation of the Group, the consultants could offer only 'a withered prune'. Their prescription was blunt: 'a total transformation of the culture in all respects'.[15] The Withered Prune's Chairman accepted their findings and agreed with Dighton on a recovery programme, inevitably christened 'Breakout'. It was to provide the framework for countless initiatives and management conferences over the next three years. Out of these, starting with a series of strategy reviews from around the network and a seminal gathering of the senior managers at a south London venue in July 1989, there emerged another fundamental change of direction for the Group. It marked, in effect, a reversal of the turn taken at that Hyde Park Hotel conference in 1975. A formal 'Purpose Statement' made this unambiguously clear:

> Standard Chartered is a multi-domestic bank gathering funds through strong franchises in Africa and Asia, financing foreign trade supported by strong Treasury products, an extensive network and relationships with financial institutions.[16]

Here was a business model not much different from the commercial proposition put to the Chartered Bank's very first shareholders in the initial stock market prospectus of 1852 (proclaiming the bank's intent 'to extend the legitimate facilities of banking to the vast and rapidly expanding trade' of the East). The geographical focus – albeit with the addition of Africa – and the stress on trade finance, networking and relationships amounted to a reaffirmation, for the late twentieth century, of the guiding principles that Howard Gwyther had asserted tirelessly through thirty years of the Victorian era. Gwyther had turned the bank of the nineteenth century into one of the strongest sinews binding the City to Britain's

Empire in the East. As their 'Corporate Goal', Galpin and his colleagues spelled out an aspiration to make Standard Chartered into 'the bank of choice between the developed and developing world' – which sounded like a sensible bid for more than a passing degree of historical continuity. Of course there was irony in this. Despite all the criticism levelled at the old Chartered bankers and their anachronistic colonial ways, it was the Eastern franchise served by them so doggedly that was now identified as the best basis for a corporate recovery.

For the region's trade could be seen without much exaggeration as 'vast and rapidly expanding' once again. The Asia Pacific Rim had accounted for 13 per cent of world trade in 1980; now its share was up to 20 per cent, and rising fast. Over the same period, intra-regional trade had risen from $65 billion to $111 billion – with Hong Kong's trade with China

Map 10. The bedrock of the Asian franchise, c. 1990

now accounting for half of it. (The June 1989 massacre in Beijing's Tiananmen Square cast an untimely shadow over this part of the general picture, but few observers expected it to have long-term economic consequences.*) Growth rates through the decade had averaged less than 3 per cent for the developed countries of the OECD, and under 2 per cent for the developing countries of Africa and Latin America, but across the Asia Pacific region they had reached 6.5 per cent, and were heading higher in 1989 for Thailand, Singapore and Malaysia.[17] The single most optimistic – and persuasive – paper submitted to the London executive in 1989 came from David Moir, a Rhodesian by birth whose own career had begun with the Standard Bank in Zambia in 1958 and had flourished in the Far East. (He was that rare bird, a former Standard man whose career had prospered in both Africa and Asia – 'I went from the least populated country in the world to the most populated: from Botswana to Hong Kong.'[18] After a successful stint in Hong Kong – where, like all Standard men, he encountered an often less than wholly inclusive Chartered Bank culture – he had worked for three years as head of the bank in Zimbabwe before returning to management posts in Kuala Lumpur and, most recently, Singapore.) Moir pointed out to his peers in London that trade and investment opportunities in south-east Asia had grown enormously over the 1980s. The region had hitherto been largely dependent on commodity exports, with an entrenched ambivalence towards foreign direct investment and a reliance on public-sector growth that had long entailed steadily rising levels of external debt. Now the private sector was emerging as the real engine of growth: foreign investors were being eagerly courted, Japanese and European multinational corporations were building vast labour-intensive assembly plants on the fringes of many of the region's largest cities – enlisting hundreds of small and medium-sized companies as their local suppliers – and manufactured exports were storming ahead. Moir might also have added, had he been pitching his case nine months later, that turmoil in Tokyo's financial markets had embroiled the Japanese banks in a crisis deep enough to curtail their activities across the region, for at least the next couple of years. It was another reason to see trade finance in Asia as a rapidly expanding opportunity for Standard Chartered.

Tilting the Group's geographical balance back towards Asia was a

---

* The tanks had just rolled into Tiananmen Square when Galpin arrived in Beijing for a long-scheduled meeting with Deng Xiaoping and his advisers. The timing was awkward for the bank, but the political background scarcely encroached on the talks. 'They said very little about it, quite honestly, and didn't seem to be unduly embarrassed.' (Galpin, interview with author, 14 July 2011.)

fundamental step, but the Breakout reorientation of 1989–91 also involved another, and subtler, shift of almost as much importance. Ever since the days of Gwyther's ascendancy, top executives had talked of networking between the principal branches of the bank as its single most powerful asset. That, anyway, had always been the theory. In practice, the commitment to a consensual approach had generally been more honoured in the breach than the observance. Telegraphy and ship mail had given way to telex, telephone and jet travel. Modern technology, though, had so far changed inter-branch communications rather less than might be supposed.* Nor had it done very much to mitigate the tendency towards decentralization, deeply engrained in the DNA of the Group. Turf rivalries and professional egos had long ensured a disdain for Head Office in most of the network's biggest cities, and not just Hong Kong. Few branch Managers could ever entirely resist preferring to be a big frog in a little pond rather than the alternative; and, over the years, some had been quite infamous croakers. McWilliam had calculated, with his federalism, that ceding semi-autonomy in a formal way to just a few main branches as regional centres might actually enhance their willingness to co-operate with each other (and would be a price worth paying, to reduce the number of ponds across the network). In the conference sessions of 1989, this was deemed to have been a mistake. Newly appointed Directors like Patrick Gillam were stunned to discover how little the major offices – especially Hong Kong and Singapore – made any real effort to work together.

Federalism was quickly consigned to the past. As a big step in the opposite direction, two Banking Directors were appointed in 1990, one based in Singapore for 'Asia Pacific' (which essentially covered all territories east of India), and the other in London for the (Western) rest. Respectively David Moir and David Brougham, they were seen as heavy hitters capable of dismantling the barriers between the traditional country franchises. At the same time, Galpin and his colleagues insisted some activities were not only 'core businesses' but also quintessentially

---

* Routine contacts in the pre-internet era could still be surprisingly old-fashioned. As late as the mid-1980s, some branches had still not acquired fax machines. In 1986, a nineteen-year-old Tracy Clarke was working in the Nottingham branch of the UK bank. 'I was a relationship manager for a company that was part of the Courtaulds Group. They had a textile division in Shanghai and had run into a problem in financing a particular trade between their Nottingham office and Shanghai. I figured we could help them, since we had offices at both ends of the trade. But I had to type a letter to the branch Manager of Shanghai which took two weeks to get there; and when he decided that joint action could be a good idea, he wrote me a letter and that took two weeks to get back.' (Interview with the author, 3 October 2013.) Communications with China had been notoriously difficult for years, though, so Shanghai's problems were rather exceptional.

dependent on linkages across the Group. 'Several businesses had been identified as having improved potential for management or coordination on a "global" basis. It was felt that development of these would enable the value of the Group to exceed the sum of the individual components.'[19] The long-standing Mocatta business belonged in this category; as did the correspondent-banking services run by 'FIG' ('Financial Institutions Group') which listed about three thousand of the world's largest banks as clients. At this stage, though, Standard Chartered could only lay claim to one genuinely 'global' business – its Treasury operation, which traded currencies and interest-rate products in the international money markets (the direct descendant, it could be said, of the Eastern exchange banking of the past). By the City and Wall Street standards of 1989–91, it was run on astonishingly primitive lines. This came as a shock to a new recruit, Mike Rees, hired as the UK Financial Controller in June 1990. 'It was like entering a ten-year time warp. The UK Treasury's balance sheet every month-end was literally done with a pencil as an extended trial balance on a fourteen-column piece of paper, and there was no general ledger at all.'[20] Nonetheless, its practised routines under the fierce eye of Alan Orsich and its long-standing foreign-exchange expertise – particularly in the marketplace for the more exotic currencies of Asia – at least provided the basis of a substantial operation: its annual trading profits by 1991 were fast heading for £100 million. The new emphasis on 'core businesses', to be run on a global basis, put a premium on modernizing this Treasury unit. Other consequences would follow soon.

The Breakout programme unquestionably made its mark. Staffing at Head Office was cut by a third. After two years, 40 per cent of the top three hundred positions in the Group had fresh occupants. In their bid to jettison the past, some of the new men may perhaps have shown excessive zeal on occasions.[21] (The contents of Bishopsgate's museum and library were sold off, and the Group's modest archival arrangements were simply binned, as were an unknown quantity of historical records – see Appendix A.) But the vigorous assault on the culture of the bank after 1988 had other, happier consequences, leaving it palpably less stuffy and hierarchical. Extensive interviews found middle and junior managers in 1991 generally complimentary about the adoption of less benighted attitudes to delegation, communications and training. Here were signs of the kind of break with the past that McWilliam had envisaged in 1983–5, and chased in vain thereafter. As for the fresh endorsement of growth in the Asia Pacific region as a strategic priority, Breakout certainly accentuated the gathering polarization of the Group's operations into what the consultants none too subtly termed 'the Best/old' and 'the Bad/new' territories.

Trading profits in the former group more or less trebled between 1989 and 1991; in the other, mostly comprising the UK and US operations, they dropped from £55 million to just £15 million. As a progress review in July 1991 put it, the gap between them was simply 'the difference between where we have a critical mass of franchises, clients and products to "rationalise" with hands-on talent, and where we don't'.[22]

Moreover, the momentum for change was buttressed by some critical progress, at last, over the Group's exposure to dubious cross-border loans. From 1988, this was generally referred to as the 'LDC' or 'PCD' problem (for Less Developed Country or Problem Country Debt) – or rather more graphically, in many internal papers, as 'the iceberg that could sink the ship'. When Galpin arrived, the PCD for which no provision had been made amounted to 144 per cent of shareholders' equity – the equivalent at Barclays stood at approximately 10 per cent – which was one obvious reason why the Group's predicament put so many in mind of the Titanic.[23] By 1991, the exposed portion had been cut to a rather less alarming 84 per cent, by virtue of a successful contraction of the total book, further heavy provisions – profits were hit hard by a PCD provision of £427 million in 1989 – and a judicious switch into Brady Bonds. A curious feature of the PCD aggregates is that they included loans to South African borrowers, though these had to date incurred no repayment problems at all and were assigned provisions at the rate of only 5 per cent, compared with a norm for LDC loans of 60 per cent or more. Excluding the South African debt converted the vital exposure:equity ratio from 84 per cent to 38 per cent – rendering the PCD problem no more than a chronic headache by this point.

The ties to South Africa itself, meanwhile, were being steadily reined back. Notwithstanding the Group's exemplary loan experience, South African assets were cut by a third in these years, from almost £600 million to £400 million. Nelson Mandela's release in February 1990 prompted speculation in the City that the 1987 rupture with StanBIC might somehow be reversed – and indeed, the Group received various overtures to this effect from Johannesburg. Donald Gordon several times made clear that he was a willing seller of Liberty Life's 30 per cent stake in StanBIC.[24] When Conrad Strauss himself contacted London with 'tentative suggestions for an association' in February 1991, though, Galpin told his Board that he feared this might involve effective control for Standard Bank over the Group's interests in central and southern Africa, and the opening was not pursued.[25] In truth, Galpin's executive colleagues had little or no appetite for seeking new business ties with StanBIC. Strategy papers in July 1991 suggested a joint venture in Johannesburg for pan-African business might be a sensible move if it served to pre-empt greater competition from StanBIC in southern Africa, but nothing came of it. Instead, the Group merely opened a small representative office in Johannesburg, in August 1991, to deal with cross-border trade opportunities 'as a first step in developing better knowledge about the emerging opportunities in that region' – an odd formulation by the consultants, given the Group's history.[26] Sure enough, StanBIC then became a much more substantial regional competitor, not least via acquisitions.

Several years earlier, as Standard Chartered's Managing Director in Harare, David Moir had been approached by an intermediary on behalf of Grindlays Bank (now known as ANZ Grindlays, since its takeover by the Australasian banking group in 1984). The parent had decided to sell its operations in central and eastern Africa. Moir was told in confidence that Grindlays' African managers were keen to become part of Standard Chartered.[27] With the assistance of the Group's own merchant bankers, he put together a formal proposal and submitted it to London, where it was brusquely swept aside by a notoriously autocratic General Manager for Africa. Moir was castigated for his pains, but the rejection of his initiative meant that, five years later, the way was open for StanBIC. Once the possibility of a rapprochement with London had been ruled out, Strauss and his colleagues turned to advancing their own cross-border plans. In 1993, they scooped up the Grindlays network, and StanBIC branches began appearing in many cities next to Standard Chartered's.

Taking stock of the Group's position in 1991, it might be supposed that Galpin could be credited with a barnstorming corporate turnaround. His leadership had halted the Group's decline and restored a sense of its underlying potential. Better still, many of the strategic choices that he had made were going to look fundamentally sound with hindsight. Sadly, it was by no means clear at the time that a corner had really been turned. Inside the bank, many were unpersuaded that the Chairman from Threadneedle Street was truly intent on securing an independent future for the Group. Morale sagged accordingly. Perhaps Galpin might have been more persuasive on this front had he communicated more directly with the rank and file. He certainly travelled extensively, attending countless receptions and dinners with overseas colleagues and representatives of host governments. But hobnobbing with commercial bankers was never his forte, and Galpin was often uncomfortable with the Group's distinctive brand of entertaining, not least each year's generous round of Burns Night suppers – 'it was colonial life, but very much focused on Scotland, I think'.[28] His wife Sylvia was much more adept at mixing with the spouses of overseas Managers, showing a genuine interest in their families. Directors' wives had always accompanied their husbands on tours of the network over the years, and many had proved rather demanding visitors. Galpin's wife was a notable exception and won many friends across the network. This undoubtedly helped, but could not entirely allay the problem. The Chairman had never led an executive team in his own career, and had little feel for some aspects of the role. He compounded his natural mandarin aloofness by relying too heavily on consultants, to whom he turned for policy implementation as well as advice and analysis. This distanced him not only from the frontline but also from many of his senior executives, who were left feeling oddly detached from the recovery process.

Nor was their quiet scepticism just a matter of harbouring reservations over Galpin's personal style. They came increasingly to believe that their Chairman was more adept at plotting future solutions than coping with present difficulties – and the latter, through most of 1990–91, were threatening to overwhelm the Group with all its well-laid plans. The earnings record was dismal. The dividend had to be cut by 40 per cent in 1990. Press commentaries remained at best ambivalent over the long-term survival of the bank. The market's response was unforgiving: the share price fell from just over £6 in February 1990 to within a whisker of £2 in January 1991 – prompting the Group's exit from the FTSE-100 market index – though it clawed back half of the lost ground in the following months. Galpin was deeply frustrated and sensed the lack of a properly cohesive top team. 'Perhaps we have tried to do too much at once', as he reflected in July 1991, 'and have not driven all the projects as hard as we might have.'[29] But this ignored the most obvious cause of the Group's continuing frailty: a legacy of disastrous corporate lending since 1986, most of it concentrated in what was now referred to as 'the OECD bank' – in essence, the Western operations accumulated since 1975. Forfeited interest payments and constant provisions for bad debts were running far ahead of corporate banking revenues.[30] Galpin was constantly in two minds over what to do with the OECD bank, still hoping it might be a counter-weight to the growth in Asia. Yet its mounting losses were looking almost as potentially lethal to the Group as the LDC debt at its height.

The story everywhere was much the same. In a bid to build assets and boost revenues as quickly as possible in the wake of the vanquished Lloyds bid, branches across the world had been urged to chase new business. (The strategy was code-named 'Pathfinder' in the UK.) In each domestic market, the customers they caught were all too often those deliberately left behind by the market leaders. No one had a keener appreciation of this than a newcomer hired by Galpin in October 1989. Malcolm Williamson had joined Barclays Bank in Manchester as an eighteen-year-old in 1957 and had been a lending banker for most of his life. As Regional General Manager for Greater London in the 1980s, he had managed corporate lending for Barclays in its single largest division. A decisive and cheerfully abrasive figure (undesirable loans were typically filed in a rhetorical category marked 'Just Bonkers'), Williamson had rid Barclays of entanglements with a long list of big companies familiar to Sunday-newspaper readers in Britain for all the wrong reasons. Arriving at Galpin's side, he found most of the very same names sitting in Standard Chartered's books, alongside several colourful newcomers. Williamson's formal role at the outset did not include responsibility for the UK. He was asked to oversee all of the Group's operations between Singapore and New York. This let him loose on the situation in Australia, where a helter-skelter expansion of 'Standard Chartered Finance' (SCF) since 1986 had produced write-offs in excess of SCF's equity but had put in place a physical network that would cost millions to close down. (Restructuring SCF's assets some months before Williamson's arrival, a newly installed country manager reviewed 26,000 customer accounts and judged just seven of them to be worth transferring across to the books of the publicly quoted Australian subsidiary.[31])

For eighteen months, Williamson scurried to and fro between the UK and Australia – occasionally taking in excursions to Arizona to inspect another arid patch of desert outside Phoenix hitherto classed as an asset of the United Bank – and a stable balance sheet was restored in the end, with the injection of another £46 million.[32] It was the state of the balance sheet in the UK, however, that really exercised Williamson, as he repeatedly made clear to Galpin with a Lancastrian bluntness: 'I said, "Rodney, you're busy chasing your tail, doing all sorts of things to try and change this business. But we've got something like an express train bearing down on us, if we don't fix it – and that's the UK loan book".'[33] He insisted on attending meetings of the UK Credit Committee whenever possible, offering strong support for the Banking Director, David Brougham. As the 1990–91 recession tightened its grip on the UK economy it was Williamson's tough counsels that increasingly prevailed. Galpin bowed to the inevitable in August 1991 and appointed him Managing Director in charge of everything that really mattered.

Williamson immediately recruited some of his best 'recovery experts' from Barclays and, together with Brougham, they set about salvaging as many as possible of the UK problem loans. Several borrowers were now on the brink of collapse, or indeed already in receivership. Intense media coverage of their woes ensured a steady flow of embarrassing references to Standard Chartered. Market wags had already begun to joke that no shocking story about the City's latest slippery customer was complete without a potential loss for 'the Banana-Skin Bank'. But there was nothing comic about the size of these problem loans. The extent of the maverick lending in Britain astounded long-serving managers from the East who were brought back to London in one capacity or another. Barry Northrop, a former country manager in Indonesia whose career since 1966 had included many years in the Gulf as well as Asia, had been based since 1988 in Singapore as 'Head of Credit' for the Asian network. It was a new post, established as part of the drive to make credit control into a centralized function with sufficient clout to impose rigorous disciplines in the field, even (or especially) where some branch heads resented them. In 1990 Northrop had moved to London as Global Head of Credit – only to discover bad debts on a scale he had never encountered before: 'I was seriously shocked, and I remember thinking, "I have spent two years of my life plugging the leaks in south-east Asia to keep this ship afloat and here we've got individual loans almost as big as the entire ship!" I was horrified.'[34]

The Group's ten largest customers at the end of 1991 included some blue chip companies that had been on the list for decades, such as De Beers Consolidated (£176 million), Jardine Matheson (£161 million) and Shell Petroleum (£130 million).[35] None of these rock-solid exposures came close to the £220 million lent to Brent Walker, a UK property conglomerate run by a former professional heavyweight boxer, sporting an eclectic portfolio of side-businesses from pubs and piers to betting shops and film studios, now scuppered in classic style by rising interest rates and sliding property prices. And there were other Shell-sized loans outstanding to private companies whose entrepreneurial founders had now fallen on hard times – like the De Savary Group (£132 million), owner of wildly overpriced properties from John O'Groats to Land's End (literally, since it owned both landmark sites). There were also smaller but still very substantial loans to several of the UK's more colourful business disasters of recent years such as Polly Peck International (£43 million), originally a Turkish Cypriot company making boxes for citrus fruit and latterly a conglomerate with stakes in a long line of corporate lemons.[36] The total value of these British loans put the UK beyond all other territories in the Group, even ahead of Hong Kong, in the corporate-lending league table.

Williamson launched a brutal contraction of both the UK branch network and its outstanding asset book, intervening personally in many of the most desperate situations to lead salvage operations.* Progress was being made by 1992, but the Group's public standing had taken yet another battering.[37]

2. PROJECT ELEPHANT

In one non-OECD country, it was not just Standard Chartered but the whole financial sector that had been straining since the late 1980s to make up for lost time. India's financial system had long been a monument to regulatory sclerosis. Forty years of the Licence Raj had left the country's money markets bizarrely convoluted. Among the distorting constraints on the commercial banks was a ruling that 38.5 per cent of their deposits had to be held as 'statutory liquidity ratio' assets with the Reserve Bank of India (RBI), obliging them to invest in Government securities. Enormous portfolios had been accumulated by 1988, when ministers and the RBI itself began tinkering with the rule book in ways they hoped might address the discomfort of the banks while easing the pressure on Government finances. State-owned corporations were given licence to issue their own bonds. These carried no explicit state backing – so were excluded

---

* He played a critical role, for example, in the Group's handling of its relations with Brent Walker. The issue by early 1991 was how best to set about liquidating its assets to pay off at least a slice of its debts. These amounted in total to well over £1 billion (about 20 per cent of them owed to Standard Chartered). The two biggest obstacles were the involvement of almost a hundred banks from all over the world, none inclined to take the initiative, and the combative stance of George Walker, the ex-boxer and Chief Executive, who was opposed to any radical restructuring of the balance sheet. Walker called a meeting with the Board to request a vote of confidence. Williamson insisted on attending this meeting. As soon as it started, he told the Directors he was sending in the Receiver at 6 a.m. the next morning unless by then they had replaced the Chief Executive. Then he sat down outside the Boardroom while the Directors, who included Walker's wife, argued over what to do. Each time they pleaded with him to let them suspend the meeting, saying they were all too tired to make a decision, Williamson repeated that he would be putting in the Receiver at 6 a.m. 'I think it was about 5 o'clock in the morning when they finally agreed to let George go.' (Interview with author, 9 October 2013.) The restructuring went ahead. It was to last six and a half years, but ended up as a classic of its kind. The creditor banks took charge of disposing of the marketable assets one by one, while Walker and a former Finance Director concentrated on defending themselves against criminal charges brought by the Serious Fraud Office. (Walker was acquitted, but his fellow Director was found guilty of false accounting.) The sale of Brent Walker's betting subsidiary, William Hill, in December 1997 rounded off 'the largest and most successful work-out in the Group's history'. (Board Minutes, 20 January 1998.)

from the Government's balance sheet – but were implicitly sovereign credits. They were therefore eligible as 'statutory liquidity' assets, offering the
banks a decent rate of return and a much greater variety of investments
which could be traded in the secondary market. The latter was provided
by half a dozen or so private brokers, who for years had enjoyed an importance out of all proportion to their tiny size, manipulating huge capital
sums on behalf of their banking clients. Handily, the banks and their
brokers could buy and sell between themselves without needing to
exchange physical securities, since the banks' liquidity portfolios were all
registered with the RBI. Adjustments were simply made to the accounts
at the RBI of the counter-parties – and since the RBI's antediluvian manual book-keeping inevitably trailed far behind the pace of the market, the
banks were allowed to issue simple certificates that acknowledged their
transactions. Thus, after verbal confirmation that a block of securities
would (eventually) be moved out of its account at the RBI, a selling bank
would put out a 'Banker's Receipt' (BR). This could be held by the broker
against eventual documentation of the sale. Other similar inefficiencies in
the corporate sector helped fuel the rise of the BR. When one bank sold
a registered corporate bond to another bank, for example, details of the
change of ownership needed to be confirmed by the registry of the bond's
issuer before the physical bond could be delivered; but it often took months
for the relevant registry to catch up with the transaction, so the vendor
bank could hand the buyer a BR as a promise of future delivery. None of
these BRs had any intrinsic value, nor were they legal proof of ownership.
Nonetheless, and with the full connivance of the RBI, each came to be
seen as a proxy for the value of the original deal; and, where that deal had
entailed a sale for cash, then the BR was effectively a bill of exchange
against which any self-respecting broker could raise funds for himself.
Once the trading of RBI-held securities began to heat up, temperatures
were bound to rise quickly in this wholly unregulated market for BRs –
and for phoney BRs, too, for which there existed no underlying securities
at all.

   In short, by early 1991, the ingredients were in place for a boom of tempestuous proportions, even by Bombay's standards. And in June 1991 the
government of Narasimha Rao came to power, pledged to a liberalization
of the whole economy, including the financial sector. Anxious to protect
the rupee's value, it kicked off the process with a deregulation of interest
rates. Companies were freed from long-standing caps placed on the cou-
pons they could offer on their bonds. Rates rose quickly, and the secondary
value of all outstanding Government securities dropped even faster. Nurs-
ing substantial losses on their 'statutory liquidity' assets, all the banks – both

Indian and foreign-owned – launched into desperate trading strategies to repair their portfolios, or at least disguise the dents they had suffered. New and ever more unscrupulous brokers elbowed their way into the action. Discounted BRs were soon generating cash for an unprecedented volume of secondary trading in Indian equities – a market boosted, before the end of 1991, by the first privatizations of public corporations. Trading levels rocketed for securities of every kind. It was just the sort of environment in which Haridas Mundhra had so briefly but spectacularly flourished in 1956–7, and it ended just as unhappily. On Thursday, 23 April 1992, a story appeared in the financial pages of the *Times of India* reporting that one of the most active brokers, identified only as the 'Big Bull' – real name, Harshad Mehta – had been caught short of a staggering R.500 crores (equivalent to just over £90 million) that he owed to his clients.

The next morning, Barry Northrop took a seat on his usual commuter train into London and opened his *Financial Times*. There the genial and unassuming Global Head of Credit for Standard Chartered found an article about a reported problem in the Bombay bond market. He recalled:

> It was not a long article but the problem was clearly a matter of concern in India. I remember thinking, 'Bonds? We don't do bonds. Carry on!' Anyway, I got to the office and thought, 'I'll just check this out'. So I rang my Head of Credit stationed in India. I said, 'I've just read about this. I take it we have nothing to worry about?' And I got a long silence at the other end. I didn't press him. I knew immediately that we were involved.[38]

The scale of the involvement took some weeks to become apparent. No hint of it had been picked up by Galpin himself, who by chance had only just returned at the beginning of March from a two-week tour of India and Pakistan. Not until 13 May were the Executive Directors notified of the problem. A crisis meeting of the Board followed on Sunday 17 May.[39] A working party had by then been despatched to Bombay under David Brougham's lead, to take charge of what was christened 'Project Elephant' – though not, it must be said, in any real anticipation of jumbo losses. A provision was agreed that month of just £50 million.[40] At the end of July, however, Brougham returned to London with some discouraging news. Under an ambitious country manager – Peshi Nat, the first national to be appointed as Chief Executive in India – the bank had been expanding at a record pace since 1989, piling up commercial loans and adding to its RBI assets accordingly. Its staff had then allowed the bank to become one of the most active parties in the febrile trading instigated in June

1991.* Its dealers had been drawn into a long series of nefarious transactions, in breach of all the bank's own rules, by their main broker, one Hiten Dalal. Brougham himself seems to have been none too well informed about this key individual, a relative newcomer to the Bombay broking scene whose letterhead incorporated his telegraphic code, 'Think Rich'.† As a result of its dealings through Mr Hiten, the meltdown in India's markets since April had already cost the Group £64 million.

Taking stock of Brougham's report, the Directors swallowed hard and doubled the provision against future losses to £100 million, which was more or less equal to the forecast of working profits from Hong Kong for the whole of 1992. Bombay's senior managers were removed and a task force was despatched to the city.[41] Reporting to Brougham, it was to be managed by Barry Northrop, who relocated to Bombay in September. (A newly appointed General Manager for the Middle East and South Asia, Ian Wilson, opted at around the same time to base himself not in London but Dubai, just a short flight from Bombay: this marked Dubai's real launch as a regional centre.) Northrop found himself grappling immediately with a crisis that was starting to raise questions about the very survival of the Group. Indian state banks had withdrawn all funding support for Standard Chartered in the money markets. Of an additional $400 million injected into the Bombay branch, almost half had disappeared already into liquidity deposits with the RBI. The Group had now shifted $1 billion into rupee deposits in India. At the start of October, the

---

* Bombay's other international banks, notably Citibank and Bank of America, had done the same. The difference was that their operations had been kept under intense scrutiny from the US, with internal auditors making monthly visits and regularly combing through the identity of all counter-parties to their trades. One of Peshi Nat's local counterparts would later recall for the author how he had run across the Bombay manager around the middle of 1991 on an internal flight in India. 'He said to me, "Young man, we're going into securities trading. You Americans are making too much money there." I said, "Peshi, you're welcome to join the party, but remember this is a tough space. Unless you've got the back-up, don't do it!" He didn't seem much impressed by that advice.'

† A breathless 'instant book' about the scam published by two Indian journalists in 1993 – which devoted two of its seventeen chapters entirely to Standard Chartered's ordeal – suggested a figure of mythic powers: 'Hiten was the Mr Fix-it of the securities business, the ultimate problem solver. "He was virtually running the treasury desks of almost all major banks", says a sacked Stanchart employee.' (Debachis Basu and Sucheta Dalal, *The Scam: Who Won, Who Lost, Who Got Away*, UBS Publishers' Distributors, 1993, p. 20.) There were in reality two parallel scams. One centred on the stock market and the adventures of the 'Big Bull', Harshad Mehta; the other comprised serial criminal frauds against the commercial banks, foreign and domestic. The versatility of the Bombay broking community ensured plenty of overlaps between the two of them, but it was the latter which accounted directly for most of Standard Chartered's losses.

RBI announced it was cancelling an arcane arrangement that had hitherto offered the Group foreign-exchange cover on these deposits. As the minutes of the next Board meeting noted ominously, the RBI's decision 'had placed the Group in a difficult position'.[42]

A few days earlier, in a wrenching memorandum to the Directors, Galpin had already bravely confronted the horrendous implications of the whole debacle, as he saw them:

> any further increase in our provisioning against India will, I fear, confirm [the analysts'] worst fears and throw into question our continued viability . . . [and so] we need to consider contingency plans should, unexpectedly, the situation in India require additional provisions. This might imply looking for a partner who sees value in our business and is complementary in its operations.[43]

In other words, Standard Chartered might now face very much the same ignominious fate as the Eastern Bank after the Mundhra scandal in Calcutta a quarter of a century earlier. It was a bitterly disappointing turn of events for Galpin personally. He had spent three years proclaiming the importance of a more professional approach to credit and risk management, only to see the Group humiliated by back-office skulduggery on a scale undreamt of in the ordered financial markets of the City. For his colleagues on the Board – led, ironically, by the heavy hitters brought in by Galpin himself in 1988 – it was a fateful moment that left them in no doubt that changes at the top were inevitable. Sensing the mood, and pointing out with his customary courtesy and tact that he had originally signed on for five years in 1988, Galpin tendered his resignation. By the end of November the Board had invited Patrick Gillam, Deputy Chairman since 1991, to step up as his successor after the next AGM. It was decided as well to appoint Malcolm Williamson as Chief Executive, with effect from the start of January 1993. Though Gillam was to be Executive Chairman, he and Williamson reached an immediate agreement to work closely in tandem together. Through the early weeks of the New Year, presentations by the two of them to institutional investors in the City were notably well received. Indeed, the impact of their appointments on the general perception of the Group was remarkable. Even while nemesis hovered in the sub-continent, reports began circulating in the London market about the purgative effects of Williamson's managing directorship since 1991. The outcome was a denouement to the Bombay crisis that ran entirely counter to Galpin's grim warning in October – and marked an historic turning point for the Group.

The additional provisions for India, so dreaded by Galpin, could not be long delayed. In March 1993, Brougham had to tell the Directors that a bad situation had become considerably worse. 'He reminded the Board that originally there had been grounds for optimism . . .'[44] Not any more. Adverse exchange movements, a bleak outlook for equities on the Bombay stock market, a wave of public hostility towards foreign banks in India and 'the general "disarray" of the RBI and the national banking system' were all adding mightily to the Group's difficulties (though the RBI had at least relented on its threat to leave rupee 'liquidity' deposits exposed to exchange losses). Above all, it had finally become clear that criminally dishonest brokers and accomplices on the bank's own staff had cooked the books in time-honoured fashion and pulled off a massive fraud (for which several were eventually imprisoned): for all the numbing technicalities of the Indian money markets, Standard Chartered had simply been swindled – though on a scale that put its losses, gallingly, well beyond those incurred by any other foreign bank in Bombay. After an anguished debate, the Directors settled on a new provision against them of £272 million, and this was the figure adopted for the 1992 Results presentation to the City. It was equivalent to 28 per cent of Shareholders' Capital and Reserves at the start of 1992. And this took no account of what the Group might conceivably need to pay in settlement of claims brought against it by other banks. At one stage, Northrop thought these might amount to as much as £800 million: 'it was very frightening at the time . . . it got better as it went on, but for the first six to twelve months the country manager [John Docherty] and I thought we were sitting on a powder keg'.[45] Inside Aldermanbury Square, the top men braced themselves for a ribald chorus of 'banana skin' taunts. Some old timers within the bank also felt deeply disenchanted. They were watching yet another replay of a wretched cyclical pattern that had been evident, it seemed, almost since the appointment of McWilliam as the first New Broom in 1983. Copious plans and consultants' reports had fuelled any number of earnest conferences, each hosting presentations from around the world and concluding with firm prescriptions for future success. And with a depressing inexorability, back had come results from the field suggesting time and again how very hard it would be to galvanize the workings of this complex organization in any sustainable way.

However, all now were in for a surprise. Instead of falling back when the 1992 Results were announced, on 10 March, the share price actually jumped 3 per cent higher. The next day, press commentators struggled to make sense of it. In the *Financial Times*, the widely respected Lex Column took stock of the paradox with a weary shrug:

Oh dear, oh dear! Standard Chartered just cannot seem to manage a year without finding a banana skin to tread on. The latest one – the securities scandal in Bombay – has cost more than £300 million . . . Strip away India, though, and it is easy to see why the market greeted yesterday's results by pushing the shares up . . . operating earnings are steaming ahead . . . On that basis, the shares are cheap, but only because rational analysis does not allow for the kind of nasty surprise which has become a Standard Chartered hallmark.[46]

In fact, the market's refusal to be spooked by the news from India was of great significance. Most immediately, the 1992 Results had their own silver lining. Higher profits on continuing businesses (up by £89 million), windfall gains on property sales (£111 million) and some timely revisions to the Charge for Bad Debts (releasing £65 million) more than offset the Indian provision in the Profit & Loss statement for the year. So the bottom line, while feeble at £21 million, at least ensured a modicum of Retained Earnings and none of the prior year's equity capital went missing – which marked a signal improvement on three of the previous five years.[47] (It might also be doubted whether investors fully appreciated the gravity of the remaining risks in Bombay. The small print accompanying the new £272 million provision studiously avoided any reference to Northrop's 'powder keg'.) But it is plain with hindsight that investors, for many months past, had also been quietly taking on board the Group's fresh commitment to its strengths in Asia. Returning from trips to appraise the operations in Hong Kong and Singapore, City analysts since the start of the year had been reminding financial institutions of a simple truth. The Group had branches in most of the budding Asian economies, whose governments were now generally opposed to granting additional licences for Western banks. It therefore had a franchise that could never be replicated.

Of course, all this presupposed that investors were feeling more optimistic about the Pacific Rim region – but few could doubt they were indeed warming to it rapidly. Around the turn of the 1990s, 'Emerging Markets' had been seen by traders as a politically correct euphemism for 'Less Developed Countries'. Just a few years on, the Emerging Markets brand had picked up genuine appeal and was increasingly associated with the so-called 'Tiger economies' of the East. As a bank for which those markets were not so much emerging as re-emerging – rekindling again some of the dynamism with which their export trades had helped fuel the first global economy in the Imperialist era before 1914 – Standard Chartered had, to say the least, an unusual claim on investors' attention. The stock market went on acknowledging as much. In July, the Group's shares rose a few pennies higher than the price they had last reached at the first intimation of the hostile bid from Lloyds Bank in April 1986. It had been seven lean years for shareholders – and especially for those white knights – but the stock was now advancing, as the brokers liked to say, into fresh territory.* One respected City editor called it 'the most remarkable share price recovery the banking sector has seen in recent years'.[48] In different circumstances, this might have been attributed to City investors placing their bets on the likelihood of a takeover bid. After the disclosures in Bombay, though, the prospect of any publicly quoted company taking on the risk of owning the Banana Skin Bank was remote in the extreme. So the rising share price could only mean investors were harking to that 'rational analysis' disdained by Lex, a view endorsed by the Board's own City advisers at the close of the year.[49]

An absence of further bad news from India helped the cause. Northrop assembled what was in effect India's largest private legal practice to help him untangle the mess that had engulfed the bank's back office in Bombay: 'at one stage I was responsible for eight lawyers, thirteen "forensic bankers" and a whole team of investigators trying to find out what had happened'.[50] In the end, none of the other banks pursued their claims against London – though Standard Chartered itself filed several suits in London and New York – and a Special Criminal Court was set up in India (largely at the Group's behest) to take over all civil suits arising from the scam. Funding costs were much reduced by the end of 1993, as was the Bombay branch's portfolio of public-sector bonds. Mercifully, no additions were required to the £272 million provision.[51] Northrop returned to London in February 1994 and the crisis passed, with scarcely a single reference made to it in the 1993 Annual Report published two months later. The Indian authorities imposed only relatively modest fines on the international banks.[52] By 1995, they were arresting some of the leading brokers, including Hiten Dalal, on serious criminal charges, which potentially endorsed the Group's own insistence from the start that it had been defrauded. (The legal ramifications of the whole affair dragged on for years. As late as 2010, Galpin was still taking advice from the lawyers

---

* Stock quotations for the Group can be compared over time by using prices adjusted to take account of changes in the number of shares outstanding. A graph of these adjusted prices since 1969 (see Chart 11, Appendix E) shows the price on 14 July 1993 nudging just above the level reached on 7 April 1986. Not until much later, of course, was it to become apparent that the 1986–93 range had in fact been left behind for good, and that the March 1993 resilience had presaged a dramatic re-grading of the stock over the next four years. Between July 1993 and August 1997, the share price was to rise fivefold.

about what exactly he could safely say about it in public.[53]) Meanwhile, investors had long since brushed aside the scam in keeping track of more encouraging reports on the Group's progress elsewhere. The analysts were bringing more good news from the East – but, as a Board paper explained in April 1995, most of the Group's leading shareholders were now receptive to a more comprehensive reassessment. They were 'sanguine about geopolitical risk in Asia and more interested in our management story'.[54] They were right to be so. The Group was changing in fundamental ways. The trauma in India had left many senior managers feeling shell-shocked – and even more deeply risk-averse over the next few years than Chartered bankers of old – but it did nothing to derail the Breakout agenda. On the contrary, the scam effectively handed Gillam and Williamson complete freedom to push through whatever measures they believed essential to the Group's survival.

3. BACK FROM THE EDGE

Coming from a humble background in Putney, Patrick Gillam had won a London County Council scholarship to go to the London School of Economics, where students from around the Commonwealth even in the early 1950s comprised a large percentage of the total. Aside from a brief stint with the Foreign Office, he had spent his entire working life since 1957 with BP – in an intensely data-driven, meritocratic and ethnically diverse environment that was about as far removed from Standard Chartered's pre-1988 culture as could readily be imagined. Towards the end of a brilliant executive career, he had accepted Galpin's offer of a non-executive role – BP allowed its top men each to take just one external Board position – because he was intrigued by the international profile of the Group; but he was less than prepared for the business frailties he found there. In fact, he was taken aback by them. ('You name it, all the things that enable you to run an efficient organization were, to one degree or another, derelict.'[55]) Once installed as the Executive Chairman in May 1993, he moved quickly to inject a new and far more commercial approach. This was going to see many aspects of BP's modus operandi adopted over the years ahead, and some of Gillam's former associates at BP, too. One of the first to turn up at Standard Chartered was Richard (Dick) Balzer, an adviser to the oil company in Gillam's time and another in the long line of consultants ushered into the Chairman's office since the early 1980s. A renowned American organizational guru with just a select roster of highly prestigious clients – they included the United Auto Workers union and the National Basketball Association as well as BP – Balzer was to have a formative influence on the whole process of decision-making and strategy formulation at the top of the Group, and would be at least as important to Gillam as Leslie Dighton had been to Galpin. One of Balzer's early contributions was to help simplify and focus the Group's strategic thinking. Malcolm Williamson was no great admirer of elaborate corporate plans. In fact, his idea of a good strategy was 'to make higher profits' or 'to incur lower costs' or, best of all, to do both at the same time – while of course avoiding any surprises. But Williamson deferred in this context to both Balzer and a former senior Citibank man in London, John McFarlane, whom he hired about this time to run the Group's corporate banking and capital markets activities. (McFarlane insisted on being head of strategy as well: 'I said I wouldn't join unless that happened, because I didn't just want to run a division. I wanted some influence over the shape of the whole organization.'[56]) It was Balzer and McFarlane together who urged an explicit identification of Standard Chartered as 'the Emerging Markets bank'. The Group would hitch its fortunes unambiguously to Asia's rising economies, while keeping its costs flat to ensure a steady rise in productivity. Provided it could skip over any future banana skins, the result could be a doubling of profits within three years. This was the kind of strategy that appealed to Williamson, and he adopted its tenets enthusiastically.

To help him implement it, Williamson had by his side yet another of his former Barclays lieutenants, Peter Wood, as his Finance Director. Wood and McFarlane both joined the main Board. McFarlane brought with him a former Citibank colleague, Mike Grimes, to become his Operations Director; and another recently poached Citibank executive, Mervyn Davies, was made Head of Global Corporate Accounts in November 1993. With a phalanx of tough ex-Barclays and ex-Citibank people around him – along with David Moir and David Brougham, both now appointed to the Board – Williamson was ready to exert much more control from the centre than had been available to any of his predecessors. This addressed an urgent priority: there could be no repeat of the India Scam, or the Group was finished. He insisted on adherence to tight and well-defined reporting lines, within which ample scope could exist for reconciling delegation with answerability. Williamson was fortunate, of course, that this approach coincided with the arrival, after 1993, of email and a quantum leap in communications technology that greatly facilitated the task of managing scattered businesses around the globe. But also crucial to securing a heightened control of the Group was the 'Extended Management Team' (EMT), which brought together thirty or so of the most senior managers from around the world. With Balzer's help, Williamson forged the EMT into a powerful cross-border team capable of disseminating important discussions in depth and tackling the Balkanized nature of the network.

At the same time, he turned his mind to some crucial decisions that in his opinion had been shirked before 1993. Three stood out. Fully supportive of the notion that Standard Chartered should return to its historical franchises in Asia, the Middle East and Africa, Williamson was also determined to grapple with its corollary: he agreed with McFarlane and Balzer that there was no basis at all, in that case, for struggling on with domestic banking operations in the OECD countries. He moved to close or severely curtail them everywhere, from Canada and the US to Britain, Europe and Australia. (The reining back of the deposit base made a welcome contribution, too, to the de-leveraging of the balance sheet – the ratio of total assets to shareholders' equity was to fall back through the 1990s, from a peak of just over 27:1 in 1992 to about 16:1 by the Millennium.) In a similar vein, Williamson was completely persuaded of the argument for running as many as possible of the Group's core businesses and functions as global concerns. This implied a matrix organization in which country managers would have to take a back seat to the global heads, so it was exasperating for him to read a recent consultants' report to the Board that Standard Chartered had struck them as 'a group of regional businesses with global overtones'.[57] Williamson was soon suggesting to the Board a blueprint, overseen by Balzer, for how this matrix might work better. It would entail a smaller Head Office, cross-border reporting for the key businesses – Treasury, Retail (or 'Personal') Banking and Corporate Banking – and Regional Managers in charge of much diminished country managers, except in the Middle East and Africa, where this 'segmentation' approach would be ignored in favour of the existing geographical entities. The new organizational structure was duly adopted and the result was – well, a group of global businesses with regional overtones. (John McFarlane became one of the new Regional Managers in 1994, running North East Asia from an office in Hong Kong.) A third key resolution showed again that Williamson was not a man for half measures. He had always strongly endorsed Boardroom talk of focusing ruthlessly on the Group's main breadwinners and not frittering away resources on peripheral activities. Yet as of early 1993, managers were still struggling to cope with a lingering assortment of unconsidered corporate trifles, from African leasing companies and discount houses to US properties and European fund managers. Williamson set about a comprehensive programme of disposals, quickly dubbed the 'Sale of the Tail'.

Several very much more substantial commitments were also chopped back over the next three years, a process driven ahead by Williamson as part of 'clearing the seaweed off the propellers'.[58] They included a 50/50 joint venture with Westdeutsche Landesbank (WestLB), the fourth largest bank in Germany and the biggest of its seventeen state-owned savings banks. This had been formed in 1990 by selling the European operations of Standard Chartered Merchant Bank to the Germans. The hope had been that the resulting 'CharteredWestLB' would thrive by bringing together WestLB's huge domestic franchise and Standard Chartered's Asian branches, enabling the latter 'to become dependable suppliers of the needs of German corporate customers throughout the network'.[59] Indeed, an even grander vision had been mooted in 1991, with the proposed sale of a 20 per cent stake in Standard Chartered itself to WestLB: it was to be the model of a new set of alliances in the West, which Galpin hoped might replace the abandoned 'OECD strategy' of 1975–88. This 'Project Africa' had been scuttled at the last minute in March 1991.* CharteredWestLB had since then lingered on without much conviction, and it was now given the *coup de grâce*. Williamson told the Board in February 1994 it had not been a success due to 'limited communality of interest'. The sale to WestLB of the Group's half-share marked the final demise of the merchant banking arm set up in 1970.[60]

Other jettisoned businesses included International Private Banking, a retail operation aimed at wealthy individuals, which was sold to one of the big Swiss banks. (A non-compete clause blocked the Group's return to this lucrative corner of the market for many years to come, later a matter of some regret.) Mocatta was scheduled for sale, pending the resolution of various legal complications hanging over it. Branches of the bank deemed peripheral to the core were cut back ruthlessly – and some long-standing minority stakes in associate companies were finally jettisoned, or at least substantially wound down. The most important of these was the Group's 40 per cent share in First Bank of Nigeria. Once the Nigerian economy had recovered from the oil-price crisis of the early

---

* The foreclosure of the sale of a minority stake to WestLB was a curious business. It was scheduled for announcement in March 1991 along with the annual results for 1990, and finalization of the details kept the Group's Treasury team busy up to the last minute. On the day of the results, however, Mike Rees, UK Financial Controller, arrived at his desk to find a copy of the results press release – with no mention of the sale. 'WestLB's legal team had come into the due diligence process at the last moment, had apparently misread contingent assets as contingent liabilities – and had called the whole deal off.' (Rees, interview with author, 13 September, 2013; Minutes of the Board Meeting of 26 March 1991, SCB Box 2313.)

1980s, FBN had again enjoyed some years of dramatic growth: its net profits had doubled between 1985 and 1989. But rising business volumes had outpaced the bank's management resources – especially after the departure in 1987 of Samuel Asabia, who had left to start his own bank – and had hugely exacerbated the 'accounting and administrative muddle' about which Stuart Tarrant had warned his London colleagues in 1984. FBN had reported an enormous loss in 1990. Reviewing the state of Standard Chartered's investment in 1993, Williamson was unhappy with the Nigerian bank's volatile earnings record – and even more uneasy about the political background, following the seizure of the presidency by Sani Abacha in 1993.* The Group in June 1994 reduced its stake in FBN to 9.9 per cent.

One other feature of the 1993–6 propeller-cleansing years had more of a prescriptive nature: shaken by the disastrous misjudgements uncovered in the 1990–91 recession and fearful of another big drop in property prices before too long, Williamson put a blanket veto on all commercial property lending. New loans were strictly off limits, even in Hong Kong, and existing loans were to be wound down as quickly as possible. As for the Group's own freehold property portfolio, this was targeted for some quick sales from the start. The precious gains booked to the Profit & Loss statement in March 1993 included surpluses realized on the sale of the Group's main offices in Singapore, Bangkok and even (to widespread local dismay) Hong Kong. Many gilded mansions enjoyed by Chartered managers in ages past now went under the hammer, including 'Abergeldie' on Hong Kong's Peak (purchased, with all the heated rose beds around its splendid lawns, by Peter Woo). Some resident managers had the temerity to question the wisdom of this approach. They got short shrift from the Chief Executive:

> We sold the Manager's house in Bangkok, with roughly an acre of land in the city that was worth about £50 million. The current Manager was very upset, and I asked him, 'Well, how much money have you made in Thailand in the last 100 years?' I'd checked it out – I knew we hadn't made more than about £5 million. So I said, 'When you make £50 million a year, come back

---

* Williamson viewed all the Group's business interests in Africa with a wary eye. He was sceptical of the growth prospects in most countries, impatient with constant requests for debt rescheduling and disinclined to spend time chasing profits in countries where exchange controls and dividend rules effectively impeded cash remittances to the UK. He also felt uncomfortable having to attend any functions in Africa where he was faced with displays of conspicuous private wealth. Visiting the presidential palace in Kenya for an official lunch attended by serried rows of local lady guests, each bedecked with an astonishing display of precious gems, was an experience he never forgot. (Interview with the author, 9 October 2013.)

and ask me if I'll buy you a house – and I probably will!' We packed him off to live in a condo, which I don't think he liked very much.[61]

He did not, and he resigned shortly afterwards. The circumstances were unusual, but news of one more expatriate's departure was by now a regular event. 'In the 1980s there were 800, mainly British, expatriates who held the key jobs throughout the bank', as a London Business School study would observe a few years later. (The appearance of an academic paper about Standard Chartered's revival was itself to be evidence of how dramatically the Group was being re-shaped in these years between 1993 and 1996.) 'By 1996 this had been reduced to 160, which had had a significant impact on career patterns within the bank.'[62] Here was another seminal change to follow in the wake of the India Scam. The importance of breaking completely with the Empire-staffing model had been acknowledged for years. Rodney Galpin had set focus groups to work on a solution. But it was Galpin's successor as Chairman who drove through the requisite innovations, fervently and irreversibly.

Nothing affronted Patrick Gillam more than the Group's lingering adherence to Empire-staffing, a way of seeing the world that had been abandoned by the international oil industry (as he often remarked) about half a century earlier. Since the start of the 1970s, as noted in Chapter 8, a couple of dozen graduate trainees a year had been passing through London, at least half of them non-British graduates recruited overseas. Locally sourced managers had accounted for a steadily greater proportion of the total of covenanted officers across the network. It had reached roughly half the total in most large branches by the middle of the 1980s. Yet the spirit of Empire-staffing lived on. For, crucially, the remaining expatriates included almost all of the country managers – Peshi Nat in India was a notable and not entirely reassuring exception – and this continued to imbue the culture of the Group with a post-colonial flavour that was starkly disproportionate to the bare numbers. With some justification, expatriates had always been seen as far more amenable to being assigned overseas at short notice: this element of mobility was reflected in the description of them since the 1970s as 'International Officers' (or IOs). And this in the 1980s had undoubtedly encouraged a widespread and self-fulfilling assumption that the IOs – almost all of them British – would have to go on dominating the upper ranks as part of the natural order, even though the strict divide between covenanted Foreign Staff and non-covenanted local staff had been consigned to history in the 1960s. As for the most senior ranks of management, a 1990 survey of the 293 posts in the top four salary bands had found that 214 of them (73 per cent) were UK nationals – and the 293 included, as already noted, only 20 women.[63] These findings appalled Gillam, then just preparing to retire from his career at BP. When he accepted appointment as Deputy Chairman of the Group in March 1991, he turned immediately to staffing as his first main concern. He set up a Personnel Strategy Committee in May 1991, and had himself installed as its first chairman.

The new men already heading the personnel function, under Martin Fish, had just produced a Board paper examining the implications of that 1990 survey. They had delivered a withering assessment of the IOs' shortcomings as 'the core resource for managing the Group's operations worldwide':

> [T]hey have received little formal training in strategic management to equip them for the more senior country and regional management posts in the organisation . . . [M]any of our managers have grown up in an administrative environment operating within procedures largely laid down at Head Office . . . [leading] to less emphasis than is now needed on marketing and strategic management capability . . . [This would leave them ill-suited to] a more coordinated, strategically managed group emphasising its global products and its ability to offer 'banking without frontiers'.[64]

It had also to be acknowledged that despatching IOs from Britain was no longer as straightforward as it had been in the past: as a Board discussion would later note, long-term commitment to expatriate status had lost much of its allure for the current generation of young British bankers (or for their wives, which was probably just as significant) and this posed 'a major challenge to the Group'.[65] On both counts, a fundamentally different approach seemed essential. Noting that large numbers of IOs were by chance due to retire from 1993 onwards, Gillam launched a campaign to prepare for their replacement. This entailed, on the one hand, vigorously upgrading the technical and general business training courses being provided for local employees – including the instigation of an in-house MBA course – and, on the other, going out into the local marketplace to hire mid-career bankers from the competition, who could take up the running while the Group developed its home-grown talent. Never any less forceful and decisive than Williamson, Gillam had set a clear agenda by the end of 1991:

> The Committee endorsed the view of the Bank [sic] that its future aim should be to put the most talented managers, whatever their background and nationality, into the positions where their talents were most suited. Whilst there were some signs that the expatriate domination of the Group was changing, the Committee were anxious to see that this process was accelerated.[66]

Thus began a drive to turn the network into 'a well-qualified, multiracial organisation'.[67] Gillam's instinct was to ditch the Group's dependence on expatriates almost entirely. An extensive survey of large multinational companies by his committee pointed in that direction. ('It was noticeable that none of the companies benchmarked now recruited permanent expatriates.'[68]) In the event, replacing all the expatriates proved rather harder than expected. Rival banks, it turned out, were not full of locally recruited stars waiting to be lured away as country managers for an organization only too plainly in the throes of a radical upheaval. Nor was it typically easy to persuade, say, successful Hong Kong or Singaporean Chinese that relocating to another country represented a handsome career opportunity. And, besides, there were still more than a few expatriate Brits in the field whose uncommon skills and experience remained a valuable asset to the bank – resourceful individuals in the best traditions of the old Chartered Bank, adept at promoting (or defending) the Group's interests in off-beat places and situations for which no mere executive training could have prepared them.

These individuals included men such as John Brinsden, whose career to date had already fuelled a small anthology of corporate legends. A veteran of more Asian postings than most – from Calcutta and Amritsar in the 1960s via Malaysia and Indonesia to a Teheran on the brink of revolution – Brinsden was a tall, wiry figure seemingly capable of adjusting to any business environment provided it featured a civilized supply of late-night bars. Four years in the US in the early 1980s had given him an unusual grasp of the marketing challenges facing commercial banks; and six years establishing Standard Chartered in Taiwan since 1984 had left him with a decent grasp of Mandarin, to add to his Malay and Hindi. David Moir had asked him to relocate to Saigon, now Ho Chi Minh City, in 1990 to re-establish the Standard Chartered branch so abruptly shuttered in 1974. With Moir's blessing, Brinsden had binned plans for the bank to operate as a mere agency on behalf of Western companies and had pushed ahead with trade-financing services that the Vietnamese, now bent on reopening to the West, were desperately lacking. With minimal capital and just a handful of staff, the business took off. It could also boast of zero credit losses, thanks in good part to one of Brinsden's less orthodox improvisations:

> The first thing I did in Saigon was to hire two professors at the banking university. They had been real bankers in their early days. Practically every local banker in Vietnam had been taught by them. Now, the traditional respect between student and master in Asia is just as strong in Vietnam as anywhere else. So if I wanted to know what was going on in (say) the Vietcong Bank in Haiphong, one of my professors would get on to them and

25. Some of the Chartered's staff who suffered but survived through Japan's Co-Prosperity Sphere. *Top left:* Gerry Leiper, chronicler of wartime Hong Kong. *Top right:* G. A. P. Sutherland, who kept a diary through the early weeks of his imprisonment in Changi Gaol in 1942 and wrote a report on Singapore's internment camps after the war. *Below:* a reunion in 1948 of the Fukushima Nine (with one absentee), who had endured internment in Japan for three years.

26. Celebrating the Chartered's centenary – and the new Queen's coronation – in 1953. *Left:* the illuminations on Singapore's Raffles Place branch. *Below:* Head Office managers and their spouses at the Centenary Dinner-Dance at the Empire Rooms in Tottenham Court Road.

27. Prominent pre-merger Chartered men. *Above left:* Sir William Cockburn, who joined the bank in 1911 aged twenty and served as Chief Manager, 1940–55. *Above right:* Harold Faulkner, shrewd China hand in the 1930s and Company Secretary, 1949–64. *Bottom left:* Vincent Grantham, Chairman 1940–67. *Bottom right:* George Pullen, Chief General Manager 1959–67 and Chairman 1967–9.

28. Prominent pre-merger Standard men. *Above:* (*centre*) Sir Cyril Hawker, Chairman 1962–9, (*left*) Sir Frederick Leith-Ross, Chairman 1953–7, and (*right*) Edmund Hall-Patch, Chairman 1957–62, with cigar in hand. *Left:* Cyril Hamilton, Deputy-Chairman 1963–9, who followed Hawker to the Standard from the Bank of England.

29. Chartered Bank and the Shanghainese families behind Hong Kong's textiles industry. *Above:* The chairman of the Hong Kong Spinners' Association, Vincent Woo, presenting George Pullen with a trophy (circa 1969) to commemorate the Chartered's long relationship with its members. *Below:* four sons and one daughter of businessmen who fled from Communist China – (*left to right*) Jerry Liu, Alex Woo, Eleanor Wong, the late Jack Tang and Richard Lee.

30. Leading the Chartered's expansion in Hong Kong. *Above:* Peter Graham as Manager in the Colony opens another retail branch in 1969. *Below:* his successor David Millar (*sixth from left*) at a formal dinner in 1972 to celebrate the successful flotation of Cheung Kong, the property group built up by Li Ka-shing (*standing to Millar's left*).

31. Hong Kong currency issued in the name of The Chartered Bank, before and after the merger of 1969 with Standard Bank. *Above:* a HK$100 note, issued in December 1947. *Below:* a HK$10 note, issued in June 1975.

32. Causes for celebration. *Above:* an unusual Bank of West Africa branch manager, Elwyn Williams, is welcomed as their newly appointed chief, Bobajiro of Oshogbo, by Nigerian tribal elders in 1966. *Below:* the Manager of The Chartered Bank of London, Norman Eckersley, hosts a visit to its San Francisco offices by Prince Charles in 1976 as part of the Bicentennial.

call up the manager. 'This is your old teacher speaking. How are you? Are you still brushing your teeth? Oh, by the way, I'd like to know the background to a possible transaction . . .' And the guy in Haiphong would say, 'Don't touch it! Tell your boss to keep away from it!'[69]

As it happens, Gillam and Brinsden knew each other well from the 1980s, when Gillam had been a regular visitor to BP's operations in Taiwan. Brinsden had also run across Williamson in London in the past. Over the course of 1992, it was agreed by all that Brinsden from his base in Vietnam would be given more or less a free hand to re-establish a presence for the Group in Cambodia and Burma/Myanmar (withdrawn from in 1960 and 1963 respectively) and even perhaps Laos. Remarkably, and with more than one intervention on his behalf by Gillam and Williamson, Brinsden and a handful of colleagues fulfilled this brief in all three countries over the next few years.[70] They succeeded in the face of a general move to replace expatriates, demonstrating again that the right man in the right place could still occasionally render their bank a rather special kind of institution as effectively as had the Foreign Staff in a bygone era.*

More indicative of the changes taking place across the Group, nonetheless, were a series of appointments in Asia from 1992 onwards that spelled the end of Empire-staffing. Some influential British (and American) managers would remain in the field, as a Board Minute noted in October 1995, but the trend was not to be doubted:

> It was recognized that the Bank needed to ensure proper balance between Caucasians and local nationals. The former had a role, but the overall direction should be to ensure appropriately qualified local staff who were prepared to uphold the Group culture . . . In any event, it was essential that, not only had the Bank moved away from its previous colonial image but that staff and customers recognized the change that had taken place.[71]

Retiring expatriates were no longer automatically replaced, and many were given early retirement. In Hong Kong, where the corporate banking division was probably the last stronghold of traditional staffing patterns, their numbers fell from about 130 in 1991 to just 12, eight years later. The

---

* One of those reporting to Brinsden was another expatriate, John Janes, whose own career was in some ways an even more remarkable example of the rugged individualism of an earlier age. He had spent three years in the 1980s, for example, resuscitating the Group's business in Bangladesh with a tiny staff. After running the branch in Phnom Penh in 1991–3, with occasional excursions to Vientiane in Laos and Yangon (the former Rangoon), he was assigned to Sierra Leone and spent three years in Freetown providing banking services for the international aid agencies in the midst of a protracted civil war. (Janes, interview with author, 21 October 2013.)

way was now open for ambitious executives of all international backgrounds to aspire to top jobs at Standard Chartered. An International Graduate Recruitment Programme was introduced in 1991 – with a first cohort of 150 (mostly Asian) graduates from a range of US and European universities hired for posts in their home countries – and a separate Development Programme was launched for 200 of the Group's most promising executives in their thirties.[72] (Something similar and just as drastic was happening in Africa, to which we will return.)

Nowhere in Asia was the general thrust of all these initiatives more striking in the early 1990s than in Singapore. When Gillam and Williamson began reviewing all senior staff positions in 1991, the office there already had a Singaporean in place as head of local corporate banking. Theresa Foo's career to date had epitomized the progress of the post-war generation in south-east Asia. She had joined Bank of America in 1966 as a twenty-three-year-old graduate and had worked her way up into its senior ranks. After a brief stint in a local Singapore bank, she had accepted an offer to join Standard Chartered in 1986. She had seen it 'as a good opportunity to get back into a foreign environment', but had barely survived her first year there. ('I almost quit. The then management was very colonial and hierarchical. It seemed so lethargic to me, I was used to the open American management style.'[73]) But, reassured that changes were on their way, she had stayed on and not regretted it. After 1988 it quickly became apparent that a new era was indeed at hand. Then in 1991 Williamson singled her out as a prospective CEO for Singapore. For two preparatory years she was assigned to work in a regional role – nominally based in Hong Kong, but with arrangements made for her to remain living in Singapore for family reasons – and in 1993 Gillam duly confirmed her appointment as Singapore's CEO, the first ever non-expatriate in that position. (She added to her brief by taking on regional responsibility for the countries being opened up by Brinsden, too.) She had reached the top, and had several Singaporean colleagues around her. Others working in senior positions by this point included the head of Singapore's consumer banking, Wilson Chia, and the head of its Treasury operations, Michael Wong. And there were many others in less lofty but always hard-earned roles – like Shirley Wee, who had been on that early training programme in 1970 and had been patiently working her way up the ladder ever since. Gone for ever, by the middle of the 1990s, was the post-colonial flavour of the British bank that Wee and her graduate peers had known for most of their working lives – the tiffin rooms with UK-style fish and chips, the men-only executive washrooms, the afternoon tea trolley and the Saturday morning beers on the desk. The old ways had survived a surprisingly long time. But 'indigenization' was at last reaching its logical conclusion.

4. HONG KONG SETS THE PACE

Nothing could disguise the overwhelming importance to the Group by the 1990s of its operations in Hong Kong. Whatever the vagaries of its colonial regulatory regime or the periodically acute misgivings over what the Chinese Communist Party might one day have in store for it, Hong Kong had ranked since the middle of the 1960s as *primus inter pares* among Standard Chartered's Asian territories. By the time of its 1969 merger with Standard Bank, the Chartered's branch in the Colony with its computerized retail network had long ceased playing second fiddle to the Malay combination of Kuala Lumpur, Penang and Singapore.[74] Thereafter, City of London observers were sometimes surprised to discover the scale of Hong Kong's profits and the speed of their growth. The authors of the 1982 Monopolies and Mergers Commission Report blocking the RBS merger seemed to be stretching for an exclamation mark in noting that 'profits in Hong Kong more than trebled between 1977 and 1980'.[75] By this time, Hong Kong was accounting for roughly 10 per cent of the Group's total working profits, broadly comparable with the contribution made by the Union Bank to the east and by Singapore plus Malaysia to the west.[76] (Profits from South Africa then represented around 30 per cent.) The managers in Des Voeux Road were feeling bullish and ready as ever to push for a little more independence, as they made clear in a paper for the Board in April 1982: 'The potential for growth is practically unlimited ... A major issue will be the degree to which Hong Kong becomes the centre of gravity for the Bank's operations in the Far East and what this means in terms of decentralisation from London.'[77] This took no account, however, of the Colony's political situation, and sudden doubts about China's ultimate intentions prompted a severe crisis of confidence the following year, which hit the currency hard. In 1974 the authorities had allowed the Hong Kong dollar to float on the currency markets (having already abandoned its fixed link to sterling in 1972). From around HK$6.50 to the US dollar at the start of 1983, it slipped to almost HK$10.00 by September. Badly shaken by the turmoil in the markets, the authorities had by the end of October 1983 effectively reverted to the old Currency Board style of control, whereby the stock of Hong Kong dollars in circulation had to be matched exactly by reserves of foreign currency – or, more specifically, reserves of US dollars.[78] This decision stabilized the situation, and in 1984 the successful negotiation of the Sino-British Treaty for the peaceful handover of the territory to China in 1997 appeared to have settled qualms about the long-term survival of its unique economy.

At Standard Chartered, profit levels were soon rising once again, and plans were signed off in 1985 for the construction of an imposing new building at 4 Des Voeux Road.

What followed was a remarkable surge, even by past standards. Not for the first time, the business in Hong Kong stole a march on the rest of the Group, innovating in ways that were only adopted more generally in 1993–6. It introduced a functional organization that shaped its activities around retail banking, corporate banking and a treasury operation – and it hired skilled individuals from other banks with proven expertise in their line of trade. By far the most important of these was Fred Enlow. One of Hong Kong's senior expatriates, Ron Carstairs, had been despatched to the US early in 1985 to find someone with the skills to build a world-class retail network. He found Enlow working for Bank of America and successfully lured him to the Colony. With fulsome support from Carstairs himself, who later became Hong Kong's General Manager, Enlow brought an inspired approach to the consumer market, as noted briefly already. His mass-market retail chain, with its pale green and light blue décor – initially rolled out across the Colony in defiance of endless objections from London, and subsequently adopted as the corporate colours for the whole Group – attested to shrewd leadership and lively marketing skills that were streets ahead of any to be found among the Group's operations in the West. And Hong Kong invested heavily in exemplary information systems, as part of the planning for the new Des Voeux Road offices, finally occupied in 1989.* Overseeing all this was a management cadre that even Galpin's hard-to-please consultants in 1988–9 thought more than competent (albeit, as they wryly observed, 'to some extent united by an adversarial relationship with [the rest of] the Group'.[79]) The outcome was a string of numbers that by 1991 were starting to attract the industry's attention. Without question, the star component was a residential mortgage business launched in 1985, which was already boasting an asset value of £1.5 billion, spread around 38,000 customer accounts – without a single default in six years.[80] A retail network of 120 branches underpinned the business and added a steady revenue stream of its own. By 1991 it had around £1.1 billion of loans outstanding in a marketplace where stiff competition was usefully mitigated by an interest-rate cartel, and it was toying with a range of new products that included a highly profitable credit card. The

---

* Sadly, the information systems did not extend to the preservation of archives. A substantial volume of papers bearing on the Group's history in Hong Kong seem to have disappeared during the move to temporary offices in Edinburgh Tower in 1986 and the occupation of the new premises in 1989.

ratio of costs to income was, meanwhile, falling year by year, and trading profits were rising accordingly. By 1991, they were up to around £75 million. Now that the Group had jettisoned its big US subsidiaries and lost its South African dimension, this was no mean proportion of Standard Chartered's worldwide total. In fact, when 1991's results were finalized, Hong Kong had chipped in 40 per cent at the trading level.

This, however, presented an obvious strategic dilemma. Taking the long view, it had to be wondered how far Hong Kong's prodigious growth was truly sustainable and how far it might represent a threat to the stability of the Group. The imbalance between Hong Kong and the rest of the network was scarcely a pressing problem before 1993: the crisis in the OECD countries and the implosion in Bombay left the Board little time to worry about a business making too much money elsewhere.* But the early 1990s nonetheless featured a low-key debate over possible responses to the too-many-eggs-in-one-basket worry. It was suggested, surely only half-seriously, that London might impose limits on the extent of the expansion in Hong Kong; alternatively the business might be incorporated there, as a stepping stone to finding a local partner.[81] When the gravity of the Indian disaster dawned in 1992, possible merger options were considered for the whole Group, trawling over much of the ground covered so assiduously by Michael McWilliam in the 1980s.[82] Only one option was given much credence by the Board, though, and it mooted the idea of a 'Two-Tier Group' with a sizeable chunk of the Hong Kong business floated separately on the local equity market. When this idea was brought back to the Board three months later, in February 1993, it was swiftly dismissed – and the minutes strongly suggest it was Williamson, newly installed as Chief Executive, who brushed it aside:

> The separation of the Group's strongest business would leave a residual [sic] business about which there would be significant doubts in the eyes of investors, regulators and providers of funding ... Hong Kong was the Group's centre for product, systems and management development; there was no other territory which could take on this role.[83]

---

* It might be noted, though, that the Group's lop-sided nature had already been starkly apparent even ahead of the 1990–91 recession in the West. In the 1989 budget, UK retail banking was to contribute £8.1 million, the whole of continental Europe £2.8 million, Canada £4.1 million, North America £8.9 million, Australia £9.0 million – and Hong Kong £61.9 million. Other 1989 budgeted numbers included £5.6 million for Singapore, £23.4 million for Malaysia, £7.8 million for India, £9.9 million for Kenya and £12.7 million for a revitalized business in Zimbabwe. ('Strategic Review Team Visits: Findings', Report by CRA, 16 March 1989, SCB Box 2390.)

Williamson had no doubt whatever that Hong Kong's success had to be wholeheartedly embraced – and indeed (as noted) fanfared for investors. This was not to deny that its growing dominance posed a quandary: for the whole of 1993, the Group's misadventures elsewhere left Hong Kong accounting for 61 per cent of trading profits. But Williamson was determined to tackle this in a positive manner that would build on Hong Kong's performance rather than seek to play it down. And for the next four years he and Gillam did just that – in the context of three main challenges. The first arose as a direct consequence of Enlow's progress in retail banking. Retail banking had never been of much importance to the Group anywhere else, least of all Asia, relative to its traditional trade-finance and treasury activities. The notion that Hong Kong's retail network might shortly be responsible for a fifth of total working profits, perhaps even more, was slightly unnerving, especially for those with little or no personal experience of the Colony. And recent events had scarcely been reassuring. The collapse in July 1991 of Bank of Credit and Commerce International (BCCI) had disclosed a seedy underworld of personal banking that cast many Asian banking circles in a less than flattering light. Indeed, BCCI's demise had been the cause of some unwonted excitement for Standard Chartered: it had helped trigger the first serious run on deposits ever experienced by the branch network in Hong Kong.

This was a colourful episode. A few weeks after the closure of BCCI's operations in the Colony on 17 July, the General Manager in Des Voeux Road, Ian Wilson, received a call from his retail-banking head late on Thursday 8 August to say three branches in the New Territories had seen much heavier than usual withdrawals. 'By the Friday morning', as Wilson would recall, 'there were lines of hundreds of people outside every one of our branches, queuing to withdraw their money from the bank.'[84] Rumours flew round the market that Standard Chartered's UK banking licence had been withdrawn. Wilson knew they were totally groundless, but had no option other than to start paying out the cash his customers were demanding. In principle, he could have increased the bank's notes in circulation to accommodate the crisis, making a matching deposit of US dollars with the Monetary Authority in the usual way. But in practice he faced an awkward problem. The bank's Note Issue had always been a modest operation, much smaller than HSBC's, and Wilson simply did not have a large enough inventory of printed HK dollar bills at his disposal. The only alternative was to ask HSBC to expand its Issue, making new notes available to Standard Chartered. This was agreed, and Wilson arranged with London for US dollars to be paid to HSBC in New York so that HSBC in its turn could be funded to make the necessary matching deposit of US dollars with the HK Monetary Authority. A substantial stock of crisp new HK dollars thereupon passed between the neighbours on Des Voeux Road. Standard Chartered's branches stayed open until 9 p.m. that evening, and were then restocked with cash – though not, remembered Wilson, without some difficulty:

> There were not enough armed vans from our security company to deliver cash to the whole of the network. So we got hold of all the bank's cars that we could find and stuffed their boots with cash. We had two policemen with guns riding in each of the cars, as they drove off to re-stock all our branches through the night. What wonderful staff we had! Many of them slept in their branches all night, so they could book the cash in and still be there to open up on the Saturday morning.[85]

By lunchtime on the Saturday, when the branches closed for the weekend, about HK$5 billion had been paid out to customers – equivalent to 10 per cent of all deposits – and it was obvious that another huge injection of cash would be required before the branches reopened on the Monday morning.* This was trickier, because HSBC had now to be asked to issue a second tranche of new notes late that Saturday, as large as the first, against a promise from Standard Chartered that it would make the appropriate dollar payment to the bank in New York on the Monday morning, East Coast time. For two days, HSBC would in principle be exposed to the risk of needing to stump up the necessary US dollars itself. Wilson's counterpart at HSBC asked him if Standard Chartered would be good for its cheque – but fortunately only in jest. The second tranche was made available and distributed like the first. On the Monday, no queues appeared, the crisis passed – and the New York payment was made. The neighbour's critical help was gratefully acknowledged by Galpin and Williamson.[86] Perhaps it was just as well that HSBC in August 1991 had no more notion than anyone else at that time of what was afoot in Bombay.

In truth, the bank-run drama made no difference at all to Williamson's

---

* It was reassuring, though, that small firms were not following the public's lead. Once assured by Wilson that there was no rational basis for Friday's panic, some of its longest established corporate customers on the Kowloon Peninsula acted together to flag their undiminished confidence in the Group. A dozen of them had their own exclusive club, formed in 1982, known as the KMO (for 'Kowloon Main Office', the Standard Chartered branch where most had opened their original accounts). Word spread quickly that the KMO's members were making fresh deposits at their local branches, which undoubtedly helped allay any serious concern in business circles. (William Lau and Peter Chan, interview with author, 20 March 2012.)

confidence in the potential of Hong Kong's retail banking network. He backed the rapid expansion of its mortgage book, and encouraged a series of initiatives that acknowledged profound shifts in the traditionally staid world of branch banking. New technology no longer meant just more automatic teller machines and paperless processing. It could mean telephone banking, on-line accounts, automated 24-hour branches, 'smart cards' and lap-top banking. By 1996, retail branches were accounting for 65 per cent of Hong Kong's profits, and had prompted the *Asian Wall Street Journal* to run an admiring article headlined 'UGLY DUCKLING TURNS INTO SWAN'.[87] But what encouraged Williamson almost as much as Hong Kong's success was the hope that it might somehow be replicated in other countries across Asia. The invaluable legacy of the Chartered Bank's standing among ethnic Chinese customers was a franchise to be tapped far more energetically across the whole region. Rich pickings were available in consumer markets where, as *The Economist* had noted a few years earlier, most of the wealth was held by an easily identifiable and relatively small group of customers, with an excellent track-record of low defaults and a welcome disregard for fee structures.[88] The main focus of attention in that *Economist* article was the remarkable performance of Citibank's consumer division in Asia, which had grown at almost 30 per cent a year for a decade and was run from Singapore with considerable flair by an Indian executive called Rana Talwar.

When Williamson first turned his attention to Standard Chartered's retail performance in the wider Asian region, it was the Group's poor showing compared with Citibank's that struck him immediately. In Malaysia, for example, little had really been done to build on the pre-1965 expansion of the network, to convert it from a basic repository of customers' deposits into a fully-fledged retail service. ('On my first visit to Malaysia, I said to the country manager there, "Can you explain to me why you've got twenty branches that have been long-established all over the place – and you make less money than Citibank makes with two branches?"'[89]) In the years after 1993, Standard Chartered made at least a start on providing personal banking services across the whole Asia Pacific region. Hong Kong was asked to provide systems support as well as a template for the expansion of the Group's mortgage and credit-card services elsewhere. And branch networks everywhere – even India, where two dozen branches had seen 'virtually nothing spent on them in decades'[90] – got a first taste of the kind of meticulous attention to premises championed by Enlow. In 1996, 49 per cent of the Group's trading profits were derived from Personal Banking (£288 million) and Consumer Finance

(£92 million), the one mostly powered by mortgage lending in Hong Kong
and the other, slightly incongruously, still largely based on car-purchase
loans, as it had been ever since its Hodge Group origins in Cardiff.*
(Corporate banking at £226 million represented a third of the total, and
Treasury at £137 million accounted for the rest.) A restructuring of the
Group late in 1997 saw Personal Banking and Consumer Finance consolidated together as 'Consumer Banking', and there were many who assumed
that it would remain the principal engine of growth in the years to come.
Ironically, Enlow himself had been absent from the Group since 1994,
having briefly joined a Chinese bank in Hong Kong and then returned to
the US for a spell working in its domestic credit-card industry. But he was
to rejoin Standard Charted in 1998 as head of Consumer Banking, basing
himself in Singapore. By that time, his was not the only voice exhorting
the Group to expand its retail operations. Poached from Citibank, and
appointed to the Board in April 1997 as an Executive Director, was Rana
Talwar.

The second challenge posed by Hong Kong was more conventional: far
from expanding too rapidly, its corporate banking in the early 1990s was
looking decidedly anaemic. Williamson was much less impressed than
Galpin's consultants by the (almost entirely expatriate) managers he found
in charge of this business, and made no attempt to exempt their activities
from the general squeeze of 1989–91. A Board paper from the Colony in
1992 hazarded a mild reproof for this policy: 'the process of cutting large
exposures, exiting domestic relationships and re-pricing assets has created
some difficulties for the corporate division'.[91] Of far more consequence
for Hong Kong, though, was the firm stand that Williamson took against
any post-recession revival of lending against commercial property. Since
almost every influential business figure in the Colony had a significant
involvement in real estate, this was a policy that needed some explaining – as
he duly acknowledged:

> I took the bank out of commercial-property lending in Asia completely. I
> went out to Hong Kong myself to see all the property developers. I had them
> into dinner at the bank and I said to them, 'Look, I don't like commercial
> property lending because this bank's been hurt too much already. If we get
> another cyclical downturn in the Far East, this bank won't survive it, so
> I'm going to ask you to gradually re-bank yourselves elsewhere.'[92]

---

* It was still based in Cardiff – which allowed the Group, in selling loan portfolios to a
subsidiary as part of making them available to outside investors, to christen the latter nicely
as CARS, standing for Cardiff Automobile Receivables Securitization. Its bonds were duly
issued as CARS 1, CARS 2 and so on.

Discussions with leading customers were generally good natured, but nonetheless amounted to a weakening of local banking relationships and left many people slightly bemused by the Group's attitude to property (especially after its announcement early in 1993 that it would be selling the head office building in Des Voeux Road, instinctively seen by many Chinese as most unwise). Standard Chartered's share of the local corporate lending market by mid-1992 was already looking thin: the in-house estimate was 3 per cent, quite a contrast with the 10-per-cent share enjoyed in the residential mortgage market.[93] After sterling's 'Black Wednesday' devaluation in September 1992 (slipping out of the European Monetary Union and down 26 per cent against the US dollar), the Group seemed less likely than ever to be interested in rebuilding its corporate loan-book. Within the hothouse environment of Hong Kong's financial sector, many wondered what alternative strategy, if any, might be available to compensate for this retreat. For eighteen months, it looked as though merchant banking and securities broking might be part of the answer. The Group handled more Initial Public Offerings on the local stock exchange than any other firm in 1993, with Standard Chartered Asia underwriting them and Standard Chartered Securities (SCS) handling the distribution of the new stock. But SCS was always a slightly dubious enterprise. Acquired opportunistically after the market crash of 1987 – when it was known as Chin Tung, owned by two brothers, Arthur and Raymond Lai – the business had been relaunched in 1992 with a change of name and fresh management. With a posh office and newly upgraded systems, Standard Chartered Securities was under pressure to prove its mettle in 1993 and plainly employed a few too many artful dodgers on its staff. The Hong Kong Securities and Futures Commission ruled as much in June 1994, rounding off a long investigation with an unusually sharp reprimand for both SCS and Standard Chartered Asia.* The head of one of the leading US brokerage houses in Hong Kong described the outcome as a damaging event for the whole Group that would 'leave a huge scar', a comment widely quoted in the media.[94] It was probably a fair verdict and within two years SCS had been sold, along with the Group's equity-broking arms elsewhere in the region.

The episode prompted further vexed analysis by the Group of its future in corporate banking – out of which sprang an elementary but nonetheless

---

* The firm was deemed to have resorted to post-flotation tactics for several clients that resulted in false markets. The Group's own investigation, 'Operation Hippo', overseen by Christopher Castleman, led to the departure of several senior executives in the summer of 1994. ('Operation Hippo Final Report' by Austin Allison, 20 September 1994, SCB Box 2440.)

momentous reform to current banking procedures. Alongside Treasury operations, it was the financing of international trade that, as ever, constituted the Group's bread-and-butter business. A customer of the bank in, say, Singapore, wanting to import goods from overseas needed to open a letter of credit (L/C) in favour of the foreign exporter in, say, Hong Kong and could turn to Standard Chartered in Battery Road to handle the documentation for him. The mechanics of this had changed very little in half a century – and had always allowed the branch opening the L/C to propose including a 'restrictive clause' in the papers, specifying that the other end of the transaction would also have to be handled by Standard Chartered. Thus, in our example, the Hong Kong exporter would be obliged to present the L/C to his local branch of the bank for settlement and payment on behalf of the Singapore buyer. The Singapore customer or even the Hong Kong exporter was of course free to decline the restrictive clause, in which case the Hong Kong end of the trade could be handled by any bank of the exporter's choosing. The zeal with which Standard Chartered's branches pursued restrictive clauses had become a decidedly hit-and-miss affair by the 1990s – surprisingly so, given the obvious potential of restrictive clauses for any bank with branches scattered across Asia. In simple terms, a trade handled at both ends was worth twice as much to Standard Chartered as a trade merely handled at one end or the other.

Around 1994, the managers responsible for the trade-finance departments in Hong Kong and Singapore happened to be two individuals – Gavin Laws and Simon Bush – whose parallel careers in the Group had made them close colleagues and who now found themselves for the first time in charge of 'back-office' operations. Taking stock of the L/Cs *without* restrictive clauses, they soon established that these accounted for well over half of the trade transactions being processed in each centre. Given the enhanced links between all of the Group's branches – with email communications beginning to be rapidly adopted – this looked an egregious act of omission. Laws and Bush resolved to ensure that all L/Cs between their respective offices carried restrictive clauses, and to launch a proselytizing campaign to alert colleagues across the whole Group to the fees they were missing. Two years later, their efforts were reinforced by the arrival in London of a third campaigner for the cause, Steve Wish, who joined the Group from HSBC (Wish had formerly worked for Midland Bank, acquired by HSBC in 1992, which had always been the UK clearer with the most expertise in the joys of correspondent banking.) Trade in and out of the UK comprised the third largest of Standard Chartered's markets – after Hong Kong and Singapore – and was based mostly on imports from Asia where L/Cs were still preferred as a means of payment across all business sectors. Wish was puzzled to discover that his overseas colleagues had more or less abandoned chasing restrictive clauses on L/Cs opened by their customers in favour of UK exporters: 'they seemed to think it a waste of time, since the Group had given up its High Street presence in Britain'.[95] He set out to turn this around, with impressive results. Within three years, the Group emerged as one of the Top 3 banks in the UK for L/Cs, ranked by the volume of business handled for exporters. The Gracechurch Street branch was especially successful at enhancing its links with Group offices in Africa, setting up a programme ('Out of Africa') that involved the automatic confirmation of L/Cs by the UK Head Office when they were issued by branches and financial-institution clients in Africa in favour of UK exporters. Over the next five years or so, Wish, together with Laws and Bush, effected a quiet transformation of this esoteric (to outsiders) corner of Standard Chartered's activities. By the end of the 1990s, restrict-ive clauses were being pushed so routinely that everyone in the Group had heard of the importance of capturing both ends of every trade transaction – or 'catching and throwing' as it became known ('you throw me the business and I'll catch it').

Two concurrent developments made this revitalization of the trade-finance function an especially timely initiative. The first was the arrival in Hong Kong, late in 1994, of a new head of corporate banking, Mervyn Davies, who quickly grasped its importance and gave it active support (endorsed by John McFarlane, who spent three years shuttling back and forth between Hong Kong and London). And second was the acquisition of the international trade division of a large Californian com-petitor, First Interstate Bank (FIB). The notion of a banking network that could bridge the Pacific, financing trade in both directions across the ocean, had of course been part of the rationale for acquiring Union Bank; but little had come of that in practice. This latest foray into California was to prove more successful. FIB's trade specialists brought with them a genuine link with their erstwhile owner on the West Coast, as Galpin explained in his original pitch for the 1992 acquisition. Standard Char-tered and FIB signed a Co-operation Agreement, '[which] gives us access for international business to the customers of some fifteen or so US banks throughout a network of around 1,000 branches, with product and service capabilities of a high order'.[96] This duly delivered plenty of lucrative new business with West Coast customers – including the Walt Disney Com-pany, for example, importing hundreds of millions of dollars' worth of toys and artefacts from mainland China every year – but the real pay-off was less specific and far outlasted the agreement with the FIB parent (which was to be terminated in 1996, when FIB was acquired by Wells

Fargo Bank).[97] The ex-FIB executives included local teams in Asia – comprised mostly of indigenous managers, with very few expatriates in the mix – as well as the US-based staff, plus a small merchant bank in London. (This was the former UK arm of the Continental Illinois Bank, whose continental European operations Michael McWilliam had tried to acquire in 1984.) Together they showed how tailored information systems could be used to keep track of individual transactions all over the world, handing Standard Chartered endless opportunities to facilitate matters with essential documents at both ends of any trade. 'They were tracking transactions that they weren't even directly involved in', recalled the head of the Hong Kong trade business. 'They brought tricks and ideas that we copied shamelessly.'[98] Within a year or so, the Group had picked up a reputation for its finely honed skills and was being contracted by other US commercial banks to handle international trading arrangements on their behalf.

The results of all this were dramatic. Profits on 'Trade and Correspondent Banking Services' began rising even more quickly than those of the Consumer Banking division. Shareholders keen to quantify their impact would have found it a frustrating exercise, however: after 1995, when they jumped by about a quarter for the second consecutive year, only 'Corporate Banking' profits were noted in the Annual Report. The exact contributions from trade finance – as from related areas like cash management and custodial services – were swept up into the broader category. There were sound reasons to be discreet. By bringing a focused and innovative approach to the basic financial plumbing that underpinned international trade, Standard Chartered had uncovered a rich seam of profits still apparently neglected by most of its rivals. (According to the Israeli computer company responsible for the state-of-the-art software used by the Group, known as 'IMEX', Standard Chartered was by far its single biggest customer anywhere in the world.[99]) The trade-finance teams began scouring the commercial world to identify the busiest container routes and the giant corporations behind them, all potential customers for a bank with a growing reputation for its coverage of the world's hottest economies. Once the targeted cargoes had been cotton from India, rice from Burma, rubber from Malaya, sugar from the Philippines and the like, exports all. Now they comprised not just agricultural commodities but rolled steel and cars, machine tools and consumer goods, flowing in both directions. Hong Kong set the pace, its status as the de facto gateway to China reflected in soaring trade volumes for the Colony (up 30 per cent in 1996 alone). Trading profits from the Corporate Banking division in Des Voeux Road more than doubled in the three years to December

1996 – by which time Hong Kong's corporate banking boss, Mervyn Davies, had been promoted as head of Global Corporate Banking, moving to an office in Singapore. But of course the essence of the new 'catching and throwing' approach to trade contracts was that revenues would flow into all parts of the Group. As they did so, the relative contribution from Hong Kong declined: it slipped down to a third of trading profits, as the Group totals surged ahead impressively. Here was a development calling for no undue discretion – and the 1996 Annual Report celebrated a turn-around of no little significance for the long-derided Banana-Skin Bank. 'Three years ago the management team committed to doubling our profits by 1996', wrote Williamson in his Chief Executive's review. 'We have achieved that target . . . We have made promises and we have kept them.' More prosaically, he and Gillam together had succeeded in distancing the Group from its recent past and finding a new momentum: 'Yes, we had changed the groove.'[100]

By the time the 1996 Report appeared, in March 1997, Hong Kong was just months away from being handed over by the British Government to the People's Republic of China, under the terms of the Sino-British Joint Declaration of 1984. Over the intervening thirteen years, the Declaration had not always been seen as the infallible guarantee of a happy ending. Nor could any public company with a heavy presence in Hong Kong have afforded over this period to ignore the various alternative and less palat-able possibilities. Here was the third, and most obvious, challenge to Standard Chartered posed by the success of its Hong Kong business in the early 1990s. The larger it loomed within the Group, the bigger the hole if 1997 were to end in calamity. The non-Executive Directors arranged a day's seminar in the Colony in 1990 that was chaired by the latest recruit to the Board – Ian Stewart MP, a former Tory Minister and Economic Secretary to the Treasury in 1983–7. They returned arguing for a Steady Ahead policy in Hong Kong itself, to be balanced, if possible, by the rapid growth of promising operations elsewhere in the region.[101] Eighteen months later, this looked a less than robust response to the 1997 dilemma. As a Board paper in November 1991 had to acknowledge, an attempt to build up Singapore and Malaysia as counterweights to Hong Kong had been 'disappointing': Standard Chartered was clearly seen in both as a foreign bank, in stark contrast to its status in the Colony. Other promising territories, such as Indonesia and Thailand, were going to need many years of investment. All this was pointing to just one unavoidable conclusion, and Williamson spelled it out at that November Board meeting. Prefigur-ing the stand he would take over Hong Kong once appointed as Chief Executive, he insisted that shareholders knew the risks. The Group had no choice but to make a full commitment to its business in the Colony. And the only plausible way of hedging the inherent geopolitical risk was to strengthen ties as quickly and as broadly as possible with mainland China. The Board concurred.

Ties of a tenuous kind had been sustained with China through the worst years of the Mao regime, even in the wake of David Johnston's 1968–70 incarceration. In later years the Group would be proud of an 'unbroken presence' in China, though in reality it was forced by the Chinese Government to keep open an office in Shanghai that it would probably have preferred to close. It went on being run after Johnston's wretched experience by a series of intrepid (but well paid) expatriate managers and a local staff numbering a half dozen or so individuals. Any larger headcount would certainly have been surplus to requirements. Letters of credit were handled only spasmodically for China's state-owned exporters; international companies merely sought help and advice from time to time, notably at the twice yearly Canton Fair held for foreign traders to meet prospective Chinese customers. Then, with Deng Xiaoping's rise to power in 1978, everything changed. This was not immediately apparent from the reported profits in Shanghai. Though one of only three foreign banks able to boast of a branch, the Group reported a China income of just £72,500 in 1981 – and this took no account of £31,141 in expenses incurred at Head Office on Shanghai's behalf.[102] The reality, however, was more promising. The first credit lines were being set up for mainland companies – advances were made in Hong Kong dollars to 'window companies' that represented them in the Colony, so this business is today hard to quantify[103] – and the Group was discreetly hiring representatives and expanding its network of contacts with national trading corporations in several of the biggest cities. ('To the extent that [their export] business is currently confined to the Bank of China, such "marketing" calls for some delicacy and perseverance', observed the Hong Kong Area Manager.[104]) Three new branches were opened in 1982 – in Beijing, Guangzhou (formerly Canton) and Shenzhen – the first additions since the 1949 Revolution to a 'network' that had comprised only Shanghai since 1955. A formal decision was then taken at Board level in 1983 to seek a strategic re-engagement with China. This grand objective involved at the outset a small helping of humble pie. A letter was conveyed to the Bank of China acknowledging its pre-war balances with the Chartered in New York – they amounted to £24,909 and US$35,402 – and the Group agreed to repay them (with simple interest of 5 per cent per annum).[105] Thereafter, the way was open to start reviving the Group's profile in the country. The annual IMF conference of 1985 was held in Seoul, and Michael McWilliam added China to his Korean itinerary, travelling around the People's Republic for four days with Bill Brown from Hong Kong. McWilliam was not impressed by the main branch ('a modest office on the 4th floor of a side street and not much to show for 126 years in Shanghai') but was pleasantly surprised to find himself being warmly received at official receptions in Shanghai, Xiamen, Jimei and Guangzhou.[106] He saw 'rather breathtaking opportunities', if only sufficient resources could be mobilized in time. Applications were soon being tendered for a string of representative offices to be upgraded into full branches. By the early 1990s the Group had a dozen branches and eight new representative offices. The initiative was well timed, for China was just emerging once again as one of the world's top trading nations. In 1985, she had a trade deficit of US$14.9 billion; five years later she recorded her first trade surplus in modern times, of US$8.7 billion. A pack of briefing papers for Standard Chartered's Board could suggest by 1993 that China's re-admission to full membership of the international trading community (as codified by the GATT treaty) was imminent.[107]

Those briefings were homework for the Directors ahead of a Board meeting in Shanghai, in October 1993. Before leaving London, they were also given a presentation on China by one of the principal architects of the 1984 Joint Declaration, Sir Percy Cradock. He had been Britain's ambassador in Beijing in 1978–83 and was a forthright advocate of engaging positively with the People's Republic, precisely as Gillam and Williamson were already recommending. The most interesting observation in a torrent of paperwork was that China's resurgence as an exporter had necessarily been driven by the state sector in the 1980s, but was going to rely on the private sector in the years ahead. A Hong Kong company had just completed the first direct investment in China by a foreign investor since 1949, acquiring a majority stake in a Wuhan textile firm. In a celebrated series of speeches in 1992 reaffirming the importance of his liberalizing agenda for the Chinese economy, Deng Xiaoping had talked of turning China's Guangdong Province into an export-led economy that might rank as Asia's 'Fifth Dragon' (joining Hong Kong, Taiwan, South Korea and Singapore, which were the other four – perhaps better known as Asia's Tiger economies).* Standard Chartered's Directors returned from

---

* A rising flood of direct investment from Hong Kong into Guangdong soon vindicated Deng's optimism. By 1996, it was estimated that Hong Kong companies were employing three million people in that province. One of these firms was Esquel, the prominent garment manufacturer founded in 1978 by Y. L. Yang and still a customer of Standard Chartered. (A photograph of the founder's daughter and successor, Marjorie Yang, had adorned a feature about trade financing in the Group's 1990 Annual Report.) In 1988, Esquel had bought a large spinning mill out of state ownership in Gaoming, a small city in the Pearl River delta, and

Shanghai persuaded that the door into China was open, and they were determined to use it. Indeed, by 1994 they were agreed in principle on an even bolder idea – that the Group might once again welcome some Chinese shareholders, this time as representatives of the People's Republic itself.[108] Visiting Beijing in June 1994, Gillam raised the idea with the state-owned Industrial and Commercial Bank of China. The Board seems to have been a little disappointed to hear back from him that no imminent developments could be expected. 'It was felt, however, that modest investments from central or regional representatives of the PRC could help the transition process relating to 1997 and would be seen as reinforcing the Group's own links into this region.'[109] In the event, none materialized – and, without them, the Group soon found itself a little light on well-connected local managers. In their absence, some early excursions into corporate lending in the Pearl River region came to grief over the next couple of years. Several sizeable loans made from Hong Kong to subsidiaries of the state-owned CITIC (China International Trust & Investment Corporation) began running into trouble, as if to remind the Group that no expansion in the Middle Kingdom had ever been entirely straightforward. It was the start of a thorny episode, not to be resolved until several years later.

By 1996, those responsible for China were carefully reassessing their best strategy.[110] The Board decided to treat Hong Kong as the hub for developing a Greater China region comprising China, Taiwan and Hong Kong itself. Within China, term loans would be eschewed in favour of the core businesses – trade credits, cash management and retail banking for the more affluent end of the market ('The ultimate prize [in China] is Personal Banking'). Capturing the mainland market's potential was likely to be a tortuous process: it could be many years before it emerged as a significant source of profits. But plans for a new office in Shanghai's Pudong district had been well received by the authorities, and Standard Chartered was one of eight banks selected in 1996 as the first to receive licences for some modest renminbi-based transactions.

As the 30 June 1997 deadline approached in Hong Kong, senior executives thus felt they had at least begun to build a genuine rapport with the banking authorities of the People's Republic. But the Group had also sought to protect its future position in Asia, just in case, through a significant expansion since 1990 of its administrative presence in Singapore. The first steps in this direction had been almost serendipitous: it had not been

---

Standard Chartered helped to finance an expansion of the site through the next twenty years into a 'campus' 10 miles wide that employed 30,000 workers in 2011 (and produced 46 million shirts).

an initiative launched on the back of wads of painstaking analysis. Appointed in 1990 as Banking Director for the Asia Pacific Region, David Moir had been expected to base himself in Hong Kong. To many people's surprise – not to say, the acute chagrin of those in Hong Kong henceforth required to report to colleagues on the rival island – he chose instead to work from an office in Singapore. Moir was at the time head of the Hong Kong branch, but had no sentimental British attachment to the Colony. Always his own man, he felt that establishing himself in his new role in the same surroundings would be harder than beginning afresh in Singapore. Having taken this decision more or less unilaterally, he then took every opportunity both to advance the careers of local Asian executives and to push the attractions of Singapore as the best location from which to co-ordinate the Group's core businesses – in many cases, pursuing the two goals at the same time. Thus Euleen Goh, who had joined as a qualified accountant from Price Waterhouse and had been working as Head of Internal Audit, was promoted by Moir into a worldwide role, monitoring the shape of the Group's overall balance sheet from her desk in Singapore. (She later helped to pioneer some critical risk-assessment techniques within the Group, notably Value-At-Risk accounting, and in 2000 would eventually succeed Theresa Foo as the local Chief Executive.) A regional Treasury operation in Singapore began expanding its coverage after 1994 and it soon morphed into a Global Treasury unit. In 1995, when consumer banking and corporate banking were similarly turned into centralized global businesses, they too were assigned head offices in Singapore. So, in addition to its thriving local business, still based at 6 Battery Road, the Group now had a regional head office, 'Plaza at the Park', that had taken on steadily more importance.

It was probably of no little consequence, in dealing with Singapore's regulators through these years, that Standard Chartered's senior people in the city were now mostly prominent local bankers, rather than the expatriate Scots of bygone days. And, in the course of some occasionally difficult negotiations, Theresa Foo as Chief Executive had an impressive story to set out for the authorities. As she recalled: 'I could say, "Look how important we have made Standard Chartered Singapore!" We had made it the financial centre for the Group. That was a very big plus point for the regulator.'[111] Given the dominance of earnings from the Malay Archipelago, including Singapore, for so many past generations of Chartered bankers, this promotion of Standard Chartered's operations there had a pleasing historical resonance.*

---

* Singapore was of course also the home of the Group's largest shareholder. Khoo Teck Puat had retained his stake since resigning from the Board in 1986, and had gradually increased

Nonetheless, Singapore's expanded role was largely administrative. As noted, its earnings potential still paled in comparison with the Group's operations in Hong Kong. So, however much had been done to allay the risk of a hostile Beijing-directed regime in Hong Kong after 1997, that risk could not be ignored. Asked by the Bank of England to quantify what might be at stake in the worst of all scenarios – half-yearly meetings were held with the Bank to review the preparations for 1997, under 'Project Sunrise' – the Group suggested it might lose fully a quarter of its total assets and a third of its attributable annual earnings.[112] Nor was the risk of future mayhem to be measured solely in terms of hypothetical financial losses. Not prepared to wait on the unfolding of events, a substantial number of the Group's senior Chinese staff were already emigrating with their families to foreign cities – notably Singapore, Vancouver and Toronto – where they could qualify for citizenship and fresh passports. They calculated that they would be able to resume their posts if all went smoothly, and the great majority of them duly did so, though at no small cost to their families and their own well-being.* By the time most of them returned, their fears for the future of Hong Kong had been dispelled. The colony's transition to Chinese rule at the end of June 1997 passed without incident – as by then was widely expected. Deng Xiaoping's 'one country, two systems' prescription was swallowed, for good or ill. The political effects seemed unlikely to be clear for some years to come. Tumultuous events in the immediate aftermath of the handover, on the other hand, briefly raised fears that the the financial side-effects might be all too soon apparent.

---

it to almost 15 per cent by 1992. He fired off many letters to the Board, sharply critical of the Group's disappointing results, and an always prickly relationship between him and Galpin was stretched to breaking point by the Bombay Scam. Patrick Gillam made it his business to restore friendly relations and he kept Khoo and his family well informed on Group developments from the start of his chairmanship. By 1997, the rise in the share price had helped make Khoo one of the richest men in Asia. He increased his holding to just over 15 per cent and seemed intent on further purchases, allowed under EU rules. Visiting him in April 1997, Gillam used all of his customary skill at concealing a steely hand within a velvet glove: 'The meeting had been extremely cordial but [Khoo's] future intentions remained unclear. The Chairman had made it clear that any addition to his holding would not be welcome.' (Minutes of Board meeting, 22 April 1997, SCB Box 2605.)
* It was of considerable concern to the bank, too, that many of those returning after June 1997 came back alone. In subsequent years, dozens of these employees would regularly seek leave to snatch a weekend with their families. 'They'd fly all the way to Canada on a Friday, then fly all the way back again virtually straight away, to be back in Hong Kong early the following week.' (Gavin Laws, interview with author, 20 November 2013.)

5. SURFING THE ASIAN CRISIS

On the day after China's formal acceptance of sovereignty over Hong Kong, the currency crisis that engulfed most of Asia's economies in 1997 broke with the devaluation of Thailand's baht. Some observers would later blame the crisis partly on fears over the former colony's future, suspecting that these had fed into wider concerns over the stability of the region. Most economists preferred eventually to pin the causes on a far more generalized panic among international investors, analogous in many ways to the run on a commercial bank. As 'depositors' in the Asia Pacific region, investors had backed a massive flow of capital into 'emerging-market' economies for several years. Now the growth in these economies appeared to be stalling. In July 1997 investors decided, unanimously and precipitately, to withdraw their funds virtually overnight. Subsequent analyses of this frighteningly sudden loss of confidence were divided over the extent to which the crisis marked a response to fundamental flaws in the devastated countries – booming trade deficits, structural flaws in local banking systems, inflated exchange rates that owed more to government officials' wishful thinking than any laws of supply and demand, and so on – or, alternatively, resulted from a blind financial panic to which the region was acutely vulnerable, given the prevalence of foreign investment in its main economies.[113] Whatever the cause, the result was a brutal and multifaceted correction. Over the next twelve months, local currencies across the region were to be savagely devalued against the US dollar, with percentage falls that varied from 34 per cent at best, for the South Korean won, to a calamitous 83 per cent for the Indonesian rupiah. And the astonishing growth rates notched up over recent years would give way to GDP contractions that were no less astonishing: Indonesia, for example, was 'on its way to one of the worst economic slumps in world history'.[114]

Just when Gillam and Williamson thought it was safe to go back on the offensive with public talk of a 'no-surprises culture' – the phrase popped up officially for the first time in the 1996 Annual Report[115] – here was a cataclysmic turn of events that would surely stress-test all claims by the Group to have changed its ways. Of the big international banks, after all, none was more closely identified with the trading of Asia's local currencies than Standard Chartered. Its whole history was bound up with the markets of the won and the rupiah, the baht, the Malaysian ringitt, the Filipino peso and a smattering of other even more 'exotic' currencies, not to mention the Hong Kong and Singapore dollars. And its commitment to them had been redoubled since 1992 in a conscious bid to capitalize on the historical legacy. Executives had that year confronted an unsettling development in the world of foreign exchange.[116] Having grown more or less continuously since the start of the 1950s, the aggregate volume of trades had dropped 30 per cent since 1989. Some of the causes – like the City of London's sudden aversion to anything too exotic after BCCI's collapse – were arguably ephemeral. Others looked more fundamental. The number of participants in the marketplace had fallen significantly, in the wake of the US banking industry's continuing consolidation and a retreat by smaller banks, intimidated by the cost of global dealing rooms that bore a closer resemblance to NASA's Mission Control Center than any traditional banking parlour. The number of tradeable currencies had fallen, too, with most Western European nations intent on linking their currencies to each other in preparation for the launch of a single European currency, slated for 1999.

This volume decline posed a challenge for Standard Chartered. In 1991, with most banking activities weighed down by the global recession, its twenty dealing centres around the world had accounted for 40 per cent of the Group's total revenues. The importance of foreign-exchange dealing to its profitability could hardly be overstated. The decision was therefore taken to shift the focus of its Treasury operations even further from the world's main currencies in favour of their exotic cousins. The latter already accounted for about 30 per cent of the foreign-exchange earnings being booked in the Group's four main dealing centres in London, New York, Singapore and Hong Kong. It looked sensible to assume by 1992 that this proportion could be lifted significantly higher on the back of the emerging-markets phenomenon. In most Asian countries, unlike in the West, trading volumes were rising steeply in every sector, from foreign exchange and plain fixed-interest bonds to commodity hedges and a wide range of interest-linked derivative products. Standard Chartered moved methodically to engage with all of them. As noted already, an international Treasury division was set up in Singapore in 1994. There was much talk of Treasury expertise being 'migrated' into the Asia Pacific region – the chief migrant was Mike Rees, sent out from London to join the Battery Road Treasury unit – and Asian-market operations duly grew quickly enough to shield the Group's total income when Treasury revenues dipped in the West. Trade magazines like *Euromoney* published annual league tables, ranking the banks according to votes cast by their peers. By 1997, the Group had been regularly topping the tables for most key sectors of the Asian Treasury marketplace and most currencies other than the Hong Kong dollar.

So, once the seismic nature of the 1997 crisis had become apparent, City investors were understandably alert to the possibility that another Bombay-style misadventure might lie just around the corner. Over the five months from mid-August 1997 to mid-January 1998, the Group's share price collapsed, falling by almost exactly 50 per cent.[117] This would, however, turn out to be an egregious misreading by the market of Standard Chartered's new-found resilience. Certainly the first weeks posed plenty of risks for its Asian Treasury business – but the rewards were to prove at least commensurate. In fact, the Group enjoyed something of a bonanza. By late October the Board was noting that 'up to about £50 million of the own-account contribution in Treasury was unlikely to be repeated in 1998'.[118] By the end of 1997, total Treasury profits had jumped 63 per cent, year on year, to roughly the same level as profits from Personal Banking.[119] The trade press noted that Standard Chartered had become the tenth largest bank in the world, as ranked by foreign-exchange revenues. Understandably keen to avoid appearing jubilant over what the ill-winds in Asia had done for them, Directors spared the details in the subsequent 1997 Annual Report – though it did note that 'revenues from dealing in Asia were up by 90 per cent' – but the broad scale of the Group's success was apparent.

It had been underpinned by some shrewd decisions, both before the crisis and during it. Dealing-room technologies had been standardized since 1995. Some conspicuously risky positions had been closed out. Risk-management techniques had been applied systematically before the crisis and were quickly upgraded to cope with anomalous interest-rate movements after it broke. Several of the more alarming book losses in the wake of currency depreciations had been anticipated and (very discreetly) hedged with overseas investments that rose in value as local asset values fell.[120] Above all else, Standard Chartered outmanoeuvred most of its international rivals by having Treasury departments in all its Asian markets that were essentially local operations with domestic banking licences. This was atypical of the industry: most of the world's largest banks, building Asian businesses in the 1980s, had formed regional operations as satellite units reporting to a hub office in Singapore, which took advantage of liberal regulatory regimes making little or no distinction between on-shore and off-shore activities. Standard Chartered had opted for a different strategy in the 1990s. It had had local branches for generations past in places like Jakarta (founded in 1864), Manila (1873), Bangkok (1894) and Kuala Lumpur (1888) – it had also been slow, as we have seen, to co-ordinate regional businesses in the 1980s – and it had striven since 1994 to capitalize on this string of independent franchises. The pay-off in 1997 was twofold. The Group's country managers had a far more intimate knowledge of local customers and enjoyed closer ties with the marketplace (and its regulators) than were available to any Singapore-based regional manager. And, after the July typhoon had swept through the markets, there followed a general resort to exchange controls that barricaded countries against banks effectively working as off-shore units for their Singapore parents. In this abruptly altered environment, Standard Chartered was enviably placed. As Mike Rees (promoted Head of the Global Treasury in September 1997) recalled, 'we were on the right side of the fence'.[121] It was a sequence of events best illustrated in the country at the very eye of the storm – Thailand.

Standard Chartered in Thailand had in some ways been a running illustration of the Group's wider story in Asia since 1970. That was the year it finally sold the colonial-style head office it had occupied since 1909 on the banks of the Chao Phraya next to the Oriental Hotel.* Moving into rather less decorous premises – a grim modern building known as 'Dusit Thani', far from the river's edge – the bank left behind those far-off colonial days when a loan of working capital often meant an elephant mortgage for a teak trader. It nonetheless pressed on into the 1980s in true colonial style, retaining half a dozen expatriate British officers, two hundred or so local employees – about a third of them working in a sub-branch on the island of Phuket – and a Thai compradore, Mr Krieng (whose daughter became the first covenanted Thai officer of the bank).[122] The unhappy result was bluntly acknowledged by a newly appointed Manager in 1984:

> During the last ten years the Bank in Thailand has lost market share and status, largely due to the absence of effective marketing and increasingly aggressive competition from both foreign (particularly the US banks) and local banks. The main business of our branches has been traditionally medium/large local (Chinese ethnic) business with particular emphasis on the rice and rubber industries. However, as the Bank did not respond to changes in the marketplace, with both our foreign exchange quotes and document handling service becoming uncompetitive, we lost a large number of our local customers including the rice and rubber industries.[123]

As in many other territories, the extent of the bank's dwindling stature was evident not just in sliding profits but also from a notable in-house

---

* The building was demolished shortly afterwards, possibly by the bank itself as a way of lifting the re-sale value of the precious riverside location – which was acquired by the owners of the Oriental Hotel in 1973 (at about the same time that the latter went into partnership with Mandarin International Hotels of Hong Kong). The modern hotel's Ambassador Wing extends across the former site of the Chartered Bank.

fraud: one of the local managers embezzled a large sum, which landed him in gaol eventually and knocked office morale for six. The McWilliam years in London then brought a belated effort to modernize the Thai bank, with the first computers and a first stab at professional training and career management. A key development followed, around 1986, when the Accounts Department set up a Treasury Desk to handle foreign exchange as a separate profit centre rather than as the by-product of trade financing that it had always been in the past. Thereafter, Treasury earnings usefully supplemented the core trade-finance business. Personal banking also made good progress in the post-1988 years. Credit-card services proved especially popular in Bangkok, and Standard Chartered was one of the first two foreign banks to join an ATM network established in 1996. Despite having only a few branches – Phuket had by now been closed – the bank enjoyed a high reputation for protecting the confidences of its customers. (Rodney Galpin was fond of recounting how the bank in Thailand, many years earlier, had refused bullying demands from a new, post-coup government to disclose the current account details of displaced ministers. All its local rivals handed over the requested data. Unsurprisingly, most of the newly installed ministers discreetly moved their accounts to Standard Chartered.[124])

Its prominence in the local foreign-exchange market took on a novel importance through the first half of 1997. As Western hedge funds began shorting the Thai baht aggressively – taking out baht loans, that is, to fuel sales of the currency in the belief that its fixed rate of Bt25 to the US dollar would soon be abandoned, allowing re-purchases to be made at a sharply lower exchange rate – the Government in Bangkok dug in its heels. Late each day, it used another slice of its US dollar reserves to buy millions of Thai baht, restoring its price to the official US dollar exchange rate. Many of these transactions were made through Standard Chartered. Anticipating each day's corrective purchases, the bank made some tidy profits by scooping up blocks of baht across the world for re-sale to the Central Bank of Thailand. Indeed, the Group's traders in London and New York were not afraid, by the start of July, to hold some quite large Thai baht positions overnight. On the evening of 1 July, those responsible for baht trading in New York confidently left behind a 'long' position when they headed uptown to a Bobby Flay restaurant in the Flatiron district, to entertain some clients visiting from overseas. Before the steaks arrived, Matt Sweeney and his colleagues were summoned abruptly back to their desks in the World Trade Center.[125] The morning of 2 July had begun in Bangkok with the announcement of a capitulation by the Government. The latest in a long string of short-lived finance ministers had looked into the Central

Bank's barrel of US dollar reserves and found it all but empty. The baht had been declared a free-floating currency, and its value was sliding fast. In promptly closing their baht positions, the New York traders booked losses that embarrassed them – but might have been far worse. By the close of 2 July, the baht had fallen 18 per cent against the dollar. This proved to be just the start of a protracted decline. The baht's flotation was the single event that triggered the whole Asian Crisis, and the scale of the resulting turmoil fed back into continuing pressure on the Thai currency. Those shorting it with borrowed funds were squeezed hard by the Central Bank of Thailand over subsequent months – local Thai interest rates were pushed up to punitively high levels, to try to offset the gains to be made on the currency – but to no avail in the end.* By January 1998, the baht's value had halved against the dollar.

Standard Chartered emerged from the Asian currency crisis looking as robust as any bank in the region and considerably stronger than most. It had weathered the Mexican currency's 1994 collapse without mishap; but few had attached much importance to that feat, given the Group's very limited exposure to the peso.[126] Emerging unscathed from the crisis of 1997, not to say surfing it with confidence – the Group's Treasury operations beat their budgets handsomely until well into 1998[127] – looked an altogether more significant achievement.† Most senior people in the bank drew huge encouragement from this. Malcolm Williamson, however, took a more nuanced view. As its Chief Executive, he could certainly feel proud of the ways in which the Group's competitive position in Asia had been enhanced. But as a man who had spent thirty years as a commercial banker with Barclays, he could not help feeling deeply perturbed over the

---

* A little ironically, Standard Chartered was itself in a privileged position to profit now from short sales of the baht. As a bank with a Thai domestic licence it had access to baht funds without recourse to borrowing overnight in the Bangkok money markets. Bills of exchange sold to the Thai corporate sector raised the necessary capital at 'normal' interest rates, and no attempt was made by the authorities to prevent the Bangkok branch assisting the Group's foreign-exchange activities in London and New York.

† Some were less impressed than might have been expected. A bumper summer for the Mocatta Group kindled hopes of a significantly higher price for the gold bullion and metals-trading business, which the Group had been trying to sell since 1994. Its culture had finally been reckoned incompatible with any 'no-surprises' regime. The Director in charge of the sale, Christopher Castleman, was frustrated by a determined purchaser, the Bank of Nova Scotia, whose executives clung doggedly to a price, US$26 million, which was equivalent to less than twice Mocatta's newly projected earnings for the following year and looked rather a steal by September 1997. Rather than abandon the transaction after months of tough negotiation, however, Castleman signed on the line. The sale was completed on 30 November. ('Proposed sale of Mocatta Bullion & Base Metals Businesses' by Christopher Castleman, Memorandum for the Board meeting of 30 September 1997, SCB Box 2605.)

trends now evident across the Asian corporate landscape: deteriorating credits, falling loan demand, depreciating currencies. This seemed to him a high-risk environment for all bankers – and a marketplace especially perilous for an international bank with no counter-balancing domestic profile in the West. Here was a familiar theme, for those with any knowledge of the past. Williamson was keen to back the triumphant growth of the Asian retail business; he believed in the huge potential of Hong Kong, Singapore and Malaysia; he hoped the Tiger economies could recover their poise. But the extraordinary gyrations he had witnessed in Asian markets this past year or so had left him deeply sceptical that the Group could rely on this region of the world alone to ensure itself a prosperous and independent future. In short, the time had come for another of the merge-or-go-solo debates that had been such a feature of the 1980s.

In fact the debate had been presaged even before the Asian Crisis broke. Williamson and his ex-Barclays Finance Director, Peter Wood, had proposed to the Board that a bid should be made for the National Westminster Bank. They had been monitoring the giant British clearer's decline for years, and felt confident that Standard Chartered by early 1997 had built up sufficient resources to pull off a merger successfully. A team from McKinsey had been set to work on the implications, and had submitted a detailed and highly encouraging paper on the prospects for 'Project Yorkshire'. (Since the early 1990s, McKinsey had steadily squeezed aside most of the other management consultancies employed in the Galpin era. Effectively embedded within Standard Chartered by 1997, its advisory team was formally headed by a director based in Hong Kong, Dominic Casserley, but was led from day to day by a partner in London, Peter Sands – and it was Sands who authored the final paper on 'Project Yorkshire'.[128]) Williamson recalled: 'Nat West was a badly run bank which Peter [Wood] and I felt we could knock into shape quite quickly. We could take a huge slice of costs out of it, and the merger would give us a UK haven and a solid home base.'[129] Patrick Gillam was at first supportive, but at some point in the proceedings, still fiercely protective of the Group's independence, he set his face against it. Williamson was dismayed. Indeed, their disagreement over the plan probably marked the end of the hugely successful partnership they had formed since the beginning of 1993. Williamson tried his best to bring the Chairman round, but Gillam stood his ground as robustly as usual and won the backing of a majority of the Board. By July 1997, the idea had been dropped. Then came the tumultuous events of the summer – and another, even more radical proposal from Williamson. Persuaded now that the logic of merging with a UK clearer was compelling, he set his sights not on the weakest of them all but the strongest.

The Group had spent three-quarters of the twentieth century shadowing the overseas businesses of Barclays Bank in various parts of the world. Williamson knew the inner workings of both banks better than anyone, and opened a dialogue with the Chief Executive of Barclays, Martin Taylor, to look at whether they might together create a new combined group. The idea had an obvious appeal for the clearer. As Taylor recalled:

> Barclays would have got its business internationalized in the world's fastest growing markets, which we could see no other easy way of doing at the time. Standard Chartered would have acquired much more muscle to operate on a far grander scale. It would have been, I think, a very interesting organization ... We did a lot of work on it. There was a lot of interest within Barclays and Malcolm was very keen, as I remember it.[130]

Barclays appointed advisers for the project and began to weigh the chances of capturing Khoo Teck Puat's stake in a timely fashion. Then they ran into the same insuperable obstacle that had sunk Project Yorkshire. Gillam was against it, and this time moved more quickly to assert his control over events. Quite why he opposed this second initiative so strongly is unclear. It may be that, as Executive Chairman, he was not best pleased to hear that conversations had been commenced with Barclays without his participation. Whatever the explanation, anyway, he simply refused to sanction further contacts. He declined to meet Taylor or anyone else from the UK clearer, and he refused to allow any papers on the proposal to be put to the Directors. His only concession was to ask consultants from McKinsey to examine the Group's strategic options, reporting back in February 1998.

This was an unusual stance for a Chairman to take, and there followed what must have been a difficult stand-off between Gillam and his Chief Executive. Williamson led a Board discussion in January, with a flurry of illustrative numbers on the relative merits of merging Standard Chartered (market capitalization: £6 billion) with a range of banks from DBS of Singapore (£2 billion) at one extreme to Citibank (£33 billion) at the other.[131] But no mention was made of Barclays. He sent out a New Year's letter to all employees, reminding them that he had consistently pressed the importance of operating on a bigger scale – and drawing out the implication of this in the new circumstances. 'Recent events have raised the question of whether we can achieve this sort of scale exclusively through internal growth and at least for now it seems unlikely. That is why we have been, and continue to be, interested in acquisitions.'[132] But he was still barred by Gillam from taking the Barclays idea to the Board. In the middle of February, McKinsey submitted their paper. The merge-or-go-solo arguments had never been more eloquently summarized, but as a directive for the future the paper was Delphic in the extreme – and, as consultants, McKinsey never offered definitive answers. The music was getting faster in Asia all the time, in their view, and there were ever fewer chairs left at the bankers' table. So joining forces with a bigger institution would make sense – but so too would a decision to push on alone, 'provided . . . that this choice does not simply become a less growth-oriented "sit it out" strategy'.[133] In response, Gillam set down an uncompromising statement of intent. He rejected the notion that the speed of change across Asia was strengthening the case for a merger. He insisted that the Group should pursue its own course 'vigorously . . . forging ahead, despite the risks'. It was true that 'expressions of interest' had been received from various banks – but with the share price currently so depressed (at around 700 pence compared with a high over £10 the previous summer), selling out now would make no sense at all. 'We [sic] recommend that all the overtures should be declined.'[134] This line was duly adopted at the next meeting of the Board, in the last week of February.[135] A press story (leaked, presumably by a disgruntled party, from Barclays) that same week about the possibility of a merger obliged Martin Taylor to abandon efforts from his end to take matters any further.

At some point in the next month or so, Williamson was approached out of the blue by headhunters on behalf of Visa Inc., the giant of the credit-card and electronic-payments world. Might he have any interest in the post of President and Chief Executive, based in San Francisco? They had done their homework, and found a ready response. Williamson decided he could look back with some satisfaction on a mission accomplished at Standard Chartered. He had 'cleared the propellers', and 'changed the groove'. Some of his closest colleagues were now departing. David Brougham, for example, retired in April. He himself had also reached the normal Group retirement age of sixty, and he saw no prospect of Gillam vacating the Chairmanship in the foreseeable future. His family were all in favour of a stint in the US and he decided to take the job, handing in his resignation in July. He and Gillam parted entirely amicably in the end – though there was time for one more disagreement before his final exit at the end of September. Williamson recommended that his successor should be the man who had led the Group's corporate banking business so successfully, Mervyn Davies. Appointed to the Board in December 1997 at the age of forty-five, Davies had moved back to Hong Kong after what had proven to be a relatively short stint in Singapore and had been made responsible since the start of 1998 for all of the Group's operations in Hong Kong, China and North East Asia. But Gillam pressed on instead with the appointment of that other former Citibanker on his Board, Rana Talwar. Nothing had been said publicly of Talwar's status as CEO-in-waiting at the time of his joining the Board, in 1997, but it had been explicitly agreed in private that he would sooner or later succeed Williamson.[136] And, in addition to his outstanding professional credentials – by 1997 he had clearly been one of the small group of senior figures seen as internal candidates, one day, to become head of Citibank – Talwar had, for Gillam, one other critical attribute. He was Indian. Few could doubt that the opportunity to appoint such a prominent Asian banker to the top job at Standard Chartered carried huge appeal for the Chairman. He had led the Group several steps closer to being a truly Asian/African enterprise. Talwar looked just the right man to push this vital process forward – as he was now to do, with a passion that would take many by surprise.

II

Metamorphosis, 1998–2008

1. INDIA RE-IGNITED

Patrick Gillam's categorical refusal to consider a possible merger in 1998 was a characteristically tough stand. In the first year or two of his chairmanship some had misjudged just how combative Gillam could be, and had generally regretted it.* His dominance in the Boardroom, still powerfully reinforced by Dick Balzer's work behind the scenes, was now rarely challenged – though Williamson would not be the last top executive to fall foul of it – and he had around him a loyal group of close associates including his deputy, former Tory Treasury Minister and for many years a painstaking chairman of the Audit and Risk Committee of the Board, Lord Stewartby (Ian Stewart). Two other long-serving confidants were fellow oil-industry men, Hugh Norton of BP and Keith Mackrell of Shell. Now, almost six years after the traumatic disclosures of the Bombay Scam, Gillam sensed a new confidence across the Group and resolved to back it.

Most of the Directors and senior managers alike were, in his view, keen to ditch the rearguard, defensive mindset that had so dominated the 1990s. Asserting the will to remain independent was an essential part of putting the Group back on to the front foot – or rather (taking the long view) switching it on to the front foot across all of its historic markets,

---

* In 1994, he had set aside a few days of a business trip in the Far East and asked John Brinsden to sort out an interesting itinerary for the two of them. With his customary brio, Brinsden arranged a visit to northern Laos and its capital, Vientiane. No doubt with the best of intentions, one of Brinsden's superiors then cautioned the Chairman against this, venturing that the trip was ill-advised insofar as 'it might give the Laos government the impression that we are interested in opening a branch there, which we most certainly are not'. Some weeks later, as Brinsden would recall it, Gillam showed him the message that he had sent in reply: 'My dear ------ , May I remind you that I am the Chairman and you are not. And if I choose to go to Laos, I will do so, with or without your permission.' (Brinsden, interview with author, 28 March 2012.) And by the end of 1995 Brinsden had opened a representative office in Vientiane, too.

and not just Hong Kong, for the very first time. Since its inception in 1969, after all, Standard Chartered had spent almost two decades chasing an alternative future in the West and ten years shaking off the consequences. It was Gillam's personal conviction that the growth of Asia's emerging markets over the 1990s had to be taken now as the cue for a resolute drive, at last, to build properly on the great franchises inherited from the Standard and Chartered Banks. Of course the Group might be overwhelmed by the vagaries of the capital markets. As he had acknowledged in that February 1998 statement of intent, the possibility could hardly be ignored that it might some day be snapped up by one of the world's many banking behemoths. 'The scale issue may, over time, make it more likely that we will be absorbed by a big player, whether we like it or not'.[1] But to be deterred from an expansionist strategy on this account would make no sense at all: much better, in fact, to embrace expansion all the more urgently as the best means of survival. (Shades, there, of Michael McWilliam's line in 1983.) And while none could know it in 1998, the Group was to be rewarded for Gillam's brave stance on a prodigious scale. There followed a burst of growth in the markets of Asia, Africa and the Middle East that was more remarkable by far than anything the architects of the 1969 merger could possibly have imagined. In some respects the outcome accorded the Group a gratifying sense of its own history, underscoring a continuous link with the geographical focus of its forerunner banks since the middle of the nineteenth century. Much of its successful response to the latter-day growth of its legacy territories, though, can be attributed to the thoroughness with which the Group also transformed its own culture, marking a profound break with its Empire and post-imperial past. On balance, metamorphosis probably trumped continuity. Out of the old, struggling Standard Chartered emerged a business that was more profoundly rooted in the lands of Asia, Africa and the Middle East than ever before.

Gillam (knighted in 1998) set the general direction, but much had to depend on the executive leadership of the Group – and here an auspicious start seemed to have been made with the choice of Rana Talwar as Chief Executive. The fifty-year-old Indian, fresh from his glittering career with Citibank, exuded confidence and was the very personification of Asian banking. His charisma and film-star demeanour did nothing for the share price in the short term – having recovered to pre-Crisis levels around £10 in April 1998, it perversely plunged again and fell to less than £4 by September – but they galvanized the top team. After years of retrenchment, when it had sometimes seemed that 'Sell it!' was the only phrase to be uttered with much real enthusiasm, Talwar espoused the case for expanding everywhere in Asia, and especially in the Tiger economies, with a fiery enthusiasm that excited his new colleagues. A few months into the job, he made his opening pitch to the Board, entitled 'Emerging Stronger' (yet another paper actually penned by McKinsey's Peter Sands, who by now was as steeped in the detailed workings of Standard Chartered's business as any of its own executives). Among its 'strategic principles' were 'Bold moves, not incrementalism', and 'Achieve a decisive positioning in Asia'. His objectives included not just the buttressing of core markets in Hong Kong, Singapore and Malaysia, but the cultivation of others in the region – additional markets to each of which the Group could look for at least £50 million a year of incremental profits. Above all, Talwar was determined that Standard Chartered, wherever possible, should turn itself into a truly local bank. He had no doubt that most of the Asian markets would in time recover from the 1997 Crisis – and that when they did so, their indigenous commercial banks would return to the rapid growth rates of the mid-1990s. Their expansion would then squeeze out those international banks largely restricted, like the Empire's exchange banks of old, to a concentrated presence in the main city centres. To be assured of a long-term future, foreign banks would need to have their own domestic networks – and this, given the insuperable difficulties of starting from scratch, meant there was no time to waste in pinning down successful acquisitions of existing institutions.

Here the crisis had opened up some unexpected opportunities that might never recur. Banking and finance across Asia were in turmoil. Local financial firms carrying dollar debt had in many cases been ruined by the devaluation of their local currency assets. Desperate to avert systemic failures, several governments had resorted to nationalizing many of their larger banks. Now, just a year or so later, they were looking to foreign investors for help in recapitalizing them. Just as the fences were going up to protect their currency markets, the barriers to inward direct investment were coming down. By early 1999, long-standing constraints on equity participation and management control had been suspended. Whole retail networks were available for the bold investor – but they were not on offer exclusively to Standard Chartered. As was pointed out by the head of the Asia Region's Treasury division, Mike Rees, seizing the hour had a clear defensive rationale: 'Failure to respond positively to these opportunities would lead to other banks aggressively leapfrogging Standard Chartered's position in key territories.'[2] For two months, Talwar kept several separate teams toiling over the figures to produce a sensible shopping list, all of them assisted by Sands and his colleagues from McKinsey. The teams came together in April 1999 at Pennyhill Park in the UK, one of the plushest conference centres in the Home Counties (also used regularly by the English Rugby Union for its pre-match workouts). The Board first heard from Talwar that the City institutions had fully endorsed the mooted expansion, readily subscribing to new issues of equity and debt worth more than £1 billion. Then the teams handed over their recommendations. Gillam congratulated all concerned for their work, which he thought 'represented a turning point for the company'.[3] This was no exaggeration. From now on, the Group was to lavish huge amounts of capital and management time on building local networks.

The first country to be targeted was Thailand. The Nakornthon Bank was Thailand's second oldest and was ranked twelfth out of sixteen local commercial banks, with sixty-seven branches. Loan provisions in the wake of the Crisis had wiped out its equity, and its publicly quoted shares had been hoovered up by Thailand's Financial Institutions Development Fund (FIDF). This was a vehicle set up by the Thai Central Bank – along lines suggested by Standard Chartered's own management in Bangkok – for rescuing and recapitalizing insolvent financial institutions, with which the country was only too well endowed after the Crisis. By early 1999, the Central Bank was ready to put the Nakornthon Bank's shares up for auction. Standard Chartered was not the only bidder; but its name had been known in Thailand for a very long time, and as the prospective new owner it could plausibly present itself as a powerful catalyst for higher standards across the country's whole retail sector. Officials at the Central Bank endorsed this argument – having successfully appealed to Patrick Gillam not to try pushing too hard a bargain on the detailed terms of the Group's bid[4] – and the acquisition of a 75 per cent stake was completed, after a rather tortuous set of negotiations, in September 1999.*

Assimilating the Nakornthon into the Group was a delicate task. Within a few months, the network had been cut back to fewer than thirty branches, retaining about a third of the original employees. But the integration team installed to oversee the transition was comprised largely of ten expatriates who set about it with kid gloves. Branches were 'merged' rather than closed, and the network's existing branch managers were all

---

* The conditions governing the £205 million purchase included protection for Standard Chartered against a small mountain of accrued losses, and this had to be approved by the Thai Cabinet. More than 65 per cent, by value, of a loan book totalling around $1 billion was no longer earning interest. ('Proposal to acquire majority stake in Nakornthon Bank PCL' by David Moir and Fred Enlow, Presentation to the Board, 15 April 1999, SCB Box 2607.) It was a financial mess that would take several years to resolve: after receiving several hundred million dollars from the FIDF to make good its loan losses, the Group only finally tied up matters by purchasing the remaining 25 per cent of the equity in 2005.

interviewed by Standard Chartered's Thai staff.[5] The implications of the takeover for the bank's employees were understandably a matter of concern to members of the dispossessed Wanglee family, hitherto the largest shareholders. Their anxieties were handled by David Moir, always one of the more avuncular senior figures at Standard Chartered, who took the time to fly round the country with them explaining how the integration would proceed. ('They wanted the bank to stay much as it was. That wasn't possible, but we had to make them feel better about it and let them see we weren't about to fire all the staff.'[6]) The outcome was a diversified banking business, enjoying close links with many of Thailand's largest companies, as it does to this day. Hitherto restricted to relatively modest trade-financing and Treasury operations, the Group was also able to develop at least a modest retail network and a deposit base with which to expand its corporate-lending activities.

Events unfolded less happily in Indonesia. At first glance, Bank Bali looked an ideal target for the Group. One of nine private banks nationalized by the Indonesian Bank Reconstruction Agency, it had 115 retail branches with 1.2 million customers and total assets equivalent to more than £700 million, chiefly comprised of loans to domestic banks and corporations.[7] And to the authorities in Jakarta, Standard Chartered must have appeared an equally ideal purchaser (notwithstanding a clash in the courts between the bank and a politically powerful local customer in 1996–7[8]). With a presence in the country that stretched back 135 years, the bank still had only five branches and seemed eager to run a broad network. Best of all, it was ready by early 1999 to pay as much as £160 million for the struggling Bank Bali, despite some deeply murky accounts and the growing threat of disorder on the streets of Indonesia. President Suharto, the country's ruler since 1967, had been overthrown in May 1998. The ensuing political uncertainties had been gravely exacerbated by the independence movement in East Timor, which was prompting increasingly violent opposition. Anxious to avert any further deterioration in Bank Bali's condition, buyer and seller came to an arrangement whereby Standard Chartered assumed management control before any shares had formally changed hands. If this suggested an unusual degree of mutual trust, both sides came quickly to regret it. Over the summer, and partly as a direct consequence of the Group's own due diligence work, a torrid scandal broke over the bank and the government officials responsible for its rescue. Soon labelled 'Bali-gate', it had serious political ramifications and would lead eventually to criminal prosecutions of senior figures, including the Governor of the Indonesian Central Bank. All this plainly amounted to a tricky environment for the Standard Chartered men sent into Bank Bali – most of whom, as was the case in Bangkok, were British expatriates. Sadly, they had little else in common with Moir's Thai team. With an insensitive handling of the local Indonesian staff and a conspicuous display of their own expatriate privileges, the newly installed management added immeasurably to their own problems. The result by November 1999 was a series of ugly confrontations, widely reported in the British press:

> Last week, after one person was fired and forty-seven suspended for obstructing the bank's operations, the Standard Chartered employees were forced to flee after being refused access to their offices. They were bombarded with plastic drinks bottles and other missiles . . . The [Indonesian] employees, who have demonstrated regularly against the government and Standard Chartered, claim that arrogant British bankers have been dictatorial, making their lives a nightmare . . . Newspapers and magazines have taken great delight in vilifying the Standard Chartered employees, publishing details of their addresses in expensive neighbourhoods, their favourite restaurants and what cars they drive, complete with their number plates.[9]

It took the Group fully eighteen months to extricate itself from this unedifying affair – the only consolation being that London had mercifully withdrawn its purchase offer in time to avoid any significant capital loss.* If anyone doubted that Empire-staffing should now be consigned to the Group's history, here was an episode that confirmed as much in dramatic fashion.

Rana Talwar himself needed no persuading that Empire-staffing was, if not already utterly defunct, at least shortly to be so. Indeed, he was inclined from time to time to draw this to the attention of the remaining British managers in Hong Kong and elsewhere, sometimes in front of their Chinese and Indian colleagues to the great discomfort of all present. A 1997 survey of the workforce had had to admit that 'we currently have a heavy "Caucasian" weighting'.[10] Talwar felt this survival of the Group's Britishness as an acute anomaly. It chided him to find senior management positions occupied by middle-aged Englishmen from the Home Counties, often with no university education and no Asian languages – while all around were scores of highly ambitious and multilingual Asian executives,

---

* Perhaps not quite the only consolation. The Indonesian authorities in 2002 merged Bank Bali with four other banks under reconstruction, to form Bank Permata – and in 2004 Standard Chartered partnered with the Jardine Matheson Group of Hong Kong in acquiring equal shares of a majority stake in the new bank. It was to prove a lucrative investment, once Indonesia had recovered some political stability and lifted its economy to unprecedented rates of growth.

bristling with degrees from the best business schools in the world, whose peers in other international banks (not least Citibank) were climbing quickly up the ladder. Where opportunities arose to appoint Asian colleagues to key positions – including a first Chinese Chief Executive in Hong Kong (Peter Wong), an Indian Chief Executive for India (Jaspal Bindra) and a Singaporean Chief Executive for Singapore (Euleen Goh) – he was at pains to make sure of timely arrangements. He and Gillam were at one on this, at least in principle, and by 1999 another Indian had also joined the Board as an Executive Director. Kai Nargolwala was primarily responsible both for the Group's services to corporations and financial institutions, and for its Treasury operations – a broad swathe of activities soon to be bundled together as 'Wholesale Banking', more usually described as 'investment banking' and encompassing more or less everything not included in the Group's 'Consumer Banking' division.

Against this background, with the number of Indian executives rising steadily at all levels of the bank, there was another anomaly that was starting to look conspicuous. The Group's presence in India, historically the heart of its Eastern operations, had shrivelled into insignificance since the Scam. Ironically, Gillam had probably visited the country more times than any other destination during his chairmanship – and had reportedly developed a good rapport with India's reforming Finance Minister, Manmohan Singh – but this had so far had less to do with future business plans than with ensuring no repeat of the 1992 calamity.

Then, with no fanfare at all, India popped up in the Chairman's Statement for 1999 as one of the countries that best exemplified the Emerging Markets to be targeted in the Group's newly expansionist phase. Signing the 1999 Report off in February 2000, Gillam could not yet disclose it, but there was a good reason for supposing that a fresh start for India was in the offing. Just a few months earlier, Rana Talwar had been contacted by the Chief Executive of ANZ Grindlays. This was John McFarlane, who had left Standard Chartered in April 1997 after his stint as Regional Manager in Hong Kong and a brief period back in London. He was now based in Sydney, implementing a broad strategic audit of ANZ that had concluded it should focus on its businesses in Australasia. This had put a question mark over its Grindlays subsidiary (which it had only acquired in 1984) and McFarlane had invited his old colleagues at Standard Chartered to talk about forging a joint venture in India. They had quickly persuaded him to focus instead on an outright sale. A famous name in banking since the nineteenth century – originally for its services as banker to the British Empire's Indian Army – Grindlays had been scaled down a little with the sale of its East African operations to StanBIC in 1993, but remained a real force in India and the Gulf states. Indeed, Grindlays was the only international bank regarded as their peer by Citibank and Bank of America, the two US giants whose Indian operations by now dominated the sub-continent's foreign banking sector (and were wholly managed, unlike Standard Chartered's, by Indian executives). By contrast, the business salvaged by Barry Northrop and his legal teams from the wreckage of the Scam cut a rather sorry picture. Reduced to eighteen branches, the Group's network in India made minimal profits from a mix of consumer and wholesale banking – only given a flattering gloss by the returns on a tiny but highly lucrative credit-card business. Dilapidated premises were hopelessly over-staffed, in line with social customs unique to the sub-continent and seemingly as entrenched at Standard Chartered as in any local Indian bank. (Its offices had long been equipped with air-conditioning, so the punkahs (fans) no longer whirled through the day; but every branch still retained its punkah wallahs, occupying inherited family positions and now squatting silently in the corridors.) So the chance to acquire Grindlays with its fifty well-managed branches in India – plus almost as many again elsewhere in the region[11] – was an offer that, to Talwar and Nargolwala, could scarcely be refused.

Like any good Scottish banker, McFarlane set all sentiment aside in fixing the sale price. He wanted $1.34 billion, including $734 million for the operations in India, erstwhile source of so much grief for Standard Chartered and almost its nemesis. This was all too much for some of the Group's senior executives, including the Finance and Risk Directors. Their objections alone were enough to ensure stiff resistance to the deal. With fulsome support from his Chairman, Talwar nonetheless pressed on hard with the detailed work of due diligence. Some lengthy wrangling ensued within Standard Chartered's own ranks through March 2000, and at one point in April Talwar was even obliged to pull back from his negotiations with McFarlane. This left ANZ free to entertain other bids. Consternation followed, when McFarlane announced that Citibank had offered him a significantly higher price.* But Talwar and McFarlane, both ex-Citibank officers, knew well enough how long and stoney that alternative road might prove. McFarlane was keen to grasp the bird in hand, only asking

---

* News of the Citibank offer triggered an unusually vehement debate over the Grindlays deal at the April Board meeting, which was held at a hotel in Taiwan. Christopher Castleman launched into a passionate presentation in favour of going ahead – which was interrupted by the hotel manager shouting 'Stop! Stop!' Castleman was using a microphone which had been hooked up in some way to the hotel's loudspeaker system, and his forthright advocacy of a Grindlays acquisition had been entertaining guests in all the public areas of the hotel.

for a (relatively) modest top-up to the negotiated price to help carry the
day with his own Board. An extra $50 million was agreed with a hand-
shake between him and Gillam, and the deal was done. As McFarlane
recalled, 'I actually waived hundreds of millions of dollars in favour of
the commitment I'd made to Standard Chartered.'[12]

The deal's impact on the Group was to be extraordinary. Operating
profits in India alone were to rise from $45 million in 2000 to $1.2 billion
ten years later – making it the Group's largest market by profits in 2010 –
and many within Standard Chartered came to see the acquisition as a
seminal moment.[13] Grindlays brought far more than just a physical network of branches, vital as these were. Its managers, well respected in the
industry, made a palpable contribution to the general quality of Standard
Chartered's whole performance in the sub-continent: by March 2001,
Talwar had assigned Grindlays men to run the Group's branches in Pakistan, Bangladesh and Sri Lanka. Patrick Gillam, after a brief visit to the
country that month, reported back to the Board that 'there had been a
transformation in the Group's business in India . . . [and its] reputation
had been significantly enhanced'.[14] Grindlays' managers assured the combined Group of a five-star range of corporate banking relationships in its
markets, just in time for Standard Chartered to take full advantage of the
vaulting ambitions of India's leading multinationals over the first decade
of the new century. But none of this was secured without a meticulous,
and occasionally muscular, process of integration.

The banking employees' trade unions made an outright bid to stop the
merger happening, threatening to withdraw the entire workforce across
the country if necessary. Tasked with leading the merger was India's new
Chief Executive, Jaspal Bindra. Deciding that endless and increasingly
acrimonious negotiations were getting nowhere, Bindra pulled out of them
and temporarily closed down both banks in Kolkata (Calcutta) where (as
ever) union opposition was at its fiercest. The strike lasted forty days.
Death threats were received against several members of the staff, and
Bindra himself had to be given a bodyguard. But the unions had no success
at all with efforts to paralyse other big cities in the network – and when
the strike in Kolkata eventually collapsed for lack of funds, it effectively
marked the end of a troubled era for the Group's industrial relations in
Bengal that had begun long before the Grindlays acquisition. But Bindra
still faced one further, quintessentially Indian problem on the labour front.
Once the merger was completed, the restructured bank still had to contend
with well over a thousand clerical workers for whom there were simply
no jobs – yet those affected had a contractual right to lifetime employment
that was a legacy of labour laws passed in the 1950s. A voluntary

retirement scheme (VRS) was devised, which, to no one's great surprise, failed to elicit much response. At this point, Bindra proposed a less orthodox solution. Empty warehouses were rented in the suburbs of Kolkata, Mumbai (Bombay), Chennai (Madras) and Delhi, each of them many miles from the Group's branches in the four cities. The clerical staff who had declined to accept the VRS were then relocated to these warehouses, where they were provided with benches and chairs – but had absolutely nothing to do. One insider on his management team recalled:

> It was something Bindra had to fight for very hard, inside the bank. The Board's response was 'we've never done this before'. But he said, 'There's no other way of doing it. Let me go ahead and tackle it in the Indian way.' So we did. We had hundreds of people in each place who would get one cup of tea at 10.30 a.m., a lunch served at 12.30 p.m. and another cup of tea at 3.30 p.m. Then they could go home. They remained on the payroll but didn't have to do any work for the bank. All Bindra wanted to prove was that we could do without them – and they were making a big mistake by not considering the VRS on its merits. Six months later we re-issued the scheme, and nine hundred of them accepted it. The rest we took back – but the whole episode sent a very good signal. This was not a management that was just going to wait for things to happen.[15]

Here was another dimension of the Group's metamorphosis into a locally based entity, a business more truly Asian than it had ever been in the past. The 150th anniversary of the opening of the Calcutta and Bombay branches in 1858 was to prompt a spate of celebratory events. Even the Government tipped its hat to the Chartered's contribution over several generations, with the issuance of a commemorative stamp by India Post, the state-owned postal service.

The many initiatives championed by Talwar were not restricted to the pursuit of new geographical markets. From the moment of his arrival on the Board in 1997 he had been intent, for example, on fostering the potential of the Consumer Banking unit in its existing markets. In November 2000, the Group spent over US$1.3 billion on the retail banking and credit-card operations of Chase Manhattan Bank in Hong Kong. Acquired for roughly the same price as Grindlays, they gave Standard Chartered top billing in the local credit-card market and ownership of the 'Manhattan' brand with 'a significant upscale component'.[16] It was especially popular, that was to say, among Hong Kong's affluent twenty-somethings, and not the least of its attractions for retail bankers was the scope for 'data-mining capabilities'. The purchase would soon prove to have been very poorly timed, as we shall see, but it was nonetheless further confirmation of the Group's determination to back its potential in Asia unreservedly. Helping in effect to fund the investment, meanwhile, was a parallel sale that at the same time signalled the final unwinding of the 1970s incursion into the domestic UK marketplace: Chartered Trust (the old Hodge Group's consumer-financing business) was sold to Lloyds TSB Group in September 2000 for £627 million, generally seen in the City as rather a coup.[17] And there was yet one more strand to a busy year. Talwar had not built Citibank's retail empire in Asia without acquiring a fine appreciation for the critical importance of IT facilities. Every international bank in the modern era required a plethora of hard-wiring behind the scenes, linked to systems that carried few charms for most outsiders but determined the calibre of every significant daily operation. One of Talwar's first acts as CEO in 1998 had been to instigate work on a new back office that would be capable of handling most of the Group's in-house computerized transactions in one place. The outcome was the inauguration in 2000 of a centralized processing centre in India – it went into the former Grindlays building in Chennai ('Grindlays' Gardens') – by which time the volume of data to be processed within the Group had grown so quickly that a second centre, in Kuala Lumpur, had to be unveiled at more or less the same time (and a third, at Tianjin in northern China, would follow seven years later). By now total spending on IT was running at about $400 million a year, and Talwar was encouraging innovative moves on a broad front. He urged on a 'Fit for Growth' project, warning the Board in June 2000 about 'a multi-fragmentation of systems from which the Group needed to escape'.[18]

It was an unfortunate irony that 'Fit for Growth' coincided, over the next several months, with another and even more damaging 'multi-fragmentation' – a breakdown of executive relationships at the top of the Group that did nothing at all for corporate fitness, leaving senior management in a fractious and distracted mood. This strange turn of events sprang in part from a series of well-meant debates over the future direction of Standard Chartered, and in particular over the extent to which the Group's destiny now lay with consumer banking. Talwar's sympathies were plain, and by the summer of 2001 he was quite prepared in a Board Review to talk of scaling down ('repositioning') the Wholesale Bank. It was impractical to abandon it altogether, but the Group's focus would be 'to pursue a paced transfer of capital from the Wholesale Bank to the Consumer Bank as opportunities to mobilise the capital presented themselves'.[19] Many of his colleagues were profoundly opposed to this course, and not just those executives working with corporate clients. A second grave source of tension was the sheer number of initiatives unleashed since the end of 1998. Alongside all the strategic reviews, acquisition studies and capital-raising exercises were fresh starts in technology, HR reporting, management-training procedures and a host of other intended departures from past practice. However individually justifiable, and even urgently required, these measures in toto amounted to more than the Group could manage within a limited period of time: from a governance perspective, by mid-2001 it was fast becoming overheated. And the difficulties were undeniably compounded by some mounting tensions between Board colleagues. There was growing dismay in some quarters over how fast and unmistakeably the Group seemed to be adjusting to the Chief Executive's vision of Standard Chartered as a locally managed Asian bank. And Talwar did not help his cause by pursuing it in a less-than-consistent fashion. He prided himself on speaking bluntly to subordinates. At other times, contrariwise, he could appear disarmingly detached from the day-to-day business of simply being Chief Executive. It was almost as though, after a hugely successful couple of years, he had for the moment lost his personal dynamism. A palpable sense of drift began to dog those charged with sustaining the earlier momentum. Gillam grew increasingly exasperated over all this through the course of 2001 – and it was meanwhile evident to all that the Board included a prospective successor to Talwar, an individual whose relationship with the Chairman was growing conspicuously closer by the month. This was Mervyn Davies, the Board director based in Hong Kong as head of Asia who also had Group-wide responsibility for technology and operations. Davies had built up a formidable personal reputation within Hong Kong itself. A mercurial and quick-witted Welshman, he brought to bear networking skills that stood out even in one of the most intensely networked cities on earth. His emergence as a potential new chief executive crowned a steady rise up the corporate ladder at three banks, starting at Midland Bank in his twenties and taking in ten years at Citibank, where he had made his mark with a prodigious energy and an unusual ability to empathize with colleagues at every level. He had deployed both these traits to good effect since joining Standard Chartered late in 1993. Travelling constantly round the Group's offices in Asia, he was the boss who seemed to know everyone's name and every facet of the bank's operations, from Boardroom to mail room. He had accumulated a thorough knowledge of the region's markets since relocating from London seven years earlier, and in recent years had successfully steered the Asia business through a period of acute uncertainty. He had built up a strong pool of local talent, especially in Hong Kong, and had a sure grasp of what he believed would drive the Group's operational performance in the years to come. And none doubted his ambition, least of all Patrick Gillam. In effect, Davies was The King Over the Water – and many senior executives by the middle of 2001 were covertly pressing Gillam hard for a change at the top before much longer.

How far this destabilizing situation helped to fuel renewed talk of an unwelcome bid is impossible to say. But there was no doubting a renewed perception in the City that Standard Chartered's vulnerability to a takeover was on the rise yet again. If the Asian Crisis had afforded the Group some degree of immunity – and most Western bankers had harboured fears over 1997's impact on the region for at least a couple of years – its effects were now fading fast. Investment bankers sketching the case for a bid had no difficulty portraying the Group as a business enticingly positioned for growth, yet still offering shareholders a diet of Jam Tomorrow. Heavy investment in newly acquired subsidiaries and technology had still to pay off, but many of the inherent restructuring costs had already been booked, putting a big dent in profits. In broad terms – and as reported, now, in dollars following the adoption of dollar-denominated annual accounts starting in 2001 – earnings had moved sideways at best since 1997, and the same applied to the share price. Many in the City suspected one or more of the UK clearers were already engaged in some gentle prodding, to sound out Gillam's response – and their suspicions were well-founded. Over the summer months of 2001, the Chairman of Barclays, Sir Peter Middleton, had indeed approached his counterpart about renewing the talks instigated by Martin Taylor and Malcolm Williamson early in 1998.[20] At least two discussions had followed, though on both occasions Gillam had made clear his views were unchanged. He intended to keep the Group independent. But, as autumn approached, it seemed likely that Middleton might have more to say on the matter. Then something happened in New York that changed everyone's agenda.

2. NINE ELEVEN

The Group's Manhattan head office had survived several brushes with relegation over the years. In the 1960s most of the glamour attaching to the Chartered Bank's US presence was snatched away by the Chartered Bank of London, a subsidiary of the Group being run by David Millar in San Francisco. The replacement of the separate Chartered and Standard premises – at 76 William Street and 52 Wall Street respectively – with one combined building at 160 Water Street in 1973 confirmed New York as the principal US office of the new(ish) Group, and in 1976 it was granted a New York licence to operate as a foreign bank branch. But after the

1978 acquisition of Union Bank, New York's activities were steadily eclipsed by the focus on Los Angeles and John Harrigan's efforts through the 1980s to build an interstate franchise in the West. And even after the 1988 sale of the banks in California and Arizona had restored New York as the main US branch, its primacy was still far from assured. One of the odder office-location decisions in the history of the Group saw the US trade finance business transferred to an office in Atlanta in 1992. Though many banks at the time were quitting Wall Street and the tri-state area in search of less inflated overheads, the historic link between trade finance and shipping still made a strong case for basing trade operations in close proximity to the assorted service businesses clustered round a major ocean port. Atlanta turned out to be too far from the US coast, so the deal with First Interstate Bank in 1994 was welcomed as an opportunity to relocate trade finance a second time, basing it close to the FIB head office in Los Angeles. Less than two years later, a review of the LA office prompted second thoughts about its operational efficiency – and the burden for managers of constant travelling between LA and New York – and trade finance was switched back to the East coast.* Even after 1996, the New York office had to co-exist with a large sister branch in Miami. Acquired as part of the FIB transaction, the latter took charge of the Group's growing presence in Latin America, while New York concerned itself solely with North American clients.

By this point, after modest losses in the early years of the decade, the US operations had at least been restored to profitability. And though still a tiny part of the whole, accounting for less than 3 per cent of total trading profits in 1996, their general importance to the Group was very much greater, on two main counts. First, and most critical, was the capacity of the New York office to handle cash transactions on behalf of customers anywhere in the world. Chief among these was the settlement of dollar payments through the US clearing system each night. Given that the great bulk of world trade was transacted in US dollars – and that the US Federal Reserve required any transfer of dollars between two parties, whatever their nationality and wherever transacted, to be passed through its US

---

* One of a handful of staff watching all this from her desk in New York was Lilly Levinson, who one day would become head of the US trade-finance operation. She had originally joined CBoL in 1979 as a humble teller and by the early 1990s was part of a small team that had stayed behind in New York to service the bank's commodity-trading clients. 'We had one member of the staff who moved from New York to Atlanta, from Atlanta to Los Angeles and then back to New York – only to lose her job in New York! . . . In those days we didn't really know what our strategy was supposed to be. We were all over the place – making good money, but with no focus.' (Interview with author, 30 July 2013.)

books at the close of every business day – this was a humdrum service with miniscule margins but astronomic volumes. It also had a growth rate in prospect to compensate handsomely for its lack of glamour: with the Group beginning to consolidate its status as the premier facilitator of international trade across large swathes of Asia and Africa, the flow of dollar payments through Standard Chartered in New York at a rate amounting to around $50 billion a year was starting to compare with the domestic clearing operations of the largest US money-centre banks. And, second, the Group, via its US-based staff, was offering giant American corporations a level of expertise in correspondent banking and related foreign-trade services that, as noted in the context of Hong Kong's success, was now sufficient to set it ahead of most of its peers, especially in the US. It was no longer pursuing domestic US banking business for its own sake. But it was offering vital assistance to any US multinational that needed help in crossing the continents. For heavyweight clients like General Electric, Exxon, Coca-Cola or Wal-Mart, its reliability and the spread of its geographical coverage made the Group an attractive commercial banking partner.

The same applied for leading corporate names in Latin America, where the volume of trade with Asia was rising briskly by the 1990s. Rather serendipitously, Standard Chartered found itself endowed with a skeletal Latin network well suited to this trend. Representative offices in Panama City and Rio de Janeiro were a legacy of the Union Bank that had somehow been retained despite plans to dispose of them.*The FIB executives who came aboard in 1994 brought with them a network dating back to the post-war world and comprising single offices in Mexico, Argentina, Colombia, Venezuela and Peru. Each office serviced all clients in its national territory. Then, early in 1998 and for reasons that were soon to be lost on everyone, a corporate acquisition was initiated from London that ran totally counter to the strategy inherent in such a network. The Group bought a controlling stake in Banco Extebandes, hitherto a lacklustre bank owned jointly by the governments of three Andean countries. In what was essentially a co-ordinated triple privatization, small minority stakes were retained by three state-owned enterprises while Standard Chartered took over a sprawling network of branches: Extebandes had four in Venezuela, six in Peru and thirteen in Colombia. Overly impressed,

---

* The longstanding Rio de Janeiro representative, Elizabeth Henshaw, was actually flown back to London in 1991 for a leaving party in her honour. She spent the party extolling the merits of having an office in Rio – with such eloquence that she was sent straight back to reopen it. She ran it for another twelve years.

perhaps, by some of the more sanguine Emerging Markets rhetoric in the banking industry, Rana Talwar was determined to see the Group embracing Latin America as 'a key group of emerging markets, representing opportunities for SCB to apply the products and skills found in its core geographies of Asia and Africa'.[21] Extebandes was deemed 'a clean bank of a manageable size', but neither adjective proved to be warranted. The purchase (for $165 million) was a sorry miscalculation, quickly exposed by its disastrous timing. A recession in Peru, the first real economic crisis in Colombia for half a century and a collapse in the market prices for Venezuelan crude oil soon put paid to any hope of turning Extebandes into a sound investment – and its private banking arm had to be sold under the non-compete terms of the earlier sale to the Swiss of the Group's private bank. Rather archly rechristened Banco Standard Chartered, it struggled from the start (and its constituent parts had all been sold off or closed down, with heavy losses, by the end of 2003).

How far the Extebandes misadventure prompted the transfer to New York of Miami's role in the running of the Latin American business is unclear – but by early 1999, anyway, New York was deemed ready to take on managing all of the Group's activities across the Americas. In March that year it was also asked to assimilate 'Tradewind', the trade-finance and dollar-clearing operations of the Union Bank of Switzerland, acquired by the Group for about $220 million and heavily weighted towards Latin America. This was an acquisition far more in keeping with the strategy inherited from FIB. The impact of the Tradewind purchase on New York's daily operations gives a useful idea of its scale around this time. Roughly 450 trading accounts were added. They accounted for around 7,000 payment transactions every day, together worth roughly $10 billion and yielding revenues of about $1.5 million a month. By the start of the new century, Standard Chartered's dollar-clearing operations in New York made it the biggest non-US bank in the business, and the seventh largest clearer of dollar payments in the entire US banking industry.[22]

The UBS deal also added ninety-five people to the Group's staff in New York. They would scarcely have found room in 160 Water Street, though it had five floors. Happily, the rapid growth of the office had been anticipated a few years earlier. In December 1995, management had overseen a move to one of the most prestigious addresses in the financial district – 7 World Trade Center (WTC), the most northerly of the seven huge buildings that comprised the WTC complex, with its central plaza and the two massive towers that had been an iconic part of the Manhattan skyline since the early 1970s. The North Tower, WTC 1, was just three hundred yards away, affording a spectacular view for anyone looking through the south-facing windows of the Group's new offices on the thirteenth, twenty-sixth and twenty-seventh floors of WTC 7, itself a forty-seven-storey building. The WTC 7 offices were handsomely decked out: the bank installed its valuable collection of paintings, accumulated over many years, and shipped in a fine collection of vintage wines, to be stored on the twenty-seventh floor in a secret 'cellar' with a concealed door.

Among WTC 7's many other attractions was its stellar rating on security grounds. Fellow occupants of the building included the New York branches of the FBI, the CIA and the US Secret Service. As if having these three in one place were not enough, WTC 7 also housed the Disaster Recovery Site for the office of the New York City mayor. Perhaps this star-studded cast of residents made it harder for mere corporate managers in the building to take their own emergency arrangements quite as seriously as they might otherwise have done. The Group's WTC 7 operations had a modest back-up facility at the aptly named Evertrust Plaza, across the Hudson River in Jersey City, but this was scarcely accorded much attention for the first year or so after the move into the Trade Center. Then, in April 1997, a newly appointed Chief Executive for New York, Robert (Bob) McDonald, had cause to rue this easy-going approach. The payments system at WTC 7 effectively jammed – an unfortunate episode requiring a virtually complete alphabet of acronyms for any more precise description to do it justice – and some multimillion-dollar transactions began defaulting to the Evertrust Plaza computers for them to make a timely contribution. Unfortunately, they jammed too. Back came the same transactions to WTC 7, and by the middle of the afternoon Bob McDonald was facing a tense situation and a succession of steadily more formal telephone calls from his main contact at the New York Federal Reserve. The crisis was resolved in the end, but not without the Fed's agreement to extend its normal late afternoon deadline by an hour and a half. In effect, as was explained to McDonald through a chilly meeting in the Fed's offices at 33 Liberty Street next day, the entire US dollar-payments system had been held in abeyance to accommodate Standard Chartered's little local difficulty. It could not be allowed to happen again.

A chastened McDonald soon turned to managing a substantial upgrading of the Evertrust Plaza facilities. This proved the usual thankless slog associated with projects of this kind, persuading budget-holders to part with the necessary funding on the one hand, and trained staff to part with their weekends on the other because back-up systems had always to be tested on non-business days. McDonald was fortunate, though, in one respect. Never before had the business world in general been so preoccupied with the threat posed by malfunctioning computer systems. The Millennium loomed, and there were horror stories galore about what might happen to the world's computers when the date of the year first commenced with a 20 instead of a 19. Just days after the embarrassment in New York, as it happens, the Board in London approved the launch of 'Project Y2K'. It featured a budget that ballooned only too predictably (from £35 million in 1997 to more than £180 million by the end[23]), a huge cast of consultants from half a dozen of the world's best technology and accountancy groups, including IBM and KPMG, and a temporary in-house staff running into the hundreds. In the event, the Millennium hour passed without a blip – but not before Y2K had provided an ideal pretext for many office managers around the world to plead the case successfully for a timely modernization of their local computer systems. McDonald ensured that Evertrust Plaza was one of the beneficiaries. By 2001 it was automatically recording all changes to electronic files held in WTC 7, on its own state-of-the-art systems plugged into a separate power grid. It also had a few frills, no doubt also courtesy of Y2K, one of which was a direct private telephone line from the Plaza's operatives to McDonald's own home. This was in Old Greenwich, one of Wall Street's finest suburbs on the shoreline of Connecticut. For his daily commute into Manhattan McDonald had a chauffered car, and on the morning of Tuesday 11 September 2001 it was taking him to a late breakfast meeting at the Council on Foreign Relations, on Park Avenue at 68th Street. Listening as usual to the 1010 WINS all-news station on the car radio, McDonald heard the dramatic news shortly before 9 a.m. that some kind of plane had crashed into the North Tower. He immediately telephoned Rana Talwar, who was at his desk in London staring at a TV screen. McDonald recalled: 'Rana was watching the events and described to me everything that was going on. I said to my driver straight away, "we're not going to get down there, let's get back to my house so I can access New Jersey".'[24]

While McDonald was speeding home to his private link with Jersey City, the 427 staff who had turned up for a normal day at Standard Chartered's WTC 7 offices had been engulfed in the pandemonium that followed the terrorist attack on the World Trade Towers. All would have their own personal stories of how their early morning routines were overtaken by the life-changing events of that day.[25] (Alongside them, by an unhappy chance, were forty-six individuals from other Group offices who were visiting New York for a conference.) In the first moments after the impact of the planes, many stood at the south-facing windows, staring through them in horror and disbelief. By the time that McDonald finally made contact with the Evertrust Plaza, around 9.30 a.m., WTC 7 was being hurriedly evacuated and Standard Chartered's staff were among the thousands of other office workers, many of them exhausted by the long trek down endless stairs, who were milling on to the streets. Some of the staff behaved with conspicuous bravery. Retrieving her two small children from a nursery centre below the North Tower, Helen Ocasio-Walfal realized the distraught young staff in charge of the centre's eighteen children had lost control of the situation. Single-handedly, she gathered all eighteen together and led them to safety, just moments before the collapse of the South Tower. Others, looking up from the sidewalks, were traumatized by what was happening above them. One woman managed to catch a last ferry departing to New Jersey. There she hired a car, drove west and did not stop until she reached Arizona.[26] Assessing the position with those at the Plaza Recovery Site, McDonald had no idea what was happening to most of his colleagues and could only hope they were all unharmed. (It was to take two full days to track everyone down and confirm their safety: no Standard Chartered employees were killed on 9/11.) When the first of the Towers crashed down just before 10 a.m. – the second fell half an hour later – it was clear they had to assume all was irretrievably lost at WTC 7, as indeed it was when that building collapsed at the end of the afternoon. While most were still struggling to grasp the enormity of what was happening that morning, those responsible for Standard Chartered's operations had to try to focus on what it meant for the bank's business. Quite apart from the terrible scale of the disaster in human terms, they knew the destruction of WTC 7 was potentially also a commercial disaster. Standard Chartered was the only dollar-clearing bank that morning to have lost its *entire* US operating platform. Everything was gone.* Other banks with space in the WTC complex had offices and additional facilities elsewhere in the city. Standard Chartered had none – except Evertrust Plaza.

Once Washington had declared – to the surprise of some – that the US banking system would remain open for business, the whole Group had to depend on the Plaza for completion of a full day's turnover. A prolonged shutdown – as befell more than one US competitor – would inflict serious and probably long-lasting damage on the reputation of the bank. Thanks to the work done since 1997, the upgraded facilities were potentially equal

---

* Many papers were blown out of the building during the afternoon. 'One manager was contacted by a resident in a neighbouring borough of Brooklyn [to say] that his work papers were found in the owner's garden'. ('Lessons Learned' by Bob McDonald, Memorandum to the Board, October 2001.) The only Standard Chartered artefact ever recovered from the Ground Zero site was a battered Perspex block containing one of the bank's specimen HK$ notes.

to the job. But they needed to be expertly staffed with the minimum of delay. Here McDonald was fortunate. One of the Disaster Recovery programme managers happened to be on site at the Plaza early that morning for some pre-scheduled tests; and he was very soon joined by one of the bank's key payments experts, who had caught a ferry from Manhattan within minutes of seeing the impact of the first plane during his walk to the office. With telephone guidance from colleagues outside the Wall Street area – mobile phone signals in the district were soon lost – these two were able to begin the task of linking up the Plaza to the rest of the Group around the world. It also helped that the IT Group in WTC 7, after that first impact, had seized a vital ten minutes to close down the normal systems in favour of the Recovery Site, while transferring the current trading book to London and extracting the most precious manuals, codes and computer disks from the safes. But none of this allayed the need for more hands at the Plaza. On this score, again, the planning since 1997 proved its worth. Half a dozen individuals had pre-assigned Disaster Recovery duties. They set off for the Hudson River without having to await instructions. The downtown road, rail and ferry links to New Jersey had all been suspended, but they managed to cross on police and fire boats, and at least one tugboat. Other colleagues, hearing that the 34th Street ferry was still operational, made their way uptown. Having walked three miles and joined a queue of thousands, they were asked to stand aside separately from others waiting to embark. Then a team of New York firemen – following instructions apparently aimed at countering a risk of asbestos contamination from the fallen Towers – turned on their pressured hoses and drenched the startled bankers in cold water. Sodden wet for the rest of the day, they nonetheless made their way to the Plaza by late afternoon.

What the Disaster Recovery team then accomplished was remarkable. The Head of Operations, Matt Millett, had taken the day off – he had chosen 9/11 to move house – and so was able to reach the Plaza by mid-morning. By 2 p.m. he and his few colleagues had established full communications with the Federal Reserve, which was itself now operating out of a Disaster Recovery Site. (By another odd coincidence, the Fed had decided that 9/11 was to be the day to test its own Recovery Site, which was also in New Jersey – and its principal Payments Division staff were in place from the start of the day.) Standard Chartered was in fact the first bank to resume normal payment transactions and was even able, at the Fed's request, to handle payments on behalf of several other banks through the afternoon and evening. Fed officials would later express their warm appreciation for this, and indeed the general response of the New York staff to the crisis.[27] Business hours for the Fed system were extended, eventually shifting the day's deadline all the way to midnight. Millett and his Operations staff kept going to the close. Compared with the Group's average daily payments total of about $60 billion, they completed 19,506 payments, worth just over $55 billion. Only some 500 payments remained outstanding. And this achievement, in broad terms, set the bar for what was accomplished over the following days, weeks and months. Hundreds of employees turned up at the Plaza next day – many had to be sent home by Millett to avoid complete chaos in the cramped conditions – and the Recovery Site worked round the clock for the rest of the week to establish, in effect, a temporary branch. The Plaza premises on 9/11 were never going to be adequate as a substitute for WTC 7. Indeed, this possibility had been explicitly ruled out since 1997 ('taking into account both costs and "probability". This decision was re-confirmed during the Y2K process.'[28]). But no time was wasted in registering Standard Chartered as a New Jersey bank, and a complete delegation of decision-making to McDonald on the spot helped with the timely acquisition of some highly prized additional space in the Plaza. Within ten weeks of 9/11, the New Jersey 'branch' was fully operational, with 340 staff. Another eighty occupied a 'front office' in Manhattan, in space rented from UBS on Sixth Avenue, and a fresh Recovery Site in New Jersey was up and running.

While these provisional arrangements averted serious disruption to the Group's dollar-based business, the task of finding a new home in Manhattan went ahead as 'Project Renaissance'. Its declared goal was a completed relocation within twelve months of 9/11. Finding the right new home in Manhattan was not easy. With millions of square feet of commercial space lost to the financial district, rents throughout the city had soared. And in a sombre reflection of the lasting trauma of the September catastrophe, several staff appealed to the project manager, Christine Sheehy, to make sure that the new offices were leased at or close to ground level. She recalled: 'We took a bus to show the management team all of the potential new buildings that we could select from . . . It was a very emotional tour.'[29] In August 2002 – just a few weeks after the (postponed) retirement of Bob McDonald but within the twelve months assigned for Project Renaissance – the lease was signed on a building at 1 Madison Avenue. The new office would be sited on the third floor, and staff numbers had to be cut by a third to help compensate for the high cost of the space. Thus were scarred memories and stretched finances accommodated in the wake of an event without precedent.

3. ASIAN PHOENIX

The sudden escalation of geopolitical risk in all markets left the financial world after 9/11 riddled with uncertainties, but brought Standard Chartered only the briefest of respites from City speculation over its future. If this nettled Gillam, he seems also to have been intensely irritated by the notion, mooted as part of the Barclays discussions in the summer, that Standard Chartered's current Chairman might like to retire as the result of any transaction. Fairly or not, Gillam undoubtedly construed this as part of a not very subtle campaign by his Chief Executive to speed him on his way. Rana Talwar was certainly involved in talks with his counterpart at Barclays – though, like Gillam, he wanted to find a way of somehow retaining a de facto autonomy in Asia[30] – and he was also party to discussions that the Board had instigated with a headhunter about starting the search for a new Chairman. (Gillam would turn seventy in 2002.) There was plenty of scope here for mischief and misunderstandings, and both duly surfaced over the autumn in a manner that sadly belied the contribution Talwar had earlier made to the Group's modernization. Some long-simmering acrimony at the top finally came to the boil. Gillam had no intention of stepping down. Angered by reports of intrigue in the Boardroom, and disconcerted by a stream of critical comments from senior managers about the unhappy atmosphere prevailing across the Group as a whole, he moved to resolve matters with characteristic decisiveness. On 27 November, a Tuesday, he secured a unanimous vote from his non-Executive Directors to dismiss the Chief Executive, obviating any need to involve the outnumbered Executive Directors (who might have been less than unanimous). Gillam then put through a Thursday call to Mervyn Davies in Hong Kong. By the Sunday, the Group had a new Chief Executive, already back in London, inviting executives to his hotel room for a series of meetings that lasted well into the evening.*

One of those summoned from his morning breakfast was Tim Miller, a former academic and now a slightly professorial, bow-tied Human Resources manager who had joined the bank in 2000 after ten years in the pharmaceutical industry. He had begun to inject modern HR disciplines across the Group in ways scarcely contemplated in the past and had been having considerable success – but he had become increasingly

---

* His speedy departure from Hong Kong entailed abandoning a private dinner party at the Mandarin Hotel scheduled for that Sunday evening – with Peter Sands of McKinsey and their two wives.

dismayed in recent months by the Group's plummeting morale. He recalled Davies's immediate impact:

> When Mervyn landed in London, the bank was on its knees, emotionally and behaviourally. It was not a happy place. Mervyn's genius was such that he came in, took the organization by the scruff of its neck, as it were, and announced: 'Come on, we can all work together and we can build this bank into something truly great.' He had the energy of ten men, and his infectious enthusiasm reinvigorated the entire senior management. He gave them a sense of purpose and direction.[31]

The new atmosphere was already apparent by January 2002, when a hundred or so executives assembled in Singapore for a much enlarged Leadership Team meeting, and Davies afterwards hastened to visit most of the Group's main branches over the next few months with his singular brand of corporate evangelism. He was not the first man, of course, to be brought back to the UK as head of the Group after a celebrated stint in Hong Kong. Whereas Peter Graham emerged as rather a reduced figure once transferred to the bigger stage in 1970, though, Davies seemed entirely at ease with his new role almost from the start. Head Office colleagues were struck by how quickly he adjusted to being based back in London. He did emulate his predecessor in one important respect, however. Just as Graham had quickly forged a close bond with Michael McWilliam, who brought a more analytical mind to the table and complemented Graham's own much more visceral approach, so Davies turned to the man from McKinsey, Peter Sands, as his Chief Financial Officer. This was itself a measure of Davies's own self-confidence, for it was in many ways a bold move. McKinsey had been assisting the bank since the early 1990s. Sands had been a key figure on the team almost from the start and had been leading it since 2000. None doubted his sharp brain – and he had written a string of seminal papers for the Board by this point – but he would probably have been a rank outsider on any headhunter's shortlist for the CFO job. He had never qualified as an accountant, had never spent any sustained period working in Asia and had never had executive responsibility for any business. He had never even worked in a bank before. Yet Davies, as he would later do in picking out many individuals for sudden promotion, backed his instincts. The two of them had worked together for long enough for Davies to feel sure Sands would be the perfect foil to his own working style. He was readily supported in this decision by Patrick Gillam, and the two of them together took pains to talk the rest of the Board round to it. Davies then spent months luring Sands aboard. It would therefore have been deeply embarrassing for everyone if the appointment had misfired. In the event, it was apparent well before the end of the year that Davies had been vindicated. The two men together made a formidable partnership, coping effectively with a crowded 2002 agenda.*

Much of this consisted of housekeeping issues, albeit on a grand scale. Tidying up the capital structure of the Group was an urgent item, for example. With surplus capital sitting in some pockets and a dearth of 'core equity' in others, reshaping the balance sheet kept Sands busy for months. As part of the work, long-standing plans to list the shares in Hong Kong – 'Project Victoria' – were finally realized in October 2002. (To accompany the listing, a modest issue of new stock was arranged and 33,000 prospectuses went out to prospective purchasers. Twenty of Hong Kong's top institutional investors were visited for one-on-one meetings – after which the head of the Group's corporate finance unit noted, tellingly, that 'such investors appeared unaware of the Company's Indian and African businesses'.[32]) Again, the dash for expansion since 1998 had outpaced the growth of the controls that were needed, to keep track of risk and rein it back where necessary. Much more disciplined top-level oversight was required for all credit decisions. Davies set out to find someone who could join the Board as a Director dedicated to risk and compliance issues, and soon found his way to Richard Meddings, a forty-three-year-old executive with a strong background in both areas as well as an impeccable investment-banking pedigree and a liking too for the operational aspects of retail banking. (Meddings had won plaudits as Finance Director at the Woolwich Building Society, and had been at Barclays since the clearer's acquisition of the Woolwich in 2000. He arrived at Standard Chartered in November.) While building his top team and imposing his personal style on the rituals of corporate life across the Group, Davies was quite prepared in his first year to relegate strategy to the back seat. It was Sands' advice that straightening out a long list of operational and financial inefficiencies would be the quickest way to lift earnings, and so it proved: pre-tax profits were pushed up 15 per cent in 2002.

Only one strategic issue of real importance needed a definitive answer for the moment – and Gillam, as usual, provided it. When the Directors in June 2002 turned to a discussion of the Group's merger options, the Minutes recorded that Gillam '[had] distributed a confidential paper to each Board member which summarised alternative courses of action . . .

* Mervyn Davies declined to be interviewed for this book, and his role in the story of the Group has had to be construed entirely on the basis of interviews with his colleagues and the documentary record. The author hopes the resulting account nonetheless does justice to the crucial importance of his contribution as Chief Executive (and later as Chairman) – though in all probability it understates the full measure of his extraordinary impact on the Group.

After discussion, it was agreed that the Company should not initiate any discussions with a third party.'[33] It was Gillam's swan song. He was finally to step down at the AGM in May 2003, concluding a ten-year chairmanship during which his personal impact had been crucial not just to the revived prosperity of the Group but to its very survival. From a list of more than thirty prospective candidates, his chosen successor was to be another former BP man, Bryan Sanderson. Perhaps it was supposed that the no-nonsense toughness of the oil-industry mindset, having served the Group so well in the person of Gillam, would now be granted a fresh purchase in the Boardroom – but Sanderson's engagement with the role of Chairman was never to be remotely comparable with Gillam's.

Whatever the importance of all the tasks accomplished in 2002, profits for the year were still well below those registered in 2000 – and the shares, having traded around £8.50 in January, had spent most of the year wobbling between £6 and £7. This was probably a fair reflection of a complex company that had still to recapture a real sense of its own purpose and identity. So many initiatives and objectives had been sliced and diced over recent years that employees and investors alike were struggling to make sense of a strategic soup. If the Group was to assert a unique future for itself, as Davies had been promising since his arrival – and if it was to keep predators at bay for much longer – by 2003 some plausible articulation of the Group's intentions was urgently needed. Davies and Sands set out to supply it. The result was a simplified and much more emphatic version of the corporate objectives that had been floated intermittently ever since those slightly desperate 'Breakout' sessions chaired by Rodney Galpin in 1989. Standard Chartered was to be identified wholly with its historic franchises in Asia, Africa and the Middle East. Simplistic notions about serving 'emerging markets' – a category that had been unwisely deemed to include the Andes of South America and might yet stretch (why not?) to cover Eastern Europe – would be left behind. The Group would maintain an active presence in the 'network markets' of Europe and the US insofar as it could be of assistance to clients in these regions in their management of business links with Asia, Africa and the Middle East, but domestic banking ties of any kind in Europe and the US would be ruthlessly precluded. Within its chosen continents – to be known as the 'footprint' territories – the Group would seek to be the most innovative and influential of all international banks, with a broad spread of localized retail networks and a comprehensive range of services for corporate clients – goals that it would pursue very publicly under an uncompromising banner, 'Leading The Way'.

These were brave words, but they did also mark the adoption of an idea, pushed hard by Sands, that marked a genuine break with the past and which the former McKinsey consultant, with all his knowledge of the competitive landscape, believed could transform a relatively modest bank into a genuine industry leader. The banking markets of the Western world were in general so mature that, for years past, banks intent on boosting their growth rate had generally found it hard going. This had put a premium on expanding the size of the balance sheet and slowing the growth of costs. Relentless cost-cutting had long been a feature of commercial banking in Europe and the US alike. The simple but far-reaching notion that underpinned 'Leading The Way' was that Standard Chartered should turn its back on this Western paradigm and invest in building up revenues. It would identify itself wholly with economies now growing on average at 5–6 per cent annually, whose markets were very far from mature. Millions of individuals in every large city across Asia were walking into retail banks for the first time. Countless small and medium-sized businesses were looking for new capital. Rising multinational corporations were in need of treasury services of all kinds. To respond to this growth, it would be entirely rational for the Group to accept a need for substantially higher costs, provided that as much as possible of the additional spending went into building extra capacity: new branches, better systems, larger sales forces and so on. And where costs were allowed to rise at broadly the same growth rate as revenues, the arithmetic would do the rest.* Since revenues were significantly higher than costs, applying equal growth rates to both still left profits rising more quickly in absolute terms, boosting the coffers available for investment. Sands and his financial team liked to talk of the result as a boost to 'the metabolic rate of growth'. The faster the Group was expanding, the more capital it would generate for reinvestment in its infrastructure and operational capabilities. Mobilized brilliantly by Davies from 2003, 'Leading the Way' squarely tied the Group's fortunes to the future of its target markets by proposing a heavy and sustained investment in the generation of revenues – starting immediately with a revamp of some thoroughly outdated computer systems.

Smarter technology was going to be critical to this process, for one

---

* Bankers pictured the relationship between the growth rate for revenues (or 'income' in banking parlance) and the growth rate for costs as two lines on a graph, the former above the latter. When the gap between them was widening over time, moving left to right on the graph, the result was known as 'positive jaws'. When the gap was closing, the graph showed 'negative jaws'. The prevailing wisdom in banking broadly identified the two with happiness and misery, to borrow from Mr Micawber. The Group flouted this in asserting the logic, for a bank in its markets, of letting costs grow at the same rate over time as revenues – making 'neutral jaws' the objective.

good reason that was rather peculiar to Standard Chartered. The Group was actually a relatively small bank within the confines of each of its operational territories. In order to exploit the kind of economies of scale essential to banking businesses, it had to rely on an agglomeration of the systems underlying all the separate parts of its network across the world. By 2003, a reasonable start had been made under Rana Talwar at establishing a hub-and-spokes structure that could provide for this: operational hubs had been built at Chennai and Kuala Lumpur. But those in charge of the group's technology were not steeped in the latest mysteries of the high-tech world, and new leadership was urgently needed. Peter Sands took charge of finding it, and in 2004 he recruited Jan Verplancke, a Belgian hired directly from a senior role at Dell Computers. Taking stock of what he found in his first months with the Group, Verplancke was often more than a little surprised. In a later assessment, gently couched, he thought 'Standard Chartered was all about relationships and was not really a bank accustomed to numerical efficiency.'[34] The Belgian set out to change this. Most big banks confronted with this kind of challenge typically embarked on a modernization of the systems most visible to the end-customer. Verplancke had no interest in installing what he dismissed as 'a veneer layer of technology' linked to existing and old-fashioned systems. Instead, he persuaded his new colleagues to fund an uncompromising assault on the back-end systems that would lay the foundations for a unique set of capabilities in due course.

To prepare the way, he built two new hubs in London and Hong Kong for data-collection (these were run by machines, whereas Chennai and Kuala Lumpur were run by people). Then he set about establishing three state-of-the-art capabilities. The first was a core-banking system, 'EBBS', to hold the essential data for all customers serviced by the bank – whether by Consumer Banking on the one hand or by Wholesale Banking on the other. The second was a fail-safe payments system that could process huge volumes every day without interruption. (Early in his career at Standard Chartered, Verplancke inquired about the existing payments system and was told it broke down about three times a day. Asked about the failure rate in 2014, Verplancke thought it an odd question: 'It doesn't break.'[35]) And the third was a global platform, 'Magellan', for the processing of trade documentation – allowing all transactions, wherever in the world they were completed, to be handled by a single system. These three together comprised a comprehensive architecture that was broadly in place by the end of 2006. In a metaphor often used by Verplancke, several parts of the car's engine had been successfully replaced though they had never had to stop the car. Now it motored ahead in some style. Over the five years starting in 2003, both Consumer and Wholesale Banking expanded in Asia as never before. And the share price of the Group would acknowledge as much, rising from below £7 in January 2003 to £19 in December 2007. For so long a troubled straggler in the international banking industry, Standard Chartered was now to emerge as one of its brightest stars.

Viewed in an historical perspective, Consumer Banking's performance was in many ways the more intriguing. This, after all, was a relatively new activity for Standard Chartered, at least in Asia, even though it was accounting at the start of the new century for comfortably more than half of Group profits.[36] Always a matter of geographically defined and essentially self-standing national networks, its retail arm at the end of the twentieth century had only been superficially transformed by Fred Enlow's success in Hong Kong. Retail was still, as for generations past, most truly an African line of business, with modest branch networks in and around the capitals of Botswana, Ghana, Kenya, Zambia and, above all, Zimbabwe. (These countries together sported 127 branches at the end of the 1990s.) In Asia, it remained heavily identified with the network in Hong Kong, which sceptical outsiders could still deride as a glorified savings bank, notwithstanding its extraordinary profits record. The bank in Singapore, similarly well placed with deep roots in a confined island marketplace, had made a decent fist of emulating Hong Kong over the years. But, setting these two aside, of all the other Asian countries, only in Malaysia had the Group really aspired to having any real network at all – and here the geographical spread essentially reflected the scattered locations of the business districts whose export trades it had helped to finance over many decades. (Building a consumer bank on the basic deposit-gathering facilities accumulated in the post-war decades had proved an arduous task: not until the very end of the 1990s, for example, were senior managers in Kuala Lumpur able at last to contemplate a computer system that would allow Malaysia's thirty-five individual branches to share their data on customer accounts.[37]) Rana Talwar had played his part in the Malaysian story – and his wider impact on the Group, as we have seen, had begun to transform Consumer Banking's prospects. But acquiring domestic networks and installing bigger and better computers were merely preconditions for Standard Chartered's emergence as a genuine rival to the home-grown banks in any given country. Sustaining a successful network would also require a self-confident service culture. Few observers in 2000 saw Standard Chartered's business in this light anywhere beyond Hong Kong. In the context of managing its employees, the Group had been heavily preoccupied in recent years with the momentous shift away from Empire-staffing. Most of the expatriates had duly departed. What remained was a collection of modest national banks, within each of which the atmosphere was now unmistakeably Asian.* But if the workforce enjoyed the cachet (as many evidently did) of working for a British entity, the vicissitudes of the Group in the City of London since the 1980s had left their mark. In truth, morale was at a low ebb.

Yet by 2003 the Consumer Banking division was able to respond enthusiastically to the fresh goals flagged by Davies and Sands with Leading The Way. This abrupt change in the mood of the retail organization had been orchestrated primarily by an unusual executive, appointed to the Board in May 2000 and given charge of running the global Consumer Bank from Singapore. A lean, quick-talking American with no time for false modesty, Mike DeNoma had swept through the business like a whirling dervish. His physical energy and stamina had spawned countless corporate stories about his triumphs in marathons and triathlons – for which it was said he had had to learn how to swim – and many colleagues seemed quite ready by 2003 to believe he ran up buildings sideways before breakfast. His career before joining Standard Chartered seemed no less extraordinary. He had run Kentucky Fried Chicken for Pepsico, headed Asian marketing for Citibank, worked on strategy for Li Ka-shing in Hong Kong and spent most of the 1990s building two separate nationwide food businesses from scratch in China (both of them sold eventually to big European companies). DeNoma was certainly a marketing whizz, but was much more besides. He tackled the marketing challenge for Consumer Banking as part of a broader corporate shake-up from the start. He began with a barrage of research to find out what those working in the branches really thought about their bank. ('You want to transform a company? You have to listen to the heartbeat, hear what's natural to the people in it, what's inherent, what's leverageable . . .'[38]) The replies helped him identify a set of values and beliefs – many, in his view, owing much to the personable but tough and resilient workplace attitudes of the African businesses – and these he would forcefully articulate in future as essential features of the whole organization. But the process also alerted him to what he saw as the suffocating conservatism of the organization's

---

* In this respect Standard Chartered differed profoundly from HSBC by the first decade of the twentieth century. New hires with experience of working for HSBC, where Anglo-Saxon expatriates were still predominant, could be surprised at how different the two banks had become – as was Tina Singhsacha, a Thai national of Chinese extraction, educated in Australia. 'When I joined as a manager in 2007, I expected to find a very British culture. I thought it would be much like HSBC, where I had worked earlier in my career. Instead I found myself completely at home in what felt like a genuinely Asian environment.' (Interview with author, 17 February 2014.)

bureaucratic structure. In effect, Standard Chartered's structure was little different from those of its competitors, but in a very minor key. As DeNoma would recall: 'I had rabbits reporting to rabbits, reporting to rabbits – all afraid to innovate. The only way we were going to win was to organize the business differently from the competition.'[39]

Three months after joining the Board, he swept away the old reporting lines in favour of a new structure. It resembled a honeycomb, with each hexagonal cell being a profit centre run by a 'value-centre general manager', empowered to make their own business decisions like an entrepreneur. He set in place 120 of these individuals, and all were indeed going to be as busy as bees if they were to meet some stretching profit targets and keep their jobs. DeNoma launched his new model and corporate values with a series of roadshows across the whole network. They were the precursor to a crowded annual calendar of conferences that over the next several years would regularly bring together hundreds of employees to air best practices and to enjoy the razzmatazz that DeNoma always ensured with his personal presence. One last critical change to the status quo was the introduction in 2001 of a fresh corporate logo, the first since 1973. Enlow had alighted on the blue and green colours that were already a familiar sight on many streets of Hong Kong. What DeNoma and his advisers now produced was a clever design that ran different shades of blue and green together in a 'digitized band'. This would soon become familiar enough to convey the Group's identity instantly, even stripped of any corporate lettering at all (see Plate 37).

It took longer than DeNoma expected for this string of initiatives to produce a leap in profits, for reasons over which he had no control. The timing of the Manhattan-card acquisition, it now turned out, had been unfortunate. Short of business in most other markets after the 1997 Crisis, Hong Kong's banks had all flung themselves with their usual competitive zeal into the credit-card business. Scores of new card names appeared in the market. The public obliged by using them enthusiastically – and by the end of 2001, the value of outstanding (and wholly unsecured) credit-card debts had jumped by 50 per cent in two years.[40] Alas, an essential adjunct to any healthy card market was still missing from the former Colony. It had no credit bureau allowing banks to assess the standing of applicants for new cards. As a result, nine million cards were in circulation, and many wallets contained a generous collection of them. Then the local economy dipped sharply in 2001, and the issuing banks soon found their write-off rates rising alarmingly. A recent change in the small print of Hong Kong's bankruptcy laws fuelled the crisis further: personal insolvency was now an option as never before, and those who

thought Chinese customers might be culturally averse to such a drastic
remedy were left looking sheepish. The number of personal bankruptcy
petitions soared. As the single largest card issuer in the market, Standard
Chartered incurred heavy losses as a direct result: they jumped from
$16 million in 2000 to $100 million in 2001, and almost $200 million in
2002. Charge-offs as a proportion of outstanding receivables peaked in
2002 at around 14 per cent. For a brief and chilling moment in the autumn
of 2001 the Board had to contemplate the possibility that Hong Kong's
Chinese customers would begin reneging on their mortgages as readily as
their credit cards.[41] Given a Hong Kong mortgage book valued at $12.2 bil-
lion in 2001, the consequences would have been devastating for Standard
Chartered. But the moment passed, and the mortgage book held firm. The
card losses alone, though, cut Consumer Banking's 2002 operating profits
by half in Hong Kong and left the division's global result for 2002 lower
than in 2001. The total card losses amounted to about $450 million in the
end. It was not how DeNoma or Mervyn Davies had envisaged starting
the new century.

Once this storm had been weathered, however, it seemed nothing could
hold the Consumer business back. It raced ahead at an astonishing (not
to say frantic) pace, in south-east Asia and the Indian sub-continent as
well as Hong Kong. Organic growth reflected above all the successful
transition to a genuine sales culture, backed up by an enormous investment
in IT through these years. Gone were the days when branches merely
waited upon the arrival of customers, with tellers sitting passively along
lines of counters, application forms at the ready just in case the next in
line should happen to be interested in a mortgage or a credit card. DeNoma's organization churned out literally hundreds of minutely variegated
new financial offerings every year, and it cleverly incentivized every individual in the frontline workforce to beat a path to the customer's door,
sometimes literally so. To support the selling effort, the business environment of every single branch was meticulously assessed so that managers
could be advised on the most appropriate tactics for their team members.
As a presentation to the Board explained early in 2004, 'Consumer Banking has now designed ten different styles of retail format so that each
outlet's size and functionality is appropriate to the individual micromar-
ket's potential.'[42] And the results were scrutinized just as meticulously.
From his base in Singapore, DeNoma had easy access not just to the profits
of each individual branch but to a set of 'performance metrics' showing
how well it was doing relative to its assessed potential. Inevitably, the
result was a heavily product-driven selling culture – but so long as this
did not outrun the necessary back-office support (rather an important

caveat, as things were to turn out), the benefits of scale were potentially enormous.

Therefore the logic of buying banks like Grindlays and the Nakornthon Bank weighed just as heavily after 2003. For penetrating any domestic market effectively would need Standard Chartered to become a familiar sight on hundreds of streets. There were City investors who doubted that the Group could ever accumulate enough branches to achieve a genuine 'local bank' presence in any large Asian country. DeNoma and Davies were keen to prove them wrong, and ready to contemplate another bold move if the right opportunity came along. It was a matter of considerable regret to Davies that one of the most alluring takeover prospects had been lost, by the slimmest of margins, to a rival bidder in 2002: the Indonesian government had sold a majority stake in another 1997-ravaged domestic institution, Bank Central Asia (BCA), and the Board had stopped short of a knock-out bid that might have erased memories of Bank Bali in high style. A stake in BCA acquired for several hundred million dollars in 2002 would have been worth many billions a decade later. Nor was this the only occasion on which the Board baulked over an eye-wateringly bold proposal. Early in 2003, Standard Chartered (like many other international banks) looked hard at the possibility of investing heavily in one or another of China's nascent joint-stock banks. The largest of them, and the fifth largest bank in China, was the Shanghai-based Bank of Communications (popularly known as BoCom), where a stake of perhaps 15 per cent was available. The prospect of such a direct involvement in China's growth quickened the pulse, but so did the size of the downpayment. Kai Nargolwala in May 2003 had to warn the Board that even a 10 per cent stake would cost at least $600 million.[43] The ensuing debate was intense, but the Board eventually backed away from an investment that would in effect have 'bet the farm', as bankers liked to say, but that might have rewarded the Group even more handsomely than a majority stake in BCA. (To the chagrin of many, a 19.9 per cent stake in BoCom fell to HSBC in August 2004 – and proved an historic move for Standard Chartered's traditional rival.[44])

There had been another disappointment at the start of 2004 – this time in South Korea. With supporting analysis from Peter Sands, DeNoma had been eyeing the Korean retail-banking sector ever since the government there had begun liberalizing its rules on consumer credit in 2001.[45] It was seen by 2003 as unquestionably the most attractive retail market in Asia over the next several years.[46] The Group had that year started accordingly to build an equity stake in one of the country's largest commercial banks, KorAm Bank. A large block of KorAm's shares had been picked up after the 1997 Asian currency crisis by US private equity funds that were now keen to disinvest; and by December 2003 the wheels were turning on a due-diligence study in preparation for a formal bid. Then, in February 2004, Citibank had suddenly stepped into the picture offering a much higher price, and the KorAm deal was lost. Within a few months, the Board had further cause to rue this setback when the news broke that HSBC, fresh from its acquisition of BoCom, was in the throes of acquiring Korea First Bank (KFB), a business roughly twice as large as KorAm Bank with more than four hundred branches and a 6 per cent share of the country's retail banking market. Here again a US private equity investor was unloading a large stake acquired as part of a post-1997 recapitalization overseen by the Korean government. It seemed by the autumn of 2004 that Standard Chartered's aspirations had yet again been overtaken by events (not to say, by a competing bid from Hong Kong).

Towards the end of October, though, word reached Head Office via a contact in Hong Kong that HSBC was poring over every aspect of KFB's operations and accounts in a surprisingly laborious fashion. The vendors were said to be growing exasperated enough to contemplate alternative offers. Gareth Bullock, appointed earlier in the year as Head of Group Strategy, knew how much homework had already gone into establishing that the Korean market was attractive in principle. He thought a closer look at KFB might yield some useful insights.[47] Contact was made with Newbridge Capital, the US private equity fund (part of the giant Texas-based TPG Capital) that owned 49 per cent of KFB – the rest of the equity was still held by the government – and that was effectively in charge of the sale. This led, in mid-November, to the despatch of a small team from London to go over KFB's books in Seoul. Their presence in the city was not disclosed to HSBC, nor, in truth, was the notion of buying KFB really taken too seriously by Bullock and the Board. Given the size of its assets and its deposit base, KFB's addition to the Group would in effect mean assimilating another Hong Kong. This looked an unlikely prospect, notwithstanding the keener appetite in London for acquisitions. When Bullock arranged a pre-Christmas tour of the Far East, he included a visit to Seoul on his itinerary only so that he could draw the 'due dili-gence' exercise to a close as graciously as possible. As it happened, his flight from Beijing was delayed by a severe snowstorm and he arrived at his Seoul hotel just before midnight. So it was over drinks in the hotel bar in the early hours that Bullock found himself being entreated by the due-diligence team to forget about recalling them to London. KFB, in their view, offered the Group a remarkable opportunity.

Given their obvious enthusiasm, Bullock agreed to meet next day with KFB's Chief Executive, a Frenchman with whom Bullock was happy to converse in French. (He could fluently swap his native Gloucestershire burr for a colloquial Brive accent.) Further conversations followed later in the day with the bank's Finance Director. That Friday night Bullock flew back to London, ready to convey the gist of what he had heard – that KFB was *propre comme un sou*. 'They insisted it was clean as a whistle. KFB's business had been comprehensively overhauled since 1999 – and we'd be mad not to buy it.'[48] The following Monday morning's meeting of the Management Committee, on 13 December, was the last before Christmas. Bullock broke it to his colleagues that instead of winding down for the festive break, they needed in his view to press ahead urgently with a genuine bid for the huge Korean bank. This recommendation was accepted, and secret talks were begun with Newbridge almost immediately. They lasted ten days, and took no account of holiday arrangements. The final terms had to be approved by Peter Sands, who was staying in a country cottage in a remote part of Wales. The deal was struck on Christmas Eve, committing Standard Chartered to a cash price of $3.3 billion. This would be funded partly through an issue of new shares for £1 billion in the second week of January – and the Group's advisers at investment bank UBS earned their fee by agreeing to underwrite the price of the shares (equivalent to more than 20 per cent of shareholders' funds at December 2004) three weeks in advance of their sale.* Remarkably, the acquisition was kept under wraps until 10 January – undisclosed, to their credit, by some very surprised HSBC executives who had been apprised within hours of the coup.

Its huge significance for the Group was unmistakeable from the start. Most obviously, the move acknowledged the extraordinary growth of the South Korean economy. Roughly on a par with the poorest parts of Asia in the 1960s, the country's growth rate had outpaced that of all its neighbours in the region for three decades. In 2004, its GDP had just passed the trillion-dollar mark and the South Korean economy was now the twelfth largest in the world. But the purchase of KFB had a special importance viewed in the context of Standard Chartered's own growth. The Board's willingness to move so quickly signalled a newfound confidence in dramatic style. And the acquisition itself conveyed the same message,

---

* It was to be a nerve-wracking time for the underwriters. Just two days after all the papers had been signed, South Asia's economies were rocked by the catastrophic 2004 Boxing Day tsunami in the Indian Ocean. Coastal regions were devastated, with a huge loss of life, and it was days before the scale of the financial impact could be even roughly assessed. It proved, in the end, to be much lighter than was at first feared.

for buying KFB amounted to a daunting proposition in operational terms. Its network was a wholly domestic operation, several times bigger than Grindlays in India. Despite having a French boss, and other expatriates in the top team, KFB was a thoroughly Korean bank, conducting most of its daily business in Korean. Its purchase took Standard Chartered well beyond its experience of the country to date. The Group had had its branch in Seoul since 1967, which had been restricted for many years to the handling of foreign exchange and trade credits for a handful of overseas companies and the expatriate community. Between 1985 and the mid-1990s it had enjoyed a brisk corporate finance business, placing dollar-denominated stock in Hong Kong on behalf of booming and capital-hungry Korean business conglomerates (the 'chaebols'), and had built up a modest commercial-lending business with a sizeable Korean staff.[49] But taking over a truly Korean bank – rebranded within months (and a little controversially) as Standard Chartered First Bank – represented a giant leap for the Group. And not just in Korea: the boost to the Group's self-image everywhere was a third dimension of the KFB purchase. As Gareth Bullock recalled, 'it electrified the bank, from top to bottom'.[50] The readiness and ability to snap up such a sizeable Asian bank in one of the region's fastest growing economies seemed to draw a line for good under the old image of Standard Chartered as post-colonial bank with a few prized niche markets. It could fairly be seen now, by its own staff as well as analysts and investors, as an international bank aspiring to compete with the biggest names in its industry.

Armed with this conviction, the Group embarked over the next three years on a remarkable shopping expedition. Month after month, Board meetings were repeatedly preoccupied with the arguments for (and just occasionally against) buying the latest acquisition target. A long list of commercial banks came under scrutiny, operating in countries from Turkey, Egypt and Kazakhstan in the west to China, Macau and Taiwan in the east. The belief in London and Singapore that the network across Asia had to be expanded post haste could almost be compared with the zeal shown by those Victorian and Edwardian gentlemen of Hatton Court who had built the Chartered Bank's original presence in the East, so many generations ago. Rather like their forebears before 1914, Davies and all his senior colleagues were utterly persuaded that Asia's economies offered shareholders a prosperous future. In the days of Empire, expansion plans meant adding single branches in the biggest ports. Now expansion entailed building a portfolio of well-run local banks with significant networks in their respective domestic markets. The modern quest was pursued just as single-mindedly. From time to time, reports were brought to the Board of merger proposals being floated in the Group's direction by other promin-ent names in the banking industry. Within just a couple of months in the summer of 2005, for example, the Chairman, Bryan Sanderson, told col-leagues of approaches he had received from no fewer than three Australian banks on the one hand, and both J. P. Morgan Chase and Bank of America on the other.[51] All were brushed aside.* Meeting every Monday morning as the 'General Management Committee', Davies and his executive col-leagues avoided all distractions and pressed on with their own agenda, fortified by the sight of the share price heading briskly higher. Some deals fell by the wayside, including a prospective acquisition in Saudi Arabia and at least two in Turkey, one of them as large as KFB itself. But several were landed successfully. They included the purchase (with the Group's Astra partners) of most of the remaining shares in Indonesia's Bank Per-mata. The eighth largest bank in Pakistan with sixty-five branches, Union Bank, was added to the network in September 2006, followed within weeks by Hsinchu Bank, the seventh largest in Taiwan with eighty-two branches. A variant on the usual acquisition approach was adopted in China, where a first and still solitary retail branch had been opened in Shanghai in the summer of 2002. Having spent a couple of years mulling the possibility of buying into one of the country's ten joint-stock private banks, the Group in 2005 accepted an invitation to invest $123 million for a 20 per cent stake in a new bank in Tianjin (formerly Tientsin), to which it would second some senior staff. The Bohai Bank, with a national licence to run a retail network, opened its first branch in February 2006.

The list of initiatives taken in these years was a long one – and as DeNoma's division expanded so the range of its activities broadened: resi-dential mortgages by 2008 accounted for less than 60 per cent of its total lending. Having started the century with just a few hundred branches,

---

* J. P. Morgan Chase's interest might have been harder to dismiss had the New York bank succeeded in acquiring the stake in Standard Chartered owned by Khoo Teck Puat. Khoo died in February 2004, leaving his 13.4 per cent stake as part of his estate, subsequently reduced to 11.6 per cent in the wake of the January 2005 share issue, in which the family did not take up their rights. Senior J. P. Morgan executives made repeated trips to Singapore in a bid to purchase the stake, but the family sold it in the end to Temasek, the Singaporean government-owned investment company, for a princely $2.3 billion. The news reached the Group's Directors as they gathered in Seoul for their March 2006 Board meeting. The Chair-man and Mervyn Davies set off days later to meet their new shareholder in Singapore, much relieved to know the stake was now securely held by a strategic investor – albeit not a share-holder much welcomed by the authorities in Hong Kong. (Temasek lifted its stake close to 20 per cent by 2008, and it looked briefly as though it might be intending to go further. But the HK Monetary Authority made known its insistence that this would require the Group to surrender its status as a note-issuer in Hong Kong, and Temasek pressed no further – nor, indeed, did it seek any representation on the Board of the Group.)

Consumer Banking by this point was running more than 1,400 – representing a powerful channel for distributing financial products tailored to Asian markets. Helping the more well-heeled to handle their money was proving an especially lucrative business, and for its wealthiest clients the Group now had a Private Bank once again. Set up in 2007, the new division was boosted in 2008 by the takeover of a US competitor that had been mooted in less happy times, late in 1988, as a suitor for Standard Chartered itself – American Express Bank. Integrating the latter's operations into the Group involved rewiring businesses in almost fifty countries. But by now, this kind of drastic expansion was fast becoming routine. And the combination of mergers and DeNoma's leadership had much more than doubled Consumer Banking's profits, driving them up from $740 million in 2003 to $1.67 billion in 2007.

4. BEYOND PLAIN VANILLA

It was a remarkable record – yet by 2008 it had already been eclipsed by an even more prodigious growth performance only tangentially related to the relentless expansion of the physical network. Wholesale Banking had built up revenues not far short of Consumer Banking's by 2008; and with profit margins consistently approaching 45 per cent – compared with less than 30 per cent in Consumer Banking – it had slowly overhauled its sister division and become once again the real engine of the Group's expansion. Huge effort had gone into this, led in the early years by Kai Nargolwala, appointed to the Board as the responsible Executive Director in May 1999. It was a process that amounted in a sense to the division's Americanization – closing a gap that had opened up between the Group and the big US banks in the international marketplace. The latter's pitch to corporate customers had undergone some striking changes since the 1980s. The Glass–Steagall Act prohibiting commercial banks in the US from competing in the securities industry had been steadily undermined since 1974. By the early 1990s, the Act was effectively moribund (though formal legislation to this effect was not passed until 1999). Having themselves lobbied hard to this end for so many years, the leading US banks had responded to the deregulated environment by opening up critical new lines of business, embracing a heady range of lending and capital-markets products (including securitized assets and 'derivative' products as well as plain debt and share issues) with ever greater sophistication. Standard Chartered's Board had eyed this whole process warily. Not until early 1997 were executives given formal clearance to start marketing currency and interest-rate swaps and the like, linked to Asian currencies. (A paper for the decisive Board meeting in February 1997 laid heavy stress on the role of 'Vanilla Products and Structured Products' as essentially insurance services for the client.[52] Prior to the meeting, the two individuals with principal responsibility for this area – Group Head of Treasury Paul Barker and his Singapore Regional Treasurer Mike Rees, who would have charge of the whole derivatives business – were assigned to talk through the subject matter with the Chairman, his Deputy and each Executive Director separately: by the day of the meeting itself, as the Finance Director assured the Board, each man 'will have had an individual briefing and discussion, typically of over an hour'.[53])

But the Group's approach remained deeply cautious, a stance reinforced by the devastating events of the Asian Crisis. So, when Rana Talwar and Kai Nargolwala arrived at the top of the Group, they found a Wholesale Banking operation looking threadbare and old-fashioned compared to the businesses they had seen flourishing in their previous senior roles at Citibank and Bank of America respectively. As one of their new colleagues recalled (unattributably): 'The bank was bereft of any modern product set. The Treasury division had no capital-markets activities at all and was basically a foreign-exchange house, while the corporate bank had only trade finance and a modest amount of lending.'[54] It was undeniably the case that its foreign-exchange prowess under Rees had carved out a prominent position for the Group in some specialized sectors of Asian finance, and its corporate relationships in Hong Kong had been well nurtured by Mervyn Davies. But the whole Group was far less than the sum of its parts. The Treasury handled its client relationships at arm's length from the work of the corporate bankers, and the latter similarly functioned at one remove from those dealing with banks and other financial institutions. Even the largest clients typically faced not one Standard Chartered but several, and were often exasperated by the confusion between them. With active support from Talwar in London and Davies in Hong Kong, Nargolwala faced down considerable resistance within the organization and scrapped its triplicated approach. He remodelled Wholesale Banking to offer corporate clients a streamlined relationship – and then led a substantial investment in the development of critical services, most notably cash management, in which the Group had been trailing badly behind rivals. Given its global connections for the financing of trade, the Group had one of the best potential platforms in world banking to meet the global cash-management requirements of multinational companies. This was indeed to be one of Standard Chartered's great strengths over the coming decade – and the foundations were laid by Nargolwala. Only then did he feel the division was ready to compete properly in the local debt and equity markets that were blossoming rapidly all across Asia.

They were dominated by the giant all-purpose US banks, and competing in this environment demanded a robust approach. A bank geared successfully to the marketing of everything from deposits to derivatives was not a vessel that could be left merely to glide along when the wind blew in the right direction. It needed to be powered every day with a thousand oars, to the sound of a relentless drum. Though its operating profits overhauled those earned in Consumer Banking by 2002 – for the first time in three years – Wholesale Banking made headway much less quickly than had been hoped. Within months of becoming Chief Executive, Davies moved Nargolwala to a broader role overseeing the entire governance of the Asian operations – a role for which he proved to be ideally suited, remaining in it until 2007 – and assigned a new boss to the division, someone plainly unafraid to thump out the beat rather more remorselessly. Having run the Treasury business (latterly known as 'Global Markets') with conspicuous success since late in 2000, Mike Rees was made head of Wholesale Banking in November 2002. Newly recruited to the Group as his Chief Operating Officer was a quiet South African with a fierce appetite for detail, Richard Goulding (who actually joined the same day as Richard Meddings). Two months later, Rees and Goulding assembled their top Wholesale Banking team for a planning session in the Indian city of Chennai. What happened next offered a revealing glimpse of their Chief Executive's penchant for the unpredictable. The Chennai meeting was organized by India's country CEO, Jaspal Bindra, who recalled:

> Mervyn arrived in Chennai completely unannounced. We had had breakfast at the Savoy in London the week before and I had run him through the agenda, but he'd said nothing about coming. Anyway, he landed early in the morning and I got a message from the hotel management saying 'Do you know your CEO is here?' That was interesting! But he went straight to his room, and we didn't know what to do. So we started off at 8.30 a.m. on our agenda. Then around noon Mervyn appeared at the venue where we were meeting and told us all, basically, that we were running a rubbish business. I don't remember exactly what his deadline was, but more or less verbatim his words were, 'if you guys can't get your act together then I'm really not interested in running a wholesale bank, I can do without it'.[55]

Endlessly recalled later by those present, this blatant piece of corporate theatre by Davies seems to have made a forceful impression. But his message was not intended to be negative. Before disappearing off to his room and a car straight back to the airport, Davies also sketched a vivid picture of Wholesale Banking's potential – insisting it would surprise them all, if they could seize the opportunities before them. There followed a tough several months, not helped by the 2003 Iraq War and its aftermath, but before the end of 2004 the evidence began emerging that Davies had judged their future correctly (and perhaps applied the right stage management in Chennai, too). The business model devised by Nargolwala and now rigorously applied under Mike Rees was to generate a prodigious growth in Wholesale Banking. Between 2003 and 2008, its profits were to rise threefold, from $933 million to $2.98 billion. The architects of the Group's strategic turn to the West in the 1970s had once supposed that an expansion on this scale would be critically reliant on having a large retail deposit base in Europe or the US, perhaps both. In the event, the corporate business under Rees's leadership effectively finessed this requirement by building a hitherto unimaginable network of relationships with company treasurers, winning their trust and attracting sufficient deposits globally to underpin the stability of the Group's expansion in its 'footprint' territories. The success of the strategy was boosted by the acquisition programme of these years. But its key strength was its simple segmentation of targeted markets. Essentially it viewed the world as a pyramid of clients' needs. The base comprised a solid layer of transactional business – trade finance, cash management, straightforward corporate lending and so on. A middle layer consisted of services to clients in the global capital markets, principally managing and underwriting new issues of debt and off-the-shelf derivative products. And topping off the pyramid was a broad category of investment banking advisory business that was certainly rendered a lot more palatable to the non-Executive Directors (and perhaps shareholders as well) by being labelled invariably as 'corporate finance'.

It says much about the reviving reputation of the Group after the Millennium that it was able to establish its investment banking dimension from a standing start – and probably it helped that so many within Asian banking circles had been impressed by Standard Chartered's contribution to a financing episode of particular note, concluded on the last working day before Christmas 2000. The setting was China, an emerging market that was by now of compelling interest to most international bankers. After a protracted crisis with historical echoes of the great China Reorganization Loan negotiations of 1912–13, international creditors had effectively secured a recalibration of their relations with Beijing. It had been an extraordinary saga. After the troubles of the Chinese CITIC Group had culminated in the collapse of the Guangdong International Trust and Investment Corporation (GITIC) late in October 1998, lethal doubts had arisen over the sovereign-credit status of state-owned entities in China. These doubts were brought to a head three months later, with news of the looming insolvency of Guangdong Province's main international trading arm. This was Guangdong Enterprises (GDE), a Hong Kong company with more than three hundred operational subsidiaries – from petrochemicals to pig-farming – and debts totalling almost US$6 billion, 90 per cent of them unsecured. Apparently on the orders of Premier Zhu Rongji, the Guangdong Provincial Government sought to avert a complete debacle for China's credit in the international markets by negotiating a Western-style restructuring of GDE's vast balance sheet. Standard Chartered chaired the steering committees tasked with co-ordinating 170 banks in a two-year resolution of what was China's largest ever insolvency – and certainly one of the most complex financial restructurings ever agreed outside a courtroom.*

Nine months later, the Group set out to establish a full presence in the world of corporate finance. Newly hired in September 2001 to lead the initiative was a forty-three-year-old Indian, V. Shankar, who had worked under Nargolwala at Bank of America in the 1990s. (It was actually the second time he had been recruited. In 1979 Shankar had been the first MBA graduate from the Indian Institute of Management ever hired by the Group, but had moved to Bank of America in 1982.) Setting up his office in Singapore, as part of the rapidly growing organization headed there by Rees, Shankar had no dedicated staff at the outset – but could turn for new recruits to a marketplace still mindful of the GDE success. His new operation was also fortunate a second time in this respect. As he set about a gradual cobbling together of teams in the principal financial centres, he and his colleagues landed a coup on their doorstep that gave the business a precious early momentum. A clamorous takeover battle erupted in Singapore in October 2002, when the state's plans to pull back from one of its larger 'Government-Linked Companies' (GLCs) – a conglomerate with international steel and construction interests, NatSteel – triggered an unprecedented stand-off between three parties intent on capturing control. Standard Chartered's nascent private-equity unit took a 10 per cent stake in one of the bidders, a consortium called 98 Holdings, and acted as its adviser through a well-publicized contest that had all the ingredients needed to showcase its fledgling expertise. The

---

* The courts were involved in other ways, and many of GDE's Directors ended up in prison. Key to the success of the restructuring was the Guangdong Provincial Government's privatization of the state-owned utility company providing Hong Kong with 70 per cent of its water. By injecting this huge new company into GDE, the Chinese were able to provide the banks with a future cash flow in HK dollars and equity in a business with future growth potential. (Jake Williams, interview with author, 20 March 2012.)

consortium finally prevailed in January 2003, and Standard Chartered Corporate Finance was off to a strong start.

Over the next five years, and working always within the context of a hugely confident Wholesale Banking division, it pulled together teams across the Group's franchise territories in a steady and methodical fashion that one insider likened to the assembly of a Lego model. Where appropriate, tiny 'boutique' firms were acquired for their related skills – aircraft leasing, for example, was added via the purchase of a Dublin-based business, Pembroke Group, and an oil and gas consultancy, Harrison Lovegrove, was purchased in Houston, Texas. Year by year, the unit won steadily more clients for its menu of services, which ran from Mergers & Acquisitions advice to project finance and a range of complex funding arrangements ('structured finance') tailored to clients' businesses. Its steady rise to prominence was a notable achievement. When other large commercial banks had tried competing in this corner of the financial world in recent times, the outcome had often been frustrating, not to say a little grisly. Standard Chartered's experience was different, not least because it focused from the start on a limited number of large corporations with which the Group already enjoyed close ties in trade finance and related areas. From a total client list of several thousand companies worldwide, it identified a list of 150 multinationals seen as offering the broadest opportunities. The Corporate Finance unit's approach was then to build upon these selected relationships, seeking the kind of advisory roles typically entrusted to just a few key players on a long-term basis. A Board update on the unit's progress in 2006 stressed the importance of technical expertise: 'the philosophy was to have a star team rather than a team of stars'.[56]

The result was a dramatic boost to Group revenues in many countries, and especially in India. The giant Tata Group, to take just one example, had previously been a source of very modest income, perhaps $1 million a year. Shankar's staff eventually took on an M&A role that involved them in virtually all of Tata's many global mergers and in due course helped earn substantial revenues over many years. This of course was also a reflection of the Indian corporate sector's enormous appeal by this point. Whatever the deficiencies of its infrastructure, India's economy bristled with huge private-sector companies intent on overseas expansion. The potential demand for Standard Chartered's services was rising accordingly (helping Indian firms to expand out of the sub-continent, it might be said, where the old Chartered Bank had helped British firms of the Raj to make sure that aspiring Indian rivals stayed within it). Progress in other countries often followed the same broad pattern, with large companies in modest local markets – clients like the San Miguel Corporation in the

Philippines, for example, or the Al-Futtaim Group of Dubai – building multinational profiles at a brisk pace. Consolidating deeper relationships over a number of years always entailed a willingness to remain supportive through occasional periods of crisis – and there were plenty of crises in Asia through the first decade of the twenty-first century to test the Group's credentials, for advisory work as for ordinary lending business.* But historical roots going back more than a century in many countries helped the Group to present itself plausibly as a local bank with a long tradition of standing by troubled clients. Its success in doing so underpinned its appeal as a corporate adviser. Within a decade of its launch, Corporate Finance would have identifiable stand-alone revenues approaching $2 billion a year.

Nor was the Group neglecting to nourish that most traditional of all its wholesale activities, the provision of correspondent banking services for corporate clients. Indeed, by the early years of the new century the Group was well placed to take advantage of the global reputation it had established for itself over the 1990s for its trade financing prowess. Despite its ancient pedigree in most of the key ports east of Suez, there yet remained a few conspicuous gaps in its geographical coverage of modern Asia and the Middle East – as, for example, Iran. The Group's links with Iran went back to the founding of the Irano-British Bank (IBB) in 1958. This joint venture with local Iranian interests had marked, as noted in Chapter 7, the Chartered Bank's first foray into a large country with no British colonial past. Perhaps on this account, the commercial returns over the next twenty years had been generally disappointing. But a presence in Tehran had helped Standard Chartered to eke out a place for itself on the eurodollar syndicates lending to Iranian credits in the 1970s, a time of breakneck

---

* The SARS-virus crisis that overwhelmed the Far East for several months of 2003 was a case in point. One of the senior corporate bankers in Des Voeux Road, Peter Hodges, had been diligently cultivating relations with Hong Kong's two most august corporations, Swire Group (owner of the Cathay Pacific airline) and Jardine Matheson (majority owner of the Mandarin Oriental hotel chain), neither of whom had given much business to Standard Chartered for years. The SARS epidemic closed down the travel business, emptying Cathay Pacific's planes and the Hong Kong Mandarin Oriental's bedrooms for months on end. Swire was losing US$3 million a day – but Hodges offered them a US$50 million overdraft as a token of continuing support. Help for the Mandarin took a more unusual form. Most of its housekeeping staff were put on part-time wages, leaving hundreds of them critically out of pocket. 'Jardines gave us a list of the staff it knew were not going to leave the hotel, and we in the corporate bank guaranteed personal overdraft facilities for all of them. We knew it would work out in the end, and it did. They all paid back the money.' (Peter Hodges, interview with author, 6 March 2012.) In both instances, relations with Standard Chartered grew appreciably warmer thereafter. Indeed, Jardine's Group Finance Director, Norman Lyle, later became an independent non-Executive Director of the bank in Hong Kong.

industrialization for what was still the biggest and most sophisticated economy in the Middle East. The February 1979 Revolution had brought this era to an abrupt close.* The new Islamic state had expropriated the IBB itself in June 1980 – or what was left of it, after an arson attack during the revolution that had destroyed most of the bank's working files.[57] There had been no further dealings with Iran for more than a decade – but in 1992 the Group had won permission to open a representative office in Tehran. Even then, it had been hard going. A confidential review of operations in the Middle East two years later had made no mention of the land of the ayatollahs.[58] But diligent work by the Tehran office had begun to win a modest trickle of business, and the potential for correspondent banking in the country seemed plain. Iran, after all, was accounting by the late 1990s for roughly 5 per cent of the world's crude oil production. Its crude exports were worth billions of dollars a month – by far the country's biggest source of foreign currency – and these dollars needed clearing through the US Federal Reserve system. Early in 2001 Iran's central bank, Bank Markazi, asked the Group to act as its correspondent bank, handling the clearance of all its dollar payments through the US financial system. This business, like all dollar-denominated trade with Iran, was subject to strict US sanctions against the country that had been imposed by the Clinton Administration in the 1990s. A singular feature of the sanction arrangements was the 'U-turn', a special provision allowing Iranian dollar payments to flow through New York under various terms and conditions. Standard Chartered intended to make use of this exemption. Bank Markazi's mandate was explicitly made conditional, however, on the Group's agreement to conceal the central bank's identity. An internal Group memo noted at the time, 'this account must remain completely secret to the US'.[59] The Group accepted the business on this basis. Arrangements subsequently made by the Group to conceal Bank Markazi's involvement could be seen (and certainly were seen, within the Group) as not breaching the letter of the U-turn exemption rules, but the resulting non-transparency troubled some of the Group's external legal advisers from the start.

---

* Quite how abrupt it had been for Standard Chartered is not entirely clear, but its losses were substantial. Just before the revolution, the Group had had total commitments to Iran valued at $44 million, which had been hastily reduced from a peak of $66 million (Board Agenda, 18 April 1979, SCB Box 555). Probably most of this total had to be written off – starting with an £830,000 sterling loan made directly to the Pahlavi Foundation. Substantial funds appear also to have been channelled into bailing out at least one of the bank's local investors. It was noted in April 1979 that over $10 million had been lent to unspecified parties to fund their purchase of equity in IBB from an existing Iranian shareholder. A full provision was made against the loan. (Minutes of the Board Standing Committee, 3 April 1979, SCB Box 867.)

Then, in 2003, an opportunity arose to win a share of the correspondent banking business offered by Iran's five major commercial banks and their subsidiaries in London. Those in favour of taking on the additional business were ready to accept that the same non-transparent procedures would have to be adopted for the five banks as were being used for Bank Markazi. Once again, the Group's external advisers cautioned Standard Chartered over this approach. One New York attorney warned that less than full disclosure of all details behind U-turn transactions 'could place SCB (New York) seriously in harm's way under the law'.[60] As the Group weighed its options, none could doubt the potential risk. As one of its in-house lawyers wrote at the time, resorting to non-transparency might gravely compound the seriousness of any sanctions breach:

> ...[If] the US authorities do indeed find a breach in the method of processing U-turns, there is no guarantee they will treat it as an isolated or minor incident. Taken with other issues which have come up in the past there is a risk that they may decide that a severe penalty is appropriate.[61]

Standard Chartered nevertheless decided in January 2004 that it would press ahead. Alas, the lawyers would be proved right in the end: when the US authorities much later had cause to pick apart the Group's use of the U-turn exemption, they took great exception to the non-disclosure of the Iranian parties and their transactions. The penalty would indeed be severe.

Taking Consumer and Wholesale Banking together, Standard Chartered's growth spawned so many dazzling statistics (and footnotes to the accounts) that its own Annual Report needed an index from 2005 onwards just to keep abreast of its expanding girth. (The Report had 96 pages in 2001, which had jumped to 168 pages by 2007; the 2013 Report would stretch to 340 pages.) Many aspects of the bare financial data were daunting enough – not least the compound annual growth rate of the Group's costs, which had run at comfortably over 20 per cent since 2003 (as prescribed by those 'neutral jaws'). Pre-tax profits over five years raced up from $1.6 billion to $4.0 billion; total assets went from $120 billion to $329 billion; and Shareholders' Equity roughly trebled, from $7 billion to $21 billion. No less astonishing, though, was the growth in the size of the workforce. In 2003, it had numbered around 30,000 – much the same as ten years earlier, though it had dipped lower in the intervening years. By the end of 2007 it had jumped to 70,000 (with 18,000 employees in India alone, working in more than thirty cities), and the numbers went on climbing rapidly.[62] Size was one dimension of the change; the ethnic mix was another. Some fifty nationalities were represented among the 500 most senior employees by 2006. Having dispensed with Empire-staffing, the

Group had emerged quite suddenly as a conspicuous champion of the very opposite approach, opening the door to an international career that was especially attractive to young graduates all across Asia. The International Graduate Recruitment Programme introduced in 1991 was feted everywhere: for the 327 positions advertised in 2006, the Group received 41,000 applications (19,000 of them from China).[63] All of the larger offices across the Group were now characterized by a remarkable cultural diversity. Exact numbers for the various ethnic groups were no longer recorded – but were certainly very different to those noted in 1997, when 'Asians and Africans' had accounted for only 23 per cent of the total.[64] Some of the consequences were unsettling to senior managers reaching the end of long careers. The proverbial conversations round the water-cooler were no longer invariably in English – though it had always in the past been an unspoken rule that other languages were not to be used within the office, even informally. ('Being very senior, I would take a stand in all the meetings I attended and would insist: "you must speak English",' recalled Shirley Wee of her final years in Singapore. 'Towards the end of my tenure [in 2007] the culture became a little strange to me.'[65]) The retreating protocol here was flagging a fundamental challenge for the Group. If the carefully nurtured bonds of the old expatriate-dominated management had been vital to the Group's survival through long periods of its history, what now would ensure a sufficiently cohesive culture to bind the greatly expanded Group together in the future?

This was always an issue of paramount importance to Davies. His own high-octane leadership style was unashamedly emotional and he thought it axiomatic that all employees would work harder and more effectively where they felt an emotional bond with their workplace. He himself could make a direct contribution to this, by reaching out to the rank and file of every office he visited and using his considerable skills as a showman to help forge a fresh sense of the Group's identity. But an inspiring personal touch from a Chief Executive was never going to be sufficient to shape the mood of an entire workforce in a truly sustainable fashion, and Davies also devoted a lot of time – with constant support from Tim Miller and the HR professionals – to institutionalizing his approach, with initiatives aimed at creating, as he explained to the Board in September 2003, 'a unique working environment'.[66] These fell broadly into two categories. The first comprised initiatives aimed directly at the conduct of the banking business itself – for example, by heightening employees' awareness of customers' requirements (through 'Outserve' projects) or by reducing the barriers between senior management and junior staff ('First Hand Days' put top managers into humble frontline jobs for a day).

The second category of initiatives featured those designed to help employees identify more strongly with the business by giving it a prominent philanthropic profile in which they could take a genuine pride. Davies reviewed the wide range of charities already supported by the Group and redoubled its commitment in many areas, notably for educational programmes to combat the spread of HIV/Aids in the poorest regions of the world. Local initiatives multiplied in these years, from community-support programmes in poor rural areas of Africa to charity-linked 'Standard Chartered Marathons' in several cities from Hong Kong to Mumbai and Nairobi. In preparing for the 150th anniversary of Chartered Bank's founding, due in 2003, Davies invited staff to submit suggestions for a new 'flagship' cause – and the outcome was a powerful idea that was to rally an extraordinary level of support among employees. A campaign, 'Seeing Is Believing', was launched to raise funds for opthalmic clinics, with a mission to eliminate all avoidable blindness (generally reckoned to account for about 80 per cent of all blind people in the world). Advised by a UK-based charity in the field, Sight Savers, that its medical staff could perform a life-changing cataract operation for just $30, Davies proposed a fund-raising target of $840,000 to pay for 28,000 patients. That matched the current size of the workforce. All funds donated by employees or raised by them would be matched by the Group itself. As it turned out, by the end of 2003 employees' donations alone reached the target – so the Group doubled the pot, as promised, and the resulting $1.6 million financed operations for some 56,000 patients. Thereafter, further ambitious targets were successively left behind and it became apparent that many had found the campaign compelling. Offices across the Group were busily raising funds in the hope of seeing them deployed within their own region. By 2006, more countries were involved than the original charity could embrace, and Standard Chartered entered into a partnership with the International Agency for the Prevention of Blindness (IAPB), a body lobbying governments around the world in partnership with the World Health Organization. At the Group's instigation, the IAPB agreed to take on the co-ordination of what was fast becoming a landmark programme, organizing the effective disbursement of the money raised by Standard Chartered – and within just a few years, the target to be met by 2020 had been raised to $100 million.*

---

* The prevention of avoidable blindness was also one of the principal objectives of the Queen Elizabeth Diamond Jubilee Trust, which was established in 2012 to support projects across the Commonwealth that could become legacies of the Queen's reign and which became a member of the IAPB in January 2014. The Trust and Standard Chartered joined forces on

Despite the necessary reliance on IAPB and its affiliated charities to implement much of the field work – providing operations for more than three million eye patients by 2013 – thousands of employees within the Group were taking a direct interest in the progress of the doctors and clinics that Seeing Is Believing was helping to finance. The intrinsic value of the campaign was what mattered most – but no one could doubt the incidental benefits for the Group itself, readily acknowledged in 2013 by the Chief Financial Officer, Richard Meddings, who for several years had chaired the committee assigned to oversee the campaign: he thought it 'one of those invisible cultural cements in the organization . . . a hugely powerful force and absolutely one of the best things about the bank'.[67]

The enduring power of Seeing Is Believing allowed the Group to identify itself with one principal charity over many years. (Its tenth anniversary would be marked in December 2013 with a dedicated carol service in London's St Paul's Cathedral – attended by two thousand guests, whose donations after the service and a VIPs' dinner in the crypt would add another remarkable £500,000 to the campaign coffers before all the candles were snuffed out. See Plate 39.) This consistency on philanthropy sat well with the steady adherence by the Group to a fixed set of strategic goals over the same period. The charity also chimed well with the business, insofar as most of its projects were located in India and Africa. For the Group was now fast strengthening its presence in the original lands of the Chartered and the Standard banks – or at least, in the latter case, the lands of the Standard beyond South Africa.

5. UNDER AFRICAN SKIES

The severance of all ties with Standard Bank and its parent StanBIC in 1987 – merely confirmed by those barren exchanges between London and Johannesburg in the early 1990s – had at first left Standard Chartered's future in Africa looking forlorn. It had branches in fifteen countries across the sub-Saharan continent, but just five of them accounted for almost 90 per cent of the region's pre-tax profits.[68] These were sometimes described as 'The Big Five' (comprising Botswana, Ghana, Kenya, Zambia and Zimbabwe) but their meagre profits scarcely lived up to this billing. The whole African division struggled to deliver trading profits of much more than £30 million. Nigeria scarcely featured at all: the Group still

---

their fundraising efforts, which gave Sir John Major, as Chairman of the Trust, another opportunity he welcomed to renew his links with the Group (see Plate 38).

retained a minority stake in First Bank of Nigeria but earned only very modest dividends for its pains. The macroeconomic background, meanwhile, had long been dispiriting. Real incomes across sub-Saharan Africa had been falling for twenty years. The region's exports had shrunk to hardly more than 1 per cent of all exports around the world, and foreign trade was bedevilled almost everywhere on the continent by volatile exchange rates and cross-border controls. The combined GDP of South Africa and Nigeria seemed likely soon to surpass that of the rest of the region put together. In the wake of its own management upheavals of 1988–91, Standard Chartered had to take stock of all this and decide how best to respond.

To help focus the discussion, Chairman Rodney Galpin led his Board colleagues down to Zimbabwe in May 1991 and convened their monthly meeting at a luxury safari lodge beside the Seruwi River, an hour's drive from Harare. A few weeks before travelling down there, they were sent a paper by Michael McWilliam's 'wise man of Africa', Dr Jonathan Frimpong-Ansah, who had made such a notable impact at the executives' conference in 1985. It set out a review of the post-independence era, sketching out for them the dismal failure of the 'state-centric' socialist models of the 1960s and the years of stagnation and decline that had followed in the 1970s and 1980s. But the former Ghanaian central banker had good news for the Directors. In the past few years, he suggested, government policies in Africa had been turned on their head. The continent by the early 1990s was embracing a reform agenda, driven by market realities. It was accompanied by 'the withering away of the anti-colonial and anti-expatriate attitudes' of the past, and this was opening up a radically different future for Standard Chartered. True, the Group had sorely neglected its African businesses – but even here, Frimpong-Ansah was inclined to spot a silver lining:

> One cannot avoid noting the passiveness in London towards the bank in Africa in the period of Africa's economic stagnation and decline. The benefit to the African operation is that it has developed its own character and resilience and in that sense it remains, perhaps, one of the strongest pillars of the bank's long-term future, just as it was in the founding years of the bank at the turn of the [twentieth] century.[69]

The Directors seem to have found this rugged optimism less than entirely convincing. It was acknowledged at the Pamuzinda Lodge that, as Galpin put it, those responsible for the Group's operations in Africa had been given 'no clear mandate from the Board as to a longer term strategy'.[70] But no steps were taken towards rectifying the situation, nor was there much progress in doing so over the rest of the year. Then, after the news broke in April 1992 of the Bombay Scam, thoughts quickly turned to selling all or part of the Group's African legacy, if any buyers could be found. In October it was agreed 'that initial approaches would be made to establish whether any local South African bank would be interested in acquiring a Minority Interest in Standard Chartered's African operations for cash'.[71] Malcolm Williamson, never much disposed to the idea of investing in Africa, returned to the Board a month later with the news that three of the Republic's largest banks had expressed an interest in this proposition.[72] (StanBIC seems not to have been approached, even indirectly.) The sequel might indeed have seen the beginning of the end for the pan-African network so painstakingly assembled by Cyril Hawker and his colleagues in the 1960s – but for Patrick Gillam. Appointed to the chairmanship later that May, one of his first forceful interventions saw him press the executive to think again about Africa. When in charge of BP's business in South Africa during the apartheid years, Gillam (though certainly no friend of apartheid) had spent huge amounts of time battling those who urged the oil company to quit the Republic. He believed Standard Chartered had made a big mistake disposing of its entire stake in StanBIC – 'if it had been my decision, I'd have stayed'[73] – and he thought scuttling from the sub-Saharan countries would only compound that folly. A lively debate followed over the next few months. The outcome was a compromise, and saw the appointment of a new General Manager for the Africa business – hitherto only part of 'Middle East and Africa' – with a team of about twenty London managers and a brief 'to have a good look and de-risk it and then clean it up, after which we'll decide whether we're going to keep it or sell it'.[74] The man assigned to the task was a forty-five-year-old veteran of various senior jobs in Asia, Chris Keljik.

Over the next five years, travelling constantly from his base in London, Keljik pulled off a remarkable revival of the Group's fortunes all across his vast parish. Probably just in time, his achievements rescued the legacies of the old BWA in West Africa and of the long-established banks in both Central (now to be Southern) Africa and East Africa. He greatly lengthened the odds against any sale – though disposals would remain a vague possibility well into the 2000s – and he laid the basis for a significant resurgence of all the African businesses. Their dire state at the outset was recalled by the former BWA man Bill Moore, who was a key figure on Keljik's staff from the start (and who would sit on most of the local Boards overhauled through the next few years). After thirty years as a manager in Europe and Asia as well as Africa, the Hausa-speaking Moore had no illusions about the scale of the challenge they faced:

Our internal Group auditors had just returned negative reports on 89 per cent of the network. This was our own people telling us the business was moribund. Controls didn't work, fraud was endemic and incompetence reigned supreme. There was wholesale demoralisation amongst the local staff and a widespread 'We're on a quiet run to retirement' attitude amongst the expatriates.[75]

Two broad initiatives halted the decline. The first tackled the fundamental personnel issues, starting with an abrupt curtailment of Empire-staffing. Every territory in Africa had a white British Chief Executive. Thirteen were invited in January 1994 to attend a Leadership Conference at the White House Hotel beside London's Regent's Park, along with more than fifty of their senior colleagues, including African and Indian managers as well as other British expatriates. Keljik invited each of the thirteen country heads to a private meeting late that evening – and eight of them emerged without jobs. The other five were recent appointments, so the evening completed a change of cast across the board. Among the replacements was a Cameroonian, Ebenezer (Ebby) Essoka, who had been working for the Group in his home country since 1986. His assignment, that same night, to run Standard Chartered in the Gambia marked the first appointment by the Group of an African Chief Executive, and signalled a radical new approach to African staffing. Indigenous nationals were to be given steadily more responsibility at all levels, and every opportunity to compete for the top jobs. Promising individuals still early in their careers with the bank were meanwhile to be given a chance to work for Group branches in Asia. This spiked a long-standing myth that Africans could not adjust to non-African posts. (A second myth, that African senior managers could not function properly within their own countries, would be debunked in due course.) Keljik set up extensive new training programmes for African employees, and mentoring arrangements for newly appointed African country managers. However, by 1998 the Group as a whole was still far from taking a modern stance towards its African workforce. Richard Etemesi was a young Kenyan accountant – he had been recruited as a graduate in 1991 and had been one of the first Africans assigned overseas (to work in Singapore and Vietnam) – and by the later 1990s was working his way up the management ladder in East Africa. He recalled: 'Too many people still thought Africa was a dark, inhospitable place. So we were hugely missing out on the talent we had in the Group. We were way behind the big US and UK multinationals, who had been developing their African talent for years.'[76] But at least by then a significant and irreversible start had been made.

The second of Keljik's initiatives involved an occasionally traumatic reconfiguration of the whole African business, drastically reducing the headcount and the branch networks in favour of a much more consolidated and properly commercial enterprise. The Group encountered no serious resistance anywhere from local officials or politicians – in his assessment of this changed mood, Frimpong-Ansah had been absolutely right – and the resulting upheaval swept unhindered across the continent. Loss-making operations in Lesotho, Swaziland, Mozambique and Malawi were closed down or sold, and the Group finally gave up altogether its shrunken stake in First Bank of Nigeria. (The Bank of England had insisted that even a 10-per-cent shareholding exposed the Group to full liability.) But elsewhere the restructuring was aimed at making a fresh start. The bank in Tanzania, nationalized in 1967, was restored to the Group in 1992 and began to rebuild its network. And in Kenya, as ever the driving force behind the economy of the whole of East Africa, the impact was palpable. With sixty branches in its national network, the bank in 1993 was still a sleepy organization little changed since the 1960s. Each branch was open to customers five days a week, from 9 a.m. to 12 noon. Afternoons were reserved for clerical chores (and for golf, on Wednesdays). Customers were charged for withdrawing their money and even for making deposits; but retail loans were seldom available. While each branch had its own computers, nothing had been done to link separate branches together: a customer at one branch could not withdraw money from any other without a laborious exchange of telexes. Within three years of Keljik's first visit to Nairobi, this whole world had been turned upside down. The network was halved to thirty-two branches, and all were open every weekday from 9 a.m. to 3 p.m. Modest rates of interest were paid on customers' deposits, and in 1995 Standard Chartered inaugurated Kenya's first Automatic Telling Machine, which did wonders for its nascent reputation as an innovative bank.* Above all, the Africa team pushed through a 'centralization' project that tied all the branches into one network system and allowed customers equal access to any part of it ('Any branch is your branch', ran the advertisements).

By the time that Patrick Gillam brought the Directors down to Nairobi for their monthly Board meeting in October 1996, Keljik and his colleagues had some impressive papers to present on Africa as a whole, and

---

* Richard Etemesi recalled: 'For three years it was the only ATM in Kenya. We called it Money Link and it seemed like magic to many customers. On Sundays we always had long queues, with families coming after church or whatever to stand beside the ATM and have a photograph taken of themselves withdrawing their money.' (Interview with author, 28 January 2014.)

Kenya in particular. The latter's working profits for 1996, comfortably over half of them derived from retail banking, were headed for £23 million, up from £7 million in 1993 – representing a 53 per cent return on equity.[77] Elsewhere across the Big Five countries, the 'Africanization Programme' was in full swing, with local results that were scarcely less encouraging than in Kenya. Keljik titled his own presentation 'A Hidden Jewel'.[78] By 1998, with his Africa stint coming to a close, he was happy to polish up the same metaphor again for the Board.[79] Over five years, the headcount had been cut from 8,600 to 5,700 and the network had been reduced from 230 to 128 branches. Trading profits had risen from £44 million in 1994 to £87 million in 1997, and a widespread relaxation of exchange controls meant that virtually all African earnings were now fully remittable to the UK (compared with only about two-thirds of them in 1993). The management and the credit quality of the corporate loan portfolio had also been immeasurably improved, and the Group's competitive position in all its core African markets looked strong enough to warrant serious investment in the network – along lines that Keljik himself had already begun to identify in some detail.

What the network now needed was an IT revolution. The Group's individual banks in their eleven separate countries were pushing against the limits of what could be achieved within a solely domestic context. Their operations all needed the leap in scale that could only be achieved by linking the countries together, and so expanding the potential business for Standard Chartered as a key facilitator of pan-Africa trade (Cyril Hawker's Grand Vision, no less). This brave future faced two obvious snags. The computers whirring away in the various countries employed a bewildering mix of software programmes: aligning them as one system would be like trying to assemble a transcontinental railway based on national networks with different gauges. And where any alignment was made possible, the fixed wires to deliver a reliable connection across the continent simply did not exist.

Installed as Keljik's successor to resolve these difficulties was Gareth Bullock, still new to the Group in 1996 and fresh from working for three years as head of corporate banking in Hong Kong. Bullock was no IT specialist – he was yet another ex-Citibank man, though his soft Gloucestershire burr rather belied his US banking background – but he did have a sure grasp of project management. For three years, he managed to fulfilment the two projects that mattered above all else. Software packages were standardized across all the African businesses, and their computers were plugged into shared central systems via a satellite station poised permanently over the sub-Sahara. The outcome was a pair of 'shared service centres', one concentrated on the west of the continent in Accra and the other on the east in Nairobi, that provided Standard Chartered's banks in Africa with a truly pan-continental approach – just ahead, in fact, of the wider Group accomplishing a similar objective with the opening of Grindlays Gardens in Chennai. (Bullock's success would lead directly to his appointment by Mervyn Davies late in 2001 as a first Group Head of Technology & Operations – in which role, he would apply many of the lessons learned in Africa to the wider development of the Group as a whole. He would join the main Board in 2007.)

The prospective mobilization of the separate African banks as one seamless business was now possible in theory, but little immediate progress was made down this track in practice. The country CEOs were still left to run their own operations, while considerable effort went into furthering the enlightened HR policies set in train by Keljik. Bullock in effect adopted a quota system that ensured a steadily greater number of Africans in the top jobs, and made a series of widely noted appointments. (Richard Etemesi, for example, was sent to run the bank in Tanzania.) Bullock was also intent on expanding the Group's coverage to acknowledge the rapidly growing importance of the economies of West Africa. The sudden death in 1998 of Nigeria's incumbent president, General Sani Abacha, heralded the end of more than thirty years of military rule, and was followed by the election of a plausibly democratic government in May 1999 that turned immediately to a radical reform of the Nigerian banking sector. The Board in London accepted Bullock's strong recommendation that the Group hasten to restore its historic presence there. He and Rana Talwar flew to Lagos together to attend the formal opening of the first branch of a new wholly owned subsidiary, taking the name Standard Chartered Nigeria, in September 1999.* Another crucial West African territory targeted by the Group around the same time was the Côte d'Ivoire. Ebby Essoka was despatched to set up a new bank there just before Christmas 1999, but soon found himself facing unexpected difficulties:

Three days after I got the licence, there was a *coup d'état*. But we went ahead and recruited about fifty people anyway. We had soldiers in the

---

* Nigeria's Vice-President Atiku Abubakar was guest of honour at the opening ceremony, and a red carpet was laid for him to walk up the concrete path that stretched forty yards from the car park to the front steps of the bank. A plane bringing the Vice-President back to Lagos from another city was badly delayed, so he was some hours late arriving at the ceremony – which perhaps explained why his chauffeur, to the consternation of all the other guests, drove his car up the full length of the red carpet and stopped only inches short of the lectern set out for the speakers. (Gareth Bullock, interview with author, 27 January 2014.)

parking lot while we were building the first branch. By the time we got the
bank inaugurated in February 2001, we had seen three presidents come and
go.[80]

All this activity augured well, but for the moment made no real difference to the essential nature of the Group's corporate business in Africa.
It remained, as for decades past, a portfolio of separate subsidiaries. Their
individual results from one year to the next remained quite volatile; but,
taken together, they now generated a surprisingly steady profit that
required relatively little capital – and eclipsed the contribution from any
single territory in Asia.

No two countries exemplified the vicissitudes of banking in Africa more
graphically than Nigeria and Zimbabwe. After Bullock had taken his seat
on the Board in 2007, with governance responsibilities for the Western
half of the Group that included Africa, he was able to report to his colleagues that Standard Chartered Nigeria had suffered scarcely a single
default on its corporate lending in eight years.[81] The bank launched in
Lagos in 1999 had doubled its network in 2007 (to twelve branches) and
had grown in the space of just eight years to become the Group's single
largest profit centre in Africa. Meanwhile the fortunes of the Zimbabwe
business had moved calamitously in the opposite direction. At the turn of
the Millennium, as for many years past, Zimbabwe had been the Group's
biggest earner in Africa. The Harare government's decision in 2000 to
instigate its 'Fast Track Resettlement Programme' had then triggered a
steady acceleration of the process by which white farmers were dispossessed of their land. The resulting disruption to Zimbabwe's largely
agrarian economy, and especially its tobacco industry, prompted a mounting sense of crisis. Appointed as the Group's country Chief Executive in
2001 was Washington Matseira, one of the most experienced Africans on
the Group's staff – and himself a Zimbabwean (he was the first African
CEO assigned to run Standard Chartered in his own country). Matseira
visited London in 2002 to brief the Board on events, and was thanked by
the Directors 'on behalf of his team in Zimbabwe for their courage and
spirit in a very difficult environment'.[82]

In fact the state of the business at this point was still showing remarkable resilience. Term loans to the agricultural sector had mostly been
phased out by 2000 in favour of seasonal facilities tied to the crop cycle,
and this helped to limit direct losses from the impact of the resettlements.
Demand for trade financing remained robust. As late as 2004, Zimbabwe
still ranked as the Group's fifth highest revenue-generating territory in the
world. But the collapse that followed was vertiginous. Most of the land

redistributed by the government ended up in the hands of new owners who lacked the farming and commercial skills to sustain the country's vital export crops. Overseas earnings plummeted, foreign direct investment dried up and the local currency spun out of control. A stagnating economy was soon overwhelmed by hyperinflation. By the autumn of 2006, Matseira and his senior managers were doing everything possible to protect the balance sheet – notably by investing Zimbabwean-dollar income in local real estate – but had no way of averting US dollar losses for the Group. When Matseira gave another of his remarkably stoical presentations to the Board, the Minutes recorded that he 'had coped admirably with the Central Bank Governor's requirement to reissue all bank notes and devalue the currency by 60 per cent within twenty-one days, and this was a testament to the robust crisis-management structures in place'.[83] (Chairman Bryan Sanderson 'noted Mr Matseira's calmness and leadership, which was an inspiration'.) For the next two years, the management in Harare could only try to ensure the safety of the staff, while preserving the Group's franchise as far as possible in readiness for the day when Zimbabwe's natural resources might once again fuel a flourishing economy. Updating Directors on the latest policy initiatives in Harare in July 2008 (including 'a further redenomination of its currency by deducting ten zeros'), Gareth Bullock assured them their subsidiary in Zimbabwe was doing everything necessary to comply with US, UK and EU sanctions – 'but would resist all pressures to exit the country at this time'.[84]

By a sad irony, the spiralling decline of its business in Zimbabwe more or less coincided with an awakening at Group level to the true potential of operations across the rest of Africa – and the scope for seeing them as part of a coherent whole rather than as separate constituents of a portfolio. Mervyn Davies acknowledged the need for a fuller integration of the African operations, and in 2002 embraced the logical outcome of the progress made under Keljik and Bullock by instigating a move from the traditional, geographically defined management to the matrix structure of 'segmentation' already in place across Asia. Suddenly senior executives from Singapore as well as London were flying into African capitals wearing a variety of Global-This and Global-That hats. By the same token, African managers, who had previously reported only at a local level, started travelling to the regular conferences in plush overseas hotels that had long been a staple feature of life at Standard Chartered for most of their Asian colleagues. It took more than two years to settle the new structure properly into place, but by 2005 the implications were clear. Richard Etemesi recalled:

It had a profound impact on the way people in the Group felt about Africa. Until then, it was an afterthought in most management discussions. Initiatives were always linked to other regions of the world. You often heard presenters finish off with ' . . . and in Africa as well'. But now the conversation changed. It was an interesting shift. You could hear people beginning their remarks with 'This is what we are going to do in Africa . . .' The messaging was very consistent from Mervyn and it raised the level of Africa's importance in the eyes of the Group.[85]

The obvious corollary of this was that corporate clients engaged in trading between Africa and the outside world, especially Asia, should be the focus of steadily more attention – and the prospects here were indeed eye-watering. Assisted by a worldwide boom in commodity prices, Africa's external trade links took on a new intensity in the years after 2005. The continent's trade with China had already been growing quickly for several years: valued at £55.5 billion by the World Bank in 2006, it was reckoned to have grown almost tenfold in seven years – and it jumped by a third again in 2007.[86] 'Trade corridors' began to feature heavily in the Group's corporate literature. A 'China–Africa Trade Corridor Desk' was set up in London 'to offer financial solutions to small and medium-sized enterprises venturing abroad'. And linked to the rising levels of trade was a surge in the number of direct investments being made in Africa, notably from India as well as China. The Group's Corporate Finance unit moved to position itself better for this business in 2006, acquiring a 25-per-cent stake in a small M&A advisory business with a strong pan-African presence, First Africa Group, with an option to buy the remaining equity in due course (which happened in 2009).

First Africa's offices were in Sandton, one of Johannesburg's affluent northern suburbs. For a company in its line of business, somewhere in this vicinity of Johannesburg was almost the only place to be.* International investors eyeing any part of the continent looked to professional advisers in South Africa; most trading conglomerates similarly turned there to find the marketing, legal and financial support for all their sub-Saharan connections. It was no longer quite the case that the quickest route between any two African cities passed through Johannesburg, but in metaphorical terms it remained almost as true as ever. Yet, denuded of its historical

---

* Since the late 1980s, Sandton itself had emerged as the city's premier business and financial district, largely displacing the central business district in the heart of Johannesburg – though the Standard Bank was still headquartered in the city centre, in a vast fortress on Simmonds Street to which it had moved in 1990. Previous head office addresses on Fox Street and Commissioner Street were just a few blocks away.

partner in the country, Standard Chartered's presence there now amounted to just a representative office (in Sandton, of course). Some of the Group's older hands in London, contemplating this prospect in the 1990s, had thought it scarcely credible that such an outcome would ever be accepted for long – executives like Alan Orsich, the long-standing head of Treasury who, as a young man, had joined the Standard Bank in 1950. Orsich and Chris Keljik talked informally about it on many occasions with Pieter Prinsloo, the former head of Standard Merchant Bank, who took charge in 1991 of building up the South African bank's nascent operations in the City. There was much shared bemoaning of 1987's ill-timed parting of the ways. As Bill Moore (himself a Standard man recruited in 1963) recalled:

> Many had difficulty understanding why we didn't make more effort to go back into South Africa on a proper basis, working together with the Standard. We thought we were still part of the same family. We'd been estranged, as it were, but we were still family nonetheless.[87]

The decision taken by the Standard early in the 1990s to begin building its own African franchise north of the Limpopo added a further twist to this convoluted family saga. Many, perhaps most, of Standard Chartered's branches were popularly referred to within their immediate neighbourhoods as 'The Standard'. A deal was struck over this delicate branding issue, and the Johannesburg bank settled on 'Stanbic' as its trading name outside South Africa (not to be confused – though it often was – with StanBIC, its group holding company). The arrangement generally worked well for the two banks' managers in the field.* The rising international profile of Standard Bank nonetheless left many outsiders – and not a few insiders, too – perplexed by the apparent co-existence of two Standard Banks, with a shared recent history but no surviving ties. Neither side appears to have spent any time on a formal reunion proposal.

Instead, several alternatives were explored in London after 2001. It was agreed within months of Mervyn Davies's appointment that a restored presence for the Group within South Africa would be an integral part of any attempt to establish Standard Chartered as top dog in wholesale

---

* The odd contretemps excepted. Shortly after arriving in Kampala in 1996 as the new Chief Executive of Standard Chartered in Uganda, Ebby Essoka opened his newspaper to find the solitary local branch of Stanbic Bank (Uganda) advertising itself as the Standard Bank. 'I called up their Chief Executive and said "we'll have to take you to court if you run this again". But we had a drink together and laughed about it later. We had a very good relationship.' (Interview with author, 27 January 2014.) Six years later, Stanbic acquired 80 per cent of the state-owned Uganda Commercial Bank, giving it control of by far the largest retail network in that country.

banking across the wider continent.[88] One or more acquisitions would be needed – and would somehow have to be engineered without affronting the Standard, which remained an important source of correspondent banking business. A tiny bank called 20Twenty was bought in August 2003, as a possible platform from which to build a retail network. But 80 per cent of the South African retail market was controlled by Standard Bank and three others.* A serious entry strategy would therefore have to be open to any chance of acquiring one of them – and two such opportunities popped up suddenly in the course of the following year. Old Mutual, the giant South African insurance group, suggested to Davies that it might be prepared to contemplate a sale of its majority stake in Nedbank.[89] Little progress had been made with this by September, but in-house analysis of the potential benefits certainly heightened the appetite in London for a decisive move into South Africa. Then, in September 2004, an even better idea came along. Shareholders with 56 per cent of the ABSA Group confirmed plans to sell their stake. Priced at about $3.75 billion, this would represent a purchase almost three times larger than the Group's Grindlays deal. It came at a slightly awkward moment, just as senior executives in London were steeling themselves to grab the right opportunity for a major acquisition in Asia. But ABSA enjoyed a 30 per cent share of the South African banking market. Buying it would transform Standard Chartered's profile in Africa and was an opening that simply could not be ignored. Alas, it quickly closed. Within a few weeks, ABSA announced that it had entered into exclusive talks with Barclays, and the UK clearer emerged with the prize a few months later.

The focus of the Group's attention switched thereafter to Asia, with the successful negotiation between Christmas 2004 and April 2005 of the purchase of Korea First Bank. (Indeed, the disappointment over losing the ABSA opportunity may well have disposed senior executives to take a bolder line in South Korea. In this respect, the rebuff in South Africa was probably more important than the loss of BoCom to HSBC, noted earlier.)

---

* All three were banks with histories stretching back well over a century. First National Bank was the modern descendant of the Boer Republics' National Bank that had been rescued by Barclays in 1925 as a principal constituent of Barclays DCO. Left to its own devices by Barclays' disinvestment from South Africa in 1986, it had renamed itself and become once again a wholly-owned South African bank – which in 1998 had become part of a much larger publicly quoted conglomerate, The First Rand Group. Nedbank was similarly the descendant of the nineteenth-century Nederlandse Bank, which had passed through various permutations over the decades and had long since fallen under the control of Old Mutual, South Africa's giant insurance group that now owned 52 per cent of the bank. The third was ABSA, originally formed in 1991 as an amalgam of several smaller financial firms including the Volkskas Bank, and owned by an array of institutional shareholders.

The progress of the wider economy in Africa would eventually draw management's attention back to the need for a reappraisal of the Group's position in Johannesburg, as we shall see, but not until around the end of 2007 – by which time Standard Chartered's executives had other reasons to be nervous about any big acquisition, in the face of momentous events shaking the whole world of international finance.

6. STURM UND DRANG

Given the rigours of long-distance aeroplane journeys, it might be supposed that the individuals at the top of Standard Chartered in these years spent half their working lives in a state of chronic jet-lag. Most of them travelled incessantly. (When Iceland's Eyjafjallajökull volcano erupted in April 2010, closing London Heathrow and the rest of Europe to air travellers for several days, 160 of the Group's senior employees found themselves stranded in airports all over the world.[90]) This dedication to face-to-face meetings did a lot for the Group's *esprit de corps* but rather less for executives' own corporeal well-being. A direct flight leaving London at around 7 p.m. would land in Hong Kong at about 3 p.m. (local time) the next day, in time for an early evening meeting or two and perhaps a business dinner. But of the journey's twenty hours, eight marked the jump in time between the UK and Hong Kong. So the traveller retiring to bed at, say, 10 p.m. (i.e. 2 p.m. GMT) might then have to start a busy day at 8 a.m. the next morning (i.e. 12 midnight, GMT) even though he may well have had a sleepless night. Most of those exposed to this kind of mind-warping schedule as a matter of routine seemed capable of adjusting to it in remarkable fashion, as they crossed continents on an almost weekly basis. It was by no means uncommon for UK-based executives spending time in the Asia Pacific region to fly to London and back for a weekend, just to snatch a couple of days with their families. But not all were so adaptable, and for some of the less frequent travellers – notably the non-Executive Directors, attending three or four monthly Board meetings each year in distant cities – the travel demands often posed a harsh test of their stamina.

One of those who found them notoriously difficult, unfortunately, was the man appointed Chairman of the Board in 2003 at the age of sixty-three, Bryan Sanderson. Extended and often inopportune daytime naps contributed directly over the next few years to a growing conviction among his colleagues that Sanderson's chairmanship would, sadly, have to be abbreviated. A Board evaluation to this effect was eventually handed to the Senior Independent Director, Hugh Norton, early in the autumn of 2006.

And Norton had also to contend at this point with a much more surprising Boardroom twist: telling Norton he wanted more time to care for his wife, who was seriously ill, Mervyn Davies resigned. It seems the two developments coincided by pure chance, but Norton sought to take advantage of the timing and asked Davies if he would entertain the possibility of stepping up as Chairman. This would open the way to a speedy and amicable succession. Davies could hand over the reins as CEO to Peter Sands; and Sands could be succeeded as Finance Director by Richard Meddings, while Mike Rees and Mike DeNoma remained in Singapore as the chief executives of Wholesale and Consumer Banking respectively. This would allow the Group to go on being run by those most responsible for its success since 2001, albeit as a reconfigured team. Davies agreed to consider an appointment for one term of three years. All the non-Executive Directors were acutely aware that shuffling top jobs in this way cut across the City's rulebook on such matters, however, so Norton set off to sound out the largest shareholders for their views. This proved to be no empty formality. The Group's largest institutional investors insisted that the proposed changes should be made conditional on the appointment to the Board of a genuinely independent Deputy Chairman. This was agreed at an emergency Board meeting on 20 November 2006. The requisite Deputy Chairman followed nine months later in the shape of John Peace, freshly retired as Chief Executive of a big name in the UK retail industry, GUS plc. Peace also assumed the role of Senior Independent Director, left vacant at the end of 2006 when the seventy-year-old Norton finally retired, after eleven eventful years.

What mattered most for Standard Chartered, when the manoeuvring was over, was that it now had in Peter Sands a Chief Executive who had no intention of being anyone's second fiddle – and whose approach still smacked heavily of his long career as a management consultant. Where colleagues of the two men were always quick to praise Davies's 'EQ' quotient, they were just as ready with complimentary asides about his successor's IQ rating – and this, in crude terms, captured the gist of a profound change at the top as the one gave way to the other. The corporate Evangelist was to be succeeded by the corporate Jesuit. Always thoughtful but reserved and unemotional, Sands was an executive driven above all by the importance of defining and meeting clear strategic objectives. The Group's post-2002 bearings – with the crucial recognition that higher rather than lower costs would be part of a successful expansion in the Asian markets – had been largely fixed at his behest, and annual budgets throughout his tenure as Chief Financial Officer had always placed a heavy emphasis on the broad context for individual profit targets. Even before his appointment his responsibilities had come to include IT, strategy, corporate development and risk as well as finance (explaining, of course, why most insiders assumed that he would be Davies's successor). In this sense, Sands' final elevation to the top merely confirmed an ascendancy that most of his colleagues had already acknowledged.

Although the new CEO and his charismatic predecessor could hardly have been more different in terms of their personalities, the management succession seemed to pose no problem for the Group. And with Richard Meddings at his side as an already experienced bank Finance Director – along with Mike Rees at Wholesale Banking, and Richard Goulding who was appointed now as Chief Risk Officer – Sands led a formidable senior executive team that had been together for years. He was quick to reaffirm its long-term goals, but he was not the kind of Grand Strategist who preferred leaving the details to his underlings. Before joining the Group, Sands had reached the top ranks of McKinsey, where every successful career began with years of total immersion in the painstaking analysis of clients' businesses. His emergence now as Chief Executive did nothing to diminish his appetite for grand strategy on the one hand and operational details on the other. And this was to prove more fortuitous for the Group than anyone on the Board could have appreciated at the end of 2006. In the Annual Report for that year, Mervyn Davies observed as part of his first Chairman's Statement that November's Boardroom upheaval had been 'an evolution of the Group's leadership which provides continuity in strategy at a time of rapid growth'. This may have been how it appeared at the time. In the event, it soon proved to have been just the opposite. It heralded a striking change in the style of the Group's leadership, which would soon help to facilitate a significant change of tack – at a time of crisis for every international bank in the world.

Connoisseurs of British art revere George Stubbs as the greatest of all painters of the horse. One horse in particular attracted huge attention on the eve of the Millennium, after support from the Heritage Lottery Fund had allowed the UK's National Gallery to acquire Stubbs's 1762 portrait of a magnificent Arabian thoroughbred called Whistlejacket. Perhaps this accounted for the name given by Standard Chartered to a sophisticated financial entity – known in the trade as a 'structured investment vehicle' (SIV) – that was launched in 2002. Its considerable importance in 2007 was that it began to come apart at the seams. In broad terms, Whistlejacket Capital Ltd was a cash-management device, much like dozens of other SIVs set up by the banking industry in the early years of the new century. It borrowed short-term cash from big banks and the more liquid sectors of the money markets, and invested it in long-term securitized assets bearing higher interest rates. The Group 'sponsored' it by seconding staff to set up and manage its affairs for a fee, but it was wholly separate in legal terms (it was 'off-balance-sheet') and carried a standalone credit rating. For thirty or so of Standard Chartered's largest banking clients – for whom it had been set up as an ancillary service – the SIV had two main attractions. Trusting its integrity and professionalism, clients could use it as a safe temporary haven for any surplus liquidity on their own balance sheets, in preference to placing the cash with third parties in the money markets. And by taking a stake in its equity – alongside the Group, which kept 20 per cent of the SIV's shares for itself – they could also derive a modest stream of revenues on the side (also a motive for the Group, of course).

So sensibly straightforward did this arrangement appear for the first five years that Whistlejacket's balance sheet ballooned to a value of about $19 billion (roughly in line, by way of comparison, with shareholders' equity in Standard Chartered itself). Then matters became considerably less straightforward. Early in the summer of 2007, it was suddenly apparent that Whistlejacket was having serious difficulty raising funds in the wholesale markets to complement the cash placed with it by shareholders. Its standard practice involved issuing IOUs in the form of 'commercial paper'. By the start of August, there were no takers. In unprecedented fashion, the market had simply died. This was an acute embarrassment for the SIV, since its borrowings were short-term and needed constant replenishing. Whistlejacket's plight required Standard Chartered as its manager to resort to months of salvage work in a desperate bid to avert its insolvency.

The SIV's distress gave Sands and his colleagues serious pause for thought. Named after an Arabian thoroughbred, Whistlejacket had become a humbler but more useful creature. As Richard Meddings recalled: 'it was our canary in the mineshaft'.[92] The poisonous gas, spreading rapidly, was a global illiquidity in the world's financial markets, directly attributable to the accelerating collapse of the US market in sub-prime mortgages. SIVs could no longer raise money because many were known to have invested heavily in sub-prime mortgages, which were now regarded as so toxic that market lenders were in no mood to make fine distinctions between different SIVs' varying levels of exposure to them. (Whistlejacket had no direct exposure to the US sub-prime market, and estimated its indirect exposure at less than 5 per cent of its total assets. But it needed to replace several billion dollars' worth of short-term borrowings in the months ahead – its assets could have been pure gold and would still have provided little comfort.[93]) It all came as quite a shock to

Standard Chartered. As a commercial bank, the Group was largely reliant for its funding on a broad base of customer (and especially corporate) deposits across Asia. It had no great exposure to the commercial-paper market, and might not have noticed for many more months what was happening there. Alerted by the crisis at Whistlejacket, Sands with Meddings and Mike Rees began holding daily calls to check on the state of the Group's balance sheet. Within weeks, they were ready to make some alarming assumptions about future trends in the markets, and began fortifying the balance sheet against them. In light of what was to happen later, their timing was fortunate. Sands recalled: 'we went into intense "crisis mode" from the summer of 2007'.[94] The SIV's predicament was also a critical reminder that sound assets were no guarantee of survival for any financial institution: liquidity counted above all else.

Over several months, the triumvirate in charge of the Group's response to the gathering crisis – with Sands himself heavily involved on an often daily basis – worked at increasing the proportion of the balance sheet set aside in cash or its equivalent. Standard Chartered had always been a highly liquid bank by comparison with most of its international peers and a net provider of funds to the interbank market – thanks in large part to those mountainous deposits held in its Hong Kong branches – but it resolved now, as one Director strongly urged, 'to turn on all the taps'. By attracting deposits as actively as possible and cutting back on loans, the cash ratio was raised to about a quarter of total assets. The Group had some other urgent preoccupations, too. It began reappraising carefully all those to whom it had extended credit, above all in the financial world. Some household names in banking on both sides of the Atlantic were running into difficulties. In September 2007 the UK witnessed the first run on a High Street bank – Northern Rock – for well over a century. On Wall Street, the panic over sub-prime mortgages was in full spate, wiping out some of the more reckless US hedge funds and triggering big losses for several of the industry's hitherto most respected investment banks. Standard Chartered began pulling back its exposure to some of them as quickly as the small print would allow. (One of the biggest, Lehman Brothers, owed Standard Chartered around $900 million at the start of 2008. Within six months, this had been reduced to less than $100 million.) At the same time, though, the Group decided to offer its full support to some of the names most obviously under threat, where they were institutions with which it had enjoyed a long relationship – such as Goldman Sachs, its adviser on a hundred matters since those first sessions with Bob Hamburger in 1985. An effort was made in the early months of 2008 to flag this support appropriately.

Whether the Group would also elect to stand by Whistlejacket was the focus of much attention at the start of 2008. Months of complex restructuring had cut back the size of its balance sheet to about $7 billion. Many of the shareholders, including the Group itself, had bought slices of the asset portfolio for cash, which had then been used by the SIV to retire liabilities that the managers could no longer refund. Unfortunately, the difficulty of recycling its short-term liabilities had by now been greatly compounded by a second problem – the plummeting value of its assets, in a market lit up by fire sales on all sides. This was a lethal complication. If the market value of its portfolio dropped below 50 per cent of the nominal value carried in the books, the articles of incorporation meant Whistlejacket would have to be wound up. Nothing in the rules obliged Standard Chartered to pre-empt this outcome; but the markets, the regulators and (not least) the other shareholders all supposed the Group would do so, rather than risk being castigated for allowing the SIV to collapse. And purchasing its assets, after all, would hardly strain a Group balance sheet that now topped $330 billion. Sands and his team saw the situation differently. Buying a tranche of Whistlejacket assets valued at $3.4 billion in 2007 had landed the Group with a book loss to the income statement of $116 million.[95] Absorbing another $7 billion onto the balance sheet might, in their judgment, risk losses that could raise questions in the money markets about the credit rating of the whole Group. In February 2008, to the astonishment of most third parties, they defied the general expectation of a rescue and allowed Whistlejacket to slide into receivership. ('We told people to read what it was called,' recalled Sands. 'This was an "off-balance-sheet" vehicle. It was not part of the bank, and we were going to let it go.'[96]) The decision deeply irked regulators on both sides of the Atlantic, and crystallized some immediate losses for all of Whistlejacket's shareholders. But Standard Chartered's line was vindicated in the end. The SIV was broken up with no lasting damage to the Group's reputation or credit standing (and where the assets purchased back from the receiver by the shareholders were held to maturity, most were eventually realized with minimal losses).

The contrast with what happened elsewhere in the SIV sector could hardly have been greater. Egged on by the regulators and their own fears of exacerbating a general collapse in asset prices, most other banks took the opposite approach. They took over the SIVs they had sponsored, paying off the shareholders and funding the asset portfolios, in effect, with their customers' deposits. By the middle of 2008, SIVs had virtually disappeared from the financial landscape. Far from eliminating the danger posed by their dysfunctional finances, though, the banks had seriously contaminated their own balance sheets. The consequences, for those who shipped in the largest portfolios, were disastrous. In the UK, HBOS (the bank formed in 2001 from a merger between the Halifax Building Society and Bank of Scotland) took aboard dubious SIV assets of $37 billion; in the US, Citibank's were valued at $58 billion. In the case of these and several other casualties of the crashing markets through the first half of 2008, the unknowable implications for their subsequent creditworthiness helped render them untouchable in the world's money markets.

By the middle of 2008, the banking industry of the Western world was in desperate straits – and Standard Chartered found itself once again being eyed as a prospective merger partner, though now on account of its enviable strengths rather than any perceived frailty. It had a broad international deposit base, which suddenly looked deeply attractive to some of the biggest investment-banking names on Wall Street. Many calls were taken from US bankers suggesting the start of 'a conversation'. And it had robust non-Western operations in both wholesale and consumer banking, which made the Group a highly desirable partner for UK banks close to the end of their tether. Prominent in this latter category by July were HBOS and the Royal Bank of Scotland (another victim of the SIV debacle, by way of its October 2007 acquisition of a giant Dutch bank, ABN Amro). Both of them sounded out Standard Chartered's interest in a merger, to no avail. But these and other approaches were not dismissed lightly. In fact, they prompted yet another series of intense discussions at Board level about the merits of submerging the Group into a larger banking combination. Rather remarkably in light of all that had been achieved since 2003 – but just like Peter Graham, Malcolm Williamson and Rana Talwar before him – Mervyn Davies urged his colleagues to see the potential of such a move in a positive light. As the Minutes recorded for the monthly Board in May 2008 – the first to be held in a glamorous new headquarters building at 1 Basinghall Avenue, to which the Group had just relocated from Aldermanbury Square – Davies suggested they should make a clear distinction now between the kind of incremental purchases pulled off since 2003 and something altogether on a different scale: 'this was a period of opportunity for the Company and it was important to ensure, as a result of pursuing a number of smaller acquisitions, [that] the Company did not negatively impact on its ability to consider and, if appropriate, pursue transactions of a more transformational nature'.[97] For several weeks, the perennial debate flared again, given a fresh sense of urgency now by the extraordinary events in the wider financial world. While the circumstances were without precedent, though, the arguments were entirely in line with more than twenty years of debate over the same basic issue. At the end of July, matters came to a head at a Board meeting fuelled by a lengthy strategy paper from the CEO. Before the Directors were various possibilities, each involving a putative merger (or 'grand alliance') with a leading British or Australian competitor. 'I was very resistant to this notion', recalled Sands, and the Minutes summarized a pivotal discussion:

> Several of the Directors reiterated their view that there was a window of opportunity for the Company to undertake a transformational move before its competitors recovered. Mr Sands highlighted that the Company's current strategy was successful and should only diverge from it for compelling reasons. He noted that for many potential targets [sic], it was easy to see what strategic problem a merger would solve for the other party, but harder to identify what it could do for the Company, given the Company's growth opportunities in the world's most attractive markets.[98]

This assessment was to dictate the Group's future stance. It had no need to submerge its identity into some huge new conglomerate, and had grown into a bank large enough and successful enough to take a highly selective approach to mergers. It was a timely moment for its intentions to be clarified. Sands had an intimation of this even before the usual August break was over. He took his family on a trekking holiday in the remote plains of Mongolia – where his mobile telephone rang one day as he was nearing the end of a day on horseback. A caller from the City asked him whether Standard Chartered might perhaps like to buy Bradford & Bingley, a tiny British bank relatively recently formed from a demutualized building society and now on the brink of collapse.[99] A small bank in Mongolia would probably have had more appeal. Other bizarre opportunities would crowd the months ahead.

12

Riders on the Storm, 2008–12

I. CAPITAL AND CREDIBILITY

The upending of Lehman Brothers on 15 September 2008 triggered such convulsions in the financial world that it seemed for a long while as though no good could possibly come of the crisis for any leading bank, and certainly none based in London. Yet for Standard Chartered the opposite was true. The global financial crisis (which very soon earned itself a capitalization: GFC) opened up endless opportunities, for which the transformation of the Group since the late 1990s seemed to have been a timely preparation. Over the course of the next four years, Standard Chartered revelled in being acclaimed one of the most successful, most envied and most highly rated names in world banking. This was not, perhaps, the universal accolade it might once have been – the banking industry now had few admirers, beyond its own parish, and none of its prominent names could escape some share of the obloquy being heaped on bankers in general for their perceived ethical and professional failings. Nonetheless, as competitors in the US, the UK and most of continental Europe were battered (at best) or blown away completely in the mayhem unleashed by the Lehman crash, Standard Chartered actually enhanced the status it had earned among international investors since 2003 as a prized growth stock. Given the Group's post-1969 history of equivocation over the long-term viability of a business with no domestic marketplace in the West, this was a splendidly ironic vindication of the strategy on which Standard Chartered had finally alighted.

Plainly much of its success after 2008 must be credited to the kind of business it had already become by the fateful autumn of that year. Its direct exposure to US sub-prime mortgages – and all the dodgy derivatives derived from them – was minimal, and it was uncompromisingly rooted in regions of the world that were to prove relatively immune to the contagions emanating from the sub-prime debacle: the economies of south-east

Asia were to go racing ahead through the 2008–12 period, at multiples of
Western growth rates. By the same token, the Group had minimal direct
exposure to the sovereign states of the Eurozone. (When the troubles of
the Eurozone turned into a fully fledged sovereign-debt crisis in 2011,
Standard Chartered would move swiftly and decisively to distance itself
from its European banking peers, most of them awash with Greek, Portuguese and Italian bonds. By the end of 2011, it had reduced its bank
lending in Europe from $38 billion to $5 billion in a matter of months.[1])
Above all, and thanks in part to those runes read during the Whistlejacket
episode, its balance sheet could boast capital and liquidity ratios that set
the Group apart from almost all its rivals in London and New York – and
as ever posed significantly lower levels of business risk, given Standard
Chartered's traditional concentration on the short-term financing of
trade.* (This did not provide complete immunity in the dramatic aftermath of Lehman's collapse: like so many other big banks, as we shall see,
Standard Chartered soon felt obliged to turn to its shareholders for additional equity – but it was not constrained for long.) It was true that other
banks accounted for a thick slice of its wholesale business. Of its forty
most important clients, twenty-two were financial institutions – hence a
widespread reputation for Standard Chartered as the bankers' bank – and
the revenues earned on this category of clients had doubled since 2005.[2]
Against this potential source of trouble, though, the Group seemed well
fortified. Formal credit procedures were backed up with computer systems
on which lavish sums had been expended since 2004.[3] So in a host of ways
the recent past was prologue to much of what the Group would achieve
in the wake of September 2008.

The Crisis itself, nonetheless, made a palpable difference, for it played
to the strengths of Standard Chartered in a remarkable fashion – not least
at the outset of the drama, when those at the head of the Group were
handed an extraordinarily influential role. Their involvement came in the
immediate wake of the post-Lehman meltdown, which left most

---

* Since 1988, with a plethora of incremental revisions along the way, the Basel Committee
on Banking Supervision – as the industry's top international watchdog – had been pressing
for capital adequacy to be assessed in terms of the ratio of shareholders' capital and
reserves – 'total Tier One equity' and, as a sub-set, 'core Tier One equity' – to a bank's
risk-weighted assets. Standard Chartered's total and core Tier One ratios had been reported
as 8.5 and 6.1 per cent respectively in June 2008. These figures were comfortably within the
Group's own target range and well in excess of the minimum levels prescribed as essential
by national and international regulators. (Minutes of the Board meeting, 13 October 2008,
SCB/GCS.) The ratio of deposits to assets had in fact not changed much since the end of the
1990s, even though assets had more than trebled in volume: the Group had marshalled the
surge in its Asian customers' deposits to fuel the expansion of its lending business.

policy-makers transfixed for days by the complexity and overwhelming scale of events. As Ben Bernanke, Chairman of the US Federal Reserve System, would later remark, 'out of maybe . . . thirteen of the most important financial institutions in the United States, twelve were at risk of failure within a period of a week or two'.[4] In the City of London, too, many feared a collapse of the entire banking system. It was a crisis on a par with July 1914. Money markets faltered on a global scale and asset prices went into free fall. Throttled by a dwindling access to overnight cash, many banks faced an immediate and crippling illiquidity. Those in the most obvious difficulty were also struggling to retain customers' deposits, which posed a threat to the medium-term funding of their balance sheets. Most alarming of all, where banks had to acknowledge that a vertiginous drop in asset values had wiped out great chunks of their capital, Board Directors were faced with the brutal prospect of insolvency and an immediate suspension of trading. The rush to avert catastrophe saw bankers, civil servants and politicians on both sides of the Atlantic juggling with an array of measures aimed at these three interconnected problems: illiquidity, lack of funding and insufficient capital – and the greatest of these three, or at least the most fundamental, was the shortage of capital. Or so, at least, it seemed to most of those in the UK Government charged with finding an effective policy response.

Various narratives of the Crisis chronicled since 2008 have plotted the drama in strikingly different ways, inevitably drawing different individuals to the centre of the stage. But it needs no exaggeration to set a crucial scene on the ninth floor of Standard Chartered's Head Office in the City's Basinghall Avenue. It was instigated at the behest of Shriti Vadera, a former City investment banker and for eight years an adviser at the Treasury, who by September 2008 had been serving as a minister in Gordon Brown's Labour Government for fifteen months. She and a senior Treasury official, Tom Scholar, had been working closely together through July and August to devise an appropriate government response to the mounting crisis in the UK's banking sector. It was now manifestly evident, in their view, that the banks' escalating losses made it essential there should be a massive further injection of fresh capital into the industry.[5] And the only viable provider of this capital, inescapably, had to be the taxpayer. Emerging by early September was the notion of a broad approach that would involve providing both additional capital on the one hand and extra liquidity from the Bank of England on the other – plus some (as yet unclear) scheme to put the Treasury's support behind medium-term borrowing by the banks, so that they could resume lending to businesses and home-buyers in the wider economy. Over the ten days following the Lehman collapse, contingency plans along these lines kept the lamps burning late inside the Treasury, the Bank of England and the Financial Services Authority. At the same time, though, officials in all three were being constantly distracted by emergency meetings to help avert specific disasters for one famous name after another in the banking sector. To make progress on a pre-emptive and comprehensive rescue for the sector as a whole, Vadera turned for help to the Prime Minister's officials inside Number Ten. She drew a ready response from Gordon Brown himself. Unusually well versed in financial matters after all his years as Chancellor, Brown was one of the first to see the imperative need for a broadbrush initiative. But he was also acutely aware of the risks that would be involved if Britain acted in isolation. This was awkward, for most other European leaders still appeared intent on treating the Crisis as a problem for the US and UK markets that called for no dramatic action on their part. Worse, when Brown and Vadera crossed the Atlantic on 24 September to talk to the US authorities about co-ordinated action, they found most of the key players there firmly opposed to any purchase of equity with public money (it smacked of socialism, to a Republican eye). The Americans were poised instead to use taxpayers' dollars to purchase the toxic assets held by the banks: details of the so-called Troubled Asset Relief Program (TARP) were just being finalized. Brown and Vadera, fortified by H. M. Treasury's views, were convinced that no rescue along these lines would be viable in the UK (nor, probably, in the US either). The scale of the purchases would be overwhelming for their governments, yet all too likely to leave the markets feeling underwhelmed and still critically short of confidence. After some dispiriting talks in Washington, Brown and Vadera flew back to London on the night of Friday 26 September. During the flight, the Prime Minister took the momentous decision that his Government would, if necessary, press ahead unilaterally – with capital investments that would amount in some cases to outright nationalization – while also persevering with attempts to rally support for this line elsewhere in Europe. Over the weekend, with time plainly running short and the Treasury hard at work on the rescue of yet another lender (Bradford & Bingley, no less), Brown asked Vadera to work out a detailed plan.

Vadera was not widely regarded in Whitehall as a shrinking violet, but at this point the unprecedented scope of what they had in mind rather daunted even her. The concept of a pre-emptive rescue by the Treasury was an extraordinarily bold idea. Confronting the need for a detailed plan, as Vadera herself would recall, 'was quite a frightening experience'.[6] Whitehall's officials were under intense pressure dealing with events from one day to the next, yet the Government would need to act with precision and total conviction if disaster were to be avoided. By the Monday morning, and still nervously eyeing the gap between a broad goal and a step-by-step implementation agenda, Vadera was ready to seek out the guidance of professional bankers with practical knowledge of the money markets and of how commercial lending banks, as opposed to investment banks, actually worked. There could be no question, though, of approaching any of the domestic UK banks for help. The Government's prospective intervention would have sweeping implications for their businesses; it could only be disclosed to them all at the same time, and as a finished package. So she turned instead to a tiny band of non-domestic bankers in whom she had complete trust, and asked for their assistance. One of them was Peter Sands. He and Vadera had known each other for some years, and she was well aware of the reputation that he and his Group Finance Director, Richard Meddings, had acquired in the City as commentators on the state of the industry. They were now widely seen by their peers as the boffins of the business, and were also greatly respected for the way they were running Standard Chartered. Vadera took comfort from the Group's evident strength and was immediately reassured by its Chief Executive's response, as she could later recall:

> Peter's bank was not in trouble, it didn't need funding, it wasn't making a fortune out of the funding market itself, and I could trust him. So we had two or three around-and-about conversations that didn't reveal the Government already had a scheme in mind or a timeline, and I mentioned the other key individuals that I was talking to. Then Peter just said, 'Why don't we all meet?' I thought that was a perfect next step, incredibly helpful, and I asked him if he would host it.[7]

Sands had been one of several key participants in the industry discussions under way since the middle of September. The meeting that he had so promptly suggested could hardly have been more timely. It began in the ninth-floor Boardroom at the end of the day on Thursday, 2 October. Invited along with Vadera were Tom Scholar from the Treasury, two of the City's best-known investment bankers whom she had separately contacted – Robin Budenberg and David Soames of UBS, the giant Swiss banking group – and Michael Klein, a private adviser keeping her informed of events in the US. Alongside Sands from Standard Chartered were Meddings and another colleague, Macer Gifford, who ran the Group's funding operations around the world. (It so happened that Budenburg and Meddings were intimate friends, having each been Best Man at the other's wedding, but Vadera was unaware of this link.) The session stretched late into the evening. No time was spent drafting anything on paper, but Sands and Meddings undertook at the end to turn what had been discussed into a written plan. The two of them, together with Macer Gifford and one of his staff, Averina Snow, then worked on into the early hours. Next day, Sands and Meddings duly presented a summary brief to Vadera, her Treasury team and the UBS men, setting out their recommendations. Crucially, these tackled capital, funding and liquidity all within one scheme. As Sands recalled: 'What made our approach different was that we stressed the importance of having an over-arching narrative. People in the markets needed a coherent string of initiatives they could believe in. We came up with a package that could work as a whole, as one coherent policy.'[8] In particular, they laid out how the Government might successfully provide the banks with a guarantee to facilitate their medium-term funding needs – this was the gist of what later emerged as a 'Credit Guarantee Scheme', putting the Treasury behind the banks' borrowing activities in the interbank market, a proposal that fine-tuned ideas which had been studied earlier by Vadera and the Treasury but not agreed upon – and they showed how exchanges of public capital for equity could be presented in ways that most of the banks would feel unable to refuse.

The presentation by Sands and Meddings made a critical contribution to the scheme that emerged from the Government over the next few days. In particular it gave the Government the confidence to believe its mooted triple-headed assault on the predicament of the banking industry could indeed be successful. 'They knew how the funding market worked', recalled Vadera. 'It gave us a level of confidence, talking to them as market practitioners, that we could never have had just working in the isolation of our Government departments.'[9] The Standard Chartered men thereafter had only a limited involvement by telephone with the Government's deliberations over the weekend. But they were soon heavily engaged again, despite having to attend a 'Seeing Is Believing' gala dinner in New York on the Monday evening. Rumours of some kind of official bail-out for the banking sector were now swirling in the City, and the Government had precious little time left to finalize its plans. After a few hours in Manhattan – just long enough to see off the first course and give his speech as the chairman of Seeing Is Believing – Meddings dashed away from the dinner and flew straight back to London. Next morning he was back at the Treasury helping its team to make the final preparations, while Sands participated by telephone from his hotel room in a pre-dawn New York. The plan was completed, and that Tuesday evening, 7 October, saw the heads of the UK banking industry summoned to a meeting at the Treasury to be apprised of a comprehensive rescue package – Standard Chartered itself was one of the very few London-based banks not to be participating in it – and to be forewarned of an announcement on the Wednesday morning. The package would be valued at about £400 billion and would provide short-term liquidity, medium-term funding and state injections of equity capital all at the same time.* Famously, Government ministers and their advisers refuelled through the evening on copious supplies from an Indian take-away restaurant – so ensuring that the episode passed into history as the Balti Bail-Out.

Standard Chartered's general image before the Crisis had scarcely positioned it in the mainstream of British banking at all, but the involvement of Sands and Meddings in the bail-out was widely noted in the City, prompting a subtle reappraisal of the Group. In broad terms, according to one of the Group's own brokers, their participation in the Government's successful rescue mission consolidated a widespread respect for their leadership 'and was a big driver of the high level of credibility that the bank as a whole enjoyed throughout the Crisis period'.[10] Meddings recalled as much himself: 'It helped us hugely in terms of the bank's reputation.'[11] More specifically, it confirmed a leading role for Sands and his colleagues in the intense discussions that followed for many months over the future regulation of international banking. They were drawn into constant dealings with myriad regulatory authorities – not least the FSA in London, the new Chairman of which from September 2008, Adair Turner, had himself been a Non-Executive Director of Standard Chartered for two years before his appointment (and he had been a close colleague of Sands at McKinsey in the 1990s, too). When the world's business and political elite gathered at Davos for their annual World Economic Forum in January 2009, it surprised no one to find it co-chaired by Standard Chartered, with a conspicuous platform presence for Sands. Indeed, the Chief Executive's immersion in one policy-making forum after another over these months put his own office schedules under enormous pressure – as he readily acknowledged to the Board a couple of months later. Not that any apology was needed, of course. As Sands himself noted, 'it was important for management to remain intensively engaged on these discussions in order to influence and shape the future of the industry'.[12] His colleagues were happy to concur with this – though as time passed, and his absences remained a feature of the executive timetable, the extent of Sands' heavy public-sector commitments would eventually draw less than constant internal approval ratings.

---

* Similar measures emerged, eventually, across Europe and even in the US – where the legal basis for TARP was construed so as to allow injections of capital into the banks as well as the buying of their toxic assets. Most of the funds earmarked for TARP were in the end channelled into the banks as capital.

While undoubtedly a boost to the personal kudos of its leading executives, the real significance of the Group's enhanced credibility was the
improved access it provided to shareholders' wallets. This was to be tested
sooner than expected. As noted, the Group's balance sheet in the autumn
of 2008 was conspicuously stronger than that of most Western banks.
However, these were exceptional times. The markets were eyeing the
capital positions of all banks very nervously; surplus capital as a buffer
against wholly unpredictable events looked highly desirable, not least to
anticipate a new era in banking regulation all over the world, which none
could doubt was going to be far more assertive than previous regimes; and
it might even turn out that such a surplus could help the Group take
advantage of the messy predicament in which many of its peers were evidently mired. For all these reasons a move was begun to raise fresh capital,
with the 'private placement' of new shares envisaged as the best way forward. Such a placement automatically dilutes the ownership of existing
shareholders, so must be used circumspectly even in the most benign of
markets. It seems very likely that a rumour of the Group's intentions
leaked into the City, where the mood was anything but benign. On the
last Friday of October, the Group's share price dropped 17 per cent. The
Directors were assured in a Sunday teleconference that nothing sinister
underlay this collapse; but the price fell another 10 per cent the next day,
closing at 680p (compared with 1,326p on the day before Lehman expired).
Faced with this kind of turmoil, the interest in raising additional capital
took on a new and altogether more urgent dimension. Movements in the
share price made no difference to the capital ratios in the balance sheet,
but the market's frightening volatility suggested any opportunity to raise
fresh capital ought now to be seized – ideally raising a rather larger sum
than had been previously under consideration.

The Board had no intention of chasing after wealth funds in the Gulf
or the Far East – though Singapore's Temasek might have been open to a
discussion, had it not been for Hong Kong's objections – nor were the
Directors at all inclined to seek a Treasury cash injection or to plunge into
a precipitate merger. So, while these options were being actively pursued
in half the banking parlours of Wall Street and the City, those at the helm
of Standard Chartered hung back in something of a dilemma. There was
logically only one course of action left to them: an appeal to shareholders.
No one in the Boardroom, however, could be confident of proposing
this and retaining credibility with their fellow Directors. Sands and Meddings privately acknowledged as much, but were nonetheless convinced
of the need to turn to shareholders for new capital. And a quick decision
was essential: after the start of December, the market would effectively

be closed to the Group pending the announcement of the 2008 results in March. So there was little time for debate. With the share price falling steadily lower, a conventional issue of new stock was out of the question. Sands and Meddings resolved to square the circle by offering new shares at an enormous discount to the current market price – and they would square their colleagues in the Boardroom by asking the Group's leading adviser, David Mayhew of Cazenove, to propose the whole idea. Mayhew had been regarded for decades as the doyen of City stockbrokers, and his imprimatur for the scheme would at least ensure it a thoughtful reception. So it proved. Mayhew backed the idea of an immediate rights issue, and suggested to the Board that shareholders could be offered, and would accept, new equity at a discount of up to 50 per cent to the market price. (Since all current shareholders would have equal rights to subscribe, the impact of the discount on the quoted market price would be an arithmetical adjustment only, with no implicit dilution of existing holdings – except, importantly, for any shareholders who declined to participate.)

It was hardly a propitious time to be asking investors for more money. Prices in the world's stock markets were gyrating wildly. Wall Street saw its Standard & Poor's index move by over 5 per cent seventeen times in the two months from mid-September, compared with sixteen times in the previous forty-five years.[13] And in the wider world, to judge by many press commentaries, banks and bankers seemed suddenly to be on a moral par with drug gangs and rhino poachers. But Mayhew's advice carried the day. The Directors agreed that the Group should turn to its shareholders for another $3.5 billion, in exchange for a one-third increase in the number of its outstanding shares. In the event, the issue went ahead at a 48.65 per cent discount to the existing price just before Christmas 2008 – and it closed early in the New Year with 97 per cent of shareholders (including Temasek) taking up their rights to new stock. It was a welcome confirmation of investors' confidence in the Group's special standing, and was to prove just the first of three audacious and pre-emptive boosts to the Group's equity. A second, timed to coincide with the unveiling of the half-year results in August 2009, saw $1.7 billion raised via a private placement of new shares; and another rights issue – at the Group's own instigation, taking even its own advisers by surprise – pulled in more than $5 billion in October 2010.* Within the space of less than two years, its

---

* The prime mover behind the enormous 2010 issue was Meddings, who persuaded his colleagues that the industry was unavoidably headed for a new era that would be defined in part by a regulatory insistence on altogether higher levels of equity capital. His prescience enabled Standard Chartered to move a step ahead of most of its peers in this respect. The 2008 rights issue lifted the total and core Tier One ratios from 8.5 and 6.1 per cent to 9.8 and 7.4 per

core Tier One equity rose from $19 billion to $29 billion. At a time when much of the international banking industry was actually shrinking, this handed the senior management in Basinghall Avenue a degree of firepower in the marketplace that few could rival – especially in Asia, where for the duration some of its keenest competitors, not least Citibank, were virtually shutting up shop.

Here was another consequence of the Crisis almost tailor-made for Standard Chartered. Other big banks were pulling back sharply in geographical territories where the Group was well placed to snap up discarded (or disenchanted) customers. Instances of this were apparent from the earliest days. On the last weekend of September 2008, Singapore hosted its first Formula One Grand Prix (and the first ever raced at night). It was a glitzy affair, even by motor-racing's flashy standards, on which Royal Bank of Scotland had expended a small fortune as the principal sponsor. Alas, by the time the practice laps got under way RBS was fast approaching a different kind of chequered flag. Its entire senior management and directorate had been scheduled to attend for the weekend; at the last moment, they were withdrawn. The decision was taken at Standard Chartered to weigh in with copious extra corporate entertaining to take up the slack. Four days later, the head of Consumer Banking was able to report to the Board that 'the Bank had received in excess of US$500 million in Private Banking commitments as a result'.[14] It was a colourful portent of things to come. And the blessings of an unusually favourable competitive wind for Standard Chartered in 2008–9 were timely for the Consumer Banking division, relieving some of the pressure on a business that was no longer enjoying the heady growth of revenues begun in 2003. Its product-driven culture now sorely needed to be complemented with a more painstaking approach to the less glamorous aspects of the business. Its marketing maestro, Mike DeNoma, had left the Group in June 2008. The air was thick with talk of transformational strategies, customer focus and 'market participation models' – all symptomatic of a struggle, now, to develop the kind of nuts-and-bolts infrastructure that would be needed to stitch together those ambitious networks acquired over the past five years. This was already looking a much tougher challenge than had perhaps been anticipated in the excitement of the pre-Crisis expansion, and the days were long gone when operating profits from Consumer and

---

cent respectively. By the end of 2013, the two ratios stood at 13.1 and 11.8 per cent. Insofar as the whole industry eventually underwent a broadly similar transformation, such numbers encapsulate the commercial impact on the banks of the Global Financial Crisis. Squeezing balance sheets smaller and making equity bases bigger has entailed a rapid fall in the returns on equity available to their shareholders.

Wholesale Banking were more or less on level pegging. They were $1.3 billion and $1.4 billion respectively in 2005; by 2009, they were to be $0.9 billion and $4.1 billion – a striking measure of how dramatically Mike Rees's Wholesale Banking division had already outgrown the rest of the Group. But the shock waves from the Crisis brought a welcome boost for the Consumer business, especially for those operations catering to the wealthier end of the retail market, where Standard Chartered looked a safer harbour in the storm than most of its leading competitors. The Group also had a bit of luck with its PR and advertising. The Hong Kong and Singapore offices' 150th anniversaries fell in 2009, providing the cue for lavish birthday parties with some prestigious guest lists – topped in Hong Kong by the business magnate and philanthropist Li Ka-shing. (To help along the celebrations in Hong Kong, the Group printed a special HK$150 banknote, issuing a million of them and giving the proceeds to charity. Individual notes were soon changing hands in Hong Kong for almost twice their face value.[15])

Notably absent from the anniversary parties was the man widely and justly credited for the astonishing growth of the Group since 2001, Mervyn Davies. As Chairman of one of the few large commercial banks seemingly unbowed by the events of September 2008, Davies had naturally been involved in the public-policy debates that had followed the Crisis, albeit in a rather less technical role than Sands. He had been especially active in advising government ministers on the broad issues raised by the banking industry's implosion, in the Far East as well as the UK: he was one of the first appointments, for example, to a well-publicized advisory committee set up in October 2008 by Hong Kong's Chief Executive, Donald Tsang. Then, some weeks later, he was approached by the headhunters Korn Ferry, asking if he would contemplate taking on one of the most challenging assignments to result from the wreckage of the UK banking sector. By the end of 2008, Royal Bank of Scotland had passed from being the single largest commercial bank in the world (judged by the size of its gargantuan balance sheet) to being one of the biggest disasters in world banking history. Its executive boss had resigned, its shares that had formerly traded for £20 each were now a penny stock, and its mountainous loan losses were growing more Himalayan by the day. RBS only remained in existence at all because the UK Government had taken up a majority stake in its equity, invested via an arm's-length affiliate of the Treasury christened 'UK Financial Investments' (UKFI). By Christmas it was horribly apparent that the bank's aggregate loss for 2008 would shortly have to be disclosed as yet another record-breaking item. The position of the incumbent chairman, Sir Tom McKillop, was deemed by UKFI to be untenable and a successor was urgently needed. The UKFI Board, under its Chairman Sir Philip Hampton, offered Davies the role of non-executive Chairman of the re-capitalized bank. Moving from SCB directly to RBS was probably not going to be without its complications, but Davies was soon engaged in detailed negotiations with UKFI over terms and conditions. A contract was drawn up, with incentives that were felt appropriate to the Herculean nature of the job. By the second week of January, Sir Philip and his colleagues fully expected Davies to accept it.[16] An announcement of his appointment was planned for 19 January, when the 2008 losses were to be unveiled.

With just days remaining before the announcement, however, Davies suddenly found his earlier counselling of government ministers was now going to lead to higher things: Gordon Brown invited him to join the Labour Government as Trade Minister, with a seat in the House of Lords as Lord Davies of Abersoch. News of his elevation spread consternation at UKFI.* But it certainly allowed Davies to end his celebrated fifteen-year career with the Group in some style. Word of his sudden exit surprised many of his former colleagues, but institutional shareholders reacted calmly to the news. It was surely helpful that a Deputy Chairman had been in post since August 2007, John Peace. The fact that Peace was no professional banker prompted some initial reservations in the City, given the dire state of the industry.† But a brief round of initial interviews with some external candidates soon satisfied the Board that he had the necessary blend of skills and that it need look no further for the right man.

Meanwhile, in Asia's suddenly less competitive markets the Group was faced with an almost overwhelming array of new business prospects – especially in Wholesale Banking. Months ahead of the Lehman bankruptcy, Mike Rees had already alerted the Board to a surge in his division's profits:

---

* The Treasury subsequently asked Sir Philip Hampton to take the job himself, stepping down as head of UKFI in order to take charge of its single biggest headache. His forthcoming appointment to the RBS chair was duly announced on 19 January 2009, coupled with news of 'an indicative loss' by the bank for 2008 of £24.1 billion after tax, interest 'and other charges'.

† The son of a Nottinghamshire coalminer and a graduate of the Royal Military Academy Sandhurst, Peace had cut his teeth in business in the 1970s as a computer programmer. Under his direction, an innovative data-collection agency was built up by the retail group GUS plc into a business that came to be called Experian, a leading international supplier of information on the financial creditworthiness of individual consumers. As Chief Executive of the parent GUS from 2000 to 2006, Peace oversaw an extraordinary worldwide expansion of Experian. It was demerged as a separate listed company in 2006 and went on to become a constituent of the FTSE 100 market index. At the time of his 2009 confirmation as Standard Chartered's Chairman, Peace was still chairing Experian – as well as another successful subsidiary spun off from GUS, the luxury clothing retailer, Burberry Group – and was also head of a range of organizations in the not-for-profit sector.

'there were real opportunities to win business, as many competitors had cut their lines and were not writing new business as a result of capital and/ or liquidity constraints'.[17] After the Crisis broke, Sands talked of a 'Balkanization' of international finance, with troubled Western banks pulling back from their cross-border networks in Asia to focus on their own domestic markets. A deluge of calls hit the desks at Standard Chartered, many from other banks' corporate customers seeking help with basic commercial banking needs. Across this 'bottom layer' of its Wholesale pyramid, accounting for roughly half the income earned from corporations, the Group stuck to its traditional approach. That is to say, it tried as far as possible to stand by existing clients and to deepen its relationships with each of them, rather than chasing new business. This was soon deemed to have paid off, with a significant jump in the number of global companies apparently happy in future to regard Standard Chartered as their principal banker. The Group's income from its top fifty clients grew by almost 40 per cent in 2009. Indeed, for its biggest and most cherished corporate borrowers, the Group was willing to extend loans on a scale that few, if any, of its peers were ready to countenance. This 'single-name exposure' was to become a marked feature of the Group's balance sheet over the next few years. The risks were felt to be mitigated by the diversity of the overall portfolio, straddling as it did many countries across Asia and Africa and a wide range of different industries. In this sense at least, it was reminiscent of that willingness to shoulder unusual levels of exposure to leading names in the remoter regions of Asia that had been such a hallmark of the old Chartered Bank's approach.

Deeper relationships, though, implied an ability to deliver a wider range of products and services – and, to meet this agenda, the Wholesale Banking division soon began to contemplate broadening its scope. In its capital-market activities (still essentially the middle of that same pyramid), Standard Chartered was a market leader in the issuance of bonds and derivative products, but had no involvement with equities at all. It was resolved early in 2010 that the Group should aim to be among the top five banks in all its local Asian markets, as both an issuer of new stock for clients and a secondary-market trader. Sands described this to colleagues as a potentially important fresh move for the Group – though in the event, it was slow to happen.[18] Much more immediately evident was an often frenetic expansion of the Wholesale division's pyramid-topping corporate finance operation. V. Shankar had moved to a more senior role in charge of all client relationships in 2008, and the unit was now headed by a former J. P. Morgan executive, Sean Wallace. Under his energetic direction, corporate finance revenues in 2009 jumped by almost 75 per cent. The speed of the Group's expansion was reflected in the management of the sales and marketing effort: new business was booked with a keen eye for whatever opportunities presented themselves. (It was said that in one corner of the bank, where individual sales executives were identified by their geographical coverage, the top-performing salesman was an executive known as 'Unmapped'.) Those orchestrating this performance were plainly the coming men. Wallace soon followed Shankar up the corporate ladder to take on the brief for all client coverage and business origination in the Wholesale sector. Shankar was promoted as one of the two top managers still charged with the operational running of the Group, broadly to the east and west of Pakistan. Shankar looked west, leaving Asia to Jaspal Bindra.

The new head of the western half of the Group found himself being posted in 2010 to the Gulf, to occupy an office in the Group's expanding premises in Dubai. Shankar was the most senior executive yet to have been based there, and his arrival acknowledged a dramatic growth of Standard Chartered's business in the Gulf region. Revenues in 2009 had jumped by 40 per cent. In addition to servicing the burgeoning trade flows between the Far East and Africa, the Dubai office was also thriving on the growth of the tiny Emirates themselves. Until very recently the UAE had been home to just one of the Group's top 100 clients. Now ten of them were to be found there.[19] And at the end of 2009 events had conspired to give the Group's profile another boost that was indirectly linked to its enhanced credibility in the wake of the Crisis. In November 2009, the news broke in Dubai that its main government-owned investment fund, Dubai World, was suspend-ing interest payments on debts of $26 billion. In effect, it had been bankrupted by the activities of its commercial property arm. Its collapse threatened to spark a default by Dubai itself (with total debts of around $80 billion, including the Dubai World figure). Standard Chartered had billions of dollars at stake in loans to the emirate, and quickly set up a team dedicated to protecting its position. Unreported in the media, though, was an invitation from officials in Dubai's rich neighbour, Abu Dhabi, to set up a parallel team that could help find a resolution of the whole crisis from the UAE's standpoint. Peter Sands himself flew to the Gulf, and spent a few weeks shuttling incognito between the two adjacent emirates as they inched their way to a rescue by the one of the other. (The Dubai debts were duly salvaged and rescheduled in January.) Sands' involvement put a dent in many of the Group's scheduled arrangements elsewhere; but as he sug-gested to the Board at the outset, 'the rationale for our involvement was the right one given the Group's franchise in the region'.[20] Perhaps unsurpris-ingly, that franchise went on growing briskly. By the end of 2010, Standard Chartered was reportedly the most profitable international bank in the

UAE, and a substantial proportion of its Middle Eastern and North African profits were being notched up in Dubai.[21]

Wholesale Banking's ascendancy within the Group was by this point more assured than ever. Mike Rees, as overall head of a division that in 2010 accounted for more than two-thirds of all the Group's operating profits, had unsurprisingly joined the main Board as of August 2009. Wholesale's future seemed all the more promising, insofar as several fledgling or entirely new businesses within the division were as yet merely hinting at their potential. Future profit targets were soon being dramatically upgraded for these late developers. They included, for example, a 'Structured Trade Finance' unit which made term loans to medium-sized companies, and specialized in offering larger packages with longer maturities than were generally available from other banks. It was earning well under $100 million a year, when Wallace challenged it to reach $500 million; and it would reach $600 million in 2013.[22] Commercial real-estate lending, a business with revenues of about $375 million in 2009, was challenged to double this by 2012 – and would shoot past that milestone with a year to spare. One of the most intriguing acorns of all was a commodities desk, which had been set up in 2006 to fill the (always anomalous) gap left by the sale of the Mocatta bullion business to the Bank of Nova Scotia in 1997. A team of fugitive Lehman traders was hired late in 2008 and their leader, Arun Murthy, set off to make the most of a customer network far wider than even the largest New York investment banks had ever enjoyed. He developed a sales and trading arm that was designed, essentially, to provide clients with effective protection against disadvantageous movements in the price of key commodities – notably gold, base metals and oil. This move into the commodity-trading world would soon take the Group's exposure here far beyond anything contemplated by the old Mocatta business – but if this implied a novel scale of risk for the Group, it was not much remarked at the time. Prices in almost every significant commodity market, with oil and precious metals to the fore, still seemed to be heading inexorably higher on the back of China's expansion. Over the next five years, the growth of Murthy's team would turn Standard Chartered into one of the world's top five commodity-trading banks, with revenues of more than $400 million (and make it the single biggest shipper of gold into India).

As it built up these and a string of other ambitious Wholesale businesses, the Group had no difficulty finding the additional resources it needed. It had access to supportive shareholders; it was still adding numbers to the payroll in spectacular fashion (from 70,000 in 2007, the workforce was to swell to 89,000 by 2012); and as a poacher of talented senior executives from elsewhere in the industry it was handily placed to make offers that few could refuse.* Never entirely dispelled by all this activity, though, was a question that lingered in many minds. Put bluntly, could organic growth alone be an adequate response to the extraordinary circumstances of the post-Lehman world? Perhaps luring aboard new executive stars, or even whole teams of them, would ultimately turn out to be a poor proxy for a much bolder move. The Board in the summer of 2008 had opted to stick with organic growth as the 'core driver' of the Group's expansion, in preference to the pursuit of a transformative merger. And it was demonstrably the case that, despite all the glamour of acquisitions from time to time, it was the steady accretion of basic banking revenues that had formed the bedrock of the Group's success (accounting, according to one internal analysis, for about 80 per cent of the growth in operating profits). Nonetheless, given the events of September 2008, perhaps this approach would need to make way for a much more radical departure.

2. LAST JUNCTION FOR JOHANNESBURG

Constant reviews duly followed, popping up regularly over the next five years. They got off to a breathless start in the immediate wake of Lehman's collapse. Sands, Meddings and a large team of support staff gathered in Basinghall Avenue every single weekend from mid-September to Christmas 2008 to cope with the fall-out from the Crisis. Their work was regularly interrupted by calls from other banks wanting to talk about merger possibilities. 'The weekends were more intense than the weekdays', recalled Sands. 'That was when the chairmen and chief executives of banks around the world were ringing each other up, in various states of distress, searching for deals that could rescue them.'[23] A few initial proposals were rejected out of hand. They included one on behalf of the Anglo-Irish Bank, which even in September was plainly heading for bankruptcy (effectively reached three months later, when the Dublin Government stepped in to nationalize what was left of it). But some of the banking world's most illustrious names were among the able-bodied suitors frequently dialling from New York. More specifically linked to Standard Chartered's core franchise was a proposal for it to assimilate those competing Asian

---

* The damage inflicted on the banking industry by the Eurozone crisis of 2011 left the Group looking even more enviably placed: its share price between January and September 2011 fell by less than 25 per cent, compared with the 40–50 per cent declines suffered by most of Europe's largest commercial banks. In fact, by September 2011 Standard Chartered was suddenly the third biggest bank in Europe, ranked by market capitalization, behind only HSBC and Santander. (Minutes of the Board meeting of 20 September 2011, SCB/GCS.)

operations of Royal Bank of Scotland. Also on offer was the Hong Kong business of the crippled insurance giant AIG. It was even suggested at one point that Citigroup's Asian empire might be for sale, when a forced break-up of the US bank seemed briefly on the cards until it became clear that no such outcome was ever likely to be acceptable in Washington. European bankers on the other end of the line at one time or another included Santander, and other familiar names from Britain's High Street – though there were no more calls about HBOS, a bank for which the UK regulators had been desperately seeking a new parent prior to September 2008 and which had succumbed to the Crisis almost immediately.* Huge amounts of time had to be spent on these exchanges: most approaches required at least some passing consideration. In reality, though, most were invitations to catch a falling knife and they steadily reinforced the scepticism among Sands and his colleagues about the supposed appeal of (in that dread phrase) a game-changing merger: 'we didn't buy anything, and most of the discussions were frankly a distraction'.[24]

As for many years past, organic growth looked far more likely to remain the principal driver of the Group's expansion. In a formal assessment of 'Inorganic Strategy' in April 2009, Sands largely restated the position as it had been summarized ten months earlier: the Board had been advised that any transformational deal would be 'risky and unnecessary', and this counsel 'had proved a good one'.[25] Undeniably the case could be made now – and would be made from time to time, over the coming years – for a more adventurous stance. 'The strategic logic for deals that reinforced the Group's scale and deposit-taking capability in key markets had become more compelling . . .' On the other hand, the obstacles to any successful acquisition in Asia had grown more formidable, too. The unwinding of the securitized mortgages market was just one of several factors that now made the legal clearance of any M&A proposition immeasurably trickier. Rees and his colleagues were attracted at one point to the possibility of acquiring the Asian wholesale business of Lehman

---

* The HBOS share price fell heavily on Monday 15 September in the wake of the news about Lehman, prompting fears by Wednesday of a run on the bank, which was the UK's largest mortgage lender. In a deal actively brokered by the Labour Government on the Wednesday and announced on the Thursday, HBOS was acquired by Lloyds TSB for £12.2 billion. Days earlier, in confirming to the regulators that it had no interest in any such merger of its own, Standard Chartered had confided that analysis by CFO Richard Meddings and his finance team had suggested a hole in the HBOS balance sheet of about £15 billion. Confirmation of the price paid by Lloyds so stunned Sands and his senior executives that they went back to check their sums. Later events suggested they had not been too wide of the mark. The reconfigured Lloyds Banking Group raised £13.5 billion in a rights issue in November 2009, as part of a massive recapitalization forced on it by the HBOS acquisition.

Brothers, but their interest soon fizzled out when myriad legal complications surfaced. And regulatory clearance was another barrier that looked all but insurmountable, especially in smaller countries with understandably nervous central banks – such as Turkey, where Standard Chartered briefly considered one or two acquisitions but retreated in the face of a cool official reception. As Sands rightly predicted in his 2009 paper, 'local regulators were expected to be much more intrusive and willing to obstruct deals to ensure systemic stability in their domestic markets'. Foreign banks would find it virtually impossible to expand their own networks in many countries, and almost as hard to add existing businesses instead – unless, of course, the business in question was large and lame, in which case local officials might be only too keen to welcome a foreign buyer.

The executives in Basinghall Avenue by this point had also come to a rather shrewder appreciation of the commercial difficulties of integrating local banking networks into the Group. Among the City's leading analysts of the banking industry, too, probably most were as sceptical as ever that Standard Chartered could really compete as a local retail bank anywhere in Asia. Pulling off the initial purchase was the easy part. After buying Taiwan's Hsinchu International Bank in 2006, for example, the Group had struggled with unexpectedly high loan impairments and the challenge of running a largely rural retail network of eighty-three branches, the majority of them based outside the Greater Taipei area (and not a few of them in remote fishing villages, as cynical observers were heard to remark). Jaspal Bindra had to advise the Board in 2009 that 'lessons had been learned' – and one of them was probably that erstwhile family-run banks closely attuned to strong local cultures might be best avoided in future.[26] A more severe cautionary tale already looked like emerging from South Korea. The bank acquired in 2005 had been half-renamed, as 'Standard Chartered First Bank' (SCFB), as though to suggest that a mix of Group and traditional South Korean work practices might be smoothly blended. But a pugnacious trade union was firmly opposed to switching the 6,500-strong workforce away from a seniority-based culture in favour of pay and promotions based on merit. It was even more hostile to any reduction in the workforce as part of a radical restructuring, even though the Group's ambitions in the country encompassed a gradual broadening of its product range.* The result was a rising tension that by 2009 was turning the business into a drag on the Group and a source of serious concern.

In short, whatever its appetite for acquisitions before 2008 – and this

---

* A modest acquisition in 2007, for example, added a securities-services business to SCFB. The name of the company seemed propitious: it was called A Brain.

had never really been as avid as many media commentators supposed – the Group's interest in buying more retail-oriented businesses after 2008 was heavily curtailed. They were not entirely eschewed. A string of very modest deals gave the Group ownership of some small additional operations, including the equities business of stockbrokers Cazenove in Asia, the custodial banking business built by Barclays across Africa, and a consumer finance business in Singapore bought from General Electric. (As it happens, almost all of these businesses were, in due course, to be sold or written off as unsuccessful ventures. Some hasty, unsecured lending ensured plenty of growth until 2012, but the record thereafter was to be less happy.) But the aftermath of the Crisis bore no resemblance to that of the 1997 Asian crisis. 'Inorganic Strategy' after 2008 amounted to a studied ambivalence in dozens of Board papers, with a strong bias against committing the Group to anything too 'transformational'. Few grand, eye-catching mergers were even mooted, and none survived as a real possibility for long – with just one notable exception, which for about eighteen months looked as though it might end up giving the South African dimension of Standard Chartered's history one further momentous twist.

It was over twenty years since the Group's family ties with Standard Bank had been finally severed in 1987; but memories of the old link to South Africa still tugged at many older executives, like the ache of a lost limb. And the lack of any substantial foothold in the continent's key economy seemed a melancholy confirmation of the Group's lack of ambition in Africa as a whole. The net contribution to the bottom line from Africa operations had changed very little, in relative terms, for many years. Operating profits from 166 branches in 15 countries had hovered at about 7 per cent of the Group total, helped by the positive trends in the continent's trade with the rest of the world. (This was still a portfolio performance: individual territories had seen their own fortunes rise or fall – or plummet, in the wretched case of Zimbabwe – but the net gains outweighed the declines. It was a modern version, in this respect, of the old Chartered Bank.) In fact, given a very meagre level of investment by comparison with that ploughed into Asia and the Middle East, a modest profitability had as ever implied a handsome return on equity. Just as important, now that historic difficulties over dividends and remittances had been largely resolved, Africa was able to generate a welcome stream of cash (much of which was being channelled into building the Group's branches in China). It had still been hard to discern, though, any dynamic future for Standard Chartered in Africa. Attitudes towards local African management had evolved usefully, but this had made little difference to the traditionally thin appetite for African risk. All the old reservations about retail business, in particular, remained in place. The phenomenal growth of mortgages, so central to Consumer Banking's boom in Asia, was not going to happen in Africa, East or West: the continent's lack of land registries still deterred Standard Chartered, like most other banks, from using property as loan collateral – a rather fundamental obstacle. In short, the lack of any effective strategy to replace the old ties with Standard Bank rather reflected the Group's half-hearted stance towards a continent with more than its share of intractable systemic weaknesses.

Since around the start of 2007, however, the need had become apparent for a serious reassessment. Africa's business environment seemed to be entering a period of profound change. Three novel features stood out. First was the gathering impact of oil and gas exports, which were starting to alter the economic geography of the continent. Nigeria by 2008 had emerged on the strength of them as the largest economy in the sub-Saharan region, and Angola as one of its fastest-growing economies; new off-shore discoveries in 2007 had transformed the outlook for Ghana (and would do the same for Mozambique and Tanzania in 2012). Second came a surge of inward investment from China – seemingly emboldened by the evident financial frailties of the Western world – with several of its state-owned corporations securing contracts to ship African commodities east in vast quantities, and relocating large numbers of Chinese employees (especially to Nigeria) to monitor the progress of this new trade corridor. Third, and of most direct concern to Standard Chartered, was a perceptible stirring of home-grown banking competition. Diana Layfield, who would take over as Regional Chief Executive of the Group's Africa division in 2011, could later recall being in no doubt about the longer-term significance of this: 'You were starting to see the development of local and regional banks, aspiring to capture the space dominated historically by Western institutions – much as had happened twenty years earlier in Asia.'[27] One of those regional players, as it happened, was Standard Bank. In 2006, the Standard's African business outside South Africa was a fraction the size of Standard Chartered's; by 2009 it was already on its way to becoming the larger entity. The management in Johannesburg appeared increasingly intent upon building up Standard as an African bank without undue pretensions to a wider international profile (a strategy explicitly acknowledged in 2010[28]). The logic in this had an obvious appeal, and was in effect underwritten in 2008 by the purchase of a 20-per-cent equity stake in Standard by the state-controlled Industrial and Commercial Bank of China (ICBC).

Standard Chartered's senior executives were just digesting the deeper implications of this move by the Chinese when they received a nudge from some old friends in Johannesburg. Nedbank was still 54-per-cent owned by the Old Mutual insurance group – the rest of the equity was publicly traded – and its top managers contacted the Group informally in March 2009 to say how much more effectively Nedbank might compete against Standard Bank and ABSA if only it were part of Standard Chartered's network.[29] This idea, intriguing in 2004, was now nothing short of compelling for many of the Group's old Africa hands. The African marketplace – essentially unaffected by the impact of the Global Financial Crisis – was in transition. An arm in South Africa might be of huge value to Standard Chartered in seeking to stay ahead of competitors. Buying Nedbank would double the African contribution to Group profits from 7 to 14 per cent, and would restore a dominant presence in Africa that could be marketed to the Group's commodity-buying clients across the Far East. The initiative from Nedbank was duly pursued. Initial contacts with Old Mutual were encouraging, too. Some worried that the South African authorities would be obstructive, but this turned out not to be the case, though plainly there would be tough regulatory hurdles to surmount. By early 2010, notwithstanding all the general reservations about transformative deals, the prospect of a merger in Johannesburg was fast gathering momentum. Sands thought it 'likely to be the last opportunity for the Group to acquire a major bank in South Africa and to cement a leading position on a continent which was of great and growing global importance'.[30] But it would not come cheaply. Rumours of a deal had seeped into the Johannesburg market, and Nedbank's traded shares had almost doubled in price over the course of 2009 (from a low of R6.5 to just over R12). The Board fully acknowledged the appeal of a Nedbank merger and felt confident that a purchase of Old Mutual's stake would lead many private shareholders to sell out. The price of the deal, however, was starting to cause concern. At a 20 per cent premium to the market, buying Old Mutual's stake would cost over $5.5 billion (far more, even, than Korea First Bank, which had cost a mere $3.3 billion). Soaking up stock offered in the open market might add another $2.5 billion to the total bill. This made the putative acquisition a potentially seminal move for Standard Chartered. Not since the 1981 bid for Royal Bank of Scotland, in fact, had it contemplated staking so much of its future on a bold throw of the M&A dice.

Those of an historical bent of mind can therefore have been little surprised to find the situation suddenly complicated by the rumoured emergence of a familiar counter-bidder – none other than 1981's troublesome interloper, HSBC. By the start of the summer, Old Mutual was pressing for an acceleration of the timetable. Fears of a snap bid by HSBC rang alarm bells in Basinghall Avenue, especially among those most alert to the support for the deal among investors in the Far East. By June, Jaspal Bindra was reporting to the Board on 'a dramatic shift in investor sentiment in Hong Kong, Singapore and Japan over the last twelve months. Investors considered that it was now crucial for the Group to protect and enhance its Asia-Africa corridor.'[31] Letting HSBC snatch the prize in Johannesburg was not going to impress anyone. Adding to the pressure on the Board were reports of a positive engagement at executive level: Diana Layfield had met with senior Nedbank managers in Johannesburg and found them 'if anything, of an even higher calibre than had been expected'.[32] The respect was reportedly mutual.* Meanwhile, though, the financial dilemma was only growing more acute. Reports of Standard Chartered's interest were appearing in the South African press, and Nedbank's share price was rising ever higher. Sands and his negotiating team pressed ahead into September, but were starting to chafe seriously at the price being sought by Nedbank. As a token of their concern, Nedbank was repeatedly cautioned about the intensity of the due diligence process to come. Perhaps this was counter-productive. In mid-September, anyway, Nedbank suddenly announced that it had given HSBC an opportunity to run as the exclusive bidder. The timing of this was disastrous for Standard Chartered's chances of completing any deal. Just weeks later, the Group launched its October 2010 rights issue, the prospectus for which explicitly tied the proceeds of the issue to organic growth and a strengthening of capital ratios. Media suggestions that a war-chest was being surreptitiously prepared for a bid in South Africa were firmly rebutted. At this point, HSBC dramatically pulled out of its talks in Johannesburg, leaving Old Mutual and Nedbank faced with no deal at all. Both appealed to Standard Chartered to return to the table – but, as all in Basinghall Avenue were agreed, for the Group to do so now would hopelessly compromise its integrity. Besides, the fact that HSBC appeared to have ruled out making a big strategic move into South Africa rather obviated the need to spend heavily on a deal that had come to be seen increasingly as a way of blocking HSBC's challenge. So the invitations from Johannesburg were declined, and there was to be no going back. The chance for an historic return to South Africa had slipped away.

It was undoubtedly a disappointment, but Sands and his team felt their

---

* The senior ranks of Standard Chartered by 2010 contained a striking number of women with remarkable personal backgrounds, but Layfield's was more remarkable than most. She had joined the Group in 2004 at the age of thirty-four after a career that had already embraced flying fighter planes for the Royal Air Force (and aid missions in Africa for the Red Cross), banking at Goldman Sachs, studying at Harvard's Kennedy School, consulting with McKinsey, and managing a technology business in the financial services industry.

cagey approach had been vindicated. Comfort was also drawn from the fact that many City investors welcomed the outcome: without yielding any ground to HSBC, Standard Chartered had in their view faced a fork in the road and chosen the wiser and far safer course.* Whatever the merits of the decision, the Group had reaffirmed in unmistakeable terms its commitment to organic growth rather than any merger-driven expansion. Plans were already afoot within Wholesale Banking to rely on its own resources to build Standard Chartered into the premier bank for Africa's natural resources sector. It had to be acknowledged, as the Board heard from management again in November, that Standard Bank was 'arguably the most well-positioned bank within Africa',[33] especially in view of its growing ties to China's ICBC. Standard Chartered, though, had its own strong claim to a competitive hold on the China–Africa trade routes – now to be a feature of rapidly growing importance.

3. BIGGER PLANS FOR GREATER CHINA

Through the plate-glass walls of Standard Chartered's head office in Singapore, based in Tower One of the Marina Bay Financial Centre and officially opened in January 2011, many of the bank's 6,000 employees on the island could look out across a steamy ocean strewn with dozens of ships at anchor every day of the year. Each awaited its turn to berth at what has long been the world's busiest transit port. Interviewed in his office on the twenty-seventh floor in October 2012, local Chief Executive Ray Ferguson could point out the view as a reminder of the colossal scale of trade passing through this narrow seaway between the West and the great ports of the Far East, and of China in particular. For Ferguson – a down-to-earth lowlands Scot, trained in his youth by the Bank of Scotland in a small town near Dumfries, in the best traditions of the Chartered Bank – it was also a handy manifestation of the business that provided the modern Group with such a rich stream of earnings, rather as the old 'country trade' of the nineteenth century once did for Howard Gwyther and his intrepid Foreign Staff. Then it was British woollens and machinery, Indian cotton goods and government-grown opium heading east round the tip of the island in exchange for tea, porcelain and more tea; in the twenty-first century it was an awesome

---

* The City may of course have been misguided in reaching this verdict. Nedbank's share price closed 2010 at R13, and by the end of 2013 was trading at R21. The bank's market capitalization rose 60 per cent, from R67 billion at the end of 2010 to R107 billion three years later. Earnings per share in 2013 were 71 per cent higher, based on a virtually unchanged number of shares (Nedbank Group Annual Report, 2013).

range of raw materials going east, especially from Africa – Nigerian crude oil, Zambian copper, Gabonese minerals and mahogany, Ghanaian cocoa and cashew nuts – in exchange for almost any manufactured article the African or Western importer would care to buy.

The spectacular growth of the African–Chinese trade corridor through the first decade of this century has already been noted in the context of Standard Chartered's changing attitude to sub-Saharan Africa. But the Group itself had only a relatively modest exposure to the phenomenon over most of this period. Despite its leadership during the Guangdong Enterprises saga of 1998–9 (see p. 670) and its general prominence in Hong Kong (as yet still effectively regarded as a separate market), the Group entered the new millennium as a tiny foreign bank in mainland China, too little known to play any significant role in the country's foreign trade. Its China network comprised just sixteen branches and representative offices, all reporting to Hong Kong. Its main claim to any special status was that oft-cited 'unbroken presence' in Shanghai since 1858 (authentic enough, albeit a legacy of the Communist regime's ruthless handling of exit visas for local British managers); but few businessmen in the post-Deng era had much interest in history. So once China had at last secured its entry to the World Trade Organization, in 2001, the need for Standard Chartered to rebuild a substantial base on the mainland was self-evident. How best to set about this task prompted some lively debate in Des Voeux Road, just as it had in the 1930s. None really questioned the final goal, so the arguments on this occasion were less strategic than tactical and the acrimony of the 1935–7 years was avoided. Nonetheless, the Group had been badly burned by its overly hasty expansion on to the mainland in the 1990s – those Pearl River Delta loans of 1994–6 had ended up costing the Group several hundred million dollars – and there was felt to be much at stake.

A key figure in the debate was Katherine Tsang, who had joined the bank in Hong Kong as a senior HR professional in 1992 and whose influence ten years later extended well beyond her HR brief. Though a third-generation citizen of Hong Kong, she enjoyed a broad network of connections on the mainland and was confident of the Group's future there. (Like T. V. Soong and his sisters in the 1930s, indeed, she also had a powerful family background: her brother Donald Tsang had been a senior government official in Hong Kong since 1995 and would later serve a seven-year term as its Chief Executive.) But Tsang concurred with the cautious line dictated from London. 'We saw quite a number of competitors buying their way into China by simply taking equity stakes in local banks. We took a different line. We're a conservative bank, and we believed we had to be actively involved in the management. That was a key point.'[34]

In short, growth had to be organic. This did not preclude talks with some of the ten large private joint-stock banks in China – like those talks, already noted, with Bank of Communications in 2003 – but the quest for genuine engagement with them repeatedly ran into dead ends. The four giant state-owned banks from time to time also showed a lively interest in some possible alignment. 'Bank of China had proposed cooperation', the Board was told in February 2003, 'which, if brought to fruition, could transform Standard Chartered's position in China ... [and its approach] had been officially sanctioned at a senior level within the Chinese Government.'[35] But, as so often in the past, it proved a slow burn – and the Group's position remained untransformed.

Late in 2004, having acquired a licence for limited corporate business in renminbi, it was at last decided to push ahead with an incremental expansion of the mainland network. Tsang was appointed as Chief Executive for China – though her marching orders could scarcely have been more restrained:

> I remember asking Kai Nargolwala what he expected me to do. 'So Kai, is there a vision of the business in China that you'd like to see?' He said: 'Just be a good citizen!' We had been trying so hard to lift our profile. Now we were almost resigned to believing that, as long as the general trend went our way, we would be fine in the end. But it was difficult to have high expectations.[36]

Sadly, perhaps, the opportunity to reoccupy the bank's old head office at Bund 18 had by this point been allowed to slip away. The 1923 building had been reopened earlier in 2004 to widespread acclaim, after a year-long restoration by a firm of Italian architects. The mosaic floors and marbled walls were occupied now by luxury retailers, bars and restaurants.[37] But fresh branches were opened elsewhere, to take advantage of a gradual accumulation of licences. The Group was cleared to trade in foreign currencies in 2005; it was the first overseas bank to apply for a local retail licence in 2006; it reconstituted its China business as a subsidiary in 2007; and it launched the first yuan-denominated credit card to be issued by a foreign bank in 2008. By the latter year, its 150th in China, Standard Chartered had more than fifty outlets across seventeen cities and a glitzy new office tower in Shanghai with its name in lights on the top. In revenue terms, the transformation of the bank was a prodigious achievement: from $57 million in 2004, the top line had grown under Tsang to $575 million in five years, a compound annual growth rate of 80 per cent, with a commensurate growth in the workforce. Sustainable profits, though, still remained a distant goal. Consumer Banking accounted for most of the

expansion, and developing the network had entailed heavy costs, not least
to fund innovative computer systems (for which China's small network
was made a guinea pig for the wider Group). As for Wholesale Banking,
as Mike Rees recalled, it was tough going: 'China was still all about potential. It was difficult to do much business. Most of the money at that time
was being made by investment banks doing global IPOs [initial public
offerings of equity in Chinese corporations to Western investors], and we
weren't in that business.'[38] Standard Chartered's annual reports identified
many individual countries, in summarizing the Group's business and financial performance by territory, but China in 2008 was not among them: it
was still lurking in the text devoted to 'Other Asia Pacific'. This in no way
reflected any lack of genuine interest among the senior executives. Indeed,
Peter Sands had a particular personal interest in China – his wife was a
Mandarin speaker, and they visited the country together quite regularly –
but the Group's mainland business just seemed unlikely to take off in the
absence of a radical change to the macro-economic background.

Then came the Crisis of 2008–9. It caused the Beijing Government little
real concern within a domestic context. Red tape had been the bane of
bankers' lives in China for several years – new regulations appeared literally on a daily basis – but its compensating benefits were evident now in
the system's resilient response to events in the West. The response of the
US Government to the Crisis, however, and in particular its resort to
printing dollar bills ('Quantitative Easing' or simply 'QE') as part of the
battle to fend off another Great Depression, incensed officials in Beijing.
Their initial reaction was slightly despairing. A senior man from the China
Banking Regulatory Commission, Luo Ping, caught the mood with an
unusual display of vernacular English while attending a conference in New
York in February 2009. Mr Luo publicly berated his largely American
audience over the potential impact of a dose of dollar inflation on the value
of China's immense holdings of US Treasury bonds: ' "Once you start
issuing $1 trillion–$2 trillion . . . we know the dollar is going to depreciate
so we hate you guys – but there is nothing much we can do".'[39] Perhaps
there were indeed few immediate remedies; but officials in China soon
began to reappraise their de facto dependence on the US dollar, and to
question more urgently the wisdom of a long-standing veto on any role
for the renminbi (RMB) in international markets. Since 2003, individuals
resident in Hong Kong had been allowed to convert tiny sums into local
RMB deposits, but this nascent liberalization process had scarcely gone
much further in six years. Virtually all of China's foreign trade payments,
in both directions, were still being settled in dollars. This had been looking increasingly anomalous even before the Crisis, given the stellar

performance of the Chinese economy, and now matters came to a head. A decision was taken in Shanghai to explore ways of engaging with globalization trends more positively.

The city's Municipal Government invited executives from Standard Chartered to a meeting to discuss how Shanghai might turn itself into a leading financial centre of the world by 2020. Mike Rees and his colleagues needed no second invitation to step into this advisory role ('we consider China our birth country'[40]), and they followed up a visit in March 2009 with two lengthy papers. One looked at the essential characteristics of successful capital markets around the world. The other focused on the crucial role of moves properly to internationalize the RMB.[41] Strikingly, the Chinese authorities acknowledged from the outset that they would not be able to ordain the consequences of currency reform with detailed policy directives. (The Communists of 2009 were shrewder than the Nationalists of the 1930s in this respect.) It was accepted that the markets would very largely have to be left to dictate the pace of change. That said, China was not ready to expose its mainland economy to a total free-for-all on foreign exchange, nor were officials about to open the gates to capital flows in and out of the country. The approach urged in Shanghai by Rees and his colleagues offered a carefully calibrated compromise. It would provide a way of turning the RMB into an international currency by stages while stopping short of a fully liberalized currency regime. The key would lie with fostering a sophisticated off-shore RMB market, at least initially within the confines of Hong Kong, which would draw on pools of the currency that could be created outside China by allowing the use of RMB for trade payments. (No such pools yet existed: this was far from being a simple re-run of the eurodollar market's genesis in the 1950s.) A pilot scheme, dismantling the barriers to RMB invoicing, was rolled out by the Chinese government three months later. No doubt other international banks also played advisory roles here, but the detailed research and recommendations submitted by Standard Chartered were more than evident in the subsequent reform programme overseen by Beijing, and its consequences unfolded much as Rees and his team had anticipated. The dollar value of China's trade settled in RMB rose from $530 million in 2009 to more than $75 *billion* in 2010.[42] Over the fourteen months to August 2011, as chronicled in a later study of the RMB's international emergence by two of the Group's own economists in Hong Kong, Robert Minikin and Kelvin Lau, RMB deposits in Hong Kong climbed from less than 90 billion yuan to about 550 billion yuan.[43] This accumulation of capital provided 'an attractive laboratory for capital market innovation while avoiding the risk of major financial market failures on the mainland'.[44]

It also opened up extraordinary opportunities for Standard Chartered itself. Ben Hung, the Group's Chief Executive in Des Voeux Road, never had any doubt of the phenomenon's importance: as he would later tell colleagues at a senior management retreat in January 2014, 'this has to be the most exciting currency development that any of us will see in our banking lifetimes'.[45] Within four years of the first liberalization moves, RMB deposits were accounting for no less than 10 per cent of all the banking industry's deposits in Hong Kong, and about the same proportion of Standard Chartered's local balance sheet. As one of the three dominant banks (and three issuers of HK$ banknotes) in the former Colony, along-side HSBC and Bank of China, the Group enjoyed a privileged position at the heart of the markets that were soon flourishing on the back of these deposits – from spot and forward exchange markets to a wide range of debt and equity products designed for corporate treasurers needing to invest their new RMB surpluses. The Group took a leading role in several sectors. In particular, it managed the first corporate bond denominated in RMB, issued in August 2010 on behalf of McDonald's Corporation. At a seminar hosted by Standard Chartered the following month, 170 of the Group's clients were offered a couple of nicknames as labels for this new class of securities – should they be 'Dim Sum' or 'Kung Fu' bonds?[46] ('Big Mac' bonds were apparently not on the menu.) The vote went for Dim Sum, which was surely more in keeping with the heavily Cantonese flavour of the off-shore market. In the course of 2011 alone, bonds worth 190 billion yuan were issued in Hong Kong, fifty-six of the issues managed by Standard Chartered. The internationalization of the Chinese currency was not limited to Hong Kong, and the off-shore market soon extended to include Singapore and other centres (including London) beyond Beijing's jurisdiction, but Hong Kong remained its epicentre. The potential rewards for the Group seemed obvious. Unlike the state-owned Chinese banks, it could boast a rich network of connections among the many Western companies, from McDonald's and Nokia to BP and Rio Tinto, seeking to tap the off-shore RMB markets. And, in approaching them for business, it could point to a presence in Hong Kong and China far beyond anything available to most of the Group's rivals in the West.

These dramatic developments galvanized Standard Chartered's Whole-sale Banking business on the mainland. A respectable showing there – by 'Chartered Bank', as was still its mainland trading name in Chinese script – had to be an essential component of the Group's sales pitch around the world. The bank in Hong Kong remained, as ever, the jewel in Stand-ard Chartered's crown, with excellent returns on capital, a strong balance sheet and a broad range of products in Consumer and Wholesale banking that all enjoyed a solid share of their local markets. As its ties with the mainland had proliferated, and the host city itself had begun to shed its old colonial character, so, the business in Hong Kong had come to be in many ways an effective proxy for operations in China. Whatever its sparkle, though, the ex-colony could never really be a substitute for the mainland. So, just as the Crisis prodded the Chinese authorities into reappraising their stance on globalization, it also motivated the Group to make the most of its new opportunities in Shanghai and Guangzhou, Tianjin and Chongqing (Chungking). Wholesale profits in China by the end of 2009 were still meagre, but were palpably on the rise. Updating the Board ahead of IMF meetings in September 2009, Jaspal Bindra saw no cause for understatement: China was 'a relatively young business which was growing extremely fast and could well become the Group's biggest'. This was a notable observation. The rapid expansion of the Indian Wholesale Banking book was, by this point, one of the main engines driving the profits of the whole Group. To suggest that China might supplant India within any foreseeable time frame was striking indeed. (There was not much sign, meanwhile, of the Group losing its appetite for Indian loans. Reported lending to Indian customers, which until 2011 was only booked onshore, grew by more than 20 percent each year in 2008, 2009 and 2010. Moreover, loans then booked in London to some of India's largest global companies went on growing apace, thanks to the close relationships built up over the previous decade or so with many of India's largest multinationals.)

The Group enjoyed close relationships with many of the world's largest global companies that were now increasingly intent on trading with Chinese customers. To engage effectively with both the buyers and the sellers, it needed to ensure that its own presence in the Middle Kingdom had genuine depth. To this end, in 2010 it reconfigured its operations in China, Hong Kong and Taiwan as one regional franchise, 'Greater China' (to be chaired at the outset by Katherine Tsang). The volume of trade passing between the three territories was growing at an exponential rate.* The Group would now be better positioned to service the companies behind this expansion. The original aversion to investing in a Chinese bank was dropped, too, in a modest fashion. The Group's experience as a start-up investor in Bohai Bank, in Shandong province, had been a happy one to date: profitable almost since its launch in 2007, it now had sixty branches and sub-branches in fourteen cities. The original investment of $123 million was reckoned to

---

* Trade between Taiwan and the mainland jumped almost 40 per cent in 2010. By early 2011, there were nearly 400 direct flights between them every week – where none had been allowed at all before July 2008. (Standard Chartered 2010 Annual Report, p. 8.)

be worth over $1 billion, in the event of a public flotation.[47] Bohai Bank's growth gave the Group a presence in and around Tianjin – now emerging as a future financial centre perhaps even rivalling Shanghai, the country's undisputed commercial capital – and its success, mostly in the wholesale banking sector, had helped burnish the Group's reputation with the banking authorities. (Standard Chartered had seconded six individuals to Bohai Bank's management team, led by Alan Fung as its Vice-Chairman – a Cantonese-speaking officer of the bank in Hong Kong since 1970, who like many others since 1997 had had to learn Mandarin in a hurry.[48]) Encouraged by Bohai's progress, the Group was happy in 2010 to buy a tiny stake (less than 1 per cent, though it cost $500 million) in Agricultural Bank of China, one of the country's Big Four state-controlled banks and the only one to have virtually no exposure to the international markets at all.

The investment was a useful gesture, given the Agricultural Bank's vast domestic network, encompassing hundreds of corporate clients with a special interest in trade links with Africa. The relationship seems not to have generated much business in the end, but added to the impression of ties growing with Chinese banking as a whole. Europe's sovereign-debt crisis of 2011 contributed to this in a strikingly direct fashion: as the Group reduced its interbank lending in Europe, its lending to China's local banks rose like the other end of the see-saw. China loans were up to $36.5 billion by July 2012 'as a consequence of a deliberate transfer of ALM [asset-liability management] exposures from European banks that might be affected by the Eurozone crisis'.[49] (A striking token, perhaps, of China's emerging importance at Europe's expense.) Operating profits for the China Wholesale business, meanwhile, were rising encouragingly – up from $165 million in 2010 to $361 million in 2013. These numbers were scarcely impressive by comparison with Wholesale profits in Hong Kong (up from $753 million in 2010 to $1,293 million in 2013), but how much of Hong Kong's income was now indirectly attributable to the Group's rising profile in mainland China none could be too sure, and only the accountants could decree. And the same applied well beyond Greater China: shareholders were assured in the 2011 Annual Report that 'income from Chinese clients booked elsewhere in our network grew at over three times the pace of onshore [that is, mainland] client income'.[50]

For Consumer Banking, the mainland prospects were more problematic. Here executives encountered exactly the same paradox as had tantalized generations of their predecessors, extending back into the nineteenth century. As ever, China represented a vast market with unparalleled prospects; and, as ever, hard profits always seemed so elusive. The sheer scale of the domestic economy by the second decade of the twenty-first century was breathtaking. The Group's own economists prepared a chart for City analysts that conveyed this with some elegance. It listed the ten countries that topped the standard league table of the world's Emerging Markets in Africa and Asia (omitting China and India) and set beside them the dozen largest provinces and cities in China. All were ranked with their respective Gross Domestic Product numbers for 2012. The aggregate GDP of the Chinese dozen easily exceeded that of the ten Emerging Markets ($5.6 billion compared with $4.7 billion, respectively). And all of the Chinese dozen could boast projected growth rates of 8–13 per cent annually for the next five years. Armed with charts like this, the Group's retail bankers marched on with the expansion of their network. It almost doubled in size across twenty-five cities within four years, adding its 100th branch early in 2013. The challenge, of course, was to render this a meaningful milestone in a country with a population of 1.4 billion people already served by more than 40,000 banking outlets. Probably all the foreign banks in China taken together shared less than 2 per cent of a market that was slewed against outsiders in countless ways. Unsurprisingly, many observers – including some of the City's foremost analysts – had yet to be persuaded of the case for expanding in such a difficult marketplace. (How long was the Group ready to go on accommodating substantial losses as part of a coherent strategy?) It was clearly essential to focus on some narrowly defined goals, and for Standard Chartered these would mostly relate to the delivery of exemplary products and services for the wealthiest of China's new capitalist classes.* Not the least attractive feature of this business was that it lapped across the borders of Greater China, rather like Wholesale Banking: of the 20,000 or so new customer accounts opened in Hong Kong in 2012, roughly half were owned by individuals resident on the mainland.[51] Even a disciplined pursuit of well-heeled retail customers, though, showed little sign by 2012 of stemming steady losses in Consumer Banking, running at around $100 million a year. They were heavy enough to dent the profitability of the Group's entire operation on the mainland. As Richard Meddings noted in December 2012, 'China

---

* It was also hoped that the Group might come to be seen as the foreign bank of choice for the country's small and medium-sized enterprise (SME) sector. Though tiny within a domestic context, the Group's network could offer essential connections for customers intent on cementing a role as suppliers to large overseas companies. This added another twist to the story of the Group's support for Hong Kong's textile industry, when Esquel turned to Standard Chartered for help in financing the cotton farmers of Xinjiang, to the far west of China. Nor was this the Group's only foray into some of the remoter regions of the country: it also set up an operation lending to grain farmers in China's Inner Mongolia province, and was the first foreign bank to open a branch in the provincial capital of Hohhot.

posed a particular challenge in terms of balancing a long-term strategic imperative against enhancing current inadequate returns'.[52] For anyone with a sense of China's history, that had a familiar ring about it, as did a proposal early in 2013 to concentrate Consumer Banking's expansion on just five core cities – though of course not all sat on the coast like the old treaty ports.[53]

4. SEIZING THE FUTURE, RECALLING THE PAST

For almost four years after the collapse of Lehman, Standard Chartered's executives explicitly set about stealing a march on most of their rivals in a deeply beleaguered industry. Signs of their apparent success mounted impressively. Revenues and profits went on climbing from year to year, as they had been doing since 2003. Total assets by December 2012 ($637 billion) were very nearly twice those reported before the Crisis ($330 billion in December 2007). There may have been other international banks that doubled in size over this period – though not many – but assuredly none operating at the same global level. It was a performance that seemed to defy the woes of Western banking with some élan. Investors acknowledged as much, pushing the share price dramatically higher over the first two post-Lehman years (up from about £10 at the end of October 2008 to more than £19 by November 2010). Thereafter the price fell back, but well into 2012 the market still appeared ready to settle for a consolidation of the Group's premium rating, leaving the shares trading around the £14 mark. Most analysts were happy to assess the Group's more adventurous strategic imperatives – as in China, for instance, or in taking aboard a much expanded portfolio of loans to commodity producers – in a trusting and indulgent frame of mind. Standard Chartered's business model had delivered such a strong performance for so many years that backing it had become one of the more popular ways, even before 2008, for fund managers to participate in the general enthusiasm over Asia's Emerging Markets. After 2008, the calamitous setbacks for the financial sector in the West generally, and the gathering gloom in the Eurozone over the viability of its banks in particular, only further enhanced the allure of investing in both Asia and Africa, adding steadily to the appeal of Standard Chartered's singular profile.

Singular, but far from static. Indeed, in one particular respect the years immediately after 2008 saw a significant evolution of the Group's business model. It was a development of particular interest to the new Chairman (knighted in 2011), Sir John Peace. His own business career had been built on turning assorted computerized systems into the giant Experian credit-checking business. Now he found himself taking the Chair at the start of a new era for the business, as he would recall in 2014:

> I've watched the whole industry evolving. The impact of changing technology has been extraordinary. You could pick out three milestones on the road we travelled prior to 2008: the establishment of our hub offices, the creation of one global platform for transactional banking and the integration of our Consumer Banking operations. But since the Crisis we've seen things happening that were scarcely dreamt about a decade ago. It's now a digital world and that is changing everything.[54]

When Peace joined the Board, in 2007, the initial restructuring of the Group's three most basic computer systems under Jan Verplancke's guidance had just been coming to fruition – but Standard Chartered's total investment in online banking had scarcely reached $3 million for the year. This had left the Group trailing some distance behind those in the van of online retail services, which had been growing rapidly since the mid-1990s. Verplancke was the man charged with ensuring it caught up – while at the same time watching over a global telecoms network of daunting complexity. (To sustain the network across the Group's branches, in forty-six countries, as the Belgian pointed out to the Board in 2010, the Group had 12,000 servers that stored more than 2.4 petabytes of data in support of 80,000 staff computers and 10,000 mobile devices. People across the network sent and received about 2.25 million emails *daily* – and were saved from 1.7 million spam emails and the attempted intrusion each day of no fewer than 70,000 viruses.[55]) Verplancke's own favourite metaphor would apply throughout the next few years – the car could not be stopped, while the engine was being radically overhauled – but he pulled off this magical feat of mechanics to some acclaim, turning Standard Chartered by 2012 into a much more plausible exponent of internet banking.

Nothing exemplified this success better than the Group's bold embrace of the dawning mobile era. During 2010, Verplancke caused a stir in the digital marketplace by aligning Standard Chartered with Apple, when most other banks were still tied to BlackBerry. It was a shrewd move, given the Group's focus in most retail markets on well-heeled customers and aspiring young professionals, as opposed to the broader mass market. That same focus was at the core of Apple's brand – and iPhone and iPad were also designed to be simple and fun, which was how Verplancke wanted Standard Chartered's mobile product to be seen. 'Our customers basically needed just two functions: to look at their money, and to move it. So they had no need of dozens of other features, cluttering up the screen. We cut all the frills and went for style instead.'[56] The result was Standard Chartered Breeze, launched in Singapore. It was an instant hit, and an early winner of several industry awards for mobile banking. Within a few years, about 30 per cent of all the Group's retail transactions across the world would be passing via mobile channels – roughly the same proportion as was handled online. From the start, several apps were also launched on the iPhone and iPad for the use of the Group's own staff, tailored to in-house systems. This brought an unexpected bonus. When Apple in 2011 launched a series of advertisements that profiled large corporations working with its products, it chose Standard Chartered to show what was happening in Asian banking. A three-minute video captured young executives on the hoof, usually pausing against spectacular urban backdrops, to summon the numbers they needed at the touch of a button. One of the apps provided live foreign-exchange data – quoting currencies as easily as the time of day, where long ago hundreds of clerks and telegraphy stations had once laboured to report a range of the previous day's rates. As narrated by the softly spoken, polo-necked Verplancke, the digital environment was now a working platform for 'commerce that is enabled in a different way'.

There was speculation in the City by 2012 that the location of the Group's Head Office might also be 'enabled in a different way', with technology facilitating a move away from the UK. Historically, the British overseas banks had been based in London in order to tap the capital resources made available by the City. This rationale continued to apply for much of the second half of the twentieth century, given the importance of the City's foreign exchange markets, the growth of the eurodollar sector and Big Bang's transformation of the City's competitive environment. Once the leading capital markets of Asia had begun emerging as fully-fledged rivals, by the turn of the millennium, Standard Chartered had been happy to extol the value of London as a neutral base that precluded any need to choose between other possible locations (meaning, in practice, Singapore and Hong Kong). By the end of the new century's first decade, though, the notion of domiciling the Group within Asia ceased to be quite as far-fetched as hitherto. Most of the additional 60,000 people recruited to the workforce since 1999 were citizens of Asian countries. In a host of ways, Standard Chartered had become essentially an Asian business, with a supporting presence in Africa. Less fundamental but rather more newsworthy, at least to the media based in London, was the adoption by the UK Government in 2011 of a new tax on banks, to be calculated – in the case of UK-based banks – on the value of their global balance sheets. The percentage rate applicable under 'the UK bank levy' climbed steadily higher in each of the next four years, and added materially to Standard Chartered's business costs – or, to be more precise, to the cost to the Group of doing business as a UK company.* These developments led some observers to wonder whether a move to Asia might really be in prospect – a line of speculation that was encouraged by an announcement from HSBC in April 2015 that it was formally considering the relocation of its head office, transferred from Hong Kong to the UK in 1993 (an option HSBC ended up rejecting a year later). Might not Singapore, especially, soon be as eligible an anchor as London for the network as a whole? Perhaps, however, the very concept of an anchor was now outdated. Senior executives could be in constant communication with any part of the network they chose, subject only to the constraints of the clock. In a digital world, the Group effectively answered to a *virtual* head office in the electronic ether – the ultimate embodiment of the concept behind those Inspectors of Agencies who travelled so intrepidly round the Chartered's Victorian network. So, in weighing answers to the domicile question, sophisticated technologies would count for less than the entrenched legal structures of the Group. And with so many of its businesses long established (unlike HSBC's) as subsidiaries of the UK parent company, this implied a strong case for remaining in the City.

The arrival of the digital era had one other intriguing dimension. For Standard Chartered (and all its rivals), enabling customers to access its services via new media posed a formidable marketing challenge. A bank's image and reputation were more critical than ever in winning and sustaining the loyalty of customers, in a ferociously competitive digital marketplace. But cultivating brand identities now involved a lot more than letter fonts, branch designs and colour schemes, given the fast-dwindling importance of physical premises. Every commercial bank in Asia needed to find more effective ways of flagging its name in front of huge audiences on a frequent basis. The challenge was especially acute for Standard Chartered, competing in most national markets against far better known domestic rivals with bigger local networks. For some years past, like other giant international banks, the Group had at least been able to offer

---

* The levy was not tax-deductible. Introduced in 2011 at a rate of 0.078 per cent of total liabilities (subject to various exemptions), the levy in its first year cost Standard Chartered $165 million, equivalent to 3.7 per cent of post-tax profits. By 2014, the rate had risen to 0.156 per cent, costing the Group $366 million, equivalent to 13.5 per cent of post-tax profits. The cost in 2015, according to mid-year estimates by the Group, would be around $540 million. By way of comparison, the Group paid total taxes (i.e. not including the levy) in 2014 of $1,530 million, implying a tax rate of 36.1 per cent. Of this global bill, the UK tax charge for 2014 was $161 million.

products and services less readily devised and marketed by local banks lacking global scale and expertise. This was still true as of the immediate post-Crisis years – but seemed unlikely to remain so for much longer. Digital technology would be the great leveller, leaving the smaller local banks in effect equally well resourced and posing a far greater threat. (Especially potent might be some of the nimbler regional banks – like Asia's ANZ Bank and Africa's Standard Bank (alas!) – that could combine a strong national expertise with a useful cross-border presence in neighbouring countries.) Nor were local banks likely to be the only beneficiaries of the digital upheaval. Banking was fast turning into a business open in principle to any large company with well-organized data covering a broad client base, from supermarkets to mobile phone operators. In short, Standard Chartered was in need of some bright marketing ideas in the aftermath of the Crisis if it was going to sustain its push into consumer banking since the 1990s, especially in its core Asian markets.

At a tactical level, the bank had been open for some time to the notion of a more active marketing of its name. This had already reaped an unexpected reward. Out of nowhere in May 2009 had come an approach from Manchester United Football Club – arguably the most famous football club in the world – asking if the Group would like to bid $40 million a year for the privilege of sponsoring its team shirt.[57] To date, the Group's sports sponsorship had been restricted to support for a handful of marathons around the world – a worthy cause, but not one with mass appeal. The phenomenal following for the English Premier League across the whole of Asia put the concept of a football-shirt logo into, well, another league. Regular television coverage of English club football reached several hundred million homes worldwide; it was beamed into more or less every late-night watering hole from Hong Kong to Singapore at weekends. For all its instant appeal, though, the lasting value of a shirt logo would depend on a genuine sense of partnership with the sponsored club. Weeks of tough negotiation with MUFC brought interminable nitpicking over the contract details, and in the end the Group was outflanked by a rival bid.[58] Despite this frustrating outcome, the project left all those involved at Basinghall Avenue, including the Board, totally persuaded of the charms of having Standard Chartered's logo on the TV screens of Asia on most weekends of the English soccer season – so the hunt was on for another eligible club. Chelsea and Arsenal had just been crossed off the list when word reached the sponsorship team in July that Liverpool FC was in the market. Word spread even faster round the whole of the Group, when an initial meeting between the two sides at Basinghall Avenue was attended by Kenny Dalglish, a former player (and then player-manager) widely believed by Liverpool fans to have walked on water for most of the 1980s. By the middle of September, the Group had signed on with the famous club from Anfield for a four-year contract – the price remained confidential – kicking off in the 2010–11 season. The success of the arrangement, later renewed well beyond 2014, surpassed all expectations. On the pitch, the Group struck gold: in February 2011, the club signed a new Uruguayan star, Luis Suárez, who over the two seasons starting in August 2012 would score more goals than any other Premier League player by some distance. (And starting in 2015, under the management of Jürgen Klopp, the club would enjoy one of the most successful eras in its history, winning many trophies including the English Premier League in 2019–20 – see Plate 40.) The link with Anfield led to a high level of staff engagement with the Liverpool team's league performance. 'When we had a dress-down day in Indonesia,' recalled the Group's main negotiator, Gavin Laws, 'many of the employees would come to work in a Liverpool shirt!'[59] It helped to foster a busy programme of community work and without doubt boosted awareness of the Group's brand in Asia hugely over the next few years: independent research completed early in 2015 suggested that, across Consumer Banking's targeted retail markets, those individuals aware of the Liverpool sponsorship were roughly 50 per cent more likely to consider using Standard Chartered for their banking needs.[60]

Running in parallel with the football-sponsorship negotiations in 2009, meanwhile, was a more strategic debate over the fundamentals of the Group's marketing stance. Winning more attention for the name was a simple matter compared with deciding what that name ought ideally to convey, if Standard Chartered was to sustain a world-beating brand. Competing advertising agencies were invited to pitch their ideas. Sands and his colleagues went for a campaign proposed by TBWA, part of the Omnicom Group and a large international branding consultancy with a long list of illustrious corporate clients (including Apple). It put forward what it called 'a lighthouse strategy', asserting the Group's ability to stand out starkly amidst the gloom pervading the rest of the industry. In differentiating Standard Chartered from the rest, there was an obvious tool to hand. Few of its peers enjoyed anything like its historical pedigree. Somehow turning this to the Group's advantage would be central to the campaign. And, for those charged with the task, there were two echoes of the past in particular that, in the taut circumstances of the post-Crisis world, had a special resonance. TBWA presented the Group with a marketing logo that caught both with a useful (not to say insouciant) pun, 'Here for good'.[61]

The first involved the old Chartered Bank's traditional image of itself as an organization sprung from the Victorian perception of the City's overseas banks, as institutions that combined business realities with a sense of civic responsibility. In the days of Empire, City grandees could see the transfer of capital and the extension of trade-financing skills to the agrarian economies of Asia and the colonies of southern Africa not just as an attractive investment but also as an enlightened and socially laudable activity, too. And as the early chapters of this history illustrated at many points, the Chartered's role overseas was often treated as a hybrid of commerce and quasi-public service by the bank's staff and customers alike. After the events of 2008 – and after the protracted changes wrought in the City itself through the twenty-five years or so that followed the Big Bang of the mid-1980s – a bank openly proclaiming such an image of itself ran the risk of being ridiculed. Nonetheless, a sense of the Chartered's past had undoubtedly lingered on within Standard Chartered. It still retained, even (perhaps especially) after the Crisis, a notion of itself as an intermediary between the world's capital markets and the capital-hungry businesses of the Emerging Markets world – a bridge between East and West, as advertised regularly in the Group's corporate literature. It was a self-image reflected in the employees' impassioned support for Seeing Is Believing, a charity construed by most people inside the Group as an entirely appropriate expression of their desire to see it do more than just make money. Building on this consensus, Peter Sands and his colleagues wholly endorsed the notion of defying the prevailing hostility towards the banking world and asserting the values that in their view still made Standard Chartered a unique institution. They would seek to draw on a shared sense of the past as a way of regaining some of the high moral ground closed to so much of the competition. As a first practical step, towards the end of 2009, they commissioned a rigorous documentation of the ways in which the Group's activities across Africa and Asia were 'Here for good', contributing materially to the well-being of local economies. Two independent economists were asked to present quantitative assessments of the Group's impact in selected countries.* Their first reports examined the evidence in Ghana and in Indonesia, and were published in 2010. Subsequent reports, produced in 2012 and 2014, looked at the record of the Group in Bangladesh and in sub-Saharan Africa.[62]

The other aspect of the Group's history caught in 'Here for good' also featured a conspicuous trait of the old Chartered Bank, namely the

---

* The authors were Professor Ethan B. Kapstein, a luminary of the INSEAD international business school and author of numerous books and academic papers on economic policy-making, and René Kim, a Dutch economist and partner in a private consulting firm in the Netherlands, Steward Redqueen. A disclaimer in all the reports would note that they expressed the authors' views, not those of Standard Chartered or indeed INSEAD.

Chartered's long-standing aversion to abandoning any geographical market in which it had once established a presence – or, indeed, any customer once an account had been opened. (The proposed logo accorded well with the Group's long-standing espousal of customer-oriented banking, as opposed to the transaction-driven approach adopted by so many of its peers.) Of course, Standard Chartered since 1969 had abandoned both its Western strategy and its South African legacy, so 'Here for good' was not to be taken too literally. But it fairly caught the spirit of the Chartered's past in Asia and sub-Saharan Africa. From its earliest days, Chartered had always set great store by its reputation in the East as a bank that would stand its ground and protect customers' interests, however inclement the political or economic weather. For generations this had simply been a commercial necessity in most of its port-city domains, where several foreign banks jostled for business and none could afford to risk being seen by customers as a fair-weather friend. In post-war times, the same mindset had endured despite the vicissitudes of the shrinking Empire. In those few cases where hostile governments had eventually forced its withdrawal – as in Burma and Iraq in the 1960s – the bank's final exit had followed years of discomfort and occasional danger for Chartered's resilient men on the spot. Nowhere saw the bank clinging on more desperately than in China after 1949 – and the threadbare presence that had survived there since 1955 was regularly cited in later decades as entirely characteristic of the bank's stubborn reaction to political adversity.

Standard Chartered since 1969 had had its own list of hardship postings, and its own record of banking in places torn apart by civil war – from South Vietnam in the early 1970s to Sierra Leone in the 1990s. Certainly the Group believed itself, not unreasonably, to have inherited a genuine propensity for running branches successfully in risky and unfamiliar locations. This had once meant islands and archipelagos without roads or railways. In the twenty-first century it generally meant territories long closed to outsiders but gradually reopening – from Angola and Mozambique to Cambodia and Indonesia. In some territories, civil war was still an all but insuperable obstacle, but Standard Chartered was prepared to explore the scope for a return quicker than most. In Iraq after the US-led invasion of 2003, many large multinational companies, in civil engineering and telecoms as well as oil and gas, had a pressing need for local banking services. The Group was a founding member that year of the Trade Bank of Iraq, a consortium of foreign banks offering facilities for international trade. In 2006, it opened a representative office in Erbil, in the Kurdish region of the country. As of 2010, it was awaiting a suitable opportunity – only finally realized three years later – to reopen a branch in Baghdad. In other places, notably Myanmar (formerly Burma) and Iran, the critical difficulties sprang less from current fighting on the ground than from the complexion of the ruling regime and the refusal of the international community – meaning essentially the authorities in the US – to countenance any full revival of banking relationships pending serious changes in that regime's stance towards the outside world. (Standard Chartered had more than once found itself accused of sustaining a presence on the ground that was rejected by the world at large as an unacceptable degree of complicity.* Here was an awkward product of its historical disposition to extend its operations in Asia and Africa to embrace places avoided by most other Western banks, or only served by them intermittently.)

'Here for good' was not adopted lightly. In the event of some seriously damaging disclosures about this or that aspect of its banking activities, the scope for public derision was obvious. Some executives worried that adopting the logo for general advertising purposes would indeed amount to a leading of the corporate chin. Even assuming an unblemished record of blameless banking for years to come, it might smack to some of hubris and self-regard. (The Group already had its critics in the City of London, by 2011, for making presentations that verged on the hubristic.) But soundings among both staff and customers satisfied the top team that the risk was worth taking. The response internally was seen as highly encouraging. Many felt strongly that Standard Chartered was indeed a different animal from its peers, and ought not to be afraid of asserting so. And the logo played to the fact that the Group still retained a lively sense of its past – perhaps oddly so, given the explosive growth of the workforce since the 1990s. Longevity was seen all over the network as a mainstay of the Group's reputation, even by those to whom ancient banknotes and faded ledger books in glass cases here and there were something of a mystery. (This awareness probably owed something to the unusual continuity of Standard Chartered's customer base. Inevitably, many of the largest companies in each of its host countries had had dealings with the Group over many years – but these reminders of the past probably carried less weight

---

* Thus, after a thirty-year absence from Myanmar's capital, it had opened a representative office in 1994, confirming letters of credit opened by local Myanmar banks. But US and European Union sanctions had obliged the Group to withdraw in 2004. By the start of 2010, renewed hopes of liberalization and an easing of sanctions suggested another reopening might soon be possible (though, in the event, the bank chose in 2014 not to apply for one of the licences issued to foreign banks in a first wave of liberalization). In Iran, Standard Chartered's correspondent banking role after 2001 had boosted its business. Disquiet in US regulatory and legal circles over the compatibility of its role with US trade sanctions had led the Group in March 2007 to discontinue its dollar-based business with Iran (and business in any currency by August 2007). It was to pay a heavy price, though, for past transgressions that would surface later.

When businesses succeed, livelihoods flourish.

In 2009, we took the initiative to be first to align with the World Bank Group in boosting global trade flows. Since then, we have continued to be proactive in encouraging growth across our markets. As trade is the lifeblood of the local economy, our commitment does more than protect businesses. It stimulates the communities that depend on them.

Here for good

Advertising copy for the 'Here for good' campaign launched in April 2010

with employees than the many private clients who were apt to remind younger Standard Chartered managers that they kept an account with the bank because their father and their grandfather had done so before them.) Longevity was a feature of many individual careers within the Group, too. Despite the addition of many outsiders hired from other (mostly American) banks in recent times, around a fifth of the top 300 echelon of managers in 2010 had worked at Standard Chartered for more than twenty years – another variant, perhaps, on the theme of 'Here for good'.[63]

In short, as a branding campaign 'Here for good' exactly matched the aspirations of Sands and his senior colleagues – and by April 2010 they were ready to unveil it. Office walls all over the Group, in stairwells and reception areas, were adorned with mounted boards that proclaimed a robust manifesto ('Can a bank really stand for something? Can it balance its ambitions with its conscience? To do what it must. Not what it can. As not everything in life that counts can be counted . . .') A television, print and digital campaign rolled out the newly assertive image of itself that the Group would now seek to foster. The impact was immediate and gratifying. Marketing data gathered over the first six months of the campaign suggested a much improved awareness of the Group's brand, especially in Hong Kong, and the staff reaction was overwhelmingly positive. As Peter Sands could later recall: 'The sentiments behind the "Here for good" campaign were and remain a much bigger motivating factor for the bank and its staff than many outsiders might appreciate.'[64] The publication of the first of the 'Social and Economic Impact' papers a few months later gave Sands himself the chance in his own words to place the new marketing tag in the context of the Group's operations on the ground – and its fast-rising ambitions:

> Given the uncertainties [in the post-Crisis] world about the prospects for sustainable growth, not surprisingly public trust and confidence in banks and political support for the [banking] industry has declined sharply. In this context, we know we must play our part in restoring trust in the financial system and in supporting recovery in the real economy. This requires honesty and rigour in acknowledging what has gone wrong . . .
>
> In Ghana and across all our markets, we are committed to being 'Here for good'. We have a clear strategy – to become the world's best international bank, leading the way in Asia, Africa and the Middle East. We have a powerful culture, with a pervasive sense of shared values and shared stories. Standard Chartered is committed to building a sustainable business as a bank, simultaneously creating value for our shareholders, supporting our clients and customers and contributing to the communities in which we live and work.

The Ghana paper inevitably attracted scant media attention, though its appearance was at least noted by the *Financial Times*. ('The initiative comes amid public criticism of banks and bankers for their role in causing the financial crisis, and a subsequent debate about the social usefulness of banks' activities', noted its banking correspondent, dutifully adding for the record: 'Mr Sands denied that the 43-page report . . . was a publicity stunt.'[65]) But the Chief Executive's Preface was a fair measure of the prevailing mood inside the Group over the next couple of years. The notion that Standard Chartered might indeed become 'the world's best international bank' did not seem fanciful. The vibrant internal culture spawned by a decade of growth was now attracting coverage in the academic world as well as the business and financial media: Peter Sands was profiled (along with Mervyn Davies) by *Harvard Business Review*, among a clutch of prototypes supposedly exemplifying a new class of successful corporate bosses.[66] Three months later, at the end of 2011, the Group featured prominently in a second *Harvard Business Review* article with nothing but praise for its business model, and a warm endorsement of the claims behind 'Here for good': 'SCB is part of the fabric of the communities in which it operates.'[67] Meanwhile, the operating results continued to extend the powerful run enjoyed by the Group since 2003. Operating income rose by 6 per cent in 2010 and another 10 per cent in 2011. On 1 August 2012, Sir John Peace and Peter Sands were able to announce record earnings for the first half of the year, for the tenth consecutive year. This remarkable feat was hailed by them as a vindication of the Group's consistency and attention to the mundane details of commercial banking ('It may seem boring in contrast to what is going on elsewhere,' declared Sands, 'but we see some virtue in being boring.'[68]). Apart from a few warnings about the dangers of executive hubris, the financial press was broadly unanimous in acclaiming the Interim results as further proof of the Group's ascendancy. Indeed, it seemed to many commentators that Standard Chartered had begun to acquire a sheen of invincibility. It was the stock market's favourite Western bank, powering ahead in the world's fastest growing economies with a much envied business model and a distinctive internal culture, while preserving a cool detachment from the turmoil in the rest of the banking world. As some of the more ebullient broking reports by the summer of 2012 came close to asking explicitly, what could possibly go wrong?

Postscript

Things began to go awry for the Group rather dramatically within days of the 2012 Interim Results press conference, and events thereafter greatly compounded its difficulties in a multitude of ways. By the spring of 2015, after a vertiginous drop in the share price, the Group found itself drawing a line across the years since 2003 and heading for another fundamental reappraisal of its business model. As in 1974 and again in 1988 – albeit within an immeasurably grander and more robust operational setting – a change in the leadership of the Group seemed likely to result in a new set of bearings for the future. This was a sudden and wholly unexpected turn of events that demands a brief summary.

Five days after the 2012 Interims press conference, just as the City was starting to shut up shop for its August summer break, an order was issued in Manhattan by the Superintendent of New York's Department of Financial Services (DFS), Benjamin Lawsky. It charged the Group with flouting US sanctions against Iran, and alleged that it had 'left the US financial system vulnerable to terrorists, weapons dealers, drug kingpins and corrupt regimes, and deprived law enforcement investigators of crucial information used to track all manner of criminal activity'.[1] This did not sit well, to put it mildly, with the tenets of 'Here for good'. Employees across the world were stunned. The impact on the Group's share price was also immediate and severe: in London the next day, it dropped by 25 per cent before recovering slightly by the close. To most of the staff, as to the outside world, the DFS statement appeared to have struck as lightning from the blue. In fact, it marked the breaking of a crisis that had been several years in the making. The Group's correspondent banking services for Iran's central bank and largest commercial banks between 2001 and 2007, noted earlier (see pp. 673–4), had always been subject to US government sanctions against dollar-denominated trade with Iran. Two internal reviews conducted in 2004–5 and in 2005–6 had given rise to serious concern within the Group over its past record on compliance issues. After further internal investigations, senior executives had concluded that the Group had indeed conducted transactions in violation of US sanctions. Several other banks had already reached out-of-court settlements with the US authorities for sanction transgressions. The Group had decided in January 2010 'to self-report its conduct'.[2] This had now led to the charges being brought by those authorities.* The Manhattan branch handled transactions worth around $195 billion every day – it was in fact the seventh-largest dollar clearer in the world – so none could doubt the gravity of the matter.

The immediate outcome, finalized for signature on 21 September 2012, was a settlement with the DFS that included a civil penalty of $340 million, along with terms and conditions for the appointment of a 'Compliance Monitor', a third party to be accommodated within the New York branch and charged with conducting a wide-ranging review of compliance matters.[3] A resolution had still to be reached with all of the other relevant US authorities, notably the Department of Justice (DoJ) and the New York County District Attorney in relation to possible violations of both Federal and New York State law. Further negotiations ensued. On 10 December, a press release from the DoJ confirmed that a 'Deferred Prosecution Agreement' (DPA) had been agreed on the basis of concurrence about what had actually happened during the period under investigation. This DPA meant the Group would not have to face indictment in a Federal court, in exchange for agreeing to a forfeiture of $227 million and accepting 'responsibility for its criminal conduct and that of its employees'. Other regulatory issues were settled as part of this agreement, involving a civil monetary penalty of $100 million, imposed by the Board of the Federal Reserve. (A fourth fine of $132 million, imposed by the Office of Foreign Assets Control, would in effect be deemed to have been paid by settlement of the DoJ/Federal Reserve figures.) So the cost to Standard Chartered by the end of 2012 ended up at $667 million – without taking account of the many millions incurred as the cost of the Group's own internal inquiries. It was enough, as one senior US regulator wryly opined, to 'make clear that trying to skirt US sanctions is bad for business'.[4]

---

* The authorities comprised both prosecutors and regulators. The prosecutorial bodies were the Department of Justice and the Office of the District Attorney for New York. The regulatory agencies were the New York Federal Reserve and the New York State Department of Financial Services, which was a recent creation amalgamating New York's State Insurance and State Banking departments. Also involved was the Office of Foreign Assets Control (OFAC), a department of the US Treasury responsible for the authorization and enforcement of US trade and economic sanctions.

All large international banks, especially those based in London and New York, had meanwhile had to adjust after the Global Financial Crisis to a sea-change in their regulatory environment. The Group's Legal & Compliance (L&C) function at the start of 2008 had employed fewer than a thousand people, with barely a dozen working at the centre of its Consumer Banking business.[5] New professional managers had subsequently been hired externally, and staff numbers had begun to rise. But 'Conduct of Business' – that is to say, ensuring a proper adherence to the rules and conventions of the financial marketplace – was not the only discipline needing urgent attention. The Compliance function also embraced all things relating to the increasingly fraught world of regulation and the prevention of financial crime, most notably money laundering and the financing of terrorists. Here, as was made graphically apparent by the 2012 charges brought against the Group by the US authorities in relation to Iran, new resource investments and a general strengthening of financial crime controls had yet to become a major priority for Standard Chartered. For years, most of the impetus for tougher regulation of the banking industry had stemmed from the work of government agencies in the US: the big American banks had responded to these regulatory pressures by expanding their in-house compliance departments accordingly. Having disposed of its pre-1989 physical banking network within the US, Standard Chartered had not followed their example, and had not yet undertaken sufficient efforts to upgrade its sanctions and money-laundering compliance and controls. This leisurely approach, it transpired, had taken too little heed of the global role of the dollar and the readiness of the authorities in New York and Washington, especially after the Crisis, to enforce their regulatory regime on a similarly global basis. As a direct result of its 2012 settlements in the US, the expansion of the Group's L&C function from early in 2013 took on a new momentum and intensity.

A fresh executive post was created to provide stronger leadership for the in-house legal team, bearing the US-style moniker of Group General Counsel. The first man appointed to the role, David Fein, was a former United States Attorney for the District of Connecticut, so there was no mistaking the message.* He was to take charge of advising the Board and senior management 'on all material legal issues'.[6] On the Compliance side

---

* Nominated by President Obama in 2010, Fein had previously been Vice Chairman of the US Attorney General's Advisory Committee's White Collar Crime Sub-Committee. Among various other prominent jobs held in Washington, he had served as Associate White House Counsel under President Clinton.

of L&C, a huge (and hugely expensive) effort went into ensuring that the Group's operations lived up to the spirit of the 'Here for good' manifesto that had just been adopted. The Conduct agenda also saw the rise of the Operational Risk function, and the adoption of much more rigorous controls on lending across the network. Indeed, the governance of operational risk was rapidly coming to be seen as one of the most critical issues facing the Group.[7] But it was undoubtedly in the context of regulatory affairs and financial-crime prevention that the Group's changed approach from 2013 was most apparent to the workforce at all levels. Professional compliance experts appointed in 2008–9 had been pressing hard for their function to be treated as a priority by top management. Now their urging was heeded as a major transformation of Standard Chartered's financial-crime controls was undertaken. All banks were having to adjust to a regulatory environment in which it was no longer sufficient for them to have investigated the integrity of their business contacts: 'Know Your Customer' needed bundling with 'Know Your Customer's Customer'. Like so many of its peers across the banking industry, Standard Chartered reacted by pressing into service large numbers of internal 'watchdog' personnel. They included dozens of compliance professionals and trained lawyers with extensive in-house experience from other financial institutions, as well as auditors, ex-regulators and even a smattering of former Group operations executives and frontline staff. The L&C function's headcount by the end of 2014 was 2,500, and still rising. And, *pari passu* with all this busy recruiting, regulatory compliance was steadily transformed into an integral part of the daily business of banking. Under new management the L&C function acquired a wholly altered status, which was impressed upon the rest of the Group via a flurry of seminars and conferences through 2013–14.

In short, the shock of the charges relating to the Iranian business – coming on top of the wider regulatory storms that had followed the Crisis – had by 2014 prompted important changes to the structure and culture of the organization that could be seen to have marked a radical break with the past. Unfortunately, the operational performance of the Group had meanwhile suffered a parallel break with the past that was even more disruptive. The self-esteem of the Group and its prestigious standing with investors had been knocked hard by the US disclosures. But evidence had also mounted steadily over this same period that the much acclaimed 'stealing-a-march' strategy of 2008–12 had been implemented at a heavy price. The market's trust in the fundamental profitability of Standard Chartered's business model had been severely shaken.

The first signs of trouble surfaced late in 2012, when margins began to shrink on the day-to-day business of financing trade customers and the volume of questionable corporate loans suddenly soared: impairments for 2012 rose by 30 per cent over the previous year. Thereafter, the Group increasingly found itself running foul of a reversal that unfolded with a terrible logic. China's growth rate slowed abruptly, putting a drag on regional economies across Asia. As Far Eastern demand for all basic commodities fell away, the long boom in world commodity prices gave way to a precipitous collapse: most fell by 50–80 per cent. Inevitably, the scale and suddenness of the turn caught a good many Asian companies ill-prepared, and some of the very largest corporate names were soon in desperate trouble, notably in the commodity sector itself. It all amounted to the proverbial perfect storm for a big bank that had made a heavy commitment to Asia's growth, expanding its presence rapidly in the commodity-related world and showing a readiness to accept 'single-name' exposures in its lending portfolio (especially in India) well beyond the levels acceptable to most of its peers. The result was a double blow to profits. Revenues declined as the Group's Wholesale business shrank: 'Operating Income' fell from not far short of $19 billion in 2012 to just over $15 billion in 2015. And loan impairments (exacerbated by losses in 2012–14 on excessive unsecured lending in the Consumer Banking division) weighed ever more heavily on the income statement, rising from little more than $1 billion in 2012 to almost $5 billion in 2015. Given that fixed costs for the Group remained stubbornly around $10 billion, the result was inevitably a splurge of red ink for 2015 – the bottom line finally emerged showing a loss of $2.2 billion. It was Standard Chartered's first loss since 1989 and the distant days of the Withered Prune.

Faced with this unfolding crisis over the post-2012 years, the executive management struggled in vain to arrest a steady haemorrhaging of investors' confidence. At the outset, a lively debate ran through most of 2013 over how effectively the Group might be able to grow its way out of trouble. A raft of new businesses had been launched since 2008, many of which had yet to deliver a return even equivalent to the cost of the capital they employed. Some on the Board still saw them as key to a renewed period of growth, reinventing the surge of 2003–12. Others regarded this as a rather Panglossian view of the Group's predicament. The sheer speed of the economic downturn in Asia, and the raft of additional costs imposed by the transformed regulatory climate, were seen as compelling grounds for retrenchment. The simple arithmetic, too, suggested the growth option might be unduly optimistic. Growing Standard Chartered's total assets by 10 per cent back in 2004 had implied adding a mere $14 billion to the balance sheet. With assets approaching $700 billion by 2013, the same rate of growth would require finding new business worth another $70 billion – and against a background of rapidly rising loan impairments, it was none too clear that the Group had anything like the managerial resources to cope with such an expansion. The details of this protracted debate went undisclosed at the time, but a succession of three downward adjustments to officially projected earnings through 2013 conveyed a sense of indecision at the top that without doubt unnerved the market. The share price, which had topped £18 at the start of March 2013, began to slither downwards.

Some egregious setbacks helped it on its way. One involved a blow to the balance sheet from the business in South Korea. This was an episode that seemed in many ways to encapsulate the reversal in the Group's fortunes. It arose from a problematic acquisition that had surely received less urgent attention than it deserved in recent years. When Standard Chartered had acquired Korea First Bank in 2005 – making it the single largest foreign investor in the country – it had entered a marketplace surging with confidence and bolstered by a sympathetic regulatory framework.[8] Since mid-2009, however, it had been apparent that government ministers in Seoul no longer had much interest in the notion of a fully liberalized financial-services sector. The country's largest domestic lender had lost more than a billion dollars in the US sub-prime mortgage market. A savage depreciation of the Korean currency since 2007 had reduced the won's value against the US dollar by approximately 40 per cent by February 2009. The government opted for a full-blown retreat: the regulatory burden on all banks in South Korea was soon mounting alarmingly and new laws were passed that took little heed of their interests. (One especially damaging change in South Korean law allowed hard-pressed private householders far more leeway to write off their mortgage debts.) By 2011, Standard Chartered's chances of sustaining a growth strategy in the country were dwindling fast.

The Group at this point began flagging to the City its deflated expectations for the Korean business, but the Board remained committed to reversing the decline rather than opting for a much-reduced commitment, which, with hindsight, might have been the wiser course. Increasingly sceptical investors were assured that steady progress could be made, and a huge effort went into proving it. Perhaps the optimists were unduly encouraged by the growth of profits on business conducted with Korean customers elsewhere in the world, and certainly these were expanding impressively. Whatever the reasoning, the Group pressed on with tough local reforms. Nothing, though, could effectively shelter it from the harsh macroeconomic winds blowing through South Korea's banking sector, as through most others in the region. All were awash with cash as a direct consequence of the remorseless injection of dollars into the global economy since 2008, under the US Federal Reserve's programme of Quantitative Easing (QE). Interest rates were at rock bottom, and wafer-thin margins in South Korean retail banking were further squeezed by fierce competition among the domestic banks. By early 2013 it was apparent that Standard Chartered Korea (as the local bank had been re-named) might struggle to make any profits at all for the coming year. The original acquisition had entailed a huge accretion of goodwill to the balance sheet, so there was little option now but to write down a substantial part of it. The resulting $1 billion dent to the Income Statement was not of much concern to the institutional investors of the City – it was a non-cash item that made no difference to the critical numbers – but when announced in August 2013, it certainly helped to prompt harsh media commentaries that contrasted starkly with the press coverage of earlier years. Reporting back to the Board on his customary round of mid-year meetings with City shareholders, Finance Director Richard Meddings noted that 'overall investor sentiment had been more challenging than it had been for several years'.[9]

The Korean write-off – and another $726 million loss would later accompany the 2014 results – was especially disconcerting insofar as it raised the possibility of other hidden misadventures to come. It was also a measure of the sea-change in the Group's business environment. There followed a market reappraisal that transformed perceptions of the Group within a matter of months. Investors had long been accustomed to expert commentaries from Peter Sands and Richard Meddings that had seemed to render the Group's business as transparent as an international bank could reasonably hope to be. Suddenly the future seemed to be growing rather opaque. A first significant reorganization of the Group for ten years was announced in January 2014. Regardless of its intrinsic merits, the timing of the news – two months after a City presentation on long-term strategy that, inevitably, had had to stop short of disclosing the full extent of what was being planned – shook the market. Even more puzzling to City folk was the impending departure, also announced in January 2014, of Meddings himself, Group Finance Director since 2006 and a key architect, with Mervyn Davies, Sands and Mike Rees, of Standard Chartered's glorious decade up to 2012. Meddings was genuinely liked and much respected in the City. After delivering his presentation of the annual results to a City audience in March 2014, he was given a rousing ovation by the assembled brokers and analysts – emphatically not a common occurrence in the Square Mile. But this affectionate farewell did nothing to assuage City speculation about the true reasons for his decision to leave.*

The 2014 reorganization entailed a significant reshaping of the Group's operations. The split between Wholesale Banking and Consumer Banking was swept away as part of a move to stem a perceived drift towards a potentially corrosive silo mentality in recent years. Alongside this and other divisional realignments, the top management hierarchy was redrawn, with a new business committee under Peter Sands – generally to be chaired each week by Mike Rees, freshly promoted as Deputy Group Chief Executive. (Of its twelve members, no fewer than five were women, though there was never any question of a gender quota.†) Every effort was made to promote a fresh start, under the banner 'One Bank', intended as a catalyst for re-energizing the Group, rather as 'Leading the Way' had been in 2003. Alas, it was to no avail. By this point, the perfect storm was well under way and within months there was little choice but to adopt the retrenchment option. The previous year's debate over cost-cutting was now resolved in brutal fashion: having spent so many years defying the banking industry's general preoccupation with cost-reduction, the Group embarked on sizeable cuts of its own. 'Too little, too late' caught the City's broad response. Suddenly it counted for nothing that the Group could boast a modern track record outpacing that of most other banks in the world, and of all its peers in the City. In terms of both profitability and total return

* Some wondered how far it reflected a clash of views over cost-cutting, the impending reorganization and future Group strategy. Meddings himself could only insist that, at the age of fifty-six, he wanted the opportunity to take on another big challenge. And, as he told a hotel ballroom full of colleagues at a Singapore management conference in January 2014, he was tired of getting up at five minutes to five every morning. After eight years of working for a business weighted to Asia's time zones, he needed a change.

† The five comprised the heads of Commercial and Private Banking (Anna Marrs), Retail Banking (Karen Fawcett) and Wealth Management (Judy Hsu), plus two operational executives (Pam Walkden and Doris Honold). The prominence of women in the Group's senior ranks was striking by 2014, even beyond Mike Rees's Executive Committee. In addition to the Africa division (Diana Layfield), the bank in China was run by a woman (Jerry Zhang), as also was the bank in Hong Kong (May Tan). Several of the fastest-growing countries in the network had female chief executives, including Nigeria (Bola Adesola) and Thailand (Lyn Kok), as also did the embryonic operations in Myanmar (Tina Singhsacha). Nor were the high flyers restricted to Africa and Asia. In London, the Group Chief Credit Officer was a woman (Roselyne Renel). On the US regional management team in New York, women filled the top departmental roles in Operations, Risk, Legal & Compliance, and Corporate Affairs; and the three latter functions were also headed by a woman at Group level (Tracy Clarke). Across the managerial ranks of the Group as a whole, women only accounted for approximately 15 per cent of the total – reflecting the fact that commercial banking remained overwhelmingly a man's world. But this only made the unusual number of leading women at senior levels in Standard Chartered all the more conspicuous.

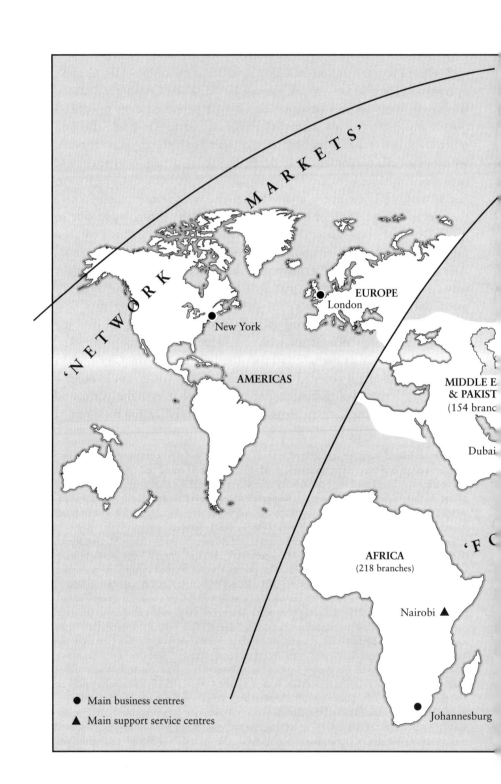

'M A R K E T S'

'N E T W O R K

EUROPE
London

New York

AMERICAS

MIDDLE E
& PAKIST
(154 branc

Dubai

'F (

AFRICA
(218 branches)

Nairobi ▲

Johannesburg

● Main business centres
▲ Main support service centres

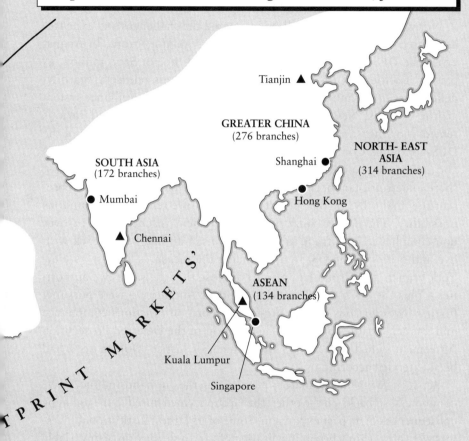

Map 11. Standard Chartered's regional structure, June 2014

Tianjin ▲

GREATER CHINA
(276 branches)

NORTH- EAST ASIA
(314 branches)

SOUTH ASIA
(172 branches)

Shanghai ●

● Mumbai

Hong Kong ●

▲ Chennai

ASEAN
(134 branches)

Kuala Lumpur

Singapore

FOOTPRINT MARKETS

Notes
1. 'Branches' comprise all retail branches, electronic banking centres, agencies and wholesale banking branches.

2. The total of 1,268 branches excludes Indonesia's Bank Permata (with *c.* 730 branches) in which the Group has a 44.56 per cent stake.

3. Representative offices not shown.

to shareholders – a measure combining the performance of the share price with the value of dividends paid – Standard Chartered had handsomely outperformed every other UK-based bank since 2002. But that now afforded the Board little cover as anxious investors went on voicing their dismay over present trends and future prospects.

Nor were Sands and his colleagues spared the challenges and expenses associated with yet another setback on the regulatory front. In August 2014, the DFS in New York imposed a further fine of $300 million, as part of a settlement (in the words of a Group press release) 'regarding deficiencies in the anti-money laundering transaction surveillance system at [the Group's] New York branch'. The settlement embraced various remediation measures, including a two-year extension to the term of the DFS-appointed Compliance Monitor. These events meant that sanctions and anti-money-laundering compliance-enforcement actions had now cost shareholders not far short of a billion dollars. Even this might not represent the final tally: further penalties in the future remained an ominous possibility. The earlier $667 million settlement reached in 2012 over non-compliance with trade sanctions against Iran had been struck with five authorities in the US. In announcing the measures against its New York branch, the Group had also to disclose that the same five authorities – plus the UK's own Financial Conduct Authority – were pursuing further investigations into its pre-2014 record on sanctions compliance and financial-crime controls. (The duration of the Deferred Prosecution Agreement signed with the US Department of Justice (DoJ) in 2012 had been extended accordingly.)

Between swingeing regulatory penalties on the one hand and successive commercial setbacks on the other, the Group seemed mired in the unhappy consequences of its past expansion. Some of its largest institutional investors were now plainly becoming disaffected, and a steady drip of (invariably anonymous) criticism began to seep into the press coverage of its affairs. The gathering media attention did nothing for the share price, which by mid-December 2014 was well below £10. It was not a helpful backcloth as the Board approached the task of finding a successor to Peter Sands. Had it been initiated a couple of years earlier, this process might perhaps have been a little easier to orchestrate. Now events rather seemed to have overtaken Sir John Peace and his colleagues. No obvious internal candidates were at hand, and the search for an external appointee had been delayed by Sands' spirited commitment to resolving the difficulties with the US regulators and his evident determination to set the Group back on the path to renewed growth. By the end of 2014, the Group's apparent failure to identify the Chief Executive's successor had become the focus of increasingly hostile comment in the financial media – predictably enough, given the abject performance of the share price, which had fallen almost 25 per cent over the calendar year. By February 2015 investors had seen the shares trading for more than twelve months at levels below those seen in Sands' first year at the helm. This was scarcely the indictment some commentators suggested, given the traumatic events in the financial world over the intervening years, but it cannot have been the finale to his career with Standard Chartered that Sands would have wished for.

There was a palpable sense, both within the Group and across the City, that a changing of the guard was overdue. It finally arrived on 26 February 2015, with an announcement by Sir John Peace that the Board had alighted on the choice of a new leader, well known and respected in the market-place – Bill Winters, a fifty-three-year-old Anglophile American and former luminary of J. P. Morgan Chase & Co, the largest bank in the US. After a brief hand-over period, Sands retired from the Group in June 2015 and turned to focus on other professional roles for which he had always been in so much demand.* His successor was openly acclaimed by many of the Group's largest investors and his arrival prompted a 5.4-per-cent jump in the share price, lifting it back over £10. The fact that no less than five other members of the Board were to step down in due course – including Sir John Peace himself, who would vacate the chairmanship in 2016 – added to the general perception that a whole new era was at hand.

Like others before him, Winters was soon immersed in a fundamental reappraisal of the Group's future. The gist of the 2014 restructuring was left in place, but several changes were announced at Board level, and the senior executive ranks saw a significant reshuffle and several departures over the next several months. Mike Rees, essentially the last of the old guard, remained at Winters' side to assist in the transition process, but did eventually announce in January 2016 that he also would be retiring from the Board before the next Annual General Meeting. The new Chief Executive lost no time establishing his personal credibility within the Group, and soon enjoyed at least a degree of rapport with the media that helped to begin restoring the bank's battered image. But the honeymoon in the stock market nevertheless proved cruelly short. From April 2015 the price of the Group's shares slid remorselessly. The market's disquiet was not hard to fathom. The macroeconomic background remained bleak: assessing relative

---

* Among various other Board memberships, he had for some years been the lead non-executive member of the UK Department of Health's main Board, and was also a co-chairman of the India/UK CEO Forum, set up in 2012. In the autumn of 2015 he took up a Senior Fellowship at the Mossavar-Rahmani Center for Business and Government, part of Harvard University's Kennedy School.

prospects for the medium term, investors in their droves were switching back to Western markets in search of bigger and more immediate gains than now looked available in Asia. Equities in Emerging Market companies were falling heavily, and Standard Chartered fell with them. More specifically, huge uncertainty lingered over both the underlying weaknesses of the loan portfolio that had been expanded so rapidly in 2008–12, and the likely outcome of the troubling investigations by the US and UK authorities that had been publicly hanging over the Group since August 2014. Few, if any, fund managers were much disposed any longer to give the Group the benefit of any doubts. For years, the share price had enjoyed a premium that reflected the management's starry reputation; now it was stuck with a discount that reflected the City's disillusionment, and which seemed likely to endure for a while. Above all, and of most direct concern to the market, few in the City doubted the Group's need to raise additional capital as a matter of some urgency.

This, at least, was one concern that Winters and his colleagues could address directly, and they moved to do so with a substantial rights issue early in November 2015. With the shares trading at around £5, new stock (on a 2-for-7 basis) was made available to shareholders at just £4.65. This raised new capital of $5.1 billion, to which 97 per cent of existing shareholders fully contributed. It was enough to satisfy the UK regulators that the Group would be able to meet its capital-ratio requirements even in the most adverse of circumstances, and despite plans to spend up to $3 billion on an extensive restructuring of the Group over the course of 2016. An outline of the strategic implications accompanied the announcement of the rights issue, with a flurry of targets for the next three years. The cost base would be curtailed, the head-count would be reined back, the loan portfolio would be rendered leaner and fitter – and a generous budget would be found for new technology and better systems, not least in aid of a stricter compliance regime. (Total regulatory costs were going to top $1 billion for 2015 alone, up 40 per cent on the previous year's bill.)

Its continuing legal problems over past compliance failures weighed heavily on perceptions of the Group over the next few years. Given the size of the fines paid in 2012 and the breadth of the further investigations disclosed in 2014, there was inevitably a sense – among staff, business partners and clients as well as investors and the media – of waiting for the other shoe to drop. By the end of 2018, Winters and the new senior team around him could fairly claim to have accomplished most of the financial goals set out in a Three Year Plan at the time of the rights issue. The working environment across the Group had also been transformed. Staff morale, undoubtedly shaken by the events of 2012–15, had made a steady recovery.

As important, a profound change had been wrought in the Group's whole approach to the management of compliance issues and the battle against financial crime. (The headcount in this hugely sensitive area of operations had grown six-fold since 2012, accompanied by extensive organizational changes since 2015.) Until it could be announced that a final settlement had been reached of the issues under investigation since 2014, though, the Group's recovery would remain unfinished business. Then, in April 2019, the news broke that terms had at last been agreed with the US and UK regulatory agencies. Under a revised version of the original Deferred Prosecution Agreement of 2012, amended several times since 2014, Standard Chartered accepted full responsibility for 'violations and control deficiencies' (mostly pre-dating the 2012 settlement), which included a criminal conspiracy run from its Dubai branch between 2007 and 2011 for the ultimate benefit of Iranian customers. The Group escaped prosecution, but only at the cost of penalties even higher than the $667 million imposed by the US agencies a little over six years earlier. The fines this time amounted to $947 million – in addition to which a charge of £102 million was imposed by the UK's Financial Conduct Authority. The 2019 settlement did promise, though, to dispel at last the grave uncertainties that had hovered over the Group since 2012. The Monitor arrangements imposed by the DoJ and the DFS were brought to an end. The settlement also included a public acknowledgement of the scale of the Group's efforts in the compliance field. The Group, as it were, was now free to go.

Welcoming this outcome, Winters alluded to the Group's legacy of a trust built up with its customer base over the course of more than 160 years. Its history, as ever, could offer the Group a comforting sense of its own unique identity. The 2019 settlement, as it happened, had its own resonance with the past, by coinciding almost exactly with a notable anniversary. It was fifty years since the agreement struck in May 1969 to form Standard Chartered via a merger of its two predecessor banks. The culture of international banking had changed profoundly over that half-century, but the distant origins of the Group still had a relevance to its modern business that was well worth recalling.

Here was an enterprise, after all, that in broad terms had prospered as an adjunct to the British Empire, eked out a post-colonial existence for much longer than might have been expected, undergone its own transformation as part of the sweeping Americanization of the international banking industry later in the twentieth century and then prospered as an integral part of the newly resurgent economies of Asia in the twenty-first. It was a past that illustrated a key dimension of the Empire – the financing of trade links that extended British influence via most of the principal ports of Africa and Asia – and equally illuminated a complex aspect of the old order's demise, as long-standing financial institutions of the Empire were re-jigged or cast aside. The emergence from these events of a leading international bank reflected the Group's success (eventually) at changing its own culture and organization more radically than had once seemed possible. It had evolved into a robust multicultural institution, justly proud of its special niche in the international industry and endowed with a commercial logic that was both compelling and impossible to replicate. Reaching its half-century mark, it was a huge and resilient business that had more than lived up to the vision of its architects in 1969 – let alone the modest aspirations of those who founded its precursor banks in the distant but unforgotten past.

Appendix A

Chartered Bank's Centenary History

It was in late 1948 that the notion was first mooted of commissioning a history of the Chartered Bank. It was thought that a book timed to coincide with its centenary in 1953 might add nicely to the occasion. Much had happened that surely deserved a permanent record; and with memories of the staff's wartime traumas still fresh in the minds of many senior managers, the idea of capturing a sense of the camaraderie within the bank had a strong appeal. One of its keenest champions was Harold Faulkner, Manager of the bank's branch in Manchester since 1938, who a couple of years earlier had penned a lengthy article for *China Trade & Engineering* on the history of the bank in China – where he had served as political liaison officer for three years from 1934 – and who was about to step into the role of Company Secretary.[1] With more than a touch of the *de haut en bas* style for which he was renowned, Faulkner wrote to the bank's Chief Manager, William Cockburn, on the last day of 1948:

> The story of the Chartered Bank is a story not so much of Silver Crises and Currency Reforms as of men. We should not aim to produce a highly ornamental volume which will gather dust in bank bookcases but a story which everyone interested in the British achievement in the East will read and re-read . . . Our historian should try to imprison in the printed word something of the tradition most of us understand, and something of that spirit of loyalty to the Service [*sic*] which all but the most insensitive and boorish of us feel.[2]

Cockburn agreed, and the project moved forward – albeit at a less than frenetic pace. In addition to a well-stocked library and museum at 38 Bishopsgate, the bank held voluminous archives in London that it was assumed would provide much of the raw material for the history. In line with his advice to the Chief Manager, Faulkner was also determined that it should draw on lively contributions from the bank's staff, past as well as present. With assistance from historians at University College London, and perhaps a little optimistically, he compiled a list of twenty-one questions for his colleagues across Asia. (Thanking the scholars for their help, he made it clear again that a dry academic tome was not what he envisaged. 'We do not intend to follow the conventional pattern of bank histories; we shall try to record the rise and development of the Bank, and the adventures of its officers and servants, against a background of the British endeavour in Asia during the past hundred years.'[3]) A Centenary Commemoration Committee held its first meeting on 2 November 1949 and a week later Faulkner's brave questionnaire went off as Head Office Circular No. 530a to all branches, with a note to the heads of the larger offices 'asking them to appoint suitably-qualified officers to undertake local research'.[4]

The Committee then turned to the task of finding its historian. Several names were put forward. The preferred candidate was Arthur Bryant, a columnist on the *Illustrated London News* and a prolific popular historian who had written acclaimed biographies of Charles II and Samuel Pepys before the war. A writer with a decidedly romantic view of English history but a fierce disdain for the City, Bryant would have been an odd man for the job. Perhaps fortunately, he turned it down, and in November 1950 the Committee confirmed instead the appointment of A. S. J. Baster (who that month attended the second meeting of the Committee). Author of two definitive works on international banking and the leading academic authority in the field, Baster was indeed the obvious choice. Appointed as his assistant to help with a serious trawl through the archives was a thirty-one-year-old Oxford history graduate, John Leighton-Boyce, who had spent four years as a German prisoner-of-war and was still struggling to establish a career. To help with sketching out the commercial background, Faulkner had also commissioned the Economist Intelligence Unit, a sister company of the weekly magazine, to research a set of historical papers on the various industries with which the bank had been most closely involved. Ten of these were to be completed by March 1951.[5] By the time these EIU papers came in, serious problems had been encountered with Baster. He had been working for the United Nations in Beirut when his contract was agreed, and a six-month sabbatical had been envisaged to allow him to research the history in London during 1951, delivering a final manuscript in the summer of 1952. But he appears to have had second thoughts once the scale of the project became apparent, and announced his intention of returning to the US – rather absurdly, given the extent of the records held in London – and tackling the book from his home in New York. He also wanted paying in dollars, an expensive proposition for the bank given sterling's devaluation in 1949. These terms were unsurprisingly turned down by Faulkner, by now the Company Secretary and (at his own instigation) the overall director of the project. Having already been impressed by Leighton-Boyce's energy and diligence, Faulkner at some point in 1951 asked the younger man to take on writing the history himself.

Initial responses to the November 1949 questionnaire had meanwhile been disappointing. Over the course of 1950–51, Faulkner had to follow it up with a stream of letters about the importance of responding. Most branches complied, eventually – but their replies varied dramatically in content. Some managers rather disarmingly claimed to have nothing of any note whatever to report: 'As far as this Office is concerned', wrote the Madras Manager, forwarding a desultory list of recent pensioners, 'nothing of any particular interest to a historian seems to have occurred during the fifty years [that] the Bank has been operating in Madras, nor do we possess any photographs of the bank building.'[6] The Karachi Manager noted that their Chief Cashier had worked at the branch since 1907 – 'but he is unable to supply us with any interesting anecdotes which would be of value'.[7] The oldest serving employee of all was a Mr Mak Poi Hee, in the Cash Department of the Hong Kong branch. He had joined the bank in 1888. But even he could offer no assistance, as his Manager explained: 'Unfortunately, Mr Mak's memory is failing and he cannot be relied upon for items of historical interest.'[8] (For items of daily interest to the bank, apparently, he was still going strong.) Several branches, including Hong Kong, lamented the fact that all their records had been destroyed by the Japanese during the war. The Penang branch Manager said he had written to more than sixty firms and individuals in and around the city asking them for their help, to little avail. ('Most of these persons and firms had also lost their records during the Japanese occupation . . .'[9]) The Saigon Office's Accountant explained that, as the office junior in 1936, he had been 'delegated to destroy as much of our records as possible [to facilitate an office relocation] . . . Anything I missed was dealt with by the Japanese.'[10] But more than a few branches did distinguish themselves, sending home long and well-researched answers – none more so than Bombay, which submitted a Memorandum by H. C. MacColl that was eighty-six pages long.[11] In many instances, it was left to retired officers to tackle the questionnaire – some of them in their seventies by 1950, or even older – and they provided several first-hand accounts of bank life in the pre-1914 era. Long letters were received, too, from a number of former Indian Chief Clerks. A second circular from Head Office was despatched directly to all pensioners of the bank, and this prompted a number of other elderly gentlemen to submit memoirs, some extending back to the middle of the 1880s.[12] These latter alumni notably included W. S. Livingstone, a former Manager in Shanghai, F. Bennett, who had served in several Asia posts through a career lasting forty years (he had retired as long ago as 1923), and J. A. Macgill, whose 106-page memoir took the form of an affectionate letter to the friend with whom he had trained in the Hatton Court Head Office in 1898–1901.[13] (The friend was sent a copy and dismissed it with a flippant aside that wounded the seventy-one-year-old Macgill deeply, as he admitted in a poignant letter to Faulkner: 'You are at liberty to do anything you jolly well please with my MS copy – you can put it in the fire if you like, for I am past caring now . . . and yet I was hurt.'[14])

While the replies and reminiscences trickled back, Leighton-Boyce embarked on a meticulous trawl of the bank's official records, most notably the half-yearly reports from its branch Managers, the reviews submitted by its travelling Inspectors and the Head Office Correspondence files, begun in the very earliest days of George Ure Adam's team in the 1850s. He took copious notes, fair copies of which were then typed out by the bank; and he added his own handwritten summaries here and there, especially on background developments which he gleaned from the well-stocked shelves of the bank's library. As the months passed, he accumulated papers for both countries and individual branch locations, eventually amassing more than fifty separate files.[15] His typed summaries of the half-yearly reports alone ran to several hundred pages. (Many of these 'JL-B notes' have been drawn upon for the earlier chapters of this book.) Leighton-Boyce also had access to what were described as the bank's 'Posterity Files' – hundreds of packets of miscellaneous documents dating back to the 1850s that had been stored in the Secretary's Department until 1933, then transferred into archival boxes. The packets had been carefully indexed as part of this operation, with each envelope numbered and its contents given a brief description, and he drew heavily on this material.[16] Much of it inevitably consisted of dull banking documentation; but in among the plethora of loan agreements, mortgage deeds, lawyers' letters and powers of attorney were plenty of more personal papers with a strong flavour of the bank's rich past.

Then Leighton-Boyce turned to penning his own history. When he started is not clear, but by the summer of 1952 he was well-advanced on it, with a manuscript of 150,000 words. Unfortunately, his text seems to have been reviewed by the Centenary Commemoration Committee only at a very late stage – and when the committee members read it, there was a mighty sucking of teeth. Alas, the author had told a story dominated for long stretches by exactly those Silver Crises and Currency Reforms that Faulkner had specifically suggested the history should avoid. Of 'the adventures of its officers and servants', the traditions and spirit of loyalty, there was almost nothing. An exchange of pained memos ensued. The manuscript was heroic in its scope, all could agree – but there was far too much on the background and far too little on the bank, and all those who had worked for it. As for many long passages on technical matters, these were so far from being 'highly ornamental' that even the professional bankers found them impenetrable.

Matters were thus delicately poised, at the end of October 1952, when a letter arrived out of the blue for the Chief (now Chief General) Manager. It came from a literary agent based in Chelsea, one Edward (Ted) Liveing, 'specialist in corporate histories'. He had noted that the bank was approaching its centenary year. Would the Board have any interest, he wondered, in the services of one of his foremost clients, Sir Compton Mackenzie? Cockburn sounded out Faulkner, who thought some kind of stand-by arrangement might indeed be a good idea '[in case] we run into disappointment with Leighton-Boyce's manuscript'. Liveing and his distinguished client were hastily invited to lunch. Mackenzie had been a literary celebrity since before the First World War, and had since then churned out books at the rate of more than one a year. Now almost seventy, he was as famous as he had ever been. His novel *Whisky Galore* had been published in 1947 and turned into a very successful Ealing Studios film, featuring the larger-than-life author himself as a larger-than-life Scottish trawler skipper. Knighted earlier in the year, he no doubt swept into 38 Bishopsgate that November like few guests before him.

A brilliant raconteur and mimic, Mackenzie was the kind of captivating personality for whom a lavish income would be assured in the television age and our modern celebrity culture. Before the advent of either, however, he had to rely instead on his pen for the sizeable earnings demanded by a notoriously extravagant lifestyle. In addition to a stream of novels, he was therefore ever ready to turn his hand to a commission. In 1951 alone, he had produced a survey of the National Trust, a history of Coalport China and a long chronicle of the Indian Army's exploits in the Second World War entitled *Eastern Epic*. But he had just purchased a new house in Edinburgh's Georgian New Town in the autumn of 1952, and was urgently in need of funds. By the time lunch with Cockburn and Faulkner was over, he had another commission in the bag. The publishers had been promised a text by April 1953, but Faulkner was soon writing to them to explain that 'an author of national repute' had now been taken on, meaning publication might have to be postponed into 1954. Then the Company Secretary had to break the news to Leighton-Boyce. He did so in a letter just after Christmas. 'I have to convey to you the congratulations of the

Centenary Commemoration Committee upon the completion, in so competent and scholarly a fashion, of the first draft of the official history of the bank', wrote Faulkner diplomatically.

> Although the Committee have decided to entrust to Sir Compton Mackenzie the writing of a popular account of the Bank's origin and development, your own work must always be regarded as the authentic version and, in due course, it will be made available to the numerous authorities and others who may wish to consult it.[17]

A few misgivings were voiced inside the bank when the news broke of Mackenzie's appointment. It was remarked that he appeared to know nothing about finance, and to care even less. (Profiles of the great man invariably cited his quip that whenever threatened with bankruptcy – which was not infrequently – he would go off and buy a new suit.) But he was renowned in the book world for his professionalism and was trusted to deliver on his word, though the challenge was obvious. So when Faulkner ventured to inquire in April 1953 as to how things were going, he was taken aback to hear from Mackenzie that he had delegated the task of producing a précis of Leighton-Boyce's text – to his agent. A few weeks later, Faulkner received a note from Ted Liveing that left him utterly confounded. Mackenzie, he was informed, would be starting work on the book at the beginning of June, and would hand over a finished draft by the end of September at the latest. This must have seemed scarcely credible to Faulkner; but then, he would probably have found most of the writer's working routines well-nigh unbelievable. (His own were a little unusual: he took a nap in the Head Office every afternoon, during which his departmental staff had to observe a strict silence.) Fuelled by serial draughts of Ovaltine, Mackenzie often toiled through the night and slept by day, immersing himself in the book at hand to the exclusion of all else for weeks on end. In this way, starting early in June as promised, he now pulled off his latest assignment, producing a handwritten text one third shorter than the original.[18] He posted it off to Faulkner a full fortnight before his deadline in September, observing for good measure in his covering note: 'I don't believe I ever worked so hard in my life as I have over this book for the last seven weeks'.[19]

It must have been tough for the typists, too: Mackenzie's handwriting was quite as wild and indecipherable as any graphologist might have predicted. The first clean chapters, with heroic efficiency, were handed to Faulkner a few days later. Their contents confirmed his worst fears. He was aghast to find long sections quite as unintelligible as anything in Leighton-Boyce's narrative. In fact, Mackenzie appeared simply to have

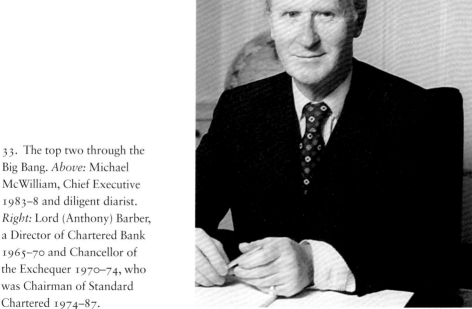

33. The top two through the Big Bang. *Above:* Michael McWilliam, Chief Executive 1983–8 and diligent diarist. *Right:* Lord (Anthony) Barber, a Director of Chartered Bank 1965–70 and Chancellor of the Exchequer 1970–74, who was Chairman of Standard Chartered 1974–87.

34. The statue of James Wilson in the banking hall of the main branch in Calcutta in the 1980s, where it stood for thirty years before being shipped to London in 1985 to adorn the atrium of Standard Chartered's new head office in Bishopsgate.

35. The Three White Knights whose support allowed Standard Chartered to defeat the hostile takeover bid from Lloyds Bank in 1986. *Above left*: the Hong Kong shipping magnate, Sir Y. K. Pao. *Above right*: the Singapore-based banker and property developer, Tan Sri Khoo Teck Puat. *Left*: Australia's first billionaire businessman, Robert Holmes à Court.

36. Architects of Standard Chartered's revival in the 1990s. *Above left:* Rodney Galpin, formerly a Director of the Bank of England and Group Chairman 1988–93. *Above right:* Malcolm Williamson, Chief Executive 1993–8. *Bottom left:* Sir Patrick Gillam, Executive Chairman 1993–2003. *Bottom right:* Rana Talwar, Chief Executive 1998–2001.

37. Two typical branches of Standard Chartered's modern retail network in Asia. *Above:* a branch in Central Shanghai. *Below:* the branch at the Bandra Kurla complex in Mumbai.

38. Standard Chartered's leaders in the new millennium. *Above*: Mervyn Davies (*right*), Chief Executive 2001–6 and Non-Executive Chairman 2006–9, and Peter Sands (*left*), Group Finance Director 2002–6 and Chief Executive 2006–15, welcoming former Prime Minister Sir John Major to a Group management conference. *Bottom left*: Mike Rees, Chief Executive of Wholesale Banking 2002–14 and Deputy Group Chief Executive 2014–16. *Bottom right*: Richard Meddings, Group Executive Director 2002–14 and Finance Director 2006–14.

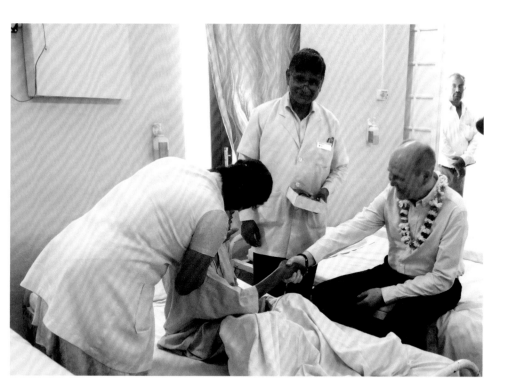

39. *Above*: Group Chairman Sir John Peace visiting Dr Shroff's Charity Eye Hospital in Delhi, India in March 2015. *Below*: St Paul's Cathedral in London in December 2013, lit with Standard Chartered's brand colours for a fund-raising carol service in aid of 'Seeing is Believing', the Group's campaign in support of the fight against blindness in poor countries of the world.

40. Promoting the brand: the Senegalese footballer Sadio Mané celebrates another goal at Anfield as one of the Liverpool FC team that won the English Premier League Championship in 2019–20.

copied out great stretches of the original in his own hand. Faulkner wrote immediately to Cockburn with the glum news.

> I have not yet read the whole of the manuscript . . . but I confess to be very very disappointed with the chapters I have seen. The book as it stands smells of the lamp – Mackenzie finished it last week at a single sitting of twelve hours. It contains a few asides, not strictly relevant to the theme, which have been 'lifted' from *Eastern Epic* but I have not so far been able to discern more than half a dozen or so original observations and these are rather commonplace.

Liveing had negotiated a handsome fee for his client and the Company Secretary had his qualms about paying it. 'Having delivered the manuscript he is, I suppose, now entitled to draw his money but I should like to have your authority to pay the [next] instalment he wants.'[20]

So Leighton-Boyce found himself pressed into service once again. For six weeks, he had to labour on extensive revisions to the Mackenzie text, while key technical passages were handed to the appropriate Directors for amendment. The result just about passed muster with Cockburn, who took a stoical view of the affair: 'with the suggestions proposed, it is throughout a worthy effort'. But Faulkner could not contain his bitter disappointment over the outcome. 'Quite frankly, I am horrified by the style,' as he confided to Cockburn at the start of November 1953.

> The shorter sentences usually written for dramatic effect are often slangy, while the longer sentences tend to become incredibly involved with verbs popping up in the most extraordinary places. If Mackenzie insists upon my restoring the original constructions where they have been altered to avoid the Bank's being made to look silly I shall, of course, defer but I do not think he will. He must realise that the book was written with indecent haste on a subject about which he knew nothing until we briefed him and he should be very glad, for the sake of his own reputation, that experts have taken sufficient trouble to preserve him from serious error.[21]

Mackenzie was indeed happy to let the Bank make what it wanted of his work. Doubtless he had plenty to keep him busy on other current projects. (He had already produced histories of Buckingham Palace and the Savoy Hotel in 1953, and there were three more books on the go for publication in 1954.) Squaring all the changes with the publishers, Routledge & Kegan Paul, was a slightly more fraught affair. Plans to include a lavish set of photographs and charts with the text had to be abandoned, and there was a final glitch over acknowledgements. Faulkner had insisted there should be no mention of his role or Leighton-Boyce's, which Mackenzie had accepted. But Cockburn was adamant at the last minute that the two men should be properly credited for their labours, and an Author's Note was belatedly added in front of the Contents. Entitled *Realms of Silver*, the book was finally published in March 1954. (Mackenzie had earlier suggested *Eastward, Ho!* but this had been passed over in silence.) None could pretend it was an easy read. Faulkner was understandably incensed that the author of *Whisky Galore* had short-changed the bank, as he saw it, and left them with something well short of expectations. But this may have led him to be overly critical of the outcome. At least it preserved a substantial part of the historical record pieced together by Leighton-Boyce. And there were paragraphs here and there that crackled with Mackenzie's unmistakeable voice – as in these lines bidding farewell to Chartered's presence in China, so recently foreclosed:

> In Shanghai, Tientsin, Canton, Peking and elsewhere the Chartered Bank throughout its history had always taken a prominent part in assisting the flow of foreign trade and the development of the Chinese economy. The great services of the Bank to the Chinese Government and to the Chinese people in helping to defend the national currency against Japanese malfeasance in the 'thirties had added lustre to the bright record of the oldest foreign bank in China and confirmed the esteem in which it was held by British, Chinese and other nationals alike.[22]

How far Mackenzie's efforts had actually improved Leighton-Boyce's original draft is difficult to say.[23] Despite Faulkner's blandishments, most of Leighton-Boyce's text vanished.*

After the centenary history's publication, the Chartered Bank's archives lost some of their former glory. Replying to those of his correspondents who had expressed their regrets at not being able to offer more help, Faulkner had consoled them by remarking on the riches held in London. As he wrote to the Singapore Manager in 1951:

---

* Leighton-Boyce himself bore no grudges. To console him for any disappointment over the book, he was offered a permanent job as head of the bank's research, a post he gladly accepted. He was able to combine his duties at the bank – which included being editor of *Curry & Rice*, the staff magazine – with his interest in banking history, and a few years later received a Houblon–Norman Fellowship from the Bank of England to help fund research into another book. His *Smiths the Bankers, 1658–1958* was published by the National Provincial Bank in 1958. He remained fully committed to the Chartered, though, and eventually became Faulkner's successor as Secretary (1964–6). He resigned to join Pilkington Brothers, where he became Finance Director and eventually Deputy Chairman. In retirement he acted as a Trustee of the Pilkington Family Trusts. His death at the age of eighty-nine in 2007 was recorded in a copy of the Family Trusts' newsletter, *Newslink*, in its Winter 2007 edition.

When we circulated our questionnaire, we realised that through no fault of their own we could expect little information as to their early history from those branches whose records had been destroyed [by wartime enemy action], but, fortunately, we have at Head Office a large quantity of records comprising minutes, memoranda, correspondence and reports which will go a long way towards filling in the gaps in our knowledge of the overseas history of the Bank.[24]

This comprehensive archive, according to Cockburn's elegant preface to *Realms of Silver*, contained 'material sufficient for a dozen books'. Indeed, the pre-1914 Head Office Correspondence files, along with the related Half-Yearly Reports and the Inspectors' Letter Files – all (or at least many of them) evidently still available to Leighton-Boyce in 1950–52 – might have been invaluable to historians of the pre-1914 Asian societies in which the bank laid down its branches, much as the correspondence files of South Africa's Standard Bank have survived as a rich source of material for historians of nineteenth-century South Africa. Alas, they were to disappear, along with perhaps a third of the Posterity Files re-boxed in 1933. It seems likely that they were destroyed at the time of the 1969 merger between the Chartered Bank and Standard Bank. (Letters held in the branches also disappeared at some point: the MacColl Memorandum from Bombay, for example, confirmed the retention there in 1951 of complete sequences of outward correspondence from 1884 and inward correspondence from 1911 – all now untraceable.) Ten years after the merger, the enlarged Group commissioned the Business Archives Council to survey what was left of the Head Office records: the BAC's report, in April 1980, ran to thirty-five foolscap pages, but included only seven on the Chartered itself and these made no reference to the missing correspondence and reports.[25] An Archives Unit was then established under an Archives Officer, J. A. Packman, and it took charge of pulling together the surviving archives of the Group that had hitherto been held in several separate locations around the City. Some archives appear also to have been sent back to London around this time from various overseas branches, including Manila.[26] All were transferred in October 1981 to a records depot in Wapping. Packman noted the following year that a substantial portion of the inherited post-1960 records 'has regrettably been destroyed'.[27]

This still left Wapping in possession of a substantial collection, though, and there existed a working index which appears to have been based on categories defined by the BAC's 1980 report. An historian researching the history of Britain's overseas banks, Professor Geoffrey Jones, had access to the archives in the late 1980s: he and an assistant, Frances Bostock, drew extensively on them for a book on Britain's overseas banks published in 1993.[28] By the time it appeared, unfortunately, further calamities had unfolded. Plans were laid in 1988 for the Wapping archives to be moved to a new depot near Redhill in Surrey, which prompted some debate over a need to cull the records.[29] In July that year, the Curator was writing to the Corporate Services Department to pass on a colleague's inquiry 'if he could now destroy the Inward & Outward Correspondence held by [the] Secretary's Department at Wapping dated before 1978'.[30] The Department wrote six weeks later to someone responsible for the Redhill move, confirming 'that, for the present, we do not wish to dispose of any of our historic archives' and seeking some assurance that sufficient space had been set aside for them.[31] But the Redhill plans were later scrapped in favour of a more radical approach. In the summer of 1989, the Standard Chartered Group was at the nadir of its fortunes and its Directors were bent on cutting costs wherever possible: the Archives Unit was disbanded, the records depot at Wapping was closed down and its historical contents were hastily divided between the City of London's Guildhall Library and the bank's external record managers, Iron Mountain. An unknown, but certainly substantial, quantity of material had to be destroyed for lack of space at the Guildhall. No time was made available for any proper indexing of the transferred archives, but the catalogue system used at Wapping was abandoned. This effectively spiked the index used by Jones and Bostock and made it impossible thereafter to trace any of the references included in their published work.[32] Then, late in 1990, Standard Chartered sold its headquarters building at 38 Bishopsgate and the Head Office was relocated to a significantly smaller building in the City's Aldermanbury Square. This left no space for the Chartered Bank's library and museum, which had hitherto housed many valuable historical artefacts. Most of the museum's contents were promptly sold off, though Rodney Galpin as Chairman insisted that the Group should retain a collection of the Chartered's banknotes. (They can still be seen in Standard Chartered's atrium at Basinghall Avenue.) Finally, and to cap a generally sad tale, a number of the bank's boxes at Iron Mountain were subsequently destroyed in a fire in July 2006.

At least the story can end on a happier note, however: the Board of Standard Chartered in 2011 commissioned the staff of the London Metropolitan Archives, part of the City of London Corporation, to begin a formal cataloguing of all the papers held in the Guildhall Library – a task pursued in parallel, and close co-operation, with the writing of this book's early chapters.

Appendix B

The Staff of Standard Bank's Kimberley Branch in December 1877

(Extracted from 'Inspection Report: Kimberley Branch, 31 December 1877' by Rees Williams, pp. 189–201. Held in the archives of the Standard Bank, INSP 1/1/84, 442/Kimberley. See Plate 6.)

[The Standard's principal branch in the diamond fields was opened for business on New Year's Day 1872 at Kimberley, then a prospectors' canvas township still known as New Rush. Its rapid growth in the 1870s made it an important destination for the bank's travelling Inspectors. Rees Williams was by 1877 one of the longest serving of these resilient figures. (He would end his career as Assistant General Manager of the bank in 1896–7.) His commentary on the staff of the Kimberley branch in December 1877 appears to have been based in part on his experience of working there for four weeks from 20 March to 24 April 1877, 'it having become apparent that a gross fraud had been perpetrated on the Bank'. Rees had to break off his inquiries to open Standard Bank's first branches in the Transvaal, annexed by British forces during 1877, but he returned just after Christmas that same year to complete his earlier investigations – and to compile for Robert Stewart this typically meticulous assessment of the men working for the bank at Kimberley.]

Officers

John Whitfield Harsant, Manager, Age 32 last birthday. Salary £1,000 per annum and House rent-free. Has signed the usual Declaration of secrecy, and his fidelity is guaranteed by the Colonial & Foreign Banks Guarantee Fund for £1,500. Was formerly clerk for three years with Messrs. A. Kroll & Co Merchants Port Elizabeth. Joined the Bank's service at Port Elizabeth in August 1863 and was appointed Manager at Kimberley in August 1872. Salary last increased on 1st January 1876. Mr Harsant is steady, active, punctual in his attendance at the office, and is I believe thought well of in the town generally. He is one of the oldest officers of the Bank, and is zealous intelligent and capable. His memory however is not one of the most retentive and he somewhat lacks a closely observant eye. After a good deal of observation of him, I believe him to be faithful and truthful: I have endeavoured to weigh well these important points, and I believe that conclusion to be right and just. Portions of his correspondence may seem to have a tinge of slimness in the way he makes the most of what may appear to justify or excuse anything commented upon, but he would not make a statement knowing it to be at the time untrue, nor wilfully and intentionally conceal facts. He is not so frank & communicative, clear open and decided as perhaps could be desired; on the other hand he is not, in his intercourse with the public, talkative and indiscreet. Although he is as a rule careful, the missing £1,000 bag of gold some years ago and again the great loss occasioned by his inattention to the reply of London Office to his own enquiry about Davis' diamonds, are painful instances of negligence or carelessness. Although past experience will, it is to be hoped, cause him to be more observant generally, and to keep a more constant 'look out', on board, it may not be inadvisable to impress upon him in forcible terms from time to time as circumstances suggest, the absolute necessity of being 'careful'.

Diamonds advanced against are made up in parcels and sealed by Mr Harsant himself and the parties bringing them in. It is his intention to write up the 'Discount Progressive Ledger' himself henceforward, as his time is not now so much occupied as formerly, and as the clerks who have hitherto kept it have not done so with the care and accuracy they should have.

[*J. W. Harsant moved on to another branch in May 1878, and Williams's reservations plainly did his career no harm: he was to be Assistant General Manager, 1902–7.*]

John Strachan Goodall, Accountant, Age 26 last birthday. Salary at £300 p. Ann. last increased in June 1877. Has signed the Declaration of secrecy, and his fidelity is guaranteed by the Colonial & Foreign Banks Guarantee Fund for £1,000. He was for eight years in the employ of the Union Bank of Scotland, first at Errol and afterwards in Glasgow. States he entered the Bank's service on the 27th September 1875 at the London Office and came straight on to Kimberley, and received his present appointment in July 1877. The principal work Mr Goodall does is the checking of the books and of all Interest and Discount calculations, drawing out of the Forms and Drafts connected with Diamond transactions, the writing up of the Weekly Form & Vo. 11 [?] and counting the Cash weekly. So far as I have observed he appears to be fairly accurate. He is quick, intelligent, useful, and writes an excellent hand. Is steady, honest and punctual in his attendance at the Office. Has good general abilities, and sufficient self-confidence. His manner and address are straightforward but appear at first rather abrupt until he is better known. He is impulsive rather than thoughtful. If his attention is directed to something he will see to it at once, but he seems as yet to be rather lacking in that steady constant watch and thoughtfulness which alone can keep the work of an office up to the mark of thorough efficiency and good order. He will however, I think, improve in that respect. Upon the whole I consider him to be a good and reliable Officer, and could be safely left in charge of the Branch during any temporary absence of the Manager. I also think him capable and fit to manage permanently an ordinarily sized Branch. I understand from him that he is not desirous of leaving Kimberley for another six months or so. He has no knowledge of the Dutch language. He has since date of this report resigned the post of Accountant to the Kimberley Mining Board, the extra work being more than he could accomplish either to his own or the Board's satisfaction – the Secretary's mode of keeping the books being, I understand, unsystematic and causing a correct Balance Sheet to be almost impossible. He is Lieut. and Adjutant of a local Volunteer Corps.

Percy George Williams, Senior Teller, Age 25 last birthday. Salary £275 last increased in August 1877. Has signed the Declaration of secrecy, and his fidelity is guaranteed by the Col. & F. B. G. Fund for £1,000. States he was clerk to J. W. Hobbs Insurance Broker, 31 New Broad Street EC for 3½ years; with Leech Harrison & Forward, Merchants, 30 Great St Helens, for one year; with W. M. Smith, Underwriters, London for one year; and afterwards, as Senior Clerk, with Messrs Smith Payne & Smith, the Bankers, for one year. Entered the Bank's service at Grahamstown on 23rd December 1874 and received his present appointment of Teller in August 1877 but had been acting Teller for about three months previously. Mr Williams's work is confined to Telling, and copying the Notes he receives and pays across the counter [;] his Cash Book is now written up for him by the Second Teller 1875. At times the Counter work is heavy – more especially on Mondays and Saturdays. Mr Williams is steady and correct in his habits, performs his duties upon the whole fairly well apparently, is I believe honest, and judging from his remarks when spoken to, seems very desirous of giving satisfaction. He does not however impress one as having more than very ordinary abilities and gumption. He gets rather nervous and excited on busy days, and there is a frequency of 'surpluses' and 'shorts' of small amounts in his Cash. His handwriting in the books is somewhat poor and indistinct. Having diseased lungs he is

frequently unwell, and obliged to absent himself from duty for a day or
so from time to time; he is otherwise punctual in his attendance at the
Office.

John Albert Tetley, Second Teller, Age 23 last birthday. Salary £225,
last increased in December 1877 on his arrival here. Has signed the
Declaration of secrecy, and his fidelity is guaranteed by the Col. & F. B. G.
Fund for £1,000. He states he was Clerk for six years with Given &
Braddyll Cotton Brokers of England, and entered the Bank's service at
Port Elizabeth in December 1876[;] from there he went to the Grahamstown Branch and came here in December 1877. Mr Tetley is one of
the 5 officers who stay on the Bank Premises at night. Having only
very recently come here, he has scarcely yet had time to show what he
is made of. He appears to be quite steady and to conduct himself respect-
ably. His work at this Branch has been to write up the Teller's Cash Book
and draw Drafts and to attend to the Counter work when the Senior
Teller is absent on sick leave. Can write quickly and well, but if he took
more pride in his work, his books would present a better appearance.
While attending to the Counter, during the present fortnight's absence of
the Teller, he did not display any marked aptitude for that special work:
press of customers making him rather nervous and excited and his manner not so courteous to them as it should be. His cash balance also was
not always correct. He is however rather new to the place and people yet
[?]. With a little kindly advice from the Manager from time to time I see
no reason why Mr Tetley should not become a good and useful Clerk in
every way.

John Joss, Correspondence Clerk. Age 23 last birthday. Salary £220, last
increased in June 1877. Has signed the Declaration of secrecy, and his
fidelity is guaranteed by the Col. & F. B. G. Fund for £1,000. Was clerk
in the Chartered Mercantile Bank of India, London & China, London,
for two years; and entered the service of the Standard Bank, in London,
on the 23rd of January 1877 and came straight on to the Kimberley Branch.
Mr Joss was offered the post of Second Teller here lately, but preferred
not to take it. His work is to write the letters, and the Monthly Returns.
He is steady and correct in his habits, useful and intelligent, regular and
punctual in his attendance at the office, and performs his duties to the
Manager's and Accountant's satisfaction. He writes a quick and fairly
good hand, and takes an interest in understanding the Bank's system of
bookkeeping. He would seem to have made up his mind to make headway
in the service. He is I think the best Clerk in the office and stands next to

the Accountant in point of ability, reliability and general usefulness. He sleeps on the Bank Premises at night.

William Macbean, Ledger Clerk. Age 29 last birthday. Salary £250, last increased 13th April 1876 on his removal here from another Branch. Has signed the Declaration of secrecy, and his fidelity is guaranteed by the Col. & F. B. G. Fund for £1,000. He states he was Clerk in the Caledonian Bank, Inverness, for three years, and subsequently in the National Provincial Bank of England London for three years; and that he entered the service of the Standard Bank at Port Elizabeth in March 1873. For some little time previous to July 1877 Mr Macbean attended from 10 to 1 o'clock daily at the Du Toit's Pan Agency, but from that time – having had the misfortune to break one of his legs while walking in the streets here one evening – he has been one of the Ledger Clerks at this office. His work is confined to keeping the Current Account Ledger I to Z and the Pass Books relating thereto. He is still lame & cannot walk far without the aid of crutches. He is, I believe, steady [sic], and is punctual in his attendance at the office. His handwriting is indifferent and slow, but he keeps his Ledger and Pass books with a very fair amount of neatness. His capabilities generally as a Bank officer appear to be small, and I would not like to entrust him with an office of responsibility, because I have an impression that he would neglect his duties and let youths placed under him do just what they pleased. Mr Macbean sleeps at night on the Bank Premises.

Richard Mullins Roberts, Ledger Clerk. Age 21 last birthday. Salary £220, not increased since appointment on 1st March 1876. Has signed the Declaration of secrecy, and his fidelity is guaranteed by the Col. & F. B. G. Fund for £1,000. He states he was Clerk to Messrs. Hoole & Co Grahamstown for about 2½ years and entered the Bank's service at Kimberley on 1st March 1876. He lives with his father Mr R. M. Roberts, Diamond Buyer etc of this place. Mr Roberts keeps the Current Account Ledger A to H and the Pass books relating thereto. He is a fair average Clerk. Can write a neat hand, and quickly, but his books shew unnecessary haste and incompleteness – painting [?] of figures and omission of dates etc. He is a steady respectable youth and is regular and punctual in his attendance at the office. With good training he would be likely to become a good & efficient Officer.

Colin Charles Campbell, Teller at Du Toits Pan. Age 24 in December 1877. Salary £240, last increased on 1st July 1877. Has signed the Declaration of secrecy, and his fidelity is guaranteed by the Col. & F. B. G. Fund for £500. He states he was Clerk to W. Peacock & Co of Grahamstown for three years; to Black & Darwell Grahamstown for two years; after that at a Boer shop in Bethulie O.F.S. [Orange Freee State] for a short time; and entered the Bank's service at Kimberley on 29th July 1875. Mr Campbell attends daily and alone from 10 to 1 o'clock at the Du Toits Pan Agency, bringing up his cash and books to the Kimberley Branch after 1pm and afterwards writing up the Current Accounts Cash Book at the latter office. He is a somewhat present Master of the High Court here, [--?--], correct in his habits, and, I believe, quite honest. He appears to possess fair abilities, but they want cultivation. He has the drawback of being slightly shortsighted, and his Cash has not been quite free of mistakes – his largest deficiency – £10 – referred to under the heading 'Cash' in this Report, he has since made good. Writes quickly, and also very <u>well</u> when he chooses, but <u>portions</u> of his books are, I regret to say, not such as a <u>careful</u>, reflecting Clerk who has set by much [of] his own time to write them would look back upon without a blush.

<u>Hegard Glenney Christison, General Clerk</u>. Aged 19 last birthday. Salary £200, last increased in December 1877 on his removal here from Port Elizabeth. Has signed the Declaration of secrecy, and his fidelity is guaranteed by the Col. & F. B. G. Fund for £500. He states he was Clerk in the City of Glasgow Bank, Arbroath, for three years; and entered the service of the Standard Bank at Port Elizabeth on 1st May 1877. He has only been here a short time. Writes a poor hand but is fairly quick at his work. Is a good-looking young man, and is I believe steady, but is in the <u>habit</u> of using very low language in the company of his fellow clerks after business hours. He sleeps on the Bank's Premises at night. The bent of his mind is towards Music and not Business. He has, I think, quick parts generally, but I have a misgiving, so far, as to his ever turning out a thoroughly reliable, good and trustworthy Officer. He is young and precocious and will require looking after.

<u>Arthur [-?-] Hawkins, Clerk</u>, Aged 20 last birthday. Salary £200, last increased in July 1877 on his removal here from Port Elizabeth. Has signed the Declaration of secrecy, and his fidelity is guaranteed by the Col. & F. B. G. Fund for £500. He states that on leaving school he entered the Bank's service at Pietermaritzberg, in January 1875, which he left about January 1876 for a clerkship at an Engineer's Office at Panmure in the Cape Colony. That after a period of six weeks, he re-entered the Bank at Cradock & was subsequently removed to Adelaide and Port Elizabeth. Mr Hawkins keeps the Bill books, Clean Cash Book (exclusive of the Current Account portion), General Ledger, writes the Weekly State and

Form No. 22. The Discount Progressive Ledger which he has also been keeping will henceforth be kept by the Manager. He sleeps on the Bank Premises at night and is steady and I believe correct in his habits. He is fairly quick at his work, and could if he tried, write a very passable hand, but his books are not very neatly kept and they contain a considerable number of mistakes. He is wanting in carefulness, accuracy and zeal, and he would not appear to have more than very ordinary abilities.

<u>William Watkin Alexander, Junior Clerk</u>. Age 17. Salary £110. Was clerk for four months at the Office of the Board of Executors here, and entered the Bank's service at Kimberley on the 26th April 1877. Has signed the Declaration of secrecy, and his fidelity is guaranteed by the Col. & F. B. G. Fund for £500. Mr Alexander makes the clearances with the other Banks, collects Bills, copies & posts the letters, and does the ordinary work of a Junior. He writes a good hand, is neat, careful and attentive. Is steady & correct in his habits, and with careful training will make I believe a good, trustworthy and efficient Clerk in a short time.

The Staff is upon the whole not above an average one, I think, in point of general efficiency. The business of the Branch being more limited than formerly, one or perhaps even two might be spared, were <u>all</u> really experienced and efficient, and were it not that during the very trying summer months, there is one or another laid up with sickness.

As regards salaries, the Accountant agrees with me that taking the Staff all round they would not be better paid outside than they are already by the Bank.

There might be a little more economy effected in the use of stationery than there is. It seems to be knocking about the office rather plentifully, and unnecessarily wasteful; blank spaces are to be seen in several of the books. I have drawn the attention of the Manager & Accountant to these and similar matters, and expressed a wish that all the Clerks might be brought to take a greater pride in their work generally, and be more painstaking and earnest to <u>deserve</u> promotion.

<u>Attorney & Notary</u> – Mr R. D. Graham. I have nothing to add to the former Reports on this gentleman.

R. Williams
Inspector.

Appendix C

A Brief History of BBWA before 1914

Registered in 1894 with a two-man office in Liverpool and a five-man office in Lagos, the Bank of British West Africa (BBWA) was the brainchild of a shipping agent on Africa's Guinea Coast, George Neville. His employer was the Liverpool firm of Elder Dempster & Co., one of the three giants of the shipping world (rivalling the British India and P&O fleets); but his parish was probably the least hospitable living environment anywhere in the Empire. It stretched from the Gambia river mouth on the western edge of the continent, south towards the equator and then eastwards round the huge Gulf of Guinea via the Ivory Coast and the Gold Coast (modern Ghana) to the great river delta and waterways of what would soon become Nigeria, a vast territory whose northern borders in 1894 had yet to be defined in any European atlas. The Guinea Coast's reputation as 'the white man's grave' was still entirely warranted. In 1896, the colonial authority for Lagos stated in its annual report 'that out of 150 Europeans, 28 died within a few months of arrival'. Locals swapped macabre jokes about the mortality rate, referring to Government House in Lagos as 'a corrugated iron coffin that contained a dead Governor once a year'.[32] Nor was it just the climate that gave the Guinea Coast its fearsome reputation. Having originally asserted control over the harbour towns only as part of its war against the slave trade, Britain had been drawn by events on the ground into a steady escalation of its role as the dominant colonial power; but its authority could still be challenged in many areas, sometimes with gruesome consequences. When a Colonial Commissioner arrived in the city of Benin in 1897, planning on a frank discussion with the King of Benin about Britain's colonial plans, his stay was cut brutally short, as indeed was the Commissioner: he and half a dozen European colleagues, along with their three hundred African bearers, were all decapitated. (George Neville himself accompanied the punitive expedition later despatched to Benin to settle the score.) Not for nothing had most commercial transactions by European merchants been traditionally handled as 'floating trade', with goods exchanged in mid-river on ships with armed guards.

Unsurprisingly, traders and ship-owners had never had much luck trying to lure European bankers to the region – and indeed, George Neville of Elder Dempster was no exception. He managed in 1891 to persuade the owner-chairman of the shipping line in Liverpool, Alfred Jones, not only that a local bank might do wonders for trade and Empire in West Africa, to the great benefit of their shipping business, but also that Elder Dempster should attract such a bank by offering its own services as an agency. Unfortunately the only bank Neville could find as a partner was a brand new institution, which bravely accepted his proposal in June 1891 but decided little more than a year later that it needed to abandon the whole idea.* Never a man to admit defeat once embarked on a scheme, Alfred Jones thereupon bought out the nascent bank with his own money, and pooled its assets with those of Elder Dempster. When the British Government pointed out that the Crown Agents could only deal with a properly registered joint-stock bank, talks followed in Whitehall that led ('after considerable negotiations', as noted in a prefatory paragraph to Volume One of the bank's Minutes Books) to the creation of the BBWA.[33] Established with 3,000 paid-up shares of £4 each that were mostly allotted to Jones himself, it was still in effect Elder Dempster's house bank: it would work out of the same offices, with Neville as its General Manager at the head of a small staff in Lagos (see Plate 17). Jones would chair its small Board with three other Directors (one of whom, Henry Coke, was the powerful Liverpool agent of David Sassoon & Co.).

For several years thereafter, it was the only bank in its marketplace – its telegraphic and cable address in West Africa was 'Banking' – and it serviced a regional economy just waking up to the export opportunities of the modern world. The local climate, however unpropitious for colonial governors, proved ideal for two new wonder crops – the cocoa bean and the cultivated rubber plant. The first export samples were shipped in 1891 and 1893 respectively, weighing less than 100 lbs each, but many tons of both were soon filling up freight steamers, usually belonging to Elder Dempster, bound for Europe.[34] Cocoa exports grew especially

---

* It ought to be added, at the risk of some confusion, that the bank accepting Neville's proposal was none other than the African Banking Corporation. Launched at the end of 1890, two months after the October collapse of the Cape of Good Hope Bank which it went on to acquire, the ABC had alerted investors to its pan-African ambitions from the start. 'Although the intention is to commence operations in South Africa ... the bank will be extended to other parts of Africa when circumstances seem to justify the establishment of additional branches' (*The Times*, 20 December 1890). But the complexities of business in West Africa and the challenge of competing against the Standard in the Cape had soon left it hopelessly overstretched.

quickly, with the Gold Coast and Nigeria shipping out 10,000 tons a year by 1906. The BBWA would in time come to be known as the Cocoa Bank. Both crops took several years to establish, and the European owners of freshly laid plantations relied heavily on advances from the BBWA. The bank was also crucial to the funding of rapid growth in several other exports, notably of cotton, hard timber, palm kernels (for crushing to make margarine, mostly in German mills) and groundnuts. The profits for City shareholders were modest in the 1890s, but the prospects for the new century were obvious. Some of the region's leading traders were anxious to see a rival for the otherwise ubiquitous BBWA/Elder Dempster combination, and with their encouragement the Bank of Nigeria (known at first as the Anglo-African Bank) was established in 1899. It brought competition into some agricultural sectors, but there was one area of the economy where Alfred Jones's bank continued to enjoy a complete monopoly – the provision of silver coins. Minted in Britain, sterling florins, shillings and sixpences constituted the bulk of the region's money for the simple reason that native West Africans would accept nothing else. Cheques and even bank notes had a growing circulation among European merchants on the coast, but inland they never made any headway at all. Whatever the inconvenience, a stiff jute bag containing £100 of silver sterling coins was the standard means of exchange for large sums; and if thousands of pounds had to be taken from a town branch into the interior, say for seasonal crop purchases, then dozens of heavy bags would make the journey accordingly. Ensuring a timely and suitably distributed supply of specie across a huge area was no mean task – and had, of course, been a principal reason for establishing the BBWA in the first place.

While acting as a stimulant for local commerce in general, its monetary role brought the BBWA itself two bonus endowments. The first was a quasi-official status in West Africa, not unlike Standard Bank's at the Cape in earlier days. This was reflected in a series of appointments around the turn of the century as the Colonial Governments' banker in most of the territories on the West African Coast, from Bathurst in the Gambia to Old Calabar in the south-east of Nigeria. The second was a tidy income from 'seignorage' – that is, the difference between the face value of silver coins and the value of their bullion content – which waxed as the sterling value of silver waned. The BBWA's right to this income, which it shared with the Royal Mint, was a perennial source of grief to the Colonial Governments. It also irked the Bank of Nigeria, which badgered the Colonial Office to reform the whole arrangement. This eventually provoked a long and tortuous wrangle between the two banks, the Colonial Secretary Lord Crewe and a long list of other interested parties across Whitehall and West

Africa that lasted from 1906 to 1909. It pitted more or less all of the Colonial Secretary's advisers against Alfred Jones, who had personally watched
over every aspect of his bank since 1894 and was a formidably tough
character. Crewe finally agreed in August 1909 to receive a private delegation led by Jones himself, and three weeks later – for reasons that were
never clear to contemporaries, and were still a mystery almost seventy
years later to the BBWA's official historian – decided to override the advice
of his officials.

> Some historians have assumed that Alfred Jones dazzled Lord Crewe with
> his famous personal magnetism, or that he used irresistible new arguments . . .
> It seems just possible that the Minister, taking a wider and longer view than
> the experts, felt in his bones that the time was not yet ripe for changing a
> system which had introduced a great deal of stability into West Africa.[35]

Whatever his rationale, anyway, Crewe decreed that the BBWA's coin
monopoly should be left in place.

But the real denouement followed over the next three years. Jones
himself died a few months after his productive meeting with Lord Crewe,
in December 1909; the Board and management structure of the bank were
overhauled, with the Head Office moving from Liverpool to Leadenhall
Street in the City; and the Directors elected a new Chairman, Lord Milner,
who was as smooth and magisterial as Jones had been blunt and dictato-
rial. The Bank of Nigeria's Directors, apparently discouraged by their
defeat in the battle over the coinage and skilfully wooed by Milner,
accepted a takeover by the BBWA in 1912. This pleased all those in Whitehall for whom a single bank in West Africa was infinitely simpler than
two; and the existing monetary arrangements were in the same year
scrapped in favour of a West African Currency Board with a new West
African silver coinage that pleased the Colonial Governments, not least
because it left them rather than the BBWA with a share of the seignorage.
The net outcome for the bank itself was that, by the outbreak of the war,
it was once again unambiguously the 'national bank' of the region, enjoying the full confidence of the British Government.[36] (Its London Chief
Manager, Leslie Couper, a likeable Glaswegian, was the only non-official
member of the new Currency Board, for which the bank acted as agent
in the field.) It had also consolidated its unique franchise as an overseas
bank with some thirty-four branches in West Africa – with wonderfully
exotic names from Axim to Zungeru – and no serious competitor.

Appendix D

Annual profits/losses per branch of Chartered Bank, 1895–1953
Current sterling values

Agency or Branch	1895	1896	1897	1898	1899	1900	1901	1902	1903	1904	1905
Bombay	12,508	17,963	23,833	19,106	8,406	16,601	14,567	24,228	3,098	26,248	19,559
Colombo	12,508	17,963	23,833	19,106	8,406	11,466	15,057	10,686	13,070	19,060	21,725
Calcutta	5,984	18,883	34,708	2,430	8,750	23,205	28,252	22,734	32,694	35,588	26,382
Rangoon	3,407	11,230	10,054	9,043	3,192	9,931	11,257	8,827	14,091	23,968	19,266
Penang	4,429	8,350	32,417	39,956	24,288	30,057	22,658	15,586	13,962	30,556	21,611
Singapore	10,619	-6,523	40,828	44,473	37,528	18,134	14,876	15,269	-3,175	-362	16,584
Batavia	20,965	12,305	10,050	11,367	8,592	7,976	14,441	7,750	4,266	9,019	9,114
Hong Kong	9,062	7,518	4,306	20,732	33,467	24,078	21,209	15,230	30,588	17,867	26,761
Manila	3,787	15,723	10,181	17,212	18,973	-3,105	14,380	26,904	2,800	13,941	5,174
Shanghai	19,225	1,956	9,979	5,430	-7,773	17,810	15,109	19,482	28,659	-3,596	34,565
Yokohama	19,225	1,956	9,979	5,430	-7,773	22,327	20,339	23,745	19,176	34,728	34,519
Madras	0	0	0	0	0	45	5,512	4,401	3,826	5,290	7,436
Bangkok	0	0	0	0	0	355	7,515	9,657	16,070	15,485	13,755
Tientsin	0	0	0	0	0	0	0	4,335	-5,114	-3,665	11,717
New York	0	0	0	0	0	0	0	-1,571	-1,258	2,294	9,836
Saigon	0	0	0	0	0	0	0	0	0	1,163	2,528
Hamburg	0	0	0	0	0	0	0	0	0	-900	6,505
Kuala Lumpur	0	0	0	0	0	0	0	0	0	0	0
Karachi	0	0	0	0	0	0	0	0	0	0	0
Peking	0	0	0	0	0	0	0	0	0	0	0
Overseas total	121,719	107,324	210,168	194,285	136,056	178,880	205,172	207,263	172,753	226,684	287,037
Head Office	-8,755	5,992	15,300	0	-18,163	-5,634	79,131	15,427	-2,064	55,581	37,216
TOTAL Branches + HO	112,964	113,316	225,468	194,285	117,893	173,246	284,303	222,690	170,689	282,265	324,253
No. of full branches	11	11	11	11	11	13	13	15	15	17	17

1906	1907	1908	1909	1910	1911	1912	1913	1914	1915	1916	1917	1918
22,921	22,897	24,819	19,085	15,002	12,387	25,729	37,069	31,893	27,763	15,591	35,098	14,398
26,162	30,799	29,526	20,711	34,864	29,579	27,059	30,514	45,921	40,605	53,716	57,040	40,582
38,608	42,031	47,584	30,785	36,026	42,813	46,984	50,919	72,067	56,581	72,096	44,435	98,984
22,803	13,690	17,919	19,867	1,697	16,829	24,604	23,061	27,046	18,270	19,181	25,407	12,100
33,085	35,009	28,335	7,833	24,003	12,912	19,473	11,646	25,066	24,951	56,377	63,455	71,176
14,259	19,680	15,063	8,047	19,521	7,836	9,605	8,067	17,249	38,697	49,138	63,056	78,914
2,719	5,137	2,772	-522	-1,192	4,727	1,896	6,809	11,472	5,968	59,415	13,671	26,052
22,504	10,459	15,903	-7,764	2,780	12,281	13,773	9,209	-22,442	1,982	22,598	64,729	134,714
6,020	8,402	19,262	16,310	27,710	27,015	33,372	20,038	18,780	32,843	25,998	15,165	8,925
7,904	-17,364	17,264	5,510	9,682	-3,356	10,925	18,787	6,536	8,805	92,876	56,224	65,851
6,524	15,041	-32,099	4,028	2,465	8,974	5,643	9,055	5,873	30,582	27,333	58,294	122,968
626	3,733	4,617	6,971	8,472	9,053	9,884	15,198	11,819	14,701	26,745	13,432	7,815
18,396	18,925	12,120	9,094	11,156	8,702	15,620	21,126	22,325	22,216	20,127	21,738	29,250
4,677	-5,322	-16,741	-991	2,207	-1,752	8,647	2,808	1,774	3,735	0	0	0
602	1,598	-1,547	-3,991	-3,471	-1,076	2,732	779	5,774	11,343	2,842	6,386	11,238
2,711	-2,317	16,370	9,109	3,345	6,267	3,814	2,291	43,362	57,637	-8,055	37,994	25,356
4,053	5,768	671	2,716	4,455	3,767	5,263	8,179	2,065	0	0	0	0
0	0	0	0	12,418	14,468	26,640	26,686	13,833	22,557	24,075	8,926	4,863
0	0	0	0	0	0	-4,049	-3,111	1,849	574	3,807	8,560	5,916
0	0	0	0	0	0	0	0	0	0	-4,317	-7,184	-10,590
234,574	208,166	201,838	146,798	211,140	211,426	287,614	299,130	342,262	419,810	559,543	586,426	748,512
29,681	75,018	95,690	20,320	41,865	55,158	97,009	105,361	52,873	18,584	71,151	105,570	160,400
264,255	283,184	297,528	167,118	253,005	266,584	384,623	404,491	395,135	438,394	630,694	691,996	908,912
17	17	17	17	18	18	19	19	19	18	18	18	18

Source: Directors' Book of Profits (reference: LMA: CH04/02/02/001)

Annual profits/losses per branch of Chartered Bank, 1895–1953
Current sterling values

Agency or Branch	1919	1920	1921	1922	1923	1924	1925	1926
Bombay	96,204	179,392	117,640	70,803	54,796	139,439	10,288	33,544
Colombo	42,566	84,919	61,294	41,885	40,803	42,911	60,718	80,272
Madras	48,160	-5,660	32,827	15,075	19,382	27,344	7,707	6,052
Calcutta	-65,348	364,774	140,358	98,733	90,979	53,866	140,501	73,045
Rangoon	85,362	-51,958	12,150	30,494	12,735	-17,090	14,730	7,976
Penang	92,374	180,199	28,361	-10,948	21,888	23,382	43,213	73,161
Singapore	186,132	177,161	113,719	47,489	76,936	72,366	148,269	183,505
Bangkok	-3,356	-320,788	294,823	71,628	181,596	18,603	28,777	34,050
Batavia	-95,525	101,706	45,277	6,265	-25,547	-26,529	-33,894	-17,990
Hong Kong	17,177	263,830	155,457	47,185	85,561	16,837	56,530	112,271
Manila	119,718	-130,074	57,675	25,264	15,375	37,188	21,719	8,265
Shanghai	-272,455	100,081	2,792	52,876	-2,363	24,160	17,185	20,417
Yokohama	257,988	469,184	91,846	16,482	43,552	0	0	0
Kobe	0	0	0	0	0	97,638	-103,098	-47,980
Tientsin	0	-4,436	21,906	30,250	-7,535	29,830	8,432	-1,138
New York	22,978	39,509	-103,566	-31,307	-543	-6,537	-8,253	1,710
Saigon	120,073	18,971	-68,892	2,041	-16,236	-11,020	-27,898	-9,208
Hamburg	1,436	-366	-1,427	-1,763	-3,689	-5,413	-5,990	-15,307
Kuala Lumpur	96,353	86,406	23,727	10,970	37,629	33,200	82,329	122,349
Karachi	20,799	-157,494	840	8,651	13,376	25,401	-10,492	-8,689
Peking	-11,167	-10,123	-6,384	-5,559	-7,488	-7,639	-7,478	-7,246
Medan	-7,578	11,624	29,279	11,046	2,448	-575	6,162	12,663
Delhi	0	-4,093	4,076	-6,462	-7,239	-7,641	-7,850	0
Amritsar	0	0	0	-792	5,014	12,994	6,015	1,598
Cawnpore	0	0	0	-665	-226	-3,084	-2,069	-3,700
Kuching	0	0	0	0	0	-1,230	3,673	4,840
Harbin	0	0	0	0	0	0	0	0
Ipoh	0	0	0	0	0	0	0	0
Manchester	0	0	0	0	0	0	0	0
Fairlie Place (Calcutta)	0	0	0	0	0	0	0	0
Chungking	0	0	0	0	0	0	0	0
Jesselton	0	0	0	0	0	0	0	0
Cochin	0	0	0	0	0	0	0	0
Aden	0	0	0	0	0	0	0	0
Overseas total	751,891	1,392,764	1,053,778	529,641	631,204	568,401	449,226	664,460
Head Office	-51,780	35,031	224,948	559,857	316,015	389,477	410,868	210,110
TOTAL Branches + HO	700,111	1,427,795	1,278,726	1,089,498	947,219	957,878	860,094	874,570
No. of full branches	20	22	22	24	24	25	25	24

1927	1928	1929	1930	1931	1932	1933	1934	1935	1936
21,331	-9,438	21,150	27,044	-15,129	18,572	28,089	14,388	-257,687	-23,443
28,454	28,682	48,263	39,194	15,877	-56,284	14,850	42,873	-14,830	1,854
13,646	2,246	10,890	11,151	-11,930	66,617	10,209	17,095	17,506	25,784
14,221	-45,529	-22,121	-17,568	-89,175	-112	40,987	35,564	56,482	63,610
-10,506	20,665	2,957	10,122	-39,215	-2,043	-6,527	-3,897	-4,790	-2,231
41,894	45,158	31,261	22,622	-31,224	51,110	7,435	20,436	20,400	15,540
84,940	82,001	61,105	9,192	24,900	-44,086	4,439	33,293	21,098	47,397
52,864	26,951	46,209	38,409	-127,608	122,243	-5,496	-4,994	-28,333	-12,086
-15,423	-3,956	1,127	-4,767	-394,178	-97,526	-73,381	-165,481	33,073	18,634
62,217	38,504	162,338	39,093	-122,981	143,677	49,102	28,425	103,878	72,891
-919	19,981	23,740	42,888	7,716	70,551	79,236	35,125	21,713	35,141
-24,070	-6,191	-2,152	15,397	-87,898	216,480	280,886	182,606	2,089	72,478
0	0	-12,072	-11,915	-9,202	1,124	546	-7,240	-9,057	-5,114
-6,311	23,255	-3,960	-5,188	-25,845	55,453	-3,228	19,683	10,567	7,338
30,348	3,073	49,609	2,170	-46,787	86,167	14,328	43,381	39,269	25,387
-31,054	-12,095	-22,442	-17,268	-9,716	-20,593	2,339	-5,056	-22,954	15,690
-22,444	-14,534	4,317	7,429	54,997	10,524	-5,746	-10,669	2,358	20,905
-10,383	-12,354	-10,645	-10,089	-11,026	-9,750	-7,560	-4,441	-618	-119
22,206	80,752	102,980	28,368	4,346	-108,644	15,945	19,916	30,099	26,654
-10,803	4,326	-1,578	-2,685	-10,494	6,923	234	13,955	-89,876	-2,997
-6,595	-6,995	-5,440	-4,373	-5,116	-3,977	-4,122	-3,226	-2,282	-1,914
2,691	4,553	11,408	9,035	-7,042	-22,276	-10,831	-9,010	-26,323	-9,854
0	0	0	0	0	0	0	0	0	0
2,930	4,940	3,531	1,305	-1,902	586	936	1,652	3,168	1,580
-3,772	-1,737	-1,564	-223	-9,887	-5,302	2,141	1,889	214	1,774
270	2,689	2,480	2,106	3,358	-1,608	-1,088	862	2,407	3,567
0	-2,243	-28,515	-28,462	-37,571	-33,405	7,405	-900	-850	649
0	0	5,386	12,266	12,908	-35,817	4,821	-1,980	7,869	1,372
0	0	0	0	0	0	0	0	0	0
0	0	0	0	0	0	0	0	0	0
0	0	0	0	0	0	0	0	0	0
0	0	0	0	0	0	0	0	0	0
0	0	0	0	0	0	0	0	0	0
0	0	0	0	0	0	0	0	0	0
235,732	272,704	478,262	215,253	-969,824	408,604	445,949	294,249	-85,410	400,487
329,547	359,039	271,948	381,724	6,385	250,064	197,791	629,192	315,320	387,190
565,279	631,743	750,210	596,977	-963,439	658,668	643,740	923,441	229,910	787,677
24	25	27	27	27	27	27	27	27	27

Source: Directors' Book of Profits (reference: LMA: CH04/02/02/001)

Annual profits/losses per branch of Chartered Bank, 1895–1953
Current sterling values

Agency or Branch	1937	1938	1939	1940	1941	1942	1943	1944
Bombay	10,087	-20,798	33,045	57,115	-12,100	107,316	65,879	61,617
Colombo	15,438	17,997	-16,432	56,254	19,080	46,872	26,586	36,108
Madras	26,446	13,050	16,122	21,676	16,922	24,939	15,028	12,853
Calcutta	22,430	38,304	41,449	90,642	100,804	147,391	66,368	79,483
Rangoon	9,690	7,338	6,593	231	33,547	-14,443	-16,531	-18,147
Penang	-15,555	-56,444	7,850	25,032	14,540	0	0	0
Singapore	44,699	53,787	64,508	208,041	103,276	0	0	0
Bangkok	-1,035	6,921	14,234	13,626	22,786	0	0	0
Batavia	-15,906	-7,952	-35,137	35,301	21,092	0	0	0
Hong Kong	6,440	14,402	103,912	116,619	25,307	0	0	-18,000
Manila	64,614	62,354	62,955	28,312	10,152	0	0	0
Shanghai	-22,230	-31,226	88,465	131,972	47,956	0	0	0
Yokohama	2,329	-5,111	2,132	2,112	0	0	0	0
Kobe	6,384	-2,524	6,723	-7,661	-976	-676	-681	-2,251
Tientsin	13,727	79,303	23,244	15,926	6,988	0	0	0
New York	24,344	19,330	-87,635	-123,610	88,412	67,221	41,367	24,669
Saigon	13,227	-12,685	23,993	13,955	-1,709	0	0	0
Hamburg	2,531	189	322	0	0	0	0	0
Kuala Lumpur	17,891	53,227	7,077	69,083	12,044	0	0	0
Karachi	-4,809	-5,745	1,479	15,119	7,569	5,500	4,003	-5,680
Peking	-2,107	-1,771	-1,323	-1,211	-1,105	0	0	0
Medan	-1,819	-1,016	4,437	4,843	7,820	0	0	0
Delhi	-2,012	-3,168	-2,230	-2,805	-1,871	4,129	737	-5,549
Amritsar	-3,403	1,446	-2,049	-1,590	-675	2,965	-8,775	-4,100
Cawnpore	1,729	3,314	6,285	7,559	9,207	10,114	11,587	7,204
Kuching	5,589	4,369	-834	4,319	4,391	0	0	0
Harbin	-545	5,028	-1,928	-3,194	-1,824	0	0	0
Ipoh	5,555	8,629	1,489	21,327	-1,965	0	0	0
Manchester	-1,066	106	243	5,904	13,599	886	-808	-5,730
Fairlie Place (Calcutta)	0	0	14,925	10,327	38,498	21,058	17,298	38,444
Chungking	0	0	0	0	0	-2,235	-8,609	-7,335
Jesselton	0	0	0	0	0	0	0	0
Cochin	0	0	0	0	0	0	0	0
Aden	0	0	0	0	0	0	0	0
Overseas total	222,663	240,654	383,914	815,224	581,765	421,037	213,449	193,586
Head Office	570,415	148,376	118,231	438,436	324,375	366,944	576,480	559,062
TOTAL Branches + HO	793,078	389,030	502,145	1,253,660	906,140	787,981	789,929	752,648
No. of full branches	29	29	30	29	28	14	14	15

1945	1946	1947	1948	1949	1950	1951	1952	1953
47,934	107,760	62,170	31,081	164,183	156,787	168,296	138,957	97,983
32,308	23,582	33,101	67,563	35,623	62,097	90,106	50,577	-52,317
22,405	46,638	18,418	19,287	40,726	50,335	57,033	43,308	30,953
76,540	128,549	57,625	73,778	130,975	124,389	144,519	131,005	92,928
-17,111	-9,893	10,272	22,769	13,752	40,364	49,674	51,727	47,473
45,826	104,309	14,438	11,453	19,257	34,595	98,127	86,592	99,906
113,355	73,557	216,564	207,439	286,636	309,026	616,029	498,902	415,643
0	74,421	103,173	102,294	124,326	155,294	154,173	262,446	123,550
0	9,029	63,010	54,594	111,929	47,151	125,387	241,970	357,529
-67,135	-51,369	115,767	105,415	262,901	148,918	172,363	155,823	258,338
-38,035	-19,726	-48,990	3,664	59,186	89,375	71,855	72,254	69,857
-58,917	-14,951	-93,464	1,577	-77,459	-34,762	-79,703	-76,424	-142,394
0	0	0	0	0	0	0	0	0
-1,301	-5,777	0	0	0	0	0	0	0
0	-35,522	-2,529	3,617	0	0	0	0	0
17,104	47,503	8,273	65,359	53,507	19,421	48,402	89,597	66,236
0	-1,337	2,445	22,417	63,427	46,545	86,388	110,956	91,630
0	-40,756	0	-1,645	-4,572	1,916	5,648	7,968	19,312
84,132	-7,496	59,164	-16,898	49,816	50,696	149,382	118,651	292,566
1,623	8,468	11,207	23,559	-91,683	166,728	103,162	71,356	14,607
0	0	0	0	0	0	0	0	0
0	0	0	0	0	0	0	0	0
-2,977	1,869	5,527	-4,565	7,727	-4,233	1,699	1,870	-5,002
-3,344	1,452	5,406	-543	3,651	-13,735	6,660	-4,254	-7,344
10,166	30,083	12,975	20,833	21,544	33,761	21,028	12,120	10,078
0	0	0	-10,541	5,537	10,921	37,468	34,301	40,025
0	0	0	0	0	0	0	0	0
-28,064	-20,197	-5,293	-43,800	-22,991	4,135	33,436	10,822	36,229
-171	518	8,383	12,283	16,245	11,908	13,577	10,392	4,939
0	0	0	0	0	0	0	0	0
-293	-310	0	0	0	0	0	0	0
0	0	0	0	-2,245	2,217	18,940	20,110	13,936
0	0	0	0	0	0	0	0	33
0	0	0	0	0	0	0	0	-2,303
234,045	450,404	657,642	770,990	1,271,998	1,513,849	2,193,649	2,141,026	1,974,391
598,896	844,746	767,339	730,746	862,180	834,622	893,681	844,655	384,251
832,941	1,295,150	1,424,981	1,501,736	2,134,178	2,348,471	3,087,330	2,985,681	2,358,642
20	25	22	24	24	24	24	24	24

Source: Directors' Book of Profits (reference: LMA: CH04/02/02/001)

Annual profits/losses per branch of Chartered Bank, 1895–1953
Summary percentages

Agency or Branch	1895–1913 s/total	Percentage	1914–18 s/total	Percentage	1919–26 sub/total	Percentage
Bombay	366,026	8.1	124,743	4.1	702,106	8.6
Colombo	402,094	8.9	237,864	7.8	455,368	5.6
Madras	85,064	1.9	74,512	2.4	150,887	1.9
Calcutta	575,360	12.7	344,163	11.2	896,908	11.0
Rangoon	264,736	5.8	102,004	3.3	94,399	1.2
Penang	416,166	9.2	241,025	7.9	451,630	5.6
Singapore	290,329	6.4	247,054	8.1	1,005,577	12.4
Bangkok	177,976	3.9	115,656	3.8	305,333	3.8
Batavia	138,191	3.0	116,578	3.8	-46,237	-0.6
Hong Kong	289,963	6.4	201,581	6.6	754,848	9.3
Manila	284,099	6.3	101,711	3.3	155,130	1.9
Shanghai	190,198	4.2	230,292	7.5	-57,307	-0.7
Yokohama	203,282	4.5	245,050	8.0	879,052	10.8
Tientsin	806	0.0	5,509	0.2	77,309	1.0
New York	4,927	0.1	37,583	1.2	-86,009	-1.1
Saigon	45,281	1.0	156,294	5.1	7,831	0.1
Hamburg	40,477	0.9	2,065	0.1	-32,519	-0.4
Kuala Lumpur	80,212	1.8	74,254	2.4	492,963	6.1
Karachi	-7,160	-0.2	20,706	0.7	-107,608	-1.3
Peking	0	0.0	-22,091	-0.7	-63,084	-0.8
Kobe	0	0.0	0	0.0	-53,440	-0.7
Medan	0	0.0	0	0.0	65,069	0.8
Delhi	0	0.0	0	0.0	-29,209	-0.4
Amritsar	0	0.0	0	0.0	24,829	0.3
Cawnpore	0	0.0	0	0.0	-9,744	-0.1
Kuching	0	0.0	0	0.0	7,283	0.1
Harbin	0	0.0	0	0.0	0	0.0
Ipoh	0	0.0	0	0.0	0	0.0
Manchester	0	0.0	0	0.0	0	0.0
Chungking	0	0.0	0	0.0	0	0.0
Fairlie Place (Calcutta)	0	0.0	0	0.0	0	0.0
Jesselton	0	0.0	0	0.0	0	0.0
Cochin	0	0.0	0	0.0	0	0.0
Aden	0	0.0	0	0.0	0	0.0
Overseas total	3,848,027	84.7	2,656,553	86.7	6,041,365	74.3
Head Office	694,133	15.3	408,578	13.3	2,094,526	25.7
TOTAL Branches + HO	4,542,160	100	3,065,131	100	8,135,891	100
Sub-continent s/total	1,686,120	37.1	903,992	29.5	2,153,107	26.5
China incl HK s/total	480,967	10.6	415,291	13.5	711,766	8.7
'South East Asia' *	1,432,254	31.5	1,052,572	34.3	2,379,510	29.2

* comprising Malaysia, Singapore, Indonesia, Thailand, Vietnam and Philippines

1927–29 sub-total	Percentage	1930–38 sub-total	Percentage	1939–45 sub-total	Percentage	1946–53 total	Percentage
33,043	1.7	-218,877	-5.4	360,806	6.2	927,217	5.4
105,399	5.4	76,969	1.9	200,776	3.4	310,332	1.8
26,782	1.4	175,928	4.3	129,945	2.2	306,698	1.8
-53,429	-2.7	150,522	3.7	602,677	10.3	883,768	5.2
13,116	0.7	-31,553	-0.8	-25,861	-0.4	226,138	1.3
118,313	6.1	34,320	0.8	93,248	1.6	468,677	2.7
228,046	11.7	194,719	4.8	489,180	8.4	2,623,796	15.3
126,024	6.5	-11,979	-0.3	50,646	0.9	1,099,677	6.4
-18,252	-0.9	-707,484	-17.4	21,256	0.4	1,010,599	5.9
263,059	13.5	334,927	8.3	160,703	2.8	1,168,156	6.8
42,802	2.2	419,338	10.3	63,384	1.1	297,475	1.7
-32,413	-1.7	628,582	15.5	209,476	3.6	-517,580	-3.0
-12,072	-0.6	-43,640	-1.1	4,244	0.1	0	0.0
83,030	4.3	256,945	6.3	46,158	0.8	-34,434	-0.2
-65,591	-3.4	-13,884	-0.3	27,528	0.5	398,298	2.3
-32,661	-1.7	80,340	2.0	36,239	0.6	422,471	2.5
-33,382	-1.7	-40,883	-1.0	322	0.0	-12,129	-0.1
205,938	10.6	87,802	2.2	172,336	3.0	695,881	4.1
-8,055	-0.4	-95,494	-2.4	29,613	0.5	307,404	1.8
-19,030	-1.0	-28,888	-0.7	-3,639	-0.1	0	0.0
12,984	0.7	62,640	1.5	-6,823	-0.1	-5,777	0.0
18,652	1.0	-79,136	-1.9	17,100	0.3	0	0.0
0	0.0	-5,180	-0.1	-10,566	-0.2	4,892	0.0
11,401	0.6	5,368	0.1	-17,568	-0.3	-8,707	-0.1
-7,073	-0.4	-4,351	-0.1	62,122	1.1	162,422	0.9
5,439	0.3	19,562	0.5	7,876	0.1	117,711	0.7
-30,758	-1.6	-88,651	-2.2	-6,946	-0.1	0	0.0
5,386	0.3	15,623	0.4	-7,213	-0.1	-7,659	0.0
0	0.0	-960	0.0	13,923	0.2	78,245	0.5
0	0.0	0	0.0	-18,472	-0.3	-310	0.0
0	0.0	0	0.0	140,550	2.4	0	0.0
0	0.0	0	0.0	0	0.0	52,958	0.3
0	0.0	0	0.0	0	0.0	33	0.0
0	0.0	0	0.0	0	0.0	-2,303	0.0
986,698	50.7	1,172,625	28.9	2,843,020	48.8	10,973,949	64.0
960,534	49.3	2,886,457	71.1	2,982,424	51.2	6,162,220	36.0
1,947,232	100	4,059,082	100	5,825,444	100	17,136,169	100
109,783	5.6	47,964	1.2	1,490,062	25.6	3,128,904	18.3
263,888	13.6	1,102,915	27.2	387,280	6.6	615,832	3.6
681,035	35.0	132,241	3.3	926,952	15.9	6,781,586	39.6

ANNUAL RESULTS

	1900	1901	1902	1903	1904	1905	1906	1907
TOTAL Branches + HO	173,246	284,303	222,690	170,689	282,265	324,253	264,255	283,184
Unexplained adjustments	2	10,732	1	1	7,329	22,220	2	2
Profits of A&B as reported	173,248	273,571	222,689	170,690	289,594	302,033	265,257	283,182
Income Tax provision	-	-	-	-	-	-	-	-
Excess Profits Tax	-	-	-	-	-	-	-	-
Corporation Profits Tax	-	-	-	-	-	-	-	-
Total Tax	-	-	-	-	-	-	-	-
Tax as % of Profits of A&B	-	-	-	-	-	-	-	-
Net moves in/ out of Reserves etc	-		-	-	-	-	-	-
Net Profits as reported	173,248	273,571	222,689	170,690	289,594	302,033	265,257	283,182

	1918	1919	1920	1921	1922	1923	1924	1925
TOTAL Branches + HO	908,912	700,111	1,427,795	1,278,726	1,089,498	947,219	957,878	860,094
Unexplained adjustments	186	2,542	1	73,000	30	1,998	2	-
Profits of A&B as reported	908,726	697,569	1,427,796	1,205,726	1,089,468	945,221	957,880	860,094
Income Tax provision	112,894	149,839	152,836	175,792	184,299	130,915	150,165	128,829
Excess Profits Tax	294,825	43,403	429,377	123,681	15,879	-	-	-
Corporation Profits Tax	-	-	53,813	68,285	42,703	31,600	37,000	-
Total Tax	407,719	193,242	636,026	367,758	242,881	162,515	187,165	128,829
Tax as % of Profits of A&B	45	28	45	31	22	17	20	15
Net moves in/ out of Reserves etc	91,786	56,980	115,000	49,900	57,056		-	24,888
Net Profits as reported	409,221	447,347	676,770	788,068	789,531	782,706	770,715	756,153

	1936	1937	1938	1939	1940	1941	1942	1943
TOTAL Branches + HO	787,677	793,078	389,030	502,145	1,253,660	906,140	787,981	789,929
Unexplained adjustments	1,298	2	10	-	1	755	215	2
Profits of A&B as reported	786,379	793,080	389,040	502,145	1,253,661	906,895	787,766	789,931
Income Tax provision	69,697	58,399	53,731	151,796	304,388	272,870	158,298	245,891
Excess Profits Tax	-	-	-	50,000	-	-	-	-
Corporation Profits Tax	-	-	-	-	-	-	-	-
Total Tax	69,697	58,399	53,731	201,796	304,388	272,870	158,298	245,891
Tax as % of Profits of A&B	9	7	14	40	24	30	20	31
Net moves in/ out of Reserves etc	220,000	243,615	-	38,000	549,113	281,160	332,805	229,801
Net Profits as reported	496,682	491,066	335,309	338,349	400,160	352,865	296,663	314,239

1908	1909	1910	1911	1912	1913	1914	1915	1916	1917
297,528	167,118	253,005	266,584	384,623	404,491	395,135	438,394	630,694	691,996
31,834	6	1,809	2	500	300	21	21,850	2	-
265,694	167,124	251,196	266,582	385,123	404,791	395,114	460,244	630,696	691,996
-	-	-	10,495	10,006	14,108	23,034	40,374	55,437	60,576
-	-	-	-	-	-	-	-	100,000	91,624
-	-	-	-	-	-	-	-	-	-
-	-	-	10,495	10,006	14,108	23,034	40,374	155,437	152,200
-	-	-	4	3	3	6	9	25	22
-	-	-	-	50,000	40,000	-	-	94,000	137,001
265,694	167,124	251,196	256,087	325,117	350,683	372,080	382,721	381,259	402,795

1926	1927	1928	1929	1930	1931	1932	1933	1934	1935
874,570	565,279	631,743	750,210	596,977	963,439	658,668	643,740	923,441	229,910
994	10,000	46,510	128	-	-	1,000	31,890	-	1,248
873,576	575,279	585,233	750,338	596,977	963,439	659,668	611,850	923,441	231,158
95,000	117,694	114,038	88,741	42,822	45,257	50,915	144,383	57,397	64,355
-	-	-	-	-	-	-	-	-	-
-	-	-	-	-	-	-	-	-	-
95,000	117,694	114,038	88,741	42,822	45,257	50,915	144,383	57,397	64,355
11	20	19	12	7	5	8	24	6	28
-	266,453	156,068	-	80,188	1,390,483	154,254	-	400,000	331,840
778,576	724,038	627,263	661,597	634,343	381,787	454,499	467,467	466,044	498,643

1944	1945	1946	1947	1948	1949	1950	1951	1952	1953
752,648	832,941	1,295,150	1,424,981	1,501,736	2,134,178	2,348,471	3,087,330	2,985,681	2,360,912
1,570	1,915	4,478	10,303	54,165	56,364	18,372	58,216	25,052	24,145
754,218	831,026	1,299,628	1,414,678	1,555,901	2,077,814	2,366,843	3,145,546	3,010,733	2,336,767
168,139	241,581	452,456	456,620	776,455	897,222	834,036	1,284,619	1,349,615	687,158
-	-	-	-	-	-	-	-	-	-
-	-	-	-	-	-	-	-	-	-
168,139	241,581	452,456	456,620	776,455	897,222	834,036	1,284,619	1,349,615	687,158
22	29	35	32	50	43	35	41	45	29
265,079	263,182	468,539	510,010	312,335	665,000	900,000	1,163,830	962,336	955,811
321,000	326,263	378,633	448,048	467,111	515,592	632,807	697,097	698,782	693,798

Appendix E

Standard Chartered's Growth, 1992–2014

All figures are derived from Standard Chartered PLC's annual reports, except those incorporated in Chart 11. The financial statements were denominated in £ sterling until 2000, and in US$ thereafter. The 1992–2000 figures used in these charts have been converted at the year-end £/$ rates for each of the nine years in this period.

Chart 1. Revenues and pre-tax profits (US$bn)

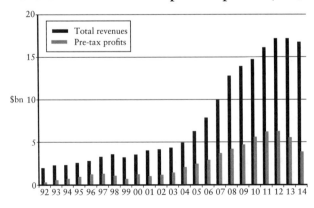

Note: 'Revenues' equate to the 'Operating Income' line of the P&L, aggregating the items described as net interest income, fees and commission income (less fees and commission expense), net trading income and other operating income.

Chart 2. Breakdown of total assets (US$bn)

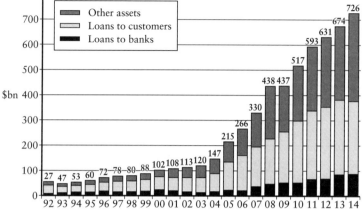

Note: 'Banks' comprise virtually all financial institutions; 'customers' comprise all non-bank borrowers, within both the personal and corporate sectors. 'Other assets' chiefly comprise Treasury and other eligible bills, debt securities and miscellaneous other financial instruments.

Chart 3. Loans to customers and customers' deposits

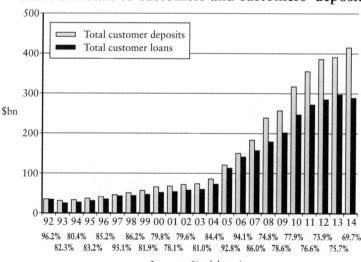

Loans as % of deposits

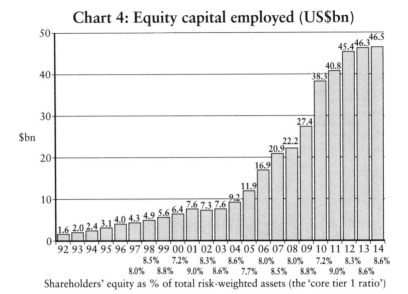

Chart 4: Equity capital employed (US$bn)

Shareholders' equity as % of total risk-weighted assets (the 'core tier 1 ratio')

Note: Shareholders' Equity represents the sum of Capital and Reserves. The 'core tier 1 ratio' follows guidelines laid down by the Bank of International Settlements in 2006 and reported by the Group accordingly. The ratio percentages for 1997 to 2005 have been calculated retrospectively.

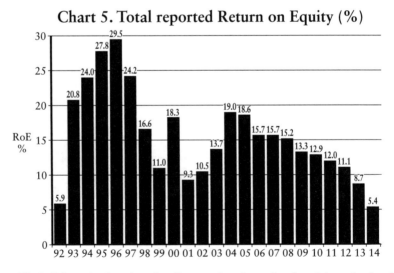

Chart 5. Total reported Return on Equity (%)

Note: The RoE figure is a function of profits earned on the one hand, and the scale of capital deployed on the other. Thus the Group's very modest capital base through most of the 1990s meant a revival in profits was reflected in a sharp increase in the RoE, while the dramatic expansion of the Group's capital base between 2008 and 2014 produced a steady decline in the RoE despite steadily rising profits.

Chart 6. The business mix:
'Consumer' and 'Wholesale' profits
100%= pre-tax profits (US$bn)

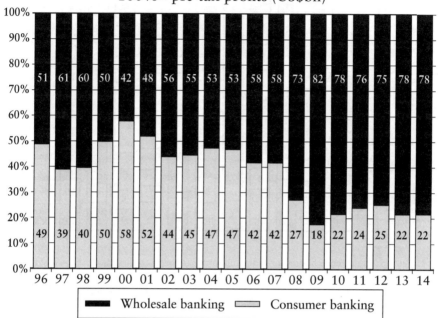

Note: The Group only adopted the Consumer Banking (CB)/Wholesale Banking (WB) structure in 2000, but that year's Annual Report set down pro forma figures for the 1996–9 years, and these are included here. Where any annual figure was restated in a subsequent report, the restated figure has been used. The total of CB and WB pre-tax profits approximated to each year's aggregate pre-tax profits for the Group, but differed marginally due to the inclusion at Group level of other minor items. For 2014, when the CB/WB split was abandoned, proxy figures have drawn on 'Retail' and 'Private Banking' (for CB) and 'Commercial' and 'Corporate & Institutional' (for WB) from p. 36 of the 2014 Annual Report.

Chart 7. The geographical mix: revenues by region, %

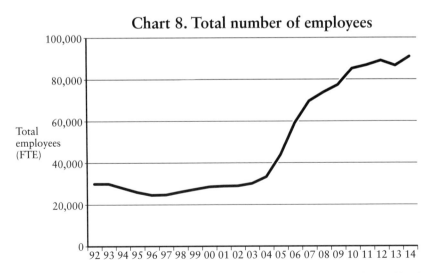

M/E & South Asia
(incl Malaysia
and India)

	1992	1994	1996	1998	2000	2002	2004	2006	2006	2010	2012	2014	
	5	7	8	8	7	9	9	9	12	13	8	8	India
Singapore & Asia Pacific (excl. Hong Kong)	28	25	32	34		16	17	17	12	13	12	21	M/E & South Asia (incl Malaysia)
					11	11	10	7	9	11	12	11	Singapore
					13	13	15				30	16	Asia Pacific (excl. Hong Kong)
Hong Kong	30	26	30	27	29	31	26	34	32	30			
		8										23	Hong Kong
Africa	11		9	9	9			19	16	16	18		
						7	11		7	8	8	10	Africa
Americas, UK & Europe	26	34	21	22	18	13	12	7	12	9	12	11	Americas, UK & Europe

Note: Separate revenue figures for India and for Singapore were first disclosed in 2001(with comparative figures provided that year for 2000 as well). The two territories were previously included with 'Middle East & South Asia', and 'Other Asia Pacific' respectively. When the geographical breakdown of 2000's revenues was restated in dollars in 2001, the Group reassigned approximately $264 million from 'Other Asia Pacific/Singapore' to 'M/E & South Asia/India'. The restated dollar figures for 2000 have been used here.

Chart 8. Total number of employees

Total employees (FTE)

Note: The figures in the graph represent 'Full Time Equivalent' totals for the worldwide workforce.

Chart 9. Total number of branches

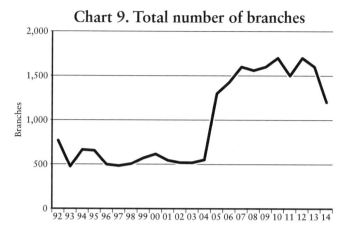

Note: 'Branches' comprise all retail branches, electronic banking centres, wholesale banking branches and corporate offices, including up to a dozen or so representative offices with no licensed banking facilities. The Group ceased reporting exact numbers in 2006, thereafter indicating approximate base numbers (as in, 'more than 1,600'). These have been used in this graph, which may marginally understate the totals for 2007–14 accordingly.

Chart 10. Total number of pages in the Annual Report

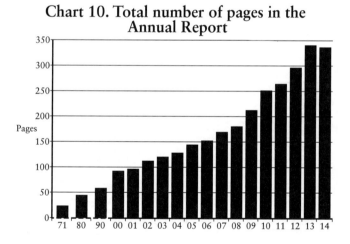

Chart 11. Group Share Price since 1969

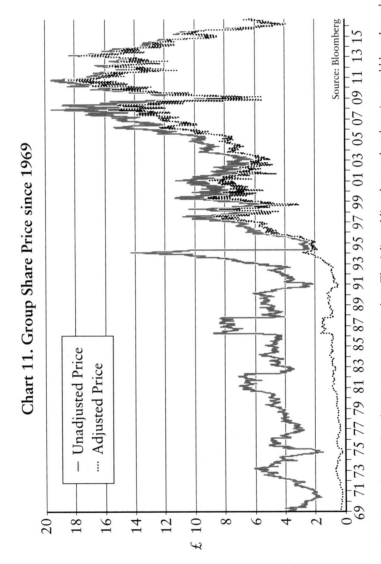

Source: Bloomberg

Note: The Unadjusted line shows the quoted trading price at any given date. The Adjusted line shows what the price would have been, had the number of shares issued at that date been in line with the number outstanding at the end of June 2016, allowing for all new issues of stock to that date. Pro forma prices for 1969 are based on those of Standard Bank and Chartered Bank prior to their merger.

Appendix F

The Board Directors of Standard Chartered Group

Sylvester Gates	1970–72
Cyril Hamilton	1970–74
Sir Cyril Hawker	1970–74
Edward Hellmuth, CBE	1970–77
The Rt Hon. The Earl of Inchcape	1970–87
Roger Leigh-Wood	1970–71
Sir Charles Miles	decd. Oct 1970
George Preston	1970–79
George Pullen	1970–72
Michael Robson	1970–82
Victor Rockhill	1970–75
Eric Tansley	1970–72
Sir Robert Taylor, CBE	1970–83
Derek d'Anyers Willis	1970–71
Sir Leslie Fletcher	1972–89
Sir Hugh Mackay-Tallack	1972–83
Sir Denis Wright	1972–81
Sir Tom Hickinbotham	1973–74
Sir Andrew Maitland-Makgill-Crichton	1973–81
David Mitchell	1973–88
Lord (Anthony) Barber	1974–87
William Davidson	1974–76
Sir Julian Hodge	1974–75
Murray Hofmeyr	1974–80
Ronald Lane	1974–83
Sir William Luce	1974–77
John McCall	1974–81
Harry Reed	1974–75
William Bowden	1975–88
Sir Peter Graham, OBE	1975–88
Alexander Robertson	1976–79

Malcom Wilcox	1976–79
Sir David Barran	1978–82
Charles McCulloch	1979–81
Sir Michael McWilliam	1979–88
Sir Derek Mitchell	1979–90
Sir Idwal Pugh	1979–88
Sir Charles Hamilton	1982–88
John Page	1982–89
Lord (Raymond) Pennock	1982–91
Robin Baillie	1983–95
James Louden	1983–90
David Millar, OBE	1983–86
Stuart Tarrant	1983–86
John Harrigan	1986–88
Robert Holmes à Court	1986–90
Sir Y. K. Pao, CBE	1986–88
Phillip Robinson	1986–95
Richard Stein	1986–96
Peter Woo	1986–89
William Brown, CBE	1987–94
Peter Macdougall	1987–88
Alan Orsich	1987–94
Rudolph Agnew	1988–97
Rodney Galpin	1988–93
Sir Patrick Gillam	1988–2003
Sir Ralph Robins	1988–2003
Paul Rudder	1988–93
Geoff Armstrong	1989–92
John Craig, OBE	1989–94
Malcom Williamson	1989–96
Sir Ian Stewart (later Lord Stewartby)	1990–2004
Geoffrey Williams	1990–94
Christopher Castleman	1991–2001
Keith Mackrell	1991–2002
Cob Stenham	1991–2004
David Brougham	1993–98
John McFarlane, CBE	1993–97
David Moir, CBE	1993–2003
Peter Wood	1993–2000
Ronnie Chan	1994–2004

Hugh Norton	1995–2007
Rod Olsen	1995–99
Philippe Paillart	1995–98
Michael Green	1996–2000
Ho Kwon Ping	1996–2006
Sir C. K. Chow	1997–2008
Lord (Mervyn) Davies, CBE	1997–2009
Rana Talwar	1997–2001
Fred Enlow	1998–2000
Christopher Keljik	1999–2005
Nigel Kenny	1999–2002
Kai Nargolwala	1999–2007
Mike DeNoma	2000–08
Rudolph Markham	2001–14
Barry Clare	2002–03
Richard Meddings	2002–14
Bryan Sanderson, CBE	2002–06
Peter Sands	2002–15
Ruth Markland	2003–15
Paul Skinner, CBE	2003–15
Jamie Dundas	2004–14
Oliver Stocken, CBE	2004–15
Val Gooding, CBE	2005–13
Lord (Adair) Turner	2006–08
Gareth Bullock	2007–10
Sunil Mittal	2007–09
Sir John Peace	2007–16
Steve Bertamini	2008–14
John Paynter	2008–14
Mike Rees	2009–16
Jaspal Bindra	2010–15
Richard Delbridge	2010–13
Simon Lowth	2010–16
Dr Han Seung-soo, KBE	2010–19
Margaret Ewing	2012–14
V. Shankar	2012–15
Dr Lars Thunell	2012–16
Om Bhatt	2013–19
Dr Kurt Campbell	2013–17
Dr Louis Cheung	2013–Present

Christine Hodgson	2013–Present
Dr Byron Grote	2014–Present
Andrew Halford	2014–Present
Naguib Kheraj	2014–Present
Gay Huey Evans	2015–Present
Jasmine Whitbread	2015–Present
William Winters, CBE	2015–Present
David Conner	2016–Present
José Viñals*	2016–Present
Ngozi Okonjo-Iweala	2017–Present
Amanda Mellor	2019–Present
David Tang	2019–Present
Carlson Tong	2019–Present

* A former Deputy-Governor of the Bank of Spain and senior official at the IMF, José Viñals succeeded Sir John Peace as the Chairman of Standard Chartered in December 2016.

Sources and References

Almost all the surviving archives of Chartered Bank, and those of Standard Bank of South Africa not held in Johannesburg, are deposited at the London Metropolitan Archives (LMA), part of the City of London Corporation. All references in the LMA's catalogue to the papers of Chartered Bank and of Standard Bank – as also to the records of Eastern Bank and the Bank of British West Africa – are prefixed with 'CLC/B/207'. In the references cited here and elsewhere in the book, this prefix has been dropped for the sake of brevity and each catalogue reference simply begins with 'LMA: . . .' Unless otherwise stated, this should be read as 'LMA: CLC/B/207 . . .'

Most of Chartered Bank's early correspondence and half-yearly reports from the branches have been lost, but were evidently still available in 1949–52 to those researching the centenary history of the bank. Detailed notes were made of them at the bank's instigation by John Leighton-Boyce, who prepared the first draft of what eventually emerged as *Realms of Silver* (see Appendix A). Several hundred pages of these notes remain in the Chartered Bank archives. Where they have been used as a proxy for the originals, they are cited as 'JL-B notes'.

References to papers held in the Standard Bank Heritage Centre in Johannesburg are prefixed with 'SBSA: . . .' The name of SBSA's holding company formed in 1969, Standard Bank Investment Corporation, is given throughout as StanBIC, and any direct quotations referring to SBIC have been amended accordingly, to avoid confusion.

Most post-1969 papers relating to Standard Chartered Bank are held in the Group's own archives, and references to them are prefixed with 'SCB'. Papers dated before 1999 are cited with their archival box number. Papers post-1999 are still held by the Group Corporate Secretariat and are cited as SCB/GCS.

INTRODUCTION

1. This was the view of Harold Musker, who with various titles ran the British Bank of the Middle East from 1952 until his retirement in 1966. (Quoted in Geoffrey Jones, *Banking & Oil, The History of the British Bank of the Middle East*, Cambridge University Press, 1987, p. 96.)   **2.** Adam Tooze, *The Deluge, The Great War and the Remaking of Global Order*, Allen Lane, 2014, p. 374.   **3.** Chartered Bank Vietnam Zone Office Rules, LMA: CH03/01/06/121.

I. A DOUBLE PROVENANCE

1. E. I. Barrington, *The Servant of All: pages from the family, social and political life of my father James Wilson: twenty years of mid-Victorian life*, 2 vols, Longmans, 1927. It includes a touching account of Wilson's last months, when he showed an almost wilful disregard for the risks to his health. Having despatched his wife to the cooler climate of a hill station, Wilson wrote to her in June 1860: 'The rains began last week and the air was very damp. I had an attack but Dr Macrae soon subdued it, and I am now again very well, taking quinine and port wine every day. I never was so hard worked but everything goes on well and cheerfully.' (Vol. 2, p. 295.)   **2.** Ruth Dudley Edwards, *The Pursuit of Reason*, Hamish Hamilton, 1993, p. 220.   **3.** See, for example, Anthony Webster, *The Twilight of the East India Company, The Evolution of Anglo-Asian Commerce and Politics 1790–1860*, The Boydell Press, 2009, pp. 136–42. In an otherwise excellent summary of Wilson's career and of the political background to the founding of Chartered Bank, the author oddly fails to mention that Wilson was one of the bank's founding directors.   **4.** The investigation was carried out by the Economist Intelligence Unit in 1951 (see Appendix A). The resulting analysis, *Original Directors of the Chartered Bank of India, Australia and China: an investigation into their commercial connections*, can be found at LMA: CH03/01/15/024. The director with direct experience of the East was John Bagshaw (1784–1861), who had worked as a banker and a merchant in Calcutta.   **5.** Tirthankar Roy, *The Economic History of India, 1857–1947*, Oxford University Press, 3rd edition 2011, p. 48.   **6.** Roy, *The Economic History of India*, p. 58.   **7.** Webster, *The Twilight of the East India Company*, p. 115.   **8.** Some years later, Wilson penned a tart description of what had happened, for the benefit of colleagues with no technical knowledge of the City: 'Houses in Calcutta drew upon their own houses in London, and the houses in London to cover themselves drew upon their houses in India or the Indian houses drew new sets of bills, and with the proceeds of such bills, purchased other bills upon other houses (of a similar character) and transmitted them to the houses in London to pay former bills of their own drawing. And thus an enormous amount of cross bills became current, representing no transactions.' He circulated his analysis as a private memo, 'Banking in India', dated 12 June 1853. (Quoted in Webster, *The Twilight of the East India Company*, p. 141.)   **9.** It survived in a small packet of papers apparently handed on from one chairman to the next in subsequent years and bequeathed to the Secretary's department by Sir Montagu Turner when he retired in October 1932. The draft is inscribed 'Drawn up by G.H. in March 1852' and is dated May 1852. (LMA: CH03/01/10/58/08/A.) **10.** Wilson to Gladstone, 17 May 1853, City of London, LMA: CH01/01/01/008/004. **11.** EIU Report, *Original Directors of the Chartered Bank of India, Australia and China*, p. 21, LMA: CH03/01/15/024. **12.** A copy of this final prospectus bears a faded ink inscription 'drawn up by James Wilson Esq MP'. It carries no printed date, but a signature on the back is dated 14 October 1852. (LMA: CH03/01/10/58/08/A.) **13.** *The Economist*, 9 October 1852. (LMA: CH03/01/10/58/08/A.) **14.** All the minutes of the Chartered Bank's Court meetings, from the very first on 18 October 1852, are held in the archives of Standard Chartered Bank. **15.** East India Company to the India Board of Control, 11 November 1852, quoted in A. S. J. Baster, *The Imperial Banks*, P. S. King & Son, 1929, p. 108. **16.** The register can be found in LMA: CH02/02/001. The first certificate went to a Mr R. Watt. **17.** Court Minutes 22 December 1852, Vol. 1, SCB Box 271. **18.** Wilson to Gladstone, op. cit. n. 10. **19.** Wilson wrote to the Board of Control on 2 July 1853 to confirm that the Treasury would be happy to see the Chartered Bank's new application given due consideration; and he wrote to the Colonial Secretary on 15 August 1853 explaining the great difficulties the bank had had to surmount. In neither letter, rather oddly, did Wilson make any mention of his role as the inaugural chairman. (LMA: CH03/01/15/002.) **20.** A copy of the Royal Charter can be found in LMA: CH03/01/09/305, a bundle of documents relating to the original and six 'Supplemental Charters' over the next half-century. The 1853 text, *inter alia*, specified 'that the whole of such houses, offices, buildings and hereditaments so held by the said Company in our United Kingdom shall not exceed the yearly value of £2,000 at the time of acquiring the same'. This was to pose a problem when the time came for the bank to purchase a sizeable new head office in 1905–7. **21.** Court Minutes, 15 March 1854, Vol. 1, SCB Box 271. **22.** George Hope to William Purdy of the Bank of South Australia, 5 December 1854, LMA: CH03/01/10/58/08/A. Hope pointed out that his bank now owned a Royal Charter that was unlikely to be replicated, opening up far grander possibilities than anything that could be contemplated by the Australian bank, which had simply grown prosperous 'from the purchase of Gold Dust'. **23.** *The Bankers' Magazine*, Vol. 15, 1855, pp. 223–6. Interestingly, Mitchell insisted in his address that he was not himself the instigator of the bank. 'When it was proposed to him to join the bank (and he might observe that it was the first institution of the kind he had ever been connected with), he agreed to become a member of the Board of Directors.' Perhaps Wilson had slightly understated his own role, in his letter to Gladstone. **24.** *The Bankers' Magazine*, Vol. 15, 1855, pp. 522–6. The merger seems to have been a real possibility, to judge by a hoard of Bank of North-West India papers retained in the archive, see LMA: CH03/01/08/019. **25.** Wilson's help was sought, for example, over the application for a 'supplemental charter', the first of many. Court Minutes, 16 September 1856, Vol. 1, SCB Box 271. **26.** Court Minutes, 16 September 1856, Vol. 1, SCB Box 271. **27.** The papers relating to the January 1857 Agreement can be found at

LMA: CH01/03/02/001. That the City Bank's loans to Macnaughton, Nelson Smith and Fraser were very far from being routine advances to third parties was spelled out explicitly in Clause 3 of the private memorandum: 'The total amount of such advances by the City Bank will be credited to the Chartered Bank of India, in a separate deposit account, bearing interest at one half per cent less than will be charged from time to time to the individual accounts, and this [deposit] account will not be drawn against for two years, except to such extent as may be set free by the repayment, meanwhile, of the City Bank's advances to those individual parties on this account.' The shares changing hands were meanwhile to belong to the City Bank, and could be sold in the market 'at par when obtainable' unless the 'individual parties' had by then paid back their loans. This gave the City Bank an asset to balance against the liability represented by the new deposit account for the Chartered. In effect, the three individuals' loans were being made by the Chartered out of its deposit account, with one half per cent payable to the City Bank as a management fee for its agreeing to be the conduit for the loans.   **28.** *The Bankers' Magazine*, Vol. 17, 1857, pp. 251–7.   **29.** Quoted in D. S. Savkar, *Joint Stock Banking in India*, Bombay, 1938, pp. 43–4.   **30.** T. M. Devine, *To the Ends of the Earth, Scotland's Global Diaspora, 1750–2010*, Allen Lane, 2011, p. 78. Remarking on the deep roots of this Scottish influence, Devine notes that 'twelve of the first seventeen trading partnerships set up [in Singapore after 1819] . . . were predominantly Scottish'.   **31.** Court Minutes, 9 September 1857, Vol. 1, SCB Box 271.   **32.** Details of the early staffing arrangements can be found at LMA: CH03/01/14/016. J. W. Maclennan would spend the next thirty years in Shanghai, becoming one of the best-known figures in the International Settlement. He was editor of the *North China Daily News* for three years, 1886–9, before returning to England (LMA: CH03/01/14/020).   **33.** 'The Story of the Chartered Bank in Calcutta', August 1951, LMA: CH03/01/14/030.   **34.** The distinction was set out on pages 8–9 of the original Charter. Forty years later, under the terms of one of many supplemental charters, provisions were inserted to allow for the general conversion of agencies into branches. Little notice was taken of this until 1912, when a letter from the bank's lawyers, Linklaters, reminded management of the conversion option. It went on to explain, though, that the bank would need to secure the prior permission of the appropriate government department, for example getting clearance from the Secretary of State for India in order to convert the Bombay and Calcutta agencies. Perhaps not surprisingly, the Chief Manager of the day, Thomas Whitehead, scribbled across the bottom of the letter 'Better leave matters as they are.' (LMA: CH03/01/10/47/22.)   **35.** Head Office to Iggulden, 10 April 1860, JL-B notes, LMA: CH03/01/14/062.   **36.** LMA: CH04/05/02/MS31519/001.   **37.** Court Minutes of 16 March 1859, Vol. 1, SCB Box 271.   **38.** *The Times*, 1 January and 27 June 1860. There is a slightly confused reference to the incident in JL-B notes, LMA: CH03/01/14/062. The Court received a telegram from Iggulden in Galle dated 5 June, which was received in London on 9 July. Court minutes, 11 July 1860, Vol. 1, SCB Box 271.   **39.** Court Minutes, 25 May 1859, Vol. 1, SCB Box 271.   **40.** Head Office to Iggulden, April 1860, JL-B notes, LMA: CH03/01/14/043.   **41.** *The Bankers' Magazine*, Vol. 21, 1861, p. 872, and Vol. 23,

1863, p. 524.   **42.** *The North-China Herald*, 2 May 1863. I am indebted to Peter Hibbard for his trawling of the Shanghai newspaper archives for this and other early references to the Chartered Bank and to Howard Gwyther.   **43.** Srinivas R. Wagel, *Finance in China*, Shanghai, 1914.   **44.** *The Bankers' Magazine*, Vol. 23, 1863, pp. 358–62.   **45.** His letter of resignation was dated 15 September 1862 in Shanghai, and was received towards the end of November. It clearly upset the Court, prompting it to write back to Iggulden that 'the Directors must decline to reply to the further contents of your letter, now acknowledged, until you withdraw altogether the charges made in it'. The original correspondence is lost. (JL-B notes, LMA: CH03/01/14/016.)   **46.** On the early growth of the rice trade, see Cheng Siok Hwa, *The Rice Industry of Burma 1852–1940*, Institute of South East Asian Studies, 2012, pp. 12–14. 'Some accounts have it that there was no rice trade of any significance before 1869 but once the [Suez] Canal was opened a flourishing rice trade at once sprang up ... [In fact, from 1852] production and exports increased by leaps and bounds. By 1866 364,000 tons were exported from Lower Burma. The rice trade continued to grow at a phenomenal speed and by 1870 about 484,000 tons were exported.' None of which is to say that the opening of the Canal was other than a dramatic development.   **47.** 'The Early History of the Chartered Bank in Burma' (author unknown, but probably D. A. Blunt), LMA: CH03/01/14/037, pp. 4–5. The Court's instructions for a Rangoon office to be opened are set out in accompanying notes by JL-B. The existence of the Rangoon office was noted by *The Times* of 8 October 1863, in reporting the announcement of an imminent branch opening in Batavia. In a separate text dated May 1951 ('The Official History of the Bank – Rangoon Branch', Memorandum by D. A. Blunt, filed with the Early History) a foundation date 'as early as 1858' is cited – but this sits oddly with the 1861 Court instruction and is probably just an educated guess, based on the incursion of substantial British forces into Burma in 1857. This latter memorandum, though, provides many excellent details on the subsequent history of the branch.   **48.** The February 1864 Power of Attorney can be found in LMA: CH03/01/06/008. As of 1989, the Standard Chartered's head office in London still held three contracts confirming leasehold arrangements in Rangoon, dating from 1866, 1879 and 1889. They are recorded as 'Sundry Documents' in the inventory of the bank's museum, SCB Box 144. They were lost before the end of 1989 when the museum was discontinued and its contents were sold off.   **49.** EIU Report, *The Cotton Boom in China During the 1860s*, 1950, LMA: CH03/01/15/024.   **50.** Quoted in Raymond J. F. Sulivan, *One Hundred Years of Bombay: A History of the Bombay Chamber of Commerce 1836–1936*, Times of India Press, 1937, p. 74.   **51.** Sherwood to the Court, 19 February 1866, JL-B notes, LMA: CH03/01/14/030.   **52.** *The Bankers' Magazine*, Vol. 25, 1865, pp. 1277–9.   **53.** Court Minutes, 8 February 1865, Vol. 2, SCB Box 271.   **54.** We know of Gwyther's continued presence in Shanghai through 1862 and 1863 because he was a diligent committee member of the Shanghai Library. Its members voted early in 1864 to thank him 'for his constant attention to the duties of his office during the past two years' (*North-China Herald*, 16 January 1864). He ran his bill-broking business with a partner, Rowley Miller, as the Hong Kong press would one day recall in acknowledging his retirement (*North-China Herald*, 3 March 1905). **55.** *The Bankers' Magazine*, Vol. 49, 1889, p. 833, and Minutes of Board meetings, 1 March and 19 April 1865, Vol. 2, SCB Box 271. His biography in *The Oxford DNB* incorrectly dates his rejoining the bank to 1868. **56.** Quoted in A. S. J. Baster, *The International Banks*, P. S. King & Son, 1935, p. 40. **57.** Court Minutes, 11 June 1866, Vol. 2, SCB Box 271. **58.** Details of the bank's early City premises can be found at LMA: CH03/01/15/006. **59.** The Ordnance Survey map of the City for 1896 still included Hatton Court, with its buildings marked 'Bank' on two sides (Bank of England archives 10A272/1 Plan 2). **60.** *The Bankers' Magazine*, Vol. 28, 1868, pp. 557–62. **61.** Gwyther and representatives of the Oriental Bank and the Hongkong Bank were among those who attended a public meeting at the Shanghai offices of Messrs Matheson & Co. in March 1870 to discuss the state of Western trade with China (*North-China Herald*, 15 March 1870). **62.** *The Bankers' Magazine*, Vol. 29, 1869, pp. 585–8. **63.** For the Chartered Bank's annual high and low share prices for 1860–1914, see LMA: CH03/01/14/014. **64.** *The Bankers' Magazine*, Vol. 31, 1871, pp. 448–53. **65.** They were so described at the Annual General Meeting of 17 April 1872. *The Bankers' Magazine*, Vol. 32, 1872, pp. 413–21. **66.** J. N. Scott to the Directors, 15 April 1871, LMA: CH03/01/10/71/01. A pencilled scribble on the letter notes: 'Handed by Mr Gwyther into the Secretary's department for preservation.' **67.** William Macnaughton to Thomas Mitchell, 21 April 1871, LMA: CH03/01/10/71/01. **68.** Thomas Mitchell to Howard Gwyther, 24 April 1871, LMA: CH03/01/10/71/01. **69.** William Macnaughton to Thomas Mitchell, 24 April 1871, LMA: CH03/01/10/71/01. **70.** Court Minutes, 26 April 1871, Vol. 2, SCB Box 271. **71.** *China Express*, 21 April 1871, recorded in JL-B notes, LMA: CH03/01/15/004. **72.** JL-B notes at LMA: CH03/01/14/077. 'Communications' contains a valuable account of the revolution wrought by the cable networks. JL-B collected much of his chronology from reports in contemporary editions of the *New China Herald* newspaper. **73.** See for example A. C. M. Webb, *The Roots of the Tree, A study in early South African banking*, First National Bank of Southern Africa Ltd, 1992. 'The imperial banks arrived in South Africa set on maintaining an image of nineteenth century banking respectability . . . [By the end of the 1860s] the cuckoo chick had cleared the nest of fledglings' (pp. 44–5). **74.** *Dictionary of South African Biography*, Vol. 1. **75.** Column by R. W. Murray Senior, quoted in Pamela Ffolliott and E. L. H. Croft, *One Titan at a Time*, Cape Town, 1960, pp. 118–19. **76.** Webb, *The Roots of the Tree*, p. 46. **77.** Lewis Michell, 'Sixty Years In and Out of South Africa', unpublished memoir, pp. 6–7. A copy of Chapters 4–10 of the memoir are held in the archives of the Standard Bank, ARCH 2/5/Michell. **78.** They included the London Chartered Bank of Australia (1852), the Bank of Egypt (1856) and the Chartered Mercantile Bank of India (1857) as well as the Chartered Bank of India, Australia and China. **79.** The report of the meeting appeared in the *Eastern Province Herald* on 22 March 1859, quoted in Ffolliott and Croft, *One Titan*, p. 139. **80.** E. H. D. Arndt, *Banking and Currency Development in South Africa (1652–1927)*, Johannesburg, 1928, p. 253. **81.** Stuart Jones, *The Great Imperial Banks in South Africa, A Study of the Business of Standard Bank and Barclays Bank 1861–1961*,

University of South Africa, 1996, p. 16. **82.** J. A. Henry, *The First Hundred Years of the Standard Bank*, Oxford University Press, 1963, p. 2. As the author notes, however, no trace of a prospectus from 1860 has ever been found. **83.** Minutes of the Standard Bank Board, 18 October 1862, ARCH 1/4/GMO. **84.** *The Times*, 18 October 1862, p. 5. **85.** Ibid., and G. T. Amphlett, *History of the Standard Bank of South Africa Ltd, 1862–1913*, Glasgow University Press, 1914, p. 8. Amplett also provides the data on the existing banks in the Cape Colony. **86.** Minutes of the Standard Bank Board, 31 October 1862, ARCH 1/4/GMO. **87.** Minutes of the Standard Bank Board, 16 January 1863, ARCH 1/4/GMO. **88.** Minutes of the Standard Bank Board, 23 January 1863, ARCH 1/4/GMO. **89.** Minutes of the Standard Bank Board, 30 January 1863, ARCH 1/4/GMO. **90.** Durban Branch Letter Book, LMA: ST07/03/001. **91.** James Alexander to Francis Searle, 3 June 1863, Durban Branch Letter Book, LMA: SBSA/0519 **92.** Amphlett, *History of the Standard Bank*, p. 11. **93.** *The Bankers' Magazine*, Vol. 23, 1863, pp. 863–8. **94.** *The Bankers' Magazine*, Vol. 24, 1864, pp. 523–7. **95.** Minutes of the Standard Bank Board, 11 December 1863, ARCH 1/4/GMO. **96.** In a letter advising Tudhope how to take advantage of an imminent rise in demand for sterling in the colony, the Board Secretary gave him a scarcely veiled warning: 'I am further instructed to acquaint you that the Court will consider and appreciate as a measure of your ability, the manner and extent in which you carry out this instruction'. (Searle to Tudhope, 19 September 1864, GMO 1/1/1 LO-GM Letters Received 1863–5.) **97.** Minutes of the Standard Bank Board, 9 July 1863, ARCH 1/4/GMO. **98.** Searle to Tudhope, 9 January 1865, GMO 1/1/1. **99.** 'A Communication [was submitted] from the Manager at Cape Town, enclosing [a] Copy of [a] Resolution of the Directors there stating their disapproval of the appointment of a General Manager . . .' (Minutes of the Standard Bank Board, 24 March 1865, ARCH 1/4/GMO). **100.** *The Bankers' Magazine*, Vol. 25, 1865, pp. 634–8. **101.** Minutes of the Standard Bank Board, 19 May 1865, ARCH 1/4/GMO. **102.** Stewart to Searle, 10 April 1865, LMA: ST03/01/02/001. **103.** Searle to Stewart, 23 May 1865, GMO 1/1/1. **104.** Minutes of the Standard Bank Board, 21 July 1865, ARCH 1/4/GMO. Paterson's refusal to sign these minutes a week later prompted another serious disagreement among the Directors. **105.** Minutes of the Standard Bank Board, 11 August 1865, ARCH 1/4/GMO. **106.** *The Bankers' Magazine*, Vol. 25, 1865, pp. 1303–7. **107.** For the L&SAB branch names, see Carolyn Terry, *A Pioneer Bank in a Pioneer Land*, Flesch & Partners, 1979, p. 106. Terry was Head Archivist of the Standard Bank, and her book reproduces a wealth of primary material from the bank's records for the period from the late 1850s to the start of the twentieth century, although it unfortunately includes no archival references. **108.** *The Bankers' Magazine*, Vol. 26, 1866, pp. 731–7. **109.** Quoted in Terry, *A Pioneer Bank*, p. 32. Tudhope would resume his career with the Standard eight years later. During the interim, he served as manager of a small bank in Fort Beaufort. When the Standard Bank's local branch acquired it at the end of 1873, the two were merged and Tudhope was appointed as manager. Reconciling this with his dismissal in 1865, Stewart wrote to London: 'He did not then give satisfaction and circumstances occurred which led to his leaving our service – but . . . what I have lately heard of him has been altogether in his favour. I have very little doubt that he will prove a useful officer . . . [and] he will be on the same footing as other members of our staff.' (Terry, *A Pioneer Bank*, p. 93.) **110.** Stewart to Searle, 28 December 1865, LMA: STo3/01/02/001. **111.** Geoffrey Wheatcroft, *The Randlords*, Atheum, 1986, p. 25. **112.** Quoted in Alan Mabin and Barbara Conradie, eds., *The Confidence of the Whole Country, Standard Bank reports on economic conditions in Southern Africa 1865–1902*, Standard Bank Investment Corporation, 1987, pp. 6–9. **113.** Ibid, p. 17. **114.** Stewart to Searle, 16 August 1869, quoted in Mabin and Conradie, eds., *The Confidence of the Whole Country*, p. 20. **115.** William H. Worger, *South Africa's City of Diamonds, Mine Workers and Monopoly Capitalism in Kimberley, 1867–1895*, Yale University Press, 1987, p. 18.

2. DIAMONDS, SILVER AND GOLD

1. A table showing all the bank branches in the Cape from 1865 to 1890 can be found in E. H. D. Arndt, *Banking and Currency Development in South Africa (1652–1927)*, Johannesburg, 1928, p. 293. There existed 89 branches in 1881. **2.** Stewart to Searle, 15 February 1878, quoted in Alan Mabin and Barbara Conradie, eds., *The Confidence of the Whole Country, Standard Bank reports on economic conditions in Southern Africa 1865–1902*, Standard Bank Investment Corporation, 1987, pp. 65–7. **3.** *The Bankers' Magazine*, Vol. 32, 1872, pp. 582–4. **4.** Stewart to Searle, 28 February and 14 May 1870, quoted in Mabin and Conradie, *The Confidence of the Whole Country*, pp. 24–5. **5.** Allister Sparks, *The Mind of South Africa, The Story of the Rise and Fall of Apartheid*, Jonathan Ball Publishers, 2003, p. 119. **6.** Stewart to Searle, 13 September 1870, quoted in Carolyn Terry, *A Pioneer Bank in a Pioneer Land*, Flesch & Partners, 1979, p. 49. **7.** William H. Worger, *South Africa's City of Diamonds, Mine Workers and Monopoly Capitalism in Kimberley, 1867–1895*, Yale University Press/ A. D. Donker, 1987, p. 13. **8.** Quoted in Terry, *A Pioneer Bank*, p. 109. **9.** Stewart to Searle, 16 December 1870 and 15 February 1871, quoted in Mabin and Conradie, *The Confidence of the Whole Country*, pp. 30 and 32. **10.** *The Bankers' Magazine*, Vol. 28, 1868, pp. 1227–32. **11.** Geoffrey Wheatcroft, *The Randlords*, Atheum, 1986, p. 36. **12.** Stewart to Searle, 1 March 1871, quoted in Mabin and Conradie, *The Confidence of the Whole Country*, pp. 32–3. **13.** Mabin and Conradie, *The Confidence of the Whole Country*, p. 36. **14.** See A. C. M. Webb, *The Roots of the Tree, A study in early South African banking*, First National Bank of Southern Africa Ltd, 1992, p. 73. **15.** Stewart to Searle, 10 December 1874, LMA: STo3/01/02/013. **16.** Stewart to Searle, 22 March 1875, LMA: STo3/01/02/014. **17.** *The Bankers' Magazine*, Vol. 32, 1872, pp. 582–4. **18.** Quoted by Terry, *A Pioneer Bank*, p. 91, who dates the comment to 'the early 1870s'. **19.** Stewart to the Secretary's Office, 4 December 1875, LMA: STo3/01/02/015. **20.** Terry, *A Pioneer Bank*, p. 147. **21.** The London and Johannesburg archives of the Standard Bank each retain many volumes with the complete correspondence in both directions (see note on Sources, above). **22.** In the Standard Bank archives in Johannesburg, see the series GMO 2/1/- for letters to Port Elizabeth from the branches, and GMO 4/1/- for letters from Port Elizabeth to the branches. **23.** Stewart to Searle, 22 March 1875, LMA: STo3/01/02/014. **24.** Quoted by Terry, *A Pioneer Bank*, p. 42. **25.** Stewart to Searle, 27 February 1875, LMA: STo3/01/02/014. **26.** Terry, *A Pioneer Bank*, p. 81. **27.** Ibid., p. 79. **28.** G. T. Amphlett, *History of the Standard Bank of South Africa Ltd, 1862–1913*, Glasgow University Press, 1914, pp. 91–2. **29.** See Terry, *A Pioneer Bank*, pp. 60–70 for a collection of graphic first-hand accounts of life in the branches at Kimberley and Beaconsfield in the 1870–1900 era. **30.** 'Inspection Report: Kimberley Branch, 31 December 1877' by Rees Williams, Standard Bank archives, INSP 1/1/84, 442/Kimberley (1877). **31.** Lewis Michell, 'Sixty Years In and Out of South Africa', unpublished autobiography, p. 20. Curiously, Michell misremembered the date of his joining the Standard Bank as 1869. A copy of chapters 4–10 is held in the Standard Bank archive, Arch 2/5/Michell. **32.** Stewart to G. M. Kiell, Chairman of the Week, 31 July 1874, LMA: STo3/01/02/013. **33.** Their travels on at least one occasion prompted some concern in Port Elizabeth: 'Mr White and Mr Stewart are now supposed to be somewhere between Natal and the Diamond Fields but nothing has been heard from either for a fortnight.' (H. C. Ross to Searle, 23 October 1874, LMA: STo3/01/02/013.) **34.** Stewart to Searle, 18 February 1874, SB Archives, GMO 3/1/4, GM-LO, No. 8/74, f. 17, p. 529. **35.** Stewart to Searle, 4 September 1875, LMA: STo3/01/02/015. The full passage is also quoted in Mabin and Conradie, *The Confidence of the Whole Country*, p. 54. **36.** Minutes of the Standard Bank Board, 24 September 1875, SCB Archives, Box 1185, Vol. 3 **37.** Stewart to the Secretary, 29 October 1875, LMA: STo3/01/02/015. **38.** The first was dated 22 August 1876 (LMA: STo3/01/01/004). They continued regularly thereafter, with a break only from mid-September to the end of October 1876 when Stewart perhaps finally took a holiday. **39.** Stewart to Searle, 5 January 1875, LMA: STo3/01/02/014. **40.** On the role of the City's general managers, see Youssef Cassis, *City Bankers, 1890–1914*, Cambridge University Press, 1994. 'Their social origins, education, careers and even, to a large extent, the way they exercised their professions, were radically different . . . As a general rule, the manager was less affluent, lived in less aristocratic districts, frequented less select company and received fewer decorations and titles than the other members of the [City] community. His activities in the City were also of a lesser order' (pp. 131–3). **41.** Stewart to Farie, 26 April 1877, LMA: STo3/01/01/004. **42.** Stewart to Farie, 17 May 1877, LMA: STo3/01/01/004. **43.** Stewart to Farie, 25 October 1877, LMA: STo3/01/01/005. **44.** Stewart to Farie, 4 May 1878, LMA: STo3/01/01/005. **45.** Stewart to Farie, 17 October 1878, LMA: STo3/01/01/005. **46.** Extracted from 'General Remarks' in the Half-Year Report, 6 August 1880, quoted in Mabin and Conradie, *The Confidence of the Whole Country*, pp. 94–5. **47.** The figures are taken from Amphlett, *History of the Standard Bank*, p. 47. **48.** Court Minutes, 21 December 1872, Vol. 2, SCB Box 271. The Chairman had written in September to one of Adam's close friends, explaining that the Directors felt a change at the top was essential and asking the friend to break the news as 'the best mode in which we can make to him the necessary announcement, to spare him as far as possible' (T. A. Mitchell to C. S. Skinner, 5 September 1872, LMA: CH03/01/10/71/01).   **49.** Profiles of Gwyther were published by *The Bankers' Magazine* in 1889, Vol. 49 (p. 833) and in 1905, Vol. 79 (pp. 219–20).   **50.** John Darwin, *The Empire Project, The Rise and Fall of the British World-System 1830–1970*, Cambridge University Press, 2009.   **51.** Dr Bennett to the Secretary, 1 May 1872, LMA: CH08/08/001. This is one of a cache of 240 letters, numbered sequentially by their date. Dr Bennett seems occasionally to have been torn between his loyalty to the bank and his professional obligations to his patient. Reporting on a Mr James Mackintosh in March 1872, he formally notified the bank that 'his general "physique" is not exactly what one would select for an Indian life'. Only in a separate letter, intended for the Secretary's eyes alone, did he disclose that the man was suffering 'from secondary symptoms, the consequence of a syphilitic attack . . . He informed me frankly of his state & does not expect me to reveal what he told me.' Mackintosh was posted to Singapore.   **52.** Darwin, *The Empire Project*, p. 61. Many histories of the British Empire until well into the twentieth century took a view of the world that was not so different from that of Gwyther and his contemporaries. See for example *The Cambridge History of the British Empire: Vol. III The Empire–Commonwealth 1870–1919*, eds., E. A. Benians, J. Butler and C. E. Carrington, 1929: 'In the dependencies [of the Empire], peace, order and security must be maintained under the British flag. That was the British tradition – the benefits it brought to harassed lands and peoples' (p. 183).   **53.** Quoted in Maurice Collis, *Wayfoong, The Hongkong and Shanghai Banking Corporation, A Study of East Asia's Transformation, Political, Financial and Economic, During the Last Hundred Years*, Faber & Faber, 1965, p. 22.   **54.** For a table of the Hongkong Bank's changing capitalization from 1865 to 1985, see Frank H. H. King, *The History of the Hongkong Bank*, Vol. 1 *In Late Imperial China 1864–1902: On an Even Keel*, Cambridge University Press, 1987, p. 7.   **55.** 'Reminiscences' by F. Bennett, LMA: CH03/01/15/006.   **56.** Head Office to Yokohama branch, 17 October 1884, JL-B notes, LMA: CH03/01/14/025.   **57.** Sherwood to Head Office, 23 September 1865, JL-B notes, LMA: CH03/01/14/031. JL-B's notes continue: 'The agent in question, Douglas, had subsequently been put in charge at Bombay and even then he had not mastered the mystery of any two accounts called Outward and Inward respectively.'   **58.** Whyte to Head Office, 23 October 1872, JL-B notes, LMA: CH03/01/14/028.   **59.** Harper to Head Office, no date, JL-B notes, LMA: CH03/01/14/043.   **60.** Head Office to Whyte, 10 May 1872, JL-B notes, LMA: CH03/01/14/016.   **61.** Amiya Kumar Bagchi, 'Anglo-Indian Banking in British India: From the Paper Pound to the Gold Standard', *Journal of Imperial and Commonwealth History*, Vol. XIII, No. 3, May 1985, p. 103.   **62.** See for example a report of 23 April 1880 from T. L. Mullins, the Manager of the branch in Batavia, who had recently begun to take on duties as an acting Inspector: commenting on the operations of the Singapore branch, he thought 'it was difficult for the Bank's officers to learn Malay seeing that all the native staff and many of the native constituents [i.e. customers] spoke English fluently'. (LMA: CH03/01/14/042.)   **63.** Bagchi, 'Anglo-Indian Banking', p. 104.   **64.** Letter from Hormusji Curstaji

SOURCES AND REFERENCES PP. 96–105807

Khan to the Bombay branch, 1950, included in the MacColl Memorandum, LMA: CH03/01/14/029. **65.** Head Office to Bombay branch Manager, 18 January 1888, JL-B notes, LMA: CH03/01/14/016. **66.** Letter from Janardan Krishna Pathare to the Bombay branch, included in the MacColl Memorandum, LMA: CH03/01/14/029. **67.** The review was published as an editorial in the *China Mail*, 19 June 1871. Its contents were summarized by Carl T. Smith at a Symposium of the Royal Asiatic Society (Hong Kong) on 25–26 November 1972. I am indebted to Bill Brown for a copy of the relevant section of the proceedings. **68.** 'When visiting Colombo, [W. C.] Main discussed the advances given by the Bank on the security of shares in Tea Estates. He formed the opinion that prices for these shares were too high even allowing for their current prosperity and suggested that this was due to too liberal advances made by the Bank.' (Main to Head Office, 10 May, 1893, JL-B notes, LMA: CH03/01/14/039.) See also Compton Mackenzie, *Realms of Silver, One Hundred Years of Banking in the East*, Routledge & Kegan Paul, 1954, pp. 47–9. **69.** 'The Early History of the Chartered Bank in Burma', LMA: CH03/01/14/037. **70.** 'Chettiar capital financed, in long-term loans, the reclaiming of the [Irrawaddy] delta and the preparation of the land for cultivation: and then, in short-term loans it financed each rice crop, from planting through to harvesting.' Ian Brown, *Burma's Economy in the Twentieth Century*, Cambridge University Press, 2013, pp. 8–9 and 15–17. **71.** '[The premises on the Strand] in 1885 were reported as being in such a dilapidated state that their appearance both inside and out was "disgraceful". The owner had died and his executors in England neglected to carry out even the simplest repairs. No new furniture had been bought for sixteen years, and most of what had survived was broken and dangerous to use.' ('The Early History of the Chartered Bank in Burma', LMA: CH03/01/14/037, pp. 4–5.) A new building on a fresh site, at the corner of Shafraz Road (now Bank Street) and Phayre (now Ponsodan) Street was nonetheless only finally commissioned by the Court at the end of 1898. **72.** Sarah Rooney, *30 Heritage Buildings of Yangon: Inside the City that Captured Time*, pub. Association of Myanmar Architects and Serindia Publications, 2013, p. 96. **73.** Hong Kong branch report to Head Office, 17 August 1892, JL-B notes, LMA: CH03/01/14/051. **74.** A currency exhibition at the Hong Kong Museum of History in 2012 prompted the publication of a comprehensively illustrated catalogue that includes (pp. 162–211) photographs of the notes issued by the Chartered Bank and latterly Standard Chartered Bank from an undated pre-1865 note to a unique $150 note issued in 2009 to commemorate the 150th anniversary of the bank's arrival in Hong Kong. **75.** Mackenzie, *Realms of Silver*, p. 110. **76.** From John Cameron, *Our Tropical Possessions in Malayan India*, London 1865, quoted in JL-B notes, LMA: CH03/01/14/042. **77.** T. L. Mullins to Head Office, 23 April 1880, JL-B notes, LMA: CH03/01/14/031, CH03/01/14/042. **78.** Penang report to Head Office, 22 May 1883, JL-B notes, LMA: CH03/01/14/043. **79.** Caleb Lewis to Lord Ripon, Secretary of State for the Colonies, 18 March 1895, LMA: CH03/01/09/135. **80.** Extracted from F. Bennett's memoirs, LMA: CH03/01/14/045. Bennett added a colourful aside on the social life of the day: 'There were two clubs in Kuala Lumpur in my time, the Selangor and the Luha ... The game of cricket was very popular and the Selangor Club had a good pitch on the Maidan. Clerks who were good at the game had a somewhat better chance of securing posts in Government and mercantile offices than indifferent players.'   **81.** T. L. Mullins to Head Office, 3 July 1885, JL-B notes, LMA: CH03/01/14/042.   **82.** See Collis, *Wayfoong*, pp. 95–6. The Hongkong Bank's withdrawal of support is also noted in a corporate history of The Straits Trading Company, K. G. Tregonning's *Straits Tin*, Tien Wah Press, 1985, p. 11.   **83.** The Mullins report from Singapore in July 1885 cited Whitehead explicitly as a manager whose approach exemplified one of the bank's weaknesses: 'Whitehead in Hong Kong in particular was apt to be over bearing and to treat his colleagues ... as subordinates, an attitude which made it difficult for Dougal [in Singapore] to work amicably with him'. (Op. cit., n. 81, JL-B notes, LMA: CH03/01/14/042.)   **84.** E. H. H. Green, 'Rentiers versus Producers? The Political Economy of the Bimetallic Controversy, c. 1880–1898', *English Historical Review*, Vol. 103, July 1988, pp. 588–612. See also A. C. Howe, 'Debate: Bimetallism, c. 1880–1898: a controversy re-opened?', *English Historical Review*, Vol. 105, April 1990, pp. 377–91 for a critique of the original article, and E. H. H. Green, 'The Bimetallic Controversy: empiricism belimed or the case for the issues', *English Historical Review*, Vol. 105, July 1990, pp. 673–83, for the author's rejoinder. **85.** *The Bankers' Magazine*, Vol. 36, 1876, pp. 452–3.   **86.** *The Bankers' Magazine*, Vol. 39, 1879, pp. 406–7. Net profits for 1878 were £42,446 if adjustment is made to the declared figure to restate it *after* the write-off of bad and doubtful debts, and *before* below-the-line transfers to reserves, in line with modern practice.   **87.** Head Office to Mullins and his reply, 16 September 1885, JL-B notes, LMA: CH03/01/14/026.   **88.** For example, when it was decided to establish a full branch in Bangkok instead of relying on the agency services of A. Markwald, an announcement of the bank's inauguration noted that all of its business would be conducted from the outset on a gold basis (*Bangkok Times*, 21 March 1894). **89.** A useful summary can be found in 'The Silver Crisis 1870–1900', EIU Report, LMA: CH03/01/15/024.   **90.** The figures are taken from Cassis, *City Bankers*, p. 76. **91.** See Cassis, *City Bankers*: Gwyther, suggests the author, was one of many names on the Bimetallic League's City Committee of whom 'we may wonder to what extent they simply thought the bimetallist system more rational without really believing that it had any chance of success in England' (p. 110).   **92.** Stewart to the Secretary's Office, 1 December 1875, quoted by Terry, *A Pioneer Bank*, p. 96. **93.** Half Year Report, 9 February 1877, quoted in Mabin and Conradie, *The Confidence of the Whole Country*, p. 62.   **94.** J. A. Henry, *The First Hundred Years of the Standard Bank*, Oxford University Press, 1963, pp. 78–9.   **95.** Most notably, the commentaries provided by the bank's staff locally and at Head Office on the evolution of the diamond industry are a principal source for the definitive account of that extraordinary story, Worger's *South Africa's City of Diamonds*. Mabin and Conradie, *The Confidence of the Whole Country*, is an edited and much abridged collection of the bank's reports on economic conditions for 1865–1902.   **96.** Minutes of the Standard Bank Board, 21 December 1880, SCB Archives, Box 1185, Vol. 4.   **97.** Farie to the Secretary, 21 January 1881, LMA: ST03/01/02/025.   **98.** Quoted by Terry, *A Pioneer Bank*, p. 75.   **99.** Gilbert Farie to the Chief Manager's Office, 11 March 1881, LMA: ST03/01/02/025. **100.** Half Year Report, 14 October 1882, quoted in Mabin and Conradie, *The Confidence of the Whole Country*, p. 133. The author, almost certainly Michell himself, suggested to London that much more might usefully be said in public of the bank's South African identity, particularly on the staffing front. 'Our Colonial staff of 30th June last numbered 399 of whom we have discovered . . . exactly 200 were born and brought up in this country. Even a larger number speak the Colonial "Dutch" language and our ranks include a large number of officers bearing . . . thoroughly Dutch names . . .' **101.** 'Being fully and constantly advised of the position of matters, we are quite alive to the necessity of exercising extreme care in advancing the Bank's money to parties speculating in scrip of this class [i.e. issued by diamond companies] . . . Being fully satisfied that sooner or later matters would become much involved, we determined so far as this Bank was concerned to restrict advances, and this course appears to have resulted in good.' (Farie to the Chief Manager's Office, 2 June 1881, LMA: ST03/01/02/025.) **102.** Quoted by Terry, *A Pioneer Bank*, p. 76. **103.** Stewart to the Chairman of the Week from Port Elizabeth, 16 May 1884, LMA: ST03/02/33/001. Most unusually, this letter is in Stewart's own handwriting. **104.** Michell to Sir Henry Barkly, 20 April 1885, ARCH 2/5/Michell. **105.** Michell, 'Sixty Years In and Out of South Africa', p. 54. **106.** Michell to R. W. H. Giddy, 21 April 1885, ARCH 2/5/Michell. **107.** Michell to C. T. Green, 20 May 1885, ARCH 2/5/Michell. **108.** Michell to Edward Thomas, 25 April 1885, ARCH 2/5/Michell. **109.** Michell to C. M. G. Mills, 1 June 1885, ARCH 2/5/Michell. **110.** Michell to H. C. Ross, 15 May 1885, ARCH 2/5/Michell. **111.** Michell also used his correspondence with Ross to vent some of his recurrent frustrations over the aloofness of the London Board. In 1888, he was appalled to find that an application to the Directors for a period of home leave in England had been turned down because he had failed to cite any specific 'reasons' for his request. He wrote to Ross: 'It is a disappointment to me to see what slight consideration the Board as a whole are inclined to give to an application made by one of the General Managers . . . Were I on the Board I should attach some importance to seeing the General Managers at rather frequent intervals.' (Michell to H. C. Ross, 29 February 1888, ARCH 2/5/Michell.) **112.** The Kimberley manager's view in 1881, relayed to London by the General Manager's Office, was that a healthy industry would require 'foreign capitalists . . . [to take] the place of weak Colonial proprietors'. Quoted in Worger, *South Africa's City of Diamonds*, p. 52. **113.** See Worger, *South Africa's City of Diamonds*, p. 193. **114.** A takeover vehicle was launched, called Unified Diamond Mines Limited. See Worger, *South Africa's City of Diamonds*, p. 195. 'Although supporting the Unified scheme, the Standard Bank's officers remained sceptical as to its chances of success.' **115.** A Standard Bank inspector's report in February 1887 claimed operations within the De Beers mine were being directed with a 'reckless disregard for human life'. (Quoted by Worger, *South Africa's City of Diamonds*, pp. 216–17.) There is no evidence this report was ever seen by Rhodes or his company, but it seems not unlikely that they were made aware of the gist of the inspector's views. **116.** See Worger, *South Africa's City of Diamonds*, pp. 223–5. 'In the final week of

September [1887] . . . the Standard's head office in London, believing that the Central had inadequate collateral, and going against the advice of its Cape Town manager, refused to make the loan.' Two months later the Central's chairman personally travelled to London to try again: 'Baring-Gould sailed to England in a vain attempt to persuade the Standard Bank to loan him money so that he could try to take over De Beers.'   **117.** Lewis Michell, *The Life of the Rt Hon Cecil John Rhodes*, Edward Arnold, 1910, vol. 1, p. 253.   **118.** Ibid.   **119.** See Worger, *South Africa's City of Diamonds*, pp. 225–6. This is the author's summary of a speech by Rhodes a year earlier, in which he had proclaimed the objectives for the new company.   **120.** According to Terry, *A Pioneer Bank*, p. 175, 'gold output [in 1890] was valued at £1,837,000, of which the Standard Bank shipped £903,000'. **121.** Quoted in Wheatcroft, *The Randlords*, p. 114.   **122.** Michell, 'Sixty Years In and Out of South Africa', p. 70.   **123.** Henry, *The First Hundred Years of the Standard Bank*, p. 113. Michell confessed to Sir Hercules Robinson that this assessment was 'not far out, as will appear later on. For one thing we escape publication of statements by our Branches separately and this is a great gain, checking curiosity and concealing our country operations from rivals . . . Our <u>combined</u> statement will make all others look small.' (Michell to Robinson, 19 October, 1891, ARCH 2/5/Michell.)

3. AT THE CREST OF THE WAVE

1. A collection of internal examination papers from 1882 and 1891 can be found in LMA: CH03/01/10/01/005.   **2.** *The Bankers' Magazine*, Vol. 79, January–June 1905, pp. 716–18.   **3.** The impact of the new city on the Standard's staffing requirements was felt almost immediately. 'During 1889 the pressure of work [on the Rand] was so great that other branches throughout the service were drained of all available men to strengthen Johannesburg and, in all, 75 experienced officers were sent there during 1889.' (Carolyn Terry, *A Pioneer Bank in a Pioneer Land*, Flesch & Partners, 1979, p. 172.) It is striking that Terry's rich potpourri of a book, which includes brief profiles of dozens of the Standard's early managers, has just a single reference to an individual returning home to Britain – Robert Stewart.   **4.** W. H. Young, *A Merry Banker in the Far East*, John Lane The Bodley Head, 1916, pp. 4–5.   **5.** C. A. Bayly, *The Birth of the Modern World, 1780–1914*, Blackwell Publishing 2004, p. 456. 'Even if the historians' arguments over continuity and change remain relatively evenly balanced up to about 1890, there is very good reason to think that change ought to win out decisively in any analysis of the years thereafter.'   **6.** Jurgen Osterhammel, *The Transformation of the World, A Global History of the Nineteenth Century*, Princeton University Press, 2014, p. 728. The author cites Gregory Clark, *A Farewell to Alms, A Brief Economic History of the World*, Princeton, 2007, p. 309, as his source for this remarkable comparison.   **7.** P. G. Wodehouse, *Psmith in the City*, 1910, Everyman edition p. 167. Psmith's cricketing friend Mike Jackson is comforted on his first day at the New Asiatic Bank by a fellow clerk who assures him: 'It's not like one of those banks where you stay in London all your life. You only have three years here, and then you get your orders, and go to one of the branches in the East, where you're the dickens of a big pot straight away, with a big screw [salary] and a dozen native Johnnies under you. Bit of all right, that.' Wodehouse joined the London branch of the Hongkong and Shanghai Bank aged nineteen in 1900 and worked there as a junior clerk for two years. But he never had any interest in being posted to the East, and left the bank to embark on his career as a writer. (See also Frank H. H. King, *The History of the Hongkong Bank*, Vol. 2 *In the Period of Imperialism and War 1895–1918: Wayfong, the Focus of Wealth*, Cambridge University Press, 1987–91, pp. 178–81.) **8.** Frances Hutchins, *Illusion of Permanence, British Imperialism in India*, Princeton 1967, pp. 107–8. **9.** Young, *Merry Banker*, pp. 7–8. **10.** Head Office to Agents and Managers, 'Rules and Conditions of Furlough', 19 October 1906, LMA: CH03/01/10/37/010. **11.** Memoir by W. S. Livingstone, submitted to the Centenary Commemoration Committee in 1950, LMA: CH03/01/14/036. **12.** See LMA: CH03/01/14/063 on the Philippines War 1898–9. It contains an eye-witness account written in 1931 by one of the bank's staff, possibly the Manager himself describing his actions in the third person. **13.** Memoir by W. S. Livingstone, LMA: CH03/01/15/011. **14.** 'Some Reminiscences' by Eric Nelson Sinclair, submitted to the Centenary Commemoration Committee in 1950, LMA: CH03/01/14/083. **15.** 'Report on the sanitary conditions of the Shanghai Premises', February 1899, LMA: CH03/01/09/066. **16.** Bombay Agent to Head Office, 30 December 1896. 'The Agent wrote later that there had been three cases of plague amongst the Bank's servants at the Agent's House in Malabar Hill and as a number of dead rats were discovered he had closed the bungalow [where the staff lived] and sent the surviving servants to the country.' JL-B notes, LMA: CH03/01/14/029. **17.** 'Several Europeans [in Bombay at the end of 1896] contracted the disease and I recall at least two cases where death resulted. One morning a Native clerk came to my office and reported finding a dead rat under his desk . . . he was very frightened and I had some difficulty in pacifying him.' Memoir by F. B. Bennett, submitted to the Centenary Commemoration Committee in 1950, LMA: CH03/01/14/016. (Bennett joined the bank in 1883 and retired in 1923, so must have been about eighty-five when he handed in his 49-page Memoir.) **18.** Extracted from F. Bennett's memoirs, LMA: CH03/01/14/045. **19.** J. A. Macgill to Faulkner, 27 January 1950, LMA: CH03/01/14/088. This letter accompanied Macgill's submission to the Centenary Commemoration Committee of a memoir running to 106 pages, and written in the form of a personal letter to a fellow trainee at Hatton Court in 1898–1901. Born in Tain, a small town in the Scottish Highlands, Macgill was seventy-one when he wrote it and spent ten months at the task, with constant encouragement from Faulkner. **20.** Memoir by J. A. Macgill, Part 4, p. 11, LMA: CH03/01/14/088. **21.** Gwyther to Forrest, 11 November 1889, LMA: CH03/01/10/026/01/A. **22.** The following account of Gibson's career has been reconstructed from letters to be found in LMA: CH03/01/10/47/09. **23.** Fraser to Head Office, 18 July 1901, LMA: CH03/01/10/47/09. **24.** Fraser to Head Office, 29 August 1901, LMA: CH03/01/10/47/09. **25.** Hong Kong Manager to Head Office, 10 November 1907, LMA: CH03/01/10/47/09. **26.** Hoggan to

Gibson, 3 April 1908, LMA: CH03/01/10/47/09.   **27.** Details relating to the aftermath of Rennie's suicide and the unwinding of the bank's position can be found at LMA: CH03/01/10/26/02. The godown stocks appear to have been sold in short order, at a substantial loss, but disposing of HKM's fixed assets proved much harder. The story was recalled in the 1930s by a popular columnist, V. H. C. Jarrett, writing in the *South China Morning Post*. A 4-volume collection of Jarrett's columns, *Old Hong Kong*, is held in the Hong Kong Public Record Office. According to Jarrett, 'the Chartered Bank, who held a mortgage on the mills [at Junk Bay], took possession of the place: and in February 1925 this bank sold the property to the Hong Kong government, who have now called for tenders to have the buildings demolished' (pp. 859–61).   **28.** Hoggan to Gibson, 27 August 1908, LMA: CH03/01/10/47/09. Gibson's explanatory letters were dated 5 May and 22 August 1908.   **29.** *The Bankers' Magazine*, Vol. 50/1, 1890, pp. 806–9, and Vol. 51/2, 1891, pp. 853–5.   **30.** Court Minutes, 3 February 1892, Vol. 5, SCB Box 271.   **31.** A profile published three years earlier in *The Bankers' Magazine* had been gushing, even by the normally eulogistic standards of personal profiles in the City's house journal. 'Mr Gwyther . . . [is] one of the most respected men in the City of London . . . The remark has often been made and echoed, that it would be well for the City of London if there were more bankers in it like him.' (Vol. 49, 1889, p. 333.)   **32.** See Philip Ziegler, *The Sixth Great Power: A History of One of the Greatest of All Banking Families – The House of Barings, 1762–1829*, Harper Collins, 1988.   **33.** The cashier's confession, ruled Mr Justice Princess, was insufficient grounds for a conviction. Even more oddly, the judge instructed the jury 'that they must be satisfied that the accused had embezzled [the total sum of money estimated to have been lost by the bank] . . . on one occasion or in one sum and that on or about the date charged in the Indictment'. Since it was well established by the end of the trial that the money had been trousered over a long period of time, the jury had no choice but to acquit the defendant, prompting the bank's solicitors in Calcutta to opine afterwards that 'there can be no other opinion than that in this case there has been a most complete failure of Justice '. (Watkins & Co. to the Calcutta Agent F. C. Marshall, 24 September 1890, LMA: CH03/01/09/303. A substantial bundle of papers on the episode includes a verbatim transcript of the trial.) Shama Churn Sen apparently died not long after the trial, of natural causes.   **34.** *The Bankers' Magazine*, Vol. 79, January–June 1905, pp. 716–18.   **35.** Department heads to Gwyther, 8 January 1891, LMA: CH03/01/09/194.   **36.** For a summary of the Chartered Bank's annual finances from 1890 to 1969, see Geoffrey Jones, *British Multinational Banking 1830–1990*, Oxford University Press, 1993, Appendix 5.   **37.** Court Minutes, 15 January 1902, Vol. 6, SCB Box 271.   **38.** The Association was inaugurated at a meeting in the London offices of the P&O Company in April 1889. Among those present who agreed to make up its inaugural General Committee were Sir Robert Jardine, William Keswick, Sir Alfred Dent and John Swire – and from the banks, Thomas Jackson and Howard Gwyther (*North-China Herald*, 25 May 1889).   **39.** Copies of the nineteenth-century supplementary charters and of correspondence between the bank and the Treasury about them can be found at LMA: CH03/01/09/305.   **40.** Caleb Lewis to Lord

Ripon at the Colonial Office, 18 March 1895, LMA: CH03/01/09/135. The episode is summarized in Compton Mackenzie, *Realms of Silver, One Hundred Years of Banking in the East*, Routledge & Kegan Paul, 1954, pp. 215–16 – and is one of many (unreferenced) passages in the book that show its original author, John Leighton-Boyce, making use of the surviving archives of the bank. (See Appendix A.) **41.** J. A. Swettenham of the Straits Settlement Government to Lord Ripon, Secretary of State for the Colonies, 27 June 1895, LMA: CH03/01/09/135. **42.** Downing Street to the Manager of the Chartered Bank. 6 August 1895, LMA: CH03/01/09/135. **43.** Caleb Lewis to Edward Fairfield at the Colonial Office, 14 November 1895, LMA: CH03/01/09/135. **44.** Gwyther to the Secretary to the Admiralty, 16 December 1896, and the reply of 18 December 1896, LMA: CH03/01/09/147. **45.** Philip K. Law, 'The Dent Family', in the *Oxford DNB*. **46.** Stephanie Jones, *Two Centuries of Overseas Trading, The Origins and Growth of the Inchcape Group*, London, 1986, quoted in T. M. Devine, *To the Ends of the Earth, Scotland's Global Diaspora, 1750–2010*, Allen Lane, 2011, p. 82. **47.** See P. Cain and A. G. Hopkins, 'Gentlemanly Capitalism and British Expansion Overseas', *Economic History Review*, No. 39, 1986, and the same authors' *British Imperialism: Innovation and Expansion, 1688–1914*, Longman, 1993. Their interpretation challenged a still influential view of the New Imperialism that ascribed it to a largely reluctant expansion of the Empire promulgated by Ministers and civil servants ('the official mind'), generally with a weary heart, in defence of Britain's (or, more often, of British India's) strategic interests: see R. E. Robinson and J. Gallagher, 'The Imperialism of Free Trade', *Economic History Review*, New Series, 6, 1, 1953, and *Africa and the Victorians: The Official Mind of Imperialism*, Macmillan, 1961. One of the most intensely debated issues in modern British historiography is succinctly summarized in John Darwin, *The Empire Project, The Rise and Fall of the British World-System 1830–1970*, Cambridge University Press, 2009, pp. 83–92. His balanced view – 'The sheer scale of Britain's global activity from China to Peru [and] the inevitable intermingling of political and economic interests . . . make any overview a heroic abstraction' (p. 88) – would seem to be well borne out by the mixed views within the Chartered Bank. **48.** J. A. Macgill worked in the Secretary's department in 1898–1901 and recalled: '[Gwyther] not only kept "tabs" on all Branch operations and correspondence but also ran a sort of secretariat of his own . . . It was this interference that hurt my boss Mr Hoggan [the Secretary] so sorely, and many a storm did blow up in our Department, I can assure you.' (Macgill to Faulkner, 6 January 1950, LMA: CH03/01/14/083.) **49.** 'The formal issuer was the Chartered Bank . . . but the man behind it was Cassel, emerging as the City's foremost international financier. The detailed background to this loan is shrouded in mystery.' David Kynaston, *The City of London, Vol. 2: Golden Years 1890–1914*, Chatto & Windus, 1995, p. 126. **50.** Mackenzie, *Realms of Silver*, pp. 203–4. **51.** Robert Bickers, *The Scramble for China, Foreign Devils in the Qing Empire, 1832–1914*, Allen Lane, 2011, p. 324. The author presents a fresh and persuasive account of China's despoilation by the rival colonial powers, though he makes few references to the world of banking and finance. **52.** Whitehead to Gwyther, 12 May 1896, LMA: CH03/01/09/221. A little more of the letter seems worth quoting as a measure of Whitehead's breathtaking self-regard: 'I fail to realize how [my spare time] and my surplus energies could be otherwise or better employed. Occupied they must be as the energetic disposition and the mental vigour with which I have been blest cannot remain idle without running the risk of stagnating . . . This full occupation and the exercise from an hour's Polo in the evening enables me to keep myself mentally and physically in the very pink of condition.' **53.** Gwyther's EGM speech, 19 October 1898, *The Bankers' Magazine*, Vol. 66, July–December 1898, pp. 631–2. **54.** Whitehead's letter and Gwyther's remarks are quoted in Mackenzie, *Realms of Silver*, pp. 205–6. **55.** Gwyther's AGM speech, 18 April 1900, *The Bankers' Magazine*, Vol. 69, January–June 1900, pp. 771–2. **56.** See, for example, the account in J. A. Henry, *The First Hundred Years of the Standard Bank*, Oxford University Press, 1963, p. 120. **57.** Michell to the Chairman of the Week, 18 October 1895, ARCH 2/5/Michell. **58.** Michell to Ross, 22 August 1895, ARCH 2/5/Michell. **59.** Michell to Ross, 29 November 1895, ARCH 2/5/Michell. **60.** Michell to Ross, 2 December 1895, ARCH 2/5/Michell. **61.** Lord Loch remained on the Board, which he served until his death in 1900. After Rhodes visited London in April 1899 and attended a meeting of the Board to talk about banking arrangements for Rhodesia, Loch was given the job of talking to him privately about a future agreement. (Minutes of the Standard Bank Board, 18 April and 6 June 1899, SCB Archives, Box 1189, Vol. 8.) **62.** Quoted in Terry, *A Pioneer Bank*, p. 184. **63.** Michell to Rhodes, 24 February 1896, ARCH 2/5/Michell. Confirming the payments, Michell added his own impression of Rhodes's standing in Johannesburg. 'People here are saying that you have blocked the Suez Canal to demonstrate the value of the Cape route. No doubt you are also responsible for the explosion [recently in a dynamite store] at Johannesburg and for the locusts!' **64.** Terry, *A Pioneer Bank*, p. 185. **65.** Michell to Rhodes, 8 January 1897, ARCH 2/5/Michell. **66.** See 'Diary of Sir Lewis Michell's Visit to Rhodesia in 1897', ARCH 2/5/M. The expedition with Rhodes was the highlight of his life, as Michell readily confessed, and his lively account of the eight days they spent together on the veld has often been quoted for the picture it drew of Rhodes's extraordinary impact on all those around him. Michell incorporated much of the diary into a two-volume biography, *The Life of the Rt Hon Cecil John Rhodes* (pub. Edward Arnold, 1910), that he wrote a decade later, and into his own unpublished autobiography, 'Sixty Years In and Out of South Africa', now held in the national archives in Cape Town. (A copy of Chapters 4–10 is held in the Standard Bank archives at ARCH 2/5/Michell.) Michell's frankest declaration of his feelings for Rhodes is to be found in the autobiography, where he writes of wishing 'to shew to those who come after me that Rhodes had a great capacity for friendship and of inspiring affection in lesser men. I have never [been] ashamed to own that I loved him as I have never loved any other man and his faults were as spots on the sun to all those who came within his orbit' (p. 86). **67.** Michell to Rhodes, 10 January 1899, ARCH 2/5/Michell. **68.** Minutes of the Standard Bank Board, 31 October 1899 and 2 January 1900, SCB Archives, Box 1189, Vol. 9. **69.** See Stuart Jones, *The Great Imperial Banks, A Study of the Business of Standard Bank and Barclays Bank, 1891–1961*, University of South Africa, 1996, p.

161: 'Army pay bills passing through the Standard Bank in Cape Town and Piet-ermaritzberg totalled £64,500,000 in the three year period from July 1899 to June 1902, bringing an income to the bank of £524,750.' This equated to 66 per cent of the aggregate dividend payments to shareholders for the four calendar years 1899–1902. **70.** Minutes of the Standard Bank Board, 8 January 1901, SCB Archives, Box 1189, Vol. 9. **71.** See Terry, *A Pioneer Bank*, Chapter 13, pp. 199–226, for a rich trove of anecdotes about the war's impact on the bank and the experiences of many individuals on both sides of the Anglo-Boer divide. **72.** Michell to Sir Gordon Sprigg, 4 January 1901, ARCH 2/5/Michell. Replying to the offer, Michell wrote: 'I regret to say that, after giving the matter full consid-eration, I do not feel at liberty to sever my connection with the Bank in the present critical state of public affairs.' **73.** Minutes of the Standard Bank Board, 3 January 1902, SCB Archives, Box 1189, Vol. 9. The Directors climbed down and assured Michell they were 'anxious to assist Cape Government in every safe way' – but ten days later they were equivocating again: 'Standard Bank Board of Directors con-sider it impossible to believe Government Cape Colony expect them to risk an indefinite amount solely to be regulated by balance creditor Receiver General. Is it intended to reduce overdraft Paymaster General . . . and to limit overdraft definite amount?' (Telegram noted in Minutes of 13 January 1902.) **74.** The Board Min-utes of 29 April 1902 note receipt of a Private Official letter from Michell, but the volume of his collected Private Official Correspondence (ARCH 2/5/Michell) con-tains no letters after late 1901. The Board voted on 6 May 1902 to accept his resignation, and to award him 'pension on the ordinary terms . . . and a special grant of £5,000'. **75.** G. T. Amphlett, *History of the Standard Bank of South Africa Ltd, 1862–1913*, Glasgow University Press, 1914, pp. 182–3. Smart had been the Joint Manager of the Johannesburg branch at the time of his appointment as London Manager. He had won some celebrity as a young man in 1880, when as the manager of the Standard's Potchefstroom branch he had refused to hand over cash demanded by the Boers in the brief war of 1880–81. It was said that Paul Kruger himself had encountered Smart in the street and shaken his hand 'to show his regard for an Englishman who stuck to his post'. (Henry, *The First Hun-dred Years of the Standard Bank*, p. 55.) **76.** Michell to H. C. Ross, 29 May 1885, ARCH 2/5/Michell. **77.** See A. C. M. Webb, *The Roots of the Tree, A study in early South African banking: the predecessors of the First National Bank, 1838–1926*, pp. 152–60. The Standard Bank was restrained by its memory of earlier heavy losses in Johannesburg, its traditionally conservative attitude towards lending capital for project development and its concern over the political edge enjoyed by its state-backed rival. 'In contrast, the National Bank held surplus funds and [had] a pair of German general managers whose philosophy of bank-ing differed radically from Michell's' (p. 153). **78.** Jones, *The Great Imperial Banks*, p. 135. The value of the Standard's shipments from the Transvaal peaked at £12.5 million in 1908 and drifted lower thereafter. The National's rose from £12.2 million in 1909 to £19.3 million in 1914. **79.** Jones, *The Great Imperial Banks*, p. 35. **80.** Michell to H. C. Ross, 15 May 1885. Michell added: 'were he now there and in robust health the purchase of the Bank of Africa would

follow'. **81.** *The Bankers' Magazine*, Vol. 73, January–June 1902, pp. 733–4.
82. The top ten at the end of 1913, ranked by the size of their balance sheets, were:
1. London & River Plate Bank (£39.8 million); 2. Hongkong & Shanghai Bank
(£39.5 million); 3. Standard Bank of South Africa (£29.6 million); 4. Chartered
Bank of India, Australia and China (£27.2 million); 5. Bank of Australasia
(£25.9 million); 6. London & Brazilian Bank (£22.3 million); 7. National Bank of
India (£19.8 million); 8. London & Tarapaca Bank (£19.0 million); 9. English,
Scottish & Australian Bank (£10.1 million); 10. Mercantile Bank (£8.2 million).
(Source: Jones, *British Multinational Banking*, Appendix 5.) **83.** Marcello de
Cecco, *Money and Empire, The International Gold Standard, 1890–1914*, Basil
Blackwell Oxford, 1974, p. 71. **84.** The father, also Marcus Samuel, had actually
been described in the 1851 Census as 'Shell Merchant' (Daniel Yergin, *The Prize*,
Simon & Schuster, 1991, p. 63). **85.** The Chartered Bank's archives include a copy
of the agreement between the seven firms in November 1891, and of the Articles
of Association for the resulting Kerosene Association ('To enter into any arrangement for sharing profits, union of interests, cooperation, joint adventure, reciprocal
concession or otherwise with any person or partnership or Company . . . buying
or selling, importing or exporting petroleum or other inflammable oil . . .'). A
pencilled note records that 308 of the 437 shares in the Association are being held
for the owners by the bank. (LMA: CH03/01/09/050.) **86.** *The Times* obituary,
2 August 1947. Mitchell also served as a director of Shell Transport & Trading.
87. No bank records of the 1897 Loan episode have survived, but a note was made
of it by JL-B: 'the [Yokohama] agency and the firm were to collaborate closely over
the issue of the 5 per cent Japanese Gold Bonds in 1897 and other similar transactions' (Mackenzie, *Realms of Silver*, p. 215). Unfortunately, the early papers of M.
Samuel & Co. have also been lost. **88.** Quoted in the EIU Report, *Initiation and
Development of Rubber Planting in Malaya, Netherlands East Indies, Ceylon & S.
India*, 1950, p. 17 (LMA: CH03/01/15/024). **89.** Circular letter from the Secretary, 2 June 1911, LMA: CH03/01/14/041. **90.** Letter from the Secretary to
selected branches, 9 June 1911, LMA: CH03/01/14/041. **91.** Main had joined the
bank in 1868, and had worked for two long stretches of his career as the Manager
in Rangoon. He died at the age of sixty-one, his obituary noting that he 'had for
some time past suffered from a failure of the digestive organs'. (*The Bankers' Magazine*, Vol. 74, July–December 1902, p. 81.) **92.** Whitehead to Main, 28 February
1902, LMA: CH03/01/09/221. **93.** *The Bankers' Magazine*, Vol. 109, January–
June 1920, pp. 796–8. **94.** '[T]he Chartered was for long represented in Kobe by
Messrs. Browne & Co. It was not until February 1895 that a branch was opened
at No.81 with Mr A.S. Harper as agent; he died very shortly afterwards and was
succeeded by Mr James Archer, brother of Mr William Archer the well-known
writer . . . the present fine premises erected, being opened in 1913.' (*The Japan
Chronicle*, Jubilee Number 1868–1918: 'History of Kobe', included in LMA:
CH03/01/14/027.) **95.** Richard Steyn and Francis Antonie, *Hoisting the Standard,
150 Years of Standard Bank*, publ. by The Standard Bank Group, 2012, p. 67. Some
customer records and other papers relating to Standard Bank's pre-1914 operations
in Hamburg can be found at LMA: ST03/05/01. **96.** JL-B notes, LMA:

CH03/01/14/042. **97.** Carl Wolter to Mr Mohr from Chemulpo, 22 November 1902, LMA: CH03/01/10/19/36. The letter, written on notepaper headed 'E. Meyer & Co, Korea', was archived by the bank alongside a letter from Mohr of December 1919 giving instructions for the handling of his sizeable cash deposits with the Chartered's branch in Colombo. **98.** 'It was decided that no agreement should be entered into for the time being by Shanghai regarding guaranteeing payment to the Corean Government of [i.e. for] ginseng crop' JL-B notes, 11 July 1900, LMA: CH03/01/14/020. **99.** The Yokohama Agency in 1909 sent home to Head Office copies of two remarkable papers on the financial assimilation of Korea by the Japanese, titled 'Report of the Progress of the Reorganization of the Finances of Korea, November 1905' and 'State of the Progress of the Reorganization of the Finances of Korea, July 1906' (LMA: CH03/01/09/277). They read today like Bank of England commentaries and must certainly have been penned by a knowledgeable British expatriate, perhaps one of the several Britons who worked at this time for the Korean Customs Service. The author seems, anyway, to have been clear about the obvious direction in which events were going: 'Recently, the Industrial Bank of Japan despatched numbers of its staff to Seoul to make an investigation respecting business conditions in Korea and necessary matters arising in relation to the loan of 10,000,000 Yen to the Korean Government ... The Korean Government intends to afford every possible convenience to the Bank for its investments in Korea' (1906 Report, p. 8). Japan's formal annexation of the country followed under a treaty of 1910. **100.** The *Korean Daily News* advertisement was carried from August 1904 to February 1905. I am indebted to Dr Jim Hoare of the School of Oriental and African Studies for first alerting me to it and for background details on the career of Carl Wolter. (He had arrived on the Korean coast around 1884, apparently taking over the local business of Jardine Matheson – even they had found it difficult to drum up much business in Korea.) The text of the newspaper advertisement is quoted and discussed in Lee Seok Ryun, *A History of Korean Currency and Finance*, Park Young Sa, 1984, p. 474. I am grateful to Ms Yu-jin Jung of the Bank of Korea for her translation of the relevant passages from the original Korean. **101.** The Court Directors in London deferred consideration of the firm's request, 'pending receipt of further particulars from Mr Wolter through the Hamburg Agent and a copy of the firm's balance sheet'. Court Minutes, 17 April 1912, SCB Box 515. **102.** 'Considered the representations made by Carl Wolter & Co, Chemulpo, with regard to the labour involved in making up the monthly returns required from them in connection with Trust Receipt facilities and decided that no modification can be allowed.' Court Minutes, 30 April 1913, SCB Box 515. **103.** G. C. Hampshire to F. G. Hunt, 4 September 1951, LMA: CH03/01/14/016. Hampshire joined the staff in Hatton Court in January 1908. **104.** Inspector's letter to the Managers, 31 December 1904, LMA: CH03/03/07/001. (Whitehead scribbled an irascible note at the bottom: 'This letter is not sufficient. What is required is a report dealing with each account – exhaustively and thoroughly with any irregularities met with and the nature of these!' But he did not demur over the accommodation issue.) **105.** Two large volumes of correspondence and a mass of miscellaneous papers on the bank's relocation can be found at LMA: CH09/05/35/003–004.   **106.** An architect contracted by the bank to assess 4 Crosby Square's suitability reported back: 'On the whole I am of opinion that the site, supposing the Directors consider the position desirable, could be rendered very suitable for the purposes of the Bank.' (Charles Jones to St Quintin & Son Surveyors, 3 December 1906, LMA: CH09/05/35/003.) The sale to another party was completed in May 1907, while the bank's lawyers were still immersed in their negotiations with the Treasury.   **107.** A lengthy account of the Crosby Hall saga can be found at LMA: CH03/01/15/006. Correspondence on the sale of Hatton Court and acquisition of Bishopsgate is included in LMA: CH03/01/09/162.   **108.** According to a centenary publication produced by the bank in Bangkok in 1994, the new building was opened for business on 3 May 1909 – ten years after the original purchase of the underlying land in 1899.   **109.** Report to Head Office, 1908, LMA: CH03/01/14/053.   **110.** 'Rex' column, *Capital* magazine, p. 547, 1907, included in press cuttings in LMA: CH03/01/10/27/05.   **111.** Note by Thomas Fraser, 25 March 1907, LMA: CH03/01/10/27/05.   **112.** 'Report by J.S. Bruce on a Visit to Baghdad and Basra, 30 January 1909', LMA: CH03/01/10/26/10. All quotations in this and the following paragraphs are extracted from the report and from correspondence enclosed with it.   **113.** The passage of Bruce's report, sub-titled 'Proposed Mesopotamia Irrigation Scheme', closes with an endearing caveat: 'I do not know if Sir William meant what he told me as confidential as he did not say so, but in any case this is a Private & Confidential report so it does not matter.'   **114.** A copy of the prospectus is at LMA: MS39001. It was published in *The Times* on 21 December 1909.   **115.** The figure was provided to shareholders by the Secretary in response to a question towards the close of the inaugural General Meeting. (Minutes of 13 April 1910, LMA: MS39004.)   **116.** Papers and correspondence relating to the 1911–13 opium crisis can be found at LMA: CH03/01/10/47/13. Copies of several of the Private & Confidential Circulars despatched from Bishopsgate in 1912 by the Secretary, William Hoggan, were retained by the bank's Agent in New York and can be found at LMA: CH07/06/001.   **117.** The letter endorsing the Memorial by E. D. Sassoon was signed in December 1912 by Chartered Bank and Eastern Bank, along with the Hongkong & Shanghai Bank and the International Banking Corporation: 'We the undersigned . . . being largely interested in the finance of the Opium Trade of India and China have read with deep interest and concern the memorial of the Merchants . . . and we desire to urge upon your Lordship that . . . [it] should be granted in the best interests of the State, the Memorialists, and indeed of all who are in various ways connected with the trade' (LMA: CH07/06/001).   **118.** The advances, secured against more than 700 chests of opium, were valued at £24,450 in Shanghai, £18,500 in Hong Kong, £17,239 in Singapore, £50,000 in Calcutta and £128,300 in Bombay (LMA: CH07/06/001).   **119.** *The Times*, 6 March 1914. The merchants' accumulated stocks in Shanghai and Hong Kong were largely hoarded until 1915, when special sales terms were agreed with the Chinese government. The last of them – the stocks, not the merchants – were ceremoniously burned in Shanghai in January 1919. Unfortunately, the continuing political turmoil in China precluded effective policing of indigenous producers, whose output was soon rising again. The ban on Indian exports to China held firm, though continuing legal exports to Singapore, Hong Kong and elsewhere in the region ensured a steady pipeline for the smugglers. (See EIU Report, *The Opium Trade Between India and China*, LMA: CH03/01/15/024.)   **120.** Central Government Manifesto, 26 December 1912. W. S. Livingstone, who had begun his Eastern career in Burma in 1890 and was now the Manager of the Shanghai branch, forwarded a copy to Head Office on 4 January 1913, describing it as a 'vague and wandering publication . . . likely to do more harm than good' (LMA: CH03/01/10/47/13).   **121.** David Sassoon & Co. to the Under-Secretary of State at the Foreign Office, 4 December 1912, LMA: CH03/01/10/47/13.   **122.** These were Société Générale of Paris and Banque d'Outremer of Belgium. It was an arrangement highly unusual in the world of exchange banking, see Jones, *British Multinational Banking*, pp. 76–7. The Eastern's flotation prospectus, unlike the Chartered's, said the bank would pursue 'the business of banking in all its branches and departments' – and this was explicitly defined to include issuing, underwriting and dealing in stocks and bonds. **123.** Chartered Bank to the Foreign Office, 26 April 1912, LMA: CH03/01/10/47/06. This packet contains a selection of what must originally have been a far more voluminous correspondence on the issue, lasting through the whole of 1912.   **124.** The offer comprised an invitation merely to participate in the underwriting of the Reorganization Bond. This implied no ranking for the Chartered Bank among the managers of the bond, whose names would appear on the prospectus and who would reap all the public kudos for the issue – always a matter of intense importance to investment bankers, since new mandates relied heavily on track records. The Chartered, complained its Directors, 'would be severely and unwarrantably slighted if excluded from appearing on the prospectus . . . an injustice to which they are bound to offer strenuous resistance'. (Chartered Bank to the Foreign Office, 26 April 1912, LMA: CH03/01/10/47/06.) This attitude seems genuinely to have surprised the Foreign Secretary, Sir Edward Grey, who made no effort to hide his exasperation. A formal letter from officials to the Court explained that Sir Edward 'fails to understand why your prestige will suffer if you do not participate in this particular loan, inasmuch as you have hitherto evinced no desire to participate in the previous loans to China' (Foreign Office to the Chartered Bank, 22 June 1912, LMA: CH03/01/10/47/06). Extensive correspondence relating to the row over Chartered's non-participation in the Reorganization Loan, and its pursuit of the Crisp Loan, can be found at LMA: CH03/01/14/018.   **125.** 'The bold and independent manner in which the new China five million sterling loan was issued by Mr Birch Crisp was made the subject of a good deal of rather hysterical comment in some of the newspapers last week, and it was only to be expected that the landing of the underwriters with about 60 per cent of their obligations should be exaggerated into what was called failure, fiasco, and so forth.' (*The Economist*, 5 October, 1912.)   **126.** 'Throughout the raising of the money to pay the loan, they [the Chinese] played fast and loose with me . . . which added to my difficulties. You had to watch your step and put a padlock on your tongue, as every eye was on you.' (Memoir by W. S. Livingstone, LMA: CH03/01/15/011.)   **127.** 'His Majesty's Government still adhere to their intention of giving their exclusive support to the

British group [i.e. the Hongkong Bank] . . . pending the final issue of the Reorganization Loan. Their future policy is now under consideration and, pending a decision being reached, Sir Edward Grey trusts that you will take no steps in the direction of negotiating loans to China.' (Foreign Office to Chartered Bank, 11 June 1913, LMA: CH03/01/10/47/06.)   **128.** Report by R. W. Robertson on Visit to Tsing-tao, August–September 1913, LMA: CH03/01/10/47/29.

4. WINNERS IN A SHAKEN WORLD

1. *The Great Illusion* by Norman Angell was widely read as a pacifist tract, expounding the irrationality of war in an age of global economic interdependence. In fact the book put forward a subtly different thesis, arguing that any resort to war would be hopelessly irrational *for Germany* and that the world would be best served by an unfettered continuation of global hegemony for the British Empire. See Niall Ferguson, *The Pity of War*, Allen Lane, 1998, pp. 21–3.   **2.** Colonel Edward House's observation, made in a report to President Woodrow Wilson, is quoted in Christopher Clark, *The Sleepwalkers, How Europe Went to War in 1914*, Allen Lane, 2012, p. 214.   **3.** *The Bankers' Magazine*, Vol. 98, July–December 1914, p. 321.   **4.** William Lawson, *British War Finance 1914–1915*, 1915, pp. 27–8, quoted in Richard Roberts, *Saving the City, The Great Financial Crisis of 1914*, Oxford University Press, 2013, p. 24.   **5.** *The Economist*, 1 August 1914, p. 219.   **6.** *The Bankers' Magazine*, Vol. 97, January–June 1914, pp. 47–8. The quoted figures come from the balance sheet as of 31 December 1913, but there is no reason to believe they would have changed much over the following half-year. They were published with a commentary in the magazine towards the end of June 1914 and no note was made of any significant change in the intervening months. **7.** Quoted in Nicholas A. Lambert, *Planning Armageddon, British Economic Warfare and the First World War*, Harvard University Press, 2012, p. 160.   **8.** Barbara Tuchman, *The Guns of August*, Macmillan, 1962, p. 105.   **9.** Secretary's Circular, 20 August 1914, LMA: CH03/01/15/008.   **10.** Head Office tried in vain to secure their repatriation, pressing the Foreign Office for help unsuccessfully on at least two occasions (William Hoggan to the Under-Secretary at the Foreign Office, 23 June 1916 and 6 May 1918, LMA: CH03/01/01/020).   **11.** Details of the Hamburg story are taken from 'A History of the Branch' written by Walter Neill in 1934, when he visited the branch as an Inspector (LMA: CH03/01/14/075). See also Inspector's Letter from Hamburg, 22 May 1936, LMA: CH03/03/07/007.   **12.** F. A. H. Goddard to Harold Faulkner, 18 March 1950, LMA: CH03/01/14/051.   **13.** File of 1914 Papers, p. 8, LMA: CH03/01/15/008.   **14.** 'Some Experiences of a Banker in the Far East', LMA: CH03/01/14/025. West opted to write his account in the third person, changing his own name to 'East' and Carl Wolter & Co.'s name to 'Hans Schmidt & Co.' (though he slipped up at one point of the typescript and wrote 'Walther' by mistake). The text is undated, but refers obliquely to the Ashes 'bodyline' Test matches of 1932–3.   **15.** Court Minutes, 4 November 1914, SCB Box 262.   **16.** Court Minutes, 11 November 1914, SCB Box 262.   **17.** Sir Charles

Addis to the Treasury, 18 August 1914, LMA: CH03/01/15/008. **18.** Treasury to the Secretary of Chartered Bank, 1 August 1914, LMA: CH03/01/15/008. **19.** Circular to all Agencies & Branches, 21 August 1914, LMA: CH03/01/15/008. **20.** Lambert, *Planning Armageddon*, p. 223. **21.** Court Minutes, 24 March 1915, SCB Box 262. **22.** T. H. Whitehead to Walter Runciman MP, President of the Board of Trade, 11 November 1914, LMA: CH03/01/01/020. **23.** William Hoggan to Under Secretary of State, Home Office, 12 November 1914, LMA: CH03/01/01/020. Another similar letter followed just a week later – though Hoggan was this time able at least to report that the bank had itself stopped payment of the mailed drafts 'until after peace is restored'. **24.** Quoted in John McDermott, 'Total War and the Merchant State: Aspects of British Economic Warfare Against Germany, 1914–16', *Canadian Journal of History*, Vol. 21, April 1986, p. 64. **25.** McDermott, 'Total War and the Merchant State', p. 65 n.16. **26.** This caused problems for more than a few non-German businesses with German-sounding names, especially some large Swiss clients of Chartered Bank with operations in south-east Asia. See Christof Dejung and Andreas Zangger, 'British Wartime Protectionism and Swiss Trading Companies in Asia during the First World War', *Past & Present*, No. 207, pp. 181–213. **27.** Thomas Fraser to Sir Thomas Holderness, Under-Secretary at the India Office, 16 May 1917, LMA: CH03/01/01/020. **28.** Foreign Office to CBIAC, Bombay, 17 April 1917, LMA: CH03/01/01/020. **29.** Ferguson, *The Pity of War*, p. 331. **30.** See Appendix 5 of Geoffrey Jones, *British Multinational Banking 1830–1990*, Oxford University Press, 1993. **31.** Report of Annual General Meeting, 1 April 1916, from *Money Market Review*, filed in LMA: CH03/01/18/004. **32.** Report of Annual General Meeting, 3 April 1915, from *Money Market Review*, filed in LMA: CH03/01/18/004. **33.** Report of Annual General Meeting, 12 April 1919, from *Money Market Review*, filed in LMA: CH03/01/18/004. **34.** CBIAC Secretary to Walter Hume Long at the Colonial Office, 1 May 1918, LMA: CH03/01/01/020. **35.** Report of Annual General Meeting, 5 April 1917, from *Money Market Review*, filed in LMA: CH03/01/18/004 **36.** Court Minutes, 20 October 1915, SCB Box 262. **37.** News of the Singapore Mutiny prompted the mobilization of volunteer militias in Kuala Lumpur, for example. One of the bank's younger men there recalled in his retirement that 'half the Officers were by turns out on military duty, and still the Office work went on'. (A. C. Times to Harold Faulkner, 7 January 1950, LMA: CH03/01/14/028.) **38.** 'The Mutiny of the 5th Light Infantry at Singapore, February 1915 – an Eye-witness Account by G.N. Allen, 24 June 1915', LMA: CH03/01/14/042. **39.** Obituary, *The Bankers' Magazine*, Vol. 105, January–June 1918, p. 204. **40.** Jones, *British Multinational Banking*, Appendix 5. **41.** He would finally step down in May 1920. 'To his intimate friends the announcement did not come as a surprise . . .' *The Bankers' Magazine*, Vol. 109, January–June 1920, pp. 796–8. **42.** Adam Tooze, *The Deluge, The Great War and the Remaking of Global Order*, Allen Lane, 2014, p. 178 and p. 198. **43.** Quoted in David Reynolds, *The Long Shadow, The Great War and the Twentieth Century*, Simon & Schuster, 2013, p. 85. **44.** Philip Woodruff, *The Men Who Ruled India*, vol. 2 *The Guardians*, Jonathan Cape, 1954, pp. 228–9.

45. J. W. Thomson to George Gordon, 13 April 1919, LMA: CH03/01/14/033. This same file includes the letter from the Head Clerk, Radha Kishen Sadjeh, to the Karachi Agent, 11 April 1919.   **46.** LMA: CH03/01/10/50/15/B.   **47.** Liaquat Ahamed, *Lords of Finance: 1929, the Great Depression, and the Bankers who Broke the World*, William Heinemann, 2009, p. 165.   **48.** Chairman's speech to the AGM, 17 April 1920 (LMA: CH01/03/05/001).   **49.** H. W. Phillips, *Modern Foreign Exchange and Foreign Banking*, 1926, pp. 54–5, quoted in David Kynaston, *The City of London, Vol. 3: Illusions of Gold 1914–1945*, Chatto & Windus 1999, p. 99.   **50.** Tooze, *The Deluge*, p. 28.   **51.** The tax payments and transfers into reserves account for the difference between the Total Branch and Head Office profits shown in Appendix D and the Published Net Profits quoted in Jones, *British Multinational Banking*, Appendix 5. Thus, in 1920 operating profits of £1,427,795 were reduced by taxes of £636,024 and a transfer of £115,000 to produce a Published Net Profit of £676,771.   **52.** Reynolds, *The Long Shadow*, p. 92.   **53.** 'Regarding Bagdad [*sic*], as far as I can remember we were closed down by the Turkish authorities about the 2nd of November [1914]. Our cash and keys were taken from us later about the beginning of December . . .' (Inspector L. F. Tucker to Young, 29 July 1923, LMA: MS39066).   **54.** Quoted in Rodney Wilson, 'Financial Development of the Arab Gulf: The Eastern Bank Experience, 1917–50', *Business History*, Vol. 29, No. 2, 1987, pp. 178–98. My account of the Eastern's early moves in Bahrain draws heavily on this article, itself based largely on material from the India Office archives.   **55.** Inspector's letter to Head Office from Amara, Mesopotamia, 1 April 1920, LMA: MS39107.   **56.** Head Office to L. F. Tucker, Acting Inspector, 21 February 1921: 'There would seem to be little use our commenting upon each individual paragraph of your report [on misdemeanours in the Basra City office] as in all cases we agree . . . The whole report is distinctly unpleasant reading and reflects little credit upon the Manager or his Assistants' (LMA: MS39109).   **57.** Inspector's letter to Head Office from Baghdad, 12 April 1920, LMA: MS39107.   **58.** Wilson, 'Financial Development of the Arab Gulf', p. 191.   **59.** Head Office to Eastern Bank Manager, Bahrain, 14 June 1923, LMA: MS39064.   **60.** J. A. Henry, *The First Hundred Years of the Standard Bank*, Oxford University Press, 1963, p. 167.   **61.** See Jones, *British Multinational Banking*, Appendix 5. In this summary of the annual figures for a sample of twenty-five British 'multinational' banks – including the four forerunners of the Standard Chartered Bank – the methodology used for the calculation of 'real profits' is only very sketchily explained. But the author and his research team, notably Frances Bostock, spent some years assembling the relevant data and presenting it consistently across the banks. As they themselves warn in an accompanying note, 'the figures need to be treated with caution', but the Appendix nonetheless represents the only readily available source of its kind, compiled by acknowledged authorities in the field of banking history.   **62.** The claim is made in the publicity material of today's National Bank of Malawi, for which the Standard's Blantyre branch can fairly be seen as a foundation stone.   **63.** 'A History of the Bank in East Africa', Memoirs of J. J. Swanson, 1954, LMA: ST11/03/003. The title is overblown and should really have been 'An Account of My Journey to Kampala'.   **64.** Memoirs of J. J. Swanson, LMA: ST11/03/003.   **65.** Swanson also set down reminiscences of his time at Kimberley – quoted at length in Carolyn Terry, *A Pioneer Bank in a Pioneer Land*, Flesch & Partners, 1979, pp. 64–70.   **66.** Memoirs of J. J. Swanson, LMA: ST11/03/003. The new branches he mentions included Bukoba (1919), Moshi (1921) and Kigoma (also 1921).   **67.** Mackenzie to the Chairman of the Week, 15 February 1918, LMA: ST03/01/07/058.   **68.** Chairman of the Week to Mackenzie, 14 June 1918, LMA: ST03/01/03/002.   **69.** Minutes of the Standard Bank Board, 4 December 1918, SCB Archives, Box 1211, Vol. 16.   **70.** Report on the AGM of Standard Bank, 28 April 1920, *The Bankers' Magazine*, Vol. 109, January–June 1920, pp. 853–7.   **71.** 'Net Profits & Estimated Value of Branches', LMA: ST04/03/01/009. Other newly opened branches recorded in 1919 included Kisumu and Nakuru in Kenya, and Okahandja and Omaruru in South West Africa.   **72.** Mackenzie to the Chairman of the Week, 5 December 1919, LMA: ST03/01/07/061.   **73.** Memoirs of J. J. Swanson, LMA: ST11/03/003.   **74.** Report by John Jeffrey on his visit to the bank's branches in Kenia Colony & Protectorate [i.e. Zanzibar], Tanganyika Territory and Nyasaland, 28 October 1920, LMA: ST03/01/07/065.   **75.** The ensuing correspondence and memoranda can be found at LMA: ST03/01/58/002.   **76.** General Managers to the Secretary, 4 July 1911, LMA: ST03/01/58/002. The cablegram concluded: 'disadvantages and risks of our amalgamating with ABC greatly outweigh possible advantages'.   **77.** Richard Steyn and Francis Antonie, *Hoisting the Standard, 150 Years of Standard Bank*, publ. by The Standard Bank Group, 2012, p. 77.   **78.** Quoted in Stuart Jones, *The Great Imperial Banks in South Africa*, University of South Africa, 1996, p. 38.   **79.** 'The Board approved the Draft of a Letter to be sent by the London Manager . . . in connection with the proposal to acquire the African Banking Corporation and the Bank of British West Africa', Minutes of the Standard Bank Board, 3 March 1920, SCB Archives, Box 1211, Vol. 16.   **80.** The other two investors were the London County Westminster and Parr's Bank (later to become the National Westminster Bank) and National Provincial and Union Bank of England (which would become the National Provincial and subsequently part of National Westminster). The three of them purchased one-third each of 100,000 shares, at a paid-up value of £4, lifting the BBWA's paid-up capital to £1.2 million. Three new seats were created on the BBWA Board, the Standard's going to the Director Robert Dickinson – though it was the Standard's new London Manager, Francis Shipton, who as William Smart's successor had patiently co-ordinated much of the process. (Papers on the transaction, including a copy of the Circular to BBWA shareholders, 6 August 1920, LMA: ST03/01/58/005.)   **81.** Writing in 1929, the historian A. S. J. Baster acknowledged the clearers' disdain: 'It is not so very long since any adventure in overseas business on the part of the English banks proper was regarded with suspicion, – when the so-called "Exchange" banks of the East were not looked upon as banks at all.' (*The Imperial Banks*, P. S. King & Son, 1929, p. 220.)   **82.** Paper given at SOAS, 4 March 1919, LMA: CH10/01/003.   **83.** Minutes of the Standard Bank Board, 29 July 1920, SCB Archives, Box 1211, Vol. 17.   **84.** *The Bankers' Magazine*, Vol. 114, July–December 1922, pp. 251–3.   **85.** Gibson to the Secretary, 9 September 1921, quoted in Jones, *The Great Imperial Banks* *in South Africa*, p. 43. His footnote incorrectly attributes the letter to Hector Mackenzie. **86.** The Standard's Directors had first noticed this a few weeks before the Armistice, when they sent a cable to Cape Town warning that Barclays had reportedly struck up an agreement with the National Bank 'for the purpose of securing control of Exchanges, and other business with South Africa' (Minutes of the Standard Bank Board, 23 October 1918, SCB Archives, Box 1211, Vol. 16). **87.** For a detailed account of the courtship see Julian Crossley and John Blandford, *The DCO Story, A History of Banking in Many Countries 1925–71*, publ by Barclays Bank International Limited, 1975, pp. 1–19. **88.** Gibson claimed he had been told by the Deputy Chairman of Barclays DCO, Sir Herbert Hambling, that the Union Government had actually opposed the takeover. (Gibson to the Secretary, 26 March 1926, cited in Jones, *The Great Imperial Banks in South Africa*, p. 49.) **89.** A detailed account of these discussions is set down in Chapter 14 of Henry's centenary history – though Henry's own suggestion that the chapter 'can be skipped without loss by readers not greatly interested in purely financial questions' ought not to be taken lightly (Henry, *The First Hundred Years*, p. 178). **90.** Gibson to the Secretary, 1 August 1924, quoted in Jones, *The Great Imperial Banks in South Africa*, p. 45. **91.** Minutes of the Standard Bank Board, 7 September 1927, SCB Archives, Box 335, Vol. 21. See also Jones, *The Great Imperial Banks in South Africa*, p. 49: 'banking harmony [within the Union] was encouraged by the speed with which Sir Herbert Hambling [Deputy Chairman of Barclays DCO] welcomed the formation of a banking cartel and accepted the force of the argument that it was necessary for the banks to cooperate with "rigid adherence to arranged rates" if fair profits were to be earned, though this should not be too obvious'. **92.** *The Bankers' Magazine*, Vol. 113, January–June 1922, pp. 701–3. **93.** 'The Story of the Chartered Bank in Calcutta', August 1951, p. 15, LMA: CH03/01/14/50/30. Few spoke out against this approach to business, though one memorandum in 1900 voiced a striking private view: 'Speaking personally, I am dead against all [inter-bank] arrangements, excepting the few unimportant ones which can be observed with ease and without friction. It has come to my certain knowledge that the National Bank of India has in many cases evaded the terms of the few existing arrangements . . . I think the less said by me on this subject the better. I think we fare much better where we have an absolutely free hand.' (Report by J. B. Lee to Head Office, 25 May 1900, LMA: CH03/01/09/097.) **94.** Letter from Mr Keenan to the Directors, reproduced in Head Office Circular No. 703a, 25 May 1922 (Head Office Circulars, Hong Kong branch collection, 1928, LMA: CH07/01/001). **95.** See Jones, *British Multinational Banking*, pp. 158–9. **96.** The architect was G. L. ('Tug') Wilson of Palmer & Turner, and the contractor was Trollope & Colls of London, who had put up 38 Bishopsgate and who shipped over from Britain almost all of the material needed for the project, even including – after some initial misgivings about the Chinese workmen's reaction – the scaffolding. Now known as Bund 18, the imposing neo-Classical building was opened by Shanghai's British Consul in May 1923. The Hongkong Bank's branch was opened one month later. For a beautifully illustrated and detailed account of the two banks and all the other buildings along the Bund, see Peter Hibbard, *The*

Bund Shanghai: China Faces West, Odyssey Books & Guides, 2007. **97.** Turner et al. to C. J. Scott, 11 March 1920, LMA: CH03/01/09/301. Slippages to the initial construction schedule and a misunderstanding over the proposed rental payment led, after a rather tense correspondence in the summer of 1921, to the P&O's withdrawal. **98.** Ryde to Buckley, 25 September 1926, LMA: CH03/01/10/16/06. **99.** Buckley to Head Office, 30 September 1926, LMA: CH03/01/10/16/06. **100.** Memorandum by J. S. Duncan, March 1931, LMA: CH03/01/10/40/08. **101.** 'Mr Gwyther's jottings re Gold Standard for India & establishment of a State Bank', LMA: CH03/01/09/055. **102.** *The Times*, 18 January 1928. Details of the bid were published on 18 October 1927. **103.** Speech to the Annual General Meeting, 31 March 1928, LMA: CH01/03/05/001. **104.** Head Office Circular No. 378a, 22 January 1925, LMA: CH07/01/001. As so often in papers from the 1920s, the Circular also had an anti-Semitic flavour disconcerting to the modern reader: 'their Jew element will not hesitate to belittle our existence in the eyes of Government or elsewhere, if they can get an opportunity . . .' **105.** Saigon Manager to Head Office, 20 February 1924, LMA: CH03/01/10/53/10/A. **106.** See Jones, *British Multinational Banking*, p. 172. **107.** Half-yearly reports, as paraphrased by JL-B, are at LMA: CH03/01/14/027. **108.** Half-Year Report from Kobe, 8 July 1910, LMA: CH03/01/14/027. **109.** Yokohama Half-Yearly Report, 14 January 1918, LMA: CH03/01/14/026. **110.** Sir John Jordan to Lord Curzon, 5 September 1919, quoted in W. Roger Louis, *British Strategy in the Far East 1919–39*, Oxford University Press, 1971, p. 23. **111.** *The Times*, 15 September 1925: 'None favoured more heartily the substitution of the new Quadruple Pact for the Anglo-Japanese Agreement, though he had always set great store by the friendship of Japan . . .' **112.** Chairman's speech to the AGM, 5 April 1924, LMA: CH01/03/05/001. **113.** Memorandum by JR, memoirs of Amritsar, 1923–35, LMA: CH03/01/14/033. **114.** Speech to the Annual General Meeting, 31 March 1928, LMA: CH01/03/05/001. **115.** Lewis Wallace (who served from 1903 to 1929) was succeeded by a fellow Director of Wallace Brothers, Sir Henry Macnaghten (1928–49). The Directors of Ogilvy, Gillanders & Co. who joined the Court were Henry Gladstone (1897–1909) and Henry Bateson (1925–9); a third, Arthur d'Anyers Willis (1929–53), would chair the bank from 1933 to 1940. Three ex-Presidents of the Bank of Bengal joined the Court: Sir Duncan Carmichael (1918–23), J. M. G. Prophit (1919–24) – who died of malaria in Calcutta – and (again) Henry Bateson. The Boustead & Co. directors on the Court were Jasper Young (1898–1907) and his son Jasper Bertram Young (1926–48). Other later 'family appointments' to the Court included that of the 2nd Earl of Inchcape (1933–9).

5. HOLDING FAST

1. *The Bankers' Magazine*, Vol. 128, July–December 1929, pp. 432–6. **2.** *The Bankers' Magazine*, Vol. 129, January–June 1930, pp. 815–17. **3.** 'The Great Slump of 1930', *Nation and Athenaeum*, 20 and 27 December 1930, quoted in Liaquat Ahamed, *Lords of Finance: 1929, the Great Depression, and the bankers* *who broke the world*, William Heinemann, 2009, p. 374. **4.** AGM of 25 June 1931, 37th Annual Report of the BBWA (LMA: MS28515, which includes the reports for 1910–37). Unusually, the BBWA produced annual reports that included a verbatim record of each year's June AGM as well as the summary financial statements for the year to March, along with a useful map and a few photographs from the field. From 1935, the report's generally khaki-coloured cover sported as a corporate logo on its front a little engraving of an elephant standing in a palm grove. **5.** The bank's 'Posterity Files' hold hundreds of packages devoted to individual customers, each typically a rolled bundle of legal documents and official correspondence, sprinkled here and there with personal letters that usually mark a serious turn for the worse in any continuing negotiations. For one collection of packages from the early Depression era, see LMA: CH03/03/05/009, 033, 035, 054 and 057. **6.** For an authoritative account of the Depression's impact on the Burmese rice trade, see Ian Brown, *Burma's Economy in the Twentieth Century*, Cambridge University Press, 2013, pp. 53–60. **7.** See Appendix D. The £963,439 compares with a 'real' loss of £715,872 recorded for 1931 in Appendix 5 of Geoffrey Jones, *British Multinational Banking 1830–1990*, Oxford University Press, 1993. It has proved impossible to reconcile the two figures, not least because the original sources used by Jones cannot now be traced. The references provided in his Appendix (viz, 'Standard Chartered Bank Archives, files SC228, 259–61; P25, P/34, P76; R/21; R/29) relate to a cataloguing system that was abandoned when the SCB archives were broken up and relocated in 1989 (see Appendix A). **8.** See Appendix 5 of Jones, *British Multinational Banking* and also above, Ch.4 n. 72. **9.** J. A. Henry, *The First Hundred Years of the Standard Bank*, Oxford University Press, 1963, p. 252. **10.** Head Office to General Managers, Cape Town, 2 June 1932, LMA: ST03/03/12/001. **11.** General Managers to Head Office, Cape Town, 6 October 1932, LMA: ST03/03/12/001. **12.** General Managers to Head Office, Cape Town, 2 February 1933, LMA: ST03/03/12/001. **13.** Head Office to General Managers, Cape Town, 23 February 1933, LMA: ST03/03/12/001. **14.** Richard Steyn and Francis Antonie, *Hoisting the Standard, 150 Years of Standard Bank*, publ. by The Standard Bank Group, 2012, p. 80. **15.** Lord Selborne returned from one such trip early in 1930 with a radical idea that was duly conveyed to the managers at the Cape: 'The country over which the activities of the Bank now extend is so vast that, even with modern travelling facilities, the old idea of corporate centralisation of the business becomes more and more difficult, and the Board incline to the view that it may become necessary in, possibly, the not very distant future to appoint a Superintendent for North and South Rhodesia as was done in the case of East Africa, where the system is working satisfactorily.' Head Office to General Managers, Cape Town, 1 May 1930, LMA: ST03/03/12/001. **16.** See Julian Crossley and John Blandford, *The DCO Story, A History of Banking in Many Countries 1925–71*, Barclays Bank International Limited, 1975, p. 73: 'By the beginning of 1935 . . . the general manager in London not only had a working knowledge of the South African business himself, but invariably had some senior men from South Africa working with him in his London team, both in Head Office and at Circus Place and elsewhere.' One of the Standard's London Directors, Lord

Balfour, notably observed after the war: 'it must always be remembered that Barclays' local autonomy [in South Africa] is more apparent than real. It is an undoubted fact that our General Manager in South Africa has far greater discretion and does, in fact, come to important decisions more quickly . . .' (Memorandum to Committee of the Board, July 1947, LMA: ST03/01/51/005.)   **17.** J. Caulcutt to E. L. Jackson, 15 February 1929, enclosed in a letter from Head Office to General Managers, Cape Town, 21 February 1929, LMA: ST03/03/12/001.   **18.** The Directors were often at pains to soften this implication, as here: 'While it is not suggested that the system of the big Banks here [in London] in examining applications for credit facilities would in all respects be suitable for the business of this bank in South Africa, it seems to the Board that the general lines adopted by those banks are worthy of consideration . . .' (Head Office to General Managers, Cape Town, 9 November 1935, LMA: ST03/03/12/002).   **19.** The grading and pay of staff received special attention, as for example: 'We are in accord with Barclays (DCO) that it is necessary that the General Managers in South Africa of the two banks should confer in order that a joint scheme may be formulated and that agreement may be reached as to the procedure to be adopted with the object of bringing it into effect.' And again, eight months later: 'As you are aware, the Board view with some anxiety the prospects of falling revenues in South Africa, as against the high administrative expenses, and they will be glad if you will again consider, in conjunction with the General Managers of Barclays (DC&O), this important question of the Grading Award.' (Head Office to General Managers, Cape Town, 18 November 1932 and 25 July 1933, LMA: ST03/03/12/001.)   **20.** Stuart Jones, 'The Apogee of the Imperial Banks in South Africa: Standard and Barclays, 1919–39', *English Historical Review*, Vol. 103, 1988, pp. 892–916.   **21.** Jones, *British Multinational Banking*, p. 137.   **22.** The proportion of the Standard Bank's deposits sourced from the Transvaal rose from 33 per cent in 1932 to 51 per cent in 1937. See Jones, 'The Apogee of the Imperial Banks in South Africa', p. 903.   **23.** AGM of 27 June 1935, 41st Annual Report of the BBWA, LMA: MS28515.   **24.** AGM of 29 June 1939, 45th Annual Report of the BBWA, SCB, Box 2573.   **25.** AGM of 23 June 1936, 42nd Annual Report of the BBWA, LMA: MS28515.   **26.** See Richard Fry, *Bankers in West Africa, The Story of the Bank of British West Africa Limited*, Hutchinson Benham, 1976, pp. 103–6.   **27.** Ibid., p. 137.   **28.** Ibid., p. 145. '[Wilson] offered the UAC reduced rates in return for an understanding that the company would not compete with the banks in future . . . [There] is no detailed record of what happened, but an agreement was eventually reached on some such terms. He had been asked by Barclays not to mention that the two banks had discussed this scheme beforehand, so that no suspicion of a joint threat could arise; in the event the agreement covered both banks.'   **29.** Memorandum by Sir Roy Wilson, 8 February 1939, Selected Minutes of the BBWA Board, LMA: MS28521.   **30.** Memorandum by Sir Roy Wilson, 8 October 1935, Selected Minutes of the BBWA Board, LMA: MS28521.   **31.** EB, Bahrain branch correspondence, LMA: MS39073.   **32.** EB, Inspector's reports on branches, Baghdad and Bahrain, LMA: MS39106/017 & 026.   **33.** The numbers quoted in this paragraph are taken from Home Staff Salary Lists 1930–36 (LMA: CH04/09/04/003) and Eastern Staff Books for 1930 (LMA:

CH08/01/002 & 003). **34.** *The Times*, 11 November 1929. **35.** Frank H. H. King, *The History of the Hongkong Bank*, Vol. 3 *Between the Wars and the Bank Interned 1919–45: Return from Grandeur*, Cambridge University Press, 1988, pp. 257–9 & 461. 'Home Staff' comprised sixty-eight men in 1938. **36.** The Board of the BBWA began employing African managers on a highly selective basis as early as 1916 (see Jones, *British Multinational Banking*, pp. 218–19). But all such appointments were exceptional events, as their citation in the Minutes of the Board would suggest. **37.** William MacQuitty, *A Life To Remember*, Quartet Books, 1991, pp. 28–9. **38.** S. L. N. Simha, *History of the Reserve Bank of India (1935–51)*, Reserve Bank of India, 1979, p. 67. While the number of exchange banks remained stable at 17 or 18, the number of Indian joint-stock banks went on climbing sharply: there were 105 of them by 1934, with several hundred branches across the country. **39.** R. W. Buckley to Head Office, 7 February 1930. The financing of foreign trade was one of three primary topics on the Inquiry's agenda. The others were the Indian bullion market and relations between the country's co-operative banks and the Imperial Bank. **40.** Head Office to R. W. Buckley, 6 November 1930, LMA: CH03/01/10/52/J. **41.** Colin Campbell to Sir Montagu Turner, 13 April 1931, LMA: CH03/01/10/04G. **42.** Colin Campbell to M. M. Gubbay, 14 April 1931, LMA: CH03/01/10/04G. **43.** Quotations in this paragraph are taken from a lengthy summary of the Inquiry's Final Report published in *The Times of India*, 16 September 1931. **44.** 'Business in Calcutta' by Isaac Sykes, 29 September 1932, LMA: CH03/01/10/40/08. Sykes observed that other foreign banks, including the P&O Bank, actually did more business with Indian firms than with European firms. **45.** Alex R. Smith to H. Denning, Assistant Secretary in the Finance Department of the Indian Government, 9 June 1932, LMA: CH03/01/10/52/J. **46.** Calcutta to Head Office Half-Yearly Report, 21 July 1932, JL-B notes, LMA: CH03/01/14/030. **47.** Calcutta to Head Office Half-Yearly Report, 27 July 1933, JL-B notes, LMA: CH03/01/14/030. **48.** Calcutta to Head Office Half-Yearly Report, 27 July 1933, JL-B notes, LMA: CH03/01/14/030. **49.** Calcutta to Head Office, Letter No. 292/a, 2 August 1934, LMA: CH03/01/02/033. **50.** Head Office Circular No. 451/a, 17 October 1935, LMA: CH03/01/02/033. **51.** In rejecting Meldrum's proposal, one colleague threw an interesting light on the conduct of foreign-exchange business: 'Each item of exchange business offered demands a determination of the relative values of the exchange and interest factors. The rate of exchange at which a Manager is willing to do a particular bit of business is determined by the <u>net</u> gain after taking interest and exchange into consideration. What then is gained by holding a post mortem?' (Memorandum by J. B. White, LMA: CH03/01/10/15/A.) **52.** Memorandum by John Meldrum, 21 November 1935, LMA: CH03/01/10/15/A. **53.** *The Times*, 31 January 1935. **54.** Letter to the Chairman and Court of Directors from members of the Committee of Probationary Foreign Staff in London, 8 January 1936, LMA: CH03/01/10/01/28. **55.** M. B. Oliver to Head Office, 30 July 1936, LMA: CH03/01/10/34/03/A. **56.** Quoted in Jan Morris, *Pax Britannica, The Climax of an Empire*, Faber & Faber, 1968, p. 140. **57.** Amiya Kumar Bagchi, *Private Investment in India 1900–1939*, Cambridge University Press, 1972, p. 166.

58. The largest firms in the Indian Jute Manufacturers Association in 1954 were Jardine Henderson, Thomas Duff & Co., Mcleod & Co., Andrew Yule & Co., Bird/Heiligers & Co., Macneill & Barry, and Mackinnon Mackenzie & Co. (Report of the Jute Enquiry Commission, 1954, Government of India: GC560, pp. 184–5, held in the Reserve Bank of India library.)   **59.** Calcutta to Head Office Half-Yearly Report, 13 January 1939, JL-B notes, LMA: CH03/01/14/030. On the resilience of the foreign banks, see Jones, *British Multinational Banking*, p. 200. 'In British India, the Exchange banks . . . saw their share of deposits of the modern banking sector decline gently from 34 per cent to 29 per cent between 1919 and 1937 . . . [and] there appears to have been no precipitate decline in their exchange business because of this competition [from the Imperial Bank].'   **60.** Amritsar to Head Office Half-Yearly Report, 11 January 1933, LMA: CH03/01/14/033. The past tense in this passage suggests it is a JL-B paraphrase of the original.   **61.** It can be found in LMA: CH03/01/14/022.   **62.** It seems appropriate, for the record, to note here that the Directors eight years later were urging the sale or lease of the building, if possible, so that the business in Tientsin could be completely closed down. (Head Office to Tientsin Manager, 15 March 1934, LMA: CH03/01/10/43/05.)   **63.** Walter Neill, one of the two Hamburg officers interned in Germany throughout the Great War, was serving as a Sub-Accountant in Hankow in 1927 when the British Concession in the city and all its municipal assets were handed over to the Nationalist Government. He saw it as 'an agreement whereby a great Power has made an undignified surrender to an upstart Government who obtained recognition by resorting to violence and mob law, a Government that cannot be trusted and one that is admittedly anti-British and dominated by Russian influence . . . our Concession had been handed over with no guarantees beyond that of a Government who incited the mob to filch it'. (Letter to Head Office, 21 March 1927, LMA: CH03/01/10/04/B.)   **64.** Man-han Siu, 'British Banks in China after 1914: the Shanghai Branch of the Chartered Bank', Paper presented to the 16th World Economic History Congress in Stellenbosch, South Africa, 9–13 July 2012.   **65.** Robert Bickers, *Empire Made Me, An Englishman Adrift in Shanghai*, Allen Lane, 2003, p. 188.   **66.** The newcomers were Colin Campbell, later Lord Colgrain (served 1923–52); Archibald Jamieson (1925–36); Edward Fairbairn Mackay (1925–43); Archibald Rose (1926–52); Jasper Young (1926–48); Sir Henry Macnaghten (1928–49); and Arthur d'Anyers Willis (1929–53). Leaving aside Henry Bateson, who retired from the Court in 1929 after four years' service, those appointed since 1925 stayed on average for just over twenty-one years – so continuity was to remain as strong a feature of the Court as ever.   **67.** An obituarist wrote of him: 'A lovable and saint-like man. His dandiacal appearance and his taste for drollery were unsure guides to his true character, in which the dominant strain was a sort of earnest but unobtrusive chivalry.' (*The Times*, 9 March 1961.)   **68.** Seventeen letters, between October 1929 and February 1933, are at LMA: CH03/01/10/04/B. Others can be found at LMA: CH03/01/10/58/08/B (January 1929, November/December 1932 and May 1934) and at LMA: CH03/01/10/58/13 (August 1935). The archive must originally have contained many more, now lost.   **69.** Archie Rose to Arthur d'Anyers Willis, 16 January 1934,

LMA: CH03/01/10/40/07.   **70.** Archie Rose to Sir Montagu Turner, 7 January 1929, LMA: CH03/01/10/58/08/B.   **71.** A review of 'Students from Chartered Bank', on SOAS stationery, is included in correspondence between E. F. Mackay of the bank and John Swire & Sons (LMA: CH03/01/10/58/24). Other papers about tuition arrangements in Hong Kong and Peking in 1928-9 can be found at LMA: CH03/01/10/43/05.   **72.** Archie Rose to Sir Montagu Turner, 15 February 1930, LMA: CH03/01/10/04B   **73.** Archie Rose to Sir Montagu Turner, (?) April 1931, LMA: CH03/01/10/04B   **74.** Archie Rose to Sir Montagu Turner, 5 May 1930, LMA: CH03/01/10/34/02/A. He had to follow up with a second letter to Turner, 29 May 1930, before drawing a response.   **75.** Their letters responding to the proposal – and the comments of the Court Directors – can be found in 'Correspondence from China Branches re Chinese-British Bank', LMA: CH03/01/10/34/02/A.   **76.** Archie Rose to Sir Montagu Turner, 15 November 1932, LMA: CH03/01/10/58/13   **77.** F. D. West to Head Office, 7 July 1930, LMA: CH03/01/10/34/02/A.   **78.** Archie Rose, Diary, 19-20 September 1931, LMA: CH03/01/10/04/B.   **79.** He had been hugely impressed by what he saw and heard on a trip to Japan in November 1929 to attend a conference of the Institute of Pacific Relations. 'I do not think that the strength of Modern Japan is fully appreciated in the West. Her leaders are men of vision, tenacity and courage' – which he readily acknowledged was not good news for the Chartered, since the Japanese had so little interest in turning to foreigners for assistance. (Letter to Sir Montagu Turner, 18 November 1929, LMA: CH03/01/10/04/B.)   **80.** Archie Rose to Sir Montagu Turner from the SS *Maloja*, 23 December 1932, LMA: CH03/01/10/58/13.   **81.** Memorandum of Proceedings of the Managers' Committee, 18 January 1933, LMA: CH03/01/10/58/B.   **82.** Archie Rose to Arthur d'Anyers Willis, 16 January 1934, LMA: CH03/01/10/40/07.   **83.** William Cockburn to Head Office, 2 August 1935, LMA: CH03/01/10/02/01.   **84.** Archie Rose to Arthur Willis, 30 August 1935, LMA: CH03/01/10/02/01.   **85.** 'The close relationship between the bank and the Chinese business community was one of the main reasons for the expansion [after 1928] in the scale and scope of the Shanghai Branch.' Man-han Siu, 'Foreign Banks and the Chinese Indigenous Economy: the Business of the Shanghai Branch of the Chartered Bank of India, Australia and China 1913-37', in Hubert Bonin, Nuno Valério and Kazuhiko Yago (eds.), *Asian Imperial Banking History*, Pickering & Chatto, 2014, Ch. 5.   **86.** See Niv Horesh, *Shanghai's Bund and Beyond – British Banks, Banknote Issuance and Monetary Policy in China 1842-1937*, Yale University Press, 2009, p. 59. Based on the author's analysis of local Chartered Bank balance sheets, an excellent graph ('CBIAC Note Circulation: Regional Disaggregation, 1883-1939') shows the annual totals of new notes issued by the Chartered Bank in Mainland China, south-east Asia (i.e. Singapore and Penang, with a tiny showing for Siam) and Hong Kong.   **87.** The total value of the Chartered's notes in circulation in Singapore and the Straits dropped from $4 million in 1898 to $150,000 in 1913 (Compton Mackenzie, *Realms of Silver, One Hundred Years of Banking in the East*, Routledge & Kegan Paul, 1954, p. 190). True to its title, the centenary history devotes many pages to the critical ups and downs of silver and the currencies of the East.   **88.** The weight of remittances flowing into Hong Kong from the mainland, and the exposure of the Hong Kong dollar to the unnerving volatility of silver's bullion price, prompted various official inquiries into the Colony's policy on banknotes – including, in 1931, a Hong Kong Currency Commission. (One of its three Commissioners was W. H. Clegg, the Reserve Bank of South Africa's first Governor.) For the Chartered Bank, J. S. Bruce in London and A. H. Ferguson in Hong Kong gave extensive oral evidence. Papers relating to the Commission fill three files, to be found at LMA: CH03/01/10/34/04/B. **89.** Details can be found at LMA: CH03/01/14/017 and LMA: CH03/01/10/15, comprising papers on the China Stabilization Fund of 1939–44. **90.** Memorandum by R. D. Murray, 25 May 1935, LMA: CH03/01/10/07/05. **91.** Memo by Mr White on R. D. Murray's Views re Shanghai, May 1935, LMA: CH03/01/10/07/05. **92.** H. E. Faulkner to Head Office, 15 April 1935, LMA: CH03/01/10/07/05. Faulkner's assessment of the Japanese threat was especially prescient: 'It is quite clear that Japanese imperial policy has undergone no fundamental change since 1915 . . . [Hence] a collapse of the European system created by the Treaty of Versailles would instantly provoke a spirited attempt on the part of Japan to usurp the position of leadership in the East that she claims as her right.' **93.** R. D. Murray to J. F. Duncan, 8 June 1935, LMA: CH03/01/10/07/05. **94.** R. D. Murray to A. H. Ferguson, 3 September 1936, LMA: CH03/01/10/07/05. **95.** Parks M. Coble, Jr, *The Shanghai Capitalists and the Nationalist Government, 1927–37*, Harvard University Press, 1980, p. 12. **96.** 'Discussion of:- R. D. Murray's letter of September 3rd, 1936, addressed to A. H. Ferguson', initialled by W. B. White but undated, LMA: CH03/01/10/07/05. **97.** A. H. Ferguson to R. D. Murray, 20 October 1936, LMA: CH03/01/10/07/05. If Leith-Ross was as forceful on this point as Ferguson reported, he must have decided to set aside the warning he had been given by Chiang Kai-shek in person just before he left China. 'Speaking slowly, and with much emphasis, [Chiang Kai-shek] said, "Tell your government that I regard war with Japan as inevitable, as absolutely inevitable . . .".' (Frederick Leith-Ross, *Money Talks, Fifty Years of International Finance*, Hutchinson, 1968, p. 223.) **98.** Head Office to R. D. Murray, 24 October 1936, LMA: CH03/01/10/07/05. **99.** Faulkner gave a hint of his feelings after the war, in correspondence with one of the bank's pensioners: 'My official relations with the [Chinese] Ministry of Finance and the Waichiaopu [the Ministry of Intelligence and Publicity] from 1934 to 1938 were complicated by my loathing of the political corruption that was then already apparent, and by my opposition to the so-called "currency reforms" of 1934. I worked hard for the Chinese and against the Japanese because it was a British interest for me to do so, but I had many private misgivings and there were times when I felt that the Japanese had a good deal of justification for some of the things they alleged.' Faulkner to J. A. Macgill, 3 January 1950, LMA: CH03/01/14/083. **100.** R. D. Murray to Head Office, 23 April 1937 (Shanghai Academy of Social Sciences, Chinese Business History Resource Centre, M151), quoted in Man-han Siu, 'Foreign Banks and the Chinese Indigenous Economy'. **101.** R. D. Murray to Head Office, 30 June 1937, LMA: CH03/01/10/02/03. A more immediate reason for shelving the proposal was that the Nationalist Government was not prepared to let the bank take up a site inside the walled city. The officially approved site outside it, said Murray, 'is extremely squalid and unsuitable for our purposes in every way'. Any move into the old city that summer would have preceded its destruction at the hands of Japanese troops, the 'Rape of Nanking', by just six months. **102.** R. D. Murray to Head Office, 12 August 1937, LMA: CH03/01/14/020. **103.** The two most senior Germans on the staff of the Standard Bank were left in control of its Agency after the outbreak of the war. They were still there in 1945, though by then the BBWA building in which the Agency was based had been gutted by fire and they were housed 'in a most primitive brick structure built among the ruins'. They resumed working for the Standard after the war was over, prompting the Secretary in 1947 to voice concern over 'the privations with which they are faced in common with other German nationals'. (Secretary to General Manager, Cape Town, 26 September 1947, LMA: ST03/03/12/005.) **104.** Walter Neill to Head Office, 6 July 1934, LMA: CH03/03/07/007. Neill took the occasion of his visit to write a history of the Hamburg Branch, now at LMA: CH03/01/14/075. **105.** William Haydn Evans to Walter Neill, 24 January 1935, LMA: CH03/04/01/012. **106.** Head Office to William Haydn Evans, 15 September 1939, LMA: CH03/04/01/012. **107.** Head Office to R. A. Camidge, 28 February 1940, LMA: CH03/01/10/19/54. **108.** A. J. Bird to R. A. Camidge, 5 February 1940, LMA: CH03/01/10/19/54. **109.** Head Office to R. A. Camidge, 14 February 1940, LMA: CH03/01/10/19/54. **110.** The Standard's total staff on 31 March 1940 comprised 3,643 men and 526 women, and 1,350 of the bank's men enlisted. The branches were learning by then to rely more heavily on women, a change '[which] has of necessity been speeded up to provide for essential wartime replacements' (1940 Annual Report, p. 184, GMO 3/2/1/13). **111.** Nick Grantham (son), interview with author, 3 June 2014. **112.** He had been a member of Bombay's Legislative Council, a trustee of the city's port authority and a Justice of the Peace (Obituary, *The Times*, 3 August 1968). **113.** Fry, *Bankers in West Africa*, p. 151. **114.** 'History of Head Office during the War 1939–45' (unsigned and undated), LMA: CH03/01/14/008 (Miscellaneous Head Office papers). The author was clearly someone with direct experience of the Blitz, perhaps as a firewatcher: 'to be perched precariously many feet above Bishopsgate under a hail of shrapnel and with bombs falling and with burning buildings all around, was an experience that had to be undertaken to be believed.'

6. MIRACLE AND MIRAGE

1. T. L. Christie to Head Office, 1 September 1942 (from Lorenço Marques, now Maputo), LMA: CH03/01/07/002. **2.** G. A. Leiper, *A Yen For My Thoughts, A Memoir of Occupied Hong Kong*, South China Morning Post Publications, 1982, pp. 24 and 28. **3.** Volumes 1–4 have been catalogued as LMA: CH03/01/07/001 (vol. 1), LMA: CH03/01/07/002 (vol. 2), LMA: CH03/01/07/003 (vol. 3) and LMA: CH03/01/07/005 (vol. 4). The contents of the War Testimonies (W. T.) relate to the Chartered's fortunes in every country overrun by the Japanese. Volume numbers are quoted below in place of full catalogue references. Two notable personal recollections catalogued separately are those of W. A. Cruikshank, dated December 1945 (LMA: CH03/02/04/012) and G. A. Leiper, dated February 1946 (LMA: CH03/02/04/013). **4.** H. F. Morford to W. D. Brown in Madras, 4 August 1943, W. T. vol. 2. **5.** Leiper, *A Yen For My Thoughts*, pp. 17–18. **6.** H. C. Hopkins to W. R. Cockburn, 4 August 1942, W. T. vol. 2. **7.** Memorandum by F. C. Lundie, Edinburgh, January, 1946, W. T. vol. 1. **8.** Memorandum by F. C. Lundie, Edinburgh, January, 1946, W. T. vol. 1. **9.** R. J. S. Davies to Head Office, 29 May 1942, W. T. vol. 2. **10.** Yokohama Specie Bank to R. J. S. Davies, 14 February 1942, included among Davies's papers held in W.T. vol. 2. **11.** E. W. Bilton to Head Office, 2 September 1942, W. T. vol. 2; R. S. J. Davies to Head Office, 29 May 1942, W. T. vol. 2; T. L. Christie to Head Office, 1 September 1942, W. T. vol. 2 (citing the payments made in Saigon of 'a monthly allowance by the Japanese Navy of $500 per family, besides the $500 per mensem paid to them by the Swiss Consul'); and Memorandum by F. C. Lundie, Edinburgh, January, 1946, W. T. vol. 1. **12.** M. G. Gordon et al. to Head Office, Letter 40, 7 January 1946, W. T. vol. 4. **13.** Memorandum by F. C. Lundie, Edinburgh, January, 1946, W. T. vol. 1. **14.** 'Memorandum from G. P. Cooke concerning Manila Agency', June 1942, W. T. vol. 2. **15.** W. D. Brown to the Chief Accountant, 27 April 1943, W. T. vol. 2, and Report by A. D. Mackintosh, 26 November 1945, W. T. vol. 1. **16.** The Accountant thought it best not to apprise HSBC of their plans, and would later note: 'a conversation, subsequent to the destruction of the notes, with the late Sir Vandeleur Grayburn, confirmed my opinion that, had our intention to destroy the notes been disclosed, permission to use the furnace would have been withheld' (Report by W. A. Cruikshank to Head Office, 22 December 1945, LMA: CH03/01/06/107). **17.** Leiper, *A Yen For My Thoughts*, p. 138. Despite their diligent burning of unissued notes in Hong Kong, there still remained supplies worth about $3 million, and four months after conquering the Colony the Japanese set Leiper and his colleagues to signing them. **18.** Leiper, *A Yen For My Thoughts*, p. 112. **19.** Report by G. A. Leiper to Head Office, 23 February 1946, LMA: CH03/01/06/107. **20.** G. A. Leiper, 'Some Recollections of Duress Banking', Part 6', *Curry & Rice*, Vol. 18, No. 4, Spring 1968, p. 11. **21.** Leiper, *A Yen For My Thoughts*, p. 161. **22.** M. E. Columbine to Head Office, 27 April 1942, W. T. vol. 2. **23.** J. G. Sellar to Head Office, 20 April 1942, W. T. vol. 2. **24.** 'The Columbine memorandum', undated but probably May 1942, W. T. vol. 2; see also Memorandum by J. C. Kyle, undated, W. T. vol. 1; D. Peacock to Head Office, 3 November 1945, W. T. vol. 1. **25.** 'On the day following the Fall . . . I learned that current account balances and other essential records had been despatched by every available steamer and that every endeavour had been made to despatch telegraphic transfers and wired instructions before the cable services were suspended.' (J. L. Kennedy to Head Office, 2 November 1945, W. T. vol. 4.) **26.** J. A. Hamilton to Head Office, 22 July 1942, W. T. vol. 2. **27.** M. E. Columbine to Head Office, 27 April 1942, W. T. vol. 2. **28.** Ten men got away on 13 February: W. D. Brown, M. E. Columbine, J. A. Hamilton, D. W. Henderson, D. Lowdon, D. M. Millar, B. M. Purser, W. M. Ritchie, J. G. Sellars and G. A. Johnson (though the latter succeeded in reaching Sumatra on his own, only to end up interned there until the end of the war – as he recounted in a lively letter to Head Office dated 6 November 1945, W. T. vol. 4). The young wife of D. Lowdon, married just two days earlier, was killed by one of the bombs that landed on the Clifford Pier as she was waiting to board her evacuation ship.   **29.** Stafford Northcote to the Secretary, 12 November 1945, W. T. vol. 1. Northcote submitted a Private & Confidential Report, twenty pages long, with a covering letter to say it set down 'my version of a sorry story of Singapore office in February '42'. He thought all should have stuck together until the actual surrender.   **30.** Report by L. W. Dixon to Head Office, Letter 52, 2 November 1945, W. T. vol. 4.   **31.** Undated memorandum by J. C. Kyle, W. T. vol. 1.   **32.** J. Scott to Head Office, 20 November 1945, W. T. vol. 1. **33.** Report by J. H. Delacour, Letter 28, 5 November 1945, W. T. vol. 4.   **34.** T. H. Gwyther (no relation) to Head Office, Letter 36, 26 November 1945, W. T. vol. 4.   **35.** J. M. Stewart to Head Office, 1 April 1942, W. T. vol. 1.   **36.** 'Memorandum relating to the evacuation of Burma', C. J. H. Browning to Head Office, 1 October 1943, W. T. vol. 2.   **37.** 'With a total floor space of over 32,280 square feet, the [1941] building boasted a spacious banking hall lit by high windows and a skylight as well as a basement with state-of-the-art vaults and the city's first underground parking lot.' (Sarah Rooney, *30 Heritage Buildings of Yangon: Inside the City that Captured Time*, pub. by Association of Myanmar Architects and Serindia Publications, 2013, p. 97.) The building still stands today, and houses the state-owned Myanmar Economic Bank 2.   **38.** C. M. Clamp to Head Office, 10 June 1943, W. T. vol. 2.   **39.** C. J. H. Browning to Head Office, 1 October 1943, W. T. vol. 2.   **40.** Detailed accounts of their perilous journey can be found in 'Memorandum relating to the evacuation of Burma', C. J. H. Browning to Head Office, 1 October 1943, W. T. vol. 2; 'Burma Episode', report by C. M. Jenkin, undated, W. T. vol. 2; 'Evacuation from Burma – Memorandum', undated, by A. McKechnie, W. T. vol. 3.   **41.** The repatriated Foreign Staff came from the offices in Peking, Hankow, Tsingtao, Canton, Saigon, Haiphong, Bangkok and Manila in addition to Kobe and Yokohama.   **42.** 'The Things I Choose To Remember' by Frances Dodds, *Curry & Rice*, Vol. 19, No. 2, Summer 1969, pp. 27–32. **43.** 'Report on Experience in Japan Since the Outbreak of Hostilities', undated, J. C. Marks, W. T. vol. 3.   **44.** 'I spent the first six or seven weeks in Durban and since then have travelled quite extensively . . . as well as spending three weeks on a farm in the Karroo. At most of these places I met some of the senior officers of the Standard Bank of South Africa and found them at all times most helpful and obliging.' J. A. Hamilton to Head Office, 22 July 1942, W. T. vol. 2.   **45.** R. S. J. Davies to Head Office, 25 November 1942, W. T. vol. 2. Sadly, a year later Bilton was among nine Foreign Staff listed as having died since the outbreak of the war (J. F. Duncan to C. D. Cox, 11 October 1943, LMA: CH08/01/003). The others were D. M. Millar, Isaac Sykes, W. Park, J. M. Houghton, C. C. W. Willson (of Shanghai), D. A. Bruce (of Colombo) and Graham Taylor (of Singapore).   **46.** A list of the internees and their locations, drawn up by Head Office in November 1942, can be found at LMA: CH04/09/06/001.   **47.** A. J. B. Dickson to Head Office, Letter 49, 26 September 1945, W. T. vol. 4.   **48.** The ten survivors were I. M. Scott, W. G. Smith, R. Hanking, D. A. Blunt, M. R. Currie, D. M. Soward, B. C.

Henderson, A. B.(?) Druce and W. E. Mackay (Ian Scott to Head Office, 19 November 1945, W. T. vol. 1; W. E. Mackay to Head Office, 17 December 1945, W. T. vol. 1). The casualty was Graham Taylor, who died of diphtheria in February 1943 (D. A. Blunt to Head Office, Letter 41, 6 November 1945, W. T. vol. 4). **49.** D. A. Blunt to Head Office, Letter 41, 6 November 1945, W. T. vol. 4. **50.** 'Treatment of the Internees in this Camp' by Joseph Miller, November 1944, included with two other memoranda from Fukushima in letter to A. G. Read, W. T. vol. 4. **51.** Sutherland to Head Office, Letter 29, 1 November 1945, W. T. vol. 4. **52.** Copies can be found at LMA: CH03/01/07/001/A and LMA: CH03/01/07/004. **53.** The original handwritten November 1945 report, 'From Internment March 1942 to Release, September 1945', is Item 26 in W. T. vol. 4. A typescript copy of the report is at LMA: CH03/01/14/042. **54.** Leiper, 'Some Recollections of Duress Banking, Part 6', *Curry & Rice*, Vol. 18, No. 4, Spring 1968, p. 15. **55.** Phuah Kim Chuan to Head Office, Letter 11, 23 September 1945, W. T. vol. 4. Someone, probably the former Kuala Lumpur Manager A. D. Mackintosh, later scribbled on the bottom of the letter 'This young man is worth his weight in gold.' **56.** See, for example, letters relating to four of the largest offices. For Shanghai: 'I have discussed with Mr Suzuki – our liquidator – the question of the Bank's records and securities and have received his assurance that everything is intact' (Letter No. 3). For Singapore and Malaya: 'The Singapore staff . . . found the bank's books stored in the Hongkong Bank strong room. I went down a few days later and found all the Kuala Lumpur current account ledgers (1941 and 1942) intact' (Letter No. 28). For Hong Kong: 'Safeguarding the Bank's records and property at Queen's Road and other sundry places called for a fair amount of coolie work on the part of Anderson and myself . . . Later we were joined in the office by Messrs Camidge and Leiper . . . The securities, bonds, share scrip, small parcels and packets were checked and placed in order by me before leaving Hong Kong on 7th October' (Letter No. 33). For Batavia: 'On the 6th October we took our ledgers and other books from the Japanese liquidators before a final balance had been taken out . . . Our safe custody, bill books and a considerable quantity of old files were taken to the Hongkong Bank Treasury when the first move was made and there they remain' (Letter No. 34). Other letters relate to records being found intact in Peking (No. 2), Taiping (No. 21), Tientsin (No. 30), Kuching (No. 5), Medan (No. 36), Penang (No. 53), Sumatra (No. 54) and even Rangoon (No. 9). (W. T. vol. 4.) **57.** It greatly annoyed H. F. N. Paull to find, on returning to Saigon, that he had to deal with a 'less than helpful' Financial Adviser to the British Military Administration in the liberated city: 'he did not appear to realise the important British interests represented by the Chartered Bank, and . . . appeared to put us in the same category as the Yorkshire Penny Bank'. H. F. N. Paull to Head Office, 3 January 1946, W. T. vol. 1. **58.** Rooney, *30 Heritage Buildings of Yangon*, p. 97. How many of the doors – including those to the bank's record rooms – had remained locked since 1942 is not recorded. The replacement handles, locks and keys 'had to be ordered from the original supplier, Messrs James Gibbons, one of the UK's most reputable locksmiths'. **59.** Manila Agent to Head Office, 26 September 1945, LMA: CH03/01/06/106. The Agent enclosed the report with his letter – 'and as he [Hollyer] prepared and initialled it in duplicate we send you herewith the original for your records'. **60.** R. M. McGregor to A. J. McIntosh, 4 March 1945, LMA: CH03/01/06/106. **61.** A. P. Mustard to P. R. Wait, 10 July 1945, LMA: CH03/01/06/106. **62.** Leiper, 'Some Recollections of Duress Banking, Part 6', *Curry & Rice*, Vol. 18, No. 4, Spring 1968, p. 11. **63.** Chairman's Statement to Shareholders, 29 May 1946, SCB Annual Reports. **64.** Its aggregate operating income for 1930–39 was £482,293, just over 10 per cent of the total (compared with the 15 per cent earned in Shanghai). See Appendix D. **65.** P. R. Wait, 'Reconstruction of Manila Accounts', 31 August 1945, LMA: CH03/01/07/010. **66.** Reports by Sycip, Gorres, Velayo & Co., 22 February and 8 May 1956 (LMA: CH03/01/07/010). **67.** Memorandum, 'Philippines War Damages Claim', 14 February 1955, LMA: CH03/01/07/007. **68.** 'The Philippine National Bank today won a refund of $1,387,000 from the US War Claims Office representing the amount it allowed American depositors to draw in 1946 against pre-war deposits . . . although the Japanese took their money during the war. The case was almost given up by the PNB after years of seemingly fruitless fight.' *Manila Times*, 29 April 1956. **69.** 'While provision was made [in 1945] in respect of interest [payable] for the Occupation Period on all these accounts, it has not been applied [on dormant accounts] as in the case of accounts still operative.' (A. J. Bird to Head Office, 13 December 1949, LMA: CH03/01/07/008.) **70.** Memo dated 31 December 1952, from 'Losses, Jap. Occupn.', LMA: CH03/01/07/008. **71.** Malayan War Damages Claim, LMA: CH03/01/07/006. **72.** See Appendix 5 of Geoffrey Jones, *British Multinational Banking 1830–1990*, Oxford University Press, 1993. **73.** A. C. Hopkins to Head Office, 23 August 1945, W. T. vol. 4. **74.** W. R. Cockburn to R. W. Roberts, 31 July 1945, LMA: CH03/02/05/001. **75.** HSBC Archives, UK0252/0251-0257. The Midland Bank men were E. Hellmuth, C. Gates and A. Allan. They together compiled a series of reports dated between August and October 1948 (though Gates appears not to have accompanied the other two to Bangkok and Hong Kong). Their itinerary embraced Hong Kong (File 0251), Shanghai (File 0252), India, Pakistan and Ceylon (File 0253), Singapore (File 0254), Bangkok (File 0256) and the Dutch East Indies (File 0257). I am indebted to HSBC's Global History Manager, Sara Kinsey, for drawing these records to my attention. **76.** LMA: CH03/01/10/06/07/C, G and I. **77.** See Jones, *British Multinational Banking*, Appendix 5 – but see again also Ch. 4, n. 61. While the 'published profits' set out in Jones's compendium match those recorded in Appendix D, there is no way of deriving his 'real profits' from the operating profits in Appendix D, even after adjusting the latter for tax deductions and transfers into/out of reserves. **78.** See Chairman's Statement of April 1950, presenting the 1949 accounts. Total assets at the end of 1949 were £151.5 million, up £13.1 million on the year earlier figure. Had sterling not been devalued, they would have been up £8.7 million. **79.** See Richard Fry, *Bankers in West Africa, The Story of the Bank of British West Africa Limited*, Hutchinson Benham, 1976, p. 169. 'The new [marketing] boards decided not to pay the buying merchants any longer against fortnightly declarations of tonnage bought and held in warehouses awaiting shipment, but to pay only after loading on board against shipping documents. This meant that the traders needed more finance, and the bank had to provide it.' **80.** Ibid., p. 178. **81.** J. A. Henry, *The First Hundred Years of the Standard Bank*, Oxford University Press, 1963, pp. 314–15. **82.** Ibid., pp. 292–3. **83.** Branch numbers for the Standard are given as 309 in 1945 and 376 in 1953, in a table set out in Stuart Jones, *The Great Imperial Banks in South Africa, A Study of the Business of Standard Bank and Barclays Bank, 1891–1961*, University of South Africa, 1996, p. 222. Oddly, Jones himself quotes 390 and 600 as the two respective totals elsewhere in his text (p. 219), which are the numbers quoted by Henry, *The First Hundred Years*, p. 321. But Henry gives no source for them, and it is hard to see how the bank could possibly have accumulated 600 by 1953, even including agencies and embracing Central and East Africa in the total. **84.** W. Roger Louis, *The British Empire in the Middle East 1945–51 – Arab Nationalism, the United States, and Postwar Imperialism*, Oxford University Press, 1984, p. 188. **85.** One of the Eastern Bank's Directors was also Deputy Chairman of Barclays DCO, and corresponded regularly with Barclays colleagues about the Eastern's activities in the Gulf. 'I can tell you in confidence that we [i.e. the Eastern] have had a look at Dhahran [in the Saudi Eastern Province] from time to time and shall probably be sending a Representative over there to have a further look around in the near future' (A. C. Barnes to Charles Gringell, 3 January 1949, LMA: MS39015/001). Five years later, according to the Chairman's Annual Statement of 1954, the bank was still waiting to receive a formal licence to open in the kingdom, though permission had been granted by the Saudi Government in 1952. **86.** John Basford to Charles Gingell, 3 January 1949, LMA: MS39015/001. Gingell was the Barclays representative in New York, and Basford its man on the West Coast. **87.** John Darwin, *Unfinished Empire, The Global Expansion of Britain*, Allen Lane, 2012, p. 352. **88.** The export statistics are quoted in Jones, *British Multinational Banking*, in an excellent summary of the adverse structural changes in the post-war world of the overseas banks, pp. 246–55. **89.** The seven comprised the Chartered Bank itself, Hongkong & Shanghai Bank, Eastern Bank, Grindlays Bank, Mercantile Bank of India, Lloyds Bank and Thomas Cook & Sons (Bankers). Nine others in the exchange banking category included National Bank of India, Bank of China, Bank of Communications, National City Bank of New York and American Express. **90.** Head Office to C. O. Tasker, 8 March 1947, LMA: CH03/01/10/16/24/C. **91.** Niall Ferguson, *Empire, How Britain Made The Modern World*, Allen Lane, 2003, p. 356. **92.** Appendix A to Karachi reply to Centenary Questionnaire, 1950, LMA: CH03/01/14/031. **93.** Margin note by R. W. Buckley on letter from Calcutta Agent to Head Office, 12 December 1947, LMA: CH03/01/10/50/33. **94.** Report of the Midland Bank visitors, September/ October 1948, HSBC Archives, UK0252/0253. Presumably the Report's authors put 'assets' in quotation marks because they had no idea what the Reserve Bank meant by the term. **95.** L. W. Dixon to Head Office, 16 March 1950, LMA: CH03/01/10/52/T. **96.** 'Report of the Jute Enquiry Commission', 1954, Government of India: GC560. A full list of the managing agencies and their loom strengths is given in Annexure I, pp. 184–5. **97.** N. Ramachandran, 'Foreign Plantation Investment in Ceylon, 1889–1958', Central Bank of Ceylon Research Series, 1963, Appendix 1. **98.** *The First Hundred Years, 1865–1965, The Story of The*

Allahabad Bank Ltd, pub. by Allahabad Bank, 1965 (filed in the Reserve Bank of India in Bombay). In seventy-two pages, the history makes just a single reference to the Chartered Bank (p. 41), noting how it 'secured an interest in India's oldest joint-stock bank' in 1927. **99.** To be found in LMA: CH03/01/14/029. See Appendix A. **100.** Quoted in Michael W. Charney, *A History of Modern Burma*, Cambridge University Press, 2009, p. 58. **101.** Charney, *A History of Modern Burma*, p. 81. **102.** Certificate to R. S. Wilson, 19 February 1950, LMA: CH03/01/15/010. In all probability it was forwarded to London that same year along with the Rangoon branch's response to the Centenary Questionnaire. The latter was written by D. A. Blunt – one of the ten Chartered men to have survived working on the Burma–Siam Railway as a Japanese PoW, and Wilson's successor in Rangoon. **103.** Jonathan Fenby, *The Penguin History of Modern China, The Fall and Rise of a Great Power 1850–2009*, Penguin Books, 2009, p. 330. **104.** Unsigned report from Tientsin Branch, 30 September 1946, LMA: CH03/01/10/32/09/G. The Russians used Japanese prisoners to help with a comprehensive dismantling of the region's industrial infrastructure, which was packed into railway wagons and despatched west of the Urals. 'They dismantled and took away some 6,000 electric light pylons . . . [which had] supplied nearly all Manchuria with electricity . . .' **105.** Rose to Grantham, 8 April 1947, LMA: CH03/01/10/05/B. **106.** Rose to Grantham, 'China Tour March & April 1947', 19 April 1947, LMA: CH03/01/10/05/B. **107.** The account of his experience that follows is based on an interview with the author, 26 January 2012. **108.** Hew Liller, interview with author, 26 January 2012. **109.** A. J. Bird to Head Office, Half-Yearly Letter No. 2, 8 July 1950, LMA: CH03/01/01/017. **110.** It is documented in twelve weighty files, at LMA: CH03/02/02/014, 015, 018 and 025–034. **111.** Memorandum attached to letter from Head Office to Shanghai Manager, 26 January 1953, LMA: CH03/02/02/025. **112.** Macfarlane to Head Office, 12 February 1953, LMA: CH03/02/02/025. **113.** 'The Present Situation Relative to the Bank's Interests in China', Report by V. B. West, 16 February 1953, forwarded by A. J. Bird to Head Office, 20 February 1950, SP&C Letters to Head Office, 1937–53, private papers of W. C. L. Brown. Details cited earlier about developments over the 1950–53 period are taken from this report. **114.** Their passage through Hong Kong en route for home was recorded in the *Curry & Rice* edition of March 1955, p. 8. **115.** 'Mr Grantham mentioned in course of conversation that Mr Pullen was back from China and they have slightly revised their ideas. Although they have no intention of doing deposit business in China they think it will prove wise to maintain some office there and do some international trade with Bank of China.' Bank of England Governor's Note, 20 December 1954, BofE C48/158. **116.** F. J. Hill to Head Office, 23 April 1955, LMA: CH03/02/02/033. **117.** Chairman's Statement to accompany the 1951 Annual Report, issued March 1952. **118.** Sports teams, of course, were of huge importance to the Chartered's culture, as a profile of The Wilderness had made clear at the time of its acquisition by the bank: 'A very high percentage of the London Staff is new and the first thing to do is to get to know one another, for never in the history of the Bank have we been, individually, so remote and such strangers. "The Wilderness" will give us an opportunity of meeting away from the office under conditions which will foster a sense of comradeship.' (*Curry & Rice*, Vol. 6, No. 2, January 1949.) **119.** Lecture by W. R. Cockburn (venue unspecified), 30 October 1950, LMA: CH03/01/14/074. **120.** 'The Centenary of the Bank', introduction to *Curry & Rice*, Vol. 10, No. 3, December 1953. **121.** Jones, *British Multinational Banking*, p. 273.

7. WINDS OF CHANGE

1. John Basford to A. T. Dudley, General Manager of Barclays DCO, 8 February 1949, Correspondence of Anthony Barnes, LMA: MS39015/002. **2.** 'The [Eastern staff's] accommodation is most primitive. There are fans, but the Electricity Supply is at present restricted . . . Air-conditioning is out of the question – there are too many apertures, and the sanitation is "dry". Water as Messrs Norman and Scott have already reported is very short. A piped supply from 15 miles westwards is contemplated.' ('Notes on Mukalla Visit, 18–22 November 1955', Memo by Sir Evan Jenkins, Eastern Bank Chairman, 29 November 1955, LMA: MS 39015/003.) Few bank chairmen, surely, would have exerted themselves to make such a visit, let alone submit a report on the plumbing. **3.** 'The Eastern Bank Ltd', Board memorandum, 12 November 1952, Correspondence of Anthony Barnes, LMA: MS39015/002. It was thought a cash offer might cost over £900,000, compared with the £380,250 that had been spent on amassing the 25 per cent stake since 1939. This was less of a deterrent than the politics: 'We should have to consider very carefully what would be the effects of running the business of the Eastern bank in our own name.' **4.** For a review of his career and character, see Geoffrey Jones, *Banking & Oil, The History of the British Bank of the Middle East* vol. 2, Cambridge University Press, 1987, pp. 37–9. **5.** Cyril Warr, interview with Christopher Cook, 16 September 1983, HSBC Archives, HQ 1670/0009/C. Warr recalled how one of the Directors, a partner of Lazard Brothers, would joke about their General Manager's firm hand. 'In fact [Mark] Norman used to come in and say "Ah, when I get my tax, it's always labelled O. H. M. S. and I never know whether it's On Her Majesty's Service or On H. Musker's Service".' **6.** Cyril Warr, interview with Christopher Cook, 16 September 1983, HSBC Archives, HQ 1670/0009/C. The Directors visited by Musker were all in their seventies. E. M. Eldrid and F. Hale had been long-serving managers in the Imperial Bank of Persia, Sir Kinahan Cornwallis was a former diplomat and had been the wartime British Ambassador in Iraq. (See Geoffrey Jones, *Banking & Empire in Iran, The History of the British Bank of the Middle East* vol. 1, Cambridge University Press, 1986, Appendix 9: Biographies, pp. 362–70.) S. J. Pears was the senior partner of Cooper Brothers, the eminent City accountants. **7.** Minute by Kenneth Peppiatt on Governor's Note, 20 December 1954, BofE C48/158. **8.** On holiday in Italy in 1958, he wrote to a fellow Director: 'I am quite sure that we are right in our policy of expanding through mergers. Don't lose sight of the BBME.' (Grantham to Sir John Tait, 12 May 1958, LMA: CH03/02/03/001.) **9.** Cable from Reserve Bank of India, Bombay, to Eastern Bank via RBI, London, 5 March 1956, LMA: MS 39130/001, File B.

The cable stressed 'presence of Rushton your Calcutta manager required in India . . .' **10.** Memorandum by Evan Jenkins, 1 May 1956, LMA: MS 39130/002, File D. **11.** Memorandum by Evan Jenkins, 12 June 1956, LMA: MS 39130/002, File D. **12.** W. A. Rushton to H. Barden, General Manager, 2 June 1955, LMA: MS 39130/001, File A. **13.** A stream of encomiums can be found at LMA: MS 39130/001, File A. **14.** W. A. Rushton to Head Office, 16 April 1955, LMA: MS 39130/001, File A. **15.** 'Notes on Calcutta Visit', by David Gordon, 28 May 1956, LMA: MS 39130/001, File B. **16.** In March 1956, the Mundhra companies had overdrafts of R.171.5 lacs at the Eastern, R.80 lacs at the Chartered, R.65 lacs at the National Bank of India and R.35 lacs at the Allahabad Bank (L. R. Goldsmith to Head Office, Eastern Bank, 13 March 1956, LMA: MS 39130/001, File B). **17.** Governor's Note, 29 April 1957, BofE C48/158. The Governor, Lord Cobbold, was grudging in his support for the Chartered's chosen strategy. 'In leaving, Mr Grantham asked what I thought about their taking an interest in the Middle East. I said that if they were a London bank starting out overseas afresh, I should think it was doubtful, but in their circumstances I saw the argument for spreading the risk.' **18.** Minutes of Meeting at Barclays DCO, 6 June 1957, LMA: CH03/02/03/002. **19.** A copy of the formal Offer Document can be found in LMA: MS 39011. In addition to the 20 per cent premium, the Chartered's shares offered Eastern shareholders a 15 per cent annual dividend, worth 27 shillings, compared with the Eastern's 8 per cent dividend, worth 16 shillings. **20.** Note for the Record, 2 July 1957, BofE C48/158. **21.** David Weatherson, interviews with author, 24 August 2012 and 12 March 2013. **22.** Correspondence and notes on the Mundhra Affair fill twenty-one boxes of the Eastern Bank's archives, to be found under LMA: MS 39129 to 39135. **23.** Lombard Column, *Financial Times*, 13 September 1957. **24.** Post-Merger Review of the Eastern Bank (undated), LMA: CH03/02/03/003. **25.** Geoffrey Jones, *British Multinational Banking 1830–1990*, Oxford University Press, 1993, pp. 258–9. Jones refers in his footnotes to an 'Eastern/Chartered Merger File' in the archives of the Standard Chartered Bank. The file was evidently consulted during the research for his book, but it has not survived and was probably lost when the group's Archival Unit was closed down in 1989 (see Appendix A). The official history of Barclays DCO makes no reference to the episode. **26.** *Quarterly Review* of the Guernsey Society, Autumn 1968. I am indebted to Stephen Foote for drawing this obituary to my attention. **27.** Much of it can be found at LMA: MS 39016/001–004. **28.** Edna Carr Green, *Just Keep a Bag Packed, A Memoir*, Author House, 2013, p. 50. **29.** Neville Green, interviews with author, 19 May and 1 June 2011. **30.** A. (Sandy) Findlay to A. E. M. Finlaison, 4 March 1966, LMA: MS39018/001. **31.** LMA: MS 39016/003. **32.** Quoted in 'Notes for a brief history of the early days of the Irano-British Bank' by James Fenwick, 23 May 1963. Fenwick was installed as General Manager in Tehran late in 1958 and remained there until his retirement some years later. I am indebted to David Millar for providing me with a copy of this 10-page memorandum. Millar himself set down a colourful account of the 1959 launch that was published in the April 1960 edition of *Curry & Rice*. 'A month before the Bank opened there was no Bank counter, no furniture, and no staff . . . two hours before the official opening no cheque books had arrived and all the lights fused.' He thought his time in Tehran 'probably my most exciting assignment'. (Note to author, 6 October 2014.)   **33.** The Persian-speaking British staff sent into Tehran by the BBME in 1959 did not rate the Irano-British Bank's record very highly. One, a subsequent General Manager of the BBME, recalled: 'They were at an immense disadvantage because they didn't know anything about Persia . . .' (Gordon Calver, interview with Christopher Cook, 26 November 1983, HSBC Archives, HQ 1670/0005/C.) But this airy dismissal may have owed something to the fact that, by the time the BBME set about reopening, several of its best Persian officers from its pre-1953 days had already been snapped up by Chartered Bank. Two of the Eastern Bank men who served in Iran during the 1960s, Ralph Winton and Alan Wren, rose later to become General Managers in London.   **34.** SCB Box 568, Files, A, B and C.   **35.** V. B. West to David Beath, 7 October 1966, SCB Box 568, File B.   **36.** Hew Liller, interview with author, 26 January 2012.   **37.** *Curry & Rice*, Vol. 10 No. 2, July 1953, pp. 4–6. The following edition of the house magazine carried a note about the happy months experienced by K. R. Venkitaraman and C. A. Krishnan from Bombay. 'The hospitality they received in and around Hatton Court touched them deeply. The neighbourhood evinced its kind feelings in a thousand ways and the local Station Master had a cheery greeting for them at all times.' (December 1953, p. 9.)   **38.** 'Conditions of Service. Asian Officers', No. 79(a), 4 November 1954, LMA: CH03/01/02/035.   **39.** A full list of the Eastern Staff was published at the back of each edition of *Curry & Rice*. I am indebted to David Millar for his kind loan of two bound volumes of the house magazine, running from 1948 to 1972.   **40.** Memorandum on the Hong Kong Branch, 17 September, 1951, JL-B notes, LMA: CH03/01/14/019.   **41.** His story has been recorded in *CC Lee, The Textile Man* by Jasper Becker, edited by Richard Lee, pub. privately by TAL Group in 2011. Lee died in 2008 aged ninety-seven.   **42.** 'There are at present working in the Colony over 750 knitting and weaving mills whose average consumption of cotton yarn has recently been 5,000 to 6,000 bales per month . . . When in full operation, the established 6 [cotton-spinning] mills will have to import every month about 3¼ million pounds of raw cotton in order to spin 7,200 bales . . . Against the total cost of production of some [HK]$7 million per month the mills may obtain from sales [HK]$10 million provided that the current price of [HK]$1,400 per bale can be obtained.' (*Far East Economic Review*, Vol. 4 No. 14, 7 April 1948.) This contemporary analysis plainly implies a substantial reliance by the early Shanghainese mills on domestic rather than export sales and supports the contention of leading scholars of Hong Kong's history that the role of local Cantonese industrialists has too often been overlooked in the past. See, in particular, Leo F. Goodstadt, *Profits, Politics and Panics: Hong Kong's Banks and the Making of a Miracle Economy, 1935–1985*, Hong Kong University Press, 2007, where 'the myth' (p. 102) that Hong Kong had no textile industry until the Shanghainese arrived is persuasively laid to rest. I am indebted to the author for his clarification of this issue – and also to Alex Woo, himself the son of one of the leading Shanghainese entrepreneurs, whose diligent inquiries of the Cantonese Weavers' Association and among veterans of the post-war textile scene unearthed further evidence that domestic demand for yarn was not insignificant.   **43.** A. J. Bird to Head Office, 8 July 1950, LMA: CH03/01/01/017.   **44.** D. J. Gilmore to Head Office, 29 October 1948, LMA: CH03/01/01/015.   **45.** Goodstadt, *Profits, Politics and Panics*, pp. 104–12, provides an excellent summary of the Hong Kong banks' response to the Shanghainese. His analysis points up the role played by the Colony's foreign-owned banks – though he makes no specific reference to the Chartered Bank per se. As for Hongkong Bank's stance, as Goodstadt judiciously puts it, 'lending to local industry was an innovation that did not come naturally to this very British banking institution. The obstacle was not commercial considerations but the powerful influence on its executives of the expatriate culture of the China treaty ports.'   **46.** A. J. Bird to Head Office, 8 April 1949, LMA: CH03/01/01/016.   **47.** G. A. Leiper to Head Office, 6 October 1950, LMA: CH03/01/01/018.   **48.** Leiper to Head Office, 23 December 1950, LMA: CH03/01/01/018.   **49.** 'I clearly recall my father's story that as there was no worthwhile market for [his company's] yarn production, the warehouse was full of it and the company was running out of operating capital.' (Jack Tang to Alex Woo, 7 June 2013.)   **50.** Biographical sketches of many of them were included in *40 Years of the Hong Kong Cotton Spinning Industry*, pub. Hong Kong Cotton Spinners Association, 1988.   **51.** Parks M. Coble, Jr, *The Shanghai Capitalists and the Nationalist Government, 1927–37*, Harvard University Press, 1980, p. 17.   **52.** Jack Tang, interview with author, 8 March 2012.   **53.** *A Glance at the Hong Kong Cotton Spinning Industry*, pub. Hong Kong Cotton Spinners Association, August 1975. It was sent to members as a diary for 1976.   **54.** Circular No. 422a, 17 November 1955, LMA: CH03/01/02/035.   **55.** Correspondence relating to half-yearly accounts between 1950 and 1958 suggests that profits remitted to London rose from about £100,000 in 1949 to perhaps £300,000 or more. (LMA: CH04/05/07/020.)   **56.** Derek Hewett, letter to author, 29 January 2012.   **57.** Agnes Pullen, interview with author, 25 November 2011.   **58.** Jack Tang, interview with author, 8 March 2012.   **59.** Between 1955 and 1961, according to the Hong Kong Cotton Spinners Association, spindle numbers climbed by 101 per cent, the workforce by 47 per cent and annual yarn production by 161 per cent.   **60.** 'I remember him coming to my father's office and consulting him. He wanted to hire a Shanghainese compradore to deal with all these Shanghainese families.' Tang, interview with author, 8 March 2012.   **61.** Sally Wong and K. C. Ma, interview with author, 9 March 2012.   **62.** Eleanor Wong, *T. Y. Wong & A Family of Textile Entrepreneurs*, published privately by Harmony Day Services, 2014.   **63.** Eleanor Wong, interview with author, 19 March 2012.   **64.** For sharing their memories of the Chartered, I am greatly indebted to Jack Tang (son of P. Y. Tang, founder of South Sea Textile Manufacturing Co. Ltd), Eleanor and Sally Wong (daughters of T. Y. Wong, founder of Hong Kong Spinners, Ltd), Richard Lee (son of C. C. Lee, founder of the TAL Group), Alex Woo (son of Vincent Woo, founder of Central Textiles (H. K.) Ltd) and Jerry Liu (founder of South Textiles Ltd). Thanks are also due to Margie Yang (daughter of Y. L. Yang, the founder of Esquel), and to Madeline Wong, whose mother, the sister of Jerry Liu, married Cha Chi Ming, the founder of the Cha Textiles Group.   **65.** The new Western Malaysian branches were at Petaling Jaya (1955), Kuantan (1955), Jalan Ampang (1956), Kangar (1958), Port Kelang (1961) and Port Dickson (1962). Two addresses were also added to the network in Kuala Lumpur in 1963, at Jalan Ipoh and Jalan Pasar. I am indebted to Ong Chong Hye, a long-serving manager of the bank in Malaysia, for his research into its history on my behalf.   **66.** Michael Brown, 'Reminiscences from the East', private memoir, p. 8.   **67.** Li Ka-Shing, interview with author, 22 March 2012. **68.** See Catherine R. Schenk, 'The Origins of Anti-Competitive Regulation: Was Hong Kong "Over-Banked" in the 1960s?' *Hong Kong Institute for Monetary Research Working Paper No. 9*, July 2006, pp. 14–15. 'HSBC and Chartered Bank took the opportunity to lobby the Financial Secretary for anti-competitive regulation, arguing that there were too many banks in Hong Kong and that this excessive competition was undermining the stability of the system as a whole.' Schenk's own detailed analysis concludes that this was a misreading of the crisis: 'the threat to banking in Hong Kong was not the number of banks or their size, but the interlocking ownership of banks and other businesses that were prone to asset market shocks, combined with poor governance'.   **69.** W. C. L. Brown, interview with author, 15 & 20 September 2011. My account of the computerization project is drawn from Brown's own private memoirs of his career (Chapter 11, Hong Kong 1966–1969).   **70.** F. E. King to E. Clifton-Brown, Chairman of Committee, 2 July 1934, LMA: ST03/03/14/001.   **71.** The Directors in London wondered whether it might be prudent – especially given the precarious state of the British war effort – 'to broaden the basis of our administration' in the Union (Lord Balfour to Milton Clough, 6 February 1942, LMA: ST03/02/34/005). After watching the course of the debates in Pretoria nervously for three months, the Directors were relieved to hear this was 'a question which can well be left in abeyance for the present' (Milton Clough to Lord Balfour, 8 May 1942, LMA: ST03/02/34/005). **72.** As of March 1946, there were 4,774 staff in South Africa, 301 in East Africa, 70 in New York, 82 in two London branches and 344 in Clements Lane. Women accounted for 40 per cent of the clerical staff within the Union. (Annual Report & Accounts 1946, LMA: ST01/04/04/003.)   **73.** 'He greatly admired the intellectual range of its prime minister, J. C. Smuts, but found little else to admire in the politics and society of that country.' (K. E. Robinson, *Oxford DNB*.)   **74.** Lord Harlech to Sir Jasper Ridley, 3 November 1945, LMA: ST03/01/51/005.   **75.** John Gilliat to Jasper Ridley, 6 June 1945, LMA: ST03/01/51/005.   **76.** Lowndes' predecessor was Francis Shipton, who had been appointed to London as Secretary of the bank in 1903 (G. T. Amphlett, *History of the Standard Bank of South Africa 1862–1913*, Glasgow University Press, 1914, p. 185). Shipton's role remained essentially unchanged but his title became London Manager after the end of the First World War. Lowndes occupied this position from 1924 to 1936, and was succeeded by Ralph Gibson.   **77.** 'The Case for a Permanent Chairman', Memorandum by John Gilliat, 3 June 1947, LMA: ST03/01/51/005.   **78.** Lord Harlech to the Secretary, 21 October 1946, LMA: ST03/01/51/005.   **79.** 'Hogg's 1947–8 Travel Notes', from Historical Archive Box 1946–8, LMA: SBSA/0656.   **80.** Secretary to General Manager, Cape Town, 19 March 1948, LMA: ST03/03/12/005.   **81.** Loans totalled £4.3 million vs £2.3 million, and £1.2 million in 1942. Profits were £89,030 vs

£28,291, and £17,288 in 1942. Report to the Board by Michael Berry, July 1948, LMA: STo3/o1/51/oo5. **82.** Richard Gray to Ralph Gibson, 22 May 1950, LMA: STo3/o3/o7/oo1. **83.** Trading profits in each of the three years 1948–50 were roughly £5 million, with the Union accounting for 50–54 per cent of the total ('The Bank's Organisation', Memorandum by Head Office Manager, 27 March 1951, LMA: SBSA/o876, File 1). **84.** The Secretary, W. G. Hall, went on an extended tour in 1949 and devoted several paragraphs of his subsequent 36-page report to recruitment problems. He remarked on an almost complete lack of branch officers in their twenties, and found the bank had been hiring about a hundred school-leavers a year where it needed three times as many. 'We are still continuing our [recruitment] efforts in London to help in filling these gaps but . . . the outlook is not promising for the present as the competition of the home banks is increasingly intense.' ('Report by the Secretary on his tour to South and East Africa, 1949', LMA: STo3/o1/53/oo2.) **85.** Secretary to General Manager, Cape Town, 13 May 1949, LMA: STo3/o3/12/oo6. **86.** Secretary to General Manager, Cape Town, 19 March 1948, LMA: STo3/o3/12/oo5. **87.** Richard Gray to Sir Jasper Ridley, 23 March 1950, LMA: STo3/o3/o7/oo1. The correspondence over his future lasted from February 1949 to August 1950. The Directors resented what they regarded as a discourteous tone in Gray's letters, but were anxious to avoid losing the services of a senior man with a formidable local following. Gray early on set down a punchy statement of his own views, which would probably have been endorsed by not a few men serving in remote parts of the Standard's network over the decades: 'One of our troubles on this side is that we never have enough time for all that we have to do. If the position were otherwise I dare say that we could practise the construction of the smooth, elaborate, flowing passages that are a feature of letters from London and sometimes from Cape Town. But our business here has more than doubled . . . [and] the work has become very heavy. I told Mr Gibson that our hurried, vigorous Colonial advices must of course seem brusque when compared to London office letters, but that for my part there had been no change of feeling' (Gray to Lord Balfour, 10 March 1949, LMA: STo3/o3/o7/oo1). This was slightly disingenuous of him. After finally retiring in 1952, Gray broke all conventions by trying to set up in business privately, in competition with the bank. A briefing memo drawn up for a visiting Director noted drily: 'some of Gray's acts are unhappy' ('East Africa – Personal & Private Notes for Sir Frederick Leith-Ross', 1952, LMA: STo3/o1/51/oo5). **88.** He reflected on the incident in conversation a few months later with W. G. Hall, the Secretary, who was on another extended tour of the country. ('Report by the Secretary on his tour to South and East Africa, 1949', LMA: STo3/o1/53/oo2.) **89.** 'Some Notes on a Visit to Africa', July–August 1950, unsigned, LMA: STo3/o1/51/oo5. **90.** A useful chronology of all the Board's machinations can be found in Gibson to Leith-Ross, 8 January 1954, LMA: STo3/o3/o7/oo4. **91.** Sir Dougal Malcolm to Ralph Gibson, 15 May 1952, LMA: STo3/o1/57/oo1. **92.** Leith-Ross to the Chairman for the Week, 2 February 1953, LMA: STo3/o3/o5/oo1. **93.** Gibson to the Chairman for the Week, 19 March 1953, LMA: STo3/o3/o5/oo2. **94.** The number of branches in South Africa grew from 457 in 1952 to 642 in 1957. This pleasingly reversed the pecking order between the Standard and Barclays DCO whose numbers went from 485 to 627 over the same period. (McKellar White to Hall-Patch, 23 May 1957, LMA: ST03/03/07/008.) **95.** Leith-Ross to Gibson, 4 March 1954, LMA: ST03/03/07/004. **96.** 'Formation of a Subsidiary Company in South Africa', Memorandum by Antony Acton, February 1954, LMA: ST03/03/07/004. Acton's shrewd observer was Dr Hendrick van Eck, the Chairman of the Industrial Development Corporation of South Africa – and the bank's first target as Chairman of its South African Board. **97.** Henniker, *Oxford DNB*. **98.** Hall-Patch was approached by a researcher on behalf of the Institute of Race Relations, seeking support for a study into 'the more general affects of industrialization on African societies and individual reactions of Africans in supervising and managerial jobs. I know that you have been extremely interested in this . . .' (Guy Hunter to Hall-Patch, 1 October 1959, LMA: ST03/03/07/010). Recommending later in the year that the Standard Bank's East Africa Superintendent be asked for assistance, he wrote of him: 'Certainly, we have found that his standing in the community is very high and that his views on race relations, while obviously very liberal, have earned the respect of many of the "diehards" who are the people who are likely to cause the most trouble' (Hall-Patch to Guy Hunter, 24 December 1959, LMA: ST03/03/07/010). **99.** R. G. Ridley to Leith-Ross, 26 March 1957, LMA: ST03/03/07/008. **100.** 'History of the Hiving-Off, 1951–61', August entry, LMA: ST03/03/20/001. **101.** Edmunds to Hall-Patch, 28 January 1960, LMA: ST03/03/07/010. **102.** Inward Letters from the South African Board Chairman, 1959–64, LMA: ST03/03/01/003 & 004. **103.** 'The Bank's Operations in Africa – Change of Title', Memorandum by G. H. R. Edmunds, 4 November 1960, LMA: ST03/03/20/004. **104.** One of the bank's problems in the Afrikaner heartlands was the way in which pastors of the Dutch Reformed Church actively promoted the Volkskas Bank. When two officers of the Standard visited branches in the Free State a couple of years later, they reported back on the travails of one English-born manager called (perhaps unfortunately) Mr Bishop. '[He and Mrs Bishop] attend the Dutch Reformed Church regularly, devote all available time in visiting clients, speak no English in the company of others and generally conform to the way of life prescribed by the predikant. In spite of this they are unable to break down the prejudice against their partially English background or prevail upon the predikant to discontinue his practice of enjoining his congregation from the pulpit to support Volkskas.' See Richard Steyn and Francis Antonie, *Hoisting the Standard, 150 Years of Standard Bank*, publ. by The Standard Bank Group, 2012, pp. 85–7. **105.** The papers of the Special Working Party can be found in LMA: ST03/03/20/005, Hall-Patch Private Files 1961–2. It held seven meetings over the course of 1961, between 16 January and 1 December. Of the Directors, only Hall-Patch and John Hogg were starting members, with Leith-Ross attending later in the year. In South Africa, only Edmunds was informed of its existence. Its advisers included Henry Benson of the accounting firm Cooper Brothers, who visited South Africa in February and quickly concluded 'that nothing less than the formation of a Union-domiciled subsidiary would satisfy our local Board'. (Letter from Benson of 29 February, quoted in the minutes of the 10 April Meeting.) A 13-page report from Coopers to Hall-Patch on 29 March 1961 spelled out the legal and accounting options – or lack of them. **106.** Hall-Patch to Edmunds, 5 May 1961, LMA: STo3/03/01/006. **107.** Memorandum by A. Q. Davies, 26 May 1961, in Edmunds to Hall-Patch, LMA: STo3/03/01/003. **108.** That this weighed heavily on their minds was evident in many of their presentations to the Board. Thus, Hall-Patch warned early in August: 'whatever initial steps we took in that event [i.e. hiving-off] to retain control in London, it was inevitable that in due course control of our South African business would move to the Republic. Thereafter, our standing as a British overseas bank in the City of London would be greatly reduced.' ('Note of Discussion by the Board on 9 August 1961', LMA: STo3/03/20/001.) **109.** Hall-Patch to Edmunds, 3 July 1961, LMA: STo3/03/01/006. **110.** 'Report on Discussions in Johannesburg and Pretoria, August 26–30 1961: The Bank's Name' by Hall-Patch, 13 September 1961, Confidential Strategy Memoranda, LMA: STo1/03/09/003. **111.** Hall-Patch to Edmunds, 14 September 1961, LMA: STo3/03/01/006. **112.** Edmunds to Hall-Patch, 18 September 1961, LMA: STo3/03/01/003. **113.** Hogg to Hall-Patch, 14 September 1961, 'Directors' Correspondence', LMA: STo3/03/13/001. **114.** Edmunds to Hall-Patch, 18 September 1961, LMA: STo3/03/01/003. **115.** Hall-Patch to Edmunds, 7 October 1961, LMA: STo3/03/01/006. Given the unambiguous advice received earlier in the year about the full implications of setting up a subsidiary, this letter would seem at best a case of wishful thinking: 'The arrangement whereby formal control of an overseas subsidiary lies with the subsidiary, but control of matters of importance in practice remains with the parent, is quite common amongst UK companies. The essential feature of any such arrangement is a modus operandi which is thoroughly understood both by parent and subsidiary. By working out carefully the appropriate procedures within the Bank, we can perhaps hope to get the best of both worlds.' **116.** Cyril Hawker more than once stressed his readiness to accept SBSA's quasi-autonomy, as here: 'I am writing to you personally and privately because I have no wish to interfere officially, or even semi-officially, in the running of the Standard Bank of South Africa which is the job of yourself as Chairman, the Board, and the General Manager . . .' (Hawker to Edmunds, 14 September 1962, LMA: STo3/03/01/006). **117.** This calculation was made by the Treasury, in an appraisal of the financial consequences of the hiving-off: 'It would be very disadvantageous to the bank to have to <u>freeze</u> part of its capital resources by keeping the additional £10 million in South Africa . . . but he saw no escape from this' (Memo from Sir Frank Lee to the Bank of England, 11 October 1961, BoE C48/157). The Treasury satisfied itself that the reduction in the Standard's UK tax payments would be very modest – perhaps as little as 10 per cent, at the outset anyway – and so had little hesitation in assisting the bank to overcome some initial objections from the Inland Revenue, whose consent was required for the reorganization. **118.** Edmunds to Hall-Patch, 15 January 1962, LMA: STo3/03/01/004. The Deputy Manager in London, Lance Martin, scribbled a slightly obsequious note to Hall-Patch on the front of the letter, in which Edmunds had written of no longer being able to tolerate complacency in the business: 'At last the full truth, which you and other Directors have not infrequently spoken about <u>and</u> written about, is coming home to him. His blood is up, and he is really doing something about it.' **119.** *Financial Times*, 6 November 1961. **120.** Note by Humphrey Mynors, 9 February 1959; Note by James Bailey, 11 February 1959, BofE C48/157. **121.** Private Minutes of Board meeting, 8 July 1959, LMA: STo3/o3/15/oo1. **122.** Private Minutes of Board meeting, 15 July 1959, LMA: STo3/o3/15/oo1. **123.** Charles Villiers, Private Minutes of Board meeting, 29 July 1959, LMA: STo3/o3/15/oo1. Later in the discussion, Leith-Ross expressed some scepticism that the authorities in South Africa would approve any link with the Chartered – but he conceded that it was worth an exploratory chat. **124.** Hall-Patch to Grantham, 17 August 1959, LMA: STo3/o3/07/o1o. Grantham was in California, en route back from Hong Kong where he had attended the formal opening ceremony for the Chartered's new head office in Des Voeux Road. Hall-Patch was suitably complimentary about the building: 'Somebody who was in Hong Kong recently told me that your new building would be even higher and more imposing than the new building of the Bank of China. Good luck to you.' The discussions at the Bank of England were the subject of Notes by the Governor on 21 and 27 July 1959 (BofE C48/157). **125.** Note of Conversation with Mr Grantham on Thursday 10 September 1959, LMA: STo3/o3/15/oo1. **126.** Nick Grantham, interview with author, 3 June 2014. **127.** The Governor, Lord Cobbold, told Grantham: 'if he and Hall-Patch were to come and tell me they were contemplating amalgamation I should welcome it'. (Governor's Note, 24 September 1959, BofE C48/157.) **128.** Note of Conversation with Grantham on Monday 23 November 1959, LMA: STo3/o3/15/oo1. **129.** The British Governor in Nairobi, for example, turned to Hall-Patch for help over compensation. 'You have given us such tremendous help in the vital matter of the future of the East African Civil Service that I am wondering whether I can enlist your further help in one of our other major problems – that of reassuring our settlers and agricultural industries about the future of their land titles and property rights? . . . Something must be done quickly if our economy is not to be very badly damaged indeed.' (Sir Patrick Rennison to Hall-Patch, 21 June 1960, LMA: STo3/o3/07/o11.) Hall-Patch had to write back explaining that any notion of compensation from the UK Treasury was a non-starter. **130.** When Hall-Patch attended the IMF meetings in Washington late in September 1960, the Bank of England's Executive Director responsible for Commonwealth affairs passed on some of the Bank's unhappiness. '[Sir Maurice Parsons] asked to see me and said he was frustrated and almost in despair at the attitude of the Colonial Office to the impending financial crisis in East Africa.' (Hall-Patch to John Hogg, 27 September 1960, LMA: STo3/07/o14.) **131.** Forrest Capie, *The Bank of England, 1950s to 1979*, Cambridge University Press, 2010, p. 49. When appointed Executive Director in 1954, Hawker had actually filled the vacancy left by the departing Harry Siepmann who went on to write the first draft of the Standard Bank's centenary history. **132.** Board Discussion, 24 January 1962, LMA: STo1/o3/o9/oo3. Leith-Ross argued with characteristic caution that the bank was 'presently engaged on what might be regarded as a major surgical operation and he thought this was not the proper time to contemplate another'. **133.** Lord Cromer to Hall-Patch and to Sir George Bolton, 6 June 1962, BofE C48/157. **134.** Leith-Ross ('Leithers' to all his City friends) died aged eighty-one in 1968. His autobiography was published a few months before his death, but gave only a couple of paragraphs to his Board-room career at the Standard. He did not disguise in the book his sadness at the turn of events in South Africa and disdain for some of the Republic's critics. Its apartheid policy, while 'perhaps carried out too inflexibly', was nonetheless 'an honest attempt to solve an almost insoluble problem. While the Africans are not allowed political rights, they are in most respects as free as in the Southern states of America.' (*Money Talks, Fifty Years of International Finance*, Hutchinson, 1968, p. 347.)   **135.** *Financial Times*, 20 February 1962. In fact he only appeared once for Essex in a first-class game, in 1937 against Lancashire (scoring 26 runs in his two innings).   **136.** 'Discussions with Mr Edmunds on 16 July 1964 – Interference from London in the affairs of the subsidiary company', LMA: ST03/03/13/002. A prime example of this heated correspondence was to follow just three months later: 'I have seen the cables about your capital and liquidity troubles and urgent replies are being drafted. I must confess that we are genuinely disturbed by the over-strained position which the cables show and we are particularly con-cerned that there is no indication that corrective action is being taken on your side so as to avoid any possibility of matters getting out of hand . . . As we see it, the real answer can only be to cut back on lending and to put pressure on recalcitrant borrowers to repay. If you do not do this you will certainly be in real trouble . . . I am sorry to write in these terms but think you yourself must see that something should be done to put on the brake.' (Hawker to C. S. ('Punch') Barlow, 16 October 1964, LMA: ST03/03/01/006.) Edmunds was in hospital for an operation and Hawker wrote to Barlow as his deputy. This rather belies the fact that Hawker generally labelled as 'Personal' his letters to Johannesburg with stiff advice of one kind or another.   **137.** Memorandum on Meeting at the Midland Bank, 20 Decem-ber 1962, LMA: ST01/03/09/003.   **138.** Memorandum 'Midland Bank' by Lance Martin, 8 March 1963, LMA: ST01/03/09/003.   **139.** 'The Chairman has written to the Governor of the Bank of England telling him of these deliberations and the present halt to progress in the hope that, possibly, some official pressure may be brought to bear on the Chartered Bank.' Memorandum 'The Board's Future Policy' by Lance Martin, 25 March 1963, LMA: ST01/03/09/003.   **140.** Note for the Record, 29 April 1964, BofE C48/157.   **141.** Three conferences on 'Future Pros-pects and Policy' were held at the Standard Bank under the aegis of R. E. Williams and his deputy, Lance Martin, in October and November 1962. One result was a paper titled 'An International Banking Alliance' by H. D. Roberts, 15 November 1962. The consortium banking concept was then pushed strongly in a separate paper, 'Some Notes on the Bank's Future Prospects and Policy' by a Mr Eley, 4 March 1963. Both in LMA: ST01/03/09/003.   **142.** 'There is no record of the choice ever being formally discussed or a decision formally taken. The fact that the bank chose to throw its resources into the attack rather than to retreat before the tide of history was probably more a matter of temperament than of logical decision. After all, that is how most historic events come about.' Richard Fry, *Bankers in West Africa, The Story of the Bank of British West Africa Limited*, Hutchinson Benham, 1976, p. 187. My summary of the BWA's transformation draws heavily on his excellent account. **143.** Fry, *Bankers in West Africa*, p. 185. **144.** Ibid, p. 197. **145.** Bill Moore, interview with author, 10 March 2014. Moore joined the BWA in 1962 after graduating from university in the UK. He went from the BWA to Standard Bank and thence to Standard Chartered – where he worked until his retirement in 2013. **146.** Fry, *Bankers in West Africa*, p. 239. **147.** Bill Moore, interview with author, 10 March 2014. **148.** Thirty years later, as a retired Welsh hill farmer, Williams produced a privately published memoir on his African career: *Oyinbo Banki, A White Chief's Nigerian Odyssey*, Elna Publications, 1996. **149.** Bill Moore, interview with author, 10 March 2014. **150.** 'Visit by the Chairman, Accompanied by L. A. Martin to East and Central Africa, September 9th to October 2nd 1963', paper presented to Standing Committee, 6 November 1963, LMA: ST01/03/04/013. In addition to meeting Nyerere and Kaunda in person, Hawker met with senior advisers to Milton Obote in Uganda and Jomo Kenyatta in Kenya. He also talked in Southern Rhodesia to Prime Minister W. J. Field and the Finance Minister who would succeed him in April 1964, Ian Smith. **151.** Confidential Strategy Memoranda, LMA: ST01/03/04/013. A Secret Note of a discussion with the Westminster Bank on 22 January 1964 records that one of those attending the meeting was Sylvester Gates, Chairman of the BWA. A subsequent meeting with the Chairman of Lloyds Bank was recorded in Hawker to Sir Harald Peake, 12 August 1964, LMA: ST03/03/15/001. **152.** Annual profits from the East African branches averaged £724,000 over the period 1951–60, of which a third represented an estimate of the interest earned in the City on their remitted earnings. ('Profits of East African Branches', LMA: ST03/02/37/007.) The BWA published net profits of just over £600,000 in the year to March 1964, continuing a fairly steady upward trend since 1945. But its published profits had for years been little more than half of its real profits, and sometimes far less than that. **153.** For the best summary account of this dimension of the City's post-war history, see Jones, *British Multinational Banking*, Ch. 8, pp. 246–84. **154.** The BWA had published reserves in March 1964 of £4 million and hidden reserves of £5.2 million (the late disclosure of which surprised the Standard and obliged it to improve its terms). The Standard's reserves in March 1964 stood at roughly £19 million and £11 million respectively. **155.** Patrick Serjeant in the *Daily Mail*, 2 March 1965. **156.** He had a lunch with Chase Manhattan's Eugene Black in June 1963, and he and Hawker afterwards crafted a subtle invitation to the Americans to open serious talks about partnership – to which they readily responded. (Hall-Patch to Eugene Black, 4 July 1963, LMA: ST03/03/07/012; Hall-Patch to Hawker, 9 October 1963, LMA: ST03/03/07/013.) **157.** 'Preliminary Observations Covering African Trip, November 19 to December 18 1965' by Charles E. Fiero, 19 January 1966, LMA: ST03/03/17/011. **158.** David Rockefeller, *Memoirs*, Random House, 2002, p. 205. **159.** Gino Cattani and Adrian E. Tschoegl, *An Evolutionary View of Internationalization: Chase Manhattan Bank, 1917 to 1996*, Working Paper of the Wharton Financial Institutions Center, 2002, p. 18. **160.** Hawker to George Champion, 4 March 1965. The letter is quoted in a 61-page in-house memorandum 'The Standard and Chartered Merger' (authorship unknown), dated 18 January 1972, to be found in SCB, Box 2573, File A. **161.** Report on Cyril Hawker's Visit to South Africa, April–May 1965, LMA: STo3/03/13/002. **162.** There are several references in Jones, *British Multinational Banking*, to letters in a 'Grand Design File, South Africa Box, Standard Chartered', but no such file has been traced in any of the extant archives. **163.** *The Times*, 6 March 1967. **164.** The hit to the consolidated balance sheet was said by *The Times* on 6 March 1967 to be around £55 million – but there is no evidence of any such write-down in available data on the bank's finances. **165.** The resulting loose consortium was christened Intercontinental Banking Services, which had a brief and inglorious existence, curtailed in 1970. See Jones, *British Multinational Banking*, p. 267, which cites an evidently revealing letter from Chuck Fiero to George Champion of 21 September 1967, now lost. **166.** Hamilton to R. E. Williams, C. E. Fiero, J. C. Read, H. R. Reed, L. C. Hawkins, 25 March 1968, LMA: STo3/03/15/001. **167.** Hamilton to Hawker, 2 April 1968, LMA: STo3/03/15/001. **168.** In 1962, for example, the Chinese Government had demanded the repayment of almost $1 million held on behalf of the Bank of China in a Chartered Bank account in New York. The account had been frozen by the US authorities since 1949. The Chartered's Court decided it was prepared to remit the sterling equivalent to the Bank of China in London, even if this entailed the loss to the Chartered of the dollars held in New York. But lengthy deliberations followed with the UK Treasury and the Foreign Office over whether or not such an initiative would constitute an unlawful breach of US sanctions by the bank. The remittance was made in the end – though whether the bank did in fact forfeit the dollars in New York is unclear. ('China: Blocked Dollar Balances of Chartered Bank', File Notes, 13 June, 15 June and 10 July 1962, BoE C48/158.) **169.** Preston wrote a 7-page memorandum in February 1977 about his move into the Standard Bank, which incorporated comments by both Hawker and Hamilton. He thought his International Division 'was a major profit earner and occupied a leading position in the London market' by the end of 1969. The paper can be found at SCB, Box 2573, File C. **170.** 'In order to ensure that these relative percentage interests are not disturbed, I am sure you will agree that there should be a mutual understanding that direct purchases made by any of the banking partners should only be made after prior consultation between them. The Chairmen of the Midland, National Provincial and Westminster Banks, to whom I have shown this letter, say they would be very happy to cooperate.' (Hawker to George Champion, 4 March 1965.) This letter and all other details of the narrative in this paragraph have been taken from a 1972 memorandum 'The Standard and Chartered Merger', SCB, Box 2573, File A. It was compiled by the Standard's Secretary, Derek Turner, who was determined to leave behind a full record of an episode that he and others at the Standard had watched with some distaste. (The Memorandum is unsigned, but its authorship was confirmed by Michael McWilliam in a note to the author, 11 April 2013.) **171.** Rockefeller, *Memoirs*, p. 206. **172.** 'The Standard and Chartered Merger', SCB, Box 2573, File A. **173.** Rockefeller, *Memoirs*, p. 206. **174.** 'Early in 1972 Sir Cyril Hawker met Kenneth Keith [who in 1969 had been a Director of the National Provincial Bank and of the merchant bankers Hill Samuel] and in conversation the latter . . . divulged that informal talks had in fact taken place at private dinner parties over quite a lengthy period prior to the Meeting [of 24 March 1969] and well before the National Provincial/West-minster merger.' Two of the people involved in these talks had been Sylvester Gates, the former Chairman of BWA, and V. E. Rockhill of Chase Manhattan. Since both were Directors of the Standard throughout 1968–9, 'the ethics of these gentlemen . . . might be thought to be questionable'. 'The Standard and Chartered Merger', Appendix B, SCB, Box 2573, File A.   **175.** 'The Standard and Chartered Merger', SCB, Box 2573, File A, p. 17.

8. TRIAL AND ERROR

1. These details and the account that follows of the transaction are mostly drawn from an anonymous 61-page memorandum compiled soon afterwards by someone closely involved in it, 'for the benefit of historians'. Its author was the Standard Bank's Secretary, H. D. M. Turner (see Ch. 7, n. 170). Additional details are taken from a shorter memorandum by Leslie Fletcher, who in 1969 was the head of the advisory team from merchant bankers J. Henry Schroder Wagg that acted for the Standard. (SCB Box 2573, Files A and D respectively.) Fletcher was to join the Board of the merged banks in 1972 and would eventually serve as its Deputy Chairman from 1983 to 1989.   **2.** SCB Box 2573, File A, p. 28. The 26 September 1969 meeting at the Federal Reserve Board is noted in the Fletcher Memo, File D.   **3.** SCB Box 2573, File A, p. 56.   **4.** 'About four of us went at a time and were sat behind a chair and table, with assorted wine glasses, knives and forks and so on. Then we were told how to use them.' (Gavin Laws, interview with author, 3 October 2013.)   **5.** The Standard man was Sir Michael McWilliam (interview with author, 13 May 2013).   **6.** Hawker to Hamilton, 11 December 1970, LMA: ST03/03/15/001.   **7.** The Standard retained Peat, Marwick, McLintock while the Chartered retained Deloitte, Haskins & Sells. Remarkably, this extravagance was not abandoned until June 1988, when Deloittes agreed to bow out.   **8.** The Standard's sports centre in Beckenham was called Elmer's End. It was highly functional and very focused on rugby. The Chartered's was 'The Wilderness', the seventeen-acre estate at East Molesey, surrounding a 1920s country mansion with its own ballroom, twelve residential bedrooms and extensive panelled corridors lined with trophy cabinets that brimmed with silverware. (*Curry & Rice*, Vol. 6, No. 2, January 1949.)   **9.** Anthony Barber, *Taking the Tide, A Memoir*, privately pub. 1996, p. 158.   **10.** 'By the time the merger with the Chartered Bank was arranged . . . the International Division of the Standard Bank was a major profit earner and occupied a leading position in the London market.' Memorandum by L. T. G. Preston, 2 February 1977, SCB Box 2573, File C. A covering note by Preston confirmed that both Hawker and Hamilton had read and approved of his account.   **11.** 'Report on Merger Possibilities for the International Divisions' by L. T. G. Preston and A. T. Hobbs, 19 January 1971, S&CBG Board paper, SCB Box 363.   **12.** 'Expansion in the UK' by R. A. S. Lane and H. R. Reed, S&CBG Board paper, 5 June 1973, SCB Box 356.   **13.** South Africa chipped in 42 per cent of net profits in 1971 (£9 million out of £21.2 million) and 46 per cent in the year to March 1973 (£15.2 million out of £33.1 million), as presented in papers for the S&CBG Board dated 6 April 1971 and 3 April 1973 (SCB Box 363).   **14.** See, for example, Hawker to Edmunds, 6 January 1964: 'I agree that South Africans would dearly love to get their hands on a few SBSA shares and if only for political reasons we may have to do something about this in the not too distant future, but I would not like to rush matters.' (LMA: STo3/o3/o1/oo6.) Chase Manhattan's Chuck Fiero had been struck by the strength of local feelings on this during his first visit to South Africa: 'we were subjected to continual pressure from both Standard and Chase people to consider a local distribution of SBSA stock (say 25 per cent). The locally-owned South African banks . . . are making more and more use of Standard Bank's foreign ownership to publically embarrass it among nationalistically oriented audiences.' ('Report on Trip to Africa' by Chuck Fiero, 19 January 1966, LMA: STo3/o3/16/oo3.) **15.** The Johannesburg talks followed an earlier meeting in London, in April 1971. The discussions had been at times rather tetchy. A Confidential Note recorded some tension between the London Directors and Bill Passmore, generally regarded as a slightly overbearing figure: 'Passmore resented what he claimed was a personal criticism that he had not initiated remedial action to reverse the falling profit trend. He said this matter was receiving full attention. We said we were very glad to hear of this. London had received no prior indication to this effect.' (South Africa Memorandum, 23 April 1971, S&CBG Board paper, 5 May 1971, SCB Box 363.) It was agreed at the Johannesburg meeting that, if any issues arose under 'abnormal circumstances', the chairmen of the two banks would resolve them – 'and, in need, the London Chairman will attend a [StanBIC] Board Meeting with a view to reaching mutual agreement'. (Memo on Discussion of 7 June 1971, S&CBG Board paper, 16 June 1971, SCB Box 363.)   **16.** It was actually the third report of the Franzsen Commission looking at fiscal and monetary policy in South Africa. **17.** Quoted in Richard Steyn and Francis Antonie, *Hoisting the Standard, 150 Years of Standard Bank*, publ. by The Standard Bank Group, 2012, pp. 125–6. **18.** 'Foreign Control of South African Banks' by Cyril Hawker, Memorandum for the S&CBG Board, 13 June 1973, SCB Box 356.   **19.** 'Visit to Africa, November–December 1965', Report by C. R. P. Hamilton, January 1966, LMA: STo3/o3/17/oo9.   **20.** Evan Campbell to Cyril Hawker, 20 May 1966, LMA: STo3/o3/o4/oo3.   **21.** Hawker to Campbell, 22 December 1965, LMA: STo3/o3/o4/oo4.   **22.** Memorandum from Preston to Hawker, 16 November 1971, LMA: STo3/o3/o4/oo5.   **23.** 'Employing the Bank's Resources in East, Central and West Africa', unsigned Memorandum to the Board, 6 September 1965, LMA: STo3/o3/15/oo1.   **24.** 'Assessing Capital Risk in Africa' by M. McWilliam, 16 February 1968, LMA: STo3/o2/37/oo8.   **25.** H. R. Reed, Memo for S&CBG Board, 7 September 1971, SCB Box 363.   **26.** 'Head Office Administrative Organisation' by H. R. Reed, 31 March 1971, Memorandum for the S&CBG Board, SCB Box 363.   **27.** Hawker to Hamilton, 11 December 1970 (from Hong Kong), LMA: STo3/o3/15/oo1.   **28.** 'Regional Profit & Loss Analysis', Paper for the S&CBG Board, 6 June 1972, SCB Box 363. The equivalent paper for the following year was submitted for the Board, 5 June 1973, SCB Box 356. The analyses unfortunately list *post*-tax profits by region and add one lump sum for 'local tax charged in the accounts' to present an aggregate Gross Profits figure of £9.0 million in 1971 vs £9.1 million in 1970. The post-tax figures inevitably flatter the territories with low-tax regimes, like Hong Kong. (Pre-tax trading profits in Bishopsgate amounted to £5.0 million in 1971 vs £3.5 million in 1970. The resulting Total Gross Profits of £14.0 million vs £12.4 million for the Chartered can be compared with £21.2 million vs £18.5 million at the Standard Bank, as per Note 13.)   **29.** In addition to those noted in Chapter 7, n. 65, several were opened in Sabah and Sarawak, on the island of Borneo. Both states were assimilated into the Federation of Malaysia in 1963.   **30.** Geoffrey Jones, *British Multinational Banking, 1830–1990*, Oxford University Press 1993, p. 286. Jones notes that the branches of domestic banks in Malaysia outnumbered those of all the foreign banks by 1966 (p. 290).   **31.** 'Eastern Bank: Integration with the Chartered Bank' by E. Hampden Smith, 19 January 1971, Memorandum for the S&CBG Board, SCB Box 363.   **32.** Head Office Circular No. 714, 26 November 1959, LMA: CH03/01/02/036.   **33.** 'Korea – Chartered Bank, Seoul', by R. A. S. Lane, 6 June 1972, Memorandum for the S&CBG Board, SCB Box 363.   **34.** It owned 45 per cent of the Anglo-Nordic Bank in Switzerland and 9 per cent of Arbuthnot Latham Holdings in the City, and had become a limited partner in the private banking firm of Conrad Hinrich Donner of Hamburg. The latter association led to the establishment in 1973 of a jointly owned bank in Panama, Banco Promotor del Comercio Latinoamericano – the first of several curious flirtations with the notion of adding Latin America to the historic franchise in Asia.   **35.** 'Expansion in Europe' by C. R. P. Hamilton, 4 January 1972, Memorandum for the S&CBG Board, SCB Box 363.   **36.** 'Expansion in the UK', two memoranda by R. A. S. Lane and H. R. Reed, 22 May and 5 June 1973, S&CBG Board papers, SCB Box 356.   **37.** 'Bruno' by W. G. Pullen, 9 October 1973, Memorandum for the S&CBG Board, SCB Box 356. 'Bruno' was the codename given to the Hodge Group by the merchant bankers (with 'Sylvie' for S&CBG). Pullen was alert to the possibility that the business might seem a little anomalous in the context of the Chartered's distinguished history. The proposal, he said, 'inevitably raises the issue as to whether there could be any adverse repercussions on the status or standing of the Group'. The City advisers were quick to reassure the Board otherwise, and to agree it was 'an obvious and sensible way' of achieving S&CBG's growth goals.   **38.** 'The Hodge Group Ltd' by R. A. S. Lane, Memorandum to the Board, 15 January 1974, SCB Box 356.   **39.** Memorandum for the S&CBG Board, 3 April 1973, SCB Box 356.   **40.** A proposed purchase of a 40 per cent stake in 1970 fell foul of a belated disclosure by Johnson Matthey Bankers (JMB) of some bad debts related to silver trades in the US. Preston and one of the Group's best corporate finance men, George Copus, then joined the Board of JMB to assist with a recovery programme, which was closely followed by the Bank of England. ('Johnson Matthey Bankers' by L. T. G. Preston, 6 April 1972, SCB Box 363.) An agreement for S&CBG to take a 60 per cent stake in JMB was about to be signed in July 1972, when a telephone call the night before the signing informed Preston and Copus that Maxwell Joseph's Robert Fraser & Partners had acquired a 50 per cent stake in JMB and would be merging it with their merchant bank, Henry Ansbacher & Co. (George Copus, interview with author, 24 August 2011.)   **41.** 'The Mocatta Group of Companies' by L. T. G. Preston, 9 April 1974, Memorandum for the S&CBG Board, 3 April 1974, SCB Box 356. In addition to setting out the details of the transaction, Preston was able to point out that the cost to the bank of its purchase of Mocatta & Goldsmid had already been 99 per cent recouped in profits, while the investment in MMC had returned a yield of 11.6 per cent.   **42.** Henry Jarecki, interview with author, 31 July 2013.   **43.** 'Chartered Bank of London' by R. A. S. Lane, 3 April 1973, Memorandum for the S&CBG Board, SCB Box 356.   **44.** 'Expansion in California' by M. D. McWilliam, 8 August 1973, Memorandum for the S&CBG Board, SCB Box 356.   **45.** 'The Chairman referred to the sale . . . which he considered was a very satisfactory arrangement from the point of view of the Group . . . It was agreed that Mr Rockhill be invited to lunch with the Directors following the meeting on 1 July and that a subsequent farewell dinner be arranged in his honour.' (Minutes of the Board meeting of 3 June 1975, SCB Box 347.)   **46.** Peter Graham, interview with Frank King, 1986, HSBC Archives, HQ1671/0013D.   **47.** Barber, *Taking the Tide, A Memoir*, p. 134.   **48.** Interview with author, 5 December 2011. Millar made a strong impression on his colleagues. 'It was the first time he had been seen by the rest of us. He was used to public speaking and intervened quite a lot – and everyone nudged their neighbours and said, "Aha, here's the next Chartered Bank star!".' (McWilliam, interview with author, 17 May 2013.)   **49.** The episode came as rather a surprise to Geoff Williams, who arrived in Kuala Lumpur for his first assignment as the commotion over the 1968 year-end accounts was still reverberating. (Interview with author, 29 June 2012.)   **50.** 'We have decided . . . that in future the managers of our parent branches will be granted discretionary power to allocate such duties to the Asian probationers, Staff Assistants and Staff Officers on their establishment as they consider [appropriate] . . . without prior reference or report to us [at Head Office].' Circular 573a, 9 May 1956, LMA: CH03/04/01/018. **51.** *Curry & Rice*, Vol. 15, No. 4, November 1959.   **52.** Chartered Bank Annual Report & Accounts, 1959. 'The Chartered Bank can claim to have pioneered the creation of opportunities for Asian clerical officers to advance to positions of responsibility in British overseas banking . . . The Court of Directors and the General Managers have long recognized not only the justice, but the advantages to the Bank, of this policy.'   **53.** *Curry & Rice*, Vol. 19, No. 2, Spring 1969. The ratio was rather lower in the Eastern Bank, which had nineteen Arab and Asian names on its list of sixty-six.   **54.** John Janes, for example, arrived at The Wilderness in East Molesey as part of the September 1971 intake. The fact that a dozen British recruits were matched by a dozen Officer Trainees from overseas prompted some concern among the British contingent about their future prospects – echoing the concern expressed in the early 1950s over the first Assistant Officers. 'We used to worry about where we would get posted – given the growing number of national officers appointed and the difficulty of getting work permits for foreign expatriates and so on.' (Interview with author, 21 October 2013.)   **55.** Shirley Wee, interview with author, 5 September 2013.   **56.** Johnny Tan, interview with author, 1 November 2012. Tan was Senior Manager, Consumer Banking when interviewed by the author in 2012 – and could still recall almost half a century of Singapore's local staffing arrangements in astonishing detail.   **57.** Interview with author, 24 June 2013.   **58.** 'Corporate Objectives and Staff Policy' by M. D. McWilliam, 27 November 1972, MMcW Papers.   **59.** Having graduated in PPE from Oriel College, he was a graduate student at Nuffield College and took a B.Litt. degree in 1957 with his thesis, 'The East African Tea Industry, 1920–56: A Case Study in the Development of a Plantation Industry'. A chapter on labour relations and child labour in the 1930s did not go down well with the Kenyan Tea Board, which managed to persuade the University that a twenty-year embargo should be placed on public access to the copy held in the Bodleian Library.   **60.** Or, at least, they would have been in the files, had these survived. How many have been retained in the Standard Bank's own archives in Johannesburg is unclear – but McWilliam kept many in his own personal papers, generously made available to the author.   **61.** I am indebted for these numbers to John Rivett, who from 1973 to 1986 worked in Clements Lane on the management team responsible for marketing the Group's services in Nigeria. The statistics on the Nigerian economy quoted in this paragraph come from official papers retained by him in his retirement.   **62.** Aide Memoire for the Chairman by M. D. McWilliam, 16 December 1974, MMcW Papers.   **63.** 'Visit to Nigeria, 8–12 October 1975' by M. D. McWilliam, MMcW Papers.   **64.** Michael McWilliam, note to the author, 19 October 2013.   **65.** 'Visit to Nigeria, 25 January–7 February 1976' by M. D. McWilliam, MMcW Papers.   **66.** 'Revised Financial Plan', Memorandum for Board Meeting of 14 November 1978, SCB Box 347.   **67.** Michael McWilliam, interview with author, 11 May 2011.   **68.** W. C. L. Brown, interview with author, 15 September 2011. 'I sympathized with the bank. They certainly had a problem and they couldn't make up their minds.' In the event, Brown and his bride ended up in Bangkok – and never encountered any anti-Japanese feelings at all.   **69.** McWilliam, interview with author, 11 May 2011.   **70.** Neville Green, interviews with author, 19 May and 1 June 2011.   **71.** 'Visit to India – October 13–17', Tour Reports 1980–82, MMcW Papers.   **72.** 'Banking on Imperfect Arabic & Other Memories' by Neville Green, a personal memoir, p. 12.   **73.** Peter Cameron, interview with author, 5 April 2013.   **74.** McWilliam Diary, 5 March 1977, MMcW Papers.   **75.** Jack Tang, for example, openly shared his doubts about the wisdom of the merger. 'When I went to London [in the 1970s] I would always go to the bank and have lunch with him in the Boardroom. He was always about to go off to Africa, flying around in these little planes. I said to him, "Gee, you're spending too much time on it." ' (Interview with the author, 8 March 2012.)   **76.** 'I did a lot of work on that. Then instead of going with the Magna Carta to California, I was asked by Barber to go with him to the IMF meetings in Manila. That was extremely hard work, but a great experience.' (Sir John Major, interview with author, 9 October 2013.)   **77.** Barber, *Taking the Tide, A Memoir*, p. 153.   **78.** McWilliam Diary, 5 March 1977, MMcW Papers.   **79.** 'When we bought Liberty National Bank [in 1973] I was holed up for a week in the Fairmont Hotel in San Francisco, negotiating the deal.' (McWilliam, interview with author, 11 May 2011.)   **80.** 'Corporate Development Activities', Memorandum for Executive Committee by R. J. Kimmis, 17 November 1976, SCB Box 381.   **81.** Barber recalls his mention of the Crocker talks in his autobiography. One of the two

Midland Directors was Malcolm Wilcox, who was later to be personally involved in the negotiation of the Crocker deal with the Chief Executive of the Crocker Bank, Thomas R. Wilcox (no relation). (*Taking the Tide, A Memoir*, p. 151.) **82.** Lex Column, *Financial Times*, 10 June 1978. Standard Chartered's shares were trading at an historic price/earnings multiple of 5.5x, compared with the P/E of 20x put on the Union Bank by the bid.   **83.** Graham, interview with Frank King, 1986, HSBC Archives, HQ1671/0013D.   **84.** In 1981 pounds, the Union Bank reported almost £30 million for both 1980 and 1981, compared with £31 million from Hong Kong in both years (excluding some windfall profits on foreign-exchange revaluations). Curiously, Malaysia and Singapore together also reported £30 million for 1980, and £34 million for 1981. Only StanBIC in South Africa contributed more than this (£64 million and £69 million respectively). The total for the Group was £273 million in both years. ('Annual Working Profits before Debts and Tax', Memorandum for the Board, 9 March 1982, SCB Box 867.)   **85.** Ian Wilson, interview with author, 4 October 2012.   **86.** Business Day, *New York Times*, 19 May 2000.   **87.** Graham, interview with Frank King, 1986, HSBC Archives, HQ1671/0013D.   **88.** General Management memorandum for the Board, 13 May 1980, SCB Box 353. The paper noted Tarrant would be starting work on 1 July, 'following a short period in the USA in the nature of a familiarisation tour to meet senior officers and to brief himself on aspects of the Group's business in the USA'.   **89.** *Los Angeles Times*, 26 February 1985.   **90.** *Glasgow Herald*, 23 April 1984.   **91.** Graham, interview with Frank King, 1986, HSBC Archives, HQ1671/0013D.   **92.** 'They could see a great deal of value in bringing home to Britain one of the big UK banks which was 90 per cent overseas. They could see the competitive side to it which also appealed to them. So they did give us a good welcome.' Graham, interview with Frank King, 1986, HSBC Archives, HQ1671/0013D.   **93.** Lord Sandberg of Passfield, *Hurrahs and Hammerblows*, privately published, 2012, p. 156.   **94.** 'He told me that he could not accept competing bids, and that we must look elsewhere. Where that might be, he could not say. He looked decidedly cross, if a bit embarrassed, when I said the bidding price was so low . . . [Afterwards] I was summoned back to the Bank of England where the Governor again verbally beat me up.' (Sandberg, *Hurrahs and Hammerblows*, p. 157.)   **95.** Documents and papers relating to the RBS bid can be found in SCB Box 1579.   **96.** Graham, interview with Frank King, 1986, HSBC Archives, HQ1671/0013D.   **97.** In addition to the business logic and prospect of seeing a 'fifth force' in UK domestic banking to set beside the Big Four clearers, the BofE contended that a merger with RBS 'would reduce Standard Chartered's vulnerability to takeover bids unwelcome to both it and the Bank'. But the MMC concluded, albeit with two dissident minority reports, that the effect of either merger, if passed, 'on career prospects, initiative and business enterprise in Scotland would be damaging to the public interest of the United Kingdom as a whole'. (*MMC Report on the Proposed Mergers*, January 1982, HMSO Cmnd. 8472.)   **98.** Graham, interview with Frank King, 1986, HSBC Archives, HQ1671/0013D.   **99.** Michael McWilliam, note to the author, 19 October 2013.   **100.** 'Mocatta Metals Corporation' by Michael McWilliam, Memorandum to the Standing Committee of the

Board, 2 October 1979, SCB Box 555.   **101.** Minutes of the Board Meeting, 9 October 1979, SCB Box 555.   **102.** 'HJ Talk at M&G', October 1982, MMcW Papers. The narrative of the 1979–82 takeover discussions draws heavily on the text of this speech.   **103.** 'Provisional Working Profits (Before Debt and Taxes) for the Year to December 1983' by Stuart Tarrant, Memorandum for the Board Meeting of 14 February 1984, SCB Box 1721.   **104.** Graham, interview with Frank King, 1986, HSBC Archives, HQ1671/0013D.   **105.** 'Provisional Working Profits (Before Debts and Taxes) for the Year to December 1983' by Stuart Tarrant, Memorandum for the Board Meeting of 14 February 1984, SCB Box 1721. Almost as noteworthy as the scale of the Western profits was the abject performance of the Group in the Indian sub-continent, where profits reached just £2.8 million. **106.** Other 1981 gains were made on a sale of StanBIC's head office in Johannesburg (£20 million) and of the old Standard Bank Head Office in Clements Lane itself (£20.6 million). None of these properties were scheduled for disposal, so the aggregate gains, worth £240 million, incurred no tax liability and went straight into the balance sheet. ('Revaluation of Bank Premises' by Stuart Tarrant, Memorandum for Board Meeting of 9 March 1982, SCB Box 867.) Another notable property gain was made on the sale of Union Bank's Los Angeles head office in 1982, which yielded a tax-free profit of more than $60 million. By way of comparison, retained earnings in 1981 and 1982 together came to £247.7 million. **107.** 'Forecast of Working Profits' by Stuart Tarrant, Memorandum for Board Meeting of 8 February 1983, SCB Box 1721.   **108.** 'Whilst contributory factors [behind a £3 million provision for Bad & Doubtful Debts in the UK for 1979] were a lack of precise instruction and control from Head Office, the main cause was inexperience and ignorance of responsibilities at Branch level. The Directors . . . supported the decision to reduce the rate of expansion in the UK, pending an improvement in the staffing position.' Minutes of Board Meeting, 12 February 1980, SCB Box 353.   **109.** Papers for Special Board Meeting, 20 April 1982, SCB Box 867. Thus, a paper on the situation in California noted: 'We have to recognize that we have expanded too quickly and a priority will be to put our offices outside New York on a sound footing to ensure longer term viability . . . Emphasis will be placed on improving the quality of staff and training requirements. The policy of employing expatriates outside California will be replaced by a policy of employing quality American bankers.'   **110.** 'Report on the Implementation of the Arthur Andersen Consultancy on Group Computer Systems' by Michael McWilliam, Memorandum for the Board Meeting on 14 June 1983, SCB Box 1721. **111.** Papers for Special Board Meeting, 20 April 1982, SCB Box 867.   **112.** Minutes of Audit Committee meeting, 13 December 1983, SCB Box 1721.   **113.** The first Chartered Bank man to go to Africa was Neville Green, in 1979. At the end of his time as Chief Manager in India, he was reassigned to the First Bank of Nigeria in Lagos. To learn about his new territory, Green immediately took a ten-day tour across the north of the country. 'I visited as many branches as I could – we had 169 of them – and came back and announced that we had an enormous payroll of ghosts. This didn't go down well at all. My deputy, who was recently retired from the Central Bank and was of royal blood, said "This is not your business" . . . So

I simply sent a message back to my General Manager, a Standard Bank man, and said "this is not going to work".' (Green, interview with author, 1 June 2011.) Within three weeks of his arrival, Green was on his way to reassignment in Kuala Lumpur. Meanwhile, his replacement in Bombay was H. J. Watson, who had served in West Africa since the age of twenty-one with BWA and the Standard Bank. He had adjusted in his time to postings in Oshogbo, Onitsha, Calabar, Kano, Accra and Apapa – but he lasted less than nine months in India. He was brought back to Clements Lane and ended his career as General Manager for Europe. **114.** City verdicts on the financial performance were mixed in 1984. Bullish analysts pointed to the dramatic increase in pre-tax profits since the 1970s – up from £170 million in 1979 to £290 million by 1984 – and enthused over the bank's future prospects. The more sceptical noted that total assets had jumped over the same period from £13 billion to £34½ billion, yet earnings per share had dropped heavily for three consecutive years (reaching 64.4 pence in 1984 compared with 101.5 pence in 1980). An ever expanding balance sheet, it seemed to them, was being turned to ever less advantage.

9. A STYMIED TRANSITION

1. See for example 'Bishopsgate Redevelopment' by Peter Graham, Memorandum for the Board Meeting of 11 March 1980, SCB Box 353. **2.** *Daily Mail*, 17 September 1983. **3.** 'HJ Talk at M&G', October 1982, M McW Papers. **4.** 'Address to General Management', 2 June 1983, M McW Papers. **5.** Diary for 1 September 1983, M McW Papers. Just a few weeks before taking over as Managing Director, McWilliam had diarized a slightly alarming conversation with another of his senior colleagues in Clements Lane: '[He] Says PAG has openly commented that if I do not perform, an alternative will be found. RC [Reg Casey] feels PAG will try to continue to control people and events' (29 April 1983). **6.** The six annual diaries' contents were subsequently typed up by his secretary at the bank, a process completed as part of the research for this book. Covering the 1983–8 period, the diaries comprise what must be one of the more remarkable eye-witness accounts of life in the City of London from any era. **7.** 'Address to StanBIC Review Conference – Johannesburg, 6 March 1982', M McW Papers. **8.** The arguments were outlined first by McWilliam himself in 'Pegasus – The Case for Independence', Memorandum for the Board, 22 February 1982, M McW Papers. **9.** To be exact, all banking operations were transferred into the Chartered Bank – which was then renamed the Standard Chartered Bank, so allowing the Group to retain its 1853 Royal Charter (which required an Act of Parliament, authorizing the changes with effect from 1 January 1985). At the same time, the Standard Chartered Bank plc was renamed Standard Chartered plc and became a holding company for the bank and all other subsidiaries. (Letter from the Chairman to Shareholders, 14 October 1983.) **10.** 'Leeds Weekend: Confidential Summary of Impressions' by Henry Jarecki, 18 September 1984, HJ Papers. McWilliam noted in his diary on 3 September 1984 that he had received a long letter from Jarecki 'including some robust recommendations as to what I should do to consolidate my authority in the Group'. **11.** Notes on discussion with John Mackenzie, Hong Kong Review Session, 25 July 1984, SCB Box 2387.   **12.** Notes of discussion on Inspection Report, Audit Committee meeting of 11 September 1984, SCB Box 2387.   **13.** Pan-Electric Industries had been ailing for months when an attempt to launch a rights issue in November 1985 brought to light a raft of fraudulent share dealings by its senior managers. The ensuing scandal forced a three-day closure of the Singapore Stock Exchange. Speculative dealing in securities for delivery at a future date, illegal in Singapore, had been partly financed by Standard Chartered's local merchant bank and this led to the prosecution of the executive responsible for its operations.   **14.** Minutes of Audit Committee meeting of 10 September 1985, SCB Box 2387.   **15.** Diary for 26 August 1984, MMcW Papers.   **16.** Diary for 27 August 1984, MMcW Papers.   **17.** 'Head Office Reorganisation', by Michael McWilliam, Memorandum for the Board Meeting of 13 November 1984, SCB Box 2387. Other significant moves included the combination of the successful Treasury and International operations into a single entity, the International Banking Division (IBD) under Alan Orsich, who since the late 1970s had effectively taken on the mantle of George Preston as co-ordinator of the Group's trading activities in the foreign exchange and money markets.   **18.** 'Of Chameleons, Apes and Coelacanths', speech given on 19 November 1981 to an audience of bankers, some of them quite possibly unfamiliar with coelacanths. (MMcW Papers.)   **19.** Diary for 10 July 1984, MMcW Papers.   **20.** Diary for 16 January 1985, MMcW Papers. McWilliam actually succeeded some days later in persuading the Board to change its mind, only for the Continental Illinois management in Chicago to back away from a sale at the last moment.   **21.** 'Strategy Considerations' by Michael McWilliam, Memorandum for the Board Meeting of 2 May 1984, SCB Box 2387.   **22.** Of course South Africa appeared far more prominently in the Group's P & L statements; but that was a function of consolidated accounting. (Figures at a pre-tax level included the whole of StanBIC's profits, with approaching half of them stripped out below the line as a Minority Interest.) Taking account only of the StanBIC income really owned by UK shareholders, and subjecting it to some fairer distribution of central overheads, South Africa's share of Group pre-tax profits for 1984 emerged in one analysis at about 22 per cent, compared with 17 per cent for Black Africa (Diary for 10 July 1985, MMcW Papers). The rest of this analysis showed 23 per cent for North America and 26 per cent for the UK. The 12 per cent share left for the territories of the East, including Hong Kong, must have seemed a dramatic vindication of the decision to move the Group's focus to Western markets.   **23.** 'Annual Results for 1983' by Stuart Tarrant, Memorandum for the Board Meeting of 27 March 1984, SCB Box 2387.   **24.** It contributed £16.0 million in 1984, compared with £8.6 million for Zambia and £14.5 million for the rest of Africa ('Provisional Working Profits for 1984' by Stuart Tarrant, Memorandum for the Board of 12 February 1985, SCB Box 2387).   **25.** Diary for 11 July 1985, MMcW Papers.   **26.** The General Manager in Harare at this time, Alan Wren, had the previous year given his seniors in London a candid assessment of the bank's position, which set its healthy finances in the context of a less than reassuring general situation. 'The problem of top level white emigration (most middle and lower ranking whites have already left) could become acute, depending on Government policy . . . The financial sector is virtually the only one to be making significant profits, with Standard Chartered Group's operation in the country being the most profitable.' (Notes on the 1984 Zimbabwe Annual Review, 12 January 1984, SCB Box 1721.)   **27.** Diary for 12 and 13 July 1985, MMcW Papers.   **28.** Report of Ad Hoc Committee on Trade Investments by D. L. d'A. Willis, L. T. G. Preston and W. Bowden, 5 March 1971, S&CBG Board Papers, SCB Box 363.   **29.** 'Proposal to Acquire MAIBL' by Peter Graham, Memorandum for the Board Meeting of 9 November 1982, SCB Box 867.   **30.** 'Post-Investment Appraisal – MAIBL PLC' by P. L. Macdougall and A. N. Sperryn, paper presented to meeting of the Audit Committee on 29 July 1986, SCB Box 2384.   **31.** Chris Keljik, interview with author, 24 November 2011.   **32.** Willie Mocatta, whose extensive family ties included not only the Mocattas of the London gold market but also a link by marriage to the Kadoories, joined Schroders and Chartered in 1982 on a six-month internship. 'We were looked on as more of an independent entity than Wardley's or Jardine's, and Win Bischoff built up a corporate finance department that I think at one time was earning more for Schroders in Hong Kong than their business in London.' (Interview with author, 22 March 2012.)   **33.** Li Ka-Shing, interview with author, 22 March 2012.   **34.** Payment of dividends in the UK incurred an 'Advanced Corporation Tax' (ACT) which could later be offset against mainstream corporation tax on UK income. Where a company's ACT exceeded its mainstream tax liability – as in the case of any overseas business with limited operations in the UK – the deficit had to be written off against current profits, unless the auditors could be persuaded that an opportunity to use the 'unrelieved ACT' was 'reasonably certain' to arise in the next accounting period. For a large company like Standard Chartered, this posed a potentially significant problem, as the Group Chief Accountant, R. E. Landon, regularly reminded his colleagues: 'ACT paid [on the final dividend for 1984] is not budgeted to be fully relieved . . . and this highlights the urgency of increasing Group profits subject to UK tax' (Group Profits and Assets Budget, February 1985, SCB Box 2387).   **35.** 'Strategy Considerations' by Michael McWilliam, Memorandum for the Board Meeting of 2 May 1984, SCB Box 2387.   **36.** Diary for 21 December 1983, MMcW Papers.   **37.** Diary for 3 January 1984, MMcW Papers.   **38.** Diary for 11 January 1984, MMcW Papers. It probably did not come as much of a shock to McWilliam. Geoffrey Taylor, Chief Executive of the Midland, and he had been to the opera together six months earlier, and the Midland man had dropped a heavy hint of his thinking. 'Presumably it was not chance that he mentioned the good "fit" of SCB and Midland. I pointed to the complications.' (Diary for 27 June 1983, MMcW Papers.)   **39.** Diary for 22 May 1984, MMcW Papers.   **40.** The City editor of *The Times*, Kenneth Fleet, wrote in December 1983 that their union had been 'merely put back seven years'. The Royal Bank's shareholders could at least be thankful, he suggested, that they had not exchanged their stock for shares in HSBC in 1981, given the crash of the Hong Kong market which 'would have left them as sick as Glaswegians after Hogmanay'. (*The Times*, 2 December 1983.)   **41.** Diary for 10 April 1984, MMcW Papers.

42. Diary for 2 May 1984, MMcW Papers.   **43.** 'Leeds Weekend: Confidential Summary of Impressions' by Henry Jarecki, 18 September 1984, HJ Papers.   **44.** Diary for 3 May 1984, MMcW Papers.   **45.** 'SST went round to the BofE this a.m. without my knowledge to "expound" [on] the capital adequacy [position] . . . Needless to say this does not seem to have been presented helpfully and I had a concerned Peter Cooke on the phone in the afternoon' (Diary for 6 February 1985, MMcW Papers).   **46.** Diary for 11 February 1985, MMcW Papers.   **47.** Memorandum from Tarrant to McWilliam, 11 February 1985, copied to Barber, Graham, Fletcher, Millar and Baillie, SCB Box 2387.   **48.** Diary for 28 March 1985, MMcW Papers.   **49.** Diary for 3 April 1985, MMcW Papers.   **50.** Diary for 26 June 1985, MMcW Papers.   **51.** Diary for 9 July 1985, MMcW Papers.   **52.** After tax and Minority Interests, profits for 1983 were £113.7 million. Contributions came from South Africa (£40.1 million), North America (£24.0 million), UK & Europe (£21.7 million), south-east Asia (£21.6 million), Africa excl. RSA (£20.6 million) and the Far East (£5.2 million). The Middle East and the Indian sub-continent accounted for a loss of £2.8 million and central financing costs were £16.7 million. ('Annual results for 1983' by Stuart Tarrant, Memorandum for the Board Meeting of 27 March 1984, SCB Box 2387.)   **53.** The Bank of England was deaf to requests for a distinction to be made between loans to SBSA and to South African third parties. In fact, the Group had the worst of both worlds, in its dealings with the Bank on this topic. It had to consolidate its South African operations like any other majority-owned business – even though the markets effectively treated StanBIC as a stand-alone credit risk – yet the Bank of England also insisted on treating loans to SBSA as straightforward inter-bank lending, rather than as intra-group funding which might have borne fewer regulatory constraints.   **54.** 'South Africa' by P. A. Graham, Memorandum for the Board Meeting of 14 October 1980, SCB Box 353.   **55.** Graham to the Registrar of Banks in Pretoria, 22 September 1976. The commitment was given in response to the 1976 Financial Institutions Amendment Act, which revised the rules governing foreign ownership of South African banks that had prevailed since the 1965 Banks Act. The Registrar of Banks, Wynand Louw, replied to Graham in an undated letter confirming that the commitment was acceptable. 'The [Finance] Minister has also asked me to convey to your Board his appreciation of the Bank's cooperation in this matter.' (SCB Box 353.)   **56.** Diary for 9 June 1983, MMcW Papers.   **57.** 'Brought Lord Barber up-to-date on developments and found that he [had] had a testy phone call with Mackenzie over the 1986 issue. Ian Mackenzie has procured that he lunches with [Minister of Finance] Horwood next week and had hoped to be the intermediary to 'settle' the matter. Lord Barber not amused.' (Diary for 21 June 1983, MMcW Papers.)   **58.** Diary for 16 August 1983, MMcW Papers.   **59.** For 1983, StanBIC's return on gross assets was 1.71 per cent, compared with 0.79 per cent for Union Bank and 0.71 for the rest of Standard Chartered. At the pre-tax level, StanBIC's wholly consolidated profits accounted for 38 per cent of the Group total in 1983. Even at the post-tax level, after deduction of the profits attributable to minority shareholders in South Africa, StanBIC's contribution to the Group still amounted to 35 per cent. ('Annual Results for 1983' by S. S. Tarrant, Memorandum for the Board Meeting of 27 March

1984, SCB Box 2387.) **60.** Diary for 27 August 1983, MMcW Papers. **61.** McWilliam noted of one encounter, on 15 May 1984: 'An important meeting with [Peter] Cooke, BofE, on the South African exposure issue. BofE are concerned with our total S. A. exposure which they consider to be our direct lending plus SBSA external borrowings and guarantees. This total is miles ahead of BofE's notion of a control figure based on our shareholders' funds . . . Fortunately Cooke also realises that any heavy handed adjustment is not practical politics and we separated to think further.' (Diary for 15 May 1984, MMcW Papers.) **62.** 'De V. phoned to say that [Peter] Cooke has apparently expressed a view to the Reserve Bank that we should sell down in StanBIC . . .' (Diary for 5 October 1984, MMcW Papers.) **63.** 'Capital Expenditure Budget, 1985' by Stuart Tarrant, Memorandum for the Board Meeting of 11 December 1984, SCB Box 2387. **64.** Diary for 5 July 1983, MMcW Papers. **65.** In Donald Gordon's official biography, the climactic meeting in 1983 is remembered by StanBIC's Chairman Ian Mackenzie as including 'four or five highly emotive and frequently acrimonious hours' – though the account suggests 'Barber caved in' which is surely incorrect. (Ken Romain, *Larger than Life, Donald Gordon and the Liberty Life Story*, Jonathan Ball Publishers 1989.) **66.** For a fuller account of Donald Gordon's evolving association with StanBIC, see Richard Steyn and Francis Antonie, *Hoisting the Standard, 150 Years of Standard Bank*, pub. Standard Bank Group, 2012, pp. 157–67. **67.** As per StanBIC's 1984 Annual Report. **68.** A detailed analysis of the balance sheet was part of a proposal tabled at this point by McWilliam to acquire a small family bank in Belgium, CBSA. ('CBSA Acquisition Proposal' by Michael McWilliam, Memorandum for the Board Meeting of 12 February 1985, SCB Box 2387.) **69.** 'Improving Capital Adequacy in South Africa' by Michael McWilliam, Memorandum for the Board Meeting of 19 February 1985, SCB Box 2387. Details of the ratio analysis are taken from this paper. **70.** Diary for 18 February 1985, MMcW Papers. **71.** Diary for 14 March 1985, MMcW Papers. On a visit to Los Angeles, McWilliam was dismayed to learn in a telephone call to Strauss that Graham, Tarrant, Fletcher and Baillie had concocted a scheme whereby the Group could take up its rights and disinvest them at a later date. They had presented it to StanBIC without reference to the Managing Director. 'All this had caused surprise and concern [in South Africa], which I shared.' Fully supported by Barber, McWilliam ditched the idea immediately. **72.** 'The Chairman reported on his visit to South Africa and informed the Board that much regret had been expressed at the prospective reduction in the Group shareholding in StanBIC below 50 per cent . . .' Minutes of the Board Meeting of 11 April 1985. StanBIC's own Board Minutes of the 2 April meeting made a careful note of the future position: 'Lord Barber explained the position of Stanchart and stressed that there was no question of Stanchart wishing to divest in South Africa. He had written to the Minister of Finance and Registrar of Banks and had indicated to them that Stanchart intended to sustain a continuing major business relationship with StanBIC as its largest individual shareholder.' (1985 Board Minutes, StanBIC BRD1/1/4.) **73.** *Financial Times*, 21 August 1985. **74.** Diary for 4 September 1985, MMcW Papers. **75.** This fear was well-founded. StanBIC had had the greatest difficulty rolling over a £40 million loan, raised a few years earlier from just a handful of banks. Sixty banks had been approached in July, and only £31 million had been forthcoming. 'In the circumstances,' as a Board paper in Johannesburg noted, 'StanBIC had decided to withdraw from the medium-term market for the time being. (Minutes of the StanBIC Board Meeting, 6 August 1985, StanBIC BRD 1/1/4.) **76.** Minutes of Board Meeting, 10 September 1985, SCB Box 2387. **77.** The Africa Private Enterprise Group had been established in 1963, in response to the impact of independence movements all across Africa. It provided a forum for its members to discuss how best to respond to incoming post-colonial black governments. Issues related to South Africa loomed large, as did the problems of Nigeria. Luminaries from the Foreign Office, academia and the media were regular guests. It petered out in 1997. **78.** Diary for 30 October 1985, MMcW Papers. **79.** Diary for 27 November 1985, MMcW Papers. **80.** 'Specific Bad & Doubtful Debts Provision' by Michael McWilliam and David Millar, Memorandum for the Board Meeting of 10 June 1986, SCB Box 2384. **81.** Diary for 17 December 1985, MMcW Papers. **82.** 'The 1986 Budget and Working Profits' by Stuart Tarrant, Memorandum for the Board Meeting of 14 January 1986, SCB Box 2384. **83.** Diary for 17 January 1986, MMcW Papers. **84.** Diary for 14 February 1986, MMcW Papers. **85.** Diary for 15 February 1986, MMcW Papers. **86.** Memorandum for Board Meeting of 8 July 1986, SCB Box 2384. Demolition was to start in July 1986 and completion of the building was scheduled for mid-1989, ready for its occupation in December 1989. **87.** 'Proposed Acquisition of 80 per cent of Mocatta Group' by Michael McWilliam, Memorandum for the Board Meeting of 11 February 1986, SCB Box 2384. **88.** 'Partial Takeover Bid for BHP by Bell Resources' by Michael McWilliam, Memorandum for the Board Meeting of 31 January 1986, SCB Box 2384. An oddity (by international standards) of Australian law allowed raiders to make partial bids for corporate targets. Holmes à Court's Bell Resources already owned 13 per cent of BHP, and planned to acquire another 20 per cent on the open market. (With furious lobbying from BHP, a change in the law to prohibit partial bids appeared imminent – so Holmes à Court was in a hurry.) **89.** Minutes of the Board meeting of 7 January 1986, SCB Box 2384. **90.** Diary for 25 March 1986, MMcW Papers. **91.** Anthony Barber, *Taking the Tide, A Memoir*, privately published, 1996, p. 154. The memoir devotes about thirty pages to his time at Standard Chartered without once mentioning Michael McWilliam, whose name accordingly does not appear in the index. **92.** McWilliam, interview with author, 11 May 2011. **93.** Diary for 19 May 1986, MMcW Papers. **94.** Diary for 23 and 25 May 1986, MMcW Papers. **95.** Diary for 8 June 1986, MMcW Papers. **96.** 'A terrible day with Lord B . . . It took more than an hour to secure my point of view again and, of course, it opened up the old wounds . . . I really feel very sore with Barber for machinating in this way.' (Diary for 13 June 1986, MMcW Papers.) **97.** Diary for 17 June 1986, MMcW Papers. **98.** Diary for 18 and 20 June 1986, MMcW Papers. **99.** Ian Wilson, interview with author, 4 October 2012. **100.** Subsequent recollections of the June crisis for the defence leave no doubt of the rift between Tarrant and McWilliam towards the close. '[Non-executive director Philip Robinson] was revealing at lunch over Tarrant's exultation last June, that he had got me on the run, so his backing off and then signing on the final defence documents is all the more odd.' Diary for 24 February 1987, MMcW Papers. **101.** Diary for 24 June and 4 July 1986, MMcW Papers. **102.** All details are taken from Michael McWilliam's diary. **103.** Diary for 10 July 1986, MMcW Papers. **104.** Diary for 13 July 1986, MMcW Papers. **105.** Diary for 28 July 1986, MMcW Papers. **106.** 'Asia Pacific Strategy and the Wing Lung Bank, Hong Kong' by Michael McWilliam, Memorandum for the Board Meeting of 14 October 1986, SCB Box 2384. The other target under consideration was the Dah Sing Bank. The Wing Lung, controlled by the Wu family, was much the more lively prospect. **107.** 'Group-Wide Systems Planning Project – Final Report July 1986', Board Papers of 9 September 1986, SCB Box 2384. See also 'The Group-Wide Systems Plan' by David Millar, 9 October 1986, SCB Box 2384. **108.** *Financial Times*, 1 December 1986. **109.** Diary for 20 November 1986, MMcW Papers. **110.** Derek Hewett arrived as the Manager 'with a cook, a grand piano and a polo pony' and helped build a flourishing polo fraternity in Brunei in the early 1970s – the precursor to the Royal Brunei Polo and Riding Club. (Interview with author, 15 October 2013.) Colleagues thought him the best Malay speaker of all the bank's expatriates, with full command of the local idioms. He retired to a farm in Johor, the southernmost of the Malay states, and endowed a student bursary for the National University of Singapore. **111.** Diary: Review of 1987, MMcW Papers. **112.** *Financial Times*, 4 February 1987. A fuller feature article followed on 10 February. **113.** The inspectors were Peter Gerrard of City lawyers White, Lovell & King and Brian Smouha of accountants Touche Ross. There can be no doubt that the Bank leaned heavily on Barber and Graham to ask for an inquiry. McWilliam later noted in his summary of the year: 'It was made clear to them that if they did not cooperate the Bank of England was minded to proceed anyway . . . [Robin] Baillie and [Leslie] Fletcher opposed the idea and events have shown that they had the better judgement.' (Diary, 1987 Review, MMcW Papers.) **114.** There were nonetheless some individuals out in Asia who thought the inspectors could have reached a prompter conclusion. In Singapore, Colin Holland was the Standard Chartered man with the most direct ties to Khoo Teck Puat and his family. Holland died in the 1990s, but had shared his view with John Janes, a close friend and colleague ever since 1971 when the two of them passed through the bank's training programme together. 'It was his contention that the rumours of illicit loans could have been dispelled much sooner if the inspectors had put the right questions to the right people.' (John Janes, interview with author, 22 October 2013.) **115.** Diary: Review of 1987, MMcW Papers. **116.** Graham greeted the announcement with predictable relief. It was 'a strong vindication of our decision nearly a year ago to request an investigation . . . [It] has been lengthy and thorough and we can all be very pleased at the clarity of the conclusions. The episode is now behind us.' Press release, 19 January 1988, SCB Box 2381. **117.** 'Perpetual Floating Rate Notes issued by the banks' by Richard Stein, Memorandum to Directors of 27 August 1987. Stein was the bearer of (relatively) good news, insofar as a succession of skilful trades in the derivatives market had by that date reduced the portfolio's value to £15 million with a loss to the P&L of just under

£10 million – substantially less than had at first been feared.   **118.** Minutes of Audit Committee meeting, 14 April 1987, SCB Box 2381.   **119.** Diary for 15 July 1987, MMcW Papers.   **120.** 'SCB of Canada', undated Board paper (December 1987?) by Bill Brown, SCB Box 2381. An earlier account of the problem was included in a review of commercial debt provisions by David Millar, Memorandum to the Board, 7 August 1987, SCB Box 2381.   **121.** A few weeks before Citicorp's move, the Bank of England had in fact told Standard Chartered and the clearers that it wanted to see them lift their cross-border provisions to 25 per cent over the course of the next three years. (Diary for 29 April 1987, MMcW Papers.) This prompted objections from all the banks, and a series of difficult discussions – which Citicorp's decision effectively foreclosed.   **122.** Shareholder Review, paper for Board Meeting of 25 April 1995, SCB Box 2506.   **123.** *Financial Times*, 26 May 1987.   **124.** Robin Baillie, interview with author, 10 September 2013. **125.** 'Cross-Border Provisions' by Michael McWilliam, Memorandum to the Board, 8 July 1987, SCB Box 2381. When the full-year accounts for 1987 came to be filed, another £119 million was added.   **126.** 'Cross-border Provisioning' by Alan Orsich, Memorandum for the Board Meeting of 11 August 1987, SCB Box 2381.   **127.** Diary for 7 May 1987, MMcW Papers.   **128.** The terms of an offer were presented to Midland's Chairman, Kit McMahon, on 28 May: 'he accepted our offer with alacrity and expressed himself confident of being able to take it through his board tomorrow . . . It all seems a little too good to be true and I hope there are no stumbles. One worry is that PAG seems to have lost his old ebullience and self-confidence and I hope he has the grit to carry the Board when it meets.' (Diary for 28 May 1987, MMcW Papers.) The Midland Board duly went along with its Chairman's recommendation, and the Bank of England raised no objections to the deal in a subsequent meeting.   **129.** Diary for 9 June 1987, MMcW Papers.   **130.** 'Managing Capital Adequacy' by Michael McWilliam, Memorandum to the Board of 9 February 1987, SCB Box 2381. The crucial measure was the 'Risk–Assets Ratio' (RAR). The Bank required all assets to be risk-weighted by a set of standard multiples. For instance, cash carried a zero multiple (producing a zero risk asset), while property carried a multiple of 2x (meaning a £10 million building represented a £20 million risk asset). The Bank at this date was advising that the total value of the risk assets should be at least 9.5 per cent of the capital available for the absorption of losses, itself a category not without its complications. The target RAR was of course subject to change, and it rose to 10.5 per cent later in 1987.   **131.** McWilliam's proposition in February had been that the Group should issue a substantial tranche of convertible preference stock – but, as with most proposed initiatives in 1987, he soon ran into endless objections from the white knights.   **132.** 'He was somewhat taken aback but will consider', noted McWilliam. Strauss indicated in October that the idea was certainly of interest but he eventually declined the offer. Diary for 1 August, 18 October & 1 November 1986, MMcW Papers.   **133.** 'Dr Strauss mentioned that he was going overseas in a few days' time and he had found it difficult to get appointments at appropriate levels with overseas banks. The only one, apart from the Union Bank in the USA, to show the same kind of interest as previously was Morgan Guaranty Trust Company.'

(Minutes of StanBIC Board, 3 June 1986, StanBIC BRD 1/1/4.)   **134.** It is possible that the 39 per cent stake may have weakened the Group in terms of the Bank of England's metrics, given a rather metaphysical claim on the former parent investor by creditors of the South African business in the event of its failure. But contemporary records made no reference to this.   **135.** A book loss did indeed emerge eventually, recorded in the Profit and Loss statement for 1987 as an Extraordinary Item of £49.5 million. This went into the Retained Deficit for the year of £459 million, which in turn was the principal cause of a 49-per-cent reduction in the Group's reserves over the year.   **136.** 'Cross-border Provisioning' by Alan Orsich, Memorandum for the Board Meeting of 11 August 1987, SCB Box 2381.   **137.** Diary for 2 June 1987, MMcW Papers.   **138.** 'I told him about the disposal situation which he took very well and [he] had some very interesting thoughts about reserving some shares for blacks and for management.' Diary for 4 June 1987, MMcW Papers.   **139.** Diary for 13 July 1987, MMcW Papers.   **140.** Diary for 4 August 1987, MMcW Papers.   **141.** The resulting ownership of the Standard Bank was shared between Donald Gordon's Liberty Life (30 per cent), Old Mutual (20 per cent), Gold Fields South Africa (10 per cent), Rembrandt Group (10 per cent), the Standard Bank's own pension fund (5 per cent) and assorted customers and staff (the remaining 25 per cent).   **142.** Notes written for the author, 10 September 2013.   **143.** 'As regards StanBIC's future relationship with Standard Chartered it was noted . . . that there had been no hesitation on the part of the SC executives in committing themselves to continuing with the present relationship.' Minutes of the StanBIC Board, 1 September 1987, StanBIC BRD 2/1/18/2. In particular, it was agreed that the regular exchange of junior personnel should go on – and later in September two young British managers were duly despatched to Johannesburg. One of them was Gavin Laws, whose later career would finish with a long stint as Group Director of Corporate Affairs. (Interview with author, 3 October 2013.)   **144.** Quoted in *Hoisting the Standard* by Steyn and Antonie, p. 130. The Standard Bank's Chairman, Henri de Villiers, sounded a similar note in his statement for the 1987 Report and Accounts: 'Strong and stable South African institutions are now the major shareholders in StanBIC but we nevertheless regret the termination of a formal association with London.'   **145.** 'It is this special relationship which has given rise to the exceptional opportunity to acquire United Bank of Arizona.' 'Union Bank Acquisition Proposal – United Bank of Arizona' by Michael McWilliam, Memorandum for the Board Meeting of 3 September 1985, SCB Box 2387.   **146.** Minutes of Board Meeting, 17 November 1987. Harrigan finally resigned in February 1988.   **147.** Diary for 30 July 1987, MMcW Papers.   **148.** Diary for 17 November 1987, MMcW Papers.   **149.** 'Following an informal approach . . . I met with [Brian] Pitman to bury the hatchet, [and to] note the way a sensible business structure could be created, but mutually to feel [*sic*] inhibited by capital and cross-border considerations. Perhaps more to come.' (Diary: Review of 1987, MMcW Papers.)   **150.** Diary for 25 January 1988, MMcW Papers.   **151.** Diary for 3 December 1987, MMcW Papers   **152.** Diary for 1 December 1987, MMcW Papers.   **153.** Robin Leigh-Pemberton to the Chairman and Directors, 3 February 1988, MMcW Papers.   **154.** Peter Graham to Robin

Leigh-Pemberton, 29 February 1988, M McW Papers. **155.** 'Governor's Note of Conversation with Sir Peter Graham on 3 February 1988', BofE 13A281/4. **156.** 'Having been vindicated, and received a contribution from the *Financial Times* to its legal costs, Standard Chartered was content . . . [and the newspaper] said it regretted any damage and embarrassment caused to Standard Chartered by the article.' (*Financial Times*, 4 March 1988.) McWilliam sought and was given a written assurance from the Bank that his removal had nothing to do with the Inquiry. **157.** Sylvia Galpin, interview with author, 27 March 2014. **158.** Diary for 11 May 1988, M McW Papers. **159.** *The Times*, 5 March 1988. **160.** Even in retirement more than twenty years later, and in characteristically elliptic fashion, Galpin insisted his move was at least a semi-private matter, clinched at his instigation. 'I had built a relationship with Peter Graham and it seemed clear to me that it would be something he would be prepared to accept. I got the sense of things and I discussed it with Blunden who said "Yes, why not?" and finally it happened . . . I didn't feel that I was actually under any pressure from the Bank to do it. I think I'd decided that I would like to do it, and they were happy that I should.' But he made no bones about the fact that his appointment was pressed on Standard Chartered by the Bank of England: 'It had happened before . . .' (Interview with the author, 14 July 2011.) **161.** M McW Papers. **162.** Diary for 3 March 1988, M McW Papers. **163.** Memorandum from Michael McWilliam, 12 October 1987, M McW Papers.

10. RE-EMERGING MARKETS

1. Many retired Chartered men still had some post-war copies of the house magazine. Pre-war copies were already very rare, but at least the bank's own museum had a bound volume of *Curry & Rice* that started with Vol. 1 No. 1 from 1930. ('Bank's Museum', SCB Box 144.) **2.** McWilliam diary for 27 April 1988, M McW Papers. Jarecki thought the situation called for a creative solution from an investment bank and even pondered whether he and McWilliam 'could have a role here'. **3.** Galpin, interview with author, 14 July 2011. **4.** *Daily Telegraph* obituary, 30 October 2013. **5.** This perspective on the merger landscape was endorsed for the Board in July 1990 by investment bankers from Morgan Stanley. Their Managing Director, Ted Dunn, told Galpin and his colleagues that squeezed profits and rising costs had driven international banks to focus much more intently on asset quality and market share. 'Against this background, he felt that it was unlikely that a predator would seek a hostile takeover of Standard Chartered at this time . . . Mr Dunn also reviewed the other major UK, Continental and Australian banks and concluded that in his view these banks had other priorities on which to concentrate and were unlikely to seek a contested bid for a bank such as Standard Chartered.' (Minutes of the Board meeting of 17 July 1990, SCB Box 2390.) **6.** 'He asked to come and see me . . . [so] I started talking to him when I was on gardening leave, sitting in my little office and not doing any Bank of England stuff.' (Galpin, interview with author, 14 July 2011.) **7.** The Earl of Inchcape had joined the Board in 1969, having served on the Court of the Chartered Bank since 1952. Sir David Mitchell, the ex-Treasury mandarin, and Sir Idwal Pugh had been Directors since 1973 and 1979, respectively.   **8.** Holmes à Court indicated to his fellow Directors in September 1988 that it was his intention to step down soon. The same meeting heard that Alan Bond had asked for a seat on the Board. This request was turned down. (Minutes of the Board Meeting of 13 September 1988, SCB Box 2383.)   **9.** That left only three survivors from the Board of 1986. Philip Robinson and The Lord Pennock, who succeeded Fletcher as Deputy Chairman, retired in May 1991. Robin Baillie remained a Director until May 1994.   **10.** A court in Arizona in 1992 awarded Standard Chartered damages of $338 million on six counts. This was gratifying for the Group, but awkward questions arose from the start over Price Waterhouse's ability to comply, even assuming success in the appeals process. 'The award . . . is the single largest such award in the history of Arizona and believed to be the largest ever made against an accounting firm . . . [But] there are serious issues which will have to be addressed in any settlement negotiations as to the ability of Price Waterhouse to pay a figure approaching this order of magnitude. It is not in our interests to push Price Waterhouse into Chapter 11 and put at risk stage payments which will inevitably be part of any settlement.' ('Litigation against Price Waterhouse' by Martin Hayman, Memorandum for the Board Meeting of 20 May 1992, SCB Box 2422.)   **11.** The decision to abandon Bishopsgate was not taken lightly, though. 'The Board recognised . . . the effect of any announcement [of its sale] on the morale of staff and the importance of sensitive handling of staff interests.' (Minutes of the Board Meeting of 28 February 1989, SCB Box 2383.)   **12.** Minutes of the Board Meeting of 13 December 1988, SCB Box 2383.   **13.** Annual Report 1988, pp. 8–15 and p. 24.   **14.** 'Strategic Review Team Visits: Findings', Report by CRA, 16 March 1989, SCB Box 2390.   **15.** 'Background to the Breakout Review 1988–91', Paper 1, Section 1 ('The Scene as it was in October 1988'), Report by CRA, July 1991, SCB Box 2313.   **16.** 'Strategy Review', 17 July 1990, SCB Box 2390. Galpin's introduction to the 1990 Review provided an eloquent summary of the 1989 conference's outcome.   **17.** The statistics were included in a key section, 'The Global Economic Scene', of CRA's July 1990 Strategy Review, SCB Box 2390.   **18.** David Moir, interview with author, 19 December 2011.   **19.** 'Strategy Review', 17 July 1990, SCB Box 2390.   **20.** Interview with author, 13 September 2013. One of Rees's first presentations at Board level, in November 1990, pointed out that the Treasury operation had no market-risk monitors, no trading limits, no management-information systems, no transfer-pricing rules and very few front-office dealing systems. His Personal Assistant suggested this level of candour might be a career-limiting move, to which Rees had a ready reply. 'I said, "if I don't wake them up, I don't want to be here".'   **21.** Insisting on a brutal contraction of the UK network, for example, they closed down the flagship branch in Manchester – disregarding the invaluable connections it had forged over the past fifty years with Chinese customers, most of whom were instantly lost to HSBC.   **22.** 'Chairman's Progress Review', Report by CRA, 17 July 1991, SCB Box 2313.   **23.** 'Chairman's Progress Review', Report by CRA, 17 July 1991, SCB Box 2313.   **24.** Malcolm Williamson, interview with author,

9 October 2013. 'Donnie used to come and see me regularly, trying to sell back the rather large investment he had made.'   **25.** Galpin naturally took a slightly different line in explaining the decision to Strauss. 'After consideration he had advised Standard Bank that a closer relationship with South Africa at this stage carried potential political risks for the Group and that there was consequently no purpose in pursuing the discussions further.' Minutes of Board Meeting, 26 February 1991, SCB Box 2313.   **26.** 'Strategy Review', 9 July 1991, SCB Box 2313.   **27.** The approach to Moir was made by David Smith (formerly Zimbabwe's first Finance Minister), who set out the proposition from the Grindlays staff. 'I asked why, and he said, "Well, the chaps there, they know you and they want it to be kept confidential – but they want the bank to go to you guys, are you interested?"' (Moir, interview with author, 19 December 2011.) The anecdote is especially of interest, given the later story of Grindlays in India.   **28.** Galpin, interview with author, 14 July 2011.   **29.** 'Strategy Review', 9 July 1991, SCB Box 2313.   **30.** The mid-year forecast for 1991's results showed a net loss for Corporate Banking of £51 million. This compared with encouraging predictions for Retail Banking (£88 million), Treasury/FIG/ Mocatta (£110 million) and Trade Finance (£63 million). ('Strategy Review', 9 July 1991, SCB Box 2313.)   **31.** 'Standard Chartered Australia – Strategy' by Peter McSloy, Memorandum for the Board, May 1989, SCB Box 2390.   **32.** An additional £5 million was spent on buying out the minority shareholders of SCB Australia – at a 32 per cent premium to the current share price. Minority holders of the preferred stock landed an even bigger premium, of 43 per cent. ('Australia', by Malcolm Williamson, Memorandum for the Board Meeting of 26 February 1991, SCB Box 2313.)   **33.** Williamson, interview with author, 9 October 2013.   **34.** Barry Northrop, interview with author, 31 August 2011.   **35.** 'Credit Management' by Malcolm Williamson, Memorandum to the Board, 25 May 1993, SCB Box 2440.   **36.** Other well-publicized debtors of the Group included Isosceles (£140 million), Magnet (£106 million), Heron (£36 million) and Tiny Rowland's Lonrho (£134 million). (Minutes of the Risk Review Committee, 31 March 1992, SCB Box 2422.)   **37.** By the start of 1993, corporate outstandings in the UK amounted to £3.2 billion, compared with £3.0 billion in Hong Kong. The next biggest territory was Singapore with £1.3 billion. 'Credit Management' by Malcolm Williamson, Memorandum to the Board, 25 May 1993, SCB Box 2440. **38.** Northrop, interview with author, 31 August 2011.   **39.** The Sunday meeting brought together 'available Directors and Advisers'. Details were provided in the Minutes of the Board Meeting of 20 May 1992, SCB Box 2422.   **40.** 'India' by Malcolm Williamson, Memorandum to the Board, 20 May 1992, SCB Box 2422.   **41.** Minutes of the Board Meeting of 29 July 1992, SCB Box 2422. **42.** Minutes of the Board Meeting of 6 October 1992, SCB Box 2422. The funds committed to India comprised $800 million at the RBI and $200 million at the State Bank of India. The cancelled arrangement was known as the Foreign Currency Bank and Other Deposits Scheme (or FCBOD).   **43.** 'Strategic Direction', Note to Board by Rodney Galpin, 1 October 1992, SCB Box 2422.   **44.** Minutes of the Board Meeting of 3 March 1993, SCB Box 2440.   **45.** Northrop, interview with author, 31 August 2011. The only acknowledgement of this 'counter-claim problem'

in the 1992 Annual Report came deep in the Notes to the Accounts, as Note 19 (d), which stated that the Group was 'aware of claims against it amounting to £12 million'. Of course any reference to the kind of numbers being countenanced by Northrop would have been calamitous. **46.** *Financial Times*, 11 March 1993. **47.** Shareholders' funds had been depleted by 45 per cent in 1987, 17 per cent in 1989 and 2 per cent in 1991. Standing at £1,004 million at the end of 1992, they were still 22 per cent short of the £1,295 million held at the end of 1986. **48.** Peter Rodgers in the *Independent*, 12 August 1993. **49.** According to a presentation made by a joint Schroders/Goldman Sachs team, 'The recent rise in the share price could be explained almost entirely by investors' growing interest in the Asia Pacific Region and, in particular, Hong Kong.' Minutes of the Board Meeting of 21 December 1993, SCB Box 2440. **50.** Northrop, interview with author, 31 August 2011. **51.** The provision covered 80 per cent of the Bombay branch's estimated losses, leaving £70 million to be recouped from arbitration and court proceedings. ('India: Full Year Report 1993 and Joint Parliamentary Committee Report' by David Brougham, Memorandum for the Board Meeting of 25 January 1994, SCB Box 2440.) This approach was vindicated over the next few years: by April 1996, the Board was being told that £100 million had been recovered. The success of this modest mop-up operation, though, does little to mitigate the enormity of the illicit gains that must have been made by some individuals in 1992–3. As the Parliamentary Committee in Delhi pointed out, 'monies stolen have yet to be traced'. And Standard Chartered's losses were just part of the story. The total value of the securities involved in the India Scam was estimated by the Committee, according to Brougham's summary, at between £783 million and £1.8 billion. **52.** Twenty-five banks were fined a total of £31 million for regulatory breaches. Standard Chartered received the second largest fine (behind Citibank) and paid out £7.6 million on a 'without prejudice' basis that implied no acceptance of guilt. ('Standard Chartered India' by Martin Fish, Presentation to the Board in Bombay, 13 November 1994, SCB Box 2576.) **53.** 'For many years I had special words written out for me by Standard Chartered, that I had to put in place to cover accusations that I might have been involved.' (Interview with author, 14 July 2011.) **54.** 'Shareholder Review', Memorandum for the Board, 25 April 1985, SCB Box 2506. **55.** Sir Patrick Gillam, interview with author, 29 November 2011. **56.** John McFarlane, interview with author, 22 January 2014. **57.** 'Progress Report on Organisation Re-Structuring' by KPMG Management Consultants, presented to the Board, 1 December 1992. As the Minutes made clear, it provided a less than rousing valedictory for Galpin, who confirmed his retirement that same day. 'By way of background, the [KPMG] team had noted that certain of the key strategies had not been implemented. The existing top management structure was complex and the role of Head Office unclear; some major management processes appeared to be weak, and parochial attitudes continued.' **58.** Malcolm Williamson, interview with author, 9 October 2013. **59.** 'WestLB Profile', unsigned Board Paper, 26 February 1991, SCB Box 2313. **60.** Minutes of the Board Meeting of 22 February 1994, SCB Box 2440. **61.** Williamson, interview with author, 9 October 2013. **62.** 'Standard Chartered Bank', Case Study by Aidan Douglas, Jessica

Spungin, Norman Kurtis and Scott Hockett under the supervision of Sumantra Ghoshal, London Business School, 1996, p. 12. **63.** 'Management Succession' by Geoff Armstrong and Martin Fish, 26 February 1991, Memorandum for the Board Meeting of 26 February 1991, SCB Box 2390. It incorporated the findings of the 1990 Survey. **64.** 'Management Succession' by Geoff Armstrong and Martin Fish, 26 February 1991, Memorandum for the Board Meeting of 26 February 1991, SCB Box 2390. **65.** Minutes of the Board Meeting of 23 February 1993, SCB Box 2440. **66.** Minutes of the Remuneration and Personnel Strategy Committee, 17 December 1991, SCB Box 2313. **67.** Minutes of the Board Meeting of 25 February 1992, SCB Box 2422, recording discussion of a Board Paper 'Management Succession' by Martin Fish. **68.** Minutes of the Remuneration and Personnel Strategy Committee, 31 March 1992, SCB Box 2422. **69.** John Brinsden, interview with author, 28 March 2012. **70.** A Representative's Office was established in Myanmar (Burma), for example, following a visit by Patrick Gillam in April 1995. (Minutes of the Board Meeting of 4 May 1995, SCB Box 2506.) **71.** Minutes of the Board Meeting of 31 October 1995, SCB Box 2506. **72.** 'The People Challenge' by Andrew Hunter, Presentation to the Board, 13 July 1997, SCB Box 2605. **73.** Theresa Foo, interview with author, 9 November 2011. Though Singaporean by nationality, she was actually from an Indonesian-Chinese family and had only moved with them to Singapore when she was thirteen years old. But English was her first language, and American management was her background. **74.** For the year to December 1971, Hong Kong reported working profits of £2.32 million, which compared with £1.22 million from Singapore and £1.26 million from Malaysia including Sarawak, Sabah and Brunei ('Regional Profit & Loss Analyses', Paper for the S&CBG Board Meeting of 6 June 1972, SCB Box 363). **75.** *MMC Report on the Proposed Mergers*, January 1982, HMSO Cmnd 8472 **76.** 'Annual Working Profits for 1982' by Stuart Tarrant, Memo for the Executive Committee, 23 February 1983, SCB Box 1721. **77.** Papers for Special Board Meeting, 20 April 1982, SCB Box 867. **78.** To be more precise, Standard Chartered and HSBC as the two commercial banks issuing bank-notes in the Colony were required by the Hong Kong authorities to purchase matching 'certificates of indebtedness' using US dollars at a fixed rate (of HK$7.80 to US$1) – and to sell them back at the same rate in the event of cutting back their notes in circulation. This same modus operandi is in place today, with the addition of the Bank of China (from 1994) as a third bank-note issuer. The Standard Chartered's share of the issuance market was around 12 per cent in 1983, and at the end of 2014 stood at 10.8 per cent (compared with 26.5 per cent for the Bank of China and 62.7 per cent for HSBC). It might be noted here that no interest is payable on the certificates of indebtedness. The right to issue HK dollars may be regarded as a useful way of promoting the good name and quasi-official status of the bank, in other words, but it amounts to a marketing expense. As for the wider implications of the arrangement, 'the monetary system functions exactly as it would, were the Monetary Authority, rather than the note-issuing banks, to be the sole issuer of currency'. (Tony Latter, *Hong Kong's Money: The History, Logic and Operation of the Currency Peg*, Hong Kong University Press, 2007, p. 58.) **79.** 'Strategic Review Team

Visits: Findings', Report by CRA, 16 March 1989, SCB Box 2390. **80.** 'Hong Kong' by A. Nicolle, Memorandum to the Board, 26 November 1991, SCB Box 2313. **81.** 'Hong Kong' by A. Nicolle, Memorandum to the Board, 26 November 1991, SCB Box 2313. **82.** 'Options for the Group' by Richard Stein, Memorandum for the Board Meeting of 1 December 1992, SCB Box 2422. **83.** Minutes of the Board Meeting of 23 February 1993, SCB Box 2440. **84.** Ian Wilson, interview with author, 4 October 2012. **85.** Ian Wilson, interview with author, 4 October 2012. **86.** 'The Run on the Bank – Hong Kong' by Malcolm Williamson, Memorandum for the Board Meeting of 1 October 1991, SCB Box 2313. A special award was also made by Galpin to the staff in Hong Kong 'in recognition of their excellent performance'. Most of the funds withdrawn by customers had by then been re-deposited. The Hong Kong branch was left holding a huge surplus of HSBC-styled HK$ notes, which it had effectively purchased but for which it now had no further use. They were returned within days to HSBC and credited to Standard Chartered's HK$ account there. **87.** 'Hong Kong Country Overview' by Ian Wilson and 'Personal Banking – New Values' by Doreen Chan, presentations to the Board, 23 April 1996, SCB Box 2506. **88.** 'Eastward, look – Citicorp in Asia', *The Economist*, 24 October 1992. **89.** Williamson, interview with author, 9 October 2013. **90.** 'Standard Chartered Bank India' by Martin Fish, Presentation to the Board, 13 November 1994, SCB Box 2576. **91.** 'Hong Kong', unsigned Memorandum for the Board Meeting of 5 November 2992, SCB Box 2422. **92.** Williamson, interview with author, 9 October 2013. **93.** 'Hong Kong', unsigned Memorandum for the Board Meeting of 5 November 1992, SCB Box 2422. **94.** 'Schroff' column, *Far East Economic Review*, 7 July 1994. **95.** Steve Wish, interview with author, 22 July 2014. I am indebted to him for clarifying this business. **96.** 'Strategic Direction' by Rodney Galpin, Note to Board, 1 October 1992, SCB Box 2422. **97.** FIB was acquired by Wells Fargo Bank, which cancelled the Co-operation Agreement and paid Standard Chartered $15 million in compensation. (Minutes of the Board, 26 February 1996, SCB Box 2506.) **98.** Gavin Laws, interview with author, 20 November 2013. **99.** The company, SureCorp, did the Group a favour around 1994 by pointing out, at the behest of the former First Interstate staffers, that their software could deliver far broader benefits that the trade teams in Hong Kong and elsewhere yet realized. 'We said "don't be silly", but they showed us then what we could really do, and the results were very powerful.' (Laws, interview with author, 20 November 2013.) **100.** Williamson, interview with author, 9 October 2013. **101.** Minutes of the Board Meeting of 26 June 1990, SCB Box 2390. **102.** 'China Report' by G. G. Janes, Memorandum for the Board of 13 May 1982, SCB Box 867. **103.** Two of the first borrowers, according to the G. G. Janes Report, were Guangdong Trust & Investment Corporation and Fujian Investment Enterprises Corporation. **104.** G. G. Janes Report. **105.** Minutes of Standing Committee of the Board, 17 April 1984. **106.** Diary for 10–14 October 1985, MMcW Papers. **107.** 'China Business Briefings', compiled by the Group with assistance from Baker & Mackenzie, Batey Burn and Deloitte Touche Tohmatsu, 1 May 1993, SCB Box 2440. China's negotiations to sign up to the GATT were in fact to collapse before the end of 1994, and were not finally completed until 2001, by which time the GATT community had been superseded by the World Trade Organization.   **108.** 'The Board discussed the possibility of a PRC investment in the Company. It was reported that the Chairman, Chief Executive and Mr David Moir would each be making separate visits to China in the following months and the issue would be reconsidered once these visits had taken place.' (Minutes of the Board Meeting of 22 February 1994, SCB Box 2440.   **109.** Minutes of the Board Meeting of 28 June 1994, SCB Box 2440.   **110.** Presentations to the Board on China and Hong Kong by John McFarlane, Ian Wilson, Lance Browne and others, 23 April 1996, SCB Box 2506.   **111.** Foo, interview with author, 9 November 2011.   **112.** McFarlane presentation, April 1996, and 'Project Sunrise' by David Brougham, Memorandum for the Board Meeting of 17 December 1996, SCB Box 2506. Brougham's commentary in December emphasized that he did not attach much credence to the worst-case scenario. In fact, 'one couldn't ask for a more favourable economic platform off which to launch this economic union'.   **113.** For overviews of the various analyses, see Ramon Moreno, 'What Caused East Asia's Financial Crisis?' *FRBSF Economic Letter*, Federal Reserve Bank of San Francisco, August 1998; and Giancarlo Corsetti, Paolo Pesenti and Nouriel Rubini, 'What Caused the Asian Currency and Financial Crisis?', paper published by the Federal Reserve Bank of New York, April 1999.   **114.** Paul Krugman, *The Return of Depression Economics and the Crisis of 2008*, Penguin, 2008, p. 92.   **115.** Group Chief Executive's Review, 26 February 1997, from the 1996 Annual Report, p. 7. 'Our key strategic aims for 1997 . . . [include maintaining] rigorous controls and effective compliance, in order to sustain a "no surprises" culture . . .'   **116.** 'Review of Strategic Initiatives Programme (SIP)', unsigned paper for Board Away-Day, 7 July 1992, SCB Box 2422.   **117.** From a high of 1082p on 7 August 1997 to a low of 543p on 14 January 1998.   **118.** Minutes of the Board Meeting of 21 October 1997, SCB Box 2605.   **119.** 'Treasury Strategy' by Mike Rees, Presentation to the Board, 29 September 1998, SCB Box 2605.   **120.** 'Group Taxation and Corporate Treasury Report' by Charlotte Morgan, Memorandum for the Board Meeting of 21 October 1997, SCB Box 2605. Off-shore selling of currencies that were under mounting pressure ran the risk of incurring fierce rebukes from their guardian central bankers, as this report carefully acknowledged. 'We need to distance ourselves from any potential criticism which might jeopardise our relationship with governments and regulators.'   **121.** Rees, interview with author, 13 September 2013.   **122.** I am indebted to K. Thippakorn, who joined the staff of the bank in 1971, for her recollections.   **123.** 'Thailand Annual Review' by K. N. Radford, 4 September 1984, SCB Box 2387.   **124.** Galpin, interview with the author, 14 July 2011. His source was Bill Brown, who had managed the Bangkok branch from 1973 to 1976.   **125.** 'We gave our overseas friends our credit card to pay for their evening because we were the hosts, and told them just to mail it back to us. We said "something has come up, we have to leave!".' (Matt Sweeney, interview with author, 31 July 2013.)   **126.** 'Mexico' by David Brougham, Memorandum for the Board Meeting of 7 February 1995, SCB Box 2506. The deal with First Interstate Bank had bequeathed the Group representative branches in Mexico City and Monterrey. At the time of the peso's collapse, it had outstanding commitments of

$455 million, mostly related to short-term trade credits. The impact on the Group was 'expected to be neutral'. **127.** Treasury income was budgeted at £24 million a month through the first quarter of 1998. The outcome for the three months was £72 million, £48 million and £40 million. ('Status of the Budget and Latest Forecast for 1998' by Malcolm Williamson, Memorandum for the Board Meeting of 7 May 1998, SCB Box 2605.) **128.** Peter Sands, interview with author, 15 December 2014. **129.** Williamson, interview with author, 9 October 2013. **130.** Martin Taylor, interview with author, 27 November 2013. **131.** Board Strategy Discussion Papers, 20 January 1998, SCB Box 2605. **132.** Letter to employees, 13 January 1998, SCB Box 2605. **133.** 'Strategic Options in a Changed Environment', McKinsey Memorandum to the Board, 17 February 1998, SCB Box 2605. **134.** Gillam to the Board Members, 18 February 1998, SCB Box 2605. **135.** It is possible that the subject of Barclays was broached at this meeting, for a discussion of Group Strategy was recorded – but only as a Confidential Minute, which is not included in the archived Board papers. (The minutes for 23 February 1998 are included in the papers for the 21 April 1998 Board meeting, held in Kuala Lumpur.) **136.** 'It was a handshake without a legal commitment, but there was basically a very clear understanding that, when Malcolm left, I would take over from him.' Rana Talwar, interview with author, 28 January 2014.

11. METAMORPHOSIS

1. Gillam to the Board Members, 18 February 1998, SCB Box 2605. **2.** Mike Rees, quoted in Minutes of the Board Meeting of 15 April 1999, SCB Box 2607. **3.** Minutes of the Board Meeting of 15 April 1999, SCB Box 2607. **4.** Salinee Wangtal, Assistant Governor at the Central Bank, spoke by telephone to Gillam and conveyed a succinct message from the Governor: 'Don't try to be stingy'. (Salinee Wangtal, interview with author, 17 April 2013.) **5.** Atchara Petchsangroj, interview with author, 18 April 2013. **6.** David Moir, interview with author, 19 December 2011. **7.** 'Proposal to acquire PT Bank Bali Tbk' by David Moir and Fred Enlow, Presentation to the Board, 15 April 1999, SCB Box 2607. **8.** The Jakarta branch froze the account of a customer, Yee Mei Mei, whose substantial cash transactions – supposedly as the agent for a bank based in Vanuatu, Dragon Bank International – it believed to be improper. She sued the Group and was awarded £4.5 million in damages. This triggered a bitter legal feud, with the local country manager accused of embezzlement and threatened with imprisonment. One of the non-executive Directors, Cob Stenham, visited him in Jakarta to help defuse the situation – which a few months later was essentially overtaken by the collapse of the Indonesian currency. In his report back to the Board on the affair, Stenham 'complimented the Country CEO, David Hawkins, on his judgement and steadfastness through a very difficult and unpleasant situation'. (Minutes of the Board Meeting of 22 April 1997, SCB Box 2605.) **9.** *Guardian*, 25 November 1999. **10.** 'The People Challenge' by Andrew Hunter, Presentation to the Board, 13 July 1997, SCB Box 2605. **11.** Grindlays offered the chance to expand the

Group in India (50 branches), Bangladesh (9), Pakistan (12) Nepal (8), Jordan (11) and Palestine (3). Duplicated branches in other countries, including Sri Lanka and the UAE, were to be merged together.   **12.** John McFarlane, interview with author, 22 January 2014.   **13.** Annual Report 2010, p. 7.   **14.** Minutes of the Board Meeting of 26 March 2001, SCB/General Corporate Secretariat (GCS).   **15.** Senior executive, interview with author, 5 September 2013.   **16.** Memorandum to the Board by Rana Talwar, 13 June 2000. Both Visa and Mastercard were issued under the Manhattan brand. Its operating profits, forecast at about US$40 million for 2000, compared with around US$90 million forecast for the Group's existing credit card. **17.** Minutes of the Board Meeting of 19 September 2000, SCB/GCS.   **18.** Minutes of the Board Meeting of 20 June 2000, SCB/GCS.   **19.** Minutes of the Board Meeting of 19 June 2001, SCB/GCS.   **20.** Rana Talwar, interview with author, 28 January 2014. His recollections are the basis for much of the narrative in this paragraph.   **21.** 'Latin-American Proposed Acquisition', unsigned paper for Board Meeting of 10 November 1997, SCB Box 2605. The full title of the bank was Banco Exterior de los Andes y de Espana SA.   **22.** 'Update on UBS Acquisition' by Roland B. Bandelier for Board Meeting of 19 September 2000, SCB Box 2507.   **23.** Minutes of the Board Meeting of 22 April 1997, SCB Box 2605 and of 21 September 1999, SCB Box 2507.   **24.** Interview with author, 1 August 2013. I am indebted to Bob McDonald for copies of the memorandum that he prepared for the Board in the aftermath of the crisis, 'Lessons Learned', and other internal papers relating to 9/11, all of which I have drawn upon heavily for my account of events. **25.** Many were collected for a 26-page 'Corporate Memory Booklet' produced by the New York office's External Affairs department, edited by Rattana Promrak and illustrated with photographs by staff members John Biscette, Michael McVicker and Werner Lederer.   **26.** Matt Millett, interview with author, 30 July 2013.   **27.** The Minutes of the Board Meeting for 25 January 2002 recorded that the Chief Executive, Mervyn Davies, had visited the New York Fed, where its President, W. McDonough, 'had been very complimentary about Standard Chartered's performance in the aftermath of 11 September 2001'.   **28.** 'Lessons Learned' by Bob McDonald, Memorandum to the Board, October 2001, p. 6.   **29.** Interview with author, 31 July 2013. **30.** Talwar, interview with author, 28 January 2014. 'I was firmly of the view that we had far more potential to create value as a business focused on the emerging markets than by becoming a mish-mash with a very London-centric British institution.'   **31.** Tim Miller, interview with author, 30 May 2013.   **32.** 'Project Victoria' by David Stileman, Presentation to Board, Minutes of 28 October 2002, SCB/GCS.   **33.** Minutes of the Board Meeting of 18 June 2002, SCB/GCS. **34.** Jan Verplancke, interview with author, 11 July 2014.   **35.** Verplancke, interview with author, 11 July 2014.   **36.** In 2000, Consumer Banking Profits before Provisions were £625 million, compared with Wholesale Banking Profits before Provisions of £558 million. The net provisions for the two divisions were £121 million and £189 million respectively. (Annual Report, 2000.)   **37.** Ong Chong Hye, interview with author, 11 February 2014.   **38.** Mike DeNoma, interview with author, 28 January 2014.   **39.** DeNoma, interview with author, 28 January 2014.   **40.** 'The Growth of Consumer Credit in Asia', *Hong Kong Monetary*

Authority Quarterly Bulletin, March 2005, pp. 16–20.   **41.** Minutes of the Board Meeting of 25 September 2001, SCB/GCS. DeNoma presented his analysis of the bankruptcies problem in Hong Kong, and its likely impact on revenues. As the Minutes drily noted of the ensuing discussion, 'There was concern that mortgages may also be affected in future.'   **42.** Minutes of the Board Meeting of 29 March 2004, SCB/GCS.   **43.** Minutes of the Board Meeting of 8 May 2003, SCB/GCS.   **44.** Richard Roberts and David Kynaston, *The Lion Wakes, A Modern History of HSBC*, Profile Books, 2015, pp. 476–8. 'HSBC ROARS: THE BANK GRABS THE LEAD OVER RIVALS IN CHINA' was the galling (for Standard Chartered) headline on the front cover of the *Far Eastern Economic Review* on 19 August 2004.   **45.** Minutes of the Board Meeting of 19 February 2001, SCB/GCS. **46.** Minutes of the Board Meeting of 8 May 2003, SCB/GCS. Commenting on a Board presentation by DeNoma, Sands observed that City investors were likely to be disappointed if the Group made no move into the Korean market.   **47.** Gareth Bullock, interview with author, 7 October 2014. My account of the KFB acquisition story is largely based on his recollections. I am also indebted to Sir Thomas Harris for recalling the significance of the episode.   **48.** Bullock, interview with author, 7 October 2014.   **49.** Alan Plumb was hired in 1985 as a Director of Standard Chartered Asia in Hong Kong, to be resident in Seoul and head of the merchant banking business there. 'With Korean staff on the ground we had better access to the market than most of the foreign banks. We were capturing a couple of mandates a week for new issues in Hong Kong.' (Interview with author, 12 March 2012.) The bank was ranked fourth out of thirty-seven foreign banks in the country in the early 1990s but its profit performance by then was patchy at best. ('East Asia Overview' by Tony Mauger, Presentation to Board Strategy Session of 23–25 April 1995, SCB Box 2506.)   **50.** Bullock, interview with author, 27 January 2014.   **51.** Minutes of the Board Meetings of 14 June 2005 and 1 August 2005, SCB/GCS. **52.** 'A "Customer Risk Management" Business Strategy' by Paul Barker and Peter Wood, presentation for the Board of 24 February 1997, SCB Box 2605. It was accompanied by a 24-page 'Introduction', replete with graphs, charts and diagrams to illustrate the difference between Vanilla Products and Structured Products. **53.** Peter Wood to All Members of the Board, 12 February 1997, SCB Box 2605. **54.** Off-the-record interview with author, January 2014.   **55.** Jaspal Bindra, interview with author, 5 September 2013.   **56.** Minutes of the Board Meeting of 12 September 2006, SCB/GCS.   **57.** A former British diplomat, working as a banker in Tehran by 1979, wrote an account of the revolution in which he recalled paying a visit to the head of Standard Chartered's foreign-exchange department after the attack. 'He and his staff had been left with only scattered files and papers. There they were, sitting on the floor out in his makeshift office, trying to sort out charred and crumpled documents and preparing telexes for banks abroad to ask them what payments or transfers were due so that they could begin to reconstitute their records.' (Desmond Harney, *The Priest and the King: Eyewitness Account of the Iranian Revolution*, British Academic Press, 1997.) My thanks to David Millar for alerting me to this memoir.   **58.** 'Middle East and South Asia – An Overview', presentation to the Board by Jim Allhusen, Minutes of the Board Meeting of

13 November 1994, SCB/GCS.   **59.** Quoted in the Factual Statement accompanying the Deferred Prosecution Agreement reached between the Group and the US authorities in December 2012, para. 23.   **60.** Ibid, para. 31.   **61.** Ibid, para. 36.   **62.** 'People Strategy' by Tracy Clarke, Presentation to the Board, 1 April 2008, SCB/GCS.   **63.** Minutes of the Board Meeting of 27 February 2006, SCB/GCS. Managers interviewed 950 applicants who survived a searching programme of online tests. The 2006 Annual Report noted that 70,000 graduate applications had been received over the year, presumably including those for regular positions as well as the training programme.   **64.** 'The People Challenge' by Andrew Hunter, Presentation to the Board, 13 July 1997, SCB Box 2605.   **65.** Shirley Wee, interview with author, 5 September 2013.   **66.** Minutes of the Board Meeting of 16 September 2003, SCB/GCS.   **67.** Richard Meddings, interview with author, 4 December 2013.   **68.** 'Africa' by D. G. Grant, Presentation to the Board Meeting of 23 May 1991, SCB Box 2313.   **69.** 'Overview of Africa and Standard Chartered Bank's African Development' by Jonathan Frimpong-Ansah, 19 April 1991, SCB Box 2313. Frimpong-Ansah reminded the Board that a new era of 'reform and restructuring' had effectively restored relations between the IMF and Africa's debtor countries in recent years ('here Standard Chartered Bank played an important pioneering role in providing bridging finance in a number of cases') and suggested the Group was 'better prepared than most' to benefit from the changed mood across the continent.   **70.** Minutes of the Board Meeting of 23 May 1991, SCB Box 2313.   **71.** Minutes of the Board Meeting of 6 October 1992, SCB Box 2313.   **72.** Minutes of the Board Meeting of 5 November 1992, SCB Box 2313. They included Nedbank and First Bank – but emphatically not SBSA. **73.** Patrick Gillam, interview with author, 29 November 2011.   **74.** Chris Keljik, interview with author, 24 November 2011.   **75.** Bill Moore, note to author, 11 March 2014.   **76.** Richard Etemesi, interview with author, 28 January 2014. **77.** 'Kenya' by Tony Groag, Presentation to Board Meeting of 22 October 1996. **78.** 'Standard Chartered in Africa – The Hidden Jewel' by Chris Keljik, Presentation to Board Meeting of 22 October 1996. His numbers profiled a doubling of working profits in 1996, compared with 1993, with contributions from four regions: West Africa (£19 million), East Africa (£29 million), Zimbabwe (£25 million) and Southern Africa (£9 million), the latter comprising Botswana, Zambia and South Africa. **79.** 'Standard Chartered in Africa' by Chris Keljik, Board presentation, March 1998, SCB Box 2605.   **80.** Ebby Essoka, interview with author, 27 January 2014.   **81.** Minutes of the Board Meeting of 1 April 2008, SCB/GCS.   **82.** Minutes of the Board Meeting of 16 April 2002, SCB/GCS.   **83.** Minutes of the Board Meeting of 12 September 2006, SCB/GCS.   **84.** Minutes of the Board Meeting of 30 July 2008, SCB/GCS.   **85.** Richard Etemesi, interview with author, 28 January 2014.   **86.** SCB Annual Reports 2006 & 2007.   **87.** Bill Moore, interview with author, 10 March 2014.   **88.** Minutes of the Board Meeting of 10 December 2002, SCB/GCS.   **89.** Minutes of the Board Meeting of 8 January 2004, SCB/GCS. **90.** Minutes of the Board Meeting of 21 April 2010, SCB/GCS.   **91.** Minutes of two Board Meetings of 20 November 2006, SCB/GCS.   **92.** Richard Meddings, interview with author, 26 November 2013.   **93.** Minutes of the Board Meeting of

11 September 2007, SCB/GCS.   **94.** Peter Sands, interview with author, 27 November 2013.   **95.** Annual Report 2007, note 52, p. 155.   **96.** Sands, interview with author, 27 November 2013.   **97.** Minutes of the Board Meeting of 7 May 2008, SCB/GCS.   **98.** Minutes of the Board Meeting of 30 July 2008, SCB/GCS.   **99.** Sands, interview with author, 27 November 2013.

12. RIDERS ON THE STORM

1. Minutes of the Board meeting of 7 December 2011, SCB/GCS.   **2.** 'Financial Institutions Strategy' by Papadopoulos and Shankar, Presentation to Board, Minutes of 17 June 2008, SCB/GCS. Revenues from the business conducted with financial institutions accounted for 30 per cent of the total for Wholesale Banking, and this excluded fees earned from banks as counter-parties in trade-financing contracts.   **3.** 'Technology Update' by Jan Verplancke, Presentation to Board, Minutes of 27 October 2009, SCB/GCS.   **4.** Quoted in Anat Admati and Martin Hellwig, *The Bankers' New Clothes, What's Wrong with Banking and What to Do about It*, Princeton University Press, 2013, p. 11.   **5.** Shriti Vadera, interview with author, 12 June 2014. The following account of the post-Lehman events draws heavily on her recollections, as well as those of the Group's own executives.   **6.** Vadera, interview with author, 12 June 2014.   **7.** Vadera, interview with author, 12 June 2014.   **8.** Peter Sands, interview with author, 10 March 2014.   **9.** Vadera, interview with author, 12 June 2014.   **10.** Tim Waddell, interview with author, 28 March 2014.   **11.** Richard Meddings, interview with author, 26 November 2013.   **12.** Minutes of the Board meeting of 31 March 2009, SCB/GCS.   **13.** Minutes of the Board meeting of 10 December 2008, SCB/GCS.   **14.** Minutes of the Board meeting of 2 October 2008, SCB/GCS.   **15.** Minutes of the Board meeting of 15 September 2009, SCB/GCS.   **16.** 'I thought that Mervyn was going to take the job; he seemed certainly very positive and very interested in it . . . [The contract] was designed around [the] input he'd made about what sort of incentive arrangement he thought would be appropriate . . .' (Sir Philip Hampton, interview with author, 28 January 2015.)   **17.** Minutes of the Board meeting of 1 April 2008, SCB/GCS.   **18.** Minutes of the Board meeting of 25 January 2010, SCB/GCS.   **19.** Minutes of the Board meeting of 22 March 2010, SCB/GCS.   **20.** Minutes of the Board meeting of 8 December 2009, SCB/GCS.   **21.** Minutes of the Board meeting of 24 January 2011, SCB/GCS.   **22.** Sean Wallace, interview with author, 15 January 2014.   **23.** Sands, interview with author, 10 March 2014.   **24.** Sands, interview with author, 10 March 2014.   **25.** Minutes of the Board meeting of 22 April 2009, SCB/GCS.   **26.** Minutes of the Board meeting of 31 March 2009, SCB/GCS.   **27.** Diana Layfield, interview with author, 22 January 2014.   **28.** 'Towards the end of 2010, the Standard announced that it no longer had ambitions to set up a universal bank on other continents or in countries such as Brazil, Russia or Turkey. Instead, it would focus on its "calling card" of Africa.' (Richard Steyn and Francis Antonie, *Hoisting the Standard, 150 Years of Standard Bank*, published by The Standard Bank Group, 2012, p. 216.)   **29.** Minutes of the Board meeting of 31 March 2009, SCB/GCS. **30.** Minutes of the Board meeting of 7 May 2010, SCB/GCS. **31.** Minutes of the Board meeting of 23 June 2010, SCB/GCS. **32.** Minutes of the Board meeting of 25 May 2010, SCB/GCS. **33.** 'Africa Strategy', paper by V. Shankar, Minutes of the Board meeting of 2 November 2010, SCB/GCS. **34.** Katherine Tsang, interview with author, 15 March 2012. **35.** Minutes of the Board meeting of 17 February 2003, SCB/GCS. **36.** Tsang, interview with author, 15 March 2012. **37.** See Peter Hibbard, *The Bund Shanghai: China Faces West*, Odyssey Books & Guides, 2007, pp. 186–93. In 2006, the restored building was recognized with an Award of Excellence in the UNESCO Asia-Pacific Heritage Awards. The original head office of HSBC at Bund 12 similarly fell into other hands after restoration – though it did at least remain a bank, as the headquarters of the Pudong Development Bank. **38.** Mike Rees, interview with author, 31 January 2014. **39.** *Financial Times*, 11 February 2014. **40.** Letter from Mike Rees to Vice Mayor Tu Guangshao, 23 June 2009. **41.** 'Considerations for further developing Shanghai as an International Financial Centre through RMB Trade Settlement', Paper by SCB – China, June 2009, SCB/GCS. **42.** 2010 Annual Report, p. 8. RMB invoicing would settle at around 15 per cent of the total, by 2014. **43.** Robert Minikin and Kelvin Lau, *The Offshore Renminbi: The Rise of the Chinese Currency and Its Global Future*, John Wiley & Sons Singapore, 2013, pp. 65–100. The market volumes are more precisely defined in Chinese yuan outside the mainland, customarily quoted as 'CNY'. **44.** Ibid., p. 53. **45.** Ben Hung, interview with author, 16 January 2014. Hung presented a paper on the renminbi's rise to the Executive Leadership Team conference in Singapore's Shangri-La Hotel that same month. **46.** Minikin and Lau, *The Offshore Renminbi*, p. xv. **47.** 'Update on Bohai Bank', paper by Ben Hung, Presentation to Board (in Shanghai), Minutes of 21 March 2012, SCB/GCS. **48.** Alan Fung, interview with author, 6 March 2012. **49.** Minutes of the Board meeting of 26 July 2012, SCB/GCS. **50.** 2011 Annual Report, p. 9. **51.** 'China Consumer Banking Update', Minutes of the Board meeting of 15 April 2013, SCB/GCS. **52.** Minutes of the Board meeting of 13 December 2013, SCB/GCS. **53.** 'China Consumer Banking Update', Minutes of the Board meeting of 15 April 2013, SCB/GCS. The five cities comprised Beijing, Chengdu and Shenzen as well as Shanghai and Guangzhou. **54.** John Peace, interview with author, 12 June 2014. **55.** 'Technology and Operations Update', presentation to the Board by Jan Verplancke, Minutes of the Board meeting of 2 November 2010, SCB/GCS. **56.** Jan Verplancke, interview with author, 11 July 2014. **57.** Minutes of the Board meeting of 7 May 2009, SCB/GCS. **58.** Gavin Laws, interview with author, 20 November 2013. The contract went in the end to Aon, one of the world's largest insurance broking groups. **59.** Laws, interview with author, 20 November 2013. **60.** Repucom Standard Chartered Football Research Report, May 2015, p. 6. **61.** 'Building a Lighthouse: Finding a Voice for the Standard Chartered Brand', presentation by TWBA Group, 24 September 2009. **62.** 'The Social and Economic Impact of Standard Chartered Ghana', 2010; 'The Social and Economic Impact of Standard Chartered in Indonesia', 2010; 'The Social and Economic Impact of Standard Chartered in Bangladesh', 2012; 'Standard

Chartered in Africa', 2014. All published privately by Standard Chartered Group. **63.** At an Executive Leadership Team conference in Singapore in January 2014, 54 (17 per cent) of the 314 participants had been with the Group for twenty years or more; 72 (23 per cent) had served less than five years. **64.** Sands, interview with author, 9 February 2015. **65.** *Financial Times*, 4 October 2010. **66.** Nathaniel Foote, Russell Eisenstat and Tobias Fredberg, 'The Higher Ambition Leader – How a new breed of CEO delivers extraordinary economic and social value', *Harvard Business Review*, September 2011. **67.** Douglas A. Ready and Emily Truelove, 'The Power of Collective Ambition', *Harvard Business Review*, December 2011. **68.** Peter Sands, quoted in the *Guardian*, 1 August 2012.

POSTCRIPT

1. Consent Order of the New York Department of Financial Services, 6 August 2012. **2.** Quoted in the Factual Statement accompanying the Deferred Prosecution Agreement reached between the Group and the US authorities in December 2012, para. 105. **3.** Consent Order of the New York Department of Financial Services, 21 September 2012. When the independent monitor, Navigant Consulting Inc., submitted its findings to the DFS in June 2013, its report contained 142 separate recommendations. The Group was given three weeks to respond, and came back with elaborate action plans. (Minutes of the Board meeting of 18 June 2013, SCB/GCS.) **4.** Statement by Ronald C. Machen Jr., US Attorney for the District of Columbia, quoted in the Department of Justice press release, 10 December 2012. **5.** Jamie Kelly, interview with author, 17 November 2014. **6.** Standard Chartered press release, 19 September 2013. **7.** Richard Goulding, the Group's Chief Risk Officer since 2006, was spending ever more of his time on the governance dimension. 'Increasingly, my own agenda has revolved round the governance of risk management, rather than risk management itself.' (Interview with author, 10 September 2014.) **8.** The following two paragraphs owe much to a conversation on 10 February 2015 with Richard Hill, the Group's Chief Executive in Seoul in 2009–14, for which thanks are due. **9.** Minutes of the Board meeting of 19 September 2013, SCB/GCS.

APPENDICES

1. A 3-page reprint of Faulkner's unsigned history 'The Oldest Foreign Bank in China', published by *China Trade & Engineering* in 1946, can be found at LMA: CH03/01/14/017. **2.** Harold Faulkner to William Cockburn, 31 December 1948, LMA: CH03/01/14/079. **3.** Harold Faulkner to Professor G. C. Allen, 9 November 1949, LMA: CH03/01/14/081. **4.** The following account of the Centenary-book project is based on papers and correspondence in nine different files at LMA: CH03/01/14/078, 079, 080, 081, 082, and 085; CH03/01/17/006 and 007; and CH03/01/10/57/A. The latter includes the minutes of the Centenary

Commemoration Committee, starting in November 1949. **5.** They have survived and can be found in LMA: CH03/01/15/024. They comprise: (1) 'The Silver Crisis, 1870–1900'; (2) 'The Development of the Eastern Trade'; (3) 'The Failure of Coffee and Development of Tea in the Subcontinent'; (4) 'Initiation & Development of Rubber Planting'; (5) 'The Opium Trade Between India and China'; (6) 'The Cotton Boom in China during the 1860s'; (7) 'Development of Jute Growing & Manufacturing up to 1914'; (8) 'Tin and the Technical Age' (2 vols); (9) 'Oil in South-East Asia' (3 vols); (10) 'The Original Directors of the Chartered Bank'. **6.** I. G. Stewart to Faulkner, 16 May 1950, LMA: CH03/01/14/032. **7.** LMA: CH03/01/14/031. **8.** A. J. Bird to Harold Faulkner, 4 September 1951, LMA: CH03/01/14/019. **9.** Penang Branch Manager to Harold Faulkner, 24 July 1951, LMA: CH03/01/14/043. **10.** F. E. H. Goddard to Harold Faulkner, 18 March 1950, LMA: CH03/01/14/051. **11.** MacColl Memorandum, 27 July 1951, LMA: CH03/01/14/029. **12.** The circular to pensioners can be found at LMA: CH03/01/14/085, and many of their replies are at LMA: CH03/01/14/083. **13.** See W. S. Livingstone's memoir in LMA: CH03/01/14/036; 'Reminiscences' by F. Bennett in LMA: CH03/01/14/045, CH03/01/14/056 and CH03/01/15/006; and J. A. Macgill's memoir in LMA: CH03/01/14/088. **14.** Macgill to Faulkner, 6 January 1950, LMA: CH03/01/14/083. Macgill, who was physically unable to walk to his local Post Office without assistance, had toiled on his memoir for ten months. **15.** They can be found in LMA: CH03/01/14/025, 026, 027 and 051 (Japan, Yohohama, Kobe and Saigon respectively); CH03/01/14/028, 029, 030, 031, 032, 033, 035, 036, 037, 038, 040 and 052 (India, Bombay, Calcutta, Karachi, Madras, Amritsar, Delhi, Burma, Rangoon, Akyab, Colombo and Siam respectively); CH03/01/14/041, 042, 043, 044, 045, 047, 048, 049, 053 and 054 (Malaya, Singapore, Penang, Kuala Lumpur, Klang, Taiping, Ipoh, Seremban, Bangkok and Phuket respectively); CH03/01/14/055, 056, 057, 058, 059, 060, 061, 062, 063, 064, 065, 066, 067, 069, 071, 072, 073 and 075 (Java, Batavia, Surabaia, Sumatra, Semarang, Pedang, Macassar, Sarawak, Philippines, Manila, Zamboanga, Iloilo, Cebu, Zanzibar, New York, Manchester, Liverpool and Hamburg respectively); and CB219, Files 1–8 (China – General, Shanghai, Hankow, Foochow, Tientsin, Amoy, Canton and Loans – General). **16.** The indexes survive and can be found at LMA: CH03/01/12/001–004. Many, though not all, of the document packets have also survived and are archived at LMA: CH03/01/09–11 and /13. **17.** Harold Faulkner to John Leighton-Boyce, 29 December 1952, LMA: CH03/01/17/006. **18.** The entire handwritten MS can be found at LMA: CH03/01/17/005. **19.** Compton Mackenzie to Harold Faulkner, 13 September 1953, LMA: CH03/01/17/006. **20.** Harold Faulkner to William Cockburn, 18 September 1953, LMA: CH03/01/17/006. **21.** Harold Faulkner to William Cockburn, 2 November 1953, LMA: CH03/01/17/006. **22.** Compton Mackenzie, *Realms of Silver, One Hundred Years of Banking in the East*, Routledge & Kegan Paul, 1954, p. 306. **23.** A first draft of Leighton-Boyce's opening chapter (LMA: CH03/01/17/001) survives – and bears little resemblance to the opening chapter of *Realms of Silver*, for which Mackenzie appears to have radically reorganized material drawn from later chapters. **24.** Faulkner to Maurice Gardner, 10 May 1951, LMA: CH03/01/14/042. Faulkner wrote in the same vein to the Manager in

Rangoon, D. A. Blunt, another colleague who had sent an anguished apology for his long delay in replying to the questionnaire – but who in the end sent back a 13-page essay on the bank's history in Burma (CH03/01/15/016). **25.** A copy of the BAC Survey can be found in SCB Box 399, File 1. **26.** Correspondence re Manila's despatch of archives in September 1981 can be found at LMA: CH03/01/06/117. **27.** J. A. Packman to E. A. C. Stride, 7 January 1981, SCB Box 399, File 1. **28.** Geoffrey Jones, *British Multinational Banking 1830–1990*, Oxford University Press, 1993. **29.** The acquisition of a 25,000 sq ft property in Redhill on a twenty-five-year lease allowed the Group to dispose of leases in Clements Lane, Old Broad Street, Lloyds Chambers and Wapping's Cole Street. (Minutes of Board Standing Committee, 29 March 1988, SCB Box 2383.) **30.** Ron Dyke to R. J. Seaman, 21 July 1988, SCB Box 399, File 1. **31.** R. J. Seaman to B. D. Lawrence, 6 September 1988, SCB Box 399, File 1. **32.** For a more detailed account of this episode, see S. G. H. Freeth, 'Destroying archives: a case study of the records of Standard Chartered Bank', *Journal of the Society of Archivists*, Vol. 12, No. 2, Autumn 1991. **33.** Richard Fry, *Bankers in West Africa, The Story of the Bank of British West Africa Limited*, Hutchinson Benham, 1976, p. 10. My account of BBWA's early years draws heavily on Fry's excellent history. **34.** The new bank signed a contract with Jones and his two partners for the purchase of the West African business on 13 July 1894. A copy of the contract is held in SCB Box 399, File 3. **35.** Fry, *Bankers in West Africa*, pp. 31–2. **36.** Ibid., pp. 50–51. **37.** As part of the process that culminated in the launch in 1912 of the West African Currency Board, a public inquiry was held into the monetary arrangements of the region. The Emmott Committee listened to a wide range of evidence, and its final report confirmed the status of the BBWA: 'The Bank of British West Africa has aimed at being, and in reality is, the National Bank in British West African colonies. It has been supported by the Colonial Office and the different West African Governments, and now holds the confidence of the populations, European and Native. It is known to be the custodian of Government funds, and has played an important part in the development of business methods and the growing prosperity of the West African colonies.' (The Emmott Report, June 1912, Cd. 6426, quoted in Fry, *Bankers in West Africa*, p. 73.)

Bibliography

PRIVATE PAPERS AND BANK PUBLICATIONS

Brown, Michael, 'Reminiscences from the East'
Brown, William C. L., 'Autobiography'
Green, Neville, 'Banking on Imperfect Arabic & Other Memories'
Green, Edna Carr, 'Just Keep a Bag Packed: A Memoir'
McWilliam, Michael, Diaries, 1983–88
Standard Chartered Bank: A Story Brought Up To Date, 1980

BOOKS AND ARTICLES

Admati, Anat and Hellwig, Martin, *The Bankers' New Clothes, What's Wrong with Banking and What to Do about It*, Princeton University Press, 2013.

Ahamed, Liaquat, *Lords of Finance: 1929, the Great Depression, and the Bankers who Broke the World*, William Heinemann, 2009.

Amphlett, G. T., *History of the Standard Bank of South Africa Ltd, 1862–1913*, Glasgow University Press, 1914.

Arndt, E. H. D., *Banking and Currency Development in South Africa (1659–1927)*, Johannesburg, 1928.

Bagchi, Amiya Kumar, *Private Investment in India 1900–1939*, Cambridge University Press, 1972.

Barber, Anthony, *Taking the Tide, A Memoir*, privately published, 1996.

Barrington, E. I., *The Servant of All: pages from the family, social and political life of my father James Wilson: twenty years of mid-Victorian life*, 2 vols., Longmans, 1927.

Baster, A. S. J., *The Imperial Banks*, P. S. King & Son, 1929.

— *The International Banks*, P. S. King & Son, 1935.

Bayly, C. A., *The Birth of the Modern World, 1780–1914*, Blackwell Publishing, 2004.

Bayly, Christopher and Harper, Tim, *Forgotten Wars, The End of Britain's Asian Empire*, Allen Lane, 2007.

Bickers, Robert, *Empire Made Me, An Englishman Adrift in Shanghai*, Allen Lane, 2003.

— *The Scramble for China, Foreign Devils in the Qing Empire, 1832–1914*, Allen Lane, 2011.

Bonin, Hubert, Valério, Nuno and Yago, Kazuhiko (eds.), *Asian Imperial Banking History*, Pickering & Chatto, 2014.

Brown, Ian, *Burma's Economy in the Twentieth Century*, Cambridge University Press, 2013.

Brummer, Alex, *Bad Banks*, Random House Business Books, 2014.

Buettner, Elizabeth, *Empire Families, Britons and Late Imperial India*, Oxford University Press, 2004.

Campbell-Smith, Duncan, *Masters of the Post, The Authorized History of the Royal Mail*, Allen Lane, 2011.

Charney, Michael W., *A History of Modern Burma*, Cambridge University Press, 2009.

Cheng Siok Hwa, *The Rice Industry of Burma 1852–1940*, Institute of South East Asian Studies, 2012.

Coble, Jr, Parks M., *The Shanghai Capitalists and the Nationalist Government, 1927–37*, Harvard University Press, 1980.

Collis, Maurice, *Wayfoong, The Hongkong and Shanghai Banking Corporation, A Study of East Asia's Transformation, Political, Financial and Economic, During the Last Hundred Years*, Faber & Faber, 1965.

Crossley, Julian and Blandford, John, *The DCO Story, A History of Banking in Many Countries 1925–71*, Barclays Bank International Limited, 1975.

Darwin, John, *The Empire Project, The Rise and Fall of the British World-System 1830–1970*, Cambridge University Press, 2009.

— *Unfinished Empire, The Global Expansion of Britain*, Allen Lane, 2012.

Davenport-Hines, R. P. T. and Jones, Geoffrey (eds.), *British Business in Asia since 1860*, Cambridge University Press, 1989.

Devine, T. M., *To the Ends of the Earth, Scotland's Global Diaspora, 1750–2010*, Allen Lane, 2011.

Farrell, Brian and Hunter, Sandy (eds.), *A Great Betrayal? The Fall of Singapore Revisited*, Marshall Cavendish, 2009.

Fenby, Jonathan, *The Penguin History of Modern China, The Fall and Rise of a Great Power, 1850–2009*, Allen Lane, 2008.

Ferguson, Niall, *The Pity of War*, Allen Lane The Penguin Press, 1998.

— *Empire, How Britain Made the Modern World*, Allen Lane, 2003.

— *The Ascent of Money, A Financial History of the World*, Allen Lane, 2008.

Ffolliott, Pamela and Croft, E. L. H., *One Titan at a Time*, Cape Town, 1960.

Fry, Richard, *Bankers in West Africa, The Story of the Bank of British West Africa Limited*, Hutchinson Benham, 1976.

— (ed.), *A Banker's World, The Revival of the City 1957–1970, The Speeches and Writings of Sir George Bolton*, Hutchinson, 1970.

Goodstadt, Leo F., *Profits, Politics and Panics: Hong Kong's Banks and the Making of a Miracle Economy, 1935–1985*, Hong Kong University Press, 2007.

Green, Edna Carr, *Just Keep a Bag Packed, A Memoir*, Author House, 2013.

Henry, J. A., *The Standard Bank's Early Days in Johannesburg*, Standard Bank, 1956.

— *The First Hundred Years of the Standard Bank*, Oxford University Press, 1963.

Hibbard, Peter, *The Bund Shanghai: China Faces West*, Odyssey Books & Guides, 2007.

Horesh, Niv, *Shanghai's Bund and Beyond – British Banks, Banknote Issuance and Monetary Policy in China 1842–1937*, Yale University Press, 2009.

Hunt, Tristram, *Ten Cities That Made An Empire*, Allen Lane, 2014.

Jones, Geoffrey, *British Multinational Banking 1830–1990*, Oxford University Press, 1993.

— *Banking & Empire in Iran, The History of the British Bank of the Middle East*, vol. 1, Cambridge University Press, 1986.

— *Banking & Oil, The History of the British Bank of the Middle East*, vol. 2, Cambridge University Press, 1987.

Jones, Stuart, *The Great Imperial Banks in South Africa, A Study of the Business of Standard Bank and Barclays Bank, 1891–1961*, University of South Africa, 1996.

Keswick, Maggie (ed.), *The Thistle and the Jade, A Celebration of 175 Years of Jardine Matheson*, Jardine Matheson, 2008 (revised edition).

Keynes, John Maynard, *Indian Currency and Finance*, Macmillan, 1913.

King, Frank H. H., *The History of the Hongkong Bank*, 4 vols., Cambridge University Press, 1987–91.

– Vol. 1 *In Late Imperial China, 1864–1902: On an Even Keel.*

– Vol. 2 *In the Period of Imperialism and War 1895–1918: Wayfoong, the Focus of Wealth.*

– Vol. 3 *Between the Wars and the Bank Interned 1919–45: Return from Grandeur.*

– Vol. 4 *In the Period of Development and Nationalism, 1941–84: From Regional Bank to Multinational Group.*

Kinsey, Sara and Green, Edwin, *The Good Companions, Wives and Families in the History of the HSBC Group*, HSBC, 2004.

Koh, Angela, *Chang Yun Chung, Steering through the Storms*, Focus Publishing, 2012.

Kynaston, David, *The City of London*, 4 vols., Chatto & Windus, 1994–2001.

– Vol. 1 *A World of Its Own, 1815–1890.*

– Vol. 2 *Golden Years, 1890–1914.*

– Vol. 3 *Illusions of Gold, 1914–1945.*

– Vol. 4 *Club No More 1945–2000.*

Lambert, Nicholas A., *Planning Armageddon, British Economic Warfare and the First World War*, Harvard University Press, 2012.

Latter, Tony, *Hong Kong's Money: The History, Logic and Operation of the Currency Peg*, Hong Kong University Press, 2007.

Leiper, G. A., *A Yen For My Thoughts, A Memoir of Occupied Hong Kong*, South China Morning Post Publications, 1982.

Leith-Ross, Frederick, *Money Talks, Fifty Years of International Finance*, Hutchinson, 1968.

Louis, W. Roger, *British Strategy in the Far East 1919–39*, Oxford University Press, 1971.

Mabin, Alan and Conradie, Barbara (eds.), *The Confidence of the Whole Country, Standard Bank Reports on Economic Conditions in Southern Africa 1865–1902*, Standard Bank Investment Corporation, 1987.

McDermott, John, 'Total War and the Merchant State: Aspects of British Economic Warfare Against Germany, 1914–16', *Canadian Journal of History*, vol. 21, April 1986.

Mackenzie, Compton, *Realms of Silver, One Hundred Years of Banking in the East*, Routledge & Kegan Paul, 1954.

MacQuitty, William, *A Life to Remember*, Quartet Books, 1991.

Marozzi, Justin, *Baghdad: City of Peace, City of Blood*, Allen Lane, 2014.

Moorhouse, Geoffrey, *Calcutta, The City Revealed*, Weidenfeld and Nicholson, 1971.

Morris, Jan, *Pax Britannica, The Climax of Empire*, Faber & Faber, 1968.

Osterhammel, Jurgen, *The Transformation of the World, A Global History of the Nineteenth Century*, Princeton University Press, 2014.

Porter, A. N. (ed.), *Atlas of British Overseas Expansion*, Routledge, 1991.

Read, Donald, *The Power of News, The History of Reuters 1849–1989*, Oxford University Press, 1992.

Reynolds, David, *The Long Shadow, The Great War and the Twentieth Century*, Simon & Schuster, 2013.

Richards, John F., 'Opium and the British Indian Empire: The Royal Commission of 1895', *Modern Asian Studies*, February 2002.

Roberts, J. M., *Twentieth Century, A History of the World 1901 to the Present*, Allen Lane The Penguin Press, 1999.

Roberts, Richard, *Take Your Partners: Orion, the Consortium Banks and the Transformation of the Euromarkets*, Palgrave, 2001.

— *Saving the City, The Great Financial Crisis of 1914*, Oxford University Press, 2013.

Roberts, Richard and Kynaston, David, *The Lion Wakes, A Modern History of HSBC*, Profile Books, 2015.

Rockefeller, David, *Memoirs*, Random House, 2002.

Romain, Ken, *Larger than Life, Donald Gordon and the Liberty Life Story*, Jonathan Ball Publishers, 1989.

Roy, Tirthankar, *The Economic History of India, 1857–1947*, Oxford University Press, 3rd edition 2011.

Sandberg, Michael, *Hurrahs and Hammerblows*, privately published, 2012.

Savkar, D. S., *Joint Stock Banking in India*, Bombay, 1938.

Schenk, Catherine R., 'The Origins of Anti-Competitive Regulation: Was Hong Kong "Over-Banked" in the 1960s?' *Hong Kong Institute for Monetary Research Working Paper No. 9*, July 2006.

Simha, S. L. N., *History of the Reserve Bank of India (1935–51)*, Reserve Bank of India, 1979.

Siu Man-han, 'Foreign Banks and the Chinese Indigenous Economy: the Business of the Shanghai Branch of the Chartered Bank of India, Australia and China', *Journal of Osaka University of Economics*, vol. 64, no. 3, September 2013 (reprinted in Bonin, Valério and Yago (eds.), *Asian Imperial Banking History*).

Siu, Susanna et al. (eds.), *Hong Kong Currency*, Hong Kong Museum of History, 2012.

Spalding, W. F., *Foreign Exchange and Foreign Bills*, Pitman & Sons, 1915.

Sparks, Allister, *The Mind of South Africa, The Story of the Rise and Fall of Apartheid*, Jonathan Ball Publishers, 2003.

Steyn, Richard and Antonie, Francis, *Hoisting the Standard, 150 Years of Standard Bank*, The Standard Bank Group, 2012.

Studwell, Joe, *Asian Godfathers: Money and Power in Hong Kong & South-East Asia*, Profile Books, 2007.

— *How Asia Works: Success and Failure in the World's Most Dynamic Region*, Profile Books, 2013.

Sulivan, Raymond J. F., *One Hundred Years of Bombay: A History of the Bombay Chamber of Commerce 1836–1936*, Times of India Press, 1937.

Terry, Carolyn, *A Pioneer Bank in a Pioneer Land*, Flesch & Partners, 1979.

Thant Myint-U, *The River of Lost Footsteps, A Personal History of Burma*, Faber &Faber, 2007.

Tharoor, Shashi, *Inglorious Empire, What the British Did to India*, C. Hurst & Co., 2017.

Tooze, Adam, *The Deluge, The Great War and the Remaking of Global Order*, Allen Lane, 2014.

Wagel, Srinivas R., *Finance in China*, Shanghai, 1914.

Webb, A. C. M., *The Roots of the Tree, A Study in Early South African Banking: The Predecessors of the First National Bank, 1838–1926*, First National Bank of Southern Africa Ltd, 1992.

Webster, Anthony, *The Twilight of the East India Company, The Evolution of Anglo-Asian Commerce and Politics 1790–1860*, The Boydell Press, 2009.

Welsh, Frank, *A History of Hong Kong*, HarperCollins, 1997 (revised edn).

Wheatcroft, Geoffrey, *The Randlords*, Atheum, 1986.

Williams, Emlyn, *Oyinbo Banki, A White Chief's Nigerian Odyssey*, Elna Publications, 1996.

Wilson, Rodney, 'Financial Development of the Arab Gulf: The Eastern Bank Experience, 1917–50', *Business History*, vol. 29, no. 2, 1987.

Wong, Eleanor, *T. Y. Wong & A Family of Textile Entrepreneurs*, published privately by Harmony Day Services, 2014.

Woodruff, Philip, *The Men Who Ruled India*, vol. 2 *The Guardians*, Jonathan Cape, 1954.

Worger, William H., *South Africa's City of Diamonds, Mine Workers and Monopoly Capitalism in Kimberley, 1867–1895*, Yale University Press, 1987.

Yergin, Daniel, *The Prize*, Simon & Schuster, 1991.

Young, W. H., *A Merry Banker in the Far East*, John Lane The Bodley Head, 1916.

Index

Bank names are generally abbreviated as CB for Chartered Bank, SB for Standard Bank, EB for Eastern Bank, BBWA or BWA for Bank of (British) West Africa and SCB for Standard Chartered Bank. Bold entries in main headings denote past and present companies within the Group. Individual branches of the banks are indexed by their location. Where indexed items have sub-entries, these are generally listed in broadly chronological order. Group personnel are listed alphabetically under 'Board Directors' and 'Managers' entries that follow entries/sub-entries for their respective banks. References in italics relate to plates, maps, charts and illustrations.